Deconstructing
Mormonism

Deconstructing
MORMONISM

An Analysis and Assessment
of the
Mormon Faith

Thomas Riskas

With a Foreword by Kai Nielsen

American Atheist Press
Cranford, New Jersey
2011

Published 2011 by American Atheist Press
ISBN-10: 1-57884-007-4
ISBN-13: 978-1-57884-007-6

American Atheist Press
P.O. Box 158
Cranford, NJ 07016-3214
Voice: (908) 276-7300
FAX: (908) 276-7402

www.atheists.org

Edited by Frank R. Zindler

Library of Congress Cataloging-in-Publication Data

Riskas, Thomas.
  Deconstructing Mormonism : an analysis and assessment of the Mormon faith / Thomas Riskas ; with a foreword by Kai Nielsen.
  p. cm.
  Includes bibliographical references.
  ISBN 978-1-57884-007-6 (alk. paper)
  1. Church of Jesus Christ of Latter-day Saints--Controversial literature. 2. Christianity and atheism. I. Title.
  BX8645.R57 2010
  289.3'32--dc22
2010040084

Printed in the United States of America

Dedications

I dedicate this book to Dr. Kai Nielsen, Professor Emeritus at the University of Calgary, to my wife and companion Deborah, and to all my beloved children and grandchildren.

To Kai, this work would not have been possible without your important work to draw from. Your intelligent and compassionate analysis of theistic religion in the context of "naturalism without foundations" has been both enlightening and therapeutic.

To Debbie, you have my profoundest love, respect and gratitude for suffering with me through my recovery from theistic belief to my natural atheism, and for being the ballast I needed to stay emotionally afloat during the difficult times of separation from my deeply rooted – and toxic – faith.

To my beloved children, my hope is that you will come to know how deep and well-informed my faith was so you might better appreciate the significance of my complete rejection of it and departure from it; and that you will one day carefully and thoughtfully read this book and come to consider it the gift to you and to your children and loved ones it was intended, in part, to be.

.

Acknowledgements

I want to acknowledge the invaluable assistance of Frank Zindler, my editor and the Editor in Chief of AAP. I have learned much from Frank, both as an accomplished Editor and a Scholar. Thank you, Frank for your valued insights and suggestions, and for your enduring patience in dealing with my seemingly endless changes and revisions.

"I hope that you will develop a questioning spirit. Be unafraid of new ideas for they are the stepping stones of progress. ... [B]ut I caution you that your thoughts and expressions must meet competition in the marketplace of thought, and in that competition truth will emerge triumphant. Only error needs to fear freedom of expression. Seek the truth in all fields..."

- Elder Hugh B. Brown

"Let us not have the heart breathe defiance to the intellect."

- Elder B.H. Roberts

Contents

* Suggested Prerequisite Reading

Contents

FOREWORD

Kai Nielsen
Department of Philosophy
University of Calgary and Concordia University

Tom Riskas is well positioned to write about Mormonism and Mormon theology. For over twenty years he was a loyal and informed member of the Mormon priesthood. But the wolves of disbelief gradually began to take hold. After a seven year struggle with his faith, Riskas finally resigned from the Mormon Church and that only after an intense struggle both emotionally and intellectually. He has looked carefully and honestly at his religion and its doctrines, including theological writings of its most distinguished theologians, including their responses to unbelief. But he has also carefully studied the philosophy of religion, particularly on its analytical side. He has a good grasp of the central issues here. The bottom line for him, as far as his position in the philosophy of religion, has become to articulate, with care and dispassionately, a pragmatic fallibilistic naturalism and a secular humanism.

These two not unrelated capabilities yield two unique strengths which together serve him well in articulating his account in this volume: (1) an understanding of Mormonism, its doctrines and the Mormon intelligentsia's theological efforts to elucidate and defend them and (2) an excellent knowledge of the philosophy of religion and of conceptual analysis which gives him a perch from which to critically but still impartially, objectively and cogently, to examine the doctrines of his erstwhile faith. We can learn much from this book about the belief structure of a particular religion and its rationale that I conjecture many of us are not very familiar with, and to portray it in an account that is both impartial and religiously sensitive. (I should remark in passing that Riskas gives us an excellent bibliography of the relevant works.) Yet it is an account which, without departing from its impartiality, powerfully shows us the deep-seated incoherences of Mormon theology and the religion it is supposed to buttress.

While it is an account of a particular belief-system, the most central religious conceptions that Riskas characterizes and criticizes are (or most of them are) not just a part of Mormonism but crucial elements of the belief structure of Judaism, Christianity and Islam: doctrinal strands that are common to them all. He does this with critical force while still giving us a balanced, firmly argued, clearly articulated and fair-minded account of what is at issue here. A Catholic or Calvinist could feel the impact of it as well as a Mormon.

Riskas adroitly deploys arguments developed with a certain reliance on my own more generalized account aimed at establishing the incoherence of non-anthropomorphic conceptions of God-the so-called transcendent Deity.[1] He also argues, as I do, for the falsity of anthropomorphic conceptions of God (e.g., the God of the Old Testament).[2] Moreover, he speaks of the distinctive quasi-anthropomorphic conception of the God of Mormonism which he takes to be an incoherent blend of anthropomorphic and non-anthropomorphic conceptions. This 'blending' enables Mormon theology to have it both ways: to portray God anthropomorphically in a way that is intelligible but plainly reveals such a belief as false (indeed obviously false) and, in a non-anthropomorphic way, which makes of God

xi

an unintelligible mystery. To avoid belief riddled with superstition, or at least plain falsity, we must try to conceive of God as transcendent to the universe or at least – and even more questionably – a Being (note the Scholastic jargon) which is not an empowered being to speak pleonastically. God, that is, is not an object, not even a 'transcendent object'. But even if we think we can make sense of 'transcendent object' or 'transcendent Being', how can such a 'reality' be a person, be our Heavenly Father? But, all that aside, with God, conceived as transcendent to the universe, we get unintelligibility and to get intelligibility we must have straight out anthropomorphism – but then we get something that is plainly false. By shuttling back and forth so overtly between these two conceptions of God, Mormon theology only adds to the implausibility and incoherence of such conceptions. On the anthropomorphic side it yields plain falsity while on the non-anthropomorphic side it has all the incoherences of developed orthodox theism. To try to escape this – to try to have it both ways – Mormon theologians came up with a quasi-anthropomorphism. This distinctively Mormon doctrine contributes a further at least putative incoherence which saddles us, just where we need insight, with what at worst is a further incoherence and at best a muddle.

Riskas rightly notes that I use 'incoherent' and 'unintelligible' is four different ways. He rightly finds this at times confusing and carefully and usefully distinguishes these four ways. He wonders if that was intentional on my part or inadvertent. I wish I could say it was intentional but it was, unfortunately, inadvert. Having carefully distinguished them, Riskas goes on to show how these different uses apply in different contexts and how they all count toward showing that non-anthropomorphic God-talk, the very concept of God conceived as transcendent to the world, is, in one way or another, incoherent. (The different uses of incoherence' are not, however, without a family resemblance.) Moreover, the different ways this concept may be incoherent point to the complexity of the concept of God. I am grateful to Riskas for pointing this out to me.

Riskas soundly critiques appeals to revelation, faith and religious experience. All three of these appeals are rendered problematic by the incoherence of the very concept of God and they do not provide us with an escape from the wolves of disbelief. But he also shows that these conceptions have free-standing difficulties that render such appeals non-starters or for that matter nothing that could be a last court of appeal. Riskas also shows that we do not need a religious morality (Mormon, Jewish, Christian or Islamic) to make sense of our lives or to ground our morality. These different criticisms of religion apply to anthropomorphic, quasi-anthropomorphic conceptions of God as well as to the appeals to the transcendent God of developed theism. These arguments given by Riskas against the soundness of an appeal to the alleged superiority and the necessity of religious morality, to revelation, faith and religious experience are all freestanding arguments. They do not presuppose his or my arguments that belief in the so-called transcendent God is incoherent. Moreover, they apply all along the line to the different conceptions of God. We can and should be secularists all the way down.

Finally, Riskas confronts the issue of the alleged need to believe-to believe, that is, in some religion. (Mormonism, and most other faiths as well, would say that it is not enough to believe in some religion or other but to believe in the right one, namely (for them), the Mormon one. The ecumenical spirit comes hard. But it is pretty vapid to proclaim 'Go to any house of faith, I don't care which one, and commit yourself.') Riskas recognizes that many people, including reflective, sensitive people, are, psychologically speaking, driven to and then by religious belief; they would feel their lives utterly meaningless without religious belief. But he stresses that that is a contingent matter of certain people living under certain conditions. It may be felt by them to be something they deeply need. But that a person feels he/she deeply needs something does not entail or establish that he/she actually needs it. They should come to recognize that there are many people, some of whom are also reflective, sensitive and caring, who feel no such need. Some of them may even be religiously attuned, though it is important to remember that you can be religiously attuned without being religious. These secular people (religiously attuned or not) can make sense of their lives and indeed have as much happiness (perhaps more), achieve as much (perhaps more) self-realization, experience well-being at least as fully, and relate as well with others without any religious belief or feeling a need for religious belief at all. Solidarity among people does not require religion. It is plainly false that if God is dead, nothing matters.

Deconstructing Mormonism should be required reading for Mormons. It is, however, not only something for Mormons or ex-Mormons, but for anyone who would seriously think about religion and wonder what its relation should be to their lives or about whether they should be religious believers or not.

Some say that we moderns live in a disenchanted world where many, experiencing the poverty of it, are being re-enchanted (or are trying to be). I say, sadly, that we – the populations of the contemporary world, even the rich nations of the North – have never lived in a disenchanted world. Unfortunately – or so I say – it is true that there are some signs (though conflicting ones) that our insecurely and uneasily and partially disenchanted world is becoming re-enchanted. However, we should recognize that we (collectively) have never lived in a secular world: a disenchanted world.[3] Some of us live without discontent utterly secularly and, as modernity marches on, an increasing number of us. But that there is such a world is a myth of certain intellectuals. Religion of some sort or other (though often of radically different sorts), whatever its waning and waxing, has always been with us. So we cannot say accurately (as some do) that we live in a post-secular world that is in the process of being re-enchanted. What we can say – perhaps mistakenly – is that one condition for our world to be a better world is that it be deeply disenchanted without angst. A disenchanted world (pace John Gray) need not be a world without meaning. Both Riskas and I believe and (more importantly) argue that we can have disenchantment without angst or a feeling that life is without meaning.[4] Of course, we may be wrong. That, however, is only to recognize, as I like to say, that fallibilism is the name of the game. But both fallibilism and what are the sociological facts notwithstanding, there is (pace Charles Taylor) no viable normative reason why the need for enchantment should be, let alone must be, a need for the human animal, But to say that enchantment is something many people seek and say they need is a sociological fact is not to depart from a naturalistic and secular humanism. That something is at present a sociological fact is not to show, or plausibly give to understand, that at another time and in another situation a secular world could not, and desirably, obtain.[5] Indeed, it could very well both be desired and desirable. That may well be an empirical possibility that may become an empirical reality. The ought-implies-can maxim has not been violated.[6]

NOTES

1   I hope this connection does not render my account too *parti-pris*. I don't think that it does but that is for others to decide.

2   I don't say only the Old Testament or that *all* the claims made in the Old Testament should be so understood.

3   As a matter of sociological fact a disenchanted world may not be in the cards.

4   Kai Nielsen, "Linguistic Philosophy and 'The Meaning of Life'," originally published in 1963, and Kai Nielsen, "Death and the Meaning of Life," originally published in 1978. Both have been reprinted in E. D. Klemke, ed., *The Meaning of Life*, second edition. New York, New York: Oxford University Press, 1999. See 153–59 and 233–56.

5   Leaving out the 'desirability' bit, that would hold for any sociological fact.

6   An ardent secular humanist could say sadly, "It's just a sociological fact that many people feel a need for religious belief without contradiction or even the slightest conceptual or moral anomaly." Moreover, setting aside the explicit or conscious commitment to naturalism and secular humanism, it may be increasingly the case with younger people in the rich North (remember that the United States is somewhat of an exception here) that they feel little or no need for enchantment. This is an empirical question that should be investigated.

Important Note

For this book to be fully appreciated and have its intended effect, it is suggested that it be read – with all substantive footnotes – beginning with the essential prerequisite reading of the Introduction, Foundational Preface and Chapters 1 and 2, followed by reading in sequence Chapters 3-8 through the Epilogue and Personal Postscript to the Appendices and list of References offered for further study.

Beyond the Betrayal of Doubt: An Important and Personal Introduction

"Prove all things, hold fast to that which is good. Only if you are unafraid of the truth will you find it."

—*Man's Search for Happiness*
Mormon Proselytizing Film

Prefatory Note: This important *Introduction* creates an essential context for the entire book, and provides crucial information and perspectives related to various important topics, including the importance, betrayal, and resolution of doubt; anticipated reactions to the book and answers to these reactions; and both general and personal background information. It is, again, and along with the *Foundational Preface* and *Chapters 1 and 2* which follow, necessary and indispensable prerequisite reading.

A favorite Christian hymn – "How Firm a Foundation" – assures Mormon believers that their god is a "firm foundation" on whom they can rely for truth, justice, mercy, deliverance, and salvation. But how firm *is* the foundation of the Mormon faith? Is it indeed, as Mormon Apostle John A. Widtsoe asserted, a "Rational Theology?" As a way of life, does living in accordance to the teachings and dictates of Mormonism truly contribute to the mental health or well-being of its adherents? As we shall learn through the painstaking analysis and assessment which follow, the answers to these three questions are not what Mormon believers might suspect or hope for.

There is admittedly a certain familiar hominess and visceral appeal to Mormon theistic discourse. It speaks of being 'spirit children' to a loving and wise 'Heavenly Father' (and 'Heavenly Mother'), with an 'Elder Brother' or 'Savior' (in Jesus Christ) and 'brothers and sisters.' And it speaks of a divine 'Plan' which promises 'eternal blessings,' 'forever families' and a return to our 'Celestial home.'

Such familiar 'God-talk' can — for those in need or to those who are, by nature, more superstitious and/or not inclined to be critical or skeptical of religious beliefs — speak comfort, security, and apparent sense to the human mind. Further, such beliefs, shaped by family and cultural conditioning and personalized by 'spiritual experience,' might seem to unquestioning believers to be comprehensive, internally coherent and wonderfully consistent with what they do on a day-by-day basis and with life and creation as they know it.

When such believers live their religion, they engage – orally or in thought – in God-talk. They tacitly assume, and consciously think, speak, and act or behave as if the existence of their god was a foregone conclusion or self-evident fact — as if they actually know what they are talking about when referring to their god or some aspect of it, or to what their god is really like or really wants, expects, or thinks. They do so even if, as some in their wisdom might say, no one can possibly know what a god's thoughts or purposes are. Yet beyond perhaps making it easier for Mormons or any theistic believers to circularly assume what they wish to believe or claim regarding their god's actual existence and the validity or justification of their faith, such familiar hominess, believed understanding, and apparent coherence cannot, even for devout believers, forestall – at a deeper level – profound, troubling questions and *real* doubts[1] and concerns.

Theistic believers typically exist on a continuum with respect to their knowledge of and commitment to the scriptures, doctrines, or beliefs of their particular religion of inheritance or choice. Mormon believers are no exception. Many if not most of the Mormons I have known personally over the years have been raised in the Mormon Church and are at least somewhat active in or committed to their faith, participating periodically if not regularly in Sunday services and Temple worship and serving regularly in assigned Church work, or 'callings.' Among these and other more active Mormons, including those in lay leadership positions and those who have served on two-year missions for the Church, I would conjecture – and I think reasonably so – that relatively few have actually read, much less repeatedly read and/or actually studied, *all* of the Standard Works (or canonized scriptures) of the Church *cover-to-cover*. Most have likely only a superficial knowledge of Mormon theology as taught in their scriptures or by the more renowned Church theologians and General Authorities of the Mormon Church such as Joseph Smith, Brigham Young, John Taylor, Orson and Parley P. Pratt, John A. Widtsoe, James E. Talmage, Brigham H. Roberts, Joseph Fielding Smith, and Bruce R. McConkie to name a notable few.

Moreover, and for the most part, I think it is reasonable to say that with respect to Mormon theology, most (if not all) members of the Mormon Church — whether active, less active or inactive — are, like believers of other theistic faiths or no particular organized religion at all, what is colloquially referred to as "salad bar" believers. Such believers essentially 'cherry-pick,' modify and embrace those beliefs or authoritative interpretations of their faith that best suit their life-style and self-interests, with little-to-no imposition of guilt and very little-to-no disturbance of the intellect (which leads to real doubt) or of what is comfortably familiar. Although all their religious beliefs and practices arguably hinge on the fundamental concepts and teachings they have been so deeply conditioned to uncritically accept as 'Truth,' most Mormon believers I have known are not theologically inclined or interested in the rigorous study of the theology of their faith, or of their Church's history. For the most part, they only know and accept what they hear and agree with at Church or in semiannual General Church Conferences, or read in Church books, periodicals, manuals, and/or periodic and superficial perusal of the scriptures. Most (if not all) of them have very likely invented and uncritically accepted as true their own personal version of what their 'God' is like, and what the 'gospel' (or *'good news'*) of their faith entails, promises, or requires.

Even so, all Mormon believers – particularly those who are more informed, thoughtful and formally educated in the natural sciences and philosophy – might at times naturally wonder (and understandably so) how, as twenty-first-century moderns, they or anyone can justifiably or reasonably claim to *know* – or even know what it *actually* means to say

---

1 'Real doubt' as used here and throughout this book is, in a Peircean context, taken to mean doubt that actually affects our lives; that has practical consequences for our actions and beliefs. In a religious context, it persistently or recurrently disturbs and rattles or threatens the faith of believers and stimulates serious inquiry. Such doubt, and the sincere questions that express it, are to be distinguished from the state of merely being 'skeptical,' or from mere Cartesian, universal, or 'paper,' doubt.

– that their god *literally* exists in its fullness as commonly or doctrinally described. What does it mean when one says that a god — who allegedly abides in another world, universe or dimension of space and time — *literally* hears and answers prayers? They might also wonder, or question, what it would actually mean for man to be an 'eternal intelligence' — or for man's eternal intelligence to be *literally* 'co-eternal' with 'God.' What does it mean for man's 'spirit' to be *literally* procreated by 'heavenly Parents'?

In their more sober moments, reflective Mormon believers might question whether there really was a *literal* 'pre-existence' and 'war in heaven.' Or whether the 'Creation,' the 'Fall,' and the 'Atonement' are *literally* true – or even possible – as doctrinally claimed and understood. They might also question if there really is a *literal* resurrection and 'life hereafter' with *literally* 'three kingdoms of glory.' Can we *literally* dwell in the presence of 'God' in the highest degree of the Celestial Kingdom as tangible, resurrected beings?

Finally, more rational Mormon believers might reasonably wonder how it is that Church ordinances of salvation can be performed by proxy for the dead — or how marriages and families can *literally* be 'sealed' together 'forever' as an 'eternal family unit,' where each family member may ultimately and *literally* become a 'God.'

Still, beyond such theological questions and concerns, there are no doubt many more faithful Mormon believers who might also wonder (and sincerely question with concern) why, notwithstanding the alleged eternal existence and necessity of free will, and given the alleged attributes and personal qualities of the god they worship, there is *so much* suffering and pre-mature death in the world caused by human and natural evil. Why are divine intervention or miracles in answer to the pleading prayers of the suffering and those in need of deliverance and healing for themselves and their loved ones or innocent babies so selective and infrequent, if indeed they truly exist at all? Why, given the supposed eternal stakes involved, the alleged fact of revelation, and 'God's' alleged power and greatest desire for man's salvation, is there *any* confusion, ignorance, contradiction, and resulting unbelief, disbelief, nonbelief, or wrong belief at all regarding his existence and the truthfulness of his 'only true Church'?

Then there are those who might also wonder, as I do, why faith in 'God,' or in 'Christ,' would be necessary for those who claim with certainty and sincere conviction to 'know' their god exists. (After all, one does not need faith – or sincere conviction for that matter – in the known existence of fire, wind, gravity, or death.) How could such an epistemic claim have any warranted assertability merely on the basis of allegedly revealed subjective and interpreted feelings – or so-called properly basic 'spiritual experiences' – that cannot possibly be objectively confirmed or disconfirmed as such, or empirically differentiated from the same reported and differently interpreted feelings of disbelievers, nonbelievers, or believers of different faiths. Why is faith required and tested by this god (if such a god could even possibly exist)? Why, again, is it even necessary, given the believed eternal stakes involved, the alleged attributes and greatest desires of this god, and the proven insufficiency of faith for so many in weathering the storms of doubt and affliction? Why would speculative Mormon scriptural exegeses and apologetics be necessary given, again, the putative stakes involved and the believed fact of personal and institutional revelation? For many, in spite of their faith, much of what they say they believe *literally* makes little or no sense when subjected to sustained dispassionate, critical reflection or conceptual analysis. For others, like me, who are totally without belief in *any* god, such faith and belief are utterly incoherent, and therefore impossible to hold, or even seriously entertain.

Believers, of course, may – and often do – treat their religious questions, doubts and concerns like we all do most of our other troubling doubts and mental and emotional disturbances and concerns. Most simply ignore and suppress them, and/or minimize them or deny they exist. Others compensate for them or otherwise dissociate from them. They deceive themselves, through denial and rationalization, into holding their beliefs as truth — no matter what the evidence or analysis might show or how sound or valid the challenging or refuting counter-arguments to their defenses might be. One thing seems certain: It is *impossible* to choose to believe – or assert that one knows – that which is unbelievable – or unknowable – without *real* doubt.

The Betrayal of Doubt by Suppression and Denial

Pierre Abelard wrote: "The beginning of wisdom is found in doubting; by doubting we come to the question, and by seeking we may come upon the truth." Elsewhere – and from a different, though not unrelated perspective – we have the cautionary if not stinging words of William Clifford, who wrote: "If a man, holding a belief which he was taught in childhood or persuaded of afterwards, keeps down and pushes away any doubts which arise about it in his mind, purposely avoids the reading of books and the company of men that call in question or discuss it, and regards as impious [or inappropriate] those questions which cannot easily be asked without disturbing it – the life of that man is one long sin against mankind."

Real religious doubt which comes from, or is revealed by, a type of inner conversation – or inner conflict between the rational and non-rational (or irrational) functions of our brain – is, as we shall learn, unconsciously suppressed by certain anxiety or fear-inducing teachings and related beliefs. These have been deeply embedded in the believer's psyche by programs and methods of authoritarian conditioning. Moreover, it is also betrayed, or exposed, by different types of symptoms, reactions, and evasions, some of which shall be exposed in some depth later in this *Introduction*. Such methods of suppressive control are insidious. Such symptoms, reactions, and evasions can be — and usually are — disguised, denied, compensated for, and normalized by the culture. Still, they can be, and are, nevertheless seen, recognized, and exposed by an honest, trained, and skilled listener and observer, whether such an observer is oneself or another.

Sooner or later our suppressed and denied real doubts and needs catch up with us and take their terrible toll, whether we admit it or not. Such, as I shall argue in Chapter 8 and the *Epilogue* of this work, is the unavoidable handiwork of all theistic religion. It is, I fear, the undesired yet ultimate fate of those theistic believers — committed or otherwise — who have been deeply conditioned and wounded in their families and in their religious life by the *shaming[2] discipline of the inherent moralistic core of their faith; a*

---

2 The terms *shame, shaming,* and *shameless* are used frequently in this book and require some explanation beyond their mere mention. As used in this book, 'shame' refers to what has been characterized as 'toxic shame' (Bradshaw 1988). According to Bradshaw, it is different from *healthy guilt* — the ability to recognize, admit, and accept personal responsibility for mistakes. It differs also from *healthy shame* — "embarrassment and blushing" due to exposure and "the source of creativity and learning" due to the realization of our human limitations, fallibility and fallibilism. In contrast to both healthy guilt and healthy shame, "[t]oxic shame, or the shame that binds you, is," according to Bradshaw, "experienced as the all pervasive sense that I am

discipline that requires them to abide by the oppressive, life-negating rules of their faith's implicit code of patriarchy and to never give head-room to real doubt concerning their fundamental religious beliefs.

In his book *Holding Fast: Dealing with Doubt in the Latter Days*, Brigham Young University professor of ancient scripture and author Robert L. Millet perversely (and I think suspiciously, for reasons which will become evident below) disparages religious doubt. Also, I think, he unwisely advises questioning or doubting Mormons to put their unanswered questions and unresolved doubts "on the shelf." He counsels them to simply say, in those areas where there are substantive questions or real doubts, "I don't know," while putting their unqualified and unquestioned trust and confidence in Joseph Smith and his successors. He then, as I see it, shamelessly and shamefully demeans *a priori* questioning or doubting believers by implicitly and presumptuously accusing them of

---

flawed and defective as a human being. Toxic shame is no longer an emotion that signals our limits, it is a state of being, a core identity. Toxic shame gives you a sense of worthlessness, a sense of failing and falling short as a human being [or as a good and loving child or sibling, or a dutiful, committed, faithful and loving spouse or parent, or, in a religious context, a faithful and righteous believer]....Toxic shame is [a neurotic disorder wherein the 'shame-based' personality considers itself as 'not (good, smart, lovable) enough'... [It] becomes an object of its own contempt [and assumes either too much responsibility for failure or too little, or none]....There is," according to Bradshaw, "shame about shame. People will readily admit guilt, hurt or fear before they will admit shame. Toxic shame is the feeling of being [self-alienated,] isolated and alone in a complete sense [, both when alone and in the company of others]. A shame-based person is haunted by a sense of absence and emptiness" (7–10).

"Both the neurotic and characterological syndromes of shame" (10–23), or toxic shame, "...[are] primarily fostered in *significant* relationships" (25) and are caused by various forms of authoritarian (or even benevolent-authoritarian) abuse inflicted by the 'shaming' attitudes and behavior of shame-based parents, caregivers, and authority figures in dysfunctional family systems and in those other organizations and institutions which consciously or tacitly embrace and recapitulate the inherently shaming, perfectionist, and moralistic ethic of cultural patriarchy. Shaming behavior is, in this sense, deliberate or reactive behavior that attacks another's *core* sense of autonomy, self-esteem, or self-worth as a person and causes or otherwise fosters, reinforces, and/or deepens toxic shame. Those who engage in such behavior either advertently or inadvertently do so 'shamelessly,' or without primary (or any) concern for the other's core psychological well-being. Usually those who are shameless are themselves either without a sufficiently strong sense of healthy shame (*i.e.* the realization of their own limitations and fallibilism), or are themselves neurotically and/or characterologically shame-based. Attitudinally they display an at times disguised sense of humble, righteous, or arrogant superiority and self-importance. Behaviorally they tend to shame others – for various and typically unconscious psychodynamic motivations – to control them (to possess them and keep them in line), or merely to vindictively or sadistically tear them down.

Given the above conceptual framework as context, it is important to distinguish between 'shameless, toxic shaming' and the shaming intended to *expose* it.

The *former* is intended to control or possess or tear down others to keep them in line with – or subordinate and in servitude to – some higher being, cause, purpose, or authority. This is done through the use, for example, of authoritative displays of disciplinary disapproval, disappointment, and condescending correction and counsel. This diminishes our core sense of autonomy, self-esteem, and self-worth as human beings.

The *latter* is shaming, through criticism, confrontation, and condemnation, and is intended to *expose* such shameless, toxic shaming. Toxic shaming tears down the individuals and keeps them in fearful servitude, while constructive shaming through the critical exposure and condemnation of toxic shaming seeks to stop the abuses and call the shaming offenders and their neurotic victims to their suppressed sense of healthy shame (or embarrassment) and to the pursuit of personal autonomy and well-being. In other words, not all shaming is toxic or shamelessly administered. At times it is necessary to invoke healthy shame through exposure and resulting embarrassment in order to break through the egocentricity of shameless abusers and the laziness of their shame-based victims who perhaps have found it quite advantageous to love their suffering or to obediently fall in line without question, doubt, or protest.

having such doubts because: (1) they lack faith or refuse to "see…through the eyes of faith," or (2) "they refuse to accept the demands of discipleship" and are therefore guilty of "gradual apostasy" and of disguising their "spiritual laziness" as doubt, or (3) "they have paid little to know" the truth (presumably because, again, they are 'spiritually lazy'), or (4) "they are living in a state of unrepentant sin" (2008, 29–33).

Millet's attempt to answer the question "why do people doubt?" by offering the above four causes as sources of religious doubt, conveniently (and I think disingenuously) leaves out an obvious *fifth source*. Some sincerely doubt the truth of their beliefs because of intellectual honesty and integrity!

This fifth source of doubt functions on the basis of "belief's own ethics" (Adler 2006), where the person *simply can no longer believe* without question (or at all) what doesn't make sense or is otherwise unbelievable without self-deception.[3] Doubt originating from

---

3 There is a tacit belief underneath each and every regressive fantasy or superstitious, wish-based belief known to man: a belief that *anything* is possible. This belief is perhaps founded, at least in part, on the defensively applied self-evident fact of human limitation and fallibilism. It is, as I see it, at the heart of both our expansive scope of imagination and our collective stupidity, gullibility, and epistemic irresponsibility as a species. It is, moreover, asserted defensively in justifying the indefensible and absurd belief in the actual existence of spirits, angels, demons, and gods.

Clearly, of course, not *everything* is possible, and not everything imaginable can be "proven" to be impossible or even needs to be proven impossible to be known to be so. As mature, rational adults, we all know without the need for "proof" that certain beliefs or truth claims are both false *and* impossible, based on what we know to be true about our world and the universe. We know, for example, that the childhood belief in Santa Clause is false; that it is impossible for reindeer to fly and for every home with children (with or without a chimney) to be actually visited by an ageless old man with requested gifts every Christmas eve. Likewise, we know it is both false and impossible, without the need for proof, for a fairy to place a coin under the pillow of a child who looses a tooth, for a goose to lay golden eggs, or for wishes upon a star to come true. We know as well that it is impossible for a square to be round or a married man to be a bachelor (as we commonly understand such terms). And we know it is impossible for a man to fly by flapping his arms, or breathe naturally and without assistance under water.

It cannot be "proven" of course that all the above examples, and all others like them, are in fact impossible. But we again know them to be so nonetheless. And as we shall learn and come to better understand in the pages that follow, we also know *a priori*, or without the need for proof by logical argument or hard evidence, that if we stop and really think about it, it is *impossible* to "know" as being *objectively*, *actually* or *literally* true any claim that is either considered to be utterly unintelligible (e.g. 'Jim drinks melancholy like peanut butter'), or that is both broadly (widely) considered to be *non* self-evident and utterly without truth conditions that would enable such a claim to at least in theory or in principle be empirically verified or falsified as being actually true (or probably true) or false (or probably false). Such unintelligible or factually vacuous truth claims can neither be proven nor disproven, for there is literally *nothing* intelligible to be known or empirically proved or disproved. It is therefore *impossible* to know that these claims are actually or literally true as claimed. Moreover, and significantly, it is reasonable to assert under the same conditions that what is being claimed *is* impossible *as stated*, for the same reasons.

We all know this, or should know this upon reflection. Still, though belief in mere possibility can be applied coherently and rationally to some areas of human concern, it alone, or in concert with invalid argument, cannot rationally or justifiably be invoked to accept as true those assertions, claims, or chosen and desired beliefs that are either utterly without truth-conditions (and therefore are not even *in principle* capable of being either proven or disproven because there is simply *nothing* to prove or disprove), or that contradict our best or most basic, common knowledge about the world and the universe and how they work.

Nor can the 'anything-is-possible' belief or sentiment be judiciously applied to matters which carry with them real personal and social consequences. For example, to gamble one's rent money in a casino on the belief that anything is possible could (and most likely *will*) result in bitter disillusionment or even homelessness. To take certain personally or socially consequential actions called for on the basis of, for example, believed revelations or commandments from a god could have the same effect. In most if not all human endeavors it

this source would make belief in the Mormon god and, consequently, the concepts of 'divine intervention,' 'discipleship,' and 'sin' in relation to 'God's commandments' impossible as even *probable* truth. Moreover, it would make such belief irrational as well, because to believe that which is impossible to believe would be incoherent.

To avoid or evade such doubt believers — following Millet's counsel — would need to deceive themselves by denying their doubt and/or rationalizing or explaining away the problem. This they could do by incoherently appealing to the mere *possibility* of their god's existence. In making this appeal, believers essentially assert that their god exists because the existence of their god is *not impossible, or cannot be proven to be impossible*.[4] The problem, of course, with such an appeal is two-fold. First, the move from something being 'not impossible' as an actual existent to being *certain*, or even *probable* is a *non*

---

is therefore clearly more reasonable and prudent to dispassionately or objectively apply the fact of human fallibilism *on the side of caution* and reasonable skepticism. One must factor in the odds or the likelihood or probabilities of certain desired outcomes based on what is *known*, *not* on the irrational, wish-based belief that anything is possible. Still, in matters of giving one's life to a god, mere possibility is clearly not enough for believers. While their ultimate defense of their faith might entail making the weak claim that "anything is possible" (which of course is arguably false in this case and would work against them as well), staunch believers must, in fact, consider their otherwise unbelievable beliefs as 'Truth' to believe and act on them at all, or to find any *real* (not illusory or self-induced) comfort in them. This, of course, and as stated above and throughout, requires self-deception. (For more information on the subject of self-deception, see Glymour 1991; Grossman 1996; Pears 1984; Rorty 1991; and Trivers 1985.)

4 There are, of course, familiar variations to this defensive appeal. First is the classic 'ontological argument' that 'God' actually exists because it is *possible* to conceive of such a being, and because to deny the actual existence of a being we can mentally conceive of would be incoherent. According to this argument therefore, and quoting George H. Smith (2000), "...if we can possibly conceive of an absolutely necessary being (God), then God must necessarily exist. Why? Because it would supposedly be contradictory to deny the existence of a being whose existence is absolutely necessary." Moreover, Smith continues, "[i]f it is possible for the most real being to exist, then it must necessarily exist, because existence is part of what it means to be 'most real'" (169). This argument and its variants have of course serious problems, and have been soundly criticized and challenged by various thinkers such as Aquinas, Gassendi, Hobbes, and Kant (see Smith 2000, 149–72).

While an in-depth analysis of this argument is beyond the scope of this particular work, and is not particularly relevant to either a defense or refutation of the Mormon faith, it is relevant in the context of this note. Suffice to say, for this *a priori* variation of the 'not impossible' argument to even get traction, believers and Atheists must possess an idea of 'God' that is intelligible, coherent, and factually meaningful, not merely imaginable or conceivable in a familiar sense. As George Smith correctly puts it: "No version of the Ontological Argument can hope to succeed if it must begin with a 'befogged' idea of God" (161). Moreover, even if, for the sake of argument, Mormon believers can somehow sensibly conceive of the existence of their god in its doctrinal fulness (which they most likely cannot do beyond mere assertion), such a conception does not necessarily translate to *cognitive* meaning. And either way, – with or without cognitive meaning – such a conception, if it did intelligibly exist in the minds of believers, would not necessarily establish the *actual* existence of such a being. See also Nielsen's treatment of this argument in his *Reason and Practice* 1971, pp. 146–67.

A second variation of this defensive 'not impossible' appeal is the familiar resort to the defense that 'God' exists because no one can prove otherwise. This defense, which holds that one cannot prove a negative, is addressed in Chapters 2 and 7 in this work. In fact, this dictum can only be applied in a narrow *empirical* context. In a *conceptual* context, however, it *is* possible to prove a negative on the basis of incoherence. Moreover, the inability to empirically prove the non-existence of a god does not either logically or empirically prove its existence. Any argument to the contrary would be invalid. The most a theistic believer of any faith could expect to gain by making such an argument is the admission from the Atheist that some being in the shape of a man who possesses intelligence, knowledge and power which exceeds man's, and who refers to himself to humans on earth as 'God' or 'Jesus Christ,' *might possibly* exist *somewhere* in the universe. Would this admission of unlikely possibility satisfy such a believer?

sequitur. Clearly, as used, to argue that something is not impossible is to argue merely that the something in question is possible. But the mere *possibility* of their god is not where highly invested and committed Mormon believers want to be. Second, the assertion that their god is not impossible makes their concept of 'God' factually vacuous, since within the realm of 'possibility' their god could be *anything* at all, even – 'God forbid!' – the god of a different faith.

Alternatively, believers could attempt to deal with the problem of their god's existence by begging the question of the issue at hand through a circular appeal to the putative existence of revelation from 'God' or faith in 'God.' The problem here, of course, is that both faith and revelation are necessarily dependent on the existence of their god — but that is the issue at hand! Moreover, if there is doubt concerning the actual existence of the Mormon god, how could there possibly be no doubt concerning the need for faith in that god and actual existence of revelation from that god?

Millet's implicit shaming of those with real doubts and explicit disparagement of religious doubt as something to be eschewed is not only wrong-headed and abusive (even if not intentionally so), but inconsistent with his own Mormon tradition. Regarding the inconsistency of his position, he (and others of like mind) need only pause to ponder or imagine what the consequences might have been if the founder of the Mormon Church, Joseph Smith, and his successors had followed the advice and admonition to "hold fast" to their pre-Mormon faith, put their religious doubt "on the shelf" and "doubt their own doubts" and contrary experiences, regarding them as "unnecessary" or counterfeits of the truth, inspired by Lucifer. Clearly he can't have it both ways without begging the question.

Further, regarding Millet's and other theistic apologists' disparagement of doubt as essentially the enemy of faith, they (and the reader) would do well to consider the fact that even the most devout fideists would admit to the salutary role of doubt in strengthening their own faith. Moreover, it is noteworthy to consider, in the words of Jennifer Hecht, "[t] he explicit idea that there *is* a history of doubt, one of great antiquity and global expanse" (2003, *xx–xxi*). As Hecht further states (with the addition of my bracketed interpolations) in the introduction to her notable book *Doubt: a history*:

> A few things about religion become visible from the history of doubt. One is that there was belief before there was doubt, but only after there was a culture of doubt could there be the kind of active believing that is at the center of modern [or developed] faiths. Until the Greeks filled libraries with skepticism and secularism, no one ever thought of having a religion where the central active gesture was to believe. Another is that doubt has inspired religion [*i.e.* religious invention and innovation] in every age: from Plato, to Augustine, to Descartes, to Pascal, religion has [been] defined [and invented] …through doubt's questions. Of course, this extends up to today [as evidenced, for example, by the advent of the Mormon faith through the doubts and resulting opportunistic inventiveness of its founder Joseph Smith].
>
> Doubters have been remarkably productive, for the obvious reason that they have a tendency toward investigation and, also, are often drawn to invest their own days with meaning. Many scientists and doctors [and philosophers] have been doubters of religious dogma, including the physicist Galileo Galilei, the Jewish theorist and doctor Maimonides, the Muslim philosopher and doctor Abu Bakr al-Razi,…the physicist Marie Curie [and the depth-psychologist Sigmund Freud, to name a select few]. Sometimes scientific [and naturalistic and analytical philosophical] methodology causes doubt by its example of questions and proof [or reflective

equilibrium], sometimes doubters are drawn to the sciences, sometimes both. Many ethicists and theorists of democracy, freedom of speech, and equality have also been doubters; in the modern period alone, these include Thomas Jefferson, John Stuart Mill and Harriet Taylor, Frederick Douglass and Susan B. Anthony. Great poets, too, from Lucretius and Ovid to John Keats and Emily Dickenson, have often written because they doubted God and an afterlife and had to work out the question with diligence.

The earliest doubt on historical record was twenty-six hundred years ago, which makes doubt older than most faiths [including, certainly, the Mormon faith]…Doubt has been just as vibrant [as belief] in its prescriptions for a good life, and just as passionate for the truth. By many standards, it has had tremendous success. (*xxi*)

In her chapter on "The Joy of Doubt" Hecht concludes by writing:

The story of doubt…has a relationship to truth that is rigorous, sober, and, when necessary, resigned – and it prizes this rigorous approach to truth above the delights of belief. Doubt has its own version of comforts and challenges. From doubt's beginnings, it has advised that if you create your own desires and model them after what you actually experience, you can be happy. Accept that we are animals, but ones with special problems [and evolved capacities to deal with those problems], and that the world is natural, but natural is just an idea that we animals have in our heads [most accurately, I think, without metaphysical foundations]. Devote yourself to wisdom, self-knowledge, friends, family, and give some attention to community, money, politics, and pleasure. Know that none of it brings happiness all that consistently. It's best to stay agile, to keep an open mind…In a funny way, the one thing you can really count on is doubt. Expect change. Accept death. Enjoy life…The only thing…doubters really need, that believers have, is a sense that people like themselves have always been around, that they are part of a grand history. (493–4)

Clearly, *pace* Millet, doubt regarding significant matters and decisions – and religious commitment is certainly not exempt – is neither "unnecessary" nor something to "put on the shelf" or otherwise dismiss the importance or existence of. The fact is, in matters affecting the significant commitments in one's life – as one's faith-based commitments to sacrifice, obedience and consecration are in the Mormon faith – doubt is not only impor-tant, but crucial to the exercise of epistemic and ethical responsibility.[5] There are in fact, when considering the commitments and suggestive power of religious belief and faith, high stakes and risks involved to personal and social safety and well-being.

Millet and other educated Mormon leaders and apologists, of course, know all this, including the grand history and necessary role of doubt in all areas of human endeavor, including their own faith. So what are they afraid of? If their commitment is to personal integrity and the honest pursuit of truth (as they would no doubt confirm) and they are convinced beyond a reasonable (or any) doubt that the Mormon god actually exists, that the Mormon faith is a "rational theology" (Widtsoe, 1915) and that the Mormon concepts and doctrines of 'God' and 'Salvation' are intelligible, coherent, and factually meaningful, then why condemn or otherwise block doubt by referring to it as a sin or threatening with damnation those who doubt? Why not rather extol doubt as the necessary virtue that it is

---

5 Regarding the importance of doubt on epistemic responsibility, John Dourley quotes C. G. Jung, who wrote: "Wherever belief reigns doubt lurks in the background. But thinking people welcome doubt: it serves them as a valuable stepping-stone to better knowledge." (1984, 18)

and welcome rigorous objective inquiry and analysis from those with sincere questions?

Furthermore, – to take this line of reasoning further – if they believe (as they must) that their god is a loving and powerful god who greatly values truth, integrity, and reason, as well as faith, and whose greatest desire is for all of his children to come to Christ of their own free will and endure in the faith until the end of their mortal lives so that they might return with honor to his presence and enjoy eternal life, then surely such a god, if he does in fact exist, would not – *could* not – allow those of his faithful sons or daughters who have sincere, legitimate questions and real doubt to sacrifice their integrity or fall away from 'The Way, Truth and The Life' — especially if this is a result of their sincere quest for answers to their questions or their honest pursuit of reasoned and revealed resolution of their doubts. Surely faith is not so fragile. If it is, why would it be required or even be deemed necessary by an all-loving and all-powerful god — particularly given the stakes involved? What good is a faith that cannot endure the skeptical eye of reason, or the critical scrutiny of an informed believer or investigator?

Moreover, according to revealed promise, such a god, if he actually exists, would intervene, as needed, where he knew it was the sincere desire of those with troubling questions, concerns and doubts to know the truth. He also would know that they were struggling in their faith and that their faith would not endure the weight of universal ignorance, skeptical inquiry, and reason. Surely, the Mormon god — who putatively possesses the quality of truth, and who is also allegedly just and merciful —would not, if he exists, judge harshly or condemn those of his children who, in the sincere exercise of their alleged 'eternal' or 'God-given' faculties of reason and volition, choose to question their faith. How could he condemn them for concluding after extensive, objective investigation, analysis and informed reflection, that none of the doctrines of deity or salvation in Mormon theology make sense (separately or as a whole) or cohere with our best justified knowledge about the world and the universe? If so with all the above, then why fear?

In light of the above, it would seem that the attitude of Millet and others toward doubt and their stated or implicit fears and concerns regarding believers rationally working through their questions and doubts through objective investigation seem incongruent with their own beliefs and faith. Perhaps – at a deeper, psychological level – their concerns betray their own unfounded judgments and assumptions regarding the causes (Millet's "sources") and motives of believers' questions and doubts. Perhaps their concern relates to the believers' competency and/or maturity in objectively and critically investigating the truth of their faith from all sides of the question. Perhaps, as I suspect, at an even deeper level, their unacknowledged disdain for the doubter is a *projection* and their fears betray *their own* suppressed or repressed doubts. Such suspicions are at least reasonable and plausible in theory, if not in actuality. In any case, it seems at least likely that authoritarian concern and hypervigilance in stamping out doubt betrays the doubt of the faithful. This is particularly so, I suspect, when those eschewing doubt as sinful, or threatening the questioning believer with damnation (or negative eternal consequences) also insist (with evoked sincerity, conviction and feeling!) that their own faith is unshakable.

Alternatively, if we acknowledge the simple truth of self-interest inherent in any patriarchal institution, another possible answer to the above question regarding what these Mormon defenders of the faith are afraid of becomes obvious. To allow and encourage doubt – and the objective, rational working through of such doubt – is essentially to threaten faith, which in turn can and often does compromise or undermine their power and authority and destabilize institutional credibility and commitment. These potential consequences of doubt place the very structure and existence of the institution at risk of radical transformation or dissolution.

Finally, and relatedly, let us consider again the above question, "why not extol doubt as the necessary virtue that it is?" It might be instructive to consider that by extolling and tolerating doubt Church leaders and members place their own and other believers' faith in jeopardy. Religious belief is a mutually interdependent phenomenon, where one's belief strengthens and sustains the belief of others and, conversely, the doubts of some weaken the beliefs of others. Doubters, dissenters and skeptics tend to break the spell of superstition and institutional group-think and are therefore not welcome among believers. If skeptics or doubters are open or vocal with their sincere questions and real doubts they are often excommunicated from the believing community, either officially or socially. Why? Perhaps in part, and as we shall learn, it is because for Mormon believers the preservation of their faith is not, in reality as they would like to believe, a testament of their steadfastness and valiancy. Rather, at a core biological level, it is a *perceived* matter of "life and death" (Faber 2004).

Notwithstanding, the best efforts of religious authorities to control or manage doubt, or of faithful Mormons to suppress, discourage and/or deny their own and others' religious doubts, neither can eradicate them by shaming or threatening the doubter, or (by following Millet, 2008) "leaning on others," "using the shelf," "doubting [their] doubts" or by merely making "the decision" to have faith no matter what.

The Betrayal of Doubt by Unintended Exposure

Those with real doubts cannot entirely obscure them from reflective insight or perceptive and objective observation. If we are truly honest, we will all admit – like it or not – that as Emily Dickenson so concisely yet insightfully put it: "*Faith is Doubt.*" At some level all believers are *questioning* believers. And again, all believers – admit it or not – have real doubts. This is so, as we shall learn, because belief is not knowledge,[6] and even

---

6 'Knowledge,' as conventionally understood, is that representation of reality – or rather those statements or propositions *about* reality – that is both justified and true. To be *justified* is, briefly, for statements or assertions about what is factual or true to be widely considered, on the basis of critically achieved overlapping consensus, as coherent with existing knowledge and objectively confirmed beyond a reasonable doubt on the basis of sound argument and — where indicated — reliable and valid evidence. To be *true* is, for such a representation of reality or claims or statements allegedly indicative of reality, to be *actually* so, or *actually* the case on the basis of such objective justification. Clearly both aspects of knowledge must be present for something to be *actually* known. Lucky guesses that happen to be true don't count. Nor does a justified statement that is not actually the case. Moreover, knowledge is only provisionally true, given, again, the fact of human fallibilism. So there is no such thing as 'absolute truth.'

'Belief,' – as distinguished from "[belief as] a psychological act of assent" (G. Smith 2000, 64) — however, is to be understood here as a proposition that is at best an intelligible, reasonable and, in principle at least, justifiable opinion, viewpoint or considered thought, assumption, or judgment. At worst, a belief is a warrantless assertion or opinion which is neither justifiable nor rational, or which is arrived at through flawed reasoning, invalid evidence, or unsound argument. It is held stubbornly in supposed virtue of one's alleged right to believe whatever one *wants* to believe, without any regard for reason or epistemic responsibility. At best, a belief is merely a reasonable and seemingly evident (or apparently self-evident) opinion or viewpoint that is not *known* to be actually true, and is moreover acknowledged as being neither formally justified nor

knowledge, given the fact of human fallibilism, is provisional and cannot coherently be regarded as absolute truth.

Accordingly, even if the doubts of Mormon believers are not admitted by honest confession, they are very likely to be betrayed in a variety of ways, too numerous to list in their entirety.[7] Consider then, for example, the following ways in which Mormons and other theistic believers might betray and thereby expose their doubts:

- Believers' doubts are likely betrayed by their fears and feelings of anxiety, uneasiness or, alternatively, by stoic indifference when their beliefs are seriously challenged.

- Believers' doubts are unknowingly and paradoxically betrayed when they are — as I was — drawn by curiosity to that which challenges or threatens their faith, as well as by an attitude (stated or not) that conveys a stubborn 'head in the sand' reaction to avoid serious challenges to their beliefs and those feelings that constitute their faith. Such an attitude in the latter case might be expressed in statements such as "I don't want to know your thoughts about religion," or "That's just how I feel," or "I don't care what you think; I believe (or feel) what I believe (or feel) and *nothing* you or anyone else says can change that." Either way, the believer's doubt is betrayed.

- Believers' doubts are also likely betrayed by their ultimate faith-based appeal to *certainty*[8]

---

necessarily true.

Metaphysical concepts of 'God' are, as we shall learn, highly problematical and *a priori* unjustifiable in principle. Religious beliefs that hinge on such concepts would necessarily fall in the worst-case category and would therefore be most subject to questions and real doubts, even if such questions and doubts are suppressed or repressed.

7 It can and should be admitted, of course, that this shoe fits on the foot of the nonbeliever or disbeliever as well. Certain attitudes and behavior might betray *their* doubts regarding their rejection of the putative existence of a god or the truthfulness of religious belief. In making such an admission, however, it must be acknowledged that for the religious skeptic or Atheist questions and doubt regarding their disbelief or nonbelief in a god are expected and welcomed in virtue of their acceptance of the fact of human fallibilism and the provisional nature of all truth. For Mormon believers (and perhaps other theistic believers as well), however, such questions and doubts regarding their belief in their god's *actual* existence are neither welcomed nor tolerable. The skeptic's *a priori* acceptance of the mere possibility of the existence of a god, as well as the fact of fallibilism and the provisional nature of all 'justified truth' (a *pleonasm*) cannot be shared by the devout, fundamentalist theist without making his or her faith in 'God' (or certainty in the absolute truth of their god's actual existence) incoherent. For the theistic believer, the mere possibility (or even probability) and provisional truth of their god's existence is not possible while claiming otherwise with certainty, even if the fact of human fallibilism is conceded.

8 Beyond neuroscientific and psychological explanations of the feeling of being "certain" about the correctness of wrong beliefs (Burton 2008 and Tarico in Loftus 2010), the expression of *certainty* — with either contained or expressed conviction — might be (and often is) a reaction formed defensively to suppress or repress doubt from exposure to self and others. Such an unconscious, self-deceiving defense mechanism is known technically as a *reaction formation* and may be considered or regarded, as suggested in Chapter 6, as being synonymous with the phenomenon of faith-as-certainty and conviction. It is also known – as we shall learn in Chapter 8 – as a *conditioned fear response* which unconsciously alters, in this case, the feared *truth* of the believer's real doubt to the *lie* of no-doubt. Moreover, a turn to faith in the mere possibility of religious truth claims – which turn is evident in the common forms of 'It's possible' or 'You can't prove it's *im*-possible' – naturally raises the question to believers of why they would be content with *mere possibility* when so much is required of them, when so much is at stake, and when so much more evidence could so easily be provided by their god.

or, alternatively, mere possibility when an informed challenge is made to their belief in the *actual* reality of their god, an afterlife, or the god's *actual, direct* involvement in their lives.

- Believers' doubts are likely betrayed by their experience of uneasiness or the gnawing persistence of unanswered questions when asked or expected to believe what doesn't make sense, or when confronted by a violation of some foundational expectation that results in apparent contradiction, confusion, disappointment, and disillusionment.

- Believers' doubts are likely betrayed when they experience some contradictory state of affairs such as loss of faith, nonbelief, wrong belief, or extreme suffering and loss through premature death, and they cannot conceive of *any* reason or purpose that would possibly explain or justify their god's failure to intervene — or at least to clearly and convincingly explain why the needed intervention did not occur as promised and in response to a real need and sincere petitionary prayer.

- Additionally, and more subtly as suggested above, believers' doubts are likely betrayed by the critical *projection* of their own uncertainty and doubts on other doubters, as evidenced by their negative *reaction* toward doubt in principle and the doubts of others, as well as the doubting believers themselves.

- Moreover, believers' doubts are likely betrayed by their turn from institutionally mandated belief in literal, legalistic, and fundamentalist scriptural interpretation and Church orthodoxy to a personal belief in a more developed, complex, and progressive (or liberal) theology with more metaphorical, esoteric, or metaphysical concepts of 'God,' salvation, and cosmology.

- Alternatively, believers might betray their doubts by picking and choosing or inventing what they *want* to believe, or feel *comfortable* believing, as, for example adopting a simple, child-like faith in a loving, kind god and a blissful, happy afterlife stripped of formal theology, doctrine, or requirements and expectations for salvation except simply believing and being 'a good person with a good heart.'[9]

- Another likely betrayal of believers' religious doubt is their exercise of moderation in living their religion where great zeal and commitment are called for and expected. Such a betrayal of doubt would be a rationalizing turn achieved by reframing luke-warm religious commitment to 'sensible' religious practice by denying certain strict doctrinally mandated, performatory requirements for salvation or exaltation." Alternatively, doubt might be betrayed by picking and choosing among the various interpretations or opinions of what it means to be a 'true believer.' It may be betrayed by diluting or watering-down certain doctrinal or performatory caveats regarding the disposition of certain 'gospel blessings,' therefore relativizing or minimizing — through rationalization, generalization, simplification, and modification — authoritatively established obedience requirements for divine acceptance and salvation.

This question is addressed in Chapter 6 in relation to the problem of faith as 'a way of knowing' and Chapter 7 in relation to the 'problem of prayer' and other irresolvable problems.

9 This version of theistic belief (or the simple faith of simple believers) actually reveals its own theology (and likely pathology as well) with its own concept of 'God' and set of 'dos-and-don'ts' for getting into heaven. It is a belief system usually based on a set of cherry-picked doctrines and moral imperatives from the scriptures and orthodox theology that make it easier for believers to avoid their doubts and continue to believe in spite of such doubts.

- Relatedly, believers might betray their doubts by humbly and meekly lowering their expectations of prayer. Instead of engaging in frequent, 'mighty prayer' – as scripturally exhorted to do — to 'draw down the powers of heaven' in pursuit of specific, promised blessings, faithful believers would instead opt to simply 'make their lives a prayer' and make their actual prayers rote, infrequent, general, simple (or child-like) and self-fulfilling, seemingly (if not actually) insulating their expectations from further, or possible, disappointment and their beliefs from further, or possible, disillusionment. Alternatively, believers likely betray their doubt by superstitiously praying obsessively and formulaically, and with exactness in form and language, as if to (incoherently) make sure their *certainly* 'all-loving' and 'all-knowing' god doesn't ignore or overlook their petition for mere lack of proper form and decorum, or somehow get it wrong for lack of exactness.

- Still another likely betrayal of believers' doubt might be their retreat to faith when confronted by the unintelligibility or incoherence of their beliefs, or alternatively their persistent use of trite generalities, known reasoning fallacies, and an evasive resistance to detail or specificity in either defending or explaining their beliefs to questioning believers or skeptical outsiders.

- Further, believers' doubts might be betrayed by their question-begging appeal to putative revelation to provide absolute or certain authoritative answers to troubling (unanswerable) questions challenging the existence of their god. Conversely, by the assertion of 'human fallibilism,' 'informed opinion,' and 'progressive revelation' they may try to explain away or relativize fundamental revisions to, or denouncements and disavowals of, prior doctrines, teachings and revelations believed to be authoritative and binding.

- Further still, the doubts of Mormon and other believers — as educated moderns — might be (and often are) exposed by their *incongruous behavior*. For example:

  - *Doubt is exposed* by existential anxiety manifested in many (perhaps countless) ways, such as refusing (as many believers no doubt do) to take sensible or necessary risks in life (as, for instance, traveling by air or by sea to transact business, vacation, or visit loved ones for fear of crashing or drowning and dying) rather than trusting in their god for safety, deliverance, or the fulfillment of his will. Believers may turn (with instinctive urgency and often greater confidence!) in times of actual or immanent danger or life-threatening illness to the 'arm of the flesh' (*i.e.* the police, the military and medical science) instead of 'legions of angels' or merely prayer or 'priesthood blessings.' They may desperately cling to life (and extremely costly and often painful life-support) — for themselves or loved ones — by seeking out costly and questionable healing options and fighting against death to the bitter end when confronted by confirmed, terminal illness. (Curiously, they do so in spite of their alleged certain belief in the 'better place' that awaits them after death — knowing full well that there is not one shred of valid or reliable evidence that would support the existence (and incoherent concept) of such a better place, or the likewise incoherent (and absurd) claim that 'God works or answers prayer *through* people.' They know the serious limitations of human knowledge, the inability of human beings to apply with consistent effectiveness or competence what little knowledge they have, and the obvious fact that human intervention has, overall, an abysmal track record at best in saving lives or alleviating suffering by force, remedy, or cure.)

  - *Doubt is exposed* by resisting the total, wholehearted commitment to living the religion as clearly and authoritatively prescribed or counseled. For Mormons this would mean *literally* 'hungering and thirsting after righteousness and truth' by 'feasting daily on the words of Christ (or scriptures),' engaging daily (or regularly) in 'mighty prayer,' 'following, both in spirit and to the letter, the counsel of the Brethren' (or General Authorities of the Church), and fulfilling *all* 'covenants with God' by sincerely striving to 'keep *all* the commandments' with '*exactness* and *honor*.'

- *Doubt is exposed* by refusing — on the false pretence of honoring the *decision* to believe and be true to the faith — the challenge (made below) to subject their religious faith to the same objective, skeptical, analytical scrutiny they would subject other questionable non-religious truth claims and other religious faiths to in the pursuit of truth.

- *Doubt is exposed* by explaining away, or rationalizing the incongruous behavior in all the above points through the *selective* and *question-begging* turn to scripture or putatively inspired statements made by those religious authorities who agree with or justify such behavior as being prudent, wise, or merely indicative of the 'God-given human instinct for survival.'

As alluded to earlier, doubt is paradoxically exposed by the *very assertion of faith or belief*. This suspicion is supported, at least analogically, by the following hypothetical example shared by Dan Barker, a former Christian Minister: "Truth does not demand [or require] belief. Scientists do not join hands every Sunday, singing, 'yes, gravity is real! I will have faith! I will be strong [and faithfully obey the law of gravity]! I believe in my heart that what goes up...must come down....Amen!' If they did, we would think they were pretty insecure about it" (Huberman 2007, 30). So too, I would argue, with religious believers who testify that they know the tenets of their faith are true. As we shall learn later on, the very existence of faith in 'God' is unintelligible, and its requirement as a necessary principle of salvation makes the concept of the Mormon god — or any god likewise requiring faith in its existence — incoherent. This conclusion, I submit, is at some level acknowledged by believers who ever so confidently speak of the putative truth of their *beliefs*, or retreat to their *faith* when their believed knowledge of the truth is seriously questioned.

Finally, doubt might be behaviorally betrayed by engaging, as Ernest Becker reveals in his *Denial of Death* (1973), in the unconscious (and theologically unnecessary) human pursuit of those 'immortality projects' that expose the religious defense against the unconscious terror of death for what it is — the 'great illusion' of man. Such defensive pursuits of immortality in the Mormon religion involve devout religiosity expressed in different ways. Examples include the 'single-minded' quest for righteousness or perfection through 'dedicated' Church service, Temple work for the living and the dead, missionary work, church and Temple-building, 'family-building' through Temple marriage (and — at one time — the practice of simultaneous plural marriage) and the procreation of as many children as possible, and the observance of religious traditions which, like all traditions, are perhaps best defined in the end – quoting Woody Allen in his film *Deconstructing Harry* – as merely "the illusion of permanence."

Imagine all of *this* energy expended by faithful believers just to *avoid* the lived truth of mortal existence — to *conceal* religious doubts and *preserve* imperfect or weak faith to preserve their illusion of divine purpose and actual immortality and eternal life. All this is done in the face of the clear cosmic meaninglessness and ultimate extinction that weighs on them *despite* their adamant denials and claimed beliefs and attestations to the contrary.

Of course, it does not necessarily follow that the actual existence of doubt in any way *proves* that the religious truth claims of the Mormon faith regarding the existence of the Mormon god are false or incoherent. Nor, conversely, does it necessarily follow that a *regressive* turn to an illusory god in a time of crisis, or the calm assertion of certainty or absence of doubt regarding the putative existence of the Mormon god, in any way indicates a belief in 'God,' or *proves* there is such a god, or that the Mormon faith is true. Both such assertions are clearly *non sequiturs*.

The point, again, is that doubt – *real* doubt – is an important state of mind which needs to be attended to, not suppressed or repressed. Such religious doubt in any form — suppressed, repressed, denied or not — can, from both a psychological perspective and common sense as well (in a broad, naturalistic context),[10] be considered a symptom that points to an inner conflict. It not only gradually exhausts the believer through more or less constant resistance to the experience of cognitive dissonance, but can — with certain personalities if suppressed and left unattended to fester — become sufficiently acute (even if *without* awareness) to catalyze aberrant behavior indicative of suppressed doubt. Such behavior can, at more extreme levels, be appropriately characterized as religious 'acting-out' (obsessive-compulsive and/or other-abusing behavior) and/or 'acting-in' (self-abusing/defeating/alienating behavior).

At very least, and significantly, religious doubt in my view needs to be attended to and resolved to allay the anxiety caused by cognitive dissonance. Beyond that, and pursuant to the arguments made, again, in Chapter 8 and the *Epilogue* regarding what I consider to be the inherent toxicity of the Mormon faith, the resolution of such doubt is necessary to (hopefully) free the questioning Mormon believer from his or her faith in 'God' (and Christ) and therefore from the likely or potentially harmful and dangerous effects of such faith.

Resolving the Dilemma of Doubt

The dilemma, of course, in attending to and resolving religious doubt, is that in virtue of our most stifling and stultifying beliefs and corresponding unresolved doubts and concerns "we are all," to quote the late M. Scott Peck, "trapped inside of a box, and the instructions on how to get out of the box are written on the outside of the box." This dilemma pertains, of course, to all believers — of *all* religions — who suppress or deny their doubts and refuse, for whatever reasons, to seek after the best justified knowledge

---

10 "[C]ommon sense," as David Eller (2007) correctly observes, paraphrasing Clifford Geertz in Geertz' essay "Common Sense as a Cultural System," "has much in common with religion: in fact, much of religion *is* common sense as far as the members are concerned....For most people in most religions, including most Christians [and Mormons] their religion amounts to their learned and inherited common sense" (420-21). Still, while, according to Eller, "...common sense...is not formal or organized, let alone creed-like" (420), it is not, *pace* Eller," what everyone knows'," but rather what everyone embedded in a particular life-form *thinks* (or believes) they know on the basis of what is culturally *familiar* to them in the narrow context of their particular belief system. This would suggest that when placed in the broader or *widest* possible context of common *knowledge*, metaphysical religious belief considered by believers to be 'common sense' is, nonetheless, nonsensical. It is in this broad or wide naturalistic (or Peircean) context that I use the terms 'common sense' and 'commonsensical' throughout this book.

they can acquire.

For those questioning believers — and again, all religious believers are, at some level and to one degree or another, questioning believers — looking for answers, the paradox here seems hopeless. How, after all (as the paradox goes) can anyone metaphorically *ever* get out of a box they're in if the instructions for getting out of the box are on the *outside* of the box? What if what is outside the box is unknown and evokes fear and anxiety? These, of course, are two separate questions. Clearly, in response first to the second question, the motivation to get out of the box is very personal. For some, the motivation to break out in spite of fear and anxiety might be the promise of personal freedom from experienced oppression of thought, feeling, individuality, and instinct. For others it might be the need to end the pain of self-alienation or the need to individuate. For others still, it might be the need to reclaim self-respect, or to reclaim the lost sense of epistemological responsibility and intellectual integrity suffered in consequence of self-denial, and of believing the unbelievable.

The answer to the first question is more straightforward and common to all who desire (or need) to get out of the box of confining religious beliefs — and to do so without socially acting-out. Hopeless as it might seem, there is a way to resolve Peck's dilemma. One such resolution consists of four requirements. Instead of putting unanswered questions and doubts "on the shelf," as Millet perversely suggests, theistic believers must *first* be willing to courageously – and with integrity – honestly confront and work through their real doubts and accept the fact of *human fallibilism*. In other words believers must be willing to relinquish (or at least suspend) their incoherent belief in the existence of 'Absolute Truth' and their claim to 'the *only* truth.'

The other three requirements are possible only if the first requirement has been sufficiently satisfied. *Second*, they must be willing to openly revisit their conceptions of *facts, knowledge, truth,* and *rationality* — topics treated in some depth in Chapters 1 and 2. *Third*, they must be willing to consider their *real* questions, doubts, concerns, and uneasiness about their religion *not* as shameful weaknesses (or ploys of "Lucifer") that should be denied, suppressed, or otherwise avoided. Rather, they must consider them as symptoms of — or 'calls' from — a troubled mind needing to be attended to and resolved. *Fourth*, they must engage in a rigorous, critical analysis of their religious beliefs (or truth claims) for intelligibility, coherence, and factual significance to determine if such beliefs are even *justifiable* as truth claims.

The first three requirements are more or less easily fulfilled, in my experience, if, again, the doubt is *real* or if a crisis in faith has ensued as a result. Alternatively, if real doubt is not a felt or acknowledged concern to believers, they might instead consider the fact of fallibilism in the first requirement and apply the prescribed approach of the fourth requirement to either test their beliefs or respond to the challenge to do so as an apologist or defender of the faith. *In either case*, the fourth requirement will require background information (provided, again, in Chapters 1 and 2), as well as critical thinking, hard, intellectual work, and honest self-examination.

Still, in either case, how specifically can such requirements be fulfilled from *inside* the box? One way to do so is provided by a former evangelical Christian minister turned Atheist, John Loftus. Fulfilling the requirements in the above paragraph would, as Loftus suggests, require believers — and particularly, I might add, those Mormon believers who

Philosophical principle that human beings could be wrong about their beliefs, expectations or understanding of the world.

are more deeply conditioned or indoctrinated — to "test [their] religious faith with the presumption of skepticism…" Or, in other words, "as an outsider… [or] disinterested investigator who [doesn't necessarily] think the religious faith in question is true since there are so many different religious faiths in the world" (2008, 66–67).

This approach is termed by Loftus the "Outsider Test for Faith" (66–77). Such a test, which is contrary to an *insider test* which is made circularly with the presumption of the truthfulness of theistic belief in 'God' and the historical and theological truth claims of their faith, would, I think, help believers constructively confront and resolve their acknowledged or unacknowledged and denied (though betrayed) 'real' doubt. In my estimation, and as shall be argued in the pages which follow, such an approach is beneficial to all believers, and is therefore important enough to present at some length below, and to reference repeatedly throughout this book as a reminder and invitation to readers.

To elaborate on this "Outsider Test for Faith," we can do no better than to let Loftus speak for himself (with a few context-relevant and hopefully enhancing, bracketed interpolations from me). Regarding such a test Loftus asks: "Why take such an extreme stance?" And then answers:

It's because that's how religious people approach all other religious faiths but their own. People approach other faiths this way all the time [particularly Mormons], so why not do that with one's own religious faith?

I'm arguing that [the religious believer of a particular faith] should adopt the presumption (or presupposition) of skepticism. If [you, as a religious believer,] simply cannot do this, then let me suggest [that you hypothetically] consider your faith from the perspective of an outsider. At the very minimum, a believer should be willing to subject her faith to rigorous scrutiny by reading many of the best-recognized critiques of her faith.

The outsider test challenges believers to examine the social [psychological] and cultural conditions of how they came to adopt their particular religious faith in the first place. That is, believers must ask themselves who or what influenced them and what the actual reasons were for adopting their faith in its earliest stages. Nearly all believers in an overwhelming number of instances simply end up believing what they were taught to believe by their parents [or what they – by nature, nurture, circumstance and need – are psychologically disposed and conditioned to wish for and believe]. The reason they adopt their faith in the first place is because of social, [psychological] and cultural conditions.…[J]ust ask yourself if your initial experiences [in adopting your faith] could be explained by a different, skeptical hypothesis [rather than by your religious presuppositions] and whether the initial reasons you had for your [adopting] your faith [including the subjective interpretation of certain feelings] were strong ones [in the context of more economical and commonsensical, naturalistic explanations].

For the Christian [or Mormon] theist the challenge of the outsider test means there would be no more [bearing witness or testimony, or] quoting the Bible [or Standard Works and the teachings and testimonies of the 'Prophets'] to defend the [claims] that ['God lives and Jesus is the Christ,' that the Mormon Church was 'restored' to the earth through Joseph Smith and is the only true Church, or that] Jesus' death on the cross [or suffering in Gethsemane] saves us from sins [and that his subsequent resurrection conquered death and consequently ensures immortality for all]… Why? Because [the believer] cannot start out by first believing the Bible [or other Standard Works], nor can [he or she] trust [Church leaders or other believers] to know the truth, nor can [the believer] trust [his or her] own anecdotal religious [or spiritual] experiences, since such experiences are had by people of all religious faiths who differ about the cognitive content learned as the result of these experiences. [Instead, the believer] would want evidence and reasons for these beliefs [assuming they made sense and were justifiable to begin with]. (67–71)

When employing the outsider test for faith the investigator or questioning believer (Mormon or not) essentially and necessarily adopts a particular *worldview* which, as Daniel Harbour succinctly and simply defines it, is "a set of assumptions about the nature of the world, on the basis of which one can begin to attempt to understand other aspects of the world" (2001, 9). Such a worldview, or set of acquired or chosen and developed "control beliefs…that control how we view the evidence" (Loftus 2008, 58–61) or interpret reality has, in this case, for Loftus and others applying the proposed outsider test for faith, "…an antidogma and antisuperstitious bias" which "must begin with skepticism" as "the default position" and place the "burden of proof" on those "making a positive knowledge claim" (59).

Harbour, incidentally, would likely refer to Loftus' suggested worldview (or 'control beliefs') as characteristic of — or perhaps even a subset of — what he terms "Spartan meritocracy," or simply the "Spartan" or "Meritocratic" worldview. This worldview, which might more appropriately and distinctively be termed a meta-worldview, or simply a 'meta-view,' is opposed, according to Harbour, to what he calls the worldview of "Baroque monarchy," or, similarly, the "Baroque" or "Monarchic" meta-view.

In his book *An Intelligent Person's Guide to Atheism* (2001), Harbour thoughtfully and, I think, correctly (as far as he goes) argues that the *meritocratic* (or Spartan) meta-view is superior — for a variety of reasons — to the *monarchic* (or Baroque) meta-view. This, he posits, is so "in the sense that only one [of the two meta-views] presents a plausible way to gain understanding" and, relatedly, "to build a [sensible and coherent] explanation and [justified] understanding of the world" (8, 11).

Paraphrasing Harbour, the *Spartan* (or meritocratic) meta-view essentially favors a *minimal* number of assumptions about the world and insists that *every* assumption *at least* make sense and, moreover, "must work and be seen to work" (10) in explaining the world consistent with other assumptions which also at least make sense and which work and are seen to work. I would add, they are, at least in principle, verifiable and falsifiable (or *justifiable*) as factual statements *about* reality, and ultimately are *coherent* with what we know (albeit provisionally and fallibilistically) about the world and the universe and how they work.

The *Baroque* (or monarchic) meta-view holds, by contrast, that "a certain set of assumptions [or beliefs]" is *presupposed* to be a priori true and, in Harbour's words, "is privileged in that one must accept them as [a priori] true" or as *properly basic* or *self-evident* without the burden of proof or justification. Moreover, in the *Monarchic* meta-view, "[if] one's [or others'] experience or commonsense or intuition or logic contradicts [that which is assumed to be a priori true] then the fault lies, not with the privileged beliefs, but with experience, commonsense, intuition and logic" (10). "The kernel," Harbour again informs us, "is that there are two ways [or meta-views by which] to look at the world. One starts with minimal assumptions and [acknowledging and accepting the *fact* of human *fallibilism*] recognizes that [existing beliefs or knowledge] may be wrong and need revision. The other starts with a rich [extravagant, and unjustifiable or unjustified] view of the way the world is and forbids revision of the basic assumptions (11).

"Recall," Harbour reminds us, "what the purpose of adopting a worldview is: to provide the basis on which to build [a pragmatic, intelligible and coherent] explanation and an understanding of the world. It should be clear," in this regard and as Harbour sees it, "which [of the two meta-views] is better placed to meet our urge to explain. The desire to [correctly and coherently] explain things [or to know how things *truly* hang together] is an admission of ignorance. So, the starting position is infected with ignorance. It is inevitably wrong. So, we should be prepared to recognize it as such and to revise it when it is possible to increase its accuracy. In order to minimize the scope for error, and in order to locate the source of such errors when they emerge, initial assumptions [or beliefs] are best kept to a surveyable minimum [and must be at least, in principle, justifiable]. Alternatively, it is either arrogance or folly to assume that an uninformed guess at the nature of Nature will be or should be beyond the need of [critical inquiry or] revision. Commonsense therefore commends the Spartan meritocracy as a sensible [meta-view]. In the quest for understanding [and explanatory value], it is clearly superior to the Baroque monarchy" (11).

Consistent with the meta-view of 'Spartan meritocracy' (and with Loftus' 'control beliefs,' or worldview), the proposed outsider test for faith does not beg the question by presupposing the falsity or factual non-reality of religious truth claims as a premise to the preconceived conclusion that religious truth claims are false, incoherent or factually unintelligible. Nor is the questioning Mormon believer (*pace* Millet) using this test to address only "seeming incongruities that pop up here and there" (Millet 2008, 132) or practical questions such as "whom we should marry, what job offer we should accept, what counselors we should choose, what we should do to deal most effectively with a wandering child…" (13). Rather, the Mormon believer, in this case, is challenged here to apply this outsider test to the bedrock religious beliefs and questions that represent his or her *real* doubts concerning the *core* concepts and doctrines of the Mormon faith. In doing so, significant questions are asked to determine whether or not the fundamental concepts of 'God' and the doctrines of deity, salvation, revelation, and faith are intelligible, coherent, and factually meaningful such that they might even be widely considered to be, at least in principle, justifiable as truth claims. Such a determination is obviously quite different than the *false choice* Millet resorts to when he, again, counsels questioning believers (from the inferior Baroque meta-view) to "exert every effort to ascertain whether the matter under consideration is of the Lord or of Lucifer" (105). By substituting "true (or probably true)" for Millet's "of the Lord" and "false (or probably false)" for Millet's "of Lucifer" we can bring his perverse counsel more in line with reason and with the superior Spartan meta-view which undergirds both the objective and methodology of Loftus' proposed outsider test for faith.

Like Loftus, combining his words with mine, I have "…investigated my [previous, Mormon] faith from the inside as an insider with the presumption that it was true. Even from an insider's perspective [and notwithstanding my own conversion, spiritual experiences, and persistent fastings, prayers, and faithfulness] I couldn't continue to believe. Now from the outside, it makes no sense at all. Christians [and Mormons] are on the inside. I am now on the outside. [They] see things from the inside [and appeal to those on the outside to see as they do and to accept their beliefs as factual and true]. I see things from the outside [and as a now skeptical outsider, and evaluate their insider beliefs, which are claimed to be as true on the outside as on the inside]. From the inside, [such claims] seem true. From the outside, [to the dispassionate, skeptical outsider who is not emotionally vulnerable, needy or excessively superstitious, they] seem untrue" (66). Clearly, as Loftus correctly observes, "[t]here are many religious faiths from which to choose." So how then, he asks, "does one actually choose to be on the 'inside' of any of them if from the 'outside' none of them have any plausibility? Unless one is on the inside as an adherent of a particular religious faith, she cannot see. But from the outside, the adherents of a different faith seem blind." If so, he concludes, "[b]elievers are truly atheists with regard to all other religions but their own. Atheists just reject one more religion" (66). This is particularly true among believers in the Mormon faith, and it is certainly true in my case regarding the Mormon faith.

Even so, it is worth noting in this regard that, according to Loftus, "[t]he basis for the outsider test challenge" — and the answer to the question of how it is that one chooses to be on the 'inside' of *any* faith – "can be found in a statement by [Christian apologist] John Hick," whom Loftus quotes as saying: "'[I]t is evident that in some ninety-nine percent of the cases the religion which an individual professes and to which he or she adheres depends upon the accidents of birth. Someone born to Buddhist parents in Thailand is very likely to be a Buddhist, someone born to Muslim parents in Saudi Arabia to be a Muslim, someone born to Christian [or Mormon] parents in Mexico [or elsewhere] to be a Christian [or Mormon], and so on'" (67). Hick's view is supported by certain notable works cited by Loftus in his book, including his reference to Hick (76). As for the converts, or the remaining *one percent*, including those without a previous faith and those who change their faith, the so-called accidents of birth likely include a variety of socio-psychological factors. Such factors and others (enumerated in Chapter 8 regarding the question of why faith exists and persists) no doubt combine with personal circumstances and emotional conditions to make the person more or less open, receptive and vulnerable to a particular faith. They no doubt appeal at the right time in the right way to that person's needs (or neediness), and also set-up the projective transference that establishes emotional faith (trust, love) in the 'Parent-God' (Faber 2004) of the new or different theistic belief system.

In the context of the above thoughts and observations it is worth repeating that the application of the suggested outsider test of faith would require Mormon, Christian, and other theistic believers to engage in the critical, conceptual analysis and critical thinking suggested in this book and in other notable atheological works cited and referenced throughout this book and in other books as well. In the end, Loftus concludes, "If after having investigated your religious faith with the presumption of skepticism it passes intellectual muster, then you can have your religious faith. It's that simple. If not, abandon it" (71).[11]

---

11 Loftus revisits his 'Outsider Test of Faith' (OTF) in his follow-up work *The Christian Delusion: Why Faith Fails* (2010, 81–106). After answering seven category objections to the OTF, Loftus addresses the initial objections of Christian philosopher and believer Victor Reppert who, at the end of his written criticism wrote, as still a believer: "If what it is to be skeptical is just to entertain skeptical questions about one's beliefs, to subject them to scrutiny, to take seriously possible evidence against them and to ask what reasons can be given for them, then I have been performing the outsider test since 1972" (102). To this seemingly dismissive statement, and its implicit argument that the OTF is nothing new and does not make a difference to true believers like him, Loftus presents his "Final Argument."

As context for this argument, Loftus reviews the supported conclusions of earlier chapters in his book

Unfortunately not everything that is simple is easily done. On the contrary, when it comes to certain beliefs it is very difficult to examine them critically, much less abandon them. What we are up against in dealing with Peck's dilemma is not merely a lack of liberating information or even its inaccessibility, but rather a common and misunderstood human condition. This condition, as is I think correctly understood by James Welles in his "Analysis of premaladaptive beliefs and behavior" (1995), entails essentially, and in the words of Welles, "…the learned corruption of learning" through the unconscious or willful disregard of important information (2, 3).

To understand why or how it is that otherwise intelligent and reasonable people do not access or utilize important information which is readily available to them is — as Welles puts it in the title of his book and throughout — to understand *human stupidity*.[12] For Welles

---

from anthropologist David Eller ("The Cultures of Christianities"), psychologist Valerie Tarico ("Christian Belief through the Lens of Cognitive Science"), and psychologist Jason Long ("The Malleability of the Human Mind") and then asks: "So on what basis do nearly all believers around the world, including Reppert, think they are the exceptions if [the supported conclusions of Eller, Tarico, and Long that we are all "enculturated" by "assumptions and premises;" we all tend to misinterpret evidence from a strong, built-in "confirmation bias;" and we, as humans, are only "partly rational," that "bias is our default setting, and most of the distortions happen below the level of conscious awareness" (102) are] the case?" Loftus then asserts "They CANNOT all be the exceptions! Believers are simply in denial when they claim their religious faith passes the OTF. Psychology has repeatedly shown us that people, all people, seek to confirm what they believe, and we also have an intellectual attribution bias to explain away what we intuitively know to be true. We do not come to our conclusions based solely on rational considerations. Because of these biases, *believers should be just as skeptical that their particular religious faith passes the OTF as they do when other believers in other different religions claim the same thing*" (103). This would entail, as Loftus points out, that instead of subjecting one's "own religious merely faith 'to scrutiny' as Reppert claims to have done," or, in other words, seeking "to subsequently understand, confirm, and defend what they believe," — which "…is not conducive to testing what one believes, so long as he or she has faith in the first place" — that the believer consciously and deliberately "repudiate such a faith stance," which is the basis of all theistic apologetics and theologizing, and which "can ONLY increase the level of confirmation bias people already have….Until believers repudiate such a faith stance," Loftus points out, "they cannot claim with a straight face that their faith has passed the OTF." In other words, and in "the language game of Christianity: *Faith is not something Christians can have while seeking to examine [and confirm] the religion that was given to them, since that is not how they approach any of the other religions they reject*" (103–4).

12 "When considering 'stupidity,'" Welles informs us, "it is important to distinguish between the term and the phenomenon. The term may be used to designate a mentality which is considered to be informed, deliberate and maladaptive. However, because of the existing taboo, this is seldom done. Usually, the term is used like an extreme swear word — a put-down for those deemed intellectually inferior, although this tactic normally reveals more about the attitude of the user than the cognitive abilities of the designate(s).

"As" — combining Welles words and mine — "a disparaging term for members of [either] an outgroup [or those who are known or assumed to 'know better' than what they believe or claim to be true] the word 'Stupidity' [, like 'idiocy,' 'stupid,' or 'idiot,'] often indicates little more than a biased [and/or exasperated] evaluation of [beliefs and] behavior [, and is often used either as a put-down for personally or politically expedient purposes, or as a tacit or intentional *ad hominem* strategy used to express annoyance, disapproval and frustration to shake others to critical self-evaluation].

"As a phenomenon, stupidity is most often a limited and limiting experience pattern (or, sometimes, one that is overexpanded and overextending). In any case, it is caused by a belief blocking the formation or function of [knowledge] more relevant to given conditions. Something going on in the environment is not matched in the cognitive world because the existing schema [or 'self-sustaining cognitive paradigm'] is too emotionally entrenched to permit an accurate appraisal of incoming data…

"There are really two dependent aspects to schematic stupidity: one is that a schema induces stupidity, and the other is that a schema is stupid. Almost every schema induces stupidity in that the schema is a belief "[t]he answer [to 'why people do not use certain information readily available to them'] has to be that some facts are emotionally disturbing and would be emotionally/socially disruptive if permitted to pass through the cerebral word processor. The emotional element throws off judgment — or provides a shifting basis for analysis. It is also the source of the 'Motivated ignorance' which characterizes the human propensity to be not just uninformed about ego-defining issues but biased by the values implicit in the linguistic system used to process data" (8).

Welles continues:

> It is this emotional factor which precludes objectivity within any linguistic system. Hence, stupidity is best construed as a social defense mechanism parallel to the Freudian defense systems which protect individuals from an overload of awareness. Just as many Freudian defense mechanisms are generated within individuals who fear self-knowledge, stupidity develops within a society to inhibit unacceptably accurate cognitions of both personal and institutional ineptitude. Along with idiosyncratic forms of individual stupidity, members of a society [or religious faith] exhibit collective forms of idiocy within the context of — or reaction against — social values [for, as examples, knowledge, reason, rationality, and psychological criteria of well-being].
>
> The induced subjectivity underlines the essential social nature of stupidity. Society defines awareness of reality as it funnels fictions into our consciousness. The mind is really a socially conditioned filter which a given experience may or may not penetrate, depending on the value structure of a particular society.
>
> In virtually all cases, stupidity is perpetrated subconsciously, in that the agent cannot sense, with his value system, that his actions are [nonsensical or] counter-productive in terms of that set of values. What he does sense is an emotional satisfaction that precludes any objective analysis on his part (and which is incomprehensible to any outside observer) because one does not consciously engage in self-analysis when cognitions are successfully shunted into

---

system which inhibits the formation of competing beliefs, hostile ideas and discomforting perceptions. Oddly enough, even a schema of 'Open-mindedness' can be stupid if it inhibits the development of clearer perceptions and an appreciation [through necessary discrimination] of the better ideas among those available. This is the chief drawback of the liberal schema, which tends to treat all cognitions, beliefs, forms of behavior and everything else equally (26, 27).

Earlier in his book, Welles elaborates: "In an epistemological context, stupidity is the failure to gather and use information efficiently. Traditionally, self-deception has been considered only in terms of the use or abuse of information present within a cognitive system – that is, a person would have to 'know' something in order to deceive himself about it. However, [and apropos to this and other atheological works,] we must acknowledge it is also self-deceptive (*i.e.* misleading) and usually stupid for one to *refuse* to gather [and critically evaluate with the presumption of skepticism] new, relevant information [or truth claims] about matters of importance....In virtually all cases, stupidity is perpetrated subconsciously, in that the agent cannot sense, with his value system [for, as an example, reason and rationality], that his actions are counter-productive in terms of that set of values. What he does sense is an *emotional satisfaction* that precludes any objective analysis on his part (and which is incomprehensible to any outside observer) because one does not consciously engage in self-analysis when cognitions are successfully shunted into emotionally acceptable if irrelevant categories" (2).

It is in the above epistemological context of 'stupidity' as a 'phenomenon' that I use the term herein or elsewhere, although I at times admittedly — and out of either sheer exasperation or with the at least tacit intent to hopefully shake the believer into critical self-appraisal — use this term as an *ad hominem* expression to attack what would commonly be considered by objective outsiders as stupid beliefs; *i.e.* those beliefs which are clearly or at least seemingly incoherent or inconsistent with common sense related to our best common knowledge about human nature, the world, the universe and how they all work. (See also Pitkin, 1932.)

emotionally acceptable if irrelevant categories. (8)

Apropos to our subject at hand, we further learn from Welles that "Contributing greatly to the culture of stupidity is the willingness of people to submit to higher authorities in matters requiring intellectual effort." Moreover, "[t]his willingness provides the psychological basis for the church and state….In their self-serving ways," and as we shall learn in our psycho-social assessment of the Mormon faith in the later chapters, *Epilogue* and *Personal Postscript* which follow, "these institutions feed on the weaknesses of people, making them weaker and keeping them from learning and doing things they might comprehend and accomplish [in their best interests]" (91).

In relation to religion in particular, Welles I think correctly observes that "One of the peculiar things about all religions, be they supernatural or superhuman, is that so much of their substance is demonstratively false [or incoherent]. Nevertheless," Welles sadly concludes, "religious beliefs are the driving force of society. People would really rather [stupidly] believe than know" (95).

Given the above perspective, it would seem that if theistic believers — Mormon or otherwise — cannot, will not, and therefore *do* not make a good faith effort to get out of "the box" of their "premaladaptive beliefs" (and there can be, to my mind as a hard determinist[13], neither blame nor praise either way in this regard) it will most likely be because of the *phenomenon* of 'stupidity' that Welles insightfully sets forth in his seminal work noted above, and the 'Motivated ignorance' that results from it.

The Therapeutic Path

Our affirmative, analytical, and then creative response to our symptoms — or religious doubts, concerns, and uneasiness in this case — is, again, necessarily therapeutic. It urges and enables us to maturely and responsibly create our *own* meaning and make our *own* moral decisions for our *own* life in *this*, our *only* life. Such an effort can seal the breach from reason revealed by our questions, doubts, and uneasiness. It can establish (or restore) personal integrity, or congruence, with our intellect and natural instinctuality, and with reality as we *really* – at some level beneath our well-protected illusions (or delusions) – know it to be. To this end the therapeutic path offered implicitly yet purposefully in this book is primarily philosophical in nature — *philosophical*, that is, with a small '*p*' denoting an approach that is pragmatic and anti-metaphysical. It is an approach that appeals to our needs for rationality, congruence (or integrity) and common sense, as well as to the related desire to truly know if, and how, our religious beliefs *actually* hang together. It helps us see how they cohere with the best knowledge we have about this physical world and the universe and how they *actually* work to create, sustain, and perpetuate existence as it really is, and as we *know* it (not believe it) to be.

Accordingly, and as we shall learn in Chapter 1, the analysis offered in this book is conducted primarily as a question consisting of many questions regarding the sense and rationality of commonly professed and accepted doctrines and beliefs which constitute — albeit informally — Mormon theology *however* it might be conceived. These analytical questions are raised to stimulate serious and critical reflection about Mormon beliefs in particular and, to the extent of any conceptual overlap, all other theistic beliefs as well.

---

13 The "hard determinism I endorse and espouse is perhaps best explicated and argued for by Derk Pereboom (2001), who refers to such a condition as "hard incompatibilism."

In asking such questions the intent, in part, is to offer the reader a provocative, sensible, and hopefully therapeutic way to work through questions and real doubts and concerns with intellectual rigor and integrity.

Moreover, by participating honestly as reflective, objective outsiders in this *analysis* of the Mormon faith, interested readers will be better able, if so inclined and motivated, to honestly entertain the socio-psychological *assessment* of their faith presented herein. Then they may perform — through additional study, inquiry, reflection and insight — their own more personal assessment of their religion (or any religion) to evaluate its rationality and fitness as a belief system, and to make sense of their religious inclinations, beliefs, and experiences.

In other words, by first engaging in this conceptual analysis of their faith, Mormon believers will necessarily deconstruct or 'unpack' the *idea* of their 'God' — *whatever* it might be — and all other truth claims which necessarily hinge on this central concept and related belief. In the end, after all the unpacking or analysis is done, intellectually honest believers, again as skeptical outsiders, will most likely, if not assuredly, find *nothing* intelligible, knowable or of factual significance to their idea of 'God' and therefore nothing *literal* to believe or have faith in. (This will necessarily be so for intellectually honest believers of *all* theistic faiths as well.) This inevitable realization will likely either gradually or more immediately break the spell of the religious transference. And the eventual occurrence of this likely outcome would then in turn (assuming, again, sufficient intellectual honesty, sufficiently honest introspection, and sufficient ego strength) free up dis-illusioned believers to retrospectively assess the social and emotional risks and once believed benefits of their faith. Importantly, they will discover more sensible and plausible *naturalistic* explanations for why and how it is they believed and felt as they did — as well as why their faith existed and persisted *in spite of* their nagging questions, concerns, and real doubts.

As with all such worthwhile efforts, the two-pronged task of *analysis* and *assessment* prescribed and conducted in this book (and referenced in its title) is neither simple nor easy. It will require considerable courage, mental effort and reflection, as well as the temporary suspension (to the degree possible) of both belief *and* doubt to make room for critical analysis. I can only say in this regard, as one who has made such an effort, that the beneficial outcomes and benefits of such analysis and assessment far outweigh the time and effort expended, and even the anxiety that might be experienced.

Reactions, Evasions and Deflections

The suggestion to skeptically test the religious beliefs or truth claims of one's faith as an objective outsider, particularly the core concepts of the god of one's faith, might be objected to at the onset as being, in some sense, inappropriate or improper. The objection in this case might be that although deconstruction *per se* (the process of taking something apart and examining it analytically in order to determine what it is or is not, or to expose biases, flaws, or inconsistencies pertaining to the claim of its existence) is certainly indicated in various secular areas or matters of concern requiring different forensic disciplines, it is neither relevant nor appropriate in understanding, evaluating, and adjudicating religious knowledge or truth claims.

But to this objection it might reasonably be asked: Why not? If the reason is that religious knowledge is established and evaluated on the basis of revelation and faith, then one might reasonably ask, — as shall be done (along with many other questions) in Chapters 5 and 6 respectively — revelation from *whom* or *what* exactly, and faith in who or what exactly? If the answer to both questions is "God," and the claim is made that such a god, as a putative being, *literally* or *actually* exists as conceptualized, then such a claim, as an assertion of actual fact, must be warranted or justified to be rationally accepted as such, or committed to if such is allegedly required.

One way to approach such justification – and arguably the only intelligible way – is, again, to deconstruct the *concept* of 'God' (the way the term *God* is used or represented in statements of doctrine or belief) to determine whether or not it is intelligible, coherent, and factually meaningful and, if so, whether or not it logically fits or coheres with our best, current knowledge about the world and the universe. To get to such a two-part question without relying presuppositionally on faith or revelation requires the use of some pragmatic method of analytical *philosophizing* to get to the bottom of the matter — if indeed there is anything at all to get to the bottom of. Inasmuch as theists insist on regarding their concept of 'God' as *actual* truth, and inasmuch as such a claim is not widely accepted (among believers, nonbelievers, and disbelievers) as being foundational or self-evident as specified, then as with all such truth claims, justification through deconstructive conceptual analysis is indicated.

To argue otherwise, on the sole basis of mere assertion, is to do so invalidly and to no effect. When we play the game of truth-telling by asserting as actual truth the *literal* existence of some existent (or experience), we are playing in a domain in the *natural* world. We must, if our assertions are *not* widely acknowledged as basic or self-evident, play by the justificatory rules which establish *knowledge* in that domain. Again, analytical deconstruction is commonly used and respected in every area of the natural domain where knowledge of or about a particular aspect of reality is sought after and valued. There is no good reason I can conceive of that would exempt the quest for religious knowledge from such a practice — particularly since religious beliefs are held by believers to be actually, literally true. Any argument for doing so would seem, to me, both arbitrary and unwarranted.

Beyond this likely initial objection, the conclusory remarks made throughout this book will likely evoke a variety of different reactions. One common reaction to critical assessments of religious faith in general comes in the form of a *tu quoque* ('You too') argument — an evasive strategy that is, as we shall learn in Chapter 2, employed by believers to argue for the existence of their god and their faith. Such an argument seeks to evade critical arguments and assessments of their personal faith, or of faith itself, by turning the tables on the disbeliever.

Three examples should suffice. First, to the argument that religious believers invalidly presuppose the existence of their god in asserting the truthfulness of some questionable aspects of their faith, believers simply evade the issue or concern by arguing that the disbelieving critics of their faith also invalidly beg the question by presupposing the non-existence of 'God' in questioning the validity of the beliefs at issue. Secondly, to the argument that religious believers rely on faith to believe without valid reasons things that are unreasonable, believers evade the issue of faith as an illegitimate way of knowing by arguing that even disbelievers, or Atheists, rely on faith. Thirdly, to the argument that religious believers likely betray their doubt through particular attitudes, behaviors, or actions

xlii   Thomas Riskas: Deconstructing Mormonism

(or inactions), believers evade the possibility or likelihood of their own doubt by arguing or asserting that critical disbelievers are really unrepentant or wounded believers who doubt their own atheistic position. Or, more pointedly, it may be claimed that disbelieving critics of religion in fact betray their belief in 'God' through their misdirected criticism of the faith, and refuse — because of pride and/or the pain of perceived abandonment and betrayal by 'God' or his chosen leaders — to humble themselves before their god for forgiveness and the renewed witness of the Holy Spirit. This turning of the tables seeks to put outspoken religious critics on the defensive by exposing the alleged incoherence of their position. It asserts that it is an impossibility for them to be both critical of the faith (and therefore angry with 'God') and an Atheist.

In all three examples the issue or concern at hand is evaded by attempting to turn the tables on the disbelieving Atheist or critic. But this will not do. The strategy itself is a thinking fallacy at best, and a specious argument at worst. Below, we will look at each example separately.

In the first example, the issue or concern is with the theist's lack of justification in believing and claiming a particular belief as literal truth. For the Mormon believer to assert his knowledge of truth, for example, that the Mormon god exists because revelation from that god has somehow established it to be so, is to beg the question, or invalidly argue for a god's existence on the basis of revelation from the god by assuming or presupposing the same god's existence as the revealer. A believer may, however, accuse the Atheist of doing likewise in arguing for the falsehood or incoherence of the belief in question — of presupposing, in other words, the non-existence of 'God' by asserting that the believed concept of 'God' — the way the term 'God' is used in a particular faith — is unintelligible or inconsistent with what we know about the world and how it works. This is not only false or not necessarily so at its face, but entirely misses the point. It evades entirely the question at issue, *i.e.* the justifiability of a seemingly unjustifiable belief.

In the second example, the undiscriminating use of the term *faith*, together with the unjustified conflation of theistic faith with atheistic 'faith,'[14] invalidates the theist's

---

14 The unjustified conflation of theistic faith with atheistic 'faith' is akin to the likewise unjustified conflation of religious faith with 'faith in science.' This *tu quoque* maneuver is invalid on the basis of competing methodologies for acquiring knowledge. Religious faith is a trust based on the believed actual existence of a god and revelation from 'God' about 'God,' and his putative relationship to man and the world. It is a trust based on, and allegedly confirmed by, human feelings and the fallible, subjective interpretation or exegesis of such affective experiences or scripture. It is based on a self-sealing and self-referential hermeneutic. According to Eller (2004), the religious 'methods' (of exegesis and mysticism) "violate the standards of reason and therefore cannot yield trustworthy knowledge. Exegesis [of scriptural texts or authoritative discourse] commits the fallacy of appeal to authority; why should we take that source as an authoritative source in the first place? It is interpretation, nothing more, and therefore only as valid as the original source and interpreter. That is why," Eller correctly observes, "we find so many — and conflicting interpretations of any original source or scripture.... [M]ysticism," on the other hand, "commits the fallacy of appeal to personal experience, whether it takes the form of intuition (making the 'discovery') or revelation ([confirming the 'discovery' or] having the 'discovery' handed to us). How do we know," asks Eller, "a real intuition or revelation has taken place, and why should we accept one over another? A report of a mystical [or spiritual, religious] experience is nothing more than a testimony...which still needs to be verified. And that raises the even more damaging empirical problem: mysticism does not produce consistent, objective, verifiable experience [which can be verified by objective, definitive criteria for verification or falsification, because such criteria do not exist] (196–7).

'Atheistic faith' (if such words can be coherently used together) is merely a conviction that there are no gods, or that the Atheist is justified in not believing in the existence of any god. It is based primarily, and according to George H. Smith (2000), on at least three methods of argument:

(1) "*onus probandi, i.e.,* the onus (or burden) of proof...which states that the burden of proof falls on

argument. As David Smalley writes in his article "The Faithful Atheist," published in the February, 2009 issue of *American Atheist*: "We must remember that all seas are at the same level, regardless of depth. On the surface, they appear to be the same — but once you're in the water, the bottom can mean all the difference in the world! Simply because two people have faith [in the lexical sense of 'complete trust, especially with strong conviction'], it does not make them equally blind to facts [sense and reason]. Faith [in this particular sense] can be both *justifiable* and *unjustifiable*.

"Since," according to Smalley, "… Atheists do not have all the answers, some level of justifiable faith [or reasonable confidence or trust,] is required, in the literal sense [in order to take necessary action]….But…when a greater amount of knowledge is [acquired], a smaller amount of faith is required….The Atheist [unlike the theist], has not made a single claim to require faith, except that all supernatural claims are without sense, coherence, or proof. If an Atheist has faith in anything, it's that theists [incongruously and selectively] accept fallacies as evidence [to justify their unjustifiable beliefs]" (25).

In the third example, the *tu quoque* strategy fails on other grounds. For a former believer to be critical of a particular religion does not necessarily entail a passionate criticism of, or anger toward, the god of that faith *per se*, or a tacit admission of belief in 'God.' A disbelieving critic very well might have been wounded in and by a particular faith, or religious belief system, and even bear, at some level, contempt for himself and others in that faith for indignities suffered because of self-abandonment to the toxic beliefs of that faith and mistreatment by others in the faith. Such a person might consequently be passionately critical of a particular faith (and those who are part of it), including the *idea* or *concept* of the god in that faith, while disbelieving the claimed existence of *any* god on the basis alone of the impossibility of such belief due to its falseness and/or incoherence. The *tu quoque* argument that belief is betrayed by passionate disbelief is simply a

---

the person who affirms the truth of the proposition, such as 'God exists'," and not on the Atheist, in this case, who, given the failure of the theist to provide such proof, affirms the truth of the proposition that the theist's claim is unproven. It constitutes a false and consequential move that would have the "treacherous implication" of immunizing all beliefs from any and all criticism and bestow upon beliefs which are not (or cannot) be proven true "the same cognitive status as a belief that could be proven true" (31–4);

(2) 'conceptual analysis,' which is the method of determining whether or not the concept of 'God,' the way the term *God* is used in a particular religious language-game, is intelligible, coherent and, in principle, factually (or cognitively) meaningful, and therefore whether or not the proposition 'God exists' is justifiable as a truth claim (34–38).

(3) 'Occam's Razor;' a principle that suggests that "mental entities (*e.g.*, concepts and explanations) should not be multiplied beyond necessity, *i.e.* beyond what is minimally required to explain the phenomenon in question….The [Atheist's] argument from Occam's Razor," according to Smith, "does not appeal to the logical impossibility of God's existence; rather, it claims that God does not exist because the concept serves no explanatory function. Naturalism is at once a necessary and *sufficient* mode of explanation, so we have no need to invoke the existence of supernatural causes" (38–43).

Finally, 'faith' or trust in science, on the contrary, is not based on the believed absolute truth of the products or findings of science (as many religious believers and apologists wrongly or disingenuously assert), but rather on its methods of observation, skepticism, analysis, and self-criticism. These are methods which, though conducted fallibilistically, are not self-referential or self-sealing, but are of necessity subject to rigid rules of evidence and subjected to rigorous, critical, and skeptical peer review and continuous challenge and revision. Clearly, trust and confidence in knowledge derived through conceptual analysis or methodological naturalism is justified, whereas knowledge asserted merely on the basis of religious faith is neither justified nor – as argued herein – justifiable. As shall be argued in Chapter 6, religious faith is simply not a legitimate way of knowing.

non sequitur.[15] Even if, solely for the sake of argument, the proclaimed Atheist was, in fact, a wounded believer, that fact alone — together with the fact that the same or other wounded or offended believers might have made false accusations about the Church or the faith in the past — would not necessarily invalidate the *present* reasoned arguments made for the non-existence of a god. To argue for such a conclusion would be to do so invalidly on the basis of a *genetic fallacy*.

Another common reaction of those Mormon or otherwise religious readers who have real questions and doubts but nonetheless will not or refuse to apply the outsider test for faith, might be expressed confidently, defiantly or dismissively — if not perhaps somewhat anxiously — by the assertion that they *cannot* doubt their faith or approach it as a skeptical outsider. They cannot do that because they *know* it to be true in virtue of what they have personally experienced and felt as evidence of their 'God's' or 'Savior's' existence. Alternatively, such a resistance to objectively test their faith might be expressed in the question: "What if your analysis of Mormon theology is wrong and there really *is* a God and the Mormon Church really *is* the only true Church of Christ on the Earth?"

The first variation of resistance is, as we shall learn primarily in Chapters 6, 8, and the *Epilogue* of this book, indicative of the transferential hold the faith has on the enthralled and conditioned believer (or so-called *convert*), as well as the conditioned interpretation(s) the believer places on his or her putative spiritual experiences. The second variation of resistance is, in the sense intended here, indicative of stultifying superstition instilled through (and reinforced by) deliberate conditioning derived from up-bringing and religious mind-control. It is not indicative — in the form of the above paradigm question asked — of a Pascalean wager suggesting the need to make a choice for religious belief on the basis of upside benefit and downside risk. Rather, the implication here, with this particular question, is that something very bad or sad will happen to doubting or questioning believers if they turn away from 'God,' religion, and the Mormon Church — if not in this life then the next. What if they are *wrong*? It doesn't matter in this case that there is not a stitch of evidence to support such a belief or fear, or that such a fear makes no sense and is utterly absurd and irrational. Such a fear, though absurd and irrational is nonetheless very sincere and real to deeply programmed, superstitious believers who are asked to objectively analyze and assess their faith.

There are, of course, no ready or compelling answers or arguments for such believers. They most likely acquiesced to religious belief for essentially the same reasons they hold to it — social conditioning and pressure, personal circumstances, co-dependence, guilt,

---

15 In this regard, George H. Smith writes that "It is understandable why the personal atheist [or former believer turned disbeliever] is sometimes hard on his former religion. This militant posture is the natural reaction to the deceit of antiatheistic propaganda. The personal atheist has no problem with the [believer] who rejects the case for atheism after careful consideration [with the presumption of skepticism]. But this is a rare occurrence, as the personal atheist well knows. Rarely does the [theistic believer] regard atheism as credible, so he dismisses it outright as unworthy of further investigation. And it is this [smug and cowardly] contempt for atheism [and judgment of Atheists] that generates a counter-contempt in the personal atheist, who knows that doubt will not land one in the [moral] abyss depicted in [religious] propaganda" (2000, 27). There are, of course, other understandable explanations for militant personal Atheism, including a natural resentment toward those beliefs and believers who might have inflicted harm on the personal Atheist, as well as Nietzschian contempt for the offence that Christianity in all its forms is upon the nature and intellect of human being. (For the author's personal treatment of this topic, see the *Personal Postscript,* and its related footnotes.)

anxiety. or fear. Shame-based co-dependence and related hypnotically induced dissociative transference are very common psychopathological phenomena, as are the obsessiveness and auditory and visual hallucinations and delusions that accompany them. Likewise, superstition, as a false belief, is a primitive irrational response to the unknown, rooted in ignorance, fear, and trust in chance, luck, and magic. It is, in essence, our evolved tendency to anthropomorphize and attribute magical powers and agency to random and/ or correlated affects, events, and circumstances. We have a tendency to see, assume, or predict intentional and magical (or divine) causality and consequences where none exist.

Perhaps, in the end, and on a sincere note, the only and most effective remedies for these forms of resistance are higher education. In more severe cases, where higher education, reason, common sense, and *necessary* social embarrassment cannot break the stubborn, transferential spell of religious belief — or where superstition combines with death anxiety and morbid dependency to form an also stubborn obsessional neurosis — an appropriate regimen (or more) of cognitive therapy is indicated for the treatment of fears and anxiety caused by superstitious beliefs. Psychodynamic psychotherapy may be needed for the treatment of co-dependency and existential anxiety associated with shame, guilt, and the fear of separation or death. In both cases, such therapy would best be administered by a *non-religious* and *qualified* psychotherapist.

Yet another common reaction by believers challenges atheistic arguments by asserting that the existence of their god and supernatural spiritual phenomena are at least *possible*. This reaction was addressed earlier in a different context as an evasion of religious doubt and in a note related to the ontological argument for the existence of 'God.' In this particular context, however, this reaction has two parts: "What if I'm right?" and "What if you're wrong?" Both defensive reactions, apart from the soon-to-be-argued incoherence of the concept of 'God' in *all* forms of theism — and therefore the irrelevance of these questions. What *exactly*, in actuality, and after all is there to be 'right' or 'wrong' about? These questions trade on the currency of 'possibility.' They assert at least implicitly that "It's *possible* that what I (as a believer) believe is true and what you (as an Atheist or Agnostic) believe is not true."

It shall be argued and concluded that the conditioned interpretation of *all* religious (or spiritual) experience is believed in spite of more plausible and parsimonious naturalistic explanations to make room for the hoped for possibility of the otherwise questionable existence of a god that is, at some level, doubted. However, this retreat to possibility nevertheless, and perhaps ironically, does not (cannot) provide the needed support or comfort to the theistic believer whose beliefs regarding the *actual* existence of a god and his 'Plan' and 'Word.' These are held presuppositionally with certainty as Absolute Truths, not as mere possibilities or even probabilities. Nor does it provide license to believe as exclusively true any particular theistic (or non-theistic) version of reality. For clearly, beyond the impossibility of having a "point of view from nowhere" (Nielsen 2001, 214), once the door of possibility is open to one view of reality, it is open to all, regardless of how diverse or seemingly absurd or contradictory all others might seem.

Believers cannot have it both ways here. For if their particular faith is possible, then *all* competing and alternative faiths are necessarily also possible, making the claim of exclusive religious truth for one possible faith among all other equally possible yet different or contradictory faiths incoherent. More specifically, *none* of the self-regarded possibly-true religions could coherently regard themselves — as the Mormon faith does — as the only true Church (or Religion), a fact which is certainly not acceptable to Mormon believers or theistic believers of other faiths for that matter.

Further, while in response to the question "Isn't it possible that you might be wrong?" the Atheist or Agnostic will (if intellectually honest) admit, on the basis of human fallibilism, that it is certainly *possible* (though not likely) that he or she is mistaken, the Mormon believer in particular cannot respond likewise to the same question. For as we shall learn in Chapter 5 and explore further in Chapter 8, the fact of human fallibilism may only be adopted by Mormon believers insofar as their fundamental beliefs in the existence and absolute truth of their Godhead, their Gospel, their Church, and their scripture is not brought into question. In other words, for Mormon believers the fact of human fallibilism may only coherently be used apologetically to account for revealed changes or corrections to, and/or disavowal of, prior and putatively inconsequential teachings, and revelation. They cannot, as I shall argue, do this for once-regarded authoritative and binding foundational revelation which, at one time, was believed by the President and General Authorities of the Church (or anointed 'prophets, seers and revelators') and Church members to have salvational consequences. Again, as with the problem with possibility above, Mormon believers cannot coherently have it both ways. To insist otherwise would be to create thereby, out of an arbitrary and indefensible double-standard, a double-bind which threatens their faith either way.

Still other predictable reactions from Mormon leaders, apologists, and other believers who might read this book would include at least the four following paradigm deflections that are followed in each case by a brief reference to the relevant Chapter(s) of this book.

"In the eternal scheme of things, none of the questions asked or conclusions reached in such an analysis are important. It is only important to believe that God lives, that Jesus is the Christ, and that Joseph Smith was and is a true Prophet of God, called in these latter days to restore the fulness of the gospel and the priesthood to the earth in this 'the last dispensation of the fulness of times'." But as we shall learn in Chapters 3 and 4 there are serious problems with Mormon doctrines regarding 'God, the Father' and 'Jesus, the Christ,' the divine act of 'Atonement' and the other two so-called 'pillars of eternity' — the 'Creation' and the 'Fall.' These, along with other fundamental 'doctrines of salvation,' comprise their god's putative 'Plan of Salvation.' Moreover, there are very serious historical problems concerning the claim that Joseph Smith was who he said he was and is who he is believed to be by faithful Mormon believers. (See, for example, Anderson 1999; Brodie 1995; Vogel 2004; Palmer 2002 and resources noted in *Appendix B*.)

"Pay no attention to the philosophies or theories of men. The 'mantle of the Prophet' and the 'power of the Spirit' are far greater than the intellect. The things of God can only be known and understood by the Spirit of God through revelation from God." But as we shall learn in Chapters 1 and 2, the questions asked and conclusions reached regarding the intelligibility, coherence, and factual significance of first- and second-order Mormon discourse and the rationality of Mormon theology are based on common sense, common practice, and sound reasoning. They do not depend upon any particular or arbitrary theory or formal 'Philosophy' of meaning (with a capital '*P*'), knowledge, or truth. As we shall

also learn in Chapters 5 and 6, there are serious problems with regarding perceptions and feelings as reliable indicators of knowledge. More specifically, there are serious problems with the Mormon theological concept and doctrine of divine revelation and the concept of 'spiritual confirmation' of truth — and also with the concept of faith as a legitimate 'way of knowing' truth.

"God's ways are not man's ways and God's timetable is not man's timetable. Some things cannot be understood in this life or are not for man to know at this time or in this life. The main thing is to not question your faith, but rather surrender to His timetable, keep reason in its place and, through the prayer of faith, hold fast to your faith in God and in Jesus Christ." The assurances typically offered by Mormon Church leaders and apologists are typified by Millet: "He [God] knows us best. He knows when and how and under what circumstances an answer [to a troubling question, need or concern] should be given, when we are prepared to receive it, and at what point the divine response and counsel will be most cherished and then followed" (2008, 13, 14). This is, however, very problematic, if not utterly incoherent, given the problem with the Mormon god's putative attributes addressed in Chapter 3 and the problem with the doctrine of 'revelation from God' addressed in Chapter 5. Further, as we shall learn in Chapter 7 there is much to be troubled about concerning the extent of suffering and premature death in the world due to human and natural evil. There is also the problem of prayer and the extent of religious confusion and theistic nonbelief, disbelief, and wrong belief (or religious apostasy) within and among the numerous faiths, nonbelievers, and disbelievers in the world. As we shall also learn in Chapter 6, there are serious problems with the theological concept and Mormon 'first (and fundamental) principle' of faith in 'God' and in Jesus Christ — not the least of which are that such faith exists and is even required and tested.

"God our Father does not expect perfect knowledge on the part of those who love and serve him; he who knows all things knows that we do not. What he does ask of us is not to surrender to our doubts. What he does call upon us to do is to pursue answers to questions with unconditional and unqualified trust in him and his anointed servants, and not to allow those questions to fester and morph into doubts" (Millet 2008, 36). But if the question concerns whether or not the Mormon concept of 'God' as taught and believed is intelligible, coherent, and factually meaningful (the central question addressed in Chapter 3), then this particular paradigm reaction, like the others, is likewise problematical. It *begs the question* of 'God's' existence, which invalidates this reaction as an argued for position. Moreover, the premise of this argument, or reaction, that "God does not expect perfect knowledge" is similar to the related arguments that "Not every statement made by a Church leader, past or present, necessarily constitutes doctrine" and that, accordingly, "A single statement made by a single leader on a single occasion often represents a personal, though well-considered opinion, but is not meant to be officially binding on the whole Church" ("Approaching Mormon Doctrine," LDS news release issued 2007-May). These are deflecting arguments that employ, in this case, what I refer to as a *reverse straw man* fallacy that also invalidates the argument.[16] The claim made here and by other atheological

---

16 Mormon apologists often accuse (and perhaps rightly so at times) Mormon critics of employing the straw man fallacy to attack the legitimacy of the Mormon faith by taking out of context comments made in prior

authors in this regard is *not* that Mormons are expected to possess perfect knowledge of their alleged gospel truths, but rather that the assertion of *any* knowledge by Mormon believers concerning the alleged *factual* reality of their god (as conceptualized) or of the truth of their god's plan of salvation (as a whole or in part) is not knowledge at all. This is so because, as shall be pointed out in Chapter 1 and argued in Chapters 3 and 4, such putative knowledge is neither self-evident, nor justified as a non-self-justified truth claim. Nor are the truth claims inherent in such putative knowledge even possibly *justifiable*. Further still, the same straw man premise is disingenuous, if not incoherent, given the fact that Mormon's *do*, in fact, claim a perfect (or 'sure') knowledge of the *fundamentals* of their faith. This perfect knowledge, moreover, is necessarily and putatively established by the 'pure' and 'perfect' witness of the Holy Ghost (Spirit) through direct personal and institutional revelation and spiritual confirmation — a serious problem addressed, again, in Chapters 5– 8.

---

published discourses by present, former, or deceased General Authorities of the Church and then representing such comments as official or authoritative revelation from 'God' that was binding on the Church — later to be changed, repudiated, or disavowed by a different Church President or General Authority. In this regard, the "like" deflective, *reverse* straw man fallacy would be to argue, in reverse, that *all* critics of the Church argue from the premise that *every single* statement made by *every single* Church President or General Authority was considered at the time by the Church to be authoritative and binding (or "official") revelation from God.

This fallacy is employed, for example, by the Church in its official press release dated 5/4/2007 and titled "Approaching Mormon Doctrine." Its purpose is to side-step questions concerning what constitutes Mormon doctrine and when statements from Church leaders can be considered as authoritative and binding revelation from their god. If applied to this work, it would likewise be disingenuous and irrelevant. The claim made in this work is *not* that every single statement made by every single Church leader on every single occasion is to be considered authoritative and binding revelation from 'God' or considered absolute truth. Rather, the claim made and argued for in Chapter 5 is that the concept of revelation, both in relation to the concept of the Mormon god *and* in itself, is unintelligible, incoherent, and factually vacuous as used or represented in Mormon discourse. Moreover, the claim is made in Chapters 5 and 8 that Mormon believers cannot coherently claim *both* the fact of human fallibilism and the infallibility of absolute truth regarding the fundamental, allegedly revealed doctrines of the Mormon faith. They do this to explain the subsequent authoritative disavowal, revocation, or modification of prior proclaimed (and regarded) authoritative and binding teachings and revelations from former Church leaders on matters also regarded at the time to be of fundamental importance to the salvation of man. Any attempt to apologetically or authoritatively do so will, as shall be argued (again in Chapters 5 and 8), ultimately destroy the very core of the Mormon faith through death by incoherence and a thousand qualifications.

Clearly, to quote George H. Smith, "Whether a revealed religion lives or dies will depend, first and foremost, on its claim to possess infallible knowledge..." (2000, 59). To appeal to human fallibilism and progressive revelation in an effort to appease mounting social criticism and member embarrassment and doubts concerning certain beliefs and doctrines of the Church, or evade or avoid deeper questions and doubts regarding the subsequent authoritative (revealed) revocation, disavowal, and modification of prior authoritative and fundamental teachings and revelation, while at the same time appealing to the infallible, unchanging or absolute truth of other authoritative and fundamental revelation, is ultimately self-defeating. Not only does it raise more questions and doubts as a result, it is, in both cases, a betrayal of the very doubt it seeks to allay. Such an appeal, in other words, gives birth and sustenance to a fundamental doubt that threatens the faith of believers and the very foundation of the Church itself. Narrowing the boundaries of legitimate, authoritative, and binding discourse and revelation to merely "well-considered opinion" while speculatively and fallibil-istically applying a broad hermeneutic to Church doctrine to create a "broad and complex context" makes it evermore elusive to criticism and acceptable to members; and outsiders will not spare the Mormon faith from valid criticism and serious doubt and rejection.

The problems and concerns referred to above and presented in this book are serious indeed. In fact, if this critical analysis hits even near its mark, the reasoned conclusions will make belief in the Mormon god and Plan of Salvation impossible without self-deception. There simply is no way that I can see for Mormon believers to dig out of this hole. Further, any attempt to do so will — if Mormon apologetics to date are at all predictive — most likely be not only futile, but disingenuous and intellectually dishonest as well.

As we shall learn below and in the chapters that follow, such attempts typically employ a variety of evasive tactics. One such tactic entails circular appeals to authority, revelation, faith, and a rather conveniently designed 'broad and complex' 'doctrinal context' (see note 16). Another tactic entails the declaration of warrantless or unjustified assertions as certain truth. A third tactic involves the solipsistic appeal to personal conviction established and supported only by arbitrarily classified and subjectively interpreted affective experiences. A fourth tactic entails the use of the three types of evasive possibility strategies presented in Chapter 2, and the various common (and favored) defensive reasoning fallacies presented below and elsewhere. All four types of evasion, of course, seriously compromise the credibility of the believer and invalidate the apologetic arguments made. Moreover, I shall argue, they sink Mormon theology — as presently or foreseeably constituted — deeper into the abyss of utter nonsense and incoherence.

Common Reasoning Fallacies in Defending the Faith

Reasoning fallacies are found in arguments (and counterarguments) where argument is indicated to establish the reasonableness of a particular position or conclusion or to defend or justify a particular position or point of view that has been questioned or challenged. Such fallacies are legion in all forms of theistic criticism and apologetics, including the work of Mormon critics and apologists. Essentially they undermine rational thinking and arguments made in pursuit of knowledge, and when knowingly and persistently used and denied, they often, and again, betray the real, albeit suppressed, doubt of the user. Ironically, such fallacies are often invoked — intentionally or not — by the very believers who profess to be committed to the truth or to metaphorically wielding the 'sword of truth' in defense of their faith.

Edward Damer, in his well-reviewed and highly regarded text *Attacking Faulty Reasoning* (2001) has this to say about reasoning fallacies:

> A [reasoning] fallacy is a violation of one of the criteria of a good argument. Any argument that fails to satisfy one or more of the four criteria is a fallacious one. Fallacies, then, stem from [1] the irrelevance of a premise, from [2] the unacceptability of a premise, from [3] the insufficiency of the combined premises of an argument to establish its conclusion, or from [4] the failure of an argument to give an effective rebuttal to the most serious challenges to its conclusion or to the argument itself…
>
> Fallacies are mistakes in reasoning that typically do not seem to be mistakes. Indeed, part of the etymology of the word "fallacy" comes from the notion of deception. *Fallacious arguments usually have the deceptive appearance of being good arguments…Such* deceptiveness, of course, may be unintentional on the part of the arguer. But it really doesn't matter whether the mistake was intentional or not; a mistake is a mistake, regardless of the arguer's intention. (42–3; emphasis mine)

These fallacies are, therefore, at times difficult to spot. Often they go unnoticed as parts of arguments which, on the surface, seem to make sense. But to spot them and expose them by name is to effectually eliminate or neutralize them. It exposes arguments based on them as being fundamentally unsound. Indeed, there is a responsibility to do so, since, as Damer correctly points out, both "…those who construct or present arguments for our consideration" (in this case Mormon apologists) and "…those to whom such arguments are addressed" (in this case Mormon believers, nonbelievers, disbelievers, and investigators) are — or may be — "guilty of faulty reasoning if they [make or] accept the conclusion of a faulty argument…[and then make] the same argument" (43).

So, given the importance of correct reasoning — even, implicitly, to Mormon believers in alleged discourse with their god (see Doctrine & Covenants 50: 10–12) or in authenticating putative revelation — let us expose a few of the more common reasoning fallacies.[17]

At the top of the list is the fallacy referenced earlier as *begging the question*. To argue, for example, and again, for the existence of 'God' and Christ from one's religious experiences, or from scriptural authority or personal or authoritative testimony is to *beg the question*, a common reasoning fallacy employed in religious apologetics. With this particular fallacy arguers (or believers) assume or presuppose, in the premises of their argument, the affirmative answer to the question at issue.

The question at issue in this case is the existence of the Mormon god and savior, Jesus Christ, but it can also be any historical or theological claim or position in question. In defending, first of all, the position or truth claim that 'God exists,' the argument might take the form of: 'God exists because the Bible (or *Book of Mormon*) says he does.' Or, 'God exists because he answers my prayers.' Or alternatively, 'God exists because he *revealed* himself to me,' or because 'He *confirmed* the truth of his existence to my heart by the power of the Holy Ghost.' The same would hold for the claim that 'Jesus is the Christ,' where the argument might be framed as, for example, 'Jesus is the Son of God because God revealed that he is,' or because 'He…has forgiven me of my sins and changed my heart.'

In these simple, illustrative instances, as in others like them, the believer is essentially arguing with premises (or 'because clauses') that *presuppose* (or *assume* up front as commonly accepted or self-evident truth) the affirmative answer to the question at issue. In other words, the arguer — in this case a defender of the faith — begs for the uncritical acceptance of the question at issue (*i.e.* the existence of 'God' and Christ) by offering premises (or 'because clauses') in his argument which presuppose, in this case, the questionable existence of that god and Christ. But, again, it is the very *existence* of 'God' and Christ that is the question at issue. So to essentially assert or argue that 'God and Christ exist because the scriptures say they do,' or because 'God and Christ did thus and so' or revealed themselves through this or that experience, and therefore they could

---

17 While an in-depth treatment of the subject of critical thinking is outside the scope of this book, the ability to recognize certain common reasoning fallacies is nonetheless essential to enable the reader to adequately assess various apologetic counterarguments made throughout this book and elsewhere in the works of Mormon authors who seek to defend or promote the Mormon faith. Beyond the cursory treatment of those few common reasoning fallacies offered in this Introduction, those readers not adept at critical thinking (and few people are), would do well to consult various sources for additional information and a more in-depth treatment of the subject. Browne and Keeley (2004), for example, suggest eleven critical questions for consideration in evaluating truth claims. Other notable resources in this regard include Lipps (2004); Damer (2001); Dewey (1997); Gilovich (1991); Flew (1998); Ruchlis (1990); Fisher (2001); and Eller (2004, Chapters 2–5).

not have done any of this if they did not exist, is to say essentially *that what 'God' and Christ allegedly said (revealed) or did proves they exist.*

More starkly stated, the argument made is essentially that 'God and Christ exist because God and Christ exist.' Such an argument is, of course, circular and neither says nor proves anything intelligible, much less true. Obviously, we cannot validly argue for the existence of something whose existence is neither basic, evident, or self-evident — and is therefore legitimately in question — by offering as reason(s) to accept the truth of its existence something which actually or logically *assumes* or *presupposes* its existence. To argue therefore — as the believer essentially does when *begging the question* — that 'God exists because *I know* (in virtue of reasons which presuppose or assume God's existence) that God exists' is, again, to assume what we wish to prove. Therefore, it says *nothing* of probative value or factual significance, no less of what is (or can be) *actually* known.

Alternatively, in defending the position that 'the *Book of Mormon* is the word of God,' or 'Joseph Smith is a Prophet,' or 'the (Mormon) Church is true,' or 'the (Mormon) Gospel (or *Plan of Salvation*) is true,' Mormon leaders, believers, and apologists — like apologists in other faiths — must "start," as Loftus puts it, citing renowned Christian apologist James D. Strauss, "'from above' by presupposing that God exists and then [argue] that God's existence makes better sense of the [historical and theological claims] and the world than the alternatives. Again," Loftus informs us, quoting Strauss regarding how Christians do apologetics, "'if you don't start with God, you'll never get to God'" (2008).

This form of question begging, when used by Mormon believers or apologists, also argues circularly. It essentially asks questioning believers or skeptics to accept all of the above questionable or doubtful historical and theological claims as true because the Mormon god exists and we know, after all, that God must exist because if he did not exist none of the aforementioned historical and theological claims would make sense or could sensibly be claimed to be true. In other words, from the perspective of Mormon believers and apologists, the claim that Joseph Smith is a true Prophet of God (or that the *Book of Mormon* is the word of God, or that the Mormon Church and Gospel are true) can only make sense if we *presuppose* the existence of the Mormon God and then reason from the presupposed existence of the Mormon God to the sensibleness or likelihood (or certainty) of the particular claim.

But these and all other ancillary Mormon historical and theological issues of concern miss the point and are merely incidental to the *meta-question* of concern at issue, which is the fundamental question of the Mormon god's putative existence. Thus, presupposing this god's existence to make sense of other Mormon historical and theological truth claims (which can only make sense or be true if this god exists) is still essentially begging the question at issue, in this case the fundamental meta-question of the Mormon god's existence.

Substituting this meta-question of concern for an ancillary and incidental question (*e.g.* the truth claim that 'Joseph Smith is a true Prophet of God') and then arguing that the incidental question at issue makes sense only if we start "from above" by presupposing (or assuming) as true the literal existence of the Mormon god is essentially (again by substitution) to argue *for* the likely (or certain) existence of the Mormon god *from* the premise that the Mormon god exists. It is to argue, in other words, and essentially, that the Mormon god most likely (if not certainly) exists because the Mormon god in truth exists, or the Mormon god's existence makes sense because the Mormon god in truth exists.

Again, as before, to argue circularly for the sense and likelihood or truth of questionable or controversial Mormon historical and theological truth claims by starting from above, or by presupposing the existence of the Mormon god, is to engage in an apologetic, argumentative sleight of hand. Such a tactic not only results in an invalid argument, but in a meaningless tautology that again says *nothing* of probative value or factual significance, still less of what is (or can be) *actually* known.

Beyond begging the question, other reasoning fallacies abound to be sure. To suggest or argue, for example, that the membership and financial growth of the Mormon Church since its inception *proves* that 'Joseph Smith was a true Prophet of God' and/or that 'the Mormon Church is true' is both a *non sequitur* and a deductive fallacy which *affirms the consequent*. A *non sequitur* is a conclusion that does not necessarily follow from anything previously said, or, alternatively, an inference that does not necessarily follow from the premise. To *affirm the consequent* is to argue

> If A then B.
> B is true.
> Therefore, A is necessarily true.

These two common reasoning fallacies essentially invalidate the actual theistic arguments being made. Clearly such conclusions (*i.e.* 'Joseph Smith was a true Prophet of God' and 'the Mormon Church is true') do not necessarily (or even reasonably) follow from the evidence (*i.e.* the growth of the Church since its inception) and can be alternatively and adequately explained by a variety of more plausible cultural and socio-psychological factors.

Additionally, to also suggest, as some Mormon apologists are wont to do, that there is no body of doctrine regarded officially as Mormon theology or, as perhaps some readers might do, that the doctrinal representations in this book are either not totally accurate or not what Mormons *really* believe is, given the central argument of this book, a *red herring*. A 'red herring' is an attempt "…to hide the weakness of a position by drawing attention away from the real issue to a side issue" (Damer 2001, 195). It is a reasoning fallacy that is both disingenuous and deflective.

What is important here – and one significant argument of this analysis – is that *whatever* Mormons believe *about* their god and, by extension, their Savior and Plan of Salvation circularly *begs the question* of — or assumes and presupposes as true — the very question at issue, *i.e.* their god's existence. Moreover, and as we shall learn in Chapter 3, *whatever* the concept of the Mormon god might be, it will be either *false*, because merely a grossly superstitious non-reality (like Zeus or Wotan), or it will be *incoherent* at its metaphysical core. So too, necessarily, will be the case with their beliefs in 'divine revelation' and 'faith.'

These arguments and conclusions, in turn, make the putative existence of the Mormon god — *however conceived or imagined* — not only a *logical impossibility* due to certain fundamental, or primary, internal contradictions (Chapters 3, 4, and 6) and an *inductive improbability* in relation to certain presently irresolvable secondary and relational contradictions with the facts of human existence (Chapter 7), but a *factual non-reality*[18]

---

18 Inasmuch as the term 'factual non-reality' is used frequently in this work, it seems important to clarify its meaning up-front. Essentially, to assert that 'God is a factual non-reality' is to assert that the concept of God, the way 'God' is used in statements of belief or doctrine, is cognitively empty, or factually meaningless.'

as well. And this meta-conclusion, as shall be argued in Chapter 2, necessarily makes the belief in the *factual* existence of such a god — as well as in the truthfulness of Mormon theology as a whole — utterly irrational.

Consequently, splitting hairs on the accuracy of doctrinal representations made in this book is a deflection. Mormon doctrine *per se* is, by its very nature, suspiciously complex and open to endless interpretation, which makes it elusive to criticism through *ad hoc* speculative deflections and evasions.[19] Still, this book deals primarily, if not exclusively, with those fundamental doctrines and beliefs which are widely considered to be beyond the reach of speculative theologizing and apologetics. These doctrines and beliefs — even in their broadest interpretations — are seriously problematic.

Moreover still, to characterize, for example, (as Mormon leaders, believers and apologists are wont to do) skeptics, critics, or Atheists offering naturalistic arguments against their faith as being like the paradigm *Book of Mormon* characters Korihor (the 'antichrist'; Alma 30) and Zeezrom (the 'lawyer'; Alma 10) is to commit yet other deflective and evasive common reasoning fallacies, including, most notably, an *attack of a straw man* and the *ad hominem* attack.

An "attack of the straw man" entails, again according to Damer, "…misrepresenting the opponent's position for the purpose of making it easier to attack" (191). In using this particular reasoning fallacy Mormons might, for example, liken Korihor's *un*-substantial and *un*-substantiated atheistic accusations and attacks on religious believers and beliefs to the substantive and valid arguments made (and conclusions reached) in this book or elsewhere on the basis of critical, conceptual analysis and common knowledge. Or they might likewise liken Zeezrom's disingenuous inquiry regarding the existence of the Mormon god to the honest analytical inquiry conducted herein or elsewhere. In both examples legitimate, critical arguments that question the Mormon faith are *misrepresented* as being, like Korihor's and Zeezrom's arguments, unsubstantial, unsubstantiated, and merely disingenuous and contentious criticisms.

"Indeed," as George Smith correctly points out, "a concept may be [familiar and] logically possible and yet cognitively empty, if it is impossible to conceive what it would be like to [actually] experience such a being [in its conceptual fullness as described or defined]" (2000, 169). Questions regarding what 'facts' are and whether or not putatively factual statements can reasonably be considered to be 'factually meaningful' (or factually intelligible or significant) are addressed in depth in Chapter 1.

19 It is interesting, if not perhaps ironic, that when it comes to Mormon and Christian apologetics, reason must come to the rescue of faith. This is ironic since reason is, in matters concerning religious knowledge (or as a religious way of knowing), considered subservient, if not irrelevant, to revelation. As shall be treated in depth in chapter VI, some, like Mormon Apostle Dallin Oaks (1991), have argued that, although both reason and faith are essential means for obtaining knowledge, they are not co-equal. Faith has primacy over reason in matters concerning theology, even though reason has an important role in secular matters and is useful to authenticate revelation. But if reason has an important role in authenticating (or testing) and, moreover, in apologetically explaining and defending revelation, then the rules governing reason must be employed and reasoning fallacies must be avoided. If so, then if the question at issue is a god's existence, and if presupposing or assuming a god's existence is begging the question at issue, isn't therefore the exercise of using reason to either explain, defend, or authenticate revelation — revelation that necessarily depends on the existence of that god to exist — simply intellectual wheel-spinning? Stated differently — and employing a different metaphor — aren't *all* well-reasoned apologetic defenses of theology essentially question-begging, and therefore like building a fortress on a foundation of sand? To continue the metaphor while adding yet others: isn't such a 'fortress' itself, constructed as it is with the employment of questionable material (facts) and faulty workmanship (reasoning fallacies) itself merely a house of cards?

An "*ad hominem* attack" on the other hand, is a common reasoning fallacy which "… consists in attacking one's opponent in a personal and abusive way as a means of ignoring or discrediting his or her criticism or argument" (191). In using this reasoning fallacy Mormon believers might, to continue the above example used as a straw man, liken this author, like all critics of the Mormon faith, to the paradigm characters of Korihor and Zeezrom. Here the skeptical naturalist is *mischaracterized* as being a conniving, rebellious, prideful, and sinful (or evil) individual like Korihor and Zeezrom, who therefore offers spurious and specious arguments against the Mormon faith which are *knowingly* untrue — merely out of spite or to get revenge or gain. This particular fallacy is used to discredit the opposing argument on the basis of a personal attack of the critic.

Often the *ad hominem* attack is coupled in Mormon apologetics with yet another reasoning fallacy known as the *genetic fallacy*. As Damer puts it, "[t]he genetic fallacy occurs when one attempts to reduce the significance [or validity] of an idea, person, practice, or institution merely to an account of its origin or genesis, thereby overlooking the development, regression or difference to be found in it in the present situation. One who commits this fallacy," according to Damer, "typically transfers the positive or negative esteem that he or she has for the thing [or idea, person, practice] in its original context or earlier forms to the thing in its present form…. The genetic fallacy," therefore, "thus exhibits a pattern of reasoning that fails to meet the relevance criterion of a good argument — that the premises must have a bearing on the truth or falsity of the claim in question" (56).

This particular fallacy would be evident in any argument (or counterargument) made which would, for example, attempt to discredit the arguments and conclusions of this or any critical work — atheistic or otherwise — on the basis of the critic's past endeavors, ideas, or practices which might bring his or her present work into question or disrepute. Alternatively, it may be argued that the practice employed in critiquing the faith is not credible on the basis of earlier versions of such a practice which have been criticized. Another example would include the attempt to discredit *any* secular criticism of the faith on the basis that the means for such criticism(s) are merely the 'theories of man,' which are provisional and therefore unreliable. This argument implies that because man is fallible and his 'theories' have often been proven wrong, this or any other present criticism of the faith will also be wrong, or eventually proven wrong, and is therefore not worth considering. This particular example, of course, would be incoherent given the *fact* of human fallibilism, and disingenuous given Mormon apologists' reliance on such fallibilism to defend their faith from accusations of opportunism and internal inconsistency related to *ad hoc* interpretations of scripture and doctrine, as well as their changing, minimalizing, and disavowing of prior, putative revelation once accepted as essential, absolute truth.

Other common and insidious reasoning fallacies pertain as well, including the use of *false dilemmas*, *faulty (or false) analogies*, *invalid analogical predication*, *post hoc reasoning*, and *poisoning the well*.

Browne and Keeley (2004) define the "false dilemma" (or "Either-Or") fallacy as "assuming only two alternatives exist when it is possible that there are more than two" (92). This fallacy was used, for example, by the late Mormon President Gordon B. Hinckley when he said in a PBS interview that the Mormon faith is "either right or wrong, true or false, fraudulent or true." Clearly the fallacy here is that the Mormon faith might, for example, be conceptually incoherent in relation to its core beliefs about its god, revelation, and faith, and that therefore assertions by believers of the putative truth of their god's existence — as well, necessarily, as the existence of revelation from, and faith in, such a putative god — are *neither* true nor false, right nor wrong. Such concepts are merely factually vacuous, or cognitively meaningless. The Mormon faith might also be false (or wrong) where superstitious in nature, and false *and* incoherent in relation to its meta-beliefs, or its believers' beliefs *about* their beliefs.

Hinckley sets this up so that if the listener or reader is not certain of (or cannot somehow *prove*) that the Mormon faith is false or wrong, he or she *must* conclude that it is therefore *necessarily* true, or right. This, it seems to me, is a disingenuous ploy to force a *false choice* by framing the argument as a false dilemma.

Finally, Hinckley compounds this fallacy with his distracting use of *emotional appeal* (another reasoning fallacy; 84) in using the term 'fraudulent' as equivalent to being 'false,' or as the only alternative to being 'true.' Again, the false dilemma here is used to force a false choice. But clearly the Mormon faith might certainly be false yet *not* fraudulent, or *neither* fraudulent *nor* true. Clearly as well, the alternative to its being true or false is certainly not necessarily its opposite, but might, again, be neither. Again, the way Hinckley sets this up, if the listener or reader cannot conclude that the Mormon faith is at least possibly true, his only alternative is to conclude that Mormons are "engaged in a fraud." Moreover, the listener or reader who does not, or is not inclined to, question Hinckley's sincerity or Joseph Smith's motives as being fraudulent *must* conclude, in virtue of this false dilemma, that the Mormon faith is at least possibly true. In either case the called for conclusion is a false choice.

"False analogy," according again to Damer, "consists in assuming that because two things are alike in one or more respects, they necessarily are alike in some other respect" (193). Applying this reasoning fallacy to our previous *Book of Mormon* example, it might be falsely assumed, for example, that the cumulative naturalistic argument presented in this work against Mormon theology is *analogous to* Korihor's arguments merely on the basis of Korihor's *like* challenge of the nature and validity of religious belief (vs.12–18) and corresponding denial of his belief in the Mormon god (vs. 37&38). Or, it might be assumed that the atheistic challenge to the existence of the Mormon god argued in this book is analogous to Zeezrom's *like* challenge of the belief that there is a 'God' (vs. 26–30). Beyond these very limited likenesses, however, there is no valid comparison, primarily because substantive and developed naturalistic or atheistic arguments in both fictional cases are not presented or developed in the *Book of Mormon* and, therefore, cannot be compared with the substantive arguments of this (or any like) book. The analogy doesn't hold up beyond the mere similarity of the conclusions reached — conclusions that might or might not result from the same argument, or from any substantive or valid argument at all.

Another example of this oft and ill-used fallacy would be to argue, as has in fact been done elsewhere, for the legitimacy of the truth claim 'I *know* by the witness of the Holy Spirit that God exists' on the basis that just as one *knows*, for example, *what* salt tastes like without knowing how to *explain* what specifically salt tastes like, so too one can *know* what the 'spirit of truth' feels like even though one cannot *explain* what specifically and distinctively such a spiritual feeling is like or how specifically it differs from the purely natural feelings identically described by nonbelievers or disbelievers. Such an argument can be very persuasive in disarming skeptical enquirers who might question how believers can assert that they know of their god's existence through the sure witness — or confirming feelings — of the Holy Spirit. It is particularly persuasive when used by a respected and admired authority in the faith, as is the case with its persistent use by Mormon Apostle Boyd K. Packer. (See my treatment of Packer's anecdotal use of this argument in Chapter 5.)

To argue thusly is to argue invalidly on the basis of false analogy. Such an argument implicitly and invalidly argues that because the inability to *explain* the taste of salt when tasting salt may be likened to the inability to *explain* the feeling of the spirit of truth when allegedly feeling the spirit, that therefore one attuned to the spirit of truth can and does in fact *know* what the spirit feels like when allegedly feeling the spirit just like one *knows* what salt tastes like when actually tasting salt; that *knowing* in both cases is analogous and therefore equally legitimate in virtue of an allegedly basic experience in each case.

For this analogy to produce a valid argument, however, there would need to be a likeness not only between the *inexplicability* of 'knowing' related to both sensory experiences in the analogy (*i.e.* the *inexplicably* of knowing what salt tastes like *when actually tasting salt*, and the *inexplicably* of knowing what the spirit feels like *when allegedly feeling the spirit*), but also a likeness between: (1) the existence, in this case, of two universally and uncontroversially recognizable (or 'known') *types* of sensations related to the compared experiences in the analogy (*i.e.* the *actual taste* of salt, which is universally and uncontroversially recognizable *and* the *actual* feeling of the spirit, which is neither universally nor uncontroversially recognizable as such); *and* (2) a likeness between the *known* factual existence of the *objects* of *both* experiences in the analogy, *i.e.* of *salt* (a known, knowable and specifiable substance) and *the spirit* (an unknown, unknowable, and non-specifiable substance). Since there can be no established likeness in 'knowing' *vis-à-vis* the two *types* of sensations and *objects* related to such sensations, the argument by analogy in this case fails, even though both sensory experiences are alike in respect to their inexplicability of knowing.

The fallacy of invalid 'analogical predication' will be addressed in greater depth in Chapter 1 and referenced throughout in different analytical contexts. According to John Bowker in the *Concise Oxford Dictionary of World Religions* (1997), "Most theological discussion of analogy has been concerned with analogical predication, a mode of predication in which terms familiar in one context are used in an extended sense elsewhere. Thus it is claimed that terms like 'love,' 'wisdom,' ['goodness'] and 'living,' which are learnt in everyday contexts, are applied to God by analogy because of some relationship (*e.g.* likeness, exemplarity, participation, and causation) between God's perfections and these human attributes."

When used to convey familiar sense or *cognitive* meaning to the transcendent or supernatural attributes and qualities of gods, analogical predication fails because it falsely assumes that we know (or even *can* know) something *literal* or *nonanalogical* about the infinite and eternal attributes and qualities of a biologically and spatio-temporally transcendent and supernatural being. It fails, in other words, and more specifically, not only because it tacitly begs the question of a god's literal existence (which it does), but because it argues invalidly, if not disingenuously, from the implied premise that the nature of such a transcendent being can be *actually* understood and appreciated through the putative resemblance of its alleged *divine* attributes and qualities, which — as shall be analytically argued for and concluded in Chapter 3 — are without cognitive meaning, to analogous *human* attributes and qualities.

But such an implied premise is the problem. For as we shall learn in our prerequisite reading of the *Foundational Preface* and Chapter 1 which follow, *all* human knowledge *about*, and understanding regarding, *any* existent is totally dependent on the use of *justifiable* predicative language in general, and on the *justification* of those justifiable declarative and indicative statements or assertions which are made to establish such knowledge and understanding as actual truth in particular (where 'actual truth,' as used herein, consists of justified statements or, in other words, statements which are *actually true*, as opposed to statements which are merely asserted without warrant to be true).

Further, as we shall again learn in Chapter 3, *any* predicative language used propositionally to claim or assert and describe the *literal* existence of the Mormon god as fully conceptualized in *any* version or interpretation of the Mormon faith is highly problematic. Such problematic religious language, or 'God-talk,' — *whatever* it might be — makes therefore *any* effort to assert the *actual* existence of such a god (or to *know* or convey *any* knowledge *about* such a god in its conceptual fullness) highly problematic as well, if not arguably impossible. This in turn, as we shall learn again in Chapter 1 and Chapter 2 as well, would make *any* and *all* believed understanding of the meaning and nature of 'God' through analogical predication necessarily empty of cognitive meaning since, again, we know nothing, or *cannot* know *anything*, literal or nonanalogical about his putative metaphysical attributes and qualities as conceptualized and expressed.

The *post-hoc* reasoning fallacy assumes "…that an event that occurs *after* another event therefore occurs *because* of that event" (Damer 2001, 153). In using this reasoning fallacy it might be argued, for example, that just as Korihor and Zeezrom were critical of Church leaders and beliefs and (as the story goes) were also in 'sin,' therefore all those who are critical of the Mormon faith and its leaders are, *post hoc, ergo propter hoc*, likewise (and necessarily) critical *because* of sin. Such an argument, of course, would also be a *non sequitur*, for it does not necessarily follow, either *causally* or *logically*, that *sin* (as Church-defined apostasy from the faith or moral transgression) *causes* one to be critical of religious beliefs, values, and practices. Alternatively, by logical extension, it does not necessarily follow that if current or former believers are critical of their own current or prior faith it is simply *because* they are in sin.

Other examples of the *post-hoc* fallacy abound, including the invalid claims (as arguments for the legitimacy of the faith) that: (1) religious belief (and living) results in emotional or psychological well-being; (2) righteous living brings joy and happiness; (3) faithfully paying tithes and offerings results in prosperity (or deliverance from financial destitution); (4) sincere prayers offered in faith by the faithful are always answered; (5) the growth of the Church is indicative of the fact that Joseph Smith was a true prophet of the Mormon god, and that his Church is Christ's only true Church. These claims-as-arguments, and many others like them, wrongly and conveniently conflate selective correlation and causality.

Finally, 'poisoning the well' is a reasoning fallacy which "…consists in rejecting a criticism or argument presented by another person because of that person's special circumstances or improper motives" (194). Applied to this book, for example, the arguments and conclusions offered against the believed existence of the Mormon god and Plan of Salvation might be — on the force of this fallacy — unreasonably discredited and rejected without a hearing merely on the basis of the circumstances surrounding the author's resignation from the Mormon Church and his stated Atheism and motives in discouraging belief in the Mormon religion.

But the attribution of motives other than those admitted to is, in any case, very problematic in its own right — and irrelevant and invalid in assessing the soundness or validity of arguments. To assert, as many Mormon believers do, that critics of the Mormon faith who were former members are motivated by bitterness due to offense, pride of intellect, the desire to hide their own sin, or deception by 'the spirit of the adversary' is not only to poison the well and commit the red herring, *ad hominem*, and genetic fallacies in response to the critic's arguments, but is to also engage in the common form of 'twisted thinking' identified in cognitive psychology as 'mind reading.' Moreover, the arguer's motives, circumstances, and status *vis-à-vis* the Mormon Church do not *necessarily* determine or affect the *validity* of arguments made and offered, and, moreover, motives cannot reliably be determined merely on the basis of the circumstances, or *vice-versa*.

"The Last Lines of Defense"

Predictably, works of this nature mobilize what R.D. Gold refers to in *Bondage of the Mind* as "Fundamentalists' Last Lines of Defense" (2008). Appropriating from Gold, there are three lines of defense which devout, orthodox Mormon believers will ultimately retreat to in defense of their beliefs.

First, they will finesse the facts on the basis of their belief that their god, being omniscient and omnipotent, can and does (and can only) work within natural laws (known and unknown) to fulfill his purposes, 'Plan' and will. Therefore, all things on earth and in the universe testify or bear witness to the existence of 'God' (Alma 30: 41&44). Moreover, there can be no contradictions between the cosmological claims of Mormon theology and natural law, or between its god's apparent inaction and his divine nature. There can be no inaccuracy of revealed historical fact, either. Furthermore, if there is contradictory evidence or apparent incoherence in their theological claims, Mormon missionaries, teachers, leaders and apologists will insist that their god can and perhaps does change his mind or even remove or alter the evidence to test the faith of believers. Alternatively, if there is no evidence to support Mormon claims regarding the existence of their god or his workings or the historical claims in scripture, this first of the last lines of defense simply asserts that no one can prove there is *no* 'God' or that 'God's' revealed works are *not true* (as in Alma 30: 40).

Secondly, they will argue that any or all conceptual unintelligibility is merely apparent, and clarifying explanations will be revealed to man by their god *at* the appropriate time, *to* the appropriate people and *in* the appropriate way. Moreover, this god in his wisdom keeps 'meaning' and his 'will' and 'purposes' hidden at times either for the welfare of his 'children' — in order to cultivate a more perfect faith — or because his reasons for silence, hiddenness, and mystery are beyond man's *ken*, or ability to understand or know.

Finally, if the 'hidden-meaning gambit' doesn't work in forestalling doubt or deflecting troubling questions, the last line of defense is to point to human fallibility or immaturity (lack of readiness). Or — and to me this is not only evasive, but possibly psychologically damaging or at least condescending, demeaning, and dismissive — it will be suggested to the questioning believer, unbeliever, or nonbeliever that "[if] you can't see or understand the Truth, it's *your* fault, not ours" (172). In other words, that it is because you are prideful (or in sin) or, again, just can't handle or understand the Truth at this time or stage of your spiritual development. Therefore, it would be useless or harmful for 'God' to reveal the Truth to you.

A variation of this third defense, as practiced in the Mormon faith, is applied to critics of the religion who are both inside the Church and who, like me, are former insiders and are now ex-Mormons. The inside critics and dissenters are, again, often regarded and labeled as faithless intellectuals who are on the road to apostasy and need (are told) to repent and remain silent. Their views are thereby discredited as being false or as false doctrine and they are either threatened with excommunication or actually disfellowshipped or excommunicated if they do not cease and desist from their 'sinful path.' The critics who are former insiders who have left the Church to join another church or who have abandoned religious faith altogether, are regarded as apostates and are discredited as having 'lost the Spirit' and as harboring the 'spirit of Satan' as enemies of the Church who, having left the Church cannot leave it alone.

As with the related reactions and deflections above there are serious problems for the believer with each of Gold's three lines of defense, some of which will be addressed substantively (albeit not by direct reference) in the pages which follow. Suffice to say, the *ad hominem* attacks made in the third line of defense (like those mentioned earlier) cannot be taken seriously. Are those in pursuit of truth who in good conscience sincerely question, doubt, reject and/or dissent from questionable truth claims necessarily enemies of the truth, or does their refutation of false or incoherent or potentially harmful truth claims diminish or undermine the truth or its pursuit? And are all those who in good conscience *persistently* and *passionately* inveigh against religious beliefs and practices they sincerely and justifiably deem harmful to the welfare of society in general and to existing or prospective believers in particular likewise necessarily enemies of the truth (or of the Church) who cannot leave the Church alone?

Clearly, when applying the above referenced *ad hominem* attacks against all those converts who left their previous faith to join the Mormon Church, — including former Mormon Presidents and General Authorities — such converts would be considered by their own standards, and by those of their previous faith, as doubting sinners or apostates who were seduced by Satan to believe a lie. They would also be judged as being 'without the Holy Spirit' because they wrongly rejected their previous faith, considered by its believers to be the *only* Truth and True Church of Christ. Finally, they would be said to be possessed by an evil spirit because they are critical of their former Church and could not leave it alone. Moreover, the serious *conceptual* problems with the Mormon doctrines of deity, salvation, revelation, and faith,[20] the serious *evidential* and *reasoning* problems with certain core Mormon cosmological claims regarding the existence of the Mormon god, the creation of the earth and biological life on earth,[21] and the crucial Mormon historical

---

20 Presented and addressed in Chapters 3, 5, and 6, respectively

21 Presented and addressed briefly in Chapter 4.

problems as well,[22] essentially strip all three lines of defense of force and credibility and make them indefensible, ineffectual and transparent for what they are, *i.e.* merely desperate, defensive strategies of evasion and control designed and employed to suppress doubt and free thinking, and deepen self-deception.

All of the above caveats regarding reasoning fallacies and lines of defense are not made to say that there is no warrant for objection to this or any argument made against Mormon beliefs or any religious belief system, or that there are no legitimate lines of defense against these or any atheistic arguments or attacks made against the truthfulness of any theistic belief. On the contrary, no argument is infallible and such objections and defenses are many and would be welcomed and seriously and respectfully considered — but not in the invalid forms presented above.

Again, invalid arguments are not, by commonly accepted epistemological standards, legitimate or respectable objections or lines of defense. Such arguments can be known by the deflective and evasive reasoning fallacies their authors employ. To summarize, invalid arguments commonly strive to turn the tables by mere assertion or through *tu quoque* evasion. Or, they circularly *beg the question* of a god's putative existence or the truthfulness of certain beliefs about a god on the basis of revelation through faith in that god. They may invalidly *affirm the consequent* or *appeal to authority* or testimony as properly basic knowledge. They may offer *ad hoc* (or arbitrary) solutions as actual fact, or argue evasively from *false analogy* and/or invalid *analogical predication* to establish truth through *mere* familiarity and likeness, or similitude. They can *poison the well*, make *post hoc, non sequitur,* or *red herring* arguments, not to mention *ad hominem* attacks and *attacks of the straw man.* Finally, as we shall learn in Chapter 2, they may employ the evasive possibility strategies of *ignorance, isolation,* and *inflation.*

Whatever the reaction to this book might be, the hope is there will be sufficient resolve and interest to stick with the project at hand. Continue, in other words, to stay in the conversation by attending to real questions and doubt by moving beyond this book to the other listed resources as well. Do so critically, deliberately, and carefully as, again, a skeptical outsider in pursuit of one's own reasoned and tentative conclusions.

General Information Regarding the Structure, Style, and Scope of this Work

This offering, which began as a personal, therapeutic working-through of certain questions, evolved into a paper and then, with some encouragement first from Evan Fales at the University of Iowa, and then from Kai Nielsen at Concordia University and the University of Calgary, into this book. In one important sense, on-going and intertwined analysis and assessment of the Mormon faith occurs throughout the entire corpus of this work. In another important sense, however, this book essentially consists of two books in one: my formal, more objective *analysis* of the Mormon faith and my formal and more personal *assessment* of the Mormon faith.

The first 'book' within this book involves my conceptual analysis of Mormon theology, as foundationally and methodologically described in the *Foundational Preface* and

---

22 Regarding, for example, those historical problems with Joseph Smith's alleged 'first vision,' the putative authorship, coming forth and historicity of the *Book of Mormon,* and the legitimacy of the "Book of Abraham" in the *Pearl of Great Price,* to name a few. (See well-documented sources referenced, in part, in the *Foundational Preface* and cited in the *References* section of this work, as well as in *Appendix B.*)

Chapter 1, and as conducted in Chapters 3 through 7. The second involves my assessment of the rationality of Mormon beliefs, as prescribed in Chapter 2, and the likely psychological and socio-cultural implications and consequences of the Mormon faith on the believer and society.

The second book within this book is informed by my own and others' reported personal experiences, the reliance on an extensive body of theory and work in applied depth-psychology, neuroscience, and socio-cultural anthropology, and extensive primary and secondary research and studies regarding the nature and abuses of authoritarianism in families and both religious and nonreligious institutions. It focuses on the nature and prevalence of various forms of psychopathology in the Mormon faith specifically.

This assessment is, again, integrated throughout the book, but primarily in the following five areas: *First*, the Mormon faith is assessed earlier in this *Introduction* in relation to the shameful caricature of doubt and the shaming condemnation and diminishment of those believers who have troubling questions and real doubts regarding their faith. *Second*, the Mormon faith is assessed toward the beginning of Chapter 5 regarding the pernicious doctrinal requirement of revelation for salvation and damnation. *Third*, it is assessed at the end of Chapter 6 regarding the framing of faith as an irreversible *decision*. *Fourth*, and perhaps most significantly, it is assessed at the end of Chapter 8 regarding the question of whether or not the Mormon faith might reasonably be regarded as a toxic belief system. *Fifth* and finally, there is a likewise important assessment of the Mormon faith in the *Epilogue* in the context of the authoritarian family system and as creative illusion.

The style of the analytical parts of the book is, for the most part, more formal and scholarly, with at times extensive footnoting, quotations and, in places, the use of elaborative sentences and redundancy. This is so both deliberately and necessarily, given the nature and implications of the arguments made, the conclusions reached, and their importance to the overall purpose of this book. More specifically in this regard, the nature of this work is necessarily complex, and the central argument made is sophisticated and, in certain aspects, nuanced and even counterintuitive. These facts required a necessary level of detail and, again, redundancy, not only to offer as clear and unambiguous an explication as I could economically provide, but also to anticipate and forestall, as best I could, inappropriate generalizations and irrelevant counterarguments. In taking this approach I realize that I have taken the very different risk of perhaps losing a certain group of readers who either do not enjoy such writing, or who might find this style of writing too cumbersome, difficult, or demanding given their level of interest, or perhaps given their need for an excuse not to engage in the necessary work required.

The *analysis, per se* utilizes the methodology presented and justified in Chapter 1 and consists primarily of the extensive use of probative, analytical inquiry, expressed, in parts where I deal with particular areas of intense personal concern, in a tone which tends perhaps to be more provocative, polemical, and perhaps, regrettably (and I hope minimally), even dogmatic. Additionally, in relation to the published words of others, the reader will encounter the not infrequent use of bracketed interpolations where required to extend the relevance of quoted material to the Mormon faith. Moreover, it should be noted that the use of both referenced and quoted material is to *propose* different concepts, perspectives and arguments for consideration and reflection, and to relevantly *explain* and *reinforce* the critical ideas presented, arguments made, and provisional conclusions reached.

Conversely, the writing in the *assessment* parts of the book tends to be more general and, in places, more personal and anecdotal. In my psychosocial assessment of the Mormon faith I argue — passionately at times — for the conclusion that the Mormon faith, as a belief system, is both psychologically harmful and dangerous to both believers and society. I also criticize and condemn what I consider to be the shameful and shaming views, teachings, beliefs, and authoritarian practices and behavior of Mormon leaders, apologists, professors of religion, and other staunch, self-righteous and dogmatic believers who, as I see it, attempt (intentionally or not) to control, manipulate, and bind the minds of questioning believers and children through guilt and shame and the promise (or threatened loss) of illusory blessings.

Such argument, criticism, and condemnation, which naturally spring from my Freudian hermeneutic of suspicion and my Nietzschian contempt for life-negating religious beliefs and practices, admittedly rely primarily on the subjective interpretation of my own and others' reported experiences and my use, limited though it might be in this particular work, of applied cognitive, psychoanalytical, and family systems theory in assessing the culture and authoritarian practices in the Mormon faith. Moreover, the central argument made in this assessment can, I think, be reasonably supported by reported accounts of authoritarian (and sexual) abuse in the Mormon Church (and other theistic faiths), published reports concerning the prevalence of psychopathology in the Mormon Church (and other theistic faiths as well), and the extensive body of theory and research in the study of religious and institutional authoritarianism and authoritarian abuse. Finally, my critical and at times condemnatory approach in making this argument as I have is justified, as I see it, by the stubborn resistance of religious ideas, transference, denial and obsession, and by, again, and significantly, what I soberly consider to be the high stakes involved, both to believers and society at large.

In offering this assessment I acknowledge fully that each believer no doubt perceives, conceptualizes, and experiences faith differently, according to his or her conditioning, inclinations, needs, desires, and preferences. In making this admission I also acknowledge (and argue) that with religious life, as with all other life-forms, it seems self-evident that there is a certain universality to all personal human experience. As renowned psychotherapist Carl Rogers observed, "That which is most personal, is most universal." If this is so (and I think it is), then I would argue, notwithstanding any denials to the contrary, that I am not alone in how I personally experienced the Mormon faith, or in how I have retrospectively analyzed and interpreted those experiences. Moreover, I would also argue that apart from how I or others have experienced or have been (and are) negatively affected by the Mormon faith, my assessment of it — including its beliefs, processes and practices — is neither actually or necessarily unreasonable nor implausible. On the contrary, given all that we know about such social systems — how they originate and operate, and how they affect people's minds and lives — this assessment of the Mormon faith is more likely than not to be very accurate in its overall approach and conclusions.

Returning to the structure of this book, it should be emphasized yet again that for this book to be fully appreciated and have its intended effect, it is recommended that it be read, with all substantive footnotes, beginning with this *Introduction*, and then proceeding to the *Foundational Preface* and then each Chapter in sequence through the *Epilogue, Personal Postscript* and *Appendices* to the list of *References* offered for further study. Moreover, and significantly, it is *essential* that the *Foundational Preface* and Chapters 1 and 2 be carefully read and understood *before* reading the remaining chapters in sequence. These foundational, prerequisite readings present the defining background and focus of this book, the methodology of conceptual analysis used and the criteria for critically evaluating rationality respectively. They establish collectively therefore, the necessary context for understanding and appreciating the full implicative weight of the analyses performed and conclusions reached.

Finally, regarding the scope and reach of this work, it should be briefly noted, as Kai Nielsen mentioned in his *Forward* that although this book focuses on the Mormon faith in particular, its reach necessarily extends beyond Mormonism to *all* theistic faiths. This is so, as shall be evident in Chapters 3–8 in particular, because the Mormon life-form, apart from its rather unique aspects and crucial differences (differences, incidentally, which are believed by Mormons and non-Mormon theists alike to make a real and significant difference), is founded – as are all the sects of Judaism, Christianity, and Islam – on core metaphysical concepts of 'God,' salvation/redemption (and damnation), revelation, and faith. These are concepts that, in connection with also common superstitious beliefs and tendencies, function for believers of all theistic faiths as the theological foundation of, hermeneutic for, and moral justification for their most fundamental or basic beliefs, religious experiences, and authoritarian practices as patriarchal social systems.

Given this fundamental, overlapping intersection, therefore, and the fact that the concepts of 'God' in all theisms — including the materialist, physicalist theism of Mormonism — are *primarily* built on an unintelligible metaphysical foundation; and given as well that all the major theistic faiths of the world are inherently superstitious and patriarchal in nature, in the end, *all* these various gods of theism — orthodox or not, and Mormon or not — shall, again, along with their derivative and related theological concepts, beliefs and practices, necessarily face the same challenges and share the same conclusory outcomes of this analytical and psychosocial assessment of the Mormon faith.

Personal Background Information

Beyond the above general background information (and for those who might be interested) I think some relevant personal background information might be in order to provide necessary context for the reader and to establish my bonafides as the author. As an essential prelude to the personal disclosure that follows below, I will say up-front, and unequivocally, that I know first hand what it actually means and feels like to be a fully converted and committed Mormon and Christian believer. The profound, affective experiences I had at the beginning of my involvement with the Mormon faith and throughout my years of religious activity, including, as referred to below, my so-regarded conversion to Jesus Christ, cannot be denied. Nor can I deny that I felt with great conviction and unwavering certitude that what I experienced was what I then wholeheartedly believed it to be on the basis of my theologically informed interpretation of those experiences.

This is, of course, the way it is with all such profound, affective experiences, religious or otherwise. They deeply affect us and cannot be denied. Even so, the fact that one has had such experiences does not necessarily mean that the subjective *interpretations* of these experiences, or our *beliefs* regarding them, constitute *knowledge* or are *actually* true (or even intelligible or cognitively meaningful), even if they are believed with sincere conviction to be so by the experiencing believer, or by those in the community of which he or she is a part.[23] In this regard, this much seems reasonably certain: While one cannot deny one's profound, affective experiences, one should — to be epistemically responsible and prudent — nonetheless critically (and with due psychological suspicion) question his or her (or others') fallible and subjective *interpretations* of such experiences. This is so in part because, as human beings, we all choose — with or without awareness — to interpret our experiences in a way that reinforces our self-image (making us feel good about ourselves), confirms, defends or protects our valued beliefs (those we wish to be true, or hope are true), or brings us the greatest comfort. More importantly, this is so because such interpretations might have real-life consequences and require binding commitments to a way of life that might present negative consequences to one's well-being or the well-being of those who might be affected by such interpretations.

Such is the case, I will argue, with the theological interpretation of conversion experiences derived from the Mormon or any theistic faith, where the acceptance of such an interpretation as *knowledge* and *actual truth* effectually results in a binding (and arguably self-confirming) commitment — a commitment, in the particular case of Mormonism, to a life of unwavering (and expected) servitude to a putatively revealed plan and church program. It results in a commitment, moreover, that requires — notwithstanding the alleged acknowledgement of, and superordinate value for, free will — the unquestioning subordination of one's will to putatively authoritative counsel and commandments.

My initial acceptance of and decision to join the Mormon Church in 1974 was born of my own innate superstitious nature and metaphysical inclinations, my primary identification with a protective, loving yet authoritarian Greek father, a shame-based personality forged by years of patriarchal abuse "for my own good," and an illness-induced terror of disease and death established at a young age as a child and again as a young man. My faith was initially based on the allure of certain wished-for promised blessings offered by the Mormon religion and was sustained by the foundational meta-belief that the scriptures, theology, and official history of the Mormon religion were *literally, absolutely,* and *objectively* true. This belief, false or incoherent as it was and is, was nonetheless a belief that I doggedly held. I held it, I would argue, primarily because I *wanted to believe*, and because that is the way the Missionaries, members, and leaders of the Mormon Church presented it then, and present it now.

Later, in 1981, I sought, perhaps in response to latent doubts and anxiety in my life at the time, to strengthen and perfect my faith in Christ and, as the result of extending myself in prayer and fasting over a three-day period, experienced on July 21st of that year what was personally regarded at the time as a conversion to Jesus Christ as my personal savior and as Savior of the world. This dramatic and profoundly emotional experience was, in my view and the views of others in the faith who knew of it, akin to the scriptural conversion experiences of two central *Book of Mormon* characters — Alma the Younger and Enos, presented in Mosiah 27 and Enos 1 respectively. It was documented and shared with a few very intimate friends who in turn shared it with many others. The interpretation of this experience was supported presuppositionally and in virtue of its experienced effects in my life — effects that signaled significant change in my attitudes, emotions,

---

23 For an interesting and provocative treatment of the subject of belief in relation to knowledge and truth, see Eller 2004, 131–151; and 2007, 395–426; and also George H. Smith 2000, 61–79.

desires, commitments, and behavior. This became, and was so considered, the cornerstone and centerpiece of my faith. (Note: For a more detailed and personal account and present-day retrospective, analysis and assessment of this paradigm conversion experience see *Appendix A*.)

Such an experience could only be described within this particular religious life-form (and the larger Christian life-form as well) as a genuine 'born-again experience,' a 'spiritual rebirth' or 'mighty change of heart.' In virtue of such an experience I became, to use William James' term, a "twice-born" religious believer. With this experience, total commitment to living the religion predictably ensued and an enlarged set of expectations formed, consisting of certain promises, assurances, and scriptural entitlements which I also accepted as being literally and absolutely true.

In consequence of my religiously interpreted conversion experience, I willfully 'put-off the natural man' (consisting of human desires and instinctuality deemed in Mormon theology as 'carnal, sensual and devilish') and 'put-on Christ' (or the 'divine nature,' consisting of the expected, idealized personality attributes and desires deemed worthy and acceptable by the 'Heavenly Father'). Having done so, I continued to serve faithfully within the Mormon Church for over twenty years as an active, 'Temple-worthy' member of the Mormon Priesthood. Specifically, I was an ordained High Priest who served as a High Priest Group Leader and, before that, an ordained Seventy in the Melchizedek priesthood who served as a Stake Missionary, Ward Mission Leader, and Stake Mission President for a total of seven consecutive years. I also functioned faithfully as a 'home teacher' in service to assigned members of the local congregations (or Wards) of which I was a part, as well as, at times, a priesthood quorum instructor, Gospel Doctrine teacher and Sunday school teacher as assigned or needed.

Moreover, I was, by any standard within the Church, dedicated and theologically well informed through my extensive and continuous study of all the Standard Works (scriptures) of the Mormon Church, as well as the scriptural commentaries, doctrinal teachings, writings, and official discourses and proclamations of Church Presidents and General Authorities (regarded by Mormons as 'Prophets, Seers and Revelators'). I was also engaged, at a personal level and as a missionary, in Mormon apologetics. I regarded myself, in a very limited sense, as one of many self-appointed, lay defenders of the faith. I read and rebutted published anti-Mormon arguments in personal journals, writings, and missionary conversations, as part of my own preparations to serve effectively in the priesthood.

Notwithstanding all of the above, including participating in numerous religious ('spiritual') experiences over the years, I struggled personally, and privately, with many of the questions addressed in this book. I also struggled with a very deep albeit vague sense of real doubt, existential anxiety, and disconnectedness with myself and others, all of which worked beneath the surface of my strongest and most sincerely held beliefs, convictions, and asserted certainties at that time to fuel my often obsessive and dogmatic commitment to the faith.

I was, of course, like so many other faithful members of the Mormon Church, very well-defended regarding my beliefs and so-called spiritual experiences, and in complete denial regarding my doubts and concerns. I rarely admitted or voiced them, even to myself, and felt guilty on those occasions when I did so.

The palliative for me when concerned or in doubt —indeed, and in retrospect, the betrayal of my doubts and concerns — was the very commitment or zealousness that established and defined my faith.[24] Specifically, it was the obsessive compulsivity evident in my own religious rituals, daily scripture and gospel study, personal daily prayer, weekly church attendance, weekly Temple worship, and stricter obedience to the commandments and to the counsel of General Authorities of the Church which provided relief from anxiety related to unanswered questions and doubts. Through the ritual of prayer in particular (as prescribed specifically in Enos 1:4 in the *Book of Mormon*), I always thought I received comforting and assuring answers and confirmations from 'God' in the form of positive feelings in response to affirming questions. Such confirming and comforting (self-generated and induced) thoughts, assurances, and feelings seemed — at least for a while — to quiet the doubt or discomfort which had broken through my defenses. Nevertheless, the doubts, anxiety, and sense of self-alienation remained — betrayed, again, and unknowingly at the time, by my dogmatic, rigid, and obsessive-compulsive religious behavior.

Ultimately and predictably, with the help of certain difficult life experiences (perhaps, in retrospect, orchestrated by deep, psychological needs at play) I found myself religiously acting-out and consequently in a crisis of faith. This crisis lasted for several years and eventually led to the deep realization that I had been living a lie as a Mormon believer and that my commitment and corresponding faithfulness in this aspect of my life was rooted — as I think it is with many if not all committed theistic believers, to a greater or lesser degree — in religious (or 'spiritual') experiences which are, like all such conversion experiences, and as shall be argued in some depth in *Appendix A*, indicative of mental illness. My resignation from the Church of Jesus Christ of Latter-day Saints (which followed my excommunication and subsequent reinstatement to full-fellowship) was tendered and finally (in the Church's way) granted[25] in 2002, after my refusal to cooperate and comply with my local Church leaders' insistence in convening a church court to determine if there was 'sin' involved sufficient to warrant excommunication. (Why, after all, — or so Mormons believe — would *anyone* in right mind want to resign from the *only* true church of Jesus Christ, if not because of sin?)

In an important sense, I could say that I was not only deconverted from the Mormon faith in particular, but from belief in all gods in general. Such deconversion, which was nothing less than my own dramatic *peripeteia*, cannot, in my case, be exclusively or even sufficiently explained, as is typically (and incorrectly) assumed and stated by others, by a particular, unintended personal offence taken from a Church leader or merely as a result of being overlooked by Church leadership for increased responsibility in the Church hierarchy, or by Church disciplinary action (although, as I explain in the *Personal Postscript*, that was perhaps the proverbial 'icing on the cake'). It cannot be explained, moreover, as it might also be assumed, because I was living a sinful life (and therefore had lost the Spirit and been 'deceived by Satan') and/or was not in the mainstream or not sufficiently

---

24 Beyond the existence of doubt, religious commitment and zeal might also betray the unconscious existence of personal shame, guilt (both personal and/or existential guilt), and existential anxiety underneath the denial of death. All of these conditions — and likely others as well — were certainly at play in my life (as in the lives of all believers to one degree or another) during my religious years as a faithful Mormon.

25 Presumably by excommunication decreed in my absence, although to this day I am not sure since I neither had the curiosity nor the desire to read the follow-up notification from the Church regarding my formal request and later final, formal refusal to attend the church court.

grounded and faithful as a believer.[26]

---

26 Such an explanation or charge, if it is made in any case, requires some careful examination. It is always easier for some (if not most) devout believers in the Mormon or Christian faith to *a priori* assume or believe that someone who has left the faith and is critical of it was either never truly converted or suffers from some unrepented sin (or transgression of God's mind, will and laws) and has been consequently seduced and deceived by Satan or the devil and lost the companionship of the Holy Ghost or Spirit. Easier that is, in the sense of being less disturbing, safer and more convenient than critically and skeptically reflecting on the *non presuppositional* sense and truth-value of such an assumption or belief, and easier as well than asking with a sincere desire and intent to deeply understand, from an outsider's perspective, the reasons, views and perspectives of the one who has chosen to leave the faith and is critical of it.

Moreover, such an assumption or belief is a conditioned judgment inbred in all believers of that faith as a necessary deterrent and mind-control tactic, and as a way to insulate the faith from question and doubt. How, after all, can one who is a long-standing believer in good standing with the faith, and who is converted to the faith, knowledgeable of Church doctrine and teachings, assertedly faithful and obedient to the 'commandments' to the best of one's ability, and — by all standards in the faith — actively involved in living the religion as prescribed and counseled, possibly be able to question, doubt, and 'fall away' from the faith and be harshly critical of it, if not for unrepented sin? Such a possibility would pose a fatal contradiction to the faith and expose it — and all its teachings, requirements and judgments — for what they are, a house of cards consisting of falsehoods and illusions. (Clearly a *tu quoque* objection would likely be offered here, and I think fairly so. There are to be sure some [if not many] former believers-turned-critics of their former faith who are guilty as well of taking the easy way. This they do by merely, and reactively, characterizing the faith as false or harmful, and devout believers as self-deceived and delusional without seeking to truly understand the history or teachings of the faith, listening to believers' reasoning for believing as they do, and providing rational grounds for their assertions and criticisms of theistic faith and its believers views. Even so, it seems self-evident to me that such an objection would only be valid in strict comparison if theists accepted that their faith was primarily based on the authority of reason, not revelation, subjective interpretations of feelings, and appeals to religious authority and/or the believed 'proper basicality' [or self-justifying status] of *non self-justifying* religious belief through religious experience, for to offer one's 'reasoning' for regarding one's *non self-justifying* beliefs as truth implies *reasoning* and/or *evidence*, not mere assertion. Moreover, this *tu quoque* objection would seem to only be valid *in a specific case* if: (i) the former believer turned critic referred to was never a well-informed, converted and devout believer of the faith being analyzed and criticized; (ii) the former believer turned critic has not truly sought to non-defensively or open-mindedly understand the theistic truth-claims of the faith from the believer's point of view; and (iii) the former believer turned critic has *only* or *merely* and *unjustifiably* resorted to *ad hominem* attacks, with no substantive resort to reason or sound, valid argument or evidence in support of his or her criticisms.)

Consequently, the charge of unrepented sin — false or incoherent as such a notion is in a literal sense, given (as we shall learn in Chapter 3) its dependence for meaning and significance on the existence, mind, and will of a factual non-reality, *i.e.* 'God' — must be the default position for the "faithful" in explaining why a once faithful believer has left the faith and is critical of it. But the belief that a once faithful believer who leaves and criticizes the faith does so *because of* satanic deception, the commission of sin, and the consequent loss of the Holy Spirit is not only false as mere superstitious nonsense, but incoherent and factually meaningless as well.

Previous believers leave their faith and become critical of it for various reasons, including those disclosed in this author's case here in this *Introduction* and in the *Personal Postscript*. Examples include exhaustion (and depression) at trying to live according to all the standards and expectations *of the faith*; resistance to being dictated to or pressured to conform to the standards and expectations *of the faith*; self-alienation through the pressure to conform to *the faith's* at least tacit or implicit standards for conduct, and suppress essential parts of one's personality to be accepted *in the faith*; offence taken at the words, actions and behavior of other members *of the faith* or its leaders; loss of confidence in, or respect for, the leaders *of the faith*; faith-induced shame and guilt associated with falling short of the standards and expectations *of the faith*, or with behavior or actions condemned as sin *by the faith*; and doubt, dissent from, and disagreement with the teachings, policies and dictates *of the faith*. These reasons and others simply are what they are: psychological and/or intellectual reasons pertaining to the person's relationship to or with *the particular faith involved*, nothing more or less.

While certain reasons are certainly rational and justifiable on intellectual, moral, and psychological

Primarily, I think my deconversion and resulting life-reorientation began naturally and unavoidably as a result of over twenty years of persistent, cumulative affronts to my personality, integrity, faith, and intellect as a committed believer and member of the faith. These affronts, as I see it, were set-up in large measure by 'pre-conversion' life-experiences, particularly in relation to the aforementioned authoritarian abuses incurred in my patriarchal family of origin, and those superstitious and supernatural biases cultivated by highly superstitious parents and a strong metaphysical itch to get to some ultimate 'Truth' or 'Power' which I could retreat to or acquire to deal with my existential angst and deep sense of powerlessness. They were also set-up by the aforementioned unwavering meta-belief that the fundamental truth claims and explicit earthly promises of the Mormon Gospel and history of the Restoration were, again, literally, absolutely, and objectively real and true. This clearly false or incoherent foundational belief, superstitiously and irrationally strengthened to the level of certainty through my dramatic conversion experience and subsequent spiritual experiences over the years, was the primary source of my doubt. Moreover, such a belief was not — and could not be — the sure foundation it was believed to be.

Ultimately this meta-belief, built on a superstitious belief in the Mormon god and a tacit belief in the existence of divine revelation and human infallibility regarding the accurate communication and interpretation of putative revealed truth, could not survive the persistent and continuous assault to my faith made by the very doubts it was fashioned to create. Nor could it stave off or eradicate those doubts or resist the persistent, uncon-

---

grounds, certain other reasons might not be. At worst, they might be determined to be (to the detriment, I might add, of the reactive believer who has not intellectually or therapeutically dealt with, or worked through, his or her questions, doubts, concerns, grievances, and personal reasons for believing) illogical, unfounded, reactive, or even psychopathological in nature. Still, and in either or any case, such reasons for leaving and criticizing the faith, *whatever* they might be, are clearly *not* the handiwork of the 'devil' or indicative of 'sin,' 'unworthiness,' or the "loss of the Spirit' *except in the narrow sense and context of the beliefs and worldview of the faith.* Outside of the particular faith in question (in this case the Mormon faith) such shaming or guilt-inducing characterizations of the reasons for leaving and criticizing the faith have no objective meaning or significance at all, and *inside* the faith such characterizations (if deemed literally, actually true as objective realities) are, again, false and/or incoherent. So if in fact the faith in question is fundamentally based on false and/or incoherent propositions and factually meaningless concepts of god, salvation, revelation and faith believed to be literally or actually true (as is argued for and concluded in this work), then the *judgments* of believers *in that faith* regarding the faith-based reasons for a believer leaving and criticizing the faith are likewise, and necessarily, confined to the false, incoherent and cognitively meaningless belief system from which such judgments take form and are given literal, 'eternal' (and consequently *ersatz*) significance.

The sad and contemptible fact is, as we shall learn in Chapter 8, that the entire man-made characterization of certain human values, views, thoughts and behavior at odds with religious dogma as sin, and the related teaching of man's sinfulness and need for continual obedience and repentance are essential aspects of what has been identified and exposed as part of the abusive dynamic of Mormonism and all theistic faiths. Such a teaching, as a taught formula for peace, happiness, freedom, righteousness, and perfection in the Mormon faith is, in my view, and assertions to the contrary notwithstanding, merely a prescription for regressive dependency, divisiveness, and the sickening and weakening of the human mind and will (or instinct) for healthy and truly ethical living.

Finally, as to the second charge, there might be some validity to the thought that I might not have been sufficiently grounded in the Mormon faith, if by 'grounded' it is meant *conditioned.* Clearly, as a relevant aside, it was I think to my advantage that I was not raised in the Mormon faith since childbirth and that therefore my lack of grounding (or conditioning) in the faith was a likely factor in explaining my *ability* to get out with my right mind and, in an important sense, my life.

scious existential anxiety and sense of self-alienation that were exacerbated by numerous disappointing and disillusioning experiences.

These disappointing and disillusioning experiences, again, compromised my faith as well as my intellectual integrity in ways I was not aware of at the time. They included, first, experiences with unanswered prayer[27] and questionable or bogus revelation and prophecy in those cases where it was believed (and felt) that prayers were answered or priesthood blessings were received from the mouth of those with authority to speak for 'God.'

Secondly, they involved discovery of disillusioning doctrinal, or theological, contradictions, including changes to prior, allegedly revelation-based, official Church policy, doctrine, and practice.

Thirdly, they included disappointing encounters (through the published and spoken word) with various Church leaders, including many General Authorities and so-called Prophets, Seers and Revelators — encounters which, in my mind at the time (and even now), betrayed their pettiness, *ersatz* spirituality, and lack of intellectual and spiritual depth, gospel knowledge, and theological understanding.

Finally, my experienced disappointment and disillusionment involved disturbing and unresolved historical questions and contradictions in official Church history, as well as the authoritarian disparagement of intellectuals and the suppression through threat and Church disciplinary action of certain scholarly publications and voiced conscientious dissent which allegedly threatened the faith of believers.

There were, to be sure, other disappointments and inadvertent offences, abuses, and bruised feelings as well over the years involving interactions with various church leaders and members, but these matters were neither primary nor decisive.[28] While they were

---

27 Regarding the problem of unanswered prayer, it is important to note that the natural and stated, or unacknowledged and perhaps unconscious doubt regarding the possibility and/or efficacy of prayer is often met, even among faithful believers, with various common psychological defenses associated with self-deception. Of the numerous ego-defenses known, the following are, I think, relevant to the problem at hand: isolation, intellectualization, rationalization, moralization, compartmentalization, turning against the self, and, at a primary level, denial. (A more in-depth treatment of the problem of prayer is presented in Chapter 7. See also McWilliams (1994) for information regarding the meaning of the aforementioned defenses.)

28 Violated theological expectations and ecclesiastical and social offenses and abuses are often, if not always the parent of crises of faith or confidence in the truthfulness of one's beliefs, as well as subsequent anger (deflected or otherwise) toward the faith and those in it. To suggest, as Mormon leaders and apologists often do, that believers' pride is the cause of such disappointment, disillusionment, and offense is, as we shall learn in Chapter 8 and the *Epilogue*, one example of a shaming mind-control strategy (or double-bind) employed by toxic authoritarian religions to subjugate free-thinking and judgment to authoritarian control. To further suggest, as is also frequently done, that believers' faith should be based on their relationship with 'God, the Father' and 'Jesus, the Christ' and on the truthfulness of the *Book of Mormon* and the 'Restoration of the Church and the Priesthood,' and not on the imperfect leaders and members of the Church is, in my view, incoherent and utterly perverse. They are all necessarily connected in a vital way as a *whole religion* or belief system, and each part represents, reflects and therefore validates or invalidates the whole. Even so, as we shall find, the theological foundation of the Mormon faith alone is anything but solid and is incapable of sustaining rational belief except through self-deception. Moreover, there are perfectly sensible and compelling naturalistic explanations which account for both the growth of the Mormon Church since its inception in 1830 and the variety of so-called spiritual experiences that bind believers to their faith — explanations in both cases that have nothing whatsoever to do with the *post hoc* conclusion that 'Mormonism must be true.' (See, for example, Tice 2001 for a social psychological perspective of Mormonism and Faber 2004, Piven 2004 and Schumaker 1995 for a depth psychological perspective of religious experience and belief).

undoubtedly part of the cumulative assault on my personality, they never alone, or as isolated experiences, damaged my fundamental faith in the existence of 'God' and Jesus Christ or in the truthfulness of the Church. And they never resulted in personal inactivity in the Church or a diminution of commitment, even for a day.

In the end, it was the cumulative effect of my own well- defended, obedient, and inauthentic life, coupled with persistent doubts and anxiety working beneath the surface of awareness and admission, that plunged me (also unconsciously) into a self-orchestrated crisis of faith which broke the spell. This cumulative violation of my personal integrity and foundational theological expectations, together with later, more extensive education in philosophy and the sciences, and intensive psychotherapy — both in working through my own self-crisis and as part of my doctoral work in depth-psychology — enabled me to finally break free (or individuate) from the superstitious, morbid dependency and delusional obsessiveness driving all my religious beliefs and commitments.

Certain of my theological expectations of the Mormon god and his putatively called and anointed servants, the prophets, might arguably be regarded by certain Mormon believers as being excessive or unreasonable within the context of mainstream thought within the Church. This observation is not disagreeable to me in general or in my case specifically. Still, I would nonetheless argue that, notwithstanding the questionable rationality of *all* theological or religious expectations, for those *in the faith* as I was, *whatever* beliefs and expectations are required to sustain their faith are, for those persons, necessary. I for one certainly could not commit to a faith, for example, which taught that often times Church leaders (or 'prophets, seers and revelators') disagree among themselves or get it wrong in important matters concerning Church history or doctrines, or the interpretation of scripture. How could I deal with the fact that the sincere prayers of the faithful are often not answered at all (or according to specific appeal)? Or that prophecies are often unfulfilled, and revealed Truth is subject to change or revocation? Or that priesthood blessings often do not work as specified, or at all?

For me, the allure and appeal of the Mormon faith were again based on those explicit, foundational promises and related expectations, made or derived scripturally and by authoritative decree through believed Prophetic discourse. Moreover, they were based on the believed receipt of personal revelation and the administration of priesthood blessings by the laying on of hands of those putatively authorized to speak for the Mormon god and 'bind the heavens.'

Further, my unequivocal and unqualified meta-belief in the objective, literal, and absolute theological truths of Mormonism undergirding such explicit, foundational promises and related expectations (irrational as such a belief was) was nonetheless a fact which could not have been otherwise for me to believe *at all*. And this fact, together with all the inevitable disappointment and disillusionment it fostered through the necessity of endless exceptions and qualifications, ultimately provided to me the needed space for education, reason, and psychological insight to work in the service of analytical self-analysis, individuation, and conceptual re-evaluation. Today I am now what I consider to be a naturalist and recovering Atheist. I have, at the age of 62 years, come full circle to return to the natural humanity and Atheism of my birth.

My more personal reasons for writing this book are, again, shared in some depth in the *Personal Postscript*. Suffice to say here, and apart from the intent mentioned above, this work has been instrumental in furthering my own therapeutic journey to bring more complete psychological closure to this part of my life by publicly exposing as best I can, through analysis and assessment, what I regard as the deep incoherence, error, and harmfulness of Mormon theology and all theistic belief.

Moreover, I have also written this book in hope that it will be likewise therapeutic to questioning believers and 'closet disbelievers.' And that it will further provide to questioning nonbelievers and investigators of the Mormon religion in particular an essential counterpoint to the false and incoherent Mormon claim that theirs is a divinely restored and rational theology. (See also *Appendix B* at the end of this book if you are currently investigating the Mormon religion or if you're not familiar with the Mormon religion and desire to explore other views and counterclaims to Mormon claims and teachings.)

I have also written this book as an invitation and challenge to all *unquestioning* Mormon believers (and all other religious believers as well) to honor their doubts by critically questioning their own religious doctrines, beliefs, and commitments from a meritocratic perspective as a skeptical outsider. Such an invitation and challenge is, in my mind, justified, not only by the need for sound (non *a priori* and question-begging) reason applied in the pursuit of knowledge which will benefit humanity, but by what I consider to be the widespread personal and social need for psychological well-being and disabuse through the pursuit of progressive disillusionment from regressive or childish religious or superstitious illusions. This latter pursuit, as I envision it, would be in the service of greater rationality, moral and emotional maturity, personal congruence, intellectual integrity, epistemic responsibility, and self-acceptance in the ethical (or conscious) experience of our human instinctuality. It would also be in the service of the rational pursuit, *not* of 'Absolute Truth,' which is an incoherent notion, but rather of "the fullest and best [justified knowledge] we can get," realizing fully that "fallibilism is the name of the game" (Nielsen 2006, 19).

Finally, I have written this book with a plea to all religious believers, my own children included, who are or perhaps one day will be, parents of young children, that they might at least pause and reconsider their commitment or efforts to indoctrinate their children in the beliefs of their faith, or *any* faith. As shall be argued elsewhere in this book, I consider all forms of theistic conditioning or indoctrination to be harmful in fundamentally shaming the personality of children through, for example, the conditioned, implicit association of doubt and/or disobedience with disloyalty, weakness, faithlessness, sinfulness, and therefore unworthiness. Alternatively, it harms them through the conditioned, implicit association of the natural human instinct for autonomy and free thinking with the dangers of wandering from the fold, or with the sins of pride, rebellion, apostasy, and ultimately wickedness. In yet another example, it shames them through the conditioned, implicit association of developing desires for sexual pleasure (from self or others of the opposite and/or same sex) as being bad, shameful, or inappropriate.

The list goes on in relation to other forms of 'invisible child abuse' associated with the religious upbringing of children, including, according to David Smalley, the "inducement of psychosis" (*i.e.* a psychiatric disorder that is marked by delusions, hallucinations, incoherence, and distorted perceptions of reality; see "Induced Psychosis: The Invisible Child Abuse," *American Atheist*, May/June 2009, pp. 32–3). This particular form of child abuse entails, in Smalley's words, "Making children believe there are things watching them at all times, that evil and demons exist in unstoppable spiritual form, or that they themselves are inherently evil and must fight their instincts….The journey begins," he writes, "when the child is taught at just three years old to repeat specific chants and songs in 'Sunday School'…which create the beginnings of brainwashing" (32).

Such brainwashing for Mormon children, as we shall explore in more depth in the *Personal Postscript*, continues in earnest with the use of religious language in the home and teaching of faith in a factually unintelligible, supernatural being (or Heavenly Father), and continues through the teaching and encouraged superstitious practice of prayer as actual, two-way communication with this invisible, incomprehensible, and factually non-existent being. From here, the developing child is further conditioned by the authoritative endorsement as fact of the fictional faith-promoting stories in the holy scriptures of righteous men and women (mostly men) who reportedly talked and saw 'God,' and entertained angels and divine messengers from that god.

As Mormon children approach the age of eight years, they are then encouraged by parents to superstitiously participate in religious 'ordinances' which somehow magically bless them and enable them to be saved and to return to Heavenly Father and live together as a family forever. And they are also encouraged, from the time they can talk, to publicly testify that they know what cannot possibly be known except by the conditioned interpretation of self or language, ritual and environment-induced subjective feelings, *i.e.* that 'God lives, that Jesus is the Christ, that Joseph Smith is the Prophet, that the *Book of Mormon* is the word of God, and that the Mormon Church is true.'

But this is not all. These children are also taught by their parents and teachers at Church of the magical outcomes to prayer, including the special feelings and promptings from the Spirit (and even spoken words from the Mormon god to their minds) which can guide them and direct them in their life. Add to this the parental, institutional, governmental, and societal pressure to embrace belief in, and obedience to, a particular god (or any god) as good and nonbelief or disbelief as bad or even evil, and we indeed *do* have the making of a psychical culture for psychosis; a psychical culture evident in all mind-controlling cults, including *all* theistic religions which are merely widely accepted cults.

As I have previewed earlier and shall argue repeatedly throughout the pages which follow, I have conducted a rigorous, conceptual analysis of Mormon doctrines and beliefs according to the *philosophical* premises and methodology presented in Chapter 1, and in accordance with "a nonscientistic, fallibilistic, contextualist, historicist, pragmatic and antimetaphysical naturalism without being subjectivist, relativistic, or nihilistic" (Nielsen 1996, 25–55).[29] In doing so I have come to the personal view that as is the case with *all* theistic religions, the Mormon faith is, at a strictly anthropomorphic level, superstitious and false. At its essential nonanthropomorphic, metaphysical core, it is conceptually unintelligible, incoherent, and factually meaningless — making it, in virtue of the criteria of rationality presented in Chapter 2, utterly irrational.

Moreover, I have also concluded, on the basis of both conceptual analysis and the intrinsic, *conceptual evidentialism* of "belief's own ethics" (Adler 2006), that not only is it irrational to hold Mormon (or any) theistic beliefs as truth, it is impossible to do so

---

29 For a list of the different species of naturalism, see Nielsen 2001, 136, and for an important understanding of the various crucial modifiers of Nielsen's *foundationless* naturalism, as well as those statements which characterize his naturalism, see Nielsen 1996, 25-55.

without evasion and self-deception. On the basis of personal experience and observation, as well as the commonsensical application of both psychodynamic principles and family systems theory, I have concluded that the theology and culture of the Mormon religion is — despite alleged benefits — at least potentially (and likely) psychologically detrimental and essentially life-negating to believers. Potentially, if not actually, it is dangerous to society.

Given the above, for reasons that will become evident throughout this book, I have further concluded that the very concept of a 'Father/Mother (or 'Parent') God' – institutionalized or not – is, from certain psychological perspectives, a very bad idea. When belief in the literal existence of such a Parent-God is coupled with the religious concepts (and doctrines) of revelation, faith, 'chosenness,' divine acceptance and approval, and 'praise and/or blame-worthiness,' then such a faith, or religion, makes a very bad idea even worse.

In this regard, and for specific reasons summarized and enlarged upon again in the *Personal Postscript*, I have therefore finally concluded that not only is Mormonism, like all other theistic faiths, ultimately an incoherent, irrational, and harmful belief system, but that at its darkest and most fundamental core, it shares and represents what I consider to be the *worst* in *all* theistic faiths. It is potentially, if not actually, one of the most socially damaging and dangerous theistic religions of all. Clearly this is a very serious charge and, as I shall argue in parts of Chapters 5, 6, 8, and in the *Epilogue* and *Personal Postscript*, a justified one as well.

This final conclusion — which invokes in me at times the greatest indignation and contempt toward the Mormon faith and certain of its believers (not all shaming is toxic shaming)[30] — will certainly be contested by certain devout Mormon believers. They no doubt will charge that my allegedly unrepresentative and entirely self-caused experiences in the faith and my so-called apostasy from the faith have distorted their faith beyond recognition. They will say that my conclusions are unreliable and of no import or consequence. To these believers I would say two things.

First of all, to your argument that my alleged misrepresentative and self-caused experiences *in* the faith, and status as a disenchanted and sinful apostate *from* the Mormon faith, have distorted my view *of* the faith, I would remind you that the use of such an *ad hominem* attack as a *red herring* to defensively (and disingenuously) *poison the well*, evades and deflect the arguments being made by shifting attention from the substance of the analysis and assessment of your faith and their conclusions to the arguer, and therefore invalidates your argument from the start. My personal background, weaknesses, motives, and intentions are, to the degree deemed relevant, honestly disclosed. In part this is to establish personal credibility as a former insider to the Mormon faith and provide human connection with the reader and a personal context for my impassioned indictment of the Mormon faith as a damaging and at least potentially dangerous belief system. In this regard, my woundedness and imperfections as a human being and my responsibility for my interpretations of the Mormon faith, and those self-inflicted wounds inflicted before, during, and after my involvement with the Mormon faith, are neither obscured nor denied. On the contrary, I readily and openly admit to them and analyze them in text and footnote to a sufficient degree throughout the book.

Still, such disclosures and admissions are, in the end, irrelevant to the substantive

---

30 See note 2.

arguments made in virtue of the actual analysis and assessment performed in this work. So too are my desires and motives. Clearly, even if my own woundedness functioned as a lens that amplified the abusive pattern of control and shame in the Mormon faith beyond what might be typically experienced by believers who either are too conditioned to notice or too much in denial to admit, it would not hold that my critical analysis of Mormon beliefs is consequently flawed. It would not hold that the conclusions reached and argued for herein are consequently invalid or without merit. Nor would it necessarily or actually hold that my assessment of the Mormon faith and its aforementioned moralistic core and related code of patriarchy are therefore not actually abusive or harmful as adhered to and practiced. Nor would it hold — necessarily or in fact — that my hermeneutic lens, even if very different than the corresponding lens of the believing reader's, is therefore distorted or wrong *merely* on that basis. In no way would it establish that it does not enable me to see a reality which others cannot — or will not — see because of their own fears and anxieties.

Accordingly, I would advise Mormon readers in particular to stay focused on the *substance* of the arguments being made and the specific questions being asked, not the arguer's motives or precise understanding of the basic tenets of the faith — especially since 'precise understanding' does not even exist among Mormons. Instead, allow yourself at first reading to be naturally intrigued and perhaps even troubled by the author's questions, analysis, assessment, and passionate judgments and invective against your faith as an informed and once faithful insider. Then seek to objectively reflect on the questions, and more deeply understand, consider, and test the arguments made on their merits.

If as with *all* arguments — given the fact of human fallibilism — there are substantive, warranted, and sound (and also fallible) counterarguments to be made, make them. Again, any and all valid criticisms and sound counterarguments are welcomed by this author and will be seriously, critically, and respectfully considered on their merits. Otherwise, I respectfully suggest that you think long and hard about what you read here and in the various sources cited, and hold your critical judgments. Keep your opinions and unwarranted beliefs (are there any other kinds?) in tension until you have, as an objective outsider with a presumption of skepticism, reached a well- informed, studied, and carefully reasoned conclusion on the matters at hand. This advice goes for non-Mormon (and even anti-Mormon) theistic believers as well, to the extent that such questions and arguments might pertain to *their* faiths.

Secondly, to your argument, if it be made, that I have distorted your faith beyond recognition, I simply say, look deeper as an objective and skeptical outsider. Look beyond yours or others opinions, into the *entirety* of your standard works and the comparative, authoritative teachings of your prophets past and present. And look more deeply and critically as well into your Church history, beyond and beneath its authorized or faith-promoting versions (see, for example, Quinn 1994, 1997, 1998, Abanes 2003, Palmer 2002, and Brodie 1995). In both doctrine and Church history, what you might *think* you know or understand to be the case might not be the way things really are, or were. Your *personal* eliefs as a Mormon might not square with the basic theological tenets and requirements of the moralistic core of Mormonism as it really is — notwithstanding its recent and current revisionist content.[31] Finally, I would respectfully ask that you also courageously and

---

31 In this regard, as former Mormon author Latayne C. Scott incisively points out in her article published in the Summer 1992 Issue of the Christian Research Institute (CRI) Journal titled *Mormonism and the Question*

honestly look more deeply into yourself. Look into your own experiences in the faith, as well as your personal psychobiography and the psychodynamics which might explain the existence and persistence of your own personal faith in the Mormon god and your perhaps stubborn and/or anxious resistance to a critical analysis and assessment of your faith and your religion. Evaluate your religious experience as an objective outsider.

It would seem, in the end, that man's 'four errors' have found their home in theistic religion, and Mormonism is no exception. As Nietzsche so clearly saw it, "Man has been educated by his errors. Firstly, he never saw himself completely; secondly, he bestowed fictitious attributes upon himself; thirdly, he placed himself uppermost in a false scale of rank in relation to animals and nature [and, I would add, other men who did not share his beliefs and values]; fourthly, he invented and reinvented new tables of [religious] goods and always presumed them, at least for a time, to be eternal and unconditional [and absolute]" (Metcalf 1996, 34).

Accordingly, in this book I attempt to offer (at times passionately and confrontationally) yet another corrective for these four errors. The corrective I propose applies analytical philosophy and psychoanalysis — as well as good common sense and human sensibility — to the doctrines, beliefs, and practices of the Mormon faith. I do so, again, following Loftus (2008, 2010), by inviting readers to look *beyond the betrayal of their doubt* with a presumption of healthy-minded skepticism to test, as an objective outsider, their own religious beliefs. I ask them to acknowledge the known (at some level) incongruence of those beliefs so ultimately they may turn back to their natural Atheism with a wholehearted affirmation of their humanity.

It is my view that if we do not avoid, ignore, or neglect our questions, doubts, and concerns, but rather stay courageously, reflectively, and honestly engaged in the various critical and difficult inner conversations hopefully stimulated by this book, we will likely come to realize that our putative reasons for believing cannot continue to breathe defiance to both our intellect and our instinctual nature. They cannot survive without considerable harm and danger to both our selves and society.

With this I shall close this lengthy *Introduction* first with a personal realization and then with the words once more of Yalom's Nietzsche. The realization, while perhaps not profound, might nonetheless be important to those readers who are impressed or enthralled by the convictions of others or the testimonies of those in their faith who seem so certain of the truth of their beliefs —those upon whom they or less certain believers might lean

---

of Truth, "A Mormon sees truth as (1) constantly changing, (2) as going, in culture and practice, far beyond written doctrine, (3) as determined by subjective feelings, and (4) as often divorced from its history. (5) The Mormon approach to truth is compromised by a heritage of deception as practiced by leaders from founder Joseph Smith to today's Elder Paul Dunn. In addition, (6) truth to a Mormon is 'layered' in the way that it is presented to prospective converts [and members]. And (7) the Church itself routinely edits both its own history and doctrine to make it seem consistent and palatable. In practice, therefore, (8) truth often yields to what the Church views as expedient. In the final analysis, (9) the Mormon concept of truth depends upon the character of its god, who as defined by LDS doctrine is constantly changing and himself ultimately human in nature" (24). This characterization of Mormon truth merits careful consideration and, as shall be learned in reading this book and the other cited works referenced herein and elsewhere, is not without considerable, and verifiable, merit, regardless of Mormon apologetic responses and authoritative justifications offered in attempting to explain-away these and other problems. (*See*: http://www.iclnet.org/pub/resources/text/cri/cri-jrn/web/crj0110a.html)

for strength in the face of their own unknown or unadmitted doubts.

As an insider of the Mormon faith I was at times impressed (and at times even some-what intimidated) by the deep sense of self-confidence, conviction, peace, and equanimity projected by certain Mormon leaders and believers regarding their professed knowledge of what they believed to be true. This observed state of mind was to me, at that time in my life, worthy of respect and emulation, particularly in my own personal, secret struggles with uncertainty and inferiority. To be utterly without questions and doubt regarding the existence of the Mormon god and the next life, as well as the other basic beliefs of the Mormon faith, was, as I then saw it, *prima facie* evidence of such truths. Moreover, it was proof of the god-likeness and chosenness of those allegedly called by 'God' who possessed such seemingly powerful personal qualities and testimonies of the truth. I remember feel-ing at times like a child in their presence. In retrospect, I thought and reacted as a child as well. Such, for some, is the regressive influence of those who claim to authoritatively and absolutely *know* or to have a personal relationship with their God.

Now, as a more mature, experienced, and informed outsider of the Mormon faith, I have come to realize a very simple and important truth in this regard. This truth seems to me so obvious or self-evident that I am frankly amazed, and even admittedly a bit embarrassed, that I did not realize and apply it years ago as an able-minded and educated investigator and adult member of the faith. Simply put, certain ideas, and the language used to express them, have transformative power with those who, consciously or not, *need* and *want* to believe. In other words, certain people —all of us at some point in our lives — can be so entranced and profoundly affected by and convinced of the seeming absolute truthfulness of an idea that they are personally transformed by it. And yet, powerful as the idea might be in appealing to one's deepest yearnings, hopes, needs, and desires — and notwithstand-ing one's personal conviction of its truth — such an idea, if stated and believed as *actual*, *literal* truth, might very well be utterly unintelligible and without factual significance as such. It might be entirely false or without justification as even provisional knowledge.

Such of course is the case with all who have ever been deluded and self-deceived regarding something they once with certainty thought they *knew* was true — and so much wanted to be true! — only to later realize it was not. It is the case of all who have experienced a dramatic peripeteia, or complete reorientation in life, in which they came to realize that all they had once thought to be real and true was, in reality, false or merely an illusion. Finally, it is the case of all who have experienced a very vivid dream which, while sleeping, they 'knew' to be real, only to realize upon awakening that what they had experienced was, alas, only a dream that merely *felt* real.

Such, as I have learned and argued in this book, is also the case with all the ideas, or concepts, of gods and the afterlife in general, and of the concepts of the Mormon god, Savior, and Plan of Salvation in particular. For these metaphysical ideas to be representa-tive of reality they must, at minimum, be widely and objectively considered to be intel-ligible, coherent, and factually meaningful as stated truth claims with clearly established truth-conditions which can, in principle at least, be empirically confirmed or disconfirmed as being true (or probably true) or false (or probably false). If they cannot meet such minimal, *a priori* requirements they cannot *even possibly* represent that which literally or actually exists or is true as stated or believed, even if such concepts or ideas have had an actual transformative and salutary effect on those who have been captured by them or conditioned to accept them as such on the basis of their *feelings*.

Nor does perception related to, or derived from, these ideas affect and effect establish reality. Not all that *affects* us for better or worse (for example an evocative lyric, verse, memory, impression or hallucination) has a literal, objective reality independent of its perceived, believed, or wished-for existence and conditioned interpretation. Finally, perception simply does *not* equate to, or represent, reality — even if it does reflect the perceiver's *subjective* reality. As we all know so well, desires, hopes, fears, defenses, and conditioning unquestionably affect and distort our perceptions and interpretations of subjective experience. The mental existence and personal *effects* of ideas and perceptions (and their wholly subjective interpretations) that *affect* us are therefore *not* reliable arbiters of truth or evidence of the actual truth or factual reality of such ideas and perceptions.

All this is to say that *perceiving* and/or *feeling* something is so, and *saying* and/or *believing* it is so, does *not* necessarily or actually make it so. This rather self-evident truth, of course, goes both ways, making the claim that something *isn't* so just as suspect as the claim that it is. Still, and this also seems at least apparently self-evident, what is crucial in *either* case is that we know and therefore can intelligibly and coherently elucidate with sufficient specificity what we are talking about when we make such assertions — even if only to ourselves. Moreover, — and only if we can so elucidate such putative knowledge — we must show that we are, given our best collective knowledge to date regarding our world and universe and how they work, in fact warranted, or justified, in making such assertions as *literal* and *provisional* (*i.e.* non-Absolute) truth claims.

And now at last from Yalom's Nietzsche: "Truth is arrived at through disbelief and skepticism, not through a childlike wishing something were so!" And yet, "It is not truth that is holy, but the search for one's *own* truth!" In such a search, we might all profitably query with Nietzsche, "Can there be a more sacred act than self-inquiry?" …If not, then perhaps we might conclude as he might, that "[t]he real question is: How much truth can I stand?"

Thomas Riskas
Las Vegas, Nevada 2011

Foundational Preface

"This is not just another Church. This is not just one of a family of Christian Churches. This is the Church and Kingdom of God, the only true Church upon the face of the earth."

—*President Ezra Taft Benson*

Prefatory Note: This *Foundational Preface* creates an essential context for this analysis of the Mormon faith and establishes the fundamental nature of and justification for the analytical work performed in this book — as well as what such work does and does not entail. It differentiates the evaluative approach taken in this analysis from the more common approach used in other atheological works. Finally, it defines and explains the repeated use of some crucial evaluative terminology that must be understood before moving forward. As such, this preface — along with the preceding *Introduction* and Chapters 1 and 2 which follow — is essential prerequisite reading.

Although the analytical methodology and conclusions of this work necessarily extend and pertain to the gods and related beliefs and practices of *all* theistic faiths, this work entails primarily, and as titled, an analysis and assessment of the *Mormon faith*. As such, and for the uninformed or non-Mormon reader in particular, there is very likely a need for essential background. Accordingly, it is appropriate that we begin this foundational preface with the words of the eminent Mormon theologian, historian and General Authority, B.H. Roberts regarding the believed divine 'restoration' of the Church of Jesus Christ through its founder Joseph Smith.

> It is a most startling announcement with which the Prophet Joseph Smith [the founder of the Mormon Church, or 'The Church of Jesus Christ of Latter-day Saints'] begins his message to the world. Concerning the question, he asked God — 'Which of all the sects is right, and which shall I join?' he says: 'I was answered [by God] that I must join none of them, for they were all wrong, and the personage who addressed me said that all their creeds were an abomination in His sight: that those professors [of religion] were all corrupt: that 'they draw near to me with their lips, but their hearts are far from me; they teach for doctrines the commandments of men: having a form of godliness, but they deny the power thereof' (History of the Church, Vol. I, p. 6).

"This is a tremendous arraignment of all Christendom. It charges a condition of universal apostasy [or 'falling away'] from God." In fact, Roberts asserts, "Nothing less than a complete apostasy from the Christian religion would warrant the establishment of the Church of Jesus Christ of Latter-day Saints," for "if men through apostasy had corrupted the Christian religion and lost divine authority to administer the ordinances of the Gospel, it was of the utmost importance that a new dispensation of the true Christian religion should be given to the world" (Roberts 1976, 213–14).

The effect of Joseph Smith's putative vision upon "the accepted theology of Christendom" (215) can be summarized, according to Roberts, as follows:

First, it was a flat contradiction to the assumption that revelation had ceased, that God had no further communication to make to man.

Second, it reveals the errors into which men had fallen concerning the personages of the Godhead. It makes it manifest that God is not an incorporeal being without form, or body, or parts; on the contrary, he [God] appeared to the Prophet in the form of a man, as he did to the ancient prophets. Thus after centuries of controversy the simple truth of the Scriptures, which teach that man was created in the likeness of God — hence God must be in the same form as man — was reaffirmed.

Third, it corrected the error of the theologians respecting the one-ness of the persons of the Father and the Son. Instead of being one person as the theologians teach, they are distinct persons, as much so as any father and son on earth; and the oneness of the Godhead referred to the unity of purpose and will; the mind of the one being the mind of the other, and so on as to the will and other attributes.

The announcement of these truths, coupled with the other truth proclaimed by the Son of God, *viz.*, that none of the sects and churches of Christendom were acknowledged as the church or kingdom of God, furnish the elements for a religious revolution that will affect the very foundations of modern Christian theology. (215)

With the above background and summary as context, we turn now to the pre-1990 version of the educational film presented as part of the Mormon Temple Endowment ceremony,[32] where a 'Sectarian Minister,' who is in the employ of Satan and who represents all other theistic religions and admittedly teaches the 'orthodox religion,' asks the man 'Adam' if he believes that God is "that great Spirit, without body, parts, or passions; whose center is everywhere and whose circumference is nowhere; who fills the universe, and yet is so small that he can dwell in your heart." Adam, who represents at once the biblical Adam, the Prophet Joseph Smith and all of 'God's elect' and foreordained adult male children, responds to such teaching by saying, "I cannot comprehend such a being… To me, it [such a teaching] is a mass of confusion."

Adam is warned of damnation and then pitied by the Sectarian Minister and later commended by a 'true messenger from God,' who agreed with Adam's assessment and then proceeded in the film to cast out Satan and convert the Sectarian Minister to the *true* 'God' and Gospel of Mormonism. The clear implication here is that to Mormons, the god of the orthodox religion is false and incoherent; a non-reality unworthy of rational belief.

Later in the film, three apostolic messengers named Peter, James and John stand in the presence of two divine beings up in heaven: *Elohim* ('God the Father') and *Jehovah*

---

32 The Mormon Temple endowment ceremony was putatively revealed to Joseph Smith by the Mormon god after his exposure to the Masonic rites of free masonry. It has been modified or changed numerous times over the years since then. This is a fact which no doubt has been more or less disturbing to many faithful members of the Church as at least an apparent contradiction to the Mormon belief in the literal revelation of absolute truth. This ceremony, along with all the other rites and rituals performed in Mormon Temples, has always been regarded as sacred and therefore not disclosed publicly. To a rational and skeptical outsider, such a ceremony would be considered strange at best and deeply disturbing at worst. I would venture the guess that even the most faithful Mormon believers would feel a twinge of embarrassment and shame at exposing the Temple garments, clothing, ceremony, rites, rituals, and their meaning and significance, to uninitiated outsiders. Today, the complete content of the Mormon Temple ceremonies, rites, and rituals over the years are in the public domain (see *Appendix B* at the end of this book for internet sources) where they may be examined by interested Church members or investigators.

('Jesus the Christ'). These two embodied male gods with white hair and beards and clothed in white robes, direct the three messengers to "go down" to Earth and visit the man Adam in the "lone and dreary world." The three messengers go down to Adam and Peter tells him that they are true messengers from the Father, come down to give him "further light and knowledge." Adam asks Peter: "How shall I know you are true messengers?" to which Peter replies: "By our giving you the token and sign you received in the Garden of Eden." At no time in the film, or in the prior or subsequent versions of the Temple endowment drama or ceremony, do these or other "true messengers from the Father" share the 'true' meaning of 'God' with Adam, except through the images of the purely anthropomorphic male gods, Elohim and Jehovah, as they interact with Peter, James, and John at a place somewhere in the heavens that is transcendent to the world in which Adam dwells.

Now, instead of offering Adam the "token and sign," let's level the playing field a bit and imagine having Peter, referring to Mormon doctrine found in the standard works (canonized scriptures) of the Mormon Church and the teachings and writings of the Prophets and Apostles of that Church, ask Adam:

> "Do you believe in a *revealed* God who is the One Supreme and Absolute Being and the Supreme Governor and Ultimate Source of the Universe; who is an infinite, eternal, self-existent and independent spirit and intelligence of the highest order, housed in an immortal, bloodless body of flesh and bones in the form of a man and animated by spirit element; who is temporal and finite as a transcendent, perfected, procreated and resurrected spirit being with body parts and spiritual passions, yet eternal as an independent, self-existing intelligence and infinite in knowledge, power, wisdom and dominion; who physically dwells on a celestial planet in another plane of existence and therefore transcends this world in space and time, yet who is everywhere and fully present in and through this world and all things in this world by the light and power of his spirit which emanates from his material being to fill the immensity of space?"

What might Adam say if this was the first time he was exposed to such a representation of 'God'? Or what, for that matter, might an objective, unindoctrinated, rational, and open-minded adult, with a well-rounded, higher education, and without any belief in a god say or think about such a concept of 'God'? Would such a doctrinal concept of 'God' likely be more or less confusing to Joseph Smith as a young boy in Manchester, Ontario County in New York prior to receiving his alleged 'first vision'? This is a particularly interesting question — given the fact that in Smith's own words, as recorded in the canonized version of his history, his "mind was [already] called up to serious reflection and great uneasiness" about the diverse and conflicting teachings about 'God' by the various Protestant sects vying for new converts. Is this concept of the Mormon god any more comprehensible than the 'Sectarian God' or any less confusing? Or are both gods equally incoherent?

In this book, I argue that the only rational response a seriously reflective skeptical outsider could give regarding such an allegedly revealed, doctrinal representation of the Mormon god is the same one given by Adam in the Mormon Temple film regarding the theological god of orthodox Christian religion. Such a response could only be: "I cannot comprehend such a being....To me it (this Mormon god) is a mass of confusion."

More specifically and inclusively, I shall yet again argue that the central tenets, or doctrines and beliefs, of the Mormon faith (and all theistic faiths) simply make no sense at all as conceptualized and believed, and cannot therefore be believed without self-deception.

As the analysis in this book shall demonstrate, the non-codified body, or collection, of official and unofficial authoritative pronouncements, teachings, and assertions made by Joseph Smith and subsequent General Authorities of the Mormon Church — as well as the canonized Mormon scriptures themselves — are unjustified as truth claims and therefore without warranted assertability.

More significantly, as we shall learn, the very concept of the Mormon Godhead — consisting allegedly of three separate and distinct beings including God the Father, Jesus the Christ, and the Holy Ghost — is itself, in each of its parts and in its totality, both false and deeply incoherent. So too is the case with the concepts and beliefs comprising the Mormon Plan of Salvation and the Mormon concepts of divine revelation and faith in its god and Christ. These conclusions will lead us necessarily to the factual impossibility of the Mormon god and the utter unintelligibility of the Mormon faith in its entirety.

In presenting this analytical argument, I will not attempt to *prove* the non-existence of the Mormon god on the basis of conclusive, empirical evidence or formal, logical proofs,[33] or at all. While (as argued in Chapter 7) I do think it is reasonable, in certain cases, and in a certain limited sense, to assert the truth of a negative (*e.g.* the non-existence of a god or gods) beyond a reasonable doubt, I am convinced that such an assertion cannot be justified conclusively in this or any other atheistic work in the foreseeable future — if ever or at all. This is because such a claim, notwithstanding the fact of human fallibilism, can be, and is, avoided (not refuted) by believers. As we learned in the *Introduction* (and shall learn in Chapter 2 as well), they do this through the use of a variety of reasoning fallacies and evasive tactics.

Nor will I attempt to discredit the Mormon faith merely, or at all, on the basis of argumentative scriptural exegeses (which are all question-begging), specific historical inconsistencies and omissions, historically objectionable social practices and actions, and/ or intra- or inter-faith doctrinal differences and disputes. All these concerns and others have been extensively and compellingly addressed and defended elsewhere by other competent and questioning physicians, social scientists, scholars, historians, skeptics, theologians, philosophers, believers, disbelievers, and nonbelievers both inside and outside the Mormon church. They are beyond the scope of this book.[34]

---

33 As Nielsen (1971) I think correctly points out in this regard, and in regard to the practice of philosophy in particular, "We have good reasons for saying there are no proofs in philosophy, but this does not entail that there are no good arguments, good reasons, or plausible reasoning in philosophy. There are. But the attempt to make philosophy into a deductive system with self-evident axioms, postulates, and so on, simply will not do. In that very rationalistic sense of 'proof,' there are no proofs in philosophy" (123–4). Earlier, Nielsen tells us why he thinks this is so: "For one thing," he states, "proofs require premises. Whenever such premises have been set up in the past, even tentatively, the discussion at once challenged them and shifted to a deeper level" (121). Moreover, as Nielsen writes elsewhere (1993), given the incoherence of the nonanthropomorphic and/ or even quasi-anthropomorphic concepts of 'God' in developed theistic faiths of Judaism, Christianity, Islam, and Mormonism, "there is no point in…trying [*à la* Moreland, Craig, Swinburne, Plantinga, and others] to give proofs, evidential or otherwise, for God's existence. Until we understand the truth-conditions for 'There is a God' or 'No God exists,' we cannot intelligibly set about trying in any sense to prove that God exists" (265). See also Nielsen 2006, 23–35.

34 Regarding the scriptural and doctrinal inconsistencies, errancy, and changes, see Vogel 1990, 2002; and Banister 1988. Regarding internal and external (interfaith) doctrinal concerns and disputes, see White 1987; Beckwith 2002; and Blomberg and Robinson 1997. Regarding official historical and biographical gaps,

Rather, (primarily in Chapters 3 through 6) I shall follow the lead of renowned philosopher Kai Nielsen by questioning the intelligibility, coherence, and factual significance of the Mormon *concept* of 'God,' as well as the doctrinal *concepts* of the Mormon 'Plan of Salvation,' 'Revelation' and 'Faith in God and in Jesus Christ.' Nielsen's *a priori* argument for the incoherence of the concept of 'God' (the way 'God' is used in religious language-games) on the basis of the unintelligibility and factual (or cognitive) meaninglessness of metaphysical 'God-talk' is in stark contradistinction to the customary *a posteriori* atheological arguments for the necessary impossibility or improbability of 'God.' Such *a posteriori* arguments are based on formal deductive and inductive reasoning and proofs, or on rational demonstration through hypothesis testing.

For Nielsen, formal deductive or inductive arguments are ultimately futile, even if "sound" or "valid" (2006, 23–35). This, again, is because there is always wriggle room for dispute regarding the theological premises of such formal arguments and nothing can be ultimately resolved, even if, "…when taken together [such proofs, as part of a cumulative argument] …give sufficiently plausible arguments to make belief in the existence of God problematic to say the least" (26).

Moreover, Nielsen simply does not regard — as purely or predominantly rationalist, Atheists do — the claim that 'God exists' is a hypothesis that can be tested by the application of the scientific method (or methodological naturalism) to determine whether or not it is true or false merely on the basis of logic or evidence. Such an approach, as Nielsen sees it, is not indicated in challenging concepts inherent in religious language, or 'God-talk,' which, in principle, simply cannot sensibly be regarded as verifiable or falsifiable hypotheses that can be tested.[35]

Moreover, as shall be expanded and elaborated on in Chapter 1, it seems self-evident that all the claimed truths and related facts *about* reality as we know them are entirely *language dependent*. So too, necessarily, is the entire conceptual framework and affective

---

misrepresentations and exposés concerning the life and character of Joseph Smith, see Brodie 1995; Vogel 2004; Waterman 1999; and Quinn 1998. Regarding the problematical history of the origins of Mormon Church and the coming to power of the Mormon Hierarchy, see Palmer 2002; Abanes 2003; Quinn 1994, 1997; and Marquardt 1994. Regarding the *Book of Mormon* as psychobiography of Joseph Smith, see Anderson 1999. Regarding the authenticity of Mormon temple rituals, scriptures, and revelation, see Madsen 1992; Persuitte 2000; Southerton 2004; and Buerger 2002. Regarding the falsity and incoherence of Mormon scientific claims, see Anderson 2003. And regarding the widely considered morally questionable or objectionable Mormon social practices and actions performed either in the past or presently in the name of their god, see Bagley 2004; Van Wagoner 1992; and Brooks 1991. (See also, as referenced in the preceding *Introduction*, and *Appendix B*, which is included by permission from its author Richard Packham at the end of this book. This *Appendix* provides an interesting overview of what the Mormon Missionaries and Church authorities probably will and will not tell you about the Mormon religion and provides as well a comprehensive source of information for questioning investigators, believers and nonbelievers.)

35 Nielsen's Atheism — and the type of 'strong Atheism' embraced by myself and others — is, as Nielsen suggests, "a deeper kind of atheism, a kind…which rejects a certain conception of God, not because it is false that there is such a God, but because such a conception [as in the case of the Mormon concept of God, as well as the traditional concepts of the various Gods of Judaism, Christianity and Islam] is incoherent." Nielsen continues by noting that as plausibly argued elsewhere by Susan Stebbing discussing A.J. Ayer, "this is even a more deeply probing atheism than the traditional kind because instead of denying the truth of 'God exists' and the like, it denies that such a sentence could possibly be used to make a true statement, where 'God' is used [primarily, if not entirely] nonanthropromorphically" (1993, 263).

justification of all forms of theistic religion. This is so, I would argue, even if the justification of such conceptual frameworks and religiously interpreted emotional experiences are not dependent on the existence of hard empirical evidence or are elusive of empirical hypothesis testing. The Mormon faith, of course, is no exception to this basic fact. Like all other theistic faiths, the very conception of Mormon reality, Mormon religious experience and the Mormon 'eternal' worldview is *entirely* language dependent.

More specifically in this regard, and apropos to our upcoming analysis of the Mormon faith, it can reasonably be asserted that without language the receipt, interpretation, and communication of propositional Mormon revelation would not be possible. Relatedly, the translation, interpretation, understanding, and communication of Mormon scripture and doctrine would not be possible without language. Nor would it be possible without language to interpret and testify of the interpreted subjective feelings associated with putative personal revelation or spiritual experience. Additionally, the preaching and teaching of the Mormon historical narrative and Gospel Plan is dependent on language, as is the performance of the Mormon rites, rituals, and ordinances of salvation.

Given the above, it can then also reasonably be said that the Mormon faith as a religious belief system consists of those declarative and indicative statements or truth claims about the Mormon god and all that such god has putatively revealed to Mormon founder Joseph Smith and his successors. These statements, which are embedded in the larger Judeo-Christian life-form and language-game, comprise again the conceptual framework of the Mormon religion as commonly understood by practicing Mormons. They serve moreover as the hermeneutic lens for all Mormon religious experience and therefore, in virtue of the testamentary function of such experience, as the very foundation of the testamentary statements of faith (or testimonies) of all Mormon believers.

As acknowledged in Chapter 1 and again in the concluding chapters of this book, it is certainly the case that physical and even theoretical realities actually exist in the world (or universe) independent of language. It is, however, also true that we would not and could not know *anything* at all *about* such realities or existents *without* language. In this sense, our knowledge *about* any and all of existence is entirely language-dependent. For such stated knowledge to be considered *actually* true as stated, it must, if it is not self-justifying, be justified.

Such, however, cannot be the case — or so it has been argued by Nielsen and others — with the stated fundamental constituents of developed, metaphysical, and nonanthropomorphic versions of theistic cosmology and theology. Nor can it be the case, as shall be argued in Chapters 3 and 4 of this book, with the stated fundamental constituents of Mormon metaphysical and quasi-anthropomorphic cosmology and theology. Such fundamental constituents of the Mormon faith include, for example, the putative literal (material or physical) realities of procreated and/or eternal spirits (or spirit procreation); eternal spirit matter and energy; infinite and eternal spiritual consciousness; eternal intelligences; eternal laws; infinite and eternal exalted beings; the infinite and eternal transpersonal omnipresence of exalted beings; sanctification (or purification) of the spirit of man by the Holy Spirit by virtue of the literal shedding of the blood of an alleged man-god (Jesus Christ); the literal resurrection of the decomposed physical body to a glorified, immortal (non-biological) state; and the exaltation (or deification) of the soul of man, which consists of the glorified resurrected body and sanctified and exalted spirit.

As we shall come to understand in more depth through the essential prerequisite thoughts and information presented in Chapter 1, for these putative infinite and eternal and biologically and spatiotemporally transcendent realities (which are not even theoretical realities) to be considered *actual* facts as stated, they must meet *at least* three basic or commonsensical requirements. Firstly, they must, *at minimum*, be nondeviantly represented linguistically in a way that is widely considered to be intelligible. Secondly, as factual propositions or truth claims, such stated facts must *make sense*, or fit with and not contradict what we *actually* know (albeit provisionally and fallibilistically, and not merely assume or can imagine) about the natural realities of the world and the universe and how they work. Finally, such truth claims must have *truth-conditions* which can, at least in principle, be directly or indirectly (*i.e.* theoretically) identifiable and verifiable or falsifiable as being true (or probably true) or false (or probably false).

But the metaphysical realities of Mormon cosmology and theology cannot possibly satisfy these basic requirements for establishing them as actual facts. They are not intelligible as stated to those outside the Mormon (or theistic) language-game. They are not coherent in relation to what we know. They have no truth-conditions that can be pointed to or otherwise identified, verified or falsified. Neither directly by valid empirical evidence or hypothesis testing, nor indirectly, as with theoretical existents, can they be tested by the confirmed realization of predicted empirical consequences in causal relation to other known realities for required confirmation or disconfirmation — even in principle.

With such metaphysical realities, therefore, Mormons (as all theists) must necessarily and very problematically (as we shall learn in Chapters 1 and 2 which follow) rely primarily, if not *entirely*, on certain *non*-justificatory measures for the justification of their beliefs. Specifically, such measures include the use of modified or more familiar religious language, false analogy, and invalid analogical predication to communicate such ideas, and the mere question-begging assertion of truth through the appeal to scripture and logic based on scriptural premises. Moreover, (as we shall also learn in Chapters 5 and 6) it is equally problematical, if not more so, for such believers (especially Mormons) to rely on the experience of purely subjective feelings (a.k.a. 'personal testimony')[36] for their *acceptance* as truth. Such assertions, inclusive of their *ersatz*-justification and testified acceptance, can only be made and obtained with and through the use of language, consisting as they do of declarative and indicative statements *about* believed reality.

In the end, when it comes to acquiring religious knowledge or establishing religious assertions about 'God' as knowledge or truth, language is all there is. There simply is nothing else. There is no knowledge by ostension or in virtue of hard, objective, verifiable or falsifiable empirical evidence — neither direct evidence nor indirect evidence through predictive empirical consequences. Even *religious experience* is totally language-dependent for inducing conversion (by the 'preaching of the word') and for interpretation and communication.

---

36 Such testimonies of the alleged truthfulness of the Mormon faith, which are derived from putative revelation or religious ('spiritual') experience, are declarative statements that would be regarded as 'properly basic' by religious proponents of so-called 'Reformed Epistemology.' The argument for the so-called *proper basicality* of religious experience, known as the 'parity argument,' is addressed, along with attending footnotes, in Chapter 2. Moreover, the problem of regarding spiritual experience and feelings as justification for the truthfulness of Mormon or any religious belief is addressed in the content and footnotes of Chapters 5, 6, and 8, as well as in the *Personal Postscript* and *Appendix A* which follow.

Given this seemingly irrefutable fact, if there is a problem with religious language — or in this case the intelligibility, coherence and factual significance of first and second order Mormon 'God-talk' — then there is necessarily a serious problem with the truth claims of the Mormon faith or *any* theistic faith or religion. Simply stated by Nielsen (1993), "if we do not understand what we are talking about in speaking of God, we will not understand whether inferences we make from [personal experience, history or scientific data point or] lead to God" (265). More specifically and technically stated in relation to Mormonism: if we do not know what it would *actually* mean, or be like, to *actually* confront or in any way empirically confirm or disconfirm, *in principle*, the truth (or probable truth) or falsity (or probable falsity) of non self-justifying truth claims such as 'eternal and/or procreated spirits exist,' or 'eternal spirit matter and energy exist,' or 'eternal intelligences exist,' or 'infinite and eternal exalted beings exist' *etc.*, then we cannot say that such statements are *actually* true and can be *known* to exist or be true. That would be to make an unwarranted assertion that is neither justified nor justifiable at *any* time and in *any* world. In other words, we cannot say — and therefore justifiably claim to know — what *specifically* such putative existents would or could *possibly* stand for or *actually* mean.

If this is the case (and it shall be demonstrated through analytical inquiry that it is), then inasmuch as the Mormon god's primary attributes, as conceptualized in the Mormon faith, consist of such literal existents (or other metaphysical existents, *whatever* they might be), then (as it shall be argued and concluded) the claim that 'the Mormon god (actually or factually) exists' would necessarily be considered *a priori* incoherent because factually meaningless. As such, this alleged entity would necessarily be a factual non-reality. In other words, the *concept* of the Mormon God, having been found unintelligible and incoherent would therefore and necessarily make any claim of such a god's literal existence factually vacuous.

Simply put, if something allegedly known to exist cannot *possibly* be known as *fully* conceptualized either *directly* through objective and controlled observation or *indirectly* through either the controlled observation of confirming predictive (and predicted) empirical consequences or at least by specific reference through literal description or valid analogical predication (not merely imagination), then such a putative existent — in this case the Mormon God — simply *cannot* be *known* to *actually* exist. Moreover, because of the language-dependent nature of all we know *about* reality, such a being as conceptualized cannot possibly exist *period* if the language describing it is either nonexistent (because ineffable), or is utterly unintelligible, incoherent, and factually meaningless as stated. To insist otherwise, *i.e.* to insist that such a being *actually* exists in spite of the inability of *any* language to tell us *anything* cognitively descriptive or meaningful about its metaphysical or supernatural attributes and qualities, is to do so by mere subjective and unwarranted assertion. Clearly this cannot actually or necessarily make it so. Such truth claims cannot possibly be justified as such by *any* means, least of all by mere assertions based on subjective, personal religious experience and hoped-for existence.[37]

---

37 Mormon leaders, scholars, and apologists have attempted in more recent years to neutralize this rather obvious problem in two ways. First, they have tried to modify Mormon God-talk in a way that is more familiar, literal, and acceptable to believers, nonbelievers, and investigators and which strives for greater agreement with mainstream Christian faiths, and second, they have tried to avoid or marginalize the mention of, or reference to, the putatively revealed metaphysical attributes and qualities of the god embedded in Mormon theology.

Regarding the first approach, it is common practice in Mormon God-talk to semantically characterize the Mormon god in very general and familiar terms. For example, he is merely a 'Heavenly Father,' or a 'Holy Man,' and Jesus Christ is 'the Firstborn of the Father,' or 'our Elder Brother' or the 'Savior and Redeemer of the world.' This move essentially homogenizes Mormon language with mainstream Christian language and has

It seems fitting, then, in the absence of any airtight logical proof or valid confirming or disconfirming empirical evidence that might conclusively prove or disprove beyond at least a reasonable doubt the claimed actual existence of the Mormon god (*however* it might be conceptualized) that the best way — and perhaps the *only* way — to effectively and definitively *test* the validity of shifting Mormon truth claims would be to submit such stated claims to the rigorous conceptual analysis advocated and described in Chapter 1 and applied, again, in Chapters 3–6. Any other approach from *outside* the faith that would employ, for example, the scientific method and inductive reasoning to empirically verify or falsify Mormon or any theistic metaphysical truth claims, or an approach from *inside* the faith that relies on authoritative pronouncements, believers' subjective feelings or reported faith-promoting outcomes would necessarily fail — either through linguistic and methodological reductionism or through circular and self-referential argument and invalid appeals to authority and testimony.

In relation to the above, Nielsen's respected contribution to the philosophy of religion consists, in part, of his rigorous conceptual analysis of developed forms of Judeo-Christian and Islamic God-talk conducted within the framework of a sound, "coherentist view" of justification referred to as *wide reflective equilibrium*.[38] And he does so, in part, and from

the benefit of obscuring the problematic *sui generis* concepts of the Mormon faith from the critical scrutiny of simple or unquestioning believers. Thereby it sidesteps controversy and enables Mormon apologists to label the critical reference to the more arcane, differentiating Mormon language authoritatively used in theological statements about the Mormon god and Christ as mere speculation, opinion, or hyperbole. However, such a move does not — as we shall learn in Chapters 1 and 3 — eliminate the problem it seeks to avoid when the primary, secondary, and relational (and putatively 'revealed') referents or attributes of the Mormon god (and, by association, 'Son of God') inherent in such familiar, undifferentiated language are exposed, unpacked, and subjected to critical conceptual analysis.

Nor, in regard to the second approach (and as shall be argued in Chapters 5 and 8), does the avoidance or marginalizing of classical Mormon God-talk regarding Mormon cosmology in general, and the Mormon concept of 'God' in particular, rescue the Mormon believer who honestly if not evasively replies with "I/we don't know" or "we don't know much (or anything) about such things" when confronted with the necessary, critical inquiry regarding such God-talk. To reply in such ways to questions regarding, for example, what certain metaphysical attributes of this god actually mean by offering vague, ambiguous, or unintelligible descriptions, as likely some well read Mormon believers do, is to say nothing that is cognitively meaningful or of probative value. Likewise, to avoid the risk of getting tangled up in further nonsense, to reply, as other Mormon believers surely do, that "we don't know, for the Lord has not seen fit to reveal such things to us yet" is to create even more problems, not the least of which is begging the question at issue, the question of 'God's existence.'

Finally, even if this second approach were to evolve to the point of disavowing and eliminating altogether such metaphysical concepts and terms, Mormons would still be faced with troubling questions regarding their god's referents and what such referents are or in turn refer to. In other words, Mormon believers cannot expect to avoid the question of what specifically the Mormon god consists of, or what *specifically* would count for or against the Mormon god's *actual* existence as fully conceptualized. Arguably such a question, and others like it or derived from it, makes all forms or versions of Mormon and theistic theology very problematic to say the least. As we shall learn, attempting to answer such questions through the use of false analogy or by employing some other reasoning fallacy will not help.

38 Such a justificatory approach — endorsed, appropriated and adapted by Nielsen, following Rawls and Daniels (1995, 1996, 2006) — is a "context-relevant" and "practice-relative or at least practice-contingent" (In Seymour & Fritsch 2007, 51–62) process without metaphysical foundations that gets us *objectively* (through "extensive and coherent intersubjectivity" (1996, 15) and *reliably* (though fallibilistically and provisionally) to the best *knowledge* of *truth* we can hope to achieve as human beings. The approach itself entails, according to Nielsen, "…[getting our beliefs] …into a consistent and coherent pattern with all [our] other beliefs, and all the relevant beliefs reasonably available in the world (the cluster of societies) in which [one] lives or stands

my reading, by relevantly and competently attending to two seminal, overarching questions:

First, can the concept of 'God,' or the use of the term *God* in the developed or putatively revealed forms of orthodox theistic religion, be reasonably considered, as a result of critical, rigorous, linguistic or conceptual analysis, to be coherent, intelligible, and factually significant or cognitively meaningful? Stated more succinctly, are religious truth claims that assert the *actual existence* of such a god justifiable even in principle?

Second, are such allegedly *justifiable* truth claims (if indeed they are such) actually *justified* through the achievement of "wide reflective equilibrium?" Was such wide reflective equilibrium (or both straight and overlapping consensus) achieved through the required and informed rigorous testing of asserted beliefs against established common knowledge through dialogue, discussion, debate or argument? Where appropriate or indicated, was there rational demonstration using the scientific method following generally accepted or standard rules of evidence[39]?

If the answer to the first overarching question is "yes," that is, if the concept of 'God' in the statement 'God exists,' as used in the God-talk of nonanthropomorphic and/or quasi-anthropomorphic theistic religions, is commonly considered to be *justifiable,* in principle, through critical and rigorous conceptual analysis, then, according to my understanding of Nielsen's work, the belief that 'God' *might possibly* exist would be considered a rational belief for rational, educated people to hold.

Further, if it can be determined, albeit fallibilistically, through the achievement of *wide reflective equilibrium*, that the assertion, or truth claim, 'God exists' is *justified*, or at least provisionally true, then the belief that 'God *probably* exists' would be considered a rational belief for rational, educated and intelligent people to hold *provisionally*. Conversely, if the answer, under the same conditions, to the first question is "no," then the concept of 'God' is considered to be incoherent and the statement 'God exists' is *unjustifiable* and therefore, neither true (or even probably true) nor false (or even probably false). This makes 'God' an unintelligible concept and a *factual non-reality*. Given the above, it is Nielsen's considered judgment, on the basis of his conceptual analysis, that the answer to the first, overarching question is indeed "no," thereby making the concept of 'God' incoherent at its metaphysical core. The assertion or belief that 'God exists' thus is both unwarranted and irrational. This makes it irrational for those well educated in Western philosophy and the natural sciences to hold such a belief.[40]

---

in contact with, including, in this wide reflective equilibrium, the commonsensical and scientific (including social scientific) beliefs readily available on [one's] society....To get [one's]...convictions in such a pattern of coherence is to square them with (render them logically consistent with) everything that is reasonably known in such societies at such a moment in time....This will justify [one's] beliefs,...if anything will, for [such wide reflective equilibrium] appeals to everything that could be reasonably known at a given time. Indeed," Nielsen concludes, "this is the only thing that a full justification could come to" (1995, 235). For an excellent exposition of, and argument for, this subject *vis-à-vis* religious belief in general, and standard theism in particular, see Nielsen (1996), 13–19; and 79–109. For a thoughtful defense of this understanding and approach to justification against the criticisms of Alvin Plantinga and Nicholas Wolterstorff, see Nielsen's treatment of Plantinga (1996, 115–146), and Wolterstorff's criticism of Nielsen and Nielsen's reply in Seymour & Fritsch (2007), 37–62.

39 For an exposition and explication of the "six rules of evidential reasoning," see Eller 2004, 68–81.

40 Nielsen's conclusion, which is shared and extended in this work, is that religious belief is unjustifiable because religious, metaphysical god-talk, including as we shall learn, Mormon god-talk, is unintelligible, and because religious truth claims — including, again, Mormon truth claims — regarding the existence of

Clearly, Nielsen's argument and resulting conclusions, albeit widely considered to be intellectually and critically balanced and respectable, are not without question, limitations, controversy, or criticism.[41] And they are not — even to Nielsen, who devoutly accepts,

---

the Mormon god and man's relationship to that god are incoherent and factually meaningless. But even if metaphysical god-talk was intelligible, and religious truth claims were factually meaningful (which they are not), they could not be placed in wide reflective equilibrium. This is so, according to Nielsen, for at least two reasons.

"First," Nielsen writes, "we will not get the needed overlapping consensus concerning religion in our intractably pluralistic societies" (1996, 144). In this regard, Nielsen continues, "Not only is there the traditional (for many of us) divisions between Jews, Christians, and Muslims, but, as well, divisions between Hindus, Shintoists, Buddhists, Confucians, Taoists, believers in native religions, and various cultists….[T] here is no possibility at all that there will [or could] be [any overlapping] consensus concerning belief in God and related matters. And the dissensus here will, for a time, possibly grow as our world…becomes more and more a global village….This lack of consensus by itself is sufficient to show that in our present circumstance religious convictions, as well as areligious or antireligious convictions, cannot be justified on the holistic basis of wide reflective equilibrium *where we try to appeal to society-wide considered judgments* in our intractably pluralistic societies. However, where the appeal to wide reflective equilibrium (including their considered judgments) is to what Hume called "men of letters" in societies such as ours, a strong case can be made for secularism" (144–5).

"Secondly, even if by some magnificent social transformation of such a society a wide social consensus came into being, something which short of a very considerable and sustained coercion, and probably not even then, could not happen, still we could not get standard theism or any theism or supernaturalism into wide reflective equilibrium. We need to gain wide reflective equilibrium, to get an ensemble of our beliefs into the best possible fit, the most coherent, economical, and perspicuous arrangement that we can, for a given time, muster. But our religious beliefs, with their supernaturalistic metaphysical claims, fit badly with the physical system that constitutes our physics. Similar things obtain with our biology and our psychology-cum-physiology. The assumptions made and the way of proceeding and viewing things in these domains are very different than those that are part of supernaturalistic belief systems" (145). Simply put, "[t]here isn't the tight, neat, economical fit between the religious beliefs of theism and the scientific beliefs of our society that wide reflective equilibrium seems to require or at least seeks….Perhaps the various beliefs, from different domains, cannot be squared with each other or can only be squared by constructing artificial and arbitrary [*ad hoc*] epicycles (*deus ex machina*), utilizing arcane conceptions [or mere speculations], whose only purpose is to achieve the fit. Shotgun marriages (to switch the metaphor) might be the appropriate metaphor. But, when these beliefs are viewed more straightforwardly, there is no fit; the plain most economical thing would place secular beliefs in place of religious ones, thereby gaining a tighter and more economical fit" (146).

"For at least these two reasons," Nielsen concludes, "religious beliefs do not, and for modern societies cannot, stand in wide reflective equilibrium with our other beliefs [or knowledge]. I have mentioned scientific ones, but, as well, many other beliefs and ways of thinking of our common life, including our morality, fit badly with them. If to justify beliefs [as knowledge] is to get them into wide reflective equilibrium, then our religious beliefs are not and cannot be justified. If it is responded that the failure in the religious case is good evidence that the method of wide reflective equilibrium should *not* have the fundamental role that I and others have given to it, then to this it should in turn be responded that (a) in arguing philosophically more conventionally (perhaps *sans* method), as I have in [demonstrating the unintelligibility, incoherence and factual meaninglessness of metaphysical theistic beliefs], I have at least made a strong case for antisupernaturalism, and (b) that something like wide reflective equilibrium seems at least to be how we do reason in domain after domain (including many commonsense domains of our common life) and that to reject wide reflective equilibrium because it does not produce the results, in reflecting about religion, that theists and other religious people want, is suspect, given the antecedent, and independently established, problematicity of religious beliefs and the pervasiveness and at least seeming good sense of such holistic reasoning" (146).

41 There are no doubt many theists — Mormon believers in particular — who, like Calvinist Christian apologists Alvin Plantinga and Nicholas Wolterstorff, would not, as Nielsen correctly notes regarding Plantinga (1996), "…accept the method of wide reflective equilibrium, at least as I deploy it, as a method of justification for theistic beliefs and probably not even more generally. In particular, in arguing, say, for Christian

without reservation, the indisputable fact of fallibilism (including his own fallibility) — considered to be the last word.

---

beliefs, the 'we' concerning whose considered judgments a consensus must be gained, and then set in reflective equilibrium, would not for him [– or for other theistic believers or apologists –] be those of the critical intellectuals (Hume's "men of letters") of our time or even just the philosophers, but, by contrast, *Christian* [or in this case Mormon] philosophers and (perhaps) other *Christian* intellectuals [or, for Mormons, Church authorities] or even the *Christian* community (suitably Orthodox) at large."

"Plantinga," Nielsen reports, "regards philosophy as a communal enterprise, but, consensus or no consensus, Christian philosophers are perfectly in their rights, says Plantinga, in taking belief in God to be *properly basic* [see Chapter 2 and related footnotes] and in just starting there in philosophizing: that is, in 'systematizing, developing, and deepening' this religious belief — this 'prephilosophical opinion' — in relation to other prephilosophical opinions without at all trying to show, to nontheists, that this belief is reasonable, let alone warranted. But, *pace* Plantinga, the issue is not what they have a *right* (even an 'epistemic right') to do or to believe, but what is *reasonable* for them to do or to believe [or what is *epistemically responsible* for them to assert in keeping others in the faith or persuading nonbelievers to believe]….[W]hat is at issue [here] is the reasonability [and epistemic and ethical warrant] of believing [and asserting, or proclaiming] as he does, particularly when he is placed as intellectuals are placed in our societies, in our time" (154, n67).

Wolterstorff likewise "…argues that standard theism 'is to be justified with reference to those intellectuals who are theists' [or, in the Mormon faith, with those in authority]. The reference class, he has it, shouldn't be present-day Western intellectuals generally or present-day Westerners generally, but theistic intellectuals. Indeed only to those who he says believe in what he calls standard theism. But that, to put it mildly, seems at the very least to be ethnocentric and arbitrary and since contemporary Western theists are the ones at whom justification is aimed they will end up saying either that theistic belief is justified or must be just accepted fideistically, on faith. In any event, a lot of people just get arbitrarily excluded. Wolterstorff admits that theistic belief can't be justified if we take present-day Western intellectuals or present-day Westerners to be the reference class" (Seymour & Fritsch 2007, 54).

Nielsen agrees with Wolterstorff assertion that "a belief is not justified *tout court* but [perhaps] always and only with reference to a certain group…or specific class of person — a 'reference class,' as he calls it." Clearly, as Nielsen correctly points out, "Reflective equilibrium is *practice-relative* with its distinctive aims…for attaining justification of considered judgments in wide reflective equilibrium. … [There] is only… justification *vis-à-vis* some particular practice or cluster practices — justification, that is, only with respect to their distinctive rationales and with respect to certain purposes. But then," Nielsen asks, "isn't Wolterstorff plainly right in maintaining that justification for Christian belief is for and to Christian believers and that it can't be anything else? Indeed, he [Wolterstorff] insists, justification, even for and to Christian believers, works only if they are standard theists. That is and must be, so the claim goes, the appropriate reference class *vis-à-vis* Christian belief."

To this claim Nielsen responds simply, "No it isn't, for many Christian believers, and particularly reflective ones, including standard [and Mormon] theists, want to show that Christian [or Mormon] belief in standard [or Mormon] theism would be justified for any reasonable person living in a culture such as ours — perhaps even for any person, period. Christ is said to be the Truth and the Way. It is not enough for them to show that it would be justified for those who already believe…. Philosophers, and what G.E. Moore calls many plain people as well, thinking and feeling through about religion — skeptics and believers alike — want to see if it could be ascertained whether it is more reasonable or better (everything considered) to believe in God than not to believe in him…. Many people living in the circumstances in which we live are able to communicate with each other and not infrequently want to ask that question. It is not an unreasonable thing for them to be concerned with. Wolterstorff is just being arbitrary in blocking it off and setting it aside. Given the importance of belief/nonbelief — a religious commitment versus a purely secular one — in our lives, it is important to see, if only we can, what would be more reasonable for informed people, but people still caring for others and caring as well about their own lives, now living in relative security in the rich capitalist democracies, come to believe, and indeed should believe, about God. We know what the explicitly Christian community believes, but what about the reference class just specified: What do they believe and what should they believe [apart from having the 'right' to do so] about God and religious commitment? Wolterstorff, whatever his intent, just evasively leads us away from this crucial question and he does nothing to show that, appearances to the contrary, it is not a crucial question with which many reflective human beings want to come to grips" (54–5).

While certain common criticisms regarding Nielsen's approach will be raised and addressed somewhat in the pages that follow, it is nonetheless not my intention to argue at length in defense of Nielsen's work or conclusions. His work simply makes good sense. Moreover, it stands for itself, having been, as we shall learn in the chapters that follow, adequately defended in the corpus of his work and justified against all serious objections to date. Nor is it my intention, looking beyond his analytical approach, to address or defend Nielsen's "naturalism without foundations" or suggested methodology of justification through "wide reflective equilibrium." He very capably and effectively does so himself. (Nielsen 1995, 1996, 2006) Suffice to say that I consider his conclusions and methodology to be sound, sensible, relevant, and of considerable weight and merit as a necessary and invaluable context, or backdrop, for my own analysis and conclusions regarding the rationality of Mormon theology.

Although Nielsen does not address Mormon theology or doctrine in particular, his *conceptual analysis* of the orthodox gods and religions of developed Christianity, Judaism, and Islam is transferable. Given the perhaps unintended, yet nonetheless real, therapeutic role of Nielsen's work for me personally, and the prominence of Nielsen's work as a respected philosopher of religion, my principle task here is to effectively make that connection in the service of *critically analyzing*[42] Mormon theology.

Accordingly, given that my analysis of Mormon theology is based primarily on Nielsen's methodology and approach, as I apply it to Mormon theology I will, again, frequently, and at times extensively and appropriately, turn to Nielsen's own words throughout this book for the necessary context, amplification, and exemplification of various key points, ideas, and core arguments. Moreover, I will also, where appropriate, likewise cite and quote other notable authors, allowing each of them, as well, to speak from their own work, rather than attempting to paraphrase or restate their words.

The conclusory remarks made and conclusions reached as a result of the critical analysis and assessment performed in this work are reasonable answers to questions asked — questions specifically designed to serve both the believer's and nonbeliever's quest for knowledge and personal well-being. It shall be evident that given the concept of *truth* and the concept of *consistency* with its related concept of *coherence* — concepts which, as Nielsen correctly points out, independently and collectively *cut across all cultures and societal structures and languages*. That being the case, Mormon theistic doctrines and beliefs simply do not and *cannot* make sense from what Nielsen refers to as a "coherence view" of truth. More fundamentally, it shall be abundantly clear to all who do not abandon critical thinking or broad-based and objective common knowledge and common sense, that on the basis of conceptual analysis, the concept of the Mormon god — which is, again, the way the term 'God' is used in Mormon doctrine and discourse — is clearly false in its peripheral, purely anthropomorphic sense, and utterly unintelligible, incoherent, and factually meaningless at its metaphysical core. As metaphysically conceptualized,

---

42 The word *critical* in relation to the term 'critical analysis' is used definitionally to denote the exercise of "careful judgment or judicial evaluation" (Webster). And the word *analyze* denotes the deconstruction (or 'unpacking') of alleged statements of fact, or truth claims, into their *specific* component parts and critically examining the parts for sense, coherence, and cognitive meaning (or factual intelligibility) in the context of the concepts being analyzed. Chapter 1 provides an essential and pre-requisite understanding of the meaning, premises, methodology, and process of conceptual analysis used in this work, as well as its philosophical context.

there simply is no such 'God' to believe or disbelieve; to prove or disprove; to affirm or disavow; or even to argue for or against, much less to 'know,' worship or 'have faith in.'

These evident conclusions shall be the ultimate outcome of this book. They bear significantly and relatedly on yet another necessarily repeated conclusion. As noted repeatedly throughout this book, I will also argue and conclude, in virtue of my own informed personal assessment of the Mormon faith,[43] that Mormonism is largely and fundamentally an innovative and opportunistic outgrowth of the authoritarian cultural undercurrents inherent in Judeo-Christian and Islamic patriarchy. It is psychologically damaging and dangerous as a belief system. Clearly such an assessment is largely subjective and anecdotal, though not without sound theoretical support and empirical basis beyond my own personal experience. It is not, I would argue, without reliance on credible secondary sources of research and psychological sense and plausibility from a psychodynamic perspective.[44]

In the end, all arguments and conclusions considered, I will finally argue that Mormon believers and investigators should, for the sake of their own intellectual integrity, as well as their own (and their children's) psychological well-being, reject the Mormon faith and *all* theistic religions, regardless of how much good it seems to be doing in their lives. This argument is made passionately — on the basis of my own experience and regrets. It is, I think, reasonable given the facts as I understand them to be.

In making such arguments and arriving at such conclusions, it is important to note that the various representations of Mormon theology made throughout this book are derived from the aforementioned collection of authoritative sources. Specifically, and again, these sources include the Mormon 'Standard Works' (Scriptures) and the published teachings and discourses of Presidents and General Authorities of the Mormon Church. These appropriated and often paraphrased representations of Mormon theology, though not formally referenced to one or any particular source (to avoid evasive, hair-splitting exegeses), will be nonetheless regarded by well informed Mormon believers as sufficiently accurate *in concept and principle,*[45] even if not always in tone or expression, for the work at hand.

Even so, where there are disagreements as to particular doctrinal representations of the Mormon god — and there are always disagreements, even among Mormon believers

---

43 This assessment is, again, addressed briefly in Chapters 5 and 6 and more extensively in Chapter 8 and the *Epilogue and Personal Postscript.*

44 The assessment of the Mormon faith offered in this book relies necessarily on the use of certain depth-psychological concepts and terminology applied primarily from a psychoanalytical perspective. Although the use of such terminology is often avoided by to make the concepts more accessible (or 'reader-friendly') to readers, I consider its use important in conveying the *gravitas* and substantiveness of the assessment. It would therefore be a grave mistake, in my judgment, to dismiss such terminology as so much psycho-babble or to dismiss depth-psychology as merely folk-psychology without sound philosophical and scientific basis. (This is an erroneous charge which I will briefly address, with references, in a later note). Rather, I encourage readers to exert themselves intellectually to learn more about these terms and concepts to better appreciate the seriousness of this assessment in their lives.

45 For those Mormon readers who either dispute or are not familiar with the theological representations presented in this book, it is advisable to objectively consult the various and relevant resources listed in the *References* section (including, more specifically, the *Standard Works* (or scriptures) of the Mormon Church, Smith, Joseph, Jr. (2005), Smith, Joseph Fielding (1954, 1976), Roberts, B.H. (1976, 1995, 2000), McConkie, Bruce R. (1979), Talmage, James E. (2003), Widtsoe, John A. (1915), and the *Journal of Discourses*), and do the necessary background study.

and authorities (an interesting fact alone, given the Mormon belief in on-going revelation from 'God' to man) — it shall be argued that such differences are typically, if not entirely, mere differences of opinion regarding the meaning and scope of *secondary* and *relational* attributions to 'God.' As such they are irrelevant to the central analysis performed and conclusions reached. This is so because the putative existence of the Mormon god's secondary and relational attributes ultimately, and necessarily, depends on the intelligibility, coherence and factual significance of the Mormon God's putative *primary* attributes.[46]

Accordingly, as we shall learn in the chapters that follow, the conclusions reached as a result of this analysis are based, again, on the incontrovertible *metaphysical core* of Mormon theology. This core consists, most fundamentally, of the *primary* attributes of the Mormon god (and of 'man') and are therefore also *fundamental* (if not foundational) to the very essence and uniqueness of Mormonism as a religion.

Without such a metaphysical core, Mormonism *as such* would not exist, or would exist merely as a false and childish fairy tale or purely anthropomorphic superstition. With such a core, Mormon theology as a whole — consisting of its teachings about 'God,' the 'Plan of Salvation,' 'Revelation from God to man about God,' and 'Faith in God and Christ' — is unintelligible, incoherent, and factually meaningless. This will become clear on the basis of the analysis described and prescribed in Chapter 1 and performed in Chapters 3–7. This will make Mormon beliefs regarding this core unjustifiable and, therefore, on the basis of the criteria established in Chapter 2, utterly irrational and unworthy of belief.

To establish my initial perspective in support of this particular conclusion, I offer this initial and fundamental summary perspective from Nielsen:

> [Though] in our ordinary language there is a use for God-talk, just as there once was a use for witch-talk and goblin-talk, when we look at God-talk [including Mormon God-talk] even moderately carefully, we will come to see that, after all, it is incoherent — its current claims

---

46 "The following definitions [apply] to the kinds of attributes an existent has which comprise its overall identity:

(1) Primary Attributes—or fundamental character of a thing may be defined as the basic nature a particular thing is composed of. What a thing is, specifically, that it may do particular things or affect those around it in a particular way. The following two types of attributes provided below can only be applied to a thing if they can be related to an existent's primary attributes and the primary attributes are positively identified.

(2) Secondary Attributes—the character traits or abilities a particular thing may enact or possess. Examples: being generous, kind, powerful, wise.

(3) Relational Attributes—…the ability of an entity to relate to other things; to interact, affect, or be connected in some such way.

"In regards to the statement in (1), the inquirer may ask why it is that (2) and (3) are dependent upon the recognition of (1). As mentioned, this is because no possible relation could be established between a concept and its properties if the existent's [fundamental] identity, or primary attribute, remains unidentified" (Excerpted from the Internet article: "The Argument from Non-Cognitivism" located at www. strongatheism.com).

In the context of the above definitional framework, the primary attributes of the Mormon god would consist of the specific, predicative constituents of the Mormon god, *i.e.* what, allegedly, the Mormon god, as a putative being, would *basically* or *fundamentally* and *specifically* consist of or *be*. Such primary attributes are distinct from the Mormon god's secondary attributes, or what the Mormon god, as a putative being, allegedly or putatively *knows* or can *do* and what specifically he would be like in *character* or *personality*. Such primary attributes would likewise be distinct from the Mormon god's relational attributes, or how specifically he (as a putative being) uniquely *relates with*, or is *related to*, man and all other matter and living things.

are either such as we can know they could not be true in any possible world or, alternatively, that they are such that we have no understanding of what would establish, with any probability at all, their truth or falsity. Given their incoherence, there is no point…trying to give proofs, evidential or otherwise, for God's existence. Until we understand the truth-conditions for "There is a God" or "No God exists," we cannot intelligibly set about trying in any sense to prove that God [in his putative fulness] exists.… If we do not understand what we are talking about in speaking of God, we will not understand whether inferences we make from such data lead to God. (1993, 265)

Relatedly,

If the concept of God is really incoherent, then we know [*a priori*, or] *ahead of time before even considering the arguments* that there can be no proof of the existence of God, for no premise or no conclusion with 'God' in it could be true (a requisite for sound argument), since the term is of an incoherent concept. We could also not, if that is really so, just take God humbly on faith, for you can only have faith in X if you have some understanding of X. But, if X is incoherent, then you cannot understand X at all, and thus you cannot understand what it is you are supposed to have faith in, to take on trust.… Only if you have some understanding of God can you accept God's word humbly on faith. But if the concept of God [in its doctrinal or theological fulness] is incoherent, you have no understanding of God — there is literally nothing to understand — and thus you cannot have faith in God. (1993, 252)

Nielsen's serious charge of "incoherence" is significant in its own right, as well as for this analysis of the Mormon god.[47] It is, according to Jonathan Adler, "the strongest

---

47 Elsewhere Nielsen elaborates, in relation to the concept of 'God' in developed forms of Christian God-talk: "In arguing that the concept of God is incoherent, I am not claiming that 'God' is utterly meaningless. Surely 'God' has a use in the language; there are deviant and nondeviant bits of God-talk. If I say "God is a ride in a yellow submarine" or "God brews good coffee" or even "God dieted," I have not said something that is false; I have not even succeeded in saying something blasphemous; I have rather indicated, if I make such utterances with serious intent, that I do not understand God-talk. In saying something such as "God is a ride in a yellow submarine" I have said something closer to "Quite grounds calculated carefully" or "Elope sea with trigonometry." In short, my utterances are without a literal meaning. "God is a ride in a yellow submarine" could indeed be a metaphor. In the context of a poem or song it might be given a meaning, but taken just like that it does not have a [literal] meaning. But even out of context — say in the middle of a commencement address — "Pass me a peanut butter sandwich" would be perfectly meaningful, would have a literal meaning, though the point, if any, of uttering it would remain obscure. However "God brews good coffee," like "Elope sea with trigonometry," are immediately recognized as not even being absurdly false like "Humphrey walked on water" but as being without any literal meaning. "God is a ride in a yellow submarine" or "God brews coffee" is immediately and unequivocally recognized as deviant by people with a participant's grasp of God-talk, while other bits of God-talk are immediately recognized to be nondeviant and do so in fact have a use in the language, *e.g.*, "Oh God be my sword and my strength" or "God so loved mankind that he gave the world his only son." Even agnostics and atheists who understand how to use Jewish and Christian religious talk do not balk at such nondeviant utterances. If they are reading a religious novel or sermon, they keep right on going and do not balk at these nondeviant sentences, *e.g.* "God protect me in my need," as they would at "God lost weight last week." Philosophically perplexed as they are about nondeviant God talk, they do not balk at it, while they do in a quite ordinary way balk at "Procrastination drinks grief" or "God makes good coffee." There are absurdities and absurdities. Thus it is plainly a mistake to say that God-talk is meaningless.

"However, in saying that the concept of God is incoherent, I am saying that where 'God' is used nonanthropromorphically, as it is in at least officially developed Jewish and Christian God-talk, there occur sentences which purportedly have a statement making function, yet no identifiable state of affairs can be characterized which would make such putative religious statements true and no intelligible directions have

criticism one can make of a set of (purported) beliefs. It implies that they must fail of their own claims to truth, requiring no additional assumptions [evidence or proofs]" (2006, 98).

To conclude this foundational preface, it seems important and timely to do a bit of necessary linguistic housekeeping. First, the term *critical analysis* referred to above and in various places throughout this book, is used at times synonymously or together with the terms *conceptual analysis* and *linguistic analysis*. All of these terms require the 'deconstruction' of concepts and statements made as putative facts or truth claims. Further, the word 'critical' is used herein, and also in reference to conceptual or linguistic analysis, as a modifier which denotes careful or judicious evaluation, *not* the animadversion or negative criticism that is directed in places to the toxic practices and harmful and dangerous effects of fundamental Mormon doctrine and belief .

Additionally, for Nielsen, the word 'incoherence,' as used in his above quoted introductory remarks, as well as throughout the body of his work, and in this work as well, means or implies a *contradiction* in seemingly *four* discrete senses of the term. *First*, a statement or concept is incoherent if it is logically self-contradictory such as a 'round square' or 'married bachelor.' *Second*, a statement is incoherent in the sense of being a

---

been given for identifying the supposed referent for the word 'God.' Religious believers speak of religious truth but "religious truth" is a Homeless Watson.

"God, as Hepburn points out, cannot be pointed to, but must be identified intralinguistically through certain descriptions, if He can be identified at all. But the putative descriptions Hepburn mentions will not do. If in trying to identify God we speak of "that being upon whom the world can be felt utterly dependent," nothing has been accomplished, for what does it *mean* to speak of "the world (the universe) as being utterly dependent" or even dependent at all. (And if we do not understand this, we do not know what it would be like to *feel* that the world is utterly dependent). If we are puzzled by 'God,' we will be equally puzzled by such phrases. We know what it means to say a child, an adult, a nation, a species, a lake is dependent on something. We could even give sense to the earth's being dependent on something, but no sense has been given to the universe's being dependent on anything. What are the sufficient conditions for the universe being dependent? What would make it true or false or what would even count for the truth or falsity of the putative statement "The universe is dependent" or "The universe is not dependent."

"To answer by speaking of 'God'…is to pull oneself up by one's own bootstraps, for talk of the dependency of the universe was appealed to in the first place in order to enable us to identify the alleged referent of 'God.' And to speak of a *logically* necessary being upon whom the universe depends is to appeal to a self-contradictory conception, for only propositions or statements, not beings, can either be *logically* necessary or fail to be logically necessary. Yet to speak of a "factually necessary being" upon whom the universe depends is again to pull oneself up by one's bootstraps; for what would count toward establishing the truth or falsity of a statement asserting or denying the existence of such an alleged reality.

"Nothing has been specified and no directions have been given for identifying "a self-existent being" or "a self-caused being" or "a necessary being" or "a totally independent being." All these expressions purport to be referring expressions, but no rules (implicit or explicit) or regulations have been discovered for identifying their putative referents. With them we are in at least as much trouble as we are with 'God' and unlike 'God' they do not even have an established use in the language.

"It is indeed true that Jews and Christians do not think of God as something or someone who might or might not exist. If God exists, He somehow exists necessarily. But given the self-contradictoriness of the concept of a logically necessary being or existent, it cannot be true that there can be anything which must exist simply because its existence is logically possible. Moreover no sense has been given to the claim that there is something—some given reality—which categorically must exist" (2006, 120–124).

These thoughts, while again directed to traditional forms of nonanthropomorphic Judeo-Christian God-talk, are nonetheless apropos to the metaphysical aspects of Mormon God-talk as well, as we shall learn in Chapter 3 and the pages which follow.

linguistic contradiction where words are strung together in a way which contradicts (or abuses) the way we typically use the English language to convey an idea or make a statement as, for example, a statement that 'Jim sleeps faster than Todd,' or 'procrastination drinks melancholy.' *Third*, a statement is incoherent if it expresses a (causally) impossible assertion or truth claim which contradicts established and common knowledge about the world and the universe and how they work as, for example, the assertion that a human being can fly off a cliff by flapping his arms or physically be in two or more different places at the same time. And *fourth*, a statement or belief is incoherent if it asserts or holds that something is factual or actually and literally true which is logically devoid of cognitive meaning (factual significance) or is without truth-conditions. Finally, as in the above quoted summary passages, Nielsen's use of 'incoherent' seems to imply a comprehensive contradiction in all the above senses of the term to designate a concept as being wholly incoherent and therefore, necessarily impossible or illegitimate.

In connection with the designation of incoherence is Nielsen's corresponding designation of certain concepts or statements being "unintelligible." For something to be intelligible is for it to make rational sense. Something, in turn, makes rational sense if it 'fits' or 'hangs together' or coheres with what we consider to be common knowledge, *i.e.,* what we as twenty-first-century moderns *know*, albeit fallibilistically and provisionally, to be *true* about this world and the universe and how they came to be and work.

To be *unintelligible* is to be incomprehensible, nonsensical, and not understandable. In other words, if some proposition is unintelligible it doesn't fit with what we know, and therefore doesn't make rational sense. Also, a word without lexical, or definitional, meaning might be unintelligible as, for example, the words "Somorlo" or "Irlig." The alleged *factual* existence of some incomprehensible being or entity might be unintelligible as, for example, "Irlig exists." Finally, certain putatively factual, indicative, or declarative statements might be considered unintelligible: for example, "Irlig is all powerful, loving and wise" or "To be saved, mankind must believe that Irlig is their personal Savior." Stated concepts are unintelligible because they are semantically, logically, or actually incoherent — wholly or in some sense.

Corresponding to the four senses of incoherence above, we may have alleged concepts or statements that are *logically unintelligible* because self-contradictory; *linguistically unintelligible* because semantically incoherent; *causally unintelligible* because actually or causally impossible or in contradiction to what we know or is actually the case; and *factually unintelligible* because factually insignificant or cognitively meaningless.

While I initially found Nielsen's varied uses of the terms 'incoherent' and 'unintelligible' confusing at times, I came to find therapeutic value in reflecting on the various ways or senses in which his uses of these terms applied in his analysis or characterization of particular theological concepts or statements. For these reasons, I have chosen to continue Nielsen's intentional or inadvertent practice to at times use the words 'incoherent' and 'unintelligible' in all of the above ways, while also at times opting to use their different aspects or connotations separately or together for emphasis, as when I group the terms *unintelligible, incoherent* and *factually insignificant* (or *meaningless*) together.

Finally, it is also important — indeed *crucial* — to understand up-front something about the meaning, premises, and methodology of the critical, conceptual analysis referred to above and used in subsequent chapters to deconstruct the conceptual framework of the

Mormon faith and assess the justifiability and rationality of Mormon God-talk and beliefs. In this regard then, we will address in Chapter 1 the questions: what is *conceptual* analysis, what are its premises, how is it used or performed, and why is it relevant to the questions of fact, truth, knowledge, and rationality — in relation to religious beliefs in general and to Mormon theology in particular?

Chapter 1

Analytical Framework and Methodology

*"Intelligent people cannot long endure...doubt. It must be resolved...
After proper inquiries, using all the powers at our command, the truth
concerning the subject becomes known, or remains unknown...As the
results of inquiry appear,
doubt must flee."*

—*Elder John A. Widtsoe*

*"To be known, the truth must be stated, and the clearer and more
complete the statement is, the better opportunity will the Holy Spirit
have for testifying to the souls of men that the work is true."*

—*Elder B.H. Roberts*

Prefatory Note: This chapter, which has been referenced in the *Introduction* and *Foundational Preface* preceding it as essential pre-requisite reading, explicates in greater depth the method of critical, conceptual analysis used in this book. Both this chapter and the next, concerning the question of rationality, are perhaps the most technical and challenging chapters of this book. Although the subjects of 'conceptual analysis' and 'rationality' presented in this chapter and the next respectively might be foreign and even counterintuitive to the way we typically think about the concepts of *truth, facts, knowledge, reality*, and *rationality*, it is nonetheless very important to make the effort necessary to carefully and critically understand them. Only by doing so in earnest can the significance and implicative weight of the questions asked, analyses offered, arguments made, and conclusions reached in subsequent chapters be sufficiently understood and appreciated.

Utilizing the words of Widtsoe and Roberts quoted above, it is in the pursuit of "the [stated] truth concerning the subject" of Mormon theology — as well as the resolution of the real doubts of Mormon believers and nonbelievers which "must be resolved" — that our "proper inquiries" are directed in the chapters which follow. But what is the meaning of the concept of *truth*, the way the term 'truth' is used and understood semantically and non-metaphysically, as well as by Mormon believers in relation to their beliefs? Is the Mormon concept of truth correct, or even coherent? Has the putative truth of the Mormon faith been *clearly* and *completely enough* "stated sufficient to be known?" What specifically constitutes 'proper inquiries' and how might such inquiries most profitably be made? What analytical questions in particular might reasonably be asked by "intelligent people" so that "doubt must flee" and *the* truth — for or against the alleged truthfulness and rationality of the Mormon faith — might "become known"? Is such a state of affairs even possible? If so, how so? If not, why not?

These questions are fundamental and relevant to critical, philosophical methodology in general and conceptual analysis in particular. In this regard, Nielsen follows renowned pragmatic philosopher Richard Rorty in making a critical distinction between '*philosophy*' and '*Philosophy*' which is relevant here, and which I quote at length below:

> What Rorty calls *philosophy* [with a small '*p*'] is "the attempt to see how things, in the broadest sense of the term, hang together, in the broadest sense of the term." *Philosophy*, by contrast, is the attempt, either in the grand metaphysical tradition, in the tradition of foundationalist epistemology or in the philosophy of logic and language, to construct a systematic *a priori* theory which, as part of an autonomous discipline, would, in one way or another, critique the various forms of life. Plato, Descartes, and Kant...gave different, but in each case classical, articulations and defenses of *Philosophy*.
>
> ...*Philosophy* I regard as an impossibility.... It is something to be set aside as a house of cards... But *philosophy* should go right on rolling along, as an attempt, common to all critical intellectuals, and rooted in no discipline, to see how things hang together... The various articulations by *Philosophy* are taken [here and elsewhere] to be illusory. There are no foundational truths, no such 'rational foundations' or even a need for them; and there is no genuine discipline called *Philosophy* which could articulate and justify such "foundations."
>
> ...So construed *philosophy* is not *a priori* purely conceptual investigation. It will be broadly empirical and historicist and rooted in a consideration of the problems of the epoch in which the *philosopher* philosophizes. In doing *philosophy*, such all-purpose critical intellectuals (*philosophers*), coming from all over the place, with a heterogeneous bunch of skills, notions and sensibilities...will try to see how things hang together and they will, in doing so, and quite properly, ask critical questions concerning religion or any other practice, including philosophy itself. They will most particularly ask questions about how these beliefs fit together [or cohere] with our other beliefs, if indeed they do. Repairing the ship at sea, including sometimes throwing overboard some rotten planks, they will try for a time, but only for a time, and thoroughly fallibilistically, to see how things hang together. In doing so, the *philosopher* will not infrequently reject certain beliefs and conceptions — and indeed sometimes, though rarely, very fundamental ones — as not being conducive to our being able to forge a coherent picture of how things hang together and thus to a gaining of a better understanding of our lives and perhaps, as well, to a coming to understand a little more adequately how we might best live our lives both together and as individuals. (1996, 539–41)

Given the understanding of *philosophy*[48] established by the above quoted passages,

---

48 To regard philosophy in a disparaging sense as, for example, the secular alternative to revelation in relation to knowing truth would not apply to the use of the term here. As used here, in the words of George Smith, "...philosophy is the most fundamental of cognitive disciplines....[It] is first and foremost the personal quest for understanding....[It] is refined common sense. By this I mean the philosopher deals with the common experience of mankind... [it] is the systematic analysis of common experience." It is, in other words, and according to Smith, "...the quest for wisdom; [the] sustained and systematic effort to understand ourselves and the world in which we live" (2000, 98-9). As used here, what philosophy is *not* is the pursuit of absolute truth regarding ultimate reality. Such a metaphysical pursuit would be regarded as *Philosophy*, not *philosophy*. And such a pursuit would be what religionists might characterize disparagingly as "the Philosophies of men." Such '*Philosophizing*' does indeed compete with the practice of religious metaphysical *Philosophizing*, and the '*truths*' derived from secular metaphysical *Philosophizing* is indeed an alternative to putative revelation. But none of this produces knowledge or is relevant to the practice of *philosophy* advocated and used herein. We are not engaged here in some metaphysical pursuit of the 'Truth.' Rather, we are engaged in the pragmatic

it now seems appropriate to articulate, as best I can, the type of conceptual analysis used in this particular *philosophical* investigation. Before doing so, however, it is important to note that such analysis, as *philosophical* methodology, is embedded in a naturalistic, anti-metaphysical view of reality which is neither subjectivist, relativistic, nihilistic, objectifying and absolutist, nor scientistic or mind- or language-independent. Rather, it is fallibilistic, contextualist, historicist, pragmatic, non*scientistic* (not anti*scientific*)[49], and mind- and language-dependent (Nielsen 1996). Such a view of reality eschews (I think with good reason) 'metaphysical realism' as false or conceptually incoherent. It provides an essential context for understanding and appreciating the ancillary concepts of *facts*, *truth,* and *knowledge* employed in the type and methodology of analysis performed and the evaluative conclusions reached in this work.

Regarding, therefore, the fundamental question of reality *per se*,[50] I turn again to Nielsen (2001) who, in defending naturalism in his chapter "Naturalism Under Challenge," provides a sense of the naturalistic view of reality or, perhaps more accurately, of what is relevant in *thinking* about reality. Such a naturalistic view is inherent in the type of conceptual analysis used and advocated herein. It provides a strong argument as well against the type of metaphysical realism embraced implicitly or explicitly by all theistic religions in general — including, I would add, Mormonism.

The Problem of Reality

According to Nielsen, following J.L. Austin, "…it is nonsense to speak [as, for example, Christian analytic philosopher Jean Hampton (1998) does] of 'the materialist characterization of *the real*' or of 'the idealist characterization of *the real*' or 'the theistic characterization of *the real*.' [Or, I might add, of the Mormon characterization of truth

---

pursuit of a common understanding and knowledge of human experience and actual (natural) reality. (For an excellent treatment of this subject, see also Nielsen's "On Transforming Philosophy: A Metaphilosophical Inquiry," 1995).

49 By *scientism* Nielsen means "the belief that what cannot be known by science – and particularly by the 'hard' sciences – cannot be known. …My nonscientistic naturalism is, of course, not antiscientific and it full well recognizes the enormous importance of science in our lives and in any coherent modern view of the world. Moreover, I think, as I also believe any naturalist should, that when we come to make claims about what things, processes, states of affairs there are in the world, it is to science that we should turn for our best answers. …But saying this," Nielsen continues, "is not to take a scientific worshipful attitude toward science. We will not attain certainty or a 'final theory,' [through science or by the 'scientific method'] anymore than we will attain either any place else. Fallibilism is the name of the game. … [For example,] science does not tell us that it is wrong to exploit people, that we should keep the faith with our friends, that knowing the truth about our situation is often a good thing …that women have a right to the control over their own bodies, and the like. Our moral knowledge is not scientific knowledge, and it often does not wait on science for its validation, though sometimes scientific knowledge [– as an evidence-supported 'considered judgment' offered in pursuit of wide reflective equilibrium –] is very relevant to ascertaining what we should believe and do. *The belief that all our knowledge is scientific knowledge is just a dogma that no naturalist should accept.* … [Likewise] the belief that what science cannot tell us humankind cannot know is utterly unwarranted dogma. Russell and Quine to the contrary notwithstanding, a sound naturalism should eschew scientism" (1996, 26-7).

50 For a well-resourced, naturalistic yet non-philosophical treatment of the topic of reality as it is constructed in its various forms through religion, hypnosis, and psychopathology, see Schumaker 1995, particularly Chapter 1: "The Problem of Reality." See also Weiner 1995, 2005 and Rawcliffe 1959.

as 'things as they *really* are' (Jacob 4:13)]. No sense has been given to 'the real' here, and it is unclear that any nontendentious sense can be given to it. It is as bad as talk of 'being' or 'being-as-such' or of the 'ground of being.' We have something sensible when we talk of 'real beer' as distinct from 'beer without alcohol,' or 'real butter' as distinct from 'margarine,' or 'real philosophy' as distinct from 'the philosophy of sport,' or a 'real hike' as distinct from a 'stroll.' *Persuasive* definitions of 'real' are, of course, at work [by metaphysical realists], but still we do have a genuine contrast and, not infrequently, a contrast with a point, a contrast that is clearly not arbitrary…But when we just, *sans contexte*, speak of an investigation of, or reflection on, *the real*, there is no contrast with the unreal. What is the difference between a materialist characterization of the real and a materialist characterization of the unreal, unless the characterization we have in mind is to speak of trees, seas, lemurs, and human beings in contrast with gods, *noumena*, pure spirits, ['spirit matter' or 'spirit element'], bodiless intellects, ['intelligences'], entelechies, the *élan vital*, [the 'Light of Truth'] and the like? (Note again the trouble — or at least the apparent trouble — with completing 'the like.') But the latter cluster of terms in their comparison with trees, tables, *etc.* is of dubious, or at the very least problematic, intelligibility. It is not, for example, clear that we have said anything intelligible when we speak of pure spirits, ['spirit matter,' 'spirit element,' 'intelligences,' or the 'Light of Truth']. It is not at all like comparing 'real cream' and 'nondairy creamer.'…But the crucial point here is that there is no sensible talk of 'the real' except in a *determinate context for determinate purposes* (Hagerstrom 1964, 41-74, 313)…Put otherwise, *contra* scientistic forms of naturalism, a nonanthropomorphic [or even quasi-anthropomorphic] naturalism is for me at least both unwelcome and unnecessary.… It has all the ills of metaphysical realism (Putnam 1992a, 80–133; Rorty 1998, 43–97). Again, language has gone on a holiday (212–213; all citations Nielsen's).

Metaphysical realists, including, I would add, Christian and Mormon believers, apologists, and philosophers, are, as Nielsen sees it, "…in search of 'the only true description of the world,' but such a quest is incoherent (Putnam 1990, 1992a, 80–133; Rorty 1991). There is, of course," he continues, "a deep and persistent metaphysical temptation to try to speak of the way the world is just in itself or of how things just are anyway. But it is incoherent to speak of how the world [is] or of how [all] things [really] are independently of any choice of vocabulary, independently, that is, of how it can be described by a particular language answering to determinate interests, or how a vocabulary we have, or can come to adopt, characterizes the world or will come to characterize it. The metaphysical illusion is to have a picture of nature as having something like 'her own language': to think (incoherently think) of nature [or 'God'] as speaking to us revealing just how things [really] are (Putnam 1990, 301–302). The idea here is, of course, incoherent, but it is all the same possible [to conceive of], where our metaphysical craving to be able to grasp how the world [really] is in itself — to finally get things right — is so very great that we will not recognize the incoherence. We will not see what is obvious to the person without the cravings. We blind ourselves here with a metaphysical picture. But, given what we want, to wit to know what the world is like in itself, it can be, humanly speaking, a compelling picture, but something which is incoherent all the same. It can be very difficult for some of us to free ourselves from the grip of such a picture" (213; all citations Nielsen's).

"It is terribly important," Nielsen further points out, "to be careful how we put things here, for even the reference to 'it' [or 'things'] in 'of how it can be described' [or 'how things really are'] in the previous paragraph can mislead. There is no 'it' [or 'things'] there to be identified, taking different specifications, but mysteriously somehow standing apart from *all* these descriptions making various specifications of something allegedly *independently* identifiable and knowable apart from these or any other specifications. It is pictures as 'something' of which an understanding is gainable without some language (Putnam 1990, 301–302). The picture — a metaphysical picture — is that we have some language-independent way of knowing or of understanding things" (214, citation Nielsen's).

"This is not," Nielsen importantly asserts, "linguistic idealism for it does not suggest or in anyway imply absurdly that, [for example], there were no stones or trees around before there were humans with their languages to describe them. But it does claim," Nielsen continues, "that we cannot think about them or understand what they are and, of course, talk about them without having a language. Similarly," he concludes, "though they [*i.e.* the stones and trees] exist quite independently of what we say or think, there could be no *truths* about them without a language. Truth is in this way *language-dependent* in the way most objects [*e.g.* stones or trees] are not. *There is no truth without language.* And relatedly, but still distinctly, we cannot without having a language know or understand anything about them or anything else" (214).

"In cold sobriety," Nielsen concludes, "we need to recognize that it makes no sense to try to discover the way the world is apart from any linguistic description of it: linguistic descriptions which will vary from context to context, changing with our differing purposes, interests, and situations (Putnam 1990, 1994)… [Metaphysical realists and theologians or theistic believers and philosophers, including, again, Mormon believers, philosophers and apologists,] cannot have [their] one true [language-independent] description of the world [or cosmos]. There can be no such thing for such talk makes no sense (Putnam 1990, 1992a). Rather descriptions [including religious descriptions of 'God' and the spiritual or supernatural nature of existence,] answer to [basic] human needs, interests, and purposes and are structured by them. They reflect the problems and resulting perspectives that people inherit or otherwise come to have. There is no intelligible 'point of view from nowhere,' …or 'an absolute [factual] conception of the world,' that is, a point of view or a conception that is interest-free, particularly perspective-free, and could yield the one true description of the world, so that, free of some determinate human interests, scientific or otherwise, we could just say — describe how — the way the world is *anyway* quite apart from any human interests and resultant ways of describing and conceptualizing things. There is…*no just finding out about reality* [by revelation, mystical or spiritual experience or otherwise] *so that we could discover whether, after all, it — Reality Itself — is really naturalistic or otherwise*" (214; all citations Nielsen's).

The Analytical Task

With this perspective of *realism* or *reality* in mind as context — a naturalistic perspective again at odds with the views of metaphysical realism — we are ready to better understand the analytical task at hand and what such analysis involves or amounts to. Therefore, as I understand and apply it here, such critical, conceptual analysis involves the methodical deconstruction and evaluation of Mormon God-talk and theological (doctrinal) statements about 'God,' god's alleged 'Plan of Salvation,' the existence of 'Revelation from God to man about God', and the epistemic legitimacy of 'Faith in God and Jesus Christ.'

The purpose of evaluating such declarative, allegedly true, or factual, first- and second-order sentences as, *for example*, 'God lives and hears and answers my prayers' and 'God is the Supreme Ruler and Governor of the Universe,' respectively, is – consistent with the naturalistic view of reality espoused – to determine whether or not such *non-foundational*[51] truth claims are intelligible. It is to determine if they have truth-conditions, or are, in principle, *justifiable* as statements with cognitive meaning and therefore, not irrational propositions or beliefs. In other words, by conducting this analysis we want to know whether or not Mormon believers are justified in believing that the putative truths and related facts asserted in their religious discourse are *actually* — albeit *fallibilistically* and therefore *provisionally* — true and factual as *the best justified knowledge* we can get on the subjects involved and assertions made.

The implications of our analytical deconstruction of the Mormon faith are, I think, far-reaching, significant, and stark. Imagine the surreal and deeply disconcerting experience of taking apart — with a strange sense of urgency and foreboding — a familiar, highly valued yet mysterious 'object of great price' piece by piece — only to discover that once the object had been entirely dissembled and subjected to critical examination to determine its nature, it no longer existed! Such an occurrence, if experienced as a disturbing, perhaps recurring dream, might reasonably be broadly interpreted as the manifest representation of a troublesome latent reality in the dreamer's life. The reality might be perhaps that the dreamer is deluded and self-deceived regarding some crucially important and consequential matter which is not what it appears to be and needs to be taken apart, critically examined, and exposed for what it is — a harmful and potentially dangerous illusion. This is essentially what we will be doing, why we need to do it, and what we shall experience, though not surreally, as we methodically deconstruct the core theological concepts and beliefs of the Mormon faith by subjecting them to critical analysis and assessment. Arguably, it is what we would also experience if we were to likewise deconstruct the concepts and beliefs of all other theistic faiths as well — a work which I think has already competently been done in part by others and, again, most notably and comprehensively in my view by Kai Nielsen (1971, 1982, 1989, 1993, 1996, 2001, 2006).

Perhaps we might gain, up-front, a better sense of the analytical work we are about to learn more about, and how we might envision and engage in such work, by framing it as an instructive 'deconstructive conversation,' and by participating passively yet thoughtfully and honestly in both sides of this conversation. Doing so will also provide a helpful perspective and context for what will follow in the remainder of this important chapter, as well as provide a preview of Chapters 3–8.

In participating in this instructive conversation, I invite you to first imagine in earnest that you are an intelligent, rational person from another world who has a mastery and

---

51 A 'non-foundational' statement is non-self-justifying, as distinguished from a 'foundational' or, more accurately, *fundamental* statement (or belief) that is considered apparently 'self-evident' and true at face value *without* the need for interpretation or justification. Statements such as 'air, thoughts and feelings exist,' 'dead people aren't alive,' 'red is a color,' 'water is wet,' or 'unmarried men are bachelors' are considered examples of typical 'foundational,' 'basic' or commonsensical and apparently self-evident statements which are self-justifying.

understanding of all languages and scientific knowledge of the earth as one of innumerable natural worlds within the universe. Yet, for purposes of this particular experiment, you have *no* familiarity with God-talk of *any* kind and are utterly without *any* concept of, or belief in, *any* god in *any* likeness to what religious believers on earth think they understand 'God' to be.

Imagine also that while in this role you, as this non-religious objective outsider, are engaged in a mutually respectful exploratory conversation with a well-informed conversationalist on earth who is a committed theistic believer. The two of you have met together to help you better understand human culture and history in this world. Finally, as you assume this role in the beginning, and then reverse your role to that of the theistic believer at the end, you are asked to allow — again as a passive observer — the conversation to unfold as it does and follow along thoughtfully and self-reflectively in whatever role you are in, taking honest note of your thoughts and related feelings as you do so.

An Instructive 'Deconstructive' Conversation

During the course of this imagined, exploratory conversation your earthly conversationalist has occasion to share his belief in the existence of his god. After sharing his belief, you, as the non-religious outsider from another world, recognize the term 'God' as used as a referring expression and curiously ask this person what specifically he is referring to when he speaks of 'God.' His reply, if he is a Mormon, is that "God is the Creator and Supreme Governor and Ultimate Source of the universe," and that he is also the literal "Father of all the spirits" of men on earth whose ultimate concern and greatest desire and purpose — his "Work and Glory" — is to "bring to pass the immortality and eternal life of man."

Although this instructive conversation will involve a representative Mormon believer, it is nonetheless a *paradigm* conversation that could involve representative theistic believers of *all* other faiths and *all* believers regarding their respective concepts of 'God' as believed to exist. Whatever the reader's faith might be, if indeed he or she is a theistic believer, this experiment would apply. The same conversational construct could profitably be used to test the conceptual intelligibility, coherence, and factual significance of the theistic beliefs in question.

Putting aside for a moment what you consider to be a premature scientific inquiry into the implied naturalistic implications of such a cosmological claim, you stay focused on the believer's language and what such an indicative, descriptive statement about 'God' might actually mean. Accordingly, you then ask the other person if he is representing and regards such a 'God' metaphorically or as an actual being that literally exists. You also curiously ask, regarding this god's alleged "Work and Glory," what the term 'eternal life' means. His reply, again as a Mormon, is that he believes his god to be an *actual*, physical being, or "personage;" a "Holy Man" with "body, parts and passions" in the shape of a man who *literally* exists and resides temporally in another world or universe, or in another dimension of space and time. He defines eternal life as "the kind of life God lives; a godly life enjoyed by exalted men and women in the next life."

Intrigued yet still unclear regarding what such a being would be like, and hence, by association, what eternal life would be like, you, as an otherworldly outsider, take your inquiry further by asking this Mormon believer about the fundamental nature of his god. You start by enquiring into his god's *primary attributes*, asking what specifically — besides a tangible body in the shape of a man with body, parts, and passions — his god fundamentally consists of as a "Holy Man."

"I'm not sure I know why you're asking such a question or what you mean when you speak of primary attributes," he asks. "Are you asking about God's character traits and capabilities, and his ability to interact, affect, or be connected to man in this world?"

"Not quite," you reply. "What you are referring to would be what I regard as your god's secondary and relational attributes. By 'primary attributes' I am referring to the *fundamental* character of your god — his basic nature or what specifically such a being actually *is*, or would consist of as an actual being. For example, the basic nature of a man, or *'Homo sapiens'* as you classify such beings, could be, generally speaking, primarily characterized as follows: 'Man is primarily or fundamentally a biological, bipedal, and sentient being which, generally speaking, walks upright on two legs, is capable of ratiocination and the use of language, and consists anatomically of certain clearly descriptive and *observable* musculoskeletal characteristics, internal, external and reproductive organs, biological systems and essential substances, and a body chemistry consisting specifically of twenty-eight elements, approximately 99% of which are oxygen, carbon, hydrogen, nitrogen, calcium, and phosphorous.' These primary attributes, if you will, establish the basis, in this example, of a human being's secondary and relational attributes (*e.g.* the ability to walk, think, talk, communicate, work, reproduce, *etc.*), as well as the specific and particular truth-conditions which must, at least in principle, be sufficiently satisfied in order to determine, at a fundamental level, whether or not the assertion that human beings actually exist, or whether or not a particular being is 'human,' is in fact a warranted assertion.

"For such a determination to be made, anyone from another world who had no knowledge regarding the putative existence of human beings, or whether or not the beings on a particular planet are in fact 'human' beings, would, in seeking both to understand what specifically the concept of 'human being,' the way the term 'human' is used, actually means as a referring expression, and to evaluate whether or not the assertion that such beings do in fact exist – or a particular being *is* in fact human – is warranted, would need to know the reference range of such a putative being, or what specific empirical criteria (*e.g.* attributes and qualities) of such a being are. More specifically, the otherworld inquirer would need to first understand what the primary attributes of a 'human being' are or refer to so that such a putative being could be (at least theoretically, if not directly) identified and differentiated from other beings in relation to like secondary and relational attributes, and so that the truth-conditions of the claim 'humans exist' might in turn be determined such that one might know whether or not such conditions could, in principle, be satisfied sufficient to regard such a truth claim as being true (or probably true), or false (or probably false) in relation to what is widely and actually known about the earth and the universe.

"In relation to human beings, this latter determination would amount to knowing, for example, that a biological human being consists in part of a substance known as *blood* — a substance that is essential to human life and which in turn consists of, and can be specifically identified by, certain chemical properties and other descriptive and functional referents through direct observation and/or predictive empirical consequences. Moreover, by knowing that blood is one of many primary attributes of a human being, an otherworld inquirer also knows one of the essential truth-conditions which must be satisfied for a being to be truly considered as 'human.' In other words, any non-human inquirer from another world might know that a being is human *if and only if* it contains and circulates blood throughout its body, and *if and only if* it requires such blood to live. Moreover, it would be known that a given substance found in a being's body is truly 'blood' *if and only if* it consists of certain defined and observable chemical properties and other descriptive and functional characteristics. This essentially and analogically is what I am referring to and why when I ask about your god's primary attributes. I am trying to establish, at a primary or fundamental level, the reference range of your concept of 'God' and the truth-conditions of your claim of its literal existence so that I might know if in fact its putative existence as an *actual* being makes sense, or is factually intelligible or coherent, in relation to what is commonly or widely known about life forms in the universe, and if, again, such a claim can be, at least in principle, confirmed or disconfirmed as being true (or probably true) or false (or probably false) as stated, and given how your god is conceptualized."

"Well," the Mormon believer remarks with a smile, "I am quite sure that I will not be able to express God's basic nature in such terms or detail as can be done with human beings. But I do think I can get at what you are asking for using different terms and concepts." Then, pausing to think for a moment, and recalling the teachings and believed revelations of the Mormon faith's founding 'prophet' Joseph Smith regarding the Mormon doctrine of deity, the well-informed Mormon believer replies that fundamentally, or primarily, "God is a sentient, non-biological being who consists of *infinite and eternal spirit matter and intelligence of the highest order*, organized through divine procreation and perfected over time to become a *finite and exalted spirit personage and intelligence clothed in a glorified, tangible body which is animated by spirit element.*"

(Take a moment now and try to imagine how you, again as an intelligent, rational outsider from another world, who is completely knowledgeable of the natural realities and laws of this world, might react to such a statement. And remember in doing so that you have *no* familiarity with God-talk of *any* kind and are utterly without *any* concept of, or belief in, *any* god in *any* likeness to what religious believers think they understand 'God' to be.)

Puzzled, yet still curious, you temporarily set aside the at least apparent unintelligibil-ity of the above stated primary attributes of the Mormon believer's god or what, if any, possibly satisfiable truth-conditions might apply to such asserted referents and, realizing that such stated attributes must at least be cognitively meaningful for the existence of secondary and relational attributes to even be possible, you nonetheless grant for a time — in hope of contextually gaining a fuller conceptual understanding of the basic nature this being — that they are, and now proceed to ask about its believed secondary and relational attributes. "What," you ask, "are the related abilities and character traits of your god and how is it that such a transcendent being can interact with, affect, or connect with man?"

The Mormon believer responds again from the authoritative teachings of his faith by stating that his god is an *all*-powerful, *all*-knowing, *all*-loving, *all*-good being who is *perfectly* just, merciful, and truthful. He says that relationally, beyond being the literal 'Father' of all the 'spirits' on earth, he knows and loves each person — each of his spirit children — *perfectly* or *completely* and hears and answers their prayers according to their needs and the righteous desires of their hearts. Moreover, by the power of his spirit, or the

'Light of Truth' which emanates from his presence to fill the immensity of space, 'God' is present *personally* and in *all* his knowledge, power, and love *everywhere* in the universe, to organize and govern or rule the universe and all his creation, and to reveal to *each* of his children personally, and to *all* his sons and daughters collectively through his servants, the prophets of his restored church, his mind and will, and all truth which is necessary for them to know to have joy in this life and enjoy salvation and eternal life in the next life.

(Once more, try to step outside the familiarity of the Mormon believer's words and honestly and objectively put yourself in the place of this curious and respectful, yet naturally and reasonably skeptical, outsider who is utterly without any familiarity with God-talk, or any religious belief, and who is really trying to understand this apparently open and well-informed Mormon believer as he speaks with such certainty and conviction of his faith's concept of 'God' — a god that he sincerely believes to be an actual, literal being as described. As such a non-religious outsider what might you be thinking at this stage of this imagined conversation?)

Summarizing in your mind what you have heard from this person so far, you say to yourself: "Here is a sincere and otherwise seemingly intelligent and rational person who talks of a god who is believed to be the *literal* Father of man's *spirit*, whatever that might actually mean or literally entail, and who is himself, in his basic nature, a *finite* and *exalted spirit personage* and *infinite and eternal intelligence* of the *highest order*, whatever such apparently contradictory referents could actually mean as well. Moreover, such a being, according to this person, is clothed in a physical, *non-biological*, *immortal* and *glorified* body in the shape of a man — which body is animated *not* by blood, he says, but by *spirit element*, whatever such 'spirit element' could possibly be or consist of.

Finally, this supernatural being who is putatively '*all*-knowing, powerful, loving and good' — and who is not physically in or of this world — is yet *everywhere* present in the universe and to all his creatures through the 'light of truth,' whatever that could actually be or mean. He has, moreover, as a finite, spatio-temporally transcendent being, a *personal* relationship with all who believe in him. He communicates directly with all mortal men in this world — in word or by vision, dream or inspiration — through his *spirit*, whatever, again, such term could actually mean or imply. "What on earth, or in any world," you would no doubt ask yourself, "could any of this possibly mean, and how can I possibly make any rational sense of it?"

Determined to understand, you put aside, as you did earlier your scientific concerns regarding the naturalistic and cosmological implications of this alleged being's role as the 'Creator' and 'Supreme Governor and Ultimate Source of the Universe.' You put aside your doubts regarding the existence of a 'next life,' or afterlife. You defer judgment of the at least apparent contradictions between this god's putative secondary and relational attributes and qualities and certain seemingly irresolvable contradictions — including the existence of widespread nonbelief and disbelief in the world (even among believers), and the existence of so much senseless suffering and premature death caused by preventable or at least reducible and relievable human and natural evil. Instead of pursuing such problems, which you regard as very troubling yet still premature, you continue your analytical inquiry. Now more deeply and incisively, you seek some cognitive understanding of what has been stated regarding this alleged being's basic nature.

"Regarding the primary descriptive referents of your god," you ask, "can you explain to me what *specifically* these stated primary referents — *i.e.* spirit matter, intelligences, spirit element, glorified matter, the light of truth, *etc.* — themselves *actually* refer to and what their truth-conditions are? Stated contextually, can you tell me what it would *actually* mean for a 'finite, tangible being' to be an 'exalted spirit' and an 'infinite and eternal intelligence'? Can you tell me what it means for such a being's physical body to be 'glorified' and animated by 'spirit element'?

"What I am trying to do here," you explain, "is understand your concept of 'God' by unpacking, if you will, its descriptive referents or attributes to determine whether or not the stated existence of such referents is factually intelligible and therefore justifiable in principle as a literal fact or as statements which are or might be actually true. More specifically, I am seeking a perspicuous, intelligible understanding of your terms and stated truth claims. I seek an understanding of the truth-conditions of such truth claims so I might somehow make sense of what you are referring to when you speak of your god. I wish to know, moreover, if your statements regarding the *literal* existence of such a being are at least justifiable as truth claims that can, in principle, be known to be actually true (or probably true) or false (or probably false). To get to this level of cognitive meaning and justifiability I will need to know what specifically, empirically, and unambiguously would count for or against the *actual* existence of a being with such putative primary and secondary attributes and qualities. I will need to know how the stated existence of such a being in its metaphysical fulness could, in principle, be empirically confirmed or disconfirmed, or otherwise objectively and uncontroversially determined."

Listening intently and respectfully to the questions asked, and explanation offered, regarding the stated Mormon concept and doctrine of 'God,' the Mormon believer sits back, ponders the questions asked separately and as a whole, and then leans forward and says: "God in his wisdom has not yet seen fit to reveal the answers to such questions to man. Simply put," he continues, "I do not know the answers to your questions, and I would venture to say that no one does or could know. Any attempt to answer such questions would entail mere speculation at most, and would be foolish and futile at least. Ultimately, beyond the general statements made, and informed theological speculations made about them, the fundamental nature of God is inconceivable to the human mind and is beyond human understanding and knowledge.

"What I do know, however," he continues, "is that such questions are ultimately not important to our salvation and that God's existence cannot be empirically or analytically known as you might expect or require. Rather, what *is* important is that God can only be known to man by *faith*, through *revelation*. In other words, it is only through *spiritual experience* that we can know, as I do, that God does *in fact* exist and that we as his *literal* spirit children can have a *personal* relationship with him."

"But respectfully," you continue as the objective outsider, "I think such questions *do* matter if, for example, it is your sincere desire — and the sincere desire of all like believers — to in fact know your god actually exists as you say you do. Such questions would also matter if you desire that others, like me, who are not of your faith, or any faith, at least understand what you actually mean by the term 'God' or the statement 'God exists,' or — even more desirable still — accept as *actually* true that which you claim to be true regarding the alleged *actual* existence of this *literal* being you refer to as your god and our alleged relationship to him.

"Now you say that you know by faith through personal revelation that your god actually exists, and I assume that you believe that I can likewise know of your god's actual existence and have a personal relationship with him as well, correct?

"Yes, but only if you humble yourself before him in prayer and ask God with a sincere heart and real intent to know if these things are true."

"Fine, but how can I do what you say is required if I have important questions (at least to me) and real doubts regarding even the possible existence of your god as described and believed? For without a perspicuous, cognitive understanding of what you *actually* mean when you speak of your god, what exactly would I be praying to except perhaps some wished for fantasy or imagined image of a father-like person in my mind? Further, what would it *actually* mean to either of us — or to anyone for that matter — to have such a transcendent being reveal itself in person, or 'through the spirit'? What would it *actually* mean to have a *personal relationship* with such a being?

"As a relevant aside related to the stated importance of having such a relationship with your god, what could it *actually* mean for a *finite* and *tangible* being as conceptualized in your faith to be *fully* present *everywhere* in all its personal attributes and qualities through the 'light of truth'? Further still, what specifically would such *sui generis* omnipresence be like?

"Finally in this regard, how, given our best knowledge of this (or *any*) world and universe and how they work, and assuming we understood what the 'light of truth' actually *is* and could objectively and reliably isolate and confirm its actual existence, could such believed literal omnipresence be possible, or even conceivable?

"My point is this: if I, as an outsider to your faith, cannot make sense of the *concept* of your god, or what it would *actually* mean to *literally* encounter such an unintelligible being as conceptualized in your faith, either through the spirit, whatever that means, or in person, how could I accept even the *possibility* that such a being *actually* exists as claimed — much less the possibility that I could have a *personal* relationship with it? You might as well ask me to believe in the existence of, or have a personal relationship with, 'Irlig' or 'Somorlo' simply on the basis of faith. That I cannot do, for I would not know what it is specifically that I was being asked to believe or have faith in. [Note: The terms *Irlig* and *Somorlo* are appropriated from the works of George H. Smith and Kai Nielsen, respectively. To my knowledge they are purely invented and meaningless terms, adopted to make the points argued in this instructive conversation.]

"Moreover," you continue, "your statement that your god can only be known through 'revelation' or 'spiritual experience' raises to my mind more questions than it answers. First, if you were to argue for the existence of your god on the basis of receiving a confirming revelation from your god, then we both know that such a circular, or question-begging, argument would be invalid. But putting that aside for now, what can you tell me about what you call *revelation*?"

"Well," he says, pausing for a moment and then recalling the words of Mormon Apostles Boyd. K. Packer and Dallin Oaks, "revelation is both a process and an event which can be explained through the experiences one has. While revelation can be subtle, yet potent, as a feeling or impression, it can also come in more obvious and dramatic ways to the recipient, as in a voice, a vivid dream or vision, or even, as with Joseph Smith, a visitation by heavenly messengers or even God and Jesus Christ. In most cases, however, revelation is typically experienced as an impression which imparts information, communicates restraint, or impels one to do something, or as a confirming feeling or a prompting that is good, and that makes one happy or gives one a feeling of comfort."

"So as a process, revelation can dawn on someone gradually, and as an event it is experienced typically as a sudden insight, prompting, impression or good feeling, is that correct?"

"Yes, it comes both ways, and usually with a burning in the breast and a tingling feeling throughout one's body — a feeling of love, peace, comfort, and a sense that all is well and that everything meaningfully fits together into one eternal whole."

"Yes, yes!" you affirm. "Although I cannot speak of a so-called 'eternal whole,' for I haven't even the slightest idea what that actually means, I know of these ecstatic, transformative feelings and have experienced them personally at times. I have also experienced such impressions, promptings, insights, illumination, and restraint — all seemingly out of the blue. They are wonderful feelings and experiences, to be sure. Still, I must say that such feelings and experiences that are common and natural to me are also reportedly common and natural to many others I know intimately. I would venture to guess that such feelings are most likely common and natural to many in your world too — to those who, like me, do not believe in your god, or any god. Would you agree?"

"I couldn't say," the Mormon believer cautiously replies in turn, "but I would think such feelings and experiences would be fundamentally quite different in one regard."

"How so?"

"Well," he continues, "the feelings or experiences I am referring to are associated with revelation from God and testify *specifically* of the *true* God's existence and his mind and will in relation to our lives. They are *spiritual* feelings or experiences which come from our spirit in response to God's self-revelation by his spirit."

"Interesting, although your answer seems again to beg the question at issue, which is how an objective and naturally skeptical outsider like me can know of the actual truth of your claim that your god literally exists as fully conceptualized in your faith? You seem to be saying, essentially, that the only way to know if such a claim is actually true is to experience those unique feelings that come from your god — who, to you, is the only true god — and that those feelings therefore reveal to one's mind and heart that he exists. But your assertion of the existence of revelation from your god necessarily presupposes the existence of your god — which is the question at issue.

"Moreover," you continue, "your implied truth-condition for distinguishing a confirming revelation from your god regarding his existence from otherwise identically described common and natural feelings or experiences does not, I'm afraid, get us any closer to understanding what it could possibly mean for 'an infinite and eternal spirit and intelligence to be revealed by the spirit of truth.' More on that later.

"For now, and returning to the nature of revelation as you have described it, can you tell me what specific, objective, widely accepted, reliably validating and non-question-begging human criteria exist which would differentiate what you refer to as a 'revelation' or 'spiritual experience' from an exclusively neurological or psychological experience originating from the human brain?"

Waiting for an answer, but receiving none, you ask for permission to resume your line of inquiry regarding the Mormon believer's earlier implied truth-condition that natural, revelation-like experiences which are commonly experienced by all — believers or not — could only be regarded, in the context of this conversation, as proper 'revelation' *if and only if* such experiences *confirmed* the existence of *his* god, which is, as he believes, the only '*true* God.' After receiving an affirming nod you proceed.

"As you stated earlier, you cannot conceive of the basic nature of your god as fully conceptualized in your faith. You cannot conceive of its or his primary and secondary attributes in particular. Now if these putative non-self-justifying attributes of your god are without valid analogical predication (we cannot, after all, possibly know anything literal or non-analogical about an 'exalted spirit and infinite and eternal intelligence that is all-powerful, loving, knowing and good') or if they lack a specifiable, intelligible reference range and related specific truth-conditions that could, at least in principle, be satisfied under controlled conditions to establish even their *theoretical* existence (either through direct observation or indirectly through the observation of predicted empirical consequences related to their existence), then how would you explain *what* specifically *caused* such a so-called 'spiritual' or 'revelatory' experience — beyond asserting again that it was your God? This of course would be unwarranted and explain nothing. How, for that matter, could you or anyone possibly know that what actually caused one's experience was a being at all, much less the being you regard as your 'God'? It would seem to me that the *most* one could rationally or credibly say regarding one's experience would be that one simply had a real and personally impactful, yet precisely indescribable human experience which cannot be explained, and that *something somehow* caused this experience which also cannot currently be explained."

"In this life, the Mormon believer retorts, "we walk by faith. But in the next life we shall all know with a perfect knowledge that God exists as we stand before him and see him with our eyes and hear him with our ears and touch him with our hands and in sacred embrace. In this life we see through the glass darkly, but in the next life we shall see him face to face."

"Your reference again to faith intrigues me," you reply, "but let's first play out your line of thought about knowing of 'God's existence' in the next life and suppose, solely for the sake of furthering our conversation, that we find ourselves actually in the presence of a physical being in the shape of a man who introduces himself as your god. How, in such a case, and beyond the mere assertion made by such a being regarding his identity, could we or anyone independently and objectively know that such a *perceived* transcendent being is *in fact* a being with the believed and assumably necessary primary and secondary attributes you ascribe to your god, and which you admit are inconceivable or beyond human understanding?

"To say in this regard that we would somehow know *then* what we cannot know *now* would be to raise the obvious question, know *what* exactly? 'That this being is God, our Heavenly Father,' you might say. But *how*, I would ask, would we *actually* know such is in fact the case if not through language? You might say 'By recognition through prior association or some spiritual faculty and experienced affect.' But again, recognition of *what* specifically? What, in other words, would we recognize — assuming again for the sake of our conversation that there *was* any existence before birth and after death and that we as physical, thinking, feeling 'spirit beings' (whatever those are) *were* in the presence of some other being? What could we perceive beyond merely the physical presence of a human-like being with certain accentuated human-like qualities? Moreover, how beyond mere assertion would we know that such an alleged 'experienced affect' was caused by anything other than merely a hypnotically induced projective transference, or that such a putative 'spiritual faculty' actually exists as even a theoretical faculty or attribute?

"'I cannot answer such questions,' you might once again reply. But your hypothetical replies would essentially ask me to *presuppose as true* the actual existence of the very being, and also some spiritual faculty, whose claimed existence are now *both* in question. For me to understand or appreciate that what you are saying could even possibly be so, you will have to very carefully explain things to me in terms I or anyone can understand. How, in virtue of specific objective and widely accepted human criteria, could we differentiate such an alleged affect-laden recognition from, say, a powerful projective transferential experience? How, empirically or otherwise, could we *know* that the appearance of such a being — whether in this life or (as you believe, the next) is in fact an 'exalted spirit' and 'infinite and eternal intelligence of the highest order'? How could we know that his body is 'glorified' or likewise 'exalted' and animated by 'spirit element' and that he is, moreover, 'all-good, knowing, powerful, loving and perfectly just and merciful'? How could we know it is not merely a powerful, hypnotically induced dissociative hallucination? Such a thing can also seem real or substantive to the touch. Alternatively, how could we know it isn't an immensely powerful, knowledgeable, and benevolent being from another world or universe who was somehow able to present himself to us as your god?

"You see where this is going, I'm sure. Without an *intelligible, coherent,* and *cognitively* (or *factually*) *meaningful* concept of your god, and without objective, widely accepted and verifiably reliable human criteria for differentiating natural from so-called 'spiritual' experiences and phenomena, there is no possible way, as I see it, for *anyone* to ever *know*, in *any* sense or in *any* world, that such a putative being, as fully conceptualized, could even *possibly* exist. There is no possible way to tell that what one has experienced is anything other than, at most, an unexplained *natural* or *neuro-psychological* phenomenon.

"What you are claiming to be a true though ultimately inexplicable, revelatory experience — in somehow knowing *that* you know your god exists without being able to explain exactly *what* or *how* you know — is clearly not self-evidently true to everyone as such. Nor are such alleged 'spiritual' experiences, in fact, properly basic in parity with other basic experiences common to all people — such as, for example, the experience of knowing what pain feels like or what salt tastes like. Therefore your claim in *knowing* that your god literally exists in virtue of some confirming revelatory experience from that god must be, with all due diligence and to the degree possible, objectively *justified* to be regarded widely as actual knowledge — particularly by those *outside* your faith whom you might seek to convince or convert. For this to be so, your statements regarding *what* your god is and *what* revelation is, as distinguished from common, merely neuro-psychological experiences, must also be justified. Justification in both cases would of course require much more than mere assertion — or even sincere assertion made with felt conviction. You cannot merely assert that you *somehow*, inexplicably *know* your god exists because of a special feeling or some other purely subjective (and subjectively interpreted) experience you refer to as a 'confirmation' or 'special witness.' Indeed, as we both know in relation to any other truth claim, merely *saying* something is so, and *feeling* that it is so does not, in either case or together, actually make it so. It is curious — if not suspicious — that one should think that only religious claims can violate this rule."

"When you speak of a truth claim being justified," the Mormon believer asks, "what specifically, from your perspective, would such justification entail to establish knowledge or warrant an assertion that something is actually known or true?"

"As I understand it," you reply, "justification would require *a priori* that the actual existence of your god be fully conceptualized. It requires the existence of actual revelation from that god to be derivatively conceptualized. Both, in principle, must be *justifiable* as claimed or stated. This *a priori* requirement would require in turn that the *terms* and declarative and indicative *statements* of your faith be *unambiguous, specific,* and *intelligible* or *coherent.* It requires that such statements or beliefs have specifiable *truth-conditions* that can in principle be empirically confirmed or disconfirmed as being actually or even theoretically true (or probably true) or false (or probably false). Finally, to be justified as actual knowledge, the stated *facts* of your justifiable truth claims would need to be broadly or widely regarded — on the basis of established common knowledge, valid argument, and/ or rational demonstration — as legitimate facts that *fit* or *cohere* with all that we actually *know* about the world and the universe and how they work."

At this point, and now changing roles in this exercise, imagine how you as a Mormon believer might reply to such a barrage of sincere questions, concerns, and criteria for justification in making legitimate knowledge and truth claims. Chances are, you would most likely admit again that neither you nor anyone has answers to such questions. You would then inform your otherworldly conversationalist that his 'way of knowing' does not apply to the realm of spiritual truth, reminding him that knowledge and understanding of God and a saving belief in God's existence can ultimately only be received and experienced by revelation from God through faith. You would then likely inform him that such faith is a gift from God, received through study and prayer, and is a sacred trust in God's existence, goodness, and purposes for our life based, again, on special feelings experienced when praying to God for a witness of his existence and when living his gospel as restored in these latter days.

Finally, and without further recourse, you would likely conclude by bearing your solemn testimony in hope that the Spirit would attest to your words and deeply touch the heart of your distinguished guest. Accordingly, you sit up, look the skeptical outsider in the eyes, and say with resolved and sincere conviction and emotion, that you *know* by faith, through personal revelation and sacred, spiritual experience, that God *lives*; that Jesus *is* the Christ; that Joseph Smith *is* the Prophet of this, the last dispensation of the fulness of times; that the *Book of Mormon* is the word of God; that the Church of Jesus Christ of Latter-day Saints (or Mormon faith) is the *only true* Church of Jesus Christ on earth which is recognized as such by God, and that, therefore, its teachings and doctrines regarding God's nature and existence are true.

Imagine now our objective outsider with a troubled look on his face and a furrowed brow, as he listens intently to your words, after all that has been discussed, admitted, and asked to this point.

Collecting his thoughts, he finally speaks and says to you — who are now in the role of the believer — "I truly appreciate the sincerity of your heartfelt convictions and certainly respect your right as a sentient being to feel and believe as you do. But again with sincere respect, none of what you have just said makes any sense to me. You speak again of revelation through the prayer of faith as the only way to know of the actual existence of your god, but again the very concepts of 'faith in God,' 'prayer to God' and 'revelation from God' necessarily depend on the existence of the being whose existence is in question. They depend on the actual existence of the 'spirit of God,' or what you refer to as the 'light of truth' — which also depends for its existence on the actual existence of your god.

"How then can you or anyone justifiably or even reasonably claim to know that you have faith in, pray to, and receive revelation from a being that cannot even be known to exist — a putative being which is, on the basis of the inconceivability or unintelligibility of its primary, secondary, and relational attributes, factually meaningless or at least nonsensical? If the fundamental nature of your god is, as you admitted earlier, ultimately inconceivable as metaphysically conceptualized, then, it also seems to me, the assertions of having faith in, praying to, and receiving revelation from your god would, again, necessarily be incoherent.

"But even if," the outsider continues with an afterthought, "and solely for the sake of argument, your god is given to be conceptually intelligible and known to exist as fully conceptualized (which is admittedly not so in the first case and therefore necessarily cannot be so in the second case), how can you or anyone honestly make any sense — given all we know about this or any world and universe and how they work — of *actually* communicating with a transcendent, finite yet infinite and eternal being who physically resides in another world in this or some other universe or alternate dimension of space and time?

"From a like perspective, what could it possibly mean or how could you or anyone honestly make sense of a being that could be *fully* present in personality and with all knowledge and power *everywhere* in the universe and be accessible to *everyone* individually and collectively in worlds without end? How could that being be 'the light, law, and power which animates, sustains, and orders all life'? It would seem that even analogy or analogical predication could not possibly help us here. Quite honestly," he states reflectively with a sigh, "I simply cannot conceive of *any* of this, and to me it is all a mass of confusion."

Still, more questions are asked — specific and incisive questions which, again, probe into the conceptual constructs and related implications of the Mormon concepts of 'God,' faith, and revelation in particular. Notwithstanding, however, the respectful tone of the inquiry and the sincere curiosity and desire for dialogue demonstrated in asking such questions, no substantive answers or agreements are forthcoming.

Sensing your growing discomfort and defensiveness under the weight of his direct inquiry, and desiring to create common ground through shared and empathic perspective, the skeptical outsider finally decides to try a different approach by rhetorically turning the tables.

"Let's look at this problem from a slightly different angle," he suggests. "If I told you, for example, as an intelligent being from another world, that in virtue of my faith, I *know* that Somorlo exists and has a divine purpose for *your* life, and that if you believe in his existence and have faith in him, and turn your life over to him in obedience to his will, you will find eternal happiness and salvation, you would likely out of mere curiosity and/or courtesy ask me what a Somorlo is, would you not?

"And if I then told you in seriousness and with sincerity and conviction that Somorlo is a biologically transcendent and finite supernatural being whose indestructible body is animated by *botir*, who lives in another dimension of space and time, and who is fundamentally an exalted *parcept* and infinite and eternal *gibling* of the highest order, who is present everywhere in his omnipotence, omniscience, and omnibenevolence through his *lobod*, what would you then want to ask me, assuming you knew and respected me well enough to take me seriously and not dismiss me out of hand as being a delusional lunatic? You would, I would guess, likely be totally puzzled, perhaps even speechless. And then you would likely want to know, at least again out of curiosity, what the terms 'botirs,' 'parcepts,' 'giblings,' and 'lobod' mean or specifically refer to, would you not?

"And what if, after offering some vague, general definitions which raised more questions than they answered, I then admitted that *I* did not know what they were specifically or what specifically they referred to, and that such things were fundamentally inconceivable to humans, but that the meaning, sense or understanding of such realities were ultimately not important? What if I then asserted that what was important was only that you believe and have faith in Somorlo, that you turn yourself over to his goodness and purposes for your life?

"Could you do so? Why not?

"In part, I conjecture, because even though you might not believe in a different deity, the term Somorlo would not be familiar or cognitively meaningful to you. You would not, therefore, be able to projectively or tranferentially anthropomorphize and emotionally relate to it. (By the way, this might perhaps naturalistically explain much about the existence and nature of what you refer to as *faith*.)

"You would also, no doubt, not be able to do so because — apart from your lack of familiarity with the term *Somorlo* — you would not know with sufficient specificity *what it was that you were being asked to believe or have faith in*! Without knowing what the primary attributes of a being actually mean or specifically refer to, you could not possibly know what its secondary and relational attributes and qualities are related to — much less what they might actually mean or even if they could possibly exist at all. To you, as a prudently skeptical outsider, the concept of Somorlo's fundamental nature, as defined, would be utterly incoherent and cognitively meaningless. Not only could you not conceive or make any sense of such a being, you might at least wonder — and justifiably so — if I really knew what I was talking about when I engaged in such 'Somorlo-talk.'

"But even if you granted me the benefit of the doubt regarding Somorlo's existence and basic nature, and became sufficiently familiar with the term to find meaning in the way 'Somorlo' was colloquially used in my life and join the 'Somorlo faith,' you still would not know — even if you thought you did — what *specifically* 'Somorlo,' as a referring expression, *literally* referred to. You would not know what its primary and secondary referents *literally* and *specifically* referred to. That would leave the truth claim of Somorlo's existence as vaguely defined — without truth-conditions which could, in principle at least, be empirically verified or falsified. You would not even be able to construct a hypothesis regarding Somorlo's putative existence, for the very concept of 'Somorlo' would be fundamentally or primarily incoherent, or factually unintelligible. In other words, 'Somorlo' as a term and concept would be *cognitively* meaningless to you, even if familiar as a term. You would not be able to responsibly, I dare say, without self-deception accept as *actually* true — or even probably true — the claim of Somorlo's *literal* existence merely on the basis of my assertions to that effect, or any feelings you might have in relation to your hope or desire that Somorlo might somehow or possibly exist."

With this said — and still in the role of the Mormon believer — you reply: "Perhaps so. But we are not speaking of Somorlo. We are speaking of God, and I cannot deny what I know to be true."

"And this allegedly sure knowledge consists of your personal experience of sure feelings which confirm the truth of your beliefs, correct?"

"Yes," you reply, "it comes from the sure feelings which arise through fasting and sincere prayer and which attend so much of what I do and experience when I am living my faith. I cannot deny what I have felt, and what I am feeling even now as I say these words to you."

With these final remarks, our skeptical conversationalist from another world sits back and looks first closely at you, then pensively into the distance. Then, after a few moments of silence, he finally leans forward and speaks again, saying: "I certainly would not ask that you or anyone deny that they have experienced something, or that they have or have experienced certain feelings. Clearly *that* you have had such feelings must be accepted as fact at face value, and accepted moreover with certainty by one who has actually had such affective experiences. Still, and with respect, it is nonetheless seems quite self-evident that while *having* such experiences is one thing, *explaining*, *characterizing* and *interpreting* them is, for all intents and purposes, quite another.

"It would seem therefore that from my now more informed perspective as an objective and I think empathic and reasonably skeptical outsider (I do, after all, acknowledge the importance of my own and others feelings and the possible or actual truth of many things which seem at least to probably or self-evidently exist as claimed), you and like believers have made the category error of *a priori* or *presuppositionally* considering your concept of 'God' as being *cognitively* meaningful and *objectively* and *literally* true.

"It also seems — and significantly so on the basis of all that is known in the biological and social sciences — that you and like believers have very likely mistakenly regarded purely naturalistic, self-induced and subjectively interpreted feelings and emotions as evidence of the wished-for existence of a supernatural being in the image of an ideal, perfect parent.

"So your religious language, or 'God-talk,' might have personalized meaning to you and other like believers perhaps in unconscious relation to primary biological relationships and how you have individually and collectively been conditioned in your families and by your religion to believe what you believe, explain, and interpret your experiences, and live your lives. It might even have some lexical meaning to others on earth through mere linguistic and cultural exposure and familiarity. But your metaphysical declarative and indicative statements *about* your god — or I would venture to say *any* like 'God' of *any* faith — are nonetheless at least apparently incoherent, without cognitive meaning or factual significance, and in error when represented as *literal*, *objective*, and *absolute* truth."

This somewhat lengthy, yet nonetheless abridged, analytical conversation is, as we shall learn in the chapters that follow, far from over. Even so, it provides a basic sense of the core analytical task before us — as well as a perspective and context for, and preview of, what is to come. It also provides us with a foretaste of the central analytical argument of this book, *viz.*, that beyond its limited boundaries as a life-form, the Mormon faith (like all other theistic faiths) — because it is an entirely language-dependent belief system intended to be regarded as literally and objectively true — is conceptually problematic and therefore deeply problematic, if not utterly false and incoherent at its metaphysical core.

This central argument is primarily an *a priori* argument that is made through analytical inquiry. It can therefore be envisioned, engaged in, and experienced as a rigorous and difficult deconstructive conversation at several levels. At its most personal level it is a conversation between a former believing and committed insider and now disbelieving outsider of the Mormon faith. It is also, at another level, a conversation between the reader, as a questioning believer, nonbeliever, and investigator of the Mormon faith and the author as someone who was completely *in* the Mormon faith for many years and managed to work his way out through his woundedness and doubts. Lastly, at an outside level, it is a confrontive conversation between devout, Mormon or other theistic believers and an impassioned Atheist intent on not only discrediting all theistic beliefs and "breaking the spell" of theistic faith, but of exposing the real harmfulness, abuses, and potential social dangers inherent in such faith. Believers who have the ego strength to read this book and to understand and appreciate the implications of the arguments being made will no doubt find their reading to be very difficult — though hopefully a fruitful conversation and experience.

At whatever level this conversation takes place, it is, in its most fundamental form a therapeutic conversation which can be productively imagined to take place to some degree *within* the mind of the reader. It is, in this sense, a type of *inner* conversation that would account for the *real* doubt which consciously or unconsciously affects or afflicts believers. Figuratively speaking, it is a conversation between the believer's stated beliefs and his unstated, perhaps even unconscious, albeit real doubts. It is, moreover, an inner conversation that might take place with awareness, even though for many devout believers who complete this book it will very likely take place beneath the surface of awareness.

Beyond the above 'instructive deconstructive conversation' and perspective, in further serving the need to better understand the analytical task before us and the threshold of justification which must be met in our analysis of the Mormon faith, it is important to note up-front that while the underlying theological propositions of many beliefs expressed by various indicative statements in Mormon discourse might, in a certain minimalist or purely semantic sense, have 'truth-value' in the sense that they are statements that *can be* either true or false, such truth-value does *not* establish the statements' *actual* truth or falsity as propositions or beliefs. It certainly does not establish anything like 'Absolute Truth.'

So, for example, the Mormon belief statement 'God is the Heavenly Father of all mankind on earth' has truth-value as a *candidate* for truth or falsity, where *truth* in the minimalist and trivial sense requires merely that this belief is not linguistically unintelligible or incoherent and is *contingently* true '*if and only if* God, the Father *is* the Heavenly Father of all mankind on earth.' However, such truth-value (and contingent truth or falsity) if it exists, does not *ipso facto* establish the *actual* truth or falsity of the statement or belief that 'God, the Father' *actually* exists and is, in *fact*, the *literal* 'Heavenly Father of all mankind on earth.' Nor does it do so absolutely or with anything like certainty. For this belief statement or truth claim — or any stated truth claim with truth-value — to be considered as *justified knowledge* of an actual, provisional, factual truth, both alleged facts *that* 'God exists' and *that* he is 'the Heavenly Father of all mankind on earth' would need first to be intelligible or coherent so as to actually fit or make sense with what we *actually* know about the world and the universe and how they work. These beliefs would also need to have *specifiable* and *determinative* 'truth-conditions'[52] which would be widely regarded by believers, disbelievers, and nonbelievers as being empirically satisfied beyond a reasonable doubt. This, of course, is a tall order to fill.

The Qualifications of Familiarity, Usefulness, Use, and Imaginability

It is also important to note up-front that there are other important qualifications to the determination of the truth of religious (and Mormon) discourse. First, as pointed out in the instructive conversation between the Mormon believer and the objective outsider, the understandability of religious statements on the basis of mere *familiarity* is not, for obvious reasons, necessarily or actually indicative of the rationality or the intelligibility, coherence, and cognitive meaningfulness of asserted or declarative factual statements, or truth claims if they are not commonly accepted as basic or self-evident common knowledge. Neither do the *usefulness* and *use* of religious language in *living* a particular religion (*e.g.* in worshipping, supplicating, preaching, teaching, serving, exhorting, testifying, witnessing, admonishing, rebuking, commanding, and counseling) nor the mere *imaginability* of cognitive meaning pertaining to religious beliefs render them rational or coherent. Finally, as we shall find, the above problems with the particular concepts of the Mormon god, the resurrected Mormon Christ, and the Mormon Plan of Salvation are not resolvable in the *next life* or by spiritual *confirmation* and *revelation* obtained in this life through *faith*.

Regarding the *familiarity* of religious language, the first-order paradigm statement, for example, that 'God is my Heavenly Father and Jesus Christ is my Savior and Redeemer,' while certainly familiar to Mormon or Christian believers and meaningful and useful in their lives, is, nonetheless, according to Nielsen, "…just a formula [believers] recite, if they are genuinely theistically religious, with great conviction and sometimes with intensity of feeling. But that does not, and cannot, turn it into sense, into an intelligible utterance" (2001, 355).

Furthermore, "we only, if we do not think, have the illusion of understanding [such statements] by extension from some familiar utterances we do understand" (354). Because we are familiar, for example, with the terms 'father,' 'plan,' 'marriage,' 'family,' and 'forever,' we can easily convince ourselves that we understand what it means to say "Through our Heavenly Father's plan, families can be together forever." But, as we shall find, if we objectively deconstruct such a statement, or any like statement such as, for example, 'Through the blood of Jesus Christ we may be cleansed of all our sins' and submit such statements to critical inquiry, we will find that they simply make no sense, and that our believed or alleged understanding of them is an illusion, and our merely expressed conviction that we do understand is merely an evocative expression and is not in itself indicative of intelligibility, cognitive meaning, or factual reality.

As Nielsen asks in this regard, "…is familiar nonsense…less nonsensical than unfa-

---

52 'Truth-conditions' are identified, as in the illustrative and instructive conversation above, as '*x*' in the statement '*p* is true if and only if *x* obtains,' where *x* is the *specific determinant* (or *condition*) of truth which must be either widely accepted by believers, disbelievers, and nonbelievers as being common knowledge or self-evidently true, or that can be, in principle and beyond a reasonable doubt, empirically confirmed or disconfirmed as being true (or probably true) or false (or probably false).

miliar nonsense? Perhaps it is," he acknowledges, "if what is unintelligible and what is not just comes down to what is familiar and what is not. But that itself," he objects, "… is a very problematic view. Assuming it is not just a matter of that, I put it to us: reflect on the fact that when we read of the religious conceptions of primitive tribes that they often — indeed typically — seem to us fantastically absurd, often even unintelligible, while it takes a certain kind of cultivation, a certain kind of taking thought, to so view the religious conceptions of our own tribe [or religion]. Yet, if we can bring ourselves to look at them [*i.e.* our own religious conceptions] with a cold, clear eye, and, abstracting from the soothing effects of their familiarity, are they not just as absurd, not just as good candidates for unintelligibility, as those primitive societies? It seems to me," he concludes, "that it is plain that they are (280)."

As noted in the *Introduction*, familiarity is often invoked by Mormon leaders and apologists through the use of *analogical predication*. This is done particularly when trying to justify the rationality of a particular theological concept or cluster of concepts (as, for example, the Mormon Plan of Salvation), or explain what the character, personality, and workings of 'God' are like. It is done to otherwise make more clear and understandable what is unclear, confusing, or difficult to comprehend. But such "analogical predication,"according to William Blackstone, "will not do the job for which it was devised …"[53] This is because, continues Blackstone, "…if one is to know analogically something of God, then one must know something of God *literally*.… Otherwise the analogy conveys no meaning" (1963, 65). "Clearly," argues Blackstone, "unless we have some *nonanalogical* (*i.e.* literal) knowledge about the meaning of 'goodness,' 'knowledge,' 'wisdom,' and so on when applied to God, we would not know that certain analogies involving such qualities in man are appropriate ones to apply to Him. But this, of course, is the problem. We don't know, except by presupposition and bald assertion, if God's 'infinite goodness' for example is, in reality, anything like man's goodness, or if any other of the putative attributes and qualities of God's 'divine nature' are anything like the actual attributes and qualities of man's 'human nature.' This is so because God and man are theologically different not in *degree*, but in *kind*." Because of this, we cannot understand the Mormon concept of

---

53 The problem of 'analogical predication' presented here is not equivalent to the problem of arguing from 'false analogy' — presented and illustrated in the *Introduction*. In the use of *false analogy* the arguer attempts to argue invalidly against a particular objection or for a particular conclusion or point of view by equating two or more *known* realities. For example, parenting children and managing adults may be analogized because they are similar in some known respect (*i.e.* parents, like managers are responsible for teaching, directing, motivating, and controlling or supervising, others). But, however, they are *dissimilar* in other, more crucial ways (*e.g.* children are *not* adults). This is done to justify a conclusion (*i.e.* that to get results managers must manage their adult direct reports like they would parent children). This makes the alleged analogy false with respect to the particular point being argued — in this case the best way to manage for results.

In contrast, *analogical predication* is used to facilitate the understanding of a particular concept (*e.g.* 'God') or conceptual reality or state of affairs (*e.g.* the deification of man) by describing through analogy what the concept means or what the particular conceptual reality or state of affairs is like. The problem with analogical predication, however, unlike the problem with faulty (or false) analogy, is with the *absence* of that which is *nonanalogical*, or literal, in the analogical predicate, or analog — which makes analogical predication *per se* impossible. By not knowing what the analogical predicate is *like* and *not* like, specifically and literally, a description by analogy (through likeness and contrast) adequate to establish a conceptual understanding of that which is being described is not possible. We cannot conceptually understand anything about the Mormon god by the comparison of the Mormon god to man without a *literal* understanding of what specifically it is about this concept of the Mormon god that is like man.

'God' on the basis of analogical predication because (as we shall learn in Chapter 3) we cannot know anything literal (nonanalogical) about what the Mormon god is like sufficient to liken any metaphysical aspect, attribute, or quality of such a putative being to man.

An example of invalid analogical predication in Mormonism would pertain to the Mormon belief that through the putative truth of the 'Great Law' of *eternal progression*, man might ultimately be 'exalted' and thereby become a 'god.' This belief, captured poetically in the familiar Mormon couplet "as man is, God once was; as God is, man may become," attempts to liken man to the Mormon god in *kind* through the analogical equivalency of the theological concept of 'eternal progression' to human development and biological evolution. But this attempt at analogical predication in attempting to justify the rationality of the belief in this god's and man's likeness and man's actual, potential, or prospective deification is hopelessly flawed. This is because, again, 'God' and 'man' are not alike in kind and therefore, we can know *nothing* nonanalogical (or literal) about 'eternal progression' or 'God.'

Even so, such impossible analogical predication is often attempted to make the Mormon god *familiar* and therefore *appear* cognitively meaningful. For if — so the reasoning goes — 'God' and man are alike in kind, and man is, as Mormons believe, 'a God in embryo,' then we can know something about the attributes and qualities of the Mormon god by making his putative attributes and qualities analogous to man's. But such analogical predication can only be attempted by begging the question at issue and cannot, even without such presupposition, possibly do the heavy lifting it is required to do — *even if the language is familiar*. For if, as will be argued in Chapter 3, the concept of the Mormon god in its putatively 'revealed' fulness is, on the basis of conceptual analysis, deemed to be factually unintelligible or without cognitive meaning, any attempt at establishing understanding and cognitive meaning through analogical predication is defeated outright and in principle. This leaves mere familiarity alone of no import or consequence in any serious quest for justified knowledge. We simply cannot make sense out of nonsense or justify an unjustifiable belief by attempting — even if sincerely and with conviction — to make an otherwise incoherent and factually unintelligible concept somehow coherent and intelligible through the use of evocative and familiar referral language or analogical predication.

Regarding the *usefulness* of religious language, it must be noted that because such language is comforting, inspiring, and motivational in the lives of believers, and it is meaningful or significant *in that sense*, such meaning is nonetheless *noncognitive* in nature and therefore not to be confused with *cognitive* meaning. Neither should cognitive meaning be confused with meaning established by the *use* (as opposed to the *usefulness*) of religious language. The idea of *meaning-as-use*, it has been argued (on the basis of the seminal work of Ludwig Wittgenstein in his *Philosophical Investigations* published in 1951), is that meaning *is* use. It is argued that the meaning of terms or statements is established contextually *only* by how (or in what particular way) such terms or statements are *used* or practiced as a 'language-game' in a particular way (*i.e.* according to its own unique rules, or 'grammar') within a unique socio-cultural context, or 'form-of-life.'

The argument from meaning-as-use essentially holds that the meaning of first-order Mormon religious statements such as 'My Savior suffered, bled and died for me,' or 'We are all spirit children of a loving Heavenly Father,' or 'Because of God's Plan families can be together forever' would not, in Wittgenstein's thinking, be established by logic or doctrine, or by some universal theory of meaning, but rather by how such statements are *used* by believers. In other words, meaning is determined by what particular role or function such statements play in religious life and discourse. Such an argument attempts to place religious language-games beyond the reach of critical linguistic analysis.

This, of course, would be so for terms or statements used idiomatically or non-cognitively within a given language-game. Consider, for example, the statement 'Go get the slab' expressed by a construction superintendent to a laborer on a construction site with the intent of obtaining a necessary 'slab' of concrete. Or consider, alternatively, the term 'Witch' in the statement 'The Witches are out tonight!' when used by children in Western society today to evoke the spirit of Halloween. The meaning of the first statement, according to Wittgensteinian thinking, is established by a current practice, or 'language-game' used within a particular societal activity, or 'form-of-life,' where the term 'slab' is understood to mean a piece of concrete by those who are familiar with this particular language-game and the way it is used in this particular form-of-life. In the second example, the *use* if the term 'Witch,' as practiced (used) in this particular culture or form-of-life is understood to mean, again, merely a fictional old woman who casts magical spells on children and flies on a broomstick on Halloween. As with the previous example, the meaning of this statement is in its use.

As shall be emphasized throughout this work, however, if the same term ('Witch') were used in a sentence to assert the existence of such a fictional or imaginary being as an objective, literal *fact*, then such a sentence, as a truth claim, would be subject to conceptual analysis. The use of the term *Witch* in such a sentence would be in this case — as in the case of using the Mormon terms *Savior* and *Heavenly Father* and *God* in the sample statements above — a *language-neutral concept* denoting the existence of a literal, *factual reality*. Such a concept (like the concepts *Savior* or *Heavenly Father* or *God*) is intended to be *non-specific* to *all* language-games and purports to be cognitively meaningful to *all* people everywhere and in *every* form-of-life. Therefore, the Wittgensteinian argument that meaning-is-use does not entail that all statements that have a use in a particular language-game within a particular form-of-life are necessarily coherent or factually intelligible when used to assert the *actual* existence of some putative reality.

This is particularly relevant in the present analysis of Mormon theology because Mormons and most, if not all, Christian believers are *external realists* with respect to their metaphysical theistic beliefs. They state them as external, objective *facts* which are actually *true* and which regard the Mormon god and Jesus Christ as literally *real* beings somewhere out there in space and time, not merely as metaphysical, symbolic, or metaphorical concepts. Moreover, Mormon believers are also *metaphysical realists* in virtue of their beliefs *about* their beliefs (*i.e.* their *meta*-beliefs) in their Godhead and their putative Plan of Salvation. As such, they reify or objectify such beliefs, and regard them as being *objectively* real with *literal*, or cognitive, meaning, *not* merely figurative or expressive-evocative (*i.e.* non-cognitive) meaning. Consequently, the putative cognitive meaning of such beliefs, as concepts, would be subject to conceptual analysis, for the theological terms used in the Mormon language-game denote an intended *language-neutral* (and language-independent) reality which is believed and attested to by believers as being *literally* and *factually* true. Such believed and stated realities therefore, according to Nielsen, are subject to "[the] concept[s] of [*facts* and] *truth* and the concept of *consistency* with its related concept of *coherence*," which are also language-neutral concepts and "not utterly form-of-life dependent" (1982, 129).

Finally, regarding *imaginability*: anyone is capable of imagining all manner of false existents such as Santa Clause, fairies, poltergeists, winged horses that can fly, talking animals, and lightening bolt-hurling gods like Zeus. As human beings we are all capable of deceiving ourselves into believing anything we want to believe or can imagine without justification. Such imaginings, like the gross anthropomorphic aspects of the Mormon Godhead, cannot be rationally believed. Although talking animals and grossly anthropomorphic Zeus-like gods with body parts in the shape of a man (or woman) are not factually meaningless, the belief that there actually *are* such gods is simply a false superstition. It is *false* because it is devoid of any *reliable* empirical evidence anywhere and at any time *in this world* to confirm their material, observable existence — and thus to disconfirm or legitimately falsify and refute their existence (Stenger 2007, 26–7). It is a *superstition* because it is a supernatural notion based on magical thinking and is held as true despite lack of confirming evidence or evidence to the contrary. It seems self-evident that the fact that a particular concept is imaginable does not make it true, still less cognitively or factually intelligible or meaningful.

Fundamental Premises: On the Meaning (use) and Analytical Implications of 'Truth,' 'Facts,' and 'Knowledge' about 'Reality'

The method employed for — and the conclusions reached by — evaluating the truth-value-status of non-foundational (non-self-justifying) Mormon truth claims for their justifiability are based on and justified respectively on the basis of the following five fundamental premises regarding the concepts of *truth, facts, knowledge* and *reality*[54]:

(a) *Truth*, in the deflationary sense used herein and as defended by Frege, Tarski,

---

54 In proposing these analytical premises for consideration I do not argue for their acceptance as irrefutable, *a priori* truth. Nevertheless, I do hold that such premises are both reasonable, widely accepted as valid, and capable of standing up under reasonable, critical scrutiny. I do, moreover, implicitly argue from them to what seems to me – as a reasonably skeptical outsider and informed and once converted insider to the Mormon faith — to be also reasonable and at least apparently self-evident conclusions. That some might disagree with and perhaps even dismiss these premises out of hand is of course very likely, particularly among those who are not philosophically informed or inclined. Still, it would seem reasonable to ask for good reasons for such disagreement and dismissal — and to expect reasonable answers in response. Moreover, even in the absence of what might reasonably be considered "good reasons" for disagreement and dismissal, the conclusions reached and argued for in virtue of these premises (or at least tacitly so) can easily enough be refuted (as, for example, and specifically, in relation to our analysis of the Mormon concept of 'God') by treating at the start the believed primary referents of the Mormon 'God' as fully conceptualized in Mormon doctrine as theoretical entities. In doing so we would establish their actual existence as we have the actual existence of sub-atomic particles that are likewise not directly observable, i.e. through the replicable confirmation of those empirical consequences which are specifically indicative of their existence as theorized. Moreover, and alternatively, we might simply, perspicuously, and non-evasively answer the analytical questions asked regarding them in Chapter 3 of this book in a way that is intelligible, coherent, and cognitively meaningful to an objective, reasonably skeptical outsider. And we would do so in a way that is not question-begging, does not rely on false analogy or invalid analogical predication, and does not result in further confusion, logical inconsistencies, or additional and likewise unintelligible metaphysical speculation.

Ramsey, Ayer, and Quine to name a notable few, is merely what a true statement states and is so, *as stated*. As Nielsen puts it, following the formula of Alfred Tarski, "A statement 'p' is true *if and only if* p;" or… "'Ten plus ten equals twenty' is true if and only if $10 + 10 = 20$;" or "'God loves his children' is true *if and only if* God loves his children. It is *sentences* or perhaps *statements* that are [in this minimalist or deflationary sense] true. Take the quotation marks off a sentence (or the formula 'p' is true *if and only if* p) and there, *voilá*, the truth on the righthand side is revealed" (2006, 17, emphasis in part mine).

This *minimalist, disquotational,* or *deflationary* conception of truth is needed, according to Nielsen, to "escape being clouded by metaphysics," which I, as Nielsen and others, including "Wittgenstein, J.L. Austin, Burton Dreben, the logical positivists, Richard Rorty and, in effect, W.V.O. Quine and Donald Davidson [regard and] reject as nonsense or as Austin said, 'cackle'" (11). "In one way," Nielsen comments elsewhere, "[this simple yet profound conception of] truth is not very important for it is not a means of establishing anything" (2008, 33).[55]

Elaborating on this point, Nielsen continues: "If we accept [even tacitly so, this] kind of disquotational, minimal, and deflationist conception of truth, then it makes perfectly good *sense* to say of *any* well-formed indicative sentence that it is true (or false): that the truth predicate can be appropriately applied to it. We can say of 'God loves his children' or any other religious utterance in the indicative mode that, if we can intelligibly say it, we can also intelligibly say it is true or that it is false: that 'true' is not being misused when we say that. But that we can say that of our or anyone's saying something (uttering some indicative sentence) that it is true — saying, that is, that the sentence ('It is true') is intelligible — doesn't in the slightest make for or establish or justify, *even with the slightest probability*, that what we are saying in making that utterance [even if on the basis of conditioned familiarity and common sense, or putative revelation from God] is *actually* true [or accurately representative of reality].… Calling it true [by mere assertion or on the basis of presupposition or perceived (or argued-for) 'proper basicality'] adds nothing

---

55   In his reply to Cheryl Misak's essay "Truth and Our Practices: Why the Naturalist Can't Do without Truth" in Michael Seymour and Matthias Fritsch's *Reason and Emancipation: Essays on the Philosophy of Kai Nielsen* (2007), Nielsen resists "… [the] idea that we need, or can intelligibly construct, a robust or substantive conception of truth and the related belief that truth is a useful justificatory or explanatory concept." Moreover, he asserts that "[w]e as pragmatic naturalists should be deflationists concerning truth and, where workable (as it typically is), disquotationalists about truth. Truth," Nielsen continues, "cannot be, or so I say, conventional wisdom to the contrary notwithstanding, the aim of inquiry. We should not aim at what we cannot get — at what we do not, and arguably cannot, understand. We should aim at getting right whatever we are investigating, which is to say getting as fully justified (in the various ways we justify things) a belief or beliefs as we can concerning whatever is under consideration at a given time. To ask in addition "Shouldn't it also be true?" is to ask for the color of heat…. Justification — the fullest justification we can get at a given time — is what we should aim at. Whether it adds up as well to ['truth'] is something we will never know or even be able reliably to surmise…. There are…no norms of truth as distinct from norms of justification. We don't even know what it would be like to have such distinctive norms of truth…. To say we have 'norms of truth' to get objectivity just uncritically invokes a reified conception of objectivity. But 'objectivity' can be taken to be wide and carefully investigated intersubjectivity: again, something we would gain from wide reflective equilibrium." Even so, Nielsen concludes, such justification — or wide reflective equilibrium achieved "…by the widest, most diversified community possibly obtainable in which the people were with sincerity and care conversing and reasoning with each other" — is not aiming at truth. But that is so *not* because "aiming at truth is optional — something we should seek instead — [but rather because] that very idea is incoherent" (155–9).

of justificatory interest or import" (2006, 18, 20, certain emphases mine).

Importantly in this regard, as Nielsen correctly points out, "…truth and knowledge of truth are crucially different. What we're after, and the only thing we can coherently be after, in seeking *knowledge* of what is true, is to get the best justified beliefs we can get at any particular time in any particular circumstance. But what is so justified at time t_1 may not turn out to be justified at time t_2," (18).

This, of course, suggests that while *truth* in a deflationary sense is appropriately conceived or understood as merely (or minimally) what disquotational (or true) statements state, *actual truth* — or non-foundationalist, non-self-evident or non-self-justifying statements that are understood as being truly or accurately representative of physical reality as we actually *know* it to be — *consists of justified statements*, or statements that have been adequately and appropriately justified through the achievement of wide reflective equilibrium. But given the fact of human fallibilism and the provisional status of human knowledge, *all* such justified statements (or 'knowledge of what is true') are necessarily space-, time-, mind- and language-dependent. This understanding makes 'truth' *per se* of minimal-to-no significance or import, and a provisional knowledge of truth the most we can achieve, or should seek after. Moreover, this renders the putative existence of, and belief in, 'Truth' (in other words, reified, objectified, or 'eternal' and 'Absolute' truth) false or incoherent. To quote Nielsen in this last regard, "There is nothing that can be established to be absolutely true or that can have an unconditional warrant. What is justifiable and what is not is time and place [and language] dependent" (2006, 21);

(b) *"Facts,"* following Xinli Wang (2003), and related to premise *a* above, "are specified and can *only* be specified by true statements [*e.g.* 'God exists' is true *if and only if* God exists]," and… "hence…are nothing but whatever true statements specify."…Therefore, they (facts) "…do not exist [*per se*] *in* the world as mind-independent, extra-linguistic entities" (11).

It could not be otherwise, for, as Wang states, "…there is no other way to specify a fact except by means of some true contingent statement. Facts are abstract and are not perceivable, *per se*, as things or events are. 'We note,'" Wang continues, quoting Austin, "'that when a detective says "let us look at the facts" he does not crawl round the carpet, but proceeds to utter a string of statements.' Facts cannot be specified by descriptive expressions… [They are] not concrete particulars" (10, 13). Rather, facts are complex, contextually derived linguistic entities functioning as *conceptual* representations — or concepts — of objects, events, properties, relations and states of affairs.

Specifically, facts are identified (or specified) as *that*-clauses explicitly or implicitly embedded quotationally *in* a contingently true sentence. For example, in the paradigm sentences presented earlier, *i.e.* 'God lives and hears and answers my prayers' and 'God is the Supreme Ruler and Governor of the Universe,' the putative *facts* in each case are the implicit *that*-clauses in each statement. Specifically, in the first statement, the facts are '*that* God lives' and '*that* God hears and answers my payers,' respectively. Likewise, in the second statement, the facts are '*that* God exists' (which is implicit) and '*that* God is the Supreme Ruler and Governor of the Universe.' Whether or not these putative, yet contingent facts can be justifiably or rationally considered as being truly representative of objective realities (*i.e.* objects, events, properties, relations, and states of affair), and hence, as being, in effect, *factual realities*, depends, of course, on whether or not the *contingent* truth statements ('p' *if and only if* p) which specify the facts are justified as being *actually* true, *i.e.* 'p' is *actually* p.

This conception of 'facts' may seem counterintuitive to some. But with reflection we can come to realize, with Nielsen, as with Wang and other notable thinkers on the subject, such as Wittgenstein, Putnam, Strawson, Davidson, Rorty, and others, that "we need," according to Nielsen, "to recognize that it makes no sense to try to discover the way the world is apart from context to context, changing with our differing purposes, interests and situations....There is," in other words, "no intelligible [factual] 'point of view from nowhere,'...or 'an absolute [factual] conception of the world,' that is, a point of view or a conception that is interest-free, particularly perspective-free, and could yield the one true [factual] description of the world" (2001, 214).

Therefore, as implicit or explicit *that*-clauses within contingently true sentences, facts *necessarily* depend on *justification* for rational acceptance as *actual* truth, where, 'actual truth' consists of justified statements or, in other words, statements that are actually true. They cannot be statements that are merely asserted without warrant to be true in the minimalist sense. Consider, for example, the truncated statement or truth claim 'Jesus Christ is the Son of the living God and the savior of mankind.' This truncated statement is taken from the entire contingent truth statement: "'It is true *that* Jesus Christ is the Son of the living God and the savior of mankind' *if and only if* Jesus Christ *is* the Son of the living God and savior of mankind." If this truncated statement is shown to be *actually* false (unjustified) or incoherent (unjustifiable), then such a truth-statement is also *factually meaningless*. This is so notwithstanding its truth-value-status as a candidate for truth or falsity. This conclusion would necessarily make the implied facts embedded in such a statement — *i.e.* the implicit *that*-clauses (*e.g.* '*that* Jesus Christ is the Son of the living God,' '*that* God lives' and '*that* Jesus Christ is the savior of mankind') — *factual non realities*.[56]

(c) For a declarative, indicative truth statement to be *actually true* as linguistically representative of something that *really*, objectively, or spatio-temporally exists *extra*-linguistically, like a particular person, object, event, or state of affairs, it must: (*i*) minimally (or logically and sensibly) hang together as an intelligible sentence, given the way our language is commonly used and understood; (*ii*) be internally consistent (*i.e.* not self-contradictory); (*iii*) fit with (not contradict) other essentially related and interdependent concepts (as statements) or previously justified, true beliefs (knowledge) with which it is to be integrated, and (*iv*) have specific *truth-conditions* which, in principle, can be empirically satisfied through verification.

(d) An allegedly true, factual statement which does not (cannot) satisfy the conditions of *c* (*i-iv*) cannot, given *a*, be rationally known, regarded or asserted as being actually true and therefore, cannot, given *b*, specify a fact or have factual meaning or significance.

(e) A putative, or alleged, fact which cannot, given *c*, be legitimately specified, because

---

56   Regarding the use of this term, see note 18.

the sentence which is given to specify it is not, given *c* (*i*) *intelligible*; or, given *c* (*ii* and *iii*), *coherent*; and/or given *c* (*iv*), cannot possibly be empirically known to be either true (or probably true) or false (or probably false). It is, as indicated in *b* above, a *factual non reality*.

The implications of the above premises for conceptual analysis are two-fold. Firstly, justified statements which hang together coherently as cognitive expressions *about* reality are the most we can intelligibly or reasonably strive to get. This is so where such statements constitute, *at best* — given fallibilism — *provisional* and *contingent* knowledge of truth about reality, or knowledge which is always subject to revision. Secondly, non-foundational, or non-self-justifying, *contingently* true statements, which are not commonly (and widely) considered self-evidently true, can *only* be *provisionally* known to be true as valid, linguistic expressions about reality *if and only if* they are, as concepts, both *justifiable* and *justified* through what Nielsen refers to as "wide reflective equilibrium." (See notes 38, 40, and 41) Otherwise, such putatively true, factual statements, if justifiable but not justified, are false. If they are not justifiable, they cannot be known to be either true (or probably true) or false (or probably false). Therefore they must be regarded as factually vacuous, empty statements indicative of a *non-reality*, as specified in premises *b* and *e* above. This understanding makes sense of the notions stated above, that *actual* facts are specified by true statements that are *actually* (not just minimally or disquotationally) true, and that *actually* true statements (*i.e.* those statements which are either *justified* or widely regarded as *self-evident* or *self-justifying*), given the facts of human fallibilism[57] and the natural constraints of space-, time-, mind-, and language-dependence, are provisional at best.

In relation to the work at hand regarding the Mormon faith, the above understanding of premises *a–e* and their stated implications, challenges the Mormon conception of, and emphasis on, truth *as* sure knowledge and foreknowledge of reality, as emphasized in Mormon scripture. Specifically, from the perspective of the Mormon faith, "Truth is knowledge of all things as they [really] are, and as they [really] were, and as they [really] are to come" (D&C 93:24, with interpolations from Jacob 4:13), and fundamental religious truths are considered or believed to be objective and literal realities which are both "absolute and eternal" (D&C 1:39; 88:66) and can be *known* with certainty by faith, through the receipt of revelation from God made possible "by the power of the Holy Ghost" (Moroni 10:3–5, see also McConkie 1979, 810–12).[58]

---

57 The self-evident fact of human fallibilism, as we shall learn with respect to Mormon theology in chapters 5, 6, and 8, necessarily cuts both ways in the human pursuit of religious 'truth' and creates a space for *uncertainty* and *doubt* which can only be attended to *provisionally* and to the extent of 'beyond a reasonable doubt' at a particular point in time. This conclusion requires — demands — by definition and also necessarily, the exercise and ultimate authority of *reason* and the possibility of *doubt*. Both of these make revelation from 'God' and theistic 'faith-as-certainty' impossible in its own right and incoherent in relation to the believer's apologetic acceptance of fallibilism as a fact of human existence.

58   The problem of religious knowledge as adduced from religious experience, mystical experience, revelation, historical occurrences, and miracles is examined competently and persuasively by William T. Blackstone. He concludes (in concert with other scholars cited in his work) "… that certain key religious sentences — when interpreted as being 'analogically true' or 'symbolically true,' or when interpreted as purporting to refer to an unobserved and unobservable object though they cannot possible be falsified [or confirmed or disconfirmed] by any data — not only do not constitute knowledge, but are also not cogni-

But 'truth' *per se* — as implied by Mormon scripture in relation to the believed and asserted fundamental and "Restored" 'truths' of the Mormon faith regarding the putatively revealed existence and nature of 'God,' the Plan of Salvation, the relationship of the Mormon god to man, and as minimally and deflationally conceived in *a* above — "is not," Nielsen informs us, "an *epistemological* notion [or something which is necessarily 'known' or even knowable]. In speaking of the *meaning* (or *use*) of 'true,' we are not speaking of how a truth claim is confirmed, warranted, established, or legitimized [and therefore justified or known]; we are not even necessarily asserting that it is establishable or legitimizable [*i.e.* knowable or justifiable]. It may even be verfification transcendent. To say something is true," Nielsen continues, "is to say that if it is really true, it is time-independent; if *p* is true it has always been true and will always be true, *e.g.*, if there were rocks some places at the bottom of the Mississippi in 1592 then it was, is, and always will be true that there were rocks at the bottom of the Mississippi in 1592. In this way the truth is time-independent, eternal if you want to reify things" (2008, 33).

But "want to" or not, — and I think Nielsen would agree that to "want to" so "reify things" is, given the incoherence and error of metaphysical realism, ultimately perverse and irrational — this logical view of 'truth' as being time-independent is, in theistic religious belief systems in particular, an incoherent, metaphysical view that objectifies or reifies believed religious concepts as being eternal, literal, objective, and language- and mind-independent factual reality. Such an objectifying, metaphysical view — known and referred to in the Mormon faith as 'eternalism' — is, as we touched on earlier in relation to Nielsen's perspective on metaphysical realism and, as we shall explore further in relation to his proposed 'error-theory' of religion, an error. It would make false or incoherent, for example, the Mormon *meta-belief* that certain of its fundamental religious concepts (such as free agency, faith, hope, love, law, and evil, *etc.*) are objective and eternal realities.

Instead, the view of truth as being time-independent is merely a logical extension of the deflationary theory of truth. It holds, essentially, that if truth is what true statements state, then such truth, *in relation to what is stated*, was always true and will always be true *in relation to what is stated*. Following Nielsen above, if *p* — given the statement '*p*' is true if and only if *p* — then *p* in specific relation to '*p*' is necessarily or logically time-independent. But such a logical conclusion regarding truth does not justifiably reify truth *per se* and certainly cannot be coherently interpreted to mean or imply that such semantic, disquotational truth is, *ipso facto*, an actual, objective, eternal reality as metaphysically conceived and believed.

Further, as Nielsen correctly observes, returning to an earlier point, the logical conclusion that truth is time-independent "…says nothing about how we confirm, establish, legitimize, or in any way ascertain the [actual] truth of a proposition [to arrive at *justified* knowledge]. That, unlike truth itself, is time and domain specific. *Taking* or establishing something to be [actually] true is always time-dependent, and what we take to be true [as human beings, again given the fact of human fallibilism], no matter how carefully justified, how well warranted, or even ideally rationally acceptable, may always turn out to be false…. This is why," Nielsen concludes here and elsewhere, "I (along with many others) say that truth is *not* an *epistemic* notion" and "is not important while justification

---

tively [or factually] meaningful" (1963, 167).

is" (33, additional emphasis mine; 2006, 19).

Specifically, the conceptual analysis conducted herein consists in determining if the *allegedly* true and factual metaphysical sentences, truth claims, or statements comprising Mormon doctrine, testimony or God-talk may legitimately be considered *actually* true and *factual* as justified (or even justifiable) truth claims about reality and therefore, sensible or rational beliefs. Can we determine, in other words, if the putative facts (*i.e. that* clauses) of the non-foundational statements of Mormon God-talk (*e.g. 'that* God lives and *that* God hears and answers my prayers') are *intelligible, coherent,* and *factually meaningful* such that they can possibly be *known* (or justified) as being *actually* (even if provisionally) true and therefore, actually factual? More succinctly and simply stated, the task of conceptual analysis applied to the semantically true (and hence factual) indicative sentences of Mormon theology would, again, consist in trying to determine if such sentences are *justifiable* truth claims which make rational sense.

Methodology

In this book, I apply the evaluative procedure of conceptual analysis through a type of Socratic inquiry,[59] engaging the reader — in a way reminiscent of the instructive conversation between Mormon believer and objective outsider presented above — in a type of deconstructive Socratic dialogue. In it I, as a former insider, and now informed outsider, ask you the reader, as either an unquestioning Mormon believer, or as a questioning Mormon believer, non-believer or investigator of the Mormon faith, questions designed to provoke critical thinking and assessment of Mormon and other theistic beliefs and practices. Such inquiry entails asking, from the skeptical perspective of an outsider, those leading and at times rhetorical questions. Hopefully, they will stimulate an *inner* conversation or dialogue among the rational, non-rational, and irrational aspects of the reader's mind that will test and either confirm or disconfirm the putative justifiability and rationality of the Mormon faith as a belief system.

To achieve such an outcome, I invite Mormon believers to reflectively and critically participate in such an informal deconstruction of their faith as skeptical outsiders — just as they would do if conceptually analyzing *other* faith claims and beliefs. In doing so, they would evaluatively determine, with the presumption of skepticism, whether or not allegedly factual *first-order* God-talk, or personal beliefs and testimonies — as well as *second-order* doctrinal statements *about* their god and Plan of Salvation, and *about* the Mormon concepts of 'Revelation' and 'Faith in God and Christ' — are *justifiable* as *actual* truth claims and are rational as beliefs.

My implicit intent in asking such questions is embedded in the astute observation, to

---

59 The nature of the inquiry performed throughout this work is relevant to the task of testing the sense, coherence, and related justifiability and rationality of the religious truth claims that comprise Mormon theology. Should the justifiability of a given truth claim be determined through conceptual analysis by establishing that it can, in principle, be regarded as an intelligible, coherent, and cognitively meaningful (not merely familiar or imaginable) statement of fact which is capable of being justified, a different set of questions would then need to be asked in pursuit of wide reflective equilibrium to actually justify the truth claims. These questions would necessarily employ the essential critical thinking, evidential reasoning, and critical assessment of authority and evidence required to determine whether or not the justifiable truth claims are in fact justified (see notes 38 and 39).

quote John Wisdom, that "[every] philosophical question, when it isn't half asked, answers itself; when it is fully asked, answers itself." My hope is that at least a critical few of the important questions asked in each of the eight chapters of this book will answer themselves in the minds of thinking Mormon and other theistic believers. Beyond this intent and hope is my conviction, perhaps best expressed by Immanuel Kant, that "The great test of sagacity and insight is in knowing what questions might reasonably be asked." The power of any analysis requires to be sure, a 'meritocratic' worldview, an outsider perspective, and a presumption of healthy skepticism. But it also requires, no less importantly, the ability to ask the *right* questions, and the trained ability to listen, observe, and reason *critically*.

Accordingly, concerning any religious statement or truth-claim regarding a god's existence, to be on sound epistemic footing we can and must ask certain questions to establish whether or not such a non-foundational or non self-evident or justifying statement is understandable and justifiable as a truth claim. We must consider whether or not such a statement could *possibly* qualify as an *actual* truth and therefore, as something which could *possibly* be *known* as true, be held as a *rational* belief and in principle be *justified* as knowledge about reality.

If, then, a person makes a claim regarding the factual existence of a god, it is appropriate — if not essential — to subject such a claim (*e.g.* 'God lives,' or 'God exists') to critical analysis by asking the following *types* of questions to make sense of the claim:

First, given the concept of 'God' or the use of the term 'God' in religious discourse, we might reasonably ask "what *specifically* does the term *God* actually mean?" What we're after here is a perspicuous and coherent understanding of what 'God' as a referring expression actually means, or *specifically*, *positively*, and *primarily* refers to as it is used in first- and second-order religious discourse. To get to this level of necessary understanding — necessary because we logically cannot attribute what *something* can or cannot do or what its relationship is to something else unless we first know *specifically* what that 'something' *is* — we are obliged to further ask: "What is 'God' *actually* like?" More specifically, we may ask "What does 'God,' as a referring expression, *specifically* refer to or stand for and what do its primary descriptive referents or attributes *actually* specify?" The emphasis on specificity is crucial in any serious and credible analysis. With the analysis of theological truth claims, in particular, the proverbial devil is *truly* in the details!

These questions are not asked to divert the focus of attention from the issue of 'God's existence' to a broader issue of the meaning of the word 'God' — as with the now infamous Clintonian reply regarding what "the meaning of the word *is*, is." Though the term 'God' is certainly colloquially 'familiar' – or meaningful – and can be non-deviantly used among theistic believers and nonbelievers as a general *term*, or as commonly or formally defined, the *use* (or function) of the word 'God' in first- and second-order religious discourse within and among various and differing theistic language-games, is nonetheless *not* common to all or commonly and consistently understood by all — particularly by or among most Mormon believers. It is particularly *not* a specific, complex, and language-neutral *concept*.

The underlying actual and logical implications of the complex *concept* of 'God' in its *metaphysical fulness* — as, for example, 'an infinite and eternal spirit and intelligence' — is rarely if ever objectively and rigorously questioned or examined for intelligibility, coherence, or factual significance. Typically, such a concept isv *circularly* asserted to be coherent by appealing to religious authority, subjective religious experience, and mystery

— all of which are highly problematical, as we shall learn in the chapters that follow. If the concept of 'God' is deemed incoherent, it is typically defended by *ad hoc* theological speculation and innovation or, as Adler would suggest, by "exploiting" the "possibility [of God]" through the evasive strategies of "ignorance," "isolation," and "inflation." These are strategies that will be explored in some depth in Chapter 2. Because of the above considerations, such questions are required for conceptual analysis and are therefore fundamental to it.

To ask, therefore, 'what is God like?' or 'what, primarily and specifically, does the term *God* actually mean?' in response to the claim 'God exists' is to ask what the *non-foundational* concept 'God' (the way the term 'God' is used) *literally* means, refers to, or is like, in a *fundamental* sense. If the answer is, for example, that 'God' is an omniscient being, then the question 'what *specifically* does the concept 'omniscience' refer to?' may be asked. Alternatively, 'what *specifically* would an omniscient being be like?' might appropriately be asked. In other words, how can the concept of 'God' as an omniscient being be understood in relation to what is relevantly known or understood as being real or true? What can the claimant of the claim 'God exists as an omniscient being' *specifically* refer to? Either by ostension (*i.e.* by ostensive definition, through pointing and similar devices), description, *valid* analogy or analogical predication, or established (self-evident or justified) fact, what would make such a claim intelligible and coherent in relation to other *known* truths or facts, or make it factually significant and therefore justifiable as a putative truth claim? Nielsen elaborates on this important aspect of conceptual analysis below by appropriately referring to the work of P.F. Strawson:

> Indeed, in using language we must not forget what Strawson has called the *Principle of the Presumption of Knowledge* or the *Principle of Relevance*. Of all speech functions to which this applies, it applies most appositely to the making of statements, which is indeed a central speech function if anything is. That is to say, when "an empirically assertive utterance is made with an informative intention" there is the standing *presumption* on the part of the speaker that "those who hear him have knowledge of empirical facts *relevant* to the particular point to be imparted in the utterance." Moreover, statements have topics, they are in a sense about something, and reflect what Strawson calls a "centre of interest." To understand a statement we must understand the topic or center of interest [what the statement is about] involved in its assertion…[Further, we] need a Principle of Relevance to pick out, in terms of the topic in question, the proper kind of answer [given by the speaker to the question of] what a statement is about. This is integral to our understanding of how to take (understand) the statement in question. (2006, 116, emphasis mine)

Nielsen continues by pointing out that

> 'God'…is what Strawson calls a referring expression, though this shouldn't be taken to imply that it is *simply* a referring expression. In asserting that [it is a] referring [expression], I am giving you to understand that presumably [this expression makes] identifying reference. Referring expressions may be names, pronouns, definite descriptions, or demonstrative descriptions. In using referring expressions in identifying descriptions to make identifying references, we do not, Strawson points out, inform the audience of the *existence* of what our

referring expressions refer to. Rather the very task of identifying reference can be undertaken "only by a speaker [or writer] who knows or presumes his audience to be already in possession of such knowledge of [God's] existence…"

Similarly, when a religionc [believer] utters ['God is my Heavenly Father' or 'Jesus Christ is the Only Begotten Son of the living God' or 'God is the Creator and Supreme Ruler of the Universe' or 'God is omniscient and omnipotent', *etc.*] there is the presumption that the speaker understands 'God' and knows or believes in the reality of what is being talked about…In asserting [these paradigm religious statements], the religious [believer] *presupposes* that there is a God and that this God has a certain character [with primary, secondary and relational referents].

…Judaism, Christianity, and Islam [as well as Mormonism] are not by any means constituted [merely] by the making and accepting of certain statements. Rather the making and accepting of certain statements [like those bracketed above] are cornerstones on which all the other type of religious utterances in such religions depend; and they in return presuppose that the statement 'There is a God' [or 'God exists'] is true, and that in turn presupposes that 'There is a God' [or 'God exists'] is a genuine statement and that the concept of God is a viable concept. The *most crucial question* we can ask about Judaism, Christianity, and Islam [and Mormonism] is whether these religious presuppositions are justified. (117–18, last emphasis mine)

This perspective enables us to differentiate the question 'What is God like?' or, more relevant to the subject of this book, 'What is the Mormon god like?' from, for example, the questions 'What is air like?' or 'What are thoughts and feelings like?' The concepts of 'air,' 'thoughts,' 'feelings,' and the like are not equivalent to the concepts of 'God' or any of God's descriptive supernatural referents in any theology. This is so because, as implicitly suggested earlier, 'air', 'thoughts', and 'feelings' are *a priori* foundational (or fundamental) realities with actual existence. As concepts these realities are self-justifying and self-evident on the basis of *the entirety* of human experience. With 'God,' or any particular version of 'God,' it is clearly different. Neither the putative existence of any 'God' nor any of its alleged primary metaphysical referents, or attributes, constitute *foundational* realities or are considered self-justifying or self-evident concepts on the basis of real consensus among all theistic believers and nonbelievers alike.[60] From my perspective then, it is precisely this "most crucial question" referenced by Nielsen in the above passage — *i.e.* whether the religious presuppositions of Judaism, Christianity, Islam, and Mormonism are justified — that justifies (indeed mandates) the rigorous conceptual analysis advocated and applied in this work. This is particularly so, as I shall argue, given the psychological and social risks and consequences of theistic belief in general, and the Mormon faith in particular.

Continuing with the nature of inquiry employed (or types of questions asked) in the critical analysis applied herein, for each apparently unfounded, non-specific, or non-specifiable, questionable, vague, contradictory, incredible or apparently nonsensical descriptive referent, it would be appropriate to ask further questions such as: "How, or on the basis of which *specific* evaluative criteria, could the *actual* truth of this asserted factual descriptive

---

60 The theistic argument that the existence of 'God' *is*, in fact, foundational, or 'properly basic' (*i.e.* self-evident and self-justifying) through, or in virtue of, spiritual (religious) experience is addressed and adequately refuted in Chapters 2, 5, and 6.

referent be *objectively* determined?" If it is claimed that a particular god's existence is self-evident, we may appropriately ask: "What *specifically* is it, for example, about such a putatively 'supernatural,' 'infinite,' 'eternal,' and 'transcendent' being that is self-evident?" "Moreover, how is it that the alleged existence of such a putatively self-evident being is *not* self-evident to all theistic believers and nonbelievers alike?"

Further, we might ask, "How does this alleged fact (*e.g.* of one of a god's primary attributes) square or fit with other known facts (or truths) — such as (another apparently contradictory or incompatible fact or attribute)?" Or "how does one sensibly reconcile the apparent internal contradiction between (concept '*x*' about 'God') and (concept '*y*' about 'God'), or the apparent contradiction(s) between (alleged fact '*f*') and other known truths or related alleged facts, such as ($'f_1,' 'f_2,' 'f_3,'$ etc.)?"

Still further, we would want to ask, "How could the existence of this alleged fact about 'God' be actually or causally possible or true, given its self-contradictory nature in relation to other stated facts or its factual unintelligibility and/or our best justified knowledge about what is real and what is not, and how the world and universe actually (or naturally) work?[61] How can we holistically, or even hypothetically, make sense of such a concept or

---

61 The question of how a putatively existent religious fact (*e.g.* 'God') could be possible, given what is actually known to be true (or justified) at this time and in the natural domain (world and universe), is legitimate, even if our actual knowledge of truth in the natural domain is limited due to innumerable known and unknown gaps, provisional beyond a reasonable doubt at best, and even possibly false. This is also so, it seems to me, in virtue of the religious believer's move to reify or objectify the theistic truth claim — thus moving it from the mere semantic (propositional) realm to an empirical claim subject to verification or falsification. This move, in virtue of the error-theory of religious belief noted earlier (and presented, again, and as a relevant aside at the end of Chapter 3), makes the objectified religious truth claim, like the objectified claims of morality and free will, false or incoherent (Mackie 1977; Joyce 2001; and Double 1990).

By asking how could the existence of a god (as conceptualized in its metaphysical fulness) actually be possible given what is actually known, we are not arguing for the nonexistence of god from ignorance. Rather, we are asking, in effect, how the claimed existence of such a being or entity could even be understood as a hypothesis to be tested as an actual truth capable of being empirically confirmed or disconfirmed, much less claimed to be so with certainty. In other words, we are asking essentially how such a claimed Truth makes sense, given the fact of human fallibilism, or how its alleged truth fits with what we currently know or can even predictably (and responsibly) hypothesize about the world and universe and how they work. How could anyone possibly know, now or ever, that such a god actually (factually) exists, given the unintelligibility and self-contradictoriness of its putative primary and secondary and relational attributes? These questions not only put the burden of making sense of theistic claims on the theist (where it rightly belongs), they put the futile attempt to hypothesize the existence of 'God,' the triviality of semantic (or merely stated) truth, the crucial difference between truth and knowledge of truth, and the unintelligibility of Absolute Truth into focus. For as Nielsen again reminds us, and as we learned above in this chapter and shall revisit in the chapters that follow, standard theistic claims about god's existence "are not empirical claims...or hypotheses to be tested" (2006, 12), and "[i]n [thinking and] speaking about truth ['disquotationally, minimally, and deflationally,' and as opposed to 'knowledge of truth'] we should not worry about correspondence, coherence, or warranted assertability," (17) or "seek[ing] the Unconditional, the Absolute, the Truth" which is, given the fact of fallibilism, "something we cannot even make intelligible" (19). Rather, we should concern ourselves with getting "the best *justified* beliefs we can get at any particular time in any particular circumstance" (18, emphasis mine), realizing that in the end, and again, what we are after, and "the *only* thing we can coherently be after," is *knowledge* of what is true, *not* truth *per se* (or 'Truth') itself (18-19, emphasis mine). As Nielsen stated more recently, "What is crucial in religion (as elsewhere) is how we *warrant* or *establish* (if we can warrant or establish) a religious claim to be true. Perhaps we cannot do so," he says. "Perhaps" as well, "we can articulate neither truth-conditions nor assertability-conditions for religious claims. We have in effect seen," he continues, "...that [appropriately constructed] indicative religious utterances [or propositional truth claims] have a truth-value. But it does not seem at least that they — more accurately the more nonanthropomorphic ones — have either truth-conditions or assertability-conditions. But it remains the case — and trivially so — that "God exists" is true [in the minimalist, semantic sense] if and only if God exists" (2008, 33). It also remains the case, as

alleged reality? How would it (could it) work, or even be possible, given what we *know* — or can sensibly conceive of, not merely imagine or speculate — about how the world and universe actually work?"

Finally, in evaluating a declarative truth claim's *actual* truthfulness, the following questions may profitably be asked to determine if the statement or claim is even a *justifiable* candidate for truth or falsity:

"What, if they exist, are the specific truth-conditions for determining whether or not this concept of 'God' or a statement about his existence is true?" "What would possibly count for or against the truth (or probable truth) or falsity (or probable falsity) of this truth claim?" "What would, in principle, empirically confirm or disconfirm the factual claim being made about this god's existence?"

With each and every stated answer to the above questions, it will be apparent to both the serious inquirer and the responder whether or not the answer really makes sense or is factually significant. Is the answer cognitively understandable — and not merely imaginable? Is it free from internal contradiction, and does it literally hang together, or fit, with common sense and/or common (established or justified) knowledge? If not, then it is appropriate and necessary to repeatedly ask the above or similar questions until it can reasonably be determined whether or not that the statement makes sense and is, at least in principle, *justifiable* as a truth claim and is possibly rational as a belief.[62]

Essentially, in this book, we are following the earlier imagined deconstruction of the 'object of great price.' We are taking apart each of the essential parts (*i.e.* core concepts) of the valued and familiar 'object of great price' (*i.e.* the Mormon belief system), including the concept of 'God,' the concepts of the Mormon gospel, and the concepts of revelation from the Mormon god to man and faith in 'God and Christ.' We do this in order to actually understand the *fundamental nature* of such concepts, to see what they actually *are* or *refer to* as represented in Mormon statements of belief and God-talk. As each part (or concept) of the 'object' (or belief system) is dissembled it is subjected to critical, analytical inquiry. Specific questions are asked in pursuit of clear, specific answers.

The answers given — if any indeed *can* be given besides 'I don't know' — determine whether or not the parts of the object, or what the object is said or believed to consist of, may legitimately be regarded to be factual realities as conceptualized or believed. If no clear, specific, intelligible, coherent, and/or factually meaningful answers are (or can be) given, then the parts of the object are deemed *factual non-realities*. Any claim made regarding the object's *actual* existence, *cannot possibly be determined* to be either true (or probably true) or false (or probably false). After deconstructing the 'object of great price' (or Mormon faith) *nothing remains*. Any assertion that the Mormon god exists and that, therefore, the 'Son of God' exists, 'revelation from God' and 'faith in God and Christ' exist — and that the 'Creation,' 'Fall' and 'Atonement' actually occurred as believed, is

---

stated earlier, that saying "God exists" — even if with utmost sincerity, emotion, conviction, and semantic truth-value — doesn't in the slightest make such an utterance actually true, or even possibly true, much less 'True' in an absolute sense.

62 These kinds of questions get at Nielsen's four criteria and corresponding category questions for determining the rationality or irrationality of belief presented in the next chapter — criteria and questions which recapitulate the method of conceptual analysis presented above.

unjustified as a truth claim and is irrational as a belief.

In such an endeavor in search for intelligibility and factual significance in pursuit of knowledge, it is important to keep in mind, as Nielsen clarifies, that "it is not a question of [the believer] proving his statements to be true; but showing that they have *the kind of meaning* he believes them to have — of showing that they have *factual* content, for if they are devoid of factual content, religious claims are (1) not what believers have thought them to be and (2) they are then, at the very least, without the kind of veracity that mankind has generally thought they possessed" (1982, 146).

Distinctions and Qualifications

The task at hand —which, to me, accurately reflects the generally accepted procedure of conceptual analysis as I conceive it to be — "…is not, " according to Wang, "[merely] to make sense of some unfathomable, [metaphysical] entity or concept [or to prescribe alternative statements to achieve greater sense or meaning] …but of knowing when we are entitled to proclaim something as a fact [and to therefore rationally regard a statement regarding the existence of something to be actually true]" (2003, 29). In performing such a task it is critical to keep in mind that, as Wang correctly states, *"If a fact is whatever is specified by a true statement, and whether or not a statement is true is language-dependent, then a fact turns out to be language-dependent"* (26, emphasis mine). Furthermore, according to Wang, "…our employment of the notion of facts depends upon both the existence of an objective world around the speaker… [which is] specified by the language… and the speaker's ability to make true statements." But this requires language. This makes truth, and therefore facts, language-dependent and, from Wang's philosophical perspective, "relative to… theoretical languages, such as scientific languages [and religious languages]" (26, 27).

Even so, Nielsen cautions us against the error of radical linguistic relativism: "We must not take one language-game or linguistic practice, or even a localized cluster of them, standing by themselves. … We need to look at the language more broadly and try to gain a perspicuous representation of how various language-games in various domains of our talk and thought, of our discoursing with each other, go, or fail to go, together. Thus we might come to recognize," Nielsen concludes, "that religious talk (or God-talk) could have… [its own unique] grammar… [or logic]…*and still be incoherent because of the way it stands with other parts of our talk*" (2001, 421, emphasis mine). In this regard, it is important to keep in mind, regarding the conceptual analysis of God-talk in particular, what Nielsen states elsewhere:

> There is no 'religious language' or 'scientific [or secular] language.' There is rather the international notation of mathematics and logic; and English, French, Spanish and the like. In short, 'religious discourse' and 'scientific discourse' *are part of the same overall conceptual structure*. Moreover, in that conceptual structure there is a large amount of discourse, which is neither religious nor scientific [or secular], that is constantly being utilized by both the religious man and the scientist when they make religious or scientific claims. In short, they share a number of key categories. (1982, 83, emphasis mine)

While religious language, like the language of physics, automechanics, or poker, has its own distinct vocabulary that is specific to its interests, and while the use of certain 'terms-as-facts' in first- and second-order religious discourse is naturally and self-evidently language- (and specific language-game) dependent, the languages or language-games used to express or communicate such terms *as facts* are not (*pace* Wittgenstein) balkanized. They are not isolated from their overall conceptual structure as alleged truth claims. Therefore, such concepts (or uses of terms) in putative truth claims are essentially language-neutral and subject to analysis.

If this is so, Nielsen asserts, then "…conceptual analysis reveals that [metaphysical] non-anthropomorphic religious claims — claims which purport to be literally or actually [factually] true or false and to be *tellings that*, not *tellings to* — are not empirically testable. That is to say, they do not have the logic of statements used to make [factual] assertions about what is [in truth] the case" (1982, 138).

Now if this is also the case, then beliefs — or, more specifically, 'beliefs *that*' rather than 'beliefs *in*' — that are derived from or related to such assertions would be of questionable rationality, where the conditions for regarding a belief as rational or irrational are consistent with Nielsen's four criteria presented in the next chapter. Plainly put, *beliefs comprised of putatively truth-stating sentences which, through conceptual analysis, are deemed to be unintelligible, incoherent, or without factual significance and therefore, neither true nor false, are also, in virtue of the four criteria of rational beliefs, necessarily irrational.* Stated differently in relation to premise *d* in an earlier paragraph above, *beliefs that factual non-realities actually exist are, by any criteria or language-game, nonsensical and incoherent, and therefore cannot be rationally believed.*

Significantly, conceptual analysis is not — and cannot properly result in — a criticism of language. Nor is it intended to be regarded or used as a prescriptive corrective to the putative inadequacy or incompleteness of a language (in this case the English language), or as a call for the development and use of a more highly developed language. Such criticism and corresponding linguistic idealism, as Alice Ambrose argues in Black's *Philosophical Analysis* (1950), would be incoherent on several fronts. According to Ambrose:

> In all the philosophic criticisms made against language we find operative what appears to be a perfectionist ideal. The case is the same with the charge that inexactness in language [rather than the concepts expressed through language] is responsible for vagueness [unintelligibility or apparent incoherencies]. Here again…attainment of the ideal situation is logically impossible. Vagueness is a source of complaint only if there is a standard which the existence of this phenomenon shows language to fall short of. Now, the ideal is exactness, an exactness such that we can always discriminate verbally between things having [a particular attribute, quality or property] and those not having it. (35)

This is particularly relevant to our task at hand, for metaphysical, religious language is said to be exact and real — with a type of 'Platonic realism' that is putatively beyond the pale of human language. The idea is "that beyond language there exists a realm of universals" which impose "standards of exactness of which language falls short…" (1950, 35). To the charge that "vagueness resides in language," while "precision [resides] in what it [language] designates," is based on the "assumption…that a word can be vague [or unintelligible] while the universal it designates is sharp [or intelligible]." But the asserted possibility of this assumption is challenged by Ambrose, who contends that "Since the universal is the meaning of the word, the assumption is that a word can have a vague application though its meaning is nonvague. But the application of a word," concludes Ambrose, "is fixed by its meaning, so that the application could not be less sharp [or intelligible] than the meaning" (37). Consequently, we cannot coherently blame language for the incoherence of our core religious concepts. We will therefore accept here the adequacy of the English language as being sufficiently complete for its intended use in all language-games in which it is applied — in this case, the Mormon language-game.

Conceptual analysis, as used in this book, is fundamental. Therefore it is relevant to the determination of the possible (actual) truth and rationality/irrationality of religious beliefs — particularly where such beliefs are considered by believers to be actually true and the truth claims implicit or explicit in such beliefs are purported to specify facts and reality. As a procedure, such analysis, according to Nielsen, serves the quest for "truth and knowledge of truth" through pursuit of "…the best justified beliefs we can get at any particular time in any particular circumstance," realizing, given human *fallibilism*, that "a statement may be ever so well justified [confirmed, established, corroborated], justified, that is, as well as it could possibly be done at any particular time, and still be false." We must remember that, while "…metaphysical impulses may drive us to seek the Unconditional, the Absolute, the Truth," such an endeavor "…is something we cannot even make intelligible" (2006, 18, 19).

The Question of Factual Significance

It should be noted that Nielsen's criterion for *factual significance* is neither arbitrary nor self-refuting or question-begging. Nor is it intended by Nielsen, or by me, to be the primary or exclusive tool of conceptual analysis or test of rationality. Rather, such a criterion is, to quote Nielsen, to be regarded "as a *proposal* justified on pragmatic grounds and not itself [an analytic or empirical claim, or] a putative statement of fact [which is itself untestable]" (2008, 32).

Moreover, Nielsen's criterion is "intended to help us sort out (provide a kind of litmus test for) sentences used to make claims about the world: what the world (universe) is like (including things in the universe) and what realities transcendent to the universe are like, if such there is or even can be, and, on the other hand, which sentences are unintelligible or incoherent verbal formulas" (2006, 22). Elaborating on this point in an earlier published work included in *The Logic of God* (1975) Nielsen explains: "We use verifiability to demarcate *within the class of meaningful sentences* those sentences that are used to make factual statements. Thus where we assume that *p* has *some meaning* and then say that *p* is a factual claim only if some *E* would count as verifying *p*, we are not pulling ourselves up by our own bootstraps, not doing anything that is logically inappropriate, but only developing a test to determine whether a purportedly factual statement is indeed factual. (236)

"I have not," Nielsen insists, "tried to do the impossible, *e.g.*, to discover whether a given statement is verifiable before I have at all understood its meaning; but where *p* stands for a statement utilizing a linguistic unit that is part of a corpus of some natural language and thus, in one plain sense, meaningful, I have tried to show, by setting out a test, how we can determine whether *p* actually makes a factual claim by determining whether *p* is verifiable. 'The square root of three is tired' is not part of the corpus of English; we do not understand it. It is not part of some scientific discourse attached to English, and native speakers cannot think of discourses (philosophical or linguistic ones apart) in which it would naturally occur. But 'There is a God' plainly is a part of the corpus of English, native speakers can paraphrase it, and they can readily think of discourses in which it would naturally occur. But nothing that I said denies the intelligibility [or *linguistic* understandability or meaningfulness] of religious utterances…Yet religious people claim that it is a fact that there is a God, but if it is a fact, then 'There is a God' must have factual intelligibility, but if it has factual intelligibility [significance] it should be verifiable in principle, and…attempts to show that it is verifiable fail…" (237)

Furthermore, Nielsen concludes, "Religious people…believe that it is a fact that there is a God. If it is not a fact their faith is in vain; but if it is a fact, then to assert that there is a God is to make a factual statement, but then the statement must be verifiable in principle, *i.e.,* there must be some empirical evidence that would count for or against its truth. But given the way in which 'There is a God' is actually used by believers, or at least by many contemporary believers, its truth or falsity seems to be equally compatible with anything and everything that could conceivably occur. But if this is so, it can hardly be a genuine factual claim. This is the challenge raised by the theology-and-falsification issue…Perhaps someone can show that such religious statements can be verified and thus show that they actually have factual intelligibility, or perhaps someone an show that…I [am] mistaken in thinking that a statement, to be factual, needs to be verifiable (confirmable or disconfirmable) in principle. [No one] has shown neither of these two things, but until either such claim can be made out, I persist in my challenge and persist in my contention that even first-order God-talk is incoherent and conceptually confused" (238).

Given the above, and within a larger 'coherence view' of human knowledge about the world, the universe, and how they work — as understood scientifically and commonsensically in any and every life-form and language-game — such a criterion, for Nielsen, "has a point…and very well might be essentially right" (2006, 23).

I think it *is* right — as do the notable philosophers of religion cited in this and other works. Responding, for example, to an earlier challenge by Nielsen for anyone "to give a case of a statement whose factual status is accepted by all parties as quite *unproblematic* which is not at least confirmable or disconfirmable in principle" (1982, 182), Michael Martin writes: "I know of no clearly agreed upon case in which a sentence is not confirmable and yet is considered factually meaningful or in which a sentence is confirmable and is not considered factually meaningful. …I [therefore] conclude that a strong *prima facie* case can be made for the thesis that if some theistic language is not confirmable or disconfirmable, it is factually meaningless… and there is independent reason to embrace such a theory… [and] to adopt this criterion…" (1990, 54–5). Later, after conducting a thorough analysis of the meaningfulness of religious language in which he presents Nielsen's critique of God-talk and evaluates objections made by Swinburne, Tooley, Hick, Kavka, and Crombie, Martin further concludes that all criticisms fail, and that Nielsen's criterion for factual significance "…is not arbitrary, since it is justified by how well it accounts for certain data. Moreover, the theory can be formulated in a way that neither allows every sentence to be meaningful nor excludes the sentences of theoretical science as meaningless" (1990, 77).

Nor is Nielsen's use of the criterion of factual significance question-begging through the alleged presupposition of a particular theory of meaning or of an alleged metaphysical naturalism which arbitrarily disqualifies metaphysical religious discourse as nonsense. As Nielsen himself has stated in an earlier work, such "a criterion for factual intelligibility" does not depend on, or advocate, any particular theory of meaning, but merely "brings out the procedures which are actually employed in deciding whether a statement is indeed factual. *It makes explicit an implicit practice…*and can be used in deciding on borderline and disputed cases…[where] certain utterances are allegedly bits of fact-stating discourse yet function in a radically different way than our paradigms of fact-stating discourse," thereby providing us with "good grounds for questioning [or asserting] their factual intelligibility" (1982, 41, 42, emphasis mine).

"Moreover," we are reminded —again addressing the criticism of arbitrariness — that "religious concepts are not problematic because of the acceptance of some contentious epistemological or semantical theory or other but are widely sensed to be problematic by many moderns quite independently of their adopting any such theory. …They are, as it were, *pre-analytically* problematic though certain theories may enhance and conceptually direct our sense of their being problematic" (Nielsen 1989, 8, emphasis mine). This suggests, according to Martin, that from Nielsen's perspective, "we can legitimately suppose that there is something amiss in religious language because many religious practitioners suppose there is. Often, [Nielsen] says, religious believers themselves have doubts about whether they are believing anything that is true or false. This is not because of some [arbitrary] externally imposed theory of factual meaning that they have accepted. [Rather, Nielsen] urges that the difficulty is intrinsic to [metaphysical] God-talk" (1999, 208).

Furthermore, although Nielsen is admittedly a secularist embracing "a nonscientistic, contextualist, and historicist naturalism without being subjectivist, relativistic, or nihilistic" (1996, 25) and without metaphysical foundations, his advocacy of a pragmatic, holistic, coherentist model of justification through "wide reflective equilibrium" invites *all* considered judgments, convictions, and beliefs (including metaphysical religious beliefs) to the table for contextual, critical examination and evaluation of their sense, coherence, and factual significance — acknowledging, as Nielsen is wont to say, that "Fallibilism is the name of the game. And that isn't positivist dogma" (2006, 19)[63].

Nielsen's emphasis on the factual intelligibility of God-talk, as I take it, is a critically reflective move toward factual integrity, rationality, and common-sense broadly conceived. The methodology and criteria for evaluation of certain theistic beliefs are sensible and neither absolute, dogmatic, nor esoteric. That we cannot possibly know what cannot *possibly* be known (putative revelation and eschatological verification to the contrary notwithstanding) is hardly a metaphysical premise — or a controversial and objectionable

---

63 As Nielsen states elsewhere (1993) in reply to a critique of his *a priori* argument for Atheism, although such an argument "…owes a lot to Logical Positivism, which in turn owes a lot to traditional empiricism, it does not make the characteristic claims of Logical Positivism — namely, to claim to a sharp distinction between empirical propositions and analytic ones, or to argue that an utterance only has cognitive meaning if it is at least empirically testable and it does not claim…that all meaningful discourse must be recastable in an empiricist language. In my view," Nielsen asserts, "not all was dross in Logical Positivism, and I use some of its least challengeable conceptions in a way that I believe is unexceptionable and free of what was in effect an empiricist metaphysic. My arguments…about reference, however, do not depend on the verification principle or on any attempt to construct an empiricist language" (263–4). Regarding the question of verifiability in particular, and its evolution in philosophical thinking and practice, see Nielsen 2001, pp. 470–88, and for a defense of Nielsen's verificationist challenge to theism, see Martin 1999.

one at that. My understanding is that Nielsen is *not* arguing from a premise that what cannot possibly be known does not exist, but rather that the *alleged existence* of what cannot possibly be known to exist is unintelligible and incoherent. It is therefore either probably untrue or incapable of being determined to be either true or false. This makes such a putative existent, in the latter case, a factual non-reality, and makes any belief that such an existent actually exists — in both cases and by common understanding — irrational. Whether or not the statements of metaphysical religious doctrines can possibly be known or rationally believed to be true are the crucial questions on the table for critical, conceptual analysis.

To summarize: the use of the criterion of factual significance makes perfect sense in the limited role in which it is used, in which it has a point. In its limited use as a litmus test to determine whether or not an allegedly true, or alleged factual statement with truth-value is justifiable as an actual truth claim, it is therefore essential to the critical, conceptual analysis performed in this book and to its primary purpose as described above.

Further, its use is advocated by Nielsen *in connection with* the necessary acceptance of human fallibilism and a broad contextualist and historicist perspective (or 'coherence view') regarding what it makes sense to say, or how putative truth claims or factual statements hang together (cohere) with *both* established, justified beliefs *and* unverifiable, fundamental common sense and knowledge. It cannot be legitimately labeled, or dismissed, as mere positivist dogma or reduced to simple verificationism. It cannot be rightly regarded as advocating a particular theory of meaning or a metaphysical system or program for single-handedly or conclusively determining or evaluating absolute truth regarding the disposition of theistic discourse or doctrine.

The criterion of factual significance is merely a proposed criterion — one important tool in a *philosophical* tool-kit — for separating factually meaningless statements from factually meaningful ones. It is an evaluative criterion, *wholly consistent with our natural intuitions and common practices.* At the very least, it can (and effectively does) raise reasonable doubt regarding putative statements of fact specified by dubious or questionable truth claims — doubt that can therapeutically work to free the mind from the grip of false or incoherent beliefs. Consequently, I regularly invoke the criterion of factual significance, as well as other criteria of intelligibility and coherence, to analyze and determine the coherence and possible rationality of the putative truth claims or claimed factual statements that comprise Mormon theology. By association — and to the degree there is legitimate overlap — this applies to all other forms of orthodox theism as well.

Chapter 2

Conditions of Rationality

*"...a rational theology is founded on truth...A man should therefore use
his reasoning faculty in all matters involving truth, and especially as
concerning his religion."*

— *Elder John A. Widtsoe*

Prefatory Note: Extending from — and implicit in — the reasoning fallacies referred to and
enumerated in the *Introduction* and the set of representative analytical questions presented in the
previous chapter is the role of reason in the Mormon faith and the question of rationality of Mormon
beliefs and believers. Unlike the Protestant Reformer Martin Luther, who declared that "reason
is a whore" and cautioned believers to "part with reason...tear out the eyes of reason...and even
kill it...else one will not get into the kingdom of heaven," Mormon leaders and believers at least
openly profess to value reason and with it rationality. It is therefore to the foundational question of
what we are justified in regarding as reasonable and rational *vis-à-vis* Mormonism and all theistic
faiths to which we now briefly and importantly turn in this chapter.

Regarding the importance of reason in the Mormon faith we can turn to no greater
authority than Mormon scripture itself. Accordingly, in the Mormon *Doctrine and
Covenants* (D & C) reason is established as at least apparently essential for understanding
truth. It is the natural means by which the Mormon god establishes man's understanding
of his 'revealed Truth' (D & C 50: 10–12). Moreover, as we shall learn through the words
of Mormon Apostle Dallin Oaks presented in Chapter 6, reason is considered essential
for authenticating revelation, although it is subordinate in authority to revelation in establishing 'God's Truths.' But, as we shall learn in Chapter 5, this is unintelligibly the case.

Rationality is significant and important to Mormons, and they collectively take great
comfort and pride in the believed reasonableness and rationality of their faith and personal
beliefs. But is such a characterization of their faith and personal beliefs justified? This, of
course, will ultimately be left to readers to determine after carefully reading this book and
reflecting on its contents and sources as a skeptical outsider to their faith. Still, in doing so
it seems important and at least uncontroversial to point out three important considerations
— the first two of which seem rather self-evident in such a determination, and the third
of which is supported by significant research in human cognition, as well as by personal
confirmation by those who are sufficiently self-aware and honest.

First is the consideration that belief that is derived from, or defended by, invalid arguments (in virtue of flawed or faulty reasoning) is both unreasonable *per se* and unreasonable to hold — much less to assert as either actual or necessary truth or as knowledge of
truth. Second, as we shall explore in more depth below, is the consideration that false,
unintelligible, incoherent, or unwarranted beliefs that are held, asserted, and defended with
conviction as knowledge or actual truth (much less Absolute Truth) on the basis of *mere*

possibility and/or subjectively interpreted personal experience are irrational *per se* and are irrational to hold. Certainly these two considerations would very likely be considered pragmatically uncontroversial and even commonsensical in determining the reasonableness and rationality of secular beliefs or of the superstitious and religious beliefs of primitives or other more civilized people. Why not then for one's own religious beliefs as well?

This last question leads us to the third consideration. In the words of psychologist Valerie Tarico in her sufficiently sourced chapter in Loftus (2010), "…research on human cognition suggests that…[o]ur brains have built-in biases that stack the odds against objectivity, so much so that that the success of the scientific [or any other rigorous, analytical and empirically-based justificatory] endeavor [of rationality concerning the verification or falsification of putative truth claims] can be attributed to one factor: it pits itself against our natural leanings, erects barriers across the openings to rabbit trails, and systematically exposes faulty thinking to public critique….One of the strongest built-in mental distortions we have," Tarico continues, "is called *confirmation bias*. Once we have a hunch about how things work, we seek information that fits what we already think. ... This bias optimizes for efficiency over accuracy. It allows us to rapidly sift through the information coming at us and piece together a meaningful story line. But in situations where emotions [or feelings] run high or evidence is ambiguous, it also lets us go very wrong" (50-1; interpolations mine).

Clearly it would seem in this third regard, and as the research also bears out, that we are, in Tarico's words, "only partly rational" (52). And it would also seem, as we shall learn in the pages ahead, and as we have hopefully learned through experience, that the part of us which *is* rational, in the limited but important sense presented in this chapter, is the part of our mental functioning which has been trained and conditioned in perceived matters of personal importance or consequence. It functions to consciously and willfully (albeit deterministically) keep such biases in awareness, while acknowledging the fact of fallibilism and deliberately adhering to the *authority of reason* as skeptical outsiders in pursuit of the best knowledge we can muster as fallible human beings.

With these preliminary thoughts and considerations in mind (as well as the last question above), we will now return to the larger question at hand: "Do the beliefs and doctrines of the Mormon faith truly amount to a rational theology?

Mormon Apologetics

Attempts by Mormon Church authorities and apologists to definitively and affirma-tively answer this question fail to do so. This is so on both methodological and substantive grounds. From a methodological standpoint, attempts to demonstrate the rationality of Mormon beliefs fail because of the use of a deeply flawed apologetic strategy or approach that I think disingenuously employs various reasoning fallacies and "evasive possibility strategies" (Adler 2006) in attempting to justify Mormon truth claims as rational. Moreover, attempts to demonstrate the rationality of Mormon beliefs simply ignore what is widely and reasonably held to be established commonsensical criteria for rationality. They appeal (wrongly I think) with theists of other faiths to the 'proper basicality' of religious beliefs and experience. In this last regard, neither the Mormon Prophet and founder Joseph Smith nor the most renowned liberal *and* conservative Mormon doctrinal authorities, including

John A. Widtsoe, James E. Talmage, Brigham H. Roberts, Joseph Fielding Smith, and Bruce R. McConkie could resist the metaphysical urge to assert, with infallible certainty, a knowledge of what is not commonly known by all and cannot be known by science or reason. All alike have tried to pass off their speculative cosmology and synthetic *a priori* propositions concerning reality as Absolute Truth.[64]

John A. Widtsoe, for example, an ordained Apostle of the Mormon Church, as well as a man of letters with a doctorate in the natural sciences, was one of the more liberal theologians of the Church who wrote the book *A Rational Theology As Taught by The Church of Jesus Christ of Latter-day Saints,* published by the Church in 1915. This book, written to appeal to an educated membership of the Church, asserted that "The Gospel of

---

64 As pointed out in the previous chapter, Mormon metaphysics, like all speculative philosophical and theo-logical schemes and alleged *a priori* knowledge or truth claims are highly problematical where they purport to provide a systematic account or one true description of how the world is and indeed must be, and/or "… synthetic *a priori* truths — [*i.e.*] truths [about reality] whose truth is independent of experience, propositions which are established to be true by pure thought, holding for all possible worlds, but still extending our knowl-edge of reality and not merely unfolding our understanding of what we already know" (Nielsen 1995, 41).

With speculative metaphysics "[o]ne difficulty," according to Nielsen, "is in ascertaining what it could mean to say, and, beyond that bare claim of intelligibility [a minimal requirement which metaphysical God-talk cannot satisfy], to give any warrant at all for claiming, that such entities [*e.g.* intelligences, spirit matter, spirit energy] are the finally real things of which the world is constituted. But how can, or can," Nielsen asks, "such propositions be established and can there be any evidence [even in principle] or [*non a priori* and *non question-begging*] reasons in their favor? It seems at least," Nielsen observes, "that we have no idea of what it would be like to have evidence or reasons here. Some…will say that ultimate reality, final actuality, all truly real being, is changeless or eternal.…But no hint at all has been given as to how we can [possibly] ascertain which of these claims about ultimate reality is true or even probably true. We can paint various word-pictures here, give different narratives, but we have no idea at all of how to establish which of these claims, if any, are true or even probably true.…Speculative [metaphysical philosophy and/or theology] purports to give us… knowledge [of ultimate truth or reality], but there is no good reason to believe that it actually succeeds. If philosophy [or theology] is identified with metaphysics [as Mormon cosmology and its doctrine of deity cer-tainly are], or taken essentially to be *a quest* [or understanding] *of ultimate reality*, then we have good reasons to be skeptical indeed about [such speculative philosophy or theology — or even fundamental particle theory in physics] as a cognitive enterprise and to be very doubtful if it has any intellectually sustainable future" (30). This is so even given, as it must be, that our current knowledge about the world and the universe and how they work is uncertain and provisional, for even with such a concession we are still confronted with the question of how it is at all plausible to think that we can, by merely ontologizing, or otherwise engaging in speculative metaphysics, give an absolutely true account of the world, or somehow actually go beyond natural science in doing so? For Nielsen, "[e]ven to ask [such a question] is to make metaphysics look absurd" (30–1).

Regarding metaphysical propositions as synthetic *a priori* truths, Nielsen likewise argues that "we have no good reasons for believing that there are any such truths and that there are not even any sound reasons for believing there could even be any" (44). The argument offered in this regard is not that there are no *a priori* truths, but rather that the alleged metaphysical truths of philosophy and theology are mistakenly (if not incoherently) held as being analytic, or self-evident. In this sense, Nielsen I think correctly argues that "…all claims to self-evident, synthetic *a priori* truths are all themselves less than self-evident," and that "to believe that there are such truths is very implausible indeed [;] [on]… no occasion – no matter what dialecti-cal gyrations we may make – do we reach a point where we have some absolute self-evident presupposi-tions which tell us what reality must be like and which are beyond all question so that finally we would have an Archimedean fulcrum rooted in self-evident certainty" (44–5). This is particularly so," Nielsen correctly points out, "even with the given transcendental, ontologizing arguments made and offered which attempt to prove the existence of absolute, eternal existences from purely conceptual premises — premises which are, for the most part, presuppositional and lack wide reflective consensus as to their truthfulness" (45–6). (For a more complete assessment of philosophy as metaphysics in general, and speculative metaphysics and metaphysics and *a priori* knowledge in particular, see Nielsen 1995, pp. 19–84, and Nielsen 1971, 1996.)

Jesus Christ [*i.e.* Mormon Theology] is a system of doctrines and practices *founded* on *unvarying certainties*."

In the first preface to the book, Widtsoe states that "This volume is an exposition; it is not an argument. The principles of the Gospel, as held by the Church of Jesus Christ of Latter-day Saints [Mormon Church] are stated briefly, simply and without comment, to show the *coherence*, *reasonableness* and *universality* of the Gospel philosophy." Later, in Chapter 2, the author cautions that all knowledge "should be carefully examined in the light of *reason*" and then counsels that "A man should therefore use his *reasoning* faculty in all matters involving truth and especially as concerning his religion," concluding this chapter with the assertion that "The Gospel, a *rational* theology, is founded on *truth*, on *all* truth…" (1915). From here Widtsoe proceeds to present a highly questionable and problematic metaphysical treatise that makes numerous unjustifiable truth claims comprising anything but a "rational theology."

The apparent strategy of Widtsoe's book — even if perhaps without his awareness or intention — is very common to other explicit apologetic attempts at justifying metaphysical religious truth claims as actual truth and reconciling unknowable religious beliefs with established or 'possible' knowledge of the physical world. Such an apologetic strategy represents verisimilitude as truth and typically consists of the following basic approach: *First*, present *known* and/or *knowable* naturalistic truth regarding certain realities in the physical world. S*econd*, presupposing the factual existence of 'God' and an eternal, spiritual realm of existence, present the believed existence of *unknown* and/or *unknowable* metaphysical realities as known and/or knowable truth. And *third*, engage in the following tacit reasoning process to connect known truth with religious beliefs and thereby justify the treatment and acceptance of such beliefs as knowledge:

I. Liken the alleged and unknown or unknowable supernatural truths and *metaphysical* realities of religious belief to known natural truths and *physical* realities (or *vice-versa*) by analogy or through analogical predication. Six paradigm examples from Mormon theology include: (1) the likening of 'spirit matter' to physical matter and 'spirit energy' to natural forms of physical energy (*i.e.* nuclear, solar, biological, electro-magnetic); (2) the likening of 'spiritual communication' between the Mormon god and man to the way a radio transmitter sends communications to a radio receiver through the medium of radio waves; (3) the likening of the so-called 'Great Law' of 'spiritual evolution' – or 'eternal progression' from 'eternal intelligence' to 'God' – to natural or biological evolution; (4) the likening of a 'spiritual' relationship between man and the Mormon god to the human relationship between a biological parent and child or, alternatively, the likening of the putative Parent/child relationship (between 'God' and his spirit children) in the alleged 'pre-mortal' stage of life to a loving parent-child relationships on earth; (5) the likening of the 'basic biological situation' between mother and child (Faber 2004) to the putative basic primordial situation between the Mormon god and man in the pre-mortal estate; and (6) the likening of knowing 'God and Christ through prayer' and 'spiritual' experience to knowing our mortal father, brother, or friend in this life through intimate communication and shared physical experience.

II. Assert explicitly or by implication — given the apparent likenesses between natural and supernatural realities — that if the asserted or claimed knowledge of natural, physical realities is rational, then, on the basis of apparent similitude established by analogy and analogical predication, belief in putative supernatural, or metaphysical, spiritual realities is also rational.

III. Assert that there is no physical or rational reason to deny the implicit or explicit assertion in **II** above, and — in anticipation of such an assertion being challenged (as surely it must be) — appeal preemptively to the need for and reliance on: (a) greater faith in 'God' and putative scriptural, authoritative and personal revelation; (b) the faithful and patient suspension of doubt in this life; (c) the certainty of the Mormon god's putative existence and purposes through verification in the next life (*i.e.* eschatological verification); and (d) defensive arguments from 'possibility' and 'parity.'

The above Mormon apologetic approach and related process of argumentation start with (or presuppose) the actual existence of the Mormon god and revelation from that god to man. It then essentially claims, or argues, that the gospel is a rational theology. This it does on the premise that that which is in heaven (*i.e.* theological 'reality') is analogous (or essentially so) to that which is on earth (*i.e.* naturalistic reality) — and *vice-versa* regarding naturalistic realities which allegedly correspond to theological or eternal realities. Such an argument, however, is clearly invalid and — for someone like Widtsoe who knows (or should know) better — disingenuous for at least three significant reasons. *First*, it assumes, or presupposes, without warrant or justification, the *a priori* and non-self-evident *actual* existence of certain eternal beings and realities such as eternal laws, principles, spirit matter, intelligences and realms of existence. Such things cannot possibly be justified.[65] *Second*, it begs the primary and ultimate question at issue, which is the Mormon god's *actual* (not imagined, speculated, or perceived) existence. It is a truth claim which, given the metaphysical concept of the Mormon god, is likewise not self-evident (or even apparently so) nor is it even justifiable without possible assertability or truth-conditions. *Third*, the argument is made primarily by appealing to putative revelation from (and faith in) the Mormon god. But these are also unwarranted assertions that beg the primary question at issue. These appeals also employ false analogy or invalid analogical predication.

---

65 Nielsen states what seems obvious when he writes: "We cannot sensibly ask whether [or how it is that] a being [or any reality] which is eternal actually exists [or came to be]." For "[i]f it is an eternal being [or reality] it must exist. Still there may be no eternal beings [or eternal realities of any kind]" (2006, 34). This seems self-evident, suggesting that such putatively eternal beings (gods) and other putatively eternal realities (such as spirit matter, intelligences, principles, laws or realms of existence, whatever such might actually mean, if anything) might *or might not* actually exist and that their putative or claimed existence may not therefore, be validly assumed or presupposed or even asserted without warrant or justification. This must be established methodologically either by the appropriate application of the scientific method or, as Nielsen prefers, following Rawls, on the basis of wide reflective equilibrium (31–35; note 38). Moreover, since such putative metaphysical realities, as concepts fundamental to the Mormon doctrine of deity, are not — Mormon attestations of 'common sense' to the contrary notwithstanding — self-evident (or 'basic') and are neither justified nor justifiable (because, as shall be argued in Chapter 3, they are, on the basis of conceptual analysis, unintelligible, incoherent and factually meaningless), they have no warranted assertability and can only be considered conceptually as *factual non realities*.

All of this raises the question of what reasonably can and should be said about (1) the rationality/irrationality of belief; (2) the argument for rationality on the basis of 'analogy,' 'possibility' and 'parity'; (3) the employment of faith (and putative revelation) as a source of knowledge; and (4) the validity of eschatological verification. To the first and second parts of this question regarding the determination of rationality (or irrationality) of belief and the argument for the rationality of religious beliefs on the basis of possibility and parity, I appropriately turn to both Adler and Nielsen for context and quote them extensively below. The third and fourth parts of this question regarding the arguments for revelation and faith as a legitimate source of knowledge and the verification of the Mormon god's existence in the next life will be addressed in some depth in later chapters of this book. But we must first consider what reasonably can and should be said about rationality in general and the rationality/irrationality of belief in particular.

Conditions of Rationality

"Presumably," according to Nielsen, "a rational human being will have rational *principles of action* and *rational beliefs*. Moreover, to have rational attitudes is at least to have attitudes that square with these principles and beliefs, and to be irrational is — though this is perhaps not all that it is — to not act in accordance with these principles and beliefs. But what are they" (2006, 230)?

Rational principles of action, as Nielsen sees it, include, "*ceteris paribus...* [taking] the most efficient means to achieve one's ends...; [seeking] to make one's judgments impartially...; [attending], where relevant, to the results of a well-conducted experiment...;" and "not [ignoring] disconfirming evidence" (2001, 140, 141). To this partial list of "general principles of rationality" (140) I would add: not ignoring or dismissing out-of-hand well-reasoned argument and incisive, critical inquiry into the underlying assumptions, implications, and relations of one's beliefs to other beliefs (2006, 230) or, more crucially, to common knowledge and at least apparently conflicting beliefs and justified truth claims.

"*Rational beliefs* [generally speaking] are typically beliefs that can withstand the scrutiny of people who are critical of [such] beliefs: that is to say, they are beliefs typically held open to refutation or modification by experience and/or by reflective examination" (230). More specifically, again from Nielsen:

A belief [religious or otherwise] is in most circumstances irrational if the person holding it knows or has very good grounds for believing that it is either (1) inconsistent, (2) unintelligible (does not make sense), (3) incoherent [contradicts or conflicts with what we know about the world through the achievements of science, philosophy and a wide, cross-cultural and inter-disciplinary consensus of considered judgments about reality] or (4) false or very probably false...

In asking whether the Judeo-Christian [or Mormon] belief in God is rational, or at least not irrational, we are asking:

1. Is belief in such a God free of [internal] inconsistencies or contradictions?
2. Is belief in such a God intelligible? [Does such a belief make sense on the basis of what is commonly known to be true?]
3. Is belief in such a God a belief in a coherent conception? [Is such a non-foundational

(or non-self-evident) belief incoherent in the sense that it is regarded as knowledge even though it is neither justified nor justifiable, and it conflicts with our best, most complete knowledge about the world and the universe?]

4. Is belief in such a God a belief in something that we have very good grounds to believe not to be the case? [Is such a belief false or probably false, given either the absence of verifiability, or the lack of supporting evidence and/or the existence of falsifying evidence, if justifiable?] (2006, 241–242)

If the answers to the above four questions are *no, no, no,* and *yes* respectively, "then belief in [an infinite, eternal, and transcendent, or other-worldly and supernatural] God is irrational for a [person] who recognizes any of these things or for a [person] who is in a position where he could, but for self-deception, recognize these things. If this is so, we can say derivatively that the beliefs are irrational beliefs" (2006, 242).

These four criteria and four related sets of category questions point us back to conceptual analysis. There is a necessary connection here which, as with conceptual analysis itself, cuts across all cultural life-forms and language-games and can be conceived of as follows: unfounded, non-self-justifying truth claims, or beliefs that are found to be *justifiable* — through conceptual analysis or through *critically* derived positive answers to the first three of four category questions above — are considered herein to be *possibly rational*. Such beliefs, or truth claims, that are found to be *unjustifiable* through conceptual analysis are considered herein to be *unintelligible* and/or *incoherent* and/or *factually meaningless*. Therefore, they are *neither true nor false*, making the subject of the putative truth claim a factual *non-reality*. It makes belief *in* such a non-reality — or belief *that* such a non-reality exists — irrational. Finally, such beliefs, as factual statements or truth claims that have been found to be *justified* through a confirmable, negative answer to the fourth category question above and have been derived by a coherentist method of rational justification, qualify as knowledge and are considered herein to be *provisionally true* (or probably true) as well as *rational*. Those found to be *unjustified* are considered to be *false* (or probably false) as well as *irrational*.

Given this context for analysis and evaluation, as well as other relevant analytical questions and considerations to be presented throughout this book, we can reasonably and rightly examine for rationality Mormon beliefs about their god, their Plan of Salvation, revelation from the Mormon god to man *about* that god, and faith in God and Jesus Christ. The Mormon theological explanations for certain apparently irresolvable contradictions will be presented in Chapter 7.

The Authority of Reason

Before doing so, however, it is important to explicitly acknowledge, up-front, Nielsen's (and my own) acceptance of 'the authority of reason' as well as his reasoned objections to the rationality of religious beliefs on the basis of religious experience and putative revelation. First, inasmuch as *reason* is crucial to the critical analysis and conclusions presented in this book and for an appreciation of Nielsen's contribution to my own thinking, I will allow Nielsen to again speak for himself:

What…does my commitment to reason come to? Well, it comes to rejecting the supernatural and transcendent and accepting instead the ultimate authority of reason. But what is it to accept the authority of reason? Well, it comes to rejecting, as being incoherent or in some other way illegitimate, any appeal to a "reality transcending what we [can or do] empirically comprehend." It comes (a) to rejecting any claim to have access to a realm of truth or an order of facts which are even in principle empirically inaccessible, and (b) to rejecting any claim to such a "non-empirical realm of fact" as being conceptually incoherent. There is and can be no gnostic [hidden] knowledge. (1989, 229–30)

The authority of reason is derived from its reliability. Its reliability is established by the *a priori* acceptance of the basic (foundational) rules of reasoning and the *justification* of *justifiable* (*i.e.* coherent, factually intelligible and non-analytical) propositions, or truth claims, where such justification is achieved through the deductive and inductive validation of predicted empirical consequences and the corresponding achievement of wide reflective equilibrium. Such 'authority,' of course, is not considered to be infallible. Following Nielsen, with the pursuit of justification, fallibilism is "the name of the game." Nevertheless, the authority of reason is the best authority we have as fallible human beings. The achievement of justification — albeit fallible — is the best we can hope for in our pursuit of truth, given an acceptance of a naturalistic worldview without metaphysical (or supernatural) foundations.[66]

Importantly, the necessary constraint that Nielsen places on the authority of reason is that which is "*logically* possible empirically to detect and comprehend and not just [that which] in fact we can observe or otherwise empirically detect, or…what is technically possible to observe or otherwise detect. Without such a [constraining] construal, we would be taken to be rejecting the belief that there really are, or even can be [for example], photons or neutrinos since they in fact cannot be observed [yet do exist as confirmable theoretical entities]. But I am not," Nielsen insists, "rejecting such *de facto* unobservables. What I am rejecting is any conception of there being any fact of the matter, any objects, relations or processes that are not, *even in principle*, empirically accessible. I am rejecting any *logical ban* on their being observed." Consequently, Nielsen asserts, responding to those who think his construal of empiricism too narrow, "…there is nothing in the very idea of accepting the authority of reason which requires that there can be no appeal to facts which are not [directly] empirical facts (*i.e.* those facts specified by supportable theoretical statements). In that way, there is nothing prioristic about my approach. It is all a matter of what, appealing this way to the authority of reason and carefully reasoning and investigating, we discover or conclude." Furthermore, Nielsen elaborates, "In speaking of what is reasonable and sensible I have not invoked any special conception of rationality. … I am appealing here, quite unexceptionally, to our *ordinary* and, if you will, somewhat loose

---

66 This admission of the underlying authority of reason from a naturalistic perspective or within a naturalistic context opens the door to questions regarding the origin of our faculties for reason and the coherence of asserting the reliability of reason given a purely naturalistic origin of such faculties. These questions — and the reasoned answers from them — form the basis of the theistic argument for the inadequacy (incoherence) of naturalistic explanations and the self-consistency of theistic explanations — an argument made and defended by Plantinga (1991) and critically assessed and refuted by Everitt (2004, 185–190). It is directly countered by others referenced by Everitt, as well as indirectly by Steven J. Conifer in his "Argument from Reason for the Non-existence of God" (2001).

use of 'reasonable' and 'sensible,' captured in part by our dictionaries and employed, by believers and nonbelievers alike, in our stream of life. ... [Specifically, in assessing the rationality of religious beliefs], I am inviting the person of faith to consider whether or not it would be reasonable for us moderns — after all, the contemporary educated religious believer is also a modern — to appeal in such a single-minded way to what he takes to be Divine Revelation, given that there are a multitude of often conflicting candidate revelations" (1989, 230–33, emphasis mine).

Instead of such a one-sided and problematic appeal to revelation *per se*, and as 'a way of knowing' (topics subjected to critical analysis in Chapters 5 and 6 respectively), Nielsen espouses both a *negative* and a *positive* alternative to acquiring knowledge as part of his previously noted deep commitment to a thoroughgoing "nonscientistic, contextualist, holistic, historicist and pragmatic naturalism without metaphysical foundations" (1996).

The *negative* alternative, referred to previously as a 'coherence view,' helps us recognize nonsense and weed-out irrational, metaphysical beliefs and truth claims. Essentially, from this view, or perspective, for a putatively factual statement to make rational sense and be at least justifiable as a truth claim, certain minimum criteria would need to be satisfied. First, the words of a statement would need to hang together logically in a way that is understandable. Next, the *truth-conditions* of the statement would need to be determinable such that it could, in principle, be known what specifically would or could empirically count for or against the truth or falsity of the claim. Also, the claim could not be self-contradictory (like a round square) and would need to fit, cohere, or hang together with the 'facts on the ground' — or rather with our best and most current knowledge (not unfounded speculations) about how the physical universe *actually* works. *If any, some, or all* of the foregoing criteria are not or could not be satisfied, then the statement would be considered *incoherent*, as well as *unintelligible* and *factually meaningless*. It would be non-cognitive as a statement and irrational as a belief, making the belief in such an irrational belief, according to Adler, incoherent and therefore, conceptually impossible. (2006, 25–32)

The *positive* alternative, also referred to earlier and above as the coherentist, justificatory method of wide reflective equilibrium, is a naturalistic method of *philosophical* inquiry which "start(s) from specific, or relatively specific, real live doubts and not...from mere methodological doubts...and (contextually and fallibilistically) goes for the best approximation we can get to maximal coherence of considered convictions, beliefs about what is the case, and observations about what is the case." This alternative recognizes that "[it] is rational generally to seek to maximize the coherence of our beliefs and convictions, remembering that we justify beliefs and convictions principally by establishing a consistent and coherent fit," and accepting, in spite of our human yearnings for solutions to our existential problems and uncertainties, that "[we] should not seek timeless [eternal and absolute] solutions to problems arising in determinant problematic situations" (1996, 57 & 59).

Extending the above positive alternative to the question of 'proof' as justification for belief or nonbelief, Nielsen writes:

[There] is a confusion of proof and justification and a melding of them together (p.14). But proof is not justification. Justification, as John Rawls well puts it, is argument, not typically deductive, though it may have deductive elements, "addressed to those who disagree with us, or to ourselves when we are of two minds" (Rawls, *A Theory of Justice*, p. 508). He goes on to add that it "presumes a clash of views between persons or within one person and seeks to convince others, or ourselves, of the reasonableness of the… [beliefs] upon which our claims and judgments" relative to our beliefs concerning religion (as well as other things) are founded (p. 508). Being designed to be reconciled by reason, that is careful reflection, impartial characterization, deliberation, and scrupulous argument, "justification proceeds from what all parties to the discussion hold in common. Ideally, to justify [a conception of 'God' or to give reasons for rejecting such a conception] to someone is to give him a proof of its principles from premises that the parties to the discussion accept, these principles having in turn consequences that match our considered judgments. Thus mere proof is not justification. A proof simply displays logical relations between propositions. But proofs become justifications once the starting points [*i.e.* premises] are mutually recognized, or the conclusions so compelling as to persuade us of the soundness of the conception expressed by the premises" (p.508)…

[Therefore], "justification rests upon our entire conception [consisting of all relevant premises and facts] and how it fits in with and organizes our considered judgments in reflective equilibrium. … Justification is a matter of the mutual support of many considerations, of everything fitting into one coherent view" (p.507)… [Such a view] relies on many diverse elements (including deductive elements [and, more specifically and where indicated, valid evidence]), but is quite different from a purely deductive model. (2006, 31–33)

In this regard, it is one thing to have, as Alvin Plantinga asserts, the 'epistemic right' to believe in 'God' without "evidence, or reason to think there is evidence" (1983, 30), and another to be intellectually and ethically *justified* in proclaiming such a *belief* as *knowledge*, in asking others to believe likewise, or in even being able to hold such a belief. Such a position hangs on not only the "extrinsic ethics of belief" regarding what one ought to believe on the basis of traditional evidentialism (Adler, 2006), but also, on a larger concept of justification itself; It is a concept that rests on a genuine consensus among believers and nonbelievers regarding how well any considered judgment, proposition, or truth claim reasonably fits — without metaphysical foundations — into a well established and widely accepted body of knowledge about the world and how it works.

Justification, according to Nielsen, depends not only on what is extrinsically *justifiable*. That is, it depends on what we know or *can possibly* know — albeit subjectively and provisionally — given our best contextual and critical reasoning and most complete, current, common, and relevant knowledge about what the world consists of and how it works (1996, 25–155). It also, according to Adler, depends on what is *intrinsically justifiable* — on "what the concept of belief demands." This notion of belief's *intrinsic* demand for justification — or intrinsic evidentialism — suggests that certain putative truth claims, as beliefs, such as, for example, 'The number of stars is even' or 'God, as a material, infinite, eternal, and transcendent being is immanent with all-power, all-knowledge and perfect love in and through all things, and governs all things by the Light of Truth,' cannot, in principle, be held. This is due to "the crucial fact that it is not possible [without self-deception] to regard oneself as both holding a belief and holding that one's reasons for it are inadequate" (2006, 25 & 26).

Of related significance to the question of rationality are Adler's objection to "evading *intrinsic* evidentialism" (*i.e.* what the concept or belief itself demands) to exploit the possibility of what can be conceived of, or imagined — which in this case would pertain to the putative existence of 'God' — and Nielsen's and others' objections to the religious parity argument of Reformed Epistemology. To Nielsen, the explicit charge of irrationality hangs primarily on the intrinsic incoherence and factual unintelligibility of the orthodox, nonanthropomorphic concept of a god (or the uses of the term 'God') in the first- and second-order God-talk of developed forms of Judaism, Christianity, and Islam.

To Adler, the implicit charge of irrationality pertains to the incoherence (and hence conceptual impossibility) of *believing* concepts that are unbelievable. Such incoherence, Adler contends, necessarily requires believers — in this case those who hold the belief *that* the 'God' of orthodox theism or Mormonism exists as a factual reality — to unreasonably or irrationally deceive themselves. They must *refuse* to be *explicit* about their beliefs and then sustain their self-deception by evading 'intrinsic evidentialism' to exploit the mere *possibility* of their god's putative existence through the strategies of ignorance, isolation, and inflation.

Adler's objection and arguments are crucial to the question implicitly asked throughout this analysis of Mormon theology and explicitly asked in the analysis of faith itself — *i.e.* 'how is it possible for otherwise rational or reasonable people to hold as *fact* or *truth* that which is *factually unintelligible* and therefore *unjustifiable* as putative truth?' Consequently, I will treat each evasive 'possibility strategy' separately and in some depth — relying heavily on Adler's own words. It should be noted that in doing so I am not conflating the *a priori* atheistic argument derived from conceptual analysis and the *a posteriori* rationalistic argument for Atheism based on modal logic and extrinsic, scientistic evidentialism. There are, to be sure, very real issues that divide these two arguments (see Nielsen 2001, 275–282). Still, the quasi-anthropomorphic conception of 'God' in Mormon theology warrants — on the anthropomorphic side — the invocation of both extrinsic and intrinsic evidentialism as an essential (albeit subordinate) part of an overall effective, cumulative, atheistic argument. Adler's argument from the incoherence of believing the unbelievable — given the demands of intrinsic evidentialism inherent in beliefs themselves — is pertinent to and supportive of the primary argument from the conceptual incoherence and irrationality of certain theistic beliefs. This argument is based upon linguistic conceptual analysis and constitutes a naturalistic coherence view without metaphysical foundations.

The Evasive Strategy of Ignorance

With this in mind we return then first to Adler's analysis of the evasive 'strategy of ignorance.' This strategy enlists ignorance, or 'absent evidence,' in support of the *possibility* of what we claim to know on the basis of the mere *conceivability* of our claims. Regarding such a strategy, Adler argues that "conceivability (or the appearance of conceivability) does not establish genuine possibility; that what we take ourselves to conceive is really a way that the world could be [or could work], or that what we take ourselves to conceive is compatible with physical laws and conceptual necessities." Clearly, as Adler points out, citing Hilary Putnam on the basis of Saul Kripke's work, "We can conceive that water is not H_2O, even if it is. Yet, nothing could truly be water, however similar its ostensible properties, unless it's H_2O" (Adler 2002, 109).

"Once the distinction between conceivability and *real* possibility is drawn," suggests Adler, "it becomes hard to understand how the two could be confused. One is about us and what we know and believe; the other is about the world (what's really possible in it). Nor is it apparent how a lack of evidence or possible verifiability against a 'possibility' can be recast as evidence supporting the existence of possibility. Steven Yablo rightly wonders, 'do I acquire evidence in *favor* of a proposition's possibility, by finding myself *without* evidence against its truth? That would be very strange, to say the least. Among other things it would have the result that there is a necessary limit on how bad my epistemological position can get: the poorer my evidence for *p's* truth, the *better* my evidence for its possibility. ...Yet the fact is that I can be *completely* in the dark about truth and possibility simultaneously' (1993:8).

"In general, we cannot infer from 'It is not the case that the evidence shows that *p* is impossible' to either '*p* is possible' or 'The evidence shows that *p* is possible,' for, as we shall learn below, such inferred or asserted 'possibility' (taken by believers as sufficient reason to believe) is isolated from [actual or possible] testability and therefore, too weak to count as a genuine reason or evidence in support of belief, or to compel and sustain belief without self-deception" (110, 124). Moreover, the question of possibility in relation to what Loftus refers to as the theist's "merely possible defense" (*i.e.* the "retreat to the position that what they believe is 'possible,' or that it is 'not impossible' and therefore, they have a right to believe it) places his belief on "shaky ground" (2008, 61). "Why? Because," Loftus asserts, "we [as believers and nonbelievers, with allegedly so much at stake] want to know what is [at least] probable, not what is [merely] possible" (61).

This, of course, presents a real dilemma for the theist. According to Loftus, "If we ask Christians [or Mormons] to defend a particular believe and they argue that such a belief 'isn't impossible,' then this is a tacit admission that instead of the evidence supporting what they believe, they are actually trying to explain the evidence away" (61). It is also, as I see it, a tacit admission that they have deceived themselves in believing what is either absurd or unbelievable and unknowable, and are not willing — either because of fear or sheer stubbornness — to admit that they have done so and that there is no rational basis for their beliefs or for their faith, which is tacitly supported by the biblical definition of faith in Paul's *Epistle* to the *Hebrews* as "the substance of things hoped for, the evidence of things not seen" (11:1).

Nor can we reasonably invoke what Adler refers to as the "blank check assumption" by taking the position that something is possible because *anything* is possible (110, emphasis mine). This position is typically taken in response to the objection that, given the existing and known laws of physics, a particular claim is actually, or causally, impossible.

Consider, for example, the particular claim in the *Book of Mormon* that the putatively resurrected 'Jesus Christ' physically appeared to his chosen people on the American continent as a "Man...clothed in a white robe" after having descended "out of heaven" to the Earth in the midst of his people, the Nephites (3 Nephi 11:8). Or, consider the alleged visitation of two divine personages, 'God the Father' and 'Jesus Christ,' to the young boy Joseph Smith in Palmyra, New York from their Celestial abode in another world, universe, or dimension of space and time. According to Smith's scriptural or official account, they appeared in a "pillar of light" and actually stood "above" him "in the air" (Joseph Smith — History 1:17). If such claims and others like them are judged to be impossible because they are in violation of the known physical laws of the universe, the rejoinder is made that "just because [such divine 'personages'] defy our laws of physics does not mean there are not further laws of physics we have not as yet discovered or do not as yet comprehend (Bryan 1995:422)" (110).

Such a rejoinder makes a disingenuous appeal to "open-mindedness" and "attempts to protect the hypothesis [or, in this case, the claim of putative celestial visitations] from the reach of massive undermining background evidence. Yet," Adler argues, "in a crucial way it actually weighs it down [for however] implausible it is to hypothesize [or claim divine visitations], it is vastly more implausible to claim that they [*i.e.* 'Gods' and 'angels'] obey new, undetected laws of physics" (110). Furthermore, as Adler correctly asserts, the appeal to keep an open mind, as invoked in arguments from ignorance, "is the wolf in sheep's clothing, trading on the... ambiguities we [find] in the use of possible." In this regard, is something 'possible' because of the absence of disproving evidence *or* 'possible' because not internally inconsistent or inconsistent with other (justified) beliefs, or established knowledge? "In fact," Adler argues, "contrary to the usage suggested [*i.e.* that 'open-mindedness' is the willingness to accept as 'possible' that which is 'conceivable' and therefore, not required to be either justified or disproved by evidence or reason], 'open-minded' should be applied to one's *procedures* for belief, *not* to the content of what is believed." In this context, "what marks an open-minded person is not what he regards as live possibilities. That is a conclusion to be reached. It is," rather, "the *way* the conclusion is reached that marks an open-minded person. *The open-minded person follows where the evidence leads*. If the evidence against [heavenly visitations] and against many other supernatural and paranormal conjectures is overwhelming [or if such conjectures, as assertions of fact, are factually unintelligible or otherwise incoherent], an open-minded person must reject them" (111–12, emphasis mine).

The Evasive Strategy of Isolation

Next, the evasive strategy of *isolation* attempts to dodge possible testability or justification by isolating beliefs in order to protect them from criticism or critical analysis. For example: "In an article promoting experiential validation of religious beliefs, [William] Alston (1983) begins by dismissing [Anthony] Flew's dilemma [that the assertion of the existence of a non-falsifiable being makes such a being no different than an imaginary being or no being at all] .

"The Christian beliefs that Alston considers 'say that God will manifest Himself in certain ways in our individual and corporate experience. From time to time we find such manifestations in our experience. This provides empirical confirmation for the beliefs in question (1983: 105).' However, if confirmation involves the risk of falsification, then the absence of these manifestations should be disconfirming. But Alston's formulation leaves no room for disconfirmation: 'our examples,' Alston writes, as further quoted by Adler, 'are not decisively disconfirmable by experience. They are markedly unspecific. They do not say *how* God will provide for His people, *when* or *under what conditions* one can expect a particular fruit of the spirit, just *what* Christ is going to do through his church, and what the *timetable* is. These "somehow-somewhere-somewhen" statements are so formulated that whereas any positive instance will be confirming..., there can be no negative instances...' (1983: 106). Alston's response to the not 'really serious challenge' of testability is that although his favored hypothesis is protected from decisive disconfirmation, it is clearly open to confirmation by his god's manifestation. (125).

"We should expect, however, that Alston's strategy to circumvent testability has serious costs. To diminish testability is to diminish possibilities for confirmation. If we drop Alston's artificial protective devices, all but logically or observationally decisive disconfirmation is readily available" (125). Consider, as Alston does, the hypothesis that there are unicorns. If that hypothesis is unadorned with the 'somehow-somewhere-somewhen' qualifier, then it is amply refuted by the absence of positive evidence. It is because we do treat the hypothesis as unadorned that the existence of unicorns is disconfirmed, a result that Alston [and other theistic apologists] no doubt [endorse]" (125).

The idea here supports Nielsen's contention that a purely anthropomorphic concept of 'God' — including the anthropomorphic aspect of the quasi-anthropomorphic concept of the Mormon god analyzed in the next chapter — is *false*, even if not incoherent, and even if it is further claimed that such a being is always *hidden*, yet material and real. It is, echoing Adler's application of this principle to unicorns, because we *do* treat the hypothesis of an anthropomorphic god as unadorned by 'somehow-somewhere-somewhen' statements that the existence of a physical, or material god is disconfirmed.

Additionally, Adler continues, "[the] 'somehow-somewhere-somewhen' protective device is self-defeating in another way. The absence of specification of conditions for repeated occurrences reduces opportunities for replication, a crucial check on the acceptance of an experiential or experimental report." (125) Moreover, the theistic believer's evasive isolationist claim that, for example, *all* so-regarded true (non-self-contradictory) and personally edifying religious experiences are self-confirming and therefore cannot possibly be otherwise disconfirmed as an experience *of* and *from* 'God' makes such a faith-based claim *factually vacuous*. This is due, as we shall learn in Chapter 5, to an absence of determinative criteria which would enable a skeptical, objective observer to definitively *contrast* the recipient's claim of having received a 'spiritual experience from God' from a purely naturalistic claim that such an experience was merely a self-or suggestively-induced neuropsychological phenomenon.

"If the key step in Alston's isolationalist strategy is the appeal to what is 'decisively disconfirmable,' then, once again, the culprit is the ambiguity of 'possibility,' this time in the service of evading falsification [instead of the absence of confirming evidence]. Its service in this role," Adler notes, "is particularly prominent in Wittgensteinian attempts to isolate beliefs of radically different cultures from criticism of their fundamental assumptions" (126). This topic was introduced in Chapter 1 in relation to conceptual analysis and will be further discussed in the context of 'faith in God' in Chapter 6.

In this regard, "[Norman] Malcolm [a prominent Wittgensteinian] takes science and religion to constitute different 'frameworks' with their own distinctive goals. Scientific evidence is appropriate to scientific claims, but not to religious beliefs: 'there can be evidence for the particular doctrines of a faith only within the attitude of religious belief' (1992:101). But why," asks Adler, "accept the assumption that if a belief is testable, its function must be scientific? ... Applying the notion of testability does not deny that the intended purposes of the practice are other than prediction and control. ... Contrary to isolationist assumptions, trial-and-error testing and testability are not parochial to scientific inquiries. The attempt to restrain the application of scientific methods [like the attempt to balkanize religious language from conceptual analysis] is hopeless, because the rudiments of these methods are merely, as Quine claims, 'self-conscious common sense' (1960: 3)" (128).

The Evasive Strategy of Inflation

Finally, "[the evasive] strategy of *inflation* deflects focus from a manageable topic to broader issues, not usually germane to the problem at hand or in violation of its presuppositions. Inflationary strategies append ostentatious theses [or apply *false analogies* and invalid *analogical predication*] to a doctrine. Criticisms are then directed to these theses [or analogies and analogical predicates], though misconstrued as challenging the doctrine itself. Correspondingly, the objection to inflationary strategies is that they are distractive, introducing irrelevancies. (129, emphasis mine)

"There is nothing wrong," Adler correctly notes, "with redirecting attention from a focal question to its assumptions or presuppositions [as, for example, in redirecting attention from the question of a god's putative existence as a factual reality to an analysis of the assumptions and presuppositions regarding what a 'fact' is and what reasonably constitutes factual significance or intelligibility]. Often the redirection is progress. But since to question assumptions and presuppositions is to shift discussion, the minimal demand is simply to be explicit about the proposed shift and one's reason for it. (129)

"Arguments from ignorance are inflationary, tacitly maneuvering us to the issue of skepticism; for if a bare epistemic possibility is a reason in support of a claim, then it is likewise adequate as a reason for doubt. But this is just the key step in radical skeptical arguments [that nothing can be objectively known and that therefore any truth claim is as valid as any other]. ... [Such a] skeptical shift is found in Malcolm's isolationist apologetic [where, for example, in response to a proposal to empirically test the validity of belief regarding the reality of vanishing objects, Malcolm would counter-propose the relativistic criterion that] '[e]ach position is compatible with ordinary experience' (1992:93), [suggesting that *both* the belief that objects can vanish in thin air and that they cannot — or do not — simply vanish are justified on the basis of 'ordinary experience']. That is, Malcolm invokes the bare possibility standard, which would render any empirical testing worthless. (129)

"The exploitation of epistemological loopholes is another characteristic inflationary strategy. ... A frequent form of [such] exploitation...is through attempts at parity of reasoning or '*tu quoque*' ('You too!') arguments. ... Those influenced by Wittgenstein [for example] hold that science and religion, as each constitutes a framework, are both groundless — they neither have nor need grounding. Malcolm writes: 'But we should not expect that there might be some sort of rational justification of the framework itself' (1992: 98). The great advances of chemistry count for naught as empirical support of its assumptions. Support according to assumptions of the framework cannot [in other words] be support for the framework. The proposal is seductive only if we treat it as spatial metaphor, where a self-enclosed world can be held up only by something that is *outside* that world [*e.g.* 'God'] and so does not share its framework principles. (130–31, emphasis mine)

"Another Wittgensteinian *tu quoque* argument claims that religious believers may look on their beliefs as akin to our belief that 'material objects exist when none of us perceive them.' Although 'most people have [not] justified these claims,' it is 'certain' that 'we are nonetheless entitled to believe these claims' (Gutting 1982: 79–80)." But Adler rightly rejects Gutting's assumption that our belief that material objects exist when none of us perceives them lacks grounds. Such an assumption, to Adler, "is exactly the opposite of the truth, as we all know. (131)

"The rejection suggests the fallacy inherent in (inflationary) uses of the *tu quoque*. Abstractly, there is no formal fallacy. If [as in the above example] doctrine D is accepted [*i.e.* that 'objects exist'] despite property r [*i.e.* the fact that 'none of us see them'], then we should not refuse to accept a different doctrine E [*e.g.* that 'God' or 'spirits' or 'spirit matter' exists] just because it has [the same] property r. However, consider how defenders of hypotheses overtly at variance with accepted scientific beliefs actually use this strategy. They identify their claims with the latest, most far-out reaches of scientific thought or speculation (*e.g.*, telepathic ESP [or 'spiritual' communication] with quantum field theory) and then argue that if we accept one theory with far-out consequences, such as a breakdown in causality, we should therefore accept or at least not reject another. But these *tu quoque* reasonings require a hidden assumption: Doctrine D has no additional support that does not hold of E. The fallacy is evident. We accept the far-out claims of the favored theory [*i.e.* 'Doctrine D'] only as a tolerable price to pay for a fruitful theory with massive experimental verification and predictive success. The huge difference in background support blocks this consistency or parity *tu quoque* reasoning. (131–32)

"The chief fault in inflationary maneuvers," according to Adler, "is usually their implicit preemptive claim — that the original problems cannot be addressed before we address the inflationary ones. That claim is always suspect. ... [Yet, despite] the failure to defend their preemptive claim, inflationary strategies are often persuasive. The strategies are difficult to reveal because their claims are expressed in the very terms of the issue under discussion or dispute, which hides the shift in focus to broader issues... [Their] failure is a failure to be distinctively or selectively relevant to the claim being made or supported, while pretending otherwise. (132)

"Ultimately," Adler concludes, "these three kinds of argument — ignorance, isolation, and inflation — are facades, even when sincere. No one believes that ignorance is sufficient for belief, or concedes the skeptical conclusions that would follow. No one believes that if he jumps from the Eiffel Tower, the *possibility* that he will survive is at all a reason to believe that he *will* survive. No one treats everyday hypothetico-deductive reasoning as merely a parochial method of scientists. No one rejects rational argument, analysis, or logic on the ground that it is culturally bound. No one thinks that religious beliefs can just be taken for granted on analogy with our taking for granted such evident beliefs as that there are cows. Representing one's beliefs or thoughts otherwise is pretense, and, if sincere, a case of distraction [and delusional self-deception] by abstract reflection or argument. For in full awareness the alleged beliefs cited above cannot really be [rationally] believed or thought" (132–33, emphasis mine).

The Parity Argument

Nielsen's treatment of the 'parity argument'[67] referenced earlier and as part of Adler's above exposure of the inflationary *tu quoque* strategy, is presented below, beginning with

---

67 For other respectable analyses of the parity argument made by Plantinga, as an advocate of 'Reformed Epistemology,' see Everitt 2004, 17–30 and Martin 1990, 266–277. See also Nielsen 1996, 115–131.

the argument itself, which he fairly and accurately characterizes as follows:

> The parity argument, in its most general form, has at its core the claim that, epistemologi-
> cally speaking, religious beliefs are no worse off than the beliefs of common sense and science,
> since all these beliefs rest on assumptions that cannot be rationally justified. We cannot, they
> claim, rationally justify our belief in the past, in other minds, in the general regularity of nature,
> or in the reality of even the most stable and precious of our moral beliefs. We are not justified
> in accepting these beliefs as rational or reasonable to believe without proof while at the same
> time rejecting equally central religious beliefs as groundless or irrational. Both sets of beliefs
> are groundless and since it is not unreasonable even in the face of philosophical skepticism to
> accept the groundless commonsense and scientific beliefs, it cannot then, by parity of reasoning,
> be reasonable or justifiable to claim that groundless religious beliefs are irrational. (1989, 5)

In other words, it is argued that:

> Believers have just as much right to believe in God without grounds or philosophical
> articulation as naturalistic philosophers (or for that matter anyone else) have a right to believe
> in the external world or in other minds, matters which, Reformed Philosophers claim, cannot
> be evidentially or argumentatively established either. ([Alvin] Plantinga 1997; [Nicholas]
> Wolterstorff 1997) But such a response, currently popular though it be in some circles is, for
> at least three reasons, off the mark. Belief in God is not pervasively accepted across cultures
> in the way that belief in other-minds and the external world is; there can be no just relying on
> some putative revelation for they are many and frequently conflicting and we have no basis
> for picking out the real thing from the merely putative. Moreover, the appeal to such a basis
> paradoxically takes us away, if we think about it a little, from a straight appeal to revelation
> as the basis for belief. For we need criteria, independently of the alleged revelation, to judge
> whether a putative revelation is a genuine revelation. Finally, and thirdly, as we have already
> seen, there are questions about the very intelligibility of talk of God in a way that there is
> not about the external world or about other minds. The idea that anthropologists might, and
> indeed actually do, come across cultures without a belief in God is a commonplace; the idea
> that anthropologists might come across a culture that does not believe that there is an external
> world or other minds is a patent absurdity (3–9).

Nielsen, following G.E. Moore and W.V.O. Quine, addresses this third reason in
an earlier work where he argues that "Many of our commonsense beliefs and scientific
beliefs can be shown to be justified on…a coherentist basis. We can know, as we bloody
well ought, that [for example] the earth has existed for many years past and that cats do
not grow on trees, while still having very good reasons for being skeptical of religious
beliefs such as that God speaks to us, God created us, God shows providential care for
us and, indeed, that God exists." He concludes that "Whatever we want to say about the
justifiability of the general accusation about [the] irrationality [of religious beliefs about
'God'], the parity argument, if my above argument is near to the mark, cannot be deployed
to protect the believer (1989, 7)."

Stating this elsewhere, for greater emphasis, as "the most fundamental claim against
Plantinga's and Wolterstorff's claim for parity between certain key religious beliefs and
[the] inescapable [natural beliefs we hold to be basic, or self-evident]," Nielsen asserts
that "…religious beliefs, even the most fundamental ones, are not…inescapable." They

are not like the basic beliefs — or certain knowledge (not 'absolutely' so) — we have regarding, for example, the existence of other minds, material objects, the external world, and the reality of the past. "… All peoples at all times and at all places have such [basic, or certain] knowledge of the natural world. No one, except when he is doing philosophy or has gone very plainly insane, ever tries to question them. … They are, as… Quine might put it, such deeply embedded beliefs because they are implicit, as background assumptions, in everything we know or warrantedly believe. They are so deeply embedded that we have no idea of how we could give them up and go on making sense of our world. They could in no way be problematic unless everything is and, if everything is, then nothing is."

Conversely, Nielsen points out, in relation to religious beliefs, "Some people in our culture have them and some do not. Outside our culture there are whole cultures of people, with long-established religions, Confucian culture or Theraveda Buddhist culture, to take key examples, which do not have them. These various religious beliefs, as well as antireligious beliefs opposed to them, unlike these inescapable beliefs (belief in the reality of the past, for example), are the subject of real-live doubts and assertions and counterassertions and arguments and counterarguments. Moreover, … there are serious questions about the very intelligibility or coherence of such religious beliefs" (1996, 127–8).

"Given these differences," Nielsen concludes, "it is not reasonable to say, as Plantinga and Wolterstorff do, that we are justified…in taking, or are even being reasonable in taking, [fundamental] religious beliefs as basic beliefs, or any other kind of acceptable belief, where we have no evidence for them or other grounds for believing them, to say nothing of claiming to know that they are true. Plantinga [like other devout theistic believers, including Mormon believers who claim their religion is true] claims that he has *immediate knowledge* that there is such a person as God, but we have no reason at all to believe him [or others like him]. He, like his mentor Calvin, who says the same thing, is just proclaiming. But saying it firmly with [sincere conviction or] Christian self-confidence will not at all help" (128). "Faced with these difficulties," Nielsen points out in a later note, "it is way off the mark to say, as Plantinga does, that [fundamental] religious beliefs [concerning the existence of 'God'] are not 'groundless or gratuitous'. It is understandable," given such a baseless assertion, "that some people in thinking about the basic belief apologetic began to speak of analogies with belief in the Great Pumpkin" (151–2, n41).

`Nor will it help for Plantinga or Mormon apologists or believers to assert the existence of some 'spiritual faculty' in humans which *basically* and *uncontroversially* enables the awareness of divinity. Nor will it help to likewise assert that religious 'awareness-based belief' — such as 'God is speaking to me' or 'God [approves] or disapproves of what I have done' — is self-justifying like belief in the external world and in other minds and is therefore *beyond controversy* on the basis of being *genuine awareness* of a spiritual reality— which putative reality is also taken to be self-justified, or properly basic, as something which is also *beyond controversy* (154–5, n67).

The problem here, of course, is that such allegedly *properly basic* religious beliefs are, in Nielsen's words, "…clearly not so inescapable as…natural beliefs. Many people do not have this [genuine] awareness, including some genuinely religious people, *e.g.* Zen Buddhists, and, since its being a genuine awareness is extensively controverted by reflected and informed people, among others, it is *not beyond controversy*. Unless," as I think Nielsen correctly points out, "one simply wants to stick one's head in the sand and dogmatically fix one's belief by the *method of authority*, one must go to the intellectual community at large [to seek for justification on these matters by the method of wide reflective equilibrium,] and not merely to the community of Christian ['authorities,' 'apologists,' and] philosophers or Christian believers more generally" (155, n67).

The above objections to 'evading evidentialism' and to the 'parity argument' also have significance to a related argument for 'rational relativism' which asserts that there are different notions of rationality and each one depends on a different conceptual perspective and context of discourse. Such an argument, which perversely holds (at least implicitly) that all notions of rationality are of equal merit and worth, is addressed briefly, and in different contexts, by Nielsen in Chapter 1 as a caution against radical linguistic relativism related to conceptual analysis, by Adler above in his treatment of isolation and inflation as evasive strategies for exploiting possibility, and again in Chapter 6 by Martin and Nielsen in response to Wittgensteinian fideism.

Regarding the question of rationality presented in this chapter, however, this argument is especially problematical. Nielsen's criteria and related category questions for determining the rationality of beliefs are based on cross-cultural evaluative concepts of intelligibility, contradiction, coherence, and factual significance. This fact, along with his fallibilistic, contextualist, historicist, perspectivist, nonscientistic, anti-foundationalist, and holistic or coherentist method for justification through the achievement of wide reflective equilibrium (1996, 2001), make this argument not only incoherent per se, but irrelevant to the concept of rationality that is espoused by Nielsen and adopted in this particular analysis and assessment of the Mormon faith.

Chapter 3

Deconstructing the Mormon
Concept of 'God'

*"We have seen that among the most conclusive proofs of the existence
of a Supreme Being, is that some knowledge of the attributes and
personality of God is essential to any rational exercise of faith in Him.*

*"We can but imperfectly respect an authority whose very existence is
a matter of uncertainty and conjecture with us; therefore, if we are to
implicitly trust and truly love our creator, we must know something of
him."*

— *Elder James E. Talmage*

Prefatory Note: If you have carefully read the pre-requisite readings including the *Introduction*, *Foundational Preface*, and Chapters 1 and 2 as suggested, then you will likely be prepared to better understand and appreciate the remaining chapters of this book, including the implications and conclusions presented therein. If you have not done this prerequisite reading as suggested, then you are again urged to do so before continuing on with this crucial chapter.

This chapter is crucial to our analysis and assessment of the Mormon faith particularly and primarily because the concept of the Mormon god — *i.e.* what such a god is doctrinally conceived and believed or stated to be in the Mormon faith — is fundamental to our corresponding analyses and assessments of all related and necessarily dependent concepts and doctrines of the Mormon faith presented in Chapters 4 through 6. Consequently, in this chapter I will take great care to unpack the familiar doctrinal assertions or truth claims about the Mormon god (or 'God, the Father') found in both first- and second-order Mormon God-talk in hope of performing the necessary fine-grain, conceptual analysis that hopefully will be helpful in enabling questioning believers and investigators deal with any questions or real doubts they might have regarding this god's putative existence. In doing so, we will have also, of course, deconstructed the concept of the 'Son of God' as well.

As we shall discover below, the results of our analysis will be the same whether the Mormon God is conceptualized among the leaders and members of the Mormon Church as, for example: (1) a *finite*, procreated being with a procreated spirit and tangible body of flesh and bones who exists as part of an *infinite* lineage of like Gods, who possesses finite (limited) – albeit sufficiently perfected – attributes and qualities, and who is eternally progressing in knowledge and power; or (2) an *infinite*, *eternal* and (biologically and spatio-temporally) *transcendent* being with *infinite* (*i.e.* all, or unlimited) knowledge and power who is *immanent* (*i.e.* everywhere present personally — though not physically — through the power of his spirit); or (3) some combination or synthesis of these two concepts. This is so because the theological differences within the Mormon religion regarding the concept of 'God' primarily focus on such a god's alleged *secondary* and *relational* attributes — or character traits and abilities, as well as on his relation to (and relations with) man. They do not focus on those *primary* referents which essentially define or specify what the Mormon god, as a referring expression, actually refers to or fundamentally consists of in its conceptual fulness.

What the analysis in this chapter will reveal, and what I shall argue and conclude, is that the *primary* metaphysical constituents of 'spirits,' 'intelligence(s),' 'spirit matter' (or 'spirit element'), and 'glorified' or 'exalted matter' common and essential to both the so-called *orthodox* and *neo-orthodox* (White 1987) theological concepts of the Mormon god render both (or all possible) theological versions identical and, in fact, incoherent and factually unintelligible. After all, both essentially and fundamentally conceive of 'God' as *'a finite, perfected spirit personage (comprised of spirit matter) and eternal (self-existent) intelligence of the highest order housed in an exalted, resurrected and bloodless body of flesh and bones in the shape of a man which is animated by spirit element.'*

Such a conclusion would, in turn, make the differences or disagreements regarding the Mormon god's putative *secondary* and *relational* attributes and qualities (or *omni-*traits, capacities, and dispositions) in relation to man, according to so-called Mormon *neo-orthodoxy*, likewise incoherent and factually insignificant. This is so apart from or in relation to other doctrines of Mormon theology or actual realities in the world such as the existence of excessive suffering, premature death, and nonbelief. But this is not all, for the concept of the Mormon god of so-called Mormon *orthodoxy* — with necessarily *limited* knowledge and power who is eternally learning new truths and whose power is subordinate to or circumscribed by putative eternal laws, eternal material existence, and 'free agency' — is also arguably insufficient, according to Mormon founder and Prophet Joseph Smith, as a worthy or adequate object of faith and worship (Smith 2005). It is also arguably inconsistent as well with numerous characterizations of the Mormon god in the Standard Works (scriptures) of the Mormon Church and with the god most praying Mormons likely pray to.

Either way, there at least seem to be serious problems. For while the tenets of Mormon theology *per se* might not be taken seriously by many believing Mormons because they raise questions the Church does not yet have 'revealed answers' to, it is nonetheless reason-able to argue that the faith of Mormons in their god indeed does rest on *some* version of theology, or on *some* theological concept of the Mormon god which is subject to rigorous critical analysis. This would be so particularly if the *meta-beliefs* regarding such *primary*, *secondary,* and *relational* attributes and qualities of 'God' are that such putative truth claims are objectively true.

Consequently, Mormon believers and investigators will necessarily be asked repeat-edly and importantly — with an appeal to critical common sense and rationality — to be *very specific* about the *actual* meaning of those descriptive statements and terms which are formally or informally used in their faith (and by them personally) to best explain their concept of 'God.' In all of this, the disturbing and inconvenient truth — or proverbial devil — is in the details. For if specifics cannot be produced, or if the offered specific descrip-tive attributes of the Mormon god are determined, as previewed above and concluded below to be unintelligible, incoherent, and factually vacuous, the Mormon believer has serious problems.

This book and this chapter in particular will not take sides on the question of which conception (either the so-called orthodoxy or neo-orthodoxy versions) of the Mormon god is dominant or more accurately constitutes Mormon theology. Rather, I have chosen a third option; a middle path which I think effectually synthesizes, in concept, both aforementioned versions and which, I also think, most accurately represents the most common and comprehensive view of Mormon theology. This middle path, or *synthesized version* of Mormon theology, classifies the concept of the Mormon god as that of a quasi-anthropomorphic being. Such a conceptualization of the Mormon god combines both the *physical* (*i.e.* material, finite, and spatiotemporal) and *metaphysical* (*i.e.* supernatural, infinite, eternal, and transcendent) aspects of this putative 'Being-in-human form' in a comprehensive list of undifferentiated primary, secondary, and relational referents within the larger conceptual framework of Mormon theology as commonly understood among the informed believers of the Mormon faith.

The "Only True God"

As was initially pointed out in the *Introduction*, it is important to note that all theistic believers (and Mormons are no exception), regardless of their particular faith of choice, are, to one degree or another, 'salad-bar' believers who worship or believe according to their own personal concept of 'God.' Stated differently, those who believe that there is a god have their own at least tacit idea of that god which appeals to them at various levels. And it is this personal 'God' of private invention and/or interpretation that is for each believer the "only true god."

At a level which John Allen Paulos (2008) suggests might be more "intellectually palatable," *God* has been and continues to be redefined in various ways — as, for example, nature, love, or the laws or structure of the universe. Such an act of redefinition or equivocation can take the form of the following, rather humorous, yet nonetheless implicitly offered sketch of an argument:

1. God is really this, that, or the other thing.
2. The existence of this, that, or the other thing is somewhat plausible, if not obvious.
3. Therefore God exists" (100).

"Announcing," for example, "that God is Love and that you believe in Love so you believe in God is not [at all] compelling….More thoughtful redefinition takes God to be the incomprehensibly complex, a [metaphysical] redefinition that may even allow [intellectual] agnostics and [certain] atheists to aver that they believe in God….Quite conceivably," for example, "the true 'theory of everything,' the holy grail of modern physicists, might…be beyond our collective complexity horizon….In any case," observes Paulos, "the verbal trick of defining God as the incomprehensibly complex, a variant of the God of the gaps, has the appeal of getting something — God, in this case — for nothing" (100–101). Clearly, beyond perhaps serving to ease cognitive dissonance through such equivocation, this approach to God-redefinition conveniently allows the salad-bar believer to avoid (though not unproblematically) criticism through arbitrariness and, as we learned in the previous chapter, the employment of "evasive strategies of possibility" (Adler 2006).

But apart from such minimal and contrived *intellectual* appeal (which Mormon innovators and apologists certainly resort to in their metaphysical redefinitions of, and speculations about, the 'true' nature of their god), believers' ideas of 'God' forcefully appeal to them at an *emotional level.* This is arguably so because their own personal concept of the Mormon god has, even beneath the powerful and inescapable conditioning influences of family, societal and cultural experiences and expectations, a deep and abiding psychological source. This source is, from a depth-psychological perspective, the internalized *ideal parent imago*, along with the powerful relational affects attached *to* it, and the primary (and regressive) need and desire for reunion *with* it.

According to this naturalistic explanation, under special circumstances this parent imago (or idealized mental image), is (or can be) projected and encountered as the omnipotent, omniscient and omnibenevolent Parent or Parent-like presence we all once experienced as infants. Such a transferential encounter – which can be facilitated by cognitively formed assumptions and beliefs that act as hooks for the projection, and triggered by certain hypnotic cues (*e.g.* words, statements, symbols, music, appearances, *etc.*) used and encountered in the environment – is motivated unconsciously by a primary need and desire for affective re-union or symbiosis with the *internalized* Parent or Primary Caregiver. The state of primal fusion or attachment accompanying such a projective transference (or 'faith-state' in 'converted' theistic believers) recapitulates our 'basic biological situation' (Faber 2004) as infants, and naturalistically explains, from a psychodynamic perspective, the emotional appeal and attachment to the believer's personal idea of 'God.'[68]

As I shall argue later, a believer's notion of 'God' merely makes *subjective* sense to the desiring and conditioned believer because, at a deep level, the very *idea* of such a being is *seductive, feels right,* and is *familiar* and *imaginable* as at least indicative of a *possible* (much less than desirable or needed) being. This is so (in relation to all gods conceptualized as a supernatural, metaphysically defined being) *not* because the concept itself actually makes literal sense as stated from the perspective of an objective, skeptical outsider, or as an idea which is critically determined after rigorous conceptual analysis to be intelligible, coherent, and factually meaningful. Rather, it is because it is a *familiar experience* which needs primarily to be yielded to, not understood.

The various ideas about what 'God' *is* or *actually means* as a putative *literal existent* are arguably, at a deep, primitive level, *all* similarly anthropomorphic and familiar as an archetypal parent imago. They are *not* sensible or believable to the individual believer *because* his or her own personal concept of 'God' is *objectively* sensible and believable (much less knowable) as a statement asserting a putatively *literal, actual* fact. Rather, believers' personal ideas or concepts of 'God' and their belief that their god is a *literal* being who *actually* exists, are sensible and believable to them *only though* self-deception. They *want* and *need* and *yearn* for such a being to exist. For such believers (delusional though they are) their god is a sacred object of ultimate desire and veneration who is perfect in every way and can evoke deep, primary emotions of love, devotion, unquestioning faithfulness, awe — and with such awe — dread.

---

68 Moreover, such a dynamic of transference (and counter-transference) continues to unconsciously affect and influence us all, to one degree or another, in all our primary relationships (or relational encounters) at a visceral level.

Such concepts and corresponding beliefs of 'God' are naturally *sacralized* and placed beyond the reach of *profane* (*i.e.* secular or 'unholy') criticism. Therefore, believers who are *affectively* and *regressively* attached to their concept of 'God' — *i.e.* are in a primary, worshipful and fearfully superstitious *faith-state* — have not analytically deconstructed their concept of 'God.' They have not looked at it critically as a reasonably skeptical outsider — and likely will not and/or cannot do so unless and until subconsciously compelled to do so by force of *real* doubt or need. Such believers are typically content to superstitiously believe according to a very simple and superficial, anthropomorphic concept and image of their god. They have no need or desire to look *beyond* what is familiar and imaginable to them. People can imagine anything they can describe with familiar language. They don't want to look *beneath* their own naturalistically explained needs, desires, and visceral affects of fear and love. If they did they would see the deep sociocultural, biological, and psychological realities at play *beneath the surface of awareness* that unconsciously shape and personify such a concept and image into the god they regressively (and irrationally) worship and serve.

Apart from the question of the common origins, sense, and familiarity of various personal concepts of 'God,' there are still notable differences worthy of mention, at least in general terms. For a simple, less informed, and more superstitious Mormon believer, for example, 'God' might be merely a physical, material personage in the shape of a man who has superhuman powers. Moreover, he would very likely be regarded as a kind, loving, and wise Heavenly Father. Beyond that, such a believer might say that 'God' is the Creator or sustainer of all creation, including this world and worlds without end. He is, moreover, an all-loving, all-good, all-knowing, all-powerful, and all-wise being who knows and loves all his children completely and unconditionally — and somehow hears and answers their prayers according to their best interests.

These simple Mormon believers do not typically — if at all — address the primary or fundamental nature of their god as metaphysically conceptualized in the theology of their faith. Accordingly, if they were to be curiously pressed by questions such as where their god actually lives, how he visits the earth, answers prayers from another world, universe, or dimension of space and time, and how specifically such a finite being creates and sustains the universe and worlds without end, or physically travels between and among his many worlds when necessary, there would likely be some discomfort — with either no answers forthcoming or a simple admission of ignorance. Then, if asked more specifically how tall their god is, how much he weighs, what specifically and in detail his physical features look like, whether he has internal organs, brown, blue, or green eyes, hair on his backside, blood coursing through his veins, and sexually impregnates his wife (or wives) to procreate so-called spirit children, these simple believers would likely feel even more uncomfortable — as well as perhaps a bit anxious and defensive. They would also likely dismiss such questions as being unimportant (if not inappropriate), or say that the answers to such questions are unnecessary or 'unrevealed.' This is likely even though questions about whether or not their god is animated by blood and sexually procreates offspring *have* been authoritatively answered in their faith — the first in the negative and the second in the affirmative!

But what might such discomfort, anxiousness, evasiveness, dismissiveness, and defensiveness reveal if not the tacit admission of the absurdity of these beliefs and a corresponding betrayal of doubt? Perhaps at some level even the simplest Mormon believers — if they are not grossly narcissistic and utterly delusional — can only go so far in superstitiously reducing their concept of the Mormon god to a perfect version of themselves or their own idealized father image — or to a mere Super-Man.

More theologically and scripturally informed Mormons, on the other hand, might have more sophisticated conceptions of their god's primary attributes or fundamental nature — even if such attributes are unintelligible to them when pressed beyond the standard definitions of their faith. These believers might fundamentally characterize their god, for example, as an *exalted spirit* and *infinite* and *eternal intelligence* of the *highest order* housed in a *glorified*, immortal body of flesh and bones in the shape of a man and, again, animated not by blood, but by *spirit element*. He is, moreover, a spatiotemporally *transcendent* and *finite* being who is the Ultimate Source and Supreme Governor of the universe. Among these theologically informed Mormon believers — including leaders, professors of religion and General Authorities of the Church — there will certainly be (and are) differences of opinion regarding the nature and limits of their god's secondary and relational attributes and expectations, mind, and will. As for the *primary* attributes and characterizations, however, there is widespread agreement in their believed existence — even if not in their meanings and referents.

If these believers were to be similarly pressed by a neutral and reasonably skeptical outsider as the simple believers were, the nature of the questions would of course change. Instead of being asked questions about the Mormon god's body, physical capabilities (or limitations), or bodily functions — which would also be renewed at a different level concerning what, for example, it would mean specifically for flesh and bones to be *exalted*, or for a body to be *glorified*, or for a physical body to be animated by *spirit element* — these more informed believers would be questioned differently. As was illustrated in the "Instructive 'Deconstructive' Conversation" presented in Chapter 1, they would be asked about 'spirits,' 'intelligences,' 'spirit matter' (and/or 'spirit element'), and the 'Light of Truth.' Specifically, they would be asked to clearly and unambiguously explain what such putative qualities and existences are. They would be asked what they refer to as descriptive or referring expressions, what they consist of, and how, and on the basis of what specific truth-conditions, their claimed existence might, in principle, be empirically confirmed or disconfirmed — to establish that such beliefs are either true (or probably true) or false (or probably false).

As with the simple believers, the more informed, complex believers would very likely become increasingly uncomfortable, anxious, defensive, evasive, and ultimately dismissive as the questions probed more deeply and analytically into the metaphysical core of their more developed concept of the Mormon god. Like the simple believers, the informed believers are arguably also simple, likewise superstitious believers at bottom. They would most likely retreat (again as the fictional Mormon believer did in the illustrative conversation in Chapter 1) first — and regressively — to a likewise simple faith and heart-felt testimony based on an alleged (and no-doubt quite regressive) relationship with a very simple and grossly anthropomorphic notion of a Father-God, and then, ultimately to silence — with only forced convictions remaining to shore up the exposed nonsense of their beliefs.

There is a wide disparity between the above two types of Mormon (and other theistic) believers and the types of questions that might give them pause or make them anxious. As initially proposed above, however, I think it could reasonably be conjectured that at some basic, visceral level, *all* Mormon believers — and all theistic believers as well, from the very simple, uneducated, uninformed, and purely superstitious believers to the very complex, educated, sophisticated, and informed believers — simply, regressively, and comfortably (because familiar) believe in a kind, loving, and wise Heavenly Father (or, on the *maternal side*, a Savior and/or "Heavenly Mother"). Both believe in a god who gives 'spiritual birth' (and *spirit* birth) and provides love, nurturing, protection, deliverance, relief, and sustenance ('succor') as needed and/or in answer to prayer. Arguably all these believers *tacitly* (and regressively) believe that their god is merely a very loving, kind, just, merciful, knowledgeable, and powerful person — perhaps like their own beloved father/mother or archetypal Parent-imago, only perfect in every way. They also tacitly (and superstitiously) believe that their god exists in the shape of a man with flesh and bones and a physical body just like theirs, who happens to be the *only true* 'God.' For the most part they don't go any deeper than that, and don't want to, unless they have to in order to defend or explain their faith or attend to their own intellectual curiosity, questions, and doubts. At least in the Mormon faith, believers at both ends of the intellectual spectrum have all been strongly and repeatedly warned and conditioned by authoritative counsel to leave such questions alone. They are not — or so believers are told — essential to their salvation.

In this last regard, what I think we will find in this analysis of the Mormon concept of 'God' is that while it does, *in a salvational context*, matter to theistic believers of all faiths whether or not believers (or prospective believers) believe in and worship the one true god of *their* faith or the false gods of all *other* faiths, it does not matter all that much what the fundamental nature of 'God' *means* — whether to different people inside or outside the Mormon faith or to any given faith or religion for that matter. As elaborated on in Chapter 7, this peculiar fact is significant to the cumulative atheistic argument that the multitude of different gods and religions is evidence, in a salvational context, for the non-existence of an all-powerful, knowing and loving god. Of import as well is the seemingly self-evident fact that, to quote John Massen, "all religions, and all their gods, are created by the fertile [and psychologically motivated] imagination of the minds of humans" (*American Atheist*, May/June 2009, pp. 24–27). Even so, these and other like considerations are not significant in our conceptual analysis of the Mormon god in this chapter.

Still, beliefs *about* 'God' held by all theistic believers, as varied as they might be, are nonetheless fundamentally grounded in the doctrines of their faith and, in virtue of intercultural transmission, of all other faiths as well. Given this fact, it seems reasonable to conclude that *whatever* the believer's personal *concept* of 'God' might be — whether of the Mormon faith or any other theistic faith — such a concept is very likely to be false, unintelligible, or factually meaningless beyond a reasonable doubt.

If a concept is entirely anthropomorphic — for example, as a finite, physical being in the shape of a man that is all-knowing, wise, powerful, loving, merciful and just — then such a concept is simply false as a purely superstitious belief, just as a belief in Wotan, Apollo, or Zeus would be. With such a conception of 'God,' the believer would have a lot of explaining to do, and would have to very carefully explain to reasonable people who are without any belief in any god or gods why such a god has remained physically hidden. Explanations would be needed to explain why there exists so much confusion, wrong belief, and nonbelief in the world regarding his existence and why faith is even necessary for salvation when direct observation and the demonstration of superhuman knowledge and power are possible.

If, on the other hand, the concept of 'God' is primarily or entirely *non*-anthropomorphic in terms of its fundamental referents or attributes as a putative being, then such a concept as a truth-claim is incoherent and factually meaningless, being a purely metaphysical construct. With this more developed concept of 'God' believers would also have a lot of explaining to do. They would have to very carefully, clearly, and unambiguously specify and describe to the Atheist or Agnostic what for example, a 'finite, exalted, and infinite and eternal spirit and intelligence of the highest order' would *actually* be like; what a 'celestial, glorified and immortal body of flesh and bones animated by spirit element' would *actually* be like; what such metaphysical referents in both cases would themselves *specifically* refer to; what their *specific* truth-conditions are, and what would, at least in principle, empirically satisfy such truth-conditions.

Finally, any concept of 'God' that incorporates *both* characteristics is, by association — as we shall learn through our analytic inquiry — both false *and* incoherent. This is moreover the case, and significantly so at an empirical level, when we consider again certain perennial, unresolved and, to me at least, irresolvable contradictions related to the more orthodox conceptions of 'God.' Such contradictions include, and specifically arise from, (1) the existence of the senseless, gratuitous, extreme, and prolonged suffering and premature death of so many good people, innocent babies and children, and animals in the world due to natural and human evil; (2) the absurd and unnecessary requirement of faith and faith-testing for salvation; (3) the cruel, senseless silence and hiddenness of 'God' in response to sincere, heartfelt prayers offered by the faithful on behalf of themselves and others who are in dire need of relief, knowledge or deliverance from suffering, danger, and doubt; (4) the widespread or extensive religious confusion, nonbelief, and multiple faiths in the world in spite of so many sincere, pleading prayers for answers and understanding after all human efforts have been exhausted; and (5) the likewise widespread and extensive prevalence of religiously considered wrong belief and correspondingly wrong believers who choose to wrongly believe in false gods, wrongly leave or join different faiths, or wrongly eschew organized religion entirely. Related to (4) and (5) specifically, we must pause to reflectively and critically consider how or why it is that given the putative eternal stakes involved in 'knowing' or *not*-knowing 'God' — for Mormons and Christians, Jesus Christ as well — there should be so much *conceptual* confusion, ambiguity, disagreement, and contradiction regarding what specifically 'God' is, or what the term *God* as a referring expression *actually* refers to.[69]

---

69 It seems rather expedient — if not quite fashionable and even evasive as an understandable reaction to prolific and thoughtful atheological criticism — for many faiths and theists to have become increasingly liberal and innovative in conceptualizing their various gods, taking what has been referred to earlier as a salad-bar approach to religious belief in 'God and his Gospel.' To be sure, differentiating one's personal or institutional god from what is most troublesome or objectionable to believers and skeptics alike is, beyond being a rather obvious betrayal of doubt, certainly a pragmatic (if not disingenuous) tactic of evasion to defend and preserve the faith from blatant contradictions and cognitive dissonance. It is an understandable reaction as well to strengthen self-deception in protecting one's illusions — or delusions as the case might be. But it is more than all that to be sure. For it would seem at least intuitively so that the very act of making

With these thoughts as prelude, we will begin in earnest with a brief overview and analysis of the Mormon doctrine of *deity*. From here we will deconstruct and critically consider in some detail the various Mormon concepts of *God*, the *Godhead*, and the *Immanent God*, or *Light of Truth*. We will also treat the Mormon strategy of likening the mortal and resurrected Jesus to 'God' in an effort to legitimize the anthropomorphic concept of the Mormon god. Finally, we will conclude this chapter with a consideration of error theory as it might be applied to religious beliefs and meta-beliefs *about* 'God.'

The Mormon Doctrine of Deity

Unlike the concept of the invented 'sectarian God' of developed Christianity, something that is immaterial and essentially nonanthropomorphic, the *concept* of the invented Mormon god is both *anthropomorphic*[70] and *nonanthropomorphic*[71] in nature. This makes

the concept of 'God' personally or socially more palatable, acceptable, and believable or less contradictory is indeed — and paradoxically — a tacit admission of a problem existing regarding the incoherence and therefore non-existence of 'God' as believed.

Clearly, in the salvational context of Mormonism and all salvational faiths that require a correct understanding of, and unwavering allegiance to, the one and only true 'God,' the 'correct idea' of such a god would not be something that needs to be figured out by man's puny intellect alone — or even modified, refined, or corrected by progressive revelation or inspired apologetics. (Why after all, according to Mormon beliefs in particular, would revelation need to be progressive to the 'spirits' of all human beings when such putative spirits are believed to be capable of having the premortal 'veil of forgetfulness' lifted and can receive and understand all the 'mysteries of Godliness' in virtue of 'sanctification' (McConkie 1979, 675), 'transfiguration' (803), and 'revelation' (643) from the Mormon god by or through the 'Holy Ghost' and 'Light of Truth'?) As all orthodox theistic faiths teach and insist, what *God* actually means, *i.e.* the fundamental idea or concept of 'God' inclusive of his personal nature (or qualities and attributes), is not subject to private interpretation. Rather, such meaning is, as also taught and believed, necessarily an Absolute Truth which can only be known in virtue of direct revelation from 'God' through scripture, religious experience, or, in some faiths like Catholicism and Mormonism, those called and anointed to authoritatively receive and interpret such revelation. To suggest otherwise simply makes no sense in a theological context if one truly thinks about it.

If, as believed, there is a *literal* god who is claimed to be an *actual* being with specific qualities and attributes, then the *idea* of such a being would necessarily correspond to what such a putative being *really is*. As such, the idea of God simply is what it is. Given the believed abilities of such a being and the necessity for all human beings to have a correct idea of him in order to know him and be saved (else what's the point of knowing or believing in the existence of a god at all?), such a 'correct' and presumably intelligible, coherent, and factually meaningful idea could be — and logically *would* be — directly revealed and taught to all people with sufficient clarity and coherence so as to be at least minimally cognitively meaningful and universally understood. There would be no need for prophets, theologians, or apologists to present and interpret it, much less change it. And yet it is not. Any explanation for why it is not — or for why there are so many diverse, contradictory, and factually unintelligible or incoherent concepts of 'God' extant today, even within the same faith — would seem necessarily to circle back against it as a blatant and self-evident contradiction.

70 Anthropomorphism, as conceptualized here, attributes human shape and personality traits to a nonhuman being, including a finite physical body — with 'parts and passions' — like the putatively resurrected Jesus Christ or the mythological Greek gods Zeus or Apollo. The anthropomorphic image of the Mormon god at play in the Mormon mind is perhaps best characterized in the Mormon Temple film shown in the endowment ceremony, where 'God' and Jehovah are represented as beings with physical bodies in the shape of men with white hair and beards wearing white robes. This attribution of human shape and characteristics onto the Mormon concept of 'God' is held by Mormon believers to be not only an attribution, but, beyond the concept itself, a literal fact considered to be actually true (Crowther 2007, 132–4).

71 Nonanthropomorphism, as theologically conceptualized here, attributes *metaphysical* — or transcendent/

him essentially (for lack of a better term) a *quasi-anthropomorphic* being. Like the 'Sectarian' concept of 'God,' the Mormon concept of 'God' is equally and deeply problematical at two levels. *First*, it is problematic both in relation to its intelligibility, coherence, and factual significance as an overarching doctrinal scheme and in regard to its specific doctrinal, descriptive referents. *Second*, it is problematic regarding how the putative anthropomorphic and nonanthropomorphic aspects of existence could be logically compatible or coherent with reality as we *know* (*not* imagine or perceive) it to be. Consider first the larger metaphysical context of the Mormon doctrine of deity as the foundation of Mormon theology.

According to the synthesized view of Mormon theology referenced earlier in this chapter, there never was, nor will be, a time when there was not, or will not be, a 'Father God,' when 'God in his fullness' did not exist as a finite, tangible personage consisting of an exalted spirit and intelligence housed in a resurrected, non-biological, bloodless body of flesh and bones, with body, parts, and passions in the form or shape of a man. In a fundamental and limited sense, the Mormon god is scripturally considered to be eternal as a spirit (and intelligence[72]) of the highest order (Abraham 3: 18–19). And so is man, as literal spirit offspring of a Heavenly Father ('God'), whose fundamental identity, according to Joseph Smith, consists of intelligences which are co-eternal with the Mormon god and which are inherently, indeterministically free to choose and act independently in accordance with the laws regulating their sphere of existence and the 'great law of eternal progression' toward the ultimate achievement of godhood.

Further, *'God,' spirits* and *men* are considered to be actual, eternal constituents of what amounts to a metaphorical "eternal chain" consisting of an eternally recurring set of three causally interdependent links, with 'God' as the first link in the set, 'spirits' the second link, and 'man' the third. Each set of three links leads or connects causally to another set of three links beginning with a god and so on, backward and forward infinitely, from set to set, without beginning or end. 'God the Father,' who is the first link in this putative eternal chain, *somehow* incorporates the 'intelligences' of 'eternal man' into 'spirits' through a pre-mortal procreative process and then *somehow* inserts the mature, procreated spirit of man into the human zygote, fetus, or fully formed child to create — in concert with the natural process of human procreation — a mortal man, just as his Heavenly Father had done with him, and so on back throughout all eternity.

Notwithstanding the timeless nature of this eternal chain and related creative and procreative process, each link in the chain is considered to have a beginning, with the existence of each finite, developed link, *i.e.* 'God,' spirit, and man, *as a discrete personage* considered to be contingent, or dependent, on the existence of the others. Thus,

---

supernatural — properties, attributes and qualities to a being who, though experienced as a personal being, is biologically, physically, mentally, characterologically, and spatiotemporally *transcendent* to human beings.

72 Such intelligences were considered and defined — unintelligibly I think — by certain Mormon general authorities such as Orson and Parley P. Pratt, B.H. Roberts, and John A. Widtsoe, to be uncreated, self-existing, indestructible, complex, fundamental, and material entities or 'particles' that are essentially self-conscious and capable of ratiocination, judgment, and the power to choose. There are other interpretations and meanings offered by other sources as well, all of which are equally unintelligible. Amidst such confusion on the subject there is, to my knowledge — and quite conveniently — no *official* Church position on what intelligences are, or what specifically they consist of or even mean conceptually. Yet they are believed to be fundamental constituents of 'God' and man, and the building blocks of the cosmos and of all matter in the universe!

according to the synthesized view of Mormon theology, *intelligences* and *spirit matter* (whether believed to be separate or identical realities) are claimed to be the fundamental, material, self-existent (or eternal) constituents of the Mormon god and man, while *spirits*, as 'spirits,' have a beginning; *man*, as 'man,' has a beginning, and the *gods*, as 'Gods,' have a beginning. Furthermore, the existence of *spirits* (consisting of eternal spirit matter and an intelligence) is contingent on the existence of *gods*, and the existence of *man* is contingent on the existence of spirits. Finally, the existence of the 'Gods' is contingent on the existence, resurrection, *and* exaltation of man — which exaltation is further contingent on man's righteous and faithful exercise of indeterminate, or contra-causal, free will, by the 'grace of God' (or Christ), in strict obedience to the mind and will of the Mormon god. These contingencies make gods, spirits, and men — as such — contingent, or non-necessary, beings.

Now let's pause here for a moment and think very carefully and critically about all this as either a questioning insider or skeptical outsider. How can we or anyone make rational sense of the concepts of eternal intelligences, spirits, and spirit matter? What do such terms actually mean and how might their status as putative facts or realities possibly be empirically confirmed or disconfirmed to establish their claimed existence as a *justifiable* truth-claim? Further, how could intelligences (whatever they are) sensibly or coherently be said to somehow *literally* become part of spirits (whatever they are) through divine procreation (whatever that means)? Moreover, how could such likewise unintelligible spirits consisting of spirit matter and intelligence somehow *literally* come into or inhabit man from another dimension or location in space and time through biological procreation?

Finally, how can we rationally make sense of the claim that a human being, allegedly consisting of a spirit and intelligence within a biological body, is somehow *literally* resurrected and glorified (whatever that means) after the death and total decomposition of the physical body to live forever as an immortal (indestructible, bloodless or non-biological) personage — a personage who can then ultimately achieve omniscience and, through omniscience, omnipotence as a 'God?' How can we make rational sense of any of this? How can anyone seriously claim the truth of *any* of this with no reservation, doubt, or at least some embarrassment, knowing full well that none of it makes sense at its face because all of it contradicts — or fails to cohere with (or hang together coherently with) — the best *justified* and *basic* knowledge we have regarding this world and the universe and how they work?

The question regarding the problem of the Mormon god achieving omniscience and, therefore, omnipotence through eternal progression is incidentally addressed by Christian philosopher Francis Beckwith. In this regard, Beckwith validly argues and concludes (as a skeptical outsider of the Mormon faith, but likely not of his own) that the Mormon concept of 'God' is incoherent because "it is impossible [given the concept of 'infinite', *i.e.* that which is limitless,] for *eternal progression* to entail that a being of limited [*finite*] knowledge gain knowledge until his knowledge [of all things past, present, and future] is *infinite*. This is a position taught by the Mormon Prophet, Joseph Smith (1978, 6: 306–7) and Mormon Apostle and theologian Bruce R. McConkie (1979, 238–39)]" (1994, 7).

Beckwith elaborates: "Starting from a finite number [of things (or truths) to know], it is impossible [as the Mormon doctrine of eternal progression insists, or at least implies] to count to infinity [or, in other words, to acquire a knowledge of *all* things]. ... [Nevertheless, someone] may argue," continues Beckwith, "that the Mormon God receives his infinite knowledge from his own 'Heavenly Father' God all at once when he reaches a particular point in his progression…. [But this argument]," Beckwith insists, "merely places the problem on the shoulders of a *more distant* God, who acquired *his* supposed omniscience from an *even more distant* God, and so on into infinity. … Appealing [therefore] to an endless series of contingent beings as an explanation for why all the Mormon gods are omniscient explains nothing. … Whether a Mormon god 'progresses' to infinite knowledge or receives it all at once from his own superior God, the Mormon concept of God," concludes Beckwith, on the basis of this particular argument as well as others, "is nevertheless incoherent"[73] (8).

It would seem that this so-called orthodox conception of Mormon theology would seek to have it both ways. First it posits its god as a being that had a beginning, through 'spirit conception,' and then became a god through 'eternal progression.' Second, it posits that this god is an eternal and everlasting god. It is a Heavenly Father, Creator, and Supreme Ruler and Governor of the universe who has *always* existed as an *eternal* intelligence *and* fully evolved god. In other words, it is a being who could not not-exist. But Mormon theologians and believers cannot have it both ways — if, except for the sake of argument, they can have it any way at all. For the assertion of a *necessary* (*i.e.* self-existing or eternal) set of *contingent* and (pro)created realities is not only a factual non-reality because

---

73 Such incoherence is at least implicitly appealed to by some so-regarded orthodox Mormon authorities — most notably Brigham Young, John A. Widtsoe, and B.H. Roberts — and certain Mormon philosophers and apologists as well, including Sterling McMurrin (1965) and Blake Ostler (1996, 2001), who claim (*pace* Joseph Smith, Joseph Fielding Smith, and Bruce R. McConkie) that the Mormon God is, and *cannot* coherently be regarded as, omniscient (and therefore omnipotent) in the sense that he is no longer progressing or increasing in knowledge and truth, or in the sense that he knows how every one of his children will exercise their 'free agency.' Rather, they argue, 'God' is all-knowing (and all-powerful) *only* in the sense that he knows all things (and therefore has all power) necessary to *lawfully* initiate and manage the Plan of Salvation, *i.e.* ensure man's salvation and exaltation, and to *lawfully* create the necessary causal, regulatory mechanisms (or natural laws) and conditions and sustain the necessary order in the cosmos needed for life to exist and perpetuate eternally according to his will.

But this speculative position regarding the nature and extent of a god's knowledge and power has its own problems.

Firstly, it is itself incoherent (or at least unjustified, if not unjustifiable) in relation to our best justified beliefs or established common knowledge regarding the realities of the natural world.

Secondly, it is logically flawed in the premise that the claimed existence of 'God's perfect foreknowledge' is impossible given man's inalienable capacity of indeterministic free will (an argument made by Mormon apologist Blake Ostler and treated in Chapter 7 regarding the problem of evil; see also Steele 2008, 206–7 and, for a refutation of the more traditional argument that foreknowledge contradicts the existence of free will, see Everitt 2004, 289–91).

Thirdly, it is also incoherent in relation to the so-called neo-orthodox view regarding the Mormon god's *absolute* and *total* knowledge of *all* things past, present, *and* future, as well as mainstream belief and Mormon scripture — which scripture is itself arguably vague, ambiguous, or incoherent in this regard. Additionally, such a position is *factually unintelligible* in its own right — for how could the putative *fact* of a god's degree of knowledge (and power) possibly be empirically confirmed or disconfirmed such that man might *know* the extent and bounds of such 'divine knowledge' (and power) sufficient to rationally sustain belief or faith in such a god without presupposition and rationalization?

Finally, how would it be possible to specify — beyond mere speculation — what truths the Mormon god allegedly does and does not know (or what power he allegedly has or does not have) and how we might *know* this without begging the question regarding his putative existence and the putative reality or existence of revelation from him to man about the nature and extent of his believed omniscience (and omnipotence)?

it is factually meaningless and therefore objectively nonexistent as conceptualized, but it is also a logical impossibility.

Specifically, the very notion that the Mormon god, as a putatively *necessary* infinite and eternal being (D&C 20:17), is also a *contingent*, procreated and finite being is, on its face, self-contradictory. This makes the very idea of such a god at least apparently as incoherent or unintelligible as a round square. Further, to assert or suggest that a god's putative intelligence — or fundamental, primary identity — is eternal, while his spirit body and glorified, resurrected body are not, is likewise sheer and utter nonsense. Something cannot coherently be asserted as being both necessary *and* contingent, or, in this case, to have a beginning, yet be self-existent or eternal in its mature form, as the Mormon god is asserted to be. A set of contingent, causally interdependent, indeterministically 'free' and non-self-existent entities, *i.e.* 'God,' spirits, and man, cannot coherently be stated as being independent and necessarily self-perpetuating throughout eternity. One writer of an article on the Mormon doctrine of eternal progression, as it relates to the Mormon doctrine of deity, framed the problem in this way:

> This teaching about 'eternal progression,' while sounding very sophisticated in nature, always begins with the heavenly father on his planet, but ignores the most fundamental issues raised by the doctrine. The origins of man are completely ignored in the doctrine. At one time there were only 'intelligences' and matter in the Mormon universe. How did man and planets come into being when there was no God to create or organize them? How did Mormon Gods come into being in order to produce spiritual children when there were no human beings to become Gods? Where did the religious revelation regarding obedience to Mormon doctrine come from when there was no God to give the revelation and no human being to receive it?
>
> The connection between the existence of the 'intelligences" the appearance of Mormon Gods and human beings is never made or explained as to how it could occur. This connection cannot be made, because Mormon theology begins with [eternal] man as the foundation and God in a subservient position to man. Not only is God secondary in existence to man, since there must first be a man who can be exalted to Godhood, but God himself is only the end of human progression to that state of being. But there is an additional problem, because for a man to be exalted to Godhood there must be an existing God to accomplish the process.
>
> What Mormon doctrine teaches is [the eternal regress of] a circular and closed process of "eternal progression", but in that [eternal,] closed process there is no allowance for the origin or beginning of the process. There is no opening in which the eternal "intelligences" first enter the process, because there is no eternally existing physical man or God to be the first cause. (Unnamed Source)

Actually, contrary to the first sentence in the second paragraph of the quotation above, a connection *has* been made between the existence of intelligences and the appearance of Mormon Gods. Contrary to the last sentence of the last paragraph above, a 'first cause' *has* been postulated. Given that only *eternal* intelligences are alleged to be independent and self-existent (*i.e. God* is not eternal, as 'God'; *spirits* are not eternal, as 'spirits'; and *man* is not eternal, as a 'mortal man'), it follows that the alleged 'will to organize' inherent in eternal intelligences could be regarded, as Mormon Apostle Orson Pratt suggested in 1851, as the "Great First Cause." However, the theological implications of such a teaching, which Pratt later disavowed (under duress) and which the Mormon church officially proclaimed in 1865 to be "false doctrine," depersonalizes the Mormon god and makes him, as 'God,' synonymous with intelligences which are considered, in virtue of their attributes as divine intelligences, as the 'Great First Cause' — the eternal 'God' and the creator and sustainer of all that is.

This theological position logically makes the finite, tangible personage of 'God' unnecessary as a creator and a Heavenly Father of spirits. It also suggests that there was a time, contrary to orthodox Mormon theology, when there was not a personal 'God' as an exalted, spirit personage housed in a tangible, resurrected body of flesh and bones. Even without such a disavowal and official denouncement, the Mormon version of the Great First Cause, as either a logical or factual necessity, is both question-begging and factually unintelligible — as are the related and foundational concepts of *intelligences*, *spirits*, and *gods* that comprise the Mormon doctrine of deity as the centerpiece of Mormon theology.

To argue as Mormon apologist Blake Ostler does in "Necessarily God is Not Analytically Necessary" (hereafter "NGNAN"), that the claim of the Mormon god's self-existence is somehow self-justified by some putative "principle of self-existence" which holds that "[a] being is self-existent if that being never in fact fails to actually exist, and is not now, has never been and will never be dependent on anything else for its existence" (NGNAN, 13) is to argue invalidly for the self-existence of a 'Being' whose claimed existence (no less self-existence) is neither self-evident nor factually intelligible. Ostler's "principle of self-existence" is a cognitively meaningless, question-begging tautology that explains nothing and justifies nothing. Moreover, it would seem to allow *too* much. For such a 'principle of self-existence' — incoherent as it is when applied to the concept of the Mormon (or any) god — can be appealed to at its face by all faiths to justify the existence of *their* gods as well. This is a conclusion surely Ostler would not accept.

Both versions of the Mormon doctrine of deity — the Great First Cause and the orthodox versions — are without justifiable truth-conditions and therefore without the possibility of justification. This makes such doctrines, regardless of their mere truth-value as indicative statements, void of factual significance.

Returning to our primary analytical task, we might again reasonably ask of both versions: What are the *specific* truth-conditions of such claims, such that it might be reasonably determined that the truth claims made are even justifiable as being, *in principle*, empirically confirmable or disconfirmable as either true (or probably true) or false (or probably false) as indicative statements which have factual significance or reality? Additionally, how do these non-self-evident metaphysical constructs hang together or cohere with the rest of Mormon theology — and with our best knowledge of how the world and the universe actually work?

Let us accept, solely for the sake of argument, that all matter and intelligences comprising the material universe are eternal; that the Mormon god exists contingently, as believed, as an exalted man; and that man's intelligence, which is co-eternal with the Mormon god, is *indeterministically* free to choose eternal life or *not* — to become 'Gods' or *not* through strict obedience to the requirements of the Great Law of Eternal Progression (Widtsoe 1915). Then, under such a conception of things, it is reasonable in principle to conceive of *any* and *every* world or universe where *no* mortal man (created, in theory, by the lawful, willful action of pre-mortal intelligences on 'gross matter') achieves exaltation and therefore, where 'God,' as a contingent being, would not and *could not* exist in any world, universe, or dimension of space and time — including this world and this universe.

Such a state of existence is conceivable given Mormon theology and cosmology, thereby making the existence and very idea of 'God' (apart from its impossibility as fully conceptualized) unnecessary, even if perhaps logically possible. But such a state of affairs, as a logical extension of the Mormon doctrine of deity, does *not* hang together, or cohere, with the doctrine in Mormon theology which asserts that the Mormon god has *always* existed as a necessary or eternal being — as the Creator of worlds without end — thereby making Mormon theology deeply incoherent at its core.

Even more fundamentally: if, as it shall be argued later, the concept of *material intelligences* is, in the fullest sense of the term, found to be an unintelligible, factual non-reality, what then happens to the related concepts of 'God' and 'man'? They are dependent on the intelligible, factual existence of intelligences as the essential foundation to Mormon materialistic cosmology. They distinguish it fundamentally from immaterialist, orthodox Christian theology.

The Concept of the Mormon God

With the above as an important backdrop to our analysis of the Mormon doctrine of deity, let us consider now the following *descriptions* of the Mormon god that are derived from various sources, including the Standard Works or Scriptures of the Mormon Church and the generally accepted teachings of Church founder Joseph Smith and certain other notable Church General Authorities. From such sources we glean the following alleged facts, as doctrinal referents, regarding the allegedly true nature of 'God.' Specifically, we learn that according to established, orthodox Mormon doctrine, it is considered a *literal fact that* 'God' is *primarily, secondarily,* and *relationally...*

- the One Supreme, *perfect* and *absolute* (*i.e.* infinite and eternal) Being; the *Supreme Governor* and *Ultimate Source* of the universe and the *Eternal Father* who is the *Creator* of *this* world and 'worlds without end,' and who exists as the head of an infinite and eternal tri-theistic 'Godhead' consisting of three separate and distinct personages, including, as commonly understood, the *Father* (Creator), the *Son* (Redeemer) and the *Holy Ghost* (the Testator);

- an *Eternal* Being who is "from everlasting to everlasting, the same unchangeable God" who was literally procreated and born to heavenly parents as a *spirit person somewhere* at a point in time, who then lived as a mortal man born to a mortal mother with mortal parents on another planet *somewhere* in this or another universe and progressed "line upon line" throughout his mortal life and afterward to Godhood and yet who always existed as an *independent, eternal (self-existent) intelligence of the highest order;*

- an *Infinite* Being consisting of a *finite, exalted spirit* (and eternal *intelligence*) housed in a *finite* tangible, bloodless, *resurrected* and *exalted* body of flesh and bones that is animated by *spirit element* and who possesses *spiritual* passions and *infinite* (*i.e.* limitless) love, goodness, mercy, and wisdom, as well as the absolute or unlimited power to do all things which are lawfully possible to do and either the absolute and limitless knowledge of all things (*i.e.* truths, thoughts, intentions, actions, events, and states of affairs) past, present, and future; or, alternatively (and not currently and officially accepted by Church Authorities or widely accepted or believed by Church members), all such things only past and present with perfect knowledge of all possible future outcomes (not actual thoughts, choices, or actions to be taken);

• a *Holy Man* who exists in space and time within his own sphere or dimension (i.e. Kingdom) of existence, yet who is *transcendent* to *both* the space-time dimension of *this* world *and* to (biological) human life; who is at once a *finite*, physical and spatio-temporal being *and* an *immanent* being who is everywhere present (or immanent) with divine power, knowledge, wisdom and love in *this* and every world and in personal relationship with mankind by the *trans*-personal *light* of his *spirit, or the "Light of Truth (Christ)."*

These foundational, doctrinal descriptions of the Mormon god are, to quote Nielsen, "metaphysical blockbusters" with at least "distinctively metaphysical strands." They are not, at their nonanthropomorphic core, empirical claims subject to empirical confirmation or disconfirmation. They are not, therefore, hypotheses to be tested. "It is senseless," Nielsen asserts in this regard, "to talk about waiting for evidence for god so conceived. We have nothing here for which to understand what it would be like to have evidence. We literally do not understand what we are trying to assert when we say such things [as, for example, the list of metaphysical descriptions of the Mormon god above] and the 'we' here ranges over believers and nonbelievers alike. And this is not," Nielsen insists, "an *a priori* claim or the laying down of 'a meaning rule.' It is rather, an empirical claim about our use of language (2001, 275)." How, after all, can we possibly make sense of, or objectively test for, the existence of 'beings' with the *italicized* modifiers, or attributes such as 'infinite' love, goodness, mercy, wisdom and 'unlimited' knowledge and power, or for the existence of the above *italicized* descriptive referents, such as 'Supreme Governor,' 'Ultimate Source,' 'Spirit,' 'Intelligence,' 'Light of Truth,' 'spirit element,' 'spiritual passions,' 'Holy Man' or 'Immanent Spirit?' They are (*pace* Hook, Stenger, and Dawkins, *et al.*) scientifically or otherwise untestable as parts of a 'God Hypothesis.' (Stenger 2007; Dawkins 2006; Hook 1975)[74]

---

74 This is not to say, however, that given — solely for the sake of argument — the intelligibility, coherence, and factual significance of a particular concept of 'God,' certain hypothetico-inductive and formal deductive arguments for the impossibility and improbability of 'God' (see Stenger 2007 and Martin 2003, 2006, respectively) are without significant value as part of the cumulative atheistic or atheological argument for the non-existence of gods. Such is not the case.

As a more recent paradigm case in point, Victor Stenger's "…scientific argument against the existence of God," offered as "…a modified form of the lack-of-evidence argument" on the basis that it can be hypothesized that there is "…a God who plays an important role in the universe" and the assumption "that God has specific attributes that should provide objective evidence for his existence," (43) clearly has merit in this regard.

For Stenger, in this regard, the theistic evasion that 'absence of evidence is not evidence of absence' is not always the case. Although such an argument is "…a logically correct statement, history and common experience provide many examples where, ultimately, absence of evidence became evidence of absence" (18). Continuing, Stenger goes on to say that "Generally speaking, when we have no evidence or other reason for believing in some entity, we can be pretty sure that entity does not exist. We have no evidence for Bigfoot, the Abominable Snowman, and the Loch Ness Monster, so we do not believe they exist. If we have no evidence or other reason for believing in God, then we can be pretty sure that God does not exist" (18).

In his provocative and well-written book *God: The Failed Hypothesis* (2007), Stenger, himself a renowned author, physicist, and emeritus professor of physics and astronomy, argues for the non-existence of 'God' on the premise that "…if a particular god model [like the model of subatomic particles] successfully predicts empirical results that cannot be accounted for by any other known means, then we would be rational in tentatively concluding that the model describes some aspect of an objective reality without being forced to prove that god really is as described in the details of the model" (40). His 'model' of 'God' includes several empirical consequences which we might reasonably expect to be evident in our world or universe if there was in fact a god— empirical consequences which are not, as stated, entirely relevant to the Mormon faith but which can be easily modified to conform to Mormon beliefs. These include the following: 'God is the creator and preserver of the universe'; 'God steps in whenever he wishes to change the course of events, which may include violating his own laws as, for example, in response to human entreaties'; 'God is the creator and preserver of life and humanity, where human beings are special in relation to other life-forms'; 'God has endowed humans with immaterial, eternal souls that exist independent of their bodies'; and 'God has revealed truths in scriptures and by communicating directly to select individuals throughout history' — to list the critical few (41–2).

In Stenger's view, "Whatever a god's true [or actual] nature, if one exists, a god model remains the best we can do in talking about that god" (39). Moreover, rather than grapple with semantics in defining or describing 'God' to establish (elusive) premises for argument, Stenger offers a simple, direct five-step 'Generic Argument' which empirically confirms or disconfirms the possible or probable actual existence of any god whose putative existence would necessarily be evident in virtue of the existence or non-existence of the modeled empirical consequences. This argument requires not only (1) "[hypothesizing a god] who plays an important role in the universe" and (2) "[assuming] that God has specific [secondary and relational] attributes that should provide objective evidence for his existence," but also requires (3) "[looking] for such evidence with an open mind" to determine if it is rational to faith in such a God. "If such evidence is found," Stenger argues, it would be reasonable to "…conclude that God *may* exist." But [i]f such objective evidence is not found, [it would be reasonable to] conclude beyond a reasonable doubt that a God with these [secondary and relational] properties does *not* exist" (43). The task, as Stenger sees it, is to determine if such empirical consequences actually exist and, if so, if there are other purely naturalistic and more parsimonious explanations for such evidence which would not necessitate the existence of a god, or which would be most reasonably expected in a purely natural universe in which there was no god.

Still, merit notwithstanding, such a hypothetico-inductive (or *a posteriori*) argument, compelling to many as it might be, is arguably only indicated and sound if we subordinate it to the *a priori* argument proposed by Nielsen and others and concede, again solely for the sake of argument, that (1) the primary attributes and qualities, or referents, of 'God' as a referring expression and as conceptualized, believed, and worshiped are, independently and as a whole, intelligible, coherent, and factually or cognitively meaningful as represented in the God-talk of the given faith; (2) we can reasonably "[a]ssume that God has specific [secondary and relational] attributes that *should provide objective evidence for his existence*" (43, emphasis mine); and (3) such putative secondary and relational properties (43) are *independent* of that god's primary attributes. If such concessions cannot be made, as is argued in this chapter and established to the contrary in the *Foundational Preface* in relation to the Mormon faith specifically, and by Nielsen and others in relation to the developed, nonanthropomorphic faiths of Judeo-Christian and Islamic faiths in general, then even if such (or any) proposed empirical consequences could be actually confirmed beyond a reasonable doubt, such confirmation — while it might validate the hypothesis of the presumed god in question — would nonetheless *not* confirm or disconfirm the *actual* or even *possible* existence of the god metaphysically conceptualized, believed in, and worshiped. This is necessarily so because *nothing* could, in principle, confirm or disconfirm the truth (or probable truth) or falsity (or probable falsity) of a god that is conceptually unintelligible, incoherent, and factually meaningless. Alternatively, the belief that *everything* empirically observed and not observed is evidence of a god's existence necessarily makes such a concept of 'God' factually vacuous and the 'scientific model' of such a god all-inclusive to the point of being untestable and therefore irrelevant.

Stated differently, there can be no testable hypothesis by which to objectively verify or falsify the existence of a factual non-reality. Indeed, while a god's 'true nature' does not matter as stated by Stenger above, such a putative being's conceptualized nature *does* matter and is, moreover, *all* that can matter under the circumstances. For if god's putative attributes and qualities as conceptualized and asserted as actual fact are deemed to be factually meaningless, then Stenger's assumption "…that God has specific attributes that should provide objective evidence for his existence" (43) necessarily cannot apply. If so, then Stenger's entire argument necessarily collapses. This would even more compellingly be the case if a god's *primary* attributes are deemed to be factually meaningless, since the cognitive meaningfulness of an entity's *secondary* and *relational* attributes are necessarily contingent on the cognitive meaningfulness of that entity's primary attributes. All this said, I would argue, following Nielsen, that any *a posteriori* argument for the non-existence of a

On an interesting, and perhaps ironic, historical note, the above doctrinal description of the Mormon Godhead was not always so. In the initial 1832 version of Joseph Smith's putative 'First Vision,' Smith writes of *only* the resurrected Christ appearing to him and forgiving him of his sins, with no mention of 'God, the Father.' The later, revised and final, official version in 1838 refers to the visitation of two separate and distinct personages: God the Father (*i.e.* 'God') and the resurrected Son of God, Jesus the Christ. Later, in 1842 and 1843, the Holy Ghost was added as the third and final member of the Mormon Godhead who, unlike the Father and the Son, is said to have a spirit body in the form of a man, but not a tangible, resurrected body.

At a Church conference in 1844, Smith completed his innovation of the Mormon god by declaring that he was not only a supernatural, finite being, or 'Holy Man' (whatever that means, if anything) but was also, most fundamentally, an 'eternal,' or 'self-existent,' 'intelligence' which *became* 'God.' The irony here is that Joseph Smith allegedly began his religious career as a young boy troubled and confused by the incoherent teachings of various Christian sects and seeking a clear, coherent, and true conception of 'God.' He ended his career as a self-appointed Prophet, describing his version of an equally unintelligible and incoherent god while professing that his "incomprehensible ideas to some" were nonetheless "simple," "good doctrine" and "good logic" (Joseph Smith's "King Follett" discourse, Smith 1976). They are, of course, neither simple nor good logic. Nor are they intelligible, coherent, or factually meaningful.

This evolution of the Mormon doctrine of deity interestingly began with a *weak anthropomorphic conception* of 'God, the Father' in 1834–35. At this time the Mormon god was characterized as a "*personage* of spirit, glory and power in the shape, or form, of a man, possessing all perfection and fulness." From here, the Mormon doctrine of deity evolved to a purely physical, or *strong anthropomorphic conception* of the Mormon god in 1843, where the god was characterized primarily as a *physical* being with a material, non-biological, "body of flesh and bones as tangible as man's." Finally, in 1844, Mormon doctrine evolved to its fulness as a *quasi-anthropomorphic conception* of a god. That is where it stands today. In this final conception of deity, the Mormon god was and is primarily characterized as a dualistic, physical, and metaphysical being consisting of *both* a tangible, resurrected body of flesh and bones *and* a procreated spirit (and intelligence) in the form of a man.

Upon reflection from the outside, there seems in this doctrinal evolution to be an attempted conceptual integration or synthesis of both the physical and believed metaphysical aspects of human life as understood through the worldview of Cartesian dualism. Such integration was creatively achieved by the apparent working backward to a strong anthropomorphic conception of the Mormon god from the scriptural characterization of the resurrected Jesus as the literal Son of God. In 1901, Mormon general authority B.H. Roberts made this move in his renowned debate with the Reverend Cyril Van der Donckt

---

god, if not qualified as a hypothetical exception to the conclusion of that god's non-existence on the basis of conceptual incoherence reached by the primary *a priori* argument, would necessarily itself be incoherent. How, again, could it be otherwise if such a god is deemed to be a factual non-reality from the start? Still, notwithstanding this conclusion, I would also argue that given the fact of human fallibilism and the evolving and various concepts of 'God' extant throughout the world, such *a posteriori* arguments nonetheless have value as part of a larger cumulative atheistic argument for the improbability or impossibility of gods.

(see below in the section *"What think ye of Christ?"*).

What's interesting here is the progression of Mormon theology from the *weak* and then *strong* versions of anthropomorphism to the *quasi*-anthropomorphic version of the Mormon god. This is perhaps a very natural progression, given the evolved, human dispositions to unconsciously anthropomorphize (Guthrie 1993), naturalistically produce supernatural agents, or 'gods' (Atran 2002), project and attach to forms of 'internalized parents' (Faber 2004), externalize mental phenomena as external realities (Steele 2008), and seek after satisfying explanations, certainty, and Absolute Truth. Unfortunately, it is a road that leads, as it always has, to an intellectual and conceptual dead-end. In an effort to avoid the falsity and absurdity of pure, superstitious anthropomorphism and fill-out the concept of 'God' to close all the intellectual gaps while remaining true to biblical narratives, Joseph Smith and subsequent Mormon leaders and religious innovators and apologists have moved the patently superstitious — and therefore false — grossly anthropomorphic Mormon concept of its god toward metaphysical nonsense.

Concerns regarding the falsity of the putative existence of a purely anthropomorphic god to the contrary notwithstanding, it nevertheless still seems on the surface at least relatively straight-forward in meaning — as well as cognitively meaningful — to conceive of the Mormon god's putatively physical body as being in the shape of a man. But is it? Can we really make rational sense of such a concept?

Referring again to the problem introduced in Chapter 1 of asserting the rationality or self-evident truthfulness of a belief on the basis of *familiarity* evoked through analogical predication, we don't know if man is in reality *anything* like the Mormon god, as is claimed by Mormon believers. As we shall learn in more depth below, the concept of the Mormon god *transcends* man in *every* significant attribute, quality, and capacity. Therefore, we can know nothing literal and therefore nonanalogical of any significance about such a putatively exalted, quasi-anthropomorphic being, other than he allegedly has a tangible body in the *form* of a man.

But even the putative body of the Mormon god as doctrinally described is not of like *kind* with man — except, again allegedly, in its human-like shape. Biological man, mortal and imperfect in all his physical and characterological human attributes, qualities and capacities does not and *cannot*, theologically speaking, *naturally* become (or evolve into) a resurrected, non-biological god who is putatively immortal and perfect — or *exalted* — in the physical and characterological attributes, qualities, and capacities of 'Godliness' (whatever that means).

Given this alleged theological and actual biological fact, how does it follow — on the given reasoning that as the human child is naturally in the express physical image of its human parent and that the human parent is likewise naturally in the same human shape as the child — that man is *analogically* in the putative shape, or image, of 'God' and that 'God' necessarily has a human-like shape? The basis of this analogy — the mortal like the divine in shape and *vice-versa* — is itself based on the presupposition that the human shape is 'eternal.' But what intelligible, non-question-begging reasons are there that can warrant or justify such a Platonic belief other than the wholly unreliable and evocative claim that it is true on the basis of subjective testimony derived through putative revelation from the Mormon god — the proclaimed validity of which itself begs the question at issue (*i.e.* that god's existence)? This is, as we shall learn, unintelligible and factually meaningless as well. The fact is, that while we do know something about the human body (what it consists of, how its shape came to be and how it functions), we know *nothing* intelligibly nonanalogical (or literally true or self-evident) and non-question-begging about the 'resurrected,' 'glorified,' or 'exalted' body of the Mormon god. That includes its shape — making the baseline belief that the body of the Mormon god is in the shape of a man, and *vice-versa*, likewise unwarranted and certainly not self-evident.

As Nielsen suggests:

> We, in some not very clear way, know our way around when we speak of God anthropo-
> morphically, as we of course learned to use God-talk as children. That gives us the illusion
> that we understand what we are talking about when we speak of God. We are told that God
> is our heavenly Father, not a father like our real father, but our heavenly Father. And what's
> that? And eventually we move from anthropomorphic conceptions of God, which we do in
> some way understand, to nonanthropomorphic ones. When we engage in our devotions (if we
> do such things), the anthropomorphic ones reassert themselves and we feel confident that we
> understand what we are praying to, worshipping, and the like. But when we reflect, we real-
> ize that neither our religious nor our intellectual impulses will sustain the anthropomorphic
> conceptions. That way makes religion a superstition. So we are driven, when we reflect, to
> ever less anthropomorphic ones, but in doing so we pass over, unwittingly, in the very effort
> to gain a religiously adequate conception of God, to an incoherent conception. We do so
> de-anthropomorphize that we no longer understand what we are saying. Yet an anthropomorphic
> conception of God of any sort gives us a materially tainted God which is subject to evident
> empirical disconfirmation in the more obvious anthropomorphic forms, made so pantheistic
> that religion is naturalized, made into what in reality is a secular belief-system disguised in
> colorful language" (1993, 55–56).

Either way, such doctrinal beliefs are, at very least, problematical. This is particularly and significantly so regarding the question the Mormon god's putative *transcendence*. Here such a 'God' is conceptually considered to be *factually* transcendent to man *physically* (as a non-biological being) as well as transcendent to man's *nature* (as an exalted, supreme being who is omniscient, omnipotent, omnipresent, and omnibenevolent). The Mormon god is also considered to be transcendent spatiotemporally to this world as a being who putatively resides physically in another world in another universe or dimension of space-time. Now we might perhaps be able to *imagine* such a putatively transcendent being. We might be able to imagine *that* such a being acts or interacts with mortal man as a Creator, Ruler, Savior or loving Father, from another world or universe, or across dimensions of space and time through his *immanent* Spirit. But such familiar imaginings are, given our best-justified knowledge (a pleonasm) to date, nonetheless factually and causally unintelligible. Consequently, the assertion or claim that such a transcendent being *actually* or *literally* exists as conceptualized or described is therefore at least apparently incoherent. It is without apparent truth-conditions and consequently it is unjustifiable as a truth-claim and irrational as a belief.

Although believing Mormons do not typically use such formal, doctrinal statements as listed above in their *first-order* religious discourse (or first-person statements of testimony or God-talk), such doctrines remain crucial and are importantly foundational and presupposed in many things Mormon believers feel, say, and do in their daily lives — secularly or religiously. It could not be otherwise, for as Nielsen suggests, "If religion [is separated from its doctrine] and becomes [merely] moral poetry — simply a set of aspirational ideals [or imagined possibilities] — and, if it is recognized [and accepted] as such, much of its appeal, its great power to take hold of us and to transform our lives, will be irretrievably lost" (1982, 146).[75]

---

75 David Eller, in his commendable book *Atheism Advanced* (2007), argues that "…scriptures, creeds, and beliefs are not where the power of religion comes from and that "[r]eligion is not so much about belief as about discipline — being the kind of person who performs certain actions and is prone to certain experiences and interpretations of experience. Belief," as Eller sees it, "is optional and trivial [to the religious] in comparison [with doing religion]" (421–423).

In an important sense, I think Eller is correct. Clearly, as alluded to earlier and concluded in Chapter 8 of this work, it is not knowledge or actual (*i.e.* justified) truth *per se* which are important to believers, but rather the unwavering, emotional commitment to, or faith in, belief as *verisimilitude* and, following Dennett, belief *in* belief. And, moreover, what is of ultimate value and concern to believers, following, I think, Eller's intent, is how the *living* of their faith makes them *feel* about themselves and how they *feel* when they are experiencing the neurological effects, or affects, of religious worship.

Still, in another important sense, it is also correct to regard the doctrines of all theistic faiths as essential to the faith of its believers. As I see it, the term 'belief'" (as a noun) means a trusted representation of reality accepted (*i.e.* believed) or held with confidence (*i.e.* in 'faith') to be true. It would appear then that the motivating beliefs and related values and mores of the religious are, as with all people, derivative of and inextricably related to a particular worldview — or set of *fundamental* beliefs or assumed truths about the origin, nature, meaning, and purpose of human existence and the world. Moreover, these motivating beliefs, as well as the fundamental beliefs that comprise the person's fundamental worldview, are consciously, unconsciously, or tacitly held in virtue of cultural transmission and social conditioning through formal or self-education, story telling, tradition, discipline, and/or the oral and written word.

This perspective, if valid (or at least sensible), would suggest, *pace* Eller, that belief in general — and wish-based religious belief (or illusion) in particular — is the explanatory/interpretive basis of all religious experience. In this sense, the power of religion essentially comes from the *interpreted affects* of religious experience made through the lens of religious beliefs (or illusions) — affects which, as Faber suggests, are "… unconsciously grounded in the basic biological situation of dependency, succor, and love" (2004, 41). They are induced through sociocultural conditioning by familiar religious language, music, symbolism, rites, and rituals.

No one, I would argue, acts without both the motivating need (or need-based intent or desire) and the at least tacit belief — consciously held or not — that such action is true or correct *at least* in the minimal sense that it will likely satisfy the pressing need or desire. People do not consciously and deliberately do anything they actually think or believe is senseless, wrong, or unimportant where significant personal consequences are at stake and significant commitment and sacrifice is required or expected. Such belief in the at least sufficient efficacy and correctness of motivated action and behavior does not, in a religious context, need to be consciously or deliberately applied in the explicit form of a formal doctrine, creed, or set of propositions to be shaped or influenced by such formal, putative truth claims. Nor do such doctrines, creeds, and theological propositions need to be consciously referred to by the actor in order for his or her personal motivating belief in the efficacy and correctness of intended action to be efficacious in motivating such action. Nor, moreover, according to Radcliffe-Brown, as cited by Eller (421), is the "function of religion…independent of its truth or falsity" (1965: 154), if by truth or falsity Radcliffe-Brown means *believed* truth or falsity.

Given this, *pace* Eller and Radcliffe-Browne, the motivating and justifying beliefs beneath the 'function [and practice] of religion' are, to be sure, quite *independent* of the *actual* — or justified — truth or falsity of formal religious belief. However, they are not independent of the *believed* truth of their way of life — which 'way of life' is in turn founded on the tacitly or unconsciously *believed* truth of the core religious belief at the heart of the culture they are embedded in. That is, it depends on the fundamental religious belief that their god — however he/she/it might be formally or informally conceptualized on the basis of their tradition, scripture, doctrine, mystical experience, or authoritative discourse — *actually* exists and is significantly involved in their lives as a *literal* being, force, or entity, and that therefore their religion is *actually* true.

To assert that religious function, as a way of life, is independent of the *believed* truth or falsity of religious

Expanding on this last thought in a later work, Nielsen surmises how Wittgenstein, under the influence of William James, Kierkegaard, and even James himself would respond to his insistence that first-order God-talk is necessarily based on doctrinal statements or formal, theological truth claims. "There you go again," they would collectively object, "with your stubborn and even arrogant intellectualism [and rationalism], turning religion into a *theory* — failing to see what is there before your eyes that gives religion its importance. It is not doctrines or creeds that count but commitment and concern turned into action on yourself, though at the same time with a certain inwardness, and *for* others. Religion is ultimate commitment and concern. Brush aside all this sterile intellectualism [and talk of rationality]. Theorizing about religion is not the way to God" (2001, 348).

To this collective fideistic objection, Nielsen replies as follows:

> Theorizing about religion is, indeed, not the way to God, if there is a way to God. The way is in your action on yourself and for others, but, if it is done religiously, it is embedded in words integral to a form of life that would not be the form of life it is without the doctrines and the creeds. Religions are for the sake of life…but genuine religious believers, immersed in those forms of life, see and feel their commitments and concerns and deeds in terms of these very forms containing, and inescapably, these doctrines and creeds. *They do not have religious feelings which swing loose from religious concepts.* Both their very understanding and deepest reactions are tied up (internally linked) with doctrines and creeds and the distinctive concepts that go with them. And their reactions and understanding here cannot be split apart (as if there were a "cognitive" and a "noncognitive" side to them). *There is no religious understanding without the reactions and no reactions which are intelligibly religious without that understanding.* (348)

In replying directly to the self-stated objection that Nielsen "just dogmatically [asserts] that religious beliefs are incoherent and that [he compounds] the error by just assuming incorrectly that what is incoherent and what is not is context-independent," Nielsen reminds us once again (speaking for himself) that "I…explicitly stress…the context-*dependence* of concepts of incoherence, but argue against the balkanization of religious concepts and religious language-games. We should start," Nielsen acknowledges, "in analyzing religious beliefs, with religious practices and the use of religious utterances as they stand in such

---

belief is inconsistent with my understanding of the way the human brain works *vis-à-vis* motivated human action and behavior. Moreover, the implication, if it is made, that such a fundamental religious belief at the heart of religious function (or commitment to a particular religious way of life) — *i.e.* that a god exists — is entirely separate from the formal set of beliefs of a particular religious life-form seems questionable as well. The formal beliefs — or doctrines, creeds, and propositions — of any given religion are (or at least would reasonably *seem* to be) merely invented and articulated formulations (or re-formulations) of collective religious experience *vis-à-vis* the believed existence of some god. Simply put, religious action and the experiences that motivate it and come from it cannot intelligibly be separated from the religious believer's *believed* truth of their belief in a god. This in turn cannot be separated from their related religious beliefs *about* their god and *about* their believed god's relationship with and expectations of mankind and all existence. Belief, in this context and as defined above, matters, and it is neither optional nor trivial in relation to motivated religious action and behavior. This is so even though knowledge, or actual (*i.e.* justified) truth arguably do *not* matter to religious believers, at least unless it can be used (even if incorrectly) to tangentially support their secondary or derivative theistic beliefs.

religious contexts. *But religious discourse is intertwined with other uses of language.* When we see how they are related, how they fit together, and reflect *carefully* on the uses of religious terms and sentences in their live contexts in religious practices and as part of some natural language (*e.g.* French or English), they seem at least to be incoherent. Referring expressions such as 'God' or 'heaven' occur in them, but we [including believers] have no idea of how to specify, even taking them in context, their referents; some key religious utterances appear to be in some sense factual cosmological (itself a pleonasm) assertions — at least in the surface grammar — but we cannot specify their truth-conditions or their assertability-conditions; there are key religious utterances that some [believers] say we must understand metaphorically or symbolically, but we cannot say what they are metaphors or symbols of' (2001, 51–2, n3, emphasis mine).

Still, first-order God-talk remains problematic in its own right. Consider, for example, the following paradigm statements of a typical Mormon's personal testimony: (1) "I know that God lives and that Jesus is the Christ;" (2) "My Heavenly Father loves me, knows me and hears and answers my prayers;" (3) "Jesus Christ is my personal Savior and Redeemer who suffered, bled and died for my sins;" and (4) "I believe in God the Eternal Father, in Jesus Christ, his only begotten son, and in the Holy Ghost." These non-descriptive assertions of 'God' are dependent for their continued force on at least some — if not all — of the metaphysical aspects of the descriptive referents of the Mormon god established in the above *second-order* descriptive doctrinal statements *about* that god that are believed to be *factual* and, therefore, *actually true.*

Even so, as Nielsen suggests, "believers do not regard [their beliefs about their god] to be testable. Most believers just accept them as given, unassailable [truths or facts]. They do not try to [critically analyze them], prove them or try to test them… [yet]…without them their faith would be destroyed; they are the life-string to their beliefs…However, need or not, we have very good reasons to regard [such claims] as…metaphysical beliefs and as therefore, however much such believers may want to deny it, nonsense" (2006, 12). In this regard, Nielsen invites us all, believers and disbelievers, to…

Try this little experiment for yourselves: if you think of yourselves as believers, what *conceivable* turn of observable events would make you say you were mistaken or probably mistaken in holding that belief; and if you think of yourself as an atheist or as an agnostic try this experiment on yourself: what *conceivable* turn of observable events, if only you were to observe them, would make you say you were mistaken or probably mistaken in denying or doubting that it is true or probably true that there is a God?

He then goes on to conclude…

If the God you believe in, deny or doubt, is anything like the nonanthropomorphic God [of developed theistic religions, or the quasi-anthropomorphic God of Mormonism]…I predict you will not be able to answer that question. But if this is so, and I think it is, then your alleged God-statements "There is a God" or "God created the world" are devoid of *factual* significance. They are then equally compatible with anything and everything that the believer and nonbeliever alike can conceive as being experiential. (2006, 155)

There is no need for sign-seeking here. 'Signs' won't help us either way. Even if, as

Nielsen suggests, the stars in the evening sky were to rearrange themselves to spell out *God* with thousands of people watching, "such an experience," according to Nielsen, "would still not constitute evidence for the existence of God, for we still would be without a clue as to what would be meant by speaking to an infinite [and eternal] individual who is transcendent to the world. Such an observation (*i.e.* the stars rearranging themselves), no matter how well confirmed, would not ostensively fix the reference range of 'God'" (2006, 58). Nor, I would add, would the physical appearance of a being who said he was the Mormon god, or Jesus Christ, or the experiences of 'physically handling him [Christ] or feeling the wounds in his flesh' and feeling a 'piercing, burning sensation in the heart' in his presence help us out here. In any case, or with any conceivable sign or witness, the problem would be the same. "Talk of such an infinite [and eternal] individual would still," Nielsen insists, "remain incomprehensible and it would also have the same appearance of being incoherent. We do not know what we are talking about in speaking of such a transcendent reality. All we would know [or be justified in believing] is that something very strange had happened [or appeared] — something [or someone] we would not know what to make of" (2006, 58).

How then — to continue our analytic inquiry — can the above doctrinal referents or descriptions of 'God,' regarded by Mormon believers as external facts or objective realities, literally make sense as factual propositions? A "characteristic feature of purely factual assertions is that they must be confirmable or disconfirmable empirically. A statement would never unequivocally count as a factual statement unless it were so confirmable or disconfirmable, unless, some at least conceivable, empirically determinable state-of-affairs would count against its truth or count for its truth. But, if the assertion and the denial of the religious statement in question is equally compatible with any conceivable, empirically determinable state-of-affairs, then the religious statement in question is devoid of factual significance. It parades as a factual claim but in reality is not" (Nielsen 1982, 145).

Clearly, it is important to acknowledge here that "when fully stated and understood, in terms of their contextual use, what *appears* to be contradictory or paradoxical may be seen to be straightforward and non-contradictory.... [Still] where there is what at least appears to be a contradiction, or where words are put together in a way fluent speakers *cannot* understand [literally or otherwise], a case must be made out for the contention that the contradiction is only *apparent*" (90). Hence the need to ask: 'How can such an *apparent* contradiction be explained or reconciled with other related beliefs and/or with reality or truth as we actually *know* it (not as we merely experience, imagine or perceive it to be)?' As with the other questions above, the answer to this question, if it is to be acceptable, must itself make sense (or be regarded by believers and skeptics alike as self-evident) and not lead to further contradictions or inconsistencies.[76]

Regarding the above doctrinal statements about the Mormon god, what then are Mormons *positively, primarily,* and *specifically* referring to when they speak of their god? Beyond knowing how to use religious vocabulary nondeviantly, try to think very literally

---

76 Such a problem would occur, for example, if the charge of incoherence made against the concept of the Mormon god was dismissed on the claim that such incoherence is merely apparent. This is so because *the mere existence* of such apparent incoherence and the inability to conclusively explain and eliminate it — given the Mormon belief in the necessity of having a 'correct idea' or concept of 'God' and the actuality of personal, institutional, and progressive divine revelation — would lead to even further and deeper incoherence, a problem which will be addressed in Chapters 5 and 8.

about what 'God' or 'God, the Father' or 'Heavenly Father' or 'My Savior and Redeemer' positively denote or stand for. What *specifically* would the claim that a god is our *literal* Father in Heaven *actually* refer to or require? Or, what *specifically* is being worshipped or prayed to when worshipping or praying to the Mormon god? Alternatively, what *specifically* do this god's primary, or fundamental, attributes *actually*, or factually, refer to?

In answering these questions it is, again, important to distinguish the meaning of 'God,' as a referring expression, established *positively* through necessarily *specific*, descriptive referents, from meaning that is established *negatively* though what is termed the *via negativa*. The latter approach is fraught with difficulties for, as Nielsen correctly points out,

> If we can only say what God or anything else is not and if we cannot at all say *positively* what he is, then we in reality do not know what he is, for there are myriads of things and even considerable numbers of *kinds* or *types* of things that anything is not. If I ask you to believe in somorlo – to trust somorlo – but cannot ostensively teach you what "somorlo" [in its fulness] refers to, or introduce you to "somorlo" by definite descriptions, but can only say that somorlo is not this or that, you are still in the dark about what somorlo is.

> We know clearly enough what *kind* of reality "Fred" refers to [as a human being] and we have some sense of what kind or reality "2" refers to, if we want to talk about "2" in these referential terms at all. We can at least conceptually identify "2" but we can only conceptually identify "God" by using terms which are at least as perplexing as "God" is.

> This much the *via negativa* can establish. God is not on a continuum – either one way or another – with a grain of sand [or with man on one end of a natural, evolutionary continuum and God on the other]. There is a coherent logical ban on observing God [in his fulness], and if it makes no sense to speak of directly observing or experiencing God [in his fulness], it makes no sense to speak of indirectly observing God either. We must, to say anything intelligible, have a non-vacuous contrast here. (1989, 23–24)

At the very heart of all Judeo-Christian-Islamic conceptions of 'God,' including the Mormon concept, there is, according to Nielsen, "a thoroughly metaphysical belief in a reality that is alleged to transcend the 'empirical world.' It is the metaphysical belief that there is an eternal, ever-present creative source and sustainer of the universe. The problem is how we could [possibly] come to know or reasonably believe that such a strange reality [factually or actually] exists or come to understand what such talk is about" (2006, 55).

To test or experience such a dilemma, I invite Mormon believers to think very hard and very literally about what *specifically* an 'infinite and eternal spirit (and intelligence) of the highest order' really is. What *specifically* is an 'eternal, independent intelligence' like? Or what *specifically* is a 'spirit' (or 'spirit matter') like? Or what is an 'Immanent Being' like? Or what *specifically* is a 'Holy Man' like? In doing so, Nielsen cautions us, as pointed out in Chapter 1, that "[we] must not confuse what we can imagine or conceive with what is possible. We can conceive of an ice-cream cake at the center of the sun, but such a state of affairs is not possible. ... Where we have a sortal concept it is constrained by the physical laws that apply to the exemplifications of those concepts... What in fact happens is the basis of all our concepts. It constrains the conceptual connections inherent in our use of language... We have no coherent grounds," he concludes, "for thinking ourselves [or 'God'] to [have or] be [physically embodied spirits and intelligences]... [consisting of] disembodied constituents [of conscious, intelligent, and eternal spirit matter] incapable of destruction" (2001, 93).

The Mormon apologetic assertion that "the [fundamental] 'matter' of which [the Mormon god's and man's] spirit is composed is not continuous in meaning with 'matter' as it is used in modern physics" (Ostler NGNAN, 9) unfortunately tells us nothing that is factually significant or cognitively meaningful, and raises more questions than it answers.[77]

---

[77] Although Mormon cosmology is built on the philosophical foundation of materialism, it is also dualistic in relation to the nature of man and the Mormon god. To Mormons all existence is material, and man consists of both a temporal, physical body and an eternal, yet procreated physical spirit body in human shape. Both of these are material in nature, consisting in turn of 'gross matter' and 'spirit matter' respectively. In this conception of things, factually unintelligible though it is, Mormons quite conveniently — even if unintelligibly and incoherently — have it both ways and are therefore able to avoid on the one hand what Mormon Apostle Orson Pratt referred to and argued against as the "absurdities of immaterialism," and, on the other hand, the faith-destroying implications of actual mind-body identity extending from a purely naturalistic (and both scientifically and philosophically established and defensible) reductive materialism.

Regarding the "Mind-Body Identity Theory" we have the following simple and concise description offered in *PhilosophyOfMind.Info*:

Mind-brain identity theory is the theory that mental states are identical with brain states. The main challenge for materialism is that of finding physical states that can plausibly be taken to be identical with mental states. Many modern materialists answer to this challenge by pointing to the brain.

According to mind-brain identity theory, for every mental state there is a brain-state with which it is identical. For example, every pain event is identical with the C-fibres firing.

The main support for mind-brain identity theory is the phenomenon of localisation. Mental events appear to be associated with specific parts of the brain. Mental activity appears to be localised in identifiable areas of the brain. This is shown by the fact that inhibiting brain activity inhibits mental activity. Those who suffer localised brain damage also suffeer such localised damage to the mind. The most natural explanation of this localisation is that the mind is the brain.

Apart from (though ultimately consistent with) the *a priori* conceptual difficulties inherent in the faith-based propositions that spirits, spirit matter, and intelligences exist, are the likewise significant *a posteriori* factual difficulties for such beliefs imposed by the scientifically justified mind-brain identity *vis-à-vis* reductive materialism. These conceptual and scientific difficulties are significant in establishing both the fundamental falsity and incoherence of all theistic faiths, including Mormonism. Simply put, if it is both philosophically and factually the case — as analytically and scientifically demonstrated — that the concepts of *spirits, spirit matter*, and *intelligences* are factually vacuous, and that all consciousness and human mental states are both intelligibly and actually *identical* with brain processes, then the idea of 'the ghost in the machine,' or the existence of a so-called spirit located and operating inside the physical, biological body becomes actually as well as conceptually incoherent and factually meaningless. This conclusion, which is arguably at least very likely the case given rigorous conceptual analysis and recent and cumulative advances in neuroscience, would necessarily and decisively refute the believed existence of spirits and intelligences. By extension, it refutes the putative existence and survival of a factually unintelligible 'spirit self' or 'spirit being' which allegedly exists independently from the physical, biological body — and likewise incoherently survives death as an 'eternal being.'

For an extensive treatment of this subject, along with exhaustive and strong arguments and counter-arguments on both sides of reductive materialism and mind-brain identity, see the texts and cited sources and bibliographies in J.J.C. Smart's entry "The Identity Theory of Mind" (2007) found in the *Stanford Encyclopedia of Philosophy*, as well as Flanagan (2002); Schlagel (2001); Edis (2002); and Nielsen (1971), to name a critical few.

For a naturalistic analysis, explanation, and perspective on spirits and spiritual phenomena and experience in relation to the concepts of 'souls' and 'immortality' see Nielsen's "The Faces of Immortality" in his *Naturalism and Religion* (2001, 77–103) and "Perceiving God" in his *Naturalism without Foundations* (1996, 451–456); as well as Elbert's *Are Souls Real?* (2000); and Edis' *The Ghost in the Universe* (2002, 179–243)

Importantly, what *specifically is* such 'spirit matter' (not what is it *not*), and what are its properties? What are the truth-conditions of its putative existence that would make its existence, in principle, justifiable or factually significant as a truth-claim? The same questions apply as well to the meaning and putative existence of *intelligences* in Mormon theology, even if, as Ostler states, the distinction in Mormon scripture between 'spirits' and 'intelligences' "remains [*pace* Roberts] unclear" (11) or unintelligible and factually meaningless. As Christopher Hitchens correctly points out in a different context, "the razor of Ockham is clean and decisive. When two explanations are offered (Ostler's or mine in this case), one must discard the one that explains the least, or explains nothing at all, or raises more questions than it answers" (2007, 148).

Please, now, let us take a moment to seriously and carefully think skeptically and critically about what *specifically* it would really be like *to observe, touch converse with, or stand in the presence of* a being who is *literally* an 'infinite, eternal, and exalted spirit (and intelligence) of the highest order,' What would it be like *to observe* a 'finite' being with 'infinite' power?' How would (could) we possibly know we were actually in the presence of such a being rather than hallucinating, imagining, or projecting?

Let us consider what *specifically* it would be like, in principle, to *empirically confirm or disconfirm* the *literal* existence of a 'finite, spatio-temporal being that is present *everywhere* in the *fulness* of his knowledge, power, love, and wisdom, and is always 'in and through' *everything* by the light of its being or spirit.' What exactly *is* the 'light of a being or spirit' (or the 'Light of Christ')? What are its unique properties that we might be able to make sense of it or, even in principle, empirically confirm or disconfirm its *actual* presence or existence?

Further, regarding the Mormon doctrine or belief in the actual reality of 'spirit procreation': what *specifically* would it *literally* be like for an immortal, tangible female god to *actually* give birth to a purely 'spirit' being? How can we make *literal* sense of such a conception possibly taking place to begin with, if the parents are supernatural, non-human beings? As we learned earlier, the use of analogical predication cannot help us here. While we know what it is like physically and biologically for a *human* female to conceive and give birth to a *human* child, we know nothing nonanalogical or otherwise about what it would literally or actually be like for a *non-human*, or non-biological female to conceive and give birth to a putative spirit. How then can we make *literal* sense of *tangible*, non-human (*i.e.* non-biological) bodies sexually conceiving a 'spirit being' or a 'divine human being' — as in the putatively literal conception of Christ involving an immortal, non-biological being (*i.e.* 'God') and a mortal woman? What *specifically* does such a *literal* conception *actually* consist of, if not a biological union of organic sperm and egg? And how *specifically* would such a spirit *literally* develop in the womb of a putatively non-biological ('resurrected') female?

Speaking of non-biological beings, what *specifically* would a *literally* indestructible, bloodless and 'exalted' body of resurrected flesh and bones animated by 'spirit element' actually be like? What would it actually be like to observe 'spirit element' *literally* coursing through the veins of an immortal, resurrected body? What *specifically* is such 'spirit element,' *i.e.* what are its properties that its *literal* existence might, at least in principle, be objectively confirmed or disconfirmed? According to Mormon theology, 'spirit matter' is a pure, refined form of 'gross matter' and cannot therefore be observed by instruments or he natural senses. But how can anyone limited by natural senses and technology know this (except by putative revelation, which is equally problematic as we shall see in Chapter 5)?

As Loftus fairly asks Christian believers in his cogent argument against the existence of miracles: "Can you precisely describe for me how spirit and matter are the same so they can interact [either through the 'miracle' of procreation or the alleged performance of miracles by 'God' through the putative 'workings of the Holy Spirit']? ... And if spirit and matter are not different substances, then what are they? How [*specifically*] are they different? How [*specifically*] are they the same" (2008, 209–10).

Again, there seems to be a logical ban on our ability to empirically confirm or disconfirm such putative existents and events or occurrences, primarily because they are devoid of *specifiable* referents and *satisfiable* truth-conditions. Even if it is argued that such putative 'spirit element' is simply and ultimately *whatever* animates or sustains the life of a god's physical body, such an argument would not rescue the concept of the Mormon god from fundamental incoherence or factual unintelligibility. Nor would it save the belief in such a 'God' from conceptual incoherence. Rather, it would merely be another application of an evasive 'isolation' strategy to establish 'possibility' where, following Alston's argument against 'Flew's (falsification) Dilemma' presented in Chapter 2, *any* putative appearance *in the flesh* of *any* being *in human shape* who calls himself 'God' or who is taken (or believed) to be 'God' will, *mutatis mutandis*, confirm the existence of 'spirit element' or 'spirit matter,' while there can be no negative (or falsifying or disconfirming) instances.

Referring back to Adler's analysis of Alston's argument: if the hypothesis of the putative existence of 'spirit element' or 'spirit matter' (and also 'intelligences') is unadorned with the *whatever* (or the *somewhat* or *somehow*) qualifier, then according to Adler, "it is [or they are] amply refuted [like the putative existence of the quasi-anthropomorphic Mormon god itself] by the absence of positive evidence [or assertability conditions]" (2006, 125). This is so, I would add, since the existence of such putative existents (including 'God') is not self-evident, or even apparently so.

In considering the above questions it is important, in assessing the intelligibility and rationality of the Mormon concept of 'God,' that we distinguish between *theoretical entities* and *actual entities*. Concerning this important distinction I again turn to Nielsen, who writes…

> [At] the very heart of a religion such as Christianity [including Mormonism] there is a cosmological belief — a thoroughly metaphysical belief — in a reality that is alleged to transcend the "empirical world." It is the metaphysical belief that there is an eternal, ever-present creative source [or power] and sustainer [and ruler] of the universe. The problem is how we could come to know or reasonably believe that such a strange reality exists or come to understand what such talk is about.
>
> It is not that God is like a *theoretical entity*, such as a proton or neutrino in physics. Such theoretical entities, where they are construed as realities rather than as heuristically useful conceptual fictions, are thought to be part of the actual furniture of the universe. They are not said to be transcendent to the universe [as we know it]…Theoretical entities are not a different *kind* of reality [than the actual reality of the universe as we know it to be]; it is only the case that they, as a matter of fact, cannot be seen. Indeed, we have no understanding of what it would be like to see a proton or a neutrino — in *that way* they are like God [or 'Intelligences' and 'spirit matter'] — and no provision is made in physical theory for seeing them. Still, there is no logical ban on our seeing them as there is on seeing God [in his fulness]. We cannot correctly say that it is logically impossible that they could be seen.

Though invisible, theoretical entities are among the things in the universe and thus they can be postulated as causes of the things we do see [with successfully predictive empirical consequences under controlled conditions (Stenger 2007, 39–40)]. Since this is so, it becomes at least logically possible indirectly to verify by empirical methods the existence of such realities. It is also the case that there is no logical ban on establishing what is necessary to ascertain a causal connection, namely a constant conjunction of two discrete empirical realities. However, for the nonanthropomorphic [and also the quasi-anthropomorphic] conceptions of God of developed forms of Judeo-Christianity [and putatively revealed forms, such as Mormonism], no such constant conjunction [between, in the case of the Mormon theology, one or many discrete, supernatural entities and all that is in — or consists of — the universe] can be established or even intelligibly asserted between [such a metaphysical] God and the [physical] universe; thus the existence of God is not even indirectly confirmable or disconfirmable. (2006, 55; emphasis mine)

Following Nielsen, what I am repeatedly asking the believer to do is to be quite *literal* and *specific* about the above and other alleged or possible factual referents of the Mormon god. I ask them to identify and articulate the natural conditions (what others could there be?) by which the truth (or probable truth) or falsity (or probable falsity) of all the above-asserted factual referents can (or could possibly) be determined. *Specifically*, for necessary emphasis, what would count for or against the truth (or probable truth) or falsity (or probable falsity) of the asserted *literal* existence of the 'One Supreme and Absolute Being?' Or of the 'Supreme Governor and Ultimate Source of the Universe?' Or of an 'infinite, eternal and independent Spirit (and Intelligence) of the highest order?' Or of a 'finite, self-existent being with infinite power?' Or of a bloodless, 'resurrected' body animated and sustained by 'spirit element' coursing through its veins? Separately or all together, we simply don't know what such referents even mean. Still less can we try to establish their sense or truth-conditions.

From a 'coherence view,' what would it mean for a person such as 'God' to be *both* 'transcendent' in space-time *and* 'personally accessible' in real time on earth? Or for a being to be *both* 'procreated' *and* 'eternal,' or 'temporal and finite' *and* 'infinite and eternal?' How can such apparent contradictions be intelligibly explained or reconciled in a way that does not create further, deeper incoherencies? This is a core problem reflected in the argument that the theological concept of the Mormon god is incoherent. In large measure this argument is valid because it is *self-contradictory* or at least *unintelligible* and *factually* *meaningless* to claim that the Mormon God is in truth a *tangible, finite, spatiotemporal* individual who is simultaneously *infinite* and *eternal* and *transcendent* to this world (or universe) but yet is *personally* and *actively* present *everywhere in it* and *in* the lives of all mankind and of all creation as a *finite individual* who is nevertheless an *infinite, Immanent Being.*

Further, how can we make rational, literal sense of a *finite* being as the 'Ultimate Source' or 'Supreme Governor' of an *infinite* universe, where the universe is not taken to be a discrete thing but rather all of existence?[78] How can we make sense of something

---

78 Nielsen addresses the conceptual difficulty with this referent of 'God' as applied to the interpolated concept of the Mormon god: "To understand what is to speak of the reality of God essentially involves understanding the phrase "ultimate source and supreme governor of the universe." Theologians characteristically do not mean by this that the universe was created at a moment in time. To speak of such [an "ultimate source and

being *eternal* — without beginning or end — yet simultaneously being a procreated entity *with* a beginning? How could any of this be *actually* (or causally) possible?

Once again, how can we possibly make sense of a god acting in this world personally but not with his physical or spiritual body? What could it possibly mean to speak of 'action' or 'an immanent person' here? How can we possibly make rational sense of such a concept?

In those instances where it is claimed that 'God, the Father' or the resurrected and glorified 'Jesus, the Christ' *literally* appeared personally and bodily on Earth to minister to the Mormon god's putative 'anointed' or 'chosen people,' we must ask what *specifically* ould it be like, and how *specifically* would it be causally or actually possible — given what we know about the laws and properties of this world and the universe. What would it be like for such a finite, physical being (*i.e.* with weight and mass) to *literally* appear and disappear in the flesh and at will, in thin air — or in the sky *standing* on thin air? How would this be possible anywhere in this world or in any like, putatively created 'worlds without end' where gravity is a common property of existence? How can any reasonable person make rational (or even common) sense of any of the above claims or concepts?

---

supreme governor"]…involves making the putative existential claim that there is an eternal, ever present creative source and sustainer of the universe. But do we really understand such talk? We understand what it is for a lake to be a source of a river, for oxygen to be necessary to sustain life, for the winning of the game to be the end for which it is played and for good health to be the reason why we exercise. But "the universe" is not a label for some gigantic thing or process or activity. It is not a name for a determinate reality whose existence can be sustained or not sustained. Moreover, what would we have to discern or fail to discern to discover or to "see" even darkly the end, the purpose or the meaning of the universe? *A* asserts that the universe has a source or a sustainer and *B* denies it, but no conceivable recognizable turn of events counts for or against either of their claims; we have no idea what would have to obtain for either *A*'s or *B*'s claim to be so or even probably so. Yet both believe they are making assertions which are true or false. Plainly, language has gone on a holiday. We have bits of discourse which purport to be fact-stating but in reality they fail to come off as factual statements; that is to say, they do not function as fact-stating utterances. They purport to be fact-stating but they are not. But with a failure to make sense here, much more talk essential to the Judeo-Christian picture becomes plainly incoherent. Consider such key bits of God talk as:

(3) God is wholly other than the world He made
(4) God is the creator of the moral order of the universe
(5) The universe is absolutely dependent on God.

"In reflecting on them, we should not forget that "the world" ("the universe") does not denote a thing, an entity, process or even an aggregate which might be brought into existence. Moreover there is the ancient point that "to make something" presupposes that there is already something out of which it is made. If it is replied that…"make" here means "sustain" or "order," then it should be noted that this still presupposes something to be sustained or ordered; there is no use for "ordering or sustaining out of nothing." Even if we try to give it a use by saying that the universe was chaotic until ordered by God or that unless the universe is a reality ordered by God the universe would still be chaotic, we are still lost, for both "the universe is chaotic" and "the universe is not chaotic" are without a coherent use. Since the universe is not an entity or even a totality, there is no sense in talking of its being ordered or not ordered and thus, while we might speak coherently of "the moral order of his life" or "the morality of a culture or ethos," there is no coherent use for "the moral order of the universe" so (4) as well as (3) is nugatory. And again, considering (5), we have seen that no sense has been given to "the universe is dependent" so (5), to put it conservatively, is also conceptually unhappy, *i.e.* it purports to make a factual statement, but we have no idea of what, if anything, could account against its truth or falsity" (2006, 123–4).

Indeed, even thoughtful insiders can and do — if they are honest and think about such things *literally* (as they are intended by orthodox Mormon believers to be taken) — come to doubt the very sense and coherence of such talk and beliefs even if they are imaginable.

As a timely aside, it seems appropriate that we turn here again to B.H. Roberts. Roberts is particularly notable for his raw intellectual prowess as a scholar, prolific expounder of Mormon history and heology, and 'defender of the faith.'[79] Among his most formidable

---

79 As an interesting, if not troubling aside to Mormon believers (including this author while he was still in the faith), B.H. Roberts — the great Defender of the Faith — himself apparently experienced serious doubt regarding the claimed authenticity of the Book of Mormon as a translation of ancient scripture. In a brief but fair and balanced summary review of Brigham D. Madsen's *B.H. Roberts Studies of the Book of Mormon* (1992), Joel B. Groat of the Institute for Religious Research (IRR.org) writes (interpolations mine):

· Incredible as it may seem to many Latter-day Saints, Brigham H. Roberts (1857–1933), an LDS General Authority widely considered Mormonism's greatest apologist and historian,[1] expressed the grave doubt that the Book of Mormon is a translation of ancient scripture. Elder Roberts reached this conclusion after his research uncovered extensive evidence that Joseph Smith [very likely] borrowed the basic plot and many details from other books. This evidence — long suppressed because it is considered harmful to the Mormon Church — is presented in detail in three essays by Roberts, now published as *Studies of the Book of Mormon* (Salt Lake City: Signature Books, 1992).

More than fifty years after his death, Roberts is still well known through his many writings. They include the — Introduction and Notes — to Joseph Smith's seven volume *History of the Church*, the six volume *A Comprehensive History of the Church of Jesus Christ of Latter-day Saints*, *Outlines of Ecclesiastical History*, and *New Witnesses for God* (3 vols). However, in 1922 Roberts became aware of troubling evidence that Joseph Smith [apparently] borrowed much of the plot and other details of the Book of Mormon from other books readily available to him,[2] in particular Josiah Priest's *Wonders of Nature and Providence*, and Ethan Smith's *View of the Hebrews*. For instance, it is often thought the Book of Mormon claim that the American Indians are descendents of Hebrew immigrants is a novel idea that young Joseph Smith could not have invented. But Roberts discovered from Priest's book, published in 1824, six years before the first edition of the Book of Mormon (1830), that it was the almost universal opinion of the ministers of New England and the Middle States, that the Indians were the descendants of the Hebrews (*Studies*, p. 153).

In Ethan Smith's *View of the Hebrews*, first published in 1823, seven years before the Book of Mormon (and in a second edition in 1825), Roberts discovered a virtual ground plan for the Book of Mormon. In section two of *Studies of the Book of Mormon*, entitled, "A Book of Mormon Study," Roberts takes nearly 100 pages to describe the specific parallels between Ethan Smith's, *View of the Hebrews* and the Book of Mormon. Did Ethan Smith's *View of the Hebrews* furnish structural material for Joseph Smith's Book of Mormon? Roberts was forced to admit that the evidence pointed in this direction:

"It has been pointed out in these pages that there are many things in the former book that might well have suggested many major things in the other. Not a few things merely, one or two, or half dozen, but many; and it is this fact of many things of similarity and the cumulative force of them that makes them so serious a menace to Joseph Smith's story of the Book of Mormon's origin. ... The material in Ethan Smith's book is of a character and quantity to make a ground plan for the Book of Mormon" (*Studies*, p. 240).

Having established that Joseph Smith had plenty of material from which to get his ideas for the Book of Mormon, Roberts moves to a second key question: Did the young Joseph Smith have enough naturally creative ability to weave together a narrative like the Book of Mormon:

"... was Joseph Smith possessed of a sufficiently vivid and creative imagination as to produce such a work as the Book of Mormon from such materials as have been indicated in the preceding chapters ...? That such power of imagination would have to be of a high order is conceded; that Joseph Smith possessed such a gift of mind there can be no question" (*Studies*, p. 243).

One of the things that convinced Roberts of this is the testimony of Joseph's mother, Lucy Mack Smith. She wrote the following about her son's creative abilities:

"During our evening conversations, Joseph would occasionally give us some of the most amusing recitals that could be imagined. He would describe the ancient inhabitants of this continent, their dress, mode of

works are his published debate with Cyril van der Donckt, referred to earlier as the "Mormon Doctrine of Deity," as well as his "Seventy's Course in Theology" and his last work, considered by some to be his Masterwork, (Madsen 1975) entitled "The Truth, The Way and The Life." Among all the leader-theologians of the Mormon religion, I consider Widtsoe, Talmage, and Roberts the best equipped intellectually to rationally represent the doctrines examined in this particular analytical work. Of these three, I have chosen to refer primarily to Widtsoe in Chapter 2 regarding the question of whether or not Mormonism is, as Widtsoe incorrectly asserts, a "rational theology" and, more predominantly, to Roberts in this chapter and in Chapters 4 and 7 regarding his more widely accepted albeit unofficial theological expositions of the Mormon doctrines of Deity, the Atonement of Jesus Christ, and the implications of both on the problem of evil respectively.

---

travelings, and the animals upon which they rode; their cities, their buildings, with every particular; their mode of warfare; and also their religious worship. This he would do with as much ease, seemingly, as if he had spent his whole life among them" (*Studies*, p. 243).

From this testimony it is apparent that Joseph was known by his own family as quite a storyteller. And the significance of this evening storytelling, Roberts points out, is that Joseph was doing all this before he had supposedly received the gold plates from the angel Moroni (*Studies*, p. 244).

Based on this evidence, Roberts draws the following conclusion:

"These evening recitals could come from no other source than the vivid, constructive imagination of Joseph Smith, a remarkable power which attended him through all his life. It was as strong and varied as Shakespeare's and no more to be accounted for than the English Bard's" (*Studies*, p. 244).

Statements like these help us understand why LDS church leaders did not want the B. H. Roberts material in circulation. And even today, many people are still unaware of the evidence compiled by this well-known Mormon apologist and historian. Fortunately, this fascinating research is now easily accessible to any who want a fuller understanding of the true origins of the Book of Mormon."

Reviewer's Notes

[1] Roberts was ranked the greatest intellectual in Mormon history in surveys by LDS scholars Leonard Arrington in 1969 and Stan Larson in 1993 — see Leonard J. Arrington, "The Intellectual Tradition of the Latter-day Saints," *Dialogue: A Journal of Mormon Thought* 4 (Spring 1969), pp. 13–26 and Stan Larson, "Intellectuals in Mormonism: An Update," *Dialogue: A Journal of Mormon Thought* 26 (Fall 1993), pp. 187–89.

[2] Josiah Priest's *Wonders of Nature and Providence [Displayed]* was published in New York state, only about twenty miles from where the Smith family resided from about 1815 to 1830, and Ethan Smith's *View of the Hebrews* was published in Poultney, Vermont, only a few miles from Windsor, Vermont where Joseph Smith's family lived until he was ten years of age. Roberts considered it "probable" that Ethan Smith's book was "either possessed by Joseph Smith or certainly known by him, for [it] was surely available to him" — Studies of the Book of Mormon, p. 153.

*****

Although this inconvenient and disturbing truth has been explained away by certain Mormon apologists like John Welch of FARMS and others with the assertions that Roberts' questions and concerns have subsequently been conclusively addressed without harm to the faith; that he was playing devil's advocate for the Church; and that he was personally neither disturbed nor in doubt regarding the authenticity of the Book of Mormon in virtue of his rushed and uncharacteristically sloppy analysis (which, it is also asserted) he was allegedly embarrassed of. Still, notwithstanding these and other apologetic evasions, the problem remains, and much continues to be made of it — and numerous other problems regarding the Book of Mormon as well — by Mormon critics and competent scholars and historians both inside and outside the faith (see various writings and internet sources cited by Packham in the resources section at the end of *Appendix B*). These historical and scriptural concerns raise still other, more fundamental concerns regarding the Mormon doctrine of revelation and the Mormon requirement of faith, both of which are addressed in Chapters 5, 6, and 8.

The 'Immanent' Mormon God as the 'Light of Truth'

Returning then to the questions asked above regarding the sense and coherence of the Mormon god's alleged omnipresence through the co-called 'Light of Truth,' we will find that Roberts does not (*pace* Madsen) help us here when, according to Madsen, he (*i.e.* Roberts) "holds up the key to the ancient either-or-controversy: God's personal transcendence or God's immanence." As Madsen sees it, "Classical and contemporary theologians often obscure or eliminate personality from their concept of God in order to make way for 'a universal spirit.' Assuming the 'everywhereness of God,' they are led to assume that in the end they must deny him a particular personality, physical resurrection, or even spatio-temporal location. To this," Madsen opines, "Roberts answers with 'one of the sweetest messages of God to man'…what Roberts called 'divine immanence'" (1975, 20). Roberts' elaboration of this doctrine of the Mormon transcendent and immanent God, or Light of Truth, is quoted below:

> This Light then, the Light of Truth and named for us men "the Light of Christ" — "which proceedeth forth from the presence of God to fill the immensity of space," — is also God, even the Spirit of God, or of the Gods, for it proceeds forth or vibrates, or radiates from all the Gods — from all who have partaken of the One Divine Nature — hence "the God of all other Gods" — mentioned by our Prophet of the New Dispensation (Doc. and Cov. Sec. cxxi) "the God of Gods," "the Lord of Lords," proceeding from MANY yet ONE! Incarnated in all personal Deities, yet proceeding forth from them, to extend the one God into all space that He might be in and through all things; bearing all the powers in earth and sun and stars; world-sustaining power and guiding force. Bearing all the mind and spiritual attributes of God into the immensity of space, becoming God everywhere present — omnipresent; and everywhere present with power — omnipotent; extending everywhere the power of God; also All-Knowing; All-Seeing; All-Hearing — Omniscient! Bearing forth in fact all the attributes of Deity; Knowledge, Wisdom, Judgment, Truth, Holiness, Mercy — every characteristic or quality of all Divine Intelligences — since they are one; and this Divine Essence, or Spirit, becomes God in unity; and by the incarnation of this Spirit is the mind of all Gods; and all the Gods being incarnations of this Spirit, become God in unity; and by the incarnation of this Spirit in Divine Personages, they become the Divine Brotherhood of the Universe, the ONE GOD, though made of many. (1975, 20–21)

This paradigm passage raises numerous questions and numerous problems. What rational sense can we as skeptical outsiders *or* believing insiders make of it — either in part or as a whole? First, the entire passage presupposes the existence of the Mormon god but does not provide us with a reference range for 'God' or a coherent conception of 'God.' We have no better understanding of what the term *God* means conceptually after reading this passage than before. Its statements or truth claims are at least apparently without possible truth-conditions and therefore without factual significance or cognitive meaning. Individually and collectively these statements do not appear to add up to anything that could even remotely be justifiable, let alone justified as rational beliefs. If any passage ever qualified as "a mass of confusion," this one certainly does. It is wholly and completely unintelligible.

How can we rationally make sense of this putative "Light of Truth;" this "Divine Brotherhood;" this "ONE GOD, though made of many" which is "incarnated in all

Personal Deities, yet proceeding forth from them, to extend the one God into all space that He might be in and through all things; bearing all the powers in earth and sun and stars; world-sustaining power and guiding force?" What can we legitimately liken this to? What *specifically* is this Light of Truth, this God of Gods? What do these terms refer to? How *specifically* can we identify this god by differentiating it from other forms of energy that it might have its own unique non-vacuous meaning and significance? *And how specifically is the core problem of a transcendent, finite, spatiotemporal god acting personally in the lives of men resolved by the putative existence of 'Divine Immanence' other than by its mere assertion?* How, in principle, can such immanence be empirically confirmed or disconfirmed? What are its truth-conditions, that its actual existence as a putative factual and non self-evident reality might be established beyond mere assertion?

Finally, from a non-verificationist standpoint or strictly coherentist perspective, how do these doctrinal statements hang together with what we know about the world and the universe and how they work? Given what we know about the physical laws of the universe, how is it causally possible (*not* just imaginable) for a *complete personality* to be transmitted to this world, and throughout the immensity of space, from a putative being that exists spatiotemporally in a different world, universe, or dimension of space and time which is transcendent to this world or universe? Given all that we know in this world about this world and universe, how can we make rational sense of someone — some putative finite, supernatural person — being always everywhere in *all* his power, wisdom, knowledge, love, *etc.*? How can we understand this to be mediated by some form of internally generated radiant energy, or inner Light, which *somehow* vibrates or radiates, or is otherwise *somehow* projected out with intentionality or will to fill the immensity of space? Surely this is extravagant, unintelligible, metaphysical speculation at its best (or worst)! Here again we're reminded by Nielsen that

> [The] metaphysical religiosity inherent in our religious language-games makes problems for the intelligibility, and thus the justifiability, of religious language-games. After all, we cannot possibly justify something that is unintelligible, and it could not possibly be true. We can say of the indicative sentences of mathematical and moral language-games that it makes sense to say they are true or false. There are established practices in mathematics where [regardless of culture, societal structure or 'form of life'] we can show that a claim like $10 + 10 = 20$ is warranted and there are established practices in morality whereby we can justify that promises generally, but not invariably, should be kept. There is (that is) a standing presumption that if I make a promise I must keep it…We can in these domains give reasons which justify saying (sometimes with nearly decisive reasons) that something is true…There may be some wanton sentences (propositions) in morals and even in mathematics concerning which we do not know what to say and that even may be true in physics. But in all these practices, in all these language-games, including their very crucial parts, we have a critical mass of interconnected sentences that are plainly used to make justifiably true…statements. We, and more than we normally believe, also have ungrounded statements as well…that would be insane to doubt. It would be insane to doubt that live human beings have heads, that we have never been to the sun, that in most places and in all places at some times it gets dark at night and light in the morning, that it is cold in the winter and hot or hotter in the summer, that fire burns and water is wet.
>
> But in religious language-games we have (at least for us moderns) nothing or at least little like this. We have as hinge or framework beliefs those metaphysical blockbusters 'God created the world,' 'God will ensure our survival of death,' 'God is transcendent but still acts

in the world,' 'God is [Lord of Lords proceeding from many yet One, the 'Light of Truth'],' *etc., etc., etc… We have no idea what should or could justify them (confirm them or infirm them) or in any way justify them* [as true statements]. And we cannot [if we are rational or intellectually honest] just take them on faith or trust for we do not understand what we are to take on faith or trust. (2006, 21–2, emphasis mine)

All said, I think it can reasonably and unequivocally be asserted that neither Mormon believers, General Authorities, professors of religion, apologists, or missionaries know what they're talking about when they make such statements about their god or attest to such statements as being true. Neither they, nor anyone, know what specifically or otherwise they are talking about when they speak ultimately of a god (or 'Son of God') who is *fundamentally* and *factually* an 'infinite and eternal spirit person and intelligence housed in a tangible, immortal (bloodless) body animated by spirit element, who is actually *transcendent* to man and the world, yet personally and actually *immanent* in the world through the light of his spirit.' They *think* they do, will say or *testify* that they do, but in fact they do not — *cannot* — know what it would be like for such ideas or concepts to be true. They cannot say *how* it would be possible for them to be true, or to be experienced directly through putative visitation, vision, revelation, or spiritual confirmation. This is so given the necessary dependence of such putative revelation on the actual existence of the Mormon god as conceptualized either doctrinally or in the mind of the believer. This is also the case given the problems with regarding such putative revelation, or spiritual experiences, as a reliable way of knowing — a topic which shall be dealt with at length and in depth in Chapters 5 and 6.

In principle, for these putatively true and factual sentences to be regarded and asserted as even probably true, their truth-conditions must be known and articulated — even if only as empirical consequences, or predictions. Such a minimal requirement, if fulfilled, would demonstrate how such sentences, or propositions, could, in principle, be empirically confirmed or disconfirmed. If such truth-conditions cannot be known or articulated, then the sentences cannot be known or regarded as being actually true. In other words, as putative facts they are *not* testable or verifiable, and therefore *not* justifiable. This makes them *factually meaningless*. The claim that such sentences are *facts* is false or incoherent.[80]

The Mormon god, like the 'sectarian God' of orthodox religion, qualifies in its theological fullness as a metaphysical non-reality — even with its alleged *material spirit* and *tangible* body of flesh and bones. Like the nonanthropomorphic god of developed Christianity, the quasi-anthropomorphic Mormon god in its fullness is also unintelligible as a supernatural being *transcending* the naturalistic realities and bounds of biological human

---

80 This is worth repeating again and again: an *actual* fact is what an *actually* true statement states. As is commonly acknowledged, in principle and practice — and in the domain of physical, objective reality — for a truth claim to be considered *actually* and *objectively* true as *knowledge* it must be *justified* through the achievement of wide reflective equilibrium. For a statement to be *justified*, it must be *justifiable*. For a statement to be justifiable it must minimally be intelligible and coherent conceptually. It must have truth-conditions that can possibly be empirically confirmed or disconfirmed. That which is not factual cannot possibly be empirically known or considered as knowledge of objective reality. In other words, that which cannot possibly be empirically known is a *non-reality*. Belief that a non-reality actually exists is *irrational*. It can only be characterized as a delusion sincerely held with conviction through denial and self-deception. (See Chapter 1)

life and the physical universe. Moreover, its *quasi-anthropomorphic* nature makes the Mormon god *both* false *and* incoherent. This makes belief in the Mormon god, at a gross anthropomorphic level, merely an irrational and false superstition — where *superstition* is formally defined by Webster as "a belief resulting from ignorance, fear of the unknown, trust in magic or chance (luck, fate), or a false conception of causation, a notion maintained despite evidence to the contrary."

"What think ye of Christ?"

From the confusing maze of incoherent God-talk regarding the existence and true nature of the Mormon god, we are pointed first and finally by Roberts to the scriptural account of the resurrected Christ as the ultimate and definitive referent of 'God' — the true revelation of 'God, the Father.' In *The Truth, The Way and The Life*, Roberts states:

> Henceforth when men shall dispute about the "being" and "nature" of God, it shall be a perfect answer to uphold Jesus Christ as the complete and perfect revelation and manifestation of God; and through all the ages it shall be so — eternally so. For there shall be no excuse for men saying that they know not God, for all may know Him from the least to the greatest, so tangible, so real a revelation has God given of himself in the person, character, and attributes of Jesus Christ…(1975, 10)

Roberts criticized Catholic and Protestant theology, calling it "paganized Christianity" — a characterization that prompted a rebuttal from the Reverend Cyril van der Donckt. The ensuing 1901 debate, published as the *Mormon Doctrine of Deity* "forms," according to BYU professor of philosophy David Paulsen, "one of the most engaging and complete considerations of the topic ever compiled" (2000, 11).

In this published debate Roberts defends Mormon anthropomorphic beliefs about the tangible body of the Mormon god by appealing to standard biblical proof texts and rational argument. Roberts' most impressive argument for the embodiment of his god is, according to Paulsen, "ingeniously grounded on premises which Van der Donckt and traditional Christians generally would be loath to deny: (1) Jesus of Nazareth is God; and (2) Jesus of Nazareth exists everlastingly with a resurrected body. The resurrected Christ thus becomes Roberts's star witness for the defense of the Mormon understanding of God" (2000, 11).

Roberts' argument proceeds:

> I suppose that thousands of sermons every year are preached from that text ("What think ye of Christ?") by Christian ministers. And now I arraign them before their favorite text, and I ask them, What think ye of Christ? Is he God? Yes. Is he man? Yes—there is no escaping it. His resurrection and the immortality of his body as well as of his spirit that succeeds his resurrection is a reality. He himself attested it in various ways. He appeared to a number of the apostles, who, when they saw him, were seized with fright, supposing they had seen a spirit; but he said unto them, "Why are ye troubled? And why do thoughts arise in your hearts? Behold my hands and my feet, that it is I myself: handle me and see; for a spirit hath not flesh and bones, as ye see me have." Then, in further attestation of the reality of his existence, as if to put away all doubt, he said, "Have ye here any meat?" And they brought him some broiled fish and honeycomb, and "he did eat before them." Think of it! A resurrected, immortal person actually eating of material food!

He continues his argument:

"What think ye of Christ? Is he God? Yes. Is he man? Yes. Will that resurrected, immortal, glorified man ever be distilled into some bodiless, formless essence, to be diffused as the perfume of a rose is diffused throughout the circumambient air? Will he become an impersonal, incorporeal, immaterial God, without body, without parts, without passions? Will it be? Can it be? What think ye of Christ? Is he God? Yes. Is he an exalted man? Yes; in the name of all the Gods he is. Then why do sectarian ministers arraign the faith of the members of the Church of Jesus Christ of Latter-day Saints because they believe and affirm that God is an exalted man, and that he has a body, tangible, immortal, indestructible, and will so remain embodied throughout the countless ages of eternity? And since the Son is in the form and likeness of the Father, being, as Paul tells, "in the express image of his [the Father's] person"—so, too, the Father God is a man of immortal tabernacle, glorified and exalted: for as the Son is, so also is the Father, a personage of tabernacle, of flesh and bone as tangible as man's, as tangible as Christ's most glorious, resurrected body. (2000, 23–26)

This argument fails to make coherent or intelligible the doctrinal or theological concept of the Mormon god — or to make such a concept factually significant — for a variety of reasons. First, Roberts' characterization of the Mormon god focuses primarily on the anthropomorphic aspect of the god as a being with a tangible body like the resurrected Christ. Although he asserts elsewhere in his rejoinder to Van der Donckt that the resurrected Jesus, like 'God,' has a body of "*flesh and bone*, inhabited by a *spirit*," and that both have — as Joseph Smith taught (unintelligibly, I think) — "spirit in their bodies, *not blood.*" Whatever that means, he does not focus in this argument on all the essential *metaphysical* aspects of the Mormon god expounded in Mormon theology.

By anchoring the nature of his god on the allegedly revealed nature of the resurrected Christ, Roberts not only begs the question by presupposing the existence of his god and the putatively historical person of Jesus *as* "the Christ" in the truth of scripture (a presupposed assertion, it turns out, not without considerable controversy and argument; see, for example, Wells 1988 and Doherty 2005), but he also merely pushes the real problem one step removed by arguing for the truth of the Mormon god from the existence of the resurrected 'Son of *God.*' Finally, Roberts' argument presupposes that the concepts of *resurrection* in general and the putative *factual* existence of the *resurrected Christ* in particular, are intelligible, coherent, and factually significant. This is also a presupposed assertion not without significant controversy and argument. See, for example, Martin 1991 and Price & Lowder 2005.

The *first problem* with Roberts' argument has been extensively dealt with above in the treatment of both the orthodox Mormon doctrine of deity founded on 'eternalism' and the specific doctrinal beliefs about the Mormon god. The doctrine and beliefs of both the synthesized list of metaphysical descriptive referents of the Mormon god and the metaphysical notion of a putative eternal chain consisting of a set of three contingent, non-self-existent, interdependent beings are, as we have learned, unintelligible, incoherent, and factually meaningless. Therefore they are found wanting of actual truth-status and rationality.

The *second problem* refers in part to the argument from scriptural errancy and the fallacy of begging the question, which invalidates any argument to prove a god's existence or define his nature on the basis of 'God's revealed word.' This argument refutes the divine origin and credibility of sacred texts on the basis of internal errors, inconsistencies, incoherencies, absurdities, and inter-text (inter-religious) contradictions with other alleged scripture. This thereby discredits Roberts' argument from scriptural revelation and, in part, his argument from the logical problem of using the resurrected 'Son of God' to point to the true nature and existence of 'God' himself.

Regarding this last part of the second problem with Roberts' argument, Roberts *must* have known at some level that there are perplexities about the existence and nature of 'Jesus Christ' that are logically just as considerable as the corresponding perplexities about 'God, the Father.' As is well known, Jesus Christ is taken to be the literal 'Son of God.' Therefore, if the concept of 'God' is unintelligible, incoherent, and factually meaningless as doctrinally described, then the concept of the Son of God will be no less so. We can know a lot about Jesus from the scriptures, as Roberts no doubt did (scriptural errancy and fallibility notwithstanding), but this does not and cannot take us to 'God' unless we already know what *God* actually means. 'God' cannot be pointed to, as Roberts argues, by looking to the resurrected Christ, but must be identified and understood intralinguistically through certain referring descriptions, if he can be identified at all. But the putative doctrinal descriptions of the Mormon god will not do. They are, in their completeness, as nonsensical and void of factual content as are the orthodox Christian god of the good Reverend Van der Donckt.

A *third problem* with Roberts' argument involves the unintelligibility, incoherence, and factual insignificance of the 'resurrected Christ,' where such a putative being would be, according to Mormon theology, a god even as 'God, the Father' is a 'God.' Once again, we're back to the problem of this god's intelligibility and factual significance as an existing being. If the concept of the Mormon god is incoherent and thus irrational and the claim that such a god actually exists is unjustifiable, then referring to the resurrected Son of *God* cannot legitimize, or justify, the claimed existence of the Mormon god. Roberts has, to put it colloquially, put the cart before the horse. How can we know that the resurrected Christ is, in fact, the Son of God if the term 'God' as a concept is factually unintelligible? Moreover, we are confronted with the problem of resurrection itself — by the unintelligibility and cognitive meaninglessness (not un-imaginableness) of *literally* resurrecting a dead body into a living, immortal, indestructible, perfected, and bloodless physical body. In the end, if we step back and dispassionately and critically think about it, we simply cannot make rational sense of the concept of resurrection. Because this is so, historical and testamentary accounts of Jesus' putative resurrection are not only very problematical as evidence, they are factually vacuous and therefore without credibility and force to the reasonable mind.

The concern here is two-fold: *one*, with the verifiability of a resurrected, divine being (*i.e.* a Mormon God); and *two*, with the intelligibility and coherence of the claim that 'God' resurrected Jesus' dead body. The first concern questions the historical truth of the putative existence of the resurrected Jesus, as well as the possible, actual (not just imaginable) existence of an exalted, bloodless, living, once-dead body consisting of indestructible flesh and bones and inhabited by an infinite and eternal spirit and intelligence. Once again, this concern questions the possible empirical confirmability or disconfirmability of the claim that a putative resurrected body or personage is — or could possibly be — a god as described by Mormon doctrinal statements. The *second concern* questions how it could be possible for the Mormon god, who is allegedly a being beyond the spatiotemporal dimension of this world or universe, to actually *resurrect* a dead body and inhabit it with a 'spirit personage' merely through the conscious, or 'spiritual,' power of his will and spoken word putatively transmitted by the 'Light of Truth.' What all this could possibly mean and how it could be causally possible or possibly confirmed or disconfirmed empirically are serious concerns — to say the very least.

Conclusion and Closing Perspectives

Under the weight of the above analytical inquiry conducted, as Loftus suggests, with "the presumption of skepticism as an outsider" (2008, 66–67), how stand the words of Talmage quoted above at the heading of this chapter? Do we have, in fact, a "most conclusive proof of the existence of a Supreme Being" in the putative "knowledge of the attributes and personality of God" as claimed in the corpus of Mormon theology? Do we have (or can we *possibly* have), on the basis of our human understanding of such first and second-order God-talk, anything like the certainty of 'God's existence' "essential to any rational exercise of faith in Him?" Even without certainty, do we, if in our right mind, have anything we can reasonably believe — can rationally make sense of without self-deception? I think not.

Such a conclusion, made as it is on the basis of wide, common sense supported by the above argued problemicity of the concept of the Mormon god, naturally raises the questions of what religious believers are actually doing when they are talking about their god and how we might more perspicuously and correctly understand what is really going on with such talk and where such an understanding naturalistically leads us. One novel and interesting perspective is offered by James Carse in his book *The Religious Case Against Belief* (2008). From this perspective, quoting Carse, "The clue [to what is really going on with such talk] lies in…the multiplicity of Jesuses [or 'Gods']. Christians [and theists generally] have reached very little consensus on who the 'real' Jesus [or 'God'] is. … At the same time, they cannot give up the quest…. This justifies the guarded conclusion," according to Carse, "*that it is ignorance and not belief that is the source of faith's vitality.* What remains unsaid, even unthinkable, and what still inspires disagreement, is far more powerful [in sustaining and preserving God-talk and religious faith] than what is known and intelligible" (140–1).

While this at least implicitly naturalistic perspective has perhaps some plausibility as far as it goes, it nonetheless does not go far enough for our purposes — and it no doubt goes too far to suit the purposes of believers. To seriously wonder — as Carse suggests — "as an ongoing expression of *communitas* [*i.e.* the coming together of participants engaged in the poetic quest for truth in mystery]" (84) about that which is unintelligible at least tacitly presumes an erroneous belief held by such participants — and perhaps even Carse. That is the belief that, given enough thought and discussion, debate, or dialogue, what is now unintelligible as mystery is, can be, or shall be made ultimately intelligible through the authority of poetic discourse and open-minded inquiry. But surely from the undeniable literalist perspective and commitments of theistic believers — as well as from nonbelievers or disbelievers responding to their unwarranted truth claims — such a presumption, whether accurate or not, is as irrational as it is perverse. It makes the very basis of such putative *communitas* (or quest for actual truth in the ineffable and unintelligible mystery inherent in metaphysical God-talk through *poiesis*) itself unintelligible in relation to how theistic religion, in general, and the Mormon faith in particular, are actually practiced as a life form. In this regard, the legitimate question here is: How is it that one wonders thus *at all* about such things, and *why*? To wonder about the *actual, ultimate,* or *absolute* truth in religious mystery is, as I see it, merely a defense, thereby making faith (and the ignorance which Carse maintains is its source) very likely a defense as well. Moreover, it seems reasonable to conclude that the *why* (or unconscious motivation) for such a defense is, most likely, to allay the unavoidable anxiety resulting from the apparent cosmic purposelessness of existence, and the stark realities of mortality.

An alternative naturalistic perspective — for me, a more inclusive and telling one — is offered by Nielsen. He suggests that essentially this first question regarding what theistic believers are doing when they are using or engaging in God-talk has "led to what among anthropologists has been called a *symbolist* (poetic?) account of religious-talk and what has been called *noncognitive* (expressive-evocative or performatory) accounts by philosophers. According to such accounts," Nielsen elaborates,

> [In making religious statements], religious believers, whether they realize it or not, are doing something performative: they are expressing certain of their deepest feelings, feelings connected with certain life orientations [and unconscious primal memories], and, in the very uttering of these utterances, tending, as well, to evoke similar emotions, reaffirming or leading to similar life orientations in others. This expressive-evocative approach is more plausible than a purely intellectualistic naturalism, yet it also leaves out something vital that intellectualist accounts try unsuccessfully to capture, namely, the alleged (intended) cosmological claim — the putatively factual assertions with their mysterious alleged propositional content — that many religious believers believe obtains when they utter certain key religious utterances. "My Lord and my God" may very well be purely [poetic or] expressive-evocative, but…sample religious utterances [such as "Our Heavenly Father will bless us" and "I know that my Redeemer lives"] are thought by believers and by some nonbelievers to do something else as well; "God created the heavens and the earth" and "God providentially orders the world [for our experience and good]" are also so thought of by such persons. Expressive-evocative they are, but they are also *taken* to be cognitive claims (truth claims or assertability-claims allegedly with truth-conditions or assertability-conditions) about a mysterious, scarcely understandable power allegedly external to the world. But this, in reality, is a mystification. But, all the same, that claim cannot be given up by religious believers without radically transforming our understanding of such religious utterances from something they have been taken to be throughout their history into something very different [and wholly inadequate and unacceptable].
>
> Such considerations lead, if thought through, to what I shall call the *error-theory of religious discourse*, an account parallel to what J.L. Mackie called an error-theory of moral discourse (Mackie 1946, 1977).
>
> Just as believers in morals, to remain reasonably orthodox believers in morals, must have some incoherent conception of a categorical prescriptivity [or imperative] inherent in the world to give them the sense of unconsciously reified objectivity they so much — though not under that description — desire, so the believers in God must have an incoherent *metabelief* in a supernatural something, somehow beyond and independent of the universe to give them a similar sense of "religious objectivity," when in reality all that is being talked about are the conditions of human existence.
>
> An *error-theory* [then, pertaining to Mormon (and all) theistic, religious beliefs and

discourse] without departing from an utterly naturalistic basis, acknowledges the importance of the pervasive affective side of religion [inherent in religious experience], while still
accounting for the ersatz [counterfeit]-cognitive side, which is so necessary for its continued
successful functioning, though, of course, it cannot be recognized to be ersatz-cognitive [or
non-cognitive] by the person sustained in belief. It shows us how religion, with its claims to a
mysterious "higher truth," is so rooted in error that we can have no sound reasons for believing
that religious claims even could be true. But it also shows how these are necessary illusions if
the religious life is to remain intact. And it explains, as well, the strong hold that the religious
life has on people.[81] (2001, 39 & 42–4, emphasis mine)

Nielsen appropriately takes the explanation further, exposing the error inherent
in religious God-talk apart from its poetic quality and socio-psychological utility as
communitas. He concludes the last statement above by correctly remarking that, "keeping
some modern societies in mind (usually the wealthier societies with higher average levels
of education), we should qualify this [last statement above regarding the "strong hold that
religious life has on people"] by saying 'some people.' The disenchantment of the world
and the resistance to re-enchantment in such societies (Sweden and Denmark, for example)
has gone very deep" (43). Even so, the hold theistic religion and other superstitions have
on the vast majority of people in the world is indeed formidable, even if variable in
strength and toxicity.

With this concluding naturalistic perspective and proposed 'error-theory of religious
discourse' in mind — as well as the conclusions reached in this chapter — we turn now,
in Chapters 4–6, to a critical, conceptual analysis of Mormon theology in its broader
scope and context. Such an analysis will show and conclude that the Mormon doctrines
and literal truth claims of the 'Plan of Salvation,' 'Revelation from God *about* God,' and
'Faith in God' are independently — as well as in connection with the Mormon doctrine
of deity itself — likewise unintelligible, incoherent, and factually meaningless.

---

81 Nielsen takes us further in his above naturalistic perspective by suggesting that "If such a naturalistic account
of religious representations is sound…we can then (forgetting about its alleged claim to truth) appropriately
turn our attention to the social and psychological functions of religion: the roles it plays in the lives of human
beings" (2001, 43, 44). While this important turn is ancillary to the primary focus of this book, it is nonetheless
significant and relevant to it as part of the larger naturalistic context of Atheism and our analysis of Mormon
(or any) theology in particular. Accordingly, while I offer and refer to naturalistic alternatives to help explain
religious experience and phenomena in different places of this book, I also refer the reader to Nielsen's work
(2001) which attempts to help us understand the role of religion in life in virtue of "the various human needs"
it "answers to" (44–50). This excerpt, of course, points to a larger body of work (1996, 2001) that is essential
reading for all who would understand Nielsen's sophisticated representation of, and arguments for, a thorough
and sufficient naturalism without foundations *vis-à-vis* religion.

Chapter 4

Deconstructing the Mormon
'Plan of Salvation'

*"The Plan of Salvation is the fulness of the gospel. It includes the
Creation, the Fall, the Atonement of Jesus Christ, and all the laws,
ordinances, and doctrines of the gospel."*

— The Church of Jesus Christ of Latter-day Saints

According to the teachings and beliefs of the Mormon faith, its god's 'Plan' — as 'the fullness of the gospel' — essentially entails the divine creation of this world (and worlds without end) where the 'spirit offspring' of 'Heavenly Parents' can be sent to inhabit mortal bodies and experience mortality as part of their 'eternal progression' toward the ultimate goal of 'eternal life.' More specifically, it includes not only 'spirit procreation' and the physical 'Creation' of worlds fit for inhabitance by human beings, but also, as explicitly referred to in the official definition provided above, a literal and necessary 'Fall' to mortality of non-mortal beings (*i.e.* Adam and Eve), a 'paradisiacal' earth, and an infinite and eternal vicarious 'Atonement' by 'God's son Jesus Christ' for the salvation of man from the natural effects of the Fall, and *all* the sins of mankind, individually and collectively.

Such a plan — ambitiously and imaginatively conceived of by the innovative and opportunistic Mormon founder Joseph Smith — seemingly attempts to resolve theologically some of the perhaps most troubling questions of all theists (including himself) regarding who created 'God' (where did 'God' come from?), who we are and where we came from prior to the earth's creation, why we were created and required to come to earth, what becomes of us and our unbaptized deceased children and relatives after we die and are resurrected, and what could possibly justify (in terms of some ultimate reward or purpose) the trials, tribulations, and seemingly pointless suffering and premature death experienced in mortality. Moreover, it was cleverly designed to differentiate the allegedly 'restored' gospel of the Mormon faith from the gospels of all other so-regarded apostate versions of Christianity, and to offer non-believers and believers of different faiths what no other faith offered — salvation for all who have died outside the Mormon faith, and something beyond mere salvation and life after death to some nondescript 'better place.'

What the Mormon faith offers in its 'gospel' is a package of benefits unmatched, to my knowledge, by any of the theistic religions existing in the world to date. Not to be outdone by the Islamic faith, and for those who might find such a 'blessing' appealing if not crucial to their own happiness, Mormonism even includes the promise of multiple wives to faithful men — in the next life. The Mormon gospel offers not only salvation for the living and the dead from sin and sinfulness, and deliverance from death through a literal resurrection ('blessings' offered by other Christian faiths as well), but also the possibility of a more glorious resurrection to the 'Celestial Kingdom of God.' This 'higher blessing' includes the possibility of personal *deification* and the assurance of *exalted* 'forever families' who have been 'sealed' together through putatively revealed and restored Temple ordinances authoritatively performed *only* in the Mormon Temples for both the living and the dead. Such unique salvational and sealing ordinances and related blessings can, of course, only be received and ultimately enjoyed by joining and fully committing to all the requirements of the Mormon faith, since only the Mormon Church, as the believed only true faith, has the authority to administer the ordinances of the 'fullness of the gospel of God.'

Beyond the above concise representation of the Mormon Plan of Salvation is the related and corresponding plan for the lives of all the Mormon god's children on earth alluded to in the preceding paragraph. Such a life plan — which, as we shall learn in our in-depth psychosocial assessment and neuropsychological analysis of the Mormon faith in Chapter eight, the *Epilogue*, *Personal Postscript* and *Appendix A* which follow — has been deeply embedded in the psyches of Mormon believers with a *feeling* of certainty through operant conditioning, structured socialization, and systematic indoctrination as part of its "infantilizing process" (Faber 2010). It entails – in the context of its "eternal" family-centric gospel narrative – essentially six basic requirements (beyond keeping all the commandments of the faith and conforming to its policies, cultural norms, and behavioral requirements) for living one's life to receive the 'fullness of God's blessings' and social acceptance and esteem in the Church.

These basic requirements include: (1) being baptized into the Mormon Church at age eight; (2) participating in all Church services, rituals, ordinances, and programs; (3) going on a full-time two-year mission for the Church at age nineteen (or later); (4) getting married in the Mormon Temple; (5) having children and raising them to be faithful members of the Mormon faith; and (6) serving faithfully in all assignments to serve in the Church. These requirements of the Mormon Gospel Plan are essential to the salvation and perfection of Mormon believers in their quest — per the plan — to achieve and enjoy godhood and eternal life as an eternal family.

Besides the rather distasteful thought of any preconceived plan for one's life — a thought which is likely as offensive as it is disturbing to any free thinking and mature individual[82] — the core conceptual framework of the doctrines comprising the Mormon

---

82 The terms 'free-thinking' and 'mature' require some clarification, since it is very likely the case that perhaps most if not all mentally competent and functional adults consider themselves to be both. As used above — and implied throughout this book in assessing the rationality of theistic believers and the reasons why faith in a god exists and persists among otherwise educated and intelligent adults — to be a free-thinking individual does not refer or appeal to the arguably incoherent notion of indeterministic free will or free agency. Consequently, what is not being referred to here is the incoherent idea of a person with 'free will.' Rather, apropos to this analysis and assessment of the Mormon faith and all theistic religions as well, to be a free-thinking individual is essentially to be a person who is not so bound by intergenerational tradition, repeated social conditioning, and indoctrination to a particular ideology or way of thinking and seeing the world that he or she is unwilling and/ or incapable of critically thinking about and rigorously testing their core beliefs for intelligibility, coherence, and factual content. A free thinking person can function (to a greater rather than lesser degree) as an objectively critical and reasonably skeptical outsider with the intent to determine — through analysis and/or the pragmatic employment of the 'scientific method,' broadly conceived — whether or not such beliefs, as asserted truth claims, are warranted as being true (or probably true) or false (or probably false). Moreover, a free-thinking person is, as conceived of here, one who is not bound by fear, anxiety, pride, or guilt to suppress real doubts about professed and held beliefs. He or she has sufficient ego strength or is sufficiently individuated as a

Plan of Salvation is, like the conceptual framework of the Mormon Doctrine of Deity presented in the previous chapter, likewise problematical for reflective, educated, and intellectually honest Mormons. Now the doctrines and related beliefs and promises of the Mormon gospel must be found to be factually vacuous, given that their alleged truth is necessarily dependent on the factual existence of the Mormon god — which is itself a factual non-reality as officially and most likely personally conceptualized. Of what force, then, are such doctrines and related beliefs in providing meaning and comfort to sane, rational, and non-delusional believers or seekers of the truth? Of what *real* value or worth is the exquisite aforementioned package of benefits sold to millions by the Mormon missionaries and attested to by Mormon scripture? These are the two primary questions I would invite readers to keep in mind as they read the remainder of this chapter.

In this chapter then, we will deconstruct the conceptual framework of the Mormon Plan of Salvation, which 'plan' (as briefly described earlier) consists essentially of the following eight fundamental doctrines or beliefs:

A. 'God' is the eternal, *literal* 'Father' of our spirits, although not the creator of our

---

personality not only to doubt, question, and test such beliefs (even closely held or cherished beliefs), but to relinquish them as well if they do not hold-up to rigorous and critical analytic scrutiny. In considering the above, the condition of being a free thinker should not be confused with being liberally or indiscriminatingly open-minded as opposed to conservatively or stubbornly closed-minded. Neither condition is synonymous with being a free-thinking individual as such is conceived of here. On the contrary, a free-thinking person, as I see it, is discriminating, critical, and reasonably skeptical (or sensibly closed-minded to nonsense) — as well as an avid proponent of the fact of human fallibilism in the pursuit of knowledge and rationality.

The term 'mature' is likewise a different state or condition than might be commonly supposed. While a mature person is perhaps minimally and commonly understood to be a person who is, in virtue of temperament, self-restraint, and life experience sufficiently developed to function responsibly in society, such a condition, at a deeper, psychological level is much more than that. As used above, the term *mature* denotes a state of being sufficiently discriminating, individuated, and integrated as a personality to deliberately (albeit deterministically) function as needed, and in consequential matters, with sufficient independence, moral imagination, reasonable skepticism, and deep, personal analytic insight to act in one's own or others' best interests. Accordingly, a mature individual, as I understand this fuller concept of maturity, is sufficiently differentiated from both the family system and the dominant culture of which he or she is a part to function effectively *as part of* the collective without being defined or bound to their own or others' physical or psychological detriment by the expectations, demands and judgments *of* the collective. Stated with current, more common terminology, a mature person in this sense might be more completely characterized as someone who is sufficiently *independent* (individuated or differentiated) as a person to function *interdependently* without being *codependent*. Such a state of being is, of course, conceptually connected to being a free thinker. One cannot be a free-thinking individual as conceptualized above without sufficient maturity, or independence from regressive, interpersonal neediness and the emotional bondage of codependency. A person who is reflexively bound by collective (family, institutional, societal) tradition, roles, rules, expectations, demands, judgments, values, beliefs, and moral imperatives (or authoritatively established and authoritarian enforced 'shoulds' and 'oughts') and who is either liberally (indiscriminatingly) open-minded or unreasonably closed-minded would *not* — regardless of their steadfastness and integrity in living according to such requirements or commitments, or their responsible functioning in society — be considered mature as referred to above.

Given the above explanations of these two terms, and the obvious fact that such characterizations exist in degrees among different human beings, it would seem — degrees or protestations to the contrary notwithstanding — that the notion of a free-thinking, mature, dyed-in-the-wool Mormon (or theistic) believer at least *seems* to be an *oxymoron* in relation to their stubborn, lazy, or fearful unwillingness (or characterological inability) to critically and non-apologetically or presuppositionally test their core religious beliefs and unshakable loyalty and commitment to their faith as an objective, skeptical outsider.

intelligences, which are co-eternal with Him;

B. Lucifer, a *literal* 'son of God,' became Satan and a third of 'God's spirit children' became fallen spirits through rebellion and a War in Heaven;

C. 'God,' both directly and through the instrumentality of Jehovah (the premortal Jesus, the Christ) actually created and sustains the universe and worlds without end (including *this* world) by the power of his spirit through his spoken word, and *literally* created (and/or placed) man and all life on the Earth;

D. Man and all life on Earth *literally* fell from a terrestrial (immortal), or paradisiacal, state of existence to a telestial (mortal) state when an actual Adam and Eve (the first man and woman on earth) physically ingested the 'forbidden fruit' from the 'tree of knowledge of good and evil;'

E. Jesus Christ is the *literal* 'son of God' in heaven and on Earth;

F. Through the vicarious, sacrificial atonement of Jesus Christ all mankind are forgiven of their sins and *literally* 'born again,' or 'saved by grace,' on condition of obedience to the principles and ordinances of the gospel;

G. In virtue of the death and resurrection of Jesus Christ, the dead and decomposed bodies of all men are *literally* resurrected by 'God,' in the twinkling of the eye, to an immortal, tangible body of glory, thereby removing the 'sting of death' from all men;

H. Those who accept and live the fulness of the 'Gospel of God' as revealed to Joseph Smith, and endure in faithfulness and righteousness to the end of their mortal probation, will *literally* become a god, even as their Father in Heaven became a god.

In analyzing the above doctrinal assertions, or truth claims, we face, apart from differences in understanding among Mormon believers, *three* very troubling facts.

First is the fact, that *all* of the above eight doctrinal claims are completely and necessarily dependent on the Mormon doctrine of deity for meaning and significance, and they all *presuppose* the truth, or factual status of the Mormon god's existence as conceptually and doctrinally set forth in the previous chapter. Consequently, if the fundamental idea or concept of the Mormon god, as set forth in the various doctrinal, descriptive referents of 'God' in Mormon theology is incoherent or irrational, such that that god, as literally conceived, is a factual non-reality, then of necessity it follows that the above doctrinal statements are likewise incoherent or irrational. Further, to argue that that god's Plan is true on the presupposition of that god's actual existence *begs the question* of the god's existence. That makes such an argument invalid from the start — as well as incoherent and irrational.

Second is the fact that while being a Mormon consists in practice of much more than believing that the above doctrinal statements are true, what matters *most* to Mormon believers is that the promised blessings of their gospel are *real*, or factual and true. But if, after deconstructing the eternal blessings promised to the faithful in their putatively revealed Gospel Plan, we find that such a package of blessings is (like the deconstructed parts of the 'Object of Great Price' presented for illustration in Chapter 1) factually empty, or nonexistent, then the actual truth of such doctrinal statements really *does* matter. It matters a great deal it turns out, for without Mormon doctrine there simply are *no* Mormon blessings, and if the doctrines of the Mormon gospel are incoherent, the blessings simply do not exist — at least not as conceived of or believed, if at all.

In relation to this second troubling fact, the implied argument above that being a practicing Mormon (or theist) consists of much more than merely believing doctrinal statements are true is met with yet another corrective (and correcting) perspective. Being a theistic believer "does," insists Nielsen regarding all theistic faiths, "in an utterly irreducible manner, involve the acceptance of what are taken by the faithful to be certain factual beliefs. And these purportedly factual beliefs are often of vast scope [as the above Mormon gospel doctrines certainly are]; they are not only ordinary empirical beliefs such as Jesus was born in Bethlehem. The expression of such 'cosmic factual beliefs' results in the making of religious or, if you will, theological statements, [*e.g.* 'God is the eternal, literal Father of our spirits' or 'God actually created and sustains the universe and worlds without end'] and these statements are taken by the faithful to be *factual* statements. Yet they are neither directly nor indirectly confirmable even in principle and thus they are in reality, as many nonbelievers have suspected, devoid of factual content. They purport to be factual but fail to behave as factual statements. We have no idea of how to establish their truth or probable truth, or their falsity or probable falsity. We have no conception of what it would be like for them to be true (or probably true) or false (or probably false). Yet they are supposedly expressive of factual beliefs. But such a statement which is in no way confirmable or infirmable even in principle is not a factual statement…So here we have," concludes Nielsen, "at the very foundation of such faiths a radical incoherence which vitiates such religious claims" (2006, 135–6).

And *third* — apart from the at least apparent radical incoherence of the Mormon Plan of Salvation considering the second fact above — is the fact that these putative truth claims are themselves nonsensical and incoherent in their own right on the basis of their unintelligibility in relation to our best justified and true beliefs (or knowledge) about the world and universe and how they work. Further, they are internally inconsistent. The rather self-evident contradictions with what are both commonsensically and scientifically known – without, it should be noted, the false, *scientistic* belief that *all* our knowledge is scientific knowledge, or that what science cannot tell us *cannot* be known (Nielsen 1996) – leaves the doctrines or truth claims of the Mormon Plan of Salvation without warranted assertability and rational acceptability as actual truth. But beyond such contradictions with established knowledge, the internal inconsistencies in the Mormon Plan make the concept of the Mormon god, as doctrinally described and faithfully conceived, incoherent *apart from* and *in addition to* its conceptual incoherence as was established in the previous chapter. For to claim — as Mormon believers do — that a totally (indeterministically) free, omniscient, and omnibenevolent being acted to initiate and perpetuate a flawed (incoherent) plan which also (as we shall learn) ultimately defeats the Mormon god's own allegedly self-disclosed purposes (or 'Work and Glory') is to make the truthfulness of the concept of such a putative divine being further incoherent and therefore logically impossible.

Readers are invited to keep in mind — and critically and soberly reflect on — the two crucial questions asked above regarding the force and value of their comforting 'meaning of life' and treasured 'eternal blessings.' To help in doing that, the following analysis of the above-listed eight core doctrinal beliefs (**A-H**) is offered to inhibit uncritical acceptance of — and any apologetic attempt to deductively justify — the concept of the Mormon god presuming the putative coherence and rationality of the Mormon Plan of Salvation. This is also needed to further flesh-out, so to speak, what is not at least apparently self-evident about the three troubling facts above and to expose thereby the deep incoherence and irrationality of the entire Mormon belief system. Taken as a whole, as we shall see, Mormonism is, again *pace* Widtsoe, far from being a "rational theology" (1915).

As an important reminder, it is instructive to notice how seemingly sensible, understandable, and seductive to the egos and troubled or superstitious minds of us weak, flawed, infirm, needy, and powerless mortals the above narrative of the Mormon Plan of Salvation and corresponding doctrinal assertions can be made to appear. With 'culturally Christianized' people this is made possible through the nondeviant use of familiar God-talk. (Simply ask yourself whether or not you think you understood the brief description of the Mormon gospel presented at the beginning of this chapter and if what you read makes sense to you. If the answer is *yes* to either question — as it was and is to millions of others worldwide and counting! — then the point is made.) As we learned in the *Foundational Preface* and Chapter 1, to determine whether or not truth claims that seem to be sensible and cognitively meaningful actually *are* so, we must look closely, critically, and soberly — *beyond* mere imaginative conceivability or familiarity with the language and how it is used — at what *specifically* is being asserted to be *literally* or *actually* true. Where agreement and commitment are being even implicitly sought by the claimer and the stakes are high (as, for example, one's intellectual integrity and commitment to rationality and epistemic and social responsibility) we must, as we did with the Mormon concept of 'God' in the preceding chapter, submit any assertions of *literal* or *actual* truth — in this case the asserted religious truth claims of the Mormon gospel — *first* to rigorous deconstructive inquiry. Then, if in fact such claims are even *justifiable* and meet the basic requirements of rationality (see Chapter 2), they must be submitted to the pursuit of more formal *justification* through the achievement of wide reflective equilibrium.

As with the analysis of any religious truth claim, there are at least three fundamental questions that must be asked. These questions are derived from the coherence view of justification. They function as a litmus test for determining, as we learned in the *Foundational Preface*, the justifiability or warranted assertability of truth claims. They are asked once again with the presumption of skepticism as an outsider or disinterested investigator.

First, how would such a doctrinal claim be *actually* possible (*not* merely imaginable), given our best and most complete, justified knowledge (a pleonasm) of the world and the universe, and how they work?

Second, how does this particular doctrinal truth claim actually *and* logically hang together or fit with itself, with other relevant doctrinal claims or beliefs, and with *basic* common sense?

Third, what are the truth-conditions of such a claim? What, in principle, would empirically count for or against the truth (or probable truth) or falsity (or probable falsity) of such claims so that they might, again in principle, be confirmed or disconfirmed?

These questions — like those presented earlier which also point (as shown in Chapter 2) to the rationality or irrationality of beliefs and the conceptual analysis of truth claims — are not arbitrary. They bring out the procedures that are arguably inherent in all belief by its very nature. They are actually, albeit informally and perhaps unconsciously, employed in deciding whether a statement is indeed intelligible, consistent, coherent, and factual. As a whole, echoing Nielsen, such formal questions make *explicit* an *implicit* practice.

If a doctrinal claim or statement (1) is found, in relation to the three paradigm questions above, to be nonsensical as stated or contradictory with other doctrines and with relevant, generally accepted knowledge; or if (2) it is self-refuting or factually meaningless, then the statement or doctrinal claim is either logically or actually incoherent. Therefore it is irrational *as a belief* as well as false (or probably false) *as a truth claim*. Such, I conclude, is the status of *each* and all of the foundational Mormon doctrines above when carefully and *critically* subjected, through rigorous analytic inquiry, to the three category questions presented in the preceding paragraph — as well as when considered with regard to the earlier questions regarding the determination of rationality/irrationality and the quest for factually intelligibility. To justify this conclusion I present below a preliminary analysis of each doctrine separately.

A. According to Mormon theology, the essential part or constituent of man's (and the Mormon god's) being, referred to as an 'intelligence,' is independent, self-existent, conscious, and in possession of indeterministic free will. It is co-eternal with 'God.' While man's *spirit* is believed to have been procreated through the sexual union of Heavenly Parents, his *intelligence* was not. We must ask, *how can we possibly make rational sense* of such a putative eternal, complex entity referred to as an *intelligence* or even a procreated *spirit*? *Specifically*, how can we possibly know there are such intelligences or spirits? What *specifically* are they and what do they refer to? What *specifically* are they like? What — if any — *specifically*, are their unique primary, descriptive attributes, or referents? How can they *possibly* be empirically confirmed or disconfirmed as such (in this life or the next, assuming such) to establish their factual significance? If, as is officially conceded by the Church, no one knows specifically and definitively *what* they are or what they're like, how can anyone know (without circularly begging the question) *that* they literally exist? How can anyone know that intelligences are, as Joseph Smith asserts, co-eternal with 'God' and are independent, self-existent entities or — as Roberts, O. Pratt and Widtsoe assert — are conscious and capable of ratiocination and free choice? What would empirically count for or against the truth (or probable truth) or falsity (or probable falsity) of such truth claims? In other words, what *specifically* are the truth-conditions of such claims regarding the literal existence and nature of so called intelligences and spirits which could, in principle, be satisfied such that the claims could actually be justified — either through rational demonstration in a narrow sense, or, more comprehensibly, through wide, reflective equilibrium?

These questions, in my thinking, provide their own answer. The concepts of 'intelligences' and 'spirits' are incoherent because they are factually unintelligible or meaningless. Both are therefore *factual non-realities*.[83] Further, apart from the problem of the factual unintelligibility of intelligences and spirits, is the related problem of making rational sense of the concept of incorporating such putative intelligences, through non-biological conception, into spirits. What *specifically* would the claim that 'God is our *literal* Father in Heaven' *actually* or *literally* refer to or entail? Specifically, what would it be like for an intelligence — even if solely for the sake of argument such an entity is intelligible

---

83 For a naturalistic analysis and explanation of, and perspective on, 'spirits' in relation to the concepts of 'souls' and 'immortality' see again Nielsen's "The Faces of Immortality" in his *Naturalism and Religion* (2001, 77–103) and "Perceiving God" in his *Naturalism without Foundations* (1996, 451–456); Elbert's *Are Souls Real?* (2000); and Edis' *The Ghost in the Universe* (2002, 179–243).

and factually meaningful — to *actually* become a 'spirit,' *i.e.* to be *literally* incorporated in the process of divine procreation? As with other core theological concepts, analogical predication does not work here. As was pointed out in the last chapter, while we know how a human male becomes a father and how conception works biologically, given biological organisms and reproductive processes, we know *nothing* nonanalogical, or literal, about 'spirit elements' and 'divine' (non-biological) beings. We know nothing about reproductive processes that result in the conception of spirits.

B. Assuming, for the sake of argument, the intelligibility, coherence, and factual significance of the concept of the Mormon god, intelligences, and spirits as described and believed, *how can we possibly make rational sense* of the *literal* fall of Lucifer from his putative status as the 'Son of the Morning' and a *literal* 'son of God,' to Satan, the very personification of evil?

Such a fall would necessarily presume that either the potential for evil is inherent in all intelligences or spirits (including 'God'), or that evil is an eternal, external, independent, and eternal force that would be able to — and would in fact — abide in 'God' where he dwells: in the 'Celestial Kingdom.' But how could that make sense? How, given the way the Mormon god is doctrinally described, could it be *logically* or *actually* possible for evil to come from him, inhere in him or abide 'in the dwelling place or presence of God'? In the context of Mormon theology, the existence of Satan makes the existence of the Mormon god incoherent; the belief that either one exists makes the belief in the other impossible. Finally, the belief that both exist as necessarily interdependent concepts is incoherent because this is self-contradictory and therefore irrational.

Similarly, given the same generous assumption for argument regarding the possible existence of the Mormon god, spirits, and spiritual procreation, *how can we possibly make rational sense* of *literally* one-third of that god's spirit children choosing to follow Lucifer in rebellion against him and his plan and fall into perdition? These spirits are presumably endowed through conception, if not eternally, with an eternal intelligence and the capacities of godliness. They are nurtured and developed for untold (and unknown) eons of time by divine parents, abiding continually in their god's presence with free agency and without a fallen, mortal body or the temptations of the flesh. How then can the concept of such a rebellious choice and a literal 'War in Heaven' possibly make rational sense — even with the presumption of 'free agency?' How could Lucifer's alleged 'alternate plan,' which is clearly defective and morally questionable even to mere mortals, contain more compelling truth than the Mormon god's plan? How could pride, rebellion, irrationality, and evil even be possible, given the putative nature and pre-mortal, celestial living conditions of the intelligences/spirits involved? What could possibly be the logical or actual basis for such a putative rebellion?

All of this presents a potentially serious problem regarding the putative intelligibility, coherence, and factual reality of the Mormon god. For if, as Mormon doctrine alleges, evil is eternal as an actual reality and in virtue of the free agency of eternal intelligences, then the *capacity* for evil is *necessarily* inherent in *all* such eternal intelligences including, also necessarily, the intelligences in all the spirits of men, and also of 'God.'

This logically extended doctrinal belief — apart from serious refuting research and counterarguments to the claimed existence of free will[84] and the question of how it could even be possible to know what the capacities are of an 'intelligence' — makes it *at least* possible, in principle, for 'God' to do or even become evil. This, in turn, makes the *concept* of 'God' as an absolutely perfect, all-good, and all-loving being — who is believed *incapable* of doing or being evil — incoherent in the larger, cosmological context of Mormon theology.

Such a concept of evil in connection with the eternal nature of intelligences — and therefore spirits and man — makes the concept of the Mormon god unintelligible. It also makes Mormon theology in this regard deeply and fundamentally incoherent. For if the Mormon god is in fact — in virtue of the conceived inherent eternal capacity of free agency — *capable* of choosing evil, then it is logically possible that he has done so or will do so in relation to man. It is such a logical possibility that makes the concept of the Mormon god incoherent and would certainly make such a concept of this god, in principle, unworthy of unconditional faith and worship.

C. How can we reasonably or rationally make sense of a finite god with infinite power creating this world — indeed, worlds without end — by *organizing* and *governing* the 'eternal elements' through the power of his spoken word or 'Light of Truth?'

In response to such a question Ostler appeals to analogy, suggesting that "[the] analogy used in Mormon scripture is that God's spirit proceeds from his physical presence like light proceeds from the sun, for even though the sun is limited in physical extension, its scope of influence is not limited to its 'physical size' (D&C 88)." Looked at another way, Ostler further suggests, "God's relation to all reality is analogous to the relation a person has to his or her own body" (NGNAN, 16).

But such analogical predication necessarily fails us here. We do, of course, empirically and conceptually know something about the sun. We know that it exists and what it is or consists of. We know about the existence and nature of sun light and how light and heat radiate from the sun and affect biological life on earth. But while we likewise empirically and conceptually know something about how a person neurologically relates to his or her body and how the brain neurologically governs the various functions of the body, we know *nothing* literal about the metaphysical concepts of 'God' or the 'Light of Truth (Christ).' We know nothing non-analogical that would justify anyone in making or accepting such an analogical appeal regarding how a putatively finite god could create (organize) or govern a universe and 'worlds without end' by the conscious and intentional power of his 'word' or 'immanent spirit.'

Given all we *know* (not believe or can speculate or imagine) about the physical universe and how it works, how would such an act of divine creation make sense or be causally possible? What are the truth-conditions of such a belief that could, in principle, be empirically verified or falsified, confirmed or disconfirmed? Even if it were argued that 'God' worked through natural law to do so, what *specifically* would it *actually* be like for a finite being to work through, by, or with natural laws to literally organize the elements into a life-sustaining world by the power of the spoken word or through the transmission of divine will, power, and intelligence through the 'Light of Truth' (or Holy Spirit)? Most

---

84 See, for example, Double's *The Non reality of Free Will* (1990) and Wegner's *The Illusion of Conscious Will* (2002).

crucially, if the expressions 'by the word' and/or 'by the spirit' are alleged to be used meta-phorically regarding how this god created the Earth and other worlds, *what specifically are they metaphors of*? What *specifically* is such 'Light of Truth?' What *specifically* are its properties or primary constituents that its putative existence might possibly be empiri-cally confirmed or disconfirmed as true (or probably true) or false (or probably false)?[85]

Surely there are more credible, naturalistic explanations for the existence of the universe. As it turns out, there are. One explanation of several in this regard is suggested by renowned American physicist/cosmologist Lee Smolin, who posits that "As there can, by definition, be nothing outside the universe, a scientific cosmology must be based on a conception that the universe made itself. This is possible because, since Darwin, we know that structure and complexity can be self-organized…without any need for a maker outside the system" (quoted in Huberman 2007, 282; see Smolin 1999, 2001 and 2006; see also Andrei Linde's work on "the eternally existing, self-reproducing inflationary universe," and Quentin Smith's argument for a "self-caused universe" in Michael Martin 2007, 182–198, and the 2008 "Great Debate" between Quentin Smith (with Paul Draper) and Francis Collins published in the *Secular Web*, together with all source references).

Other credible cosmological explanations for the origin of the universe (or, alter-natively, "multiverse") exist to be sure, including, most recently, Stephen Hawking's published view (2010) that the universe spontaneously created itself from nothing in virtue of the necessary balance of positive and negative gravitational energy. (See also Mills 2003, 84-98; and Stenger 2006, 121-35.) What is significant here is that *not one* of these theories actually or necessarily indicates, requires, or justifies the existence of a god as such is conceptualized and believed in *any* theistic faith. The fact that some 'theistic scientists' (an oxymoron, as I see it) can speculatively and metaphysically argue for the *possible* existence of a 'god-as-intelligent designer' in any of these theories does not avoid or address the *a priori* argument against the metaphysical conceptual constructs of such speculations and putative gods. The *a priori* argument presents the problem of their factual unintelligibility and unjustifiability, and it is no comfort to theists whose faith in their god and gospel narrative requires certainty — or a least probability or likelihood and not mere possibility.

Further — inserting alternate Mormon views in parentheses — how can we reason-ably or rationally make sense of a god *literally* creating (or, alternatively, transplanting)

---

85 Warding off such questions, it is argued by Ostler, that "In the Mormon scheme of things, explanation stops with the essential and eternal nature of intelligence. Intelligence or the light of truth simply exists because it is its nature to exist" (NGNAN, 17)." To Ostler, and other so-called orthodox believers of like mind, the inherent order in the universe that ultimately accounts for its putative creation by the Mormon god, "…is ultimately explained by referring to the intentions and powers of God in relationship with the natural tendencies and propensities of eternal intelligences (NGNAN, 17)." But what could this explanation possibly and actually mean? Such an explanation — in the context of the problem with the concept of 'eternal intelligences' (see analysis of doctrine **A** above) — tells us nothing intelligible or factually significant, and therefore nothing actually true. Besides once again begging the question, it simply attempts to explain the otherwise incoherent concept of divine creation by presupposing the actual existence of another incoherent concept and factual non-reality. Unfortunately this *ad hoc* explanation — like Ostler's other speculative explanations cited throughout this book — raises more questions than it answers. It must be discarded on the basis that it begs the question and explains less (or at least nothing more) than the clear analytical conclusion implied in the questions and concerns cited above.

Adam (as a 'god' or immortal man and therefore), as the first man, from the dust of this Earth (or another world) and breathing into him a spirit to make him a living soul? And how are we to make common, rational sense of a god *literally* creating (or, alternatively, transplanting) Eve as a 'god' or immortal woman, with Adam, as one of his wives — thus creating the first woman from the rib of Adam? Given, as above, all we actually know about the physical universe and how it works — including in this case the factual reality of natural selection to account for the origin and biological evolution of species and the descent of man[86] — how would such an act of divine creation (or, alternatively, transplantation) make sense or be causally possible? What would be the truth-conditions of such a belief, so that such putative 'special creation' or 'divinely directed creation' might possibly be empirically verified or falsified, confirmed or disconfirmed? Even if it were argued that this god worked through the natural laws of biological evolution to do so, what would it be like for a finite, yet transcendent being to *literally* or actually work with (and within) such natural laws to bring about the origin of man and of all species of animal and plant life by the power of the spoken word or 'Holy Spirit?' Again, if the expressions 'by the word' and/or 'by the spirit' are alleged to be used metaphorically or symbolically regarding how the Mormon god created man and life on Earth, *what specifically are they metaphors or symbols of?*

Moreover, we must ask why a god would even be necessary if the laws of biological evolution existed *independent* of him as fundamental and eternal laws of an eternal universe. If such laws are *not* eternal and require special creation, on the other hand why would an all-powerful and all-knowing god choose to create such laws rather than more efficient and effective laws in order to create man through natural selection?

In this regard, some theistic apologists perversely and futilely attempt to deal with the problem of natural selection by, as Mattill puts it, "mixing God and evolution" (1995, 35). This move has resulted in various conceptions. One is "theistic evolution;"[87] the idea that "Evolution is God's method of creation" (35) through which the 'designer God' *somehow* directs and guides creation to fulfill his purposes. Another is 'pantheistic creative evolution,' the idea "which is quite similar to theistic evolution but stresses God's *transcendence…* and *immanence*" (36) in *somehow* directing evolutionary processes and mechanisms from afar as an intelligent, immanent force. A third notion is 'progressive creationism.' This is the idea that "[t]he world is as old as modern science claims," that "God," after *somehow* and *actually* "creating more and more complex forms of life over a period of hundreds of millions of years…*somehow* stepped in (when the earth was ready for humans) and *somehow* and *literally* created Adam and Eve" out of "the dust of the earth." Alternatively, he did *not* so create Adam and Eve's *body* (which evolved naturally), but *somehow* created and implanted their 'soul' — whatever such actually means, if anything (36).

---

86 For fundamentalist Mormon (or other theistic) believers who question the fact of the origin of species and the descent of man through natural selection, see the very readable and informative books by Mills (2003) and Smith and Sullivan (2007). For a more substantial treatment of the topic of evolution through natural selection, see Dennett (1995) and, more recently, Mayr (2001) and Dawkins (2009).

87 See also Bart Link's "The Untenability of Theistic Evolution" wherein Link argues that "Mere compatibility with science does not make [Theistic Evolution, or] TE true or even plausible," and concludes that there is at least "apparent conflict with science [which] provides grounds to reject TE, but [that] the biggest problems for TE are theological and philosophical," making "evolution and theism…irreconcilable" (2009, 2).

To these *ad hoc,* incoherent conceptualizations I would add yet another likewise *ad hoc* and incoherent idea that synthesizes some parts of the preceding ideas and is more consistent with Mormon theology. This idea could be termed 'eternal creationism.' It entails first a finite, transcendent god, as Creator, who is physically (bodily) located on this or another planet *somewhere* in this or another universe or dimension of space and time. This putative Creator then *somehow* — through the 'Light of Truth' or immanent 'priesthood power' (whatever these terms *actually* mean, if anything) — *literally* 'spoke' to the 'eternal intelligences' (whatever these *actually* are, if anything) within the 'eternal elements' and directed them to obey the natural laws he designed and/or initiated, including the law of evolution through natural selection. This he did in order thereby *somehow* to physically create (organize or assemble) all 'eternal life forms,' including plants, animals, and man. After this he then *somehow* and *actually* inserted the 'spirits' of such life forms, consisting of organized or procreated 'spirit matter' and 'intelligence,' into their *biologically* created bodies to make 'living souls.'

What this synthesized version[88] of Mormon creationism suggests is utterly absurd. Simply put, putatively conscious '*eternal* intelligences' are inherent in "the *eternal* elements.' As I understand it, this idea was speculatively if not dogmatically interpreted by some, like Brigham Young, to be fundamental to *all* 'gross matter.' These eternal intelligences chose, in virtue of their '*eternal* capacity for free will' (where *eternal* in each case means *self-existing* or *uncreated*), to cooperate with the Mormon god's expressed will and directions and *somehow actually organized themselves* — intelligently and willingly — to form (create or organize) the earth (and 'worlds without end') and all earthly life-forms, including the first man, or Adam, according to the temporal, natural laws 'God' created and/or initiated.

All of these speculative, *ad hoc* ideas which "[mix] God and evolution" (35) are, of course, evasively adorned by implied "somehow," "somewhere," and "somewhen" qualifiers to make room for possibility. Yet they all beg the question of this god's existence as well as the existence of eternal intelligences, spirit matter, and law. They are, moreover, unintelligible and incoherent in their own right and in relation to the incoherent concepts of the god that they espouse.

To the degree that they try to harmoniously mix the Mormon god with evolution, these incoherent ideas raise further problematical questions. Why would a putatively all-knowing, omnipotent, and merciful Creator prefer such a cruel and inefficient process? Arguably it results in excessive and purposeless suffering and premature death. Thereby it fosters both nonbelief and, for many, the loss of faith. Why not instead use his putative power more *directly, efficiently,* and *tellingly* to accomplish his alleged purposes and promote the required and necessary *knowledge* of his existence as theologically conceived? Such apologetic explanations, beyond again begging the question of this god's existence, simply do not make rational sense. As Mattill rightly concludes, paraphrasing White, "mixing more or less of God with more or less of evolution produces results more or less absurd" (37).

---

88 Equally absurd, as well as unofficial and controversial, are the alternative versions espoused by Brigham Young and B.H. Roberts. They vary in that all 'eternal life forms' — including Adam and Eve, who in Young's version are the 'Gods of this world,' *i.e.* our Heavenly Father and Mother — were *somehow* and *literally* transplanted from other planets and/or dimensions of space and time to *this* earth. In Roberts' version the earth was already inhabited by 'pre-Adamites.'

Of equal concern for rationality: how can we make sense of the Mormon belief regarding procreated spirits inhabiting a physical body on Earth? According to Mormon belief, an adult 'spirit child of God' leaves its celestial home (wherever that is, if anywhere) and somehow *literally* either enters into the womb of a chosen mortal woman on Earth, thereby joining symbiotically with a biological organism such as a zygote, embryo, fetus, or enters directly into the newborn child to form a 'living soul.' Can we make rational sense of such a belief? What, *specifically*, would such an event be like? Given all that we know about human biology, procreation, and cosmology, how would such a feat be *actually* possible — or even be intelligently or rationally conceivable? How *specifically* could such a belief have factual meaning, given the factually empty status of the concept of spirits? How could it, *in principle*, be empirically confirmed or disconfirmed such that such a belief could even be justifiable as a truth claim?

D. We move now to the doctrine of the alleged *literal* 'Fall' of Adam and Eve. As the Mormons believe, Adam and Eve were *literal* beings. Both had uncorrupted, 'immortal bodies' and 'celestial spirits' and lived *literally* in a paradisiacal garden of Eden in an uncorrupted (Terrestrial) world (planet Earth) where they actually walked and talked with 'God' and all creation in a state of total innocence. Enter Satan — remember him from **B** above? — who refutes everything the Mormon god told Adam and Eve to do. He persuades Eve to eat of the forbidden fruit of the *literal* 'tree of knowledge of good and evil.' Eve partakes of the fruit, and then 'beguiles' Adam, who also partakes. With the forbidden fruit now ingested, the 'terrestrial' (*i.e.* immortal) bodies of Adam and Eve actually become physically and spiritually corrupted (*i.e.* mortal). They consist now of a spirit alienated from 'God' (through sin) and a natural, or 'fallen' (*i.e.* 'telestial' or earthly, mortal) body of flesh and blood that is capable of decay, sin, and death. God chastises them both and expels them from the garden into the now 'fallen world,' which is the natural world we all now live in. How did the planet and all the animal and plant life 'fall' from a terrestrial, paradisiacal state to a corrupt, telestial state? According to certain Mormon Prophets, most notably Brigham Young, the Earth *literally fell* the instant Adam and Eve actually partook of the forbidden fruit.

Now please stop and think and ask yourself as a skeptical outsider how any reasonable person could possibly make rational sense of such beliefs? In the same context of **B** above, how could this putative temptation even occur? Consider first who Adam and Eve allegedly were — 'gods' or, at least, 'valiant spirits.' Consider also where they (as putative 'spirits') allegedly came from — the presence of the Mormon god. Then consider what their putative physical nature was (immortal), who they allegedly had access to ('God'), what their understanding likely was of that god's plan, nature, and will. Consider where they allegedly lived — in 'paradise.'

Finally, consider that they were allegedly in a condition of total innocence and purity where they regularly walked and talked with their god. How, given all the above, could such a special couple possibly be tempted? Further, given common sense and what we know about the geological, biological, and archeological history of this planet, this entire drama — like the creation story itself — makes absolutely no sense and is devoid of coherence and factual meaning. If it is argued that such a doctrine is not to be understood literally but only figuratively or metaphorically, then again we must ask what this metaphorical or symbolic story could be a metaphor or a symbol of. If the answer is that the story of the Fall is a morality tale and that in fact there was no literal Adam or Eve and no Fall, then the entire corpus of Mormon theology falls like a house of cards. As Mormon Church leaders have argued repeatedly: *no divine creation, no Adam and Eve; no Adam and Eve, no fall; no fall, no need for redemption or salvation; no need for redemption and salvation, no need for Atonement; no need for Atonement, no need for Jesus Christ; no Jesus Christ, no first vision to Joseph Smith and no Mormon religion, or even Christianity, as it currently exists.*

If our previous consideration of the concept of the Mormon god enters this equation, the house of cards falls with the rational conclusion established in the previous chapter that the Mormon god, as doctrinally conceptualized, is an unintelligible, incoherent, and factually meaningless concept. Therefore it is a factual non-reality.

E. Let us grant, however — *solely* for the sake of argument and analytical comprehensiveness — that the Fall of man actually occurred and that the Mormon god, as doctrinally conceptualized, actually exists. Let us assume — also for the sake of argument — the factual historicity of Jesus of Nazareth, which is very problematic and, by some reliable accounts, very unlikely (see Barker 2008; Martin 1991; Wells 1988; and Doherty 2005). Even if all this be granted, what rational sense can we make of the concepts of the 'divine conception,' or 'incarnation,' and 'atoning sacrifice' of Jesus Christ (see also doctrine **F** below)?

Given what we know (not imagine or speculate) about the natural laws of human conception, what *specifically* would it *actually* mean for a human female (Mary) to *actually* have sex with a God, as Mormons believe? How would such an act of fertilization be *actually* possible, given that the Mormon god, as doctrinally conceptualized, is not a biological being, but is a bloodless (semenless?) physical being who is *transcendent* (in space and time, as well as biologically) to this world? And what sense can be made of the doctrine that the Holy Ghost *somehow* prepared Mary's body and mind for the consummation of her marriage to that god? What sense can we make of the orthodox Christian belief that Mary *literally* conceived by the 'visitation of the Holy Ghost'? Beyond the apparent irrationality of the belief in the existence of the Holy Ghost, what are we to understand about Mary's preparation or literal transfiguration? What *specifically* could such 'preparation' *actually* mean? What *specifically* would such 'transfiguration' *actually* be like? Additionally, how *specifically* could it be causally possible — *whatever* it might actually mean? Finally, referring back to doctrines **A** and **C** above, how can we make rational sense of Jehovah's 'spirit body' (whatever that means, if anything) *literally* entering the womb of Mary at conception or birth? Do Mormons really know what they are talking about here? Or — as Nielsen is wont to say, following Wittgenstein — is language idling or on a holiday?

We must wonder further how *specifically* it is *logically* or *actually* possible for a human being to be wholly human and wholly divine — as Jesus Christ is believed to be. How, for example, can we make sense of the assertion that Jesus was a '*God incarnate,*' who was wholly human, capable of temptation, but not wholly human in that he could not sin? What is the factual significance or meaning of such a claim? What *specifically* are the truth-conditions that would make it possible to empirically confirm or disconfirm, under *controlled* conditions, that a man was *both* man *and* 'God,' where 'God' is the being doctrinally conceptualized in Mormon theology? Clearly, if the concept of the Mormon god is unintelligible, incoherent, and factually meaningless as argued, so too is the concept of the 'Son of God.'

F. Next, we must see if and how we can make rational sense of the concept of the 'Infinite Atonement' of Jesus Christ. What would it *actually* mean for an allegedly divine human being (whatever that means, if anything), to *literally* take upon himself *all* the sins of *all* human beings past, present, and future and *literally* 'satisfy' the demands of eternal justice (whatever that literally means, if anything)? How would that act *ransom* mankind from the bondage of sin and death? How could Christ's personal suffering, bleeding, and dying on the cross *reconcile* man to his god?

This doctrine, though charged with great emotion for "infantilized" believers and psychologically receptive nonbelievers (Faber 2010), is totally unintelligible. Answer this: how *specifically* does the suffering, bleeding, and torturous death of an allegedly impeccable, divine human being infinitely atone for all — or any — human sin? How, by suffering in prayer and dying on the cross could Jesus possibly and literally take away any or all the sins of the world? How *specifically* could such an effect be causally possible or possibly be empirically confirmed or disconfirmed to establish factual significance or meaning?[89] And how could it hang together, or cohere, with other well-grounded beliefs about the natural world and how it works? "Could there be," Nielsen asks in a personal correspondence with the author, "anything like a remotely reflective equilibrium here?"

Furthermore, why should *faith* in Christ (and 'God') and in Christ's putative atoning sacrifice be necessary or required (as it most certainly is in most Christian religions as well as in the Mormon faith) to ensure man's salvation in fulfillment of the Mormon god's allegedly declared superordinate purpose, or 'Work and Glory,' which is "to bring to pass the immortality and eternal life of man"? As shall be argued in Chapter 6, the concept of 'faith in God and Christ' is not only incoherent as trust and confidence in an incoherent god. It is both insufficient and unnecessary regarding man's need for acquiring *and* securing the necessary knowledge of and belief in 'God and Jesus Christ' to ensure 'life

---

89 This question essentially asks how we might know of the actual existence of something that is not, at least in principle, directly and empirically confirmable or disconfirmable — a question addressed elsewhere in this work. Simply answered, and assuming the factual intelligibility of the claim, we know of such things in virtue of the existence of those objective, empirical consequences which are best explained by known or theoretically plausible causal mechanisms. Faith and wishful thinking are not options here, as we shall learn in Chapter 6. Related to this particular question concerning the putative effects of the believed atonement of Jesus Christ, believers would no doubt point to their experience of divine forgiveness, or a profound feeling of love, peace of mind, acceptance, approval, joy, and personal salvation, or the transformation characterized as the 'mighty change of heart.' But these reported subjective experiences, including the empirically supported claims of behavioral change putatively caused by them, have perfectly sensible and compelling naturalistic explanations, as we shall learn in Chapters 5 and 6, and Appendix A. We do not require the existence of a Savior, or of a senseless, barbaric — not to mention absurd — and supernatural act of atonement by the suffering, blood-shedding, and sacrificial death of a 'man-God.' Moreover, the believer's argument for such a theological explanation is itself — beyond being factually unintelligible — riddled with serious reasoning problems. It is, first of all, invalid as a *post hoc* argument that *begs the question.* It is also a *non sequitur* that invalidly *affirms the consequent.* Moreover, it invalidly *appeals* to subjective *experience* and questionable *and* fallible (if not discredited or incredible) *authority* and purely subjective and fallible *testimony.* Last but not least, it certainly fails to survive the application of *Ockham's Razor.*

eternal.' Moreover, as scripturally acknowledged, "many are called but few are chosen" to be saved and enjoy eternal life and "few there be that find the Way" to eternal life. If these things be so, then the claimed *requirement* of such faith as the *necessary* 'first principle' of the gospel is ultimately self-defeating to this god's greatest purpose and so it is incoherent in that sense as well.

Beyond the problem with faith, let us accept, solely for the sake of argument, the sense and coherence of the concepts *Christ* and Christ's *atonement*. How even then could *repentance, baptism* by immersion in water and by the Holy Spirit (whatever that *actually* means, if anything), and regularly participating in a *sacrament* by symbolically ingesting Christ's flesh (bread) and blood (water or wine), be intelligibly and coherently considered as necessary and sufficient conditions for *actually* and *literally* invoking the putative effects of Jesus' believed atonement? How could that thereby save, forgive, purify, or sanctify anyone dead or alive now or in the future? According to Roberts, through such putatively essential 'gospel ordinances' as baptism and the sacrament, "we do *literally* partake not only of emanating powers, but of what Peter calls 'the divine nature,' by inviting into our systems…the elements of higher life, higher spirit, higher power — the power of Godliness" (1975, 19, emphasis mine).[90] But this further example of grandiose, metaphysical nonsense regarding the efficacy of religious ordinances yields related and serious problems — not only when applied to living, human participants on Earth, but even more significantly when applied to theologically mandated 'Temple work' for the dead. What basic, common, or rational sense can we make of *any* of this, given all the criteria of rationality? What *specifically* does all this *actually* mean? How is it logically and

---

90 Religious symbols and their unintelligible interpretations are, from my perspective, not only an essential part of the infantilizing process of all theistic faiths essential to faith and conversion (see Chapter 6 and *Appendix A*), they are invented to give legitimacy and necessity to ignorance to bind believers to their faith. The conveyance of legitimacy is accomplished by authoritatively branding such ignorance as *divine mystery*. Moreover, power is conferred to those who invent such symbols and/or claim to hold the 'keys of knowledge' of the putative mysteries they symbolize. But 'keys' or not, it seems self-evident that it is *impossible* to know that which is unintelligible (through symbolism or otherwise) and therefore *cannot* be known. Given this rather obvious point, it seems reasonable to conclude that those who claim possession of such keys of knowledge (as Joseph Smith, Brigham Young and other so-called Mormon prophets did) are simply inventing yet another layer of unintelligibility to an already unintelligible faith and are cloaking it in yet a deeper level of ignorance or divine mystery.

Such alleged mysteries, of course, serve the need to preserve the faith by subjecting believers to an authoritative double-bind. This double-bind effectually nullifies natural doubt by first making the unintelligibility of the 'sacred' necessary to protect the faith of the ignorant. Then, believers' ignorance and concomitant doubt are declared to be a function (and indicator) of spiritual immaturity, unreadiness, unchosenness, or intellectual pride. Faithful acceptance of 'divine mystery' is claimed to be indicative of humility and meekness. So believers confronted by the unintelligibility of their faith, as manifested by word and symbol, are ingeniously bound to it. This results either from the desire to avoid guilt and shame for questioning or doubting their faith — or for not being worthy enough to have its mysteries revealed to them — or from being praised for their humble and meek acceptance of their ignorance and their reliance on faith and either 'God' or Church leaders for greater 'light and knowledge' promised to the faithful in the 'due time of the Lord.'

In this particular context, the study of religious symbolism becomes a subspecialty of sociocultural anthropology. Beyond exploring the *cultural* transmission of religious ideas through symbolism, it reveals the built-in *social* mechanism (through the invention of such symbolism and its status as divine mystery revealed to an elect few) of perpetuating and preserving religious belief systems. It reveals the trading on human superstiousness, the need for belonging, and the human hunger for absolute truths that enable human transcendence and the alleviation of existential anxiety.

actually *possible*, given what it makes sense to say on the basis of sheer common sense? How does it square with all that we know (not perceive, imagine or speculate) about this world and universe and how they work?

The common analogy, employed prominently by Mormon Apostle and General Authority Boyd K. Packer in his book *The Mediator*, of the charitable benefactor mercifully paying someone's debt to release him from bondage or destitution in return for the beneficiary's gratitude, love, trust, loyalty, obedience, and commitment to good works does not work. We know what a charitable benefactor would be and what it would be like to have someone step-in and pay our debt to release us from the consequences of our inability to repay the debt. We also know how the payment of money by another repays a debt and legally ransoms the debtor from the consequences of foreclosure or lien. But we *don't* know *anything* nonanalogical or literal about what it would be like for a perfect, man-god to be a benefactor by paying for our sins — and the sins of everyone else who ever lived, lives now or will ever live — with his blood and death. We know to *whom* we owe and *what* we owe when we borrow money from someone. But we *don't* know what we owe and to whom (other than, in some cases, those we might have harmed or offended) for our so-called sins. We do not know how *specifically* our putative debt is literally repaid by the vicarious suffering, blood, and death of a putative man-god. Even Roberts' direct, metaphysical appeal below to a putatively foundational reason and purpose for an 'eternal atonement' is fraught with serious problems. Roberts himself, according to Madsen, recognized the various logical problems with what he termed "the difficult doctrine of [the] atonement" of Jesus Christ. On several counts, as he noted in *The Truth, The Way and The Life* (1995), such a doctrine did not make rational sense. According to Madsen, "Roberts saw the following contradictions arising from [what Madsen terms 'the hard and fast Aristotelian definitions of God's omnipotence, omniscience, omnipresence, and omni benevolence']" (1975, 12). He then quotes Roberts as follows:

"The atonement was the divine response to man's need." But in the creedal view God created out of nothing all men and all his environment and therefore created the need!

"The atonement is God's reconciliation to man's abuse of his freedom in and after the fall of Adam." But in the creedal view God created all the circumstances that led to, and therefore required the Fall.

"It was God's way of tempering justice with mercy." But God supposedly created and defined the law of justice and the limits of mercy. Could he not, then, reorder or abandon these demands?

"The atonement was Christ's voluntary rescue or ransom effort." But in the creedal view God could have forgiven man [Is he not omnipotent?] and dispensed his grace without requiring the awful sacrifice of his Son.

"It was God's setting a moving example through his Son." But might not that example have been set without innocent, not to say infinite, suffering?

"It was God's conquering death." But is God not able to transmit life without the suffering of his "Most Beloved" Son?

"It was God thwarting the influence of the Devil's powers of darkness." But the creeds say God created the Devil and all his hosts. Had he no alternative?"

"All in all, would not Christ himself have wondered why the Father did not in his infinite wisdom plan a better, or prevent this worst, alternative? One is led back to the very "why?" of creation. Why did God permit the knots to be tied that [only] Christ could untie?"(13)

"Roberts' fundamental response" to this last question, according to Madsen, "is that there is something *eternal* and *inexorable* about law. If God made all the laws, he can surely revoke them. But if there are some laws which even God did not originate, then he cannot. He can only find ways to master their consequences. On the other hand, mercy that is born of genuine *caring and love* cannot obliterate law, but *may somehow lawfully transform the effects of law*. Christ's power is founded on this *balance between justice and mercy*.

"In this view," according to Madsen's interpretation of Roberts, "the 'noble doctrine' of the eternal nature of individuality and freedom 'affects in a very vital way' every other question about the [necessity of the atonement]."

"Under the conception of the existence of independent, uncreated, self-existent intelligences," continues Madsen, "who by the inherent nature of them are of various degrees of intelligence, and moral quality, differing from each other in many ways, yet all alike in their eternity and their freedom — how [according to Roberts] stands it [*i.e.* the doctrine of atonement] under this conception of things?" (13, emphasis mine) To this question Roberts answers:

> [It] relieves God of the responsibility for nature and the status of intelligences in all stages of their development [because] their inherent nature and their volition make them primarily what they are…The only way God affects these self-existent beings is favorably; he creates not their freedom to choose good or evil — their free moral agency; nor is he author of their suffering when they fall into sin. (13)

In other words, such a putative infinite and eternal, sacrificial atonement was, according to Roberts' interpretation of Mormon theology, the only way the Mormon god could, as Madsen asserts, "manage (the) consequences" of the eternal law of "individuality and freedom" among eternal intelligences. But this speculative treatment of "the difficult doctrine of atonement" — and of what I consider to be the irresolvable problem of god's complicity in the extent of moral and natural evil in the world and discuss in some depth in Chapter 7 — is itself deeply incoherent. It raises more troubling and problematical questions while (*pace* Roberts and Madsen) intelligibly answering none. For example:

- Regarding the putative existence of 'eternal' and 'inexorable' law: What *specifically* is eternal and inexorable about law? Which laws? Why not other laws, or none? What *specifically* are the objective, irrefutable criteria for determining whether or not a particular law is eternal or inexorable? Furthermore, what *specifically* would count for or against the truth (or probable truth) or falsity (or probable falsity) of such a claim besides mere *ad hoc* assertion or speculation?

- Regarding the claim that "caring and love…may somehow transform the effects of law": How can we make rational sense of such a claim? We know what it means for caring and love to affect our perspectives toward and relationships with others —and even perhaps our attitudes, direction, and motivations in life. And we know as well what it means for caring and love to bring relief to the troubled and suffering mind and body of the afflicted. But what *specifically* can it mean for caring and love to *literally* "transform the effects of law?" *Specifically*, what can it mean? How could it be possible for Christ's alleged care and love for all mankind — perfected, as believed, by his 'infinite and eternal blood sacrifice' — invoke the law of mercy to *literally* satisfy (transform?) the law of justice invoked by *all* sins of commission and omission that are committed by *all* men everywhere and at *all* times? In what way, *specifically*, can such a claim in principle be justified beyond, again, mere assertion or unfounded speculation? The very concept is unintelligible.

- Regarding the claim that "Christ's power is founded on this balance between justice and mercy": What *specifically* constitutes such a 'balance' and how *specifically* can the necessity and the existence of such a balance be intelligibly explained or caus-ally explained or possibly confirmed or disconfirmed as a putative truth claim with empirically satisfiable truth-conditions? Further, if we grant, as we must, that this statement has truth-value (in a minimalist, deflationary or disquotational sense), how could it be justified? What would its implications be for the assertion of Christ's (as the Mormon god's) infinite power (as a god), considering the absolute dependence of his power on the actual realization of his infinite mercy by all this god's children through their faith in Christ and the appropriate exercise of their alleged free agency? In other words, how can Christ, like his putative Father, be all-powerful if, as Roberts asserts, his power is "founded on (the) balance between justice and mercy" and if such a putative balance is severely compromised by the existence of all people who either reject or do not accept the claim that Jesus existed or that he is the 'Christ' or the literal 'Son of God?' Under such a conception of divine power, would not the rejection of belief in 'God' and Christ necessarily and effectually nullify Christ's putative act of love and mercy in their lives? Would it not nullify his power through disbelief or nonbelief and unwillingness to repent of their sins, be baptized in water into the Mormon church for the remission of their sins and receive, at the hands of Mormon elders, the gift of the Holy Ghost? For this god's (or Christ's) power to save souls to depend on a 'freely chosen' belief in Christ is to make such power con-ditional or contingent on the exercise of man's putative free agency. This is hardly a comfort to those who *cannot* (and, out of integrity, *will not*) believe that which is utterly unbelievable in *any* conceivable world (including an inconceivable spirit world) without self-deception.

- How, given our previous analysis of the concept of intelligences, can we make sense of the "…conception of the existence of independent, uncreated, self-existent intel-ligences" which, according to Roberts, is so essential — even foundational — to this doctrine of atonement? If such a conception is, in fact, as argued, unintelligible, incoherent, and factually meaningless, what then can we make of Roberts' defense?

- Finally, how *specifically* can we know that "the *only way* God affects these self-existent beings (intelligences) is favorably" through the "mercy that is born of genuine caring and love" through the willing blood sacrifice of Jesus Christ? Such a claim is problematic at minimum in that it presupposes the existence of self-existent intelligences as conscious, free agents capable of ratiocination. It also presupposes the putative truths that: (1) 'God' exists and Jesus Christ existed and is the 'Son of God'; (2) 'justice and mercy' are eternal properties, or laws of existence; (3) we are in a position to know (not merely wishfully believe) that Jesus existed as a 'man-God' who was impeccable and whose putative life, suffering and death was, or could possibly be, intentionally efficacious in mercifully and completely satisfying the eternal demands of justice for all sins of all mankind throughout all time; and (4) that the putative existential demands of justice, if such demands are even intelligible or factually meaningful, can be determined and only be satisfied by the willing blood sacrifice of an impeccable man-God.

If any or all of these presumptive premises are questionable or invalid on the basis of their unintelligibility or lack of factual significance, as implicitly concluded above, then the rest of Roberts' attempt to make sense of the atonement fails. We are left with the contradictions or "hopeless puzzles" that arise from orthodox, creedal, theological concepts — puzzles that extend beyond the list of contradictions cited by Roberts to include the above problems with Roberts' counter-assertions as well.

The Mormon doctrine of the infinite atonement is, in summary, presuppositional and devoid of factual meaning. There is no possible way to empirically test its claims. The far-reaching (infinite!) claims of redemption and salvation through Jesus' allegedly perfect, vicarious sacrifice are totally without sense and truth-conditions. We don't know what would count for or against such claims, in large part because we (including Mormon insiders) don't know what the claims *literally, actually* mean. Consequently, the claims cannot possibly be confirmed or disconfirmed, verified or falsified as being true (or probably true) or false (or probably false). They all must, it is believed, be accepted as true on the basis of scriptural revelation and/or on the basis of *faith* and religious experience. But such bases for belief are themselves very problematical, as we shall discover in the next two chapters.

G. As we found in our previous analysis of Roberts' argument for his god's true nature from the resurrected Christ, the Mormon doctrine of the *literal* resurrection of Jesus Christ — and resurrection and immortality in general — is likewise very problematical scripturally, historically, scientifically, and philosophically in the context of the Mormon doctrine of deity.[91]

Mormons, like orthodox Christians, believe in a *literal* resurrection of Jesus' dead body. This they do in spite of the fact that the concept of Jesus putative resurrection is, again,

---

91 See Martin 1991, 73–104; Loftus 2008, 351–382; Loftus 2010, 291–315; Nielsen 2001, 77–103; Price and Lowder 2005; and Barker 2008 for well reasoned arguments against the belief in resurrection and immortality in general and Christ's putative resurrection in particular.

incoherent and factually unintelligible and that, moreover, there is no reliable historical evidence or mandate of reason that could possibly justify even the probability of such an otherwise unjustifiable event.

Moreover, these believers also claim with certainty that *all* mankind will be *literally* resurrected in virtue of Jesus' literal resurrection. This they do in spite of the fact that there is not *one shred* of *reliable* historical or scientific evidence — *i.e.* evidence that has been objectively, empirically verified or falsified under controlled conditions or generally accepted rules of evidence — to support the claim that *any* (even one) dead, decomposed human being has *ever* been *literally*, *physically* resurrected, or can, in principle, even *be* resurrected.

Beyond mere resurrection, Mormon believers claim that people will be literally resurrected to different 'kingdoms of glory' according to each person's degree of faithfulness and worthiness or righteousness in this life or in the spirit world, where those departed spirits who have not accepted the Mormon gospel in *this life* (for no fault of their own) go and are conveniently (and suspiciously)[92] given another chance to accept the gospel. Accordingly, some will, according to Mormon doctrine, inherit a 'celestial glory (body)' capable of 'exaltation' (deification) and the procreation of spirit offspring. Others will inherit a 'terrestrial glory (body)' and still others a 'telestial glory (body).' Each type of resurrected body is believed to look like the person's mortal body in its perfect form, without deformation, and is immortal (non-biological and indestructible) with different capacities and limitations for functioning and advancement in knowledge, power, and dominion (*i.e.* wives, offspring and worlds to govern).

This belief, like the generic Christian belief in a resurrection, is likewise held with conviction and is likewise factually unintelligible. Concepts such as *spirits*, *spirit world*, different *degrees of glory* pertaining to *resurrected bodies* and *kingdoms of glory* are, like the concepts of *spirit matter*, *intelligences*, and *spirit element* on which they depend for meaning, wholly without sense or factual significance. Moreover, they all, as putative existents, necessarily presuppose the actual existence of 'God' and revelation. This begs the fundamental question at issue. They also, as core concepts representing actual facts, stare in the face of serious historical, scientific and *p*hilosophical problems that challenge the credibility, validity, and coherence of those asserted truth claims which attest to their putative factual status.

"Jesus the Christ," according to Mormon theology, was *literally* resurrected as a god with the same type of body as 'God the Father.' Moreover, the resurrected Christ is, like 'God,' a *glorified* and *exalted* personage consisting of an exalted *spirit* (and *intelligence*) housed in a tangible, bloodless, immortal body of flesh and bones which is animated by

---

92 I refer above to the Mormon doctrine of a second chance in the spirit world as *convenient* and *suspicious* given that, as Mormons believe, *this life* is the time for man to prepare to meet their god and that *this life* is theologically designated as a probationary state of existence where men are proven worthy (or not) to return to the presence of their god so they can enjoy eternal life in the midst of their families and loved ones. It is highly likely Mormon founder Joseph Smith (who invented a faith which also conveniently resolves (albeit incoherently) many of the objectionable theological problems of other Christian faiths) realized that a second chance would no doubt appeal to the believers in other religions whose theologies do not provide such a second chance — as well as to those who would naturally struggle intellectually with doubt at the presentation of the claimed miraculous, yet incredible, origin of the Mormon faith and the unintelligible and either plainly false or incoherent beliefs and meta-beliefs of Mormonism.

spirit element. Such an *exalted* being, to be worthy of man's worship and sacrificial faith, must be, and *is* according to Joseph Smith, *all*-knowing, *all*-powerful, *all*-wise, *all*-loving, and *all*-good, or morally perfect. (2005, Lectures Two, Three, and Four)

But again, on the basis of conceptual analysis alone, how can we make rational sense of such a resurrected being? This question was addressed in some depth in the last chapter regarding the Mormon doctrinal beliefs about their god and the analysis there pertains to an analysis of Jesus Christ as the believed Son of God. The related question of how we could possibly know such a being objectively, through vision, revelation, or visitation, will in turn be treated in the next chapter regarding the Mormon doctrinal belief about revelation *from* 'God' *about* 'God.' This likewise would also pertain to the person of the resurrected Christ. In both aforementioned chapters it is concluded that the Mormon beliefs in question are irrational, without sense, coherence, or factual meaning.

Still, it is no doubt implicitly believed by Mormons and other Christians that the truth of the resurrection (as with the truth of all things past, present, and future) is a matter of *faith*, not history, science, or philosophy. Moreover, they believe that human beings have an innate spiritual capacity[93] that enables them, when such a capacity is unimpeded by pride, sin, or doubt, to know all truth or, more particularly, to actually *see* 'God' or recognize 'God' when they see him.

The problem of 'faith as a way of knowing' will be addressed in depth in Chapter 6. But regarding this putatively innate, human 'spiritual capacity' to see and recognize the *resurrected* 'God' or Christ, we must, as skeptical inquirers, ask what reason there is to believe such a claim is true, or even possible. What *specifically* would such a capacity be? What are the truth-conditions of the claim to its factual existence? Would it be a capacity of the brain or of the 'spirit?' If it is a capacity of the brain, then what *specifically* are its primary neurobiological properties or other qualitative criteria that would differentiate it from other notable brain functions? What would enable it to be identified or located? If it is believed to be of the 'spirit' in man, then we have a problem once again. How can we make sense of 'spirit' or establish its factual status through the identification of testable or satisfiable truth-conditions or otherwise differentiate it from the mind-brain? In either case there is a problem.

As long as such a capacity — or any imagined spiritual or metaphysical power or faculty — is honestly regarded and represented as mere metaphysical speculation or science-fiction, then the problem is relatively harmless. But when religious innovators, apologists, authorities, or lay believers assert that such metaphysical (spiritual, super-natural or transcendent) beliefs are *factual* statements, then the questions of rationality/irrationality apply and the putative factual statements, if unintelligible and without factual significance, are found to be incoherent. Therefore they are either nonsensical and false, or at least *probably* false.

H. Finally, if the orthodox doctrine of 'eternal progression' as concluded in the previ-

---

93 The putative existence of a 'spiritual capacity' (or *sensus divinitatus*) inherent in man's 'spirit,' enabling him to somehow know or remember all truth beyond the 'veil of mortal existence,' is not only highly suspect on the sole basis of common sense and knowledge, but is ably argued against and, I think, sufficiently addressed to the contrary by Everitt (2004, 178–190).

ous chapter is incoherent and factually unintelligible, and if the Mormon doctrinal beliefs about 'God' are likewise found to be irrational and without sense and factual significance, then *how can we possibly make rational sense* of the Mormon belief that man may literally become 'even as God is'? Mormon doctrine claims that man may evolve or progress as an eternal intelligence to a spirit through 'divine procreation' in the 'first estate'; then progress from a spirit to a mortal man in the 'second estate'; and then, finally, advance from a post-mortal disembodied spirit in the spirit world to become a resurrected and 'exalted man,' or 'God' in the 'third estate.' There he will forever enjoy eternal life, or 'the kind of life God lives.' The coherence and factual intelligibility of these beliefs are logically contingent on the coherence and factual significance of the concepts of 'intelligences,' 'unembodied spirits,' 'divine procreation,' 'spirit-inhabited human-beings,' 'disembodied spirits,' 'spirit world,' 'resurrection,' 'exaltation' (or deification), and 'God.'

All this raises serious questions. How, ultimately, can we make rational sense of eternal progression, exaltation, or eternal life (*i.e.* 'Godhood') without reference to 'God'? What *specifically* would such referring expressions otherwise refer to? What *specifically* would it mean to *actually* be exalted or to enjoy eternal life? If we cannot identify such terms by ostension, by pointing to an 'exalted' being — which would be an actual and logical impossibility given the described 'fullness of Mormon Godhood' — then how can they be *specifically* described such that their descriptive referents have truth-conditions that would in principle enable empirical confirmation or disconfirmation? How could we, or anyone (regardless of how 'spiritual' they might be, whatever that means if anything) possibly *know* that an exalted being ('God') *actually* exists except by begging the question, or presupposing what is at issue? How could anyone know what would empirically count as being an exalted being or what it would be like to *actually* see one or be in the presence of one? (Relatedly, we know there are no purple people or three-headed people either, but we know what it would be like to see one.) Given that such terms are inextricably related to 'God,' it is logically and actually impossible to identify their independent truth-conditions. *In the absence of truth-conditions there can be no justification for any truth claim. Claimed facts that have no truth-conditions are not facts; they are pseudo-facts, or factual non-realities.*

The concepts of exaltation and eternal life, together with the concepts of all the alleged secondary attributes and qualities descriptive of the Mormon god are unintelligible without reference to 'God.' But with reference to that god's primary, metaphysical referents, as presented in the preceding chapter, such concepts are incoherent and empty of factual significance. It is irrational to believe that man may become a god through obedience to the principles and ordinances of the Mormon Gospel — including the ordinances performed by the Mormon Priesthood in the Mormon Temple which putatively 'seal' (or record) in heaven those baptisms, confirmations, ordinations, and marriages and families which are sealed on Earth. This is irrational because, in the context of *both* Mormon theology and widely established, common knowledge, such a belief is utterly unintelligible, incoherent, and factually meaningless.[94]

---

94 Nevertheless, as Welles (1995) correctly points out, "Facts and knowledge pale before the values of established beliefs and cherished attitudes… [and contrary facts and knowledge] are routinely refuted by information [putatively] gathered by divination [and 'spiritual confirmation'] — method[s] of gathering unavailable information, a means of learning the unknowable and a source of considerable comfort and solace to those

The Problem of 'Next-Life' Verification

The doctrinal problems raised in this and other chapters through conceptual analysis often lead believers to the possibility of *eschatological (next-life) verification*. This is another evasive isolation strategy that removes the putative theological truths of the 'Gospel' from the possibility of falsification in *this* life and makes them subject to *possible* verification in the *next* life. This putative verification, in turn (and quite conveniently), is something that only those who have the 'eyes of faith to see' will be able to see. But such an authoritative or apologetic faith-based appeal — or retreat — to next-life verification to rescue the concept of the Mormon god and the above doctrines of the Mormon gospel from incoherence and factual unintelligibility comes on the heels of another difficulty. This is the tacit, if not explicit acknowledgement that such a concept and such doctrines are indeed problematical and that the fulness of truth regarding this god's putative nature and Plan of Salvation are conveniently beyond human understanding *in this life.* While the question regarding what, if anything, can be beyond human understanding will be addressed in Chapter 6, it is important to say here that the presumption of next-life verification invalidly *presupposes* the reality of an afterlife and of the existence 'God,' Jesus Christ, and the Mormon god's purposes and plan for man as described in Mormon doctrine and as believed and asserted by Mormon believers.

Mormon believers take as *fact* what they believe to be true *right now* (in this life) regarding the existence and nature of their god and his purposes and plan for mankind. But then they suggest that we will know in the *next life* what we cannot understand specifically about God in *this life.* This suggests that somehow, when we are standing in the presence of the Mormon god in the hereafter, we will finally *know* for a *fact* (not merely believe, feel, or sense) that he is, indeed, what he *was* revealed to be. We will therefore know *without question or doubt,* that the being standing before us is *in fact* the 'Supreme Creator and Governor of the Universe,' the *literal* 'Father of our spirit,' and an 'Exalted, all-knowing, all-powerful, morally perfect, and all-loving infinite and eternal Spirit (and Intelligence) of the highest order, clothed in a celestial body which is animated by spirit element.'

We shall also know, when we stand in the presence of the resurrected Christ, that, in addition to being identical in nature with 'God' as doctrinally described, he is in fact the 'Savior and Redeemer of the world,' including all of the Mormon god's creatures and 'spirit children.' We shall know, without any question or doubt that in virtue alone of his eternal sacrificial atonement and resurrection all men are saved from sin and death to enjoy immortality and eternal life. We shall likewise *know*, not merely believe, that because of his agony in Gethsemane and on the cross on Golgotha and the blood he willingly spilt, we and all men — on condition of repentance and baptism by water and spirit — are cleansed of all sins past, present and future.

But all this is exactly the problem. Let us grant, for argument's sake, that there is in fact a next life (an otherwise irrational belief) and we find ourselves — believers and nonbelievers alike — standing in the presence of two men — as Joseph Smith allegedly did in the final, edited, and official version of his notorious 'First Vision.' They seem radiant, powerful, knowledgeable, loving, and wise beyond what we have ever encountered.

---

firmly committed to the prevailing religious beliefs" (96). But still, as shall be determined in Chapters 5 and 6, where does such recourse leave the believer when beliefs in revelation and faith are deemed to be likewise incoherent and irrational, and where it is also realized that explanations for such inter-related and interde-pendent phenomena are purely and exclusively naturalistic in nature and substance, with no need to posit the existence of gods or a supernatural realm? The final recourse would seem to be in eschatological (or next life) verification, an appeal that is addressed above and determined to be equally problematic.

We Can't Know, Beyond Rational

How shall it be rationally established or verified beyond any doubt that they are, or have accomplished, in fact, all that has been doctrinally described or believed above about them? How, *at the very least*, shall it be rationally established or verified or confirmed that one of the men is *literally* the 'Omniscient and Omnipotent Creator and Ruler of the Universe and of worlds without end' and the 'Eternal Father of our spirits'? And how shall we likewise establish that the other is *literally* 'Jesus the Christ,' the Son of God and the literal 'Savior of mankind and the world? *If these and all other fundamental metaphysical, doctrinal descriptive referents lacked truth-conditions in this life, how would they, or even could they, have truth-conditions in the next?* On what bases would or could such putative metaphysical facts concerning their physical nature, qualities, and attributes possibly be empirically confirmed or disconfirmed in any possible life-time or in any possible world?

Language is still the problem. For to use problematic theological language to describe what would be experienced and verified in the next life is to fatally beg the question. It presupposes the factual reality or verifiability of the very metaphysical, doctrinal, and descriptive referents that are in question and which are at least *prima facie* (if not in fact) *cognitively meaningless*. As Nielsen correctly argues, "to impute onto next life experiences problematic metaphysical first and second-order God-talk assumes that such talk has factual meaning, which is precisely what is at issue. In doing so, [Mormon and Christian apologists and] believers are asking nonbelievers [and themselves] to "pull ourselves up by our own bootstraps" (1975, 216).

The above questions and conclusions that follow and derive from Nielsen's analysis in "The Logic of God" (1975, 209–222) of John Hick's paradigm argument for the existence of 'God' from eschatological verification in his essay from the same source (188–208) are met by Hick later (239–243) with two objections. First, "[i]f it is asked how we can be in a position to tell the difference between God existing and God not existing without fully knowing what 'God' means, the general answer is that such combined knowledge and ignorance is a very common epistemological situation" and therefore "we must not rule out *a priori* that one might be able to be aware of the presence of God, to identify an act of God, and to recognize God's rule, without being able fully to define or comprehend the divine nature" (243). And second, "[s]urely our participation in an eschatological situation in which the reality of God's loving purpose for us is confirmed by its fulfillment in a heavenly world, and in which the authority of Jesus [Christ], and thus of his teaching, is confirmed by his exalted place in that world, would properly count as confirmatory. It would not," Hick continues, "amount to logical demonstration, but it would constitute a situation in which the grounds for rational doubt which obtain in the present life would have been decisively removed. Such eschatological expectations – without the detailed [doctrinal] imagery in which earlier ages have clothed them — are an integral part of the total Christian conception of God and his activity. And they suffice," Hicks suggests and concludes, "to ensure the factual true-or-false character of the claim that God, as so conceived, exists" (243).

Regarding Hick's first objection we might first point out again what Nielsen argued against Hick initially: "if we do not understand what it would be like to stand in the presence of God now or how to individuate God [as a specific person with all the putative descriptive referents ascribed to him in Mormon theology] so that we can gain some understanding of what 'God' refers to, dying and waking up in heaven will not help us one bit (2001, 276)." We might reasonably ask in this regard what *specifically* the putative 'awareness of God's presence' would entail in the next life. How would it be different in nature than such putative awareness in *this* life that serves as the basis of believers' personal testimony of the existence and nature of 'God' and defines the concept of 'God' in *this* life? Likewise, what *specifically* would an 'act of God' or 'God's rule' be like? Relatedly, what *specifically* would count for or against the authenticity of such putative *acts* that they might accurately or correctly be identified and ascribed to a god?

To argue that true believers in fact *just know* — in virtue of the workings of the Holy Spirit — what it would be like to be in the presence of their god, but cannot put such knowledge in words is to create further problems. One problem is in presupposing the factual existence of a factually unintelligible non-reality, *i.e.* the 'Holy Spirit.' Another problem lies in presupposing as true the claim that faith is a legitimate way of knowing — by means of revelation, or religious (spiritual) experience — that which is otherwise ineffable or inaccessible through reason. This is a topic treated in depth in the next two chapters.

As with the verification of revelation in this life, so too is it with putative eschatological verification. Without valid human criteria for making such determinations, *any* perceived miraculous act or *any* perceived glorious or transcendent presence or affective experience, or perceived superhuman display of power, or 'rule' — regardless of the faithful perceivers' differing beliefs — could be attributed as an '*act* of God' or as the '*presence* of God' or the '*rule* of God.' This makes the *concept* of 'God' as propositionally represented factually vacuous and 'faith in God' *in this life* arbitrary and without factual significance.

Similarly, Hick's second objection putatively confirms the existence of 'God' on the basis of Jesus Christ's 'exalted place' (whatever that means or would be like, if anything) in 'that world' and the next life fulfillment of our eschatological expectations, or 'God's loving purpose' for us. It must be realized *first* that the Mormon believer's faith in the Mormon god is based on the Mormon concept of 'God' (the way 'God' is used in the first- and second-order religious discourse of the Mormon religion) and all putative religious experience is interpreted *in virtue of* this particular hermeneutic of 'God.' Without a given concept and hermeneutic of 'God' there would be no basis for determining that an eschatological experience would verify the existence of 'God' or of 'Christ.'

Furthermore, according to the Mormon Prophet Joseph Smith, the correctness of the concept or idea of the Mormon god in *this life* is the primary, if not exclusive, determinant of an enduring 'faith in God,' not the mere possibility or expectation of eschatological experience. For Mormons, it is 'confirmation' through the receipt of direct, personal revelation in *this* life that putatively verifies their god's and Christ's existence, not eschatological verification. If it is argued that it ultimately will not matter to believers in the next life if the theological concept of 'God' in this life was true or coherent as long as the believers' eschatological expectations are fulfilled in the next life, then why should it matter now? We may ask, what other putatively revealed truths that believers base their faith on now — in *this* life — might be wrong, incoherent, or not important to understand? What might be the impact on believers' faith in *this* life if they regarded their *present* beliefs as tentative or problematic — as apparent incoherencies which are not, as well, necessarily true or accurate, but which will be cleared-up in the next life?

Hick essentially argues that it is not necessary for believers to perspicuously understand the concept of 'God' or even to have a correct or coherent understanding of that concept in *this* life, for ultimately the truth about the Mormon god's existence and nature will putatively and presumptively be clearly revealed and understood in the *next* life. All that is required or needful in this life is for believers to have faith in their god and Christ. It is not likely that this will work for the truly committed Mormon believer, however. For simple, superstitious Christian or Mormon believers, the promise or idea of eschatological verification might indeed be sufficient, even if discomfiting at times. Their concept of 'God' requires only confessional belief or a childlike trust and belief that 'God the Father' and 'Jesus Christ' are real and know and love him. It requires as well a sincere desire and effort to live a decent, moral, good Christian life by practicing the Golden Rule and serving others.

For many devoted Mormon believers, however, their very faith or unqualified trust in and commitment to their god putatively depends on having a clear, coherent, and correct understanding of his putatively revealed nature and Plan. For the idea that their concept of 'God' might be wrong or even incoherent in this life— that, in other words, the Mormon god might not in fact exist as understood and believed on the basis of his putatively revealed self-disclosure — would definitely be a problem *in this life*, even if it would not be in the next life. Such a possibility (or eschatological fall-back position) would very likely make the unwavering faith required by Mormon believers impossible or unsustainable in this life and the burden of the covenantal relationship with their god impossible to bear.

But what if such were not the case, and Mormon and other theistic believers would not be bothered in their faith *in this life* by the possibility that their concept of 'God' was incomplete, or even incorrect or incoherent? Even if such considerations are not (or would not be) important in *this* life *or the next*, as long as the next life is a better place than this life and merely approximates eschatological expectations, there is still a problem with belief in that 'better place' after death. Clearly, if the question of what or which god — or even that there *is* a god as fully conceptualized — is not a problem for Mormon or other theistic believers, then belief in the 'true God' is not necessary to the fulfillment of eschatological expectations.

This shift of concern shifts the problem from the false or incoherent claim of the Mormon god's factual existence to the false or incoherent claim of the actual existence of a next life as a habitat *somewhere* in space-time for disembodied spirits. Still, I think it is reasonable to say that the concepts of 'God' and the 'next life' are inextricably related in the minds of theistic believers. If so, this makes the argument for the existence of their god on the basis of eschatological verification relevant to its task. It is also inadequate, given the fact that the Mormon god (like the gods of *all* putatively revealed and developed forms of other theistic religions) is a *factual non-reality*.

Second, it should be pointed out that for Mormon believers the chief or ultimate eschatological expectation is personal deification in the context of eternal marriage and family. If it holds that an expectation can only be known to be fulfilled if it is first understood, then how can the eschatological expectation of deification be known to have been fulfilled in the next life if the fulness of the concept of 'Deity' is factually unintelligible, or if the claim of such a god's literal existence in this life is false or incoherent? How can the putative realization of personal deification in the next life even be possible if believers do not or cannot understand the concepts of Deity and deification in this life? How can we understand *then* (in the next life) what is impossible to understand *now* (in this life) — even with alleged revelation from a god? If some putative being who identified himself as 'God' or the 'Son of God' told us in the next life that a particular experience or state of being or affairs was in fact a realization of those eschatological expectations held in our earthly life, then we are back to where we started. The belief that such is possible is simply incoherent.

The above two implications serve to explain why, for the Mormon believer, eschatological verification might not be an acceptable or preferred solution to the conceptual problems with their concept of 'God' in particular and their theology in general. For dyed-in-the-wool, devoted Mormon believers, other evasive strategies must be employed. They may adopt the authoritative strategy of assuring the acquisition of salvific knowledge by faith, through revelation from their god, while also authoritatively and apologetically *qualifying* such an assurance.

Such qualification is accomplished by arbitrarily (and quite conveniently, even if sincerely) invoking human fallibilism, seeker unreadiness or unworthiness, necessary tests of faith, the preservation of free agency, and the inscrutable wisdom and purposes of the Mormon god to explain away faith-threatening questions concerning apparent contradictions. But what if the bedrock theological concepts of revelation and faith are also incoherent, particularly in relation to the putative 'nature of God and man'? And how might the incoherence of revelation and faith, in conjunction with such an evasive, qualifying 'possibility strategy' plunge Mormon theology into even deeper, irresolvable incoherence? What then?

Beyond our brief analysis of the Mormon concept of 'God' conducted in Chapter 3 and our likewise brief analysis of the theological, doctrinal concepts comprising the Plan of Salvation conducted in this chapter, there is the brief — albeit crucial — critical analysis we will conduct in Chapters 5 and 6 on the coherence, intelligibility, and factual significance of the Mormon doctrines of 'revelation from God' and 'faith in God and Christ' respectively. These conceptual analyses will necessarily produce the same outcome with cumulative force, *i.e.* that Mormon theology —as a whole and in each of its parts – at its deepest core is thoroughly and utterly incoherent in the broadest sense of the term.

Chapter 5

Deconstructing the Mormon Concept of Revelation from God to Man

"...revelation signifies the making known of divine truth by communication from the heavens."

— *Articles of Faith*

"The presence of revelation in the Church is positive proof that it is the kingdom of God on earth."

— *Elder Bruce R. McConkie*

"Only those books which are held by the Church to be scripture — the Bible, the Book of Mormon, the Doctrine and Covenants, the Pearl of Great Price — ...have been accepted by the Church as containing the word of God, and these books the Elders at home and abroad should maintain as absolutely true."

— *Elder B.H. Roberts*

In a well sourced article in Meridian Magazine titled "Hard Questions and Keeping the Faith,"[95] Mormon writer and apologist Michael R. Ash writes:

It is important to understand that spiritual things must be spiritually discerned....A testimony of Christ and His Gospel cannot be transmitted from one person to another; it must come by direct and individual revelation.

...Neither the existence of God, nor the reality of the Resurrection, nor the divinity of Christ, not the authenticity of the Bible or the Book of Mormon as the word of God, can be determined strictly by secular means.

As B.H. Roberts wrote: "The Power of the Holy Ghost...must ever be the chief source of evidence for the truth of the [Mormon faith]. All other evidence is secondary....No arrangement of evidence, however skillfully ordered; no argument, however adroitly made, can ever take its place. (4, 5)

But how do these mere assertions help the perplexed and skeptical outsider who is without belief in the Mormon or any god, or even a cognitive understanding of what 'God' *is* or *means* beyond mere familiarity with the term as generally and diversely used? What can a reasonable or rational person make of such assertions? If, as was concluded in Chapter 3 of this book, the concept of the Mormon god is found to be very likely false and/or incoherent — making such a god a factual non-reality as believed — how, except

---

95 www.meridianmagazine.com/lineuponline/040318harquestions.html.

from the strict naturalistic perspective presented later, can we possibly make rational (or any) sense of the concept of a 'testimony' received by the putative transmission or communication of truth through "revelation' from the Mormon god (or any 'Parent-God') by the 'Power of the Holy Ghost?' These and other crucial questions and related concerns will be raised and explored in this chapter.

To begin our analysis of the Mormon concept of 'revelation' from 'God' to man, we might profitably turn to the authoritative words of Mormon Apostle and doctrinal authority Bruce R. McConkie in his widely accepted-as-authoritative book *Mormon Doctrine* (1979). In doing so, we find that Elder McConkie had this to say about the doctrine of revelation in Mormon theology:

Regarding the nature of revelation: "As used in the gospel…[r]evelation comes from God to man in various appointed ways, according to the laws ordained by the Almighty. The Lord appears personally to certain spiritually receptive persons; he speaks audibly by his own voice, on occasions, to those whose ears are attuned to the divine wave length; angels are sent from his presence to minister to deserving individuals; dreams and visions come from him to the faithful; he often speaks by the still small voice, the voice of the Spirit, the voice of prophesy and revelation; he reveals truth by means of the Urim and Thummim (seer stones); and he gives his mind and will to receptive mortals in whatever ways seem appropriate as circumstances require" (644). Moreover, "… Every person who is sufficiently faithful has the categorical promise that God himself will appear to him" (D&C 93:1) and, "[w]ith reference to their own personal affairs, the saints [members of the Mormon Church] are expected (because they have the gift of the Holy Ghost) to gain personal revelation and guidance rather than to run to…church leaders to be told what to do" (645, all scriptural citations McConkie's).

Regarding revelation for the Church: "Our Lord's true Church is established and founded upon revelation. Its identity as the true Church continues as long as revelation is received to direct its affairs, for the gates of hell can never prevail against that power of faith and righteousness which pulls down revelations from heaven.

"Where the Church is concerned revelation comes only through the appointed channels. No one but the President of the Church [or 'Prophet, Seer, and Revelator'], who holds and exercises the fulness of the keys [or authority of the Mormon god on earth], can [receive] or announce revelation to the Church…This system of promulgating revelations through the established head of the Lord's earthly work is so unbending and inflexible that it stands as a test to establish the truth or falsity or purported revelations" (646).

Regarding the dependence of salvation (and damnation) on revelation: "'Salvation cannot come without revelation; it is vain for anyone to minister without it,' the Prophet [Joseph Smith] taught. (*Teachings*, p.160.) Without revelation the very existence of God and of the plan of salvation [analyzed in Chapter 4] would be unknown, and without revelation there would be no legal administrators to perform the ordinances of salvation with binding effect on earth and in heaven" (647, citation McConkie's).

"[However, the] receipt of revelation by individuals or peoples does not assure salvation to the favored recipients. Salvation is gained by enduring in faith and devotion to the end; it is the reward of righteousness. …Indeed, the receipt of revelation may lead to damnation as well as to salvation.[96]…In fact the greatest of all penalties, that of being cast out with the devil and his angels in eternity, is reserved for 'those sons of perdition who deny the Son after the Father hath revealed him' (D&C 76:43)" (647–648, scriptural citation McConkie's).

Regarding the dependence of Church administration on revelation: "Since The Church of Jesus Christ of Latter-day Saints [a.k.a the Mormon Church] is the Lord's true Church; and since the Lord's Church must be guided by continuous revelation if it is to maintain divine approval; and since we [Mormons] have the unqualified promise that this Church and kingdom is destined to remain on earth and prepare a people for the Second Coming [of Christ] — we could safely conclude (if we had no other evidence) that the Church today is guided by revelation…*The presence of revelation in the Church is positive proof that it is the kingdom of God on earth.* And because the Lord is no respecter of persons he will give to any person, who abides the law entitling him to know, personal revelation of the divinity of the Church and of the fact that it is being led by revelation today" (650, emphasis mine).

Mormonism is clearly based on the principle of a conditional or qualified promise of

---

96 As an important and personal aside to be addressed in more depth in later chapters and parts of this book, this particular doctrine represents, in my view, perhaps the most dangerous doctrine of the Mormon faith. It ingeniously, if not shamefully and shamelessly, manages to control the minds of Mormon believers. It does this by effectually appealing to or playing on at once their egos — through the connection of revelation (and therefore salvation) with righteousness and worthiness — and their hopes and fears, through the connection of revelation with both salvation and damnation.

Specifically, this doctrine effectually (even if not admittedly) inflates the ego of the 'righteous' and keeps believers in check. It does so by rewarding the faithful with recognition, status, power and the assurance of divine acceptance and approval, and by reinforcing the need for humility and faithfulness to 'God' though obedience and loyalty to Church leaders and the program of the Church. Conversely, this doctrine also tacitly advocates and encourages faithfulness to 'God' in the Abrahamic (or fanatical and antisocial) tradition, through loyalty and obedience to 'God' and Joseph Smith, where *faithfulness* in this sense requires obedience and submissiveness to the Mormon god *directly*, either covertly while being faithful, in a subordinate sense, to Church leaders, or overtly and apart from the Church hierarchy.

Either way, both salvation and damnation depend on revelation from the Mormon god. This revelation is considered minimally as an unshakable testimony, born of the Spirit through faith in Christ, that 'God lives"; that Jesus is the Christ; that Joseph Smith is the Prophet of the Restoration, and that the Mormon Church is the *only true* Church of Christ on the earth. This both *requires* and *reinforces* faithfulness, or unwavering, loyal obedience to the end of one's mortal life, through *both* the *self-sacrificial* pursuit of the earthly assurance of salvation and the realization of this god's acceptance and approval (by the 'Spirit' or directly and/or indirectly through Church leaders) *and* the avoidance of personal *damnation*. This is experienced as: (1) the experience of guilt, shame, self-alienation, and rejection through authoritative (and authoritarian) chastisement and/or the judgment of unworthiness and disciplinary action, and (2) the believed or declared revocation or forfeiture of both earthly and eternal 'blessings,' or the imposition of the ultimate consequence — putatively reserved for those who *know* (not merely believe), by the sure witness of the Holy Spirit, that Jesus is the Christ and then deny such a witness through apostasy or murder. One is threatened with being 'cast out' with the devil as a 'son of perdition' for all eternity.

As shall be explored in Chapters 6, 8, the *Epilogue,* and the *Personal Postscript*, this doctrine regarding the necessity of revelation for salvation — as well as the related and interdependent doctrine regarding the necessity of 'faith in God and Christ' for salvation — has potentially grave personal and social consequences. It makes the Mormon faith, as a belief system — at least likely or potentially, if not actually — both harmful and dangerous. For many if not most Mormon believers, the safest path between the promises of salvation (or eternal life) and damnation is what I characterize as 'faithful activity in moderation.' It is, however, a path that betrays their doubts as well as their fears.

continuous revelation of 'Absolute Truth' from its god to man. Indeed the promise and putative reality of such personal (and institutional) revelation is at once the very life-blood and controlling force of the Mormon faith. For many if not most 'active' (fully participating) and 'faithful' (consistently obedient and 'selfless') Mormons, revelation as perception, intuition, thought, proposition, or insight to the mind — coupled with a 'feeling in the heart' — is the final arbiter of truth and the foundation (or 'rock') upon which they build their lives. But for Mormons — as with all Christians who embrace the 'self-authenticating witness of the Holy Spirit' (see Loftus 2008, 213–219) as their way of knowing the truth *about* their god and his mind and will in their lives — it is not the intelligibility, logic, consistency, or justifiability (and hence rationality) of the propositional content of the putative revelation or inspired teaching which finally or necessarily establishes its believed truth. Rather, it is the *experienced affect* or *feeling* associated with — or induced by — the familiar language of such content, the tone of its delivery, the personal circumstances of its receipt, and the physical performance of some sacred practice or ritual.

Such an epistemic practice, or way of knowing, is prescribed in the Mormon scriptural formula found in the *Doctrine and Covenants* (D&C) which instructs believers or investigators to study the question or subject of concern in their minds, come to a conclusion or decision regarding the matter and then 'ask God if it is right.' Then, "if it is right [*i.e.* true]," God will "cause that [the believer's] "bosom shall burn within" such that he or she "shall *feel* that it is right [or true]" (D&C 9: 8, emphasis mine). Elsewhere in the *Book of Mormon*, the prophet Alma likens the revealed "word…unto a seed" which, when "planted" (presumably by the 'Spirit') in the heart of a receptive believer, will "swell within the breast" of the recipient, or hearer of the "word," if it is "a good [or true] seed." With such a "swelling" sensation in the breast the person will "feel" and thereby know that the word (or "seed") is a "good seed," for it will "enlarge [the person's] soul" and "enlighten [the person's] understanding" (Alma 32:28). Many other instances of revelation and conversion by revelation are in the *Book of Mormon*, all of which emphasize the primary role of *affect* (or feelings and emotion) in revelatory experience.

Yet, from the perspective of a *meritocratic* worldview (or meta-view), there is no need to turn to the baroque assumptions of supernaturalism or spiritualism to explain the feelings or affects — and corresponding sense of comfort, peace, joy, 'enlightenment,' and 'truth' — associated with "asking and receiving." Such a formula, contrary to the tenets of Mormon theology, is rooted in "our basic biological situation" (Faber 2004, 2010) and can, as we shall learn below and in Chapters 6 and 7, be parsimoniously explained naturalistically with *no need at all* for 'God' or a belief in him.

Moreover, beyond the fact that the Mormon claim of revelation from its god begs the question of its god's existence, it makes no rational sense to say or suggest, as Mormons do, that their god can be known *only* by revelation and spiritual experience through faith. Such an isolationist retreat from reason to revelation, spiritual experience, and faith creates further, deeper, incoherencies. Notwithstanding the above, yet in consideration of it, I invite believers to employ Loftus' 'Outsider Test for Faith' (2008, 2010). I invite them to think very literally and critically, "with the presumption of skepticism" (66), about what is being suggested or asserted above by McConkie and elsewhere in Mormon scripture — and by other notable Mormon leaders and apologists as well — about the Mormon concept of divine revelation and about what can be 'known' with certainty.

With the above invitation three significant challenges to the concept and claim of Mormon revelation from the Mormon god to man are presented below. Of the three, the first and third challenges are the most relevant, and shall likely be the most troubling, although the second challenge will, for obvious reasons, become a prominent concern if the first and third challenges prove to be insurmountable. Moreover, the third challenge consists of a four-fold problem, each of which shall be dealt with in some depth in turn.

Three Challenges and a Four-fold Problem

First, following Valerie Tarico in Loftus (2010), we need to think about three crucial and fundamental questions. (1) How do we know what is real? (2) How do we know what we know? (53) And (3) what can we know about *anything* with certainty?

As Tarico correctly points out, "The more we learn about the hardware and operating systems of the human brain — the more we understand about human information processing — the more we glean bits of insight into the religious mind," (48) and how it works in relation to our "feeling or sense of knowing that can get activated by reason and evidence but can get activated in other ways as well" (53). She goes on to cite neurologist Robert Burton, author of *On Being Certain*, who, in his own words, writes: "'Despite how certainty feels, it is neither a conscious choice nor even a thought process. Certainty and similar states of knowing what we know arise out of involuntary brain mechanisms that, like love or anger, function independently of reason.'" (54).

"Burton says," Tarico continues, "that the feeling of knowing (rightness, correctness, certainty, conviction) should be thought of as one of our primary emotions, like anger, pleasure, or fear. Like these other feelings, it can be triggered by a seizure or a drug or direct stimulation of the brain….Once triggered for any reason, the *feeling* that something is right or real [or true] can be incredibly powerful — so powerful that when it goes head-to-head with logic or evidence, the *feeling* wins. Our brains make up the reasons to justify our *feeling* of knowing, rather than following logic [or the evidence] to its logical [and justified] conclusion." (54; emphasis mine)

"When we overstate our ability to know," Tarico concludes, "we play into the fundamentalist fallacy that certainty is possible. Burton…calls this 'the all-knowing rational mind myth.' As scientists learn more about how our brains work, certitude is coming to be seen as a vice rather than a virtue. Certainty is a confession of ignorance about our ability to be passionately mistaken" (55).

The above summary observations of course do not deal with the *philosophical* treatment of justification, provisional knowledge, the fact of human fallibilism, and the question of 'reality' dealt with briefly at the beginning of Chapter 1. Nor do they deal with the psychological mechanisms of defense and projective transference referenced throughout this work, or specific neuro-psychological mechanisms of reality formation and distortion touched on later in this chapter in relation to the natural phenomena of hallucination and dissociation. Still, all of our best thinking to date regarding the above and other considerations is fundamentally consistent (or at least not inconsistent) with Tarico's conclusions throughout her chapter that *at best*:

- "We humans are [by default] not rational about anything, let alone religion.

- "Certainty is [merely] a *feeling*, not [knowing or] proof of knowing. It can fail to materialize even when evidence is enormous, and can manifest itself independently of any real knowledge.
- "Social insularity protects a community consensus. Repetition of ideas reinforces a sense of conviction or certainty. Forms of [theistic belief] that emphasize right belief have built-in safeguards against contrary evidence, doubt, and assertions of other religions.
- "The 'born again' [or theistic conversion] experience is a natural phenomenon [connected to our evolved capacity to "map" invented gods and "infantilizing" theistic narratives onto our "basic biological situation," thereby creating the *felt* illusion of an *actual* god and *two people* (or selves); the imperfect, sinful or "fallen" biological person (or "natural man"), and the "spiritual," or reborn, 'spirit-child' of 'God' and 'Christ' (Faber 2004, 2010; see also *Appendix A*)]. It is triggered by specific social and emotional factors, which can [and do] occur in both religious and secular settings.
- " Given what [we know] about knowing…we can't…claim to know anything… with certainty" (47–63; interpolations and emphasis mine)

Of course, to the theistic believer such conclusions might likely be subsumed within the paradigm of Cartesian mind-body dualism which would, in a Mormon context, make the brain an instrument of man's 'spirit (and intelligence)' and the recipient of revelation by the 'Light of Truth' emanating from the presence of 'God' as the 'Immanent God' of Mormonism referred to and analyzed in Chapter 3. But the Mormon believer who retreats to such a position would have a lot of explaining to do. Beside the fact that the notion of such dualism is rapidly becoming null and passé to all but poets, song-writers, theologians, and metaphysical philosophers due to the advancement of neuroscience, such a retreat, if it is made, would encounter great difficulties. Theists would then be asked (as they have been and shall be) to justify their assertions by first making intelligible and coherent their concepts of *spirits*, *intelligences*, the *Light of Truth*, and the nature and possibility of *revelation*. They would have to show why each is not a *factual non-reality*.

Second, and perhaps of least significance to Mormon believers (except when forced to specify what their god is actually like and how they know), is the claim that 'God' is, ultimately, an ineffable mystery and that the mystical or spiritual experience of encountering 'God's presence, love, or power' (*i.e.* 'glory') is like certain transcendent human experiences such as witnessing the birth of one's child or a beautiful sunset or natural wonder. It is inexpressible, and believers say things like "I don't have the words to say how I feel or what I experienced, but I know it was God." In this sense, "The ineffability thesis," according to Nielsen, "commits one to the belief that there are things one can know which are in principle impossible, that is, logically impossible, to coherently or intelligibly express or to exhibit in any system of notation. In this way 'a true religious statement' or 'an expressed religious truth' [such as a testimony] would be self-contradictory" (2006, 130). But this thesis, which asserts on the one hand that 'God' can only be known by revelation from 'God,' but on the other hand, that one's direct encounter with him through some putative spiritual experience is sublime beyond words or conceptual understanding simply doesn't make sense.

Ask yourself how it could be possible to *know* (not merely perceive or experience) what is not coherently or intelligibly knowable, *i.e.* is *unknowable* (or a mystery), or how is it possible for someone to reveal or testify of that which is *unspeakable* (or ineffable). Furthermore, if 'God' is a *mystery* such that any attempt to rationally understand or analyze such a concept would invalidate it as a genuine religious claim, wouldn't it be better *not* to make such claims or engage in such deviant God-talk? We don't know what counts for truth or falsity or in being reasonable or unreasonable here. "Indeed," to quote Nielsen, "we do not even understand what we are saying. We are just in a fog. Nonsense engulfs us. Isn't talk of a mystery just a high-fallutin' way of saying that?" (2001, 354)[97]

Nielsen refutes the 'ineffability thesis' first through formal argument (see 2006, 130–31) and then with still simpler considerations as follows:

> [Take] note of the platitude that if you know something that is literally in principle unsayable, inexpressible, incapable of being shown [or known] or in any way exhibited, then there trivially can be no communicating it. You cannot justifiably say it is God you experience, know, encounter, love, commit yourself to in utter trust; you, on your own thesis, cannot significantly say that if you do such and such and have such and such experiences, you will come to know God or come to be grasped by God. "What is unsayable is unsayable," is a significant tautology…So, given such a thesis, there could be no confessional community or circle of faith; in fine, the thesis is reduced to the absurd by making it impossible for those who accept such a thesis to acknowledge the manifest truth that the Judeo-Christian [and Mormon] religion is a social reality. On this simple consideration alone, we should surely rule out the ineffability thesis…What is indescribable is also unintelligible. (131)

Further, while Nielsen agrees with Sydney Hook's observation that "[sometimes] despite the language of oxymoron, we can dimly discern the objectively existent reference of what the incoherent language seems to be referring to (1975, 129)," he nonetheless goes on to argue that "we can only be justified in believing this for some particular utterance or cluster of utterances when we have good reasons to believe that [what, in fact, we dimly discern as being inchoately so] is [in fact] so, or could be so. Someone," in other words, "must be able to articulate in intelligible language what it is that the persons in unintelligible speech were trying to say" (2001, 284).

Third, we must examine the assertion that "God' must be self-revealed or remain forever unknown — that as Ostler states, "We have knowledge of God's existence, but it derives from revelation and God's self-disclosure and not from logical certainties" (NGNAN, 15). This is, on its face, at least apparently incoherent. Beyond the obvious presupposition of a god's existence in such an assertion — which invalidates the assertion by begging the question at issue — there is the *four-fold* problem of: (1) knowing a god exists through revelation or spiritual experience, *i.e.* of encountering through revelation

---

97 "But what if god is mysterious and unknowable? This, alas," according to Eller (2004), "is another refuge of the confused, for how," echoing Nielsen and common sense, "can one coherently talk about, let alone believe in, the unknowable? How could one possibly 'know' that one's claims and beliefs are legitimate and founded? For example, if god 'works in mysterious ways,' how can we know for sure [or at all] that that he/she/it is working at all? If I said that my car worked in mysterious ways, in that sometimes it starts and sometimes it doesn't, that would be the definition of *not working*! If god sometimes answers prayer and sometimes doesn't, sometimes intervenes in human affairs and sometimes doesn't, how can we know which is which? We cannot. Therefore, since the very words and concepts Theists use appear to be incoherent, we may be able to dismiss their claims out of court before the argument even starts" (51).

that which is factually unintelligible (*i.e.* 'God'); (2) the concept of Mormon revelation *per se*; (3) authentication and fallibilism pertaining to Mormon revelation *specifically*; and (4) revelation and religious experience as purely *naturalistic* phenomena. Each of these four problems will be addressed in some depth below.

The Problem of 'Knowing God exists' (and 'knowing God personally and directly') through Revelation or 'Spiritual Experience'

Loftus (2010) cites an example of why faith fails from what one Mormon said in a written review about the skeptical book *Joseph Smith and the Origins of the Book of Mormon*:

> "… *[P]eople believe what they want to believe*. If you want to KNOW something, why not ask the only one who truly knows: God? That was Joseph Smith's message. That was the message of the *Book of Mormon*. It was also the message of our Savior… (Matthew 7:7). Or you can refer to the scripture quoted by the prophet himself… (James 1: 5–7).
>
> "I know Joseph Smith was a prophet of God. Not because some person told me, and not because some man showed me a book full of evidence (*there is such evidence for those who want to find it*). *I know, because like Joseph Smith, I got down on my knees, in faith, and asked my Heavenly Father if it was true.* You cannot know anything, but by God. What do you have to lose? *I'm not giving you my opinions*. I only invite those who wish to know the truth…If you want to know, ask God, and I promise you that He will answer if you honestly seek only the truth." (20–1)

This example is paradigmatic in my view of how believing Mormons think and talk, and what they believe. As we learned above in the first challenge above, as well as in Chapters 3 and 4, and as we shall learn below and also in Chapters 6 and 8, the *Personal Postscript*, and *Appendices A* and *B* which follow, this Mormon's testimony (as all others of like kind) is deeply flawed and problematical for various reasons.

Not only does this believer commit various serious and invalidating reasoning fallacies (*Introduction*) and make unwarranted assertions that are arguably irrational (Chapter 2) and false or incoherent in relation to his or her references to 'God,' 'Heavenly Father,' and 'Savior' (Chapter 3), but he or she confirms and tacitly admits, directly and through reversal, to two important facts. First, as Loftus correctly informs us on the basis of substantial evidence, in matters of religious faith "people…justify whatever they were raised [or conditioned] to believe" (21). Second, in the quoted statement above, this Mormon believer (again no doubt like all theistic believers) not only incorrectly if not incoherently conflates *feelings* of certainty and certain knowledge of Truth, which is itself problematical on the basis of what we learned in the first challenge above, but inadvertently connects the believed *divinely* sanctioned and prescribed way of knowing *all* Truth to *self-deception*. Such self-deception, as we know and learned in Chapter 2 in regard to Jonathan Alder's work (2006), is a ubiquitous psychological phenomenon which entails one believing that which would reasonably be deemed by rational and reasonably skeptical outsiders to be unbelievable. This is done primarily if not exclusively because one *wants* or *wishes* to so believe.

Mormons must and do believe that by faith, through revelation, they can know — and have a personal relationship with — an infinite and eternal Heavenly Father who, although not physically in or of this world, nonetheless can and does reveal himself and his will personally, by the Light of Truth (Christ) or the power of the Holy Ghost — as well as in person, to those who seek to know him with a pure, sincere heart and real intent. This believed way of knowing religious truth is a crucial aspect of Mormon theology. It is addressed briefly in this chapter and more completely in the next. For reasons connected to the observations touched on above, this aspect of theistic epistemology is a serious problem for thinking Mormon believers and soberly minded investigators of the Mormon faith.

In an edited transcript of Ostler's 2007 presentation at a FAIR Conference we learn that "To know God is the most important aspect of [religious] experience because to know God in this sense is eternal life. Indeed," Ostler asserts, "to know that we are accepted into relationship with God [through revelation and spiritual experience] and to invite God to reside in our hearts is a moment of justification by grace through faith, and the beginning of the life of sanctification in which the spirit enters into us and Christ takes up abode in us in the process of Christification, of being conformed to the image of Christ; a process culminating in deification. That's," insists Ostler, "the message that we offer" (2007, 5).

But what exactly does such a message actually and specifically amount to? Apart from my differences with Ostler's apparent theological interpretation of the Mormon doctrines of justification and sanctification (differences which are neither relevant nor significant to our task at hand), there are several problems with his Mormon God-talk. As a whole it seems to amount to *literal* nonsense that is cognitively meaningless.

First, 'to know God' or 'to know that we are accepted into relationship with God' and 'to invite God to reside in our hearts' (whatever that *actually* means, if anything) again *presupposes* the putative existence of the Mormon god. It also presupposes that the implied truth claim 'God exists' is both *justifiable* and *justified*, a claim which, in the context of this book and others of like kind that deal with such concepts (Nielsen 1996; 2006), cannot be uncontroversially made.

Second, how can we come to know or relationally experience a being that in its metaphysical fullness is unknowable in virtue of its factual unintelligibility? What could it actually mean, in Ostler's words, for "the spirit" to enter a human being and for "Christ to take up abode in us in the process of Christification," or of being "conformed to the image of Christ" toward "deification" (5)? What *specifically* is 'the spirit' and how *specifically* would such a thing *actually* enter a human being? How could such a non-self-evident claim possibly be known, or justified? Moreover, what could it actually mean for 'Christ,' as the putative 'Son of God,' to *literally* 'take up abode in us' — given that since the concept of 'God' is incoherent, so too is the concept of the 'Son of God'? Given that 'Christ' as a person is a tangible, resurrected man, how could he 'take up abode in us'? If the expression 'Christ taking up abode in us' is not meant to be taken literally, then in what sense exactly *does* Christ 'take up abode in us'? If by *Christ* Ostler means merely the *remembrance* of Christ, then what *specifically* and *literally* is such a remembrance indicative of? (There is in fact a sensible, naturalistic answer to this question. It will be addressed in the next chapter.)

Likewise, how can we make rational sense of the 'process of Christification' toward 'deification'? If such a process is intended to mean 'becoming Christlike,' then what would it *actually* mean for a human being to *literally* become *like* a god (Christ) — or to be deified — when the very concept of the Mormon god (and hence 'Son of God') is incoherent and factually unintelligible? Or what *precisely* is 'the image of Christ' and what would it *actually* mean for a human being to be *literally* 'conformed to the image of Christ?'

If 'becoming Christlike' or 'being conformed to the image of Christ' is intended to mean that one somehow puts on the 'divine nature of Christ' and therefore becomes *good* as Christ is 'good' or *charitable* as Christ is 'charitable,' or *forgiving, generous, compassionate* and *empathic* as is Christ, then how can we make sense of what such putatively *divine* attributes *actually mean* — except perhaps through analogical predication? As we learned earlier, this would necessarily fail us in this case since we can know *nothing non-analogical* or *literal* about such divine attributes. Accepting such as the case, what then exactly *is* the 'image of Christ' and how *specifically* is a human image *literally* transformed to conform to such an unknown and unknowable image? We clearly lack a reference range here, as well as truth-conditions regarding such a state or process that could in principle be confirmed or disconfirmed as being true (or probably true) or false (or probably false).

How can we understand what it *actually means* for an infinite, eternal and transcendent 'Person' to *literally* reveal or be able to reveal himself — and relate *personally, on a real-time basis* — to anyone in a different dimension of space and time by the 'power of the Holy Ghost'? Beyond the factual unintelligibility and incoherence of the concept of the 'Holy Ghost' as a 'spirit personage,' the third member of the Mormon Godhead, and the 'Light of Truth' analyzed in Chapter 3 as part (in Roberts' term) of the doctrine of 'Divine Immanence,' what *specifically* is the 'power of the Holy Ghost'? How can we understand what it *actually* and *literally* means for truth to be *literally* transmitted from a god through the Holy Ghost to man? If such a revelation or spiritual transmission is experienced as a feeling or 'burning in the bosom,' by what objective and universally accepted human criteria can such an affect be *actually* and *specifically* known to come from or be caused by a being unintelligibly conceptualized doctrinally as the Mormon god (or Son of God) or the recipient's literal spirit Father (or personal Savior)? Again, language seems to fail us here in establishing cognitive meaning. As we learned in the *Foundational Preface* and Chapter 1, all knowledge is language-dependent. If language fails us we have a serious problem. Simply put, it is not possible to know by the language-dependent interpretation of subjective experience that which is unknowable, since conceptually (and therefore linguistically) it is unintelligible.

In relation to both the phenomenon of revelation and particularly the revelation of the Mormon god to those who claim to have received such, the Mormon author, apologist, and Church educator Gerald Lund speaks of the Mormon belief that "The Spirit's communication [*i.e.* revelation] is unlike any other form of communication we experience in life" (2007, 26). He is forced to admit: "And therein is the problem. How do [can] we define or describe something that is different from all other things we know? How," he asks further, "do we recognize it when it comes if it is unlike the everyday experience we are used to? We may try to liken it to other experiences, but those are inadequate to describe it so clearly and so well that when it comes [if indeed it exists] we will always recognize it for what it is" (27).

Lund then suggests that "Spiritual things may be beyond the capacity of the mortal mind and tongue to express" (27) and then presents two analogies from Mormon Apostles Neal A. Maxwell and Boyd K. Packer which he implies, on the basis of his selection, adequately explain the problem of knowing by revelation that the Mormon god exists while not negating the putative reality and truthfulness of either revelation or God. But as we shall discover below, both analogies (and the arguments they were no doubt intended to make) are seriously flawed, for they not only beg the question at issue by presupposing the existence of the Mormon god and revelation, they are also false and invalid as analogies — sensible as they might seem at face value.

First, Maxwell (27) employs an analogy which likens one's 'knowing by revelation that God exists' to being able to point to a picture of one's mother among the pictures of *all* other women in her age group, even though one could not adequately or with sufficient accuracy describe one's mother to someone else who had never seen her so that the other person could correctly pick her out among all other women. This argument by analogy fails, of course. First of all, it *begs the question* of a particular god's existence. Secondly, unlike pointing to a picture of an actual human being (in this case one's mother), admittedly no one who alleges to know 'God' can reliably specify or describe *either by words or by ostention* (pointing), what *specifically* the Mormon god is or even looks like beyond merely having the shape of a man. Thirdly, no one can identify what *specific*, affective experience — among all other similar human affective experiences — may indubitably (beyond circularly affirming the consequent) be regarded as *revelation*.

Next, Packer (28) shares an experience in which, during a conversation with a fellow passenger while traveling, he allegedly had occasion to claim or testify to this person that he (Packer) 'knew that God lives.' Packer's testimony was then allegedly dismissed by the person to whom he was speaking (reportedly "an atheist") who, after claiming that no one could know such a thing, asked Packer first to explain how he could know that 'God' exists, and then to describe what this god was like and how Packer could know what he was like.

Packer was self-admittedly at a loss for words. Then, according to Lund, he received what Lund characterized as 'a revelation' and asked the Atheist first if he knew what salt tasted like. Then, upon receiving a predictably affirmative answer, he was asked to describe the taste of salt. When the Atheist was likewise allegedly lost for words, Packer then argued from analogy that even though he did not have the words to describe 'God' to the Atheist, he, like the Atheist who claimed to know what salt tasted like but could not describe the taste, nonetheless knew that his god existed by the revelation of the Holy Spirit.[98]

Unfortunately, this argument by analogy — like Maxwell's —fails for all the same reasons. Not only does it *beg the question* of a god's existence, it falsely compares the objectively verifiable and falsifiable existence of a physical substance (salt), and the sensory experience of tasting salt, with the unverifiable, unfalsifiable and purely subjec-

---

98 Packer implicitly asserts the parity argument (addressed in Chapter 2) by falsely claiming the properly basic status of knowledge putatively acquired through religious experience, in this case revelation. But while it is common knowledge that the experience of tasting something *salty* (or, alternatively, *sweet* or *bitter*) is *basic* as a common human experience, where taste is commonly known to be a natural sense which is widely experienced, and where the descriptive terms *salty, sweet, bitter*, etc. are commonly acknowledged in relation to certain tastes, such is not the case with *spiritual sense* or *spiritual experience* —including the putative 'knowing of God' through revelation. Unlike salt or tasting salt, neither revelation from the Mormon god, nor the *experience* of revelation *per se* is commonly and indubitably experienced (even among members of the Mormon faith). Moreover, the factual, objective existence of the Mormon god is most certainly *not* commonly or widely acknowledged or accepted as basic, common knowledge. On the contrary!

tive existence of 'Spirit,' 'Intelligence,' and 'spiritual experience' (or 'revelation'). Again referring to the problem of invalid analogical predication addressed earlier and in Chapter 1, we must point out that while we know something definitive about the natural substance of salt and about the biological sense of taste and the basic taste of salt (even though we can't describe it), we know nothing specifically *non-analogical*, or literal, about the putatively supernatural physical and spirit substances comprising the Mormon god. We know nothing of any alleged supernatural 'spiritual sense' in man that enables him to receive revelation from a god. We know nothing of any reported spiritual affects of 'revelation' that would enable cognitive understanding through this or any other analogy.

Consequently, Packer's simple argument from analogy is flawed on the basis of its *false* comparison of what *is* naturally and commonly known and knowable (*i.e.* the existence of salt and the taste of salt) to what is *not* naturally known or knowable (*i.e.* 'God' and the 'spiritual knowing of God through revelation'). Furthermore, it is also flawed as a way of facilitating cognitive understanding through the analogical predication of entities and phenomena that are without objectively (empirically) or even commonly known (or *basic*) non-analogical (literal) properties. It is invalid to argue, as Packer does with his faulty analogy, that the claim of knowing that 'God exists' is valid — notwithstanding one's inability to describe 'God' or explain how one knows such a god *actually* exists — on the analogical grounds that such a claim is no different from (or just like) the claim that salt exists and that one knows salt exists by taste even though one cannot describe the taste of salt.

Therefore, Packer's reported answer to the first question, *i.e.* that he knew by the Holy Spirit through revelation, is not a valid argument. The use of Packer's analogy to answer the second question, *i.e.* that he could not describe what the revealed god is like any more than he or anyone could describe what the taste of salt is like and that therefore, his knowledge that his god exists is like his knowledge of what salt tastes like likewise is not an appropriate or valid argument. The *first answer begs the question* at issue (*i.e.* the Mormon god's alleged existence) and also invalidly argues for his existence by further presupposing the existence of revelation from him and the truth of the premise — offered as basic fact — that this god can only be revealed by revelation. It then invalidly argues, and unjustifiably concludes, that since this god's existence can only be known by revelation, then the fact that the believer has reportedly received a revelation of a god's existence necessarily proves this god exists.

The *second answer*, again, argues from false analogy. But not only, as we learned above, are such answers fatally flawed, the questions themselves miss the crucial point. The alleged "atheist" in Packer's account, I would argue, should have *first* asked Packer to elucidate the concept of the Mormon god and specify the 'reference range' of his god (Nielsen 1982, 140–170) so that it could be known in principle what *specifically* might count for or against the actual existence of the Mormon god in its theological (physical *and* metaphysical) fulness. If, on the basis of a rigorous and thorough conceptual analysis of the Mormon god, it is reasonable to conclude that the concept of the Mormon god as claimed is unintelligible, incoherent, and factually meaningless (as argued in Chapter 3) — thereby reducing the Mormon god to the status of a factual non-reality — then the first question 'how do (could) you know your god exists?' is unnecessary. This would be so because the concept of revelation in Mormon theology *necessarily* depends for its very existence on the *factual* existence of the Mormon god. If therefore, the claim of the Mormon god's existence is factually meaningless and therefore unjustifiable as a truth claim, then the question of how one could *know* such a god is as absurd as it is unnecessary.

Essentially, then, the two questions asked by the Atheist would best be reversed. In doing so, the first part of the second question ('what *specifically* and *literally* is your God like?') becomes the first question, and Packer's evasive non-answer to *that* question ends the conversation with the conclusion, preferably stated by the Atheist, that neither the believer (in this case Packer) nor the non-believer (in this case Packer's "atheist") knows what is being said with the claim 'God lives' and that therefore the claim is factually vacuous and not worthy of any consideration, much less rational belief.

Be that as it may, after presenting Maxwell's and Packer's attempts to deal with the problem of "how to define or describe something [in this case 'The Spirit's communication' of the existence of the Mormon god] that is different from all other things we know?" (26), Lund apologetically concludes — with no apparent consequence for his remaining presuppositional exposition of the believed fact of Mormon revelation — by stating merely that "Our language is not adequate to the task" (29).

But this important conclusion is much more troubling than it would seem Lund realizes. It takes us back to the first problem addressed in this chapter — the problem with the claim that 'God' (and therefore revelation from him) as a putative reality is a being or process whose description is ultimately *ineffable* and therefore beyond our ability to express in human language or even understand. In this regard, it seems worthy to repeat Nielsen's earlier observations — with all the implicative weight that such observations necessarily impose — that "what is unsayable is unsayable" and "What is indescribable is also unintelligible" (2006, 131). Moreover, Lund's conclusion also takes us back to the language-dependent nature of factual discourse and reality as we know it to be and the unfounded criticism of language addressed by Ambrose, both presented in Chapter 1. It also takes us back to the evasive possibility strategy of isolation exposed and addressed by Adler in Chapter 2, as well as to the Wittgensteinian fideistic argument (presented and addressed by Nielsen in the next chapter) that some things are beyond human understanding and therefore must be taken on faith — a claim that is likewise itself, and in relation to the Mormon concept of 'faith,' both unsatisfactory and problematical for the Mormon believer.

Fundamentally, if one cannot make rational sense of what is meant by the Mormon conception of 'God, the Father' as literally (doctrinally) defined and described by alleged revelation from the Mormon god and authoritative pronouncement or Prophetic declaration — if, indeed, such a concept is incoherent and factually meaningless — then *one has no idea what specifically one must authentically encounter to experientially encounter such a god through revelation or religious experience.* What must one encounter (in this life or in the presumed and highly improbable next life) to directly or experientially encounter 'the Supreme Governor and Ultimate Source of the Universe,' or 'an infinite and eternal Spirit (and Intelligence) of the highest order,' or 'the One Supreme and Absolute Being,' or 'the unchangeable God, the framer of heaven and earth, and all things which are in them,' or 'the only…independent being in whom all fulness and perfection dwell,' or the 'Heavenly Father,' or the 'Father of Lights,' or 'Alpha and Omega,' or the great 'I AM'? What specifically would a revelation of any or all of these aspects of the Mormon god literally be like? Even if a radiant, apparently powerful, wise and loving being appeared and introduced himself as "God," how would we truly know that we were, in fact, encountering such a being as doctrinally described or scripturally referred to or believed in as *God*?

To be sure, there are still Mormon leaders, apologists, and believers who would no doubt argue, as does Christian apologist William Alston in "The Perception of God" (1988), that, *pace* Nielsen and other analytical thinkers, it is not incoherent or irrational for a person to believe that 'God' is revealing himself through personal experiences, including spoken revelation and revelation through affective perception, dreams, visions, and visitations. Alston specifically considers the arguments of Nielsen, and those many others who believe that the experiential cognition of the god of orthodox Judeo-Christianity and Islam (including the Mormon god) is impossible, to involve, in Nielsen's words, "considerations concerning the *ontology* and not the *phenomenology* of the experience" (1996, 454). He claims, according to Nielsen, "that what is at issue here is the *phenomenological* character of the experience and not whether the agent having the experience has got the ontology [*i.e.* theory (or in this case, theology or doctrine) of a god's existence and nature, or *being*] right, to wit, whether she actually has an experience of God. Phenomenologically, one can be directly aware of a unicorn or King Arthur even while being mistaken about the existence of unicorns or King Arthur. What one, in such a circumstance, is directly aware of is not what one thinks it is, rather, one is directly aware of something one mistakenly identifies as a unicorn or as King Arthur" (454, emphasis mine).

"But" — or so it seems to Nielsen — "that is not to the point in the case of God, for we could not phenomenologically, or otherwise, be directly aware of what it is not even possible to be directly aware of. Such, however, is the challenge being made to claims of religious experience. Thus, to translate into the concrete again and to argue first from analogy, if someone says they saw a colorless, shapeless figure we know that they could not have seen such a figure any more than someone can draw a round square. *This is not a matter of ontology but of what makes sense.* What we have in such instances is an incoherent attempt at a phenomenological characterization of an experience. As we shall see (*pace* Alston) — or so at least my argument shall go — perceiving God is in the same boat. God is an infinite [and eternal] individual transcendent to the universe [world], but such a being could not possibly be directly experienced any more than someone could draw a round square or see a shapeless, colorless figure. It is not, Alston to the contrary notwithstanding, at all like whether someone could see what appears to be a unicorn. The issue in the case of God, as in my two examples, is logical or conceptual and not ontological. [It simply] makes no sense to speak of perceiving an infinite [and eternal] individual transcendent to the universe" (454).

Furthermore, Nielsen continues, "…if in directly perceiving God the perceiver is not cognizant that it is God she is perceiving, the fact (if it is a fact) that she in fact, though unwittingly, is perceiving God is cold comfort to her and to us. We would like to know whether we can *sometimes* ascertain, albeit fallibilistically, that it is God we perceive. We would also like to know whether our perceiving God can provide us with a justified belief that God exists" (459). This we cannot do within the limited (and limiting) confines of Alston's argument, for on the basis of the conceptual analysis of both the orthodox Christian and Mormon concepts of 'God,' in their fullness, it is not possible to experience 'God.' The 'experiential path' defended by Alston — and by Mormon believers, leaders, and apologists on the basis of the factual existence and truth of divine revelation — has been conceptually blocked by their respective definitions of who or what their god in fact is believed to be (463, see also Everitt 2004, 165–175 for another effective, atheistic assessment of Alston's argument).

The Problem of the Concept of Revelation per se

This *dilemma of authentication* pertains also to 'revelation' itself. If one has no idea of what counts as a revelation one has no idea of what is needed to have what is called an authentic, self-confirming revelation or 'spiritual experience of (or with) God.' Ask yourself in this regard, what specifically would count as an authentic revelation, or spiritual experience? First of all, how would such revelation even be possible? *What exactly and relevantly — and without resorting to* ad hoc *explanations adorned with evasive 'somehow,' 'somewhere,' or 'somewhen' qualifiers — would it be like for a finite, personally transcendent being (a god) in a particular universe or dimension of space and time to personally communicate or reveal himself either transpersonally or in person and in real-time to another finite being (man) in a different universe or dimension of space and time? How would such personal or transpersonal communication, or self-disclosing revelation, be possible on a real-time basis or at all? How would such transcendent, transpersonal communication be possible on a real-time, two-way basis, as in prayer?* When praying, to whom or to what *specifically* are we actually or literally praying when we think we are praying to, say, an 'infinite and eternal spirit (and intelligence)' or a biologically and spatiotemporally transcendent being? (This is a crucial and important question addressed in Chapter 7 in relation to the problem of prayer and asked and answered intelligently, reasonably, and compellingly from a naturalistic perspective by M.D. Faber in his well-documented chapter "Prayer and Faith," 2004, 135–154 and in his book on the subject entitled *The Magic of Prayer*, 2002.)

Appeals to imagination and irrelevant and false analogies to current remote-communication technology aside, given that we know *nothing* non-analogical, or literal, about 'spirit-energy' or the 'Light of Christ' (whatever such might actually mean, if anything), how would such a transpersonal revelatory process be actually possible? Could it be conceivable or even imaginable? If it were realistically conceivable and clearly, non-deviantly communicated, how could the existence of such a revelatory process possibly be empirically and credibly confirmed or disconfirmed as a factual reality?

Let us assume, solely for the sake of argument, the possibility of such revelation. We must then ask what human criteria would enable the *sure distinction* of an authentic revelation (or confirmation of a revelatory teaching, belief, or course of action) from a counterfeit or false one? Distinct from — yet related to — the earlier problems with analogical predication is the problem of the vagueness and ambiguity of Mormon references to a 'burning in the bosom' or a 'swelling of the breast' or a 'feeling of rightness' (or 'wrongness') or 'goodness' (or 'badness') or the 'taste' of revealed truth as 'delicious.' All of these evocative terms or expressions are without cognitive meaning or factual significance as defining criteria. We must ask, therefore, what *specific,* unique, decisive, and widely accepted criteria (either inside or outside the faith) would enable a Mormon believer (or anyone) to *surely* distinguish a divine revelation or spiritual confirmation from merely the theological interpretation of certain naturalistic phenomena? How could we distinguish a putative revelation from the very real experience of, for example, a latent "wish"-induced visual or auditory hallucination, or from a hypnotically-induced dissociative experience or mere brain-induced optical illusion? Alternatively, how could we distinguish such a believed revelatory experience from a projective transference of the internalized parent *imago* onto the invented image of the Parent-God, or from an "implicit, affective memory" evoked by certain *familiar* cues or non conscious auto-suggestion? Or, relatedly, from a compelling associative (or stimulus-induced) affect connected to "implicitly recollected parental ministrations in infancy" (Faber 2010, 31)? Basically, how could we differentiate a so-called "spiritual experience" from simply a chemically or environmentally induced neural misfire or neurological malfunction; or from a biologically induced (and wished for) "figment of the imagination?" As Nielsen commonsensically points out in this regard, "We must have some human criteria for 'revelation,' including human criteria for the application of the term, or we could not even converse or think about the subject. There is no choice here but to define it in the terms and possibilities of knowledge open to man" (2006, 193).

Furthermore, if such criteria are claimed to exist and are themselves claimed to be authoritative as putative revelation, we are trapped in a circular argument that gets us nowhere. For if it is argued that we know by scripture or revelation from a god what counts and doesn't count as true or authentic revelation from him on the basis of criteria of authentication revealed by him, we have asserted nothing of any probative value or significance. Such a claim, given its dependence on the existence of the god as conceptualized, is not only question-begging, but unintelligible and factually vacuous as well.

Beliefs based on the content of putative personal revelation or religious (spiritual) experiences or encounters with a god are often considered by some Christian (and Mormon) believers and theologians to be self-validating in virtue of one's experiences alone — *without* the burden of proof or the need for objective, interpretive, or authenticating criteria and justification or supporting argument. As touched on in our earlier analysis of rationality and the parity argument presented in Chapter 2, there are, however, various problems with such a 'Reformed Epistemology.' Two of them are relevant to this particular chapter.

First, to suggest that alleged self-disclosing revelation from a god is properly basic is to beg the question by presupposing the existence of that being ('God') whom the self-disclosing revelation is at least implicitly attempting to establish.

Second, to reverse the burden of proof, as Reformed Epistemologists insist, amounts to the principle that we, as reasonable people or skeptical outsiders, should accept as being true or self-evident (*i.e.* 'properly basic') *any* and *all* alleged personal revelations or religious experiences regarding any god's existence, nature, mind, and will that is not conclusively or sufficiently refuted or proven to be untrue by the skeptic. This we are asked to do simply on the basis of: (*i*) the assertion that sense experience and religious experience should be accorded parity on the basis that they are, in Richard Gale's words, "analogous in cognitively relevant respects, especially in regard to both containing their own checks and tests" (1991, 299), and (*ii*) the recipient's interpretation of their personal experience, or the interpretation of any so-called and so-regarded religious experience reportedly given to *anyone* or *everyone* who claims or believes to have received one, regardless of whether or not such experiences are intelligible or coherent internally or in relation to others within the same or different faiths.

This assertion of revelatory experience being properly basic has been shown to be significantly problematical with obviously absurd consequences,[99] as has the claim made by certain so-called liberal theologians that essentially *whatever (or everything)* anyone experiences of an insightful, wondrous, ecstatic, transcendent, or transformational nature is revelation *from* and *of* a god.

Such assertions are devoid of widely accepted, objective, human criteria, required checks and tests for veridicality and necessary contrast. They are questionable at least and necessarily void of any credibility as truth claims. For if essentially every wondrous or otherwise seemingly ecstatic, comforting, or transcendent, affective (or feeling-toned) experience is revelation, or if *everyone* who claims to have received revelation about a god from that god has essentially made a 'properly basic' (self-justifying) claim, then such putative revelation essentially requires no objective human (or divine) criteria for authentication or validation. Therefore, it cannot possibly be verified, confirmed, falsified, or disconfirmed. This makes the alleged truth of the claimed revelation unjustifiable and therefore factually insignificant — as well as illegitimate as a knowledge claim according to common or widely held epistemic standards. Furthermore, disingenuous claims of religious inclusivism to the contrary notwithstanding,[100] such assertions create real problems for competing theistic positions that claim absolute and eternally binding theistic truth with eternal consequences, as the Mormon religion certainly does.

Clearly, to be credible, all such alleged self-disclosing revelation by a god, or other mystical or spiritual experiences from 'God' or the 'Holy Spirit' which purport to be literally true or to reveal actual and absolute truth from 'God,' *must* be subject to critical analysis and validation through cross-checking.[101] They cannot merely be accepted *a priori*

---

99 Regarding the problem of parity between sensory experiences and religious experiences, see Gale 1991, 285–343. Regarding the difficulties and absurd consequences of the acceptance of 'proper basicality' of religious experience, see Nielsen 1996, 115–155, and Everitt 2004, 26–29.

100 Mormons have in fact adopted religious exclusivism with respect to their foundational claim of being the *only* true Church and of all other faiths being false and an abomination to 'God.' Moreover, Mormon theology is indeed exclusive in regard to its most crucial and foundational doctrines such as its doctrine of Deity and the assertion that Mormon priesthood authority is *required* to officiate in the ordinances of salvation (or else salvation is not possible. Non-members cannot, for example, receive or enjoy the 'gift of the Holy Ghost' or live in the presence of the Mormon god in the next life. They cannot live eternally with their family without receiving the Mormon Temple 'sealing' ordinances in the Mormon Temples that putatively bind on earth and in heaven the living and the dead for 'time and all eternity.' Finally, all devout Mormon believers would no doubt agree that believers in other faiths who claimed to have received a revelation or a spiritual witness from a god that, for example, Joseph Smith was *not* a true 'prophet of God,' that the *Book of Mormon* was *not* the 'Word of God' or a 'Second Witness of Jesus Christ," or that the Mormon Church was a cult would be mistaken, or deceived by Satan, or merely self-deceived.

101 In an important article, Evan Fales argues that "[t]he problem of perception derives largely from the general truth that any effect — hence a perceptual experience — can be caused in more ways than one. Our strategy for removing this ambiguity is cross-checking. Ultimately, cross-checking involves just collecting more data, which is subject to the same ambiguity. Our implicit reasoning is that the total amount of ambiguity can nevertheless be in this way progressively reduced. The means by which science draws a bead on postulated 'unobservable' entities (like electrons) is not in principle or in practice different in kind; it is just more systematic and careful than the humdrum of everyday perceptual judgments. In everyday contexts, cross-checking is informal, and it is so automatic, continuous and pervasive that, except under duress (*e.g.*, as we try to catch out a magician), it is scarcely noticed….[C]ross-checking…is [arguably] a mandatory feature of any recruitment of perceptual experience to epistemic ends; and to show that, therefore, it is a requirement that must be met in theistic appeals to mystical ['spiritual' or 'revelatory'] experience as evidence for theism.

on the basis of faith,[102] analogy,[103] or analogical predication.[104] They cannot be accepted as being 'properly basic'[105] or considered *prima facie* probable or true in virtue of some 'principle of credulity'[106] or putatively reliable 'mystical doxastic practice.'[107] Nor can they be accepted on the basis of some version of 'language-game fideism.'[108] Further, such claims, whether made publicly or privately held, can only *reasonably* be validated through the use of *reliable* (*i.e.* non-question-begging and justified), objective human criteria.

The use of the word *reasonably* in the last sentence above is not gratuitous. Human *reason*, applied to the logical use of human language, is used *primary* in the effort to validate the substance, content, and source of claimed divine revelation. Without both human reason and language, which are critically and necessarily interdependent in establishing knowledge or truth in any domain, human criteria of validation could not be established. The knowledge claim of a 'true revelation (or confirmation)' would therefore necessarily be illegitimate as well as unintelligible.

But this is the very dilemma. Circular arguments to the contrary notwithstanding, since there are *no* such reliable objective and generally accepted human criteria for validating claimed revelations, the claims that 'true revelation exists' and that 'revelation is the Ultimate Source and arbiter of God's truth' are both incoherent. Further, if the concept

---

Finally,…this requirement has not and probably cannot be met. So,…mystical [spiritual or revelatory] experience provides hardly any useful support for theism" (2002, 2). This, I think, is true in the absence of objective and justified human criteria for identifying, and differentiating the nature and affects of purely spiritual or mystical experiences and validating the source and content of such experiences.

102 For a treatment of the problem of faith as epistemological justification for religious experience-based belief in a god, see Chapter 6 and Blackstone 1963, 140–160.

103 The argument for belief in or about a god on the basis of analogy applied to religious experience-based God-talk and 'language-game fideism' is critically and competently assessed and challenged by Nielsen 1989, 190–207 and Gale 1991, 285–343.

104 For a treatment of the problem of analogical predication as epistemological justification for belief in a god, see Chapter 1 and Blackstone 1963, 62–72.

105 For a presentation, analysis, and refutation of the theistic claim that belief in and beliefs about a god are 'properly basic' because they are grounded on religious experience, see Chapter 2 of this book, as well as Nielsen 1996, 115–156; Martin 1990, 269–277; and Everitt 2004, 17–29.

106 Swinburne (1979) asserts the a priori validity of presented religious experience on the basis of what he terms the 'Principle of Credulity,' which essentially holds that religious experiences should be trusted as *prima facie* probable as presented by the believer, unless there is good and undefeated reason to doubt their validity. For presentation, analyses, and objections to Swinburne, see Martin 1990, 166–187; Everitt 2004, 160–165; and Gale 1994 and 1991, 285–343.

107 Alston (1991) argues that "…people sometimes do perceive God and thereby acquire justified beliefs about God" (3) and that such perception is, moreover, reliable as being indicative of an actual experience-independent reality, making the belief in 'God' properly basic. For presentation, analyses, and objections to Alston, see Nielsen 1996, 79–156; 451–456; Everitt 2004, 151–9; 165–177; and Gale 1994 and 1991, 285–343.

108 Wittgenstein's thinking regarding contextualized 'meaning as use' was introduced in Chapter 1, and the Wittgensteinian argument that religious experience and belief in 'God' is epistemologically valid or justified on the basis of Wittgensteinian language-game fideism is critically addressed in Chapter 6 and at length by Nielsen 1982, 1989, 2001 and 2006, and Gale 1991, 285–343.

'God' and the use of the term 'God' are in fact incoherent, unintelligible, and factually or cognitively meaningless, then it logically follows that the very idea or concept of revelation is incoherent — even without the need for validation. This means that it is not possible that there could be a revelation *of* a factual non-reality ('God') *from* a factual non-reality ('God'). After all, as with 'God' so too with revelation: what is not possible cannot be actual. *How can the existence of 'God' — which is necessarily impossible because the concept 'God' is either incoherent or factually meaningless — possibly be actually revealed by such a non-reality to "all nations, kindreds, tongues [languages] and people?"* How is such a presumed possibility or claimed actuality even comprehensible let alone rational?

To these and other questions, "Some may counter," Nielsen acknowledges, speaking for himself and for me as well, "…that I have mistakenly talked about revelation apart from scripture and the authority of the church to *authorize* who can speak for God. But here," he replies, "we must in turn ask *which* scripture [and *which* version of scripture] — and there are many Holy Writs [and many changes to them through human translations and corrections] — on *whose* interpretation (and there are many conflicting interpretations) and which church [or Church Authority, for there are many such authorities and many contradictory teachings and putatively revealed truths among them]? To give a respectable answer that would justify making one claim rather than another, we would have to be able to [justifiably] answer the question: *who is justified in speaking for God?* More fundamentally still, a decent answer here would require our answering the question: how can we know or have good reason to believe that anyone speaks for God?" (2006, 194)[109]

---

109 Nielsen argues, as do I and others of like mind, that the core, 'revealed beliefs' of theism — this would, of course, include those of Mormonism — "cannot be so deeply mythologized that they lose their core sense [or literal status to believers]," or cannot be "…put into wide reflective equilibrium, or in any way justified, if indeed there is any other reliable way….The claim that there is or even can be a revealed truth that just must be accepted [widely, or by 'all nations, tongues and people'] as infallibly true is," according to Nielsen, "plainly incompatible with the coherentism and fallibilism of reflective equilibrium" (see note 40). Beliefs," Nielsen continues, "…have an *initial* credibility [as statements of alleged truth within a given context or practice], [but] get their fuller justification from other beliefs: from fitting into a coherent pattern of [basic or justified] beliefs [which constitute human knowledge]. But no belief, however deeply embedded [in a given faith or religious practice, or life-form], can just be accepted independently of how it fares with respect to [established knowledge on the widest scale]. Though it may have an *initial* credibility, if it does not cohere with a critical mass of the other [basic or justified] beliefs in the [larger] culture, then it must be rejected, however important it may be to the person [or religious institution] who is trying to get her [or its] beliefs in reflective equilibrium….Beliefs get their justification or warrant principally by such coherence with other [basic or justified] beliefs. On such an account, no belief [including those most fundamental to a particular practice or belief system] can be immune to the possibility of rejection, for it is always possible that it might fail such a test of coherence. But revealed beliefs — alleged 'revealed truth' — [particularly those fundamental, putatively 'revealed' truths of a given theistic or religious belief system] claim precisely this immunity. Some beliefs may in fact always stand fast — their initial credibility may always be sustained — but this can never be more than a contingent standing fast, for if they do not fit, or fit less well, with the other [basic or justified] beliefs than some alternative, then the belief in question [even if previously regarded as knowledge] must be rejected. That just is what it is for us to be fallibilists. But that is completely incompatible with appealing to revelation [and particularly fundamental or canonized revelation]" (1996, 88–9).
"Similar things," Nielsen continues, "should be said [regarding] the appeal to authority. In reasoning in accordance with wide reflective equilibrium, it is reasonable to make some appeals to authority. Indeed, I do not see how such an appeal could possibly be plausibly avoided. But it is a very different kind of appeal to authority to what we have in the religious case [when referring to a faith's most fundamental, defining beliefs]….[U]nlike the religious case, the claim to authority over…factual matters is never ultimate….But the appeal to authority in religion tells us that there are certain doctrines that we must just accept and act in accordance

This question, of course, implies the even more fundamental question: How can we make sense of *anyone* speaking with 'God' where the very concept of 'God' is factually unintelligible? In other words, *how can we make sense of anyone speaking for a factual non-reality?* Furthermore, Nielsen appropriately asks, "…why should we believe that what these men, [*i.e.* church authorities or leaders] *take* to be Divine revelation *is* Divine Revelation or that *their* Scripture [or teaching] is the *True* Scripture: the central document in which God putatively reveals himself to man [or the *true* teaching from God to man]? And if a man happens to be a Christian [or a Mormon] why should he remain one and continue to believe these things are so? [Respectable] answers are not forthcoming here. Rather there is a retreat to the allegedly self-validating, self-confirming nature of Divine Revelation.[110] But," Nielsen correctly points out, "it was because of difficulties with such conceptions [as with putative personal 'revelation' and 'spiritual confirmation'] that we were led to appeal to Scripture and the church. Now we are back where we started" (195).

The Problem of Authentication and Fallibilism Pertaining to Mormon Revelation Specifically

It is instructive to point out that Mormon scripture — which is considered the final arbiter of the truth or falsity of putative revelation — is itself problematic. This is so even apart from the various — very serious, if not decisive — other problems touched on above. The problemicity referred to involves the vagueness and ambiguity of certain Mormon scriptural guidelines and criteria for authenticating putative revelation from the Mormon god as well as the present and historical implications of such criteria in relation to conflicting Mormon claims concerning 'Truth,' 'God,' and recipient fallibility or fallibilism.

For example, revelation is considered true if it is sought for with a "sincere heart and with real intent, having faith in Christ" (Moroni 10:4), and if its content is "good" or "just and true" (Moroni 10: 6). Or if the recipient is "moved upon by the Holy Ghost" (D&C 68:4), or "quickened by the Spirit of God" (D&C 67:11). Or if the recipient's "Bosom shall burn," or he (or she) shall "feel it's right" (D&C 9:8) and not, conversely,

---

with no matter whether they seem plausible to us or not, no matter what else we may know or think we know. Again, that is incompatible with the fallibilism and coherentism of wide reflective equilibrium. No belief, on such a methodology, can stand on in such an authoritative position" (90).

"There is also the problem of the multitude of diverse, not infrequently conflicting, putative revelations. There are…different religions…[which] all have their sacred texts and their claims to revelation and authority. And these claims frequently fundamentally conflict….In short, we have many candidates for revelation with no nonquestion-begging, nondogmatic, and nonethnocentric way of claiming that one putative revelation or one set of putative revelations of any religion gives us the true revealed word: the truth about our nature and destiny and about what ultimate reality is like and how we must order [and live] our lives. Christians tell us that Christ is The Truth and The Way. But we have no good [justified and/or nonquestion-begging, nondogmatic and nonethnocentric] reasons for accepting the putative revelation that supposedly guarantees that claim, and no other religion fares any better in trying to make such appeals. There is no getting appeals to revelation in wide reflective equilibrium and, that aside for a second, it is unreasonable simply to try to ground one's faith on what one takes to be the revealed word of God or whatever is the supposed source of the alleged revelation" (90–1).

110 Evolutionary biology and neuropsychology do, however, provide a respectable, naturalistic explanation for the phenomenon of revelation in general, and diverse and conflicting revelation, whether personal or scriptural. See Jaynes 1990; Baker 1996; Schumaker 1995; and Faber 2002, 2004, and 2010.

experience a "stupor of thought" or "forget the thing which is wrong" (D&C 9:9). Or if the recipient receives "pure knowledge" which "enlarge[s] the soul" (D&C 121: 33, 42), or which "begins to swell within [the] breast" and "enlighten [the] understanding" making it therefore, "real" because "it is light; and whatsoever is light is good, because it is discernable, therefore [the recipient] must know that it is good" (Alma 32: 28, 35).

The problems with these scriptural criteria for authenticating the putative veracity of scriptural revelation are similar to, if not identical with, those addressed earlier regarding the absence of objective, universal criteria for distinguishing putative revelation from naturalistic neuropsychological phenomena as well as for authenticating the putative veracity of direct, personal revelation. Specifically, what could such general, vague, and ambiguous guidelines and criteria *actually* and *specifically* stand for, mean, or point to in a prescriptive or literally discriminating (qualifying or disqualifying) sense? What in principle would count for or against the truth (or probable truth) or falsity (or probable falsity) of such guidelines and criteria in such a way that they would be widely regarded among believers *and* nonbelievers as unquestionably reliable? How could they help in justifying and distinguishing the reported affects of putative *spiritual* phenomena (revelation) from the similar affects of purely and exclusively *naturalistic* (brain-generated, psychological) phenomena? What *specifically* are the unquestionable, non-question-begging and factually significant descriptive referents of such proclaimed discriminating or distinguishing criteria which would enable a believer to *accurately* and *conclusively* know whether or not a putatively revealed truth claim, spiritual experience, or inpouring of 'knowledge' is or was 'good,' 'pure,' 'just and true,' or is 'right' (or 'feels right') or 'wrong,' or is 'light and truth'?

Likewise, we must ask what *specifically* are the unquestionable, non-*a-priori*, non-question-begging and factually significant descriptive referents of the proclaimed discriminating or distinguishing criteria for the *recipient* of the putative revelation? What would enable the recipient to accurately or validly determine whether or not he or she was or was not in fact 'quickened by the Spirit of God' or experienced a 'burning in the bosom,' an 'enlarge[d] soul' or 'swelling of the breast' or was truly 'moved upon by the Holy Ghost'? How could we tell if the supplicant did or did not 'approach God' "with a sincere heart and with real intent, having faith in Christ" or had or had not first and adequately "studied [the matter] out in [his or her] mind" (D&C 9:8)?

To those believers who claim they can make such determinations, I would challenge them to *specifically*, *perspicuously* (*i.e.* clearly, without vagueness or ambiguity), and *non-redundantly* describe and distinguish such criteria without begging the question or resorting to false analogy or invalid analogical predication. Additionally, I would point out that clearly *every* Mormon — including excommunicated fundamentalist Mormons who have split-off from the main Church — who has ever claimed to have received revelation from the Mormon god would justify (and has likely justified) *in his or her mind* the truth and reality of personal putative revelation(s) or 'confirmation(s)' of 'Truth' on the basis of these scriptural verses and others like them. This they do even — or especially — if the veracity or legitimacy of their revelation was brought into question or was regarded as counterfeit, false, incoherent, or even dangerous by themselves or others in or outside the faith or by those with ecclesiastical authority.

What this amounts to in the Mormon faith is authentication and justification of revelation (and the interpretation of such revelation) by, or in virtue of, the experience of certain *feelings* or *emotions* that are regarded as spiritual experiences and described as manifestations or witnesses from the Holy Spirit of that which is true. Mormon believers are conditioned or indoctrinated from a very early age, as children or as new converts, to regard positive feelings experienced when attending Temple sessions, singing or hearing Church hymns, speaking or testifying in Church meetings, listening to the talks and the testimonies of others in Church meetings or conferences, studying scripture or Church literature, and engaging or participating in prayer or ritual, as evidence of 'truth.' They are likewise conditioned to regard negative feelings experienced when doing, thinking about doing, or being exposed to what they have been conditioned to regard as bad or inadvisable as evidence of falsehood or evil. "This means," as Jack B. Worthy observes, "that no evidence is required [to establish the truth (or falsity) of an experience or belief], and that no amount of conflicting [analysis or] empirical evidence could ever prove the Church [or any of its doctrines or commandments and counsel] to be false....[Mormons] are taught that no amount of information can trump these feelings, no matter how high its quality, how logical [or justified], or how plentiful" (2008, 25; see also the *Personal Postscript*).

The problem, of course, with such criteria is that the believed spiritual feelings and emotions considered to be indicative of spiritual phenomena and efficacious in judging the truth or falsity of revelation, confirmation, or spiritual experience, are nonspecific and therefore cannot be objectively differentiated from either the like (but conflicting) reported religious experiences of other theists, or the like reported non-religious experiences of Agnostics or Atheists. There simply are no objective, non-*a-priori* and non-question begging, justified (or justifiable) human criteria that are generally accepted by Mormons and non-Mormons for making such distinctions beyond merely offering unwarranted assertions and vague and ambiguous generalities.

If in response to this argument it is objected or argued that such feelings can be known and differentiated from non-spiritual feelings and emotions but that such differences cannot be expressed, then such differences would then be rightly considered ineffable and we are brought back to the problem presented earlier of asserting that which is ineffable — of saying what is unsayable. Moreover, if it is argued, as it is in the Mormon faith, that *all* positive feelings and emotions experienced in virtue of religious practices are true spiritual experiences from God (and that all revealed truth is accompanied by positive feelings of confirmation), and that all negative feelings (including a 'stupor of thought') are spiritual warnings or indicators of that which is wrong, evil, or false for the same reason, then we have no contrast between spiritual and non-spiritual feelings and emotions. This absence of contrast makes the claim of revelation and spiritual confirmation on the basis of feeling and emotion factually vacuous and incoherent as well in relation to contradictory feelings and interpretations of feelings regarding the same beliefs or truth claims.

Consider, for example, two people. One is a Mormon believer, the other an Atheist; both are emotionally overwhelmed by the beauty of nature. The Mormon exclaims with felt conviction "Behold the majesty of God's creation! There is indeed a God!" while the Atheist exclaims with felt conviction "Behold the majesty and beauty of nature! There is indeed no god!" Which one has received a bonafide spiritual experience? "Only the Mormon," some Mormons might say. "Both," other Mormons might say. "Neither," disbelievers might say. "They merely had a natural, human experience." Who among these judges is right or wrong, and how would they (or we) know without specific, justified criteria or begging the question?

Now, let's break this example down further and separate the feeling from the interpretation or the expressed thought. Let's assume, for purposes of this example that the Mormons who believe that both the Mormon believer and the Atheist *felt* the spirit of 'God' nevertheless say (as they undoubtedly would) that the Atheist's *interpretation* of the true feeling is false. Let's also assume that the disbelievers say (as they undoubtedly would) that the Mormon believer's *interpretation* of the human feeling is false. Again, how would (could) they know that such is the case without objective, justified criteria or begging the question? Do you see the problem we have here? We could extend this example to include a Mormon believer, a Catholic believer, an Evangelical Christian believer, a Muslim, and a Jew. All would be walking away from such an experience (or any transcendent experience) believing that their respective faiths have been confirmed by their feeling and interpretation of that feeling — that their God lives and theirs is the only true faith. All others are good — but ultimately false in their totality.

Clearly ineffable feelings cannot be asserted with any significance and nonspecific feelings and emotions alone are not acceptable arbiters of truth. They cannot justify beliefs (or interpretations) without objective, justified criteria for determining truth or falsity — both of the feeling in question and the interpretation. Nor can we make sense of celestial feelings 'from on high' — or of putative relationships with a god — on the basis of analogical predication by suggesting that such spiritual feelings between the Heavenly Father and his spirit children are analogous to, for example, the tender feelings between loving earthly parents and their beloved children. While we do know much that is literal about the feelings we experience in relation to our human parents, we simply do not know anything nonanalogical (or literal) about spiritual feelings *per se*. We know nothing in relation to an infinite, eternal, and biologically transcendent spirit being as a putative father of spirits that would distinguish such putative spiritual feelings from our purely human feelings toward our biological parents.

Other so-regarded authenticating criteria that true revelation will not contradict what is written in the Standard Works (scriptures) of the Mormon Church, and/or the official program, policies, and statements of the Church, and/or the teachings of Joseph Smith and the subsequent Presidents (or Prophets) of the Church are also problematical. There are in fact numerous fundamental and significant contradictions among the various books of Mormon scripture, and also among the fundamental doctrinal teachings of certain Mormon Presidents and General Authorities who allegedly and self-assertedly spoke authoritatively when allegedly 'moved upon by the Holy Ghost' to do so.

Different Mormon Presidents or General Authorities, functioning as alleged 'spokesmen for God' (*i.e.* putative Prophets, Seers, and Revelators), occasionally change, omit, minimize, explain away, disavow, or repudiate the declared revelations or authoritative and binding (*i.e.* revealed) teachings and pronouncements of prior Church Presidents or General Authorities. This has been done, for example, by authoritatively disavowing and repudiating Brigham Young's allegedly revealed 'Adam-God' doctrine, which held that the biblical Adam was the Father-God of all people in this world. Other examples include changing or modifying (allegedly *clarifying*) problematical verses or allegedly unnecessary material in Mormon scripture. Or modifying the putatively 'revealed' Mormon Temple ceremony to remove or amend socially problematical teachings and rituals, including, most notably, the binding 'penal oaths' and related physical gestures, or 'signs' of secrecy and certain 'endowment' ordinances and rituals. Or by reversing prior binding revelation, as Mormon President Wilford Woodruff did officially in 1890 in discontinuing — by putative revelation — the earthly practice of simultaneous plural (or 'Celestial') marriage.[111] Still another, more recent example is the 1978 alleged revelation to Mormon President Spencer W. Kimball that lifted the previously revealed ban on Black males receiving the Mormon priesthood, the Temple endowment and the sealing blessings of the Church for themselves and their families. This had been an *irreversible ban* established and attested to explicitly and without qualification by prior revelation to former Mormon Prophets and Apostles.

All of these putatively revealed changes were, of course, legally or culturally (and therefore institutionally) expedient at the time.[112] One might suppose that the Mormon god certainly would have known about such exigencies *before* giving such revelations in the first place. As it turns out, these have become very problematical for many believing Latter-day Saints. This situation also was and is very problematical for the belief in authoritative and binding revelation from the Mormon god, as well as for the very concept of the infallible, immutable Mormon god as doctrinally described and putatively revealed.[113] In considering

---

111 Polygamy (or more accurately *polygyny*) in the Mormon faith began in the 1830s in secrecy. It was practiced openly from 1852–1890, and it continued in secrecy with authoritative approval after the 1890 Woodruff Manifesto up until 1904. Polygyny, or 'Celestial marriage,' was declared by the Prophet Joseph Smith to have been 'restored by God,' through revelation. It was considered and officially taught by him and later Mormon Presidents, including Brigham Young and John Taylor, as well as other notable Church Presidents and Apostles (including Woodruff himself), as being a true, necessary, and 'binding' principle and practice. It was entered into under oath and covenant and was required in this life for 'exaltation,' or ultimate deification in the next life. It was regarded as a sacred obligation and privilege by all faithful Mormon men who were called to live it.

112 Institutional expediency is certainly one apparent explanation for such changes, although not necessarily the only explanation. Human motivation is, to be sure, complex, and speculations regarding the reasons for such changes are just that — speculation. Still, apologetic efforts to explain (or explain away) changes to scripture, Temple rituals, teachings, ordinances, and doctrinal teachings and declarations by prior Church Presidents — all once regarded as revelation from the Mormon god — require much more than mere speculation to resolve the problem of apparent (or likely) incoherence. But then what could such a sure resolution amount to if not merely a question-begging explanation? As I see it, a satisfactory (*i.e.* intelligible and coherent) answer to this question has not been (and most likely cannot be) provided.

113 Although it is common today for the Mormon Church to evasively argue that modified or superseded teachings, counsel, or admonitions by prior Church Prophets were not 'binding revelation' to the Church (see 5/4/2007 Official Press Release from the Church entitled "Approaching Mormon Doctrine" at www.religioustolerance.org/ldsdoct.htm), but were and are in some cases simply 'well-considered opinion,' such was not always the case. Consider, for example, in the context of D&C 68: 2–5, 11:25, and 21: 4–6, the words of President and Prophet Ezra Taft Benson who said the following in relation to the issue at hand in his February 26, 1980 address entitled "Fourteen Fundamentals in Following the Prophet" that: (1) Church members "... are to "give heed unto all his words' — as if from the Lord's 'own mouth;'" (2) "The living prophet is more vital to us than the standard works;" (3) "The living prophet is more important to us than a dead prophet;" (4) The prophet will never lead the Church astray" (including both present and past prophets); and (5) "The prophet does not have to say 'Thus saith the Lord' to give us scripture." Some Mormon believers suggest that the teachings of their prophets and other anointed General Authorities (who are also considered 'prophets, seers, and revelators) are merely their opinions and are not binding revelation to the Church unless formally canonized by the Church or given under the influence of the Holy Ghost. But they would find themselves not only in contradiction to their own scripture and the words of many of their prophets, but in difficulty as well

such allegedly revealed changes, omissions, reversals, disavowals, or departures from prior, putatively authoritative revelation it is certainly not unreasonable to ask — apart from the question of what 'revelation' actually means in the context of an incoherent concept of 'God' — *what else do the so-called Prophets, Seers, and Revelators of the Mormon Church have wrong*? Why has there been need for amendatory or clarifying revelation from a putatively all-knowing and all-powerful god at all — particularly from a god who values 'light and truth and knowledge' as the Mormon god allegedly does?

This last question, which is treated again for greater emphasis and depth in Chapter 8, is particularly pertinent, I think, to the Mormon fundamental belief that because of what is claimed by Mormon authorities and scholars to be the historical 'Great Apostasy' (or falling away) from Christ's original Church established in 'the meridian of time,' the Mormon Church — which was putatively restored by 'God the Father and Jesus Christ' through divine revelation to Joseph Smith — is the *"only true Church"* on the face of the earth today. On the basis of this fundamental belief, Mormons alone — individually in their own personal lives, and collectively as a Church through their god's anointed Prophets, Seers, and Revelators — are putatively entitled and inherently capacitated (through their lawful right as worthy members of the Church who enjoy the 'companionship of the Holy Ghost') to receive *continuous* and putatively *infallible* revelation (or Truth) from their allegedly *infallible, all-knowing,* and *unchanging* god on all matters of their faith that concern them.

This historical and deeply rooted theological position, as well as the widely believed doctrinal claims regarding revelation elucidated by McConkie at the beginning of this chapter, necessarily and unavoidably impose, without qualification, higher — if not inhuman — epistemic and justificatory requirements on Mormon Prophets, Apostles, missionaries, and faithful believers who claim to the world, with the intent of influencing others to accept such claims as 'Truth' and to accept the Mormon faith by joining the Mormon Church, to know that the various fundamental truth claims of the Mormon faith are in fact *Absolute Truth*. Such claimed certainty of knowledge and truth would seem unavoidably to make *any* appeal to fallibilism — in order to sidestep doctrinal contradictions and apologetically explain away amendatory teachings or Church policies that have essentially changed, discredited, or revoked prior revelation or authoritative teachings — ultimately incoherent and at least seemingly disingenuous.

Apparent incoherencies, include (1) doctrinal and *scriptural* inconsistencies; (2) alleged personal or authoritative revelation which corrects, reinterprets, supersedes, or disavows as false doctrine prior, official and binding revelation declared as true doctrine and taught as such by former Presidents of the Church; and (3) putatively revealed or inspired changes or corrections to canonized scripture and sacred practices, ordinances, and rituals believed to be established and required by prior revelation. All are a serious problem for

---

trying to explain how it is that progressive revelation to their prophets can exist if *not* canonized. Why would progressive revelation exist if not, in theory, to either add to or amend what was previously canonized (as the Book of Mormon did in parts with the Bible and the Doctrine and Covenants did in parts with the Book of Mormon). How specifically can they discern whether or not their Church leaders are 'moved upon' by the Holy Ghost except by their own subjective feelings? Perhaps this current official position of the Church on this matter can be best explained, in light of its problemicity, by the words of one Mormon blogger who wrote in response to this published press release: "They [the leaders of the Church] are running scared. They know the floodgates are open and there is no stopping it. It is a matter of damage control now."

the Mormon faith. They are a problem that *cannot* be coherently explained or explained away by apologetically invoking or appealing to the fact of human fallibilism or (as shall be concluded in the next chapter) the need for faith or faith-testing. These problems cannot be eradicated or minimized by question-begging appeals to 'God,' 'God's will,' 'wisdom and goodness,' 'the unknown purposes of God,' or 'the authority of the Word of God.'

Mormon believers cannot — contemporary apologetic or scholarly attempts or hopes to the contrary notwithstanding (see Vogel 1990) — have it both ways by claiming the *infallibility* of revealed truth from their god *and* the *fallibility* of their god's appointed and anointed servants, the Prophets, when receiving such putatively revealed truth while allegedly 'in the Spirit' and 'acting as the Prophet of God.' Some Mormon authorities, believers, and apologists suggest that the now regarded 'false doctrine' or incorrect teachings of previous, fallible or imperfect Prophets, Seers and Revelators was not bonafide revelation from the Mormon god because the so-called Prophets in question were simply mistaken, and/or were not acting or speaking with the Holy Spirit, and/or were not acting in their office as the Prophet, Seer, and Revelator at the time. But this is to say essentially that the only way to really, *conclusively* know if putatively revealed truth is in fact true is for any particular putative revelation *not* to be later corrected, rejected, or otherwise substantively amended or modified by the same or a different Prophet! But certainly such an argument raises the question once again of how anyone can then *ever* regard or rely on *any* putative revelation from *any* putative Prophet or Church authority as truth — much less Absolute Truth.

It also raises in a different context the question of the Mormon claim to the so-called 'Restoration of the Fullness of the Gospel' following the alleged Great Apostasy referred to above. This claim justifies the very existence of the Mormon Church, for without such an apostasy there would obviously be no need for a restoration. But how could such an apostasy even be possible if those ordained church leaders of the early church of Christ were presumably worthy *at that time* to receive the revealed 'Word of God' and if they also had access to continuous revelation *then* as the alleged prophets of this so-called dispensation do today? If the answer is that the so-called Church leaders then forfeited their right and access to continuous revelation because of pride and greed or other sins, and they made unauthorized changes to previously revealed 'Gospel Truth' (which is essentially the Mormon view), how can anyone know that such is in fact the case in the absence of credible or reliable historical evidence provided on the basis of widely accepted, time-independent human criteria? How can one argue for the truth of such a claim without begging the question and invalidly affirming the consequent?

Moreover, if, as it would be reasonable to infer on the basis of our knowledge of human nature, these earlier Church leaders no doubt believed then as Mormon Church leaders do now that they still had the *Truth* (something that cannot be refuted by Latter-day Saints without also begging the question or affirming the consequent), then what assurance would Mormon believers *today* have (again, without begging the question) that the alleged truth of Mormon theology is not likewise false? What assurance is there that Mormonism in *all* its forms is not the cult that other religious sects claim it to be? How can mainstream Mormons answer fundamentalist factions of the Mormon Church who believe that the 'mainstream Church' has lost its way or fallen away (*i.e.* apostatized) from the 'Truth' because of fundamental changes made to the putative revelations of Joseph Smith and

Brigham Young? Clearly, the 'argument from apostasy' cuts both ways.

Finally, arguments in support of allegedly true and authorized changes to prior revelation are hopelessly flawed because they are circular. To suggest that revelation from a god can only be ultimately confirmed or disconfirmed by revelation from that god is, yet again, to beg the question of the existence of that god and revelation — as well as to say nothing worthy of rational belief. To argue — as perhaps some Mormon believers or apologists might do — that the authorized changes to prior revelation is merely expansive of prior revealed knowledge (or 'further light and knowledge') and is neither amendatory nor a refutation, is to do so falsely and disingenuously. For the fundamental changes referred to above (as well as numerous others[114]) are in fact plainly amendatory and/or are in some significant aspect plainly refutations of prior revelation.

A fundamental Mormon belief is that those who enjoy 'the gift of the Holy Ghost' have the capacity to *know* and *understand* in truth "all mysteries, yea, all the mysteries of [God and God's kingdom]…even the wonders of eternity…and things to come" (D&C 76: 5–10). It seems reasonable to conclude then that, in matters of fundamental doctrine and practice, nothing that was later changed could not have been correctly and more fully revealed in its present form to prior Mormon Prophets or faithful believers to at least avoid the appearance (if not actuality) of contradiction or inconsistency — and to avoid, in no doubt many cases, the consequent loss of faith or the rejection of the faith. To assert otherwise is to do so without possible justification. To argue otherwise is to do so invalidly once again by begging the question.

All of this, of course, brings us back to the problem of human criteria for determining whether or not a putative revelation is, in fact, an intelligible, factual reality and, if so, a bonafide or true revelation. Sydney Hook, in regard to the latter problem, treats the claim of revelation as a hypothesis (a very generous, if not unwarranted, move — except solely

---

114 For an interesting catalogue of and inquiry regarding the numerous scriptural and doctrinal changes and at least apparent (if not glaring) contradictions among the authoritative ('revealed') teachings and 'revelations' of Mormon Presidents and General Authorities, see S.I. Banister's *For Any Latter-day Saint: One Investigator's Unanswered Questions*, 1988. Regarding this book, Richard Packham writes: "This compilation of materials is one of the most powerful one-volume tools available for making an iron-clad case about the self-contradictions and lies of Mormonism. If one were going to buy only one book to study the 'other side' of Mormonism, this should be the book."Banister wrote the book after she began a study of Mormonism as an 'investigator,' that is, a potential convert. Her study continued for six years. She never became Mormon. This book — essentially the questions and contradictions that the Mormons could not satisfactorily explain — is the result.

"In format, the book is a 'workbook,' with quotations from Mormon scriptures, Mormon prophets and other Mormon writers, on various topics of history and doctrine. After the reader reads various quotations from Mormon sources on a specific topic, the reader is asked a question, usually involving a choice between one statement and a contradictory statement. There are even blank lines or check-mark boxes for the reader's answer.

"Most Mormons label any book critical of their church as 'anti-Mormon.' That criticism would be difficult to justify here, since the quotations that are the real core of the book are all from PRO-Mormon writings. The only thing the author has done is to place those Mormon writings side-by-side in such a way as to make their mutual contradictions self-evident.

"And, lest the Mormon reader be tempted to claim (as Mormon apologists frequently do) that the quotations are misquoted or taken out of context, the author has provided many of them as actual photo-copies of the original (Mormon) publications.

"In all, there are over 650 such questions, arranged topically in sixteen chapters. Although one could browse around, the most devastating effect comes from working through the book from question number one to the end" (www.packham.n4m.org/banister.htm).

for the sake of a larger, cumulative argument — given the established factual unintelligibility of the very concept of revelation *vis-à-vis* the incoherent concept of the Mormon god). In doing so, he rightly puts the burden of proof where it belongs: on the theistic believer. Thus, he would correctly ask of the Mormon believer who claims to *know* a god or something *about* a god or the *will* of a god on the basis of some authoritative teaching by a Prophet: "Is this knowledge by revelation? What about false revelations? How are they to be distinguished from true ones? After all, not all revelations can be true since so many of them conflict [even within the same faith]. If you can't tell the difference between the true and false until *after* the event, whatever it may be, what good is the knowledge by revelation? And if you can tell the difference between true and false revelation [and 'confirmation'] *before* the event, how do you do it without falling back upon empirical methods [and corresponding human criteria for validation or invalidation]. What holds," Hook concludes, "for claims of knowledge by revelation or authority holds for claims of knowledge by intuition" (Nielsen 2001, 265).

The Problem of Revelation and Religious Experiences as purely Naturalistic Phenomena

Given the above three problems, how can we explain, for example, the testimony of an Emmanuel Swedenborg, the famous eighteenth-century 'beholder of angels,' who testified, according to Faber, "in response to the charge that he was imagining things, 'I have seen, I have heard, I have felt.'" (2004, 181)? How can we explain the canonized words of the founding Prophet, Seer, and Revelator of the Mormon Church, as Joseph Smith claimed to be, who solemnly testified that he "saw [Jesus Christ], even on the right hand of God; and heard the voice [of the Holy Ghost] bearing record that he is the Only Begotten of the Father" (D&C 76: 22–23)?

More specifically, when considering the testimonies of mystics and religious believers (Mormon believers in particular) concerning their asserted *knowledge* of spiritual or eternal truths (a topic we will take-up again and in more depth in our analysis of faith as a legitimate source of knowledge in the next chapter) we must ask three important questions. First, what *specifically* does the testifying believer *really* know in virtue of his or her so-called religious or revelatory experience? Second, how is it known to be *reality*? Finally: how, if at all, can we otherwise (naturalistically) explain the reported *sense* and *affect* of such alleged knowing?

To answer these three questions we will focus our attention, in particular, on the well researched neuropsychological mechanisms of transference and dissociation related to the visual, auditory, and affective hallucinatory phenomenon of personal reality formation.[115]

---

115 This particular psychological focus complements, or as Evan Fales suggests, closes the gaps of a broader explanation offered by social anthropologist I. M. Lewis in his Book *Ecstatic Religion* (1989). Although not focused on beyond this footnote, Lewis' research is nonetheless compelling on its own in appropriately placing certain types of religious experience in a larger social context.

In summary, according to Fales, Lewis "finds that mystical [or spiritual and revelatory] experiences occur primarily in two categories of persons, but are used in every case as a strategy for gaining greater access to social or political power. It is employed by disenfranchised, marginalized groups…to recruit or demand attention and concessions from those who oppress them. And, under certain competitive conditions, it is employed by aspirants to high or central status in whom involuntary possession by a central deity can confer

Given the current state of knowledge on this matter, "We are now," according to Faber, "in a position to understand naturalistically and psychologically how [such religious experiences involving the] *seeing, hearing,* and *feeling* [of spirits, angels and gods] come about, all the way from the mere sensation of God's presence to the full-blown sensorial witnessing of an angelic [or divine] visitor."

"To put it somewhat differently, we are in a position to set aside permanently any and all reliance on the 'transmundane' sphere (to use James' term), on 'energies' emanating from 'on high' [including the 'Light of Truth (Christ)' or manifestations of the 'Holy Ghost'] to 'meet' the 'demand' (supplication) of the believer who [putatively] feels, or otherwise sensorially perceives, the 'actual' presence of the Parent-God or one of His manifestations" (2004, 181). Simply put, there is no need at all for the concepts or existence of 'God' and 'revelation' to account for so-called religious, revelatory, or spiritual experience.[116]

---

authority, sanctity, and the ability to recruit followers. So mystical possession [inflates the ego], batters at the doors to power, and provides a route to social legitimization" (1996, 297–8).

Fales writes elsewhere, "Lewis shows that, at least where mystics [or Prophets and 'Saints'] 'go public' and appeal to their experiences in the social arena, mysticism [or spirituality] serves mundane interests either of the mystic him-or herself, or of some group with which he/she identifies" (2002, 6). Lewis also shows, Fales elaborates, "how the descriptions mystics give of their experiences, and the behaviors they exhibit prior to, during, and after mystical episodes, serve these social ends in quite precise and predictable ways. One of the great strengths of Lewis' theory," Fales observes, "is that it cuts across the entire spectrum of [mystical or revelatory] experiences, providing a unity of explanation that the theist cannot hope to match" (6).

Still, Lewis theory does not address with sufficient depth, the "psychology of the mystic" (which can now be explained neurologically and psychologically) or "[h]ow…social circumstances, including a particular religious ideology and iconography, get translated into a particular [initial and evolving] ecstatic content in the mind of the mystic[;]" a question addressed in brief by Fales through his consideration of "five possibilities," including: (1) calculated deception by the mystic; (2) self-deception of the mystic; (3) personal psychological conditions of the mystic; (4) mistaken interpretation of the described mystical experience by the mystic and others within the mystic's social group; and (5) social agreement among members of the mystic's social group to maintain an interpretation of the 'mystical' or 'spiritual' fiction (or revelation) which serves some social purpose or need (1996, 299–301). As a relevant aside, it would seem that the findings of Lewis' research are particularly applicable, in theory at least — if not historically in fact — to the Mormon Prophet Joseph Smith, who, along with Fales' test of the prominent Christian mystic Teresa of Avila, might be said, as Fales put it, "to provide a flagship confirming instance of Lewis' view" (1996, 298).

116 In the May 7, 2001 issue of *Newsweek* on "Religion and the Brain," Sharon Begley reports: "In 1997, neurologist Vilayanur Ramachandran told the annual meeting of the Society for Neuroscience that there is 'a neural basis for religious experience.' His preliminary results suggested that depth of religious feeling, or religiosity, might depend on natural — not helmet-induced — enhancements in the electrical activity of the temporal lobes. Interestingly, this region of the brain also seems important for speech perception. One experience common to many spiritual states is hearing the voice of God. It seems to arise when you misattribute inner speech (the 'little voice' in your head that you know you generate yourself) to something outside yourself. During such experiences, the brain's Broca's area (responsible for speech production) switches on. Most of us can tell this is our inner voice speaking. But when sensory information is restricted, as happens during meditation and prayer, people are 'more likely to misattribute internally generated thoughts to an external source,' suggests psychologist Richard Bentall of the University of Manchester in England in the book 'Varieties of Anomalous Experience.' Stress and emotional arousal can also interfere with the brain's ability to find the source of a voice, Bentall adds.

"In a 1998 study, researchers found that one particular brain region, called the right anterior cingulate, turned on when people heard something in the environment — a voice or a sound — and also when they hallucinated hearing something. But it stayed quiet when they imagined hearing something and thus were sure it came from their own brain. This region, says Bentall, 'may contain the neural circuits responsible for tagging events as originating from the external world.' When it is inappropriately switched on, we are fooled

For Faber and others, "The conspicuous presence of hallucination in our potpourri of angelic [and divine] encounters serves to underscore the thesis [that]…all religious experience is ultimately hallucinatory in nature" (180). Citing Frank Bruno, who "defines hallucinations as 'false perceptions,'" and Neil Bockian, who "says simply that hallucination consists in 'perceiving things that are not really there'" (184), Faber concludes with others that:

> Although hallucinations are commonly associated with, and present in, mental disorders such as schizophrenia and psychosis, their mere occurrence in individual cases does not [necessarily or always] indicate psychological disturbance…Indeed, odd as it may appear at first glance, hallucinations are an ordinary, everyday occurrence within the full range of human behavior and can be precipitated by such mundane factors as fatigue, hunger, solitude, [a neurological reaction to hallucinogenic or other chemical substances], a bump on the head, [anxiety, fear, loneliness], or, as we now appreciate, a heartfelt religious supplication. (183)

"Thus," continues Faber, "the inextricable tie between hallucination and religious experience in no way attests [*per se*] to the insanity, or abnormality, or instability of such experience within the world of human perceptual behavior." From this, "[the putative] presence of God in the experience of an ardent supplicator, for example, is neither more nor less than a 'false perception' [or falsely interpreted perception] called up through unconscious associations emergent in the psychodynamics of prayer"[117] (184). The clear implication here is that "Supplication is explicitly, theologically, practically designed to arouse the attractor state through the pray-er's rigorous, orthodox imitation of the early parent-child interaction" (185).

Thus, man "relies on hallucination to accomplish his astonishing purpose: the denial of separation and death. For it is 'man's' hallucinatory capacity, his unconscious potential to resuscitate through implicit, state-dependent memory the human 'immortals' [*i.e.* internalized parental care-givers] of the early time [infancy and childhood], that engenders

---

into thinking the voice we hear comes from outside us.'" In this regard, *pace* Begley, what we "believe" (*i.e.* "whether our brain wiring creates God, or whether God created our brain wiring") is irrelevant, and the preliminary findings and tentative conclusions produced by neuroscience, psychobiology, and psychoanalysis bring the belief in divine revelation into serious question.

What is relevant is what we in fact know, or can justifiably say we know. Therefore the proper question is 'what can we know?' The answer to this question requires justification, and justification requires that the presupposed truth claim in question (*i.e.* 'God exists') be justifiable in principle. But, as argued in Chapter 3 in relation to the Mormon god, it is not. Even so, substantial if not conclusive evidence *does* exist to support the *fact* of the biological evolution of the human brain through natural selection. So the belief that a god created the brain is simply false or incoherent, given our best justified knowledge to date. Moreover, assuming, solely for the sake of argument, that the concept of 'God' as stated and believed is intelligible, coherent, and factually meaningful sufficient to be justifiably and rationally believed (which it is not), how, in principle could such a putative act of natural creation take place by the divine act (or spoken word) of a transcendent god? Why (hearkening back to our analysis in Chapter 4, doctrine **C**) would a putatively all-loving, all-knowing, and all-powerful god utilize such an inefficient and wasteful natural process as a means of biological creation rather than an empirically verifiable supernatural act of 'special creation'? This would clearly demonstrate his actual and necessary existence beyond a reasonable doubt, and without the unintelligible and incoherent need for faith in his existence.

117 A more extensive naturalistic treatment of faith and prayer as a way of knowing a god and the so-called 'mysteries of godliness' is, once again, provided in Chapter 6. See also Faber 2002, 2004, and 2010.

the supreme religious 'mystery,' namely the 'mystery' of the 'supernaturals' [gods and angels] who are experientially 'there' to annul separation and expunge the terrors of death. Theological man, in a word, emerges from hallucinatory man" (185; see also Faber 2010, 19-68; Becker 1973; and Piven 2004).

John Schumaker, in *The Corruption of Reality: A Unified Theory of Religion, Hypnosis and Psychopathology* (1995), elaborates from a more fundamental, yet related naturalistic perspective:

> We have within our brains a highly sensitive *monitoring authority* that allows us to determine with great accuracy what constitutes *reasonable evidence* in support of the propositions offered to us. When this is operational, we are able to obtain what Ronald Shor labeled the *generalized reality orientation*. This he defines as 'a structured frame of reference in the background of attention which supports, interprets and gives meaning to all experiences.' Like a critical member of a jury in court, we are capable of rejecting information if there is *reasonable doubt.* Or we can accept something as probably true if sufficient evidence exists that it is. When our monitoring authority is engaged fully and when we are operating with the general reality orientation, our mental scales are quite finely balanced. At these times, we would not find someone guilty of murdering her/his boss simply because it was shown that the accused person worked for that individual. The evidence would be analyzed critically and deemed inadequate to *justify* the charge.
>
> If [likewise] a critical jury were gathered to decide about the existence of...angels [or gods], the verdict would be an emphatic *guilty* since it would be judged that they do not exist based on insufficient evidence. In fact, there would be no [uncontroversial, verifiable or falsifiable, *i.e.* reasonable or rational] evidence at all. (1995, 56)

But then how is that some people actually believe or claim to know that they have actually seen and conversed with — or even touched — 'angels' and even 'God'? Have such people lost their 'generalized reality orientation' in accepting their hallucinations as reality? Not necessarily, for under such circumstances there is a highly evolved mental phenomenon at play called *trance logic* which, according to Schumaker, provides us with "[the] ability to accept, at the same time, two completely contradictory sets of information" (54). Schumaker notes that "hypnotized subjects...provide us with some of the most dramatic displays of trance logic." To point,

> After a man has been hypnotized it is possible to illustrate this remarkable ability by suggesting to him, for example, that he will 'see' (*i.e.*, hallucinate) his wife sitting next to him in an empty chair. If the man is a good hypnotic subject [and, *pace* Brigham Young who asserted that a person who had received the Holy Ghost could not be hypnotized, all Mormon (or religious) believers are, on the basis of extensive exposure to familiar hypnotic conditioning and suggestions consisting of affect-laden language, teachings, tone, music and ritual which all serve to induce the "spiritual" trance-state (and concomitant trance logic) referred to as being "caught-up in the Spirit"], he will be completely convinced that his wife is there with him in the room. With relevant suggestions, it would be quite easy to get the man to have a detailed conversation with his wife, *or even to give her an affectionate hug and a kiss.*
>
> But what happens if we then take another empty chair and suggest that the man 'sees' his wife in that chair as well? Logic would tell us that the impossibility of having two identical wives in front of him would destroy his ability to see the second wife. Or we might expect the man to relinquish the first fictitious wife in order to regard the second wife as real. On

the contrary, he is readily able *simultaneously* to maintain the belief that both wives are real. If asked if Wife A is his *real* wife, the man will answer affirmatively. When asked the same question about Wife B, he will respond the same way. Of particular interest is the fact that such a person shows no surprise or bewilderment at the prospect of having two [identical] wives instead of one. To illustrate even further the phenomenon of trance logic, we could next bring the man's *real* wife into the room and sit her in the third chair. He will claim that she, too, is his real wife, thus giving him a total of three [identical] wives.

In a state of trance logic, people can delude themselves about a matter while also knowing the truth about it. They can be in touch and out of touch with reality at the same time. This may be seen with our hypnotized man if we ask him which of the three wives he would like to take home with him if he could choose only one of the three. Predictably, he will pick Wife C, the one who is not an illusion. He will not be disturbed at the prospect of leaving his other two wives behind because, even though they are real to him, they are also *not* real to him. [Absent a psychotic break from reality altogether, or extreme cases of self-deception and delusion, some] executive cognitive process, working outside of awareness, maintains a grasp of the overall situation, even though conscious awareness flits from one illusion to another. (54)

After presenting his survey of the extensive scientific literature on the subject of 'neodissociation theory' and the mechanics of dissociation and suggestion in relation to the unified phenomena of *hypnosis* and *psychopathology*, Schumaker folds in the third related phenomenon of *religion* into his unified theory and concludes that…

[the] main biological ingredient for religion [or alleged religious revelatory experience] is the brain-level capacity to dissociate itself into separate and largely independent streams of consciousness. In fact, the ability to achieve dissociative trance has always been a direct extension of human beings' fundamentally [or culturally conditioned] *theological* nature. When trance and suggestion are embedded solidly into a culture [as surely they are now, and as they were in the early part of the 19th Century in New York when the Mormon Church was founded in the midst of the fervor of religious revival], the combination yields religion [or charismatic and revelatory religious experience], however varied our expressions of religion might be. The historical roots of dissociation (as well as "hypnosis") lie outside psychology altogether, in the realm of religion where it *works* best. It is only a culture that has lost its way religiously that could "discover" something like hypnosis and fail to see it as a weak, skeletal version of the more powerful trances that have permitted human beings to religiously *transcend* [and thereby escape] their general condition.

Dissociative trance makes possible all types of religion and quasi-religion, as well as the powerful experiences they often entail. Without our brain's capacity to dissociate and thereby process information along parallel channels, history would not have seen any of the estimated 100,000 or so gods [including, as one of them, the Mormon god] that have come and gone…Religion and dissociation are so closely linked that one must understand them as *coevolutionary* phenomena that unite biological and cultural evolution. Dissociation, which is the result of our unique physiology, is the cornerstone of all religion [and of putative revelatory experience]. (88–89)

Schumaker concludes this section of his work by suggesting that "[what] we call religion, therefore, is in effect a cultural-level system involving *group dissociative trance induction techniques* for purposes of instilling reality-distorting suggestions that can be *agreed upon* and therefore not questioned" (90). This, I think, can induce both auditory and visual hallucination as putative revelation or religious ("spiritual") experience through the transference (or projection) of internalized care-givers to the invented *Parent-Gods* of God, the Father and Jesus, the Christ.

Such coherent and justifiable — or even justified — naturalistic explanations, according to Nicholas Everitt, "… [are] superior to a theistic explanation in two related respects:

> First, it invokes only psychological dispositions for which there is a great deal of independent [empirical] evidence. Second, it provides a much simpler explanation than the theistic explanation. It does not invoke [or speculatively invent without justifiable warrant and without confusing conceivability as possibility or invoking, in turn, favored status or familiarity through invalid analogical predication] any new entities or processes or mechanisms, but relies solely on ones which we already accept. The theistic account, by contrast, postulates a unique and completely unprecedented sort of being, with an amazing range of properties and powers which are in conflict with all that [common knowledge, sense and] science tells us - [with all that we *know* (not merely perceive or experience), albeit fallibilistically, regarding this or any world and the universe] — about what is possible, what is impossible and what is necessary… (2004, 171)

In summary, this chapter concludes that putative revelation *from* a god *about* a god is incoherent on the basis of four arguments: (1) The Mormon god, as doctrinally or theologically conceived and described, is unintelligible, incoherent and without factual meaning or significance, making him, in principle, a non-existent object of experience or source of communication; (2) revelation itself is without specific, clear, objectively verifiable and non-question-begging human criteria for identification and authentication and cannot possibly be objectively, critically and empirically verified, falsified, or authenticated and therefore, is neither veridical nor factually significant; (3) revelation (including scriptural revelation) is internally inconsistent, subject to error, change and varying (and often contradictory) interpretations, and is not universally accepted among competing or differing theistic religions as the *only true* Word of God; and (4) there are better [naturalistic] explanations of religious experience and revelation than the theistic explanation, making the theistic argument from such experience to a god's existence not only question-begging, but another *non sequitur* — for the *actual* existence of the Mormon god does not necessary follow from the occurrence of the so-called religious *experience* of revelation or confirmation. Nor, moreover, does the mere assertion of putative revelatory experience validly, as a deductive argument, affirm (or prove) the consequent (conclusion) that the Mormon god in fact exists.

All of the above problems with the Mormon doctrine of revelation from a god to man lead Mormon believers to the doctrine of last resort and ultimate retreat: '*faith in God and Christ.*' It is this core doctrine, or 'first principle' of Mormon theology, to which shortly we shall turn our analytical attention.

But before doing so, it might be worthwhile briefly to address a question underneath the question of whether or not what is affectively experienced in the putative revelatory experience of 'God,' 'Christ,' 'angels,' and 'spirits' can be rightly or rationally considered as being *real* or merely fabricated or hallucinated by the human brain. Underneath this question — for otherwise rational people questioning at some level the reality of such experience in their own or another's life — is the question of how one can tell what is real and what is not.

To address this question it is helpful to keep in mind that if something does not make sense or is unintelligible because it is conceptually self-contradictory, then, like a round square, *it cannot be real.* If something does not make sense because it is conceptually *without* factual significance and is incoherent as well with what is known to be *actually* (even if provisionally) true about the world and universe and how they work, then *it cannot be regarded as a factual or actual reality as conceptualized.*

Under such conditions, it is reasonable to conclude that if someone believes something to be real that cannot be coherently regarded as real, then at least one of the person's held assumptions about reality has to be wrong. This much seems to be self-evident. But what if the faulty assumption is the notion that what is *experienced* as real *is* real? Again, if what is reportedly taken from an experience (*i.e.* the literal or actual existence of something real) conceptually does not make sense or is conceptually incoherent and factually meaning-less, then while the *experience itself* might indeed be real (if not fabricated), what is *taken* from the experience cannot be, making a sincerely held belief that it is real a delusion.

Religious or otherwise, as long as such a delusion is (1) defended by self-deception; (2) supported by self-induced, wish-based conviction and/or social acceptance and rein-forcement; and/or (3) is made or manipulated to make sense on the basis of twisted logic, experiential or analogical familiarity, or rationalized possibility (on the basis of the erroneous belief that anything is possible, or the mere absence of decisively refuting evidence), the mind lets it go on. The primary strategy for determining whether or not something spiritually experienced *as* real *is*, in fact, *actually* or *objectively* real, is to make the questionable experienced reality *not make sense* by, again, subjecting — with the presumption of skepticism — the belief that such an experienced reality actually or factually exists to the rigorous conceptual analysis and justificatory process of wide reflective equilibrium advocated and employed in this book and, more thoroughly and competently, elsewhere by Nielsen and others.

Beyond such an outsider analytical and justificatory process, or test of faith is a more radical, therapeutic approach of pushing — with or without awareness — the delusion (or sincerely held wrong belief about the experience) past the point where it can trick the mind. This brain-initiated intervention might require one through the activation of certain unconscious, corrective defense mechanisms to go *with* the delusion to the extreme by taking the hallucination literally and acting on one's total commitment to its 'call to action,' trusting in the deep structure of the brain (referred to by depth-psychologists as 'the unconscious' and perversely — by theistic believers and even analytical psycholo-gists — as 'God') to break the spell through the creation of a crisis of faith. This approach alone has potentially grave risks and might not be sufficient,[118] making the cumulative

---

118 Certainly there are some who have taken their faith to an extreme, as in the scriptural pattern of Abra-ham's sacrifice of his son Isaac. Such believers have become, as a result of other sociopsychological factors at play, more entrenched in their delusion through pathological dissociation and self-deception. For others, however, who are, perhaps out of neediness and doubt, compelled psychologically to push their faith to the extreme and experience, in so doing, a crisis of their faith, a corrective 'enantiodromia' occurs, resulting over time in a psychotherapeutic de-conversion (characterized as a 'loss of faith') through the exposure of the self-deception and delusion, and the breaking of the transferential, dissociative trance (or 'spell'). (Re-garding *enantiodromia*, "[C.G.] Jung used the term particularly to refer to the unconscious acting against the wishes of the conscious mind" (*Aspects of the Masculine*, chapter 7, paragraph 294). As defined, "[e]

outsider test of faith, in my view, more effective and reliable, as well as less risky. In either or any case, the principle is the same. The more real and convincing the experience seems to be — while at the same time or in retrospect not making sense to skeptical outsiders and/or to the believer at another level of awareness — the more likely the experience is a hallucination and the believer is deluded and self-deceived — and the more radical the therapy might need to be to expose and break free from the delusion *that* the hallucinatory experience is real, as well as the self-deception that the delusion is *actually* true. That such questions need to be asked and measures taken in relation to spiritual experience is clear, particularly where there are legitimate and abundant reasons to question or doubt whether what one believes to be real or actually true *is*, in fact, real or actually true (and not merely a wish and need-based hallucinatory delusion), and whether or not such beliefs are at least potentially toxic and could be damaging and/or dangerous to the believer and others. That such is the case on *both counts* with the Mormon faith in particular (and argu-ably all theistic faiths in general) is argued throughout this book and others.[119]

---

nantiodromia is '[l]iterally "running counter to," referring to the emergence of the unconscious opposite in the course of time. This characteristic phenomenon practically always occurs when an extreme, one-sided tendency dominates conscious life; in time an equally powerful counterposition is built up, which first inhib-its the conscious performance and subsequently breaks through the conscious control' ("Definitions," *ibid.*, par. 709). Enantiodromia is typically experienced [therefore,] in conjunction with symptoms associated with acute neurosis [or one-sidedness], and often foreshadows a rebirth of the personality," [or what Aristotle termed *peripeteia:* a dramatic reorientation in one's life]. Finally, in support of the potential salutary effect of this radical, brain-initiated intervention proposed in the text above as a possible corrective for determining whether or not something 'spiritually' experienced *as real is*, in fact, *actually* real, is the idea shared by Jung that "… the unconscious life of the psyche is constructed… [such] that we can never know what evil may not be necessary in order to produce good by enantiodromia, and what good may very possibly lead to evil" ("The Phenomenology of the Spirit in Fairytales," *Collected Works* 9i, par. 397)" (From Wikipedia.org; see entry for "Enantiodromia").)

119 Regarding the *first count* of the justifiable questionability or doubt concerning what the Mormon be-liever believes to be real or actually true, see Banister (1988), Vogel (2004), Tice (2006), Southerton (2004), Marquardt and Walters (1994), Anderson (1999), Abanes (2003), Palmer (2002), and Brodie (1995) to name a few. Additionally, it is important to point out again, as we have learned in this chapter, that all so-called spiritual experiences (or revelations) from a god necessarily depend for their existence on the actual existence of the god. On the basis therefore, of our analysis of the concept of the Mormon god in Chapter 3 (and of the concept of the gods of developed forms of Judaism, Christianity, and Islam by Nielsen and others), the putative reality of Mormon spiritual experiences from — or the putative revelation of — such a god does not make sense. A factual *non-reality* (*e.g.* the Mormon god as conceptualized and believed to be) simply cannot produce an actual experience of such as a factual reality. To assert the contrary is utterly incoherent, as well as factually meaningless, regardless of who one is or what one might believe or think he or she knows. Moreover, when the conceptual content of the putative revelation (or spiritual experience) does not make sense, as we learned in our analysis of the Mormon Gospel, or Plan of Salvation in Chapter 4, the assertion, if it is made, that such revelation is real and true is also and likewise incoherent as well as factually unintelligible. Either way, the argument for the reality of revelation or spiritual experience is a non-starter. One simply cannot legitimately, coherently or responsibly argue for, or assert, the actual reality of a factual non-reality. And, as argued throughout, but particularly in Chapter 2, one cannot rationally believe to be objectively real or actu-ally true that which cannot be justifiably believed to be objectively real or actually true (either linguistically, logically, or empirically) without self-deception and delusion.

    Regarding the *second count* concerning the alleged harmfulness of the Mormon faith, see applicable assessments in Chapters 5, 6, 8 and the *Epilogue* and *Personal Postscript* in this book, as well as Anderson and Allred (1995, 1997); Krakauer, J. (2004); Striker, M. (2000); and Worthy, J.B. (2008), to name a few.

Chapter 6

Deconstructing the Mormon Concept and Requirement of Faith in God and Christ

"...for faith could not center in a being of whose existence we have no idea, because the idea of his existence in the first instance is essential to the exercise of faith in him."

—*Joseph Smith*

"Every man eventually is backed up to the wall of faith, and there he must make his stand."

—*Elder Ezra Taft Benson*

The cumulative force of the analysis and assessment of the Mormon faith made and offered to this point and on through the remainder of this book, does indeed, as Ezra Taft Benson predicts in the header quote above, 'back up' intellectually honest believers to the 'wall of faith.' This is understandably so, for neither evidence nor reason, self-referential claims to knowledge ('I know what I know'), or appeals to authority, ineffability, next-life verification, and/or the legitimacy of groundless religious belief, can rescue their beliefs from incoherence and irrationality. Still they have their *faith*, or so it shall be claimed — no doubt asserted with summoned sincerity, confidence, and conviction. But unfortunately (and perhaps ironically as well) for such believers, that which backs them up to the wall of faith, by forcing their *beliefs* beyond the reach of evidence, reason, and rationality — indeed, beyond the justificatory reach of wide reflective equilibrium — does so with their *faith* as well. In fact, the problem of incoherence seems to get worse for the Mormon believer or investigator when we entertain the idea of 'faith in God the Father and in Jesus Christ.'

The implied claim, or argument, if it is made, that because faith in the Mormon god is attested to, or asserted by, Mormon believers, such faith and the object of such faith ('God') must therefore exist is, of course, a *non sequitur* in both cases. But such an argument also begs the questions at issue, which involve the possible existence of both 'God' and 'faith in God' respectively, as they are conceptualized in Mormon theology.

It seems reasonable in this regard to assume that for *faith* in someone to exist as a principle and phenomenon in its intended sense, the *object* of such faith must either exist or, in the absence of its known (justified) existence, the *concept* or idea of the object of faith must at least be justifiable, or intelligible, coherent, and factually meaningful as a possible, theoretical reality. To conclude therefore that either the Mormon god or faith in the Mormon god exists merely because Mormon believers experience what they consider to be faith in their god is invalid since such conclusions would assume or presuppose that what is experienced as (and believed to be) 'faith in God' *is* such, and that what is believed to be 'God' either exists or can possibly exist as theologically conceptualized in its fulness. Contrary therefore, to what might seem obvious, the mere assertion of 'faith in God' by Mormon (or other theistic) believers does not necessarily establish either the existence or possible existence of a god or of such faith itself.

Moreover, on the basis of Nielsen's 'error-theory' of religious belief presented at the end of Chapter 3, faith as an 'eternal principle,' like 'free will' (or 'free agency'), moral principles, eternal laws and Platonic forms or other putative eternal realities (religious or otherwise), cannot be correctly or coherently objectified (reified). Therefore, it does not exist as an objective reality that transcends its natural existence as a very real, human experience. Still, as a very real phenomenon experienced by Mormon and other theistic believers, and on the basis of its important role in Mormon theology as the first principle of the Gospel, such faith, as a concept and an experience, merits careful, critical analysis and assessment. That is the task that confronts us in this chapter.

The Mormon Concept and Doctrine of Faith

Referring to such faith as simply "faith in Christ," Millet informs us that: "To have faith in Christ is to trust him. To have faith in Christ is to have confidence in him. To have faith in Christ is to rely completely, wholly upon him" (2008, 14) and to love him completely, unequivocally, and unconditionally. Alternatively, though not contradictorily, Millet quotes Elder Boyd K. Packer of the Quorum of the Twelve Apostles of the Mormon Church as "testifying" that "faith, to be faith, must [presumably as a principle and not in relation to the Mormon god or Christ] go beyond that for which there is confirming evidence. Faith, to be faith, must go into the unknown. Faith, to be faith, must walk to the edge of the light, and then a few steps into the darkness. *If everything has to be known, if everything has to be explained, if everything has to be certified, then there is no need for faith. Indeed, there is no room for it*" (37, emphasis mine). Moreover, according to Joseph Smith in his authoritative *Lectures on Faith*, faith is an eternal principle of *action* and *power*[120] in 'God' and in man, accounting for his god's ability to lawfully create and govern the universe and man's ability to 'bind the heavens' in performing miracles on earth in the name of the Mormon god. Additionally, faith, as an 'unwavering commitment,' is regarded as a *decision*, and ultimately as a feeling-based *knowledge* held with *unwavering certainty* and conviction — not merely as a feeling of trust and confidence or a belief without reasons, or a principle of action and power. Finally, encompassing all of the above conceptualizations, faith in Christ (and 'God') is, according to Mormon theology, an eternal principle that must be operative in the lives of men to ensure their

---

120 In a purely secular context this particular conceptualization of faith is relatively straightforward. It is common knowledge that we all act rationally in innumerable ways each day on the basis of our empirically established trust and confidence in predictable outcomes. It is also common knowledge to all that our *ability to act* (power) is determined, in part, by our rational trust and confidence in our own proven capacities, abilities, and knowledge of how things work and in predictable outcomes. Clearly then, this concept of faith, the way *faith* as a term is used secularly in the common vernacular of Western man, relates to the psychological concepts of *confidence* and *trust* as natural, human states of mind which enable human *action* or behavior on the basis of common knowledge established by sufficient empirical evidence and thereby increase one's natural *power* (or ability) to predictably produce certain outcomes.

salvation. As such, 'faith in Christ' is therefore doctrinally *required* and considered both *necessary* and *sufficient* as the means for both attaining the promise of such salvation in this life and enjoying such salvation in the next life by 'enduring (in faith) to the end' of their mortal probation.

The Mormon conceptualization of faith is a way of relating to 'God and Christ.' It is a way of knowing the unknown truths and mind, will, and ways of the Mormon god. It is a principle of action and power in 'God and man.' Faith is a *feeling-based* decision resulting in an unwavering commitment to 'God' and is a requirement that is necessary and sufficient for ensuring salvation and eternal life. It is itself a serious problem. As I shall argue, it is a very *bad* idea as well. Accordingly, five significant facets of this problem will therefore be addressed in this chapter.

The *first* facet entails the *impossibility* of faith as an eternal principle of supernatural power "existing in the Deity" and, by extension, in man (see Smith 2005, Lecture One, # 15, 17). The problem here is with the unintelligibility of 'faith' as an attribute of 'God' that essentially determines his existence (#16) and enabled him to 'speak to chaos' and thereby create and enable the existence of all things "in heaven, on earth, or under the earth" (#15, 16 and 22). This problem extends likewise, by association and relation, to *man*, who is believed to be enabled by faith (even if such faith is only "as a grain of mustard seed") to "move mountains" (#18), cause a change of heart in disbelievers (#19), "subdue king-doms," obtain the promises of the Mormon god, "[stop] the mouths of lions," "[quench] the violence of fire," "[escape] the edge of the sword," "[turn] to flight the armies of the aliens," "[receive] their dead raised to life," and effectually "[bid] the sun and moon to stand still," (#20, 21) as well as heal the sick and otherwise command and control the elements.

The *second* facet, alluded to above, entails the *impossibility* of faith as confidence in the existence of 'God,' and trust *in*, love *for*, and devotion *to* him and Christ, given the factual unintelligibility of the stated existence of the Mormon god and, consequently, the 'Son of God' as fully conceptualized and believed. The argument made here is *not* that faith in the Mormon god is impossible because the doctrine or notion of the Mormon god is mistaken, wrong or theologically incorrect. It is much stronger than that.

My contention here is that faith in *any* 'God' – *including* the Mormon god – is *neces-sarily* impossible, and therefore does not exist *because the object of such faith as attested to is a factual non reality as conceptualized.* In other words, and more directly and person-ally, if you are a believer and your *idea* of god (Mormon or otherwise) is reasonably considered to be – through formal analysis, refuting or disconfirming evidence, or just plain common sense – false and/or incoherent in relation to such god's defining primary, secondary and relational attributes, then what you consider to be 'faith' in your god is not what you think and say it is.

In fact, continuing on this personal note, if neither you nor anyone in your faith can speak sensibly and clearly – without ambiguity, vagueness and contradiction; without appeal to scripture and 'spiritual' feelings; and/or without employing reasoning fallacies and evasive possibility strategies – to the nature, coherence and at least possibly confirm-able or disconfirmable truth-conditions of your god's primary, secondary and relational referents as a putative being or person worthy of worship, then not only is the idea of your god incoherent and without factual significance, but so is your assertion of faith in such a god. To even *appeal* to 'faith in God' in such a case would be self-refuting. This seems obviously so because your god, if incoherent *as conceptualized* (either doctrinally or by your own invention), does not – *cannot* – possibly exist, making your faith in such a god therefore, and necessarily, nonexistent. Such an argument, of course, raises the follow-up question: "If what I have come to experience and regard as faith in my God is *not* such, then what is it?" This important question will also be addressed.

The *third* facet is the related impossibility of faith as a "way of *knowing*" God (and knowing *of* God's literal existence) through "revelation" or "spiritual experience." This particular aspect of faith, like the aspect of faith in the second facet above, is addressed from an analytical, philosophical perspective, as well as both an evolutionary and neuro-psychological perspective. In the first instance, as we learned in the previous chapter, we have the problem of the incoherence of "revelation" and "spiritual experience" *from* a factual non-reality (i.e. "God") to provide knowledge *about* a putative being (again, "God") that is conceptually unintelligible and incoherent. In the second instance, as we shall learn, we have, again, a perfectly sensible and adequate *naturalistic* explanation for "revelation" and "spiritual experience" that makes the literal existence of supernatural or transmundane gods, spirits, angels and the like unnecessary, as well as incoherent.

The *fourth* problematic facet is the resulting impossibility of the Mormon god, given this god's *requirement* of an enduring, tested *faith in Christ* for man's salvation. The problem here is (1) with the unintelligibility and incoherence of such a requirement, given the putatively revealed nature of the Mormon god and the related *non-necessity* and *insufficiency* of such faith in coming to know such a god (and "Jesus Christ whom [he] has sent"), and (2) in invoking and benefiting from the putative salvific effects of the alleged 'atonement of Jesus Christ' and 'enduring to the end' of mortal life in 'righteousness.'

And the *fifth* and final facet of the problem with faith to be addressed in this chapter involves the possible (in all cases) and likely (in many cases) *negative personal and social consequences* of regarding faith as an unshakable commitment to the Mormon god and the Mormon religion on the basis of treating such faith as a *decision* to be made on the basis of feelings without valid reasons or evidence and adhered to (again on the basis of feelings) *without* question, doubt, or equivocation. Of all five facets of faith addressed in this chapter, this fifth facet resembles the dependence of salvation and damnation upon feeling-based and subjectively interpreted revelation addressed in the previous chapter. It is the most worrisome, the most frightening and, potentially, the most harmful, dangerous, and destructive conception of faith to both the believer and society.

All of the facets of faith introduced above and treated below constitute part of the reason why, as Loftus argues *vis-à-vis* Christianity (2010), "faith fails" in Mormonism as well. It fails, as we shall learn below, because it is impossible as conceptualized. It makes the existence of the Mormon god as conceptualized impossible as well. It fails as well because, as we also learn in this book and others cited herein, it is baseless, and at least potentially (if not actually) harmful, dangerous and destructive as both a principle and state of mind in *all* theistic faiths.

The Impossibility of Faith as a Principle of Supernatural 'Power' in God and man

First of all, while the idea of faith as a *secular* principle of *human* action and power can be regarded as common knowledge and makes rational sense to all (see note 120), it is neither intelligible nor cognitively meaningful to associate such natural phenomena with Christian or Mormon concepts of religious 'faith in God' or in supernatural agents.

In a religious context, faith as a principle of action is based on the Mormon believer's belief, trust, and confidence in a conceptually unintelligible god that is based on a putative revelation from and/or revelatory or spiritual experiences with such a god. It is *not* based on the predictable, empirical consequences of human development, interactions, and physical laws. Faith requires acting on the basis of trust and confidence in, love for, and devotion to an unintelligible, factual non-reality ('God' and the 'Son of God') on the basis of putative revelation from and spiritual experience in relations with a god. But these are, in their own rights, neither 'properly basic,' factually intelligible, nor logically supportable unless one begs the question of the existence of 'God and Christ.' It is irrational even if it is psychologically understandable.

To believe, as Joseph Smith put it, that by faith "God spake, chaos heard, and worlds came into order" (Smith 2005, #22) and that "So with man also; he [man with sufficient faith] spake by faith in the name of God, and the sun stood still, the moon obeyed, mountains removed, prisons fell, lions' mouths were closed, the human heart lost its enmity, fire its violence, armies their power, the sword its terror, and death its dominion" (#22) and that therefore, "Faith…is the first great governing principle which has power, dominion and authority over all things" (#24). But it involves believing something that is not only both false *and* incoherent in relation to man, but is also indicative of gross superstition — 'magically' or in contravention to physical law believing that a god somehow, through the power of faith, orders and controls creation and natural phenomena by the 'spoken word.'

This idea of 'faith' as an eternal, *supernatural* attribute of the Mormon god and (through grace and development) of man as well, never really made rational sense to me as an insider of the Mormon Church, as hard as I tried to make it so. It still doesn't. Not only is it false or incoherent as a claimed complex of reified and deified human motivational, volitional, and effectuating biological capacities, it is inconsistent with the way *faith* as a term is typically used in the Mormon language-game. Additionally, it is unintelligible and incoherent when applied to both the concept of the Mormon god as theologically conceptualized and commonly believed among informed Mormon believers and to the factual reality of man. Moreover, it is utterly nonsensical when applied to the analyzed concept of the Mormon god presented in Chapter 3 of this book. Significantly, this particular idea of faith is, once again, factually unintelligible as a putative principle or attribute and source of supernatural power. It also does not cohere in practice with the best justified knowledge we have regarding the natural laws, causal mechanisms, and physical realities — seen and unseen — of this world and universe and how they work.

The Impossibility of Faith as Confidence in the Existence of God, and Trust in, Love for, and Devotion to God

Regarding the *second* facet of the problem with the Mormon concept of faith, it seems self-evident that to have such 'faith in God' (and Christ) and in the reality of 'God's existence' presupposes that we *first* conceptually *understand what it is we have faith in*. This not only makes good sense, but is perfectly consistent with Mormon theology, which asserts, as in the quote of Joseph Smith at the head of this chapter, that conceptual knowledge — "the idea of [God's] existence" — precedes faith. Such faith supposedly comes by "hearing the word of God" (Romans 10:17) as preached, taught and testified to by those who allegedly *know* the 'Word of God' and who themselves 'know' or have 'faith in God and Christ' by *personal* revelation *from* their god and 'spiritual experience *with* that god and Christ.

This idea of 'faith in God' suggests, in turn, that an acceptance of a god's existence is, ultimately, also a matter of faith — or trust and confidence in the truthfulness of the words, or 'witness,' of religious authority. But such faith "cannot," according to Nielsen, "insure the meaningfulness [or truthfulness] of religious utterances [about a god]; quite to the contrary, faith presupposes that the discourse in question is itself meaningful [intelligible and true]...." Consequently, argues Nielsen, "If I do not know what is meant by *x*, I cannot intelligibly say that I have faith in *x*, that I place my trust in *x*, or that I accept *x* on authority.... I *must* understand the *meaning* of a proposition before I can accept or fail to accept it on faith or on authority" (1963, 162). Other notable thinkers like for example A.J. Ayer would agree. In Ayer's words:

> People who try to justify their belief in the existence of God by saying that it rests on faith are sometimes maintaining no more than the proposition that God exists is one which they have the right to accept, in default of sufficient evidence; but sometimes they look to faith for the assurance that the words "God exists" express some true proposition, though they do not know what this proposition is; it is one that surpasses human understanding....[But] *until we have an intelligible proposition before us, there is nothing for faith to work on*....[And] if we really cannot grasp [the proposition of God's existence, or nature, with sufficient clarity and specificity to make it intelligible or coherent], if the sentences which purport to express them have no [factual or cognitive] meaning for us [beyond mere familiarity], then the fact, if it were a fact, that they did have meaning for some other [super-intelligent, celestial] beings would be of little interest to us; for this meaning might be anything whatsoever. The truth is, however, that those who take this position [that beings of super-human intelligence, if there are any, entertain and understand propositions that we humans cannot grasp] do understand, or think they understand, something by the words "God exists." It is only when the account they give of what they understand appears unworthy of credence that they take refuge in saying that it falls short of what the words really mean. *But words have no meaning beyond the meaning that is given them, and a proposition is not made the more credible by being treated as an approximation to something that we do not find intelligible.* (Joshi 2000, 96; emphasis mine)

This seems self-evident, or at least makes good sense. Mormon apostle and General Authority James E. Talmage would seem, in principle, to agree when he wrote: "We have seen that among the most conclusive proofs of the existence of a Supreme Being, is that some knowledge of the attributes and personality of God is essential to any rational exercise of faith in Him" (2003, 309).

But if: (1) the concept of the Mormon god and the assertion of its existence are unintelligible, incoherent, and factually meaningless, making such a god a factual non-reality, as concluded in Chapter 3; (2) the claimed 'Word of God' (scripture, doctrine) regarding the nature and existence of the Mormon god is arguably incoherent and of questionable origin and veracity and, as well, doctrinally contradictory, conceptually unintelligible and historically unreliable, as concluded in Chapter 5, and (3) the claims of the mystery and ineffability of the Mormon god's purposes and the corresponding need for, and possibility of, revelation from that god to man about that god are incoherent (as also concluded in Chapter 5); then the concept of faith in the Mormon god is likewise incoherent and the belief in such faith is, as a putative 'saving principle,' irrational. *How can one intelligibly have faith in (or have trust and love for) a putative being whose believed existence is utterly incoherent, unintelligible, and factually meaningless as fully conceptualized — who is therefore a factual non reality as believed, and therefore cannot possibly be known, or even believed without self-deception?*

This question presents a serious problem that has serious implications. It is a problem that is addressed *pragmatically* by both the pre-depth psychologizing of William James, in his classic work *The Varieties of Religious Experience* (1987) and the philosophizing of Blaise Pascal, as well as *paradoxically* by the existential *fideism*, or faith-based philosophy, of Søren Kierkegaard and *relativistically* by the *fideism* reflected in the philosophical thinking of Ludwig Wittgenstein. Such fideistic (faith-based) defenses of religious belief and God-talk, as well as the assertion that faith and reason are justifiably separate (yet not conflicting) and acceptable ways of gaining knowledge, require at least some treatment here as serious counterpoints to the type of critical, conceptual analysis advocated and employed in this book and by Atheists in general. Though such defenses of traditional Christian faith and God-talk are rarely (if ever) referred to in the popular writings and discourses of Mormon leaders, apologists and professors of religion, they are, in my view, nonetheless relevant to this analysis and assessment of the Mormon concept and doctrine of faith. As such, they merit at least the brief analysis of these defenses in the pages which follow. That said, let us first consider the fideism of James and Pascal, followed by the fideism of Kierkegaard and finally, Wittgensteinian fideism.

The Fideism of William James

"James admits readily," as Faber correctly states, "that we have no scientific, empirical evidence in support of religious belief. He asserts that religion is integrally bound up with the 'subconscious' mind. He is impressed by the powerful, utterly convincing nature of heartfelt religious experience, and he is sensitive to the genuine psychological and physical benefits that flow toward those who believe.[121]...In a famous *mot* James holds that [supernatural, theistic] religion doesn't work because it's true, but is true because it works. He calls this his pragmatic criterion" (2004, 43). But the assertion or claim that such putative psychological and physical benefits are *caused* by what James refers to in one place as supernatural 'transmundane energies' and in another as 'God' (1981, 467) is, like the Mormon concept of the 'Holy Spirit' or 'Light of Truth (Christ),' not only unintelligible but factually meaningless.

How can we make rational sense of such metaphysical realities and such an alleged *causal* relationship? What precisely are such putative 'transmundane energies' that they

---

121 The question of whether or not the putative sociopsychological and physical benefits of religious belief (such as a sense of self-actualization, contentment, optimism, self-esteem, security, and belonging, as well as physical health, *etc.*) are real or exceed the like benefits experienced by nonbelievers, or are sufficient in worth to offset the likely psychological risks and costs to the believer associated with the Mormon faith in particular (such as depression, anxiety, guilt, shame, regressive co-dependence, and a sense of self-alienation and oppression, *etc.*), is addressed briefly, from my own personal perspective as informed by experience, observation and secondary research, in Chapters 7 and 8, as well as in the *Epilogue* and *Personal Postscript*.

might be specified and their existence possibly verified or falsified? What are the truth-conditions of the claim that such 'energies' (whatever they might be) factually or literally exist and that they might be established conceptually as facts or as causal mechanisms of transcendent personal transformation and well-being? The actual or justified truth of propositions is not established by mere assertion, speculation, or perceived *correlations* among self-reported states-of-mind, actions, and affects, or by self-reported feelings, sensations, or alleged and subjective personal experience and benefit — regardless of how convincing they might be to the recipient.

In other words, actual truth is not necessarily synonymous with what *allegedly* 'works.' After all, delusions work when they motivate a particular, desired course of action or way of life, yet the fact that such a course of action or way of life might produce beneficial results along the way clearly does not make the delusion actually true as a stated charac-terization of reality. A statement is considered to be *rational* as a belief if, and only if, it is *justifiable* as a truth claim, and is legitimately considered to be *actually* true if, and only if, it has, in fact, been *justified*. Further, *knowledge* consists of beliefs, or propositions, which are justified and true. This makes — if the conclusions based on our analysis of the Mormon concepts *God*, the *Gospel* and *revelation* are sound — any first-order testimony of a Mormon (or a Christian) believer claiming knowledge of the truth of a god's existence, or of the truthfulness of the 'Gospel of God,' either false or incoherent.

It is to these arguments and charge that James objects when he writes:

> If you have intuitions at all, they come from a deeper level of your nature than the loqua-cious level which rationalism inhabits. Your whole subconscious life, your impulses, your faiths, your needs, your divinations, have prepared the premises of which your consciousness now feels the weight of the result; and something in you absolutely knows that the result must be truer than any logic-chopping rationalistic talk, however clever, that might contradict it. (73)

Again, "our impulsive belief [derived from putative religious conversion experience] is…always what set up the original body of truth, and our philosophy [doctrine, theol-ogy] is but its showy verbalized translation. The immediate assurance is the deep thing in us, the [theological or apologetic] argument is but a surface exhibition. Instinct leads, intelligence does but follow" (74).

In these putative belief-forming 'conversion experiences' "there is," according to James, "little doctrinal theology" (203) and "no need of doctrinal apparatus or propitiary machinery" (211). But this, as argued in Chapter 3, is absurd. All religious experience is interpreted in the context of a particular and foundational *theological/doctrinal framework or belief system* within a particular religious life-form or tradition. How else could those who have such affective experiences interpret them as religious *conversion* experiences resulting, for example, from the 'baptism of fire and the Holy Spirit' in virtue of the 'atonement of Jesus Christ' without exposure to Christian or Mormon doctrine? Or, as S.T. Joshi put it, "…why did this person not feel the presence of Allah or Apollo or Thor rather than Jesus? How else could he have 'learned' that it was Jesus unless he had been previously exposed to Christian [or Mormon] doctrine, as opposed to the doctrines of Islam or Greek or Egyptian mythology?" (2003, 42)

Nevertheless, "Faith, for James, is not," according to Faber, "merely a mentalistic, intellectual, or even an emotional position adopted by the believer after inwardly debating the theological issues. On the contrary, it is a 'biological state' by which the believer 'lives,' a biological state that reaches into his 'subconscious' region" (2004, 44). In James' words, "the theologian's contention that the religious man is moved by an external power is vindicated [presumably as a 'fact'], for it is one of the peculiarities of *invasions from the subconscious region* to take on objective appearances, and to suggest to the Subject an external control [or 'God']" (1987, 512–13, emphasis mine). Beyond the incoherence of considering 'facts' as external, objective, and mind- and language-independent entities, conditions, or states of affairs (as argued in Chapter 1), is the apparent incredibility of James' conclusions themselves. From Joshi's perspective, "The totality of James' argument amounts to this: if the subject *feels* that [his] perceptions of a 'higher' reality are external to him, then they must, in the absence of definitive proof otherwise, *be* external."

But in making this argument Joshi argues that "James totally ignores the rationalization that is constantly going on in the religious subject while he is having these 'feelings' (even though these rationalizations themselves may be partially subconscious), as well as the hopes, fears, wishful thinking, and prior [exposure to or] indoctrination into religious dogma that lead the subject to come to this conclusion in the first place" (2003, 61). Moreover, as if to at once correct and update James' otherwise incoherent conclusions, Faber asserts, while "not faulting James" for writing according to the best understanding he had at the time, that

> When we wed James' observations on 'religion experience' to our own developmental perspective, including above all the recent neuropsychological investigation of memory as it extends itself across the life-span, we can see the degree to which the 'faith-state' is tied to internalized interactions with the caregiver of the early period, the maternal provider through whom the individual's very selfhood germinates both biologically and psychologically. We can see that implicit recollections of affective *states*, triggered by retrieval cues in the environment, have the capacity to restore the *presence* of the maternal figure at the 'subconscious' levels of perception. (2004, 45–6)

Importantly, from a depth-psychological perspective, Faber relevantly convincingly concludes his analysis of James' psychological perspective on faith by suggesting that, in the end,

> The remarkable, mysterious, uncanny aspect of our 'creation' is this: the nurturing parent of the early period is not explicitly recalled by us as grown-ups in spite of the fact that she governed the quality of our inner world and mapped out the initial course of our existence. The 'biological faith-state' by which we 'live' is, then, a 'state' with a developmental history that can be aroused by present events, including the wish for symbiotic merger. *People 'get religion' not through their 'religious experience' as such but through their early internalized experience with the biological parent, the experience upon which religion operates to construct its mythic, ritualistic edifice.* When we sense the Creator within us [through affect, as well as *apparently* outside us in 'vision' or 'visitation'] and acknowledge with gratitude His delicious love and care, we don't know whence such 'experience' derives because we cannot *find* explicitly the foundational strata of our lives. *We attribute to the outside what is happening on the inside, always, and without exception.* (46, emphasis mine)

Indeed and in truth, something does 'work' in relation to the phenomenon of personal, psychological transformation — but it clearly is *not* supernatural and it is not 'God.' No causal connection can coherently be made between personal ('religious') transformational experience and supernatural 'transmundane energies,' whatever such might mean, if anything at all. On the other hand, there are completely coherent and plausible naturalistic explanations for such experiences — explanations pointing to biologically grounded psychodynamics. William James' pragmatism does not rescue 'faith in God' from incoherence.

Nor, as Nielsen points out elsewhere, does James' argument for the virtues of non-creedal or non-doctrinal religious belief even remotely establish that because they are untestable with no hard or conclusive evidence against them "…belief and disbelief… [are therefore] on a par intellectually"; or alternatively "…that man needs religion for his life to have significance"; or finally "…that belief in God is perfectly intelligible, that is, that we know what it would be like for God to exist but that we just do not know and cannot come to know whether in fact there is such an ultimate reality" (1971, 211–12). In all and in the end, Nielsen concludes that James' advocacy for the 'will to believe' is faced, at least, with "very considerable difficulties" (204–13).

The Fideism of Blaise Pascal

Neither can we accept the pragmatism of Blaise Pascal. He argues for the prudence of a 'wager,' wherein doubting nonbelievers who want (or are willing) to believe but cannot, nonetheless should force themselves to believe with the rationale that if they do and it turns out there is a god, then they will be eternally blessed and not damned by their doubt or unbelief. If it so happens that there is no god, then nothing is lost, since the believer would have lived a markedly better life. Specifically, such a wager makes it wise, in Pascal's words, for one who doubts to "convince yourself" by "acting as if [you] believed," which will "naturally make you believe and deaden your [natural, uncomfortable] senses [of doubt]" (1958, 233). Pascal's premise here is that belief follows action. It advises that if you cannot believe, act as if you do, and — by and by — you shall. For Mormon's experiencing a crisis in faith, or for questioning or doubting investigators or believers, this argument would translate to the counsel to make of faith a decision — once and for all and without equivocation — to continue, in spite of doubt, to 'keep the commandments of God' and to follow without question the counsel of priesthood leaders.

Pascal's argument is based on the philosophical (and scripturally supported) premise of 'doxastic voluntarism,' a theory which, in its strong and typically held version holds that we can and do deliberately choose our beliefs — that we believe what we choose to believe. Relevantly, committed Mormon believers, as all committed religious believers, exercise their faith in their god and Christ believing that their belief *that* 'God and Christ exist' as doctrinally conceptualized is true in the *absence* of empirical proof or evidence, or even factual intelligibility or significance. Such belief, in turn, it might be argued, is consciously, deliberately chosen on the basis of 'faith,' which is scripturally understood as "the substance of things hoped for, the evidence of things not seen" (Hebrews 11:1). But is it?

Under normal circumstances, as Adler points out, "[w]hen we [rationally] try to believe at will, we fail, and not from any mere inability. Our failure seems to mark a genuine conceivability. Pick haphazardly an ordinary proposition such as 'Plato would not like peanut butter,' and attempt to believe it directly [without reasonable or valid proof or evidence], just as a result of a decision. Also, randomly select among propositions that you do believe, and simply try to cease believing them. You cannot do either, and it would not help to imagine, in the former case, that you desire the belief, or in the latter case, that you are averse to it." Nor can we believe, Adler continues, "that the Eiffel Tower is in Central Park or cease to believe that $2 + 3 = 5$." Finally, Adler correctly asserts, even strong voluntarists "can allow that it is not possible to knowingly believe…a contradiction, let alone will it" (2002, 59).

The problem with such voluntarism in its strong form — and, by extension, with the concept of faith itself as a reflection of a personal, pragmatic choice or decision to believe in the putative existence of the Christian god and Christ (a problem in its own right which is treated below) — is that it is *normatively* and *conceptually* incoherent, as well as irrational at best and psychopathological at worst. Generally, the normative incoherence of 'faith' as a 'principle of action' reflective of beliefs chosen in the absence of empirical or sensible evidence or reason may be demonstrated by the fact that *normally*, as a matter of course, we would not rationally assert (or sanely act on the mere assertion[122]), for example, that "Flight 462 goes directly to Phoenix because I have faith that it does." Or, more extremely, "I can walk across a busy freeway blindfolded and not be hurt or killed because I have faith that I can."

Apart from the inability of such a 'prudent,' pragmatic strategy of rescuing 'faith in God' (or the concept of 'God') from incoherency, or the obvious difficulties with Pascal's justificatory premises for his wager argument (including, for example, his premise that obediently living a religious (Christian, Mormon) life entails *no* loss, but *only* gain, even

---

122 As a relevant aside, the assertion that we all act regularly in mundane matters on the basis of *unseen* evidence, or faith as a 'principle of action,' is, as addressed above, not analogous to this use of the term 'faith' in a religious context. In a *naturalistic* context our decision to act in the world each day is based on massive empirical data that give us the confidence we need to act for some reason or in pursuit of some goal or desire. The fact that the future outcome of our next act of, for example, starting our car to go to work is necessarily unknown (or 'unseen') does not mean that we act without evidence-based confidence — evidence consisting of extensive empirical data and knowledge of actual (and natural) conditions, states of affair and causal mechanisms related to our automobile and the likelihood of it starting today as it did yesterday.

This clearly does *not* hold in a religious context, for while we *do* know *that* our automobile *actually* exists and know (or have access to knowledge regarding) *how* it works, we do not and cannot possibly know *that* the Mormon god exists as theologically conceptualized, or consequently *how* such a god, as a factual non-reality (or even, for the sake of argument, as an actual finite being with supernatural attributes), could possibly do what he is believed to have done or allegedly can and does do. Alternatively, the conceptual incoherence of faith as the "evidence of things not seen" is, by contrast, established not by normative practice but (as addressed above and earlier in this chapter) by the incoherence of the concept, or putative reality, believed to be factual or true, in this case the concepts of 'God' and 'Christ' (as these terms are used in Mormon theology). Again, the allegation of doxastic incoherence holds that we cannot rationally believe what is unbelievable without self-deception. As for the claim that such belief (or faith) is based on 'unseen evidence' (*i.e.* putative evidence not subject to empirical observation or verification), the problem is *not* that evidence exists but is hidden for some reason 'known only to God,' but rather that *there can be no evidence for something which is conceptually unintelligible or factually meaningless.* What confirming or disconfirming evidence, for example, could there possibly be — or would possibly count — for proving or disproving the existence of 'an infinite, eternal, and transcendent being,' or 'spirit matter, or element,' or 'intelligences,' or 'the Christ,' or the 'Light of Truth (Christ)'?

if only in this life — a premise challenged explicitly in Chapter 8) — there is the very real and potentially serious problem of self-deception addressed below by Adler. He writes:

> Pascal acknowledges the agnostic's plea but provides no reason to actually believe there is a God. Rather, Pascal recommends an indirect way for the agnostic to induce the belief he wants. He is to convince himself by a procedure of imitation, whereby the desired belief arises in him without notice. Pascal's recommendation is for a long-term project of self-deception to evade the impossibility of straight-forward belief that there is a God. (2007, 280)

In other words, faith derived by belief in the unbelievable (*i.e.* by believing that which is fundamentally incoherent as, for example, 'God exists' and 'Jesus is the Christ, the literal Son of the living God') exists *not* because of reasonable, conscious, or deliberate choice, but rather in virtue of the natural mechanisms of projective transference, dissociation (or, more specifically, dissociative trance-logic) *and* self-deception. For Adler, such a 'project' of self-deception in the service of legitimizing, exceptionalizing and isolating religious affective and hallucinatory experience from critical analysis or the burden of proof bears significantly more risk than simply believing 'little white lies.' This is so particularly in the case of fanaticism where, in cases where "the perversion of belief is extensive [for a variety of different psychological reasons], the self-deception required is not occasional self-trickery but more of a mental fog or massive self-delusion" which can lead, in extreme cases of otherwise morally questionable or immoral behavior, to potentially serious social consequences, including — where such behavior is ego-dystonic for the self-deceived believer — "mental breakdown" (280).

But even if such belief and faith, acquired as it is through the program of self-deception advocated by Pascal, does not result in dangerous fanaticism, it certainly does raise the question — even if subconsciously — as to whether or not the self-deceived believer may trust his own confidence in his acquired faith. As Daniel Garber puts it, "Now it is one thing if, in the course of events, I [naturally, or involuntarily] find myself in [the] epistemic state [of belief]. But it would seem to be quite another if I deliberately put myself into that state. In that case, it looks as if I am deliberately going about deceiving myself, believing because I *want* to believe [or because I'm *afraid* of the social or believed personal, eternal consequences of not believing]. The process by which I attain the rational belief would seem [at some level] to undermine the rationality of the final outcome" (39). In other words, the incoherence of belief in the unbelievable is ultimately self-defeating to faith itself as a remedy to doubt. If it were not so, could there even *be* sincere religious doubt?

The Fideism of Søren Kierkegaard

Søren Kierkegaard's fideism fares no better. "Religious faith, as Kierkegaard conceives it, is," according to Martin, "a total and passionate commitment to God. It is the result of an act of will [a "leap of faith"] as it were, or a decision, and the person with this faith completely disregards any doubts" (1990, 251). Further, Martin interprets, "…it is precisely because it is not based on objective reasoning that faith has the highest virtue." Moreover, "[f]aith [by definition and its very nature] is not and should not be objectively certain; that is, it is not and should not be certain on the basis of objective reasoning."

Kierkegaard contends, according to Martin, "that, even when the Christian God seems paradoxical and absurd, even without adequate evidence for such commitment, total and passionate commitment to [or faith in] God is necessary for salvation and ultimately for [personal growth] and happiness" (252; see also Nielsen 1971, pp. 214–26).

Such views, particularly the extended popular view extolling the virtue of 'leaps of faith' in accepting baseless, absurd or consequential propositions as true, are highly problematic. This is so logically, pragmatically, and morally. Logically we still have the problem of specifying what it is exactly that a believer is to have faith in. Again, if the object of such faith is 'God', and if the concept of such a 'God' as stated and believed is unintelligible, incoherent and factually meaningless (as is certainly the case the Mormon god), then there is *necessarily* nothing to have faith in.

At a pragmatic level, the alleged call for a 'leap of faith' fails whenever the believer cannot specify what would distinguish such faith from an utterly delusional commitment made merely on the basis of feelings, ignorance and self-deception. Or, alternatively, whenever the alleged earthly necessity for such a 'leap of faith' (i.e. to enjoy personal growth and happiness) is demonstrably *not* a necessity at all; when such goods can (and are) enjoyed by many others who *cannot* and *will not* make such an intellectually debasing 'leap'.

Finally, when the utter 'leap of faith' in the putative existence and will of gods or other supernatural agents presents potentially harmful or destructive consequences to the well-being of self or others, it is morally questionable at least, if not wholly immoral. In this last regard Michael Martin understandably and accurately sees Kierkegaard's 'Knight of Faith' as a self-deceived and dangerous fanatic — like Abraham of the Bible who was willing to sacrifice his son Isaac. How, in fact, on the sole basis of faith in a god could we, in principle, differentiate a committed, Kierkegaardian 'Knight of Faith,' like Abraham, from a lucid, intelligent, and otherwise deeply religious psychopath who commits or sanctions acts of inhumane abuse, human exploitation, violence, or perhaps even human sacrifice — all mixed with acts of apparent kindness, compassion and self-sacrifice — and who justifies such inconsistent and deplorable acts on the basis of alleged revelations or divine commands from his god?

Moreover, such a concept of faith results in at least an apparent contradiction with the belief in an 'all-good God.' "How [or why]," asks Martin, "could [would] an all-good God want [or require] his creatures to have blind faith in him without adequate evidence, let alone with negative evidence? Surely an all-good God would not want [or require] his creatures [children] to [deceive themselves or] be fanatics, especially when there is good reason to suppose that fanaticism leads to great human suffering?" (252–53)

Again from Adler's perspective, these questions point to troubling social problems (2007, 266–285). According to Adler, religious beliefs in the supernatural and faith in a god enable fanaticism and extremism through the mechanism of self-deception, which is necessarily invoked to manage the incoherence of believing the unbelievable and thereby enable the exercise of faith. Faith in a god, for Adler is "fertile ground for [such] fanaticism," (266) particularly if it is believed — as in Mormon theology — that one's god is not subject to any moral code — that there is a higher moral law resting with 'God,' wherein *whatever* he commands is right and good. With such a belief, Adler writes,

The goodness attributed to God adds no restraint upon which we can rely. If biblical [or scriptural] texts are treated as authoritative, God commands what [for human-beings] is unjust and permits terrible evils. He actively orders and commits atrocities. The binding of Isaac is actually less consequential ethically than those incidents in the Bible in which God orders the slaughter of all members of an enemy or sinning community. Such tales, as ones of righteous retribution, illuminate the religious terrorist's intellectual path. (285)

Mormon scripture and Mormon history — including the personal histories of many Mormon believers in and out of the Mormon Church embracing what Quinn refers to as "theocratic ethics" (1994) — are certainly not without numerous examples of such fanaticism and related acts of atrocity, abuse, and anti-social behavior. Therefore, not only does Kierkegaardian fideism fail (like James' and Pascal's pragmatic fideism) to rescue 'faith in God' from incoherence, it makes such incoherent faith in an incoherent god (who is believed to be perfectly good and all-powerful yet responsible for committing and commanding human atrocities) potentially and likely dangerous to the believer and society.

Wittgensteinian Fideism

Very different defenders of the legitimacy of religious language-games and belief were Ludwig Wittgenstein and his followers. "According to Wittgensteinian fideism," writes Martin, "religious discourse is embedded in a form of life and has its own rules and logic. It can only be understood and evaluated in its own terms, and any attempt to impose standards on such discourse from the outside — for example from science [or philosophy] — is quite inappropriate. Since religious discourse is a separate unique language game different from that of science [or philosophy, *etc.*], religious statements, unlike scientific ones, are not empirically testable. To demand that they be is a serious misunderstanding of that form of discourse. On this view of the language game of religion, religious discourse is rational and intelligible *when judged in its own terms*, which are the only appropriate ones. Because the meaning of a term varies from one language game to another, to understand religious language one must see it from within the religious language game itself" (1990, 256, emphasis mine).

As acknowledged in Chapter 1, it certainly makes sense to say that understanding a particular language game requires an insider's perspective, or point of view. But in a cultural as well as a topical context, such philosophical if not common sense does not extend to the assertion that language games are or should be impervious to external criticism. Nor does it require that the meaning of language is "radically contextual and that it is impossible to communicate across practices or ways [forms] of life" (258).

"Suppose," Martin suggests, "each religious form of life is governed by its own standards. Then there could be no external standards that could be used in criticizing a religious form of life. However," cautions Martin, echoing Adler above and following his own characterization of the dangers of Kierkegaardian fideism, "this has unfortunate consequences. Some religious denominations practice sexual and racial discrimination [or engage in various forms of abuse, including authoritarian, physical, and sexual abuse]. For instance," as Martin correctly observes, "the Mormon Church excluded blacks from positions in the church hierarchy, and it still excludes women [and also once practiced plural marriage with other men's wives]. It is not implausible to suppose that most enlightened people today, including, perhaps, many Mormons, believe that [these] practice[s] and the beliefs on which [they] rest are wrong. Yet if Mormonism is a separate form of life, there can be, according to Wittgensteinian fideism, no external criticism of its practices" (257).

"Despite what Wittgensteinian fideists say," argues Martin, "external criticism is not only possible but essential….Although insight into a form of life may be gained by taking the participants' perspective, one cannot rest content with this, for the participants may be blind to the problems with [the content of] their own practices and beliefs, and the perspective of an outsider may be necessary if these are to be detected" (257–58).

Beyond the moral or social implications of religious beliefs and practices which, as Martin rightly argues, should be open to external moral and legal criticism and rigorous internal dissent, there are *rational* implications which address the question of what makes sense to rationally believe or assert as truth or as something that could possibly be actually true. To the appropriateness or possibility of such external *rational criticism*, as advocated and pursued by Nielsen and others, it might be apologetically argued here, as Matt Talbert has stated, that: "Neither Wittgenstein nor the contemporary Wittgensteinians hold that all beliefs are necessarily inviolate or immune from criticism." According to Talbert, "Beliefs can certainly become senseless, especially if the believer attempts to push propositions outside their proper bounds….If the believer does believe, in the realist's sense, in prayer or miracles [or, as in Mormonism, for example, in the *literal* conception of Jesus Christ, 'baptism for the dead' and the *literal* 'atonement' and 'resurrection' of Jesus, *etc.*] it seems that they are written off. For the Wittgensteinian, it appears that religious belief is fine, so long as religious propositions are kept enclosed in the purely self-referential language-game of a vague faith and trust" (Matt Talbert on "Wittgensteinian Fideism and Religious Skepticism").

In other words, as long as religious discourse is *not* asserted to be knowledge, *i.e.* is *not* taken *literally* or represented as *fact* or *truth* but is regarded *merely* as being expressive of a particular religious way of life, it remains insulated from conceptual analysis or scientific and philosophical criticism. But when, for example, Mormon believers assert, *as they most certainly do*, that their *first-order* testimonies or God-talk and *second-order* doctrinal beliefs are *factual*,[123] that, for example, their god *factually* (actually) exists, or baptisms, ordinations, and marriages can be *vicariously* performed on Earth by living proxy for the dead, all bets are off.

This is precisely Nielsen's point in arguing as he has — and as I have throughout this book — that Judeo-Christian, Mormon, and Islamic God-talk that purports to make true or false statements is unintelligible, incoherent, and factually meaningless. According to Nielsen, the very *nature* of God-talk itself, as a language-game, is problematic. In his words, "If we select for comparison with such God-talk (as, for example, 'God made the world and sent His only begotten Son to save mankind') certain [linguistic] *paradigms* such as 'There are clouds in the sky,' 'Hans caught three fish,' 'Women sometimes die in childbirth,' which are bits of discourse used pervasively by believers and nonbelievers alike, we will see that there is an important difference between them and such God-talk."

---

123 For a believer in such nonsense to simply wave-off criticisms or challenges to such beliefs by saying, for example, as one believer did recently, "That's just what we believe in our religion," is to employ a fideistic isolation strategy to evade the truth. Such assertions of belief are, in my view, at very least disingenuous in relation to the believed truth they contradict.

Clearly, argues Nielsen, "…with these core paradigms we have a norm which is common currency both in the language in question, namely English, and in the languages of the entire human family, while the very conceptions built into God-talk…are widely disputed and not currently ubiquitous. There is no one who can intelligibly deny that we can know what time it is, whether there are stones and trees or whether there is a difference between day and night, but many would deny," including Nielsen and this writer, "that *anyone*, including manifestly holy men, ever have religious knowledge or even justifiable religious beliefs, for example, know or rightly believe that there is a God and he [is the 'Creator and Supreme Ruler of the Universe' and] guards [and directs] the destinies of man.…" Accordingly, Nielsen concludes, "neither believer nor nonbeliever can show what it would be like to have religious knowledge or justified religious beliefs: to know whether religious claims are true or false or to have good grounds for believing them to be true or false" (1982, 137–39, emphasis mine).

Against this argument — and relevant to the question of faith in a god, as well as to the believer's retreat to faith in the face of conceptual analysis — is the Wittgensteinian counter-argument that some things are *beyond human understanding*, including especially things pertaining to the nature of 'God.' Regarding the *philosophical* task of evaluating the declarative factual statements concerning 'God' through conceptual analysis as well as from a 'coherence view' of human knowledge, Wittgensteinian fideists (most notably D.Z. Phillips) have attempted to show that such analysis is inappropriate and arbitrary. According to them, it essentially begs the question by presupposing that expressed mystical (or spiritual) encounters with 'God' can be humanly understood conceptually beyond how they affect the life of recipients. Nielsen's response to Phillips — which initially recapitulates his argument against the 'ineffability thesis' presented at the beginning of the previous chapter — is, as quoted extensively below, appropriate to the challenge:

[But] If God [in his metaphysical, or supernatural, fulness] is utterly beyond human understanding, then there is nothing to be said, nothing to be thought, nothing to be perplexed about, and nothing to wonder at. Accounts of encounters with God, of coming to know and love God, of living or standing in the presence of God, of sensing or feeling the grace of God, are…without sense.

Phillips might respond…that like most philosophers I place too much weight on understanding. I worry about the coherence or truth of the belief that, where God [in his fulness] is concerned, we need to understand that it is something which passes our understanding, "at least while we are on earth"; and, over-intellectualizing things, I try to see if any coherent sense can be made of that.

[Phillips] would no doubt [also] claim that in saying that (the) talk [of mystics such as St. John of the Cross or even Joseph Smith] is incoherent, that it does not make sense, I must be importing standards of rationality or intelligibility from outside the religious language-games actually played; and it is unclear where these standards could come from, what authority they could have, why we should appeal to them, or why the religious person, or anyone else, should pay any heed at all. They seem, Phillips could say, like news from nowhere, arbitrary impositions from out of the blue.

I agree with Phillips that language gets its sense from the way it enters human life. This is a lesson we have rightly taken from Wittgenstein. But language must be taken more holistically than Phillips takes it. We must not take one language-game or linguistic practice, or even a localized cluster of them, standing by themselves. It is not enough to say, "This language game is played." We need to look at the language more broadly and try to gain a perspicuous representation of how various language-games in various domains of our talk and thought, of our discoursing with each other, go, or fail to go, together. Thus we might come to recognize that religious talk ('God-talk' as I call it, as distinct from other religious talk such as the Buddhist might engage in) could have the grammar — the logic, in Phillip's extended sense of 'logic' — that he says it has and still be incoherent because of the way it stands with other parts of our talk. That something like this is the case is what I think to be so. (2001, 420–21)

Beyond the Wittgensteinian challenge to the criticism of religious beliefs, Martin further points out the "paradoxical implications" of Wittgensteinian fideism "concerning the [relative] truth of religious utterances within a language game" (1990, 258). In cases where believers in different religious sects, such as, for example, Mormons, Catholics, and Protestants, make radically different statements about the nature of 'God' and the 'Godhead' then, according to Wittgensteinian fideists, all three sets of statements are true. But if all three sets of statements about 'God and the Godhead' contradict each other, how can they all be true? Martin explains that "The answer a Wittgensteinian fideist would give is that the meaning of a religious utterance is *relative* to the language game to which it belongs," thus making the apparent contradictions merely "an illusion" (258, emphasis mine). But why, paraphrasing Martin, should we accept such a radically relativistic and contextual view of language which makes it impossible to communicate across different ways of life and different language games? "Surely," he suggests, "a more plausible view is that the Christian and non-Christian *are really* disagreeing and that the Catholic, [Protestant and Mormon] are talking about the *same thing*; in other words, that there are a common language and common categories" (258, emphasis mine).

Given the above, albeit brief, explorations and challenges by Adler, Joshi, Martin, and Nielsen, it would seem that neither James' and Pascal's *pragmatic* fideism nor Kierkegaard's *paradoxical* fideism nor Wittgensteinian *relativistic* fideism can adequately resolve the dilemma of faith presented earlier, *i.e. how a presumably rational person could possibly have faith, or trust, in an incoherent, factual non-reality and truly be rational.* None of these works answers the questions it raises. For James, we must ask what makes the object of a putative 'working faith' (*i.e.* 'God') a factual reality or a religion 'true' because it *allegedly works*? And is the fact – if indeed it is a fact – that faith "works" in helping people cope with the existential anxiety and vicissitudes of life sufficient rationale for irresponsibly believing in the existence of a factual non reality? For Pascal, the question arises 'why the need for a wager?' To Kierkegaard we must ask why he thinks there is a need for a 'paradoxical faith' in an 'absurd God'? Or, to quote Nielsen, "Why," as Kierkegaard requires, "believe in a patent absurdity?" (1971, 218) For Wittgensteinians, the question is why the need for different 'language-games' or 'relative truth' in matters of faith in gods? Not one of these philosophers answers the crucial, more fundamental questions implicitly asked in Chapters 3 through 5 and explicitly asked in this chapter and again in Chapters 7 and 8, namely: Faith in *what*, exactly? Moreover, *why faith in a god*? Apropos to the Mormon faith in particular, why *faith testing* — particularly given the Mormon god's putative nature and greatest purpose and desire ('Work and Glory') concerning man's putative eternal state and condition?

With these questions in mind and reserved for further consideration, we turn now to perhaps the most pressing question regarding this particular aspect of faith. Given the impossibility of the Mormon god *as conceptualized* and *believed* in the Mormon faith, and therefore (and necessarily) the impossibility of *faith* in such a god, what is it (or what could it most likely be) that is typically referred to by believers as "faith in god?" The answer to this question seems clear based on what we know about the evolution and workings of the human brain, and the unconscious motivations inherent in our human existential predicament and "basic biological situation" (Faber 2004, 2010). Simply and economically stated, such alleged faith in god is, at its most basic or fundamental level, an infantile, dissociated state of mind. Moreover, what faith is as an experience of "knowing" of God's existence (or "knowing" God) with *certainty* and *conviction* on the basis of induced, experienced visual and/or auditory hallucinations regarded as "visions," "dreams," "revelations," or "visitations" from God can perhaps be best and most fundamentally characterized as a delusion, and explained, as we learned in the previous chapter and shall revisit below, as merely a neuropsychological phenomenon originating in the human brain.

Additionally, as shall be enlarged upon below in this chapter, and again in the analysis and assessment of an actual conversion experience in *Appendix A*, what such faith is in relation to religious "conversion" experience can I think perhaps best be characterized as a motivated projective transference. Specifically, the believer, motivated by the "hoped (and *wished*) for" "assurance" of "salvation" and "eternal life," or simply a "personal relationship" with 'God' or 'Christ,' unconsciously projects (or 'transfers') his internalized parent image to the imagined (and *illusory*) Parent-God and the same ecstatic merging of the infant and care-giver ensues. With this experience the convert becomes utterly convinced in his belief that he has truly encountered God (or Christ) and has been literally "saved" (or "born again") and/or enlightened by the sure revelation of Truth.

Jerry Piven, in *Death and Delusion*, elaborates below on this plausible and, in my mind, important, relevant, and compelling naturalistic idea in the context of Ernest Becker's groundbreaking work *The Denial of Death* (1973):

> One transcends weakness and death through transference. For Becker, transference meant the repetition of childhood dependence on new objects that provide security. One regresses emotionally to a state of infantile dependence, *distorting reality* to relieve helplessness and fear, instilling a willingness to be hypnotized and submissive. One needs transference in order to endure life. As Becker noted, "The less ego power one has and the more fear, the stronger the transference" (1973, 147). The transference is derived from need; therefore the object of the transference is endowed with holiness. The transference object becomes an idol; it is deified and invested with tremendous power, authority, truth, value, beauty, and glory — *mana*. One depends on this immortality figure or object to deny the most stark weaknesses and fears. (2002, 240, emphasis mine)

This perspective, along with its rather technical psychological terms, is admittedly neither easily understood nor applied to one's own religious experiences without some uneasiness, if not outright defensive dismissal and denial. Nevertheless, for those who are open to an alternative (and I think very plausible) understanding of the nature and source of so-called "spiritual" experience, such a naturalistic perspective is certainly worth looking into and seriously considering. Indeed, compared with the incoherent faith-based perspective and explanation offered by theism, such a naturalistic perspective – and/or others similar or related to it – is, in my view, the most sensible way to understand such experiences.

The Impossibility of Faith as the 'Way of Knowing God' and 'Spiritual Truth'
through Revelation or 'Spiritual Experience'

Continuing with our analytical query beyond the usage of 'faith' as *confidence, trust, love,* and *devotion* (and beyond fideistic arguments in support of religious belief), how can faith in a god be conceptually tied, as it is in Mormonism, to knowledge of the Mormon god obtained by personal revelation or by an affective 'spiritual experience'[124] induced by the spoken word, scripture study, ritual, and/or fasting and prayer? Would not the content of the emotionally-toned belief or (so-called) knowledge derived from such an experience depend in large part (if not entirely) on an *interpretation* by the experient believer?

Applying Ockham's Razor, would not the best (most economical) explanation of the nature of the experience and content of the interpretation be a naturalistic one involving determining factors defined by the person's personal life-circumstances, emotional (or psychological) needs and condition, and family, Church, and socio-cultural conditioning? Returning to the preceding chapter and the three challenges and four-fold problem presented there, are not claims of certain knowledge, the ineffability of a god's self-revelation (if claimed), and 'knowing' such allegedly experienced or received revelation to be *actual* truth *all* seriously problematical in their own right? Are they not all likely unintelligible and therefore unbelievable to a reasonably skeptical outsider? It would seem, given the at least apparent incoherence of asserted 'revelation from God to man about God' established

---

124 It has become fashionable for some Atheists and Atheist writers to appropriate the word 'spiritual' (or relatedly, 'spirituality') to describe the very human or natural experiences, or feelings, of profound wonder, awe, enlightenment and the sense of being swept away, enlivened, or filled with overwhelming feelings of love, gratitude, insight, and inspiration which are thought (or asserted) to be different than 'religious experience.' This considered distinction between *religious* and *spiritual*, as well as the tendency among certain Atheists to characterize certain experiences as 'spiritual' in nature, or even suggest that spirituality is a natural aspect of human nature that is not exclusive to theistic believers is, in my view, perverse, unwise, and, implicitly at least, incoherent (particularly in relation to its connection with a dualist conception of human nature and its at least implicit connection to the concept of 'spirit' as used in various life-forms). Moreover, I consider the use of such terms, along with words such as *religion, soul, believe,* or *belief* to be inherently part of the long-established language-games of all theistic faiths. Consequently it is a practice that I think (following Eller) implicitly betrays our humanity — and perhaps even our tacit disdain for such humanity in the implied metaphysical and perhaps even superstitious quest and desire to experience its transcendence — and needs (particularly among Atheists) to be avoided and discouraged.

In Eller's words, "This talk of 'spiritual' and 'spirituality' perpetuates a profound mistake and constitutes a profound betrayal — perhaps the most profound that humans have ever committed against themselves. The mistake is the prejudice or belief or faith that life and its finer aspects, and our ability to appreciate those aspects, are not natural but must be supernatural [or biologically transcendent in function and perception] — that beauty, awe, wonder, and love [particularly the 'pure love' of a god)] are not things of this world. No, they must belong to a better world, a higher world, and they are only revealed to us [intermittently and] for a brief time. These finer, more powerful aspects of life are seen as separate from us, other than us, better than us, outside of us [as mere biological creatures of flesh and blood]. Surely we — weak puny [biological] beings — could not be capable of them on our own. (2004, 338)

"But the things that we call spiritual are precisely of this world. They are natural, and they are social. They are not *other* life but *simply more life*. They are not *other than human*, they are *more human*. They are the best of human. The spiritual is experienced as getting 'extra life' from somewhere outside ourselves [outside our human brain and bodily senses]. In reality, it is discovering deeper or better levels inside us [*i.e.* from different parts of our brain]. It is encountering human-ness at its fullest [without the need for a 'spirit,' or 'soul,' or 'the holy spirit,' or some 'spiritual realm of existence']" (338). (For a provocative and incisive treatment of this concern, as well as a competent treatment of the topics of 'spirituality,' 'speaking Christian,' and the 'language of belief,' see Eller 2004, 333–340 and 2007, 33–66 and 395–426.)

in the previous chapter, that it is reasonable to ask again in the context of this analysis of the Mormon concept of faith: *how can anyone know something that is incoherent or unintelligible by revelation which is itself conceptually incoherent*? How, following Nielsen, can faith, *especially by revelation*, insure the meaningfulness of an incoherent concept of 'God' or make it intelligible? These questions necessarily lead us to an analysis of the conflict between faith and reason, an assessment of faith as an epistemic strategy and psychological defense, and an evaluation of an apologetic defense of Mormon faith-based epistemology, all of which follow.

Faith and Reason

According to Mormon Apostle and General Authority Dallin Oaks (1991), reason and faith are both essential, although not co-equal, means for obtaining knowledge. For Oaks, faith has primacy over reason in matters concerning the sacred domain of theology and reason is essential in the secular domain and is useful in authenticating revelation by subjecting it to certain tests — while neither creating nor confirming (justifying) revelation nor superseding revelation nor supplanting faith.

But if, as Oaks asserts, reason is useful in authenticating revelation by subjecting it to certain tests, what could such authentication or justificatory tests be — if the source and content of such putative revelation is not presupposed or justifiable and the very doctrinal belief in the existence of revelation is unintelligible, incoherent, and factually meaningless? Is not the claim that revelation — which is not subject to the authority of reason — 'can only be justified by faith *through* revelation' begging the question as well as incoherent? Would not such a claim itself be unjustifiable and therefore unjustified, if not utterly irrational?

Further, unless we can make sense of the apparently unintelligible assertion that we, as human beings, are endowed with an infallible spiritual sense or capacity — what Widtsoe refers to as a 'sixth sense' and Alvin Plantinga as the '*sensus divinitatus*' — then we must regard as apparently self-evident the fact that human fallibilism makes all truth necessarily provisional. But we cannot *possibly* justify and therefore cannot know whether alleged truth claims are *actually* true (even if provisionally) if the truth claim itself is unintelligible or incoherent and/or neither factually significant (*i.e.* without truth-conditions) nor regarded as self-evident or common knowledge to all reasonable people.

The fact remains, if we cannot understand through reason the concept of 'God' (*i.e.* the use of 'God' in religious statements of belief), and if the concept of 'revelation from a god' is likewise unintelligible and without factual significance, then we do not come closer to understanding these concepts or doctrines through faith or, for that matter, through continuous or progressive revelation. How, after all, can we possibly make sense of new, expository, declarative, or clarifying revelation being possible if revelation *per se* is factually unintelligible? The same holds true with the Mormon doctrines comprising the Plan of Salvation. Once again, what is not knowable or justifiable cannot possibly be known or justified. "Faith does not," asserts George H. Smith, "erase contradictions and absurdities; it merely allows one to believe *in spite of* contradictions and absurdities" (1989, 124, emphasis mine). Similarly, believing something to be true, or saying that something is true "doesn't in the slightest," Nielsen insists, "make for or establish or justify, even with the slightest probability, that what [we believe or] are saying is actually true" (2006, 20). It would seem that the *appeal* to faith merely diverts attention from the crucial issue of justification.

To make this last point more substantive, consider the following analytical question: "How can *faith* establish, or justify, the putative truthfulness and factual significance of a non-self-evident truth claim which is devoid of specifiable and possibly satisfiable truth-conditions?" For example, how can faith establish, or justify, the putative truthfulness and facts specified in the non-self-evident truth claim: "[It is true] *that* Jesus is the Christ, the Son of the living God," when the concept of 'God,' in its metaphysical fulness, is devoid of specifiable and possibly satisfiable truth-conditions and is therefore considered to be a factual non-reality or to be factually unintelligible?

If the answer to this question is that faith establishes the truth of a god's existence through revelation from that god, we not only invalidate such an argument by begging the question, or by presupposing the existence of that being ('God') whose putative existence is in question, we also create with such an answer yet another problematical truth claim: 'It is true *that* revelation from God about God's existence exists.' But here again is another vacuous truth claim. As we discovered in the previous chapter, it also is devoid of specifiable and possibly satisfiable truth-conditions and criteria of authenticity. Therefore, it is neither justified nor justifiable as to its putative truthfulness. But if 'revelation or spiritual confirmation from God' is thus deemed as a literal reality to be factually unintelligible on the basis of such conceptual analysis, then we are back to the original question regarding the usefulness of faith in establishing or justifying the putative truthfulness of any testamentary or doctrinal truth claim.

Faith as "Epistemic Strategy" and Psychological Defense

So why then is such an appeal to faith made by believers? *"Why,"* asks Smith, *"does the Christian* [or Mormon] *employ two concepts, reason and faith, to designate different methods of acquiring knowledge, instead of just using the concept of reason itself?* In other words, why is it necessary for the Christian [or Mormon] to introduce the idea of faith at all? What purpose does it serve that is not served by reason?" (104)

These questions point to faith – apart from being a biologically rooted, neuropsychological phenomenon – as a pragmatic, epistemic strategy used by believers to legitimize their religious beliefs. Accordingly, to Smith, the answer is obvious. "[T]he Christian [and also the Mormon] wishes to claim as knowledge beliefs that have not been [or cannot be] rationally demonstrated [or otherwise justified], so he posits faith as an alternative method of acquiring knowledge. Faith permits the Christian [or Mormon] to claim the status of truth for a belief even though it [is unjustifiable and therefore] cannot meet the rational test of truth, or the generally accepted threshold of knowledge."

"Faith is required," continues Smith, "only if reason is inadequate; if reason is not deficient in some respect, the concept of faith becomes vacuous. The Christian [or Mormon] creates the need for faith by denying the efficacy of reason….If reason can tell us anything there is to know, there is no longer a job for faith. *The entire notion of faith rests upon and presupposes the inadequacy of reason*" (104). It depends as well, I might add, upon the factual existence of a god and the reality of revelation or (as for the Buddhist or Mystic) 'transcendent enlightenment.'

For Mormon believers, according to Oaks, the existence of the Mormon god is a *given* and is *not* to be questioned. Faith, as an appeal to authority, allegedly enables believers to get beyond skepticism, doubt, Agnosticism, or Atheism — none of which is a living option for the committed believer. To this end it might also be asserted that faith, as well as the appeal to faith and the pursuit of greater faith, is not only an epistemic strategy designed to validate, legitimize, or defend religious beliefs that are neither justifiable nor justified through reason, but is also a defensive reaction that has been formed without awareness against the experience and emotional, social, and institutional consequences of doubt. In this sense appeals to and pursuit of *greater* faith, the emphasis on faith as being necessary for salvation, and the practice of faith-as-"testimony" (or "witness") of the existence of 'God' and 'Christ' are, like the repetitive and authoritative appeal to eschew doubt, defensive reactions formed to avoid, suppress, or repress deeply nested doubt. They mobilize and fortify self-deception and denial, and motivate unquestioning obedience to authority and faithfulness to one's putative covenants with a god.

This understanding of faith as a psychological defense, or 'reaction formation,' was introduced in the *Introduction* and is particularly relevant to the Mormon believer who must live with scriptural injunctions to "Doubt not, but be believing" (Mormon 9:27; Matt. 21:21) and shaming and threatening teachings and exhortations from notable Church authorities like Elder Bruce R. McConkie who wrote in *Mormon Doctrine*: "Faith and belief are of God; doubt and skepticism are of the devil. There is no excuse for not knowing and believing true principles for the Lord has ordained the way whereby all may come to a knowledge of the truth. Doubt comes from failure to keep the commandments" (1979, 208).

Regardless, many modern believers will no doubt argue (*pace* Kierkegaard) that while faith differs from reason, "faith is not contrary to reason: it is an auxiliary method of gaining knowledge,…and propositions of reason do not contradict the propositions of faith — and, therefore, reason and faith do not conflict." But, Smith continues, "While it is true that the Christian [or Mormon] will never find a contradiction between the propositions of reason and his religious beliefs, this is true only because he will never permit such contradictions to exist. The apologist reduces all contradictions to *apparent* contradictions, which he claims are ultimately explainable or reconcilable [if not in this life, then in the next]" (111). This is a strategy, Tice might argue, of managing 'cognitive dissonance,' a term coined by Festinger and his associates in 1956 to explain a common psychological reaction to cognitive discomfort. In the important excerpt below, Tice first briefly summarizes cognitive dissonance theory, and then appropriately applies the theory of cognitive dissonance to a contemporary example involving a fundamental Mormon belief:

> Cognitive dissonance theory, simply stated, postulates that if an individual simultaneously experiences two conflicting cognitions, he or she will perceive that condition as aversive and will be motivated to make an adjustment in the direction of greater consistency. In laymen's terms, people want their lives to make sense. If they believe something to be true, they don't want to see or hear anything that is inconsistent with that belief. Dissonance describes the ambiguous discomfort felt by a person when there are two or more inconsistent elements among his or her thoughts, feelings, or behaviors.
>
> When an individual does not perceive inconsistency, there is no cognitive discomfort. However, when an element of inconsistency is introduced, that individual will become psychologically uncomfortable and will be motivated to return to a state of constancy…

During my research, I ran across a fascinating book that applied dissonance theory to an analysis of the *Old Testament*. Carroll (1979) postulated that biblical hermeneutics evolved as a response to dissonance. As editors worked with the texts they occasionally provided explanations that reduced some of the problems associated with the expectations in the traditions (p.124)...

When I read this book, I was reminded of a particularly dissonant experience I encountered in modern-day Mormonism. In 1835, Joseph Smith purchased Egyptian papyri at an exhibit in Kirkland, Ohio. Smith claimed the ability to translate the Egyptian and said that the papyri contained the writings of the prophet Abraham... His translation came to be known within Mormonism as *The Book of Abraham,* and it was canonized into Mormon scripture as part of *The Pearl of Great Price.* Because Smith's translation predated the deciphering of the Rosetta Stone, the claim could not be proven or disproven at the time.

... [In] 1967 the papyri used by Joseph Smith to translate the *Book of Abraham* were discovered in the basement of the Metropolitan Museum of Art in New York City. The church was initially excited about the find, but evaluations by renowned Egyptologists reveal that Smith's original translation was quite erroneous...Even more potentially embarrassing to the church was the fact that some of Smith's original notes remained, and it was shown, in some cases, that he had translated four paragraphs from a character that is now known to be a portion of one word (Heinerman & Schup, 1985; Tanner & Tanner, 1987).

The Mormon Church's original response to this 'disconfirmation' was to cast doubt on the skill of the initial Egyptologists who analyzed the papyri (Tanner & Tanner, 1987). However, as the evidence mounted, the Mormons fell back to a hermeneutical solution. The official current explanation, found in *Encyclopedia of Mormonism* (Ludlow, 1992), is that Smith's translation was never intended to be taken in a 'literal' sense; rather, it was a spiritual translation of the encrypted meaning within the papyri... There is a whole section about the *Book of Abraham* in the *Encyclopedia of Mormonism* covering a number of pages, but nowhere in that section does it mention that Joseph claimed that his translation of the papyri was literal, or that this had subsequently been proven false. Instead, the focus shifted to an esoteric red herring. The section ends by summarizing that "the numerous similarities that the *Book of Abraham* and the associated LDS doctrines share with both ancient Egyptian religious texts and recently discovered psuedepigraphical writings may confirm further the authenticity of the Joseph Smith's translation known as the Book of Abraham" (p.138). As Festinger would say, it is a rationalization that allows the Mormons to alleviate their dissonance about this situation while keeping their core beliefs (2001, 63–67)

More fundamentally, George Smith argues, "... by claiming that the 'truths' of faith do not conflict with the truths of reason, the Christian [or Mormon] begs the question at issue. Granted, if faith can arrive at knowledge, it cannot conflict with reason — but the crucial question is: *Can faith arrive at knowledge in the first place?* Is faith a valid epistemological procedure? Unless the Christian [or Mormon authority, believer, or apologist] can demonstrate *that* and/or explain *how* faith is capable [of justifying what is otherwise reasonably considered unjustifiable and irrational, or] of rationally distinguishing truth from falsity, he cannot uphold the compatibility of reason and faith" (120).

An Apologetic Defense of Mormon 'Faith-based' Epistemology

Blake Ostler attempts to offer such an explanation by arguing that for the Mormon believer in tune with the Holy Spirit knowledge comes surely in virtue of the believer's faith-invoked "spiritual experiences." These are experiences that are, according to Ostler, "most basic" (self-authenticating) to the believer and which infuse "pure knowledge" (presumably knowledge from the Mormon god) into the "heart" of the recipient. They "are so powerful that they reorient everything in [the believers'] lives" and thereby "become the bases [interpretive framework or 'lens'] through which [believers] see [and presumably come to know the truths of the Gospel]" (2007, 2–4).

In answering his own question regarding what believers know after receiving such a spiritual experience, Ostler suggests that the believer knows — on the basis of how the recipient is *affected* by the experience — whether or not the experience is 'good' or from the Mormon god. Essentially, according to Ostler, if the experience makes the recipient "feel immense love and a desire to do better" then the recipient knows that he or she is "born again" (6).

Ostler further argues that although the recipient must interpret the spiritual experience to convert it to cognitive content, nevertheless the reductive naturalistic argument that the interpretation is therefore nothing but a *human* interpretation "proves too much." "[I]f the naturalistic argument were true," Ostler argues, "there would be no possibility of new experiences that break out of the framework of existing paradigms and worldviews or our prior interpretations.…Yet," he continues and concludes, "that is precisely what a conversion experience is.…Thus, it [the conversion or spiritual experience] must be in some sense logically and experientially *prior to* interpretive experience" (6,7; emphasis mine). This conclusion leads Ostler to further conclude that "there is more than interpretation that gives content to our experience, and the [spiritual conversion] experience of the burning in the heart and the inspiration as coming from God is, in fact, good reason to believe that it does in fact, come from God; because that's how we experience it" (7).

As a relevant aside to be explored in more depth below, Ostler and other Mormon apologists of like mind are certainly not alone in this argument. As anthropologist Stewart Guthrie states, "In the past two centuries, religious writers…such as Friedrich Schleiermacher, Rudolf Otto, and Mircea Eliade, have argued that what religions share is not beliefs or practices but an experience. These writers," Guthrie informs us, "say the experience in question is [ultimately] ineffable and autonomous. It can be neither refuted by, nor related to, nonreligious experiences. At the same time, they suggest the experience consists in apprehending something, indicated by terms such as the holy, the numinous, or the sacred. This something — [like Ostler's 'burning in the heart'] — is transcendent and irreducible. Religious experience [while believed in some cases to be reducible to language, as with spoken revelation] allegedly is [at its deepest, affective level] 'prereflective, transcend[s] the verbal, or [is] in some other way free [or independent] of the [limited (and limiting) cognitive] structures of thought and judgment which language represents" (1993, 9, some interpolations mine).

Before responding to Ostler's assumptions and conclusions — and those of the other prominent writers cited by Guthrie above — it seems important to note the qualifying insistence by Mormon authorities and apologists that, in Ostler's words, "Having spiritual experiences doesn't mean that one is omniscient or knows all truth or cannot be mistaken about gospel principles"; that "[r]evelation is continuing in the Church and it must be continuing for each individual believer" (2007, 10); that, in other words, even the most devout believers are *fallible* and knowledge gained through faith by revelation and spiritual confirmation is *not perfect* or necessarily correct or clear in every detail. Nevertheless, notwithstanding such professions of Mormon fallibilism, there are some things Mormon believers say they do *know for sure* on the basis of the testimonies of their Church leaders, the prophets, and their own personal, feeling-toned spiritual experiences. Specifically, these putatively certain truths include the following:

- 'God' *literally* lives (exists) and is the *literal* Heavenly Father of all people, the *literal* Creator of this world and worlds without end and the *literal* author of the Plan of Salvation known as the 'Gospel of God.' He *literally* "knows and loves each of his children" and *literally* "wants each of us to come to a knowledge of the truth" (Millet 2008, 74).

- Jesus is the Christ, the 'Son of God' who *literally* exists and is *literally* the Savior and Redeemer of all people through his infinite and eternal sacrificial atonement, death, and literal resurrection. On the basis of Christ's atoning sacrifice, all men may *literally* be saved through faith in Christ, repentance, baptism by immersion for the remission of sins, and the receipt of the gift of the Holy Ghost — bestowed through the laying on of hands by those in authority to administer the saving ordinances of the Gospel. Moreover, in virtue of Christ's *literal* resurrection from the dead, death is overcome and all men shall be *literally* resurrected from the dead.

- The Holy Ghost *literally* exists and is *literally* the third member of the Godhead and is *literally* the Testator of God and Christ.

- Joseph Smith was and is the chosen Prophet of the Restoration of the Church of Jesus Christ on the face of the earth. Through him the *Book of Mormon* was translated by the 'gift and power of God' and brought forth as the *literal* 'Word of God' and as a 'Second Witness of Jesus Christ.' Through him the Church of Jesus Christ and Holy Priesthood were also restored in their fulness to the earth to teach the Gospel of God to "every nation, kindred, tongue and people," to administer the saving ordinances of the Gospel with the needed authority, and to minister to the 'Latter-day Saints' — or members of the Mormon Church.

- The *Church of Jesus Christ of Latter-day Saints* is *literally* and *definitively* the *one and only* true Church of Jesus Christ on the face of the earth today and those who are ordained members of the Mormon Priesthood are the *only* ones authorized to *literally* speak for the Mormon god, teach his Gospel, and officiate in the ordinances of the Gospel on the earth.

- The current presiding President of the Church is *literally* the 'Prophet, Seer, and Revelator' and spokesman for the Mormon god on the earth. The members of the Quorum of Twelve Apostles are also *literally* Prophets, Seers, and Revelators and 'Special Witnesses' of the Lord Jesus Christ to all nations, kindreds, tongues, and people of the earth.

These putatively basic Mormon truths, and certain others related to man's exaltation or deification, are believed by Mormons — on the basis of strong, putatively spiritual feelings — to have been revealed by the Mormon god to his servants the Prophets, and are considered *a priori* to be *absolutely true*. They are regarded ('testified to') as being *known* and *accepted* as such on the basis of the feeling-based 'spiritual experiences' which Ostler refers to and treats above. Clearly, Mormons (*pace* Ostler), like all other theistic believers, hold that faith — experienced as a feeling-based or spiritual sense of truth — is a legitimate source of *certain* knowledge.[125] Moreover, it is the *only* legitimate source of metaphysical *religious* knowledge.

In response to Ostler I want to focus on what I consider to be his two key points of emphasis. First, I shall consider Ostler's insistence that personal faith-induced spiritual experiences (including revelation and confirmation) in relationship with the Mormon god are, ultimately, the foundation of Mormon epistemology (way of knowing). Secondly, I want to focus on Ostler's defense above against what he considers to be "the strongest arguments" against the belief that such "spiritual experience" actually comes from his god— arguments which he refers to collectively as "The Argument from Interpretive Framework Inherent in all Human Experience" (2007, 6). These two points are necessarily interrelated, as we shall discover below.

In addressing Ostler's first point, I refer the reader to the beginning of this chapter, which addressed the question of having relational faith (trust and confidence) in the Mormon god and Christ, and the preceding chapter which analyzed the related, and also relational concept of revelation as a way of communicating with and *knowing* a god and knowing truth *about* him or the ways, mind, and will *of* a god. In these chapters the concepts of revelation and faith were not only found to be incoherent on the basis of their necessary, *a priori* dependence on the likewise incoherent concept of the Mormon god, but were also found to be incoherent and factually unintelligible in their own right for a variety of reasons.

These conclusions, I submit, are *primary* in challenging the Mormon (and Christian or other theistic) belief that knowledge of the putatively basic truths of religion can be gained in virtue of religious experience through or by revelation of *any* kind or in *any* form or, as stated differently, on the basis of faith.[126] Claims to the contrary are simply unwarranted.

---

125 It is appropriate and necessary here to refer the reader back to the previous chapter concerning the questions 'How do we know what is real?' and 'How do we know what we know?' as well as the problem of 'certain' knowledge from a naturalistic perspective. Additionally it is appropriate and necessary as well to refer back to that same chapter concerning the problem of how to specifically and intelligibly differentiate (without begging the question) *natural human feelings* from putative *sui generis spiritual feelings* induced by the Mormon or any other god or 'Spirit' as an ultimate arbiter of truth. Lastly, it is important to repeat what was noted earlier regarding the incoherence of accepting, as Ostler and other Mormon leaders and apologists no doubt do, *both* (and simultaneously) the *basic* (or self-evident) fact of human fallibilism *and* faith-as-certainty in relation to certain religious statements regarded as absolute truth. As was previously noted, the fact of human fallibilism essentially and necessarily cuts both ways in the human pursuit of truth and creates a space for *uncertainty* and *doubt* which can only be attended to *provisionally* and to the extent of beyond a reasonable doubt. This conclusion requires — indeed demands, by definition and necessarily — the exercise and ultimate authority of *reason* and the possibility of *doubt*. This, however, makes theistic faith-as-certainty impossible in its own right and incoherent in relation to the acceptance of fallibilism as a fact of human existence.

126 Regarding Ostler's (and other Mormons') solipsistic way of knowing and accepting putative knowledge obtained through spiritual experience and revelation as most basic, see, again, Nielsen's treatment of the parity argument in Chapter 2 and Everitt's treatment of Reformed Epistemology (2004, 17–30). Also, for a

Solely for the sake of argument, let us overlook the conclusions reached so far on the basis of our conceptual analysis and grant that many believers do in fact have the affective experiences which they believe attest to the truth of their faith and the existence of their god. Is there any good reason for an objective outsider working from the presumption of skepticism to suppose that the believer's faith-based, spiritual experience is, as Ostler suggests, *prior to* the 'interpretive experience' (presumably the interpretation of such experience)? Must we suppose that the interpretation of such experiences is 'transcendent and irreducible,' and necessarily 'free' or independent of explanation and the limited and limiting natural structures of cognitive thought and judgment? Further, is there any good reason to believe such interpretation is *actually* true or can even be *known* by the believer or anyone to be true?

Concerning the question of supposing the believer's faith-based interpretation of affective religious experience to be "transcendent," "irreducible" and "free of structures of [natural] thought and judgment which language represents" (9), we return now, as promised, to a brief assessment of such claims. Apropos to the writings of Mormon and other religious writers in this regard, including Ostler, I will turn again to Guthrie (1993), who rightly observes and argues, as I have also done in this work, that the thinking of such writers, "Besides being vague…are internally inconsistent." These writers "say religious experience is unconditioned, primitive, [pure], immediate, and prior to [interpretive] beliefs and concepts. At the same time, they say it is the experience of particular feelings, emotions, and sensation — such as unity, infinity, dependence, love, and awe. But such feelings and emotions do not exist in a vacuum: they implicitly are directed toward or are about something, whose existence they assume. Assuming that existence, they thus are grounded in beliefs" (9). Continuing, Guthrie adds:

> Emotions and other experiences also depend upon interpretations of sensations such as heat, cold, [burning], and nausea, and of such phenomena as sweating, shivering, [tingling], smiling. Emotions are not primitive, but are at least midlevel models, situated above perceptions of bodily states and below broad interpretations of, for example, human relationships. As such, they are based on an assumed order. In Wayne Proudfoot's example, a woodsman who mistakes a log for a bear has an experience of being frightened by a bear. When his companion points out that it is only a log, he is reassured. His fear, like other emotions, occurs not in isolation but as the product of a context and of an interpretation. When the interpretation changes, the experience changes. Since experience depends on interpretation, it cannot be prior to beliefs and concepts, but is generated partly from them. Schleiermacher [and others, including Ostler] then cannot claim simultaneously that religious emotions are simple, immediate, or unconditioned

---

thoughtful and competent treatment of the topic of "spiritual experiences," see Proudfoot (1987), as well as Eller quoted and referenced in note 124. Finally, for an interesting and informative treatment of the subject of 'The Self-Authenticating Witness of the Holy Spirit' and the problems that belief in such a solipsistic way of knowing poses to all theistic faiths (including the Mormon faith), see Loftus 2008, 213–219. What is interesting to me in this regard is that 'Holy Spirit Epistemology,' as it is known in the Evangelical Christian faith, has its identical counterpart in Mormon faith-based epistemology. Yet both faiths hold that while the other faith can receive enlightenment and, on occasion, have certain spiritual experiences from the Holy Spirit (or 'Light of Christ' in the Mormon faith), they nonetheless cannot come to a *true* (and therefore *saving*) knowledge of their god and Christ while in the *wrong* faith. This no doubt pertains to other faiths as well. It seems the 'self-authenticating witness of the Holy Spirit' is not quite as 'properly basic' as believers and apologists would have us believe.

by belief and that they constitute an experience. (9)

Moreover, as Columbia University religion professor Wayne Proudfoot himself writes in his important, careful, and groundbreaking book *Religious Experience* (1985), the arguments for the *a priori*, and therefore independent, autonomous, and irreducible nature of spiritual experience are "…a protective strategy built upon an erroneous separation of the religious life from ordinary belief and inquiry. Each of these [arguments]," Proudfoot argues, "results in an artificial block to inquiry which serves an apologetic purpose, [even if] grounded in a genuine insight….The insight that the experience must be identified from the subject's point of view is," however, "combined with the erroneous claim that the point of view is innocent of explanatory commitments. It is then employed in the protective strategy built on the claim that the proper description of the experience excludes all [naturalistic] explanations of the experience" (233–4).

Unfortunately for believers, the argument for the validity or actual truth of their interpretation (or for knowing their *interpretation* is true) cannot be based on an appeal to scripture or Church authority or other putative spiritual experiences without invalidating their argument by begging the question. Nor, for obvious reasons, would it seem sufficient for the believer to appeal to mere possibility. Ostler acknowledges the dilemma for the Mormon believer and asks: "So is it the case that all we [as Mormon believers] are really doing when we [say we] have a spiritual experience is *interpreting* it as coming from God, and it's simply up for grabs as to whether the interpretation is true or not?" (7, emphasis mine). He then challenges the implied conclusion in his question by essentially arguing, if I understand him correctly, that if our interpretations of our experiences were limited to our historical frame of reference we could not, in principle, interpret our experiences in new or different ways. In other words, because, as Ostler assumes, our interpretive frameworks are closed, our interpretations are necessarily self-sealing and therefore limited. But since Mormon believers and investigators do, in fact, interpret their experiences as conversion (or revelatory) experiences, then they must be so and must also be from a god. This is because they logically could not experience it otherwise, since such an interpretive framework allegedly did not exist in them (and could not have been learned or acquired) *before* they had the experience. Therefore, they could not possibly have *interpreted* the experience the way they did — as being from a god.

Ostler's erroneous argument, like those of Oaks and others earlier, unfortunately assumes too much and proves nothing. Millet, for example, in concert with Oaks earlier and Ostler above regarding the need for faith as a way of knowing religious truth, asserts that unlike faithful Mormon believers, nonbelievers and questioning believers or disbelievers doubt the truth of the Mormon faith "because they are not able to accept divine intervention, prophesy, or miracles. That is to say," Millet adds, "they have limited their epistemology (their way of knowing) to the natural world — what can be experienced through the five senses or what can be observed, studied empirically, or replicated. Their map [Ostler's 'lens' or 'interpretive framework'] is limited. To be straightforward," he concludes, "they are seeking directions from a deficient map. Their worldview is limited" (2008, 29).

But Millet assumes, as do Oaks, Ostler, and other Mormon religious authorities and apologists, that the spiritual, faith-based map (lens, or interpretive framework) is an objective, factual reality which is not derived naturally or which cannot be naturalistically explained, or evaluated at all. I suggest, in agreement with Guthrie and Proudfoot above, that such an assumption is wrong, and that just the opposite is the case. The implicit claim that believers (or all people) are either endowed (as putative spirits) with a spiritual frame of reference (or interpretive framework), or receive it with the receipt of the 'gift of faith' or a 'spiritual, conversion experience' from the Holy Spirit is either false, in virtue of error-theory, or it is incoherent on the basis of the previous analyses performed on other like metaphysical concepts and truth claims.

Moreover, Millet's insistence on the need for faith as essentially the only way for knowing religious truth and his imposed limitations on naturalistic ways of knowing miss the crucial point of this *philosophical analysis*.[127] Like Oaks' arguments earlier and also Ostler's above, these are simply *red herrings* which rely on question-begging language and evasive arguments from isolation and ignorance.

Significantly, Ostler's explanation for the Mormon (and theistic) way of knowing through faith (when applied to religious or spiritual truth) is itself not only conceptually problematical and naturalistically explainable (as argued above and in Chapter 5) but is superfluous and unwarranted. This is so because it does not take into account the vast body of relevant research and theorizing in relevant fields that study the human mind.

In this final regard, Ostler does not explicitly consider the explanatory value of *developmental psychology* as it pertains to the effect of parent-child dynamics on religious faith-formation (Faber 2002, 2004, 2010). Nor does he consider the *neuroscientific* research and analysis of *infantile amnesia* as it applies to the unconscious development of interpretive and projective relational schemas that recapitulate the primal parent-child matrix (Faber 2010, Restak 1986; Wilson 2002; Le Doux 2002; Johnston 2001; Schachtel 1982). Further, he does not consider the vast amount of work in neuroscience and cognitive science in relation to the *acquisition and nature of human knowledge* and *belief formation* (Fine 2000; Linden 2008; Ramachandran 1998; Burton 2008; Boyer 2001; Shermer 2000, 2002; Atran 2002), *linguistic analysis of self-transformative experience* as it relates to religious conversion narratives (Stromberg 1993), or *neo-dissociation theory* as it relates to the researched phenomena of hypnosis and psychopathology and pertains to the related phenomena of religious belief and reality formation and distortion

---

127 See also, as part of an analysis of the larger problem of religious knowledge, Blackstone's treatment of the 'appeal to religious experience' and the related epistemological argument from subjectivity which similarly holds that "faith precedes reason" as a "new way of seeing things (or knowing)" because "unless you believe you will not understand" (1963, 140–157). According to Blackstone, who echoes Nielsen and other analytical and linguistic philosophers in this regard: "The philosopher recognizes that the question of the meaning or cognitive [factual] significance of a statement [*e.g.* 'God exists'] is logically prior to the question of either the truth or falsity or the knowledge-status of that statement. Until one is reasonably clear about what is being claimed [when referring, for example, to the concept of the Mormon (or any) god in its fulness], one cannot possibly know what data are *relevant* to the confirmation or disconfirmation of the claim or if the data *are* confirming or disconfirming." Accordingly, Blackstone continues, "[t]he appeal to faith completely misses one very important point of the philosopher's question. The philosopher is really asking what he is supposed to have faith in — what is the [actual] meaning of the belief he is supposed to accept. To be sure…faith is not merely the acceptance of a group of propositions….But faith certainly does involve the acceptance of a proposition or set of propositions, even if it involves other things. The philosopher's point, a point neglected by the [believer or theistic apologist], is that you cannot justifiably ask or suggest that someone accept or believe a proposition or group of propositions unless it is made reasonably clear what [specifically] the proposition, or set of propositions, literally means. If the religious claim has no clear meaning, can we even correctly speak of it as a proposition which can be accepted?" (150–51).

(Schumaker 1995; Faber 2010). The work in these fields provide a more parsimonious and reasonable, if not compelling, alternative to Ostler's very limited and question-begging view of knowing religious truths from spiritual experience, or through the interpretive lens which accompanies such *sui generis*, or 'God-given,' experience.

To paraphrase Faber's work[128] in particular, the collective body of research in the fields of developmental psychology and infantile amnesia shows, *pace* Ostler, that the emotions, feelings and affects associated with religious spiritual experience, as well as related religious belief formation, are naturally (biologically) derivative of self-transforming and reality forming mechanisms of the 'mind-brain' which operate beneath the surface of awareness. These natural biological and psychological mechanisms are associated with forgotten non-verbal, image-based memories of primal parent-child relational experiences. They are memories that are formed in infancy and early childhood and stored in the non-verbal, image-based memory system of the brain where they are forgotten but never lost.

Although such primal memories are inaccessible to willful, conscious recall, they are *affectively* recalled by the unconscious mechanism of *association* and the consequent *transference* of the *internalized parent* to the familiar (culturally transmitted) concept of the Parent-God (*i.e.* God, the Father and Jesus, the Christ). Such a self-transforming (or converting) *transference* of internalized parent images and relations to the Parent-God is invoked by the timely expression, hearing and practice of familiar religious language (Stromberg 1993), music, and ritual. It produces the religious conversion experience and the sense of recalling and knowing that accompanies it. The transference not only evokes the sublime, ecstatic feelings and emotions of fusion (or oneness), attachment, acceptance, and security with the internalized all-loving, all-knowing and all-loving parent or care-giver, but also activates, in turn, the mechanism of *dissociation* which constructs an alternate, illusory (and hallucinatory) reality (Schumaker 1995) and accompanying meta-belief in the *actual* reality of the created illusion. In this case, it is the Parent-God.

This would suggest that *all* feeling-toned and hallucinatory religious and conversion experiences in *all* theistic faiths or religions are anchored or rooted at bottom in the primal *parent-child* matrix (what Faber calls "the basic biological situation"). The child's unconscious, non-verbal, image-based memory of the loving, nurturing, protective, and life-sustaining parent-child experiences in the first few years of life — neurologically imprinted on its brain *for* life — is the *primary* 'interpretive framework' (to use Ostler's term) which functions in tandem with the culturally transmitted religious worldview of the child to form a familiar religious frame of reference (or lens) through which all so-called religious experiences are interpreted and regarded as basic.

Given the above, there is no need or basis to assert or argue, as Ostler does, that there is no historical interpretive framework for spiritual conversion or revelatory experiences and that therefore both the religious interpretive framework and the experiences must be from God.[129] On the contrary, our best-justified knowledge to date on the subject of

---

128 I am indebted to the pioneering work of M.D. Faber (2002, 2004, 2010) which I have referred to previously and throughout this book and which I think fairly, accurately, and effectively integrates a vast amount of primary and secondary research in various disciplines to provide a plausible, synthesized, and elegant naturalistic explanation for understanding religious belief and experience in the context of the psychodynamic model of human development.

129 Such an apologetic assertion or argument cannot be made without *a priori* begging the primary and ul-

such experience provides — as claimed at the end of the previous chapter — a sensible, coherent, and parsimonious, naturalistic explanation without the need to postulate, assert, and presuppose the existence of supernatural gods. There is, *pace* Ostler, no explanatory gap here that requires the concept (or existence) of 'God.' There is no need to consider faith as a legitimate source of knowledge of a god, or as a way of knowing the truth about that god. As Faber puts it: "From the psychological perspective…we may reword the old scriptural promise "all who seek shall find" as follows: all who seek shall smoothly transfer their early, unconscious attachments and longings to the Parent-God of the mysterious, supernatural realm" (2004, 113). And once again, for emphasis:

> People *'get religion' not through their "religious experience" as such [or any putatively actual 'relationship with God,' as they believe] but through their early internalized experience with the biological parent, the experience upon which religion operates to construct its mythic, ritualistic edifice.* When we sense the Creator within us [through affect, as well as *apparently* through hallucination outside us in 'vision' or 'visitation'] and acknowledge with gratitude His delicious love and care, we don't know whence such "experience" derives because we cannot *find* explicitly the foundational strata of our lives. *We attribute to the outside what is happening on the inside, always, and without exception.* (46, emphasis mine)

This internalization and repeated invocation of the basic biological situation (through prayer, music, language and ritual) amply accounts for – naturalistically and without the need for theological explanation or speculation – the "feelings" or affects associated with putative "spiritual experience," including, again, the believed "salvational" experience of religious conversion (or "spiritual re-birth"). "To view the matter from the 'hard' neuropsychological perspective," Faber writes in his most recent work, "we might say that the [believer's] mind-brain, primed and grooved by [the] pre-subjective interactions [of his infancy], maps his early experience onto the religious narrative he encounters. … [Indeed] Christian [and Mormon] doctrine would be empty of [familiar] meaning were it not grounded in the basic biological situation of dependency, succor, and love [so essential to the success of 'religion's infantilizing process']" (2010, 28, 30).

All this said, George Smith is I think correct in asserting, as noted above, that, as the primary epistemological underpinning of Christianity (and Mormonism), faith (*pace* Oaks, Ostler, Millet *et al*) cannot deliver legitimate knowledge. Faith is believed to deliver knowledge about the Christian or Mormon god and his plan *by revelation* from him. But this, again, has already been shown to be an irrational belief given its presuppositional and unwarranted reliance on the existence of a god, and given the unintelligibility, incoherence, and factual meaninglessness of the Mormon concept of 'God' and of revelation *from* 'God' *about* 'God' established in the preceding chapters. It is also problematical for other reasons as well, including the fact that putative religious knowledge obtained by faith through revelation is often and, at times, crucially: (1) different among different people, faiths, and cultures; (2) contradictory with other 'revealed' religious knowledge within the same or other faiths; (3) not justifiable in its own right, or in relation to justified knowledge about the world and universe and how they work; and (4) without sense, coherence, and factual

---

timate question at issue, *i.e.* a god's actual (not merely perceived or imagined) existence or employing false analogy or invalid analogical predication.

significance or meaning when referring to metaphysical religious realities.

Without revelation as the Ultimate Source of knowledge of sacred, spiritual truth, the proposition that we can reasonably or rationally know anything through faith is impossible. By its very nature, faith does not (cannot) rely on or require rational justification. Therefore, whatever predictive truth or valid idea it might produce (by putative revelation or religious experience) is merely coincidental and cannot meet the widely accepted and established minimum requirement of *knowledge*. To qualify as knowledge, by generally accepted and implicitly or explicitly practiced epistemic standards, a belief which is *not* regarded as self-evident or as widely and critically accepted common knowledge (among believers *and* nonbelievers), must be *justified* and *true*. Unjustified declarative assertions or predictions might happen to be *coincidentally* true on the basis of non-foundational intuition or just a lucky guess, or even felt to be true on the basis of experience and putatively revealed interpretation. But such 'truth' is not considered knowledge. This is because it was not justified, as Nielsen convincingly argues, by the achievement of wide reflective equilibrium among believers, nonbelievers, and disbelievers.[130]

Nor can the believer's experience of 'knowing' be reasonably regarded as anything other than a *re-knowing* of retrieved, primal memories of the parent-child matrix through the mechanisms of transference and reality-forming and distorting dissociation. Indeed it seems, as Nielsen suggests, people need faith when they don't have knowledge and can't get it. Then, as Adler suggests, they deceive themselves, through the employment of evasive 'strategies of possibility,' to think that their belief in the literal existence of the believed subject or object of such faith *is* knowledge.

The Impossibility of Faith as a Necessary and Sufficient Requirement for Salvation

Beyond the incoherence of the notion that faith in a god is, through revelation and religious experience, a legitimate source of religious truth and knowledge there is the incoherent notion of faith in a god as a requirement of salvation. Why would the Mormon god — who allegedly revealed to the Mormon Prophet, Joseph Smith, that His (the Mormon god's) "Work and Glory" is "to bring to pass the immortality and eternal life of man," and who further allegedly revealed in the bible that "life eternal" is to "*know*" the "only true God, and Jesus Christ" — require *faith* in his (and Christ's) putative existence, when such faith is neither necessary nor sufficient to produce such knowledge? Faith is neither necessary for, nor capable of, acquiring either an intelligible or provisional (let alone certain) knowledge of a god or salvation, making its requirement for salvation, like the ideas of 'God' and 'revelation,' as nonsensical as it is impossible. Still, we can understand something humanly (naturalistically) strategic about such a nonsensical requirement by understanding something about what Dennett refers to as "belief in belief." Following are a few select, important, and illuminating, remarks on the subject, offered in Dennett's words:

The fundamental incomprehensibility of God is insisted upon as a central tenet of faith,

---

130 Such a state of broad consensus would necessarily involve robust interdisciplinary and inter-cultural dialogue, followed by rigorous and critical conceptual analysis and, where appropriate or indicated, *sound* reasoning applied to *valid* evidence, *i.e.* falsifiable, comprehensive, sufficient, and replicable evidence produced and replicated under controlled conditions, and objectively, honestly, and logically interpreted (see Eller 2004, 68–80).

and the [doctrinal] propositions in question are themselves declared to be systematically elusive to everybody. Although we can go along with the experts when they advise us which sentences to say we believe, they also insist that *they themselves* cannot use their expertise to prove – even to one another — that they know what they are talking about. These matters are mysterious to *everybody*, experts and laypeople alike [and are best left to God]. Why does anybody go along with this? The answer is obvious: *belief in belief.*

Many people believe in God. Many people believe in *belief in God.* What's the difference? People who believe in God are sure that God exists, and they are glad, because they hold God to be the most wonderful of all things. People who moreover believe in *belief in God* are sure that belief in God exists (and who would doubt that?), and they think that this is a good state of affairs, something to be strongly encouraged and fostered wherever possible: If only *belief in* [the right] *God* [*e.g.* the Mormon god] were more widespread! One *ought* to believe in God. One ought to *strive* to believe in God. One should be uneasy, apologetic, unfulfilled, one should even feel guilty, if one finds that one just doesn't believe in God.

People who believe in belief in God try to get others to believe in [their] God and, whenever they find their own belief in God flagging, do whatever they can to restore it. (2006, 220–21)

Succinctly put, to *believe in 'belief* in God' is to believe that 'belief in God' is a really good thing and those who *believe in 'belief* in God' behave accordingly by regularly going through the motions of religious observance. This they do by regularly or periodically attending Church meetings or engaging in Temple worship, by paying their tithes and offerings, by doing church work as assigned (or 'called'), and by trying to live a properly religious or moral life. If people *actually believed in a god*, Dennett suggests, instead of merely believing in 'belief in God' they would live their religion with total commitment and abandon, putting their lives on the line to do whatsoever their god commanded them to do — as with Abraham of old. They would, in Mormon theological terms, *completely* (or whole-heartedly and with righteous intent) honor and fulfill their covenants of *sacrifice*, *consecration*, and *obedience* with their god. They would be continuously hungering and thirsting after righteousness and 'Truth.' Such people who truly 'believe in God' tend to be extreme in their behavior and compulsive in their religious observances. They tend, according to Dennett, to do "all kinds of lunatic things." But those people who merely 'believe in belief in God' don't put their lives on the line for a god. They really don't *believe in God* in a literal sense, as Dennett sees it. They believe in 'God' as they believe in Santa Clause — superstitiously and out of habit and tradition.[131]

---

131 As a relevant aside, I have often wondered in this regard, what would happen to the faith and status of those so-called active and faithful members of the Mormon Church today — who, to use Dennett's distinction, merely *believe in belief in God* and are not, in the Kierkegaardian sense, true Knights of Faith as was the biblical Abraham — if they were asked or commanded by the President of their Church to live their lives to the full extent of the laws they once practiced or accepted as Truth as a people and covenanted to obey in their temples. This would essentially require these Church members — especially those who have been through the Mormon temple and received the higher ordinances and promises of the gospel under solemn and binding covenants — in virtue of revelation from the Mormon god to the Mormon Prophet to:
(1) accept as Truth that *only* those marriages performed in Mormon temples are recognized by that god as being lawful and binding in heaven and that *all* other marriages which are not sealed or solemnized in a Mormon temple are considered by him to be invalid and unlawful, making those married members of the Mormon Church who have not been married in the temple because of unworthiness (and those married non-members who have either rejected the Mormon faith or have not sought to accept it, knowing of its existence) adulterers in the sight of God;

That such religious believers tend to engage in some form of missionary work (or in sharing the Gospel with others) is, as implied by Dennett above, a further indicator of *belief in belief* in 'God.' And how shall those who *believe in belief* in a god get others to believe in their god or strengthen or restore their own flagging belief in God? By understanding, according to Dennett, that "[what] is commonly referred to as 'religious belief' or 'religious conviction' might less misleadingly be called *religious professing*." Furthermore, "Unlike academic professors, religious professors [not just priesthood authorities and missionaries, but all the faithful] may not either understand or believe what they are professing [as a literal truth]. They are just *professing*, because that is the best they can do, and they are required to profess (228)."

Dennett continues:

> Though lip service is thus required, it is not enough: you must *firmly believe* what you are obliged to say. How is it possible to obey this injunction? Professing is voluntary, but belief is not. Belief …requires understanding, which is hard to come by, even by experts in these matters. You just can't make yourself believe something by trying, so what are you to do? Cardinal Ratzinger's (later elected Pope Benedict XVI) Declaration offers some help on this score: "Faith is the acceptance in grace of revealed truth, which 'makes it possible to penetrate the mystery in a way that allows us to understand it coherently' [quoting John Paul II's Encyclical Letter *Fides et ratio*, p. 13]." So you should believe *this*. And if you can, believing this should help you believe you do understand the mystery (even if it seems to you that you don't), and hence do firmly believe whatever it is you profess to believe. But how do you believe *this*? It takes faith. (228–29)

In a Mormon context, *saying* or *professing* it — or, to use the Mormon expression, *testifying* of the Mormon god and the doctrines and 'mysteries of Godliness' — requires the believer to have faith that he actually understands that which is otherwise incoherent and therefore, unintelligible. In this way, saying or professing something to be true with conviction and sincerity somehow makes it so by *believing in the belief* that through faith as "the acceptance in grace of revealed truth" we are somehow enabled to understand what we really *cannot* understand (because of its conceptual incoherence) and "to understand it coherently." Such is the tacit, psychological sleight of hand at play in *believing in belief*.

---

(2) practice the principle of simultaneous plural marriage, with an understanding that *only* those who entered into such a practice could be exalted as gods in the next life;

(3) sustain the practice of 'blood atonement' in the Church wherein certain sins of members of the Church (such as apostasy, murder, and the denial of the Holy Ghost) would be 'atoned' for by the literal shedding of their blood unto death;

(4) sustain the denial (and revocation) of the 'higher blessings' of the Mormon priesthood to all Black males;

(5) live the *fulness* of the 'law of consecration' in the 'United Order' and to thereby deed over to the Church *all* their property and income (not just a paltry 10% tithe of gross income) and dedicate *all* their time and talent (not just two years for a mission and a few hours a week for a church assignment) to the 'building up of the Kingdom of God on Earth and the establishment of Zion'; and

(6) accept as Truth, and as a condition of salvation, that Adam is their god and heavenly Father and the literal father of Jesus Christ.

What would happen to these mere *believers in belief* in their god? No one knows, of course, but my guess would be that Church activity and membership would greatly diminish in numbers, perhaps to the extent of virtual extinction.

Dennett further reflects on this phenomenon by quoting Rappaport as saying: "If postulates are to be unquestionable, it is important that they be incomprehensible." And, quoting Dennett, "Not just counterintuitive, in Boyer's technical sense of contradicting only one or two of the default assumptions of a basic category, but downright unintelligible. Prosaic [or commonplace] assertions," concludes Dennett, "have no bite, and moreover they are too readily checked for accuracy. For a truly awesome and mind-teasing proposition, there is nothing that beats [an unintelligible] paradox eagerly avowed" (229).

With the help of the above and other explanatory insights, we can reasonably conclude, on the basis of our conceptual analyses in previous chapters of the theological concepts of the Mormon 'God,' the Mormon 'Plan of Salvation,' the Mormon concept of 'revelation,' and now, in this chapter, the Mormon concept of 'faith in God,' that such faith in a god is logically and actually non-existent *as understood* by Mormon believers and Christians alike, making the *requirement* of faith in a god incoherent and therefore absurd.

Even so, with all of the above analytical and naturalistic concerns and perspectives duly considered the above claimed incoherence of the requirement of faith merits further emphasis in order more fully to disqualify such 'faith in God' as a legitimate refuge for questioning believers struggling with doubts. The thrust of this additional emphasis goes in a different direction from what was emphasized earlier. Rather than concluding, as above, that the requirement of faith in the Mormon god is incoherent and therefore irrational, or that the phenomenon of 'faith in God and Christ' is coherently and justifiably explained naturalistically from a depth-neuropsychological perspective without the need for revelation, we will now examine from a reversed perspective the possibility of the actual existence of the Mormon god. We shall look at that god as conceptualized in Mormon theology *on the basis of* such a god's claimed requirement of faith and its (faith's) very existence, given the argued for *non-necessity* and *insufficiency* of 'faith in God' *per se*. To conduct this analysis we will necessarily grant, *solely* for the sake of argument, that the concepts of the Mormon god and revelation are intelligible, coherent, and factually significant.

The conclusion of our analysis, made on the basis of both inductive and deductive reasoning in the form of a formal, logical argument, is that because 'faith in God' exists and is — given the putative existence and nature of 'God' and the frailty of man — both logically unnecessary and actually (empirically) insufficient to ensure salvation (whatever that means, if anything), then the *unqualified requirement* of 'faith in God by God' as the 'first (and foundational) principle' of the Mormon 'Gospel of God' is necessarily incoherent. This conclusion would, in turn, necessarily make the concept of the Mormon god — and therefore his putative existence as doctrinally described in Mormon theology — impossible (because self-contradictory) and the belief in such a god therefore irrational.

In making this argument, it is important to acknowledge up-front that I do not consider it (or any argument) to be conclusive or decisive as a proof of the non-existence of the Mormon god. Clearly it is possible and perhaps even likely that the theological premises of this argument — regarded and presented as at least apparently basic or self-evident to the Mormon faith — will be challenged at some level.[132] Nevertheless, I readily acknowledge

---

132 From my perspective, I admittedly cannot see how or where the premises of this argument can be substantively challenged, given that they are all so well established and generally accepted as truth by well-informed Mormon insiders and therefore cannot be significantly challenged without also significantly altering the Mormon concept of 'God' to the point where such an altered god would arguably, from a Mormon

again, as I did in the *Foundational Preface* of this book, the imposed limitations of such formal arguments in producing conclusive proofs.

For me, the primary and most compelling argument for the non-existence of the Mormon god comes from the rigorous and critical conceptual analysis of the very concept of 'God' itself as presented in Chapter 3 and in all theistic theologies and related God-talk. Still, I do consider this argument essential as part of a larger, cumulative and, in my view, compelling atheological argument. It further demonstrates the logical incoherence of the concept of the Mormon god and therefore strengthens the analytical conclusion that, conceptually, the Mormon god might reasonably be considered a factual non-reality, making therefore all of Mormon theology necessarily incoherent — including the need for faith.

Consequently, given the fact of fallibilism in our conceptual analysis of Mormon theology, what we're after here is the reasoned evaluation of *first-order* testamentary and *second-order* doctrinal truth claims to determine whether or not such putative truth claims might reasonably be considered rational beliefs that are justified and true. In this context, with the above acknowledgements as qualification, we can rightly proceed with my formal argument *for* the non-existence of the Mormon god as doctrinally described *from, or on the basis of,* such a god's requirement of 'faith in God and Jesus Christ' for salvation:

1. 'Faith in' (or knowledge of, love for and trust in) 'God and Christ,' according to Mormon theology (MT), is *required, necessary,* and *sufficient, as a principle of action and power,* for satisfying the requirements of salvation and exaltation;

2. 'Faith in God and Christ,' according to MT, is accessible to all who are mentally competent as a 'gift'' from God,' through his grace as it is given to those who receive his word and therefore believe in him and in his Son — and who are sufficiently *humble* (teachable) and *meek* (open-minded and submissive to the truth);

3. The existence of 'faith in God and Christ' is, according to MT, logically and actually contingent upon the Mormon god in truth possessing certain attributes and personal qualities. Because the 'correct ideas of the character of God,' as set forth in MT, are, according to Joseph Smith, "*necessary* in order to exercise faith in Him," such 'faith in God' would not be possible if such putative metaphysical attributes and qualities were, as claimed existents, false or incoherent. (See Chapter 1 of this book and Smith (2005));

4. The superordinate *purpose* and ultimate *desire,* or 'Work and Glory,' of the Mormon god is the salvation of *all* his children; that *all* his spirit children might "fill the [full] measure of their creation and have joy therein" by coming to *know* him, and Jesus Christ whom he has sent, so that they might *all* return to his presence in celestial glory and enjoy the fruits of eternal life (*i.e.* live the kind of life that their god lives). Such a desire can only be fulfilled if *all* men *believe in the Mormon god* and will *come unto Christ* and repent of their sins, be baptized by water and spirit and receive the Gift of the Holy Ghost by the laying on of hands by those in authority and then

---

perspective, no longer remain an object worthy of worship and capable of inducing total, self-sacrificial faith.

endure faithfully in righteousness and truth (through obedience to all the command-ments) to the end of their mortal lives;

5. The Mormon god is, in fact, everything he is doctrinally described and required to be in order to be worthy of the faith and worship of men and to assure for all men their salvation. Specifically, the Mormon god *necessarily*:
    a. *knows* all things past, present and future, including, with sufficient complete-ness, the thoughts, desires, motives, intentions, and dispositions of all people (the more common and officially accepted belief);
    b. *loves* all people, as his literal 'spirit children,' with a pure and perfect love and wants as his *greatest desire* all people, all his children, to come to Christ and be saved;
    c. *knows* full well that all people who are not mentally disabled or handicapped are capable, as his 'spirit children,' of being saved when they reach the 'age of accountability'[133];
    d. has the *power* to: **(1)** 'Open the eyes of understanding' of each and all of his 'children' on Earth by somehow boosting their natural intelligence through the 'Light of Truth (Christ)' and 'lifting the veil of forgetfulness;' **(2)** reveal his existence to all people, privately and collectively, sufficient to indisputably inform all people, believers, and disbelievers, of his actual existence; **(3)** penetrate psychological resistance to the knowledge of his existence putatively caused by 'pride' or 'sin' or 'hard-heartedness'; **(4)** reveal his mind, will and purposes with perfect clarity and — given *d.(1)* above — perfect understanding, *i.e.* without vagueness, ambiguity, confusion, or uncertainty, to all people, individually and collectively; **(5)** answer — through 'revelation' — all the reasonable, significant, faith-threatening questions and concerns of all believers and disbelievers sufficient to eradicate all *real* doubt and nonbelief; **(6)** reveal perfectly all people to themselves, *i.e.* their needs, strengths, weaknesses, destiny, true desires, motives, intentions, and spiritual or psychological condition; **(7)** effectually call even the 'hardest-hearted' (prideful) sinners to repentance and bestow upon all who have faith in Christ and have repented and been baptized by those in authority the Gift and power of the Holy Ghost, as well as those gifts of the Spirit they need to fully develop and realize their salvation and eternal reward; **(8)** cause in each person a 'mighty change of heart' such that they will have "no more disposition to do evil, but to do good continually"; **(9)** guide and direct each person individually, as needed, through personal revelation to avoid error and unbelief and achieve, obtain and follow after righteousness and truth, and bring all people to a unity of understanding regarding his doctrines, mind, and will; and **(10)** deliver each and all of his children from ignorance, sin, evil, mental disability, and danger that they might not, individually or collectively, perish prematurely or before reaching the age of accountability, suffer physically or mentally (through

---

133 Those who are not at the age of accountability — eight years old — or who are mentally disabled or handicapped are not, according to Mormon theology, considered accountable and are therefore saved by grace without 'faith in God.'

mental disability or mental anguish and illness) beyond their ability to endure in faith, or be tempted to fall from grace and lose their faith and the Holy Spirit as their guide;

e. has complete, direct and instant access — by the 'power of the Holy Ghost' and through his presence by the 'Light of Truth (Christ)' — to *every* person individually at all times, and to *all* people collectively at all times to make his existence, plan, mind, will, and purposes known perfectly;

f. "*changes not*…but is the same from everlasting to everlasting" in nature and purpose and therefore never deviates from his greatest desire, 'Work and Glory' (see **4** above);

g. *cannot lie*, but is a god of truth, enabling man to have unwavering confidence in his word and purposes.

6. There are no non-question-begging and non-*a-priori* or otherwise valid or compelling theological, scriptural, logical, or naturalistic reasons to believe that the requirement of 'faith in God and Christ' is an 'eternal,' or non-god-imposed requirement of salvation, or to regard 'knowledge' as an impediment to the development of ('spiritual' or 'Christian') character or the exercise of 'free agency.' On the contrary, common sense confirms that 'knowledge' is an essential *pre-requisite* to the wise and effective exercise of such agency. Further, there is ample scriptural and recorded ecclesiastical evidence to support the assertion that the Mormon god has, on numerous occasions, intervened directly in the lives of certain men (some even *without* faith, or who were resistant to *the* 'Truth' and were once *enemies* of the faith and in grievous sin, such as 'Saul of Tarsus' ['Paul'] and 'Alma the Younger' among may others) to putatively reveal essential knowledge of his existence, mind and will.

7. Still, notwithstanding **(1)**, **(2)**, **(4)**, **(5)** and **(6)**:

a. Not *all* people who are taught the gospel and pray for a testimony of the existence of the Mormon god and Jesus as the Christ necessarily receive one or acquire 'faith in God and Christ' sufficient for salvation;

b. Not *all* who believe or have faith in the Mormon god and Christ *remain* in the faith, notwithstanding their alleged best efforts, desires, or intentions to do so. Many allegedly struggle and ultimately lose their faith in spite of their resistance to the contrary. According to scripture, relatively few will endure in the faith unto salvation and eternal life;

c. There are no non-question-begging and non-*a-priori*, or otherwise valid or compelling doctrinal or logical reasons to believe that *all* who are either **(aa)** without 'faith in God and Christ' or who **(bb)** lose their 'faith in God and Christ' are **(cc)** *necessarily* not 'foreordained' or 'predestined' to 'salvation' and 'eternal life,' or are 'sinners' beyond the reach of the Mormon god's (and Christ's) alleged perfect love and power — *i.e.* are prideful, greedy, slothful, vain, wrathful, gluttonous, licentious, or 'carnal, sensual, and devilish,' or are otherwise insincere, closed-minded, self-deceived, mentally impaired, or dysfunctional, or uninterested in knowledge or truth about the Mormon god and the Gospel of Jesus Christ.

8. If **(7.a.b.c.)**, then 'faith in God and Christ' is either *not* accessible or given to all who seek and need it and/or is *not* sufficiently resilient to doubt, temptation, or loss due to reason, human need, suffering, psychopathology, death, or circumstantial trial and tribulation.

9. If **(8)**, then faith is insufficient in eliminating all reasonable, real and significant doubt, despair, anger, and resistance to fulfill **(4)**

10. Given **(5)** and **(6)**, then **(1)** is unintelligible, since 'faith in God and Christ' is neither logically required nor necessary for the requirements of salvation to be met, i.e. for all men to 'know the only true God, and Jesus Christ whom he has sent' and their own 'fallen condition' and 'divine potential' sufficient to repent, be baptized, and receive the gift of the Holy Ghost.

11. Given **(4)–(10)**, there are, in principle, no non-contradictory theological reasons which would support the assertion of a putative 'unknown purpose' to account for the Mormon god's unwillingness to supplant faith with certain, uncontroversial knowledge regarding his true existence, nature, mind, and will. If such a god could, in theory, have some (unknown) purpose or explanation for: (a) requiring faith without giving it, or requiring faith even if it is insufficient or unnecessary, or (b) not completely or conclusively eliminating confusion and nonbelief, or not insulating faith from doubt or loss due to reason, sin, or trial and tribulation, then such 'unknown purpose' would necessarily contradict **(4)** or **(5.a.–g.)**.

12. If **(9)**, **(10)** and **(11)**, then, given **(1)–(6)**, the doctrinal claim of 'faith in God and Christ' as being required by the Mormon god and declared by him (and his putative servants, the Prophets) as necessary and, implicitly, sufficient for man's achievement of salvation is necessarily false or incoherent and unintelligible. Thereby this makes the Mormon doctrinal claim of the Mormon god's existence likewise false or incoherent and therefore makes the putative existence of the Mormon god necessarily impossible as conceptualized and attested to by such doctrine and by the faith-based testimonies of the truthfulness of such doctrines.

Finally, if **(12)**, then *any* argument to refute **(12)** on the basis of the putative existence and personal faith-based religious experience of the Mormon god is, as argued previously in this chapter and in Chapter 5, *invalid* due to question-begging and being better and more economically explained naturalistically; *self-defeating* because it is inclusive to the point of being non-specifiable and non-exclusive; and *cognitively meaningless* because it is factually insignificant, while *any* justificatory appeal to a faith-based 'testimony of the mystery and inscrutability of God's ways and wisdom' to refute or reject **(12)** is likewise problematical, incoherent, and irrational as well, given **(11)**, as well as **(3)** and **(5)** as established in Chapters 3 and 5.

The first four significant facets of the problem of 'faith in God and Christ' identified at the beginning of this chapter have, in my mind, been presented in sufficient depth to make some things clear:

First, and relevant to Mormon theology in particular, it is clear that the concept of 'faith' as a principle of supernatural power in the Mormon god and man is incoherent.

Second and *primarily*, the concept of 'faith in God and in Jesus Christ' as the putative 'Son of God' is impossible *sans* self-deception if the concept of the Mormon god is incoherent — as it has been shown to be primarily in Chapter 3 and also in 4. Moreover, 'faith in God,' which is allegedly established by putative 'revelation from God to man about God,' is likewise impossible if the concept of 'revelation' is also incoherent. It too was shown to be incoherent in its own right in Chapter 5. Additionally, we also found, in regard to this second facet, that pragmatic, paradoxical, and relativistic fideistic attempts to rescue the concept of 'faith in God' failed to do so.

Third, the theological assertion that faith through putative revelation or 'spiritual experience' is a legitimate and superior source of religious *knowledge* in its own right and in contradistinction to reason was also found to be incoherent and therefore unwarranted.

And *fourth*, we found that rational belief in the existence of the Mormon god is *impossible* if 'faith in God and Christ' is believed to be *required* by that god, since such faith is empirically neither *accessible* to all nor logically *necessary*, given the putative (and necessarily believed) purpose and nature of the Mormon god. Nor is it *sufficient* to insure salvation and exaltation, given the scriptural assertion that relatively few attain to such faith or endure in faith to the end. Simply stated, the claimed and believed *necessity* of faith, given the assumed existence of the Mormon god, doesn't make sense. The concept of the Mormon god, given the theological requirement, existence, and insufficiency of faith likewise doesn't make sense. According to this particular argument, the theology as a whole is fundamentally and fatally flawed.

In the end, following Douglas Krueger it would seem that when believers appeal to faith they are — beyond defending themselves psychologically against their own doubts and cognitive dissonance — actually asking other believers and nonbelievers to "trust [in *something* — or some putative *someone* — that is unintelligible or factually insignificant] for *no reason*, or commit [to a factual non-reality] *for no reason*. They are asking people to abandon the need for [sense and] evidence, for [coherence and] supporting reasons [or justification], for their beliefs (1998, 209)." In other words, they are asking people to believe in the alleged existence of something or someone whose factual existence, in truth, is neither justified nor justifiable by any reliable or credible means. "Faith," Krueger concludes, is believing [in the absurd] for no reason (209)." To quote Bertrand Russell in this regard: "We only speak of faith when we wish to substitute emotion for evidence" (Cited in Krueger, 208).

Moreover, as Krueger correctly observes, "[since] faith is belief in the absence of [intelligibility or valid] supporting reasons, faith cannot be used as *a reason for belief*." Elaborating, he continues:

> After being shown that there are no good [justifiable or justified] reasons to believe in gods, the religious person who says, "Ah, but you forget, that's where faith comes in!" is [*essentially*] saying nothing other than "Ah, but you forget, that's where having no [intelligible understanding and justifiable or justified] reasons comes in!" One who says, "No matter what you say, I still have my faith!" is merely [and again essentially] saying "No matter what you say, I still [do not know what specifically I have faith in, and] have no [justifiable or justified\] reasons [to claim that I know God exists as I conceptualize him to be].

To which the atheist may simply reply: "Correct!" (210)

"The strangest thing about the appeal to faith," Krueger observes, "is that it really does not disagree with most of what the atheist asserts. The atheist is maintaining that the believer has no good [*i.e.* justifiable or justified] reason to believe that there are gods. If the believer then states that it is a matter of faith, this is simply stating that the atheist's critique is correct — there are no good reasons." Further, "the theist [to be rational] should not be tempted to reply, "I will accept that there are no [good] reasons for belief in god, but I will then have faith that I am right anyway." That is simply saying," as Krueger sees it, "that he or she has no [good] reasons for his or her beliefs and no [rational] reasons to believe that he or she is right anyway. If having no [good] reasons didn't work the first time, it won't work the second time. Faith in faith is pointless (210)." Also, I would add, incoherent, even if irrationally (or emotionally) appealed to with a feeling of sure conviction on the basis of personal religious experience — and given that such non-self-justifying experiences are subjectively interpreted, unverifiable, and unfalsifiable in principle and can be justifiably and more economically explained naturalistically.

To be sure, most if not all staunch theistic believers would not be affected even in the slightest by Krueger's claim that their "faith in faith is pointless." They would no doubt (though no doubt *in* doubt) insist that ultimately everything — all knowledge — rests ultimately on faith. That includes what we know from science. They would insist that their beliefs in their god and the putative revelations from him regarding his plan and will are not subject to scientific verification. But as Nielsen correctly points out in relation to the first point: "If everything is said to rest on faith [including naturalism and science] there can be no faith at all, for there can only be systems of belief that rest on no evidence whatsoever if some systems of belief have some evidence that counts in their favor or at least that we have a conceptualization of an activity — a set of practices — where this could be so. We could not have practices constitutive of faith if we did not have practices which were not so constitutive. We need a nonvacuous contrast here. It is dramatic to say that everything rests on faith [like everything is a revelation or all things 'testify of God,' or all revelation is properly basic], but it is all the same an incoherent claim (2001, 181)."

Furthermore, regarding the second point, Nielsen would certainly agree with believers that their beliefs are not verifiable. "But," he would remind us, taking us back to the central argument of this chapter, "if I am right and [the concepts of 'God,' 'God's plan' and 'revelation'] are unintelligible, then we cannot (logically cannot) take them on trust or just on faith, for while we can take on trust something that we cannot prove or have no evidence for, we cannot take on trust or on faith what we literally do not understand.... We have to be able to understand," Nielsen insists, "the question 'What is it [specifically] that I am supposed to take on trust?' Without at least that very minimal understanding, we are not able to take something on trust, no matter how much we want to, for we do not understand what that something is (289)."

The Problem of Faith-as-Decision and Unwavering Commitment

Consider for context the following words of Millet:

Unshaken faith in the Lord. *Unshaken* faith in the work of the Lord. Isn't that what each one of us [as Mormon believers] most desires in the midst if snide cynicism and religious skepticism? Knowing the truth and knowing that you know the truth bring peace and balance, certitude and calmness in a world gone mad. Indeed, to have a testimony of the gospel, to put doubt out of one's life, is to have a settled conviction of things as they really are and thus to enter the rest of the Lord. (2008, 145)

"Unshaken faith in the Lord"? I ask again, what *specifically* do Millet and other believers *actually* have unshakable faith *in*? Stated differently, how is it even possible to have faith in the Lord *at all* (let alone *unshakable faith*), given that the concept of 'Lord,' the way the term 'Lord' is used in the Mormon religion? The Lord is the literal 'Son of God.' But the related concepts of 'atonement' and 'salvation' are actually — when taken to be an objective facts or realities — *impossible* because they are incoherent and factually unintelligible. Are rational, responsible, and educated adults being asked or counseled to have 'unshakable faith' (trust and confidence) in believed realities that are factual non-realities? Or even to have such faith if there's not one shred of reliable, uncontroversial evidence to prove even the probable *factual* existence of Jesus *as Lord*? If so, can such counsel sensibly be considered to be rational or sane? Even if, solely for the sake of argument, such a state of affairs were actually possible — which it is not — why would such 'faith in God and Christ' and 'faith testing' even be *necessary* as *requirements* of salvation?

Even if such requirements made rational sense given the Mormon concept of 'God' (which they do not), why would they (or faith alone) *really* be a *good* thing? Would it be a good thing if such faith and faith testing required you to forsake your own needs and well-being in pursuit of an illusory better life? Or would it be a good thing to deceive yourself into believing — even to the detriment of yourself and others — that which is otherwise rationally unbelievable? If not, then why? To "bring peace and balance," Millet insists. But peace and balance at what expense? Can't we achieve and enjoy peace and balance without having 'unshakable faith in the Lord' (whatever that means)? If not, why not? Millions think they can — and reportedly do. But if not, then what *specifically* are the distinctive, qualitative, and causal differences between *secular* feelings of peace and balance and *religious* feelings of peace and balance? If such differences cannot be specified and at least in principle either be empirically verified or falsified on the basis of universally accepted human criteria, or be justified through the achievement of wide reflective equilibrium, then how can such putative differences be justifiably claimed as being known and true, or as being a difference that truly makes a difference?

What else might make an unshakable faith in the Lord a *good* thing? Perhaps, as Millet states, the assurance of "Certitude and calmness (a 'settled conviction of things as they really are') in a world gone mad." But certitude in *what specifically*? And on what *objectively reliable* basis, other than by *subjectively* and *infallibly* "put[ting] doubt out of one's life" through denial and self-deception? Additionally, how can anyone coherently be said to 'spiritually know things *as they really are*? By revelation? But revelation from *which* god? How, on the basis of *which* uncontroversial or basic human criteria can we sanely rely (with "certitude" and "settled conviction") on such revelation when the putative Revealer ('God') on the basis of conceptual analysis is a factual non-reality? And how could it possibly be true (or probably true) or false (or probably false) that an infallible, finite being who is spatio-temporally *transcendent* to this world could *actually* communicate with *fallible* human beings in *this* world and convey Absolute Truth?

The very idea is unintelligible. Again, what would it *actually* mean to assert that such putative communication would be possible (or, in fact, occurs) through the medium of the 'Light of Truth' or the 'power of the Holy Ghost'? Moreover, how can one even approach certitude in *anything* not self-evident without succumbing to solipsism and self-deception or experiencing doubt? And how can *any* concepts not held commonly and uncontroversially to be self-evident or basic be anything other than merely *subjectively* and *apparently* self-evident and responsibly subject to reasonable doubt?

And what if the "madness" Millet refers to is — in the *believer's* "corruption of reality" (Schumaker 1995) through religiously induced dissociation and the corresponding irrational "certitude and calmness" associated with "unshaken faith" or delusional commitment — the product of an illusion? Perhaps it is the settled conviction of the faithful which constitutes the great illness (or 'madness') of the world and which paradoxically keeps us from greater social and scientific progress and truth. Perhaps in the end, unjustified (or baseless) convictions based merely on feelings, faith, and opinion are, as Nietzsche rightly concluded, "…more dangerous enemies of truth than lies"[134] (Metcalf 1996, 225).

Beyond Millet's indirect answer to the question "Why is faith in God and Christ *actually* a good thing?" is David Wolpe's answer to the related question "Why does faith matter?" offered at the conclusion of his book appropriately entitled *Why Faith Matters* (2008). After each passage quoted from his book below I offer my italicized replies:

---

134 Apropos to this discussion of faith, I quote at length a powerful passage from Nietzsche's *The Antichrist* (2000): "Do not allow yourselves to be deceived: great minds are sceptical.… Strength and the *freedom* which proceeds from the power and excessive power of the mind, *manifests* itself through scepticism. Men of conviction are of no account whatever in regard to any principles of value or of non-value. Convictions are prisons. They never see far enough, they do not look down from sufficient height: but in order to have any say in questions of value and non-value, a man must see five hundred convictions *beneath* him, — *behind* him…A [man] who desires great things, and who also desires the means thereto, is necessarily a sceptic. Freedom from every kind of conviction *belongs* to strength, to the *ability* to open one's eyes freely.…

"The great passion of a sceptic, the basis and power of his being, which is more enlightened and more despotic than he is himself, enlists all his intellect into its service; it makes him unscrupulous; it even gives him the courage to employ unholy means; in certain circumstances it even allows him convictions. Conviction as a *means*: much is achieved merely by means of a conviction. Great passion makes use of and consumes conviction, it does not submit to them — it knows that it is a sovereign power. Conversely; the need of faith, of anything either absolutely affirmative or negative…is the need of *weakness*.

"The man of beliefs, the 'believer' of every sort and condition, is necessarily a dependent man; — he is one who cannot regard *himself* as an aim, who cannot postulate aims from the promptings of his own heart. The 'believer' does not belong to himself, he can only be a means, he must be *used up*, he is in need of someone who uses him up. His instinct accords the highest honor to a morality of self-abnegation: everything in him, his prudence, his experience, his vanity, persuade him to adopt this morality. Every sort of belief is in itself an expression of self-denial [and a denial of *knowledge* as well, (see Eller 2004, 2007)], of self estrangement.…

"If one considers how necessary a regulating code of conduct is to the majority of people, a code of conduct which constrains them and fixes them from outside; and how control, or in a higher sense, *slavery*, is the only and ultimate condition under which the weak-willed man, and especially woman, flourish; one also understands conviction, 'faith.' The man of conviction finds in the latter his *backbone*. To be *blind* to may things, to be impartial about nothing, to belong always to a particular side ["who's on the Lord's side, who?"], to hold a strict and necessary point of view in all matters of values — these are the only conditions under which such a man can survive at all. But all this is the reverse of, the *antagonist* of, the truthful man, — of truth.…

"The believer is not at liberty to have a conscience for the question 'true' and 'untrue': to be upright in *this* point would mean his immediate downfall. The pathological limitations of his standpoint convert the convinced man into the fanatic,… - these are the reverse type of the strong [man] that has become *free*. But the grandiose poses of these *morbid* spirits, of these epileptics of ideas, exercise an influence over the masses, — fanatics are picturesque, mankind prefers to look at poses than to listen to reason" (85–7).

Wolpe: "Why does faith matter? Love of this world, of one another, is the sole hope in an age when we can destroy the world many times over."

Reply: *See my reply above to Millet's assertion that faith in God is somehow an antidote to "a world gone mad." Also, how specifically is Wolpe's concept of "love" dependent on "faith" in a god, and what role does critical intelligence, judgment, and reason play in humanity's "hope" in this perilous, faith-obsessed age? The implication here is that "love of this world [and] of one another" is necessarily and actually dependent on faith in a god. But how can Wolpe or any rational person possibly believe such an absurd assertion or validly argue for such a conclusion given both the incoherence of the concept of 'God' in all theistic religions (including Mormonism), and the empirical justification of just the opposite in the history of religion and in the existence of such love among nonbelievers and disbelievers?*

Wolpe: "There is no power that is only good, that cannot be twisted for evil. Religion is hardly an exception."

Reply: *But why isn't religion an exception? With 'God,' at least according to the Mormon faith, mankind allegedly has access to — on condition of faith in Christ, repentance, and baptism by immersion by those in authority — the 'gift of the Holy Ghost,' the various 'gifts of the spirit,' continuous 'revelation from God,' and personal transformation which ensures a 'mighty change of heart' wherein those with faith in Christ have been purified of all sin and sinfulness such that they "have no more disposition to do evil, but to do good continually." So why, even granting free will, would the Mormon religion, or any charismatic, 'Holy-Spirit' Christian religion not be an exception?*

Wolpe: "But while there are many things that can doom us, only one thing can save us. Faith. Not blind or bigoted faith, but faith that pushes us to be better, to give more of ourselves, to see glimmers of transcendence scattered throughout our lives…" (197–8)

Reply: *Faith in what, specifically? And "better" in what sense and at what cost? And better than what specifically? Better than being human? Give more of ourselves to whom (A god? Whose god? Which god?) or to what end, specifically, and why or according to what or whose standards and criteria? And why does one need faith in any god to love and give of oneself generously and compassionately to others? Many do so without belief or faith in any god. Also, does such 'giving' include giving to oneself and one's needs? Moreover, does the 'love' which putatively comes through faith and which is, according to Wolpe, our "sole hope" of survival, require self-deception, self-denial, and the suppression of self-interest to be efficacious? What 'evils' might exist because of suppressive self-denial? Is such 'love' and selflessness even advisable, much less possible? Finally, self-transcendence (if even possible or advisable) neither necessarily nor actually requires faith in a god for its existence. This makes the implicit claim that faith matters because it somehow enables man to fulfill his human need for self-transcendence (or even love) a non sequitur. Moreover, it can be argued that for such 'self-transcendence' to be healthy or not pathological in its experience or expression, one must first be sufficiently individuated and integrated as a personality — something which 'faith in God,' as a regressive phenomenon itself, works against by its very nature. So tell me again why faith matters or is a good thing?*

The self-answering questions asked and the conclusions reached regarding Millet's (and Wolpe's) above-quoted advocacy of an "unshaken faith in the Lord" (as well as all the others asked in this chapter regarding the Mormon principle of 'faith in God and Christ') bring us to the fifth and last facet of faith to be considered in this chapter. This facet characterizes faith as *a decision* — indeed *the* most important decision in one's life. This faith is a decision to trust or believe primarily if not exclusively on the basis of experiencing certain allegedly unique 'feelings of the Spirit' without reasons, or without sense or reason. It is a faith that does not question one's belief in a god or the nature of one's alleged love for, trust in, and devotion and unwavering commitment to that god. Such a characterization of faith as a feelings-based decision is, in my view, not without the significant conceptual difficulty of relying on feelings as special arbiters of truth. But regarding faith as a decision also has egregious personal or social consequences that justify both a careful treatment extending far beyond this book and a polemical tone — and even, perhaps, a bit of snide cynicism.

In his chapter "The Decision," Millet recounts a personal watershed experience while listening to an address given by Elder Neil L. Anderson, a General Authority of the Mormon Church during the April 2007 general conference of the Church. Earlier, Millet had been confronted by a friend who could not understand Millet's admission that his review of "anti-Mormon propaganda" didn't affect his faith. Later, while listening to the aforementioned conference talk, he heard Elder Anderson say: "Faith is not only a feeling; it's a *decision*" (2008, 131). "That was it," Millet writes. "That was the answer. Faith is a decision. Decades ago I made a decision: I determined that God is my Heavenly Father. Jesus Christ is my Lord and Redeemer, my *only hope* for *peace* in this life and eternal *reward* in the *life to come…*" (131, emphasis mine).

When faith consists merely of a wish-based belief in the imagined, *merely possible existence* of an all-loving, all-powerful Parent-God who offers unconditional salvation to *all* with *no* performatory or belief requirements of any kind, then such faith would be a benign, and perhaps even beneficial illusion to the believer. This Disneyesque faith — contrary as it most likely would be to the prevailing concepts of 'God' canonized and proclaimed in every theistic religion in the world today — would (as we learned from Dennett earlier) amount to nothing more than a comforting and relatively harmless *belief in belief*. It would be a faith, moreover, that would be without force or influence in inducing or otherwise compelling moral goodness or in directing and controlling the lives of believers. To be otherwise would, of course, require beliefs with specific, ego-syntonic, and guilt-inducing performatory conditions and consequences.

When the object of faith is a Parent-God who *does* (even if tacitly) impose behavioral, attitudinal, and performatory requirements ('good works') and makes at least implicit moral demands and judgments on the basis of obedience to authoritative counsel, 'divine command' and self-sacrifice — as it most certainly explicitly does in the Mormon faith — then such a belief can, if embraced as a commitment or irreversible decision, be harmful, dangerous, and even life-threatening for believers and others. This is so particularly where the believer is or tends to be superstitious by nature, not sufficiently individuated and integrated (or shame-based) as a personality, psychologically unstable, or vulnerable (in virtue of conditioning, need, or neediness) to authoritarian control and corresponding suggestion and dissociation. Such a person is prone to shame and shameful or shameless acting-out, addictive or obsessive-compulsive behavior, irrational guilt, delusion, and self-deception[135]. But then, who among us is *not* so wounded, vulnerable, or even unstable to one degree or another?[136]

Many so-called true believers — and professed disbelievers or nonbelievers as well — will, of course, exempt themselves automatically from such risk-factors and self-deceptively rely on their feelings as arbiters of the truth of their beliefs. But this will not, I fear, be without considerable risk to themselves and others.

Certainly it will be conceded by Mormon believers who are honest, psychologically sophisticated, and self-aware that their own attraction and loyalties to 'God and Christ,' and also (perhaps to a lesser degree) this loyalty to the authority figures of the Church, are likely rooted in 'the basic biological situation' of life (Faber 2004) and the dynamics of their family system (see the *Epilogue* and also Gerson 1996). Such a concession would acknowledge what is commonly known, that what is most basic to our physical and emotional lives is the sufficient satisfaction of our human needs for attachment, belonging, acceptance, and approval to provide the necessary security, love and esteem necessary for survival and personal happiness and fulfillment. It would acknowledge that we need to avoid or otherwise ameliorate the existential anxiety or fear of rejection, isolation, and annihilation or death that we experienced pre-verbally at birth, and as infants, children, adolescents, and adults due to separation and, in many cases, abuse, abandonment, or loss.

Furthermore, honest, informed and self-aware believers would also acknowledge their own personal 'demons" (or psychological complexes) and woundedness. They would acknowledge as well the fact that their own personal capabilities are rarely revealed in their extremes and that much of what we are all as human beings truly capable of doing — for good or evil — is beneath the surface of our awareness and very well insulated from consciousness by highly evolved and developed defense mechanisms.

Who is to say, therefore, that they (or anyone) honestly and coherently know perfectly well or with *perfect* certitude what they are capable of doing under *any* and *all* circumstances and situations — particularly if in need or *in extremis* and under the spell of an emotionally compelling, hallucinatory, dissociative trance (known in a religious context as a revelatory religious, or spiritual experience)? Among the most faithful and deeply converted Latter-day Saints (Mormons), who would be so presumptuous as to say — incoherently, *as believers*[137] — that their 'God' would *never* require of them some form of

---

135 The question of Mormonism as a socially and psychologically toxic faith is addressed in some depth in Chapter 8, the *Epilogue,* and the author's *Personal Postscript* which follow. Nevertheless, adequate determination of psychological risk related to theistic religious belief is clearly beyond the scope of this book and requires a correct understanding of the above noted risk-factors as well as sufficient self-knowledge obtained through honest self-analysis and/or appropriate psychotherapy. In this context, for theistic believers to wave-off such concerns in relation to their own supposed exception to such risk-factors is not only psychologically naïve, at minimum, it is, more likely, delusional as well. The fact is, *no one* can predict with *certainty* what the future might hold, or what lies beneath the surface of one's own consciousness or known capabilities for good or evil.

136 This point is made autobiographically in the *Introduction* and *Personal Postscript*.

137 Mormon or Christian believers betray their doubt at some level when they assert with certainty that their god would never require of them what was believed to be required by the 'God' of other notable characters in holy writ or in the history of their particular faith. (We may think, for example, of the scriptural characters Abraham, Job, Jonah, Jesus, and the Christian apostles and martyrs. We think also of the *Book of Mormon*

self-sacrifice (of needs, means, pleasures, preferences and even relationships or life itself) as an act or test of faith or loyalty for their own spiritual well-being or eternal reward?

At a much more extreme level, how would they suppose that their god would never require of them what he putatively required of other likewise faithful followers and so-called chosen 'saints' and 'prophets' such as Abraham from the *Bible* (in sacrificing Isaac)? Or the character of Nephi from the *Book of Mormon* (in slaying Laban)? Or Joseph Smith and numerous other Latter-Day Saints (in practicing plural marriage in secret or in public with single women, as well as with other men's wives and young girls)? Or Brigham Young (in allegedly authorizing or condoning 'blood atonement' or commanding or, at least, enabling and encouraging the Mountain Meadows Massacre)? And who among the truly faithful could say with certitude that they, in turn, would not respond likewise under the right circumstances, when to do so would be regarded by their god as an act of supreme loyalty and valiancy, resulting in great blessings on earth and in heaven, and when failing to do so would be regarded by their god as an act of disobedience and disloyalty resulting in the forfeiture of eternal blessings? Mormon history — which includes the history of Mormon fundamentalism — is indisputably replete with such extremism or fanaticism. Particularly among those who truly and completely love, trust and believe in their god, and who are committed, *by decision* and *conviction*, to do *whatever* is asked of them by their god — no matter what.

Even the average, putatively normal, mainstream ('active') Mormon is at considerable risk of personal harm and potential extremism. This is due, in my view, to the repressive and shaming forces built into the theology and the culture that can (and arguably do) block the formation of an integrated personality. Such forces can also split the personality through dissociation in times of stress (or personal distress) and block individuation through the fostering (as virtuous) of an unhealthy dependency on, and obedience to, the Parent-God and his parental surrogates. Moreover, these regressive, shaming forces can and often do incite inner conflict and, consequently, one-sided living. This in turn eventually takes a toll on the believer's mental and emotional well-being. The so-called 'happy life' for Mormons in denial of their grave predicament is — subjective protestations and assertions to the contrary notwithstanding — a life that is often characterized by self-alienation. It is a state of being that is effectuated through the dissociative splitting of the personality into good/bad or acceptable/unacceptable polar attributes and qualities in consequence of direct or indirect pressure to conform to Church-imposed standards and expectations. It is also a life characterized for some (if not many or all) by the suffering due to self- and culture-imposed anxiety, depression, shame, and guilt in consequence of living — or even occasionally fantasizing or wanting to live — outside such standards or expectations.

Other conditions or characterizations also apply. These include the denial of personal instinctual desires, preferences, and needs that are deemed by Church leaders or members as forbidden, taboo, 'unadvisable' — a softer version of forbidden — 'carnal, sensual,

---

character Nephi, and certain Mormon 'martyrs' and 'prophets' and their wives.) That doubt may concern the putative existence of their god, his putatively revealed attributes and works, the putative truth and accuracy of scripture as revelation from him (including the scriptural 'truth' indicating that 'God' proves, tries, or tests the faith of those who would inherit the fulness of the blessings of the gospel), the asserted, believed, and generally accepted accuracy of ecclesiastical history as recorded, and even concern the very existence of their own professed faith.

and devilish,' or otherwise unbecoming a true believer. They include the suppression of authentic self-expression, free thought, intellectual freedom, doubt, and dissent in matters of cultural mores, basic beliefs, religious doctrine, and policy. They require the foreclosing of those living options not in line with Gospel or Church standards, expectations, and implicit (if not explicit) requirements. Such conformity, suffering, suppression, and self-denial are, even if admitted to, sadly considered among the well-indoctrinated faithful to be a small price to pay for womb-like inclusion within the 'community of the faithful,' the comforts, security, and conditional acceptance and approval of their Parent-God and his mortal surrogates, and the factually vacuous promise and assurance of eternal reward.

Still, if Freud was correct[138] — and history and science have shown repeatedly in this

---

138 While the work of Sigmund Freud embodied in psychoanalysis has been questioned and attacked over the years and, as Faber correctly points out, "…partially superseded by biological and pharmacological approaches," it continues "to 'live' and to live vigorously, as John Horgan expresses it in *Scientific American*" (1996, 106–11). There are various reasons for this cited by Faber, quoting Horgan (1996), Webster (1995) and Liechty (1999), and various effective refutations to the philosophical criticisms of psychoanalysis offered by skeptics such as Grunbaum Crews, Cioffi, Webster and others (see Sachs in Neu 1991, pp. 309–338; Levy 1996; Robinson 1993; Wallwork 1991, 293–298). As Levy concludes in this regard, "Psychoanalysis is amply equipped to respond to the philosophical criticism that has been mounted against it thus far. No good philosophical arguments against it have been produced, and much empirical evidence supports it" (1996, 172).

Further, Philip Rieff (1987) adds to the significance of Freud's work in the context of its impact on culture. In Rieff's words "Freud's is a psychology that matters culturally. His psychology not only studies the conduct of life but seeks also to affect it. For that reason alone, it is just to call Freud's a moral psychology, whatever one's judgment as to its scientific merits." … Moreover, Rieff continues, "Freud's object was personal capacity not general cure, [and] one will not [necessarily] lead to the other. Cure is a religious category. … Freud, knowing there was no cure, in the classical sense of a generalizable conversion experience, sought an increase in human power without reference to any of the established ideals. … [His] doctrine of personal capacity [and]…the limit of [his] success: the greater freedom to choose does not cure anybody — in the sense in which…Western man yearned to be cured. … While [Freud] did not deny that the cures others might develop may be efficacious modes of therapy… [he nonetheless] proposed that all those who wanted to cure souls, or preach a saving idea, do so under a banner other than his own." This said, and as a consequence of the stated "disappointment" and even "bitterness" of "many" [who entered and are] entering analysis "innocently," as "part of their quest for 'meaning' and 'identity,' and [did not find] what they were looking for;…there are new polemicists stalking Freud throughout the land, …[and] loudly saying that he cannot 'cure' — when such a cure in the [religious] sense was never his object" (39, 87, 90, 92).

"However," Faber points out, "it is not in regard solely to philosophical [and cultural] issues that psychoanalysis has lately experienced a vindication of its approach [both to psychotherapy and as an interpretive schema for understanding religious and cultural pathology and] human behavior. On the contrary," Faber reports, "striking evidence of its [theoretical] accuracy and value emerges from the burgeoning field of neuroscience, a field that [bears directly on the naturalistic interpretive alternative offered in this book to so-called religious (or 'spiritual') experience related to conversion, revelation, faith, and prayer]. Writing in a recent issue of *Scientific American*, the cover of which announces in bold type, "Science Revives Freud," Mark Solms contends that modern biological descriptions of the brain may 'fit together best' when 'integrated by psychological theories Freud sketched a century ago.' Solms continues," Faber concludes, "in a number of pivotal sentences [included below for emphasis in support of this work]" (2004, 51, all citations referenced below are Faber's): 'Neuroscience has shown that the major brain structures essential for forming conscious (explicit) memories are not functional during the first two years of life, providing an elegant explanation of what Freud called infantile amnesia. As Freud surmised, it is not that we forget our earliest memories; we simply cannot recall them to consciousness. But this inability does not preclude them from affecting adult feelings and behavior. One would be hard-pressed to find a developmental neurolobiologist who does not agree that early experiences, especially between mother and infant, influence the pattern of brain connections in ways that fundamentally shape our future personality and mental health. Yet none of these experiences can be consciously remembered. It is becoming increasingly clear that a good deal of our mental activity is

case that he was — that which is repressed *always* returns — if not in dreams or consciously through analysis, then in symptoms of the mind and body or in relationships and various forms of deviant, damaging, self-defeating, or even destructive social behavior. Nature *always* has its day *and* its way — like it or not.

The crucial point here — revisited in Chapter 8 and again in the *Epilogue* — is not that faith-based religious excesses or atrocities did occur in the past. That is a historically undisputed fact. Nor is it the point that relatively few believers act-out neurotically or psychotically in the name of their god to harm themselves or others — which is probably statistically true as far as we know. Rather it is the point that *all* fundamentalist religions are at least *likely* harmful and *potentially* dangerous or — even stronger still, given the unknown (and even unknowable) yet certain psychological risks involved — *actually* harmful and dangerous, even with ecclesiastical safeguards[139] in place. This is so, as I see it, because such religious belief systems are founded theologically on a patriarchal concept of a god who allegedly accepts and rewards or else rejects and punishes believers (his putative *children*) in this life and the next on the basis of their faith and unwavering obedience to *all* his commandments.

I suspect that acting-out in one form or another and to one degree or another is much more common than Mormon Church authorities know or would care to admit. It can be

---

unconsciously motivated' (2004, 82–89).

139 Significantly, such safeguards, particularly in the Mormon religion, are ultimately impotent or ineffectual against those believers (among whom I was one) who obsessively and dogmatically (out of personal neediness) 'hunger and thirst' after greater 'righteousness and truth.' They are ineffectual against those who possess (or, more accurately, are possessed *by*) an active 'faith complex' and belief in personal revelation. Safeguards fail against those who truly believe (*know!*) — in spite of their questions and doubts — that they have in fact received *direct* revelation from their god who *literally* directs and requires them in the tradition and pattern of Joseph Smith to pursue a 'more enlightened' and 'true' (albeit forbidden) path than the current program of the Church. Their god expects them to disregard current Church prohibitions.

To such self-regarded devout believers in their unknown or unacknowledged personal circumstances of need, the natural impulses of their neediness are often regarded as emotionally compelling spiritual promptings from their god to pursue a particular course of action where established or codified rules and safeguards do not necessarily apply. They do not apply because, in the minds of these wounded believers, they (the believers) are regarded by their Lord (through putative revelation) as being 'faithful,' 'chosen,' and 'called disciples and servants' whom the god regards under special circumstances as 'exceptions' to the rules. In their minds, they believe that their god, having 'purified their hearts' and placed them on 'the path of righteousness' would not so prompt or direct them, or fill them with such desire, or allow them to pursue such a course of action if such desire and course of action were inappropriate or contrary to his will.

Such believers might further narcissistically exploit doctrinal loopholes in Mormon theology. They might consider themselves, in virtue of their believed revealed assurance of exaltation — or "calling and election made sure" by the "more sure word of prophesy" (McConkie 1966, 109–110) — to be members of the 'Church of the Firstborn' (which is separate and elevated in status from the Mormon Church on earth; 139–140) and therefore are subject to *higher* 'laws, ordinances, callings, and privileges.' As perhaps final justification, such believers might (and often do) rationalize their behavior by embracing 'theocratic ethics,' which regards as ethical and morally right *whatever* the Mormon god commands or requires. They might refer to what is evident to them and to all honest, well-informed members of the Church, that the ordained local Church leaders and anointed General Authorities or professed Prophets, Seers, and Revelators of the Mormon Church are either working a different agenda for the Lord and ministering, by necessity, at a lower level to the church on earth, or are, conversely, clearly fallible and flawed human beings who have fallen far short of the putative and believed 'knowledge, spiritual gifts, and mantle of authority' supposed to have been bestowed upon them by the Mormon god. All of these self-justifying rationalizations are ironically rooted in, and tacitly condoned by, the very theology that condemns them.

causally related to the repressive — and therefore toxic — beliefs of the Mormon faith. It can be tied to those beliefs (and related meta-beliefs) that infect and poison the wounded minds of those who are seeking — out of their neediness — to be regarded as special, chosen, called, empowered, privileged, blessed, accepted, and approved by the Parent-God. Such a state of affairs is not only yearned for, but believed to be obtainable in virtue of the promises made *explicitly* in Mormon scripture and doctrine and the teachings of the founding Prophets of the Church, and *implicitly* in the recorded, legendary experiences of the 'truly faithful and righteous' men and women in Mormon history and scriptural accounts.

To regard faith as a *decision* that once made should *never* — no matter what — be critically revisited, examined, or questioned (still less reversed) as a skeptical outsider is not only irrational and unwise, it is irresponsible as well. It is a feeling-based decision which is arguably not only an unethical evasion of individual and social responsibility, but very likely it is as well a decision that blocks to a greater or lesser degree the natural, psychological mandate for individuation and integration necessary for one's personal development and well-being. In that sense, I consider such a conceptualization of faith-as-decision a tacit admission of — and an inadvisable and regrettable commitment to — self-deceptively living a lie in denial of the lived truths of human existence.

As I see it, to suggest to others that faith is an irreversible decision and badge of true commitment and loyalty to a god is not only perverse, it constitutes both immoral and unethical counsel. Those like Millet and other influential men and women in the Mormon Church (especially Church leaders and prominent apologists) who advocate or profess such nonsense — while simultaneously exercising subtle forms of authoritarian mind control through the implicit or explicit authoritative promise and threat of eternal rewards and punishments — are, to my mind, *complicit* in *all* the exceptional atrocities and commonplace abuse and human suffering caused by religious parenting, need-suppression (self-neglect), shaming, extremism, and authoritarianism.

Further, to actually make faith "*the* decision," as Millet and others suggest, is nothing less than to decide — to the believers' overall detriment and well-being — to say *no* to the authority of reason and conscience in the domain of religious observance and obedience, and *no* to the right, privilege, and desire to say *yes* to the 'sanctity of dissent' (Toscano 1994) and the necessity of doubt. It is also a decision to say *no* to the full range of human needs, possibilities, and experiences in this life. To make faith a decision is essentially to give up one's life and freedom in pursuit of an illusion — in denial of the natural, existential mandate that *we* ultimately choose how *we* should live and die as purely and exclusively *natural* beings.

Such an ultimate choice clearly and necessarily requires that we *first* decide to say *Yes!* to *this, our only life* without *any* belief in a next life or concern for invented and illusory next-life rewards and punishments. It requires that we act without *any* sacred regard or anxious concern for the invented, proclaimed, and defended requirements and constraints (*i.e.* commandments, binding covenants, and Church standards and policies) that have been devised and imposed authoritatively by religious leaders who likely seek to either consciously or unconsciously forestall the return or exposure of their own suppressed doubts[140] *and* – human nature being what it is — their desire to expand, preserve, and ensure their own power, control, entitlements, veneration, exaltation, and eternal kingdom

---

140 What human being in right mind does not, after all, have *any* doubt regarding the veracity of matters of faith which are ultimately unknowable, and even unbelievable?

on earth and in heaven.

The above crucial point and the admittedly cynical,[141] subjective, and impassioned commentary aside, all arguments, concerns, and conclusions considered regarding the Mormon doctrines of feeling-based and justified 'revelation from God *about* God' and feeling-based and justified 'faith in God and Christ' are, on the basis of critical, conceptual analysis and argument, completely incapable of rescuing the concept of the Mormon god and the putative Plan of Salvation from the charge of utter incoherence and unintelligibility. Simply put, believers cannot intelligibly or rationally appeal to something *incoherent* to make what is at least apparently incoherent *coherent*.

Concluding Questions and Remarks

Considering then, the concept of faith in particular — and beyond, solely for the sake of argument, the conclusion that 'faith in God and Christ' *per se* is *impossible* (given the incoherence and factual meaninglessness of the Mormon concept of 'God' and 'Jesus Christ as God') — there are, to recapitulate, *four questions* for all Mormon and other theistic believers which demand to be answered to pass the outsider test for faith.

First, how and in what sense *specifically* is faith *a principle* of *supernatural power in* 'God' and man? *Second*, what *specifically* do Mormon believers have faith or ultimate trust and confidence *in*? Why and how, or on what basis *specifically*, is faith justified as a *legitimate* source of knowledge? *Third*, why is 'faith in God and Christ' (and faith-testing) *required* and deemed *necessary* as a principle of salvation or demonstration of loyalty, given such faith's empirically established *insufficiency* and the putatively revealed attributes, qualities, and purposes of the Mormon god? And *fourth*, why is 'faith in God,' as an irreversible *decision* (or at all), *necessarily* a good thing? Why is it not, in its theistic context, inadvisable as being at least a very risky commitment?

These four questions, like those asked earlier of Jamesian, Pascalian, Kierkegaard, and Wittgensteinian fideists, to my knowledge have not only *not* been intelligibly answered to date, but I cannot even conceive of possible, non-*a-priori* and question-begging answers that would be conceptually or empirically coherent or factually intelligible to a rational person. If this is the case, then Mormon believers are confronted with an irresolvable dilemma. For not only can they not (in virtue of the fact of fallibilism) appeal to scripture, revelation, spiritual experience or authority as sources of absolute truth, neither can they abandon their incoherent, feeling-based claim or unwarranted assertion that their 'faith in God' is a certain knowledge of their god's existence, or that faith itself is the only way of certainly knowing their god and eternal truth. To do so, again given fallibilism, would necessarily make their so-called knowledge uncertain, provisional, and subject to error and revision — something they cannot accept without making their unequivocal claim to

---

141 To be *cynical* is to hold the belief that human conduct is primarily, or at bottom, motivated by self-interest. Although self-interest, as I understand it, negates the Christian ideal of selflessness as something humanly impossible and therefore incoherent as conceptualized, it is nonetheless not synonymous with narcissistic self-absorption, selfishness, or egocentricity. It can involve the higher *human needs* of mature love, self-actualization, and self-transcendence as conceptually understood, for example, by Fromm (2006) and Maslow (1962, 1976) respectively. Perhaps with such a qualification the cynical insistence that all human action is motivated, at bottom, by self-interest is not as negative as it might seem.

be the only *true* Church in possession of *the* Way, *the* Truth, and *the* Life also incoherent.

It would seem apropos to all the above, in conclusion to return to Mormon Apostle Boyd K. Packer's qualification of faith quoted in Millet (2008) at the beginning of this chapter where he stated that *"If everything has to be known, if everything has to be explained, if everything has to be certified, then there is no need for faith. Indeed, there is no room for it."* Here, Packer's argument for faith is as disingenuous and misleading as it is invalid.

I have argued that 'faith in God (or Christ)' is impossible as conceptualized in Mormon theology and that believers who experience faith as trust and confidence in, love for, and commitment and devotion to their 'Lord and God' are not, in fact, experiencing a relationship with anything or any being which is actually real. This is not because believers do not know, as Packer insists, 'everything there is to know' or cannot *explain* or *certify* everything they say they know about their god. But I do make such an argument on the premise that for 'faith in God' to exist, as even Joseph Smith knew (and certainly Packer knows as well), those who claim to have such faith must, at minimum, have some intelligible, coherent idea or concept of such a being. But as was determined (beyond, I think, a reasonable doubt) in Chapter 3 and reiterated in all subsequent chapters to this point, that is precisely what Mormon believers do *not* have. This is because the very concept of the Mormon god in its putatively revealed, theological fullness is unintelligible, incoherent, and factually meaningless — making the Mormon god a factual non-reality that is, by definition, *unknowable, unjustifiable* as a truth claim, and *unbelievable* without self-deception.

No one who argues for the incoherence of the requirement of faith and against the need for 'faith *in* God' (as I also do) thinks, *pace* Packer, that *every* actionable premise or assumption in the secular domain has to be known, explained, or certified (*i.e.* justified) before certain mundane action is reasonably and responsibly taken. Such a position would be absurd, and would function as a *straw man* if used in arguing for the need for theistic faith and against Atheism.

Still, if considered in relation to certain choices made in matters of considerable consequence, where the risks are high regarding the sacrifices in (and even of) life which must be made — and the potential if not likely harm and danger which might ensue to self and others in making such a choice — then surely to be rational *and* responsible the justificatory claims warranting such choices *must* be *known* or justified *before* making them. Such choices, to be morally and epistemically responsible, cannot be made solely or primarily on the basis of non-specific spiritual feelings or emotions. This, it seems to me, is particularly so in relation to those putatively transmundane feelings or emotions that cannot be intelligibly differentiated beyond mere unwarranted assertion from the reportedly similar but purely mundane feelings and emotions that are experienced by nonbelievers and disbelievers, or by believers in different and/or fundamentally conflicting faiths.

As argued in this book, the 'choice' to 'follow Christ' and 'obey God' in all things constitutes a momentous choice. For most if not all believers it requires the rigorous justification of the religious claims putatively justifying such a choice (*e.g.* claims asserting the *literal* existence of the Mormon god and the *actual, absolute* truth of the Mormon Gospel and Church). Such a choice, based on 'faith in God' (which is a purely affective, neuropsychological phenomenon devoid of epistemic significance or function) is made to justify what is, in fact, *unjustifiable*. It is not only *unnecessary*, as Packer unintentionally albeit rightly suggests, it is utterly irrational and morally and epistemically irresponsible as well. Truly, I would agree — in a sense clearly not intended by Packer — that there is "no room" (and also no need) for faith in matters concerning one's considered or inclined commitments to *any* god. A sound mind, an outsider's presumption of reasonable skepticism, and plain common sense will do just fine to frame such religious commitments as they truly are — perverse, superstitious nonsense accounted for ultimately by our human fears, insecurities, foolishness, and "stupidity" (Welles 1995, 1997).

Chapter 7

Irresolvable Contradictions and Problems
In the Mormon Faith
(*And All Theistic Religions*)

*"The atheist does not have to know anything in order to say that [god
cannot exist], the atheist just has to know
what the theist says about god."*

—*Douglas Krueger*

"The only excuse for God is that he doesn't exist."

—*Nietzsche*

Non-Mormon theistic readers surely know by now, if they have been closely and reflectively following the *a priori* atheological argument so far, that the systematic deconstruction of Mormonism in Chapters 3–6 applies as well to their faith, *whatever* it might be, and that their faith, *as conceptualized*, would therefore necessarily meet the same fate. If this is so, as it surely seems to be (and no one to my knowledge has been able to substantively and legitimately answer the challenge made by such an argument or the analytical questions which comprise it), then *all* professed primary, secondary, and derivative beliefs asserting a god's existence are false and/or incoherent, and therefore *factually vacuous* as stated, and *irrational* as beliefs and as believed. Consequently *all secondary* religious beliefs which necessarily hinge on the putative existence of 'God' as institutionally or individually conceptualized (*e.g.* the 'Creation of man' and 'worlds without end' by 'God,' the 'Atonement of Christ as Son of God' for the 'salvation' of man, the 'Resurrection of Christ and all mankind by God,' a 'Last Judgment by God,' and an 'Afterlife in another world' or 'better place' with 'God,' *etc.*) are equally vacuous and irrational.

The theological claim that the revealed Father-God of Mormonism (or of any theistic faith) is, for all necessary intents and purposes, at least *sufficiently* good, loving, knowledgeable, accessible, and powerful to be worthy of worship, devotion, and faith — apart from being factually unintelligible and incoherent in all its aspects — is also *radically incoherent* in the context of at least five perennial, irresolvable problems. These problems constitute perhaps the most stark and fundamental internal contradictions inherent in all theistic faiths. They are, individually and collectively, perhaps the greatest source of unspoken and unacknowledged anxiety and doubt to believers who have not yet seriously or objectively analyzed and assessed the concept of their god and the explicit and implicit truth claims of their faith and found them to be factually empty. More than historical and doctrinal problems, which are often regarded and dismissed as mere intra- or inter-faith squabbles among the intelligentsia within the faith or among different faiths, these internal contradictions are truly troublesome because they affect all believers' faith at a primary and visceral level.

With every personal challenge or difficulty in life that requires faith — where one's god is silent or hidden and the consolations and perspectives from religious texts and leaders are vague and seem trite and empty of any real personal connection or significance — something doesn't add up. With every unanswered prayer and unrealized blessing; with every troubling question or occasional wave of doubt or existential anxiety; with every deconversion, defection or apostasy from the faith by a once-faithful believer; with every rejection of the faith by a friend, loved one or investigator; every excommunication on the basis of conscientious dissent or the public intellectual criticism of the faith; every seemingly unfair or premature loss of fortune, health, or loved ones; every dashed hope; every day of unremitting personal suffering or the suffering of a loved one; and with every natural disaster or atrocity which claims the lives of innocent victims and children, the internal contradictions of one's concept of 'God' press on the minds of the faithful the deep sense that something doesn't fit or cohere — the sense that belief in their god is *empirically* unjustified as believed.

Even if denied, these irresolvable contradictions no doubt subconsciously hound the faithful, and the elaborate, *ad hoc*, *a priori,* and *question-begging* apologetic attempts to resolve them bring no real or lasting relief. Again, the very need for such apologetics might seem suspect to more reflective believers, even if tacitly so, given the believed attributes and alleged desires and purposes of their god. Why, after all, it might be wondered, would an all – or sufficiently – powerful, loving and infallible god need to rely on limited and fallible human apologists to defend the truth of his existence and his revealed Word from the honest confusion or disbelief of reasoning and reasonable nonbelievers, or those of different faiths? Even the meek and humble retreat to faith provides only interim relief until the next contradiction is experienced, the next disappointment is encountered, and the next reminder is made as a challenge to the coherence and rationality of belief.

Ultimately, it is my considered opinion — and one which is again informed by personal experience as a once-converted, faithful, and committed holder of the Melchizedek Priesthood in the Mormon faith for over twenty years — that *all* theistic believers, regardless of education or vocation, realize *at some point* and *at some level* that the actual existence of their god as conceptualized and believed is, given these experienced internal contradictions, improbable to the point of being reasonably considered impossible. The fact that some might outright deny having such a realization — or any conscious awareness of such — has I think more to do with the power of self-deception and the resiliency of delusion than with the power and resiliency of faith. Faith is, as we have learned, nothing more than a regressive, dissociated and delusional state of mind.

Such observations and personal opinion aside, let us proceed by first briefly listing the aforementioned irresolvable contradictions and then briefly explore each one in turn. These contradictions constitute *real* problems which result in *real* doubt, and include the following:

First, there is the perennial problem of the morally repugnant existence and/or extent of senseless human and animal suffering and premature death due to so-called human (or moral) and natural 'evil' in at least apparent contradiction to the putatively revealed nature and purposes of 'God,' and without revealed, plausible, reasonable, or moral justification. (See Weisberger 1999 & 2007; Drange 1998; Gale 1991; Mackie1982; Martin 1990; Q. Smith in Martin & Monnier 2003; Q. Smith, Rowe, Martin and Metcalf in Martin & Monnier 2006; Everitt 2004; Steele 2008; Beversluis 2007; Loftus 2008, 2010.)

S*econd*, as addressed in the previous chapter, there is the problem of the Mormon god's incoherent salvational requirement of 'faith in God and Christ' and 'faith testing' in spite of its obvious non-necessity and insufficiency.

Third, related to our analysis of 'revelation from God to man' in Chapter 5, is the problem of prayer *per se* and petitionary and intercessory prayer in particular, given its incoherence, non-necessity, and unreliability.

Fourth, contrary to the putative nature and greatest desire of the Mormon god for the salvation and eternal happiness of man, there is the problem of widespread *nonbelief* (Drange 1998) due to contradictory beliefs and the existence of religious doubt, confusion, and ignorance that are caused in turn by the other four problems, as well as by scriptural errancy and vague, ambiguous, and contradictory revelation and doctrine.

Fifth, related to the second, third, and fourth problems above (as well as to the problem of revelation presented in Chapter 5 and revisited in the next chapter) is the problem of 'wrong belief' and 'wrong believers' (or 'believing apostates') among and within a multitude of differing faiths and their fundamentally different core requirements for salvation.

Focusing again on Mormonism, and suspending for the sake of argument the *a priori* unintelligibility of the Mormon concept of 'God,' as well as the corresponding and consequential problems with the related concepts of revelation *from*, and faith *in* a god as established in previous chapters, all of the above perennial problems, in some way or other, contradict the Mormon god's believed nature, power, and greatest desire and purpose to "bring to pass the…eternal life of man." Such contradictions, if at least logically justified, establish that the Mormon god could not possibly exist as conceptualized — a conclusion that will be developed in greater depth below.

In making this assertion I find myself in loose agreement with David Steele who I think correctly concludes that "We can indeed prove negatives, and we do so all the time. In fact," Steele points out — in a rather blinding statement of the obvious — "if we couldn't prove a negative, we couldn't prove a positive either, since every positive statement implies negative statements (an infinite number of them, actually)." Instead, he continues, "[what] I think people are getting at when they come out with the claim that we can't prove a negative is that, given a limited number of observations, we often can't demonstrate that something doesn't exist, because an exhaustive search is impracticable…. [But observation] is not the only way to prove the non-existence of some entity. We can prove that a square circle does not exist because it is logically impossible: it is self-contradictory. We can prove that a perpetual motion machine does not and cannot exist, because its existence would [incoherently] contravene the laws of physics. In cases like these," Steele suggests, "proving a negative may be a lot easier than proving a positive: if there is no self-contradiction or contradiction of natural laws, this doesn't show that the entity exists, whereas if there is a contradiction [with common knowledge, or a self-contradiction or conceptual incoherency], the entity [as conceptualized, or defined and described,] does not exist" (2008, 167–8).

Common Christian and Mormon apologetic defenses against the above five irresolvable contradictions lead, as argued below, to further incoherencies given the Mormon god's alleged nature, powers, and purposes in relation to a very creative and logical set of plausible human alternatives to the existing state of affairs. Indeed the very need for, and existence of, non-authoritative 'apologetics' with its accompanying rationalizations and *ad hoc* interpretations, explanations, and excuses for god and his 'Word' constitute a significant (and rather obvious) problem for the Mormon belief in continuous and progressive revelation to living prophets, or the Christian belief in the completeness of god's revelation to man.

The Problem of Evil

The classic, perennial problem of evil entails the apparent incoherence of the claimed existence of a god who is a sufficiently-to-all-knowing, powerful, loving, and morally perfect being, given the extent of nonsensical and extreme human and animal suffering and premature death in the world that can be attributed to both *natural* and *immoral human* causes. Stated differently in the context of this particular work, the troubling question indicative of this problem is how a god as conceptualized in the Mormon faith could either inflict or otherwise tolerate or allow the extreme suffering and premature death of his putative children.

Regarding the latter cause first, and under a narrower conception of this problem involving only the suffering and premature death of human beings, the bedrock apologetic 'Free Will Defense' (FWD) is particularly troublesome for both the Mormon and non-Mormon believer. This is so even if given, for the sake of argument, the reality of indeterministic free will — a 'given' which is, as noted below, arguably false or incoherent.

Regarding such a defense, how can we make sense of the Mormon doctrine that claims the existence of 'eternal intelligences' possessing free will as an inherent capacity? How could such a claim regarding the existence of such intelligences and of innate, indeterminist free will possibly be rationally justified (or even justifiable) as a truth claim indicative of an objective reality? Further, how can the very concept of eternal, contra-causal free will (or 'free agency') be considered coherent, given our best knowledge and the absence of broad reflective consensus regarding the topic?[142] In other words, what is the warrant for asserting — *with certainty* no less — the existence of contracausal (or indeterministic) free will, or of free will at all?[143] Or for doctrinally asserting, as some so-called orthodox

---

142 See, for significant, dissenting views, the work of Double 1990; Pereboom 2001; Wegner 2002; Honderich 2002; Dennett 2003; and Flanagan 2002 and their references and bibliographies.

143 The arguments on both sides of the free will debate are extensive and, from my assessment, most compelling on the side of hard incompatibilism or determinism. Recently, in the Introductory essay to *Essays on Free Will and Moral Responsibility* (2008), Editors and contributors Nick Trakakis and Daniel Cohen suggest, as "a way out" of the dilemma of circular debate on the question of "responsible action" and the existence of free will, that "...perhaps a closer look at the Wittgensteinian 'solution' to the problem of freedom and responsibility will throw new light on the matter" (xiv). Through the Wittgensteinian perspective, they argue, "...conflicts in the free will debate arise at least in part because the central notions involved in these debates have been divorced from their original contexts where they serve a primarily practical purpose, and have instead been made the basis for philosophical theories such as libertarianism and compatibilism" (xx).
This Wittgensteinian perspective on freedom and responsibility, as with religious faith, has its drawbacks and limitations, particularly in the Mormon life-form and language-game. My sense is that, all said, Wittgenstein would be no friend of a concept of free will which is embedded in the claimed literal existence of

Mormon apologists and philosophers have, that because man is indeterministically free their god does not have complete (and therefore sufficient) foreknowledge of every thought, desire, motive, intention, and decision to act of each and every person on earth? Or for asserting, as others might, that their god's putative foreknowledge necessarily (logically) contradicts man's putative free agency when it logically does not. (See Everitt 2004, 289–91)

Additionally, even if — solely for the sake of argument — such free will is, as Mormons believe, an eternal capacity *and* law which even their god cannot and would not directly limit, modify, or revoke, how is it, given that our *real* actions follow our *real* choices *in time*, that their god would not have sufficient warrant, given his *actual* degree of *knowledge* and *power,* to *somehow stop people from acting* on certain 'totally free' choices such that *sufficient* freedom of action is preserved? This question is addressed by Andrea Weisberger in *The Cambridge Companion to Atheism*, who suggests that:

> We can easily draw a distinction between the ability to choose to act freely and the commission of those acts…We all have the experience of choosing to pursue goals that never came to pass, but this does not mean that our choices were not free simply because we were unaware of the inability, perhaps even the impossibility, of our choices being actualized. It seems perfectly reasonable to claim that one can choose freely without being able to actualize that choice, and it is this that seems sufficient for the attribution of free will…If we allow that free choice not need to include "being able to do otherwise" but rather exists if the condition of "being able to choose otherwise" is met, then we can question why God does not render choices to commit heinous evil unattainable. (2007, 178)

Elaborating on the conceptual premise of Weisberger's argument in the context of the theistic FWD, Steele writes:

---

other believed realities such as 'intelligences,' 'souls,' or 'spirits' and is literally regarded, as it is in certain religious life-forms and related language-games, as an *actual*, fundamental faculty of man's eternal soul or spirit, not unlike (by analogy) the faculties of reason or perception.

Moreover, when belief in the literal or objective existence of free will objectifies (reifies) it as an *actual* reality, it is fair game to subject such a belief, as a truth claim, to analytical scrutiny, and to argue, in virtue of both 'error theory' and naturalistic realism (see Chapter 1), for the falseness or incoherence of such a claim, as well as for the naturalistic alternative of hard incompatibilism.

The *p*hilosophical task, it seems to me, is to apply the therapeutic process wisely. To do so would not require a particular theory of meaning, but would require the practice of *p*hilosophy to not only contextualize their analyses and arguments, but to take a more holistic approach to the implications of certain language-games, attending to the interrelationships of our various language-games and how they affect each other in order to determine how, if at all, they hang together and affect our lives.

For example, the concept of free will in its primary religious (particularly theistic) context crosses over to the naturalistic realm and deeply affects our lives with its relationship to 'strong accountability' and the sense of guilt and (toxic) shame which come with authoritarian judgments of sin and sinfulness; righteousness and wickedness; worthiness and unworthiness; divine judgment and blessedness or retribution; and eternal salvation and damnation. The implications are vast for believers and, in my view, negatively consequential to human personal and social wellbeing. Here, as I see it, there should be no Wittgensteinian *quietism*, but rather rigorous *p*hilosophical analysis together with, as Nielsen suggests, "… a Deweyan-Rawlsian broadly historicist and contextualist forging of a wide and general reflective equilibrium." It is in this sense that arguments for hard incompatibilism (or at least compatibilism) are both relevant and important, even if perhaps not decisively, justified.

If we're to think about the whole notion of what it might mean to deny people free will or to take away their free will, we need to look at three different aspects of free will: the *exercise* of free will, the *scope* of free will, and the *capacity* for free will. When people speak of 'taking away someone's free will,' it is often unclear which of these terms is meant. And the Free Will Defense trades on this unclarity.

The *exercise* of free will is executing a chosen course of action. If...someone forcibly prevents me doing what I want [choose] to do, then I am prevented from exercising my free will in a specific way. My capacity for free will remains intact.

A person's *capacity* for free will is only of value because of exercises of free will, but preventing a particular exercise of free will does not detract from a person's capacity for free will. That is, a person prevented from doing a particular thing still 'has free will,' just as much as if they were not prevented. *Scope* for free will refers to the general conditions which make it possible to contemplate various courses of action.

It is a fact of life that specific exercises of our free will are continually being blocked off by circumstances, including the actions of other people...Yet this normal condition, in which we find our scope for free will narrowly restricted and our conceivable exercises of free will blocked off at almost every turn, is spoken of by the proponent of the Free Will Defense as one in which we retain all our free will. It seems then, that by saying that God leaves us with our free will, the proponent of the Free Will Defense must mean that we retain our *capacity* for free will. But...nobody is suggesting [in the atheological 'Argument from Evil'] that God should take away our capacity for free will, rather it is suggested [as Weisberger does above] that God, [if he exists, should prevent those who would do evil] from doing certain things which lead to a huge amount of appalling evil. (206–7)

This he allegedly can do and has done so *directly*, according to numerous scriptural accounts, throughout the history of man, and has also done *indirectly* by allegedly creating the world as he has and then allowing — on a daily basis — such preventive frustrations to the *exercise* of free will through the natural vicissitudes of mortal life.

This argument against the Christian FWD is particularly pertinent to Mormon theology, which asserts that both evil and free agency are uncreated or eternal, and that, consequently, according to Roberts, "God is not able to prevent evil and destroy the source of it, but he is not impotent, for he guides intelligences, notwithstanding evil, to kingdoms of peace and security" (1975, 14). Yet, while theologically the Mormon god allegedly cannot act against the eternal law of free agency, he nonetheless allegedly has, according to Mormon theology, sufficient knowledge and power to intervene on a real-time basis in the lives of his children to deliver them from suffering, temptation, and evil. Allegedly, he has done so — and continues to do so regularly — in the lives of faithful believers. Indeed, as referenced earlier, it is held that such perfect, or complete, knowledge and power are essential to the nature of this god in order to enable mankind to have faith in his existence.

Juxtaposing the doctrinal assertions that (1) 'God is not able to prevent evil' and (2) 'God has the power to deliver his children from evil, and has done so in the past and present' makes Weisberger's argument relevant to our analysis of Mormon theology and supports the conclusion that such a theology is at least apparently self-contradictory or incoherent, if not actually so.

Other relevant objections to the FWD exist, three of which are suggested by Steele below, including:

- "Evil Outcomes from Non-Evil Decisions," where "Many human evils are the outcome of actions arising from mistakes due to acceptance of false theories because of limited knowledge," or because certain persons "are so circumstanced [psychologically and environmentally] that any of the alternative courses of action they select will lead to evil outcomes." This objection correctly observes that "[what] is often taken for granted by proponents of the FWD is precisely that human acts leading to evil outcomes are morally wrong acts, that if everyone behaved perfectly morally [or according to a god's mind and will], evil outcomes would evaporate. And this is not true, because people can act morally [or in their minds consistent with their god's will], though mistakenly, with appalling results [a fact born out in Mormon history and in the personal lives of innumerable Mormons — including prominent Mormon leaders — who sincerely believed they were choosing the 'right' when they took a course of action which resulted in harmful, even devastating, outcomes]. Although there is something [unethical] about [acting on] limited knowledge [about oneself and one's beliefs], virtually motivated action guided by a false but sincerely held theory [or belief], which is the best available to the person in a given situation (including that person's limited intellect [and psychological state]), [are not only preventable by a god, but] cannot be [deemed] morally wrong" (197–8).

- "Free Will and a Guarantee of Goodness," where the argument is made that "[if the Mormon god allegedly] combines," in virtue of His putative 'divine nature', "free will with a guarantee against ever committing evil, then it cannot be impossible to combine free will with a guarantee against [man] ever committing evil.... What is the quality that God possesses," Steele asks, "making it [theologically] unthinkable for him to do any evil, that could not be conferred on [or is not inherent in] humans...? Whatever it may be, it is not free will.... Theists often claim," Steele correctly asserts, "that it is God's nature that rules out the possibility of his doing anything wrong." Therefore, Steele argues, on the basis of traditional Christian theology, "God should have created humans with a nature that ruled out the possibility of their doing anything wrong" (200). This objection is not relevant to Mormon theology with respect to the implied idea that the Mormon god created man in the classical sense. Still, it is particularly relevant to Mormon theology in a different sense of the concept of 'spiritual creation,' since: (1) 'All God's children' are theologically considered colloquially as 'God's in embryo,' or eternal 'spirits and intelligences' capable of deification, and (2) the 'Divine Nature' is, according to Mormon theology, available to all humans — 'God's children' — in this life who receive and exercise faith in Christ sufficient to be baptized by water and by the Spirit through receipt of the Gift of the Holy Ghost. Those who are therefore 'baptized of fire and of the Holy Ghost' — or 'Born of God' through 'spiritual rebirth' — receive thereby 'a mighty change of heart' such that they have (according to Mormon scripture) "no more disposition to do evil, but to do good continually" (Mosiah 5:2). This theological belief raises the same basic question Steele implicitly does: Why doesn't the Mormon god transform or spiritually regenerate *all* mankind such that *every* person would 'put on Christ,' or the 'Divine Nature,' through the 'Baptism of fire and of the Holy Ghost?' Relatedly, why would such a necessary transformation need to be earned or sought after in faith, or be denied to so many who sincerely seek it, as is no doubt the case?

- "Persuasive Intervention by God," where, as Steele argues, "[there] are various ways in which person A can interact with B, and influence B's behavior without taking away B's free will. Most notably, A can supply information, A can persuade, and A can advise. It does not matter here whether A is God or someone else" (203–4). The objection here, of course, is that while according to Mormon theology, direct revelation from God to man is available to all, and while there are numerous examples in the Standard Works (Mormon scriptures) of the Mormon religion where the Mormon god *did* persuade men to change their course to avoid error, danger, and harm, there are no doubt innumerable living examples where such intervention was not forthcoming, even in reply to prayer. To invoke the FWD in such situations would be inconsistent.

Serious problems exist as well for other apologetic answers explaining why a god allows moral evil — problems which will be evident in the analytical questions asked in response to such answers below. But first, let's address briefly the cause of extreme human and animal suffering and premature death cited first above, *i.e.* the prevalence of what has come to be known and referred to as *natural evil*, or the suffering, death, and destructiveness caused by natural phenomena, including the inadvertent human actions that, by definition, are not intentionally or willfully enacted by man to do harm.

Regarding 'Natural Evil'

This aspect of the 'problem of evil' is perhaps most classically framed by the Greek Philosopher Epicurus, who wrote: "Is God willing to prevent evil, but not able? Then he is not omnipotent. Is he able, but not willing? Then he is malevolent. Is he both able and willing? Then whence cometh evil? Is he neither able nor willing? Then why call him God?"

Stated differently, but with the same ultimate conclusion, this problem of natural evil is concisely framed by Weisberger who writes: "If it is possible to show that [or even reasonably conceive of a world where] the suffering [and premature death] that exists could exist in less abundance, then some suffering [and death] is unnecessary, or gratuitous, and is unaccounted for by the [concept of 'God']. Therefore, the existence of natural evil must be somehow justified if the [concept of 'God'] is to maintain plausibility" (171).

Here we must come to terms with the at least apparent incoherence of 'God' as believed and worshipped — *i.e.* a god whose fundamental nature, or attributes and qualities, are capable of eliciting and preserving enduring love and trust — in relation to such occurrences as, for example, the unremitting and excruciating suffering of terminal illness or physical trauma. We must try to reconcile that concept of 'God' with the millions of men, women, and children who suffer and die in natural disasters like the Indonesian tsunami in 2004, hurricane Katrina in 2005, and the more recent earthquake in Haiti; or, as we shall come to later in this chapter in relation to the 'problem of prayer,' the millions of innocent babies who suffer and die terrible deaths each year in impoverished countries because of disease and malnutrition; or even the vast extent of animal suffering and death in the world.

To argue as many theistic apologists and believers do that such seemingly senseless, purposeless, and preventable suffering and death are justified for some short- or long-term good, or are necessary as a counterpart to good, or are necessary as a test of faith, or as punishment for sin, or as a necessary warning, or exist merely as a necessary by-product of the physical laws of nature or the universe — or, finally, occur for reasons we as mere humans cannot possibly understand or appreciate — is to raise more questions than answers; it effectually minimizes the 'power and goodness of God' as conceptualized and/or believed.

Ironically in relation to the first argument presented above, even the humane intervention of theistic believers on behalf of the suffering caused by natural disaster tacitly betrays their doubt and makes their belief in their god, and their belief that their god acts through them and others, incoherent. After all, if such a god, as believed, is all knowing, he would necessarily know *in advance* the occurrence of natural disaster and the extent and severity of the suffering and death which would ensue. If a god is all-powerful as believed, he would necessarily be able to *prevent* the foreknown occurrence and consequences of natural disaster, either directly by the power of his word, or indirectly by at least warning and empowering humans to avoid such imminent danger. And finally, if a god, as believed, is all-good and all-wise and acts with purpose, wisdom, and goodness in all things, then clearly when such natural disaster strikes and unknowing, powerless, or innocent people and animals suffer and die as a result, it is necessarily because he wants and chooses it to be so for reasons and a purpose which are allegedly 'wisdom in him.'

If such is the case, and it necessarily must be, given such beliefs, then it would seem — contrary to the apologetic and utterly incoherent belief commonly held that 'God' is not absent in the face of such catastrophe, but rather is present in spirit and action through the merciful efforts of faithful humans to comfort and save the suffering and those in peril — that those believers who act to alleviate human suffering and death from natural disasters necessarily do so *contrary to the will, wisdom, and purposes of their god.*

Such believed 'God-induced action' (in virtue of the incoherent notion of the 'spirit' of their 'God' working 'in and through them') makes their god utterly incoherent, and their faith in their god's goodness, wisdom, power, and love likewise incoherent. Apart from the conceptual incoherence of such beliefs, this is so in part because under such a conception of things their god would essentially have allowed such natural evil to occur with the *sure knowledge* that only a relatively *very* few of his fallible and virtually powerless mortal children would actually show up to help alleviate the terrible suffering and massive destruction of life which had *already* occurred, and which would yet *continue* to occur *even with* such human intervention. Given such a sorry state of affairs, what then could such relatively minimal and impotent (even if humane) acts of providing relief and rescue ultimately and truly amount to beyond being merely a manifestation of *natural* human compassion and/or self-interest? At bottom, isn't this once again a tacit betrayal of their own latent doubt in their god's believed existence? What, moreover, could incoherently invoking the 'hand of God' in characterizing such believed godly or Christian assistance ultimately and truly amount to? Is it not a tacit and pathetic apologetic attempt to preserve some illusion of rationality and intellectual integrity in maintaining the believer's regressive, infantile delusion that such an incoherent being could even exist, much less be worthy of worship as a celestial being in possession of *perfect* love and goodness for all?

But this is not all. Knowing the above, to counter, as many believers do, that their god allows natural disasters to occur in order, for example, to test the faith and/or build the godly character of suffering survivors or affected believers (whatever such 'godly character' could possibly mean, if anything) would be seriously problematical on at least two fronts.

First, such a counterargument would raise again the problem of the incoherence and reductive nature of 'faith in God' addressed at length in Chapter 6.

Second, it would make the putative goal of 'godly character building' utterly unintelligible given not only the cognitive meaninglessness of such a goal and its questionable incremental value in relation to its cost, but also the unarguable ability of a god alternatively to realize such a purpose (assuming, for the sake of argument, its intelligibility) *without* requiring such extreme devastation, loss, and suffering — or even *any* actual loss through death and destruction at all. To argue otherwise is to do so invalidly on the basis of *a priori* and *question-begging* assertions, including for example, the claim that if a god could accomplish such a goal without allowing such extreme suffering, death, and destruction, he would. Such a claim, if it is made, is not only invalid as an argument, but raises, as we shall learn below, serious, unanswerable questions in turn.

In short, belief in a test of faith or godly character building as moral justification for such preventable and devastating suffering, death, and loss would necessarily be incoherent, and the concept of a god who would *unnecessarily* test the unnecessary and insufficient faith of believers — at the unfathomable price of so much suffering, death and loss — to either prove their faithfulness or build godly character would also and necessarily be incoherent as well.

Beyond such obvious incoherencies, and before addressing the several aforementioned apologetic answers to the question "Why so much 'evil' and consequential suffering and loss through premature death in the world?" which follow, let us briefly examine yet another common, favored, and likewise futile attempt to reconcile the existence of a god as believed with the reality of natural evil as defined. Consider then the argument that natural evil is necessary as a counterpart to good.

To this argument we might ask, following Weisberger, "Is it *impossible* to *experience* pleasure without *experiencing* pain?" (172, emphasis mine) The implicit assertion related to this question seems, on its face, certainly false or incoherent. If it is applied to explain why a god would allow *moral* evil to exist to the detriment of others on the premise that, for example, only by allowing man to *experience* wickedness can he *experience* righteousness, the question becomes even more starkly problematic for Christians in particular. For we might reasonably ask how, through the putatively necessary *experience* of counterparts, could Christ, being impeccable or without sin as believed, experience *sinlessness* (as one who never personally sinned) without correspondingly having experienced *sinfulness* as one who *actually* sinned in act or desire? If it is objected that he need only to experience sinfulness *vicariously* or *virtually* (as Mormons believe he did in consequence of his atoning prayer in Gethsemane) through, perhaps, some mystical connection with actual sinners, then why, as believed, would *all* humans need to personally sin or even *directly* (*i.e.* non-vicariously or non-virtually) experience the effects of sin in the world in order to experience sinlessness or 'righteousness' through repentance?

If, on the other hand, this argument for the necessity of evil as a counterpart to good is, as Weisberger points out, "[i]nterpreted as an *epistemic distinction* (*i.e.*, to *know* what is good, we would need to *know* what is bad)" or, as Joseph Smith writes in the *Book of*

Mormon (2 Nephi 2: 11-15), an *existential imperative* (*e.g.* without evil, there could *be* no good), then, in either case, "it fares no better" (172, emphasis mine). This is obviously so in the first interpretation because, in the case of the suffering and destruction of animal life, such "[n]onhuman creatures [clearly]…derive no epistemic benefit from protracted and agonizing [suffering]" (172). And it is also obviously so, as we shall learn below in relation to our analysis of B.H. Roberts' use of the latter interpretation, because such a premise of existential imperative simply makes no sense as interpreted and, as an argument made from such a premise, is simply invalid both empirically and logically.

Nor do the other, above referenced arguments fare any better, where the theist is asked to explain, for example, how it is *known* (without *a priori begging the question* or invalidly *affirming the consequent*) that such suffering, death and destruction are *necessary*, or are allowed for some *unknown purpose* beyond our ability to understand or need to know? Or how is it *known*, beyond mere hopeful or judgmental speculation, inference, or arbitrary and projective attribution, that those who suffer and die prematurely because of natural evils do so to their 'eternal glory' and according to their 'foreordained' purpose, or *deserve* to do so because of sin (or conversely, how it is that those who are blatantly sinful do *not* likewise suffer, or live long lives)? What can the believer say when asked to explain how such deserts (or any reasons) apply, for example, to non-human animals that suffer and are killed in forest fires, earthquakes, or on roads by on-coming traffic? What answer can there be when the theist is asked to non-speculatively or unambiguously explain *exactly* what the putative *ends* or *goods* are which require such suffering and premature death? What justifies an all-loving, all-good, and all-powerful god's 'epistemic distance,' hiddenness, and lack of direct involvement in relieving his so-believed children of their intolerable suffering, or in delivering them from the premature death caused by such natural evils? When — minimally! — does he not clearly and definitively reveal to them *why exactly* such suffering and loss(es) are necessary or what *specific* purpose they serve or incremental goods they produce? Finally, the theist must be asked to explain, as has been asked earlier and shall be asked again below and in the next chapter, why *exactly* faith requires testing or *even exists*. These questions are problematical for the believing theist, both intellectually and morally.

Mormon Answers and More Troubling Questions

Still, as referred to above, there are additional questions and anticipated apologetic answers worthy of thoughtful consideration. To the paradigm question, then, concerning why, if the Mormon or Christian god indeed exists, is there *so much* human suffering and premature death through human and natural evil, I offer for consideration seven paradigm Mormon *answers* (**A1**–**A7**) — all of which, of course, predictably assume the coherence and factual intelligibility of the Mormon concept of 'God' and beg the question of the Mormon god's actual existence. I offer accordingly seven corresponding sets of follow-up *questions* (**Q1**–**Q7**), addressed solely for the sake of argument and sensible reflection:

A1: "Again, according to B.H. Roberts, 'Evil is not a created reality. It has always existed. … It is as eternal as goodness; it is as eternal as law; it is as eternal as [the existence] and agency of intelligences. Sin, which is evil active, is transgression of law, and so long as the agency of intelligences and law have existed [*i.e.* forever], the possibility of the transgression of law [and therefore, evil] has existed" (1995, Chapter XXVI, 6).

Q1: But the evil we're concerned with in the 'problem of evil' is the suffering and premature death caused, again, by either the *exercise* of human choice or by natural disasters and accidents or mishaps caused by human error or ignorance. We are not concerned with the putative and highly questionable 'eternal' *capacity* of human choice related to the heretofore determined factual unintelligibility of the Mormon concept of the eternal intelligence of man. Evil in the sense intended *is*, in fact, created by man *and* by natural causes and *can*, in fact, be prevented *and* stopped by the Mormon god on the basis of his allegedly and believed sufficient knowledge and power. This he can do *without* violating 'eternal laws' (whatever those are, if anything at all) or interfering with, or in *any way* nullifying, as argued above, man's 'free agency,' (or capacity for free choice) providing such a god has the *desire* to do so. And why would he not want to do so? (This last question leads to the answers and related questions which follow.)

A2: "As the Lord told Joseph Smith, '…all these things [i.e. trials and tribulations resulting from extreme suffering, loss and death caused by *moral* and *natural* 'evil'] shall give thee experience and shall be for thy good.'"

Q2: But what *specifically* and *intelligibly* is the human or eternal significance or value of such experience *over and above* the value of the goods acquired in virtue of the natural suffering experienced as part of the human condition *sans evil*? And what exactly *is* the *factually intelligible* 'good' that comes from such extreme suffering to those who suffer so egregiously, or which would morally justify, from any perspective in any possible world, the allowance of such suffering, where it could be, according to Mormon theology, prevented or alleviated? If such suffering is necessary to allegedly allow this god's children to fulfill their 'divine' potential (whatever that actually means, if anything), how can the suffering and premature death of infants, babies, and young children be intelligibly or coherently reconciled with the alleged necessity of such experience? In other words, how can those who suffer and die prematurely reasonably be said to have fulfilled their divine potential and the believed requirement for necessary mortal experience? How can we make rational sense of such a proposition?

A3: "God does not intervene to prevent human acts of evil because to do so would make 'justice' of no effect; would empty divine justice of significance and moral justification, or fairness. Moreover, it would effectually undermine human freedom, or would require God to have the type of foreknowledge which would necessarily make total freedom of choice or action impossible."

Q3: "But why is the *exercise* or *enactment* of choice necessary for justice to exist or be fair? The actual *exercise* of choice could (as argued earlier) be blocked by a sufficiently knowledgeable god, with appropriate restraint imposed and justice meted out, if indicated, or necessary, on the basis of *intention* or *choice* to do evil, as well as the mediating circumstances involved. Further (as also argued earlier), the *capacity* for free will does not necessarily depend on the *exercise* or enactment of every choice to exist. Even if, as suggested by some Mormon theologians and apologists, the Mormon god does not intervene because he does not have foreknowledge of man's choices (a minority position which is not widely accepted by Mormon believers or Church Authorities), surely such intervention to block the enactment of evil designs and choices, or, alternatively, revelatory intervention to persuade and warn, or restrain, probable offenders or warn probable victims, or convert all people to righteousness and the abhorrence of evil through the 'baptism of fire and of the Holy Ghost' does not require complete foreknowledge or nullify the person's putative free agency.

Even if such foreknowledge was, for some reason, required for the Mormon god to effectively intervene and does exist as an essential aspect of his putative omniscience (as many, if not most Mormons believe[144]), it would not logically, or necessarily, take away man's free agency. One opposing argument in this regard, if I correctly understand it, is simply that if, in fact, 'God' has complete foreknowledge, then man logically could not have the power of free will. This is so, the argument goes, because if a god had perfect foreknowledge, man's power of indeterministic free will would necessarily entail the power to change the god's past beliefs. Therefore, since no person has the power to change a god's beliefs, no person can have the capacity of free will if a god has perfect foreknowledge of man's acts and choices. (Ostler 1996)

Besides again begging again the question of all that is at issue (*i.e.* the existence of 'God' and 'eternal intelligences' and the 'eternal capacity of indeterministic free will'), this argument against the logical possibility of a god's putative foreknowledge, given the putative existence of man's eternal free will, is flawed at two levels. *First,* it is flawed because, as discussed earlier, it wrongly equates the *capacity* (power) for free choice and action with the *exercise* of such a capacity. And *second* because the Mormon doctrine of the Mormon god's omniscience and foreknowledge, factually unintelligible as it is, simply holds or presumes, as I understand it, that *whatever* a person does or chooses to do now or in the future is known by this god. In other words, this god putatively has a continuous knowledge and understanding of the *Gestalt* of all existence and therefore knows all truth homospatially or trans-temporally, or has the "knowledge of all things as they are, and as they were, and as they are to come" (D&C 93:24). Such truth, it is written, is present

---

144 Who — or so the neo-orthodox argument might go — among believing Mormons actually has faith in a god whom they really believe would fairly judge them, yet does not surely know (or cannot perfectly discern) all their deepest thoughts, needs, and desires? Alternatively, who among Mormons believes their god does not have the perfect knowledge, foreknowledge, power, or desire required to, for example, foresee and prevent every and all possible, potential or actual, immanent threats to human life, the earth, and the Plan of Salvation if he will? At a more personal level, who among the Mormon faithful believes their god does not have the knowledge, power, and love sufficient to stop them from going astray against their will or deliver them and/or their loved ones from peril, suffering, temptation, and evil? Moreover, on a more global level, who among Mormon theists believes their god cannot, in virtue of his believed omniscience and omnipotence, ultimately defeat or prevail over evil, and prevent the destruction, suffering, and premature death caused by evil and ensure salvation to all? Who thinks he does not have the power to reveal the Absolute Truth of his nature, existence, mind, and will, and the truth of all things pertaining to the salvation of all mankind to all men? Finally, from an omnibus perspective, who among the faithful who pray actually believes that the god they worship and to whom they pray is not perfect (or whole, complete) in every sense? Whose god is not *all*-knowing, *all*-powerful, *everywhere*-present and *all*-good, loving, wise, and just without limiting qualifications?

always before the eyes of 'God' [as one eternal now]. (D&C 38:2; Moses 1:6) Under this conception, this god's beliefs regarding what men will do are not 'beliefs' at all. Rather, they constitute perfect knowledge that is *not* independent of the actual choices and actions of men, *whatever* they might be.

Further, with respect to the more conventional argument that a god's putative fore-knowledge necessarily nullifies free will, Nicholas Everitt correctly argues: "If God fore-knows that I will do [or choose to do] X, then it follows that I *do* not do [or choose to do] not-X. What does not follow is that I *cannot* [or am compelled to] do [or choose to do] not-X. What knowledge of a proposition requires is the truth of the proposition known; it does not require the *necessary* truth of the proposition. ... Events [*whatever* they might be] are truth-makers for propositions; propositions are not necessitators of [choices or] events" (2004, 290–91).

A4: "Such suffering builds 'Godly character' in the sufferers."

Q4: What *specifically* and *intelligibly is* 'Godly character,' or what is it like? What *specific* attributes or qualities of character are allegedly built which can *only* be acquired, or developed, through such extreme *actual* suffering instead of, say, through less actual suffering or, perhaps, virtual suffering through, for example, 'Scrooge-like' transformational dreams or hallucinations? And what *specifically* — beyond mere assertion or presumption — is the human or eternal value of such incremental character development in any case or all cases, which would morally justify such extreme suffering? Further, and relatedly, as Steele asks and then correctly observes, "Is the amount of evil [enacted] sufficiently paid for by the noble actions it evokes? Does the perfectly benevolent God perceive a moral profit on the deal? Are the Holocaust or natural disasters fully paid for by the heroic efforts of resisters and rescuers? ... While bad events sometimes bring out the best in people, they far more often bring out the worst. ... Suffering is a school for vice more often than for virtue" (185).

A5: "Such suffering (including the anguish of not understanding why God did not — or does not — intervene), as a 'test of faith,' enables the 'faithful' to 'prove their faith' and thereby acquire a profound self-knowledge and eternal life, which could not be attained otherwise."

Q5: But what would such "profound self-knowledge" and "eternal life" *actually* and *specifically* consist of and why is such *incremental* self-knowledge *necessary*? What *specifically* is the human or even eternal value of such *incremental* self-knowledge beyond the extent of self-knowledge gained naturally through much less severe or extreme experiences? Additionally and significantly, why test believers, for example, on their unquestioning loyalty, obedience, or endurance based on personal faith rather than, alternatively, and for example, on the basis of their well-informed judgment based on knowledge and reason? Or why test *at all* if the outcome is either foreknown by a god (as is commonly believed; see **Q3** above) or even, at least, predicted with a near-certain probability (a less common and more problematical view)?

If the god in question does not have sufficient foreknowledge, for example, of whether or not a person will ultimately endure in the faith or 'believe in God, repent, and come unto Christ' and be 'saved,' how, in principle, would such a god then know with the required certainty beforehand how the person will react when he is tried or tested? How, in other words, would a god know with required certainty that any severe trial or test would or would not backfire, resulting in a total forsaking of the faith and/or a turn to wickedness? And how would a god manage such risk if he doesn't sufficiently know how the person will respond to subsequent acts of divine intervention?

If physical intervention is needed — on the basis of perfect foreknowledge or not — to stop or block a person from performing a particular act (as, for example, in the paradigm case of Abraham attempting to carry through the sacrifice of Isaac), wouldn't such a physical intervention (to be consistent with the FWD) interfere with the person's exercise of free will? If a god reveals directly or through others that the ordeal is only a test, how would he sufficiently know that such a disclosure would forestall the person's decision to forsake the faith and/or turn to wickedness? Isn't such probabilistic knowledge or foreknowledge really nothing but a well-educated or informed guess? If so, then (following Mormon Prophet Joseph Smith) is such a *limited* god worthy of worship or an adequate object of unqualified, sacrificial faith?

Alternatively, if knowledge of the person's unquestioned loyalty and unwavering faith in the face of any adversity is meant for the *person* to have and *not* for the god (because he putatively knows the end from the beginning), why couldn't such knowledge simply be revealed to the person in a way which is experienced as self-knowledge and which produces the god's putatively intended salutary affect? Further, aren't believers revealed to themselves through *all* their experiences, whether or not they are faith-based or faith-promoting? If so, then what categorical truths *specifically* do they learn about themselves (beyond what they might otherwise learn about themselves in virtue of their unexceptional life experiences) by enduring in the faith other than that their faith and hope has endured? Why would this knowledge be essential, other than for allegedly assuring themselves that they are acceptable to, or approved (or 'justified') by their god?

But if believers are tested so that *they* might know they are accepted and approved, or justified, by their god — that their faith is sufficient to him — and if he, through his omniscience, knows the extent of their faith and who they are with a complete knowledge and can moreover reveal such knowledge through what Mormon theology refers to as "the more sure word of prophesy," then why is a test necessary? Why would even a *virtual* test be necessary?

A6: "Such suffering is allowed so people will be humbled and come (or return) unto Christ and so God can prove them to see if they will keep all his commandments."

Q6: But, again, what of those who *aren't* humbled, but instead are *hardened* by such extreme and excessive suffering and loss, or are disillusioned and, in either case, lose or turn away from faith and belief in 'God'? If that god knows who will lose or turn away from faith or will not return to the faith then why would he allow them to be tested or tried through such suffering beyond their ability to endure such suffering — particularly if he knew they would turn from faith or lose their faith *because* of such unremitting suffering? If a god does not or cannot know or foreknow who will turn from faith or lose their faith, then how can he know what intervention is necessary and when to surely manage the risk of losing a single individual to an excessive test or trial?

If, as is apologetically suggested, the name of the game with 'God' is 'ultimate victory' in the cosmic chess game of life, and that while "God [as the 'Master Chess Player'] may lose some pieces [or persons] during the games" [because of the misuse of their free agency], he will nonetheless "guarantee ultimate victory" in the games, "not because of his omniscience, but because of his almighty power" (Ostler, 1996), then what *actually* and *intelligibly* constitutes ultimate victory? And how many pieces must be lost before such "ultimate victory" is lost? And how is it that such so-called *pieces* (individuals) — considered by the Mormon god, according to President Brigham Young and others as being "worth worlds" or, in other words, of being of inestimable worth to 'God, their Father' — are thus so expendable? Are you therefore expendable? Or your children? And if not you or your children, then who? And if no one of his putative "children" is truly expendable in the eyes of the Mormon god, then how can these two putative attributes of the Mormon god — his *omniscience* and his *almighty power* — be disconnected in the effectual management of risk of loss of individuals due to unforeseen choices made and actions taken in consequence of such tests of faith? Finally, how can this particular explanation intelligibly explain or morally justify the extreme suffering of those who are regarded by those in the faith as humble, meek and faithful?

And again, regarding the Mormon god's alleged intent to 'prove' believers to see if they will keep all his commandments, why would he need to test believers beyond what they must endure in the course of their natural lives? What *specific* and *intelligible* incremental benefits to him or to man could possibly accrue from such obedience or faith-testing that would morally or even pragmatically justify such testing and concomitant extreme suffering and loss? Moreover, of what real, intelligible value is such implicitly coerced or externally motivated obedience (no obedience — or failed test — no reward) as a test of the person's *internal* (incentive-free) commitment to righteousness?

A7: "God's ways are not man's ways. His purposes in allowing such tortuous or extreme suffering, premature death and nonbelief are inscrutable and ultimately unknown to (or unknowable by) man."

Q7: Apart from the incoherence of claiming that the Mormon god works in mysterious ways, we must ask how, apart from the factual unintelligibility of the concept of the Mormon god as stated and believed, can anyone know that he is working at all if his ways are a mystery? How can anyone know when he is working and when he is not? Why should anyone believe that this putative god has such secret, hidden, or unknown or unknowable purposes? Why should such putative purposes be unknown *or* unknowable to man, given their at least *apparent* contradiction to those essential divine attributes and qualities (*i.e.* knowledge, power, love, truth, and constancy) necessary to enable men to worship and exercise faith in their god's existence? How can this all be, given, as well, the alleged reality and putative existence of divine 'revelation from God to man,' and given the fact that man's putative intelligence is co-eternal with 'God' and is therefore endowed or capacitated naturally, as a 'spirit child of God,' to receive and understand such revelation? How can this all be, given, finally, that mortal man, according to Mormon theology, is putatively enabled, by 'the grace of God' (through 'spiritual transformation' — or 'sanctification' and 'transfiguration' — and the receipt of the 'Gift of the Holy Ghost') to understand the 'mind and will of God' and ultimately (in the next life) become 'even as God is'?

But even if it is conceded, solely for the sake of argument, that some 'unknown purpose' *might* exist, isn't it more reasonable to conclude that: (1) since there is *no* alleged or believed greater good than the Mormon god's putatively self-revealed Work and Glory to "bring to pass the immortality and eternal life of man;" that (2) since this Work and Glory of ensuring man's salvation is allegedly the Mormon god's *greatest* desire and that, following Victor Cosculluela's argument, given the necessary omniscience of the Mormon (and Christian) god, the obtaining of this desire is necessarily better than the obtaining of any other, incompatible state of affairs (2006, 365); that (3), given **A5** and **Q5** above, by 'God' allowing such excessive, extreme, and unremitting suffering without prevention, relief, or deliverance, he *knowingly* undermines (or places at risk) the realization of his greatest desire as established in (2) above for those who turn away from God because of a perceived betrayal of trust and/or disillusionment; and that (4), as asserted above in this chapter, there are no known or conceivable good reasons for the Mormon god *not* to intervene somehow to prevent, lessen, or relieve the excessive and extreme suffering and premature death due to human and natural evil, then again, from the perspective of orthodox Mormon theology, isn't it more reasonable to conclude that the traditional 'argument from evil' prevails?

Alternatively, isn't it more reasonable to conclude, appropriating from Krueger, following Epicurus, that "regardless of the reason, whether it is known or unknown [to man], either god does not *want* to [prevent or relieve such extreme suffering and premature death more than he wants something of necessarily lesser value], in which case god is not [by human standards] all-good; god does not *know how* to [lawfully prevent or relieve such suffering and carnage], in which case he is not *all-knowing*, or god is *unable* to bring about [a world with less suffering and premature death], in which case god is not all-powerful" (1998, 201)? If so, then given the questions in **Q6** (which are arguably self-answering), including the argued answer, or conclusion, from the question asked in relation to premises (1)–(4) above, isn't therefore, the very apologetic claim of God's 'unknown purposes' unintelligible? And doesn't such an unintelligible claim thereby further support the conclusions reached that Mormon theology, including, at its core, the very concept of the Mormon god, is incoherent and irrational?

Clearly, even when Madsen answers the question "Why, then, is there evil?" by stating, in the context of Roberts' work, "The answer is, that it is a necessary and eternal part of 'the dramatic whole [consisting of both good and evil intelligences in necessary opposition,]'" (1975, 14), we are left to conclude, or at least reasonably suspect, that Joseph Smith needed to invent 'eternal intelligences with free agency' and, by extension, 'eternal evil' as "a necessary and eternal part" of "the dramatic whole" in order to make sense of his doctrine of 'God and his Plan of Salvation.' But, ironically, and even regardless, in attempting to do so, Mormon theology (*pace* Roberts and Widtsoe) is plunged into deeper incoherency and irrationality by the doctrine of eternal intelligences and by the invalid premise that the experience of peace, security, and hope may never be realized except by the 'conquest over evil' through 'divine guidance.'

Such an assertion, as well as the alleged existence of evil as a necessary antithesis of good, is again, as a putative truth claim, wholly unwarranted, for even if divine guidance — which presupposes the factual existence of a god and revelation — was even possible, which it is not, because both the concept of the Mormon god and the concept of 'revelation from God to man' are (as we have seen) incoherent and factually insignificant as truth claims, clearly the *existence* of evil is not (*pace* Roberts) necessary to the *existence* of good or non-evil. For as Steele correctly observes: "A quality may hold for every existing thing, and its absence or opposite might hold for nothing at all." Just as, for example, "[awareness] of time, measurement of time, discussion of time's attributes [are all] entirely feasible without there being anything timeless," so too "[there] is no conceptual problem about a universe lacking in actual evil, whether or not we suppose that in such a universe anyone comes up with an idea of evil" (184).

Roberts, of course, would disagree. Expounding doctrinally on the Mormon teaching that "there must needs be an opposition in all things" such that there could not be good if there is no bad (or evil), or righteousness if there were no wickedness, and therefore, without such opposites the 'wisdom, eternal purposes, power, mercy, and justice of God' would be "destroyed" (2 Nephi 2:11) Roberts argues:

> This [scriptural teaching] may be regarded as a very bold setting forth of the doctrine of antinomies, and yet I think the logic of it, and the inevitableness of the conclusion unassailable. As there can be no good without the antinomy of evil, so there can be no evil without its antinomy, or antithesis — good. The existence of one implies the existence of the other: and, conversely, the non-existence of the latter would imply the non-existence of the former. (1976, 131)

But, as argued above, while contrast (or opposition) is essential to establish the factual significance of a statement, or an understanding of a concept, it is *not* necessary, *pace* Roberts, to establish actual existence. More specifically, and again, the actual *existence* of evil is not necessary for good to *exist*.[145] So too, it may reasonably be argued, with the putative existence of 'righteousness,' 'wickedness,' 'happiness,' 'sorrow,' or any other set of so-called 'antinomies' Roberts refers to.

Furthermore, Roberts' argument is certainly invalid since he concludes that the alleged eternal existence of such 'antinomies' (opposites) is necessarily true because 'God' and all his putative creation in fact exist. But Roberts' argument is irremediably flawed for three reasons. *First*, it begs the question by presupposing the existence of 'God' (as well as the coherence of the concept of 'God' in Mormon theology) as well as the truthfulness of the *Book of Mormon* whence comes this 'doctrine of opposites.' *Second*, it attempts to establish the validity of this doctrine by invalidly affirming the consequent, a fallacy which in this case overlooks other, more sensible naturalistic explanations for the existence of the

---

145 This refutation of the argument that "physical good (*e.g.* pleasure) is not possible without physical evil (*e.g.* pain and suffering)" is also briefly but convincingly addressed by H.J. McCloskey in Angeles (1997, 208–9). In his refutation, McCloskey argues that "pleasure and pain are not correlatives" and that "… [i]t is clear that pain is possible in the absence of pleasure. It is true that it might not be distinguished by a special name and called 'pain,' but the state we now describe as a painful state would nonetheless be possible in the total absence of pleasure." To illustrate, McCloskey asks: "Can it seriously be maintained that if an individual were born crippled and deformed and never in his life experienced pleasure, that he could not experience pain, not even if he were severely injured?"

"heavens and the earth and all things that in them are." And t*hird*, Roberts' metaphysical belief, or *meta-belief* (which is shared by most, if not all, believing Mormons and Christians alike) that 'good,' 'evil,' 'righteousness,' 'wickedness,' and other normative properties are objective realities, is false or incoherent. Such putative realities do not, according to error-theorists, exist as objective, independent, empirical realities that are inherent in the natural world. As Nielsen reminds us, "[normativity] in reality, though not in the beliefs *about* normativity of many people, is a matter of feeling and attitudes. It is not something there to be discovered as a property of actions or things. What we actually have are states of affairs (purely empirical matters), attitudes toward those states of affairs, and the actions generated by these attitudes" (2001, 40–41).

In the end, in addition to all of the above regarding the problem of evil, Loftus addresses what might be considered the final defensive appeal by Christians (and Mormons) to rescue their god from utter incoherence and resolve this contradiction once and for all. In this final appeal — what Loftus refers to as the "ignorance defense" (2008, 256) — "Theists claim everything will work out from the perspective of eternity. They claim the sufferings of this present life are not worthy to be compared with the joys of eternity. But this presupposes what needs to be shown. We are on this side of heaven and hell, and from here we want to know if there really is a heaven and hell [or different 'kingdoms of glory' (D&C 76)]. From here we just don't know" (256). Such a fact, of course, simply compounds the problem of theistic belief. For how, and for what good reason, would such a truth remain hidden to all (even to staunch believers who wrongly claim they *know*), by a god who could so easily confirm the existence of an afterlife, so that its existence could be known perfectly by all without the need for faith.[146]

Loftus continues: "In the absence of good reasons [for the extreme sufferings and losses of this life], the final state, even if pleasant for all of us, only compensates us for the evils experienced in this life. But compensation for suffering cannot [morally or otherwise] justify the suffering endured: otherwise, anyone could be justified in torturing another person so long as the victim is later compensated (257).

"Theists say God has a higher morality than we do such that God is not bound by the same ethical obligations as we are, because he has 'higher purposes.' Whatever this higher morality and higher purposes are, we don't have a clue [although certainly he could easily reveal them to us to help us make sense of our and others' suffering and pre-mature death and prevent us from falling out of faith because of his silence and doubt regarding his believed existence] (258).

"At this point, the whole notion of God's goodness means nothing to us at all…The bottom line is that the evidence of intense suffering [and premature death] in the world is an empirical refutation of the theistic conception of God [including the Mormon god, as argued and concluded above] (259).

"Is it ever rational," Loftus asks, "to believe against the evidence?" and then answers, "I don't think so…All theistic attempts to fully justify the evil in the world [including the apologetic attempts by Mormon apologists and theologians to appeal to incoherent and factually unintelligible concepts like 'eternal intelligences with free agency'] can be likened to a physicist trying to create cold fusion. The naysayers have the weight of

---

146 The question "why faith?" is addressed in Chapter 6 through the author's argument for the non-necessity of faith.

evidence behind them (259).

Loftus concludes at a visceral level, in a way which clears away all the nonsense and appeals powerfully to common sense and basic human sensibilities, through the words of Dostoyevsky, Voltaire, and John Stuart Mill.

> If the Christian [and Mormon] still wants to maintain that there is a good purpose for all human suffering [and pre-mature death], then let her also consider what Ivan Karamazov, Fyodor Dostoyevsky's character said: "Tell me yourself — I challenge you: let's assume that you were called upon to build an edifice to destiny so that men would finally be happy and would find peace…tranquility [and joy]. If you knew that, in order to attain this, you would have to torture just one single creature, let's say a little girl who beat her chest so desperately in the outhouse, and that on her unavenged tears you could build that edifice, would you agree to do it? Tell me and don't lie!"
>
> In light of all that has been said, listen to Voltaire: "The silly fanatic repeats to me…that it is not for us to judge what is reasonable and just in the great Being, that His reason is not like our reason, that His justice is not like our justice. What!? How do you want me to judge justice and reason otherwise than by the notions I have of them? Do you want me to walk otherwise than with my feet, and to speak otherwise than with my mouth?"
>
> John Stuart Mill forcefully concludes as I do: "In everyday life I know what to call right and wrong, because I can plainly see its rightness and wrongness. Now if a god requires that what I ordinarily call wrong in human behavior I must call right because he does it; or that what I ordinarily call wrong I must call right because he so calls it, even though I do not see the point of it; and if by refusing to do so [or to act accordingly], he can sentence me to hell, to hell I will gladly go." (259)

The problem of evil is a non-starter for those who accept the fact that the concept of 'God' is unintelligible, incoherent, and factually meaningless as a truth claim; that 'God' is, as conceptualized and believed, a factual non-reality. For those, however, who still consider their claims of their god's existence justifiable, the existence of evil is a real, vexing, and I think irresolvable problem — philosophically, empirically, and experientially.

At an experiential level suffering affects believers viscerally when it is *they*, or those who are closest to them, who are suffering terribly without relief or deliverance, or when *they* lose children or loved ones to premature death notwithstanding the exercise of their faith. During such times, religious apologetics avail little or no comfort. The anguish is often made worse when the sufferer suffers what seems to be a betrayal from their silent or absent god. If, through fear, guilt, dissociation and infantile regression and rapprochement induced by prayer and the apologetic and nurturing 'ministrations' of others in the faith, their faith remains intact or they return to their waning or lost faith, they will confidently assert that their god did not (in their case) and will not in *any* case try the faith of the faithful beyond their ability to endure. But if their faith — or the faith of others among the faithful — does *not* endure, what can be made of such an assertion? When do exceptions finally bring the 'certain witness' or 'testimony' of the faithful into serious question? When is doubt finally justified for the believer who hangs stubbornly and irrationally to his faith? Perhaps, again in the words of Nietzsche, "People who understand something in all its depth rarely remain faithful to it forever. They have brought its depths to light; and there is always a great deal to see that is bad" [and, I might add, false or incoherent] (Metcalf 1996, 225). If so, then perhaps there is still hope for the truly faithful believers that live their religion to its depths, for perhaps again, denials to the contrary notwithstanding, it is *in* the depths of the truly faithful theist that the greatest doubt resides in sedated repose.

The Problem of Faith Revisited

Although the problem of faith was treated at length and in depth in the previous chapter, it seems appropriate here to return again, from a different angle, to the question of why 'faith in God and Christ' is necessary as a requirement for salvation. To this question the Mormon believer or apologist would likely answer: "Because salvation requires knowing God and Christ (John 17:3) and the *only* way for man to *know* God and Christ is by faith." But apart from the fact that such an answer at least *appears* to be nothing more than an unwarranted assertion, and apart from the problem (addressed in Chapter 6) of regarding faith as a legitimate source of knowledge (or way of knowing), how can 'man' exercise faith in that which he cannot literally make sense of — *i.e.* the concept of 'God' and, by substitution, the 'Son of God'?

To this follow-up question (which was also addressed in some depth in the previous chapter) one standard answer might be that man cannot fully understand the concept of 'God' in its fulness, but needs only a *sufficiently true understanding* of 'God' to have or receive a 'saving faith in God and Christ.' But again — or so the argument must go — how is it possible to obtain a 'sufficiently true' or literal understanding of an unknown being, the concept of which in the case of the Mormon god is unintelligible, incoherent, and factually meaningless as stated and believed — and therefore not literally understandable or knowable? Even if, solely for the sake of argument, the concept of 'God' is understandable and coherent, what specifically counts as being 'sufficiently true' in relation to such required understanding?

The believer's answer to this question might be that such an understanding is sufficiently true if and only if the person has experienced and enjoys the 'gift of faith' by the grace and power of a god. But apart from assuming that the concept and claimed reality of 'divine grace' is not question-begging (which it is), and is intelligible or cognitively meaningful (which it is not), how specifically, or on the basis of what specific, objective, and generally accepted (justified) human criteria can the putative receipt of such 'faith in God and Christ' be justifiably differentiated from those alternative depth-psychological or naturalistic characterizations of faith presented in the previous chapter? If the answer to this question is given — without again begging the question or affirming the consequent (which it does) — that such differentiation can be made in virtue of the intrinsic nature and 'fruits,' or affects and effects, of the personal faith-experience itself and its 'confirmation by the Holy Spirit,' then we are brought back again *via* Ockham's Razor to the more parsimonious, naturalistic explanations and interpretations of such putative affects and effects, as well as the various *p*hilosophical problems with the concepts of revelation and 'spiritual confirmation' treated earlier.

It is clear, on the basis of our earlier analytical inquiry into the Mormon concepts of 'revelation' and 'faith,' that the claim of faith as an alleged requirement for salvation being dependent on merely *sufficient* understanding of the otherwise unintelligible concept of the Mormon god is highly problematical at least, and incoherent and irrational at worst. Even so, there is yet another problem. If, again solely for the sake of argument, it is granted that

(i) 'God' is an intelligible, coherent, and factually meaningful concept (which it is not), and that, therefore, (ii) faith in god is possible (which it is not) and is in fact necessary for man to know god as a requirement for salvation; and if, as well, (iii) those who allegedly have faith in him are said to *somehow* 'know God and Jesus Christ' and believe they are in possession of a *correct* idea and understanding of their god's divine nature (as they would likely assert with certainty and sure conviction), then how is it that among all who profess to have such faith and would claim to have been saved in virtue of their faith, there are so many different and conflicting conceptions of 'God' and the Godhead? If it is answered that though the various concepts of 'God' might differ or be in conflict among the faithful, yet they all essentially have faith in the same, 'one true God,' then all claims of 'knowing God' are essentially the same, notwithstanding the conceptual differences and conflicts. Moreover, or so the more liberal theistic answer might go, all who have faith in their god are saved regardless of how they might conceptualize or understand their god to be.

This answer would imply that the differences and errors of man regarding the concept of 'God' are of no significance or consequence to their god and that, in the end, it does not matter to their god which concept of 'God' people believe in, as long as they believe in the god of their particular faith or its scriptures. But apart from the problem of believing in something unintelligible and incoherent, or believing in the factual existence of a factual non-reality, is the problem of *faith-nullification*.

If, according to the above answer, *all* conceptualizations or private and ecclesiastical interpretations of 'God' are essentially true and acceptable to the 'one, true God,' and sufficient for the receipt of "saving" faith, then, following William James on the pragmatic insignificance of differences that make no difference,[147] the conceptual (and doctrinal) differences among the different faiths (and believers within the different faiths) regarding the character, perfections, attributes, and requirements of their gods make no real difference and therefore are not real, consequential differences at all.

Beyond the obvious problem with making all concepts of 'God' essentially true and sufficient objects of worship for salvation, thereby making the concept of the 'one, true God' factually vacuous through the absence of contrast (what, after all, would be a 'false God' under such a conception?), such a pragmatic nullification of the different God-concepts among different faiths and believers is also a nullification of the different faiths. This would particularly be so in those faiths like the Mormon faith which hold that they are the *one and only true faith* that saves souls, and that salvation comes *only* to those who worship the 'one true God' of that faith and receive the saving ordinances by those who have been duly authorized by their particular god to administer in Christ's one and only true Church.[148] And it is also a nullification of the faith of those believers of a different god, or of those theistic believers of various faiths who might be said to have never correctly or sufficiently 'known God or Jesus Christ' as conceptually understood in yet other theistic and Christian faiths.

Moreover, the existence of different faiths makes incoherent the claim 'faith is the only way to know God.' More specifically, the insistence by the adherents of different faiths

---

147 William James' unsourced saying that "A difference which makes no difference is no difference at all" certainly seems to apply here.

148 See McConkie's entry on "Worship" in *Mormon Doctrine*, 1979, p. 848.

that theirs is the only true faith and that their god is the 'only true God' and therefore, the only Way to salvation, makes their claim 'God can only be known by man through faith' incoherent, given all who profess to have faith in a *different* god within a *different* faith or theistic religion.

Finally, the very existence of different faiths, each with different and conflicting concepts of gods and revelations from them, would surely make this problem of faith-nullification — which is essentially equivalent to theistic Atheism — 'God's problem,' not man's. This fact consequently, and necessarily, makes *all* concepts of 'God' incoherent given the putative attributes and purposes of particular gods and the alleged eternal stakes involved.

The Problem of Prayer

Related to the irresolvable problem of evil and the likewise irresolvable problem of the incoherence, non-necessity, and insufficiency of 'faith in God' addressed in part above and again in far greater depth in Chapter 6, is, once again, the aforementioned problem of prayer *per se*, and petitionary and intercessory prayer in particular. As I see it, the problem of prayer can be expressed in the following three sets of critical questions, as follows:

- *First*: Regarding prayer *per se*, who or what *specifically* are believers *actually* praying to when they say they are praying to their god? Moreover, what *specifically*, and in principle, would empirically count for or against the truth (or probable truth) or falsity (or probable falsity) of the claim that 'God as an infinite, eternal, and transcendent being hears and answers prayers'? How would or could such a claim even be *causally* possible given what we *know* to be true about the physical universe and how it *actually* (not speculatively) works?

This first set of questions connects the problem of prayer to the problem of the existence of 'God' — specifically the problems with the foundational concepts of the Mormon god, revelation, and 'faith in God' respectively. Essentially, this first set of questions points to the unintelligibility, incoherence, and factual insignificance of the concept of prayer in Mormon and all theistic theology, both in relation to the established factual non-reality of the Mormon god, and in its own status as a putatively real form of communication with a god. On the basis of conceptual analysis, the idea of prayer as claimed literal communication with a god is utter nonsense. One might just as well pray to Irlig, Santa Clause, or the Tooth Fairy!

- *Second*: If given — solely for the sake of argument — the justifiability of the Mormon god as theologically conceptualized in its fulness, why would prayer be necessary to establish or strengthen 'faith in God'? Why would it be needed to confirm the existence of a god or to receive the 'blessings' needed or sought for from a god?

Surely the Mormon god, like the Christian god, knows, without the need for prayer, who needs faith and who needs faith strengthened. Or who needs his god's existence confirmed. He must know what his putative children are physically and emotionally in need of to survive and thrive in the world or endure in their faith.

To answer these questions Mormon believers might insist on the need for prayer to develop so-called godly character, including, most prominently, the traits of *humility, meekness, gratitude* and *submissiveness* to 'God.' But such insistence would not answer the questions and would raise other problematical questions regarding, for example, the possibility of 'revelation from God' addressed in Chapter 5. Besides, such an answer, as with the earlier possible claims that the existence of 'revelation and faith in God' implicitly (or even actually) 'prove the existence of God,' would be yet another *non sequitur*, for it does not necessarily or causally follow that prayer builds godly character (whatever that means, if anything) or even human character.

Further, arguing that 'the development of godly character requires prayer' not only would also beg the question at issue (*i.e.* the necessity of prayer) by arguing for the necessity of prayer on the premise that prayer builds godly character, but would likewise falsely *affirm the consequent*. For the traits of humility, meekness, gratitude, submissiveness (for example, to the authority of reason, conscience, and the laws of nature) could, in a purely naturalistic context, be effectually and more plausibly cultivated through human development, interaction, and generosity in response to one's needs — *without* the need for prayer.

- *Third*: For those believers who assert and insist that a god has actually answered their prayers and that therefore petitionary and intercessory prayer 'works' and testifies of that god's existence and love for us, two problematical questions must be confronted. Firstly, how, or by what *specific* and common, or widely, accepted human criteria, can such a putative fact be known to be true in contradistinction to the more parsimonious, naturalistic explanations involving, for example, suggestive self-fulfillment, other-responsiveness to need on the basis of observation, conversation, or informed intuition, or mere coincidence? Secondly, how can the problem of *unanswered* sincere and urgent prayers be coherently explained by believers, given the putatively revealed and believed promises — allegedly from a god – that *all* prayers will be answered?

The first question in this set of questions points us back primarily to the problem of the Mormon god explored in Chapter 3, as well as the related problem with revelation explored in Chapter 5. Clearly it can only be validly argued that the requirement for such authenticating criteria must be fulfilled by human beings to avoid begging the fundamental question at issue (*i.e.* the Mormon god's existence), and yet must also be revealed by that god to be universally regarded as absolute truth. This presents theists with what appears to be an inescapable double-bind. The simple fact of the matter is that there neither is nor can be such criteria, given the fact of fallibilism, the existence of competing and conflicting revelations in answer to prayer, and the incoherence of the concepts of 'God' and 'revelation.'

As above in the second set of questions, the possible argument that *allegedly* 'answered prayer' *proves* a god's existence would be still another *non sequitur* and would also be invalidated as an argument because it not only *begs the question*, or assumes the existence of the god in the premise that such putatively answered 'prayer to God' would therefore prove that god's existence. Moreover, it also invalidly *affirms the consequent*. It argues essentially and falsely that a god's existence is the *only* explanation for answered prayer when there are other, more sensible and plausible naturalistic interpretations of, and explanations for, such merely human experiences.

Regarding the second question concerning unanswered prayer, there are, to be sure, various apologetic answers, some of which are addressed quite competently by Loftus, who is himself a former Christian evangelist and apologist. According to Loftus, "[t]hree [common apologetic] solutions are inadequate for this problem. First, some Christians [and Mormons] simply deny that prayer ever goes unanswered if prayed in faith. This is a radical view," Loftus points out, "and has given rise to the 'name it claim it' theology. But this view leads to intense guilt if prayers go unanswered and forces some," for example, "to paradoxically claim that God healed them even when the symptoms remain [or there might be naturalistic explanations (known or not) to account for the person's recovery]! Second, others believe that God always answers prayer, but that sometimes his answer is 'no.' "

"But think about it," Loftus asks. "[H]ow is it possible that a negative answer is not considered an unanswered prayer? Someone," Loftus contends, "who says an unanswered prayer is one in which God could sometimes say 'no' is merely saying God has responded in some way. But in order for us to say that prayer was answered, we really want to know whether the request was granted or not. A denied request is one that goes unanswered, and a request granted is one that is answered. If someone wants to maintain that all prayers are answered, then we merely need to ask that person whether God says 'yes' to all prayers, and God clearly doesn't do this. *That's the whole reason why unanswered prayer is a problem in the first place*, and it *is* a problem. Third, still others rationalize things away so that they can still say God answered their prayer even though God didn't do what they requested. …While it may be true to say God gives us what is best, that doesn't mean he gives us exactly what we asked him" (2008, 221, emphasis mine). Moreover, to assert that *all* prayers are answered by God in some way or at some time — in this life or the next — is to utter a factually vacuous statement. Again, for something to have factual content there must be a meaningful contrast, in this case to the notion of answered prayer. Finally, to claim unintelligibly – as many believers do — that prayer is efficacious because it "works" is to commit what is known as the "pragmatic fallacy." According to Carroll's *theSkeptic'sDictionary.com* (updated 11/11/2008), this fallacy perversely holds that what 'works' "[a]t the least…means that one perceives some practical benefit in believing that it is true, despite the fact that the utility of a belief is independent of its [actual] truth-value."

Clearly, as Loftus further accurately observes, "[s]everal other solutions are offered to help explain the problem of unanswered prayer," including: the presence of "sin in our lives," the "wrong motives in our prayer," the "lack of faith in prayer," not asking "according to God's will," not asking for something which is "within God's power to grant," and not praying with an open, pure and receptive heart to God's will, to name a critical few"

(221).[149] Moreover, "[b]elievers demand that we see the promises of unanswered prayer as qualified ones. It's these qualifications," Loftus astutely suggests, "that lead David

---

149 Another related and equally problematical solution to 'help explain the problem of unanswered prayer' comes to mind in relation to a recently reported conversation between my sister-in-law and her brother, who is a non-denominational Christian minister (the same brother incidentally who told my wife when we first met that he would rather she be a nonbeliever than a Mormon). The brother and his wife had been suffering a severe trial of illness and economic hardship. When his sister asked what she could do to help, he reportedly asked her to pray — but in the "right way." He then explained to her the "right way to pray." To this believer it not only mattered *which* god to pray to (clearly, for example, praying to the Mormon god or assumedly the Islamic god would not do), but *how* to pray.

This comment, of course, brought me back to the Mormon faith, which also teaches that there is a 'right way' to pray, both on a conventional, daily basis, and in special circumstances in the Mormon Temples. In the first instance proper prayer consists of kneeling if possible, folding the arms, bowing the head and addressing the 'Heavenly Father,' followed by offering (in 'King James' language) thanks, then asking for 'God's aid' according to one's needs (subject of course, and conveniently, to 'God's will'), and finally closing the prayer with the words "in the name of Jesus Christ, Amen." In the second type of prayer, known and referred to in the Mormon faith as the 'True Order of Prayer,' Temple-worthy believers, clothed in the robes and garments of the 'Holy Priesthood' circle an altar in the Temple, offer up the required hand and arm "signs," clasp hands in the 'patriarchal grip, or sure sign of the nail' with the person on their right while raising their left arm to the square and resting it on the arm of the person to their left, and repeat the words of the prayer offered by the Temple officiator kneeling at the altar for and on behalf of the names of those in need of blessings placed on the altar. According to Mormon belief, the 'True Order of Prayer' employs the 'keys of the priesthood' in the prescribed way to *directly* access the throne of their god, Elohim with sure influence or power to obtain the specific blessings sought. These petitions are also made "in the name of Jesus Christ," and are also asked for (and likewise conveniently, as well as incoherently so) on a contingent basis, or according to their god's will. Such a ritual is strange to be sure (even to many Mormons who don't return to the Temple after their first visit), and I am quite sure that apart from their refusal to demonstrate such a ritual in public — clothed or not with their Temple vestments — on the stated basis of its 'sacredness,' even the most devout Mormon believers would be unbearably embarrassed to do so. Such embarrassment, of course, should tell Mormons something important, for it would be the body's betrayal of the healthy shame experienced for practicing such an utterly bizarre and incoherent ritual and actually believing it to be efficacious.

Beyond the aforementioned incoherence of talking to a factual non-reality, such insistence on precise form and decorum in praying (including the biblical instructions and example believed by Christians to be taught by Jesus in Matthew, Chapter 6) betrays the gross superstitious nature of prayer and belief in a god. It also likely betrays the unacknowledged or unconscious doubt of the believer through both the contingent nature of prayers offered in deference to 'God's will,' and deflection through an emphasis on the practice of prayer itself, and whether it is right or wrong in form and decorum. For if all prayers are subject to 'God's will,' then again, as Loftus correctly implies above, believers have a convenient — as well as incoherent and self-refuting — way out of the problem concerning the unreliability of prayer. What exactly are you doing or talking to when you pray, how could such communication even be possible, and why pray at all? Likewise, if one prays to one's god the 'right way' and his or her prayers are *not* answered, the non-answer is necessarily a *sure* answer — and therefore a tacit confirmation of their god's existence — precisely *because* the prayer was offered to their god the *right way*. Conversely, if one's prayers or the prayers *of others* are offered the 'wrong way' in form or substance and are *not* answered, it is because the prayers didn't make it to the god. Either way the doubt regarding the existence of the believer's god on the basis of unanswered prayer is conveniently deflected to the practice of prayer. By association, the believer's faith and worthiness and/or the god being prayed to are all vague, ambiguous, and incoherent criteria which amount to mere smoke and mirrors to preserve an incoherent faith in the 'grand illusion' of 'God.'

Apart from the arguments presented above regarding the various problems with prayer, from a psychological perspective, the superstitious practice of prayer as a ritual for either obtaining (or not forfeiting or losing) divine acceptance and approval from a Parent-God, or for securing (or not forfeiting or losing) divine protection and deliverance in times of need, seems clearly indicative not only of a betrayal of — and defense against — doubt, but also of a regressive obsession.

Mills[150] to argue that 'believers create the illusion of answered prayer by systematically employing the fallacy known as "Selective Observation," a perceptual error also referred to as "counting the hits and ignoring the misses."' If prayer seems to get answered, God gets the credit. But if it goes unanswered, then there was a reason for why didn't answer it. My question here," Loftus asks, "is whether the biblical promises of answered prayer [like the claim of God's existence] 'dies the death of a thousand qualifications,' so to speak" (221).

Why We Pray: A Deeper Look

Given the above three problems with prayer regarding its *incoherence, non-necessity,* and *unreliability,* how can we explain its continued importance to theistic believers? Clearly to the rational mind, it cannot be because the concept of prayer *per se* literally makes sense, or is coherent in relation to the concept of 'God' or the natural realities of the world and the universe as we know (rather than just imagine) them to be. Nor could it be because the practice of prayer is reliable or capable of producing consistently predictable and confirmable empirical consequences. So why does the actual practice of prayer persist in spite of the incoherence of the concepts of 'God,' 'revelation from God,' and 'faith in God' as concluded in Chapters 3, 5, and 6 respectively, and in spite of its logical non-necessity and clear and irrefutable unreliability?

There are, I'm sure, many different sensible, naturalistic (and therefore atheistic) answers to these questions, not the least of which is sociocultural conditioning beginning in the believer's family of origin. Beyond this rather obvious answer, there are two naturalistic explanations for prayer's enduring importance and persistent practice that appeal most convincingly to me. The first is the suggestion, alluded to at the end of the preceding footnote, that prayer is a regressive, obsessional practice accounted for by inherent human superstitiousness, existential fears and anxieties, and the "denial of death" (Becker 1773, 1975). The second suggestion, related to the first, is that prayer is the manifestation of the likewise primary human desire or yearning to recapitulate the "basic biological situation" (Faber 2004, 2002). Both of these explanations are closely related and have deep sociological and psychological roots. The former explanation will be addressed somewhat in the final Chapter and the *Epilogue*. The latter will be treated in some depth below.

In his book *The Magic of Prayer* (2002), Faber makes a compelling case, from a psychoanalytical perspective, that religious belief in general, and the practice of prayer in particular, is motivated, at bottom, by an unconscious and biologically rooted *infantile wish*. This regressive wish to merge once again with the internalized, nurturing parent-ideal is ultimately experienced by believers — in their prayer-induced and sustained 'faith-state' as a *feeling* of incomprehensible love, acceptance, protection, and 'eternal unity' (and consequently immortality) with and through the source of all life. It is a powerful, somatic sense that the loving and protecting parent, which is unknowingly projected (transferred) onto the image of the believed Parent-God (*e.g.* 'Heavenly Father' and 'Jesus Christ'), is near *and* is responsive to their needs for survival, security, love, esteem, and transcendence.

This unconscious wish and its affective fulfillment are, according to Faber, what we are really and primarily after when we pray. Those who pray do so not only as a habit developed and reinforced through family, institutional, and cultural conditioning, but

---

150 See David Mills 2003, 179.

because at a deeper, unconscious level we are all, as human beings and in relation to our degree of personal individuation, addictively (as the song goes) "hooked on a feeling [and] high on the feeling" of 'transcendent love.' Such a feeling, which is not unlike the feeling of '*falling* in love,' is embedded in the brain by the experience of ecstatic, unconditional love experienced as a total fusion or oneness with the beloved. It is initiated and reexperienced after natural, developmental separation from the mother through the subsequent, unconscious transference of the internalized protecting and nurturing parent-ideal *to* another 'object,' in this case the imagined and believed Parent-God.

Relying on the best thinking and research in the field of applied psychoanalysis, Faber compellingly connects the "rite of prayer" with the superstitious practice of "magic" rooted in "the [primal] child-mother situation." Building on the observations and conclusions of renowned anthropologists such as Frazer, Malinowski, Durkheim, and Roheim, and eminent psychologists and psychoanalytical researchers and theorists such as Freud, Mahler, Stern, Winnicott, Bollas, Rizzuto, and Neumann, Faber creates the primary relational context for understanding the phenomenon of prayer, and concludes:

> The child-mother situation in which magic is rooted is primarily a situation of asking and receiving. Accordingly, it is the soil in which the magic of prayer takes root ("ask and ye shall receive" [Mark 11:24]). The infant's cry is the Ur-prayer, prayer in its original, presymbolic expression aimed directly at the caregiver upon whom the child's survival depends. Because maternal ministration is not perfect, because the child's requirements are not immediately met, the cry that summons the object becomes invested with power, intention, will, qualities with which the word also becomes invested as the symbolical mind begins to impinge upon primal, instinctual being. The magical formula for the emergence of prayer is clear: from the caregiver to the word and back again to the caregiver. In the beginning is the word because the word calls forth the empathic parental relation from which both self and Deity are born. Nor do we relinquish our magical propensities as we mature. On the contrary, magic becomes in Roheim's words our "great reservoir of strength against frustration and defeat." Conjuring up imitatively through prayer an idealized, complexified version of the first relationship, we continue to rely upon a caring, empathic Big One who hears and responds to our calls for succor and guidance [even if not according to our specific request for tangible, observable 'blessings']. With the blessing of the social order [who does not value or speak of the virtue of prayer in our Western society] — indeed with its encouragement — we indulge our "infantile fantasy" of benign attachment to an omnipotent provider whenever the inclination to do so moves within us. We give up our "magical omnipotence" on the one hand, and we forge a personal, magical alliance with the Almighty on the other. Although we cannot control Him, we can perhaps touch His empathic heart with our prayers. (94)

Continuing, Faber concludes…

> No matter how complex and multifaceted one's conception of the deity may become, no matter how selfless and sophisticated an overall, individual supplication may be, a prayer to an anthropomorphic God who stands in personal, loving relationship with the pray-er [and in prayer the *image* of God is *always* anthropomorphic, even if the theological *concept* of God *in its fulness* is not, or is quasi-anthropomorphic as it is in the Mormon faith] must always and forever be based upon an infantile model. The reader may be thinking… "is not the putative infantile model you offer but a metaphorical or symbolic representation, an imaginative depiction of spiritual reality designed merely to guide the suppliant toward an appropriate interaction

with the Creator? Why must you insist on both its origination in infancy and its direct, causal connection to prayer?" I insist because religion [as a fundamental affective state] goes all the way down, to the unconscious strata; I insist because prayer reaches into our primal, instinctual being; I insist because for countless millions the "faith state"…is a matter quite literally of life and death…The origins of prayer are tied integrally to the origins of our biological life — in a word, to our initial asking and receiving. We don't invent prayer; we act out our passionate, unconscious concerns as they are rooted in our elemental, mind-body experience. From the soil of what psychoanalysis calls "object relations" spring the psychodynamics of what religion calls "spiritual relations." (101–2)

Each of Faber's stated reasons for insisting that prayer, like faith, originates from and is caused by, or rooted in, our basic biological situation is, again, founded on an extensive and coherent body of research consisting of well-supported biological and psychological facts. These facts make the said basic biological situation inaccessible to the concepts of a biologically and spatiotemporally *transcendent* god such as we find in Mormon, Judeo-Christian, and Islamic theology.

What theists cannot coherently or validly argue in this regard is that this psychological pattern is the result of their god's *intent* to create man such that he would *naturally* seek after him through prayer and then come to realize that the psychological pattern Faber refers to in fact *testifies* or bears witness of a god as Creator, a Creator-god who is our literal Father in Heaven. The argument which appeals to the basic biological situation as metaphor or symbol, parallels assertions by certain theistic apologists that certain metaphysical religious statements about 'God' are not to be taken literally, but merely as metaphors or symbols of, deeper truths or realities about 'God,' and man's relationship to him.

Such assertions, however, in both cases, may reasonably be met with the question: what *specifically* are these putative metaphors or symbols *actually* metaphors or symbols *of*? Specifically, if, as argued, the basic biological situation explicated by Faber is merely a metaphor or symbol, what *specifically* is it a metaphor or symbol of? Man's relationship to a god? But how is the primal relationship between biological mother and child in any way a metaphor of, or analogous to, the relationship (or 'appropriate interaction') between biological man and an infinite, eternal, and *non-biological* spirit being with body, parts, and passions, existing in the shape of a man who is biologically and spatiotemporally *transcendent* to man? Analogical predication again fails us here, for we know nothing nonanalogical or literal about a 'spiritual relationship' with a tangible, spiritual being who is transcendent to man in every fundamental way except, minimally, in shape. This question necessarily takes the theist full circle to the theological concepts that have been deemed unintelligible, incoherent, and factually vacuous by conceptual analysis and mere common sense.

Additionally, the argument that appeals to a god as the literal Creator, or Ultimate First Cause of our biological existence on earth is likewise false or incoherent (as argued and concluded in Chapters 3 and 4) and also begs the primary and ultimate question at issue, *i.e.* the existence of the Mormon god. Presupposing the actual (not merely perceived or imagined) existence of this god as the Creator who created all things to testify of the actual existence of himself gets us nowhere.[151] Moreover, given the eternal stakes involved rela-

---

151 Psychoanalytical philosopher Jonathan Lear (2005) sympathetically (and I think perversely) writes in

tive to belief and nonbelief in this god, it seems absurd to conceive of a god who would intentionally rely on *natural* phenomena to *indirectly* testify of eternal, supernatural realities — including his own existence. Would he not rather reveal himself *directly, perspicuously,* and *unambiguously* to mankind to avoid confusion, conjecture, error, doubt, and nonbelief? Why would a god create and rely on the 'basic biological situation' and other natural processes and phenomena on earth to testify of his existence, when doing so would likely lead natural Atheists[152] to conclude that there is, in fact, *no* need for religion or God to explain so-called religious (or "spiritual") experiences, phenomena or practices? Such an argument or belief simply does not make sense. Nor does it help the believer to insist that *all* things on earth and in the universe testify of a god's existence. For under such a theistic conception of reality — given the gross imperfections and flaws of creation, the extent and degree of suffering and premature death, the hiddenness of the god and the

---

this regard that a person who would accept Faber's conclusion that the 'basic biological situation' is the 'root' of religious belief "[m]ight…also [and presumably justifiably] believe that this ['basic biological situation'] is what a beneficent God would design in a well-ordered universe[.]" Further, from Lear's perspective, "[f] or such an outlook, it would not be a criticism to point out that there are infantile dimensions to religious belief" since "[f]rom the perspective of the religious person [who in Lear's example accepts both Freudian psychoanalysis and theism]…it is *marvelous* that [theistic faith and worship] has infantile roots: [that] God recognizes that we began life as infants — and [that] God agrees with Freud that we carry our infantile past with us" and that therefore, "a genuinely sacred act is able to resonate so deeply in our psyches" (206–7).

The problems with Lear's philosophizing are varied. First, as Rieff correctly points out in a related context, for Freud "…to be religious is…to be sick: it is an effort to find a cure where no one can possibly survive. For Freud, religious questions [and beliefs] induce the very symptoms they seek to cure. 'The moment a man questions the meaning and value of life,' Freud wrote (in a letter to Marie Bonaparte), he is sick, since objectively neither has any existence.' … Freud," Rieff observed, "risked the correlative implication [to the idea that 'because men are ill, gods exist'] that healthy men need no gods" (1987, 33–4, 89)

Second, Lear's hypothetical 'genuinely religious person' must presuppose the *literal* existence of an *actual* deity that is intelligible and therefore believable. But is it? Is belief in the literal existence of that which is factually unintelligible or incoherent — or personal incoherence in believing that which is false or incoherent — healthy or advisable from a psychological or even broad, commonsensical perspective? What *specifically is* the object of such religious belief? What is a rational person to make of a putatively *literal* "beneficent [and presumably transcendent] God" *literally* designing and creating a "well-ordered universe"? Can sincere, superstitious belief in, and total childlike dependence on, the *literal* existence of an unintelligible, factual non-reality or Parent-God be anything other than delusional and pathologically regressive?

Further, *pace* Lear, the "infantile dimensions to religious beliefs" (or Faber's 'basic biological situation') is not merely a criticism of religious belief (although it is that, as well), but *a naturalistic explanation of the root of religious belief* which makes such religious belief in a god unnecessary.

Finally, in reply to Lear's later and adjudged more crucial question regarding what might "mature religious commitment consist in" (206–7), the answer — as argued implicitly in the next chapter, the *Epilogue,* and the *Personal Postscript* — is that 'mature religious commitment' to the gods of Judaism, Christianity, Islam, and Mormonism, is a contradiction in terms. This is so given that such commitment requires, as Lear readily acknowledges, the regressive access of those infantile parts which enable "prayerful forms of reaching out" in childlike love, and, moreover, typically and necessarily consists in regressive obedience to an illusory Parent-God. I'm not sure which religious belief systems Lear had in mind when he wrote as an advocate for religious belief, but it certainly is not the developed theistic faiths of Mormonism, Judaism, Christianity, and Islam. Simply put, Lear's hypothetical religious believer who wants to reconcile and accept Freudian psychoanalysis and theism cannot coherently do so.

152 George Smith makes a distinction between a "natural atheist…who has never been a religious believer and so remains in his original condition of nonbelief" and a "personal atheist…who was formerly a religious believer of some kind [but has made the deliberate transition from belief to disbelief through] …deconversion" (2006, 25–6). See also Eller (2004).

unreliability of prayer in response to the cries of the suffering for deliverance and the existence of doubt and the extent of disbelief and nonbelief — their god would clearly be unworthy of admiration, still less of worship and complete devotion.

Nor does it necessarily follow, as some in the Mormon faith might suggest, that because the basic biological situation between parent and child relationally reconnects mortal man to the Mormon god through prayer, that such an archetypal situation is therefore an 'eternal dynamic' within an 'eternal scheme of things.' Such a claim, if it is made, would clearly be another *non sequitur*.

Furthermore, merely saying or believing something is *eternal* neither logically nor actually makes it so. Such an apologetic move merely invokes as an evasive possibility strategy of isolation *ad hoc* 'eternalism' to avoid questions of origin. Although saying this parent-child situation is *not* eternal likewise does not make it so, there nonetheless are no good reasons — no justifiable warrant — to think or believe it is in fact eternal, or that any putatively eternal religious or spiritual reality is an objective or actual reality as believed. Such a meta-belief would be, again, *vis-à-vis* error theory, false or incoherent, making the putative eternal reality a *factual non-reality*.

Moving now to a more fine-grained understanding of prayer, we return again to Faber who asks: "Exactly how does this interior prayer work (108)?"

> Let's get to the analytical essence of all this. What ostensibly "flows" between the supernatural and the suppliant is in reality the unconscious, feeling recollection of a vital, elemental, intimate relationship between the suppliant's nascent, genetic self and the attentive mothering figure whom he internalized into the unconscious core of his being. Because the one who prays cannot detect the relationship directly, he projects it (through the infantile model of prayer) onto the spiritual level and onto the energetic, powerful Other ['God'] who supposedly resides there… [In doing so,] the…loving, feeling ministrations [and] powerful transformational capacities [of the internalized caregiver (usually the mother)] awaken [and transform (or enliven) the suppliant]…from the deadness which the lack of mothering invariably engenders. It is not God who does this but another [now internalized] human being. A person, not a god, has this power. We pray for many reasons, of course, and among them is the longing to get back to the source of our aliveness, to feel still again the indelible, primal "hit" we felt over and over again during the early time as the caregiver focused her loving energies, her loving rays, upon us. We eagerly adopt the infantile model of supplication because we would have that, again and again, just as we had it early on — world without end. (109)

Surely, if this naturalistic explanation is even near the mark, we can understand how it is that on the basis of dissociative 'trance-logic' (Schumaker 1995) induced by prayer, the wish-fulfillment of ecstatic merger or symbiosis with, and acceptance by, the Parent-God through transference creates an alternate reality which effectually recreates the primary relational matrix of mother and child.

To extend this understanding further, it seems apropos to conclude this portion of our analysis by pointing out that while in this alternate reality or faith-state the three problems of prayer presented above — no doubt encountered by reason which is not entirely absent in this state — become 'separation concerns' that elicit a biological *rapprochement* response to restore unity and allay the familiar, infantile anxiety of alienation and fear of abandonment. Such concerns are experienced as real possibilities akin to death or extinction by the 'child-like' believer. In order to avoid the *ersatz* reality, the delusional faith-state, of the believer that has been created by prayer-induced dissociation will naturally, necessarily, and subconsciously be protected or preserved through various self-deceptive and regressive defense mechanisms.

These defense mechanisms require, as we might imagine, the expenditure of substantial amounts of energy and will remain active to ward-off the believer's unconscious or unacknowledged doubt. Unless and until, that is, the force of such doubt — growing over time through the relentless pressure to reason and integrity applied by personally experienced and irresolvable contradictions in the faith — eventually wears down the believer's resolve to defend the faith. If and when this occurs, the believer is ready to finally relinquish the 'Grand Illusion' and individuate from the Parent-God and from the need to believe in all other externalized parent-surrogates. Such is the natural course of the very few who are, as I see it, fortunate enough to grow-up and break free from the foolishness of their childish faith and say "Yes!" to the creative burden of their lives,[153] and to the bitter-sweet joy which accompanies it.

"Prayer & Babies"

The above treatment of the problem with prayer seems sufficient to raise in the mind of a believer-as-skeptical outsider some serious questions regarding the rationality of religious belief in a god. But there's more. Related to the three sets of questions addressed in regard to this problem, and the earlier problem of human suffering and premature death as an argument for the non-existence of a god, is the problem addressed by Guy Harrison in his article in the February 2009 issue of the *American Atheist* entitled "Prayer & Babies." In this article Harrison takes the problem of unanswered prayer as an argument for the non-existence of a god to both an intellectual and raw emotional level.

Harrison offers a singular perspective to this problem which narrows the focus of our attention to the primal emotional relationship between mothers and their innocent, utterly dependent and defenseless babies. Speaking personally, this particular focus on the atheological problem of evil reaches beneath my intellectual commitment to Atheism to a visceral commitment — a commitment which is itself no doubt rooted in the basic biological situation and the parent-child bond. As a human being, and a parent and grandparent in particular, I think this particular argument makes the larger, albeit secondary, argument for the non-existence of a god on the basis of suffering and premature death, and the incoherence of faith and prayer, more fully accessible and compelling.

Here then, in his own words, is Guy Harrison's report and corresponding argument:

"Every day of the year, thousands of mothers who sincerely believe in a god or gods watch helplessly as their babies die. Virtually every one of these deaths occurs despite the torrent of passionate prayers asking gods for life. The prayers are sent out to a variety of divine beings, in many languages and from many nations. They are diverse in both structure and delivery, faithful to the idiosyncrasies of numerous belief systems. Every day and night, countless prayers from Muslims, Hindus, Christians, and other believers

---

153 The question of man's need for religious illusion to deal with the existential anxiety of mortality in contradistinction to the creative and life-affirming analytic alternative is treated in some depth in the *Epilogue*.

fill the skies on behalf of impoverished babies on the verge of death. But the babies keep dying by the tens of thousands. They perish precisely as one would expect if good nutrition, clean water, medication, and access to doctors are all that matter. They die as if no gods exist or, at the very least, as if prayer does not work (18).

Harrison continues: "More than 26,000 children under the age of five die every 24 hours in developing nations, according to UNICEF. …This carnage totals more than 9 million children per year (18).

"[These babies] suffer terribly in their final days and hours, enduring high fevers, severe headaches, cramps, and nausea. Is anything in our world more unjust than their fate? ... One would think prayers for them would be a high priority for a god to respond to rapidly and favorably. Even if a god's answer is "no" to the mothers' prayers and for some mysterious reason [or unknown purpose] 9 million babies must die each year, how can we explain why that god [if he/she/it exists and is worthy of faith and worship] refuses to [at least] ease [or remove] the children's suffering before they die? (18)

In what must strike a common chord in the hearts of all mature, sane people everywhere, Harrison continues by poignantly observing that "A mother's prayer, transmitted within the life-and-death context of her seriously ill baby, must be among the most heartfelt words ever uttered by a human being. There simply is no doubting the sincerity and force of such a plea when death stalks a mother's child. Certainly these prayers, above all others, should get god's attention and inspire action. But the children keep dying. If just one version of one religion that is popular in the developing world had a true communication link to a god who responded to prayers we should see impoverished babies linked to that religion fare better than others in similar conditions. But we do not. Based on the numbers, the world's poorest babies appear to die strictly in relation to their access to adequate food, clean water, and healthcare. Nothing else seems to matter, least of all prayers (19).

"Meanwhile, as babies die by the millions in highly religious societies, children under the age of five do much better in nations with relatively high rates of Atheism such as England, France, Sweden, Canada, and Denmark. ... Of course, defenders of prayer may point to the severe imbalance of resources and healthcare between wealthy and poor [races and] societies as the reason.[154] But wouldn't that suggest that the gods [apart from

---

154 Some in the Mormon faith might still unadmittedly believe, as Mormon General Authorities Joseph Fielding Smith, B.H. Roberts, Mark E. Petersen, Bruce R. McConkie, Alvin R. Dyer and others taught, that those non-Caucasians who are born in impoverished societies were not as valiant in the pre-existence and therefore implicitly not sufficiently favored by the Mormon god to warrant the same privileges and blessings as those born in better circumstances, particularly in the United States of America, which is the home of the 'restored gospel' of Christ. Here are some interesting, if not disturbing statements excerpted from the Web-site at www.utlm.org:

Joseph Fielding Smith, who became the tenth president of the LDS Church, explained the church's position on race:

"There is a reason why one man is born black and with other disadvantages, while another is born white with great advantages. The reason is that we once had an estate before we came here, and were obedient, more or less, to the laws that were given us there" (*Doctrines of Salvation: Sermons and Writings of Joseph Fielding Smith*, compiled by Bruce R. McConkie, vol. 1, Bookcraft, 1954, p. 61).

This teaching was clearly stated in a letter written by the LDS First Presidency on July 17, 1947: "Your position seems to lose sight of the revelations of the Lord touching the pre-existence of our spirits, the rebellion in heaven, and the doctrine that our birth into this life and the advantages under which we may be born, have a relationship in the life heretofore. From the days of the Prophet Joseph even until now, it has been the doctrine of the Church, never questioned by any of the Church leaders, that the Negroes are not entitled to the full blessings of the Gospel" (as quoted in *Mormonism and the Negro*, by John J. Stewart and William E. Berrett, Horizon Publishers, 1978, p. 47).

Apostle Mark E. Petersen, speaking at the Convention of Teachers of Religion at Brigham Young University in 1954, declared:

"We cannot escape the conclusion that because of performance in our pre-existence some of us are born as Chinese, some as Japanese, some as Indians, some as Negroes, some Americans, some as Latter-day Saints. These are rewards and punishments . . . Is it not reasonable to believe that less worthy spirits would come through less favored lineage? . . .

"Let us consider the great mercy of God for a moment. The Chinese, born in China with a dark skin, and with all the handicaps of that race seems to have little opportunity. But think of the mercy of God to Chinese people who are willing to accept the gospel. In spite of whatever they might have done in the pre-existence to justify being born over there as Chinamen, if they now, in this life, accept the gospel and live it the rest of their lives they can have the Priesthood, go to the temple and receive endowments and sealings, and that means they can have exaltation. . . .

"Think of the Negro, cursed as to the Priesthood. ... This Negro, who, in the pre-existence lived the type of life which justified the Lord in sending him to the earth in the lineage of Cain with a black skin. ... In spite of all he did in the pre-existent life, the Lord is willing, if the Negro accepts the gospel ... he can and will enter the celestial kingdom. He will go there as a servant, but he will get celestial glory" ("Race Problems—As they Affect the Church," address by Apostle Mark E. Petersen at the Convention of Teachers of Religion on the College Level, Brigham Young University, Provo, Utah, August 27, 1954).

LDS Apostle Bruce R. McConkie discussed the curse on Cain:

"Though he was a rebel and an associate of Lucifer in pre-existence, and though he was a liar from the beginning whose name was Perdition, Cain managed to attain the privilege of mortal birth. Under Adam's tutelage, he began in this life to serve God. ...Then he came out in open rebellion, fought God, worshiped Lucifer, and slew Abel. ...

"As a result of his rebellion, Cain was cursed with a dark skin; he became the father of the Negroes, and those spirits who are not worthy to receive the priesthood are born through his lineage. He became the first mortal to be cursed as a son of perdition. As a result of his mortal birth he is assured of a tangible body of flesh and bones in eternity, a fact which will enable him to rule over Satan" (*Mormon Doctrine*, by Bruce R. McConkie, Bookcraft, 1958 edition, p. 102; in the 1966 and 1979 editions, p. 109).

Alvin R. Dyer, assistant to the twelve apostles and later ordained an apostle, spoke on racial issues to the Norwegian Mission. In this talk he said:

"We have talked a lot about missionary work and heard the testimonies of those who have spoken. I want to talk to you a little bit now about something that is not missionary work, and what I say is not to be given to your investigators by any matter of means. ... Why is it that you are white and not colored: Have you ever asked yourself that question? Who had anything to do with your being born into the Church and not born a Chinese or a Hindu, or a Negro? Is God such an unjust person that He would make you white and free and make a Negro cursed under the cursing of Cain that he could not hold the Priesthood of God? ... Those who have been cursed in the pre-existence were born through this lineage of Ham. ...Why is a Negro a Negro? ... The reason that spirits are born into Negro bodies is because those spirits rejected the Priesthood of God in the pre-existence. This is the reason why you have Negroes upon the earth.

"You will observe that when Cain was influenced by the power of Lucifer to follow him and to fall down and worship him in the beginning, it was then that . . . Cain rejected the counsel of God. He rejected again the Priesthood as his forebearers had done in the pre-existence. Therefore, the curse of the pre-existence was made institute through the loins of Cain. Consequently, you have the beginning of the race of men and women into which would be born those in the pre-existence who had rejected the Priesthood of God. ...Ham reinstated the curse of the pre-existence when he rejected the Priesthood of Noah, and in consequence of that he preserved the curse on the earth. Therefore, the Negroes to be born thereafter, or those who were to become Negroes, were to be born through the loins of Ham.

"All of this is according to a well worked-out plan, that these millions and billions of spirits awaiting birth in the pre-existence would be born through a channel or race of people. Consequently, the cursed were to be born through Ham" ("For What Purpose," talk by Alvin R. Dyer, Oslo, Norway, March 18, 1961, typed copy in our files. Part of this talk is quoted in *The Church and the Negro*, by John L. Lund, 1967, p. 97).

their factual non-reality], are limited in their [goodness] and powers? Do prayer defenders really imagine that their god's hands are bound by mere human economics? Is their god stumped by the challenges of inadequate healthcare infrastructure and low doctor/patient ratios in the developing world? Surely a god could overcome such trivial details [and racial/religious prejudices] and answer a mother's prayer (19).

"Those who claim that praying causes positive results are in a tough spot given the long dark shadow of [nine] million more dead babies each year. Can they explain why so many babies die in accordance to their society's global economic rank rather than how much praying is done on their behalf? Standard defenses for prayer [and the existence of gratuitous suffering and premature death in the world, presented and questioned earlier in this chapter and elsewhere] do not work so well here. Otherwise unintelligible and incoherent statements such as "God works in mysterious ways" [or] "Sometimes God says 'no,'" [or "These babies are in a better place, doing important work for the Lord," or "God did not answer the prayers of these mothers for their suffering babies because the mothers did not pray in the right way to the right God] seem trite and offensive in the face of so much pain and death. Keep in mind," Harrison soberly observes, "these dead babies had not been blasphemous or sacrilegious. Most of them barely lived long enough to learn to speak. These babies were not gay. They didn't belong to Atheist clubs, watch pornography, or listen to immoral music. They were babies (19).

To conclude, "Praying mothers and their dying babies — approximately 100 million per decade — provide a devastating blow against belief in prayer. … Personal stories of answered prayers and canned comebacks are unlikely to gain much traction before a mountain of dead infants. … When believers say praying [saved the life of a friend, acquaintance or loved one, or] brought them more money, a better job or success in love, Atheists need only bring up the 26,000 babies who were not saved by prayer yesterday and the 26,000 who won't be saved today" (20).

The Problem of Nonbelief

We now come to the problem of nonbelief. Assuming again, solely for the sake of argument, the actual existence of the Mormon god as commonly believed by Mormons, the problem of nonbelief presents believers with yet another irresolvable contradiction. This argument for the non-existence of a particular god from nonbelief (or ANB) was developed by Theodore Drange and treated extensively in his book on the subject (1998). It is paraphrased summarily in the following two slightly different forms by Steele:

1. God could easily have shown strong evidence of his existence to humans — strong in just the same way that the evidence of the existence of trees, stars, and other people is strong.

In a letter dated April 10, 1963, Apostle Joseph Fielding Smith wrote:

"According to the doctrine of the church, the Negro, because of some condition of unfaithfulness in the spirit-or pre-existence, was not valiant and hence was not denied the mortal probation, but was denied the blessings of the priesthood" (Letter to Joseph H. Henderson).

2. God wants humans to believe that he exists.
3. Therefore God must have given strong evidence of his existence to humans.
4. Humans have no strong evidence that God exists.
5. Therefore God has not shown humans strong evidence of his existence.
6. Therefore, God does not exist" (172–3).

Alternatively,

1. God could easily have arranged things so that everyone would believe that he exists.
2. God wants humans to believe that he exists.
3. Therefore God must have arranged things so that everyone would believe that he exists.
4. Many humans do not believe that God exists.
5. Therefore God has not arranged things so that everyone believes that he exists.
6. Therefore, God does not exist (173).

The common theistic responses to this argument are essentially the same as to the argument from evil presented earlier, and the objections to those responses are likewise similar, if not the same.[155] One dissimilar response to this argument entails the assertion that nonbelief is essentially a defense employed by nonbelievers to escape those moral or performatory obligations required by belief in – and covenant with – god. This, of course, is a baseless *ad hominem* argument that doesn't make sense under critical scrutiny. First, as with the Pascalean argument from 'prudence' for religious belief presented in the previous chapter, it falsely assumes the veracity of doxastic voluntarism and therefore, in this case, suggests that everyone could believe that god exists if they wanted to or simply chose to. But this notion is very problematic given, as we learned in Chapter 2, the fact that we can only coherently and responsibly "believe," or accept the truth of an assertion or claim in virtue of "belief's own ethics" (Adler 2006), i.e. because the truths we accept are *inherently* believable given their coherence with what is known about the world and universe, as well as supporting evidence and common sense. In other words, we believe on the basis of a statement's *intrinsic believability*, and *not* because we *want* and *choose* to believe. Accordingly, we cannot – except by self-deception, and to be congruent and epistemically responsible – either *refuse* to believe that which is self-evidently or demonstrably reasonable and true, or conversely believe that which is commonsensically and/or demonstrably *unbelievable* or *untrue* merely, again, because we want to or choose to. Moreover, this defense does not explain the phenomenon of deconversion, where those once devoted, converted, and committed believers have been compelled to leave their faith – or all of religion – because of persistent, *real* doubt.

The above theistic assertion takes a slightly different form in a particular argument offered by Paul Pardi (2003). He suggests that there actually is a god (although he presupposes and does not establish a factually intelligible concept of such a god) and that he

---

155 See "The Argument from Nonbelief," "McHugh's Expectations Dashed" and "Arguments from Confusion and Biblical Defects" by Theodore Drange (341–361; 369–379), and "Bolstering the Argument from Nonbelief" by Victor Cosculluela (362–8), in Martin and Monnier (2006).

('God') has given all persons a sense of himself. This alleged fact requires the Atheist to at least allow for the possibility if not likelihood that he or she "might be suppressing or rejecting or somehow failing to recognize something that is present within [him or] her [therefore involving culpability] on the part of the [nonbeliever]" (24). This fact would necessarily render Atheism a self-deceiving rationalization. To this response Philip Kuchar (2004) replies directly, and I think correctly, that:

> For atheism to be a rationalization, the atheist would have to feel that God exists and be unwilling to understand this feeling for what it is. This corresponds with the evangelical Christian's [and Mormon's] emphasis on the need for a personal relationship with God, which is something more emotional than intellectual. Until the Christian [or Mormon] can articulate the feeling of God's existence, however, without confusing it with some other feeling such as a simple wish [or transference-affect], there is little need for the atheist to reply to such an accusation. When the Christian [or Mormon] claims to speak for God [or testify of God's existence under the influence of the Holy Ghost], for example, but is incapable of distinguishing God's voice from that of her own conscience, this is just the renaming of a familiar [even if not remembered] experience, one which is at least divided on the question of God's existence.
>
> Even if there were a universal feeling that God exists, this feeling would not amount to knowledge, since feeling that p is true doesn't make p true. ANB, however, points to an absence of knowledge among many people. Conscious, rational nonbelief should be the intolerable obstacle for God, but this nonbelief can't be overcome by a feeling.
>
> … Pardi's claim [therefore,] that the atheist is self-deceptive is an *ad hoc* contrivance and thus likely false; that is, the accusation does not flow from a criterion that covers similar cases [on the basis of an assumed parity of evidence for and against the existence of God]. Even if the empirical evidence were equally split, atheism would be value-driven, not self-deceptive. When the atheist claims to have involuntary belief, it's reasonable to take this nonbelief at face value. Since rational nonbelief is incompatible with a certain characterization of God, God so characterized does not exist.
>
> What Pardi would have to show is that atheism…is based mainly on character flaws such that in interpreting conflicting evidence the atheist would be culpable. Even if there were such typical character flaws, they would be balanced by what seem to be the atheist's virtues, such as skepticism or lack of gullibility, allegiance to science rather than to dogma, secular humanism rather than guilt-ridden hatred of human nature, and so on. At the very least, Pardi would have to enter quite controversial territory in waging a pure personal attack against the atheist. (7, 11–12)

Kuchar concludes that "ANB withstands Pardi's objections" and that "[c]ertain expectations had of a loving, sovereign God are not well met by actual nonbelievers who cannot be held accountable for being bad children in the cosmic sense, given the lack of any obvious heavenly parent. Most theists," Kuchar suggests, "should be surprised by the incompatibility of blameless nonbelief with any theistic position that compares God to a human parent. At any rate, theists seem able to explain the incompatibility only in an *ad hoc*, contrived manner, which itself is evidence of God's hiddenness and thus, according to ANB, of his non-existence. A loving father doesn't systematically hide from his children" (12).

Like the problem of evil, perhaps the most evasive, widely used defense against the ANB employs the strategies of ignorance and isolation presented in Chapter 2. This ultimate defense, or "deterrent," as Steele refers to it, is labeled by Drange as the "Unknown Purpose Defense," or UPD (Drange 1998). Simply stated, the UPD asserts that 'God's purposes' are inscrutable and beyond human understanding; assertions which have been addressed in previous chapters, including this one earlier. In addition to previous responses to this defense, I offer below some pertinent remarks by Steele, who writes:

> This [UPD] is a kind of ultimate deterrent: it annihilates any argument. Yet like other ulti-mate deterrents, it annihilates assets on both sides equally. Everything the theist tells us about God, and every possible case he can make for the existence of God, appeals to our understanding of God and of his motives, character, and qualities [and purposes]. The theist tells us that there is a God, and that God is this way and that way. [But if] we cannot begin to understand [the basic nature of God or] God's purposes, then all the theist's assertions about God are in vain. Theism requires that God be comprehensible in broad outline, if not in perfect detail. (178)

According to the Mormon faith, such is required that man might believe and have 'faith in God unto salvation and eternal life,' a fact that confronts the believer again with the ultimate, irresolvable contradiction, *i.e.* that man must believe and have 'faith in God' when such belief and faith are impossible because, as argued in Chapter 3, the very concept of 'God' in his fulness is factually unintelligible.

This ultimate contradiction, if you will, of being asked or required to believe the unbelievable or absurd points again to the obvious fact that, *pace* Drange and others who pose well-reasoned deductive and inductive atheological arguments as 'proofs of God's non-existence,' such arguments are burdened by the fact that there is simply no conceiv-able way to prove either the existence or non-existence of a god which cannot, as fully conceptualized and believed, possibly exist as a factual reality. But again, if solely for the sake of argument, we take the concept of 'God' to mean a *purely* anthropomorphic being, or 'Exalted Man' who has a tangible, physical body of flesh and bones in the shape of a man and who has finite, albeit superhuman powers and an intelligent mind then, as Steele rightly concludes in his treatment of the argument from nonbelief, given these conditions, such a god "therefore could easily make his existence clear to humans" (172) so that if he doesn't, we therefore have another contradiction that cannot be coherently resolved by appealing to faith and revelation. And again, he could do so without compromising free-will, even if such does not exist.

The Problem of Wrong Belief and Wrong-Believers

Just as the existence of nonbelief, the requirement of faith, and the existence of senseless and extreme suffering and premature death for any conceivable purpose make the concepts of the Mormon or Christian god incoherent in a strict salvational context, so too does the existence of multiple concepts of a 'saving god' and the corresponding requirements for salvation established and specified by different books of believed revelation from such gods, and the authoritative, soteriological teachings based on such revelation.

The atheistic argument that the multitude of different concepts of god and different faiths — as well as the phenomenon of apostasy from the true god by theistic believers who turn to other gods or religions — is, as part of a larger cumulative argument, evidence of the non-existence of a god is usually met by theist's counterargument that such an argument is a *non sequitur*. It is claimed that all faiths worship *essentially* the same god; that the various concepts of god are not *fundamentally* different; and that the widespread belief in a god who is allegedly a being of perfect love, goodness, and knowledge with supernatural powers is, *pace* the arguing Atheist, evidence *of* his existence, and belief in such gods is a *good* thing for believers and society.

Leaving aside the *non sequitur* that the existence of widespread belief and faith in a god is evidence of its putative existence (an argument treated in Chapter 6), and also leaving aside the questionable and at least *post hoc* contention that religious belief in a god is a good thing for believers and society (an argument treated also in Chapter 6, as well as Chapter 8 and the *Epilogue*), I think it is appropriate to address here the argument that all the various god-concepts are *essentially* the same for all faiths. Certainly, there are certain faiths, like the Mormon faith, which would take issue with such an argument. In fact, it would seem that the differences among all differing god-concepts are, in fact, *fundamental* or substantive differences in the minds of believers. According to the respecive soteriologies of their various faiths, these differences *do* make a very real and significant difference to those who believe or do not believe.

Further, to argue that all god-concepts are the same in their secondary and relational referents is to state nothing factually meaningful about their primary referents. This makes the larger argument that such gods are therefore fundamentally, or primarily, the same necessarily incoherent, particularly if the believed *primary* attributes of the gods in question are — as has been argued in Chapter 3 in relation to the quasi-anthropomorphic Mormon god, and elsewhere by Nielsen and others in relation to the nonanthropomorphic Christian god — unintelligible, incoherent and factually meaningless.

But there is more, as alluded to above. The gods of the various theistic faiths are fundamentally different in virtue of their different and believed revealed requirements for salvation. For believers in different theistic faiths, it is not enough to simply believe in a god. One must believe in the *right* god to be saved. In all theistic faiths there is the 'one true God,' and then there are all the other gods. These other gods are *false* gods who, if believed in or worshipped, will cost believers their salvation — or at least the fulness of their salvation. In this regard, for a believer to be saved or enjoy eternal life, he or she *must* have faith in the '*only true* God' of their faith. Surely, if all gods are fundamentally the same, then it would not matter which god was worshipped. The fact that it *does* matter, and that there are so many different gods who are believed to be, on the basis of putative revelation, either false gods or the 'only true God,' is evidence in a soteriological context that at least seems to support the atheistic argument that *all* gods and *all* religions are merely invented by man. No concept of god exists independent of its believed revealed existence and its believed salvational efficacy.

This decisive factor — what I refer to as the *salvation factor* —as formally argued in Chapter 6 and informally above is not only that which makes the requirement of faith and the existence of nonbelief indicative of the Mormon and Christian gods' incoherence and therefore non-existence, it is *a difference that makes the difference*. It is an eternally consequential difference! Just ask believers of different faiths who consider their god to be *fundamentally different* — if not in attributes, then of existence and consequence — as being 'the one and only true God.' Clearly if *all* the allegedly revealed concepts of god in *all* theistic faiths are believed to be the 'one and only true God' by the adherents of each respective faith, and if, as is the case, *all* other gods are believed to be false gods, then the argument that, for example, one of the multitude of believed gods could still be true, or more true than the others, is incoherent given the believed concept of an 'all-loving, all-knowing, and all-powerful God' who *requires* faith in him *alone* for salvation, and who desires *above all else* the fulness of salvation for all his creatures.

Concluding Thoughts

All of the standard apologetic defenses offered to date against the five irresolvable problems referred to above — as well as the strongest rationale offered by theologians and believers in support of theistic, religious belief in a god — have, of course, been intelligently and effectively rebutted and sufficiently refuted elsewhere in the best atheistic and atheological arguments of noted and formidable philosophers, scientists, and scholars. The list is formidable, and includes notable names such as Hume, Kant, Nietzsche, Feuerbach, Freud, Marx, and contemporaries such as Russell, Kaufman, Matson, Mackie, Hagerstrom, Hook, Edwards, Nielsen, Martin, Gale, Grunbaum, Stenger, Drange, Rowe, Shellenberg, Dennett, Dawkins, Quentin Smith, Parsons, Fales, Boyer, Shermer, Eller, Everitt, George H. Smith, Carrier, Kurtz, Schlegel, Loftus, and *many* others.

Such arguments force believers and apologists alike to retreat ultimately to rationalization and ultimately self-deception through a variety of evasive strategies. Strategies of *ignorance*, *isolation*, and *inflation* (Adler 2006, 103–133) are employed, and we are offered sincere, albeit incoherent, *testimony*, which claims belief and knowledge of that which conceptually can neither be rationally believed nor known (25–53). Let us also not forget the strategies of false or *ersatz* theological inclusiveness with the sciences, false analogy or invalid analogical predication, and theistic relativizing through *ad hoc* theological apologetics and metaphysical speculation. In every case such strategies lead once again and ever more back to the problem of irrational beliefs about 'God,' the 'Plan of Salvation,' 'revelation,' and 'faith.'

For many, faith does not survive the exposed or apparent incoherencies of their beliefs, in spite of such defensive strategies. This fact has far less, if anything, to do with sin, intellectual pride, character weakness, or the weakness of their faith than with the subjective principle of evidentialism, which suggests, according to Adler, that "it is belief that requires [coherence and] proportional reasons or evidence, not any external source" (2006, 5). This therefore makes incoherent those unjustifiable beliefs which are naturally unbelievable without self-deception. (See also Rey 2007, 243–65) It is to the insufficiency of faith itself in stemming the tide of reason, as well as the vicissitudes of life and human nature, that we must look in understanding why faith does not, and cannot, survive in the minds of those who have come to reason and lost their faith.[156]

---

156 It seems appropriate here to quote George H. Smith's published insights regarding the deconversion experience of the 'personal atheist.' According to Smith, who himself was once a former Christian believer, "[t]he most passionate and forceful defenders of atheism are frequently those personal atheists who, prior to their deconversion, were enthusiastic champions [and defenders] of [their] faith. It will not do," argues Smith, "— notwithstanding that it is often done — to explain [away] this phenomenon by psychological means, as if the former true-believing Christian [or Mormon] merely shifted his dogmatic allegiance and became a true-believing atheist instead. Nor will it do to attribute the sometimes strident atheism of the deconverted [believer] to an inner crisis that was precipitated by a loss of faith. Nor can we accept the traditional explanation that attributes deconversion to a willful and malicious rebellion against God [or, incoherently, to the

To others who are more superstitious by nature or nurture, and/or are perhaps psychologically needier, less resourceful, or more deeply conditioned or embedded culturally in the religious *Weltanschauung,* the assault of reason might unfortunately drive faith deeper into the abyss of irrationality. This would occur through further unwarranted, *ad hoc* metaphysical speculation, assumptive errors and reasoning fallacies, and/or through defensive avoidance, self-deception, denial, and ultimately delusion. It would occur, essentially, in the false and empty hope and grandiose illusion of eschatological verification and ultimate vindication. To these stalwarts of faith "…the secret of keeping the faith is this: Don't stir the water! Don't stir the dust! [Be still!] Don't [question, or doubt or] investigate truth any more! Let your beliefs be set in stone from now on!" (Mattill 1995, 246)

Clearly, as has been pointed out by numerous others, this imperfect world and universe, such as they are, and all the existents and existing states of affairs pertaining thereto, are exactly what we would reasonably expect them to be if there were no gods. All the gods defined and described in doctrines and alleged revelations — and as they exist in the minds and hearts of believers — are exactly what we would reasonably expect each of them to be, given the tendency of human beings to create or invent such deities out of their deepest needs, desires, anxieties, and insecurities — and their illusions.

---

work of Satan or possession by evil spirits].

"There are better ways to explain the strident atheism of former [believers]. For one thing, no personal atheist can fail to notice a vast discrepancy between the expectation and reality of deconversion. He quickly learns that most everything he had been taught about atheism was misleading at best and fraudulent at worst. Depictions of atheism that he once accepted without question, such as referring to deconversion as a "loss of faith," now grate on his nerves. His deconversion, far from evoking in him a sense of loss, was experienced as an intellectual breath of fresh air. Atheism, by liberating him from the stern and steady gaze of an omnipresent voyeurist, gave him a sense of moral and intellectual privacy, a sphere of personal autonomy in which he need answer to no one other than himself. He was now free to think for himself — to question and criticize without moral[istic] restraint — to live and learn, succeed and fail, as an autonomous moral agent.

"Atheism as it appears to the [believer] is much different than atheism as it appears to [or is experienced by] the former [believer]. Things look much different to the personal atheist after the process of deconversion is complete. The expected crisis and internal turmoil failed to materialize, and his deconversion ended with a whimper instead of a bang. The former [believer] signed no pacts with the devil while traveling up the path to atheism — nor did he engage in licentious [or ethically irresponsible] behavior, shake his fist at heaven in defiance of the Almighty, declare war on everything good and decent, sink into the depths of spiritual depravity, or pine after a lost deity" (2000, 26–7).

Chapter 8

Recapitulation and Psychosocial Assessment of the Mormon Faith

"I will not seek to compel any man to believe as I do, only by the force of reasoning, for the truth will cut its own way."

—Joseph Smith

Prefatory Note: Before reading this final Chapter, it is again suggested that if you have not read the *Introduction*, *Foundational Preface*, and preceding Chapters, you do so first. Such prerequisite reading is again essential for understanding and appreciating the consequential conclusions and implications of this work, both in relation to the validity and viability of the Mormon faith as a belief system *independent* of the commitments of its adherents, and as a social system defined in large measure by such commitments.

It seems appropriate at this point, and prior to the recapitulation and assessment which follow, to briefly address Joseph Smith's quote above, and his apparent confidence (shared no doubt by all devout Mormons) that "the truth [of Mormonism] will cut its own way" by "the force of reasoning." Is there any reasonable basis for such confidence? If so, what is it? If not, why not, and from what alternative perspective, if any, can we correctly understand what was said?

The short answer to the first question above is *no*. *Pace* Joseph Smith, the "truth" of Mormonism can only "cut its own way" by emotional appeal, suppressed reasoning, and self-deception. What we can arguably say we know (beyond a reasonable doubt) on the basis of the analytical work performed in this work and the extensive and credible work referred to in other relevant sources, is that the most fundamental theological truth claim in Mormon theology – the claim that the Mormon 'Godhead' and 'Plan of Salvation' *literally* and *necessarily* exist as fully conceptualized in Mormon doctrine – is utterly false or incoherent, as well as factually vacuous. There is, in other words, arguably nothing intelligible in Mormonism for reason to work on, and even if there was, there is not one stitch of reliable evidence to support even the probable truth of such a claim. There is no actual "truth" in the Mormon doctrine of deity or in fundamental Mormon cosmology which could possibly – by the "force of reasoning" or otherwise – "cut its own way" in the rational mind of a reasonably skeptical outsider, or even a rational and intellectually honest insider. This of course is so for all theistic religions as well.

In fact, the so-called "force of reasoning" which allegedly 'cuts its own way' to compel belief in Mormonism (or any theistic faith) has little, if anything, to do with reason at all. And given the presuppositional nature of theistic reasoning, and the numerous reasoning fallacies and "evasive possibility strategies" commonly used in presenting, arguing for and defending theistic belief, it is fair to say that whatever Smith had in mind when he used the word "reasoning" was more akin to (if not in fact) magical and wishful or delusional thinking, and neither *sound* reasoning nor *valid* argument.

So what is it then that *compels* belief in Mormonism, if not the self-evident truth of such belief itself or the "force of reason?" As we learned in Chapter 6, what compels belief in the 'Parent-God' of *any* faith is simply and merely a neuropsychological reaction. More specifically, it is ultimately, and primarily, a powerful transference-*affect* induced by a tacit appeal to *implicit memory* formed in infancy in virtue of our "basic biological situation" (Faber 2004, 2010). In this regard, and as shall be argued in the pages which follow, only by exploiting the human condition with false or incoherent claims of 'revelation,' bogus promises (and threats), and *a priori question-begging* arguments for the existence of a 'Heavenly Father' and his 'Plan of Salvation,' can the Mormon message exert any force at all on the suffering, needy, anxious, and culturally preconditioned brain of man.

In the end, it seems Joseph Smith's words betray the very motivations he sought to deny. Everything he did was an obvious (even if tacit) attempt to essentially compel others to believe as he did, and to accept his claim that he was the chosen 'Prophet of the Restoration.' This he did then – as Church leaders and missionaries of the faith do today – through, again, the exploitative inducement of an affective, infantile state of mind characterized by submissive, 'child-like' feelings of *dependence* on, *love* for, *attachment* to, and *awe* of the Mormon 'Parent-God,' and the likewise regressive magical, wishful thinking beneath the believed efficacy of prayer and authoritatively administered priesthood rites (i.e. "blessings") and ordinances of salvation. Such an effort to corrupt reality (Schumaker 1995) by inducing a dissociative mental state of faith (not reason) through a selective appeal to scripture, and through persuasion, 'testimony,' teaching, exhortation, rite, and ritual, is clearly nothing other than a well-designed program of mind-control. This program is motivated at least in part by the desire and intent to get others to accept certain religious truth claims; to essentially compel ('convert') others to believe and have faith in the Mormon god and the "truth" of the Mormon faith, and to live their lives according to the Mormon 'Plan.' Even those authoritarian Mormon leaders today who might arrogantly and forebodingly insist (as Elder Boyd K. Packer once did in a General Conference address) that it is more important that they be "understood" than agreed with, would arguably (and transparently) make such an implicitly threatening disclosure to, at bottom, compel others to 'fall in line' and believe as *they* do (or else!) about the existence of their god and his 'revealed' purpose and will for their lives. To think or suggest otherwise is, as I see it, either naïve, dishonest or indicative of either a state of denial or a disconcerting lack of self-awareness. (Who, after all, is not at least capable of, or inclined to, at least tacitly seek truth in numbers as a way to perhaps justify one's own self-invested and fervently wished-for beliefs and related commitments and sacrifices; and/or as a way to allay the effects of suppressed doubt and deep-seeded feelings of self-betrayal?)

Recapitulation of Analytical Arguments and Concerns

With the above as perhaps a fitting prelude to what follows in this chapter and *Appendix A*, we might all do well to pause and again revisit (and perhaps more deeply commit ourselves to) the dictum that as far as we humans are concerned, "fallibilism is the name of the game." If we have learned anything as a species, we have certainly learned that with respect to our knowledge of truth human fallibilism is a fact of life; that what we know – or think we know – about the world and the universe is provisional and constantly changing, and that what we call "truth" is, apart from its minimalist, deflationary construct and what is widely or globally and cross-culturally considered "basic" or "fundamental," "self-evident" truth, often complex, and at times counterintuitive and paradoxical in nature. Moreover, as we have also learned, there is no sensible talk of "the real" *sans contexte*, or of things as they *really* are. (See Chapter 1 and Nielsen 2001, 199-233) Rather, truth *about* reality is context, time, and language dependent, and our *knowledge* of such truth (as opposed, again, to the incoherent notion of 'Absolute Truth' or knowledge of *Reality* as it *really* is) requires *justification* to be regarded as such; justification which we have referred to, following Nielsen's take on Rawls and Daniels, as "wide reflective equilibrium." This, it seems to me, is particularly so regarding the putative truths of religious beliefs in general, and Mormon and other theistic beliefs in particular.

That said, let's return to where we began in our *Foundational Preface*: with the fictional, dramatic exchange portrayed in the 1984 Mormon Temple endowment film between the Sectarian Minister and Adam regarding the intelligibility of the sectarian concept of 'God.' This exchange, of course, is still as relevant today as before. Significantly, it opens the door to a similar test for the Mormon god, confirming implicitly what we intuitively know — that *there is no truth without language*. "This is not," as Nielsen points out, "linguistic idealism for it does not suggest or in anyway imply absurdly that, [for example], there were no stones or trees around before there were humans with their languages to describe them. But it does claim that we cannot think about them or understand what they are and, of course, talk about them without having a language. Similarly," he concludes, "though they [*i.e.* the stones and trees] exist quite independently of what we say or think, there could be no *truths* about them without a language. Truth is in this way *language-dependent* in the way most objects [*e.g.* stones or trees] are not (2001, 214)."

Although, as a natural matter of course, we cannot, through our physical senses, encounter and point to a god (in his doctrinal fulness, if at all) as we can a stone or a tree, the alleged *truth* of a god's factual existence is nonetheless likewise language-dependent. It makes no sense, echoing Nielsen (and Adam in the Mormon Temple film), to try to discover or understand — either directly through ostention, or indirectly through instruction or putative revelation — what this god is, or even *that* he exists (given his alleged inaccessibility to the natural senses) without any coherent, linguistic description or "reference range (Nielsen 1982, 140-170)." Moreover, such linguistic descriptions, if they are intelligible and coherent in the Quinean sense of how well such descriptions hang together with and, in Rey's words, "[strengthen] evidential relations among the vast network of interlocking [and justified, true] beliefs [or knowledge] we have about the world" (Rey in Anthony 2007, 251; Quine 1960), are also *contextual* as well as language dependent. They are contextual, that is, in a necessarily naturalistic sense because they are asserted to be literally factual and true; and such assertions can only be justified — from a 'coherence view' — in relation to what we know *vis-à-vis* the natural world or realm of existence.[157]

---

157 Regarding the relationship among language, thought, and belief about the natural world, and apropos to our analysis, Sam Harris writes: "The first thing to notice about beliefs is that they must suffer the company of their neighbors. Beliefs are both logically and semantically related. Each constrains, and is in turn constrained by, many others. ... In fact, logical and semantic constraints appear to be two sides of the same coin, because our need to understand what words mean in each new context requires that our beliefs be free from contradiction (at least locally)." ... Therefore, "[t]o know what a given belief is *about*, I must know what my words mean; to know what my words mean, my beliefs must be generally consistent. There is just no

So where does all this leave us? It would seem, appropriating the words of Wittgenstein, that our investigation or analysis of the Mormon faith and all theistic faiths gets its importance from "destroying" that which is "nothing but houses of cards, and…clearing up the ground of language on which they stand." Accordingly, and in virtue of the necessary "critical commonsensism which would come to grips with…questions concerning the limits of intelligible discourse;" a 'commonsensism' based on certain "minimal semantical assumptions" (Nielsen 2001, 250-3), we are left, at the end of our analysis, with the destruction of the Mormon concept of 'God,' the way 'God' is used in Mormon God-talk, and with it the entire Mormon faith — the entire "house of cards." Such in part is the therapeutic value of the deconstructive, or analytical, work we have done— a work which is done by the authority of reason and common sense. It is a work, moreover, that in Wittgenstein's view is stated elsewhere. Perhaps in the end, "All that philosophy can do…[is] destroy idols."

To sum up, the Mormon concept of 'God' is, as a putative quasi-anthropomorphic being, just like the 'sectarian God' and all other metaphysical, nonanthropomorphic gods the Mormons denounce as unintelligible, incomprehensible, and a 'mass of confusion.' Such a god is, like all others of traditional and developed Christianity, Judaism, and Islam, factually unintelligible as literally and fully conceptualized and believed.

Simply put, the assertion made presuppositionally either on the basis of putative revelation or on personal 'spiritual (religious) experience' that the Mormon god objectively, literally, or actually exists is either false or incoherent. Such a truth claim is neither justified nor justifiable. Rather, it is utterly without sense and warranted assertability. To insist or believe otherwise is, on the basis of this analysis, irrational. Such is the literal status of the Mormon god and the belief about the Mormon god.

*Faith or confidence that the Mormon god actually exists, or trust that the Mormon god exists as an actual being makes sense **only if** the concept of the Mormon god, the way 'God' is used in Mormon discourse and doctrine, is at least intelligible and factually meaningful. Paradoxically it makes **no** sense as a necessary requirement of salvation if the Mormon god actually exists as conceptualized and worshipped. Consequently, Mormon believers are in a double-bind with respect to their faith. Because the concept of their god is incoherent their faith is incoherent and therefore irrational. Because they attest to having faith in their god, such faith, as well as their god's requirement of such faith for salvation, necessarily makes their god incoherent.*

These conclusions, which again pertain to all other theistic faiths as well, are reached on the basis of the critical, conceptual analysis described in Chapters 1 and 2 of this book, and performed in Chapters 3 and 6 respectively, as well as in other notable works referred to throughout. To summarize, the central, *a priori* argument of this conceptual analysis is as follows:

---

escaping the fact that there is a tight relationship between the words we use, the type of thoughts we think, and what we can believe to be true about the world." Further, and relatedly, as Harris correctly observes, "… the value we put on logical consistency is neither misplaced nor mysterious. In order for my speech to be intelligible to others – and, indeed, to *myself* — my beliefs about the world must largely cohere. … Certain logical relations, after all, seem etched into the very structure of our world" (2004, 53–4).

Summary Analytical Argument

1. If we cannot make sense of, or do not (could not) possibly know (through personal experience or the objective observation of *some relevant* – or contrasting – evidence or otherwise) (i) what the *primary*, metaphysical (or *nonanthropomorphic*) attributes or referents of the Mormon god would *actually* be like or *specifically* refer to as fully conceptualized and believed in the Mormon faith (see Chapter 3); or (ii) what the specific, intelligible *truth-conditions* are, or could possibly be, for the claim that such a god with such attributes *literally* exists as taught and believed, then beyond mere *familiarity* with the 'God-talk' used, or the *imaginability* of certain stated attributes of god as extensions of human attributes, or the *pictorial* meaning ascribed to mental images suggested by certain utterances regarding the actions of – and interactions with – god, there would be no way for anyone to make *rational* or *coherent* sense of such a putative being. Nor would it be possible to at least *in principle* empirically confirm or disconfirm (either directly or indirectly) the truth or falsity of such an existential claim. (Such a proposed requirement for establishing factual significance is *not*, again, "positivist" or "verificationist" dogma. See Chapter 1, Nielsen 1971, 406-37; 1989, 15-26; 2001, 470-88; 2006, 9-45 and 115-44, and Martin 1990, 40-78 and 1999.)

2. If 1 obtains, then the concept of the Mormon god, the way 'God' is used in the Mormon faith in relation to each member of the Mormon godhead, is incoherent, and the truth claim that such a putative being *actually* or *literally* exists is factually meaningless.

3. On the basis of the conceptual analysis performed in this work and elsewhere as referenced throughout (as well, arguably, on the basis of rational, common sense), 1 obtains.

4. Therefore, given 3, 2 necessarily obtains, thereby rendering the Mormon god a *factual non reality* as fully conceptualized and believed, and the assertion of its actual existence (as well as the existence of the 'Son of God' and the 'Holy Ghost') unwarranted because fundamentally unjustifiable as a truth claim.

5. On the basis of 4, the Mormon beliefs in the actual existence of their god's 'Plan of Salvation,' as well as 'revelation' from and 'faith' in their god, are likewise *necessarily* incoherent and without factual significance.

6. Given 4 and 5, the fundamental theological beliefs or doctrines comprising the Mormon faith cannot be rationally or coherently accepted or believed as *actual* or *literal* truths. Nor can they be legitimately argued for or defended. This is so at one level because such argument would invariably and necessarily employ the evasive "possibility" strategies of *ignorance*, *isolation* and *inflation* or resort to various reasoning fallacies which would *a priori* invalidate any arguments made. But it is also the case primarily because, in Nielsen's words, "we know *ahead of time before even considering the arguments* that there can be *no* proof of the existence of God, for *no* premise or *no* conclusion with 'God' in it could be true (a requisite for a sound argument

[or hypothesis]), since the term is of an incoherent concept." And we know as well, Nielsen states parenthetically, that "If a concept is really incoherent, [as it is with the concept of the Mormon god,] it is plainly illegitimate" (1993, 252).

The conclusions (**3–6**) of the above summary argument are reflected and reinforced in the following sets of self-answering *questions*[158] to the Mormon believer, who is asked yet one more time, as Loftus suggests, to test his or her faith "as a disinterested investigator" with "the presumption of skepticism" (2008, 66–67; see *Introduction*):

First, regarding the believed existence of the Mormon god — or of his attributes or referents — as conceptualized in the Mormon faith and presented in Chapter 3...

- What *exactly* are *eternal intelligences* or, more particularly, an *eternal intelligence of the highest order* (i.e. 'man' and 'god' respectively; see D&C 93:29 and Abraham 3: 18-21)? In other words, what *specifically* are they like, and what would *positively* and *perspicuously* count for or against the stated truth of their actual (or even theoretical) existence?

- What precisely is *spirit matter* (or *spirit element*) and what *specifically* is it like – or what *specifically* are its properties or truth-conditions – that the putative truth of its

---

158 Again, the discomforting truth — or proverbial 'devil' — is in the details when it comes to the justification of truth claims. Although, as we learned in Chapter 1, indicative statements have truth-value in a minimalist or deflationary sense, they cannot be regarded as indicative of *actual* (or justified) truth or knowledge without justification; and they cannot be justified unless they are at least *justifiable*. Finally, and commonsensically in a broad naturalistic context, justifiability in matters concerning the determination of *actual* truth requires the ostensive or linguistic specification of the claimed existent's (or reality's) descriptive referents and/or corresponding truth-conditions — specific referents and truth-conditions which can, in principle, be empirically confirmed or disconfirmed as being *actually* true (or probably true) or false (or probably false). *Ad hoc*, vague or ambiguous generalities, or likenesses established through false analogies and/or invalid analogical predication, cannot get us to actual truth, or to a verifiable understanding of what we believe, particularly where, as Nielsen points out, it is not possible "at least in principle to state certain empirically determinable states of affairs that would justify one in asserting the *existence* of a putative existent (e.g. 'God') and certain contrasting empirically determinable states of affairs in which one will be justified in asserting the *nonexistence* of such an existent" (Nielsen 1971, 433).

Nor can suffice the mere assertions of faith, revelation, spiritual (or special, mystical) feelings or ineffable experiences (see Chapters 5 and 6), which must also be justified, and which are necessarily dependent on the at least possible existence of their god as conceptualized and believed. Because Mormon believers claim the objective, *actual* truth of certain putative metaphysical or eternal and supernatural realities, the requirement of *exactness* or *specificity* (through ostension, description, or analogy) with respect to the descriptive referents and truth-conditions of such alleged realities is warranted in determining if such claims are at least *justifiable* sufficient to be considered even possibly or theoretically true as objective, factual realities with at least predictable empirical consequences in satisfaction of specific truth-conditions (as is the case, for example, with unseen, subatomic particles). If such truth claims are not justifiable because they are unintelligible, incoherent, and factually meaningless due to a lack of the perspicuous specificity of descriptive referents and truth-conditions, the putative realities they allegedly attest to, in virtue of believed revelation and faith-based spiritual experiences, may reasonably be regarded as *factual non-realities*. The belief in such realities — along with the corresponding belief in the personal experience of faith in and revelation and spiritual experience from 'God through the Holy Ghost or Light of Christ' — can reasonably be regarded as irrational (see Chapter 2) and perhaps even delusional.

actual (or even theoretical) existence might, in principle, be empirically confirmed or disconfirmed?

- What exactly are *glorified (or "exalted") flesh and bone* and what are they like or what *specifically* are their properties or truth-conditions that we might *clearly* know what, if anything, might *positively* count for or against the stated truth of their actual existence?

- What *specifically* is an *infinite, eternal,* and *exalted Spirit*? What is it like, or what in principle would empirically count for or against the *actual* or *literal* existence of such an entity or being? How exactly could one verify, falsify or in *any* way justify the asserted *actual* existence of such an entity or being?

- How can we make rational sense of an infinite, eternal and exalted being remotely – from another universe or dimension of space and time – creating, ruling and governing the Universe and worlds without end by the "Power of the Priesthood" through the spoken word or transpersonal "Light of Truth" (or "Divine Immanence")? Again, referring to the preceding questions, what specifically would count for or against the alleged existence of such a being? And what specific and indicative empirical consequences could be objectively observed or otherwise determined and differentiated from known natural phenomena to confirm or disconfirm the actual existence of such alleged *sui generis* acts or putative powers or agencies of divine creation and universal governance?

- What exactly *is* the '*power of the priesthood*' and '*Light of Truth*' and what are they like or what are their properties or truth-conditions such that the stated truth of their factual existence might, in principle, be empirically confirmed or disconfirmed?

- Additionally, what would the claim that 'God is our Father in Heaven' actually and specifically refer to or entail? Specifically, what could it *literally* mean for an immortal, material, yet non-biological being with a tangible though bloodless body of exalted flesh and bones to *literally* procreate a spirit being? How can anyone possibly conceive of such a being and such a procreative process with a like female being except through analogical predication? And how could such analogical predication even be valid if we know nothing literal about such putative beings?

- Finally, regarding the believed *personal omnipresence* of the Mormon god (or 'Immanent God'), what *specifically* would such 'omnipresence' actually mean, or *actually* be like? How would it actually be physically possible (not merely imaginable) for a spatio-temporally transcendent and finite god to *literally* be personally, willfully, and with full knowledge and power in and through *all* things as the "law" by which *all* things are created (ordered, organized), governed, and sustained (D&C 88)? Further, what are the specific truth-conditions of such an omnipresent, 'Immanent God' such that its claimed existence could possibly be objectively or empirically confirmed or disconfirmed as being true (or probably true) or false (or probably false) as conceptualized and believed?

Second, regarding the Mormon belief in the existence of Jesus Christ and the atonement and resurrection of Christ that was presented and analyzed in Chapters 3 and 4 respectively...

- What *specifically* would it entail for a human being to actually be the 'Son of God' and 'Savior and Redeemer' of the world, and what, in principle, would empirically count for or against the actual (or literal) existence of such an entity or being so as to justify the belief that such a being *actually* (or even theoretically) existed or exists? More specifically, what would it *actually* be like for a transcendent, non-biological being ('God'), whose putative tangible, exalted body is allegedly without blood (and therefore, necessarily without semen), to *literally*, biologically inseminate (through *literal*, sexual relations) a mortal (biological) woman to biologically procreate a 'man-God' (Jesus of Nazareth)? Further, what *specifically* would a 'man-God' be like, other than as a being that is simplistically and noncognitively described as wholly a god and wholly a man?

- Relatedly, and more specifically, how would it actually be possible (not merely imaginable) for this man-God known as Jesus Christ to *literally* and *vicariously* 'atone' for *all* the so-called 'sins' of mankind (past, present, and future) through personal suffering and the literal shedding of blood? How exactly (or in theory) would such a putative act of vicarious atonement actually work? What specifically would the empirical consequences of such an infinite and eternal act of vicarious atonement actually be such that the claimed *sui generis* 'spiritual consequences' of such an alleged act — *i.e.* the transcendent sense or feeling of peace, joy, love, forgiveness, and redemption experienced in virtue of faith in Christ, repentance, and baptism — could, in principle, be objectively and conclusively identified, confirmed or disconfirmed, and differentiated from the naturalistic consequences (or predicted outcomes) of known neuropsychological phenomena?

- What would it mean, or be like, and how would it *actually* be physically possible (not just imaginable) for a 'man-God' (Jesus) to *actually* die as a mortal being and be *literally* resurrected by a spatiotemporally *transcendent* god (whatever that actually means, if anything) as an immortal, exalted, non-biological being? What *specifically* does the act of *resurrection* entail? How exactly (or in theory) does the act of resurrection actually work? How would it be *actually* possible (not merely imaginable), given what we know about the physical universe, for a dead, decomposed body to be *literally* resurrected to an immortal state of existence? What *specifically* would such a state of existence *actually* be like, and how *specifically* would the putative resurrection of Jesus, as 'the Christ,' *actually* enable the like resurrection of all men?

- Finally, related to the first and third sets of questions above in this second category, what specific and objectively verifiable evidence can be offered that would *uncontroversially* justify *beyond a reasonable doubt* — *i.e.* without question-begging appeal to scripture or asserted or alleged and unverifiable instances of revelation, spiritual confirmation, vision, or visitation — the historical existence of 'Jesus of Nazareth' as either a man or 'man-God,' or the existence of a literally resurrected 'Jesus Christ' as the literal 'Son of God'?

Third, regarding the Mormon concepts of revelation, prayer and spiritual experience presented and analyzed in Chapters 5, 6, and 7…

- Granting for the sake of argument the possible existence of the god of interest, what would it *actually* be like and how would it *actually* be physically possible (not merely imaginable) to *literally* receive a revelation from an infinite, eternal and finite being (whatever that could possibly be, if anything) who is transcendent to the world in space and time?

- Moreover, and making the same concession above for argument's sake, how *exactly* — without invalidly appealing to analogy — do (or could) revelation and prayer *actually* (or even in theory) work? What specific *empirical* consequences would, in principle, confirm or disconfirm that a revelation from a god has or had in fact actually occurred as claimed? What *specific* empirical consequences would, in principle, confirm or disconfirm (beyond mere coincidence) the claim that a vocal or silent prayer to an alleged transcendent being in another universe or dimension of space and time has in fact *actually* been heard and answered, particularly if it is believed (as is typically the case) that *any* or *every* state of affairs attending the offering and aftermath of sincere supplication to such a putative being constitutes prayer received and answered?

- Finally, apart from concerns about the possibility of revelation given the impossibility of a given god's existence as fully conceptualized and stated, how or by which *specific, objective, and justified human criteria* would an objective, skeptical outsider (or believing insider for that matter) be able to *conclusively* authenticate — through cross-checking or some other form of rigorous, objective method of authentication — the existence, source and truthfulness of putative revelation? How *specifically* would one differentiate it from neuropsychological phenomena such as, for example, an auditory or visual hallucination or suggestively (or hypnotically) induced psychotic or dissociative experience? How could one objectively determine and either confirm or disconfirm that a putatively revelatory or spiritual experience was not merely the subjectively interpreted neurological effect of the human brain exclusively caused by a self or other-induced mental state or some random, naturalistic phenomenon? How could one explain (without merely defensively 'explaining away') those asserted and reported *non*-Mormon revelations or spiritual and mystical experiences which fundamentally differ from, or refute, the theological *content* or truth claims of Mormon revelation, or the authenticity of alleged Mormon spiritual experiences that confirm the truthfulness of their faith? On the basis of what specific, non-arbitrary, non-question-begging, objective, and widely accepted (*i.e.* justified) adjudicating criteria, would Mormon believers be able to warrantedly or justifiably assert that such non-Mormon revelations and religious experiences are *not* true or trustworthy, while yet their own (or their Church's) are?

Finally, regarding the Mormon concept of 'faith,' the existence of faith, and the appeal to faith presented and analyzed in Chapters 6 and 7...

- How *specifically*, or in what *specific* way, is faith an *actual* 'principle of power' in man and in god? How, in principle, can the objective or even theoretical existence of faith as both a 'principle of power' (sufficient to 'create worlds,' 'move mountains,' 'raise the dead,' 'heal the sick,' or otherwise 'bind the will of God') and an 'eternal principle of salvation' be non-circularly, objectively, and empirically confirmed or disconfirmed or otherwise justified?

- Moreover, what *specifically*, given the concept of the Mormon god in its theological fulness, are believers asked to *actually have faith in* and why *specifically*, given the putative attributes and qualities of the Mormon god (*sans* faith itself) and the irrefutable insufficiency of faith, is 'faith in God and Christ' even required and considered necessary for believing in the existence of the Mormon god and Christ, and for the attainment of salvation and eternal life?

- Finally, what *specific* objective and widely accepted (justified) human criteria would enable the *conclusive* cognitive differentiation of 'faith in God or Christ' (or the religious faith-state) from, for example, a projective transference resulting in a dissociative, hallucinatory mental state? How, and again on the basis of what specific objective and widely accepted or justified human criteria, could one differentiate alleged faith-based cognition and experience from mere wishful, 'magical thinking' and the "believer's [corresponding] hallucinatory, heartfelt conviction that his invisible, mysterious, 'transmundane' Parent-God is [*actually*] there [or present]" (Faber 2004, 65)?

If the most informed and inspired of Mormon believers or 'General Authorities' of the Church were constrained by force of personal integrity (or somehow willingly enabled through some form of chemical inducement or technology) to truthfully, specifically, and straightforwardly answer these questions and all other analytical questions asked in Chapters 3–7 — and the natural and necessary follow-up questions to unspecific (vague, ambiguous) or incoherent answers — I suggest that the *only* answer that could possibly and ultimately be given would be: "I don't know." If this is so then it would seem reasonable and not flippant to ask: *"How many admissions of ignorance in reply to analytical questions about the nature of something claimed to be known to actually exist are needed to convince a reasonable person that he or she does not in fact know what is believed or claimed to be known, and consequently does not know what is being talked about when such beliefs are unwarrantedly asserted as truth claims?"*

Moreover, such devout believers would no doubt admit under the influence of such hypothetical constraints that in virtue of the questions asked, and the complete absence of reliable evidence aside, their unpacked beliefs simply do not make sense and are in fact, by any rational standard, unbelievable. To which the following questions might reasonably and appropriately be asked from the arguments made in Chapters 2 and 6 in particular: *"Then how is it that you believe in something that is not understood or even understandable, which does not make sense, and which is by any rational standard utterly absurd?"* If, as Elder Benson suggested in his quoted words at the top of Chapter 6, when "backed against the wall" a Mormon believer "makes his stand" and appeals to faith, we must ask yet again: "Faith in *what*, specifically?" We must ask how faith (as felt and stated confidence or certainty) in the truth of such admittedly unbelievable beliefs would be possible without rationalization or self-deception. Even if solely for the sake of argument, we grant the possible existence of the Mormon god, as well as his alleged purpose or 'work and glory,' and the supposed 'eternal stakes' involved — why would such faith (as trust or confidence) even be required or necessary, not to mention be considered a virtue?

Such a requirement, given the preceding considerations and arguable insufficiency of such faith, simply makes no sense. And if the reply to such an observation is that faith is required to make sense out of *apparent* nonsense, then the objection to such a reply would be that, in the absence of any possible intelligible and coherent explanation, '*apparent* nonsense' is *actual* nonsense and cannot be made sensible by appealing to further nonsense. Given this apparently self-evident proposition, and given that, as we learned in Chapter 3, the very concept of the Mormon god itself is, in fact, actual, utter nonsense, then the initial reply to the above query "Why would faith even be required or necessary?" could essentially translate to the incoherent assertion that believers must nonsensically have faith in order to somehow make what is incoherent coherent. But what could this actually, and ultimately, amount to if not gross metaphysical speculation and self-deception?

This translated assertion, if accepted on its face as at least reasonable, would presumably make both the authoritative and assertedly consequential requirement of faith and the necessity of faith-testing questionable at least, if not disturbing and morally objectionable. They simply ensure that nonsense prevails over sense as truth, and that believers endure to the end of this life believing nonsense. Still, in light of these conclusions, the assertions that both faith in the Mormon god and faith-testing are necessary and required does make sense from a particular point of view if we ask ourselves honestly, in the context of the *secular* agenda of the Mormon faith and all theistic religions: who benefits financially or otherwise by making faith and faith-testing an essential requirement of salvation?

According to Mormon author and apologist Glenn L. Pearson, "It is impossible [for regular Church members] to learn all the pat answers one would need [to address such questions].... [and such] pat answers eventually come from our scholars."[159] To this I would reply that it is not "pat answers" we are looking for here. The questions asked above and throughout this book do not require theological research or scholarship. Nor do they require proof or authoritative and question-begging answers from Church leaders. They merely require specific, clear, unambiguous, well reasoned, and non-question-begging answers that at least make rational sense to an objective outsider and can reasonably be regarded as justifiable in principle.

It would seem, on the basis of our analysis and the unanswerable (and therefore self-answering) questions its conclusions are based on, that we are left with Mormon (and arguably all theistic) believers who claim to *know* — by *revelation* or spiritual experience through *faith* — that which cannot possibly be known. This is so because that which is alleged to be known is factually unintelligible and therefore unjustifiable. The putative 'religious ways of knowing' — through faith by revelation and so-called spiritual

---

159 Glenn L. Pearson, *The Book of Mormon, Key to Conversion*, Bookcraft, 1963, p.4.

experience — are not properly basic (or self-evident) and are not capable of producing valid or even justifiable truth claims. This makes the fruits of such *ersatz* ways of knowing factually vacuous and necessarily both incoherent and unintelligible *vis-à-vis* the likewise unintelligible concept of the Mormon god.

The above concluding argument, questions, and observations *cannot* be adequately appreciated or addressed without *first*, and *at least*, carefully reading *and* understanding the necessary information on conceptual analysis introduced in the *Foundational Preface* and presented in some depth in Chapter 1. Nor perhaps, and as an important and relevant aside, can such be fully appreciated without differentiating what Adèle Mercier refers to in her *Religious Belief and Self-Deception* (2009) as the crucial difference between "first-order" and "second-order" beliefs, and the implications of such a difference for understanding *what* it is that believers believe about god, if anything, and how it is that *no one* can have the belief that 'God exists' without self-deception.

Drawing primarily on the work of Gottlob Frege and referencing Dennett's earlier presented idea of "belief in belief" (2006), Mercier, Professor of Philosophy at Queen's University, Ontario, first points out the fact that "…believing something – let us call it having a *first-order* belief about an object or event – differs from believing that you believe it – let us call that having a *second-order* belief about your first-order belief, namely that you have it" (41). After establishing that "[f]irst-order beliefs are compatible not only with the absence of second-order beliefs, but with their outright denial," (41) and that "…believing that you believe something is not the same as believing it" (42), Mercier demonstrates that "[m]ost people don't really believe the religious claims they purport to believe" (e.g. life after death) and then concludes that "[v]irtually all religious beliefs are second-order beliefs, mistaken for first-order beliefs." (43) She then offers two "canonical ways" to believe that one believes he has a first-order belief (e.g. 'God exists') that he doesn't really have.

"One way," according to Mercier, "is to believe that you hold a belief that "turns out to be contentless or empty, that is, about nothing," like, for example, when children "think they believe in (the existence of) Santa Claus. …Whatever children believe when they think they believe 'in Santa Claus' is not a first-order belief in some [actual] thing or person, but a second-order belief…[either about the fact] that they have a particular belief about a particular person, when in fact there is no such belief to be believed, for want of any person for this belief to be about; or else at best, a belief…[that] is a (false) second-order belief that a certain *concept* [i.e. of 'Santa Clause']…is singularly instantiated in the world (44).

"Another canonical way to believe that you have a belief that you don't really have is to think you believe something that turns out to be unintelligible or incoherent, i.e. "ill-formed to even count as a belief" (44). Apropos to our analysis here, Mercier illustrates her point by asking the reader to "imagine if someone claimed to believe that slithy toves gyre and gamble in wabes, say, because they read it in a book presumed written by an authoritative author, much like we believe that $E=mc^2$ even though we don't really understand it. It's not that their first-order belief would be wrong: it's not that slithy toves don't after all gamble in wabes. It's that [unlike the belief that $E=mc^2$] there is no such belief to be had, since 'slithy toves' is an expression that doesn't even purport to make sense. It's not just that there are no such things as slithy toves (though it is that, too), but that one would not even know what to start looking for to see whether slithy toves existed or not, much less whether gambling in wabes holds of them. Since the sentence is meaningless nonsense," Mercier points out, "so too is it to purport to believe it. Even purporting to have a second-order belief about the *concept* of slithy toves is empty [of sense and factual significance] since the very concept about which one is purporting to have a belief is itself undefined [and incoherent]" (44-5).

All of this leads Mercier to the reasonable assertion (confirmed I think by common-sense and, to me personally, by my own experiences) that "[m]ost people who claim to have religious beliefs have scarcely ever analyzed the contents of their belief, and indeed are reluctant to do so even when prompted," as readers have perhaps been in this book and numerous others. "Ask a theist pointed questions about God, or about the concept of God," she writes, "and you end up with non-answers…things we really can't understand. …So their first-order beliefs have referents they can't refer to, and their second-order beliefs can't be of the sort that are about concepts, since the concepts about which they would purport to be are themselves undefined, indeed purposefully so. The concepts making up their belief are essentially vacant [of any cognitive or factual significance]" (45). These observations lead Mercier to her final – and telling – conclusion that "*[r]eligion is all about believing that one's beliefs are right, not about having right beliefs*. If first-order religious beliefs had content, their content [would be intelligible, coherent, and factually meaningful, and] could [at least in principle] be checked against the truth. It is precisely because such beliefs lack content that one can go on believing that one believes them despite [their unintelligibility and incoherence, or] any and every evidence" (47). Such a conclusion squares with the analytical conclusions of this present work, as do Mercier's closing comments that "…the price of second-order belief in vacant first-order beliefs is self-deception," and "[a]ll forms of self-deception are dangerous, but none is more cruel than that which robs one's very reason for living of its authenticity" (47, emphasis mine).

Given all the above, *any* attempt to validly or respectably refute the ultimate conclusions of the analyses performed throughout this book and recapitulated in this chapter would require much more than mere question-begging 'hand waving,' or asserting dismissively that such conclusions are not so on the basis of scripture, or revelation, or erroneously and incoherently regarding religious experiences to be properly basic. Nor will it do to attempt to discredit the premises and analytical methodology used on the grounds of previously refuted objections without responding to such refutations in turn with substantive and well-informed and reasoned counter-argument. (This, of course, will require, to be credible, a great deal more study than of this book, specifically — and minimally — the careful study of Nielsen's and others' work as cited throughout and listed as sources.)

Moreover, and as established in the *Introduction*, the above conclusions cannot be validly refuted by *poisoning the well* through an *a priori ad hominem* argument by suggesting, for example, that the author is clearly a disgruntled apostate who can't leave the Church alone, or an infidel living in sin without the Spirit. Nor can they be validly refuted by merely *affirming the consequent* — by arguing, for example, that any ex-Mormon's criticism of the faith is invalid; the author is an ex-Mormon, therefore his criticisms of the faith are invalid. Nor is available the invalid appeal to scripture or authority, which *begs the question* regarding the primary and ultimate question at issue, *i.e.* the Mormon god's actual existence. Lastly, these conclusions cannot validly be avoided or side-stepped on pragmatic grounds ('my faith works for me'), or by resorting to *tu quoque* deflections, or by employing *false analogies* or *invalid analogical predication*, or by arguing for 'eschatological (next-life) verification,' or by 'moving the goal posts' through the use of *ad hoc* theological speculation, or the retreat to those 'evasive possibility strategies' of *ignorance, isolation,* and *inflation* presented in Chapter 2 and referenced throughout, and/or by *special pleading* through invalid appeals to religious authority, revelation, faith or purely subjective 'spiritual experience' established as such in Chapters 5 and 6.

Clearly, regarding the last set of avoidance tactics and evasive strategies mentioned above, the alleged fact that some adopted way of life might 'work' at a personal level does not necessarily — or in *any* way — mean or suggest that it in fact does, or that the way of life adopted is '*The* Way,' or that its putative, subjectively experienced and interpreted effects are indicative of some revealed Truth or Law Giver. To employ such reasoning fallacies and others betrays denial and self-deception, and to retreat to such evasive strategies and implicit *special pleading*[160] betrays unacknowledged doubt. In both cases the believer betrays the failure to deeply understand and appreciate the weight and implications of the arguments made and the questions asked. Regardless, it is clear that the employment of such tactics and strategies results at best in further metaphysical nonsense. At worst, it ends in utter incoherence. Either way, nothing is made clear and we are no closer to the truth or to the justifiability of Mormon theology.

Still, notwithstanding the caveats of the preceding three paragraphs, and hearkening back to an earlier quote by Kant regarding the importance to "sagacity and insight" of "knowing what questions might reasonably be asked," it seems appropriate to wonder and question (again, following the thinking of Wittgensteinian fideists) whether or not all the questions asked above, in virtue of conducting a conceptual analysis of Mormon theology, "might reasonably be asked?" In matters of faith are such questions even relevant?

They are, I would argue, relevant where the believer avers or claims to *know* of the *actual* existence of a *literal* god with *literal* primary, secondary, and relational attributes as doctrinally described, or claims to know of *literal* or *objective* spiritual and eternal realities or phenomena — as Mormon believers do regarding the putative *eternal* existence of their 'God,' 'spirit matter,' 'eternal intelligences,' the 'Light of Truth,' and the putative *eternal* realities and phenomena of 'atonement,' 'resurrection,' 'revelation,' and 'faith.' Assuming that such alleged truths (and others, as enumerated and analyzed in Chapter 4) are important to Mormon believers, then the *philosophical* questions and challenges presented here are both relevant and appropriate, as are other formidable atheistic or atheological arguments and scientific challenges presented elsewhere. All of them pose a very serious, if not insurmountable, cumulative challenge, fallibility notwithstanding, to all forms of theistic belief.[161]

---

160 As, for example, through the mere allegation that the critical, conceptual analysis described and applied herein is *somehow* irrelevant to Mormon theology; that Mormon theology is *somehow* — or for *some* reason — isolated from such analysis or is *somehow* possible on the basis of what we *don't* know, or what might be *somehow* possible on the basis of current and unjustified scientific speculations, or on the unjustifiable belief that such a conclusion will *somehow, somewhere* and at *sometime* be decisively refuted by science or the divine dispensation of 'further light and knowledge.'

161 Such an atheological cumulative challenge or argument for the non-existence of any particular god can, as noted earlier in the *Foundational Preface* of this book, perhaps most notably (to me) be found in the clas-

Unless the believer resorts to question-begging, *ad hoc*, and *ad hominem* arguments to the aforementioned challenges, or solipsistically and incoherently holds that subjective feelings (or rather subjective interpretations of such putative feelings) are sufficient evidence to justify belief, it would seem to be both reasonable and responsible for Mormon (and all theistic) believers to further seriously ask themselves, *as skeptical outsiders*, a series of important follow-up questions.

First: *why are there so many crucial, critical, unnecessary and unnecessarily (because of the alleged reality of revelation from 'God') unanswered or unanswerable questions challenging my faith?*

Second: *why is it even possible to seriously and sincerely question or deny the very existence and necessity of my God when knowledge of his existence is allegedly so essential to the experience of joy in this life and eternal life, or salvation, in the life to come?*

Third, stated directly to believers: *How is it that your god's existence and necessity are even questionable and not compellingly or convincingly obvious to all of your god's children in the same sense that all self-justifying or justified, true beliefs and common (self-evident) knowledge are naturally compelling without self-deception or the need for faith?*

Fourth: *if your god is the only true god, and believing in, and worshipping, the right god is so important (or crucial to salvation), as it is believed to be, then why are there so many different concepts of god in the world? Why are there so many sincere believers who believe in so many fundamentally different gods, or interpretations of 'God,' particularly since the alleged 'one true God' has the power to reveal himself 'in truth' to all who seek to know him? Why should a god be hidden from the nonbeliever, the wrong believer, or the believer in crisis? Why do doubt, confusion, disagreement, and non-belief (or disbelief) even exist?*

Finally: *why is 'faith in God,' given its vulnerability to reason and doubt, necessary, required, or necessarily tested by that god for salvation? Why is there a need for faith, apologetics, and the existence and suppression of doubt, confusion, ignorance, and non-belief at all — given the putative nature and 'greatest desire of God,' and the putative eternal stakes involved?*

If the response to these follow-up questions is, once again, that answers exist, as do explanations which reconcile such apparent contradictions, yet this particular god, in his wisdom, or for undisclosed reasons, has chosen not to reveal such answers and explanations

---

sical works of Hume (1976), Kant (1949;1963), Nietzsche (1982; 2000), Feuerbach (1989, 2004) and Russell (1986), and the contemporary works of: Nielsen (1982, 2001, 2006), Mackie (1982), Martin (1990, 2003, 2006, 2007), Everitt (2004), Loftus (2008, 2010), Gale (1991), Drange (1998), Dawkins (2006), Dennett (2006), Harris (2004), Hitchens (2007), Stenger (2007, 2009), Steele (2008), George Smith (1989) and Beversluis (2007), as well as *many* others. While these works do not address Mormon theology directly, they do address those problems common to *all* theistic faiths and discoverable by those Mormon believers who choose to focus on the theological commonalities and the problems they pose to rational belief.

to man, then we must ask again: how can anyone possibly know that without retreating to revelation and faith, which are problematic and at issue? Further, why would a god *not* infallibly reveal such needed answers and explanations? Cannot, as Mormons believe, 'God,' Christ, and legions of angels descend from clouds of glory to visit, in the flesh, all mankind? Could not such an envoy — even the 'Eternal Godhead of Father, Son, and Holy Ghost' — visit the heads of all nations and faiths to establish and unify beliefs as common knowledge once and for all? Cannot, moreover, the eyes of man's understanding — as putative co-eternal intelligences and spirit children of the Mormon god — be opened by the 'power of the Holy Ghost' to see and know the Godhead and the truths of eternity in the flesh? Cannot man's eternal, God-like mind be enlightened by the 'Light of Truth'? If so, assuming solely for the sake of argument that such putative truths are even sensible and justifiable (*i.e.* intelligible, coherent, and factually meaningful), why has it not happened so that this god might reveal himself with answers and explanations?

We are not seeking for signs and wonders here. We are dealing with legitimate and appropriate questions and *real* doubt — *sincere* doubt. If revelation is, contrary to the reasoned conclusions reached in Chapter 5, indeed possible, why is it not forthcoming, together with the necessary 'spiritual boost' to the intellect that would enable understanding? Alternatively, according to Mormon belief, why wouldn't 'God' lift the human 'veil of forgetfulness' or human ignorance so that man might be re-acquainted, in sufficient fulness, with what he, as a putative eternal spirit and intelligence already knows? And if there are those who testify he has done so for them, then why not for all? Why are these and other questions unanswered or unanswerable by those who allegedly know the answers? Either way, all are in need and so many, no doubt, sincerely ask and seek in vain.

What possible purpose could a god's hiddenness and silence serve such that 'faith in God' would even be necessary? Why would faith even need to exist or need to be tested? Why would nonbelief, confusion, and real doubt be allowed to exist or need to remain until the 'next life' — which itself is highly questionable, to say the least? Moreover, if the stated reason for the Mormon god's hiddenness and silence to nonbelievers and/or disbelievers is their lack of worthiness or prior indoctrination, why would such 'worthiness' or prior indoctrination need to be a prerequisite for the revelation of this god's sure existence when such knowledge is, as taught and believed in the Mormon faith, essential to salvation? Isn't it more plausible and rational to conclude instead that there simply are no answers or explanations because there aren't any to give? Shouldn't we conclude that the incoherencies are not merely apparent, and that, given such incoherencies, the Mormon god (and all gods) as conceptualized therefore simply does not (cannot) *factually* exist?

Furthermore, if the response to the questions above is that elimination of such mysteries through the certain knowledge of a god's existence, if possible, would *force* people to believe, then the rejoinder would be to ask why belief is necessary or deemed (if it is) to be superior to knowledge, and how specifically knowledge is coercive and interferes with 'free choice' to believe instead of enabling it? The very notion that knowledge (or sure knowledge) is coercive is incoherent. How, it would be asked, given the incoherence of strong doxastic voluntarism, can providing compelling answers to reasonable questions in the form of true statements and rational justification force anyone to believe against their will?

As we have learned earlier, we do not *choose* to believe or accept as truth that which is clearly, commonly, or self-evidently known to be true. The assent of the 'will to believe' (whatever such 'will' might be) in the face of compelling knowledge and sense, is neither affirmation nor violation of will, in any sense of the term, but rather an *affirmation* of that which is either justified and true or self-evident to all. Besides, how is taking a 'leap of faith' and *forcing* ourselves to believe (or deciding to believe, no matter what) *in spite* of reason different from self-deception? How is forcing ourselves to believe against our natural inclination to doubt more virtuous than allowing ourselves to doubt, question, and disavow that which is found to be questionable or absurd under the weight of rational justification, sound *philosophical* analysis, or common sense?

Finally, the apologetic reply, if it is made, that the existence of such questions or of the non-answers to such questions is man's problem, not the Mormon god's — and that answers exist notwithstanding man's ignorance, differing interpretations of scripture and/ or disagreements regarding his nature, mind and will — is both evasive and nonsensical. This is particularly so given this god's putative secondary attributes (or powers and capacities), man's alleged relationship to him, and his putatively declared 'work and glory' (or greatest desire and purpose in relation to man), which is allegedly to 'bring to pass' man's 'immortality and eternal life.'

Such a sorry state of affairs, in light of the above, simply does not make sense. If it is then replied in rejoinder that not everything that is true necessarily makes sense and that we do not have to make sense of this particular state of affairs (*i.e.* the existence of unanswered or unanswerable questions) regarding all that we believe or feel to be true, I would reply in turn that we *do* indeed need to make sense of our ignorance and incongruence. We need to do so when by taking what is believed to be truth we are required in turn to embrace a prescribed and self-suppressive way of living, make or require real sacrifices and take or advocate real risks in return for merely hoped-for or wished-for rewards in this life or in a highly unlikely next-life. We are morally obligated to do so even if that which we believe to be true is potentially, if not actually, physically and/or psychologically harmful or dangerous to the believer or society (an argument which will be made later in this chapter and in the *Personal Postscript*). We certainly have the *right* to believe what we will, but such a right does not mean that we *should* believe what we do, or, more importantly, that we do not have an epistemological responsibility in sharing such beliefs and asserting (particularly without warrant) that they are true. We can, to be sure, eschew or neglect such an epistemological responsibility to self and others, but not without serious potential personal and social consequences.[162]

This all seems clear, reasonable, and fair enough. Still, this proposed reply, while relevant to the above rejoinder, again misses the central point of our analysis of the Mormon faith. The problem with the above rejoinders and replies to the troubling questions above is the assumption that a certain knowledge of a god's existence is, in fact, possible. But if the critical analysis of the Mormon concept of 'God' and Mormon theology suggested herein hits the mark, then such certain or perfect knowledge of a god's existence would be, on the basis of such analysis, *impossible* because the Mormon god – as fully conceptualized in the Mormon faith – is *necessarily* a *factual non-reality* as propositionally attested to and putatively experienced. So the overarching answer to the italicized questions above is

---

162 See Clifford 1999, 70–96; Krueger 1998, 207–217.

simply that it is possible to question the existence of the Mormon god, not just because of his need or desire to preserve 'free agency' in believing what one will. Nor is this because of incomplete or flawed revelation, or for some reason unknown to all but a god for that god to justifiably remain hidden and allow non-belief to exist and for him to require (or test) faith in his existence. Rather, it is because such a god does not — could not — exist as believed or doctrinally described. This conclusion, which necessarily follows from our analytical deconstruction of the concept of the Mormon god, might be — and likely would be — responded to in turn in at least three ways, each of which will be presented and replied to below.

Perhaps the first apologetic response to the conclusion that the Mormon god is a factual non-reality as conceptualized and defined or described would be that even if such were the case because of the natural limitation of our imperfect language, the Mormon god could or does nonetheless factually exist. It might be claimed that *conceptual* incoherence or the factual unintelligibility of existential statements does not necessarily equate to *actual* non-existence, and that we as humans can and do in fact know through direct personal experience alone of the actual existence of 'God.'

Such a response, of course, though perhaps persuasive to some, would also miss the point and is deeply flawed. In the first place: there is the problem of blaming conceptual difficulties on language inadequacies (see Chapter 1, and Ambrose in Black 1950, 15–37). If such a putative being actually (factually) exists *apart* from the language used to conceptualize or describe it, and if the language which doctrinally or experientially describes or characterizes the Mormon god in the Mormon faith (or in any theist's personal faith) is wholly inadequate to establish a perspicuous, coherent, factually meaningful "reference range" (Nielsen 1982, 140–170) for such a 'God,' thereby making it, as an alleged being, and as fully conceptualized, a factual non-reality, then what exactly *is* the Mormon god that it might be known and worshipped *in truth*? As we learned in the *Foundational Preface* and Chapter 1, and as has been repeated throughout and at the beginning of this concluding chapter, if, as is self-evident, we cannot know anything *about* reality without language, then what are Mormon believers actually left with if their language fails them or falls short of the mark? On what justifiable basis can they claim that their god actually exists *at all*, no less than as being the 'one and only true God'?

In the second place: apart from the problems with how religious or spiritual experiences are regarded and interpreted (see Chapters 2, 5, and 6), *i.e.* as 'properly basic' and as 'revelation,' there are the questions regarding the believed source of such experience, or 'God.' These questions, of course, bring us full circle back to the problems at hand. They are reflected in the analytical questions asked in Chapter 3 and above. There is the question of what *specifically* 'God' *is*. What does 'God,' as a referring expression, actually and specifically refer to? There is the question whether the believed and asserted conceptualization of such a putative being makes rational sense linguistically and coheres, or fits, with all that is known (not just speculated or imagined) about the world and the universe. There is the problem of what the truth-conditions are of such a being or its referents, such that its (or their) actual existence might, at least in principle, be empirically confirmed or disconfirmed as being true (or probably true), or false (or probably false). There is the question of how, if at all, the existence of such a god can be reasonably and compellingly reconciled (to the satisfaction of a neutral, informed, and reasonably skeptical outsider) with the various and at least apparently irresolvable contradictions on the ground — *e.g.,* the existence of widespread natural and human evil in the world, the requirement of faith and faith-testing for salvation, the wide-scale prevalence of religious confusion, ignorance, and nonbelief in the world, the extent of unanswered prayer offered in extremis, the existence of competing and conflicting revelation, and the extent of wrong beliefs and believers, *etc.*

Alternatively, if it is responded that the Mormon god is not as doctrinally described — he is not, in other words, a transcendent, supernatural being with all the primary, secondary, and relational attributes and qualities doctrinally ascribed to him — then Mormon believers are faced with yet another serious problem. For according to their founding 'Prophet,' Joseph Smith, "…without the *idea* [concept] of the existence of these [doctrinal] attributes in the Deity men could not exercise faith in him for life and salvation" (2005, Lecture Four). Such a god, stripped conceptually of its metaphysical attributes, or reduced in knowledge and power through apologetic redefinition or diminution to merely a purely anthropomorphic being with merely extensive yet sufficient telepathic powers of influence and an immortal, physical body of flesh and bones in the shape of a man, would not, according to Joseph Smith, be sufficiently worthy of faith or worship. Yet such a god that *is* in possession of the divine *omni*-attributes and qualities doctrinally attributed to him is, if not false or incoherent as charged, likewise not worthy of faith and worship on the grounds that the italicized follow-up questions above even exist and cannot be conclusively and compellingly eliminated as legitimate questions which can and should reasonably be asked.

Finally, related to the previous apologetic responses to the analytically-based conclusion that the Mormon god does not or could not possibly exist as believed or doctrinally described, we come to the third response which argues that what has been revealed regarding the nature of the Mormon god is, in virtue of human limitation and fallibilism, incomplete and imperfect and therefore subject at times, and to some (no doubt of lesser capacity, faith, spirituality or faithfulness) to benign, malignant, or self-serving misinterpretation, misunderstanding, and confusion. This third apologetic response, which was addressed initially in Chapter 5 as part of our analysis of the Mormon concept of revelation, has significant implications and is treated again below in greater depth.

The Problem of Mormon Revelation Revisited

To invoke the fact of human fallibilism *vis-à-vis* revelation as a way out of the problems suggested above and throughout this book is to open the door to yet one more significant argument for the incoherence of the concept of the Mormon god as doctrinally conceptualized, and therefore of the Mormon faith as a whole.

Such a retreat to fallibilism is problematic for at least four significant reasons. First, it is problematic because of the stated Mormon belief in the *perfection* and consequent *infallibility* of their god.

Second, it is problematic because of the believers' reliance on the existence and promise of *continuous* revelation from their god to man directly and through their god's anointed 'Prophets' (which revelation is itself doctrinally claimed to be the Mormon god's truth, otherwise what is the point or converting force of such a claim?).

Third, it is problematic because of the fact that such authoritative revelation has, on occasion and in historically and doctrinally significant cases, been authoritatively changed, corrected, disavowed, or omitted by subsequent or different 'Prophets' of the Church.

Fourth, it is problematic because of the fact that new official and canonized revelation has not been forthcoming to address apparent contradictions or to clear-up serious confusion or ignorance — a fact which has led (even among the faithful) to real doubt and disbelief, as well as to a multiplicity of competing or splinter faiths.

The idea here, as I see it, and as noted in the *Introduction* and in previous chapters, is that the truth of fallibilism in the context of orthodox theism cuts both ways — but more deeply, if not fatally, on Mormon believers and other fundamentalist theists. For Mormons, their 'certain faith' and 'testimony of The Way, the Truth and the Life' are built on the allegedly sure and restored foundation of definitive and infallible Absolute Truth. Such truth is established in turn by three sure sources. They are, first, the 'continuous personal revelation' from an infallible god to themselves and to their anointed Prophet-leaders; second, the 'revealed written word of God' in their canonized scriptures; and third, the allegedly sure, or certain, receipt — through the affective 'confirmation of the Holy Spirit by the power of the Holy Ghost' — of pure, perfect, and properly basic knowledge, experienced as a 'burning in the breast.'

For the honest naturalist and Atheist the truth of fallibilism naturally and logically forecloses on the possibility of certainty either through conclusive evidence or an unconditionally decisive argument or irrefutable proof that 'God' does not exist. It even prohibits the certain conclusion that any or all concepts of 'God' are decisively and absolutely unintelligible, incoherent, and factually insignificant. In this sense, the truth or fact of fallibilism necessarily fixes the outcome of the valid or sound atheistic argument to, at most, a provisional truth claim which justifiably asserts the non-existence of such a god — as currently or historically conceptualized — *beyond a reasonable doubt*.[163]

---

163 George H. Smith in his book *Why Atheism* (2000) posits the difference between *positive* and *negative* Atheism, where *positive* Atheism asserts the non-existence of 'God' and *negative* Atheism asserts merely the absence of theistic belief. In making this distinction, Smith advocates putting "the myth of positive atheism...to rest once and for all" in order to facilitate reasonable dialogue between theists and Atheists. For such dialogue to exist, according to Smith, Atheists must remove from the theist the "easy refutation of atheism" and the misrepresentation of Atheism as irrational "because no one can prove the non-existence of God" (21-5). As Smith sees it "[p]ositive atheism is a subset of negative atheism; after all, the belief that the concept of God is self-contradictory is a major reason why atheists do not believe in the existence of God"... Further, "... positive atheism is simply," as Smith sees it, "a possible justification for the nonbelief of negative atheism rather than a competing definition" (44).

From my perspective, 'positive atheism,' *pace* Smith, is the reasonable and justified conclusion that, just as 'Mickey Mouse,' 'Santa Claus,' 'Leprechauns,' and the 'Tooth Fairy' do not *literally* exist because plainly false, or just as the invented terms 'Irlig' and 'Somorlo' do not *literally* exist as supernatural beings because utterly incoherent, so too 'God' does not *literally* exist because both false and incoherent. 'God,' as conceptualized, does not actually or literally exist because 'God' *as a concept* is false in its purely anthropomorphic sense, and unintelligible, incoherent, and factually meaningless as stated in its nonanthropomorphic sense. This makes the existence of a god (in this case the Mormon god), *as conceptualized and believed*, an utter impossibility. It is the absence of the justifiability of any god's putative existence which, in my view, justifies the assertion that 'God,' as conceptualized, does not — necessarily *cannot* — exist as a literal, factual being, and is moreover false and incoherent as a belief. In this sense the Atheist may, I think, legitimately or justifiably assert that 'God' does not (cannot) literally exist as justification for his rejection of the theist's unjustifiable and therefore unjustified claim to the contrary. Even so, such an assertion could only be accepted provisionally and beyond a reasonable doubt.

For Mormon believers, however, the accepted truth of fallibilism is often appealed to apologetically to explain away both their ultimate ignorance regarding the '*why*' of apparent doctrinal incoherencies — 'mistaken inspiration,' scriptural changes, or amendatory revelations, authoritative teachings, or official pronouncements which correct, denounce, or otherwise supersede prior revelation — and the '*why not*' of revealed authoritative and belief-compelling explanations from the Mormon god. Such an appeal, in my view, necessarily results in the incoherency of regarding *with certainty* Mormon theological truth claims as 'Absolute Truth' which can be *added to* or *contextualized*, but *not* changed, amended, corrected, or denounced. The difference, I think, can rightly be accounted for on the basis of a *contextual application of fallibilism*.

Mormon theology, as I understand it to be from the perspective of an informed and experienced former insider, essentially backs the Mormon believer into a corner from which it is impossible (or so it seems to me) to coherently escape. Given the Mormon doctrines of 'God and revelation,' established by allegedly infallible revelation from a believed infallible god, all apologetic escape routes from apparent and serious incoherencies that threaten to weaken or destroy faith in the Mormon god and Christ and which imply or require human fallibilism are effectually closed.

This dilemma, I think, can be demonstrated by playing out typical Mormon reactions to two key questions. The first key question deals with the absence of revealed answers to troubling questions that give rise to real doubt. The second key question addresses the problem of fundamental changes and differences in current Church positions, authoritative doctrinal teachings and interpretations, and religious practices. To the extent that this second question gives rise to real doubt among believing Mormons, the first question again pertains.

To the first key question: 'Why no revealed answer?' to a troubling problem or inconsistency, Mormon leaders, apologists, and other believers typically offer a variety of evasive answers. These answers include replies such as: "That's just the way it is"; "That's not for man to know"; "God in his perfect wisdom has chosen not to reveal such things at this time"; "That's beyond human understanding"; "That is not important or necessary knowledge required for salvation"; "Some answers have to wait for the next life to be known"; or, ultimately, "I/we don't know, it's a mystery or a matter of faith."

Such replies can reasonably be met *in every case* with other sincere, unanswerable questions. Questions such as: 'But why so, or why not?' or 'What good, non-question-begging, non-*a priori* reason is there to believe such a reply, given your god's putatively revealed purposes, desires, nature, and abilities and man's believed eternal relationship to your god?' or 'If your god's existence and his ways are inscrutable or unknowable mysteries, how can you or anyone possibly know them or claim they are true, or even exist?' If the believer's answer to this last question is "only by faith and revelation," then the final unanswerable questions would be: 'Faith in *what*, specifically, and why the need for faith?' And, regarding the retreat to revelation: 'Revelation from whom or what, specifically?' and 'If revelation, then why the vagueness, confusion, ambiguity, apparent contradictions and unanswered questions at all?'

To the second key question: 'Why the fundamental changes and differences in current Church positions, doctrinal teachings, and interpretations and religious practices from those established by prior Prophets?' there are likewise certain typical, evasive replies.

Such replies include: "Some doctrines are more important than others"; "Modern prophets receive revelation relevant to the circumstances of their day"; "Sometimes the living prophet speaks in his role as prophet and sometimes he simply states his own opinions, and until such opinions are presented to the Church in general conference and sustained by vote of the conference, they are neither binding nor the official doctrine of the Church"; "Latter-day Saints have no inerrantist views, neither of the scriptures nor of the prophets. The scriptures are the word of God, but only as far as they are translated correctly, and prophets sometimes speak for the Lord, and sometimes they express their own opinions."[164]

But such replies themselves are neither official doctrine nor inerrant views and are met with contrary views from the prophets themselves, both in scripture and in discourse. In Mormon scripture, for example, Mormons are commanded by revelation to Joseph Smith to "…give heed unto all his [the prophet's] words which he shall give unto you" (D&C 21:4). From President Ezra Taft Benson Mormons are taught that "the living prophet is more vital to us than the standard works," "The prophet will never lead the Church astray," and "The prophet does not have to say 'Thus saith the Lord' to give us scripture."[165] From President N. Eldon Tanner Mormons are told they "…should never discriminate between these commandments [from the prophets], as to those we should and should not keep," or "[take] the law of the Lord into our own hands and become our own prophets,…because we are all false prophets to ourselves when we do not follow the Prophet of God"[166] and also "When the prophet speaks the debate is over."[167] And from President Brigham Young, Mormons have this assertion: "I have never yet preached a sermon and sent it out to the children of men, that they may not call scripture."[168] And also, as a published and circulated message to the Church: "When our leaders speak, the thinking has been done. When they propose a plan — it is God's Plan. When they point the way, there is no other which is safe. When they give directions, it should mark the end of controversy. God works in no other way. To think otherwise, without immediate repentance, may cost one his faith, may destroy his testimony, and leave him a stranger to the kingdom of God."[169]

The internal argument goes on and on with both sides of the question. But again, why so? And why, again, is there such uncertainty and disagreement in such fundamental matters of importance? Which of the teachings and revelations of prior prophets are merely opinion, and which are absolute truth? If none are inerrant truth, how so, given

---

164 These replies are taken or paraphrased from the 5/4/2007 official media release from the Church titled: "Approaching Mormon Doctrine," and from "What is Official Doctrine?" by Stephen E. Robinson found on the Internet at www.lightplanet.com/mormons/priesthood/prophets/doctrine.html.

165 "Fourteen Fundamentals in Following the Prophet," by Ezra Taft Benson, February 26, 1980.

166 *Church Conference Report*, October 1966, p. 98.

167 August *Ensign* 1979, pp. 2–3.

168 *Journal of Discourses*, Vol. 13: 95.

169 "Ward Teachers Message," *Deseret News*, Church Section p. 5, May 26, 1945. According to one source, "This message was sent out to the Church membership as the official ward teaching message and in two publications of the Church (one being the official Church publication). The message has never been rescinded in any official way and several General Authorities have made similar statements since then" (www.ldsmormon.com/thinking.shml).

the Mormon god's believed power, man's alleged spiritual capacity and endowments, and the putative eternal stakes involved? If any are in error, then why are others likewise not in error, or at least potentially so? And if *none* are inerrant, absolute truth, then how can *any* be absolute truth? If there are no absolute truths, because all men are fallible and no revelation is inerrant, then what is the point of 'revelation from God' and what then does the firm foundation of the Mormon faith consist of?

If the point of revelation is to test the faith of believers, then why, again, the need for such tests — or, yet again, for faith at all — given the nature of the Mormon god and the putative eternal stakes involved? If the firm foundation of the Mormon faith is in 'progressive revelation' and no revelation is perfect or complete in accuracy or truth, then how reliable is such revelation? How would such revelation differ from the provisional truths naturally discovered and confirmed through mere human inspiration subjected to reason and justified by valid evidence, sound argument, and the achievement thereby of wide, reflective equilibrium?

More specifically, were the alleged truths of the 'Great Apostasy' and 'Restoration' merely informed inferences? Or are they errant historical truths? If neither, how specifically are they justified beyond mere subjective confirmation on the basis of feeling and desire? Which of the revealed doctrines and practices of the Mormon faith are inerrant, if any? Why and how can such be known if all men including the prophets are fallible and no revealed truth is inerrant? And if none are inerrant, then where is the absolute truth in the Mormon faith? If certain prophets gave false revelation or were mistaken in thinking they received certain false doctrine as revelation (like the salvational doctrines of plural marriage, Adam-as-God, Blood Atonement, and the teaching that Blacks would never receive the priesthood and higher blessings of the gospel), then which other salvational doctrines or teachings did they or other prophets get wrong? More inclusive yet, how reliable is *any* putative revelation if its recipients are *all* fallible? If there is no inerrant, absolute truth in the Mormon faith, then how can the Mormon Church coherently claim to be the *only true* Church? If some truths are inerrant, what are the *specific, non-a priori, non-question-begging,* and *justified* objective criteria to be used to determine which truths are and which are not? Where would such criteria come from? If by human beings, then they are fallible and therefore the criteria are necessarily fallible. And if from putative revelation, and no revelation is inerrant, then we're back to where we began.

Beyond the fundamental conceptual problem of incoherence with the Mormon doctrine of divine revelation treated in Chapter 5, as well as the invalid question begging argument for its existence, this dilemma can only leave believers with the fallibilistic view in a double-bind. On one hand, if they believe that their prophets are fallible human beings who nonetheless teach inerrant truths as revelation from the Mormon god, and that such teachings are not merely opinion but are binding revelation from their god, then they are left in a bind in trying to explain failed prophesy and amended or revoked and repudiated prior teachings by former prophets of their Church regarded at the time as revelation. They cannot have it both ways.

On the other hand, if they believe that because all men are fallible, neither scripture nor revelation from the prophet is inerrant truth and that teachings by General Authorities of the Church which are not canonized are merely informed opinions and not binding revelation to the Church, then they must also, to be consistent, question those core doctrines and teachings of the Church, such as the 'Great Apostasy,' the 'Restoration' of the Church and the Priesthood, and the 'Plan of Salvation' which they regard as absolute truth. And they must do so, essentially, while acknowledging that they 'know' that such beliefs are 'True.' They too cannot have it both ways.

Such a double-bind makes believers on both sides of the question of the errancy or inerrancy of revelation double-minded or incongruent at their core. Such incongruence necessarily produces cognitive dissonance, requiring them to willfully or unconsciously suppress or repress such dissonance, or doubt, and force such contradictions into their minds through compartmentalization in order to live their faith habitually, blindly and blissfully through self-deception. This tacitly employed strategy of mind-control will inevitably result in mental illness, a fact which makes all faith-based religions ultimately harmful to believers, as well as potentially dangerous and destructive. It simply cannot be otherwise, as I see it.

Moreover, this dilemma makes any and every direct, apologetic appeal to faith, revelation, and/or human fallibilism among Mormon believers and nonbelievers in understanding the 'Absolute Truth' of their god's nature, mind, will, motives, and purposes utterly circular. It also renders them unintelligible as well and incoherent in the context of *both* positions and *all* current versions of Mormon theology. Plainly and summarily put, the very existence of the inevitable and ultimate non-answer (*i.e.* 'I/we don't know' and/or 'It's a mystery and therefore, a matter of faith') to the exhaustive regress of *unanswerable* belief- or faith-threatening questions expressing *real* and *significant* doubts is, as I see it, a near *decisive* argument for the incoherence of the Mormon concept of 'God' and for Mormon theology in its totality as currently and historically constituted. This is so *precisely* because Mormon theology necessarily reframes the premise of human *fallibilism* in distinction to its god's *infallibilism* to the revised (and believed 'restored') premise of man's spiritual ability as a capable recipient — through believed divine inheritance, grace, and intervention — of *infallible* revelation (or Absolute Truth) from an *infallible* god.

This reframing of the argument — from *fallible* man *in relationship* with an *infallible* god, to *godly, god-like* or *spiritual* man, or *authorized, ordained,* and *anointed* man in a *necessarily infallible* revelatory relationship with an *infallible* god[170] — sets up certain questions pointed to above. Specifically: "How then, given the high stakes involved (*i.e.* man's salvation and eternal life) is doctrinal error and incoherence, and human confusion, ignorance, doubt, skepticism, and non-belief even possible in a religion which was putatively restored by, and founded on, claimed infallible revelation given to Joseph Smith and built on the putative 'Rock' of continuous, progressive revelation from an all-knowing, all-powerful, all-loving, perfect (infallible) god?"

Further we must ask, why do real doctrinal contradictions, disagreements, and controversy exist and why are amendatory revelations and theological apologetics or authoritative scriptural exegeses even necessary in a Church where all its members putatively have the right and privilege of *direct* access to their god in such matters through the 'Gift of the Holy Ghost'? If not all Mormon believers actually enjoy such a putative Gift, for a variety of reasons arguably not in their natural ability to control or change, why give such a 'Gift'

---

170 To be otherwise would seem to make the whole Mormon notion of the 'Universal Apostasy' from, and 'Restoration' of, '*the* Truth of God's nature and Gospel' and the certain claim of being the 'One and only True Church' pointless and further unintelligible.

at all? Why not, better yet, at least apparently more consistent with the putative goodness and love of the Mormon god, ensure that *all* recipients of this putative Gift (or all mentally competent human beings for that matter) actually and continuously enjoy it? How would believers objectively and uncontroversially *know* whether or not they or others actually enjoyed such a Gift, other than by the persistence of ignorance, unanswered questions, doubts, or nonbelief? And isn't everyone — even those considered among believers to be the most righteous and faithful (whatever that means and however it is reliably determined, if at all) — troubled or at least perplexed or puzzled to some degree by unanswerable questions they have been counseled to just put on the shelf or leave alone?

Further we must wonder about the documented instances of doctrinal controversy or significant and substantive disagreement among General Authorities — and even among Presidents of the Church — who are no doubt believed to enjoy the 'constant companionship of the Holy Ghost' when officiating in their appointed calling? How is it that they can err or differ in their fundamental understanding and teachings given their *infallible* relationship with an *infallible* god?

To answer these and other vexing questions, Mormon believers can only appeal again to human fallibilism and/or the need only for *sufficient* truth (whatever that means or amounts to and by whatever human criteria such alleged sufficiency is determined, if any). Additionally, they likely appeal to the need for 'faith in God and Christ' or arbitrary, pointless, and senseless divine 'faith-testing.' But such apologetic appeals, offered to evade the implications of the apparent incoherencies suggested in the above questions and dilemmas, necessarily plunge orthodox Mormon theology further into the abyss of utter doctrinal incoherence. For according to its teachings, allegedly revealed 'Truth *from* God *about* God' and *about* the 'Gospel of God' (including the existence of divine revelation and the requirement of faith) is *nothing less* than Absolute Truth.

It is the *fact* of human fallibilism in conjunction with the *actual* existence of widespread ignorance, real doubt, skepticism, disbelief, and non-belief resulting from the unresolved and irresolvable theological problems addressed herein which makes orthodox Mormon theology even more deeply incoherent from my perspective. In my analysis, this establishes beyond a reasonable doubt that the Mormon god does not and cannot *actually* exist as presently conceptualized and believed by devout Mormon believers with unwavering, or absolute, *certainty* as Absolute Truth.

Such a god and such a theology simply do not make any sense to a skeptical outsider — or even, I would argue, to an honest insider. Even the ultimate retreat to faith is futile. For apart from the impossibility of faith in god, and/or as a way of knowing god, having faith (as unwarranted belief) that something incoherent is true, while knowing — albeit not necessarily consciously — that it is *not* true is merely deceiving oneself into believing the unbelievable because one *wants* to believe and because one *wants* what is believed to be true. How, as an aside, is this act of forced compartmentalization (which results ultimately in a dissociated and deluded mental state) mentally healthy and not psychologically harmful, particularly, as we shall learn below, when the forced acceptance of such contradictions requires self-hatred and self-sacrifice, as it certainly does in Mormonism and Christianity? This is not simply harmless wishful thinking, although it entails wishful thinking to be sure. It is self-deception with a steep price. But apart from this aside (which shall, again, be addressed below in our psychosocial assessment of the Mormon faith), and returning to the subject at hand, isn't such wishful thinking (and its accompanying doubt) effectually betrayed by both the believer's *ersatz* quest to know if it's true through 'authoritative' assurance, the resort to presuppositional argument and *ad hoc* speculation, and the retreat to prayer — and by the avoidance of the "outsider test of faith?" (Loftus 2008, 2010)

In the end, it would seem that at most all that Mormon believers can honestly and reasonably say — instead of appealing to all the above problematic apologetic assertions and evasions — is that when it comes to their religious doctrines and beliefs they really do not *really* care about knowledge and truth. They choose to believe the unbelievable on the problematic basis of conditioned feelings which have been subjectively interpreted in turn on the basis of the very incoherent doctrines and beliefs which form their interpretations and which they have been conditioned (indoctrinated) to accept as true. At a rational level they realize that these things are utterly unbelievable and without sense or coherence with anything which can legitimately be known. What is of ultimate importance and concern to them is rather how the *living* of their faith makes them *feel* about themselves and how they *feel* when they are experiencing the believed 'spiritual fruits' of their faith — the fruits of infantile comfort, peace, serenity, and acceptance by their god. Finally, they cling to their faith, not because they know it is true — because they do not — but merely because they superstitiously fear the consequences of *not* believing, and because, again, they like how their faith in an all-loving, all-powerful and all-knowing Parent-God makes them feel in an otherwise lone and dreary world. In this sense, as we have learned from Faber, Mormons are no different than Christians, Jews, or Muslims, or than any regressed human beings seeking succor – as "God's children" (2010) – from the existential *Angst* of mortality in the bosom and protective care of a nurturing parent.

Why faith (as belief in god) exists and persists

In the section "Faith and Madness" in Chapter 2 of his book *The End of Faith* (2004), Sam Harris writes, apropos to the Mormon faith, as well as all others: "We have seen that our beliefs are tightly coupled to the structure of language and to the apparent structure of the world. Our 'freedom of belief,' if it exists at all, is minimal. Is a person really free to believe [either an incoherent, senseless] proposition [or a proposition] for which he has no evidence? No. [The existence and coherence of legitimate or valid sensory or logical evidence]…is the only thing that suggests that a given belief is really about the world in the first place. We have names for people who have many beliefs for which there is no rational justification. When their beliefs are extremely common we call them 'religious'; otherwise, they are likely to be called 'mad,' 'psychotic,' or 'delusional.' Most people of faith are perfectly sane, of course, even those who commit atrocities on account of their beliefs. …" (71–2)

"[But it] takes a certain kind of person to believe what no one else believes. To be ruled by [incoherent, nonsensical] ideas for which you have no [valid or legitimate logical or sensory] evidence (and which therefore cannot be justified in conversation with other human beings [in pursuit of broad, rational consensus]) is generally a sign that something is seriously wrong with your mind. Clearly, there is sanity in numbers. And yet, it is merely an accident in history that it is considered normal in our society that [there is an infinite, eternal and transcendent] Creator of the universe [who] can hear your thoughts [and words], while it is demonstrative of mental illness to believe that he is communicating with you by having the rain tap in Morse code on your bedroom window. And so, while religious people are not generally [considered] mad, their core beliefs absolutely are. This is not surprising, since most religions have merely canonized a few products of ancient [and even modern] ignorance and derangement and passed them down to us as though they were primordial truths. This leaves billions of us believing what no sane person could believe on his own. In fact, it is difficult to imagine a set of beliefs more suggestive of mental illness than those that lie at the heart of many of our religious traditions." (72)

"The danger," Harris concludes, "of religious faith is that it allows otherwise normal human beings to reap the fruits of madness and consider them *holy*. Because each new generation of children is taught that religious propositions need not be justified in the way all others must, civilization is still besieged by the armies of the preposterous" (73).

"Sanity in numbers" aside, in the face of all the above, rational and reflective individuals might wonder how it is that *personal* belief in the Mormon god, or any god, exists and persists? In relation to Mormonism specifically, the answer we seek to this two-part question cannot, I'm convinced, be found in some incoherent conception of 'foreordination' related to a likewise incoherent notion of a 'pre-existence.' Nor can it be found circularly or presuppositionally in Mormon scripture, religious experience, or theology, or through either synthetic, *a priori* metaphysical insight or transcendental metaphysical speculation. Moreover, as I have labored to show and have come to know personally through my own experience as a former insider, the answer to why faith in Mormonism exists is not found in the putative and/or 'confirmed truth' or even believability of the tenets of the Mormon faith, or in the experienced reality of the Mormon Godhead. Nor, I would argue, is the answer to why such faith persists to be found in the alleged virtue of enduring faith, the alleged character strength, or righteousness, of the faithful, or an alleged human and 'premortal kinship, relationship or status with God,' whatever that means, if anything. And so it arguably is for all theistic faiths as well.

At a high level this two-part question points again to the need for understanding 'the learned corruption of learning' addressed in the *Introduction*, and in reference to Welles' aforementioned work in understanding human 'stupidity' (1995). What we learned there — and from all the relevant disciplines and reliable sources Welles and so many other notable scholars and thinkers have drawn on to form like conclusions — informs us here at the conclusion of this work. Applying Welles' thinking to this particular question, to generally understand why faith in a god — in any theistic religion — exists and persists (especially in otherwise intelligent, educated and rational people), we must look primarily to the learned set of 'premaladaptive' beliefs and corresponding linguistic and behavior patterns formed and reinforced by acquired and developed 'maladaptive schemata' (or mental models) and the corresponding 'Motivated ignorance' at the heart of self-deception which unconsciously tempers or blocks the desire to know "by a sense that learning more would be emotionally disturbing" (4).[171]

---

171 As Welles (1995) informs us in this regard, "However adaptive a schema may be, it will also be maladaptive to the extent that built-in biases compromise data so that perceptions will conform to expectations and desires...."

"In general, schemas tend to be conservative, with norms organizing behavioral systems into rituals that prevent effective responses to significant change. Habits may originate as functional patterns of behavior but

This very general proposal calls for a deeper look at what might be required to answer each part of the question in turn. Regarding the first part of this question concerning *why faith exists*, we might profitably turn first to the fields of philosophy, biology, sociology, anthropology, and psychology. More specifically the question of how it is that personal belief and faith in a god *exist* we might consider the "naturalistic explanations of religion" (Nielsen 2001, 29-55) and "the core philosophical errors of Western Civilization," *i.e.* dualism, essentialism, immutability, and absolutism (Eller 2007(a), 307–314), as well as the explanatory weight of neurobiology (Jaynes 1990 and Andreadis 2009), evolutionary biology (Slavin and Kriegman 1992 and Rose and Phelan 2009), anthropology (Eller 2004(b) and Roheim 1973), sociology (Becker 1973, 1975) and depth-psychology (Freud 1961(a)(b); Fromm 2006, Piven 2002, 2004; Pataki 2007; Faber 2002, 2004, 2010). We might also explore in some depth the seminal questions of how and why we believe what we believe (Shermer 2000, 2002; Boyer 2001; and Kurtz, Hunt, Pinker and Noelle in Kurtz 2003) or come to 'believe in belief' (Dennett 2006) or that we believe what cannot be believed (Mercier 2009). Additionally, we might want to look at our various cultures with their evolved and transmitted belief systems and values (Atran 2002; Guthrie 1993; and in Loftus 2010, 25–46), as well as the related "colonization of religious experience" through the religious appropriation of language, space, time, the arts, and everyday habits (Eller 2007(a), 267–303).

Last but surely not least, we might want to learn of and appreciate, at a personal as well as intellectual level, the social or interpersonal dynamics of our families and communities in understanding how we come to faith and persist in it, as well as the profound impact the psychological needs, dynamics, faculties, mechanisms, and condition of the individual have on the phenomenon of religious belief.

More specifically *yet*, in regard still to this first part of the question at hand, I think the answer we seek can be found in at least *five* interdependent areas of explanation:[172]

---

later may serve more to promote group complacence than group competence. At worst, such rituals become sacred and form the trappings of a religious system [or group-think], with the devout satisfied just to repeat habitual responses [without question or critical thought]. The rituals may then serve as reinforcing rewards in and of themselves without reference and often without relevance to the environment...."

"In the case of our own species," Welles continues, "it is primarily through misperception that we become maladaptive. Misperception is limited, distorted and/or inventive data gathering. It is a feature common to schematic systems and makes stupidity a normal part of human experience, since stupidity is based on the subjective nature of perception, which requires the observer to be actively involved in the process. ...."

Welles goes on to observe that "If stimuli fit the perceiving schema, in that they conform to expectation, they will barely register and are promptly dismissed. ... However, the perceiver will immediately pick up on any aspect of the environment which does not quite fit the schema. Anything exceptional will be noticed and, if necessary and possible, adjustments will be made. In fact, the schema may adjust itself a little to allow for future variations similar to any experienced."

"Beyond this normal range of perception and adjustment, however, the schema can be a limiting and debilitating factor when it prevents appreciation of events [and information or argument] which would be emotionally distressing if acknowledged. This is the basis for the fabled ostrich strategy for avoiding aware-ness of threats or other unpleasantries. Such selective ignorance of stimuli is characteristic of the schema as a mechanism for misperception and a program for stupidity" (66, 70; see pp. 66–89 inclusive of notes).

172 Neither these five areas of explanation, nor the sources cited in relation to each source, should be consid-ered exhaustive or definitive. They may, however, be considered as an essential part of the reading required to adequately conduct an outsider test of religious faith.

- *First*, in a multi-factorial, neuropsychological consideration of the deeply uncon-scious and ever-active "basic biological situation" indigenous to all human beings, and the "infantilizing process" of Christianity in general and Mormonism in particu-lar (Faber 2004, 2010).
- *Second*, in the related primary and ever present human needs for safety, security, belonging, attachment, actualization, and transcendence, coupled with the corre-sponding fear of condemnation, rejection, separation, isolation, death, and meaning-lessness (Becker 1973, 1975; Piven 2004; Brown 1959; Kurtz 1991; Tillich 1980; Maslow 1962, 1976; Bowlby 1988; Kirkpatrick 2004).
- *Third*, in the primitive and genetically evolved cognitive schemas and projective mechanisms or modules in the brain (Boyer 2001; Atran 2002; Guthrie 1993; Welles 1995).
- *Fourth*, in the psychological reality formation and defense mechanisms of dissocia-tion, repression, hidden memories (cryptomnesia), denial, projective identification, regression, isolation, intellectualization, rationalization, compartmentalization, re-action formation, reversal, identification, acting out, sublimation, transference, and self-deception (Schumaker 1995; Freud 1961(a); Baker 1996; Weiner 1995, 2005; Freud, A. 1993; McWilliams 1994; Trivers 1985; Grossman 1996; Pears 1984; Gly-mour 1991; Rorty 1991).
- And *fifth*, in the 'memetic' transmission — or 'differential replication' — of cultural concepts and beliefs (Dennett 2006; Dawkins 2006; Ray 2009).

Related to this fifth explanation for the existence of faith, and moving now to the second part of our question regarding how it is that personal belief and faith in gods *persist* in the face of so many troubling, unanswered questions and contradictions, we will turn first to the rather basic idea that, in the words again of Sam Harris, religious belief is both a 'social disorder' and, since such belief is embedded in a particular language-game within religious life-forms, a 'conversational disorder' as well.

As I see it, this is a two-fold problem. It is a problem, first of all, that in our society it is a fact that we cannot apply enough social pressure to those who hold religious belief — that to do so is considered a social taboo (but one that fortunately is currently being widely challenged). Secondly, as we have learned in our analysis of the Mormon faith in particular, it is the fact that religious language, though unintelligible and expressive of incoherent, nonsensical concepts, has become so familiar as a language-game within vari-ous religious life-forms, that statements made by religious believers are never questioned by believers as to their justifiability. Such statements, as putative truth claims, are made and regarded by believers as self-evident truths, even though they are neither self-evident nor warranted as knowledge of truth in a justificatory sense.

This rather obvious and compelling two-fold socio-cultural explanation for the existence and persistence of faith or religious belief in our society is accompanied, in my view, by the *psychological* conditioning of believers *within* theistic belief systems to equate *faith-fulness with righteousness and worthiness*, and *doubt with sinfulness and unworthiness*. This problem of conditioning or mind-control is, metaphorically speaking, a two-sided coin. Both sides of this problem explain, from a psychological perspective, the *feelings* that bind believers to their beliefs and faith.

How persisting in our religious beliefs and faith makes believers *feel* about themselves in relation to their god can, I think, be adequately explained by the equation of faithfulness with righteousness and worthiness in the 'eyes of God.' Clearly such a foundational belief makes persistence in the faith *ego-syntonic*. The faithful 'Mormon ego' is inflated by the consequent belief that one is loved by, acceptable to, and approved by, a Parent-God, and therefore one is worthy of the promised blessings of the particular faith on earth and in the afterlife. Such ego inflation is usually — and necessarily — accompanied by an *ersatz* humility which, if sincerely believed by faithful believers through the ego defense of compartmentalization, can be convincing to themselves and others. Such ego inflation is usually accompanied by very positive *feelings* toward themselves in relation with their Parent-God — feelings of personal esteem, worthiness, specialness, chosenness, entitlement, and power, and feelings of love for (and reciprocated love and acceptance by) the Mormon god.

The flip side of this metaphorical coin is the equation 'doubt equals sin or sinfulness and unworthiness.' In this regard, George H. Smith correctly observes that "It is the moralization of doubt — the prohibition of doubt as sinful — that makes the Christian [and Mormon] scheme of faith fundamentally dishonest at its core. I say 'dishonest' because a Christian [or Mormon believer], having committed himself, through faith, to the tenets of his religion, is thereafter prohibited [even if implicitly] from doubting his fundamental beliefs. ... Doubt is [considered] an affront to the very God in which the [theist] believes, and this God does not take such matters lightly. Doubt can imperil the [believer's] eternal soul" (2000, 51–2).

Regarding the problem of doubt itself, Smith continues: In the Christian [and Mormon] faith, "... [t]he [believer] must believe in God while somehow doubting that belief. But this can prove nearly impossible for the [believer] who, while fully aware that God is monitoring his every thought, must call into question the very faith on which his every salvation depends." (52)

"This is what makes Christianity [and Mormonism] fundamentally dishonest. The [believer], having entered into a belief system, finds that [even though the god and ministers of his faith allegedly value free will above all else], the door swings only one way, and that getting in was much easier than getting out. The [believer] is effectively precluded from criticizing his own beliefs, for such criticism is always attended by [guilt, shame and] the threat of divine retribution." (52)

"It may appear," Smith observes, "that the [believer] has forever freed himself from the danger of doubt by building a massive wall of certainty between doubt and his doctrines. His beliefs, after all, are certified by the infallible authority of God, so what has he to fear from doubt? Of what possible threat are a few human doubts when compared to the fortress of revealed knowledge? Why does the [believer], secure in his citadel of certitudes, fret so much over even the slightest doubt?" (53)

"To ask such questions is to answer them, at least in part. The [believer] is quite right to feel apprehensive about his citadel of certitudes, as if it does not provide as much protection against doubt as may first appear. Indeed, his citadel, which supposedly rests on an infallible foundation, is a house of cards that could collapse upon the slightest tremor of doubt. The [believer] is vulnerable to even the slightest and most insignificant doubt, because all his beliefs rest on a single, narrow — and very unstable — point, *viz.*, the appeal to infallible revelation. This is the foundation of his belief system, so if even one belief is called into question, if even a single, solitary doubt is permitted to invade this belief system at any point and for any reason, then the entire system can easily be thrown into a state of crisis. Why? Because if even one doubt is appropriate, if even one belief is made to seem less than infallible, then the same reasoning that justified this single doubt will apply to every other …belief as well." (53–4)

"In short," Smith concludes, "for the [believer] to doubt the truth of [the] purported revelation[s] [upon which his faith is based] is potentially to challenge the authority of the infallible God in whom she believes. It is therefore religious doubt, not atheistic disbelief, that constitutes the greatest threat to orthodox beliefs, because doubt threatens to undermine a belief system from within" (56).

It threatens as well how believers *feel* about themselves in relation to their god. Doubting is *ego-dystonic* to Mormon believers. To doubt is to sin, and for believers to sin against their god makes them sinful, weak, unworthy, and unacceptable (or at least a disappointment) in the eyes of their god, as well as in the eyes of their fellow Church members and leaders.

Such threatened and believed conditions make conditioned, doubting believers feel 'less than' those who are faithful and consequently deflated, defensive, and defeated. Doubt — along with conscientious dissent and disobedience (the three mortal sins of theistic faith) — is accompanied, through systematic family and religious conditioning, by self-deprecation and feelings of guilt and inferiority.

Doubting Mormon believers are conditioned, as we shall learn in the *Epilogue* which follows, by: (1) the authoritarian administration of what I term the 'patriarchal code' — a basic set of inviolable rules which is inherent in the patriarchal family system and recapitulated by the Mormon faith; and (2), as shall be presented below, the employment of various control strategies and mechanisms related to the *moralistic core*, which itself is also inherent in all patriarchal family systems and theistic belief systems.

Because of such conditioning, doubting believers suffer — by personal experience, observation, or threat — from the anxiety or fear of condemnation by their Parent-God and parent-Church leaders, with consequent alienation from themselves, their peers and superiors, and their Parent-God. This is a *very real* fear of rejection and isolation which threatens to leave shamed believers alone to carry the burden of self-disappointment and self-condemnation unless and until they repent of their doubt and get back in line.

This exploitive and abusive conditioning, of course — even if administered, as asserted and believed, with love and concern by authorities and loved ones — establishes or reinforces and strengthens in turn two related, primary, psychological mechanisms of control among others which are inherent in all Christian belief systems (including especially Mormonism) and which effectually bind believers to their faith.

The first psychological control mechanism is what Darrel Ray (2009) appropriately refers to as "The Religious Guilt Cycle." Essentially, this cycle begins with behavior (including thoughts and feelings) which is prohibited, forbidden, or otherwise regarded as wrong or 'sinful.' In this case such behavior is the forbidden thought-crime of doubt, which is the 'mother' of the great, unpardonable sin of infidelity and apostasy. With this behavior guilt is experienced, which creates a tension that seeks relief, either (paradoxically) through the experience of greater doubt, which results in greater guilt, or in the promise of divine help offered by confession and repentance. This help is, conveniently enough, offered by the Bishop, Priest, Minister or Rabbi who assuages the guilt by promising or invoking, through promise, witness, prayer, or blessing, divine forgiveness on condition of repentance. With this promise and invocation of 'grace' on the repentant believer's behalf comes psychological relief (in this case a regressed experience of rapprochement between parent and child). But because doubt is natural to the human mind and cannot be entirely eradicated, even if suppressed or repressed, and even if prohibited it returns in one form or another and the guilt cycle continues.

When doubt — in any of its betrayals or manifestations — results in sufficient guilt and tension, binding relief will again be sought, and the cycle will continue. So "[W]hat is the purpose," Ray asks, "of prohibiting something that cannot realistically be prohibited, something that cannot even be monitored? *The purpose is to create religious guilt.* Even though it [*i.e.* doubt] cannot be stopped, it invokes the guilt cycle *that bonds the person closer to the religion*" (91; emphasis mine).

The second mechanism of psychological control is what is well known among psychologists as a 'conditioned fear response.' Such a response unconsciously — through the defense mechanism of dissociation — alters the feared *truth* of *real* doubt into the acceptable, ego-syntonic and self-preserving *lie* of no doubt. This unconscious defense mechanism — on the basis of the conditioned fear of rejection, isolation, suffering, self-alienation, and the forfeiture of promised blessings associated with disbelief or apostasy — effectually alters or converts feared and painful emotional truths to acceptable lies. It allows doubting believers to continue to function dutifully as faithful — and believed and self-proclaimed unquestioning or undoubting — members of the religious community. The conditioned fear response triggered by the anxiety or tension accompanying doubt is neurologically induced to provide relief. But, like the relief obtained by the promise of forgiveness from the ecclesiastical parent-surrogate obtained in the regressive religious guilt cycle, it does not eradicate the doubt, but rather binds the believer to the lie or delusion of *no* doubt — and consequently to the lie of their cherished faith.

These observations and conclusions certainly have merit in helping to explain how it is that believers persist in their faith in spite of their known or suppressed doubt and consequently continue to stubbornly or defensively believe what is unbelievable to the rational mind. For Mormon believers, as argued earlier, the threat of doubt is perhaps even more severe. This is because of their incoherent belief in continuous personal and institutional revelation and the problem of reconciling their belief in revealed truth from an infallible, all-knowing and unchanging god with later amendatory revelation or the official, authoritative disavowal of prior revelation — where in both cases the claimed revealed doctrine or teaching is confirmed as truth by revelation and considered absolutely true by faithful believers. Still, given "the malleability of the human mind" through indoctrination, cognitive dissonance, impression management, psychological reactance, and confirmation bias (see Jason Long in Loftus 2010, 65-80), belief and faith persist along with secret or dissociated doubt. This doubt is betrayed in many ways — including the existence and persistence of faith itself — and it is suppressed or repressed through rationalization, denial, and self-deception. All of this is motivated in part by the often unspoken and undiscussable consideration of doubt as sin and the fear and anxiety such a consideration instills in the conditioned minds of believers.

Our final treatment of the question regarding how it is that belief and faith in gods persist deals with the mortality of the believer and the related pursuit of meaning and immortality to stave off the fear and denial of death. This last analysis begins with the paradigm belief, regarded by many religious believers as truth, that without the illusory promises and comforts of eternal life, which are inherent in religion and dependent on the persistence of faith and the special sense of transformation, love, forgiveness, protection, and acceptance from a Parent-God (Faber 2004, 2010), there neither is nor can be any enduring, worthwhile meaning, purpose, happiness, or good in life. Instead, there is only 'sickness unto death' and a deep sense of despair in the face of ultimate extinction.

Such a belief (*pace* Kierkegaard and other notable fideists) is simply groundless and wrong, as Nielsen and so many others have articulated, and as the life experiences of so many Atheists, including myself, have conclusively demonstrated. First of all, Atheism, to a naturalist or secular humanist, is not necessarily nihilism. To all of humanity, life can and does have meaning, purpose, value, and goodness without the need for belief and faith in a god. As former evangelical preacher turned Atheist Dan Barker simply yet directly and effectively puts it, "There is no purpose of life. Life is its own reward. But as long as there are problems to solve, there will be purpose *in* life" (2008, 344). In other words, as elaborated on in the *Epilogue* of this work, we create our own meaning and purpose in our lives in virtue of how we make sense of our lives in this world, what is most important to us in this, our only life, and how we should live and die in relation to our most basic and important intellectual and biological imperatives. This point is also made in the following two representative vignettes offered by renowned existential psychotherapist Irvin D. Yalom from his important work *Staring at the Sun: Overcoming the Terror of Death* (2008).

In the first vignette, Yalom writes of a conversation with Jill, "a patient who had long been plagued with death anxiety, [and who had] habitually equated death and meaninglessness" (138). At the young age of nine years, Jill had an experience involving the death of the family dog. Recalling that experience she says: "Then and there I realized that if we must all die, nothing had any point…" Employing the Socratic technique of inquiry intended to "help a student [or patient] excavate his or her own wisdom," Yalom invited Jill to first imagine her young daughter (about nine) asking her, "'If we are going to die, then why or how should we live?'" and then asks Jill, "How would you answer?" Yalom continues:

> Unhesitatingly she replied, "I'd tell her about the many joys of living, the beauty of the forests, the pleasure of being with friends and family, the bliss of spreading love to others and of leaving the world a better place.
> After finishing, she leaned back in her chair and opened her eyes wide, astonished at her own words, as though to say, "Where did that come from?" (139)

"Great answer, Jill," Yalom replied, and then observed: "You've got so much wisdom inside. This is not the first time you've arrived at a great truth when you imagine advising your daughter about life. Now you need to learn to be your own mother" (139).

The second vignette, more confrontive and apropos to this book, involved Yalom in session with an Orthodox Rabbi who, in Yalom's words, "was training to become an existentialist therapist but was experiencing some dissonance between his religious background and my psychological formulations" (192–93). This young Rabbi initially called Yalom to request a consultation with the implied purpose of resolving his dissonance, but once in session "began," according to Yalom, "to voice his beliefs with such zeal as to make me suspect that the real purpose of his visit was to convert me to the religious life" (193). Yalom replied directly and, according to him, in an uncharacteristically blunt and 'matter-of-fact' manner, followed by the Rabbi's response and most of the remaining published exchange:

> "Your concern is a real one, Rabbi," I interjected. "There *is* a fundamental antagonism between our views. Your belief in an omnipresent, omniscient personal God watching you, protecting you, providing you with a life design, is incompatible with the core of my existential vision of humanity as free, mortal, thrown alone and randomly into an uncaring universe. In your view," I continued, "death is not final. You tell me that death is merely a night between two days and that the soul is immortal. So yes, there is *indeed* a problem in your wish to become an existential therapist: our two points of view are diametrically opposed."
>
> "But you," he responded with intense concern on his face, "how can you live with only these beliefs? And without meaning?" He shook his forefinger at me. "Think hard. How can you live without belief in something greater than yourself? I tell you it's not possible. It's living in the dark. Like an animal. What meaning would there be if everything is destined to fade? My religion provides me with meaning, wisdom, morality, with divine comfort, with a way to live."
>
> "I don't consider that a rational response, Rabbi. Those commodities — meaning, wisdom, morality, living well — are *not* dependent on a belief in God. And yes, *of course*, religious belief makes you feel good, comforted, virtuous — that is exactly what religions are invented to do. You ask how I can live. I believe I live well. I'm guided by human-generated doctrines. I believe in the Hippocratic oath I took as a physician, and dedicate myself to helping others heal and grow. I live a moral life. I feel compassion for those about me. I live in loving relationship with my family and friends. I don't need religion to supply a moral compass."
>
> "How can you say that?" he interjected. "I have great sorrow for you. There are times I feel that, without my God, my daily rituals, my beliefs, I'm not sure I could live." (193–4)

After sharing in turn that he likewise could not conceive of devoting his life to "belief in the unbelievable" and to spending his day "following a regimen of 613 daily rules and glorifying a God who dotes on human praise," Yalom concludes by stating: "We ended our session amiably and parted, he heading north, I heading south. I never learned whether he continued his study of existential psychotherapy" (194–95).

So here we have two cases, two very different approaches, two very different outcomes, yet the same message in both, that there *can be* and, in fact, *is* meaning and value in life *without* belief in any god. As a relevant aside, what is also evident from the second case, by the young Rabbi's comment that "without my God, my daily rituals, my beliefs, I'm not sure I could live" is that, as Yalom correctly states earlier in his book: "Death anxiety is the mother of all religions, which, in one way or another, attempt to temper the anguish of our finitude" (5). Such an attempt, also from Yalom, "seems like an end run around death: [where] death is not final, death is denied, death is de-deathified" (188).

As for 'happiness,' I find myself in agreement with Freud, as interpreted by Wallwork, in being critical or at least suspicious of subjective and "illusory satisfactions in fantasies and delusional re-moldings of reality" for their "lack of truthfulness" (1991, 248). Specifically, according to Wallwork, "Freud did not see [the] subjective experience [of happiness] as always a reliable guide to true or authentic well-being[173] — that is to say, the smooth and mature psychic functioning that is the source of the deep, if mild, continuous self-confidence and contentment that accompany most of a person's activities" (1991, 254). More specifically, continues Wallwork:

> Subjective evidence is not sufficient, in part because people who have become fixated [stuck] at early developmental stages have no idea of what they are missing. Nor do people who neglect certain basic desires [or seeming internal mandates to necessary action] understand through introspection [alone] the deleterious psychic consequences of such neglect…It is on the basis of these and other limitations of the subjective evidence for happiness that Freud and his psychoanalytic descendants argue that some people who claim to be relatively happy are missing out on valuable experiences or that they would experience more satisfaction if their desires were different in specifiable ways. (1991, 254)

I am convinced that it is our own fears, insecurities, conditioning, and ignorance, as well as our unique psycho-biographies and the deepest, unconscious brain functions, defense mechanisms, and relational psychodynamics of the human mind, which keep us in the dark and tied to our superstitions and beliefs in faith — in spite of our reasonable doubts. Moreover, to those believers who might argue that their putative state of happiness is proof of the truth of what they believe regarding 'God, Christ, and salvation,' I would reply, in Nietzsche's words: "The proof through [the experience of some subjective definition of] 'happiness,' is [merely, and at most] a [self-referential] proof of happiness — and nothing else; why in the world should we take it for granted that true judgments cause more pleasure than false ones, and that in accordance with a pre-established harmony, they necessarily bring pleasant feelings in their wake? — the experience of all strict and profound minds teaches the reverse" (2000, 77–8).

Perhaps, after all is said, and beyond the central question of how it is that personal belief and faith in gods exists and persists, there is merit to the reductive, yet simple, psychoanalytical perspective that *belief* in the actual existence of a god — and belief *in* such belief as a source of happiness, well-being and moral goodness — is merely an *illusion* or *delusion*. '*Faith* in God,' as an affective phenomenon of trust, personal transformation, and commitment is merely a projective *transference*. The convicted appeal to and compulsive reliance on such faith is simply an unconscious ego defense, or self-deceiving *reaction formation* in response to suppressed doubt and cognitive dissonance.

Related to the above perspective, there is considerable evidence to support the conclusion, offered by Schumaker, that underlying these psychological, reality-distorting phenomena of illusion and projective transference are the twin processes of *dissociation* and *suggestion* noted above and earlier in Chapter 5. According to Schumaker:

---

173 The meaning of 'happiness' is highly subjective, and the condition of personal, psychological well-being is complex and multi-faceted to be sure. This is particularly relevant in evaluating any instrument-based, psychometric evaluation of religious belief, disbelief, and non-belief on the subject's reported states of happiness and psychological well-being. Such research is, in my view, superficial and essentially self-referential in nature. Consequently, it is of questionable value at best. Any arguments therefore, in support of religious belief as a source of happiness and psychological well-being which are based on such research are, in my estimation, invalid as post hoc arguments that, in my view, omit key evidence and therefore, and ultimately, draw the wrong conclusion, leaving them without critical, credible, or persuasive significance or validity. See also note

In general, the error pervading the human mind in the form of illusion and artificial order is not [merely] the result of passive ignorance. On the contrary, it is a complex mental operation that has two essential components. The first of these deals with the means by which the brain can disengage itself in such a way that information will be processed in contravention of its own capacity for the accurate higher order information processing. In the course of this, the person essentially prevents or blocks a conclusion that would otherwise present itself in light of available information.

The second step in the operation concerns the manner in which the person is delivered false alternatives that serve as functional surrogates to the rejected portions of reality. This process [entails] internal and external suggestion in relation to the mechanism of dissociation. Here let us introduce the concept of dissociation by asking how it is that we highly intelligent creatures are able to entertain error that should not exist given our sophisticated brains. A more succinct form of the question would be this: "How do we manage to accept, and act in accordance with, error we know to be error?" Such a question seems to imply that the human mind is multidimensional, with its different dimensions acting independently of one another. This is exactly the case and it is only this situation that makes possible all forms of reality modification, including religion and psychopathology...

Research supports [the] position [that] dissociation has been implicated in many disorders, including obsessive-compulsive disorder, phobia, paranoia, eating disorders, post-traumatic stress disorder, multiple personality disorder, psychogenic amnesia, and others. It has also been proposed that dissociation is the faculty enabling all types of trance states, possession, Faith healing, shamanism, [revelatory, seeric] and visionary experiences, age regression, glossolalia, and automatic writing...To this list I would add [religious belief] since it involves cognitive, perceptual, and affective distortions that are completely dependent upon dissociation. (1995, 35-37)

There are those, like Becker, Schumaker and others who, while acknowledging a psychoanalytical and psychopathological interpretation of religious experience, belief and faith in a god, nonetheless believe that man cannot survive the brutal realities of mortal existence without illusion. For Becker (1973), an acceptable, creative, or life-enhancing illusion would be a "positive transference" which, according to Van Harvey in Liechty's book *Death and Denial* (2002), would meet three proposed standards as follows: "the *first* is that the transference strikes a balance between the twin ontological motives [to stand out from the crowd and to fit in]; the *second* is that the transference acknowledges the limits of human nature; and the *third* is that the transference not obscure (lie about) the 'lived truth of creation'" (252).

But what could such an illusion be? How, following Jerry Piven, could such a positive transference even be possible as a "freely chosen dependence" (243) such that it would satisfy Becker's criteria while compelling acceptance and faith without self-deception or insult to the intellect?

In short, like so many others before me and as Nielsen states, I have "...come not to believe in God, not only because I am convinced that there is no evidence or good grounds for believing that God exists, but also because I believe that the very concept or idea of God (where nonanthropomorphic) is so problematic that there is nothing statable which could even be the grounds for such a belief. There is, to put it bluntly, nothing to believe. But it is a mistake to go on to say, 'But then there is nothing to disbelieve either,' for the Jew or Christian [or Mormon] is attempting to make a positive claim and this claim is being rejected as incoherent in its nonanthropomorphic [or metaphysical] forms" (2006, 77). To me, the doctrinal concept of the Mormon god (and all gods), as anthropomorphically conceived, is *false* as superstitiously conceived, and is *unintelligible, incoherent, and factually meaningless* as metaphysically or supernaturally conceived. If such a conclusion is warranted, then such a god would necessarily be a factual non-reality. This conclusion would, in turn, necessarily render the *unjustifiable* belief in such a god, or any god (*pace* Widtsoe *et al.*), *irrational* at best and, from my informed perspective, delusional, life-negating, and at worst, psychologically and socially harmful, dangerous, and destructive.

This final rendering and indictment of irrational belief in gods (Mormon or otherwise) – and the corresponding exposure and censure of willful self-deception through "belief *in* belief" (Dennett 2006) and the second-order belief *that* we believe what *cannot* be believed (Mercier 2009) – leads us to the psychosocial assessment of Mormonism that follows. Such assessment is primary to this work, with the foregoing conceptual deconstruction of Mormon beliefs a necessary aspect of it, offered as a therapeutic, analytical inquiry to hopefully loosen the grip of irrationality and self-deception through the intellectual and commonsensical appeal to reason and rationality. In the end, as the following assessment shall show, and as I shall argue for and advocate below and in the *Epilogue, Personal Post-script*, and first *Appendix*, there is a reasonable and I think compelling and sufficient basis for abandoning religious belief entirely. This is not merely because of the lack of proofs or evidence in support of such beliefs, as some Atheists argue, or, more significantly, because such beliefs are false or incoherent and without factual intelligibility, as argued herein. Rather, – and here I find myself in agreement with Tamas Pataki (2007, 2009) – religious belief in gods and revelation should be abandoned primarily, *even if exclusively*, because of the psychological reasons for such beliefs, and the consequences of such belief on the individual believer and, perhaps more importantly, the children of religious believers. As I think Pataki correctly states in this regard, "Even if there were cogent arguments for the existence of a deity [which there are not], they would in all likelihood remain disconnected from the main causes why the vast majority embrace belief. … [T[he most fundamental issues," in Pataki's informed and professional judgment, "turn on the psychodynamics of religious mentality, on the unconscious motivations to religion" (2009, 206). And, I would add, on the psychosocial implications – in principle and in fact – of theistic belief and practice in relation to the mental health and well-being of religious adherents.

Psychosocial Assessment: Is Mormonism a toxic faith?

Heraclitus, a Greek philosopher of the late 6th Century concluded that "Religion is a disease." Bertrand Russell wrote likewise, following Lucretius who, in Russell's words, characterized religion as "a disease born of fear and as a source of untold misery to the human race." Freud (1961) characterized religion as "the universal obsessional neurosis," (55) and while it might be so that, as he also wrote, "devout believers are safe-guarded in a high degree against the risk of certain neurotic illnesses" on the premise that "their acceptance of the universal neurosis spares them the task of constructing a personal one" (56), it is clear from extensive clinical case studies documented since then that religious belief and practice in general, and theistic belief and practice in particular, is associated – motivationally and causally – with certain unconscious, characterological dispositions and various psychiatric symptoms and syndromes indicative of psychopathy or mental illness.

Three examples of unconscious dispositions "in the religious domain" presented by Pataki (2009) include "[s]ome *obsessional* dispositions – which generally arise from the need to control sexual and aggressive impulses toward objects (i.e. significant others); ...[h]ysterical* dispositions, to separate or split off the lower (sexual, profane) aspects of the personality from the higher (moral, spiritual) ones; ... [and] *[n]arcissitic* dispositions, which involve more or less unconscious needs to feel special, powerful, superior...[to be] Elect or Chosen [by 'God']" (207). According to Pataki, these psychopathological dispositions and others, and the desires related to them, account at least in part for the "unconscious or other extrinsic motives for holding [religious] belief, ... [and for] our tendency to wishful thinking and self-deception" (207), a recurring phenomenon characteristic of religious belief and commitment. In Pataki's view, "religious beliefs, practices, and institutions can indirectly satisfy (or pacify) – 'substitutively or symbolically' (208) – enduring unconscious desires and other dispositions" (207); in effect feeding them, while simultaneously covering them from analytical scrutiny unless or until they are exposed by overt dysfunction or self-destructive and antisocial behavior.

Moreover, and of primary significance, psychiatric symptoms including anxiety, depression, obsessive compulsivity, and dissociation, and psychiatric syndromes such as bipolar disorder, OCD, panic disorder, post-traumatic stress disorder, schizphreniform disorders, and somatization disorder, etc. have all been causally connected to religious belief. (H. E. Jones 2006, 58-102).

There are, in this last regard, and in fact, a significant number of psychiatrists and clinical psychotherapists who, on the basis of personal experience and documented clinical case work, would concur that religion is causally related to mental illness. (See, for example, E.D. Cohen (1988), H.E. Jones (2006), Wendell W. Watters (1993), A. Ellis (1971), and "Psychiatrists' religious attitudes in relation to their clinical practice: a survey of 231 psychiatrists." *Acta Psychiatrica Scandinavica*, 88, 420 –424.[Medline]) And while there are various studies that suggest a positive relationship between "intrinsic" religious belief and mental health (Allport and Ross 1967; Bergin 1991), such studies are very problematic for various reasons (see notes 177 and 179) and are at odds with other studies that do not, and find instead an inverse relationship with religiosity (Watters 1993, 153-61; Batson and Ventis 1982). Also, the reported salutary effects of religion (e.g. sociability, happiness, physical health, positive attitude, ability to cope with stress, and a sense of security, belonging, and meaning or purpose in life, etc.) also reportedly ensue in the lives of well-adjusted or resourceful adults who are utterly *without* religious belief.

Significantly, the reported beneficial psychological effects of religious belief are contingent on a baseless and irrational belief in the literal existence of a god that is both scientifically and analytically nonexistent or incoherent as hypothesized and conceptualized, and on related *ersatz* assurances of this and next life 'blessings.' This would bring into question the *actuality* of such alleged psychological benefits. For if the perceived or believed benefits are gone when the spell of magical and wishful thinking is broken, then there weren't any *real* psychological benefits to begin with; only the *illusion* of well-being – or worse, delusion. Just as the assurances and so-called 'blessings' of religion are bogus, so too are its believed and asserted positive, psychological effects. They are arguably manufactured, self-induced, and reinforced by mental conditioning and mass delusion.

And they are believed *in spite of* the persistence of real questions and doubt suppressed and denied through fear and anxiety by self-deception. Even misery can be transformed into believed happiness and well-being through delusion and self-deception.

Moreover, reported salutary psychological effects of religious belief are also reportedly offset by arguably greater social and personal psychiatric concerns, including irrational guilt and anxiety, toxic shame, narcissistic grandiosity, neurotic one-sidedness and conflictedness through suppression and compartmentalization, and the perversion of motivation and cognition which all lead to self-hatred and self-sacrifice and their various psychiatric symptoms and syndromes (Jones 2006, 16-93). Also, there is substantial and reliable historical evidence to suggest that religious belief – and religious fundamentalism in particular – is a social disease connected to incidents of authoritarian child abuse, spousal abuse, and various other forms of damaging, destructive, and anti-social behavior.

In this psychosocial *assessment* of the Mormon faith it shall be argued that Mormonism, as well as all other theisms, is a toxic faith that can result in mental illness and, to a greater or lesser degree, personal and social harm. This is not to say, of course, that *all* devout Mormons (or other theists) are *manifestly* symptomatic from a lay perspective or to the untrained eye, although many are, and admittedly and diagnostically suffer from a variety of psychiatric symptoms and disorders *as a result of* their religious beliefs, practices and upbringing. And it is not to suggest that the Mormon faith (or other theisms), as practiced by *all* its believers, is necessarily or actually dangerous or destructive to society, although it shall be argued (and I think compellingly so) that it is at least *potentially* and even *likely* so, given the fact that revelation from its god is considered to be the ultimate source of Truth, or the mind and will of 'God,' to all Latter-day Saints, as well as indicative of their personal righteousness.

The focus of our analysis of Mormonism to this point has been on the nature of Mormon beliefs regarding the existence and nature of 'God,' the alleged Plan of Salvation, and the existence and nature of 'revelation from God and faith in God,' and whether such beliefs and those holding such beliefs could reasonably be considered rational. We also looked critically at those irresolvable problems making the concept of the Mormon god further incoherent, including the existence of gratuitous suffering and premature death due to natural and human evil, the existence of confusion and nonbelief, and the problems of wrong belief, wrong believers, multiple faiths and ineffectual prayer, to name the critical few. And earlier in this chapter we addressed why and how it is that faith exists and persists.

Now the focus is different. It is not the justifiability and rationality of religious beliefs that are in question. Nor, again, is it the reasons why faith as belief in god or gods exists or persists. And it isn't the personal or social consequence of simply believing, for example, that there is a wholly benign and benevolent god who is conceived as an unconditionally loving, undemanding, and nonjudgmental Father figure who confers 'blessings' (defined without contrast as whatever happens) in response to the needs, hopes, and requests of all people, and without requirements or expectations. Such belief, even if infantile and unworthy of respect, would be no different than a modified belief in Santa Claus, dressed up to appeal to grown-ups who can no longer believe in Santa, but who need to believe in – and/or believe in the belief in – a 'Cosmic Parent' who will love, provide, and deliver them from the vicissitudes of life and the daunting specter of death.

Beyond the subtle but very real assault on the personal intellectual integrity of the theistic believer incurred by self-deceptively believing that which is unbelievable, we must — to get to the root of the problem with theistic religion (and Mormonism in particular) — focus our attention and best thinking on the very real damage inflicted on the believer by the underlying abusive dynamic at play within the social system of all hierarchical, authoritarian institutions and belief systems. This dynamic is tacit and likely operates for many, if not most, in positions of ecclesiastical authority without any deliberate intent to inflict harm. Nevertheless, the actual harm done, as evidenced by extensive empirical evidence, and the deep cultural embeddedness of such a dynamic as an essential and fundamental practice, would seem to make its use (or at least its persistent use) suspect — notwithstanding adamant, self-deceiving denials, and sincere, justifying rationalizations to the contrary.

Regardless of the conscious or asserted intentions and motives of the abuser (which are neither relevant to this argument nor definitively determinable), the psychologically abusive dynamic at play seems to be inherent in the patriarchal world-view dominant in all forms of theism. Specifically, and for purposes here, it seems moreover to consist of what has been introduced and referred to earlier and repeatedly as the fundamental *moralistic core* of such authoritarian belief systems, and its related control strategies and derivative set of rules, or *code of patriarchy*. These related aspects of what I regard and have referred to above as the *abusive dynamic* of all theistic religions, constitute a learned and conditioned, or programmed, way of controlling and manipulating others to maintain power, control, and homeostasis or stability in an authoritarian, theistic social system. They work to preserve, protect, and perpetuate the particular death-defying, 'anti-self,' and 'anti-life' morality and dogma of that system.

The Moralistic Core of Theistic Faiths

The *moralistic core*, as I consider it to be, consists of those moral demands and performatory requirements rooted explicitly or implicitly in the religious belief system. These moral demands and requirements essentially direct and govern the lives of believers and define their state and status with their god and their relationship with others in and outside of their particular faith.

What makes such a moralistic core potentially damaging and dangerous to believers is not only the particular belief in a particular god held by members of the faith, or the unconscious desires and characterological dispositions for holding such beliefs. Nor is it solely the irrational nature of religious beliefs and practices adhered to, or the exercise of authoritarian control by religious leaders and parents (although that alone could be quite damaging). Rather, and of additional and perhaps primary significance, it is *all of the above* in relation to the conditioned *meta-belief* that this moralistic core of their faith (including its moral demands and performatory requirements — *i.e.* 'shoulds,' or 'shalts' and 'shalt-nots' — and its derivative *code of patriarchy*) is an *objective* and *eternal* reality regarded falsely and incoherently – and ultimately detrimentally – by believers as 'Absolute Truth'.

As a relevant aside, this meta-belief is most likely legitimized in the minds of believers by the corresponding, primary meta-belief in the absolute existence of their eternal Father-God and the eternal family — a meta-belief in turn legitimized in the believer's mind by the invocation of the unconscious, primary parent-child dynamic which potentiates and makes real the projection of the internalized loving, powerful, and authoritative parent onto the believed concept of 'God' and the actual authority figures of the faith. It is a meta-belief that imputes to such a believed Deity, and to the asserted mantle of authority of his alleged 'called and anointed' surrogates — together with their assessments and judgments of what constitutes worthiness and unworthiness, and the putative eternal consequences of both — the illusory legitimacy of objective reality and Truth.

But such meta-beliefs, as we have learned, are both false and/or incoherent. Moreover, the projected parent-child dynamic and experienced 'eternal family reality' — regressive artifacts of the "basic biological situation" (Faber 2004, 2010) and "evolved deep structure" of the brain (Slavin and Kriegman 1992) operating *without regard for reality* through the governing "primary process of the unconscious" (Kahn 2002) – are merely conditioned and reinforced psychological constructs of the evolved human brain which are hard-wired and culturally conditioned to affectively respond to and produce such constructs. Neither Parent-Gods nor the reified family system (and corresponding family relationships) are "eternal" in the sense believed by theistic believers of the Mormon faith. As with all religious or so-called spiritual experiences, the experience of such an 'eternal' and subjectively 'real' and 'true' quality is naturalistically explained without the need to resort to or believe in metaphysical nonsense.

When the moralistic core of a particular faith is implanted and activated in the brains of believers by the authoritative (and authoritarian) employment of the various mind-control strategies and devices, and related primary imperatives at play, it can afflict the believer with a variety of emotional problems and psychological maladies including, but not limited to, anxiety, depression, obsessive compulsivity, and self-alienating guilt, shame, conflictedness, and one-sidedness. Such is the case, I shall argue, with the Mormon faith and all theistic religions which have as their center this moralistic core and its code of patriarchy, and which tacitly employ those human mind-control strategies and devices designed to subjugate Church members and their children to authority and keep them in line with the moral and performatory code of the faith.[174]

---

174 Apropos to this assessment of the Mormon faith as an important adjunct to it is Marion Stricker's discovery and description of what she refers to in her book of the same title as "the pattern of the double-bind in Mormonism" (Stricker 2000).

"The Pattern," according to Stricker, "is the method of psychological manipulation [that] the 'Binder' [or dominant, controlling party] uses to bind another to him. This manipulation reaches a crisis in the Double-Bind" formed in Stage 4 of the process. "From that point on, the Double-Bind is then reinforced by alternate contradictions that obfuscate and deny [to] the 'Bound' [or subservient, obedient follower] his or her ability to think or feel rationally.

Stricker's nine-stage process of "The Pattern of the Double-Bind in Mormonism" has a familiar feel in both the content and sequence, and corresponds to the author's and others' personal experiences in the Mormon faith, as well as to my own. It is also – incidentally and importantly – evident and reinforced in the Bible (one of the four authoritative "Standard Works" or scriptures of the Mormon faith) in what Jungian psychotherapist and former fundamentalist Christian Edmund D. Cohen (1988) has identified as seven psychological "devices" of mind-control designed by its authors to entice and bind pre-conditioned, vulnerable and unsuspecting people to the Christian faith (see note 224 in Appendix A).

For me, the stages of this pattern reflect and represent different aspects of a tacit agenda and corresponding process designed and used in the Mormon faith to increase membership and control and manipulate its members. Although the use of stages and the way the stages are conceptualized and sequenced are helpful in communicating how the pattern works, neither the number nor sequence of the stages in the pattern, or even the notion of stages *per se*, are the intended or recommended focus of this presentation — or, I suspect, of

Stricker's as well.

Essentially, the 'double-bind in Mormonism,' as astutely identified by Stricker, is set-up in stage one of the process by those pressing problems, anxiety, and unsatisfied longings which urge us to seek fulfillment so that we can feel well and complete. This human condition becomes the personal, existential problem requiring a solution. For many, this existential problem might not be acute. For others it is, and might in some cases incapacitate them through depression or despair, making them dysfunctional and perhaps, in turn, alienating them from others and exacerbating the isolation and loneliness that make matters worse. In either case the existential anxiety exists, making fellow sufferers vulnerable in their search for answers or solutions to their condition.

The solution offered by the Mormon faith is an *ersatz* solution embedded in, as Stricker puts it, "…a closed system [designed to] keep its members in an emotional and rationally confused state of mind from which they 'choose without choosing'; they 'choose' [as investigators and members] the label that best fits their needs without being shown the [hidden requirements and implications of the choice] (32–4).

The set-up of the double-bind is followed by the tacit agreement offered in stage two of the process. As Stricker states it, "The *problem* in Stage 1 created a need for answers [or a solution]. It is in this mental and emotional [state of need and] confusion that Mormonism steps in with a formula that 'fits all problems.'… In Mormonism the key factor is an agreement based on [a packaged set of promises with hidden terms and conditions]; in short, a fraudulent contract." (39).

In stage three, "New members are caught with a psychological hook. It begins with the '*Yes*' agreement" — a 'yes' which connotes a promise to provide the needed and wanted answers and blessings sought for. This 'yes' "…is then altered by a prepositional '*But*' this is what you must do extra. … What is now to be received is a [conditional] '*gift,*' given [only] '*if*' you become *worthy* to receive [it]. A definite agreement has become a [contingency agreement with] *undefined* worthiness [clauses] in order to receive [the needed and promised 'blessings']. (39) This third stage leads to the double-bind, which, according to Stricker, is built on stages two and three.

This double-bind in Mormonism, which is established in stage four of Stricker's process, is as follows: "If you don't obey the [hidden provisions of worthiness] you will be 'guilty' of not being sincere,' not trying hard enough [or being in sin]. If you do obey, you are 'guilty' [when] you [("wretched" person that you are: Romans 7:24; 2 Nephi 4:17) continue to feel your human inadequacies and)] still haven't received the [relief and blessings you seek, *e.g.* freedom from your true, biological self (i.e. human nature), and a confirmation or "more sure" revelation attesting to a proposed course of action or needed transformation and direction], which you would have received had you done them properly (53–4)." In other words, the member of the Mormon Church is 'damned' if they do *not* obey, or comply with, the hidden, vague or ambiguous requirements of worthiness to receive the promised blessings they desire and seek, and they are 'damned' if they *do* obey or comply, both by not doing so sufficient to receive — a disappointment which even the most 'faithful" often experience (except by coincidence) with unanswered prayer and unfulfilled 'priesthood blessings' — and by the guilt and shame attending their failed effort and conditioned belief of 'spiritual inadequacy.' Here then is the classic double-bind of Mormonism which keeps the faithful bound to their faith through guilt, shame, or baseless hope and self-deception, or plunges them into a crisis of faith and a decision to leave or stay in the faith.

With either decision — stay or leave — the disillusioned 'Bound' [Church member] suffers what Stricker refers to as a type of death by suicide. If the member turns away reflectively (not reactively), there are often, at first, mixed feelings of anxiety, guilt, disorientation, and depression, accompanied by an overwhelming feeling of relief. If the released 'Bound' does not continue to chase after other gods, and gets the needed help or support, there is hope of needed psychological separation and renewal. If not, and the member repents and turns back to the 'Binder' or turns compulsively to another Binder, the self-betrayal will turn to what Stricker calls "psychological cannibalism," and the Bound's deep sense of self-abandonment will slowly, metaphorically, 'eat him or her alive,' in spite of denial and the repressed guilt and shame experienced. When this happens, the repressed always returns, and the Bound suffers a slow psychological death by the self-inflicted wounds of his or her own cowardice; a death which is bitterly ironic considering the reasons the Bound entered into the agreement with the Binder initially. Depending on whether the Bound leaves or stays in the fold, the Binder will of course frame this tragic state of affairs as either an unfortunate victory of Evil caused by the faithlessness (or sinfulness) of the Bound, or a state of blessedness for the Bound's valiancy in faithfully 'enduring to the end.'

Through the use of such mind-control strategies and devices, regardless of intent, religious leaders and parents belonging to dogmatic religions disclose and impose certain *shoulds* and *oughts* in relation to believers' thoughts, feelings, desires, needs, beliefs, motives, actions, attitudes, and behaviors. They enforce compliance with such moral imperatives by connecting them to a putatively revealed doctrinal foundation of obedience and sacrifice, sin and sinfulness, worthiness and unworthiness, righteousness and unrighteousness (or wickedness), blessedness and barrenness, chosenness and unchosenness, spirituality and carnality, and salvation and damnation.

The mind-control strategies referred to above translate in the Mormon faith to five *primary imperatives*, as follows: First, believers are taught to accept as *Absolute Truth* the existence of the Mormon godhead, the Mormon 'Plan of Salvation,' and their relationship to their Father-god as his literal spirit children. They are also taught to accept as *actual* truth the existence of *revelation* from their god to man, and to regard such revelation from the Mormon god, through both the authorized channels of the priesthood and directly to faithful believers, as Absolute Truth for the Church and for them personally as, in both cases, a necessary requirement for salvation (and damnation).

Second, Church members are instructed to regard *faith* in the Mormon god and in the truthfulness of the Mormon faith as a necessary requirement for salvation and the avoidance of damnation, and as an irreversible decision. They are also taught of the necessity of *faith-testing* and of *enduring to the end* in 'righteousness' and 'Truth' to *prove* themselves worthy of the highest blessing of "eternal life."

Third, Mormons are *implicitly* "encouraged" to facilitate the construction and confirmation of a personal reality which conforms to, and necessarily confirms, the Mormon "gospel reality" of the Church, and are *explicitly* required (as a condition of salvation and acceptance by God) to be (and remain) "humble, meek and submissive" (or "childlike") before the Parent-God, both through participation in all prescribed religious ordinances, rituals and practices, and through continual repentance.

Fourth, Church members are counseled to live a *Christ-like* life in humility and submissiveness to divine authority; to obey all the "commandments" of 'God' (including the counsel of Church leaders) and *eschew doubt* in the revealed truths of the Church, and in the divine authority, teachings, and counsel of Church leaders.

And fifth, Church members are called upon and expected to establish and strengthen their commitment to Church growth, solidarity, and survival, and to loyally defend the Church and follow, obey, and sustain the General Authorities and local leaders of the Church.

The problems and concerns related to the first two theological imperatives were addressed in Chapters 5 and 6 respectively. The third imperative involving the induced or facilitated construction of desired personal 'reality' and a regressive dependence on 'God' employs two specific conditioning programs. The first entails the indoctrination of children and converts to regard the teachings of the Mormon faith as true primarily (if not exclusively) on the basis of *positive* (or 'good') *feelings*, and criticisms or refutations of the truth claims of the Mormon faith as false primarily (if not exclusively) on the basis of *negative* (or 'bad') *feelings* (Worthy 2008, pp. 15–51; see also *Personal Postscript*). The second program is the "infantilizing process" introduced in Chapter 6 and presented in some depth in *Appendix A* in relation to a Mormon conversion experience. This process entails the repetitive, suggestive (hypnotic) induction of a regressive, dissociative, and hallucinatory faith-state (and the associated affects and feelings) through the required practice of prayer, the systematic use of familiar, evocative language, music, literature and art, the appeal to tradition, and expected participation in religious disciplines, programs, rites and rituals (Schumaker 1995; Faber 2002, 2004, 2010; Stromberg 1993; Watters 1992; and Cohen 1988).

The fourth imperative to live a Godly or Christ-like life and eschew doubt involves creating and repeatedly presenting as true a purely speculative and fictitious historical account of Jesus' life and teachings as the *literal* Son of God and as the head of his restored Church on the basis of putative revelation. This imperative, of course, appeals to the believer's ego and regressive need for recognition, acceptance and approval, and essentially commits him to a repressed, one-sided, conflicted, and inauthentic way of life. It also effectually keeps believers bound to the faith either by keeping them, through the aforementioned religious guilt cycle (Ray 2009), in a perpetual state of dependence and guilt, shame, and repentance for doubting or not living a self-sacrificial Christ-like life, or by keeping them, through the also aforementioned psychological mechanism of the conditioned fear response, in an inflated delusional state of self-righteousness, undoubting belief, and *ersatz* humility for believing they are doing so. Either way, control is maintained by requiring self-hatred and self-sacrifice, and by invoking humility and submissiveness to divine authority to obtain and sustain the acceptance and approval of peers, parent-leaders, and the Parent-Gods of the Mormon Godhead. Simply put, the injunction to be like Jesus, or to 'do as Jesus would do' — *i.e.* be *perfect*, even as the Mormon god is perfect by submitting one's will to the Father — is the assurance of emotional control and bondage.

The fifth imperative regarding the building and strengthening of believer (member) commitment and loyalty to the Church and its leaders involves the institutionalization and reinforcement of certain effective social commitment mechanisms. These include *sacrifice, investment, renunciation, communion, mortification* and *transcendence* (Tice 2001). This institution of social commitment mechanisms is essentially accomplished in two ways.

First, it is accomplished through the ceremonial and ritualistic establishment of a covenantal relationship between the Mormon god and mentally competent members of the Church. This is done initially through baptism, then (for male members twelve years of age and older) through the conferral of the priesthood, and finally, for 'worthy' men and women, through the Temple endowment. Secondly, it is done through the operant conditioning of children and adult Church members. This, in turn, is done in two ways.

First, it involves the repeatedly stated and implied threat or concern of alienation from the Mormon god, self, and Church in consequence of unrepented personal sin and, in more serious cases of transgression, formal Church disciplinary action resulting in 'disfellowship' and 'excommunication' (see *Personal Postscript*). Secondly, it is done through the repeated promise of security, love, esteem, happiness, and fulfillment through Church fellowship and the acquisition of Church status, 'priesthood power,' and 'eternal reward' on condition of *eventual* and *sufficient* faithfulness, righteousness, and worthiness as prescribed and adjudged by Church leaders.

For the above mind-control strategies and devices to work effectively or at all, a trade must occur. Essentially, this trade is initiated by Mormon missionaries, member-parents, and ecclesiastical parent-leaders first manipulatively offering to their children and to Church investigators and members an illusory and factually vacuous promise of 'joy' in this life and 'eternal life' (or the avoidance of damnation) in the next life. Then, once this seductive offer and promise is accepted by trusting, vulnerable, and naïve listeners, the hidden requirements for receiving the promised 'blessings' are disclosed.

The trade therefore, consists of the promise of illusory supernatural protection, healing, and deliverance, as well as yearned-for earthly and otherworldly blessings (such as divinely bestowed esteem, power, health, and prosperity in this life, and immortality and eternal life with family and loved ones in the next) *in exchange for* a Faustian abdication of certain human goods. These 'goods,' which are essential to their well-being, include their intellectual integrity, their personal integration, their moral imagination, their right to free-thinking, doubt, dissent, the challenging of authority, and conscientious disobedience, and their right to pursue non-sanctioned, or officially disapproved, yet personally desired or necessary living options, orientations, and preferences, whatever they might be.

This exchange effectually and often results in self-betrayal through the subordination or abandonment of one's wants, needs and internal authority to externally imposed or authoritarian 'oughts,' 'shoulds,' and ecclesiastical authority. It is a trade or exchange that is made in order to avoid conditioned guilt and shame and to acquire peer and parental acceptance and approval.

Such an exchange is made possible, from my perspective, by the vicissitudes of life and the fear of separation and death which set up or invoke the regressive yearnings and accompanying unconscious recapitulation of a submissive and regressive parent-child dynamic (Faber 2004, 2010). Such a primal dynamic, common to us all, is induced, at its most basic and compelling level, by a hypnotic, dissociative transference induced through language, music, symbol, and ritual. The transference is then characterized as a 'conversion through faith,' and the affect-based 'faith' (experienced as a primal trust and commitment) is then effectively reinforced through on-going facilitated belief formation and systematic indoctrination and operant conditioning within the culture (see *Appendix A*).

The cumulative incidents of self-betrayal very likely will eventually — even if unknowingly or unadmittedly — take their toll on both the accommodating and the committed believer. At a basic level, such an exchange will likely impair psychological individuation and integration and promote psychological one-sidedness, obsessive-compulsivity, and inner conflict in the personality to a greater or lesser degree. Moreover, the repeated acts of self-betrayal resulting from such an exchange can ultimately foster deep resentment toward oneself (for repeatedly selling-out to one's commitments, fears, and insecurities) and direct or displaced resentment and anger toward those in authority.

As a result of such resentment and suppressed anger and guilt, some degree of self-loathing and self-alienation will likely ensue, resulting at times in withdrawal of commitment or Church activity and perhaps even some form of self-defeating reactivity, intrapersonal acting-in, or antisocial acting-out. All these contribute in the end to the social, psychological, and even possibly physical detriment of believers and others. These potential, if not likely, consequences are very real and, I would argue, even predictable in the lives of those affected by this inhuman exchange.[175]

---

175 Denial of such predictable consequences is itself predictable, particularly in those who would argue that their religious life has brought them only, or on balance, great happiness, fulfillment, and psychological well-being in spite of their struggles, trials, and tribulations. But such an argument, if sincerely believed, is likely both self-deceiving and delusional. Let those among the faithful — or those who were raised in active

Accordingly, believers or believing investigators of any faith or religion might know that a particular faith is toxic if its beliefs, values, language, and authoritative requirements tend, *in practice*, to…

- require *faith in* and *revelation from* an infinite, eternal and supernatural being as a necessity for divine acceptance, approval and salvation;

- require *faith* as an unquestionable, irreversible *decision* based entirely on a *feeling* (or revealed 'confirmation' or 'witness' from the Holy Spirit);

- promote the *duality* of the self as *spirit* and *body*, where the spirit-self is godlike and the body ("natural man" or biological-self) is "carnal, sensual and devilish" and an "enemy to God," and require accordingly that believers "put off the natural man" (or one's biological instinctuality and related needs) and live Godly or Christ-like lives; to do what Jesus would do, and to follow the admonition of Jesus *to be perfect,* even as 'God' is perfect;

- require *obedience to revealed commandments*, performance up to revealed standards, expectations, or authoritative 'counsel'; the *sacrifice* or circumscribing of certain human appetites, desires, passions, and needs 'within the bounds the Lord has set'; the *consecration of time, money, and talent* for the building of the Church; and the *suspension of doubt*, skepticism, and dissent *to obtain and retain favor*, acceptance, and approval from the particular god and *from those in authority*, and *to obtain 'blessings'* (and 'blessedness') in this life and salvation and eternal life in the next life;

- *separate reason from faith* and *subordinate knowledge* through justification to knowledge by revelation confirmed by 'testimony,' or a *feeling* of the Spirit;

- *dictate to believers* (by directive or 'counsel' or scriptural admonition and explicit/implicit warning) *how they should live their lives*;

- implicitly or explicitly *advocate or require the subordination of personal conscience* to the 'revealed will of God' on the basis of the belief that *whatever* the god requires or commands his children to do is morally right;

- promote one-sided living by *proscribing certain feelings, attitudes, life-choices, and*

Mormon families — who doubt the toxic affects of the Mormon faith (or any authoritarian, theistic faith) in their lives take a troubling current or recurring symptom or problem in *any* area or relationship of their life and submit willingly and openly to either cognitive behavioral therapy or, preferably, rigorous psychoanalytical or psychodynamic psychotherapy (with, in either case, a qualified, competent and irreligious psychotherapist) and they will very likely, if not most certainly, come away with a very different psychological assessment and self-constructed life-narrative than what they ignorantly believe to be the case. Perhaps this is why such psychotherapy (particularly psychoanalysis) is frowned on or discouraged by fundamentalist Church leaders and avoided by the faithful. It is difficult (to say the least!) to confront one's symptoms and the possibility or likelihood that one's life of supposed happiness and well-being is perhaps, at its core, a lie formed and perpetuated through self-denial and self-deception.

human rights and values for living as sinful and wrong on the basis of 'God's Word' (or 'will'), or Church policy;

- *frame hardships*, suffering, loss, and required sacrifices of time, talent, means and possessions *as necessary and required tests of faith* imposed or allowed by 'God' *to prove worthiness* and loyalty to him and his 'anointed' or 'chosen' leaders;

- *foster superstitious, magical thinking* in supernatural agents, rites, and rituals *as indicative of a 'saving faith in God'*;

- ensure belief in the unbelievable by mandating *the imperative to believe and not doubt*;

- foster, by expectation and authoritative imperative, a perpetual or *life-long child-like dependency* on a Parent-God and parent-Leaders;

- require believers to essentially *abdicate the burden of their own freedom and responsibility* to fully and conscientiously engage life *by submitting to 'counsel' or 'commandments'* regarding what is right and wrong, *i.e.* what should and shouldn't be done or experienced, or how life should and shouldn't be lived;

- *require binding commitments* to the particular god and, by association, to a way of life which essentially forecloses on certain forbidden possibilities and the right and obligation of believers to ethically choose those possibilities and experiences, or that course of life or action which might be necessary for, or merely preferred by, the individual;

- promote or *provide a sense of being 'special,' 'favored,' and 'chosen'* by the 'one true God' as part of the *one and only true faith*, religion, or church;

- set up or implicitly condone or *tolerate putatively benevolent authoritarian control*;

- either explicitly or implicitly set up, or foster and perpetuate, through its belief in 'continuous revelation from God,' the potential or actual compulsive *acting-out of self-righteousness and religious extremism or fanaticism in the quest for divine approval,* favor, and special blessings;

- implicitly, if not explicitly, *require conformity to established standards* of appearance, behavior, thinking, language, and belief at the expense of one's uniqueness in order to fit in or be accepted or regarded worthy or appropriately representative of a desired image;

- *impose guilt, shame, and* — in cases of disobedience — *condemnation and the forfeiture of blessings as punishment* in this life (by censure and disciplinary action) and/ or the next (damnation) for 'sinning' by disobeying the commandments and expectations established by scripture and authoritative counsel, or by doubting, questioning, or conscientiously dissenting from authority or authoritative pronouncements, doctrines, and counsel;

- *advocate 'free agency'* and lead people to believe that they are free to choose how to live their lives *while simultaneously governing such putative freedom through a variety of different strategies designed to control such agency*, and by warning believers that their ability to 'choose the right' (*i.e.* their 'moral agency') can be lost by exercising their free agency in opposition to their god's commandments or the counsel of Church leaders.

Certainly some if not all of the above criteria apply, to one degree or another, to the Mormon faith. Many no doubt also apply to some degree to other theistic religions as well. Regardless of intent, the criteria apply. Even soft or subtle and 'benevolent authoritarianism' can be (and often is) insidiously abusive, or at least potentially so. With 'authority' — particularly when it is believed to come from a god — authoritarianism is very likely if not inevitable, given the moralistic core at play in all dogmatic theistic belief systems and the code of patriarchal control embedded in it.[176]

---

176 Those notable psychologists who are supportive of certain forms of religiosity, such as Allport's 'mature *vs.* immature religion' (or 'intrinsic *vs.* extrinsic religiosity'), Jung's 'individuating religion'; Fromm's 'humanistic *vs.* authoritarian religion,' James' 'personal *vs.* institutional religion,' *etc.* would all likely agree that all forms of institutional, dogmatic, and authoritarian theistic religion are objectionable on the grounds that they are at least potentially, if not likely, harmful to the believer's psychological well-being in one way or another (Fuller 1994). These psychologists would likely not believe in, or approve of, belief or faith in the literal existence of the patriarchal, authoritarian Parent-God of traditional or orthodox theistic life-forms. Nor would they likely approve of an institutional religion like the Mormon faith, or any of its fundamental or charismatic splinter faiths that have both intrinsic and extrinsic aspects. Nevertheless, they generally do seem to advocate a mature, intrinsic, non-institutional religious belief — a mature way of life in relationship with a mature, loving god who is conceptualized as a divine being solely committed to the individuation and integration of the personality and the humanistic values of self-direction, self-actualization, self-transcendence, and mature, loving relatedness in the service of human wholeness and well-being.

Apart from the difficulties of confirming or disconfirming the putative salutary effects of religious belief on the mature believer's psychological well-being, there is the difficulty of conceiving of religious beliefs which are wholly without potential risk of psychological harm or extremism. At *minimum*, purported belief in *any* god presents potential risk of self- and other-alienation, even where such confessed, sincere, and enduring belief is thought to be the *only* requirement for salvation, and the absence of such belief is thought to either forfeit salvation or warrant damnation. (Clearly, a concept of a god who is all-knowing, all-powerful, and exclusively benevolent — desiring only that all people are happy and ensuring immortality and eternal life for all people, without any requirements or conditions for salvation, including belief in him — does not fit with any known theology. Belief, disbelief, or non-belief in such a god would be salvifically inconsequential. Further, belief in such a god would arguably be psychologically suspect.)

With the need for faith, and the dependence of faith on affective, confirming revelation comes the potential risk and danger of induced dissociative hallucination, projective-transference, delusion, self-deception, and religious acting-out. Finally, where belief in a particular god is required for salvation and the realization of the putative psychological benefits of religious belief, there is the risk of anxiety, guilt, and shame, and with it the risk of defensive withdrawal, regression, splitting, undoing, and/or turning against the self when belief is either incongruously retained (by believing what one knows at some level is unbelievable), threatened, or lost.

Clearly, these and other risks of psychopathology, and their attending consequences to personal well-being, coupled with the fact that nonbelievers and disbelievers can and do enjoy all (if not more) of the goods of personal well-being enjoyed by religious believers (save the alleged comforts derived from the illusion of

Religious Values and Mental Health and Well-Being

To be sure, many, if not all, devout believers credit their belief and 'faith in God' as the source of their character strength, courage, comfort, and hope in the face of adversity and death. For these believers, their religious beliefs allegedly provide security in the face of uncertainty, as well as comfort, peace, serenity, and happiness in the face of the hardships and vicissitudes of life. They also allegedly provide them with a sense of meaning in an otherwise meaningless existence, and esteem and self-regard in the face of human limitation and imperfection. Last but not least, their beliefs are, for them, an alleged motivational force for good in an otherwise immoral world.

Such putative benefits are formidable indeed. However, it would certainly be false and prejudicial to suggest that *only* those with belief and faith in a god can and do enjoy them. It would also be a *non sequitur* — and a *post hoc* argument as well — to argue that such benefits and conditions necessarily follow or are caused by belief and faith in a god. Even so — and even if, solely for the sake of argument, it is granted that such benefits are, in fact, experienced and necessarily and exclusively follow faith in a god (which they do not) — I would argue, primarily on the basis of my own and others' personal experience, that these benefits enjoyed do not compensate either believers or humanity for the real damage done and losses incurred to themselves and others who have suffered at their hands as a result of any or all of the religious beliefs and practices listed above.

I would also argue, again on the basis of my own and others' personal experience, that many believers with 'faith in God and Christ' do not truly enjoy such benefits consistently, if at all. In fact, as suggested earlier, it can be argued that such putative benefits do not – and *could not – actually* exist *as such*, because they are not anchored in reality. They are instead based entirely on a believed, illusory reality; a sort of 'virtual reality' which is *factually meaningless* and created *entirely* by the wishful, magical thinking at play in the self-or-other-induced dissociated mental state (i.e. *faith-state*) of the believer. Finally, it is arguably the case that many disbelievers and nonbelievers actually and reportedly *do* in fact enjoy many if not all of the above benefits, solely on the basis of their own natural, psychological resources and the meaningful lives they live in virtue of their commitment to a realistic, 'reason-driven life' (Price and Sweeney 2006), their life work, their integrated suffering, and their relationships with others.

To my mind, the risks and losses associated with toxic religions like the Mormon faith are considerable. They far outweigh any putative or actual salutary benefits[177] and

---

divine intervention, immortality, and eternal life — illusions subject to doubt that is betrayed in numerous ways by believers' words, behaviors, and actions, as noted extensively in the *Introduction*), make the net benefit of religious belief, in my experience, nonexistent at best.

177 Assertions or arguments made by certain psychologists, on the basis of psychometric research, regarding the physical and psychological benefits of "intrinsic" vs. "extrinsic" religious orientation are, in my view, problematical for at least the following seven reasons, the first six of which are largely interrelated:

First, the self-reporting personality questionnaires (most notably the MMPI and CPI instruments) used in such research are not uncontroversially or universally accepted among psychotherapists (and psychodynamic psychotherapists in particular) in terms of their validity and actual or predictive diagnostic efficacy.

Second, such questionnaires do not address the deeper structure of personality.

Third, the indicators of mental health in such questionnaires, taken individually, in clusters or as a whole, are not universally (or uncontroversially) accepted as being either definitive of psychological well-being or

perceived or alleged happiness or self-satisfaction and sense of well-being that allegedly accrues to believers. Specifically, I consider all scripturally-based, or orthodox, authoritarian theistic life-forms, as religious belief and value systems, to be fundamentally harmful to believers and society, and life-denying or life-negating by design. This is particularly so in relation to various core "theistic values" presented, for example, by renowned Mormon psychologist Allen Bergin (1980).

Bergin, whom I know personally, proposes a "spiritual alternative" (whatever that could actually mean, if anything) to what he terms "clinical-humanistic" values. He suggests that such an alternative – which he incorrectly contrasts to an unrepresentative set of opposing values and not to what, for example, Albert Ellis (1980) refers to as a more accurate set of "clinical-humanistic-*atheistic*" values – might be called "theistic realism;" a designation which could correctly be regarded as an oxymoron. But what are these preferable alternative values Bergin proposes that I consider being psychologically harmful and dangerous? They include, in my words and in summary, belief in a supreme god, obedience to god and his chosen leaders, acceptance of absolute moral values (and presumably Truth), the necessity of self-sacrifice, commitment to heterosexual marriage and procreation, acceptance of guilt, suffering, and contrition for wrong doing (as defined primarily, if not exclusively, by the faith and its "absolute," "universal" moral code), forgiveness of those who harm or have harmed you, and making faith and "spiritual insight" inseparable from reason and the intellect in attaining knowledge, meaning, and purpose in life (6).

Such values and beliefs, and the religious "conception of human nature," "moral frame of reference," and set of therapeutic "techniques" which serve as an "orienting framework"

---

absent of counteracting or compensatory psychopathology.

Fourth, reported indicators of mental health and well-being are very likely not indicative of either the *presence* or *absence* of suppressed, somatized, or otherwise occult anxiety, guilt and shame, or repressed psychological trauma and its resulting counteracting or compensatory psychopathology.

Fifth, indicators of mental health or psychological well-being are not *causally* specific to "intrinsic" and/or "extrinsic" religious belief and practice in general, or the beliefs and practices of different faiths in particular. As Watters I think correctly (and commonsensically) points out in this regard, "The correlation of 'being religious' with being 'something else' (mentally healthy, prejudiced, or concerned about others) does not 'prove' cause and effect. If, for example, a study demonstrates that people who are religious in a certain way are also mentally healthy or unhealthy, we cannot say for sure that either state caused the other. Each could be the result of a third variable not yet identifies [or missed altogether]. Also, most of the studies in this area are based on self-report, paper and pencil questionnaires which do not always take into account the social desirability factor, the human tendency to want to respond in a way that makes one look good, however inaccurate the response" (1992, 153; see also pp. 153-161).

Sixth, reported indicators of mental health and psychological well-being are necessarily subjective and neither actually nor necessarily indicative of the person's *actual* mental state or psychological condition.

And seventh, the distinction of "intrinsic" and "extrinsic" religiosity is essentially null from a purely theistic religious perspective. Quoting again from Watters, 'The extrinsically religious person is one who presumably attends church because of the social and political advantages, whereas the intrinsically religious person is preoccupied with more internal events having to do with spiritual matters, their relation to God and Christ and the hope of salvation, or joy in being already 'saved.' When one realizes that the most powerful incentive for people to embrace Christianity [and Mormonism] was the promise of eternal bliss [life] in [the presence of God, Christ and loved ones], coupled with the threat of eternal damnation if they rejected Christianity [or Mormonism], it is very difficult to talk about an intrinsic motivation at all. Both types of religious people indulge in religious behavior for what they hope to get out of it. The expected rewards for the 'extrinsically' religious are short-term social ones; in the case of the so-called intrinsically religious, the individual's rewards are long-term ones" (27-28).

to their understanding and acceptance as truth, are derived from what Bergin refers to elsewhere as a "spiritual perspective" that "there is a spiritual reality and that spiritual experiences can make a difference in behavior [; that the] spirit of God or divine intelligence can influence the identity, agency, and life-style of human beings" (1991, 398-9). This perspective and all its related derivatives are implicitly and, as we have learned, invalidly presented as actual truth *at parity with* analytical and scientific truth. Such a move on Bergin's part tacitly condones the acceptance of such unwarranted assertions as truth or probable truth when it is neither prudent nor possible to do so without self-deception. His views are, to be blunt, utterly absurd on the basis of their necessary dependence on the believed literal existence of a *factual non reality* (god), and on the basis of asserted and believed "spiritual" experiences from god through the believed medium of the 'Holy Ghost' or 'Light of Truth' (which are likewise factual non realities as represented linguistically). Such non self-justifying views, in part and as a whole, are false or incoherent, and factually vacuous as truth claims. And they are incoherent as well in relation to the only reality we can actually or objectively *know* as mere, fallible human beings; a purely naturalistic reality *without* metaphysical foundations.

From my perspective, and as a relevant aside, for *any* psychotherapist to propose such a perspective and set of values and beliefs not only betrays his professional commitment to foster mental health and well-being, it exposes the need to sustain and legitimize his own religious faith. Moreover, such a position and proposal is professionally irresponsible. It essentially amounts to tacitly condoning epistemic irresponsibility, and professionally regarding an irrational, dissociated mental 'faith-state' and its related regressive, delusional acceptance of false or incoherent, and harmful and potentially dangerous and destructive values and beliefs, as indicative and characteristic of, and even necessary for, mental health and well-being.

Pace Bergin and other psychologists of like mind and faith, the aforementioned primary imperatives of the various mind-control-strategies and devices of Mormonism's moralistic core and code of patriarchy, along with the implicit faith-imperatives to conform one's personality to religious norms (or "theistic values") and submit to the dogmatic mandates of faith in god, repentance of sin and sinfulness, and obedience to authoritative "counsel" and "commandment," can – and likely often do – result in both the suppression of human need fulfillment and the stultification of character development. Both of these outcomes are interrelated and inevitable on the basis of fundamental beliefs that are in some fashion, and to a significant degree, common to all theistic faiths; beliefs, in the end, that promote the conditions of *self-hatred* and *self-sacrifice* that are the root of mental illness. What do these two conditions entail in the Mormon faith?

Self-hatred entails "putting off the natural man" (or the biological, instinctual self) as "carnal, sensual and devilish;" the "natural man" who is an "enemy of God." This is done through continual *repentance* (remorsefully acknowledging, confessing, forsaking, renouncing, and making amends) for *all* human imperfections and sins of commission and omission, where 'imperfections' are personal shortcomings in relation to god's expectations, and 'sins' are transgressions – by thought or action – of the commandments and requirements of god as revealed in the scriptures, by priesthood leaders or by one's conditioned conscience.

From H.E. Jones' perspective as a psychiatrist, and as shall be elaborated on in *Appendix*

A in relation to the assessment of an actual Mormon conversion experience, "Self-hate is the natural consequence of the evil morality of human sacrifice, of self-sacrifice" (2006, 38). *Self-sacrifice* entails the creation of what Jones terms a "pseudo-self," which is the "false 'religious self' [that] is…a phony, contrived, inauthentic…perfect, selfless, goody-two-shoes [self;]…too good to be believable" (36). This, again, is done in the Mormon faith in four ways. First, by committing to sacrifice all that one possesses, even one's own life if necessary, in sustaining and defending the kingdom of god. Second, by "circumscribing all appetites, passions and desires within the bounds the Lord has set," and avoiding every 'unholy' and impure practice (i.e. those practices considered profane or unseemly in the Mormon culture, such as masturbating, watching R-rated movies, telling risqué jokes, engaging in sexual fantasy, colorful language or loud laughter, making light of 'sacred' subjects, etc.). Third, by refraining from engaging in sexual relations outside the bounds of legal and lawful marriage, i.e. marriage between a man and a woman (or women, in polygamy) established and sanctioned by civil law and god's law. And finally, by 'consecrating' oneself, one's time, talents, and everything one owns for the building of the Mormon Church and the establishment of 'Zion' (or the 'United Order' of god).

Together these two conditions of self-hatred and self-sacrifice effectually stunt or abort personal individuation and integration through the fostering of regressive dependence on a Parent-God and parent-Church leaders for moral direction, acceptance, and approval.[178]

---

178 This result occurs, at least in part, and again as addressed above and earlier, by establishing, through a putatively sacred (and authoritatively binding and consequential) covenant with an illusory god, the required promise of the believer to obey the 'laws' of obedience, sacrifice, and chastity, and 'keep all [natural, human] appetites, desires, and passions *within the bounds the Lord* has set,' and by authoritatively making certain human desires and essential aspects of the believer's personality ego-dystonic through the implicit or explicit authoritarian shaming of those aspects of human nature considered to be shameful, bad, or unseemly and therefore unworthy of divine approbation. Such an arbitrary and controlling characterization of human instinctuality and personality (as good or bad) is characteristic of 'one-sided theistic moralism.' It is, in my view, at the very heart of human neurosis and the personal disempowerment and inner conflictedness which come with it. It is as well, along with the danger to self and others, at the heart of my objection to any insistence on obedience to authority.

This is to say that while the informed observance of the basic, natural principles (or 'laws') of physical, mental, and social health and well-being is both indicated and sensible to one who values such goods, such observance, as well as obedience to the natural mandates of one's evolved moral conscience as a human being, and the necessary observance of civic laws and ordinances to ensure a safe and orderly society, is *not* equivalent to the theistic requirement of obedience to a god's commandments to establish personal worthiness as a human being, and acceptance and approval by a Parent-God and the parent-leaders of 'God's only true church' who allegedly act with authority for and as gods in judging those of the faith.

Obedience in this latter sense — even if such commandments and authoritative counsel which one obeys are consistent (to the degree that they are in fact consistent) with natural principles of personal and social morality and well-being — is both harmful and dangerous (not to mention indecent and immoral). This is because the requirement of obedience is also, if not primarily, an authoritarian strategy of manipulation and mind-control, and because it ultimately serves the institution *at the expense* of the member's dignity and integrity as a human being.

The argument that the Mormon faith does not, after all, require obedience to anything which is not in some way naturally good for the obedient believer and society is both disingenuous and untrue. For such obedience brings with it an authoritarian requirement and a judgment, along with believed illusory consequences which are falsely believed to be real. It is such a conditioned authoritarian mandate, coupled with the believed authoritative judgment, and the conditioned belief in the accompanying illusory consequences and meta-belief concerning their objective reality which makes the difference. (See also the *Epilogue, Personal Postscript, Appendix A* and, for an excellent study on the dangers of obedience to authority, Milgram, 2009)

Moreover, such a cult of conformity and obedience can — and likely often does — result in the proscription of certain personally necessary experiences through the consequent (and psychologically coercive) foreclosure on many of life's possibilities.

In this last regard, I would argue that Mormon religious dogma — perhaps in part as a defense against the threat of espoused personal revelation run amuck — too often reduces and confines the complexity and profundity of human experience to binary (either-or) moral categories, value judgments, and categorical imperatives. Such dogma, in my experience and judgment, cannot accommodate the demands of our humanity for the necessary degree of psychological individuation and development required in dealing more effectively with the complex personal and social problems which confront mankind today.

Additionally, Mormon religious belief too often circumscribes life's meaning within narrowly conceived ideals or prescriptions for living derived from doctrinal interpretations of the putatively revealed Plan of Salvation, thereby foreclosing on the analytic and imaginal creation of *personal meaning* — a topic we shall revisit in the *Epilogue*. Finally, authoritatively imposed religious dogma and morality foreclose on the necessity for moral imagination to creatively or ethically resolve the moral tension inherent in life's numerous collisions of duty where the inconceivable and forbidden is mandated conscientiously as a necessary course of action for personal individuation and well-being. Such creative, ethical resolutions are too often blocked at the expense of those necessary (and religiously discouraged or forbidden) natural, human experiences sufficient in themselves to provide all the depth, mystery, drama, tragedy, comedy, and adventure necessary to live a profoundly rich and meaningful human life *without* the need for any gods.

When the possibility for experience is foreclosed by dogma, commandment, or authoritative counsel — or by the related threat of shame and guilt through *parental* censure or chastisement, disfellowship, excommunication, and damnation — following Freud, we simply do not know what we are missing. Subjective and often self-deceptive assertions of happiness and fulfillment are, by definition, both *limited* and *limiting*. They are *limited* by what is given or believed to be the good life (or putatively 'acceptable life before God') and what is rationalized in the face of intimations to the contrary. They are *limiting* through their self-sealing and self-referential reinforcement.[179] It seems to me, on

---

179 What, after all, are the objective, universally accepted *human* criteria and causal mechanisms that give cognitive meaning and predictive significance to the concepts of *right, wrong, happiness* and *fulfillment*? How are such putative values or goods to be generically or specifically defined or otherwise characterized and formulated so as to be objectively meaningful to all, without exception? And to adequately attend to the needs of all without exception? Truly, one person's moral or ethical decision might be unconscionable to another, and one person's happiness and success might be, and often is, another person's misery or failure. What if, for example, happiness or fulfillment to a nonbeliever is *not* construed as such to a believer, or *vice-versa*? Or what if what makes the believer 'happy' is not a source of happiness to the nonbeliever, or is a source of unhappiness, and *vice-versa*? Moreover, what if what is *necessary* to the physical and psychological well-being of the individual is a burden that needs to be born, or which calls for, again, ethical decisions which require the burden of holding the tension of a collision of duty between two competing goods, and ultimately acting *outside* the mandated moral code? (See in regard to this last question the important works of Beebe 1995; Neumann 1969; and Stein 1993)

How, more specifically, can any belief system claim to possess the key to happiness, or promise happiness and fulfillment to all believers, given the highly variable and subjective nature of such goods and states of mind? Moreover, what if a person who claims to be happy is really *not*, or is even unhappy and miserable? Or, conversely, what if a person who is suffering or in misery considers himself to be truly or profoundly happy in virtue of his or her suffering? Surely all of these differences and apparent contradictions are com-the basis of contrasting personal experience alone, that human life (and living) is much more profoundly complex and meaningful than what a one-sided, moralistically dogmatic, religious life can offer.

The affective demands which express our deepest, unconscious instincts, or needs and desires, as distasteful to our civilized or idealized sensibilities as they might on occasion be, define the heights and depths of our very humanity and the vast possibilities of human experience and human life and living. A *life-affirming* moral belief system is, following Freud, simply, commonsensically, naturalistically, and necessarily based on the conscious and ethical satisfaction of human needs. Such a moral belief system, if such it is considering the fact that all humans are biologically evolved to act in their best long-

---

monplace among people, making concepts of morality, happiness and fulfillment non objective realities, and making the blanket assurance of happiness and fulfillment to all believers of any given belief system a promise which can only be fulfilled by limiting the meaning of these states of mind and then conditioning believers to believe they are — or certainly shall be (or should be) — happy and fulfilled in this limited sense if they comply with, and fulfill, the necessary conditions.

Such conditioning is, of course, circularly self-fulfilling. By controlling (as is the case in the Mormon faith) the meaning of moral goodness, happiness, and fulfillment by telling believers what *goodness*, *happiness*, and *fulfillment* mean and entail, and what they need to do to be good, happy, or fulfilled, the psychological states of moral self-satisfaction, happiness, and fulfillment are effectually defined and limited to the psychological effects of living one's life in the prescribed and required way. This can effectually limit the meaning of personal goodness, happiness, and fulfillment to the subjective, religiously indoctrinated interpretation of the natural affects of *ego-fusion* and *ego-inflation* — *i.e.* 'ego-fusion' through the suggestively induced regressive transference of the internalized parent imago to the Parent-God, and 'ego-inflation' through the ego-syntonic belief (held by the believer as true in virtue of a self-induced and self-validating affect, or putative 'confirmation by the Spirit') that he or she is — in virtue of being compliant or obedient to moralistic demands of the faith — righteous, faithful, and 'worthy in the eyes of God' and his anointed leaders, and therefore is 'accepted, approved, entitled, and empowered by God' to ask for and receive desired or needed blessings on earth and in heaven.

Clearly, by limiting the meaning of moral goodness, happiness, and fulfillment to such beliefs and related affects, *i.e.* by making their realization contingent or dependent on certain ego-syntonic attitudinal, behavioral, and performatory conditions, a self-fulfilling and self-deceiving dynamic is created and put into play wherein the socially conditioned desire or wish to find genuine or true happiness and fulfillment in life, coupled with the human needs for security, love, acceptance, and esteem, are dynamically coupled through authoritative religious conditioning (or mind control) with the necessary connection between righteousness and happiness (Alma 40:12), and unrighteousness (or wickedness) and unhappiness (Alma 41:10).

This conditioning mind-control strategy essentially translates to the belief that if one is good (or repents, falls in line, and follows the program) one will be truly happy and find fulfillment in life; whereas if one is *not* good, or is bad (*i.e.* is sinful or wicked and unrepentant) one will not be truly happy or fulfilled, or worse, will be unhappy or miserable in this life and throughout eternity. This belief — which is not merely reflective of a natural, causal connection, but of an *ersatz* causal connection itself *caused by* a contrived means of control — and the resulting belief that one is truly happy and fulfilled in virtue of one's faith (something which all faithful Mormons are also conditioned to attest to) is not only self-referential, but is self-sealing as well through wish-fulfilling and/or anxiety induced self-deception.

Who, after all, among the faithful or unnoteworthy afflicted or suffering Latter-day Saints wants to publicly admit that they are not free, good, happy, and fulfilled by 'keeping the commandments,' if doing so necessarily admits of somehow and for some reason not being right with their god? I would argue, given our human propensity for delusion and self-deceit, that saying and believing one is truly morally good, happy and fulfilled does not necessarily make it so, either by the limited and limiting standards of one's religious faith, or by one's allegedly honest answer to the Socratic question of how one should live — a question incidentally, and perhaps, more appropriately answered in our time by Nietzsche and Freud than Jesus and Joseph Smith. This raises a question, moreover, whose answer, at a personal level, can only be revealed, as Joseph Campbell rightly suggests, not from above, bur rather "from way down below" — if at all.

term interests, tends, ironically perhaps, to be somewhat iconoclastic and liberal rather than traditional and conservative in nature. It gives ear to and honors *all* human demands and possibilities for individuation, development, and personal well-being. It requires *only* the more conscious and mature, or responsible, exercise of 'free-thinking'[180] and 'moral imagination' (Beebe 1995) in the creative, considerate, and rational pursuit of personal happiness through need gratification.[181]

In summary, *any* religious tradition or belief system which holds that there is a supernatural, Parent-God who directly or through others reveals his will to man and tests the required faith of believers, expecting and rewarding faithfulness and obedience and disapproving of and punishing disobedience, is at least potentially, if not actually, *dangerous* to believers and society. Furthermore, *any* religious tradition or belief system is harmful which: (1) holds that believers are chosen and favored by god, and that nonbelievers or less valiant believers or disbelievers are not, or are cursed; and/or (2) holds that an all-seeing and all-knowing god judges (or will finally judge) the thoughts, actions and behavior of human beings, judging believers as worthy or unworthy of acceptance, approval and salvation on the basis of faithfulness and righteousness; and/or (3) holds that god rewards with recognition, acceptance, privilege, and 'eternal life' or 'salvation' obedience and faithfulness to commandments, counsel and other implicit (cultural) or explicit (doctrinal) attitudinal and behavioral standards, and excludes, forbids, discourages, and punishes — through the consequential infliction of shame, guilt, and anxiety, and the withholding or revocation of privilege or membership — conscientious dissent, disobedience, and the responsible and ethical pursuit of free-thinking, free-expression, and alternative life preferences or choices, is, on the basis of my analysis and personal experience, actually detrimental to the psychological well-being of believers.

In my informed and considered judgment, the Mormon religion is on balance and at bottom not only an *irrational* faith (because it is unintelligible, incoherent, and either factually meaningless or false), but a *toxic* faith as well. This is so, I suspect, for all believers

---

180 'Free thinking' as used here implies the conscious exercise of critical thinking which is free from moralistic constraint and tradition. It does *not* imply one is free to think how one pleases or believe what one wants to believe without epistemic responsibility.

181 This perspective and argument should not be construed as an advocacy for a universal and objective set of criteria for happiness or well-being. Nor should it be construed as an advocacy for the unbridled experience of instinctual impulses (or human needs) without moral, ethical, or legal restraint to preserve and protect the property and inalienable rights of others. On the contrary, what is argued for here is the immorality of essentially taking from man, through the imposition of guilt, shame, and the threat of excommunication (rejection) and damnation (eternal punishment) the *options* for necessary or desired experience — whatever they might be — which require him to more consciously, ethically, and responsibly respond to his natural instincts for living and dying in his own fashion and on his own terms (see the *Epilogue*).

Such control is justified by the false belief that without a god and religious restraint everything would be permitted and nothing would be forbidden — that morality (and, by association, moral goodness) as such has its objective existence and imperative force in virtue of some god's existence. In other words, without a god, morality — and moral sensibility and goodness — would not exist in man. This belief — and all theological and philosophical arguments in support of it — is not only false and incoherent as a truth claim, but has been roundly and, from my perspective, decisively discredited and refuted by Dennett 1995; Flanagan 2002; Martin 2002; Shermer 2004; Eller 2004; Nielsen 1990 and 1991; Joyce 2001; Hauser 2006; Carrier 2005; and Mackie 1977 to name a critical few.

of all theistic faiths. But in my experience it is especially so for those Mormon believers who take their faith seriously and literally. For those, in other words, who strive to live the religion primarily and strictly (or with 'exactness and honor') according to its theological and scriptural requirements, and not merely according to the less exacting and demanding cultural norms of the local church community (Ward or Stake) of which they are a part. This conclusion, as I see it, is unavoidable to those Mormon believers who look critically at their faith, with the presumption of skepticism as an outsider. It is unavoidable *even if* their faith is considered on balance with the acknowledged salutary personal and social benefits derived from it — benefits incidentally which are reportedly enjoyed by many believers of other faiths, as well as by Agnostics and Atheists.

"What if you're wrong?"

Still, it might be asked of me again, as addressed in the *Introduction*, "What if you're wrong?" Of course, being wrong is always possible and often likely, given the provisional nature of knowledge and the fact of human fallibilism.

Certainly, for example, my personal assessment of Mormonism as a toxic faith, while I think it is reasonably based on personal experience, published studies, and reports of authoritarian abuse, sexual abuse, and psychopathology within the Mormon Church, correctly applied psychological and psychoanalytical principles, and extensive research on the abusive effects of authoritarianism in the family and in religious and secular institutions, is nonetheless subject to criticism based on differing points of view, different studies or research, and different theoretical orientations in the behavioral sciences. Even so, I think the research on authoritarianism (and authoritarian abuse in particular) and mind-control (Altemeyer 1996; Swartz 2000; Wolfe 1999; Milgram 2009; and Taylor 2004) supports my assessment of the Mormon faith, as do the published reports of authoritarian and sexual abuse in the Mormon Church (Anderson and Allred 1995, 1997), and published reports in the public domain in relation to the incidence of psychopathology (depression, anxiety, addiction, extremism, *etc.*) within the Mormon faith. I also find compelling the thinking of those certainly more qualified than I in making such assessments, including most notably the classic works of Feuerbach, Nietzsche, and Freud, and the more contemporary works of Fromm, Mogenson, Piven, Cohen, Ellis, Jones, and Watters to name a critical few. Finally, my own experiences, as well as the like experiences of many other former members of the Mormon faith, also tend to confirm my assessment.

When, however, this question ('What if you're wrong?') is asked as an indirect appeal to my admission of the possibility of the Mormon god's actual existence, it cannot, as I think about it, be coherently answered. This is so because it is an incoherent question. Such a question would be like asking "What if you were to find out that a square is really round?" or, more relevant to the question asked: "What if you discover in the next life that an infinite and eternal spirit and intelligence of the highest order who is all-loving, all-good, all-knowing and all-powerful really does exist?" How could I or anyone ever make sense out of such questions or come to know, in either case, of the existence of something which is unintelligible?

Even if there is a 'next life' (which is itself an incoherent and factually unintelligible idea in relation to what we know about the world and the universe and how they work) and I did find myself standing in the presence of an extra-terrestrial superior being in the shape of a man (as, for example, the fictional humanoid and Messianic character Klaatu in the science fiction film *The Day the Earth Stood Still*), how could I possibly know (except by a very unreliable and certainly fallible and inconclusive subjective interpretation of some induced, pre-conditioned affect) that such a being was 'God" or 'Christ' as fully conceptualized in the Mormon faith except by mere assertion? Surely such a hypothetical superior being could be perfectly versed in scripture and reproduce the legendary 'wounds of Christ' on its body.

Such a hypothetical next-life scenario assumes too much without offering any specifiable human criteria or acceptable and intelligible rationale or evidence to justify convincing, rational acceptance. Besides assuming the existence of an afterlife for the dead — an assumption which presupposes at minimum the actual existence of 'spirits,' 'resurrection,' and 'immortal' (non-biological) physical bodies — such a scenario assumes the actual existence of both a 'sixth ('spiritual') sense' and an alternate reality. It assumes a reality where, in virtue of our putative spiritual capacity to know such truth (a capacity believed to be inherent in all 'spirit beings') and our access to a transcendent, universal language ('God's language,' or as Mormons believe, the 'Adamic language'), we can *somehow* know as absolute truth all that is ineffable or otherwise not knowable — or is considered impossible in this life.

Aside from being very imaginative, such a scenario, along with its various assumptions, is nothing more than mere science fiction. There are, of course, no valid reasons to accept such a hypothetical scenario and *ad hoc*, fictional assumptions as *actual* or justified truth — or even *possible* or *justifiable* truth. There are no *a priori* or non-question-begging arguments to suggest otherwise. As we learned in Chapter 6, even faith cannot help us here.

"What, if anything, would convince you that there is a God, or to return to God?"

Related to the above question of 'what if you're wrong,' is the question many Agnostics and Atheists are asked, either directly or indirectly: "What, if anything, would convince you that there is a God, or to return to God?" This question has I think less to do with any genuine interest in my answer than it does in whether or not I have an open mind to the possibility that a god exists, that Jesus is my personal savior, and that the Church is true.

In either case, my initial and direct answer to this question is simply that I cannot answer such a question without first knowing what *specifically* and *exactly* I would be convinced of, or would return to. Beyond this concise yet accurate reply, my more elaborative answer is as follows: I cannot conceive of ever returning to *any* god because I do not, cannot, and will not believe in the literal existence of an illusion which is based on an incoherent concept — comforting as such an infantilizing illusion might seem to be in the face of death and loss. In my view, all such belief in a god is baseless illusion, and this pertains to the concept of the Mormon god in particular, as well as to all the various personal and institutional gods of Christianity, Judaism, and Islam. To ask anyone to believe in any of these or other like gods would be to ask them to accept as a possibility, and at very least, the existence of a round square. Such an act of acceptance simply cannot be done without self-deception and a significant loss of personal integrity.

I do not and cannot believe in the literal existence of gods for the same fundamental reasons I do not and cannot believe that Santa Claus, the Easter Bunny, the Tooth Fairy, Gremlins, Unicorns, Zeus, and spirits and intelligences literally, or actually, exist. With the first six entities, there simply is not one shred of evidence to suggest their existence, and it is absurd and incoherent to believe they do in fact exist — magically or otherwise. The belief that there is a purely anthropomorphic god like Zeus, as some Mormons and other theistic believers essentially do, is pure superstition and is therefore patently false. As mature, educated (or even uneducated) adults, we all know this, of course, if we are in possession of our faculties. With spirits and intelligences, I *cannot* believe because their believed or stated existence — is unintelligible, incoherent, and factually meaningless. It simply makes no sense and can be nothing other than a factual non-reality.

More specifically, my answer to the question above has three parts. *First*, for me to accept that there might *possibly* be a god, the concept of 'God' (and therefore the 'Son of God' as well as the 'Christ') would need to be intelligible, coherent, and *factually* meaningful, making the acceptance of the possible existence of a literal god (and Christ) at least rational on the basis of the *justifiability* of their existence. In other words, all the questions asked throughout Chapters 3 and 6 in this book would need to be satisfactorily or reasonably answered without presupposition. *Second*, for me to accept that there *probably* is a god and a Son of God (Christ), I would require that the truth claims of their physical and metaphysical existence be *justified* through the achievement of wide-reflective equilibrium, as referred to in earlier chapters of this book and in depth by Nielsen (1996). *Third*, as an integral part of the requirement for justification, the irresolvable problems cited and treated in Chapter 7 would need to be intelligibly and reasonably resolved in my mind — at least to a sufficient degree to warrant rational acceptance.

In this last regard, I would need to be satisfied with answers to the following questions:

(1) Why, if there is a god, and if belief in the existence of such a god is essential to salvation, is there such widespread non-belief and confusion, disagreements, uncertainty, and diversity of doctrine and belief among so many faiths and believers regarding the existence, fundamental nature, and putatively revealed mind, will, ways, requirements, and alleged purposes of 'God'?

(2) Why — within the Mormon faith and within and among other theistic faiths as well — the existence of conflicting and amended revelation, differing authoritative or personal interpretations of revelation, and the existence of false revelation once authoritatively held to be true?

(3) Why the necessity for, and unreliability of, prayer? More specifically, and beyond the incoherence of the concept of prayer given the incoherence of the concept of 'God,' why, given the putative existence of an all-knowing, all-powerful, and all-loving god do people need to pray? Why the at least apparent and unexplained randomness and unreliability of alleged answers to prayer — particularly among sincere and faithful believers?

(4) Given the putative foreknowledge, power, goodness, and love of 'God' for mankind (his alleged children), and the singular importance (necessity) of mortal life and experience, why the existence of so much senseless, gratuitous, and preventable or avoidable suffering, premature death, and destruction? Specifically, why the absence of divine intervention by notably and consistently stopping or even significantly reducing or eliminating and/or at least explaining, through personal revelation, this god's specific reasons for allowing

such human and natural evil? Why should sufferers need to lose their faith or will to live, or suffer in anguish with the question of *why* such suffering was not prevented or abated?

(5) Why, given the primary importance and requirement of 'knowing God and Jesus Christ' for salvation, does 'God' remain hidden in the face of global diversity and conflict of belief between and among sincere theistic believers of the same or different faiths, the extent of non-belief and confusion regarding his and Christ's existence, and the insufficiency and loss of faith for so many in the face of doubt, temptation, and suffering? Specifically and to the point in this regard, why is 'faith in God and Christ,' and faith-testing, necessary and required for salvation? More specifically, why wouldn't such a god or Savior, if his existence and divinity as conceptualized by at least one of the theistic religions or sacred texts on earth was at least in principle empirically confirmable or disconfirmable (which it is not), actually descend from the heavens in plain sight? Why wouldn't he repeat the alleged appearance of the resurrected Christ to all the "people of Nephi" as reported in the *Book of Mormon* (3 Nephi 11)? Why wouldn't he unquestionably and irrefutably, beyond all doubt, establish up front – through demonstration, coherent explanation, and facilitated understanding – god's and his existence and divinity, god's gospel, and god's mind and will and word once and for all to all mankind?

All of the above questions, like those presented earlier in this concluding chapter, add, from my perspective, decisive, cumulative force to the two-part conclusion reached in this analysis of the Mormon faith, *i.e.* that (1) the concepts of 'God' in the Mormon and all other theistic faiths are utterly unintelligible, incoherent, and without factual significance. Therefore, belief in such Gods is not and cannot possibly be justified or warranted through the achievement of wide reflective equilibrium or rational demonstration; and (2) that it is irrational for well-educated, otherwise rational and intelligent people in the West to hold such irrational beliefs, and it is epistemically and ethically irresponsible for those who hold them to share and represent them to others as actual and absolute truth. These questions, of course cannot be answered without begging the question and incoherently and illegitimately retreating to faith and subjectively interpreted religious (or so-called spiritual) experience as a way of knowing what cannot be known or justified, by cold, sober reason through rational demonstration or the achievement of wide reflective equilibrium.

Because the only answers to such questions are non-answers, the questions effactually answer themselves as, essentially, a conclusive, cumulative argument for the non-existence of gods. In virtue of the arguments implicit in such questions, the negative is proven, for me, beyond a reasonable doubt. To establish the incoherence of a putative existent as conceptualized is to essentially prove its non-existence as conceptualized. Such is arguably the case with the concept of 'God,' regardless of faith.

I would argue that for any sane, reasonable, intelligent, and well-educated person in any developed democratic nation in the West to even accept the *possibility* of *any* god's existence, the concept of such a god would need to be deemed, through rigorous conceptual analysis, at least intelligible, coherent, and factually significant or cognitively meaningful. Beyond that, each of the above questions would require, for me, a specific, sensible, non-question-begging, unambiguous, and non-arbitrary answer that makes rational sense and fits or coheres with our best justified beliefs (or knowledge) of the world and the universe and how they work. For me, there can be no question-begging appeal or retreat to revelation, scripture, or faith in answering these questions. Nor can there be an appeal to subjectively interpreted, so-called spiritual experience. Moreover, there can be no appeal to divine mystery or *ad hoc* supernatural speculation to fill in our current gaps in knowledge in an attempt to force-fit the concept of 'God' into a coherent, natural scheme of things or to make it part of the truth as we know it — provisional or contingent as such truth might be. Finally, I would need to be satisfied that such a god or faith was not demanding, judgmental, or punitive, and that belief in such a god was not, at its core, moralistic and therefore inherently detrimental to the physical and psychological well-being of believers and society.

These constraint, I would argue, are both fair and reasonable in the legitimate pursuit of knowledge of truth. They are both fair and reasonable given the way theists (and Mormons in particular) want their beliefs and their particular faith to be regarded — *i.e.*, as literal or actual truth and a way of living which is wholly beneficial to all. It would seem that the honest answer to the question of what would convince me that there is a god (or to return to a god) could be reduced to a one-word answer: "Nothing."

There is *nothing* that could persuade or convince me — as long as I am rational and of sound mind (*i.e.*, neither certifiably insane, cognitively demented nor desperate, deluded, and self-deceived) — to believe or accept as true or even possibly true the actual existence of *any* god as conceptualized by *any* faith, or theistic religion. This answer should not be considered merely a stubborn refusal to believe (or believe again), or an answer motivated out of fear, anxiety, or some misplaced devotion or loyalty to a particular belief system, principle, or worldview. Nothing would convince me to believe because nothing *could* possibly convince *anyone* to believe — in the sense 'belief' is used synonymously by theistic believers as 'knowledge' — who approached *any* theistic faith as a rational, skeptical outsider of sound mind without need, wish, or desire for regressive, superstitious solutions to existential fear and anxiety. This is not because I am immovable in my Atheism, but because, like Eller, and in the formal, technical sense of the term, I don't do 'belief,'[182] and because, moreover, the concepts of 'God,' 'Christ,' the 'Plan of Salvation,' 'revelation' and 'faith in God and Christ' as taught and believed as literal, actual truths in the Mormon faith and standard theism simply do not make any sense. They are in general, as a whole or in particular as specific beliefs, either false or incoherent and factually meaningless. They are moreover irreconcilable (without invalid presupposition) with the irresolvable contradictions of gratuitous suffering and premature death caused by natural and human evil, the requirement of faith and faith-testing, the requirement for and unreliability of prayer, and the existence of widespread and eternally consequential non-belief and apostasy to Atheism or other faiths. In short, I could not possibly accept as either *eternal truth* or *actual* (justified) *truth any* theistic claim regarding the existence of *any* god because, in my view, *all* theistic concepts of 'God,' 'revelation,' and 'faith' in *all* developed forms of theism — including Mormonism — are simply, utterly, and unequivocally unbelievable without self-deception. I would literally need to be utterly out

---

182 As referenced in a previous note, see Eller 2004, 131–151 for an interesting and provocative treatment of the problem of 'believing *vs.* knowing,' and Eller 2007, 395–426 for his provocative proposal that Atheism be regarded as a sub-category of nonbelief and part of a larger state of mind which he refers to as 'discredism,' a position requiring "the courageous and unrelenting application of reason to all questions" (402) and the rejection of *all beliefs as such*, both religious and non-religious in nature.

of my mind due to illness, grief or the terror of death and loss to turn to *any* god (either directly or indirectly through the faith of others on my behalf), and even then such a turn, if it did regrettably occur, would be utterly irrational (as are *all* such 'turns' to gods), as would *any* profession of belief. Should such an irrational turn to, or profession of, religious belief unfortunately occur in my case (and I sincerely hope it does not), make nothing of it, and remember, only our "basic biological condition," human existential anxiety, and the religiously exploited space created by mere "possibility" and human fallibility enable such irrationality to exist or persist. There is no truth in it – about me, or about the irrational beliefs I might profess in such a desperate, deranged or regressive state of mind.

Turning the tables: *"What if you, the believer, are wrong and there are no gods?"*

All said, and with my answer standing as specified above, it only seems fair to now turn the tables on the theist and ask in return: What if you are wrong and there is no 'God'?[183] and what, if anything, would convince you that there is no God? If your answers are that you are *not* wrong and that nothing could convince you that there is no 'God' or Jesus Christ, how would you justify such answers without simply and stubbornly begging the question at issue? How could you avoid invoking the mere *possibility* of their existence, or appealing to fallible authority, subjective testimony, and the purely naturalistic (psychological) phenomena referred to as *revelation* and *faith*? If you could not therefore justify your answers (because such attempts at justification would necessarily be invalid, evasive, and incoherent), how then could you explain your ability to believe such things? How could you explain why your belief and faith are even *necessary* if your god is who you say he is?

These questions on both sides of the argument may well invoke the argument or plea for mutual tolerance and respect. Why not just leave well enough alone; let believers believe without criticism, ridicule, or derision, and let disbelievers and nonbelievers disbelieve or not believe without judgment? After all, or so the argument goes, religious belief is a private matter and all are entitled to their beliefs, since all — or so the argument continues — have their 'free agency.'

Such an argument, if it is indeed made, would be disingenuous at least and hypocritical

---

183 Daniel Dennett (2006) elaborates: "There are some people — millions, apparently — who proudly declare that they do not have to foresee the consequences [of their allegiance to the allegedly toxic faith they embrace]: they know in their hearts [on the basis of their alleged spiritual feelings] that this is the right path, whatever the details [or risks]. ... If you are one of these, here is what I hope will be a sobering reflection: have you *considered* that you are perhaps being irresponsible? You would willingly risk not only the lives and future well-being of your loved ones, but also the lives and future well-being of all the rest of us, without hesitation, without due diligence, guided by one revelation or another, a conviction that you have no good way of checking for soundness. ... Do you ever ask yourself: *What if I'm wrong?* Of course there is a large crowd of others around you who share your conviction, and this distributes — and, alas, dilutes — the responsibility, so, if you ever get the chance to breathe a word of regret, you will have a handy excuse: you got swept up by a crowd of enthusiasts. But surely you have noticed a troubling fact. History gives us many examples of large crowds of deluded people egging one another on down the primrose path of perdition. How can you be so sure you're not part of such a group? I for one am not in awe of your faith. I am appalled by your arrogance, by your unreasonable certainty that you have all the answers" (50–51). I certainly share in Dennett's observations, questions, concerns, and self-disclosure, all of which pertain to Mormon believers as well.

and dishonest at most — particularly if made by those in the Mormon faith.[184] First of all, any faith that seeks to condition its innocent and intellectually defenseless children and convert nonbelievers or believers of other faiths to itself certainly does not regard religious belief a 'private matter.' Those who believe in a non-Christian god are regarded by many mainline evangelical and fundamentalist Christians as following a false deity. Such misguided, deceived, or self-deceived and delusional followers or believers of 'false gods' are not and cannot be saved, according to 'true Christians,' until and unless they repent of their false belief and believe in the '*only true* God of the Bible.' The same holds for believers in other faiths. Non-Mormon Christians, Jews, and Muslims, for example, cannot be saved until and unless they are converted to the Mormon god and baptized in the Mormon faith by those in the Mormon Church who have the authority to do so.

Moreover, it simply is not 'ok' to theistic believers of *any* faith for nonbelievers and disbelievers to eschew or be critical of religious belief. Every effort is made to convert them to the faith so they might be saved and enjoy the fruits of joy in this life and eternal life in the next. For such religions, faith is certainly *not* a private matter. Many religious believers openly share their beliefs with nonbelievers and disbelievers. They *publicly* witness or testify of their putative knowledge of 'The Truth' of their beliefs. They practice their rituals of prayer, sacrament, and baptism publicly. They engage in their God-talk *publicly*. And they teach and preach their various gospels *publicly* to all who will hear or, in some cases, are merely within earshot. Those who do not so share their beliefs are nonetheless expected and encouraged to do so. Spreading the 'Good News' — overtly or subtly — is *not* optional. Likewise, tolerance of alternate lifestyles, or even religious practices, is very limited at best and nonexistent at worst, where such lifestyles and practices are considered sinful or offensive to the god or the religious sensibilities of the faithful.

As Sam Harris (2004) correctly points out in this regard, "While all faiths have been touched, here and there, by the spirit of ecumenicalism, the central tenet of every religious tradition is that all others are mere repositories of error or, at best, dangerously incomplete. Intolerance is thus intrinsic to every [faith]. Once a person believes — really believes — that certain ideas can lead to eternal happiness, or to its antithesis, he cannot tolerate the *possibility* that the people he loves might be led astray by the blandishments of unbelievers.[185] Certainty about the next life is simply incompatible with tolerance in this one" (13).

"Observations of this sort," Harris continues, relating to his earlier explanation for why faith persists, "pose an immediate problem for [those disbelievers who are critical of religion]… because criticizing a person's faith is currently taboo in every corner of our culture…Criticizing a person's ideas about God and the afterlife is thought to be impolitic in a way that criticizing his ideas about physics or history is not" (13).

---

184 See Note 100.

185 On a personal note, it seems worthwhile to share the reaction of my wife's brother to her disclosure that I was once a Mormon. Her brother, a devout Christian minister, reportedly said that he would rather his sister not believe in any god than believe in the Mormon god. To this Christian believer, Atheism was preferred over Mormonism. The reverse is also true of many in the Mormon faith, and other faiths as well. Then there is the classic Mormon story, repeated often with pride, of the Mormon father telling his son departing on a Mormon mission that he would rather his son come home in a coffin than in disgrace because of inchastity. So much for religious tolerance!

But "[i]t is time," Harris argues, echoing independently my comments above, "we recognized that belief is not a private matter; it has never been merely private. ... It is time we admitted, from kings and presidents on down, that there is no evidence [or even possibility of evidence] that any of our books was authored [directly or indirectly] by the Creator of the Universe." Or, for that matter, that 'God' — whatever such a term, in concept, might mean, if anything — has ever spoken or revealed himself to man. With such recognition and admission, I would certainly agree with Harris that religious moderates — those who are not extremists and "do not want to kill anyone in the name of God," but "want us to keep using the word 'God' as though we knew what we were talking about... [and] do not want anything too critical said about people who really believe in the God of their fathers, because tolerance, perhaps above all else, is sacred" — are the source of "the greatest problem confronting civilization," beyond even religious extremism itself. The problem consisting of "the larger set of cultural and intellectual accommodations we have made to faith itself." Such "[r]eligious moderates are," therefore, "in large part, responsible for the religious [extremism and resulting] conflict in our world, because their beliefs provide the context in which scriptural literalism, [putative revelation], and religious violence [and abuse] can never be *adequately* opposed" (44–5, emphasis mine).

In the larger social context of the challenges to the Mormon faith made in this book, I would certainly agree with Harris that "[i]t is imperative that we begin speaking plainly about the absurdity of most of our religious beliefs" (48). Foremost, I would add, this includes those irrational beliefs about the existence of *any* god, the existence of an after-life of heaven (salvation) and hell (damnation), and the need for faith. If such 'speaking plainly' seems insensitive, intolerant, offensive, or impolitic, so be it. It is far better, as I see it, to hurt feelings and drive God-talk underground than allow the perpetuation of such rampant memetic infection to go unchecked. This is particularly so since, as has been argued, the spreading of the 'god virus' is, very likely at least, significantly harmful and dangerous to believers and society. Moreover, in my view, such intolerance of, and disrespect and disdain for, religious belief is amply justified, if not mandated, by the potential and actual abuses from and to religious believers — moderates and extremists alike.

Finally, it might be said to me, as it is, admittedly, frequently said to Nielsen and other skeptics that "I am missing the most important reason for believing in God," *i.e.*, the removal of the sting of death. To this point Nielsen responds appropriately for himself, as perhaps for all like "secularists all the way down" (2001). Accordingly, it seems fitting to allow him here one final word:

> In my atheist world, it is certain that we will die and (if we don't get cremated first) rot. I must face the fact — the unsettling fact — that this will happen to me and to those I love, as it will inescapably to everyone, if my bleak atheist conception of the world is really so...
> If my physical and mental powers are intact, I would rather not die. And I certainly do not want to lose the people I love. But I must die, and they must die, and we can all face this and, realizing that is all we have (and it is not a little), live that life to the full. Love is not worthless because the death of both lovers bring it to an end. Fastening on what we know we have (among them thick relations between people) and what, if we are not too neurotic, we, by ourselves or with others, can make something of, without distracting ourselves with things (God and immortality), which at best are just barely intelligible, we can in a Godless world have both a full moral life and really demanding and reciprocally fulfilling human relations...

> A central thing is…to cultivate the care of the self, and to… find — though without indifference to others — your happiness and human flourishing where you can. This is fully available to you even if you are, as I am, utterly without religious faith. (1993, 280)

As for me, Nielsen's words are particularly poignant. While I am also "utterly without religious faith," I can nonetheless understand how easy it is to hope beyond reason for a meaningful and joyous afterlife with those we love and cherish. Given the foregoing critical analysis of Mormon theology as part of the cumulative argument for Atheism as a whole, such hope, regressive and irrational, yet humanly understandable as it is, cannot translate for me — nor, I would argue, for anyone else — into anything worth seriously considering, much less accepting as even possibly true. This fact, in all of its stark reality, leaves us to ask perhaps one final, rhetorical question: What then could such hope reasonably translate to, if not simply wishful thinking?

Perhaps we are all best served by acknowledging that, in the minimalist sense of personal consciousness, we are all born Atheists. If we are fortunate, we will at some point in our lives (if we are believers in some theistic concept of 'God'), renounce our religious beliefs and live and die as Atheists in the end. Ultimately there can be no immortality beyond the rippling effect of our own lives on those still living who remember us or are somehow benefitted or harmed by our lives. Finally, perhaps there can be no meaning beyond the healing fictions we create in the context of a thoroughgoing naturalism without metaphysical or supernatural foundations — a therapeutic naturalism which acknowledges our utter humanness. As Becker suggests, this naturalism requires only that we "fashion something — an object or ourselves — and drop it into the confusion, make an offering of it, so to speak, to the life force" (1973, 285).

Such a consummate challenge, in my view, requires that to be fully human we all must first deliberately pass through the Nietzschian metamorphoses in *Thus Spake Zarathustra*, changing symbolically from the 'camel' to the 'lion,' and then, finally, from the 'lion' to the 'child.' These changes —symbolic for me of our individuation from a state of infantile or regressive dependency to adult independence and then to a state of more mature, creative interdependence with others and the natural world (a pleonasm) — may also be interpreted (more true perhaps to Nietzsche's intent) as a tale or allegory that more pointedly (given the context of Nietzsche's work) charts the course from theism to Atheism and beyond.

According to Eller, "The *camel* is the long-suffering Theist, and her religion is the dragon — the realm of authority, of command and commandment, of the past and tradition, of pre-existing values that one must not question. The *lion* is Atheism, the resisting spirit ['free-thinker'], the great 'No,' the denier and destroyer of old authorities and commandments. ... But notice," Eller continues, "with Nietzsche, that the job is not done with the lion's forceful nay-saying, its purely (if liberating) negative action. Something positive must follow — something innocent (of the destruction from which it was born), something forgetful and unmindful (of the traditions and 'truths' left behind and the negative escape-process itself), something creative (of new values and meanings), something 'yes-saying.' This [*child*] is Nietzsche's transcendent man and society" (2004, 325–6). But still, even for the creative 'child' — or individuated and developing individual — what is it, following Becker, that we might so fashion and offer "to the life force" (whatever that might be) which is not simply another ego-based immortality project? And how does Mormon (and

Christian) belief fare as a creative, life-enhancing illusion, or positive transference? It is these final questions that I address in the *Epilogue* which follows.

Epilogue:

Behind and Beyond the Veil of Projection and Illusion

"For life is at the start a chaos in which one is lost.
The individual suspects this, but he is frightened at finding himself
face to face with this terrible reality, and tries to cover it over with a
curtain of fantasy, where everything is clear. It does not worry him that
his 'ideas' are not true, he uses them as trenches for the defense of his
existence, as scarecrows to frighten away reality."
—*Jose Ortega Y Gasset*

"As a matter of fact, the world gets ahead by losing its illusions, and not
by fostering them. Nothing, perhaps, is more painful than disillusion, but
all the same, nothing is more necessary."
—*H.L. Mencken*

"There is something feeble and a little contemptible about a man who
cannot face the perils of life without the help of comfortable myths.
Almost inevitably some part of him is aware that they are myths and that
he believes them only because they are comforting. But he dares not face
this thought!"
—*Bertrand Russell*

According to Thomas Clark (2009), director for the Center for Naturalism, "Traditional theism (including Mormonism)…seems to specialize in defending the prospect that our fondest dreams – for life everlasting, reunion with loved ones, a purposeful cosmos headed by a benevolent intelligence – might [or will] be fulfilled. …Theistic religions," Clark continues, "make their living by offering existential reassurance, and much modern theology, however sophisticated and cognizant of current science and philosophy, is essentially an apologetics on behalf of a desired conclusion: that God exists. Likewise," Clark adds, "the standard justifications for belief in God – the authority of sacred texts and religious officiants, personal revelation and [affective] intuition, the various rationalistic armchair proofs – are all quite the opposite of science's open-ended, corrigible empiricism. They are modes not of investigation, but of confirmation. God is the vigorously defended projection of our deepest hopes onto the world" (62). Moreover, due to the "explanatory poverty" of the supernatural in general, and the Judeo-Christian god in particular (including the Mormon god), 'God' becomes, in Clark's words, merely an "ad hoc gap filler" and "a cognitive cul-de-sac…ruled out by the naturalist's desire for explanatory transparency, a transparency exemplified by science" (60), and, of course, by factually intelligible statements, or truth-claims with truth conditions that are at least in principle empirically verifiable or falsifiable sufficient to confirm or disconfirm their truth or falsity.

"The naturalist's off-the-cuff challenge to the traditional theist," Clark concludes, "might be that God is simply too good to be true [as superstitiously imagined], and too obscure [or unintelligible] to explain [as metaphysically conceived]" (63) – in all, incapable of being coherently and rationally regarded as reality. Still, the question to be asked is whether or not belief in 'God' – or other transcendent, creative illusions or myths – is, as eminent thinkers like Kierkegaard, Rank, Becker, and others conclude, necessary for humans to live well while dying — to endure the uncertainties and vicissitudes of life and thrive in spite of the consciousness and dread of our mortality, our own ultimate extinction.

In this Epilogue, I address the above question naturalistically, without supernatural or metaphysical foundations, and in the context of theism in general and Mormon theology in particular. I also offer two non-theistic alternatives, one from the psychoanalytic tradition, and the other from Buddhism. Finally, I conclude with a purely naturalistic perspective that eschews all theistic, transcendent, and commitment illusions and therapeutic solutions to our existential predicament, and opts instead – from a Freudian and Nietzschian perspective – for an "existential worldview" and related psychodynamic approach for creating personal meaning in life, and striving to live fully to die well.

Turning first to the afore-referenced question regarding the necessity for myth and illusion, it seems rather self-evident to me that the most we may reasonably say about — or ask from — 'creative illusions' up-front and pragmatically is that they work for us. They make no promises or demands and do not set us apart from others who do not share the same wish or hope, and they help us (non-compulsively) cope or they comfort us when we are confronted or buffeted by our existential anxieties. We expect them to help us make sense of, and cope with, the choices we make, as well as the difficult experiences of life and "the illness that we are" (Dourley 1984). Regarding their truthfulness, the most we can rationally say — if a particular illusion is not utterly unintelligible or incoherent — is that "Perhaps, possibly, hopefully such a wished-for eventuality is true but ultimately, and most likely, it is not. ... Either way, who knows?" Such illusions, we would acknowledge, are merely wish-based, loosely held beliefs as hopes and fantasies that do not qualify as justified or even justifiable truths.

None of this, of course, will do for committed Mormon believers or other theists. Here again it is important to note that it is neither acceptable nor permissible for believers of theistic religions to consider their beliefs about their gods as mere illusions and their saving theologies or doctrines as mere fictions without real promises for a better life after death. To sincere, true believers, their religious beliefs are *facts* specified by doctrinal or creedal statements of Absolute Truth. Nevertheless, theistic beliefs about gods (and Mormon beliefs in particular) are — believers' testimonies to the contrary notwithstanding — nothing but illusions, or *delusions* if sincerely held with unwavering conviction. From my perspective, and for reasons stated in previous chapters and others stated below, such beliefs are at least likely or potentially psychologically detrimental illusions which are neither life-enhancing nor life-affirming.

For an illusion to qualify as a "creative, or life-enhancing, illusion" it must, again, according to Becker (1973), satisfy at least three proposed standards. Such an illusion would strike a balance between the twin ontological motives of wanting to stand out from the crowd and wanting to fit in. It would acknowledge the limits of human nature, and it would not obscure or lie about the 'lived [naturalistic] truth of creation.' To these three basic, yet crucial, standards, I would add three more.

First, for an illusion to be 'creative' and 'life-enhancing,' it must *not* dogmatically and/ or moralistically dictate a particular way of living or foreclose on personally mandated ethical and/or vocational experience.

Second, it must not be harmful to human psychological well-being by in any way frustrating or blocking the natural imperative (instinct or drive) to individuate and integrate the personality.

Finally, it must foster both moral and intellectual integrity and epistemic responsibility. It must also eschew self-deception, and allow for the abdication of belief — or disillusionment — without guilt, shame, or the fear of condemnation and isolation.

These three additional standards serve the imagination without burdening it with the demands for rigorous scientific confirmation or insulting the intellect. They also provide at least the logical, if not actual, possibility of truth and rational belief without the need for defensive rationalization and self-deception, arguably necessary factors contributing to human mental health and well-being.

Perhaps in this context, as well as in the spirit of Nietzsche's *amor fati*, one way to say '*yes*' to life in spite of death — to, as Nietzsche pronounced, "Consummate your life, Become who you are" and consequently "Die at the right time," is to confront death as our *ultimate concern* and adopt, in Yalom's words, an "existential world view." Such a worldview, according to Yalom, "…embraces rationality, eschews supernatural beliefs, and posits that life in general, and our human life in particular, has arisen from random events; that though we crave to persist in our being, we are finite creatures; that we are thrown alone into existence without a predetermined [or foreordained] life structure and destiny; that each of us must decide how to live as fully, happily, ethically, and meaningfully as possible" (2008, 202) and, I would add, in response to our human needs.

We can adopt such a worldview by eschewing death-denying, life-negating salvational and immortality illusions and by cultivating instead, following Tillich (1980), the "courage to be" — the courage, in part, to confront the anxiety of condemnation, death, and meaninglessness. We need the courage moreover to accept with honesty the brutal fact that, like Tolstoy's protagonist Ivan Ilych in *The Death of Ivan Ilych*, we are "dying so badly because we have *lived* so badly," where living badly essentially amounts to succumbing to our preoccupation with avoiding the reality of death through the pursuit of immortality. Or rather, as Yalom puts it, "through [our] preoccupation with prestige, appearance, and money" (2008, 35) and, I would add, by living according to other's (including a fictional god's) standards, plans, and expectations. We need the courage as well (crucially so) to more consciously, albeit deterministically, choose to experience without praise or blame the pain and joy of life in its fulness *in spite of* the vicissitudes and cosmic meaninglessness of our mortal existence. We need courage to deal with the existential *Angst* that comes (*pace* Tillich) with the non-existence of *any* god, including, I might add, his own incoherent concept of the 'God above God' who is unintelligibly conceptualized as the 'Ground of all being.' (See Tillich, Hook and Nielsen in Hook 1961, pp. 3–11, 59–69, 270–281.)

Such a way of life-affirmation would of course, be in stark contradistinction to 'The Way' prescribed by Mormon and Christian theology. The intellectual and analytic practice of profound, ethically responsible instinctual living in a pragmatic, naturalistic context which is both antimetaphysical and without foundations can place us in a creative relationship with our condition, circumstances, needs, desires, experiences, environment, and others. It does so through our construction of subjectively meaningful narratives that provide us with a life-enhancing and life-*and*-death affirming perspective. It does so, moreover, *without* transference-based 'faith in God and Christ' or compulsive, life-negating commitment to some external or internal transcendent authority or 'salvational Plan' (Rieff 1987).[186] Such a fictional perspective — if it is truly life-*and*-death affirming — can in time open us to more life *and* to a genuine acceptance of death through both direct and sublimated instinctual gratification.

Profound living pragmatically confronts us all with the fundamental question that ought to concern us: a question which is both more relevant and productive than metaphysical questions such as 'What is Truth?' or 'Beauty?' or 'Goodness?' or even 'What is the Meaning of Life?'' The fundamental question I have in mind is the one originally asked by Socrates, and again, in a psychoanalytical context, by Jonathan Lear, which profoundly asks: 'How should one live?' (2005, 14) Such a question, in turn — if profoundly asked from a deterministic perspective — necessarily confronts us with the equally profound question: *'How should one die?'*

Such existential questions are typically answered by culture, and the communal theistic cultures of the West are all, in the words of Philip Rieff, governed by what "…we may call 'faith.' Faith," according to Rieff, "…is the compulsive dynamic of culture, channeling obedience to, trust in, and dependence upon authority" (1987, 12). Regarding this "compulsive dynamic" in relation to the profound questions of 'how one should live and die,' we find, again in the words of Rieff, that: "With more or less considered passion, men submit to the moral demand system [or moralistic core of their theistic belief system] — and, moreover, to its personifications, from which they cannot detach themselves except at the terrible cost of guilt that such figures of authority [*i.e.* parents, Parent-Gods, and parent-leaders] exact from those not yet so indifferent [or individuated] that they have [either] ceased troubling to deny them [or ceased being troubled by them]" (12).

For those who — notwithstanding the burden of *existential* guilt they willingly bear — have sufficiently individuated or detached themselves from the 'compulsive dynamic' of theistic culture and "faith," and have, to a greater or lesser degree, ceased being troubled by the authoritarian imposition of *religious* guilt concomitant with such separation, a different

---

186 Philip Rieff (1987) importantly distinguishes 'commitment therapies' from 'analytic therapies.' For Rieff, "…commitment therapies are authoritarian, whereas analytic therapies are anti-authoritarian. Moreover, commitment therapies tend to take on a sacramental symbolism; analytic therapies have an anti-sacramental bias" (76). Also, "all…therapies of commitment [following the likes of Jung, Adler, Reich, Rank and others] belong to the religious category of cure: that of souls. More modestly, Freud['s] [analytic therapy] sought to give men that power of insight which would increase their power to choose; but he had no intention of telling them what they ought to choose. He wanted merely to give men more options than their raw experience of life permitted. Where experience impoverished, Freud would enrich, and do so by interpreting the meaning of their impoverished experience, thus reversing its effect — or, at least, mitigating it. … [Freud, as an analytic therapist,] had no interest in creating a doctrine of the good life, nor one of the good society." Rather, "Freud's object" — and the object of analytic therapy — "was personal capacity, not general cure. Moreover, one will not lead to the other. Cure is a religious category. [Commitment therapists, again like Jung, Adler, Reich, and Rank] sought," according to Rieff, "each in [their] own way, a *cure*, while Freud, knowing there was no cure, in the classical sense of a generalizable conversion experience, sought an increase in human power without reference to any of the established ideals [of the required commitment]" (87).

concern emerges. For emancipated theistic believers, or those seeking to live without *faith* as "obedience to, trust in, and dependence on [external or internalized external] authority," this concern — presented as yet another question — becomes how these existential questions regarding how one should live and die might meaningfully be answered *by and for each individual* without retreating or otherwise relying on or resorting to 'faith in *any* God' or 'faith in *any* man' *as* 'God' and their corresponding *ersatz* heroic immortality projects or commitment ideologies of salvation and independent self-creation and self-sufficiency?

Perhaps one approach to answering this question — and a key to forming the creative myths, or illusions we allegedly need — is to reflect deeply on both questions as one. We can make them two separate but inseparable sides of the same metaphorical coin. In doing so we might instead come to ask "how should one live in relation to one's death?" or, alternatively, "how should one live to die well?" The word *should* in each of these questions connotes an unconsciously determined life-style and affectively justified ethical and vocational imperative rather than a moral imperative imposed by culture, faith, or external authority. Moreover, these integrated or synthesized questions effectually shift the emphasis of the philosophical enquiry to the more pragmatic pursuit of, and desire for, an accepted, anticipated, and meaningful death as the *end* of a life well lived, *not* the illusory perfectibility of life through faithful obedience to and dependence on authority toward a desirable and wished-for life after death.

At a collective level, such a shift in perspective, emphasis and approach to living would require a corresponding therapeutic shift from the commitment (or transformational) therapies of cure and salvation to the analytic (or informational and morally neutral) therapy of detached individualism. At a collective level, such a rational shift in emphasis and approach might eventually result in the marginalizing, or at least relativizing or soften-ing, of the unnatural, religious moralistic core of Western authoritarian culture. We might find the gradual emergence of a more naturalistically grounded, non-authoritarian culture that would be behaviorally characterized less, if at all, in 'terms of faith' as selfless trust, commitment, loyalty, and obedience to authority. It would be describable more, if not entirely, in terms of a *faithless* and *godless* striving for the moral achievement of personal well-being characterized by mutual self-interest and the more mature management of relational ambivalence, social risk, and ethical tensions in relation to instinctual conflict.

Relatedly, at an individual level such a rational shift in emphasis and approach — which would essentially embrace, in Rieff's term, an 'analytic attitude' (31)[187] — would necessarily shift the burden of moral responsibility from the *external* or, alternatively, *hierarchical* authority of the collective to the *internal* authority of the individuated and

---

187 The cultivation of this therapeutic attitude requires, as Rieff correctly points out, a "therapeutic re-education," which, in Rieff's words, "…teaches the patient-student how to live with the contradictions that combine to make him into a unique personality; this it does in contrast to the older [religious and moralistic] pedagogies, which tried to re-order the contradictions into a hierarchy of superior and inferior, [worthy and unworthy], good and evil, capabilities" (55). "The analytical attitude is," in other words, "an alternative to all religious ones" (36). "To maintain [it], in the everyday conduct of life, becomes the most subtle of all efforts of the ego; it is tantamount to limiting the power of the super-ego (internalized conscience of the family, culture and society) and, therewith, of culture. The analytical attitude expresses a trained capacity for entertaining tentative opinions about the inner dictates of conscience, reserving the right even to disobey the law insofar as it originates outside the individual, in the name of a gospel of freer impulse [which, although not alone to be trusted, is nevertheless to be respected]" (30–31).

integrated personality, personified *in part* by what Rieff refers to as the emerging character-type of 'Psychological man' (39).[188] It would therefore, and necessarily, result — as it did for Freud, according to Rieff — in the refusal "...even to ask the religious question [*i.e.*, "how are we to be consoled for the misery of living" and the sting of death?], or proclaim a characterological ideal" (29; 30–65).[189]

Returning to the above existential questions apropos to the subject of this *Epilogue*, this rational shift in emphasis, approach, and attitude might in turn lead, as it perhaps did either consciously or unconsciously for Freud, to the profound insight that the desire for

---

188 Rieff's idea of 'Psychological man' is derived from Freud's sober vision of man in the middle, a go-between, aware of the fact that he had little strength of his own, forever mediating between culture and instinct in an effort to gain some room for maneuver between the hostile powers" (31). Specifically, and quoting more extensively from Rieff, "Psychological man is (as an evolved "character-type" beyond the predecessor types of "political man," religious man," and "economic man"), of course, a myth — but not more of a myth than other model men around whom we organize our self-interpretations." He is, as a character-type, "the holder of the reins, to assume command of our emotional chaos. He is the sane self in a mad world, the [individuated and] integrated personality in the age of nuclear fission, the quiet answer to loud explosions." ... Such a "...modern man is not in the position of a wise man exhibiting a fool, or that of a healthy man examining the sick; we are all fools, all sick — and until we can control the shock of this recognition we shall not be able to assess the character of our age correctly. That a new myth of man is developing, at least among the educated classes, seems evident to me. It is a response to the divisiveness and destruction without and to the chaos within. But we are ourselves involved in the creation of this new myth of man and cannot be expected to see the type in clear perspective.

"Nevertheless," Rieff continues, "psychological man can already be approached with the confidence that he is alive and prospering among us, nurturing his sense of well-being, the healthy hypochondriac who rightly expects to survive all interpretation. Who," asks Rieff, "without Freud, would so well know how to live with no higher purpose than that of a durable sense of well-being? Freud has systematized our unbelief; his is the most inspiring anti-creed yet offered a post-religious culture. Throw away all the old keys to the great riddles of life; depth in psychology brings men's minds around from such simplicities to the complexity of everyday tournaments with existence, to an active resignation in matters as they are, to a modest hope, and to satisfiable desires. Balance is the delicate ethic Freud proposes, balance on the edge that separates futility and ultimate purposelessness from immediate effectiveness and purpose" (39–41; see also, and importantly, Rieff 1979, pp. 329–57).

Through the psychoanalytic therapeutic process and the achievement of freedom from "the tyranny of [the patient's delusions and] inner compulsions," narcissism breaks down, enabling the analysand to develop empathic compassion for others and moral imagination to more maturely and consciously employ the analytic attitude in the reasoned (and realistic) pursuit of self-interest. Clearly, in this more fully conceptualized character-type, 'Psychological man' as Rieff-ian 'Therapeutic,' is indeed freer and more balanced and independent, as well as 'self-serving,' 'sick' and 'foolish' in many ways. But if the therapeutic's analysis has been hard and honestly won, he is more intelligently so. He is also more insightful and honest about his condition, and naturally and morally serves humanity without intention, calling or commitment (faith) to gods or men. He serves without either the desire or need for salvation, as an atheistic, non-spiritual yet moral, individuated individual and integrated personality who knows his limitations.

189 As Rieff correctly points out, "Freud," unlike his successors such as Jung, Adler, Rank, and others, "never felt tempted to [save the suffering or offer consolation and cure for the misery of living]. His genius was analytic, not prophetic. At best, psychoanalytic therapy is devoted to the long and dubious task of rubbing a touch of that analytic genius into less powerful minds. Here is no large new cosset of an idea, within which Western men could comfort themselves for the inherent difficulties of living. Freud's was a severe and chill anti-doctrine, in which the awesome dichotomy with which culture imposes itself upon men — that between an ultimately meaningful and a meaningless life — must also be abandoned. This, then, was Freud's prescription to mankind as the patient, so that by the power of the analytic attitude a limit be set to the sway of culture over mankind" (30).

life-preservation is ultimately motivated unconsciously by the deep desire to die *only in our own fashion*. This insight, I suggest, might be what Freud came to in the formation of what Adam Phillips refers to as his 'Ur-creation' myth — the 'death instinct' (2000, 79). "The fact that we are going to die," Phillips writes, "says nothing [factual or truthful] about the future except that we are going to die. Once our death doesn't matter to anyone else but us — not to God, or Gods, or nature itself — it matters in a different way. Once there is nothing (or no one) overseeing it, it begins to look different. [Freud], as we shall see, [invented a] new [death] for us. [He had] to make our deaths matter in a secular language. And this makes the future, in its turn, a new kind of object of desire" (2000, 29). Phillips' provocative and rather unique and non-technical perspective on this controversial topic is presented here for consideration and reflective stimulation in order to offer at least one creative alternative to theism from the West among different possible myths or illusions which provide an utterly naturalistic and analytic (or individuating) perspective for living while dying. A different, yet complementary, creative perspective from the East will be presented afterward.

For Freud, according to Phillips, "Life is a tension which seeks to extinguish itself, to 'cancel itself out'... There is something unbearable about life — and perhaps by (Freud's) implication, consciousness — some 'tension' that only death can release us from... Every living creature, Freud speculates, is hungry, indeed ravenous for death... 'We have no longer to reckon,' Freud writes, 'with the organism's puzzling determination (so hard to fit into any context) to maintain its own existence in the face of every obstacle. What we are left with is the fact that *the organism wishes to die only in its own fashion*.' There is a death, as it were, that is integral to, of a piece with, one's life: a self-fashioned, self-created death. (76–77, emphasis mine)

"I think it is worth spelling out," Phillips continues, "just how drastic — and bizarre — Freud's assertion here is. Everything we might have described a life as being about — reproduction, happiness, justice, and of course survival — are all subsumed by this primary project of the organism dying only in its own fashion. We are satisfied, so to speak, only when the wish for satisfaction has disappeared (in death); and yet essential to this satisfaction is that we do it in our own way... We are, in other words, perfectionists to the end, the artists of our own deaths. Not, of course, conscious artists — the person I recognize myself to be is not plotting this — but inspired by oblivion. The struggle is to have the self-fashioned death... In Freud's mysterious Ur-creation myth, it is indeed as though life is resistant to itself; oblivion is the subject and object of desire. For Freud the original life story was a death story, a how-to-die story." (77–78)

"Freud's notion of the death instinct, controversial as it has always been — as (metaphysical) fiction of the most implausible kind, a way of starkly accounting for an apparently intransigent aggressiveness or regressiveness in so-called human nature — has seemed to many people to be Freud's most aberrant but significant fiction." Still, Phillips insists, it is crucial to keep in mind that "when Freud was talking about...what he called a death instinct, he was talking about people's natural (unconscious) furtive independence. Freud, Lionel Trilling wrote in his famous lecture, 'Freud and the Crisis of our Culture,'

> ...needed to believe that there was some point at which it was possible to stand beyond the reach of culture. Perhaps his formulation of the death instinct is to be interpreted as the

expression of this need. 'Death destroys a man,' says E.M. Forster, 'but the idea of death saves him.' Saves him from what? From the entire submission of himself — of his self to life in culture. (108–9)

"But what, it is also possible to ask, is submitting oneself to culture submitting oneself to, in Trilling's terms? Whatever else it might entail, it entails our submitting ourselves to other people's descriptions, [demands, expectations, values, beliefs, and judgments]; of which [societal and family biographies] might seem to be the crudest examples (every child [for example] begins his life being described by his parents). Nature in Trilling's interpretation is a kind of alternative to culture for Freud; as though there are two things in a sado-masochistic relationship, nature forever submitting to culture — bound and whipped and tantalized by it — but asserting its forlorn independence in something called a death instinct. The death instinct as that part of ourselves that eludes the multiple biographies we submit to — everybody's account of us, including our own — by living in culture." (109)[190]

---

190 Although, in Rieff's words, "Freud declared that the religious question, in its inherited form, as a self-abnegation achieved with moral artistry, was no longer worth asking" (1987, 48), it would not be correct to argue, as Rieff does in an earlier work, that at some level Freud figuratively "closed his eyes" (one or both) to the "repressive imperative" — or fundamental and "unalterable authority" which "splits evil and good" — by symbolically (through his theorizing) negating, or refusing to open both eyes to, the truth of a higher law, *i.e.* that which is "repressive with its ['sacred'] coda of commands," and by essentially ignoring such putative "truth" and its consequent sense of guilt (1979, 360–97). Rieff's so-called 'repressive imperative' is, most fundamentally, and at the deepest structure of the evolved human brain, nothing more, it seems to me, than the basic, biological instinct for survival triggered by culturally conditioned (and also unconscious) judgments of transgressions and experienced as death (rejection, abandonment, isolation)-avoiding restraint (anxiety) and a *sense* of existential guilt. Such is Rieff's religiously toned, moralistic authority of the 'sacred order'; the mere affect of the cultural conditioning of religious patriarchy.

Rieff was correct, it seems to me, in connecting his so-called 'repressive imperative' (along with the alleged truths of his 'coda of commands,' whatever they might be) to a 'sacred order' of 'moral authority' and 'faith.' I think he was also correct in stating elsewhere that "[n]othing in psychoanalytic therapy encourages immoral behavior," but rather "…discourages moral behavior on the old, self-defeating grounds — out of what is now called a *sense* of guilt rather than guilt" (1987, 57). But, as I see it, he was wrong in seemingly *sacralizing* such 'moral authority,' 'coda of commands,' and 'sense of guilt' as an eternal or immortal — and necessary — shaming mechanism in the service of a necessarily 'commanding culture' and the best in man. He was also wrong, as we learned earlier regarding religious beliefs, in his apparent meta-belief that such authority or law is objective, absolute, and eternal truth and therefore beyond the critical reach of reason. And he was wrong as well, I think, in his speculation that Freud compromised the success of his life's work as symbolist and therapist, condemning it ultimately to failure in terms of its desired impact on culture (396).

What is to me shameful and shameless is not, *pace* Rieff, "thinking ourselves, uncommanded" essentially by Kantian "categorical moral imperatives," but rather the religious exploitation of the evolutionary imperative for survival and the human anxiety of death and extinction we all suffer through the authoritarian administration of the moralistic core of theistic faith and the corresponding code of patriarchy which defines our culture. Moreover, the so-called *suicide* Rieff refers to in relation to those like Freud who, in virtue of self-analysis and reason, refuse to obey the 'repressive imperative' and dismiss the sense of existential guilt as irrational and unfounded by reason as necessarily right or moral action, might alternatively be understood and respected as the human will of the free — or illusionless — individual to individuate from the oppressive and repressive patriarchal culture (consisting of the paternal and maternal matrices of discipline, judgment, punishment, forgiveness and salvation) and 'die in his own fashion.'

Clearly, to 'close one's eyes' necessitates that they were once opened and that what one saw was perhaps irrationally bothersome and/or at least not worth fixating on (or being concerned about) beyond its obvious meaning. To close one's eyes in this case to such a psychological phenomenon is to dismiss it as ultimately insignificant. Freud, like all of us, was conscious of his own mortality and eventual death and extinction. And he,

"The anticipation of our own death tells us more about anticipation than it does about death. Indeed the whole notion of looking forward to something immediately becomes enigmatic in relation to death. The word itself," remarks Phillips, "is at once a stark symbol of the future as always opaque, always unknowable; a word without an obvious referent — when one [typically] thinks about death one is thinking about life after death, the word itself implying [for many] a next stage — it denoted for Freud an object of passionate desire; the lover who ultimately will not refuse us, and yet who takes everyone. (110)

"Freud's notion of the death instinct suggests, at its most minimal, that we can want (or need) something [very real and intelligible in concept that] we [nonetheless] know nothing about, and that we are [paradoxically] most drawn to what we think of ourselves as trying to avoid. That we are, essentially, idiosyncratic suicides, but not from despair, but because it is literally our nature to die. But death, in Freud's poetic fiction, is a paradoxical and therefore exemplary object of desire; it is the object of desire that finally releases us from desire. The end, in both senses, of our suffering" (110–11).

In his Epilogue, Phillips suggests, apropos to the theme of this book and this *Epilogue* in particular, that "For [Freud] the idea of death saves us from the idea that there is anything to be saved from. If we are not fallen creatures, but simply creatures [as Darwin and human experience have confirmed] we cannot be redeemed. If we are not deluded by the wish for immortality, transience doesn't diminish us. Indeed, the traditional theological conviction [apart from its incoherence] that we needed to be saved – the secular equivalent being the belief that we could and should perfect ourselves, that we are in need of radical improvement — assumed that we were insufficient for this world; that without a God who could keep us in mind — a God who, in however inscrutable a sense, knew what was going on — we were bereft and impoverished (and compared with an omniscient Deity, or magically potent deities, we were indeed lacking). If mortality was a flaw, or punishment, we were always verging on humiliation [and, if a test in relation to our perfection, we were always verging on failure]. Tyrannical fantasies of our own perfectibility still lurk in even our simplest ideals…so that any ideal can become another excuse for punishment [or failure]. Lives dominated by impossible ideals – complete honesty, absolute knowledge, perfect happiness, eternal love — are lives experienced as continuous failure" (115).

By disabusing ourselves of the "Tyrannical fantasies of our own perfectibility" — our life-negating (or *fatal*) ego-illusions of immortality and salvation — and resolutely surrendering ourselves, *not* compulsively or self-deceptively to some unintelligible god, but to the vicissitudes of life and those 'calls of our nature' which, as Joseph Campbell put so well, are deterministically and non-teleologically "running the show" from "way down below," we may indeed create something that is *truly* heroic and, as Becker suggests, worth "dropping into the confusion" as an "offering…to the life force." That *something* is our own individuation. It is a life courageously and creatively shaped by the separation

---

like all mature (and therefore moral) Atheists who utterly reject belief in gods and the moralistic, authoritarian core of theistic, religious belief and strive in good conscience, and by reason and moral imagination, to ethically create their own morality without the need for categorical imperatives or religious interdictions by external authorities, saw, and experienced the conditioned *sense* of existential guilt associated with his own symbolic (theoretical and reasoned) patricide of the 'God of his Fathers,' and needed to at once acknowledge and accept it as part of his humanity (with one or both eyes open) and dismiss it (with one or both eyes closed) for what it was and is, *i.e.*, merely a natural response to our consciousness and fear of death transformed to a *sense* of guilt by the moralistic, authoritarian conditioning of religious culture and civilization.

from our infantile transference-based attachments to loving and controlling Parent-Gods, parent-lovers, parent-institutions, parent-mores, and parent-ideologies and theologies, and the mature, realistic reintegration with and acceptance of the disenchanted world. By so exhausting ourselves in such courageous living; in living profoundly and ethically without gods and *in spite of* the existential anxiety and despair of the meaninglessness, non-being, and condemnation which burdens us, we may in fact unwittingly, unconsciously, and imperfectly "fashion our own death." In doing so, we may grow in increasing anticipation of the satisfaction of our ultimate and paradoxical desire or wish: The release from all the transient desires of living and therefore, all the suffering of life.

In my mind, such a natural return to our original inorganic or inanimate state is, from a purely naturalistic perspective, the only sense in which the concept of 'eternal rest' makes any sense at all. The memory of our life which continues to live in the minds of others still living — for good or evil — is likewise the only sense in which the concepts of 'immortality' and 'eternal life' or 'damnation' make sense. Freud's naturalistic and 'poetic vision' of death — and the 'death instinct' — is, as interpreted by Phillips, indeed one example of a life- and death-affirming illusion — a life-and-death story, if you will, with therapeutic value. It is a 'creative illusion' that serves the human need and desire for individuation, for life *and* death. It provides at least one non-death-defying, denying, and life-negating perspective which might enable those with like vision to live well — and mourn well — while dying.

Another different and complementary perspective on death is offered from the East by David Loy as "the Buddhist solution to no-self" (2002). Loy begins by quoting French playwright Eugene Ionesco asking: "Why was I born if it wasn't forever?" He suggests that "[the] Buddhist answer is that we cannot die because we were never born" (222).

"Buddhism," writes Loy, "resolves the problem of life and death by deconstructing it. Negating this dualistic way of thinking reveals what is prior to it. There are many Buddhist names for this prior, but it is significant that one of the most common is the *unborn*.

"In the oldest Buddhist scriptures, the sutras of the Pali Canon, there are many references to *nirvana*, the state of liberation, but few descriptions of it. The two best-known accounts refer to 'an unknown sphere,' which is 'unbecome, unmade, unfabricated,' where 'neither this world not the other, nor coming, going or standing, neither death nor birth, nor sense-objects are to be found' (*Udana* VIII.3, 1).

"For Buddhism," Loy explains, "the dualism between life and death is an instance of our more general problem with [Cartesian] dualistic thinking," a general problem which defines our existential problem *not* as death, but as life *against* death. "From a Buddhist perspective, then, our most problematic duality is not life against death but our sense of self versus awareness of our 'no-thing-ness.' If [then], death is what the sense-of-self fears, the solution is for the sense-of-self to die. If it is 'no-thing-ness' I am afraid of, the best way to resolve that fear is to become nothing.

"Forgetting ourselves," from the Buddhist perspective, "is how we lose our sense of separation and realize that we are [ultimately] not other than the world." Such self-forgetfulness is not achieved in 'self-less' service, sacrifice, or consecration to a god, as the Mormon and Christian traditions insist. Rather it is achieved by dying — facilitating the death of self or ego — through a type of 'meditation' which becomes, in Loy's terms, "an exercise in de-reflection." This is where "[consciousness] unlearns trying to grasp [or preserve] itself, 'real-ize' itself, objectify itself," [and] instead learns to let go of self, "become no-thing, and discover that I am, [as fundamentally part of the physical world], everything (or, more precisely, that I can be anything)" (222–227).

The 'Buddhist solution' — or fiction — to the feared annihilation ('no-self') of death is in the 'enlightened awareness' of our 'no-thing-ness' except as a manifestation of the 'whole world.' It is the profound realization that although each of us is nonexistent as a discrete, independent 'self,' we are nonetheless "grounded, not in some particular [self-concept or identity] but in the whole network of interdependent relations that constitutes the world" (226). More specifically, it is the conflating realization that "I am groundless and ungroundable, insofar as delusively feeling myself to be separate from the world; yet, I have always been fully grounded, insofar as the whole world manifests in (or as) me…" With this realization, "… [the] 'no-thing' at my core is transformed from sense-of-lack [or desire for more life] into a serenity that is imperturbable because there is nothing to be perturbed" (227).

An important and relevant point to make here, beyond acknowledging the putative human need for creative, life-enhancing illusions, is that some such illusions — naturalistic or not — might in fact be life-enhancing while others might not be. In other words, some illusions might be detrimental to our (and others') mental and physical well-being, even if seemingly or actually being pleasurable and comforting. But whatever myths or fantasies we consider, the question is the same. Do such fictions constitute intelligible, creative, life-affirming and -enhancing beliefs or illusions that enable us to intelligibly, coherently, and pragmatically answer the seminal question: *how should one live in relation to one's death*?

As indicated throughout, I generally tend to regard (*pace* Becker) those beliefs or illusions established and anchored by transference and believed to be *literally* or *absolutely true* on the basis of unjustifiable or unjustified convictions, or strong feelings, as delusions which are at least likely, if not actually deleterious to the mental health and well-being of believers. This is so particularly if such putatively factual illusions tend to promote or incite *narcissistic inflation* and *narcissistic scapegoating*, and projectively and regressively invest in human beings, as putative agents of a supernatural being (Parent-God), the authority and power to know the 'will of God,' speak for — or as — 'God' and officiate on his behalf to enjoin (command) the obedience and *self*-sacrifice of believers through binding and consequential commitments, covenants, and counsel. Such transference-induced, wish-based illusions set-up, by their very nature, authoritarian control and extremism. Tacitly, if not explicitly, they prohibit the necessary separation through doubt, disagreement, and conscientious disobedience and dissent that is so essential to personal individuation and integration. Such in part are my concerns with, and indictment against, Mormonism — on *all* counts — as well as against all theistic religions and theistically-toned 'commitment psychologies' (Rieff 1987) to an equal or lesser degree.

As we have seen from our brief conceptual analysis of Mormon theology, any attempt to make our immortality and exaltation fantasies *literal* or *factual* is utterly incoherent and irrational. The Mormon god, as all supernatural gods, is literally impossible because it is literally unintelligible and factually meaningless. It is a factual non-reality. Still, as intimated above and earlier in Chapter 8, the problem of the irrationality of Mormon theology points to deeper questions and concerns. Specifically, echoing the similar question asked in that chapter regarding why faith exists and persists, how is it that such an irrational religion — as with all theistic religions — attracts and has such a hold on otherwise rational believers? What is the personal cost of allegiance to such a faith?

There are, of course, different answers to these questions that have been offered from different perspectives within different disciplines. From my perspective, and on the basis of my particular orientation, assessment, and experience, the Mormon faith, as a relational or social system, recapitulates the authoritarian Western family system. Specifically it is a patriarchal family system characterized generally by various forms of parental control and manipulation, as well as child-sibling posturing for power, status, acceptance, approval, favor, and attention. It is a family system, moreover, where differentiation or separation from the system toward individuation is tacitly discouraged if not forbidden by those in authority. This makes such separation and individuation very difficult for some and next to impossible for most — even if the actual parents are dead or absent.

It seems rather self-evident, from a naturalistic perspective, that what *attracts*, or 'hooks,' a person to such an ideal and eternal social system (which the Mormon Church is ideologically and theologically set-up to be) is the deeply embedded and emotionally charged *idea* of 'family,' and the regressive, dissociative *transference* or projection of the internalized family imago *to* the Church. As Darrel Ray suggests in his provocative book *The God Virus: How Religion Infects Our Lives and Culture* (2009), "…religion is the infection of the mind by a religious idea [which appeals to, and interacts with, the 'personality characteristics' of those in a given environment who are naturally conditioned and vulnerable to such an idea by upbringing, human need and circumstance]" (165).

The fundamental (and invented) religious idea at play in Mormonism is the 'eternal family' in general, and a *heavenly* 'Father (God),' 'Mother,' 'Elder Brother (Jesus),' and 'brothers' and 'sisters' in particular. This idea is, metaphorically, the virus believers 'catch' because of their human condition and conditioning, and their personal needs and neediness. In other words, people get 'infected' (or psychologically hooked) by the 'Mormon virus' through, in effect, a *participation mystique* at play which projectively makes the Mormon community identical with the believer's unconscious family imago. By joining or committing to the Mormon faith the believer psychologically becomes part of an illusory, or regressively wished-for, 'eternal family.'

Accordingly, it seems reasonable to suspect that what *holds* the patriarchal Mormon social system together, in spite of its imperfections and abuses, is, in part, the believer's *cathexis* — or investment of libidinal (erotic) feeling or energy — accompanying the also *binding* participation mystique. This cathexis onto the 'Church family,' which comes about through the above-mentioned dissociative transference, is reinforced first by the *familiar* moralistic core and its related authoritarian mandate for obedience and personal sacrifice in return for authoritative acceptance, approval, and promised joy in this life and eternal life with family and loved ones in the next. Secondly, it is reinforced by the employment of social conditioning and mind-control strategies and programs designed to create and reinforce the delusion of absolute truth in the divine origin, restoration, and administration of an exalting, death-defying faith.

The "patriarchal" social system and its various recapitulating relational systems are inherently abusive because they are implicitly or explicitly governed by what can be referred to as the fundamental 'code of patriarchy,' a code that is grounded in, and derived from, the moralistic core of the system itself. Each member of the family painfully understands from childhood — on the basis of indoctrination established by edict and reinforced by consequential actions taken, attitudes discerned, and real feelings felt (not just imagined) — that this patriarchal code *must* be complied with by those who ultimately desire to be regarded as members in good standing and be considered to be (by external and ultimately internalized authority figures) worthy of love, acceptance, approval, respect, esteem, and 'blessings.'

This moralistic code of patriarchy transcends gender and is comprised of a set of implicit or explicit principles, values, and rules we are all familiar with. These principles, values, and rules include the following:

- "Families are divinely sanctioned and must stick (or stay) together — *at all costs* — to survive and ensure happiness."
- "Always put family first."
- "The authority figures (parents, caregivers, leaders) truly care for you, know better than you what is best for you and are *always* right;"
- "Trust the authority figures and *always* do what you're told. Follow counsel and obey the rules, or commandments."
- "Don't believe, feel, or act in ways the authority figures think is inappropriate."
- "Don't learn, think, communicate, teach, or do anything that might weaken your faith, commitment, or trust —or that of others — in the family or the authority figures. Do not threaten or embarrass (expose) the authority figures or otherwise undermine their authority."
- "Don't talk back, disagree with, dissent from, or disobey the authoritative pronouncements, commands, or counsel of the authority figures."
- "If, while doing what you're told (or not), anything should go wrong, mistakes are made or 'sins' are committed, blame yourself, repent, and remember: the family always comes first and the authority figures care for you, will make you 'right' with them (and/or with 'God') through the 'loving' administration of 'appropriate' disciplinary action, and they are *always* right."

Through indoctrination and operant conditioning by the promise, threat, and administration of forgiveness, rewards, and punishments, authority figures are enabled to effectually (although perhaps not always consciously or intentionally) control and manipulate members within the system. These members, as with children in a patriarchal family, function unknowingly, and to some degree, as 'narcissistic supplies' to the authority figures. They also, or instead, function to preserve the balance of power and relational dynamics in the 'Church family system.'[191] In doing so, they also function as necessary, albeit unwitting, accomplices in preserving and perpetuating the lived lies of self and immortality inherent in the system. The underlying, implicit and overarching objective of the aforementioned code of patriarchy — beneath the surface of espoused and perhaps even genuine, benevolent concern — is essentially to maintain the bonds of dependency and subordination to preserve order and homeostasis in the system. By doing so, the authority figures and co-dependent members of the patriarchal Church system effactually preserve — again through control, manipulation, and suppression — the death-denying illusion and thereby they collusively

---

191 For an interesting and accessible introduction to family system theory, see Bradshaw (1988), and for a more advanced treatment of the subject, see Herr and Bowen (1988).

serve, directly or indirectly, their own and others' unknown or unacknowledged survival interests and corresponding needs for power, status, security, esteem, and belonging, as well as the approval of, and acceptance by, *their* authoritative *Father*-God.

Both the malevolent and allegedly benevolent exercise of authoritarian control in any patriarchal religious setting essentially extorts obedience, sacrifice, and the consecration of time, talents, money, and possessions through illusory threats and promises, and fosters a morbid, regressive dependency on the authority figures of the system to ensure that such threats are avoided or forestalled and promises (or 'blessings') are realized in this life and the next. Further, such control tends to reopen or deepen — intentionally or not — those typical narcissistic wounds that are prevalent, to one degree or another, in all who have been raised in authoritarian family systems. Such wounds are caused by various forms of authoritarian abuse. More specifically and categorically, these include *deprivation* (being insufficiently esteemed, accepted and respected), *deprecation* (being used, objectified, shamed, belittled, or disapproved of), *isolation* (being misunderstood, wrongly judged, cast out or overlooked), *stultification* (being traumatized, controlled, smothered, or stifled) and *rejection* (being shunned, abandoned, neglected, or unappreciated).

The narcissistic wounds inflicted by such abuse cast a long and dark shadow. Counterintuitively yet in fact, they tend to keep those who are thus wounded pathologically bound in blind, perverse loyalty and obedience to their trusted caregivers or leaders. They also tend to recapitulate the control cycle by eventually making the controlled the controllers, and, therefore, the abused the abusers. Additionally, they dis-empower those who are wounded and keep them, through the control mechanism of the 'religious guilt cycle' (Ray 2009) introduced in Chapter 8, enslaved to their faith. They are neurotically stuck at an undifferentiated level of maturity as a result of repeated 'transgression' or 'imperfection,' and they seek relief from the tension, guilt, and shame resulting from it through the emotionally exhausting process of continual 'repentance.'

As was discussed in Chapter 8, such wounding, and the pathology it causes, invariably creates a *conditioned fear response*. This unconsciously alters the fearful, difficult, or painful truth of the believer's condition, experiences, and doubt into an acceptable lie which allows him or her, as with the mechanism of the aforementioned guilt cycle, to persist in the faith and continue to function as a believing or faithful member of his or her religious community. Such consequences, resulting from various overt and often subtle, or insidious, forms of authoritarian abuse, have been validated and confirmed in my own life, and no doubt repeatedly in the lives of countless others. (For a representative sample of documented case reports regarding sexual and authoritarian abuse in the Mormon Church, see Anderson and Allred 1995 and 1997, respectively.)

So it seems to be with the repressed and inseparable authoritarian dark-side of Mormonism and all patriarchal theistic religions or belief systems. Their theologies require the worship of a Parent-God (more specifically a Father God) and they promise, with one hand, *divine goodness* through mediated and earned salvation, beatific love and joy as part of an eternal family, and the acceptance and esteem of 'fellowship in the household of faith' for the worthy, righteous, repentant, and obedient. This they promise while threatening and delivering, with the other hand, *divine retribution* through damnation, rejection, condemnation, and the wounding, rejection, and shame of unblessedness, disfellowship, or excommunication for the actual or would-be unworthy, "sinful" and unrepentant doubters, dissenters, and disobedient 'children of God.'

None of these religions can satisfy the criteria for rationality presented in Chapter 2 or the proposed standards for qualifying as a creative, life-enhancing myth or illusion presented above. Further, the dissociating transferences they engender (the family trance or 'spell' they cast) through their language, doctrines, rites, and rituals are — as are all unresolved transferences — regressive and pathological. They undermine essential individuation and personality integration.

Finally, the package of 'blessings' offered come, as we have learned, with serious risks of personal harm and danger. They trap the unwitting investigator or member in a *two-part* double-bind where, in the first part they are taught and conditioned to believe that if they join the Mormon Church they will receive the promised blessings of the Mormon Gospel, but if they do not join the Mormon Church they will not. Then, in the second part, they are told that if they *do* join the Church and do *not* receive or enjoy the promised blessings — for example, forgiveness, prosperity, health, peace, acceptance, deliverance, sanctification, and the 'gifts and fruits of the Spirit' — it is because they are either *unworthy* because of their lack of faith or disobedience, or because they are *worthy* and are being tested for even greater blessings.

Either way, or in any case, investigators and members *must* accept without doubt or reservation that the Church is true and that they will suffer hardship and loss if they do not join the Church. Even if they do join but later sin, doubt and/or leave the faith, they will suffer. Clearly, sincere and committed (or 'active') adherents of such likely (if not actually) harmful illusions are deluded and trapped by their own pathology and denial of death in an authoritarian, patriarchal system which is difficult if not impossible to escape without crisis or analytic intervention, or both.

In the end, I am not convinced of the need for any transcendent theistic, spiritual, or psychological mythology or illusion — particularly any which foster or require belief and faith in, or obedience, commitment, sacrifice, and consecration to, some transcendent, perfect, and authoritative being, agency, archetypal affect, force, institution, moral code, characterological ideal, plan or purpose to ensure meaning, salvation, perfection, goodness, or immortality. I am, rather, personally and psychologically inclined toward humanistic, Atheistic values, and a morality that is neither a set of principles or code of rules (or 'moral imperatives') to live by, nor a 'selfless' commitment to others or a prescribed way of life. Such values and morality are, as I see it, naturally rooted in the mature, or individuated and integrated personality. And they are likewise naturally manifested in the authentic inclination or disposition to act (not act-out) reflectively (or ethically) – and at times even strategically – in one's best interests, or according to one's needs and related desires (not neediness and related impulses), and to do so by naturally taking every precaution not to carelessly or thoughtlessly hurt or alienate others, or deprive them of their right to act likewise in their best interests.

The humanistic, Atheistic values and morality I embrace and advocate necessarily, and again naturally, reject all gods and religion, and advocate the mature cultivation of moral imagination and internal moral authority. They also endorse the importance of critical thinking, the commitment to intellectual integrity and epistemic responsibility, the eschewing of irrational guilt and toxic shame (and shaming), the importance of treating others with due respect, compassion and empathy as human beings, and the right to accept or reject social norms, traditions and institutions on their merits or demerits for personal and social well-being, while being personally responsible for the consequences for doing so.

Further, I am, as a hard-determinist, of the mind that questions concerning the purpose *of* one's life, and/or the meaning *of* life, are themselves meaningless if not unintelligible and incoherent. I am also of the mind that mythologies or transference-established illusions (or delusions) are unnecessary and, to the extent they fit the profile presented in Chapter 8 – and reflect or recapitulate, in form, tone, or content, the authoritarian or narcissistic family system of the believer – they are injurious to our well-being as well. Nevertheless, as Piven reminds us, "confronting paralyzing truths or the fictitiousness of our sacred illusions may only be minutely possible." Still, Piven suggests and then asks, "If our goal is not ego-support, but profundity, not mere normalcy or happiness [whatever that means], but self-truth, then one makes a career of that. Can we live artistically, prepared to accept the world as illusion without despair but with our own art? Are we prepared to live a 'neurosis of health' for the sake of intellectual honesty, profundity, and generation?" (2002, 246)

Such questions and above preferred values and perspective can only be offered for deep, personal reflection. There are no easy or right or wrong answers. What we *do* know, again from Piven, is that "We cannot simply will a belief and then make of it [as Becker wrongly suggests] a 'freely chosen dependence.' This is neither belief nor faith" (242). Nor can we, again following Adler, believe the unbelievable without cognitive dissonance and self-deception (2006). Finally, as argued above, we cannot simply resign ourselves to such "sacred (theistic) illusions" without compromising our own intellectual integrity and credibility and incurring an even greater cost than the loss of "mere [so called] normalcy and happiness;" the cost of personal well-being and, ultimately, life itself. All said, I tend to agree with Yalom, who writes:

> I believe that we should confront death as we confront other fears. We should contemplate our ultimate end, familiarize ourselves with it, dissect it and analyze it, reason with it, and discard terrifying childhood death distortions.
>
> Let's not conclude [*pace* Kierkegaard and Becker] that death is too painful to bear [without 'faith' or illusion respectively], that the thought will destroy us, that transiency must be denied lest the truth render life meaningless. Such denial always exacts a price — narrowing our inner life, blurring our vision, blunting our rationality. Ultimately self-deception catches up with us.
>
> Anxiety will always accompany our confrontation with death. I feel it now as I write these words; it is the price we pay for self-awareness. [Nevertheless,] raw death terror can be scaled down to every-day manageable anxiety. Staring into the face of death, with guidance, not only quells terror but renders life more poignant, more precious, more vital. Such an approach to death leads to instruction about life. (2008, 276)

I endorse the above-quoted 'existential worldview' and the related human need to more modestly and consciously cultivate physical and psychological well-being without faith or commitment and surrender to any gods or men and women in authority — and without creating some substitute illusion or external, absolute, and authoritative 'plan,' 'purpose,' or 'morality.' This alternative would, as suggested earlier and in Yalom's words above, necessarily entail the mature acceptance of our condition and the progressive disillusionment and 'normal unhappiness' that naturally attend it. As noted earlier, it would also necessarily entail an 'analytic attitude,' which is, beyond Rieff's limited conception noted earlier, an attitude which values the moral and ethical pursuit of personal well-being through the psychodynamic creation of 'resonating' *personal* meanings, perspectives and narratives, as well as honest, empathic human connection in the face of the stark realities of the natural world.

Such an attitude, as I interpret and embrace it, calls for neither commitment nor obedience to either an external or internalized-external authority, ideology, or moral code. And while, through its application in the psychodynamic therapeutic process, the analytic attitude opens *all* options for living to the analysand through fantasy or opportunity, and it does so without moralistic judgment or shame — by correctly differentiating legitimate guilt from an illegitimate and irrational *sense* of guilt — it strives *only* to increase the personal capacity for moral and ethical choice on the basis of the psychodynamically developed capacities for empathic consideration of others, moral imagination, and the more conscious determination of reasoned, informed, and analyzed self-interest *in the context of* the *reality* of personal limits or limitations. Beyond such a modest goal, the analytical attitude — and the psychoanalytic process which channels it — promises *nothing*, least of all the realization of some (illusory or delusional) transcendent purpose or destiny, or a transformational cure and its concomitant and illusory goods of hope, happiness, comfort, security, and salvation. Moreover, the created narrative of our life that comes from it simply explains and makes sense of what *is*, neither moralistically prescribing nor advocating what *should* be or prophetically assuring what *will* be. Such a narrative is merely a personally meaningful interpretation of our suffering, actions, and choices made honestly through the particular hermeneutic of our own psychoanalyzed experience.

Subjectively created personal meanings, perspectives, and narratives, as developed analytically by therapeutic talk and resulting reflective insight and corrective emotional experience, because of our experienced emotional resonance with their personalized, interpretive content, would seem (to us) to accurately reflect and perhaps enable the cybernetic shaping (or perhaps even re-shaping) of those 'hidden agendas' (neuronal pathways) in our brains which account for our individual patterns of relating with ourselves and others in the world.

As Joseph Campbell insisted, these hidden agendas are effectually "running the show from way down below." Further, they would serve to help us make reasonable, *earthly* sense of our lives in the context of a naturalism without supernatural foundations — a naturalism which holds that all living (biological) organisms seem naturally to individuate and fill the measure of their *natural* existence. Such naturalism provides an 'earthly sense' which acknowledges moreover that our psychological wounds and physical limitations are never fully resolved or eradicated, but rather can be understood and thereby they can make us stronger, becoming as well the impetus of our vocational and ideological passions in life which give us personal meaning *in* our life, even if not an illusory meaning *of* life.

Such created, personal meaning in the context of a pragmatic, historicist, nonscientistic, and non-metaphysical naturalism would attest to us, by experience and rational thought, that a positive, or life-affirming, relationship with the world and others cannot be achieved by attempting to creatively transform the 'natural' world into a 'supernatural' world , or even a *christianized* world. Rather, this must emerge through analytic interaction and guidance — by making of our life a meaningful work of art. Moreover, through the more conscious exercise of 'moral imagination' we shall open ourselves up to potentially new or different types and forms of essential experience.

Finally, such personal, fictional meanings and narratives would at least seem to lend anecdotal, albeit non-factual support to the perhaps necessary social illusions of personal, indeterministic self-control, responsibility, and contribution — even as we are nonetheless deterministically (not fatalistically), cybernetically moved, as parts of an interdependent web of life, to live *and* die at the right time and in our own fashion.

Personal Postscript:

A Few Parting (and Harsh) Criticisms and Some Concluding Observations, Concerns, and Personal Disclosures

"It is not possible to be intellectually honest and believe in [any] gods."

—*Peter William Atkins*

"Contributing greatly to the culture of stupidity is the willingness of people to submit to higher authorities in matters requiring intellectual effort."

—*James F. Welles*

"No simplicity of mind, no obscurity of station can escape the universal duty of questioning all that we believe."

—*W. K. Clifford*

"Not to question, not to tremble with the craving and the joy of questioning...that is what I feel to be contemptible."

—*Nietzsche*

"Nothing is at last sacred but the integrity of your own mind."

—*Ralph Waldo Emerson*

I

At the end of his Introduction in *Atheism: A Reader* (2000) S.T. Joshi wrote: "The atheist, agnostic, or secularist...should not be cowed by exaggerated sensitivity to people's religious beliefs. ... Those who advocate...folly...should be held accountable for their folly; they have no right to be offended for being called fools until they establish that they are not in fact fools. Religiously inclined [believers] may plead that 'respect' should be accorded to [their] religious views in public discourse, but [they] neglect to demonstrate that those views are worthy of respect" (20).

Before theistic believers take offence at Joshi's rather incendiary words (if they do) they should perhaps first recall 'the Psalmist' who, as Hitchens points out with his usual flare (2007), "was obviously pleased enough with the polish and address of psalm 14 to repeat it virtually word for word as psalm 53. Both versions," Hitchens observes, begin with the identical statement that 'The *fool* has said in his heart, there is no God.' For some reason," he continues, "this null remark is considered significant enough to be recycled throughout all religious apologetics. All that we can tell for sure from the otherwise meaningless assertion [how, after all, can a person be a fool for not believing as factual a statement which is factually meaningless?] is that unbelief — not just heresy and back-sliding but unbelief — must have been known to exist even in that remote epoch. Given the then absolute rule of unchallenged and brutally punitive faith, it would perhaps have been a fool who did *not* keep this conclusion buried deep inside himself, in which case it would be interesting to know how the psalmist knew it was there [if not for the fact that he himself suffered from unbelief]" (253–4; emphasis mine).

A *fool*, as most relevantly defined by Webster for our purposes here, is simply "a person lacking in judgment and prudence." More specifically, as I define the term, a fool is someone who acts on the basis of consequential and foolish (or objectively considered absurd, ridiculous, nonsensical) beliefs, and uncritically and stubbornly holds and repre-sents such beliefs as actual truth (or worse, as 'Truth') merely on the basis of faith.

In the general sense of the term, we of course *all* lack in "judgment and prudence" in certain areas in our life, and hold (or have perhaps held at times) foolish beliefs. Just as *all* human beings undeniably act stupidly (Welles 1995) from time to time (and to a greater and lesser degree of frequency and severity), so too with 'foolishness' as we all at times act the *fool*. Both terms are closely related, though not synonymous. *Stupidity* leads to foolishness, and those who act stupidly are acting foolishly as well. To be irremediably and/or willfully stupid is to also be a fool.

In the more specific sense of the term, and for *all of us*, if the proverbial shoe of the fool fits regarding whatever superstitious or metaphysical beliefs might be held and asserted as truth about, for example, gods, spirits, angels, ghosts, goblins, the afterlife, and other supernatural and superstitious nonsense, then, by all means, we should wear it. This conventional call to personal ownership of the nature of our beliefs and assertions of fact would certainly extend to the Psalmist, whoever he was, who apparently, as perhaps an unconscious betrayal of, and reaction formed against, his own real doubt, wrongly, mean-inglessly, and defensively put the shoe of the fool on the wrong foot. It would certainly extend as well to all theistic believers and apologists who might likewise defensively use these words of the psalmist against Atheists or non-theists while ironically continuing to advocate as truth the folly of their own absurd religious beliefs.

Still, even with such arguably justified or justifiable views regarding the 'folly' or 'foolishness' (Joshi 2000, 20) of certain religious beliefs, and the characterization, as defined above, of certain theistic believers as 'fools' (not to mention the stated contempt-ibleness of many of their religious practices of mind-control and authoritarian abuse), certain readers, even if not themselves believers, might nonetheless be uncomfortable with the terms and tone of such discourse. To them, and to believers especially, such pejora-tive characterizations are considered offensive and unnecessary as ridicule. The question asked or at least brought to mind in this regard might be: 'Why ridicule, or be so harshly critical of Mormon and theistic beliefs, practices, and believers?' Moreover, other related questions might be asked as well, such as 'Why not just leave the Mormons and other theistic believers alone to worship their gods and live their religion as they please?' 'Why question and disturb their faith?' 'Why not be tolerant of others' beliefs and respectful of their right to believe what they will?' 'If their beliefs bring them happiness, joy, meaning, guidance, comfort, and peace, and they're not religious extremists or religiously abusive, why not let them be?'

When asked out of sincere perplexity and concern, and not disingenuously out of what Joshi characterizes as "rhetorical strategies [employed by believers] to stifle criticism of their beliefs and practices" (17),[192] these are all fair and sensible questions which have been asked of me, and which I asked of myself repeatedly and reflectively over the years and as I have written this book.

For those readers who have such questions and are truly desirous of answers, I will attempt — to the extent not already implicitly done throughout this work — to respond as plainly, sensibly, honestly, and directly as I can in this personal postscript. But first I will briefly say up front, in anticipation of any defensive dismissals of the answers and conclusions which might ensue, that in answering such questions, or even writing this book, I harbor no grandiose and foolish illusion that the Mormon faith, or any theistic faith for that matter, will be affected significantly, much less seriously threatened or mortally wounded, by the answers and arguments made or the harsh criticisms offered in demonstrating and calling-out respectively the patent foolishness, harmfulness, and potential danger and destructiveness of its beliefs. Such threats and related 'mortal wounding' to religious

---

192   Joshi lists six such evasive, rhetorical strategies which are presented with italicized emphasis in this note, followed in each case by a brief, bracketed paraphrasing of Joshi's reply, mingled or modified with my own for additional perspective or relevance to the Mormon faith.

According to Joshi, believers rhetorically "maintain that religion [i]*is really a matter of taste and preference* [then why does it matter which god is worshipped, or if no god is believed to exist?]; [ii] that *it is a 'way of life' rather than a set of doctrines* [then why would it matter if one was a Jew, or a Christian, or a Mormon, or a Muslim, or an Atheist? And how can a religious way of life be entirely divorced from all doctrines of a given faith, or of the religious books upon which they originate or are built on?]; that [iii] *Atheism itself is a dogmatic religion* [Atheists have no beliefs about gods. They do not believe that there is no 'God,' they simply do not believe there is a 'God,' or any gods.]; that [iv] *skeptics should not 'meddle' with people's religious beliefs* [does the right to believe as actual truth whatever one wishes to believe protect believers and their beliefs from open criticism and derision if such beliefs are reasonably and supportably deemed to be false and/or incoherent, and harmfully exploitive, oppressive or regressive to society and potentially dangerous, damaging and destructive to believers and nonbelievers alike?]; that [v] *religion nowadays has been purged of all the bad elements that polluted it in the past* [has such 'purging' of now-regarded false, absurd, harmful, or dangerous beliefs (e.g., the doctrines of the literal creation of the universe and worlds without end; the belief in the literal creation and fall of man; the belief that all people are born into a fallen state through the literal 'Fall of Adam and Eve'; the need for a literal, infinite and eternal 'atonement' of man's sins by the shedding of the blood of a 'God-man' who is the literal 'Son of God'; the belief in a literal apocalyptic end of the world and the literal destruction and damnation of unrepentant sinners; the belief in the literal resurrection of Jesus and all who have died, etc.) resulted in the necessary invalidating or discrediting of the various 'books of revelation' or scripture which are still embraced as the 'Word of God' by believers of those religions which were founded on, and legitimized by, such books, and within which certain renounced beliefs, teachings, and commandments or doctrines are still represented as 'God's word and will'?]; that [vi] *it would be cruel and unfair to 'take away' a person's religion from him when he or she finds it a comfort"* [does the realization, in virtue of sound and valid secular argument and the presentation of compelling evidence, that one's religious beliefs are false or incoherent denote or connote that such beliefs, if consequently relinquished by the believer, have been 'taken away' or removed by coercion by the secularist? Likewise, would evangelists or missionaries consider their facilitation of someone's acceptance of religious beliefs through the teaching and preaching of the 'Word of God' as "taking away" their reason or rationality? And, regarding the idea that religion provides comfort, is it better for a person to reject reality because it does not conform to his or her wishes, or to accept reality for what it is live life with a mature grasp of reality?] (2000, 17–21).

institutions and their ideologies unfortunately do *not* come through reason and charges of foolishness and of stupidity alone — regardless of how warranted and compelling the force of reason might be, or how true the charges are. Rather, the discrediting and demise of established religious institutions and their belief systems typically come only with the public exposure of egregious scandal and abuse, or wide-scale social outrage and internal dissent and rebellion; matters which are both usually well contained or kept under very tight wraps.

This said, I do think that culture *can* be changed — even if very slowly and perhaps minimally — one crucial conversation at a time, and that at an individual level certain believers are affected by meaningful discussion and well-reasoned criticism of their theistic beliefs, and do allow real doubt to have its way in bringing them to their senses and even back to their natural Atheism. There are to be sure at least some (if not many) otherwise rational and intelligent believers who do *actually* value intellectual integrity and eschew epistemic irresponsibility sufficient to seriously question their faith as a reasonably skeptical outsider. For the sake of these believers meaningful dialogue, discussion, and debate must continue.

Sadly, however, I think such believers are in the vast minority, and that with the vast majority of believers (especially those raised and indoctrinated in their faith as children) reason and rationality do not apply, and are in fact antithetical to their faith. To these dyed-in-the-wool or utterly brainwashed and rigidly uncompromising believers, dialogue, argument, and debate are futile, and they continue dutifully, stubbornly, and unashamedly to believe — and shamelessly assert as actual truth — factually unintelligible propositions, and demeaning, harmful, and potentially dangerous proposals for living. It is this latter category of believers — the staunch, devoted believers who have made their faith an unquestioning and irreversible 'decision,' and who will not even entertain (much less do so seriously) the very real *possibility* that their religious beliefs are irrational, harmful, and potentially dangerous and destructive, or that they might in fact be brainwashed, self-deceived and delusional in holding such beliefs as they do — that I have in mind as I address below the first question regarding why the harsh criticisms and pejorative characterizations leveled in this book (and in this *Personal Postscript* in particular) against Mormon and theistic beliefs, practices, and believers.

To answer this question I will say again what I stated in the *Introduction*, that given the stakes involved regarding the toxicity of the Mormon faith and the personal and social price paid for theistic belief and faith to exist and persist in our world, such criticism and characterizations have an important if not essential consequentialist purpose. To be sure, the *status* of such beliefs as truth claims needs to be continually exposed — through well reasoned critical analysis, sound argument, and, where relevant, valid evidence — for what it is, *i.e.*, absurd, wholly unwarranted assertions which are false and/or incoherent. This exposure, over time, hopefully serves to at least bring such beliefs and their corresponding practices into question. Perhaps it can even somewhat depotentiate them through well-reasoned and supported criticism.

In so criticizing the religious beliefs and practices of the Mormon and other theistic faiths (as well as certain believers themselves) it is crucial to keep three important points in mind. First, that the criticisms of such beliefs and practices as false and/or incoherent as well as harmful and potentially dangerous and damaging or destructive are, as argued throughout this book, not without ample, careful, and well supported analytical, historical, psychological, and commonsensical justification. Second, that the criticisms and harsh, negative characterizations of certain believers are not, as shall be made clear and likewise supported below, merely or exclusively *ad hominem* remarks or characterizations. While they *are* such to be sure in the narrow sense of being personal in nature, they are certainly not made to meanly or cruelly offend, or to argue for a particular conclusion or ideology. And third, that in offering such criticisms and characterizations we are not, as neuroscientist Robert Burton (2008) has rightly discouraged, "perpetuating the all-knowing rational mind [or scientistic] myth" as a deterrent to "real discussion" (196). Nor are we dealing merely with differences of opinion. If the real discussion is about what we are *justified* in *objectively* regarding as *knowledge* or *fact* about what there *actually* is in the world and how the world or universe *actually* works, then reason pragmatically and rationally applied (*i.e.*, through abduction, deduction, and induction) is fundamentally and primarily indicated as the best 'way of knowing,' and subjective, feeling-based knowing or intuition is *contraindicated*.

Differences of opinion in any endeavor or course of action can be respectable to be sure, and even beneficial in stimulating mutual understanding and progress, with neither party the worse for their differences. But beliefs in *any* domain which are demonstrably false and/or analytically or logically incoherent and therefore wholly unwarranted as truth claims, as well as harmful and even potentially dangerous and damaging or destructive in practice (as Mormon and other theistic beliefs arguably are), are neither respectable nor salutary, and harsh criticism of the loyal adherents and practitioners of such beliefs and practices *can* at times, and in certain circumstances, be therapeutic, if not moreover in society's best interest.

Additionally, I think it is also crucial to keep in mind what we all already know: that not everyone's opinions and beliefs are on par simply because everyone *thinks* their beliefs are true, or has a right to their own opinions or to believe what they will. Such a fallacy at least tacitly implies the belief that religious claims or beliefs and strong Atheistic (or Anti-theistic) counter-claims are epistemically equivalent. This belief from a *non-religious* standpoint seems obviously invalid. The claim, for example, that 'married bachelors exist' is not *epistemically* equivalent to the counter-claim that such a claim is incoherent, and that therefore 'married bachelors *do not* and *cannot* possibly exist.' The claim that 'the "Easter Bunny" *literally* exists' is not *epistemically* equivalent to the counter-claim that such a claim is false, and that therefore 'the "Easter Bunny" most likely (or beyond a reasonable doubt) does not *literally* exist.' To suggest in either of these examples that both the assertion and counter-assertion are beliefs which are of equal *epistemic* value as truth claims would be hopefully absurd to all (some children excepted in the latter case).

These simple, non-religious examples of false epistemic equivalence of belief are noncontroversial to the mature, rational mind capable of sound reasoning. But such consensus is lost when epistemic equivalency is dismissively and defensively asserted by theistic believers in relation to fundamental religious claims or beliefs and strong Atheistic counter-claims.

Take for example, the claim 'the Mormon god (or any god) *literally* exists.' This claim is not epistemically equivalent to the strong Atheistic counter-claim made throughout this book and elsewhere that '*given* the way the term "God" is used in the Mormon faith (or *any* faith), the belief that *any* such gods *literally* exist is either false or incoherent, and therefore such gods either most likely (or beyond a reasonable doubt) *do not* exist (if false), or necessarily *cannot* possibly exist *as presently and fully conceptualized* (if incoherent).' For a believer to dismissively and defensively suggest or assert, if he does, that both of the above claims are epistemically equivalent as beliefs (*i.e.*, 'my belief is just as worthy of being regarded as knowledge or truth as yours') is simply wrong as well as wrong-headed.

This is so, again, for all the same reasons that *all* non self-evident and unjustifiable or unjustified theistic truth claims will not and cannot (as argued earlier) "cut their own way" by the "force of reasoning," or at all. Conversely, the counter-claim of the strong Atheist, while itself certainly a belief, where the term 'belief' is used to denote an analytic or justified proposition reasonably thought to be true, is nonetheless arguably based on sensible, supportable, and commonly or widely used practices for acquiring knowledge (through abduction, induction, and deduction) or determining if truth claims qualify as knowledge, or as something which can even be reasonably considered — or possibly known — to be true. This would be in contrast to a religious belief as *non-rational* or *irrational* assent to a non-analytic and arguably incoherent, factually unintelligible, and wished-for proposition which is *unjustified* or unwarranted because it is *unjustifiable*.

There is a personal and social price to pay for openly representing one's foolish religious beliefs as Truth, or even probable truth. Such a price might include public disagreement, contention, and humiliation. The avoidance of that price, as well as the preservation of one's intellectual integrity (if such is important), requires — as commonly understood among sensible people — that if people cannot reasonably support such claims then they should either responsibly and legitimately seek such knowledge before making such claims, if it is to be had, or keep their foolish opinions and beliefs to themselves. Moreover, simply countering challenges to one's stated religious beliefs with "That's just what I believe" or "You have your opinion, I have mine," or "I know what I know" as rationale or defense for one's unwarranted and reasonably challenged or refuted assertions or opinions, is no rationale or defense at all, or even a tacit admission of human fallibilism. Rather, it is merely a defensive and shameful admission of willful ignorance and intellectual laziness that is not worthy of serious consideration, much less respect.

Nor incidentally, for those less informed believers who might turn to their religious leaders, professors, and apologists for answers, are such authoritative assurances or speculative apologetic counter-arguments respectable. In my experience, they are all equally nonsensical as well as unsound, invalid, and unsupportable. In this regard I think it can reasonably be suggested that exercising intellect and reason to explain or defend one's belief in a god (however one's god might be conceptualized) is not only sheer folly (how, after all, does one explain or defend a superstition or a factual non-reality?), it is a terrible misuse of one's intellect and reason. Moreover, such an effort would seem to be a tacit admission as well of both the problemicity of one's beliefs and the insufficiency of faith and revelation.

More bluntly put, simply throwing more *a priori* question-begging foolishness (including appeals to revelation and faith) at sound or valid objections to one's foolishness just makes one a bigger fool. Again, from Joshi's quote above, "*Those who advocate…folly… should be held accountable for their folly; they have no right to be offended for being called fools until they [reasonably or validly] establish that they are not in fact fools.*" This it would seem is a minimal requirement which, in my view, Mormon and other theistic believers and apologists simply (and I think obviously) *cannot* satisfy in defense of their faith or their unqualified and unquestioning acceptance of it, except in convincing other like believers who likewise foolishly embrace such folly.[193]

While I would certainly stop short of characterizing *all* Mormon or theistic believers as *complete* fools merely on the basis of holding and adhering to certain religious beliefs and practices, I would, however, so characterize those believers whose *entire life* is *centered* in their faith, and who are, or strive to be, *by admission and choice*, proudly immovable and unquestioning in their beliefs and loyalty to their 'God' and their faith *in spite of* reason or evidence which might bring such beliefs and practices (and therefore their reason for being, or living) into question. Such believers, in my view, and particularly those accomplished

---

193 Such a requirement seems reasonable, if not at least apparently self-evident, given the implicit interaction involved. Consider the following. Someone makes a strange and incredible claim to another and advocates its acceptance as actual truth. The claimant is understandably asked for either the meaning of, or support for, the claim, but none can be given, even in principle. Instead the person is asked to accept the claim merely on faith, or for no reasons which would at least make such a claim justifiable, or even intelligible. The claimant is nonetheless given a fair hearing and the judgment is finally made that the he is talking nonsense and irresponsibly making foolish, unwarranted assertions, and that he is, moreover, and also irresponsibly, asking the impossible, *i.e.*, to believe as true that which is unintelligible, incoherent, and factually meaningless. The claimant persists and is finally told, in an effort to bring him to his senses, that his belief is frankly stupid and that he is a fool for believing such nonsense. If the claimant disagrees with such a characterization of himself and his claim and desires to refute it, what must be done? The claimant must of course reasonably or validly *establish* that he is *not* advocating folly and is not in fact a fool. If he cannot, then the judgment stands by authority of reason and common sense.

It would of course be the burden of Mormon believers or apologists attempting a *tu quoque* riposte here to be specific regarding the nature of the 'folly' attributed to the atheological and personal criticisms of their faith and adherence to it presented in this book which would make this author in particular a 'fool' as Joshi specifies. If such specific rationale can be mustered, then a deeper understanding of the arguments made in this book would be called for by this author to establish the contrary, and my accuser(s), if they are such, must be prepared to carefully specify and validly argue to the satisfaction of intelligent, educated, and reasonably skeptical outsiders why my arguments and criticisms as presented fail or are insufficient as a defense against such an accusation. If such insufficiency can be established without a valid and sufficiently substantive or compelling rejoinder from me, then the accusation would stand that the conclusions of my analysis and psychosocial assessment of the Mormon faith, and my harsh criticism of its staunch believers as specified, are 'folly,' and I am a 'fool' (in both the general and specific sense of the term) for unwarrantedly asserting and stubbornly representing such conclusions and criticisms as being valid and deserved.

On the other hand, I for one, as a former insider and once staunch and loyal believer in the Mormon faith for many years, and as a student of comparative theistic religion, have paid the price to deeply understand the conceptual framework and tenets of the Mormon faith in particular and have determined on the basis of the analysis and assessment of that faith (and the other major theistic faiths as well) performed in this work that its fundamental beliefs and practices are, to use Joshi's words, sheer "folly" and its devout, unquestioning believers are therefore "fools."

This book has, I think, compellingly made such a case to an intelligent, educated and reasonably skeptical outsider. It is now up to Mormon believers or apologists in particular to reasonably, validly and sufficiently establish the contrary if they can. If, more specifically, they cannot do so by clearly, unambiguously, or coherently answering the analytical questions presented in Chapters 3–8 or, alternatively, they cannot likewise establish why such questions are either irrelevant or inappropriate and/or why therefore an inability to answer them satisfactorily if at all would not be a *prima facie* confirmation of the conclusions reached in regard to them; and if, moreover, they cannot sufficiently and convincingly refute (beyond mere subjective or anecdotal assertions to the contrary) the psychosocial assessment made primarily in Chapter 8 of this book, then the above conclusion would necessarily stand that Joshi's implied threshold cannot be crossed, and that Mormonism may therefore reasonably be considered as folly, and devout, unquestioning Mormon believers as fools.

and highly educated intellectuals who use (misuse) their developed, refined and educated minds to justify and defend their faith and their beliefs through sophistry, rationalization, and intellectualizing, should be ashamed of themselves. And their healthy sense of shame or embarrassment should extend to shamelessly *taking pride* in believing, representing and defending as 'Truth' such patent stupidity, and endorsing as rational, wholesome, good, and praiseworthy such clearly irrational, harmful, divisive, and potentially damaging, dangerous, and destructive doctrine, as is arguably the case in mainstream Mormonism, and most likely, to a greater or lesser degree, all other theisms as well.

Significantly, the above rationale for the harsh and at times angry criticisms of Mormonism and other theistic faiths offered in this work is not, as I see it, devoid of compassion for the human condition or felt need of many to believe in gods. But it *is* intolerant (and I think again reasonably and appropriately so) of that which undermines the authority of reason, the integrity of the intellect, the intellectual, scientific, and moral progress of civilization, the psychological health and well-being of believers, and the preservation of human rights and life, and does so through the absurdity and sickness of theistic faith.[194]

The insidious and epistemically irresponsible use of God-talk, and the at least tacit endorsement such talk, as religious practice, gives to the socially dangerous doctrines and harmful, destructive abusive dynamic inherent in all theistic faiths an *ersatz* legitimacy which simply can no longer be regarded by nonbelievers as harmless or merely annoying. It is, to me, neither mean-spirited nor cruel to justifiably and soberly push back against such personally and socially consequential nonsense in stark and even pejorative terms if necessary to try to disturb to an awakened sense of intellectual integrity and epistemic and social responsibility those who are in truth — sincere insistence or appearances to the contrary notwithstanding — beyond the reach of reason and reasoned discourse in such matters; those who have, in other words, made faith a decision and stubbornly and insistently stick to it. In doing so, I for one am not consciously or deliberately setting out to merely or meanly hurt feelings or to convert anyone to my way of thinking — or to *any* ideology as 'way of thinking.[195]'

---

194 I am reminded of the relevant words of Nietzsche in this regard who wrote: "Christianity [including, of course, Mormonism]…stands in opposition to all *intellectual* well-being, — sick reasoning is the only sort that it can use as Christian reasoning; it takes the side of everything that is idiotic; it pronounces a curse upon 'intellect,' upon the *superbia* of the healthy intellect. Since sickness is inherent in Christianity, it follows that the typically Christian state of 'faith' must be a form of sickness too [or that 'faith' is the sickness which causes the sickness of the Christian]….'Faith' means the will to avoid knowing what is true" (from an excerpt of the *Antichrist* in Joshi 2000, 205).

195 Such intolerance, and the critical 'consequentialist' approach which comes with it, has of course its risks and drawbacks. Faith dies hard and often galvanizes to extreme one-sidedness when suppressed or challenged by argument or social embarrassment. Such suppression can certainly result in acting out, social or relational alienation, the strengthening of ego-defenses, and a total collapse of productive dialogue, discussion, or debate, if such is even possible in this particular strain of human stupidity.

Even so, and perhaps most notably in the United States, we are clearly no longer dealing with believers who keep their beliefs to themselves and innocuously live their religion without fanfare or imposition on others or public policy. On the contrary, we are all exposed, advertently or not, to incoherent God-talk at every turn and in every medium. Familiar yet unintelligible and factually meaningless theistic language has completely saturated our public consciousness and way of thinking and talking. At every turn we are counseled incoherently to, for example, "put God and Christ at the center of our lives" or to live a "purpose driven life," where *the* "purpose" is "God's purpose" for our lives, and something we need to discover through 'spiritual'

My intent — at least when I am not in a purely reactive state (which, for reasons which shall be disclosed later, is still regrettably too often the case) — is to promote *reason*, provoke or encourage *critical questioning and doubt*, and thereby, if possible, prod believers (through a healthy dose of shame if need be) to simply *think seriously, deeply and critically*, again as skeptical outsiders, about the sense and personal and social implications of their religious beliefs.

In doing so, I have not lost sight of, as Burton puts it, of "the biological constraints on our ability to know what we know" (197). Still, notwithstanding such undeniable constraints, not all that is asserted as knowledge *is* such; not all that is known — fallibilistically and therefore provisionally — is of equal value; and not all ignorance is consequentially equivalent. Even so, Burton holds (inconsistently, I think) that a deep acceptance of human fallibilism and "the idea of provisional facts" is "our only hope" at resolving the 'faith *vs.* reason' argument (197; see 177–197). But to foster such hope requires that we all, in whatever domain of knowledge, challenge (as a reasonably skeptical outsider) what is believed so that doubt — *real, live* doubt — might flourish and call the intellect to reason (whatever reason we can muster) in pursuit of *objective* truth through the achievement of wide, reflective equilibrium. Unfortunately, such a sensible and reasonable way of knowing is, for staunch theistic believers concerning their 'faith in God,' categorically impossible without at times the intervention of not only sound argument, but harsh criticism and even ridicule[196] for believing and behaving as they do.

---

self-discovery. We are unintelligibly asked or told to pray for others and we are subjected to the likewise unintelligible testimonies or witnessing of believers of blessings from 'God' as answers to prayers. We hear of so-called miracles with every merely unexplained (albeit no doubt naturalistically explainable) natural event, and receive unsolicited and putatively authoritative counsel and incoherent apologetic references to 'God's will,' his goodness and love for mankind, and his factually meaningless greatness and expectations, as well as his purposes for, and direct involvement in our lives.

Moreover, theists today of every persuasion are politically active and very vocal about their beliefs, and they are bold in enlisting others to believe likewise. Meanwhile, missionaries and other evangelists from all faiths continue to knock on doors and crowd the airways and bookstores with their factually vacuous claims and likewise empty promises, all with a steep price to pay. Arguably all of this is so in part at least because the foolishness and idiocy of personally and socially consequential theistic or otherwise religious beliefs have not been openly exposed and confronted for what they are, and the illness and danger they engender and perpetuate. Consequently, there is no necessary corrective, healthy shame or embarrassment in the equation.

As stated, dialogue, discussion, debate, and argument certainly must continue to expose the false and incoherent status of theistic concepts and truth claims, and will do so to be sure. But the terms of engagement are shifting, and the suppressed social contempt and outrage toward theistic dogma and abuse will likely and hopefully continue to expose such religious dogma and practice for what they are. Bruised feelings or strained relationships will be, and are, in my view, a sad yet relatively small price to pay by those who truly care, given the very real stakes involved.

196 In a letter to F.A. Van Der Kemp dated July 30, 1816, Thomas Jefferson wrote, in relation to religious absurdity, "Ridicule is the only weapon which can be used against unintelligible propositions. Ideas must be distinct before reason can act upon them." While different religious faiths and believers might argue that their beliefs are exceptions to the specific beliefs listed by Jefferson, what I think is significant here is the fact that Jefferson referred to the necessary ridicule of "unintelligible propositions." Clearly, as we have learned in this deconstruction of the Mormon faith, the core Mormon beliefs about 'God,' his putative Plan, and the concepts of 'revelation' and 'faith in God' *per se*, and as a 'way of knowing God,' would all certainly qualify as being *unintelligible propositions*, as would the core beliefs or propositions of all other theistic faiths. Moreover, and elsewhere regarding the necessity of ridicule, Joshi insists that "ridicule is an entirely valid enterprise…a welcomed tool to expose religious folly, hypocrisy, and injustice" (2000, 19).

II

Turning now to the remaining sincere questions concerning, as a whole, why I don't leave the Mormons and other theistic believers alone to worship their god and live their religion as they please, especially if they are not religious extremists or religiously abusive, I would answer first by asking certain follow-up questions in turn. Specifically, to all whose religious beliefs allegedly give them happiness, joy, purpose, meaning, guidance, comfort, and peace in their lives, I would ask: Happiness, joy, purpose, meaning, guidance, comfort, and peace on the basis of which *actual* truths exactly; of what specific, actual *worth* exactly; and at *what price* to society and to you personally? More specifically, happiness and joy on the basis of what *actual facts*? I would ask? A sense of purpose in regard to what *realistic* and *intelligible* end, or from what *factually intelligible* source? And guidance from *whom* exactly, and to what intelligible end and personal cost? And similarly, and again, comfort from *whom* exactly, or on what *factual basis*? Comfort by what *reasonably* or *demonstratively* reliable assurances exactly, and on the basis of what *intelligible* and *reliable* evidence? Likewise, peace in what sense exactly; of what *objectively determinable* value exactly; and on the basis of what *intelligible* and *reliable* assurances exactly?

If the most we can say in reply to the questions about *who* or *what* it is *exactly* that gives us such putative purpose, meaning, guidance, comfort, and peace is that it is 'God,' and his Plan of Salvation, then as we have learned in Chapters 3 and 4 of this book, we have said *nothing* of any factually intelligible value or import at all. If the most that can be said is that our religion provides us with 'The Way' and 'The Truth' to live our lives such that we might find such happiness and joy with 'God' and family in the next life, then we are faced with the incontrovertible fact that there is *not one shred of reliable evidence* that such a 'next life' could even *possibly* exist as conceptualized, if at all.

All of this, of course, boils down to one final question: If the allegedly supernal happiness, joy, purpose, meaning, guidance, comfort, and peace you say you enjoy on the basis of your religious beliefs are all based on the merely *wished-for* existence of a *factual non-reality*, which the Mormon and other gods are, then of what *real* worth are they?

Moreover, as we learned in Chapter 8 and the *Epilogue*, 'happiness' and 'joy' in the Mormon faith — or any theistic faith — is particularly elusive (if not utterly *illusory*) in *this* life given the abusive dynamic and corresponding pattern of the double-bind at play. The very notions of 'happiness' and 'joy' in *this* life are likewise purely subjective as well as psychologically suspect. They are certainly nothing (*sans* objective and widely accepted criteria for determining otherwise) so special or unique that we could not naturally enjoy them (to the degree humanly and personally possible) *without* religious belief, merely on the basis of our *created* meaning *in* life in relation to our significant experiences, our relationships with others, our work or vocation, and our own physical and psychological resources. Surely we must *all* at least intuit at some level that apart from what we would like to believe (or have deluded ourselves into believing), this life is truly all there is. We intuit that our 'immortality,' as Yalom (2008) puts it so well, is in the "ripples" of our lives (the way our lives are remembered and affect the still living) when we're gone. We realize that, following Freud's realistic assessment, the *most* we can hope to experience in this, our *only* life, given its vicissitudes and the relentless, random, and indiscriminating forces of nature, is a state of "normal unhappiness," punctuated at times with pleasure and relief, and the prospect of perhaps more consciously living and dying "in our own fashion."

As for the price of believing that which is utterly unbelievable without self-deception, there is indeed a steep personal and social price exacted by religious belief. At a personal level, the price is nothing less – at the highest level – than self-betrayal and abandonment, the loss and abdication of intellectual integrity and epistemic responsibility, and the corresponding negation of life. As Joseph McCabe, Atheist and former Catholic priest put it so well, "The more man puts into God, the less he retains in himself." This, as we have learned again in Chapter 8, and as has been attested to by so many former (and no doubt current) Mormons, is especially true in the Mormon faith *whether or not* one lives or practices it according to authoritative or official requirements and counsel, and the at least implicit or unspoken expectations of other believers in one's family, circle of friends, or congregational community.[197]

---

197 There are no doubt, as initially referred to in the *Introduction* and addressed again in Chapter 3, those members of the Mormon faith who believe in their own version of god and allegedly 'live the gospel' according to their own chosen standards. These so-called salad-bar believers pick and choose their own version of the faith that suits their life style while superstitiously keeping them comfortably and happily deluded in the false or incoherent beliefs that their god is real, knows their heart, accepts the way they live their religion, blesses them according to need, and hears and answers their prayers.

These believers (and they surely exist in every theistic faith) would likely argue that there is no egregious price to pay (if at all) for their beliefs, loyalty, and commitments to their god and their faith — paltry as they are. But I think they are sorely mistaken. There is a steep, though perhaps unacknowledged, price to pay personally if they have been exposed or indoctrinated in the faith at all through the hymns, talks, lessons testimonies, counsel, and even casual God-talk conducted in Church meetings, conferences, lesson manuals, interviews with leaders, inquiries and exhortations from concerned family members and loved ones, and even seemingly benign social conversations with other members of the faith. Such exposure conveys, in various forms, the explicit or implicit expectations of the faith and exerts, even if sincerely, lightly and lovingly, the stern requirements at the moralistic core of the faith, and the expectations and doctrinal requirements for worthiness and acceptance by the Mormon god and those who are, at least ostensibly, living the faith more truly and acceptably, or righteously.

For the selective, casual believer who is considered by orthodox (or scriptural) standards to be living the faith at a lukewarm level of socially or doctrinally expected commitment, the price is steep indeed if, for example (and as is the case for all Mormons who have been 'endowed' in the Mormon Temple and taken upon themselves certain binding covenants) he or she has been conditioned to believe (even if currently rejected) that their god expects them, among other things, to keep *all* the 'commandments of God' with 'exactness and honor,' and they know they fall far short of such commitment by action and desire. The price here is experienced or suppressed guilt, which can be manifested pathologically in many different ways, and which is typically allayed by the attempted self-assurance that 'one day I will repent' or 'God knows my heart,' both of which are betrayals of their guilt and lack of faith and commitment, and neither of which removes the gnawing, superstitious fear of an eventual day of reckoning, or the guilt which accompanies the lies they tell themselves and the excuses they make for betraying both their faith and themselves for living the lie which is their faith.

If, as another example, the lukewarm or *ersatz* believer inauthentically poses as being at least apparently faithful to the satisfaction of bishops, quorum leaders, home teachers, family, friends, and other church members, or resists doing so and thereby incurs the silent yet felt judgments of others who nonetheless persist in their seemingly innocuous though actually toxic encouragements, reminders, or more overt exhortations to greater commitment or righteousness. These explicit and implicit reminders, which are relentless and omnipresent (if you are part of an active church community) impose, at minimum, implicit judgments which deeply affect even the strongest minds over time, and erode the integrity and will of both the inauthentic poser and the independent rebel, breeding a deep, even if subconscious, sense of self-betrayal and self-abandonment, and the corresponding emotional exhaustion, depression, resentment and numbness which come with them.

In either and all examples, the put-on and sincerely attested to state of happiness of such an uncommitted

III

In addition to the initial set of questions and responses presented in the first two sections above, there are other likely questions to be sure. Three distinct types come to mind.

The first type might be the evasive *possibility* question "what if you're wrong and what I believe is right, or true?" This type of question is usually accompanied by the at least implied assertion "You don't know that what I believe *isn't* possible." Next might be the evasive question "how do you know that?" in reply to the above responses. This question, when offered defensively, may be translated — without the appearance of genuine curiosity or reasonableness — to the likewise evasive assertion "you don't *know* that your conclusions are correct or factual." Also, there might be the charitably defiant, dismissive, and deflective "so what?" questions which might be asked by those Mormon believers who would lead me, others, and even themselves to believe that even if they charitably grant the philosophical and psychological validity of this analysis and assessment of their faith, they don't really care about any of this, and that none of it matters to them, or is relevant to their personal faith. Let's take a brief look at each of the above three types of questions in turn.

The 'what if you're wrong and what I believe is right or true?' question was initially addressed in Chapter 2, and yet again, regarding my psychosocial assessment of the Mormon faith, in Chapter 8. Still, it is important to state here once again in the service of necessary redundancy that neither assertability, conceivability, nor imaginability establishes genuine possibility where (*i*) explicitness or specificity in relation to a particular concept (*e.g.*, 'God') exposes incoherence or factual unintelligibility, or where (*ii*) the believed existence of such a putative being, given its coherence as conceptualized, is incompatible with, or contradictory to, established (justified) knowledge about the world and universe and how they work, and/or where (*iii*) empirical 'facts on the ground' (*e.g.*, preventable suffering and premature death, the requirement of faith and faith-testing, unanswered prayer, erroneous and contradictory revelation, non-belief, wrong belief, *etc.*) contradict

---

(or selectively committed) believer is merely a defensive and inauthentic reaction formed to avoid the truth of their misery.

There is no escape for such a believer, either from the relentless authoritative pressure to repent and be more obedient and righteous, or the insidious and likewise relentless social pressure from family, friends, and fellow church members and believers to conform, to fit in, and be more committed to the prescribed way of life. The only options, if the believer chooses to remain in the faith, are to give in — to fit in or conform more fully with others' or their religion's expectations, or to remain true to his or her own needs and standards.

Either way, such believers are living a lie as long as they remain in their inherited or chosen faith. They are consequently not only deluded, self-deceived, and irrational in adhering to false and incoherent beliefs, but — protestations to the contrary notwithstanding — they are truly exhausted, weakened, and miserable as well by maintaining appearances. They are exhausted by failing to live up to (or dutifully living up to) their own and others' *conditioned* expectations, and for surrendering reason and rationality and forsaking — likely because of their own psychological woundedness, maladaptive beliefs ('stupidity'), and/or laziness — their *authenticity, intellectual integrity*, and learned sense of *epistemic and social responsibility*, as well no less their natural *commitment and loyalty to self*, including the inherent human needs for *individuation* and *integration*, and the *existential right* of all who are sentient, free-thinking human beings *to ethically live and die in their own fashion*.

All of these fundamental human needs are essential to well-being, and all the remaining fundamental human values and rights are also arguably important, to one degree or another, and whether acknowledged as such or not, in civilized and philosophically, psychologically, and otherwise scientifically enlightened cultures.

the believed nature of such a being.

For example, while we might be able to imagine or conceive of the possibility of a finite, material 'spirit personage' in the shape of a man, the *explicit* referents of such a being, *i.e.*, what *specifically* such a spirit being *actually* refers to, and what in turn such referents themselves *actually* refer to would not, as we learned in Chapters 1 and 3 among many other examples, be factually intelligible even if imaginable. Additionally, the alleged possibility of a "'finite, procreated being' who is fundamentally 'infinite and eternal' (which the Mormon god is doctrinally thought to be) is, as we also learned in Chapter 3 among many other examples, simply absurd or nonsensical — as well as flat wrong — for the simple reason that such a being would be conceptually *incoherent*, like a *round square* or *married bachelor*, and that which is incoherent is *impossible*.

Finally, even if it is given solely for the sake of argument that a particular god's existence as a being is not incoherent or factually unintelligible, and that such a god is, moreover, both imaginable and conceivable as a purely anthropomorphic being, we still have the problem of lack of evidence; and the common claim, if it is made here, that *the absence of evidence is not evidence of absence*, is a claim which in the words of Jonathan Adler (2006) "is false both in detail and in spirit," for "[o]ne of the most important ways we accumulate warrant for our beliefs is through *'absent' evidence*" (107). Apropos then to this particular problem, I shall repeat for emphasis an important excerpt from Chapter 2. This excerpt begins again with the words of Adler and concludes with an apt observation by John Loftus:

"Once the distinction between conceivability and *real* possibility is drawn," suggests Adler, "it becomes hard to understand how the two could be confused. One is about us and what we know and believe; the other is about the world (what's really possible in it). Nor is it apparent how a lack of evidence or possible verifiability against a 'possibility' can be recast as evidence supporting the existence of possibility. Steven Yablo rightly wonders, 'do I acquire evidence in *favor* of a proposition's possibility, by finding myself *without* evidence against its truth? That would be very strange, to say the least. Among other things it would have the result that there is a necessary limit on how bad my epistemological position can get: the poorer my evidence for *p*'s truth, the *better* my evidence for its possibility. ...Yet the fact is that I can be *completely* in the dark about truth and possibility simultaneously' (1993:8).

"In general, we cannot infer from 'It is not the case that the evidence shows that *p* is impossible' to either '*p* is possible' or 'The evidence shows that *p* is possible,' for, as we shall learn below, such inferred or asserted 'possibility' (taken by believers as sufficient reason to believe) is isolated from [actual or possible] testability and therefore, too weak to count as a genuine reason or evidence in support of belief, or to compel and sustain belief without self-deception" (110, 124). Moreover, the question of "possibility" in relation to what Loftus refers to as the theist's "merely possible defense" (*i.e.* the "retreat to the position that what they believe is 'possible,' or that it is 'not impossible' and therefore, they have a right to believe it) places his belief on "shaky ground" (2008, 61). "Why? Because," Loftus asserts, "we [as believers and nonbelievers, with allegedly so much at stake,] want to know what is [at least] probable, not what is [merely] possible" (61).

The second type of question ('how do you know that?'), when asked defensively, is clearly a *red herring* used to evade and discredit the issues and concerns in question (as well perhaps as the one making such claims). No answer is possible in such a case, because the inquirer has either tacitly assumed the incoherent position of *radical*, or universal skepticism[198] or is not truly interested in *any* reasoning or empirical evidence offered in support of the above responses or conclusions. In either case, *whatever* answers might in good faith be offered in reply to such an evasive question (and they would, I am quite confident, be sufficiently convincing to merit acceptance as being at least likely true by those who are not self-deceived or in utter denial) would essentially be met with the reply "and how do you know *that*?" and so on, circularly, to no productive end.

Last but not least, the third type of question ('so what?') referred to above would, notwithstanding the at least apparent charitable concessions made by the respondent, likewise be an evasive *red herring*. Absurd examples of such questions asked in the context of the analysis and assessment of Mormonism in this book might include:

---

198 Extreme, radical, or 'universal skepticism' is quite different from ordinary skepticism which requires merely that a truth claim be at least, in principle, justifiable (*i.e.*, intelligible, coherent, and factually meaningful) and, if justifiable, then justified through the processes of wide reflective equilibrium or, where indicated, rational demonstration through the process of methodological naturalism. The ordinary skeptic responds to a questionable, fantastic, foreign, or consequential truth claim first with an inquiry into the meaning and implications of the claim, then, if necessary, into its truth-conditions for confirming or disconfirming its truth (or probable truth) or falsity (or probable falsity), and finally into valid reasons (sound argument, confirmable expert testimony, or hard evidence) why such a claim should be accepted as actual truth.
'Universal Skepticism' alternatively is an absurd, incoherent (self-refuting) position which positively asserts (or at least implicitly so) that *nothing* can be known and there is consequently *no* knowledge, and that therefore one must doubt *every* proposition. As George Smith (1989) writes in summary: "[W]e have indicted universal skepticism on two counts: first, because it cannot be maintained without contradiction and, second, because it commits…the 'infallibilist fallacy' — *i.e.*, the equation of epistemological terms, such as 'knowledge' and 'certainty,' with a standard of infallibility, which is completely inappropriate [as well as incoherent] to man and to the science of knowledge in general" (143).
The question 'how do you know that?' might betray, again, a defensive application of universal skepticism if and when the questioner is committing the 'fallibilist fallacy.' Moreover, when such a question is asked by a *theist*, it is often used, even if incoherently, to play on human fallibility and with it reason and science, and make room in so doing for faith and revelation. In this way, such universal skepticism serves the believer as it makes room for an *infallible* source of truth, and the believed *infallible*, Absolute Truth of theistic dogma, as well as the necessity for faith as the *only* sure way of knowing. Finally, when used for none of these reasons, such a question is simply disingenuous, giving the appearance of regard for honest inquiry with the undisclosed intent of evading and discrediting the claims being made, or hypotheses being offered for consideration, without a fair hearing. (For an excellent treatment of the interdependent (even if uncomfortable) relationship between skepticism and faith, see Smith 1989, pp. 125–62. Here Smith argues to and from the conclusion that: "Christianity [including Mormonism and all other theistic faiths] thrives on faith, and faith cannot exist without skepticism. Skepticism is the precursor of faith; it paves the way for faith. Through denying the efficacy of reason, skepticism creates the need for faith. If faith is the epistemological underpinning of [theistic religion], skepticism is the epistemological underpinning of faith" (127–8). From an analytical perspective, such interdependency multiplies incoherencies, for all the implied concepts involved in this argument, *i.e.*, 'God,' 'faith,' 'revelation,' 'Absolute Truth,' and 'Universal Skepticism' are all incoherent. While Smith's observation is quite true at an abstract, opportunistic level, pragmatically it is a flawed alliance from the start, and provides no relief at all to the worthless concept of theistic faith. For this alliance to be fruitful theists must presuppose the existence of their god and the coherence of faith, revelation, and universal skepticism given the incoherence of their concept of 'God.' Such presuppositions are very problematical at best, and wholly invalid as premises in arguing for the need for faith as a legitimate way of knowing.)

- "*So what* if we believe as literally true that which is unintelligible, incoherent, or otherwise impossible in relation to our best knowledge about the world and the universe and how they work?"

- "*So what* if our beliefs as stated cannot, in principle, be known to be either true (or probably true) or false (or probably false) and are therefore factually vacuous as truth claims?"

- "*So what* if we can't reasonably justify (through 'wide reflective equilibrium' or otherwise) the truth claims of our faith, or if our doctrines and beliefs cannot stand up to rigorous analytical scrutiny?"

- "*So what* if certain of the Church's revealed or official doctrines and practices have changed over the years, or if what is taught today as truth differs from, or contradicts, some of what was taught as truth by other prophets or Church leaders?"

- "*So what* if we believe and have 'faith in God' even though we don't know what specifically the concept 'our God' means or what in our language the term 'God' *actually* stands for or refers to?"

- "*So what* if the teachings and practices of the Mormon faith are considered to be likely if not actually harmful to believers' well-being and dangerous to society?"

- "*So what* (in summary) if no one can answer all or any of the analytical questions you ask, or refute your stated concerns about the Mormon faith as a toxic belief system?"

At their face, these defensive, dismissive, and deflective questions are patently absurd as presented, although to the discerning ear they clearly reflect what is essentially (even if unknowingly and unintentionally) being said. Beyond therefore what the above questions are *literally* saying, what they and perhaps other 'so what?' questions seem in reality to be *really* asking is 'Why should I, or we, as Mormon believers care about these things?' Alternatively, they seem to be admitting — defensively, I think — that they *don't care*; that such matters are at least allegedly not important to them, and that they are happy with their religious faith and nothing can change that.[199] To answer such questions directly would therefore, as with the 'how do you know that?' questions presented above, likewise be fruitless, inviting even more 'so what, who cares?' questions in return. So I will try to answer them *indirectly* by instead asking the Mormon reader (or any theistic believer of similar bent) a different set of questions of perhaps more personal and fundamental importance in a *non-religious* context.

To start, I will ask if *personal well-being, intellectual integrity,* and *epistemic and*

---

199 Regarding this defensive admission in particular, see note 175. Regarding the matter of the alleged or asserted 'happiness,' well-being, and other salutary benefits attending theistic belief and religious living, see also notes 173, 176, 177, and 179 in Chapter 8, as well as the psychosocial assessment of the Mormon faith as a toxic faith in that chapter, and note 174 in particular regarding the insightful "Pattern of the Double-bind in Mormonism" discovered by yet another former Mormon, Marion Stricker (2000).

social responsibility are important? In other words, speaking now (and below) directly to *all* Mormon and theistic believers as one, is it important to you that people (yourself included) attend to their needs for emotional well-being and be true to themselves, or be personally honest about what they *actually* need, want, value, think, and feel? Is it important to you that people *actually* know what they are talking about when they speak of *actually knowing* something important to be true? Moreover, is it important to you, again in a *non-religious* context, *not* to believe something which is false or incoherent? Is it, in other words, important to you that mentally competent, mature adults think critically, be reasonable, and not regard illusion as fact?

Further, is it important to you that people — including you — who make consequential claims which others rely on be able to *support* their claims with *valid* argument and evidence? Is it, in other words, important to you that you and others be *responsible* in making personally and socially consequential truth claims, and not represent something as true which is *not* true, or which *cannot* possibly be known to be true by *any* widely considered and accepted method of justification?

Moreover, is it important to you that when it is reasonably demonstrated to people — again, including you — that what they believe is simply *wrong, foolish,* or *stupid,* that they have the good sense and courage to let go of such beliefs and not hold on to them stubbornly or because they are afraid of losing face, or are too proud or otherwise invested to admit they are wrong? Is it important to you that people (again including you) have the courage or character strength to at least critically and reasonably question or test (as a reasonably skeptical outsider) their own and others consequential beliefs which are reasonably and widely considered to be at least questionable and potentially, if not actually, harmful and dangerous to yourself and others?

To conclude, do you consider it important, as a rule, in a non-religious context, *not* to naïvely or irrationally believe or accept as truth *important* and *consequential* non-self-justifying statements of fact without sound, valid reasons and/or legitimate, supporting evidence for doing so? Relatedly, do you consider it important to critically question, investigate, or test *important* and *consequential* beliefs or truth claims *before* accepting and committing to them? Is it also important to you that people (yourself included) *not* irrationally or immaturely 'bury their head in the sand' when their beliefs are legitimately and reasonably challenged? Is it alright for them delude or deceive themselves into believing as true something that is false or incoherent, or psychologically harmful, damaging and potentially dangerous, just because believing it *feels* right and makes them *feel* good, or because they just *want* it to be true or are too fearful to determine or admit is isn't?

If the answers to the above questions would reasonably be considered to be *yes* in a *non-religious* context, then why not in a religious context as well? If these matters are truly important in either case, then the 'so what?' questions listed earlier are indeed merely defensive, dismissive, and evasive deflections. The answers to such 'so what?' questions, if asked, are apparent in virtue of what is admittedly important in these matters.

Here then, given the presumed affirmative answers to the above questions of personal value or importance, is my *indirect* answer to the 'so what?' questions above:

"*All that has been brought into question in virtue of this deconstructive analysis and psychosocial assessment of the Mormon faith is important — and crucially so — to you as a person and as a Mormon because*:

"(1) *You*, as an intelligent and thinking person *first*, admittedly think it is important for people *not* to neglect or jeopardize their psychological well-being or live a lie, but rather to be authentic and true to themselves by attending, without shame, guilt, fear, or apology, to one's needs, and to honor and respect one's true thoughts, feelings, and values for living in one's own fashion.

"(2) *You*, as an intelligent and thinking person *first*, admittedly think it is important *not* to cowardly 'hide your head in the sand' when your beliefs are reasonably and seriously questioned or challenged, or to be (or be regarded as) foolish, stupid, or too afraid to face the real possibility that what you believe to be true is in fact foolish and stupid.

"(3) *You*, as an intelligent and thinking person *first*, admittedly do *not* want to irresponsibly believe something is true merely because you *want* or *need* it to be true, or delude or deceive yourself into believing something as true which cannot possibly be objectively known to be true, or even probably true.

"(4) *You*, as an intelligent, thinking and *moral* person *first*, admittedly do *not* want to accept as truth the consequential non-self-evident assertions of others without sound, valid, and at least in principle, verifiable or falsifiable reasons. Nor, admittedly, do you want to *misrepresent* as true something which is reasonably and demonstrably deemed to be either false, or neither true nor false, and/or which can be reasonably be shown to be harmful to others, and even potentially dangerous to society.

"(5) *You*, as an intelligent, thinking and *ethical* person *first*, admittedly *want* to be both personally and socially *responsible* in determining or asserting what you know, and how you *legitimately* came to know it, particularly in matters of grave importance or concern to you or others.

Finally, because

"(6) *You*, as an intelligent person *first*, presumably (and at least implicitly) *value* being a rational and reasonably skeptical 'free thinker,' and therefore being nobody's fool."

For the above professed core values — if in fact they are regarded as such — to be qualified as being of subordinate importance (or not important) in a religious context would require some very careful, *non-arbitrary*, *non-a priori* and *non-question-begging* explaining. To argue, for example, as Kierkegaard and Luther might, that reason, rationality, intellectual integrity, and epistemic responsibility as suggested above are unimportant, irrelevant, and inappropriate in matters of faith; that essentially to believe is absurd, and the 'leap of faith'[200] in the face of patent absurdity is a virtue necessary for salvation, is,

---

200 "Actually," as Hitchens (2007) interestingly points out, "the 'leap of faith' — to give it the memorable name that Søren Kierkegaard bestowed upon it — is an imposture. As he himself pointed out, it is not a 'leap' that can be made once and for all. It is a leap that has to go on and on being performed, in spite of mounting evidence [and sound argument] to the contrary. This effort is actually too much for the human mind, and leads

as we learned earlier in Chapter 6, an incoherent, nonsensical, and dangerous position.

Dangerous too would be the assertion that in a religious context 'knowing is feeling' and one has only to *really* 'feel it' to know it. Of course, only 'true' feelings count, even though every mystic, spiritualist, and orthodox or conventional believer of *all* different faiths and beliefs allege to have true feelings attesting to differing and even contradictory beliefs and 'doctrinal truths' and religious practices. Even though there are no specific, non-ambiguous, generally accepted, and objectively confirmable or disconfirmable human criteria or truth-conditions to uncontroversially differentiate such varied feelings as being genuine or counterfeit, or to verify or falsify any such claims, significantly, *all* such feelings can be reasonably and most economically explained as purely naturalistic phenomena. In this regard, therefore, my earlier question stands: If the above values are not relevant or equally important *in a religious context*, why not?

IV

I would like to return again as promised to the matter of the aforementioned price paid for "believing that which is utterly unbelievable without self-deception." Perhaps in no other faith, save fundamentalist Christianity and Islam, is such a price so high, or such an onerous burden to bear as it is in the Mormon faith. For honest, informed Mormons intent on truly living their religion according to the dictates of their scriptures and the doctrinal teachings of their leaders, nothing or no one is truly ever *good enough*. Mormons are exhorted to *always* strive for 'greater light and knowledge' and 'greater righteousness and truth.' Mormons are to avoid complacency and 'moderation'[201] and be always 'anxiously,' 'selflessly,' and 'zealously' engaged in good causes and good works which 'bring to pass much righteousness.' Even the stalwart, righteous and faithful Paul in the *Bible* and Nephi in the *Book of Mormon* were shamefully self-critical of their own humanity, thereby making self-derision and continual repentance an indicator of personal righteousness and spirituality, and the faith itself an effectual double-bind which controls believers through shame and dependency on an illusory God whether they are faithful or not. (See Romans 7: 14–24 and 2 Nephi 4: 17–19 respectively.) In this regard, even the most righteous, faithful, and 'blessed' among the so-called prophets and 'latter-day saints' fall short of the draconian demands and shaming judgments and criticisms that

---

to delusions and manias. Religion understands perfectly well that the 'leap' is subject to sharply diminishing returns, which is why it often doesn't in fact rely on 'faith' at all but instead corrupts [the idea] of faith and insults reason by offering [invalid] evidence and pointing to confected 'proofs.' This [bogus] evidence and these [invalid] proofs include arguments from design, revelations, punishments, and miracles" (71).

201 In an address given at Brigham Young University in 1992 titled "Our Strengths Can Become Our Weaknesses," Mormon Apostle and General Authority Dallin H. Oaks said the following in relation to the idea of moderation: "[The] idea that our strengths can become our weaknesses could be understood to imply that we should have 'moderation in all things.' But the Savior said that if we are lukewarm, he will spue us out of his mouth (see Revelation 3:16). Moderation in *all* things is *not a virtue* because it would seem to justify moderation in commitment. That is not moderation but indifference. That kind of 'moderation' runs counter to the divine commands to serve with all of our "heart, might, mind, and strength" (D&C 4:2), to "seek . . . earnestly the riches of eternity" (D&C 68:31), and to be "valiant in the testimony of Jesus" (D&C 76:79). Moderation is *not the answer* (emphasis mine)."

are implicit in the moralistic core of their own faith, and all too often are explicit in the authoritative teachings and admonitions of Church leaders. Indeed, as James Joyce so well stated: "There is no heresy or philosophy so abhorrent to the Church as a human being."

At a social level, the price of believing is divisiveness and the very real threat to human life. This social price for religious belief is exacted by those conservative, fundamentalist believers of all theistic faiths who hold that *their* god's existence and mind and will have been revealed to *all* mankind in the inerrant 'Word of God,' and that such 'Absolute Truth' — confirmed by purely subjective and self- or other-induced affects that are entirely explainable naturalistically — is binding on *all* mankind as 'The Law,' or as 'The Way, The Truth and The Life.' Such a price includes the social intolerance of religious doubt, nonbelief, wrong belief, and disbelief, as well as the at least tacitly intended and desired oppression of free thought, moral imagination, human instinctuality and dissent through the imposition of guilt and shame, and the threat of social isolation and eternal damnation (or the forfeiture of eternal blessings) in order to establish and maintain mind-control and social conformity of thought and behavior. Religious belief requires by its very nature obedience, sacrifice and consecration as the price for the sought for blessings of joy, peace, abundance, and divine deliverance in this life and salvation and eternal happiness in the life to come.

But religious belief, as we know so well, also exacts a price on society through the political activism of religiously indoctrinated and motivated fundamentalists — and also through secular law-making and policy-making by our religious elected, appointed, and hired officials. Such societal laws and policies, and the activist forces which influence them, define and dictate what is to be regarded as right or wrong, good or bad, or permissible or forbidden in the 'eyes of the law' — which are really believed to be the 'eyes of God' according to the different believed books of revelation and their accepted authoritative or personal interpretations.

To those of more moderate or liberal religious persuasion who might argue that their faith and that of others brings to pass much good in their communities and the world, I would argue that such an argument is a *non sequitur* and ask why such religious faith is necessary beyond *natural* human compassion, empathy, and self-interest. How it is that nonbelievers or even militant Atheists can perform such social goods without *any* faith in gods? And to those same believers who might also argue that such a steep social price need not be exacted by religious beliefs on the basis that secular matters can be separated from religious concerns, I would counter that not only does history seem to confirm that just the *opposite* is the case, but that it is not coherent — given what we know about the nature of belief and how our beliefs work in our lives — to argue that we can entirely (or even at all) separate our most fundamental beliefs and corresponding judgments and motivations from our decisions and actions.

Metaphorically put, our beliefs are the lens through which we interpret and justify personal experience and action and interaction, as well as natural events, situations, and circumstances in the world and in our personal lives. They are also, together with their related values and felt certainty, the basis of human motivation and action. As Sam Harris articulated so well in a recent interview with Bill Maher on the program *Real Time*, "Religious beliefs cannot be kept separate. They intrude in public policy, [in education,] in politics and in science. Insofar as somebody believes something, it inevitably shows up in the world. Beliefs are the means to organize behavior and emotion" (8/23/2009; transcript and interpolation mine).

Clearly, when we learn of leaders of the world who interpret world events through, for example, the immoral lens of the Old Testament and the apocalyptic lens of the New Testament or other believed sacred texts, we are in danger. We suffer when leaders legislate secular laws in a religious context that subordinates human rights to what is believed to be 'God's Law.' We suffer when they legislate the teaching of religious non-science in our schools as though it were science, in order to uphold the scriptural versions of the creation of the world and religious beliefs concerning the origin of life and man on the earth. The consequences of religious belief in our world are significant indeed, and can and do threaten scientific progress and personal and social well-being, if not our very existence as a human race.

This is not mere hyperbole. When religious dogma and believed prophesy become secular laws and self-fulfilling prophesy, and when leaders and people of authority and influence in our society consider their sacred books as the *literally* 'revealed word of God' to *all* men, and see themselves moreover as instruments in the hands of their god and as having been *called* and *chosen* by their god to spread his word and do his work to realize his will on earth, then we are, to be sure, *all* in very real danger.

We cannot take comfort in the practice of religious moderation. For while the social price is perhaps not directly exacted by the simple, moderate, harmless believers of a self-constructed and equally incoherent tolerant, liberal, or fairytale faith of unconditional love and free salvation for all, the social price is nonetheless paid by them — and by others, believers or not, in some measure *because* of them.

The problem with desiring or calling for social tolerance of privately held religious belief on this basis is, as pointed to in the beginning pages of this *Personal Postscript*, that the private, moderate believer must also at least implicitly tolerate, if not tacitly support, the privately held religious beliefs of others, including the beliefs of more fundamentalist and extreme religious believers. Even if private, moderate believers eschew the actions, behavior or viewpoints of certain religious fundamentalists or extremists, they do not — cannot — dare eschew these extremists' *fundamental* (as distinguished from *fundamentalist*) religious beliefs in 'God,' revelation, and faith. To do so would necessarily bring their own fundamental beliefs into question. But, as we have learned and been repeatedly reminded, such fundamental religious belief is at the heart of the problem. To sidestep or fail to critically confront such a problem (and even harshly so, where indicated) — *i.e.,* the problem of fundamental belief in a god, revelation, and faith — so as not to invoke personal doubt or direct social criticism toward *all* such fundamental belief, including one's own, is essentially and *actually* to enable the very religious extremism eschewed.

Those who therefore challenge religious beliefs or are critical of them — or of those who hold them as truth — are not being mean. Nor are they inconsiderate or intolerant of either the human right to think, believe, or speak as one will, or the human need for purpose, moral guidance, and comfort in the face of life's vicissitudes. On the contrary, as I see it, Atheists are pointing to the *only* reliable resources we have in these consequential matters and troubled times. That is to say, the natural resources of reason, common sense, imagination (including *moral* imagination), psychological honesty, science, and the scientific method unfettered by denial, superstition, and wishful thinking — uncorrupted by the pursuit of power and political advantage. They are challenging believers to realize that by uncritically, unquestioningly, and stubbornly holding to their beliefs and corresponding meta-beliefs out of superstitious fear and misplaced loyalty, they are, in a very real sense, not only being irrational and epistemically irresponsible (which have their own very real personal and social consequences), but are complicit as well in exacting the steep price for holding and tolerating such beliefs. They are helping to extort a price for something that yields no *real* returns of *any* real value in the physical or social economy of man's existence.

Harris, I think, said it well in the concluding remarks of his previously referenced interview with Bill Maher: "We are in a war of ideas that needs to be prosecuted. We can be intelligent, educated people and still believe religious bullshit because nobody challenges it. … Religious belief is a social disorder; it's a conversational disorder"… and "we need to [face the fact that] we have a problem of good ideas *vs.* bad ideas… [and] overcome…the real double-standard that religious ideas can't be criticized."

V

Moving now more specifically to the Mormon faith, I will say up-front, as I did in the *Introduction* of this book, that at its darkest, most fundamental level — which is not, incidentally, the public side (or *persona*) of Mormonism which is presented to those inside or outside the faith — I think the Mormon faith, like the Catholic, Islamic, and all other fundamentalist, authoritarian Christian faiths, is paradigmatic of what I consider to be the very *worst* in *all* theistic religions. To be sure, *all* theistic religions are in my view an affront to man's rationality and intellect as incoherent belief systems built on superstition and metaphysical nonsense.[202] *All* theistic religions are also an affront to man's humanity. Because of the irrational faith they require and the inhuman, performatory and behavioral demands they make, they shamelessly and shamefully exhibit a disguised disdain for human reason, human nature, and human dignity through various forms of abusive boundary violations, including mind-control and the moralistic intrusion into the personal lives and choices of its adherents in the name of love and concern for their temporal and eternal welfare. Moreover, *all* theistic faiths are, in addition to being utterly absurd in content, ultimately regressive in nature and tend to weaken and disempower believers. They stultify, to one degree or another, their naturally mandated individuation and the necessary integration of their personality, keeping them dependent on Parent-Gods and parent-religious leaders, priests, or ministers — and thereby stuck at a low level of psychological maturity. Such, in part, is the personal price believers pay for their stupidity and *ersatz* or illusory happiness, meaning, guidance, comfort, and peace — counterfeit personal goods derived from projections, hallucinations, and illusions that become delusions to those who are conditioned to accept such illusions or wished-for beliefs as literal and absolute truth. These counterfeit goods moreover are given form, legitimacy, and force through religious indoctrination and the self- or other-induced and affective dissociative

---

202 In reply to G.K. Chesterson's published comment in 1908 that he found "…the moral atmosphere of the Incarnation [of God in Christ] to be common sense," and the "…established intellectual arguments against the Incarnation…to be common nonsense," S.T. Joshi correctly and appropriately observes, both in his critique of Chesterson and to all theistic believers of like mind, that "To one who has indoctrinated himself [or has been indoctrinated] into believing that there is some common sense in the world being flat, the notion that the world is round will naturally appear to be nonsense" (2003, 85).

trance-states which define their faith.

All of these characteristics and problems are, it seems to me, endemic to theistic faith in general, as are the innumerable abuses and atrocities performed in the name of a god, or according to a god's will, by religious zealots or extremists of all the different faiths. The fact that such abuses and atrocities sometimes are committed by atheistic ideologues as well is irrelevant. All moralistic ideologies which are either explicitly or implicitly built in error on the meta-belief of absolute truth, and which establish the notion that its adherents are a chosen or superior people, are ultimately religious ideologies, whether theistic or not. Pointing to Atheist despots or non-theistic fanatical ideologues and their like abuses and atrocities is nothing more than a *red herring* which neither nullifies the indictment against theism, nor lessens its severity. In fact, I think it can be and has been reasonably argued (and to my mind decisively so) that *all* theistic religions, including the Mormon faith, net of any putative personal or social benefits they might boast are more or less a blight on all societies.[203] But the Mormon faith, as it *is* (again, apart from its *persona*), and as I know it to be from the inside, multiplies both actual and potential harm, abuse, and danger in at least four rather significant ways.

The *first* way is through its *meta-belief* that it *alone* is the *only* true faith, that *all* other faiths, because of an alleged Great Apostasy, are false and 'an abomination before God,' and that the Mormon faith was *literally* restored by its inventor and founder Joseph Smith through divine revelation. Because of such revelation, the Mormon Church, and all of its official teachings, policies, programs, and practices are authoritatively founded on the 'rock' of *direct* and *progressive* revelation to this day and administered by alleged 'prophets, seers, and revelators' who supposedly have been called, ordained, and anointed by the Mormon god to preside over the Church as in times of old. This unique meta-belief is what I regard as the first *multiplier* of negative effects. It is the meta-belief of *exclusive*, *absolute,* and *actual* Truth because of, and in virtue of, *apostasy* and *restoration* through divine *revelation*.

The *second* multiplier is the unique and effective system of Mormon indoctrination presented in Chapter 8 and elaborated on below. This system, like all other theistic religions, promotes and fosters mind-control, intellectual atrophy, and epistemic irresponsibility by regarding faith as a legitimate way of knowing. Relatedly, it also undermines reason and intellectual integrity by establishing the regarded 'blessedness' (or pleasure) of subjectively interpreted feelings as final and authoritative arbiters or confirmation of truth or falsity.[204]

---

203 Here, again, I join with Nietzsche in condemning not just Mormonism, but Christianity and all theistic religions as, collectively and individually, "the greatest of all conceivable corruptions" which "[have] converted every value into its opposite, every truth into a lie, and every honest impulse into an ignominy of the soul." I, like Nietzsche, regard Christianity and all of its derivatives and theistic co-horts in crimes against humanity (including Mormonism, Judaism, and Islam) "the one great curse, the one enormous and innermost perversion, the one great instinct of revenge…the one immortal blemish of mankind" (2000, 106–7).

204 The null Mormon (and Christian) proposition — that through faith the resulting manifestation of spiritual feelings reveal or confirm the Truth of one's beliefs, or the teachings and truthfulness of one's faith — was addressed in some depth in Chapters 5 and 6, and by the reasoning of Nietzsche who I think correctly observed that "…there prevails among Christians [and also Mormons] a sort of criterion of truth that is called 'proof by [the] power [of faith, which]… is actually no more at bottom than [an incoherent] belief that the effects [and *affects*] which faith promises will not fail to appear. In a formula," Nietzsche continues, "'I believe that faith makes for blessedness — *therefore*, it is true' [or Truth]. … But this is as far as we may go. This 'therefore'

The *third* multiplier, also presented in Chapter 8 and the *Epilogue*, as well as in Elizabeth Tice's afore-referenced short work *Inside the Mormon Mind: The Social Psychology of Mormonism* (2001), is the Mormon recapitulation of the patriarchal family system, together with its abusive *code of patriarchy*, and the unique Mormon system of social commitment through ritual covenant-making and sacrifice. Through such social strategies the Mormon hierarchy ensures the loyalty of its members, even to the point of self-sacrifice and self-abandonment.

Finally, the *fourth* and last multiplier, which is also common to all theistic faiths, is, again, the *moralistic core* of the Mormon faith itself, a topic also treated in some depth in Chapter 8 and elsewhere. Again, this moralistic core shamelessly, though effectively, keeps Mormon believers in line with the Church program through what Stricker (2000) insightfully refers to as "the pattern of the double-bind in Mormonism" and the authoritative imposition of performatory, behavioral, and attitudinal requirements for both earning praise and reward, and avoiding shame, guilt, the forfeiture of blessings, and ultimate rejection and isolation in this life and/or the next. Moreover, on the basis of this moralistic core, believers in the Mormon faith are conditioned to experience the inflating effects of unwavering faith and obedience, and the depressive and shaming effects of doubt and disobedience or lack of commitment invoked, in both cases, by the at least implicit approval and/or disapproval of the *parent*-God and *parent*-Leaders of the Church, or their implicit and/or explicit authoritarian judgments of worthiness and unworthiness.

Each of the above unique multipliers essentially multiplies the effects of the others and they all together produce, to a greater extent, the potential, if not actual, harm and dangers inherent in the Mormon faith. Such is the foundation of my general case against the Mormon faith. Such an indictment, well-deserved as I consider it to be, therefore warrants and demands, in my analysis and assessment, the need for thoughtful, critical inquiry at least. In certain aspects of the faith it may warrant impassioned exposure, harsh criticism, and outright renunciation and denunciation as well.

Even so, returning to the initial questions asked at the beginning, beyond their religious attitudes, practices and beliefs, I have nothing against Mormons or other theistic believers *as people*, or as individuals *per se*. Nor am I intolerant of Mormon or religious believers *in the strict sense* of being unwilling to grant to them or share with them the fundamental right of believing as they choose or expressing their religious views. The Mormons and other mostly Christian believers I have known over the years have, for the most part, been pleasant enough people (at least socially), and have done no intentional harm to me personally that I know of.

My reasons for questioning, challenging, and at times even harshly criticizing them

---

would be *absurdum* itself as a criterion of truth. ... [C]ould blessedness — in a technical term, *pleasure* [or the so-called confirming feeling of revelation and/or confirmation] — ever be a proof of truth [much less 'Truth,' which is an incoherent conception, given the fact of human fallibilism]? ... The proof by 'pleasure' [or confirming feelings]," Nietzsche concludes, "is [*merely and only*] a proof of 'pleasure' [or some ego-syntonic or belief confirming feeling] — nothing more; why in the world should it be assumed [much less believed] that *true* judgments give more pleasure than false ones [or that false ones come with no feelings or disturbing feelings], and that, in conformity to some pre-established [and a priori question-begging] harmony [with the putatively revealed Truth from a god], they necessarily bring agreeable feelings in their train? — The experience of all disciplined and profound minds teaches *the contrary*. Man has had to fight for every atom of the truth, [and has more often than not been discomforted by its discovery]" (from *The Antichrist*, quoted in Joshi 2000, 202–3; brackets mine).

and their faith — as well as their thinking and motivations for believing — have nothing to do therefore with Mormons or believers as fallible human beings. Rather, my criticism has to do with the *implicit* denial of their folly and human fallibility (through their asserted sure knowledge of, and stubborn, unquestioning acceptance of their irrational beliefs as Truth). It concerns their explicit abandonment of human nature through both their *beliefs* and religious *attitudes* and *behavior*, as well as their beliefs and attitudes *about* their beliefs.

At a more specific and personal level, my reasons for challenging and criticizing the Mormons in particular (as well as my reactive attitude to them and other theistic believers) are rooted, it would seem, in the affront that they are (in virtue of what they stand for, espouse, and aspire to be) to *my* basic humanity. They are painful reminders, through their own adherence to the faith, of the systemic, institutionally and theologically administered shame inflicted upon me and experienced over many years as a practicing Mormon. To these two personal reasons, I would add a third: at a general, collective level there is the very real danger their beliefs pose to society and the damage and indignities their beliefs and attitudes so often inflict on the mind, body, and intellect of believers, unsuspecting investigators, and, more importantly, innocent and defenseless children.[205]

VI

To better understand the basis of my concern in this last regard, it might be helpful for the reader to understand, first, something more about the way Mormons indoctrinate their children (and each other) to their faith and way of life and, second, how they formally discipline or punish believers who have committed certain sins against their god and the Church. In the first instance, I will appropriate a few paragraphs from a recent book by Jack B. Worthy entitled *The Mormon Cult* (2008). The subtitle of the book provides, in brief, the necessary context and relevance to this personal postscript: "A Former Missionary Reveals the Secrets of Mormon Mind Control." In the second instance, I will refer to Worthy's published account of his personal experience as a participant of the Mormon disciplinary process; an account which is consistent in sufficient detail with the 1998 formal guidelines of the Mormon Church.[206]

In a chapter entitled "The Indoctrination Process," Worthy (an interesting name for a former Mormon missionary and returned Atheist) likens the Mormon indoctrination process to one of my favorite films,[207] *The Truman Show*. This film is, in Worthy's words, "a movie about a television reality show of the same name... [which] was filmed inside a giant domed studio the size of a small town. The town inside the dome was an artificial

---

205 These concerns and grievances are not restricted to the Mormon faith. To be sure, all authoritarian, theistic faiths are likewise dangerous, harmful, and damaging in virtue of the inherent abusive dynamics of their respective theologies.

206 Although the Mormon Church has taken action to prevent the circulation of their official *Church Handbook of Instructions* in the public domain, it is nonetheless available in the Internet to any who are interested in reviewing it. For access, *Google*: "Mormon church handbook of instructions."

207 Other films of note which also had an impact on me after I left the Mormon faith include: *The Island* (2005), *1984* (2003), *Pleasantville* (2004), *The Shawshank Redemption* (1999), *Dead Poets Society* (1998), *September Dawn* (2008), and both the original and recent remake of the series *The Prisoner* to name a few.

world in which everything, including the ocean and the sky, was human made. Truman, the first person lucky enough to be legally owned by a corporation, was born inside the town, and was raised to believe that the human-made, corporate-owned studio he lived in was a real and natural world. Everyone in Truman's life, his parents, his friends, and his associates, were all actors, each doing their part to create his false reality. Everyone except Truman knew that his life was a manufactured reality," and Truman was indoctrinated to believe, as his role-playing wife put it at the end, that "The Truman Show" 'is a lifestyle. It's a noble life. It is… a truly blessed life.' (15–16)

"Mormon indoctrination," Worthy correctly observes, "attempts to duplicate what was done in 'The Truman Show.' Rather than using the physical dome to separate Mormons from the outside world, The Mormon Show uses a psychological dome, locking Mormons safely inside a feeling-based reality. This feeling-based reality has to co-exist alongside a contradictory fact-based reality, so keeping the dome impermeable is no easy task…. (16)

"The Mormon Show uses a very effective three-step program of child indoctrination: first, indoctrinated parents are commanded to indoctrinate their children; second, parents and others who are responsible for teaching children are given detailed instructions on how to indoctrinate them; and third, they carry out the indoctrination. Mormonism then adds one key ingredient that makes the whole process of indoctrination work very well: Mormons teach children that the truth of Mormonism is proved through feelings. This means that no evidence is required, and that no amount of conflicting empirical evidence could ever prove the Church to be false. … [In other words,] Mormon children are raised to believe that… natural human feelings and emotions are the prompting of the Spirit [or revelation from 'God'], which is telling them the Church is true. They are taught that no amount of information [or no analyses] can trump these feelings, no matter how high its quality, how logical, how plentiful. Anyone who tries to persuade Mormons that Mormonism is untrue has been influenced by Satan and his followers to say such things. And Mormons who are tempted to consider any evidence [or argument] that disproves [or challenges the veracity of] the Church are *themselves* influenced by Satan. (17)

"This powerful and effective method of mind control links the truth of Mormonism to both pleasant and unpleasant emotions. Believers have been conditioned to feel anything from calmness to ecstasy when exposed to anything even remotely linkable to the Church's truthfulness. … And at the same time, believers are conditioned to feel anything from slight anxiety to outright panic when exposed to whatever church leaders have defined as bad. … Uncomfortable feelings come from committing (or even contemplating) a Mormon-defined sin, by reading what is, or might be, considered to be 'anti-Mormon' literature, be hearing someone criticize the Church or its leaders, or, more interestingly, by being in any cultural environment that is too foreign to allow Mormons to feel the Spirit, which is equated with the pleasant feelings above. (25)

"All of an indoctrinated member's feelings, both pleasant and unpleasant, are interpreted as a form of evidence that proves Mormonism to be true." Of course, as Worthy also correctly points out, "[t]hose who end up losing their belief in Mormonism… eventually discover that their feelings prove only one thing: humans have emotions that are triggered by any number of things for any number of reasons. They discover this when those feelings interpreted [previously] as being from the Spirit continue to manifest themselves even after they have left the Church. These feelings are not Mormon; they are human. The only thing unique about Mormon feelings is the frequency and intensity with which they are [experienced,] focused on and developed, as well as, of course, the interpretation they are given" (25–6).

Worthy's account of his experience with the disciplinary process of the Mormon Church and his resultant excommunication can be found in the last chapter of his book. As a missionary of the Church, he admittedly had consensual sex with a non-member woman and was sent home in disgrace where he was required to undergo a formal disciplinary process in his 'ward' and 'stake' (or geographic church congregations). The first step of that process is confession. That is where I will pick-up his account:

> When I told my stake president I had had premarital sex, he asked me who the girl was. I was surprised that he asked and wondered aloud if I was required to tell him. He said I was.
>
> I told him who the girl was because I believed I had to… I regret having done so for the same reason I regret having confessed anything to him at all: it was none of his business.
>
> A Church court was quickly arranged and I received a letter informing me of the time and date. I arrived at the chapel with my parents [missionaries for the Church are predominantly young men between 19 and 21 years of age who still live at home]. They were not allowed to attend the court so they waited outside in the lobby. My bishop escorted me in. I wasn't prepared for what awaited me. Filling the small room to capacity were fifteen men in suits and ties, standing around a conference table. This was standard procedure: "All three members of the stake presidency and all twelve members of the high council participate in a stake disciplinary council" (1998 Church Handbook of Instructions, p. 92).
>
> My court was a stake-level event, rather than a more local, ward-level event. That is because I was a Melchizedek Priesthood holder, and I was a likely candidate for excommunication. The Melchizedek Priesthood is [conferred through the laying on of hands by another authorized and qualified Melchizedek Priesthood holder and] held by virtually every Mormon male over the age of eighteen. A member of the Melchizedek Priesthood can only be excommunicated by the stake president. Everyone else, namely all women and children, can be excommunicated by their local bishop.
>
> I was escorted to the end of the table and stood there looking at all those men, and they at me. It was the most intimidating moment of my life.
>
> The first counselor of the stake presidency led the hearing. He instructed everyone to sit. He explained the charges, after which he asked me to confirm my guilt. After going over what I had confessed, I was then subjected to questions from all the men, as if I were at a press conference. The questions involved actions going back even before my mission and were mostly related to masturbation, pornography, and sex. I went through the robotic motions of the indoctrinated and answered them all, which is something I now regret very much. My hearing was a perverted and bizarre expression of power by some men over another — in this case, me.
>
> When asked, I chose to say nothing on my own behalf and did not plead to keep my membership… I was judged guilty based on my confession to the stake president. The sentence was excommunication. (164–7)

Beyond being understandably suspicious and interested, in retrospect, at the seemingly indignant and self-righteous tone and content of the stake president's closing statement regarding his own fidelity to his wife and the requirement that Worthy likewise fulfill the same requirement for maintaining a monogamous relationship, Worthy found it "even more interesting to consider" (as well he might) "the fact that, if he (the stake president) had held me up against Joseph Smith, I would have looked pure as snow" (167). As

Worthy correctly observes, on the basis of recorded history, "Joseph Smith was a man with sexual morals that would shock most people who approve of my having had consensual premarital sex. He had," Worthy states, quoting Quinn (1994, 89), "'sexual relationships with polygamous wives as young as fourteen, polyandry of women with more than one husband, [and] marriage and sexual co-habitation with foster daughters.' Considering the behavior of the Church's founder, it is ironic," or so it seems now to Worthy, "that I was judged unfit for membership because I had sex outside of marriage" (167–8).

Although I was (thankfully!) not raised in the Mormon Church, I did raise four children in the faith and can say unequivocally that Worthy's above account of the Mormon indoctrination process is accurate in every respect. From newborn blessings and baptisms to family prayer, Family Home Evenings, Sacrament, Testimony, and Sunday School meetings, and Young Men and Young Women lessons and gospel-centered activities during the week (not to mention periodic Ward, Stake, and General Conferences), children are indoctrinated into the Mormon faith and rarely escape the effects of such indoctrination, except to an outward state of 'inactivity.' Every activity and lesson — at home and at Church — is highly programmed and regulated by tightly correlated and centrally created teaching and member manuals, films, and other resources. Children are instructed as soon as they are able to talk in the proper way to bear testimony of the putative truths of the Mormon faith — 'truths,' as we have learned in virtue of the conceptual analyses performed in this book, which are neither justified nor justifiable. Such 'truths,' because they are unintelligible, incoherent, and factually meaningless as concepts, cannot possibly be understood by children or their parents.

Additionally, young boys and girls are taught at a very early age of the need to serve a mission for the Church and marry young, *only* in the Church and *only* in a Mormon Temple. Further, they are *expected* and *pressured* to do so through relentless social and authoritative admonition and counsel. This indoctrination process has been tried and tested. And it works well if done right. I know. Three of my four adult children were married in a Mormon Temple and are more or less active in the Church. My two sons served a two-year Mission for the Church and seem to follow the program, more or less. Only my youngest daughter, Tessa remains uninterested and turned-off by the whole affair, but I fear even she remains vulnerable to return to the fold if she does not do the hard work necessary to metaphorically inoculate herself from the virulent outbreak of the Mormon virus in her brain.

I did a good enough job of indoctrinating all my children (especially the three oldest), and where I might have been lacking, there were (and are) others — *i.e.*, leaders, advisers, teachers, home-teachers, friends, in-laws — to fill in the gaps and provide the needed pressure to remain steadfast in the faith. Sadly, though they would no doubt disagree, they never *really* had a chance or a choice, and now it would seem they will likely deprive their own children of such a chance and a choice as well. Hopefully, my decision to leave the faith, and my unqualified renunciation of it, will at some level give them the implicit permission they need to eventually challenge their beliefs and perhaps ultimately do likewise.

As for Church disciplinary action, I will say again, as alluded to in an earlier footnote, that to me the practice of such a disciplinary process — which allows Church leaders to violate a person's rights, boundaries, and dignity as a human being — is deeply offensive in principle and insulting and demeaning in practice. It is, along with the process and practice of indoctrination, characteristic and paradigmatic of what is, in my view, so harmful, damaging, and immoral about the Mormon faith, or any faith or religion which employs the same or similar processes or practices. In saying this, it is important preemptively to point out that while the *practice* of such processes is clearly performed by flawed and fallible human beings, the authoritative *processes* and related *policies* and *priesthood counsel* which mandate or at least implicitly condone such processes are believed by Mormons to be 'inspired by the Holy Spirit.' Stronger still is the notion that this all is at least implicitly condoned and approved by their god. They are, moreover, inextricably connected to the moralistic core of the faith established by its official doctrine and canonized scripture, making such processes and policies, though changeable, fundamental to the faith.

The inescapable conclusion, as I see it, is that while it might be apologetically claimed that honest mistakes are made by well-meaning Church leaders and members, such a claim does not take either the members or the Mormon faith off the hook. The theologically justified and mandated practices of indoctrination, judgment and discipline, and the systematic and relentless conditioning of believers by these practices in their homes and church communities, are extensions of the officially prescribed and sanctioned processes of indoctrination in the Church. They are extensions of the foundational moralistic core of the Mormon faith and the related doctrinal beliefs associated with it.

Does all of this make Mormonism a cult as Worthy and others suggest? As I see it as an informed former insider, whether we accept the formal definition of a 'cult' as: "1. A system of religious worship and ritual. 2. A religion or sect considered extremist or false." (*The American Heritage Dictionary* (Third Edition)) or, alternatively and more broadly, as *any* group which advocates a particular belief system as exclusive 'Truth,' and employs mind control and deceptive recruiting and retention techniques to obtain followers and keep them in the group, Mormonism would certainly qualify as such by any objectively informed outsider.

VII

Not surprisingly, given my personality, being a Mormon was never easy for me, even though I lived it faithfully for over twenty years. It certainly was not worth the personal price I had to pay then, as an active, faithful believer, or the price my children had to pay (with my help) and are still paying now as a result of the real and isolated damage inflicted by the teachings, conditioning, and culture of the Mormon faith and community in which they were raised, and of which three of them are still actively a part. This damage, of course, now extends naturally and inevitably to my grandchildren, as my children keep the destructive cycle going with their Mormon spouses and their Mormon families.

The damage Mormonism inflicts on the family and its members occurs subtly, and can easily go unnoticed to the naked eye or unreflective family members embedded in the faith. In a crucial way, Mormonism, like Christianity, has contradictory values when it comes to family and faith. In one sense these two fundamental values are deeply connected and interdependent. In another they are opposed and antagonistic — even mutually destructive. Where they paradoxically converge and diverge is in the loyalty of individual family members to the faith.

The fly in the ointment is the individual family member. For Mormonism to work as a family system fostering *genuine* love, acceptance, and connectedness *all* the members of the family must remain at least *in* the faith. To ensure this outcome *all* family members must be deeply conditioned to believe that the *only* way to happiness is living as a Mormon. But what happens if a member of the Mormon family is unhappy as a Mormon? As Worthy correctly writes in this regard, "Sadly members are taught to believe that Mormonism is right for every single human on the planet — that the Church is perfectly compatible with every person who has the good traits of human nature," and that "[i]f a person has trouble fitting in, therefore, there is something seriously wrong with that person. If a member is unhappy, unmotivated, or if their life seems meaningless or unfulfilling, the solution is always the same: they need to [repent and] be more diligent in obeying the command-ments and carrying out their Church duties. This is the only path to happiness, they are told. The irony, however," Worthy rightly concludes, "is that it is the same path that led to their unhappiness" (50–1). In other words, the conditioning must reframe unhappiness as rebelliousness or sinfulness, or as the result of a way of life which must be repented of to restore the natural happiness lost.

Regardless of what might be said to the contrary, and contrary to its espoused values, Mormonism can and does divide and damage family relationships. This it does by making the family identical *with* the faith, and then subordinating family relationships *to* the faith. In his afore-referenced book *Becoming God's Children* (2010), Faber accurately addresses the subordination of the family to the faith when he writes: "Jesus makes it very clear to His devotees [(Christians and Mormons alike)] that… [they] do not merely owe Him their absolute allegiance. … they must substitute Him for their own real mothers and fathers. They must 'love' Him more than their own parents, and if they are parents, they must love Him more than their own children:

> I come to set a man at variance against his father, and the daughter against her mother. … He that loveth father or mother more than me is not worthy of me; and he that loveth son or daughter more than me is not worthy of me. (Matt. 10: 35, 37; see also Luke 14: 26)

"Jesus declares in effect that He's the crucial one, not the parent or the child [or siblings]. … So much for familial loyalty, familial order" (14).

This subordination of family to faith has been experienced in numerous cases, notwith-standing the sincere professions of love and acceptance by those family members still in the faith toward the family member who is no longer in the faith. How could it be otherwise when, in any case, the 'differentiated' family member who has conscientiously or otherwise 'left the fold' (not merely become 'less active' or 'inactive') was once a faithful believer, or at least somewhat active in the faith? Such a person, as a nonbeliever or disbeliever, is now at least tacitly or subconsciously considered to be a misguided, faithless outsider, particularly in families which have tacitly if not openly defined themselves as a good *Mormon* family and are identified personally and as a family with Mormonism, as being 'Mormons first.' With the departure from the faith of any member of an entirely *Mormon* family the family system is disrupted and is no longer in balance (abusive or dysfunctional as such a 'balanced family system' might be).

The Mormon faith is designed to create and sustain such identification and cohesion where the very idea of *family* is made identical, through relentless doctrinal conditioning, to *Mormon family*, and where the primary Mormon value for the family translates to the primacy of the *Mormon* family. As a natural outcome of such conditioning the insiders experience ambivalence toward the outsider, who, while remaining a 'loved'[208] member of the family, is also a *prima facie* threat and painful reminder to the insiders that belief is not always protected by faith; that faithfulness is not always sufficient to protect against the commission of 'sin' or loss of faith; that something is or might be seriously amiss or broken in the family (and therefore, by association, in *all* its members); and that the outsider is, lamentably and necessarily (by definition), an unrepentant 'sinner' who is a negative reflection on the *Mormon* family and a social blemish on its status in the Church. Furthermore, when the outsider has joined another faith or has, as I did, returned to his or her natural Atheism in opposition to *all* theistic faiths (including Mormonism) and their teachings and practices, the experienced ambivalence and sense of disconnectedness is even more pronounced. Strong family attachments and loyalties now conflict with Church attachments, loyalties, ambitions, and commitments, and the strain on once intimate relationships can be palpable, and unavoidably divisive and damaging.

Of course the Mormon faith provides its own solution to the problem it has created by deliberately making *family* and *Mormon family* identical. The 'Mormon family' can be restored to a 'fullness of joy and happiness' *if and only if* 'wayward outsiders' (or inactive insiders) repent and actively return to the fold. In this solution, coming back to the Mormon faith as an active member in good standing with the Church is *identical* with coming back to the *family* in 'full fellowship.' And what is the duty of the 'faithful insiders' in applying this solution? Seek *to get* the wayward or departed family members back in the faith where they belong, so everyone can all be happy again (if they ever truly were) as a *good* Mormon family. How? By praying for their return and 'loving them back' to the fold.

This solution, similar in intent and form with prescribed 'friendshipping' and 'fellowshipping' practices in the Mormon Church, usually comes with a hidden agenda, some specific and typical counsel — and implicit, parenthetic (and of course denied) qualifications. First, accept wayward family members as 'children of God' and valued members of their 'Mormon family' of origin — but *not* for who they are or have become as individuated individuals, and not the 'inactive life' they have chosen, or worse, their decision to leave the faith. Also, continually invite them to be an active part of your life and the Mormon family to which they belong — but do *not* consider yourself a part of *their* non-Mormon lives or family. Finally, and importantly, keep the lines of communication open, but do *not* seek to really understand why they left the faith or are not actively involved. Above all, do *not* open your mind to their questions, doubts, or views and arguments against the faith). In other words, love them with the conscious, tacit — or perhaps even subconscious — 'collective motive' to *get them back in the faith* and therefore restore balance to the destabilized *Mormon family system*. This of course is how all co-dependently enmeshed patriarchal family systems work, where members have not individuated or differentiated

---

208 The fact that deconverted family members who have left the faith are still loved or deeply cared about is not at issue. In truly loving Mormon families, love likely remains, where such love is characterized as natural affection, care, and a natural responsiveness to need. Such love, however in a Mormon family, is typically disconnected from a sense of real intimacy. It is this disconnectedness, or profound sense of being disconnected from the family at a fundamental level that constitutes the real damage to the family caused by a religion that effactually makes families identical with, and subordinate to the faith. In such families relationships among believers and nonbelievers or disbelievers are likely experienced by all as being generally civil and friendly, though superficial, strained, and awkward, if not at times contentious.

from the system and are conditioned by the system's dynamics and code of patriarchy not to do so. The fact that the Mormon faith exploits such a pathological condition (knowingly or not[209]) is, in my view, deserving of exposure and criticism — if not contempt.

At a personal level, what is so sad and regrettable to me is that as a once religiously committed Mormon believer, father, member of the priesthood, and local priesthood leader, I allowed myself to suffer for so long, without question or objection, the systematic insult to my intellect, personality, and fundamental nature inflicted by the authoritative (and authoritatively administered) expectations, prohibitions, and judgments inherent in the moralistic core of the Mormon belief system. By so doing I essentially abandoned myself and condemned myself to a life of servitude to an illusory Parent-God in pursuit of illusory or wished for promises of redemption and divine power, acceptance, and approval.

Moreover, I was certainly complicit, as a father, church member, and missionary, in the perpetuation of this harmful, damaging, and potentially dangerous faith. I was, as alluded to in the previous section, shamefully among those of whom Christopher Hitchens writes (2007) who "beguile[d]" and "terrif[ied]…children…with [illusory promises of unintelligible and factually vacuous 'blessings' and] horrific visions of apocalypse, to be followed by stern judgment from the one who supposedly [loves us and] placed us in this inescapable dilemma to begin with" (58). Perhaps even more egregiously, by practicing such faith I, no doubt like so many other devout believers, became one of the offended who becomes the offender. The more faithful and zealous I became in the Mormon faith, the more critical I became toward myself. The more extreme I became in my behavior, the more judgmental, critical, controlling, and at times shaming by attitude and words I became toward others — including my own family — because of my judgment of their lack of faith and faithfulness.

That I did what I sincerely believed to be right and true at the time is of little consolation for the sadness, regret, and shame I feel at times. Nor am I consoled by knowing how 'human' it is to be superstitious, or how 'natural' it is to believe in gods and care enough about one's children to 'raise them up righteously before the Lord.' After all, there are many natural and very human acts (including all social taboos) that are considered in Western civilization to be immoral, inhumane, and criminal in nature, and avoidable through reason and self-restraint by all but the utterly insane. Moreover, such harmful, hurtful and dangerous acts are often accompanied by harsh criticism and social consequences. At very least we angrily chasten those who irresponsibly engage in such behavior with disapproving words such as "Shame on you! You know (or *should* have known) better!" We all know this and likely consider such chastening appropriate. Yet we consider those who believe in a god and practice their religion to be different, and exempt from similar social criticism and chastening when they commit acts of authoritarian abuse through mind-control and other forms of oppression. But why is this so? Such violations are likewise harmful, damaging, and at least potentially dangerous and destructive to self and others.

---

209 Ignorance of family systems theory, if claimed, is neither a legitimate excuse nor excusable in this regard. Such knowledge regarding the nature, workings, and pathological dynamics and effects of the family system has been, after all, common knowledge in the public domain for some time. It is widely known and accepted among mental health professionals, and is easily accessible to Mormon leaders, psychologists, and members. See for starters Bradshaw 1988, 1995 and his sources; Napier and Whitaker 1988; Gerson 1996; Miller 1981, 1990; and, more definitively, Kerr and Bowen 1988. See also the *Epilogue* in this work regarding the code of patriarchy within the family system which shames and thereby binds believers to the Mormon faith.

Those who are epistemically irresponsible misrepresent the truth to their own or others detriment or harm. They do not exercise intellectual due diligence and are therefore guilty of at least gross incompetence and negligence. They too know better. The fact is, in my case, I *wanted* and *needed* to believe in the Mormon god and in the Mormon narrative of restoration and exclusivity as the only true Church. I did not heed my real doubts or think critically or morally about what I irresponsibly accepted and asserted as 'True,' or practiced as 'right.' Moreover, I wrongly and selfishly put my own commitment to the faith ahead of my own children — ahead of their welfare and mine. The fact is, I *irresponsibly* represented to my vulnerable, impressionable, and intellectually defenseless children (and many others) the harmful, damaging, and potentially dangerous and destructive beliefs of the Mormon faith *as Truth*, and I did so repeatedly, with the sincere and at times severe exhortation that they hold them as such without question or doubt.

It is true that such believing, teaching, and exhorting is natural to the Mormon or theistic form of life. And it is also true that such religious practice is part and parcel of being human. Even so, it is epistemically irresponsible, and therefore immoral, to represent as truth (or worse, 'Absolute Truth') consequential beliefs which are not only false and/or incoherent, but are harmful and potentially dangerous and destructive to the believer and society. The fact is, I should have known better. I should have listened to myself, to my own questions and real doubts. I should have been more critically reflective and skeptical about my religious beliefs and the teachings of the faith. And, I should have kept my beliefs to myself and kept my mouth shut until I could make rational sense of my beliefs and analytically resolve my doubts as a reasonably skeptical outsider, just as I would normally do in considering *non*-religious truth claims that didn't make sense or seemed too good to be true. But I didn't, and for that I am guilty as charged.

Of related sadness is the profoundly troubling realization — that came to me, as perhaps with others in a like situation *after* 'breaking the spell' of my faith — that in looking back over the many years I was active in the Mormon faith, and notwithstanding all the pleasant, comforting, and even, on occasion, inflating and 'ecstatic' feelings I experienced in virtue of my own conversion and indoctrination, I truly cannot recall how much of my life I truly enjoyed. More specifically, I cannot recall how much of what I did in my 'duty to God, family, and Church' I truly *wanted* to do, instead of doing it out of some sense of duty or for self-approval and the achievement and preservation of acceptance by, and approval of, a Parent-God and parent-Church leaders.

Essentially, my shame-based neediness, masked even from myself as religious commitment and devotion, drove me, as did my natural human needs for belonging, esteem, status, recognition, and power, to metaphorically sacrifice myself on the altar of superstition and wishful thinking. Looking back, I honestly do not know how much of my life was really mine, how much of what I did as a person, husband, and father I did because it was expected or required of me as a faithful member of the Mormon Church and Priesthood, or because I wanted to do so and truly enjoyed doing so.

In retrospect, I can recall with prominence only four memorable experiences during this period of religious bondage in which I *authentically* lived my life free from delusion and self-deception and did what I *truly* wanted and needed to do and not what was merely expected or required of me, doing it out of need for acceptance and approval and the avoidance of neurotic guilt. Although these experiences culminated in decisions which in the end had to be made, given the determining conditions, I *experienced* them as *mine* for *me*. I was not experiencing 'spiritually confirmed' rationalizations, or ego-syntonic, face-saving responses to religious or cultural expectations and moralistic imperatives or institutional *shoulds* or *oughts*.

The first memorable experience culminated in my final psychological deconversion from the both the Mormon faith and theism. While religious deconversion, like conversion, typically occurs gradually over time, it is often initiated, completed, and confirmed by certain significant and memorable experiences. Such was the case for me in my conversion to the Mormon faith, my complete conversion to Christ (See *Appendix A*), and my deconversion from both Mormonism and theism. In each case I had certain initiatory, consummating, and confirming experiences over time. All of them were of course subjectively and incoherently interpreted from a conditioned religious perspective. I remember them completely and vividly to this day.

My deconversion from Mormonism and theism again occurred gradually, but was completed ironically while I was kneeling in prayer during the final crisis of my faith. I say ironically because the very first prayer I uttered regarding the Mormon faith, and which initiated my conversion to Mormonism, was also a memorable experience, but for very different reasons.

Having been taught by Mormon missionaries the lesson on living prophets and the story of Joseph Smith's alleged 'First Vision' which began the believed restoration of the only true Gospel and Church of Christ on the earth and established him as the Prophet of the Restoration, I admitted at the time that the idea of a restoration through a prophet made sense the way the leading questions in the discussion were set-up and presented.[210] Still, I distinctly recall having some reservations about the claim being made. It seemed a bit far-fetched to me, even if provocative as a possibility to be entertained. Perhaps sensing my underlying skepticism, I was, as all investigators are, challenged and encouraged to pray for a confirmation of its truthfulness and I was promised, through the authority of scripture, that if I prayed with a 'sincere heart' and 'real intent,' having 'faith in Christ,' 'God' would reveal the truth of this claim to me by the power of the Holy Ghost and I would feel such a confirmation as a 'burning in my bosom.'

Interestingly, I accepted the challenge with some anxiety. That evening, while alone in my bedroom, I knelt to pray as invited. I prayed as sincerely as I could, the way I had been taught by the missionaries to pray. And I prayed specifically to know if what I had been taught was true and if Joseph Smith was indeed a prophet.

---

210 This Missionary discussion, as I recall, was built on the premises that: (1) there is a 'God'; that (2) 'God' had called and spoken to prophets according to the Bible; that (3) the Bible is literally the 'word of God'; that (4) 'God' set-up his Church through Jesus Christ in the meridian of time; that (5) Christ's Church ultimately fell away from the truth in what is referred to by Mormons as 'the Great Apostasy'; and that (6) 'God' needed to call a prophet, like all the other prophets of the Bible, to ultimately restore his Church on the earth in "this, the last dispensation of the fulness of times" for the salvation of man. Presupposing the truth of all these premises on the basis of the core premises 1–5 above, and given my familiarity with Christian terms and beliefs, it seemed reasonable at the time to at least tentatively accept that Joseph Smith might possibly be, as believed and attested to by the missionaries, the one "foreordained from before the foundations of this world" to be the 'Prophet of the Restoration' as allegedly prophesied in the Bible. The problem, of course, in retrospect, is that such a conclusion (that Joseph Smith is the prophet of the Restoration of a god's one and only true Church) is based on an invalid argument which blatantly and, I think, disingenuously begs the primary question at issue, *i.e.*, that god's putative existence — an alleged fact which I superstitiously accepted and never questioned.

I felt nothing, so I prayed harder and with greater intensity. Still no answer or feeling of confirmation as promised. I distinctly remember — and this is particularly significant given my personal disclosures about my physical and psychological condition at the time — feeling some anxiety: *not* that I wasn't getting the answer I *wanted* (which is also significant), but that perhaps something was *wrong* with *me*, or that *I* was doing something wrong which was blocking 'the spirit.' I persisted with even more intensity, determined to get not really the truth but rather the answer I *wanted* — the answer that would please the missionaries and confirm that I was one of the elect who recognized the Truth of the Restoration when presented with it — the answer that promised to bring the healing I needed.

Finally, I stopped praying and just knelt in silence, waiting for something — anything — that would confirm the truth I was taught. After several moments had elapsed, a thought came to my mind in these exact words: "*Get up off your knees; you already know the answer to that question.*" At the time, I did not even think to question the *source* of such an expressed thought, or even to ask the obvious question: "What answer?" Looking back, the thought was clearly *my* thought; the words were *my* words; and the 'answer' was what I *did* in fact know at some level *before* I debased myself by participating in this strange, demeaning, and incoherent ritual: That *none* of it was true. Still, I chose to *interpret* my thought as a 'revelation from God' which confirmed what I *wanted* to hear — what I *wanted* and *needed* to be true. My neediness distorted the message and made the unwanted truth ambiguous and open to interpretation. It provided an interpretation that served my *ego* and my *neediness* at the expense of what I *truly needed*.

With this brief account as context, I return now to the aforementioned *deconversion* experience involving my prayer during the final crisis of my faith — and to the irony which will soon become evident. As a result of my personal crisis of faith, I had exerted myself to the limit of my personal resources — which had naturally atrophied over time due to my regressed state of religious dependence and subjugation to 'God' and Church authority — and I was praying for peace, comfort, and understanding.

Upon completing my petition, the following thought came to awareness with compelling force and clarity: "*Stop praying, get off your knees, and live your life as a free man on your own two feet.*" This thought dawned on me like all my other believed answers to prayer, only this time the message was radically different. I realized then, in virtue of this experience, what I stated above in relation to my initial experience with prayer: that *this* thought, like all the other putative answers to prayer I had received over the years, including the ambiguous, so-regarded answer to my very first prayer, was not a revelation from the Mormon god or any Jamesian transmundane being, force, or agency. It was, once again, a thought just like all the others that came merely, and *exclusively*, from *my* brain, *my* mind, as exclusively *my* thought.

Beyond being clear, compelling, and unambiguous, this thought was unexpected. It had a felt force of integrity and liberation that all my other manufactured thoughts had lacked — notwithstanding the experienced, self-induced affects that are naturally and naturalistically evoked by the conflation of personal neediness, language, and the ritual of prayer. This force can only be likened to the impact of a profound, personal realization of some fundamental and self-evident, personal truth. The personal and powerful realization in this case was that there was *no* god and *no* divine revelation. *This* prayer, like *all* prayers, was merely a pious exercise in self-talk. It was a regressive, superstitious habit motivated by personal insecurity and authoritative conditioning as something that *should* and *must* be done to be righteous, worthy, protected, and otherwise 'blessed by God.' With this thought and realization I remember also, and distinctly, also realizing how silly, stupid, and pathetic this was. Rhetorically I asked myself, in so many words, "what are you doing here?!"

Immediately upon having this experience, I stopped what I was doing and stood up. I have not prayed again — or even thought of praying — since then. It was over.

I was finally, and ironically, *deconverted* and freed from my self-imposed religious bondage in the same way that I had consigned myself to such bondage over two decades earlier — by the compelling thought to "get off my knees." Only this time I understood what I was trying to tell myself. In retrospect, these realizations seemed directed and informed by a personal need and insight: the need to separate and become a more mature and integrated personality, and the insight that my crisis of faith had all been necessarily orchestrated by unconscious forces and dynamics at play while fighting for my psychological survival.

My second authentic experience came afterward, after deciding to end my marriage and leave home to start my life again. This was a difficult decision that came after enduring years in a loveless and mutually suffocating marriage. I was dying emotionally in my marriage, and so was my ex-wife. I had reached the point where I needed to leave to survive. I struggled with how to tell my children and knew how difficult it would be for them if I left. They were still very young and had already no doubt been wounded badly by the tension in the home. One day, after taking my oldest son TJ to baseball practice (he was about 13 years old at the time), I paused outside my car after dropping him off and watched as he walked away from me toward his teammates. As I watched him walk away, his head bowed, I thought I sensed the weight of the tension in the home on his little shoulders and how sad he was at the thought that I might go away. I then thought about how sad my other three children would be if I left home with them at this tender and vulnerable stage of their lives. As I thought about TJ and my three other children, I decided then and there to stay for *him*, for *them*, and for *me*. I stayed seven more years — a decision *I* made, a decision I never regretted.

The third profound, authentic experience I remember was finally ending my marriage and divorcing my wife of twenty years, in spite of my personal insecurities and culturally and religiously imposed guilt. The fourth authentic experience was when I formally resigned from the Mormon Church by requesting that my name be removed from its records and I returned to my natural Atheism — an act that forced me to confront the final vestige of religious superstition. Apart from these four experiences, nothing else stands out as having been a genuinely *authentic* expression of what *I* had wanted and *needed* to do instead of having done it because it was expected of me, or because I had been conditioned to believe it was 'right.' Rather, it was to be done because *I* truly wanted and needed to do it — and I knew it was right *for me*, independent of my conditioned, superstitious beliefs and motivations.

I had lost myself for those years, and though arguably some good might have come from my so-called and so-regarded faithfulness or righteous efforts, I cannot explain the profound sadness I now feel looking back at how I had abandoned myself for so many years. I can only say that when being oneself is not enough — when being simply human is not good enough — then sadly *whatever* one does is a waste of life and a sad rejection of oneself. The self-alienation and self-rejection I experienced to earn my way to 'the highest degree of Glory in the Celestial Kingdom' of the Mormon heaven is at once an exposure of my own shame-based personality at the time *and* an indictment of Mormon theology and the related practice of Mormonism. Mormon theology — like Judeo-Christian and Islamic theology — in concept trades on guilt and shame and the need for revelation, faith, repentance, obedience, and self-sacrifice through 'self-less service.' Such theology does so, as I see it, to effectually control the minds and behavior of the respective religion's adherents, thereby alienating them from themselves and from their own unacknowledged needs, wants, thoughts, doubts, feelings, and emotions as well. It makes them regressively dependent on an illusory Parent-God and on Parent-Church leaders for acceptance, approval, protection, deliverance, forgiveness, and the illusory promise of salvation and eternal life. All this notwithstanding, the Church is widely and well regarded for its 'positive social values' and 'commitments to family and society.'

There are many Mormon believers who would no doubt read the foregoing retrospective account of my previous experiences in their faith with mixed thoughts and emotions and perhaps feel a believed genuine sadness that such experiences and views were and are so distorted from the way they think they know and experience *their* faith or how they perceive their faith to be. Such a reaction to this personal account, as with the personal analysis and assessment of my conversion to Jesus Christ included in *Appendix A*, is of course as predictable as it is inauthentic and dishonest. Dissociation is a powerful defensive mechanism against the anxiety and suffering we experience because of our shame, guilt, and fears. So too are denial, selective inattention, dismissive deflection, and rationalization.

Clearly my painful and difficult experiences in the Mormon faith — both as the offended and as an offender — are likely more representative than many culturally conditioned and self-deceived believers would care to admit. But our condition, while often not consciously acknowledged or confessed for what it is until after the fact (and even then often only through facilitated insight), is nonetheless betrayed, as Freud and many other renowned psychodynamic psychotherapists affirm, in innumerable ways. It is betrayed through our experienced anxieties, doubts, dreams, fantasies, wishes, and slips of the tongue. It is betrayed by our words, jokes, and what we laugh at or cry about. It is betrayed by our moods, feelings, emotions, behavior, physical and emotional ailments, and relationship problems. It is also betrayed in our compulsions, reactions, projections, and defenses. It is betrayed by our resistance to self-analysis and our evasions of truth regarding our beliefs and the existence of our real doubts.

All the indicators of the harm done through a given theistic faith or belief system are plain to see with a trained eye or by those with the proverbial 'eyes to see.'[211] Dismissing (even with apparent sincerity) the honest, analyzed account of a former believer's experience in their faith as merely sad and misrepresentative (or perhaps as indicative of unrepented sin) is, in my view, psychologically suspect — given, at minimum, the established commonality

---

211 As renowned American psychologist Nathaniel Brandon correctly put it, "Anyone who engages in the practice of psychotherapy confronts every day the devastation wrought by the teachings of religion" (Huberman 2007, 51–2). This would most certainly apply to the teachings of Mormonism as well. But one does not have to be a psychotherapist to see such psychological devastation. One only need be psychologically informed and psychologically-minded by disposition and orientation.

or universality of all that is suffered personally.[212] It is suspect as well, given any anxiety that might be experienced by such sincere, dismissive believers when reflectively hearing or reading of such accounts, or when challenged directly regarding their own doubts and ambivalences in relation to their own faith and church leaders.

Such anxiety, if honestly acknowledged, would likely also be indicative of the aforementioned *conditioned fear response* introduced in Chapter 8 regarding the question of why faith persists, referred to again briefly in the *Epilogue* in connection with wounding inflicted by the intentional or inadvertent authoritarian abuses committed by parents or parent-leaders (*i.e.*, ecclesiastical authorities) of the patriarchal family system and all theistic faiths. The conditioned fears associated with the threatened mortal and believed eternal consequences of known and/or suppressed or repressed doubts and ambivalences (or feelings of offense, anger, disappointment, and hatred) would be triggered by such anxiety. They unconsciously would alter or convert in the believer the feared and painful *truth* regarding such conditions and affects (as well as the underlying truth of the hurtful acts which caused them) into the acceptable *lies* of personal exception or exemption, of warranted and benevolent chastisement or character building, or of necessary faith testing sanctioned by a loving Parent-God.[213]

In fairness, there is to be sure much to positively acknowledge about the secular achievements, characteristics, and commitments of many Mormon believers, including their industriousness and commitment to formal education, welfare, thrift, preparedness,

---

212 It must be acknowledged here that very likely for many if not most Mormon believers who were born and raised in the faith, their religion is simply a way of life without experienced contrast. For these believers being a Mormon is all they know, and is so completely integrated with their personality and day-to-day lives that they don't even notice, much less question, the underlying beliefs, meta-beliefs, and socio-psychological dynamics at play which keep them bound to their religious schema and conditioned way of life, or oblivious to the real harm it is inflicting on their psychological well-being, or others.

Simply put, they do not know any better, or what they are missing, and they have been conditioned to regard their delusions as truth, their conditioned state of mind as happiness, and any different way of life — or of being *in life* — as a perversity, or as wrong and perhaps even sinful. Still, as history and likely numerous if not innumerable clinical case files attest regarding the sad, pathological, and even tragic personal lives of self-professedly happy Mormons and other theistic believers, the fact that one *feels* regressively happy or at home in a particular belief system or life-form does not mean that such is in fact so, or that one's conditioned way of life is not in fact harmful to one's well-being and potentially or actually dangerous to oneself and others.

Nor is it necessarily or even actually indicative, denials to the contrary notwithstanding, that all is well in one's life, because of one's faith or at all, or that one has not been psychologically damaged by his or her faith or is in a state of delusion. On the contrary, the evidence would reasonably support the *opposite* conclusion, or at least place the Mormon or theistic believer's assertions of happiness and psychological well-being under reasonable analytic suspicion — particularly where the belief system itself is based on, or tied to, the moralistic core and code of patriarchy inherent in the abusive dynamic of all theistic life-forms (See, in this regard, and again, the relevant passages in Chapter 8 and the *Epilogue*).

213 What is significant in all such cases of defensive, dissociative reality distortion is the conditioned fear response itself. Such an unconscious conditioned fear response is, I would argue, created by the same various and abusive strategies of mind-control employed initially in the patriarchal family system and authoritatively in all theistic faiths, including, of course, the Mormon faith. As we learned in Chapter 8 and the *Epilogue*, all such conditioning strategies of mind-control are founded on the belief systems and, more fundamentally, the moralistic core and code of patriarchy inherent in *all* hierarchical and authoritative social systems — religious or otherwise — which recapitulate the patriarchal family system. It is the *creation* and *reinforcement* of such a conditioned fear response — as well as the inhuman beliefs, requirements, rules, and shaming abuses (and those in authority who inflict them) that create and reinforce them — which are so contemptible to me.

service, and family values. Nevertheless, I would argue that all of these values, commitments, and related achievements are *naturally* accessible to, and can be experienced by, *all* people *without* religion. They pale in significance as compared to the insidious harm inflicted by the doctrines, beliefs, and practices that shape the culture. Through the culture, they weigh upon the minds and lives of believers and nonbelievers alike.

In reading the above retrospective, it is important to note that while I readily acknowledge that I am, for all the reasons articulated throughout this book, indeed a harsh and at times angry critic of *all* religious belief, particularly the Mormon faith, it would nonetheless be incorrect to conclude that I blame the Mormon Church or certain people in the Church for my woundedness or loss of faith. It would also be false to assume that the personal abuse and indignities I suffered at the hands of certain Church leaders or the Mormon faith in general was intentionally inflicted, or is the sole or even primary reason for my writing this book. Nothing could be further from the truth.

On the contrary, I want to be clear that I do *not* blame the Mormon Church or people for my own *pre-existing* woundedness or the wounds incurred during my years in the faith. As I see it, although the Mormon faith is culpable (and least implicated) in the authoritarian abuses inflicted *post conversion* on its adherents through its teachings and practices, I was admittedly wounded *before* I joined the Mormon Church, and I will carry with me the effects of my woundedness to some extent throughout the rest of my life.

From my psychoanalytic perspective there is no 'cure' for such wounding, only the modest possibility of analytically developing an increased capacity for doing less harm to myself and to others as a result of my woundedness, and for dealing with the effects of my woundedness more productively. Accordingly, I no longer seek such cures, or illusory transformations promised by any ideology, discipline, or commitment therapy. My life is what it is, and it could not have been otherwise than what it is — all things considered. As a hard determinist, I try (with far less success than I would like at times) not to blame or praise anyone for anything, including myself. I also hold, following Pereboom (2001) and others of like mind, that the incoherence of blame and praise in a hard-incompatibilistic or deterministic context does not remove the coherent fact that we are all ultimately responsible for the choices we make and the actions we take, and that there are actual and natural physical, psychological, and social consequences for our determined choices.

As for my admitted anger — and for those readers who might be interested — there is no mystery here that warrants speculation as to its source, types, or objects. In my case the source of my anger toward all authoritarian, theistic religions and their adherents is the authoritarian abuse suffered initially in my family of origin and both recapitulated and exacerbated by my involvement in the Mormon faith. More specifically, my anger is essentially of three types. The first is a personalized, reactive anger born of my woundedness. The second is exasperation. And the third is indignation born of contempt.

As noted earlier, at its most basic level, the personalized, reactive anger of the former theist-turned-Atheist toward the prior faith and its adherents is a common counter-reaction to the explicit, implicit, or assumed judgments or accusations of theists who essentially function as stand-ins for the *internalized* 'Authoritarian Other' (or the imago of the 'dark' Parent-god) in the mind of the recovering Atheist. Simply put, such personalized, reactive anger is rooted in the shame-based personality of one who has, to one degree or another, lost his or her deep sense of intrinsic self-worth and internal authority because of parental, societal, and/or religious authoritarian abuse. It is a primal, existential defense against the internalized Authoritarian Other.

The wounds of authoritarian abuse are difficult to heal; perhaps they are impossible to heal completely. As when getting hit by a truck, the injured person might walk again, but always with a limp and perhaps never without some pain or discomfort. Raw anger or rage springing from the wounds of authoritarian abuse is rarely, if ever, productive, and it is usually self-defeating and damaging or destructive to primary relationships, social order, and even (in extreme cases) human life. Still, as we learned in Chapter 8 and the *Epilogue*, such anger is one painful reminder among others of why Mormonism and other authoritarian theisms are inherently toxic at their core and therefore are harmful, potentially destructive, and dangerous.

The second type of anger I experience is exasperation. This anger is triggered by, and directed to, human stupidity, intellectual laziness, and psychological ignorance (including my own at times). Besides creating a host of personal and interpersonal problems, ignorance collectively retards our moral and scientific progress as a species and creates the fertile ground from which the seeds of regressive, theistic faith take root.

The third type of anger — the anger of indignation — is triggered by and directed to three very troubling and related areas of concern. The first is the shaming, abusive dynamic of all authoritarian, theistic faiths. This includes, of course, the exploitive 'infantilizing process' (Faber 2010) of Christianity and Mormonism in particular which was designed to keep believers in a perpetual 'faith-state' of regressive dependency and obedience to authority. The second area of concern is authoritarianism in general and, in particular, those believers in positions of authority — including Church leaders and parents — who irresponsibly even if unintentionally afflict others through the administration of the abusive dynamic and infantilizing process of their faith. The third area of concern, which is characteristic of contempt, is the epistemic irresponsibility of those believers referred to earlier who seem to take pride in their unshakable faith, and who stubbornly, smugly, and dismissively refuse to even consider the *possibility* that what they believe, practice, and pass on to others as 'Truth' might in fact be false or incoherent as well as harmful and potentially dangerous and destructive to themselves and others — particularly to impressionable, vulnerable, and intellectually defenseless children.

While anger *per se*, apart from reactive anger and rage, seems to be widely regarded as a negative or counter-productive, self-defeating, and destructive emotion, I consider it to be a valuable and useful *human* emotion which helps us protect our physical and psychological boundaries from assault or offense, or from unwarranted personal criticism. It can also be useful as an important indicator of frustration that needs to be constructively attended to, as well as an emotion which can and often does empower us to right wrongs. In the latter case, such anger as indignation can provide a useful consequentialist purpose to society, provided it is rationally and justifiably directed, which I think is arguably so where the object of such anger is theistic religion and its shamelessly smug, authoritarian, and epistemically irresponsible adherents. This assumes as well that such anger is not reactive or merely vindictive — a tall order to be sure, even for the more psychologically informed or analyzed among us who have been the objects of authoritarian abuse.

Personally, I consider my non-reactive anger to be crucial when accessed as indicated above. It would, however, neither be indicated nor present (as is so with reactive anger) were

I meaningfully engaged in *informed* discussion or dialogue with open-minded believers who can openly acknowledge their questions and real doubts, and who are honestly and sincerely desirous of respectfully exchanging views, analytically exploring beliefs, and pursuing greater understanding and personal insight from the vantage point of a reasonably skeptical outsider. Unfortunately, such crucial conversations with devout Mormons and Christians (as well as devout orthodox Jews and Muslims) will most likely be very few and infrequent, if indeed they would or could ever occur at all.

All things considered, I think a strong case can be made (even if I have not effectively made it) that those faithful believers advocating and practicing the Mormon religion, including its doctrines, indoctrinating practices, and humiliating and shaming methods of discipline (or teaching and punishment), are also at least complicit and ultimately responsible for the abuses it inflicts — *intentionally or not* — on themselves and others. I have certainly felt the weight of my own complicity and responsibility in this regard, both for my own acts of self-betrayal and abuse, and for the lie I lived and shared with or imposed on others — as in the case of my children. Moreover, while there is no doubt much to respect and positively acknowledge about many Mormons and other theistic believers from a purely secular perspective, and while their state of mental bondage to their faith is certainly understandable and worthy of compassion from a naturalistic perspective, there is, from my informed perspective, nonetheless *nothing* either culturally necessary or worthy of admiration or respect for their beliefs or for their faith and conviction.

VIII

As must be clear by now, I neither advocate religious belief in *any* form or for *any* reason, nor do I hold in respect or esteem educated and otherwise reasonable and intelligent religious believers *in virtue of* such beliefs. On the contrary, and at the very least, I regard such beliefs as pure folly. And I regard those who unquestioningly accept, live by, and share them as truth foolish as well as epistemically irresponsible.

As set-forth in the *Epilogue*, I advocate instead an analytic way of life — a way of life that characterizes and eschews faith defined as belief and 'trust in 'God' as being a paranoid delusion and considers the religious illusion of salvation-as-forgiveness, protection, and deliverance as a defense against more life, and death. In this sense, to quote Mogenson from his provocative and profound book *God is a Trauma* (1989), "Theology [including Mormon theology] stands as a shield between mankind and trauma. A compromise with the trauma [the trauma of birth, of loss, of abuse and suffering, and of existential *Angst*], theology is a return of our exterior surfaces to the inorganic world, that is, to the spiritual world, death. To operate optimally, to protect mankind adequately, religion must be a dead [and deadening] shell — mere lip service, Sabbath after Sabbath, mere duty" (96). Religious man, in his religious 'shell,' is like "[t]he tortoise in its shell, the fish in its scales, the rhinoceros in its hide — all creatures great and small — [who] live by virtue of a protective outer crust of dead matter. The purpose of this protective crust or shield," Mogenson asserts, is, "according to Freud…for protection against stimuli" (99); for protection against experiencing the traumas and "little deaths" (97) connected with more life. As we learned in the *Epilogue*, it is for protection as well against the natural instinct to live and therefore to die in our own fashion.

I am also an advocate for children — for the preservation of our children's and grandchildren's natural Atheism and for their right to a fullness of life. In this regard, I am reminded of an unforgettable experience with one of my grandchildren. It involved my granddaughter Codie when she was seven years old. One day she came home from her first-grade class where she and her classmates shared their favorite Christmas family traditions. When we asked her if she had any questions about other traditions she admitted that she did, and then asked — with honest puzzlement at her little classmates' talk of their Nativity traditions — "Who the heck is baby Jesus?" Having raised my children in the Mormon religion and taught (indoctrinated) them all at a very early age the Christian meaning of Christmas, I couldn't help but reflect on how refreshing Codie's innocence and honesty were and how fortunate and free she was — at least for the time — from the influence and effects of theistic beliefs. This child, like her sister Chloe and all of our other precious grandchildren, was — as we all are at birth — a natural Atheist — a person without any belief in gods or Christs.

My fervent hope is that parents will think long and hard about indoctrinating their children into *any* form of theistic belief. Such indoctrination can cripple young and questioning minds with theological nonsense and dogma such as '*God*,' '*duty* to God,' '*obedience* to God and to Church authorities,' '*faith* in God,' '*chosenness*' on the basis of belief in the '*only true* God and Church,' '*sin* against God,' '*worthiness* (unworthiness) in the eyes of God,' '*righteousness* (wickedness) as *judged* by God,' and '*salvation* or *damnation* as *decreed* by God' on the basis of behavior and 'works' in this life. It can also weaken their will to more fully individuate by keeping them superstitiously and codependently or regressively attached to a 'Father God,' a 'Savior God,' and a 'Mother Church' — including its *surrogate-parent*-Leaders. Finally, it can foster psychosis through the concept and expectation of revelation and 'spiritual experience,' and neurosis through deeply conditioned inner conflict and one-sidedness in virtue of an insufficiently integrated personality due to authoritarian parental and institutional shaming. The possible psychological hazards of theistic belief (and particularly Mormon beliefs and practices) are extensive and very real, not the least of which are religious addiction and extremism.

More generally and in principle, I have come to think that parents do not have a *right* to indoctrinate their children in *any* form of religious belief. In this regard I therefore agree wholeheartedly with the strong words of psychologist Nicholas Humphrey delivered in his Amnesty Lecture in Oxford in 1997 and quoted by Richard Dawkins in *The God Delusion*:

> Children, I'll argue, have a human right not to have their minds crippled by exposure to other people's bad ideas — no matter who these other people are. Parents, correspondingly, have no God-given license to enculturate their children in whatever ways they personally choose: no right to limit the horizons of their children's knowledge, to bring them up in an atmosphere of dogma and superstition, or to insist they follow the strait and narrow paths of their own faith.
>
> In short, children have a right not to have their minds addled by nonsense, and we as a society have a duty to protect them from it. So we should no more allow parents to teach their children to believe, for example, in the literal truth of the Bible [or other scripture] or that the planets rule their lives, than we should allow parents to knock their children's teeth out or lock them in a dungeon. (2006, 326)

Joshi puts this matter in an equally strong and characteristically blunt perspective. "To my mind," he writes, "the inculcation of religious belief into the young — a process that can scarcely be termed anything but brainwashing — is religion's great crime against humanity. Billions have been prejudiced in favor of one religion or another by its kind of indoctrination, and it requires a tremendous strength of mind and will to overcome it in later years. ... One would suppose that religionists would wish their adherents to have come by their beliefs freely and of their own accord; so why do they insist that religious training begin at an age when the child is not able to think for itself and is incapable of questioning the authority of its parents or other adult figures? As H.P. Lovecraft states:

> We all know that any emotional bias — irrespective of truth or falsity — can be implanted by suggestion in the emotions of the young, hence the inherited traditions of an orthodox community are absolutely without evidential value. ... If religion were true, its followers would not try to bludgeon [or brainwash] their young into an artificial conformity; but would merely insist on their unbending quest for *truth*, irrespective of artificial backgrounds or practical consequences. With such an honest and inflexible *openness to* [reason and] *evidence*, they could not fail to receive any *real truth* which might be manifesting itself around them. The fact that religionists do *not* follow this honorable course [which is certainly the case in the Mormon religion], but cheat at their game by [shamefully] invoking juvenile quasi-hypnosis [and psychosis], is enough to destroy their pretentions in my eyes even if their absurdity were not manifest in every other direction." (17)

Children of Mormon or religious parents are not born as 'Mormon children' nor are they any particular religion's children. They are children of parents who have been indoctrinated — by choice or upbringing — in the Mormon faith or in some other religion. If we truly love our children and desire ultimately that *they* make those choices in their lives which will result in *their* greatest well-being in this life (which is the only life they or we have or know of), then it seems reasonable and moral to me that we not presuppose that what is presumed to be in *our* best interests regarding *our* religious beliefs is, in fact, also in *theirs*.

Nor need we presume that *our* choices (and how we might have made them) regarding how *we* have chosen to live *our* lives are best for *them* as well. Rather, it seems most reasonable, sensible, and moral to me to focus instead on the emotional and physical well-being of our children by appropriately educating them in the *facts of life* (*i.e.*, those naturalistic *facts* pertaining to our *knowledge* of physical, social, and economic realities) and to the ability to function morally, effectively, and responsibly in the world — to love well, reason well, interact well with others, work hard, and make the best decisions they can. None of this requires religious belief. Much of it, from my perspective, is actually impeded by religious belief. Still, this most reasonable, sensible, and moral path is one that cannot be taken by religious parents still rooted in any faith. It would seem that the only hope for the young children of believing parents is the parents' ultimate *and informed* return to their own natural Atheism — and to rationality.

Notwithstanding the above, I do not think it is possible in religious cultures to avoid *exposure* to or infection by 'the God virus.' Still, I do think it is possible and advisable, as individuals and parents, to strengthen our resistance to it, and perhaps even eradicate it over time. To do this would perhaps minimally require, following Freud, learning how to meaningfully differentiate *actual* guilt from the irrational *sense* of guilt resulting from instinctual gratification, ambivalence, and doubt, and returning to the modest and realistic goal of well-being and 'normal unhappiness' by engaging in earnest in an analytic process which, as understood by Greg Mogenson (1989), would return us to "the creative burden of [our] own existence" (84). It would also require, following Loftus (2008, 2010), Harbour (2001), and Nielsen (1996, 2001, 2006), the outsider test for faith from a meritocratic worldview with an analytical, *philosophical* methodology consistent with a non-scientific, contextualist, and historicist naturalism without metaphysical foundations.

I will conclude this personal postscript by first addressing an insightful question once asked of me by my former daughter-in-law Christa (whom I now regard simply as a daughter) as to whether I thought my experiences in religion — and with Mormonism in particular — had made me the person I am. She was implying, I suppose, that I would not be the person I am today without such experiences, and likewise my children would not be the people they are today — or shall be — and that we should therefore not regret any experience. I will then follow my answer to that question with one final reflection and an honest, personal disclosure regarding my reasons for writing this book.

To the question of whether or not my experiences in religion and with Mormonism in particular had made me the person that I am today, I would answer that I cannot deny that our experiences in life significantly shape our choices, circumstances, and personality. Even though I agree with Nietzsche that "whatever does not kill [us] will make [us] stronger," I do not conclude therefore that we are not unnecessarily harmed or psychologically damaged or crippled by certain of our choices and experiences. A different array of ideas, choices, and life experiences might very well have produced a healthier, if not better outcome — where *healthier* or *better* implies the modest goals of doing *less* harm to oneself and others, and learning to creatively and productively live one's life more fully and profoundly without childish illusions.

More specifically, I do not think that I would necessarily be any *worse* off for *not* having believed in a god or Christ or *not* having been a Mormon. Nor do I think that my children or grandchildren would or will necessarily be any worse off for retaining or regaining their natural Atheism. On the contrary, I have come to conclude on the basis of my own and others' life experiences and reflections that we would *all* be much better off without a belief in *any* god, especially the Mormon god. It is never too late (again following Nietzsche) to say *"Yes!"* to life *without* the evils of religious faith, hope, and illusion.

After much reflection and introspection, I am left with the rather sobering and self-evident realization that among all the evolved species of life on this planet, only we human beings are capable of inventing and narcissistically and superstitiously worshipping supernatural gods created out of our imagination and shaped in our own image. Moreover, only we humans — regardless of our intelligence and rationality in all other areas of endeavor — can be stupid, pathetic, and pathological enough to irrationally believe in the actual existence of such putative beings. Only we humans cling to those beliefs *in spite of* their inherent and utter incoherence and absurdity — even to the insane extreme of self-abandonment, self-destruction, and utter annihilation. Given this, it would seem that in the words of the late Zen Buddhist Nanrei Kobori, "God is an invention of Man. So the nature of God is only a shallow mystery. The deep mystery is the nature of man."

Still, where there is consciousness, the capacity for reason, and the possibility through experience, influence, insight, and corrective emotional experience of cybernetically altering the brain, there is, at least for me, a very small hope that, in the end, reason, rationality, and sanity will prevail. More and more theistic believers may eventually disabuse themselves and the world of their religious nonsense.

Even if such hope is, because of human weakness and stupidity,[214] itself based on a mere illusion with no possibility of realization, there is for me still the pressing need and desire to personally expose and depotentiate the 'god virus' wherever and however I can. Openly and boldly (even if necessarily angrily and offensively at times) I must eschew and speak out against superstition, theistic belief, and authoritarian religious dogma and abuse in *all* their forms and all their places. There is as well a very personal need to reclaim at least some of the integrity, self-respect, and human dignity I lost by superstitiously, needily — and, yes, *stupidly* — chasing after, believing in, and worshipping different gods throughout my life, and subjecting myself, my children, and those I have influenced while in the faith to demeaning and dehumanizing authoritarian mandates and judgments to my own (and their) detriment and shame.

Perhaps in the end, apart from my very modest hope that reason, rationality, and sanity will ultimately prevail over the sway of irrational religious feelings and beliefs, the pressing needs and corresponding desires of which I have written constitute my primary motivation and justification for writing this book — along with the accompanying desire to persuade others to attend *therapeutically* to their *real* doubts by more critically and skeptically testing their religious beliefs and commitments as objective outsiders.[215] To this end I will close with the words of Alexander Saxton quoted by Victor Stenger in his fine work *The New Atheism* (2009): "The truth – the hard core, 'get real' kind of truth – is that somewhere down under, by some sort of subliminal awareness, every human being really knows that believing in belief…is 'nothing but make believe.' The atheist's mission is to nourish the seed beneath the snow; to seek not escape but survival" (228).

---

214 Again, beyond its common, limited, and inapplicable use as mere lack of intelligence, the concept of stupidity, the way the term 'stupidity' is used herein and in a social-scientific and historical context, explains a common human phenomenon which affects *all* people, regardless of their degree of intelligence or education. More starkly, and I think correctly put in Welles' words (1995), "In every age, land and culture, stupidity defines the hominid condition. It is…ubiquitous, although the specific forms it may take are, of course, dependent on the misperceptions and fantasies of the particular people [in this case Mormon and other theistic believers] running themselves into the ground chasing their own [gods or] favorite rainbow" (90). See also Welles 1997 and note 12 in the Introduction.

215 My thanks again to John Loftus who introduced me to the seminal idea of "The Outsider Test of Faith" (2008, 66–77 and 2010, 81–106).

Appendix A:

Analysis and Assessment of a Personal Conversion Experience

"Except ye be converted, and become as little children,
ye shall not enter into the Kingdom of Heaven."

- Matt. 18:3

"And the Lord said unto me [Alma the Younger]:
Marvel not that all mankind, yea, men and women,
all nations, kindreds, tongues and people, must be born again,;
yea, born of God, changed from their carnal and fallen state,
to a state of righteousness, being redeemed of God...;
And thus they become new creatures; and unless they do this,
they can in nowise inherit the kingdom of God. I say unto you,
unless this be the case, they must be cast off..."

- Mosiah 27: 25-27

Prefatory Note: The most sacred and precious possession of devout Mormon believers is their personal "testimony" of the believed 'Truth' of their faith. Such a testimony typically consists of five interrelated parts. First, that God lives. Second, that Jesus is the Christ, the "Son of God," and the "Savior" of the world and of the believer *personally*. Third, that Joseph Smith was called of God as "the Prophet of the Restoration" of God's only true Gospel and Church to the Earth in "this, the last dispensation of the fulness of times." Fourth, that the current President of the Church is a true "Prophet, Seer and Revelator." And fifth that the Church of Jesus Christ of Latter day Saints (or Mormon Church) is the one and only true Church of Jesus Christ on the earth today. Such a solemn attestation of what is sincerely held and declared by the faithful to be 'The Truth' is derived and "confirmed" to the believer through some form of affective "spiritual" or religious conversion experience considered by the believer to be a transformative personal revelation from God through the "power of the Holy Ghost." It is declared not as a mere belief, but as *knowledge*, wherein the believer states that he or she "knows" *with certainty* all of the above to be *actually* "true."

Such a personal "testimony," which usually evolves and is reinforced over time with so-called "spiritual" (feeling-toned) experiences, repeated declaration and the alleged receipt of "further light and knowledge," typically establishes and sustains the faith of the Mormon believer. Moreover, it is regarded as the most effective way to attract others to the faith, and to defend their own beliefs and faith from doubt, skepticism and direct challenge from discrediting evidence or argument.

The existence of religious conversion and testimony is not unique to the Mormon religion. Other Christians, in like manner, "bear witness" to the Bible as revealed 'Truth,' and to their own 'born again' experience as evidence of Christ's love for them personally, and his power to 'save' them from sin and suffering.

Below is an account, retrospective, and analysis and assessment of the author's post-baptismal conversion experience referenced in the *Introduction* of this book. This experience was, again, formally documented at length, and as recalled, sometime after it occurred on July 21, 1981, most likely in 1982 or 1983. Moreover, it was, as all such regressive, "infantilizing" experiences are, a profound, ecstatic and fervently *wished for* experience which culminated in an ultimate and inexplicable (albeit self-induced) feeling of love, forgiveness and unconditional acceptance. Significantly, no one who had ever enjoyed such an experience would ever *want* to deny it. And I dare say, no one burdened by felt shame, guilt and existential anxiety who had learned of the possibility of having such an experience, and its alleged attending theological implications and benefits, would not fervently, even if secretly, *wish* and *seek* for it (a fact, incidentally, together with the believed 'unpardonable sin' committed through post-conversion 'apostasy' would seem at its face to rule out deconversion and resulting nonbelief or disbelief as self-deception). In the end, however, and notwithstanding such a profound personal experience, it eventually became evident to me, as it has for many others, that in the words of psychologist and former Christian fundamentalist Edmund Cohen, "The supposed renewal of the mind [through theistic conversion and devotion]… [produces the] side effects of a dissociated state of mind."

My reason for including this *Appendix*, inclusive of its substantive and essential footnotes, is two-fold. First, it was my intent to provide readers with a brief analytical and naturalistic analysis and assessment of an actual conversion experience as perhaps a paradigm case in which to summarily apply or appreciate what has been learned through the reading of this book. And second, it was (and is) my hope that the conclusions presented in my own analysis and assessment of this personal experience might provoke and encourage a like reflective examination (or re-examination) of the reader's – or others – "conversion" or "spiritual" experience(s) from a different, naturalistic perspective.

Biographical Context

The circumstances which led to my conversion to the Mormon Church, and later to my dramatic conversion to Christ, were similar and in many ways paradigmatic. Raised in a patriarchal family culture by a loving but strict Greek mother and a likewise loving but authoritarian, superstitious ("God-fearing") and at times abusive Greek father, I was conditioned from childhood to feel at home in the familiar, superstitious Mormon patriarchal culture. This, along with my own acquired superstitious nature, various serious childhood illnesses, and two traumatic brushes with death at a very young age (due to allergic and asthmatic crises respectively) made me particularly vulnerable to chasing after different "gods."

Common to all these gods, to my mind, was power and magic. And underneath them all was the God of my parents, the "God" of the Christian Greek Orthodox faith, whom I never knew about – except through the superstitious, "God fearing" attitudes and language of my parents. And underneath the God of my parents were my "parent-gods;" the unconscious, idealized (i.e. "god-like," or powerful, magical, loving, nurturing, protecting and favoring) parent imagoes internalized as a young, pre-verbal infant and child and unknowingly projected onto all the other fictitious gods I admired and followed throughout my life.

For years preceding my introduction to the Mormon faith, I had been living an incongruent, rebellious and self-indulging life. I was in college in San Francisco in the late 1960s and the rebellious, anti-establishment (anti-authoritarian) theme of "free love" and self-indulgence without rules or restraint was everywhere. I was part of it all, motivated primarily, I suspect, by desire for instinctual gratification and in part, at least, by my reaction to the suppressive authoritarian control imposed by my parents, particularly my father. I settled down after a few years, completed my undergraduate and graduate education and got married in 1973, commencing my career in a profession I hated, public accounting. The distresses of life began to accumulate with force. My life was a mess and I was chronically ill. In retrospect, my anxieties seemed to point to the fact that the early childhood terrors of death and feelings of paternal oppression and utter powerlessness were just beneath the surface of my awareness.

It was in this particular biographical context that I was introduced to the Mormon Church in early 1974. Sensing my desire for a change in my life after a bout with another serious illness, a Mormon colleague at my place of work invited me to go with him to the Mormon Temple Visitor Center in Mesa, Arizona and then afterward suggested that I meet with the Mormon missionaries to learn more about the Church.[216] I did both, and during the course of the missionary lessons, determined that I had found the right god and religion for me. I recall that my wife at the time and her parents were concerned at my decision to join the Church. They were all members of the Mormon Church, but were inactive. They knew me well enough to know how committed I would be to the religion. And they were right.

The following personal account is offered as a paradigm case of both Mormon and Christian conversion along with a brief follow-up evaluation for consideration. I think, from the perspective of a skeptical outsider (including, perhaps, other non-Mormon and Christian theists), my retrospective analysis and assessment below will generally ring true. From an insider's perspective, however, there might be varied reactions, which I will address below.

Here then, for analysis and assessment, is the actual first-person account of my post-

---

216 As an important and I think relevant aside, missionary work in the Mormon faith initiates what Stricker refers to as the "pattern of the double-bind in Mormonism" (2000). It is also, in addition to Temple work in the Mormon faith,, and as Watters (1992) correctly points out, "the most important" of the developed "strategies that enabled Christians to 'persuade' people to the faith" (35). "The stated justification for Christian [and Mormon] missionary work," Watters writes, "is the obligation to share [– out of their professed godly love for mankind –] the good news about Jesus Christ [and his 'restored' church and gospel] into the world to save us all from the consequences of [the 'Fall'] and our sins. But there may be deeper psychological motivation for this behavior [(as there certainly was in my case, and very likely with all other Christians and Mormons as well)]. The essential elements of the Christian [and Mormon] doctrine so violate human intelligence and well-being that, as a way of quieting their [suppressed,] disturbing doubts, believers are internally [(as well as externally)] pressured to serve missions and do missionary work to convince [themselves and] others of the validity of that doctrine" (36).

Such an unconscious personal and collective betrayal of doubt and corresponding motivation for doing (and pressuring others to do) 'missionary work' – coupled with the tacit or even conscious motivation to expiate guilt and win favor with god and forgiveness of sins for 'bringing souls to Christ' – may also function unconsciously, as Watters further explains, as what "Eric Fromm has called…a *folie á millions*, an expansion of a term used in psychiatry, a *folie á deux*. This is applied," according to Watters, "to the phenomenon of shared craziness between two people who live together in a relatively isolated state, tied together by blood, marriage, friendship, belief systems, or necessity. One member of the dyad develops delusions, usually of a persecutory nature, and tries to get the other to agree with his perception…. The 'sane' partner has the choice either of agreeing with the 'crazy' one or of challenging the correctness of his perceptions and thus creating conflict in the relationship. Unable to risk the rift that might follow from this latter course of action, the 'sane' partner goes 'crazy' in order to preserve the relationship in tact. …

[Another] often overlooked aspect of proselytization is that it depends on the proselytizer being 'one up' on the proselytized, who is usually disadvantaged psychologically [and therefore vulnerable and needy]. This process never takes place between equals; it is always a case of 'get 'em when they're down'" (36-7). This was certainly the case in my life, both as a vulnerable subject for Mormon missionary work and later as a Missionary for the Mormon Church. Moreover, it explains why Christian and Mormon missionary work is so effective in countries or populations where people are suffering, disabled and/or disadvantaged psychologically, physically, socially, educationally, and economically. In this regard, and all considered, missionary work (including the sharing of one's 'testimony' or 'witness' of 'Truth') is, as I see it, simply the defensive, self-interested exploitation of the seduced, superstitious, oppressed and downtrodden masses done, again, to expiate guilt from sin and suppressed doubt, win favor from an *illusory* 'Parent-God', parent-Leaders, and significant others in the faith, and engage the masses in a *folie á millions* to establish sanity in numbers by getting others to join in the madness of one's faith.

baptismal conversion to Jesus Christ, written for posterity and very limited distribution sometime between the years of 1982 and 1984 and quoted below as written:

Conversion Account

"For seven years, from 1974 until 1981 I was actively and zealously engaged in Gospel living. In 1975 I received my [priesthood] endowments and was married in the Arizona Temple. I was consumed with the desire to live the Gospel fully; to serve, teach, testify, study and pray fervently. And I did so continually. I was actively involved in missionary work, temple work and home teaching. I strived to magnify all my church callings and took my membership in Christ's church very seriously…I absorbed myself in Gospel and scripture study feeling that I couldn't read or learn enough. I indeed hungered and thirsted after righteousness and truth…

"In 1981 my life changed. … This was a very difficult time in my life. At the time I was serving as the Stake Mission President in my stake. I was immersed in my calling and was enjoying a good measure of success. But I was self-employed at the time and my consulting practice was very slow. In fact, at the time I had no clients and was financially without means to provide for my family.

"It was during this time that I was called to come to Christ. The Spirit called me one day as I sat behind my desk and prompted me to pray. I…locked myself in my office and began to pour out my heart unto God. I [fasted and] prayed that day and for two succeeding days. I prayed long and hard and for many things. But the primary intent and focus of my prayers was to know the Lord and to understand and appreciate the personal implications of the Atonement in my life.

"On the third day, July 21, 1981, I found myself kneeling again by my chair in fervent prayer to know the Lord. Suddenly I saw myself praying and the presence of the Lord was beside me. As I watched, the Lord spoke to my mind and said, "Look." I looked and for the first time in my life I saw myself as I really was, through the eyes of Christ.

"What I saw I cannot fully describe in words. My whole soul was illuminated and I saw with complete clarity and understanding the deepest recesses of my subconscious mind. I saw within the hidden nooks and crannies of my soul the effects of all my sins as well as all my sins of commission and omission which had been repressed into the hidden regions of my mind. I was completely transparent. Everything was now so painfully clear, my sinful motives, intentions and desires, all cleverly disguised and rationalized through years of self-talk. Even the good things I had done for the wrong reasons were flashed before my all-seeing eye. No act, word or deed escaped my view. I saw everything.

"As I beheld myself thus, my mind was, to use Alma's words, "racked with torment" and "inexpressible horror" [Alma 36: 14] Several times I tried to shut out the vision but the Lord would not allow it. Each time I tried to shut out the vision the Lord would not allow it. Each time I tried to turn away the Lord would say, "Look", and I continued to look into my soul. I wept and pleaded for the Lord to stop the vision. When I had finally seen everything the vision ended and there was darkness. I turned to find the Lord but He was no longer beside me.

"The scene instantly changed and I found myself behind the brush on the outside of a garden clearing. Again a voice came to my mind and instructed me to look. My eyes turned to the garden clearing and there, in the midst, I saw my beloved Redeemer. Suddenly it became clear to me that I was witnessing His act of Atonement. ...I saw the love and suffering of the Christ and am a personal witness of it. I don't know how it is possible , but I was in Gethsemane on the day of His Agony and I saw in great and terrible detail with my eyes and heard in awful clarity with my ears that which is too sacred to describe to unprepared ears.

"His sobs and His cries pierced my soul and I felt the wrenching of my heart with each audible groan or quivering convulsion of His body. Then came the revelation that broke my heart: "Behold the love of God for you and His suffering for your sins."

"I...plead for forgiveness until...the vision stopped and the voice of the Lord said unto me, 'My son, thy sins are forgiven thee.' When I heard these words from my Savior I was filled with fire [and with the Holy Ghost]. Never had I felt such love, such peace. I was overcome again unto great sobbing, but this time with joy. So intense was the outpouring of God's love through the fire of His Spirit that I felt as though my very life would end and my flesh would be consumed.

"I came to know by the spirit of revelation that my life was acceptable to the Lord; that I had been completely and unconditionally cleansed of all my sins and the effects of my sins; that I had been truly born of the Spirit to enter into the Kingdom of God; I was redeemed from the fall; sanctified by the endowment of His perfect love, even charity."

Personal Retrospective

As interpreted through the lens of my faith at the time, I had, through this experience, offered up what is referred to in the *Book of Mormon* as "a broken heart and contrite spirit" (3 Nephi 9:20); a pronounced and profound, crushing sense of contrition, culminating ultimately in an ecstatic experience which seemed to entail a literal inpouring of consuming love and an also overwhelming sense of forgiveness and acceptance. I had, in other words, literally been "born of God" by the "baptism of fire and of the Holy Ghost," and thereby received a complete remission of my sins and a "mighty change of heart." This transformational and believed salvational "meta-conversion"[217] experience changed the

---

217 It might be significant to Mormon readers, and perhaps of interest to non-Mormon Christian readers, for me to explain how I conceptually differentiated what I now refer to as a "meta-conversion" experience from my referenced earlier conversion to the Mormon faith. To this end, I have presented below an explanatory excerpt form my actual written account of this later "born again" experience:

"For me, the process of repentance began with my baptismal interview prior to my baptism.... [I was] truly contrite as I entered into the waters of baptism....I had truly been born again to see the Kingdom of Heaven. I felt the burden of my past remembered sins lifted and I rejoiced with all my heart at my membership in Christ's true church.

"Through it all I did not know that, although I had received the spirit of repentance prior to my baptism, I had not received the gift of full repentance; that while I had been born again to "see" the Kingdom of heaven through the receipt of my testimony by the power of the Holy Ghost, yet I had not been born again to "enter" into the Kingdom of God and I had not actually received the constant companionship of the Holy Ghost. While I enjoyed a sanctifying experience that lifted the burden of my past remembered sins, yet I had not been sanctified unto a complete and unconditional remission of all my sins, including the effects of those sins. My knowledge of these heavenly truths did not come until later, in July of 1981."

This experience, while only one of many significant "spiritual" experiences (i.e. believed 'miracles', 'revelations', 'visions', and answers to prayer) chronicled in my fifteen personal journal volumes written during my years in the faith, lead several years later, in virtue of my intensified commitment to the faith, to my believed and also documented receipt of what is known in Mormonism as the "more sure word of prophesy"

direction of my life, intensified my commitment to God, and became – as referenced in the *Introduction* – the cornerstone and centerpiece of my faith.

As I wrote in the *Introduction*, I *know* first hand what it actually means and feels like to be a fully converted Mormon *and* Christian. The profound, affective experiences I had at the beginning of my involvement with the Mormon faith and throughout my years of religious activity, including, as recorded above, my so-regarded conversion to Jesus Christ, cannot be denied. Nor can I deny that I felt with great conviction and unwavering certitude that what I experienced was what I then wholeheartedly interpreted and believed it to be on the basis of my theologically informed interpretation of those experiences.

This is arguably the way it is with all such profound, affective experiences, religious or otherwise. They deeply affect us and cannot be denied. To this day, as I pass a Mormon Church or Temple my body at times faintly remembers the familiar feelings associated with my life in the faith; the comforting, peaceful and serene feelings induced by, and associated with, distinctive physical spaces, architecture, symbolism, music, ritual and fellowship. Even so, and again, the fact that one has had such experiences does not necessarily mean that the subjective *interpretations* of these experiences constitute knowledge or are *actually* true (or even intelligible or cognitively meaningful), even if it is believed with sincere conviction to be so by the person, or by those in the community of which he or she is a part. Nor, incidentally and importantly, can those who have freed themselves from religious belief and who honestly pursue knowledge about life and the world indulge in such regressive feelings, or even seek or yearn to otherwise enjoy them or relive them.[218]

Significantly, as I reflect on this experience today as an objective outsider to the Mormon faith, I experience two distinct reactions: minimal remembered affect and embarrassment. The remembered affect of these life experiences, like those of all other significant, affective human experiences which leave a lasting imprint on the brain, is of course explainable neurologically as merely a function of brain physiology, and not, as some Mormon believers might perversely like to think, through "the working of the Spirit."

The reaction of embarrassment, it seems to me, is – apart from my understanding of *what* happened and *how it is* that it happened – a function of the patent absurdity of what I then believed to have actually occurred. Although I now have some understanding of how it is that I or anyone under the same or similar circumstances could believe (or *want* to believe) such nonsense, or regard it as true, I nonetheless am dismayed that I did so without question. It would seem, in retrospect, that we indeed do believe what we really *want* to

---

(D&C 131:5; McConkie 1979, 109-10).

218 In this regard I am reminded of the fictional account of a conversation between Josef Breuer and Friedrich Nietzsche in Irvin Yalom's provocative novel *When Nietzsche Wept*. In it Nietzsche responded to Breuer's desire for some immediate relief from his despair with characteristically hard and discomforting words of truth. Referring to a previous letter he had written to his sister Elizabeth, Nietzsche instructed Breuer that "...those who wish for peace of soul and happiness must believe [in God] and embrace faith, while those who wish to pursue the truth must forsake peace of mind and devote their life to inquiry. ...You must choose between comfort and true inquiry! If you choose...to be liberated from the soothing chains of the supernatural, if, as you claim, you choose to eschew belief and embrace godlessness, then you cannot in the same breath yearn for the small comforts of the believer! If you kill God, you must leave the shelter of the temple." These words had a profound impact on me when I first read them, and they still do to this day.

believe, or *wish* were true.[219] Overall, it is to me now a sad memory. It is sad because it was a very sad time in my life; a time when I was emotionally and intellectually crippled by shame, guilt, insecurity and superstition, and consequently unwilling (or perhaps unable) to examine the Mormon (or any) faith – or religious experience – critically.[220]

Also, and likewise of significance, what I felt during this particular watershed experience in my life, and in all of my other so-called "spiritual experiences" before and after, I have not felt since and do not expect to ever feel again, except perhaps in a very minimal, indirect sense as a result of some inadvertently induced brain function. This sober disclosure requires, I think, some treatment before presenting my summary analysis and assessment below, particularly given the nature of such and its implications to those Mormon readers who might have had like conversion experiences, and who might have real concerns about seriously questioning those experiences which they regard as being "sacred" and undeniable without dire "eternal" consequences.

From whence came the feeling to "sing the song of redeeming love," and whither did it go?

There is among Mormons a well-known chapter from the *Book of Mormon* found in the "Book of Alma," where the protagonist Alma speaks to members of the Church of God at that time and says: "And now behold, I say unto you, my brethren, if ye have experienced a change of heart [been "born of God"], and if ye have felt to sing the song of redeeming love, I would ask, can ye feel so now?" (5:26). The teaching in this chapter and throughout the *Book of Mormon* and other Mormon scripture is plain. If converted or "born again" members of the faith do not hold fast to their faith they will eventually fall-away and lose the Spirit and no longer *feel* the joy and peace they once did. This teaching, as I see it, is, apart from being both conceptually and scripturally contradictory as we shall learn below, part of a comprehensive program of mind-control accomplished in part through social indoctrination. Repeating an earlier quote from former Mormon Jack Worthy, "All of an indoctrinated member's feelings, both pleasant and unpleasant, are interpreted as a form of evidence that proves Mormonism to be true" (2008, 25). This particular form of indoctrination, as Worthy also correctly points out, is effective primarily *because* of its

---

219 I am reminded here of a line in an old Waylon Jennings song (appropriately entitled "I've Always been Crazy"), which cautions: "Be careful of something that's just what you want it to be." This caution pertains, of course, to all religious beliefs, and is one significant problem with "belief" (and "believing") per se. As the wise old Greek Demosthenes (384-322 B.C.E.) observed in this regard, "Nothing is easier than self-deception. For what each man wishes, that he also wishes to be true."

220 I am at times constructively confronted by my wife with the at least seeming contradiction of my at times passionate criticism of others' religious beliefs, given my own past religious commitments. I above all, she fairly and reasonably argues, should understand how it is that other people – even educated and intelligent people – could believe such nonsense. The point, of course, is well taken. I do understand. Still, my clearly passionate criticism of religious belief and *ad hominem* reactions toward religious believers, unseemly and perverse as it surely seems in one sense, is, in another sense, more understandable when appreciated in the context of Nietzsche's words, again from in Yalom's *When Nietzsche Wept,* that "Great passion is required to defeat passion! Too many men have been broken on the wheel of lesser passion." And further, when seen as perhaps more an indictment of human laziness, superstitionsness, stupidity and cowardice, and as a lament that we are collectively so unevolved, weak and pathetic as a species that we still need to invent, chase after, follow, and defend illusory parent-gods.

focus on feelings as the ultimate arbiter of truth and falsity, worthiness and unworthiness, blessedness and cursedness, and right and wrong. It is, again, in Worthy's words, the "key ingredient that makes the whole process of [Mormon] indoctrination work very well" (17).

These so-called "spiritual" feelings, or affects, as we have learned and shall revisit below, are rooted in the "basic biological situation" (Faber 2004) and are produced naturalistically – neurologically – in virtue of the transference (or projection) of the internalized parent imago (or "parent-god") onto the culturally embedded and accepted fictional deity, or Parent-God. Such dissociative transference, as we have also learned, is suggestively, hypnotically induced by familiar language (Stromberg 1993) as well as familiar music, art, rites, practices and rituals, including especially the discipline, or practice, of fasting, and the ritual of petitionary prayer (Faber 2002). It is, moreover, in certain theistic cultures, regarded as purely religious experience and linked specifically with religious worship, conversion and salvation, appropriated as such by various theistic faiths within the context of their respective canonized revelation (scripture) and formal or informal theologies.

Such appropriated and contextualized cultural beliefs enable each Church or religion within its respective theistic tradition to provide an authoritative interpretive lens to believers by which to effectually indoctrinate them to believe that such self-(or other)-induced *natural* feelings are, in fact, "spiritual experiences" from God or the Spirit. And that those experiences can *only* be given and received by the Spirit if believers remain faithful and "choose the right" (or do what they have been taught, counseled, exhorted or commanded to do). And that, moreover, such experiences will cease or be lost if the believer rebels or hardens his heart and either apostatizes or falls into sin, thereby "losing the Spirit." But apart from the problem of arguing for one's interpretation of such experiences by invalidly regarding it as "possible" or "properly basic" (problems addressed in Chapter 2), how is it that someone who once experienced the intense feelings ascribed to spiritual conversion or "rebirth" no longer experiences them and consequently is no longer able to "sing the song of redeeming love" (or bear "testimony") to the truth of Christ's existence, atonement and love?

Mormons, of course, and again, necessarily point to the "sinful" attitudes, choices and behavior or actions of wayward and former converts (see, for example, Alma 5: 27-42) – as well, ironically, to hallucination and the delusional state of the believer – to answer such questions and to argue that such an answer is true. (How, after all, could they do otherwise and preserve their own faith and likewise delusional state of self-deception?) But at a purely theological level such an answer never made sense to me as a believer, given the scriptural characterizations of the experience and effects of spiritual rebirth. For how, – except through the very convenient and wholly unsubstantiated *ad hominem* argument asserting, as a default position, the misinterpretation, prevarication, or Satanic counterfeiting of such an experience[221] – could one who had been truly converted or "born

---

221 Such *ad hominem* argumentation is, along with other forms of false argumentation employing various other reasoning fallacies, common fare among Mormon and other theistic apologists who seek to resolve apparent contradictions between or among the claims or teachings in their sacred books of revelation and the empirical facts on the ground. The problems of evil, nonbelief, wrong belief, unanswered prayer and others addressed in Chapter 7 are paradigm examples, as is the problem of deconversion and defection from the faith by once converted and faithful believers who allege to have been "born of God." One significant problem for the user of such a tactic – as well, again, as the other common reasoning fallacies used without exception by Mormon and Christian apologists who must, at minimum, and necessarily, *a priori* presuppose (or 'beg

of the Spirit;" who had, in virtue of such an experience, and according to the revealed word of scripture, "put off the natural man," received "a mighty change of heart" and been "changed from [a] carnal and fallen state, to a state of righteousness" such that he no longer had "the disposition to do evil, but to do righteousness continually;" who moreover was likewise believed to have actually received the promised "Gift of the Holy Ghost" and now enjoyed the constant companionship of that member of the Mormon godhead (including, with it, the gift of discerning good and evil, and false revelation or "spirits"); and who, also according to scripture, could not (and "doth/does not") therefore commit sin" or "continue in sin"… or…"continue *to* sin, for the Spirit of God remaineth in him" and "because he is born of God" (1 John 3: 9; and Joseph Smith's *Inspired Version*, 1 John 3: 9) *possibly* be deceived, self-deceived, or enticed to *sin* again against God, Christ, and the Holy Spirit, as well as *continue* in such sin? The very possibility of such a state of affairs – as well as the possibility of committing the "unpardonable sin" (Heb. 6:4-8; Jacob 7:19; Alma 39:6; D&C 76: 34-5)[222] – seemed incoherent to me then as a faithful insider who had such a *paradigm* experience[223] and no conscious desire to sin, and still does as

---

the question' of) the very existence of their god's existence in order to resolve any apparent contradiction or skeptical challenge to their faith – is that its use also *a priori* invalidates the argument being made and does nothing to resolve the contradictions and answer the challenges, except perhaps in the troubled minds of those who simply seek to relieve or avoid their doubts.

In this last regard, Dr. Jason Long, in his contribution *The Malleability of the Human Mind* in Loftus 2010, put it very well: "A troubled [theistic believer] might not peruse, comprehend, or even read [– no less reason through –] an entire argument offered in defense of his belief, but the mere fact that a possible answer exists satisfies him that there is a reasonable answer to the skeptical objection [or inconsistency]. Never mind the fact that anyone can cite an authority who agrees with a particular position, especially when it comes to interpreting [scripture]. Due to an innate bias to confirm what we already believe, the authority's position is not going to be scrutinized or tested against a rebuttal. The [believer] is interested in feeling comfortable with his beliefs, not in dispassionately evaluating them. People want to feel reassured that they are correct in their beliefs, especially when there is a lot of emotion, personality, history and identity at stake. If the [believer] were genuinely interested in the truth, he would analyze the argument critically and thoroughly to see if it adequately addressed the points of the skeptical objection. But he is not questioning; he is defending" (72).

222 According to Mormon doctrine, and in the words of the late Mormon Apostle Bruce R. McConkie (1979), "Commission of the unpardonable sin consists in crucifying unto oneself the Son of God afresh and putting him to open shame. (Heb. 6: 4-8; D&C 76: 34-35.) To commit this unpardonable crime," McConkie continues, "a man must receive the gospel, gain from the Holy Ghost by revelation the absolute knowledge of the divinity of Christ, and then deny 'the new and everlasting covenant by which he was sanctified, calling it an unholy thing, and doing so despite the Spirit of grace.' (Teachings of the Prophet Joseph Smith, p. 128) He thereby commits murder by assenting unto the Lord's death, that is, having a perfect knowledge of the truth he comes out in open rebellion and places himself in a position wherein he would have crucified Christ knowing perfectly the while that he was the Son of God'" (816-7).

According to this particular teaching, those who are 'born of God', or sanctified by the receipt of the Holy Ghost and the sure revelation that Jesus is the Christ, and then leave the Church and become enemy of the faith, denying that they had in fact received such a revelation, has committed the "unpardonable sin." That this teaching is in blatant contradiction to the scriptural effects of being 'born of God' is clear, as is the fact that Bible authors and Joseph Smith invented such a "sin" to place "apostasy," persecution, and the profaning (or secularization) of what they of necessity deemed "sacred" outside the reach of such a contradiction; something which is impossible to do without conveniently qualifying the meaning of the words of scripture which make such sin – or *any* sin and its continuance – impossible for one who has truly been 'born of God.'

223 For a Mormon scriptural account of such an experience, see Mosiah 27: 24-29 for the conversion narrative of one of the fictional protagonists of the *Book of Mormon*, Alma the Younger; and for another account of

an informed outsider looking back on the chain of events and nagging inconsistencies and related doubts leading to my deconversion.[224] Moreover, any attempt to evasively or apologetically equivocate on the plain, unequivocal meaning of the scriptural words referred to above in an attempt to resolve such apparent inconsistencies would not do so.

---

the same experience, see Alma 36: 3-24. See also a like account in Enos 1-8. The *Book of Mormon* is replete with examples of dramatic conversion experiences.

224 Apart from the incoherence and factual unintelligibility of 'God-talk' and putative 'spiritual experience' or 'revelation' as such, and, quoting Cohen (1988), "After taking into account the plays on words, other translation problems, and the use of hyperbole in a way foreign to Western literature, there remain the calculatedly confusing biblical [or scriptural] usages of words, making them take on conflicting or even contradictory definitions [or meaning]. The believer cannot articulate or relevantly discuss the ponderous ideas and menacing implications impinging on him; nevertheless, they register at a subconscious level. His attempts to articulate and discuss them result in his discourse becoming filled with time-consuming casuistry. Dialogue with the deeply indoctrinated goes in circles" (186).

This is clearly the case in the scriptural treatment of the "Doctrine of Christ" in Mormonism alluded to above. The "calculatedly confusing biblical [and other scriptural] usages of words" regarding what it means to be "saved," "sanctified," or "born of God" is indeed contradictory in relation to the 'reborn' individual's state of being. In the Mormon faith, the words of scripture are, from a broad or widely consensual understanding of certain words, clear that those who are truly 'born of God' are essentially and necessarily saved *unconditionally* in virtue of the "mighty change" wrought in their minds and hearts and the receipt of the gift of the Holy Ghost as a *constant* companion. To experience such a "mighty change" is not only to be "cleansed" of *all* sin and sinfulness by the "baptism of fire and of the Holy Ghost," but to have one's fundamental nature changed to the degree that the person has *no* "disposition" to do evil, but rather to do "righteousness *continually*." Yet other scripture and teachings in the Mormon faith suggest otherwise, i.e. that those who are 'born of God' (or 'sanctified') are saved conditionally and can sin and fall from grace, or even sin "unto perdition" (see note 222 above).

"The biblical [or other scriptural] assault on key words, loading them with ponderous, contrived, dissonant meanings," Cohen writes, "I call *logocide*, the killing of words [or the common meaning of words]" (186). This third of Cohen's seven "devices" of "The Evangelical Mind-Control System" (169-387) is preceded by what he terms the "attractive persona of the bible [or scriptures]" or "colossal bait-and-switch sales pitch" found in those scriptural passages promising deliverance, redemption, prosperity, and happiness in this life, and joy through "eternal life" and reunion with family in the next (device 1), and by the second device of "discrediting 'The World,' including one's human nature and secular humanistic values. And it is followed naturally (and logically) by four other "devices," including (device 4) the scriptural assault on [intellectual] integrity through insistence on believing of the unbelievable (and in spite of contradictions caused by logocide), (device 5) the inducement of dissociation through (in my interpretation) the creation of a one-sided religious self and the creation of an alternate reality – or "corruption of reality" (Schumaker 1995) – through faith for fear of being found unworthy, (device 6) the isolation from outsiders (and outsider criticism of the faith) who are *of* the World, and (device 7) the "Holy Terror" of sinning ("unto perdition") by leaving and turning against the faith.

All seven of Cohen's discovered "devices" of mind-control in the Bible are used by Christian fundamentalists and, no doubt, by all other forms and sects of revelation-based theism. They are also embedded in the other Mormon scriptures and, as noted earlier, the "pattern of the double-bind in Mormonism" discovered by Stricker (2000). But of the seven devises, and in regard to my own experience, it was the contradictions by logocide, the relentless assault on my intellect, and the force of my suppressed and shamed human needs and doubt split off from consciousness by dissociation that enabled my deconversion. This it did by first requiring me to intellectually and "spiritually" separate from the Church hierarchy in order to preserve my faith (delusion), and then by facilitating the crisis of faith which ensued when I rationalized the use of my faith to justify acting-out in an unconscious move to psychologically individuate and thrive as a person. Ironically, and from a depth-psychological perspective, by fully embracing the doctrines of Mormonism (and especially its 'doctrines of salvation') I was restored to my natural Atheism and mental health by the very teachings of the faith – and the pattern, mechanisms and devices of mind-control inherent in them – that were designed to bind me (as well as *all* believers).

It would merely strip such an essential, salvational experience of its *sui generis* doctrinal significance as the singular healing, redemptive, and empowering 'blessing' to man it was enticingly (even if incoherently) held out to be to compel belief and constancy in the faith for those who sought it. For in addition to the utter incoherence of such an *ersatz* promise and its nature, requirements and implications, if a person can sin whether or not he has been saved, sanctified, or 'born of God,' and thereby received the "mighty change of heart" and "constant companionship of the Holy Ghost," then why the scriptural emphasis on being 'born of God' as being essential for salvation, and on the promise and stated fact that such a person, in virtue of such an experience and 'blessing,' does *not* sin or continue *in* sin, or *to* sin?[225] The intentional 'bait and switch' and resulting 'double-bind' are, to me, clearly evident here.

Further, and apart from the very concept of conversion and redemption through 'spiritual rebirth' being *a priori* incoherent alone and in virtue of its necessary dependence on the actual existence of certain factual non realities such as spirits, God, Christ, the Holy Ghost, the Light of truth (Christ), revelation, faith and the atonement, as we learned in Chapters 3-6, the above *ad hominem* explanation for deconversion is also invalid as an argument. Beyond *a priori begging the question* of god's existence, it also invalidly *affirms the consequent*. This it does by implicitly arguing that since a person who has truly been "Born of God" *cannot*, according to god's revealed word, continue to sin or continue in sin, then if a person who claims to have been 'born of god' continues in sin to the point of deconversion or 'apostasy' from the faith, that person consequently and necessarily has not been truly 'born of god.' Such an argument, of course, disregards more plausible and parsimonious explanations for deconversion (and therefore, conversion); purely naturalistic explanations which have no need for god, or obedience to god.

From my perspective, the most intelligible and plausible answer to the earlier question (i.e. how is it that someone who once experienced the intense feelings ascribed to spiritual conversion or "rebirth" no longer experiences them and consequently is no longer able to "sing the song of redeeming love" to the truth of Christ's existence, atonement and love?) is not, again, the superstitious (and unintelligible) one of being "cut-off from the Spirit" or losing the capacity to "feel the Spirit" as a consequence of "sin." Rather, it is

---

225 The defensive appeal to "free agency," if it is made, cannot resolve this problem for Mormons. Apart from the arguable *non reality* of free will (agency) and the falseness or incoherence of body/spirit dualism (see note 234), its putative existence is theologically considered in Mormonism to be an inherent capacity or faculty of the 'eternal' 'spirit and intelligence' in man. Unless Mormons are willing to concede that the *agency* in the 'flesh' and the power of 'Satan' are *more powerful* than the 'free agency' in the 'spirit' and the power of the 'Godhead,' then the 'sanctified' or transformed spirit in man that has experienced *the* 'mighty change' of 'heart' – i.e. has 'put-off' the 'natural man' that is 'carnal, sensual and devilish,' and 'put on' the divine nature inclusive of the disposition, desire and motivation not to sin or continue in sin, but to do right continually – and is guided and protected from deception by the constant companionship of the 'Holy Ghost' would necessarily make it impossible for the 'saved' or 'born again' saint (or sanctified believer) to exercise (because of satanic deception, self-deception, temptation or desire) his 'free agency' to deliberately sin and continue in sin. According to Mormon and Christian theology, it is the *spirit* in man that has free agency, and it is the *nature* and *disposition* of the *spirit* in man that determines *how* such free agency will be exercised, whether for good or evil. How then could a redeemed, 'born again' spirit in a man who enjoys the 'gift of the Holy Ghost' exercise his free agency to sin if, by definition, he has no need, desire or disposition to do so (because of the 'mighty change of heart'), if he knows better (by indoctrination, warning, revelation, or the restraint of regenerated conscience), and if he cannot be deceived, self-deceived, or tempted to do so?

again a naturalistic one which would amply account for such a loss or absence of certain intense feelings physiologically and psychologically on the basis of certain changes to the brain caused by various deconverting experiences which undermine faith or no longer support religious belief. More specifically, and from, for example, a depth-psychological perspective, certain ecstatic, transformational feelings of attachment (love, trust, devotion, commitment, fusion) once experienced in virtue of a suggestively induced, regressive transference of the internalized parent onto the believed Parent-God are no longer experienced once the transference is broken, or resolved. Such feelings can also be blocked as an unconscious defense against the repeated loss or abandonment of self, or simply depotentiated through the resulting development (individuation and integration) of the personality and its internal coping resources which can naturally make regressive dissociation and transference less frequent, less likely under stress or distress and less compelling or forceful. Additionally, and significantly, such so-called "spiritual" feelings can be effectually blocked by deprogramming effectuated through the conscious and deliberate submission to the "authority of reason" in the use, for example, of Loftus' "outsider test of faith" (2008, 2010) and the adoption of a naturalistic – or what Harbour (2001) refers to as a "meritocratic" – worldview, as well as by changes in the person's basic belief structure effectuated through cognitive and behavioral re-conditioning or pre-conditioning, and the "intrinsic evidentialism" attributed to "beliefs own ethics" (Adler 2006).

Analysis and Assessment

Beyond being prototypical as a "twice born" conversion experience (James 1987), the particular conversion account above is a case, like all the others, worthy of conceptual analysis (Chapter 1)[226], discourse analysis (Stromberg 1993)[227], and

---

226 Again, as used in this work, "conceptual analysis" determines whether or not intended *factual* statements made about the *literal* existence of God and spiritual phenomena make rational sense or have cognitive meaning as *actual* (i.e. justified) truth claims. More specifically, such analysis involves the "unpacking" of core religious concepts such as God, salvation, revelation and faith to determine if such concepts, the way such terms are used in first and second order religious discourse, are intelligible, coherent and factually meaningful if stated as *literal* or *actual* "truths" or *knowledge* of "truth," and if such statements, as beliefs, can be considered to be rational.

227 "Discourse Analysis" is the specialized methodology of analyzing conversion narratives. According to Peter Stromberg, a cultural anthropologist who wrote the insightful and thought-provoking book *Language and Self-transformation* (1993), "...it is through the use of language in the conversion narrative that the processes of increased commitment and self-transformation take place[;] that... [p]ractices such as the conversion narrative arise as ritual means to reconcile contradictions in common-sense views held by an individual concerning human beings, intentions, morality, [reality] and so on. Such contradictions," Stromberg observes, "are likely to manifest themselves in our society in experiences of emotional conflict or 'mental illness,' [self-alienation] and other intense personal conflict [caused by contradictions experienced by [the individual] as confusion, guilt, anxiety and fear]" (vi, 27; interpolations mine).

In this context, such narratives "can be understood," again according to Stromberg, "as a form of ritual in which believers invoke central emotional conflicts and then attempt to resolve these conflicts by reframing them in the [grandiose, ego-syntonic] language of [their religious faith]." This suggests, as Stromberg states elsewhere, that the assumption of what he terms the "referential ideology" of meaning in language – the assumption that "...language points to an independently existing reality and that it can be used to describe that reality in terms that convey, without fundamentally distorting, its characteristics" – is "incorrect" (2). Such an "assumption is wrong," he explains, "in part because language always shapes the reality it describes. But

psychoanalytic assessment[228]. Specifically, and significantly, it entailed an experience which was suggestively and physically induced by prolonged fasting and prayer over the entirety of three consecutive days; an experience which was motivated *primarily* by personal circumstances, anxiety and emotional neediness at a time in my life when I reportedly sensed that "something was missing," and *secondarily* by an egocentric desire – born of a deep sense of personal powerlessness and unworthiness, and the believed scriptural injunctions and invitations related to "worthiness" and the acquisition of divine favor, privilege and power – to, as I put it then, enjoy a "personal relationship" with Christ, "enter into the Kingdom of God," and more fully enjoy "the blessings and gifts of the Holy Spirit."

Essentially this "conversion" experience, which, again, occurred in 1981, seven years after my conversion to the Mormon faith, involved what was then (incoherently) interpreted and believed to be a "vision" of Jesus Christ's suffering for the past sins and sinfulness of mankind; a vision which was experienced as being so real that it seemed I was somehow *actually* present as an eye witness to his atoning sacrifice and, moreover and significantly, his suffering on *my* behalf, for *my* salvation.

Over time I have come to regard my above described post-baptismal conversion experience as psychologically significant, even if not actually "sacred" in the religious

---

even more important," Stromberg continues, "is the fact that the process of referring to events and objects that transcend the actual event of speech is not the sole basis of meaning in language. Equally important in the creation of meaning are processes of indexing; language is meaningful to speakers in part because it may reflect a situation [, or unconscious psychological phenomenon and wholly subjective interpretation,] beyond the event of speech, but also because it creates a situation [or unconscious psychological reaction] in the event of speech" (2-3; interpolations mine).

"In this context," Stromberg concludes, "the important point is that [the] conversion narrative is not only or even primarily an account of [actual] events from the past, it is a *creation of a particular situation* in the moment of its telling. The way to look at [the subject's] conversion," he suggests, "is not as something that [actually] occurred in the past [as described] and is now 'told about' in the conversion narrative. Rather, the conversion narrative itself is a central element of the [situationally and psychologically self-induced] conversion. The way around the evidential problem…is to look instead at the speech itself, for it is *through language that the conversion occurred in the first place* and also through language that the conversion is now re-lived as the convert tells his tale" (3; interpolations and emphasis mine).

228 "Psychoanalytical assessment" pertains not only to the psychoanalytical (or psychodynamic) *treatment* of the religious convert, which in my view is always indicated, but to the assessment of the conversion narratives and religious literary and artistic works of religious converts or believers as an extension of conceptual and discourse analyses. Psychoanalytical assessment in this latter sense " does not," as clinical psychiatrist Robert D. Anderson informs us in his excellent psychobiography of Mormon founder Joseph Smith (1999), "deal with theory or the treatment of patients but instead [, and again,] focuses on…our *understanding* of individuals by their writings or personal histories… The techniques used in [such] psychoanalytic investigation are [, of course,] adapted from the techniques of psychoanalytic treatment [and are] rooted in the *natural* world and the body of knowledge that has accumulated about how both mentally healthy people and mentally ill patients react and think, and how the works of artists and writers reflect their personalities in one way or another" (xxix, xxxiii, 138, emphasis mine). And such techniques are in turn based on the fundamental premise of Freud's work in psychoanalysis, which, as simply summarized by Michael Kahn in his accessible and engaging book *Basic Freud* (2002), is that "We don't know why we feel what we feel; we don't know why we fear what we fear; we don't know why we think what we think; and above all, we don't know why we do what we do" (16). This premise is itself is rooted in Freud's theory of the unconscious, and is certainly reflected in the oft quoted words of renowned mythologist Joseph Campbell, who I think rightly claimed that: "What is running the show is what is coming up from way down below."

sense.[229] In the end, I have concluded, on the basis of my own conceptual analysis of my written account of this experience, that it contains, in its entirety as stated, "God-talk" which is again, both in its particularity and entirety, utterly unintelligible and cognitively meaningless as literal truth claims – even, I would argue, to honest, educated and reflective insiders of the Mormon Church.[230] I have also concluded, on the basis of the proposal for assessing the rationality of belief presented in Chapter 2, that my beliefs and interpretations as then recorded in the above account were then, and are now, in both their particularity and entirety, unquestionably incoherent and therefore irrational.

Clearly, in making certain putative knowledge and truth claims as I did in my formal written account, that, for example, "the Spirit called me," "the Lord spake to my mind," "I saw my beloved Redeemer," "I was in Gethsemane on the day of His Agony," "I witnessed his act of Atonement," "I saw the love and suffering of Christ," "I had been truly born of the Spirit to enter into the Kingdom of God," "I was redeemed from the Fall and sancti-fied by the blood of Christ" etc., I did not know then (or now) what I was talking about and neither did those who thought they did or might now think they do. As we learned in Chapters 1 and 3-5 none of these statements make literal sense as stated, or as literally believed. All are unintelligible and factually vacuous (and therefore wholly unwarranted) as truth claims, as well as utterly incoherent in relation to what is – or might be – possible

---

229 The psychological significance of this experience, from a psychoanalytical perspective, was, for me, in the intra-psychical healing of the narcissistic wound inflicted at childhood. Such self-induced healing, albeit partial, ensued, by my way of thinking, through the ecstatic reunion with the internalized and idealized maternal imago or 'object.' This affective reunion with the 'internalized parent' was reframed – by religious conditioning and delusional, wishful thinking – as a 'redemptive' reunion with the 'Parent-God' of my faith. Such an intra-psychical dynamic is, I think, likely to be the psychological reality beneath all mythological 'redemption' or 'salvation' dramas embedded in our psyche through religious indoctrination or enculturation (and perhaps even genetic transmission), including the derivative, mythic Christian drama of the suffering Christ ('Maternal Matrix') who heals or 'redeems' his children through pure, unconditional, and sacrificial love and forgiveness, and reconciles the wayward child to God (or the 'Paternal Matrix').

There is, of course, nothing at all 'eternal,' supernatural or objectively literal in such religious mythology, or of 'divine' origin (an assertion, if made, which is false and incoherent). It is, rather, simply the way the human brain evolved and works, and how it has, for many, been affected, again, through religious indoctrina-tion and/or enculturation over time. Nor is such psychological significance unique to religious experience. It is essential to note in this last regard that given the toxic effects of theistic faith in god, I and others who have had such a religious experience would have been far better off without it. Instead, it is in my view far better to experience such effects through *non-religious* human relational experiences, as so many others do in the natural course of their lives, or though, again, an indicated form of *non*-religious psychotherapy. Ironi-cally, what the religious mythology of redemption holds out as psychological benefit to the believer, theistic dogma nullifies or reverses through its "deadly doctrine" (Watters 1992) and, as we learned in Chapter 8 of this work, the "abusive dynamic" inherent in it.

230 While the language in my written and above summarized conversion account was certainly meaningful and significant to me then, as it is to Mormon and Christian believers today, it is not, as we learned in Chapters 1 and 3-6, expressive of concepts which are *cognitively* meaningful or *factually* significant. As statements or beliefs intended to be taken as *absolute* and *literal* or *actual* truths they are unintelligible and incoherent. In that sense, I did not know what I was talking about, even though I was certainly familiar with the terms and they had, for me, meaning as use. By using these terms according to the rules of the Mormon language-game I was essentially living or practicing my religion. The "meaning" of the language used was its use, and its significance was, as it is in all such religious "witnessing" or "testifying," in producing the desired effect, which was to *affect* (inspire, edify) myself and others, and thereby strengthen my own and others' commit-ment to the Mormon way of life believed to be true.

in this or any world in the universe.

Further, on the basis of both discourse analysis and psychoanalytical assessment born of my own psychotherapy and introspective self-analysis over the years, I am personally convinced that my particular conversion experience (and all others like it of any faith) was merely a hypnotically induced psychological phenomenon. Clinically stated, it might be appropriately characterized as a regressive psychotic experience[231] and accompanying "transcendence hallucination"[232] originating from a dissociated and delusional state of mind. Significantly, such a state of mind and accompanying dissociative, hallucinatory experience was in this case, as again in all others of like kind, made possible by my own personal circumstances and psychological condition at the time. And it was made all the more "real" by religious indoctrination, and the "magical thinking" and superstitious beliefs inherent in, and definitive of, Mormonism and all theistic faiths.

---

231 Such psychological experience is not necessarily indicative of acute or chronic psychopathology in all cases. As we learned in Chapter 5 from Schumaker and Faber, we all distort reality from time to time through the induced mechanism of dissociation, and we all likewise, and often, hallucinate. Nevertheless, "conversion" experiences such as this one and others of like kind involving, by their very nature, a delusional split from reality, as well as self-flagellation and despair through morbid repentance, followed by regressive rapprochement and ecstasy or mania experienced and interpreted as 'redemption' or 'salvation' from a "carnal and sensual" state of sin, are, in my view, and from a clinical psychiatric perspective, indicative of mental illness (see Jones 2006, 16-40 and 64-5; and Watters 1992, 133-52, inclusive of notes and references).

Even if, as suggested for example by the various contributors in Isabel Clarke's *Psychosis and Spirituality* (2001), certain "spiritual" or religio-mystical experiences might arguably exist on a continuum and are not all necessarily indicative of psychopathology, they are mere (and non-dualistic) manifestations of brain function (i.e. neuropsychological phenomena) and consist of at least some false, incoherent or nonsensical truth claims which are therefore *not* indicative of *actual* truth or reality. This would be so in *all* cases involving reported and interpreted religious "dreams," "visions," "revelations," and heavenly "visitations" claimed to be from gods, angels, or spirits. I think it is reasonable to suggest therefore that given the above, whenever *anyone* claims in seriousness to have *literally* seen, spoken with, or heard from any god, spirit, or angel; or to have "felt" the "Spirit" of god or received a "revelation" from god or an actual and specific "answer" to prayer, such people have experienced hallucinations which – if believed with *certainty* to be *literally* true as claimed *despite* common sense, sound argument, and valid evidence or sound, naturalistic explanation to the contrary – are very likely delusions as well. Moreover, if such claimed experience has in fact had a profound affect on the believer's life (as all true conversion experiences do by definition), that person is delusional (*at least in relation to that particular aspect of his life*) and has therefore very likely experienced a regressive psychosis (and thereby created an alternate reality) which is at least, – given the unavoidable and undeniable psychological woundedness of *all* humans and the unpredictability of human action and reaction in certain extreme circumstances – *potentially* if not actually psychopathological to some degree.

Perhaps in the end, and again in regard to affective, religious "conversion" experiences in particular and not merely irrational religious belief (a pleonasm), Nietzsche got it right when he wrote that "Not every one who likes can be a Christian [or Mormon]: no man is "converted" to Christianity [or any theistic religion], – he must be sick enough for it" (2000, 79). This was certainly so in my case, and I suspect in every other case of religious conversion as well, regardless of whatever salutary effects or *net* psychological benefits might ensue or accrue to the 'converted' believer, if any.

232 As Tarico informs us in Loftus (2010), "The transcendence hallucination" is a clinical term which applies to "an acute sense of connection with a reality that lies beyond and behind this natural plane. It typically lasts for just a few seconds or minutes but may leave a profound impression that lasts a lifetime. Transcendence hallucination can be triggered by neurological events (like a seizure, stroke, or migraine aura) or by a drug (such as psilocybin), but it also can be triggered by overstimulation or understimulation of the brain [through, for example, fasting and prayer]" (61).

More specifically, and as alluded to in Chapter 8 and note 231, I consider my conversion experience, like all others, to be a specific manifestation of mental illness. This condition may be characterized in such a case by self-hatred, superstitious, magical thinking, the compartmentalization and delusional acceptance as 'Truth' (through self-deception) of absurd, irrational beliefs, and a perversion of motivation based on a self-sacrificing moral code.

While "mental illness" is still unfortunately considered a pejorative term or attribution to many if not most people today, it need not be. The mind is merely and entirely a function of the brain, and the brain is, of course, part of our body as human beings. In this sense, to be mentally ill is to fundamentally be physically ill, and to suffer from mental illness is no different – again at a fundamental level – than suffering from a disease or illness of the heart or the liver. To be mentally ill, therefore, is to suffer from disease or damage to, or a malfunction of, the brain (note 234). Such illness is manifested in the brain's cognitive, affective, and behavioral functions, as well as in the body through somatization and distress. While mental illness can be genetically caused, or result from certain physical factors such as injury or trauma to the brain, drug and alcohol use or abuse, or disease of the brain, it can also be caused by various social and environmental factors that damage the personality (and therefore the brain) and consequently impair the ability of the person to function well (or in extreme cases at all) in relation to self and others. In relation to religion specifically, and the personality or brain function of the theistic believer in particular, we are dealing with mental illness caused primarily by social and environmental factors typically originating in the home and reinforced by the religious community and society at large. More specifically in this regard, the mental illness that believers (and arguably, to some degree, all who have been culturally infected by theism) suffer from is, in large part, and as I see it, the natural result of the toxic shaming of moralistic, authoritarian abuse (see note 2 in the *Introduction*). Someone who is "shame-based" through "toxic shaming" (Bradshaw 1988) is mentally ill, and typically, if not invariably, suffers various psychiatric symptoms, syndromes, and character disorders as a result of such abuse which explain or account for the desire for, and experience of, redemptive religious conversion.

Authoritarian abuse, whether overt or covert in the guise of 'gentle-but-firm' persuasion or character building, typically begins and does its baseline damage to the brain in the shame-based family of the individual during childhood. Such abuse is rooted in what Alice Miller refers to as the "poisonous pedagogy" of "child-rearing" in the home[233]

---

233 See Alice Miller's *For your Own Good*, 1990. This book is, in my view, essential reading for all parents. In it Miller exposes the deeply embedded values, beliefs, and implicit teachings of "child-rearing." Such a "pedagogy," for Mormons and other theists, is derived from the 'moralistic core' and 'code of patriarchy' inherent in their religion, as presented in Chapter 8 and the *Epilogue* of this work. What is crucial here from my perspective is that *regardless* of how nurturing, loving, patient and longsuffering religious parents are, or intend or strive to be (or seem to be) in raising their children, their commitment to their faith will make *whatever* they teach and do in 'raising up their children to the Lord' abusive. In other words, *regardless* of the gentleness and benevolent intentions of religious parents, *whatever* and *however* they teach their children in the faith will be a form of authoritarian abuse which eschews free-thinking and doubt regarding the faith, manipulates and conditions their children's thinking to accept the prescribed way of life and commitments of the faith, and implicitly or explicitly requires their children to be obedient to their god and priesthood authority in the home and church, and to behave in a way that reflects the values and mores of their faith and religious community. Simply put, and as we learned in Chapter 8, authoritarian abuse is *built into* the teachings, doctrines, practices, and programs of the faith, and framed (falsely or incoherently, and either ig-

and, if the parents are religious, the indoctrination to the belief system of their particular faith. This damage is essentially done through 'toxic shaming' and brainwashing – allegedly for the child's "own good" (Miller 1990) – by various forms and degrees of authoritarian mind-control and related verbal and physical abuse. And it is reinforced and made worse by 'hard' (insistent/coercive) or 'soft' (suggestive/persuasive) religious indoctrination into a particular faith or, if not, when the damaged individual is later inducted into a theistic religion (such as Mormonism) that recapitulates the abusive pattern of the family through its inherent 'abusive dynamic' (see Chapter 8 and the *Epilogue*).

In my case, the damage to my personality which initially made me ill occurred, again, in my own family of origin. Such damage was later reinforced and made worse through my indoctrination to the theistic beliefs and shaming 'moralistic core' and 'code of patri-archy' deeply embedded in the belief system of the Mormon faith. This superstitious and toxic belief system is, of course, not exclusive to Mormonism. It is inherent in all theistic faiths whose belief system fosters "magical thinking," and which implicitly or explicitly eschews or condemns the natural, biological (true) self and teaches and enforces – through its 'authoritative' teachings and various "infantilizing" (Faber 2010) mind-control and disciplinary strategies and devices – what clinical psychiatrist H.E. Jones refers to, again, as a morality of "self-hatred" which requires "self-sacrifice," and the formation of a new (false or inauthentic) "religious self" (2006, 16-39).

In this particular context, and in relation to my believed 'redemptive' conversion experience above, it is important to enlarge our perspective by turning to the words of Jones in more depth. In doing so it should be noted – as shall be further elaborated on below – that his paradigm psychiatric characterization of the internal mental landscape and processing of the religious believer is accurate in my case, and no doubt in other (and arguably *all*) like cases as well.

Accordingly, in his chapter outlining the development of the fundamentals of mental illness, Jones writes (with my interpolations added for increased relevance to Mormonism):

"The foundation for mental illness is formed by the religious indoctrination of chil-dren. The anti-self morality combined with the [regressive, irrational, and delusional faith-based] epistemology produce both emotive and cognitive mental damage. This produces the two attributes of these post-indoctrination individuals that play a role in the development of psychiatric syndromes. These are "magical thinking" and an ["anti-self"] and anti-life [ideology] and motivation" (64). Such an ideology, Jones informs us, "will not…integrate into the human mind [without force through self-deception]. The Forebrain can be programmed with religious self-sacrifice, but the Hindbrain…cannot adapt to it. However, a child [or needy, insecure and/or shame-based individual] placed under great

---

norantly or stupidly) as the 'divinely sanctioned' way to truly 'love' one's children. Merely by encouraging, involving, or requiring their children to participate in the ordinances, rites and rituals of the faith and follow the programs of the faith (i.e. Church attendance, 'Home Teaching,' 'Family Home Evening,' 'Missionary preparation,' full-time 'Missionary work,' 'Temple marriage,' 'Temple work,' etc.), faithful Mormon parents, who have themselves been made mentally ill through indoctrination and self-sacrifice, *are* in fact likewise indoctrinating their vulnerable and intellectually defenseless children to the harmful superstitious and de-lusional 'self-hating' and 'self-sacrificing' program of their faith. In doing so – even, again, with the best intentions "for their own good" – they are in fact creating the conditions of mental illness in their children, whether they know or admit it or not.

social pressure [or the pressures of life-circumstances] to adopt this...anti-self, anti-life ideology may do so by using...the mental mechanism of compartmentalization" (65).

"Using his ability to compartmentalize, the theist child [or shame-based, indoctrinated adult] will form a pseudo-self. Using his imagination he creates a phony, contrived, inauthentic...'religious self.' This false 'religious self' [– which he is taught to believe is his 'eternal,' god-like 'spirit'-self'234 –] is [inhuman and consequently] too good to be believable. This perfect, selfless...'religious self' is created by the child [or the wounded 'child' in the mind-brain of the adult] in response to attacks on his moral character. He wants to be a 'good' person. So he creates a 'self' [(which has already, in principle, been created and characterized for him by the scriptures and teachings of the faith)] that he thinks will be acceptable to his parents [(or the illusory 'Parent-God' of his faith)], his culture and himself. He has a true, natural [or biological] self in his Hindbrain, but to please his parents [, 'Parent-God'], and himself, he creates an abstract, conceptual 'self'

---

234 The basis for the false and incoherent belief that there is a 'soul' or 'spirit'-self housed in the physical body can be traced to the philosophical belief in *dualism*, as well as in the belief held by theologians and some philosophers (and accepted and argued from ignorance) that matter cannot create thought. These two beliefs have no basis in reason or fact and allow for the formation of the pseudo, religious self Jones speaks of above.

As Watters (1992) writes in regard to dualism: "From its beginnings, the [Christian and Mormon] church had taught a rigidly dualistic conception of the human being; each man and each woman consisted of a body of 'flesh' and a 'spirit,' and the two were destined [in mortality]... to be at war with each other.. ...The concept of dualism did not originate with the Christians, but has philosophical roots reaching back to Plato and beyond. However, it is safe to say that the Christian version has had the most profound impact on the lives of human beings in the Western world. ...Under the influence of a belief system that promotes such hostility and distrust between two 'parts' of the indivisible whole human being, it requires almost superhuman effort for an individual to develop any sense of unity or wholeness. Without integration of the whole person, there can be no real self, no self-esteem, and no true self-mastery. If one buys into the Christian belief system, such integration becomes impossible, and the individual becomes dependent on the authority of the church. Such a divided person," Watters informs us, "is doomed to a life-long fate of irreconcilable conflict between potential human being struggling for integration and mastery, and the Christian [or Mormon] doomed...to fragmentation and abject groveling at the feet of the Almighty Father" (37-8).

Moreover, and regarding the supporting belief that the brain alone (consisting of mere gross, physical matter) cannot create thought (and therefore there must be a soul or spirit, consisting for Mormons as 'refined, spirit matter,' whatever such could possibly mean, if anything)), neuropsychologist Chris Frith, *in Making Up the Mind* (2007) writes, as quoted in Stenger (2009): "... [The] distinction between the mental and the physical is false. It is an illusion created by the brain. Everything we know about the physical or the mental world comes to us through our brain. ...By hiding from us all the unconscious inferences that it makes, our brain creates the illusion that we have direct contact with objects in the physical world. And at the same time our brain creates the illusion that our own mental world is isolated and private. Through these two illusions we experience ourselves as agents, acting independently in the world. But at the same time, we can share our experiences of the world. Over the millennia this ability to share experience has created human culture that has, in its turn, modified the functioning of the human brain. ...By seeing through theses illusions created by our brain, we can begin to develop a science that explains how the brain creates the mind" (189). "Frith's claim," according to Stenger, "is supported by a growing body of experiments in which a subject's conscious awareness presents a false picture of reality. Some of these are already familiar, such as subliminal perception, blind-sight, and phantom limbs. Perhaps the most startling example, one that clashes with our most cherished notions of self [and indeterministic or contra-causal free will], is the evidence [produced by Benjamin Libet and collaborators in 1983, and independently confirmed later] that the brain makes decisions before our conscious awareness of deciding to do something [(see Wegner's *The Illusion of Conscious Will*, 2002)]. ... [W]e have no reason," Stenger concludes, "to make a connection between the unconscious and the soul [or 'spirit']. The main examples in Frith and thousands of other books and articles on empirical neuroscience provide convincing evidence that matter makes mind" (189-90). See also Elbert (2000), Flanagan (2002), and Edis (2002).

[– an ideal, 'one-sided' self –] in his Forebrain [that corresponds to the ideal, 'spirit'-self (as a *literal* 'child of god') specified or characterized by the faith as being like 'Jesus' and 'Heavenly Father'] (36).

"What happens inside the mind of [individuals] who internalize self-hate? ... [The individual's personality splits and he] forms a mental compartment where he can store his 'religious' self' and all the superstitious fantasy and religious nonsense he [has been socially conditioned and pressured] to believe. Mystical beliefs and fantasies of life after death, immortal beings, and supernatural realms populated with human-like [Parent-Gods] are accepted into this compartment. Saints, angels, [the 'spirits' of deceased loved ones], prophets, disciples and devils [or 'evil spirits'] all become inhabitants of this mental sphere. Here, these fantasies can be protected from reality (37).

"All mental illness begins with the identification of the true, biological self as selfish, bad, evil, unworthy, and destructive [; as, in Mormonism, the 'carnal, sensual, and devilish' fallen or 'natural man' who is an 'enemy to God' in need of redemption]. After identifying the true self as something undesirable, shameful and loathsome, the individual goes to work against his true self. All mental illness begins as a form of self-hate. The mentally ill see their self as their enemy, something within themselves [– i.e. their natural, human 'appetites, desires and passions' –] that they must work to control, imprison, disown or destroy. Or they must do things so terrible as to get somebody else to destroy their self for them (38).

"When the mentally ill individual sides with his true self, he feels guilty. He has violated his moral code of self-sacrifice [(the internalized 'moralistic core' of his faith)]. When he sacrifices his [true] self, he becomes angry. This is because he recognizes he has done something painful and stupid [by abandoning himself]. Then, feeling ashamed of his anger, he turns inward on himself, punishes himself inside his mind and becomes depressed. He spends his life vacillating between guilt and depression [for continually falling short of his own, others' and his god's expectations]. ... (38).

"Suicide is often the end result of this self-hatred. Suicide is premeditated murder of the 'self.' Self-hate is the natural consequence of the evil morality of human sacrifice, of self-sacrifice. Once a child [/individual] has developed self-hate, the escape from suicide is the [formation of the] 'religious self.' The creation of this inauthentic, phony identity establishes a way to think well of oneself. There is then a way to stimulate secretion of brain endorphins and have some ['happiness']. It is through redemption" (39).

Jones continues: "The promise of redemption, of being 'reborn' or 'born-again' post-pones total destruction of the self and relegates self-destruction to times of excessive success and happiness. Without redemption, the individual will engage in the self-destruction that religion has now programmed into his mind. ...The redemptive process must be 'extra self', or beyond or above the 'self'. Redemption must come from without, from a 'higher power'. The mentally ill believe that nothing good can come from within, the self is bad, and cannot redeem anything" (40).

Jones analysis is based, again, on his own extensive clinical case-work over an extended period of time as a practicing psychiatrist. And though his conclusions that the religious indoctrination of individuals causes mental illness come from his psychodynamic perspective, they are confirmed by other psychological perspectives as well, including those informed by family systems theory, learning theory, and cognitive-behavioral theory.[235]

Taking a Deeper Look

Renowned psychotherapist Erik H. Erikson wrote: "Christianity [including Mormonism] has shrewdly played into man's most child-like needs, not only by offering eternal guarantees for an omniscient power's benevolence (if properly appeased) but also by magic words and significant gestures, soothing sounds, and soporific smells – an infant's world." These words, coupled with the likewise provocative words of Demosthenes quoted earlier that "Nothing is easier than self deception, for what each man wishes, that he also wishes to be true," and the immortal words of Socrates that "The unexamined life is not worth living," serve I think as an apt and important preface to this section.

Given the unjustifiable and therefore unwarranted theistic truth claims made in all religious or "spiritual" experiences (in contrast to the warranted – or justified – and common-sensical, naturalistic explanations of such experiences) and their consequential impact in the lives of believers, perhaps the most significant question to consider more deeply in this analysis and assessment is: What is the nature, source and likely explanatory basis of the *certainty* experienced and asserted regarding the interpretation and believed meaning and truth of such experiences? Again, that I experienced and asserted such certainty at the time of this conversion experience and throughout my remaining years in the faith cannot be denied. It is to the nature and source of such certainty, and how it is that I came to regard my interpretation of this experience with such certainty that we now turn.

In doing so, we shall consider first the neurological phenomenon of certainty related to the interpretations of all such religious (or "spiritual") experiences. That the experience and at least tacit belief of certainty *as a fact* is common in all walks of life is uncontroversial, as is – with often qualified admission – the acknowledged fact of human fallibilism. One area of exception to this latter fact, of course, is in what theistic believers regard as the certain, unquestionable religious truths of *their* faith; truths based on, and confirmed by, their likewise certain interpretations of *their own* believed truth-confirming religious (or "spiritual") experience.

But how reliable are our subjective experiences of certainty in *any* area of human knowledge? And how "true" is our belief that our feelings of certainty are *actually* indicative of actual, infallible truth?

These questions have I think, and again, been convincingly addressed from a neuro-scientific perspective by Robert Burton (2008) and others noted and cited in his very

---

235 See Watters (1992), pp. 133-52, inclusive of his notes. Although there are, again, competently argued views on both sides of the question of whether or not religious belief is conducive to mental health and well-being (see Schumaker 1992), the research and conclusions which suggest that religion is correlated to mental health and well-being is, as addressed in Chapter 8, very problematic for a variety of reasons (see notes 176, 177 and 179). There is in my view, however, sufficiently compelling clinical and theoretical justification to suggest that "religion" – as represented by the authoritative, sacred texts, doctrines and teachings of 'revelation'-based theistic faiths – is determinative of certain psychiatric symptoms, syndromes, and character disorders, thereby establishing an at least apparent causal relationship between religion and mental illness. Still, as Watters I think correctly points out, while "rigorous scientific examination…should be tested as rigorously as research methodology will allow…[the] methodology for testing these [clinical] hypotheses is a long way from being developed; indeed, the design appropriate for studying this question may never be developed" (22). Nevertheless, and the absence of "rigorous scientific examination" notwithstanding, there is, to my mind, sufficient logical, empirical, and commonsensical support to warrant the conclusions presented in this work.

important and readable book, and referenced earlier in this work and by Valerie Tarico in Loftus (2010). Burton's stated goal in his book is to "strip away the power of certainty by exposing its involuntary roots" in hope that "[i]f science can shame us into questioning the nature of conviction, we might [as a species] develop…an increased willingness to [more reasonably] consider alternative ideas [and, I would add, more skeptically and rationally test our personal beliefs in the light of sound reasoning, valid evidence, and established knowledge]" (xiv).

Essentially, to the question regarding the nature and source of certainty, we learn from Burton and other neuroscientists that the experience of certainty originates in the *brain* (its source) and is manifested as a *feeling* (its nature). In other words, it is merely, and uncontroversially, an affective mental state or neurological phenomenon. "Are certainty and conviction purely deliberate, logical, and conscious choices, or not what they appear?" Burton answers: "For me, the evidence is overwhelming; the answer is startling and counterintuitive, yet unavoidable….Despite how certainty feels, it is neither a conscious choice nor even a thought process. Certainty and similar states of 'knowing [with certainty] what we know' arise out of involuntary brain mechanisms that, like love or anger, function independently of reason" (xiii). Later, in an effort to "dispel the notion that a *feeling of knowing* must be attached to a thought [believed to be right]," Burton points to "clinical examples…when the expression of the feeling of knowing occurs in the absence of any knowledge" as "…an isolated feeling of knowing" related to "moments of abnormal or altered brain function" (21). He concludes his survey of the state of neuroscience in this regard with the wise counsel that while "Neuroscience needs to address the physiology of mental states; we need to question the *feeling* [of *knowing* and the corresponding feeling and derived belief of being right when we're not]. And nothing," Burton suggests, "could be more basic [and I would add commendable] than to simply question the phrase, 'I know'" (219).

Going deeper still regarding the explanatory basis of *religious* certainty related to the nature, source and interpretation of so-called "spiritual" experiences in general, and "born again" or "conversion" experiences in particular, we must return yet again to our "basic biological situation" by exploring in more depth M.D. Faber's most recent work, *Becoming God's Children: Religion's Infantilizing Process* (2010); a work which complements and extends his other books (2002, 2004) which have been frequently (and extensively) quoted from and referred to throughout this work. Before summarizing the primary premises and conclusion of Faber's work, – a work which I think demands to be read in its entirety by all who are interested or in any way affected by this subject – I will begin with his initial "psychological inquiries" as context.

After presenting a few "thematic vignettes" of different Christian believers' participation in different affect-inducing religious activities (scripture reading, prayer, rituals, hymn singing, etc.) which lead to a reported sense of "spiritual" *renewal* and felt *confirmation* of the *certainty* of their belief in the *literal* existence of their 'Lord' and 'God,' Faber asks initially (and apart from the demonstrated incoherence of the believers' theistic beliefs): "What are these people doing? What are the mental and emotional processes, the mental and emotional aims that inform their behavior?" Other questions follow: "Why would someone who has already been born and parented seek to be reborn ritualistically [or "spiritually"] as the child of an invisible god whom he regards explicitly as his father, or if he follows the New Testament closely, as his 'Abba' or 'daddy' (Romans 8:15)? Why does Christianity [in general, and Mormonism in particular] consider this transformational baptism rite [by water and 'Spirit'] to be 'the basis of the whole Christian life?"

More specifically and relatedly, "Are Christians [and Mormons] always expected to [humbly and meekly] pray as 'little children'? If so, why? What does it mean to claim that a 'Holy Spirit' [or the 'Holy Ghost'] mediates the communication between the earthly prayer and the supernatural deity who presumably hears and answers? What *is* the Holy Spirit [or Holy Ghost] anyway? When people assert that they 'feel' its 'presence,' what [exactly] do they feel? What [specifically] constitutes its presence? When a Christian [or Mormon]... suggests that Jesus 'calls' upon [them – through scripture, hymn or 'prompting,' etc. –] to 'walk' with Him, ['follow'] Him, and...'talk' with Him, [does he mean to] imply that worshippers *actually* hear Jesus' voice, *actually* experience walking and talking to their Savior [or Heavenly Father]?" (4, 5; latter emphases mine)

These questions of course lead to others regarding, for example, the Christian Eucharist (or Mormon 'Sacramental' ordinance) in which the believer, if a Mormon, symbolically eats the body of Christ (broken bread) and drinks his blood (water in a cup) every Sabbath day (Sunday) in remembrance of the sacrifice of the 'Son of God,' and as a renewal of the baptismal covenant of obedience and commitment to Christ and his Gospel. In this regard, Faber asks, "Why would anyone want to (symbolically or, if a Catholic, *literally* through transubstantiation) eat the body of Jesus, or drink [his] blood?"... "Surely," Faber states, "such behavior invites close psychological scrutiny" (5).

Indeed it does. When such practices are placed in the Christian/Mormon context of "eternal salvation" through the believed sacrifice of Christ, we come to understand again what has been stated earlier; that the entire Christian (and Mormon) framework of beliefs and practices is, in Faber's words, an "infantilizing process" designed, at its most fundamental level, to "[remove] or at least [diminish] adaptively humankind's primal, instinctual fear of death, the termination of one's existence, the dreaded, inevitable end" (6). "But," as Faber also – and I think insightfully – points out, "death as human creatures perceive it, feel it, apprehend it developmentally and psychodynamically constitutes not only [existential] naught-ment, nothingness, emptiness; it also constitutes a *traumatic separation from the self and from others*, both as the self extends into others and as others are internalized into the self along the way, from the inception of one's days. Accordingly," – and this is particularly evident in virtue of Mormon Temple 'sealing' ordinances which are claimed to authoritatively and surely establish the marriage and family relationships of "worthy" believers 'for all eternity'– "heavenly salvation for [all Christian believers] is usually *social* in nature and tied conceptually to *reunion* with those they love, those upon whom they depend. ...Eternal salvation is ultimately *rescue* from the crisis of eternal separation" (7).

With the above preliminary (albeit greatly abridged) context as prelude, we can perhaps better appreciate the primary evolutionary and neuropsychological basis of feelings of certainty in the minds of religious believers regarding the interpretation of their religious experiences and the Truth of their theistic beliefs. Faber's seminal conclusion in this regard is consistent with Burton's neuroscientific position above on the experience of certainty, with the additional – and significant – aspect of positing a religious "infantilizing process" as its basis. (74-138)

Simply stated, and as I understand it in its most basic form, this process is the way

Mormons or other theists (particularly Christians) appeal to people of all ages to accept, in and remain in the faith.[236] It entails "priming" (or triggering) the "implicit" (or unconscious) memory of both investigators and believers – through evocative beliefs, promises, teachings, rites, rituals, and deliberate, supportive and inviting acts social acceptance – to hypnotically produce an *infantile* attraction to, and attachment with, the Parent-God of the faith. Psychologically such an (often overwhelming or compelling) affective infantile attraction and attachment is known, again, as a regressive, projective transference; a psychodynamic phenomenon (not unlike falling in love) that results in – or is characterized by – a *regressive, dissociated* state of mind.

Such a mental state is, from this perspective, the so-called "spiritual" faith-state of a religious believer who "testifies" of, or "bears witness" to, a believed *certain* knowledge of their Lord's and God's existence, mind and will, and various attributes of greatness and perfection. According to Faber, through the infantilizing process, all *Christianized* faiths effectually invoke the primal, "magical" *affects* of infancy – i.e. "mirroring," "evoked companions," "affective attunement," " merger," and "primary transformation" – experienced by each of us as infants in virtue of the "basic biological condition," (18-71; see also 2004, 17-47) and reframe such affects – as well as our early (and on-going) experiences as children of attachment, separation and rapprochement – as *confirming* and *defining* "spiritual" experiences of God and his "revealed" Word. This, again, is done by "the triggering of [what is known as] state-dependent memory…to associate unconsciously [the believer's] current [religious] experience with the early, life-sustaining, originative experience of parental administration and care" (28).[237]

In virtue of such an infantilizing process working in tandem with, in E.O. Wilson's words, the culturally evolved "environmental tracking device" of religion and our biologically evolved capacity for "tracking changes in the environment" through "the directedness of learning – the relative ease with which certain associations are made and acts are learned, and others bypassed even in the face of a strong reinforcement" (139-40), the [believer] "fashion[s] another, alternative identity (a version of the original one we experienced [as infants]), and place[s] it alongside the problematical, biological one with which our development has saddled us. [In doing so, believers] become [, in their own minds,] *two people*, one in the natural, 'fallen' world of smallness, separation, and mortal-

---

236 It is important to note in relation to my earlier psychosocial assessment of the Mormon faith, that the "infantilizing process" presented by Faber (2010) and in this Appendix is, from my perspective, the underlying neuropsychodynamic mechanism of Stricker's "Pattern of the Double-Bind in Mormonism" (2000) referred in that Chapter 8 and presented in note 174. As I see it, Faber's work explains and confirms, at a scientific level, from an evolutionary and neuropsychological perspective, what Marion Stricker insightfully intuited and observed from her and others' experiences in the Mormon faith.

237 "Remember," Faber writes to informed Christian (and Mormon) readers, "every major aspect of Christianity as a whole (including, for Mormons, the first principles of the Gospel of Jesus Christ), is devoted to transforming the worshipper into a 'little child' of the Lord [or God]: 'Verily I say unto you, Except ye be converted, and become as little children, ye shall not enter into the kingdom of heaven' (Matt. 18: 3). When [, in the language-game of Christianity/Mormonism,] the Holy Spirit [or Holy Ghost] reaches the Christian [or Mormon investigator or believer], it is always in this infantilizing context. Indeed, the infantilizing context is *there* in the first place [in the unconscious, or 'implicit,' 'state-dependent' memory of the early period of infancy] to facilitate the [faith's] transformational workings in the one who craves a 'salvation' that that turns out to be nothing other than *union with the Parent-God*" (2010, 11).

ity [the physical body], and the other in the 'spiritual' domain of eternal bonding, eternal security, [and] eternal innocence [and progression as 'spirit children' of our Parent-God, or 'Heavenly Father']" (142).

This understanding is significant, for in virtue of this regressive, dissociated mental state, the second, self-created "spirit/spiritual" person (or part of the brain) "affirms [with a sense of certainty] the religious realm [of experience] because, like the presubjective realm that he has internalized and transmuted into his self-structure [as an infant], it has 'the impact of singular truth' at the *unconscious* level of *implicit* recollection. Because the [believer] cannot *see* the naturalistic, psychological, developmental *connection* between his own mind-brain, his own internal world, and the transcendent, supramundane [religious] narrative to which he is now increasingly exposed at the conscious level, he is impelled to accept the truth-claims of [his faith].... Implicit memory validates cultural [and religious] myth. The perceptual, affective nature of the [believer's] inward domain is predisposed unconsciously to affirm the culture's [and his faith's] religious stories [and teachings], to say 'yes' [– with *certainty* and *conviction* –] to the supernatural landscape that looms. On the inside, the [believer]"...regards the *felt* presence of the Parent-God as being *actually* there, *actually* present in them, and in *everything* that exists (142-3).

Moreover, in this dissociated mental state the believer "can *feel* the accuracy of [his religious beliefs and interpretations of religious experience]. ...To view the matter from the 'hard' neuropsychological perspective, we might say that the [believer's] mind-brain, primed and grooved by his presubjective interactions, *maps* his early experience onto the religious narrative he encounters [or is given to believe]. ...What we have here," Faber asserts, "is a perfect or nearly perfect neurological, affective correspondence or fit, one that does not require proof because it has the inward [, certain] ring of truth, the veracious impact of the [believer's] very selfhood that has been molded by his presubjective, interpersonal dealings with his loving caregiver [as an infant], the dealings which provide the mnemonic 'stuff' of his implicit recollection. And indeed," Faber adds significantly, "if those dealings contained maltreatments or even abuses of some sort, the child's reentering process, his remapping of the early 'data,' is flexible enough to transform imperfection into wished-for ideal, the flawed god of the nursery into the wondrous, [perfect] God of [the believer's faith]" (28).

In all of the above, as elaborated on in depth throughout the remainder of his book, Faber is quick to additionally point-out that while he is not suggesting that "the whole of Christianity as it manifests itself within a given social order boils down [exclusively] to the process of infantilizing" he exposes, he nonetheless *is* suggesting that "Christianity [and likewise all salvational, theistic faiths] in its theological, doctrinal, ritualistic heart of hearts...is dedicated overwhelmingly, one might even say entirely, to the intellectual, emotional, and psychological *infantilizing* of all those who turn to it, follow it, subscribe to it for what we commonly think of as 'spiritual' reasons" (11).

He is also suggesting that while "the [psychological] 'map' of the early period [is] only the first in a series of 'spiritual' maps, a series that is characterized by increasing moral and theological complexity that mirrors our development over the years [of] an entire lifetime,...all the [later] spiritual maps that are devised and entered with time's passage are [nonetheless] based upon the first one, which reflects the early period. The initial, unconscious, internalized experience with the [actual or imagined] loving, care-giving provider holds the primal, 'eternal' source of Christianity's [and Mormonism's] affective power, the primal, foundational source of its compelling, persistent appeal, its mystery, its resistance to logic and reason. The initial map in the depths of the mind is the powerhouse. ...Although one can grow 'spiritually,' there is no growing out of the infantile stage. ...I am writing," Faber reminds the reader, "[not about theism, but] about emotional, heartfelt belief in an anthropomorphic...God [; the] kind of belief [which] is a natural, projective outgrowth of implicitly recollected [actual, wished-for, or fantasized] parental ministrations in infancy" (31).

The above perspective makes it clear that given our "basic biological situation" and evolved capacity for "directional learning;" and given as well (i) our personal circumstances and emotional condition; (ii) "religion's infantilizing process" as an "environmental tracking device;" (iii) the culturally embedded religious ideas of 'God', 'Savior', 'Sacrifice' and 'Salvation' and our religious conditioning or indoctrination at home and in our communities; (iv) the common tendency to believe with certainty one is right even when one isn't, and to do so on the unreliable basis of *feeling* certain (Burton 2008); (v) the false and/or incoherent (and therefore unjustified or unjustifiable) religious truth-claims assuredly known with certainty by believers to be actually true; (vi) the fact that "spiritual" knowing on the basis of religious experience cannot be uncontroversially or widely accepted as "properly basic" (see Chapters 2 and 5); and (vii) the "malleability of the human mind" and its inclination to seek *confirmation* for what one *wants* to believe (note 221), it would seem again, as concluded in Chapters 3, 5 and 6, *at least* very likely – if not beyond a reasonable doubt – that believers' faith-based 'spiritual' experiences and "testimonies" of the allegedly "revealed," "certain" knowledge of the Truth of their God's existence and of the faith they embrace are neither "knowledge," nor "certain," nor "revealed" by god and "known" by "faith in god." Finally, for believers to trade on the above qualifications of "very likely" or "beyond a reasonable doubt" in order to cling onto such harmful, potentially dangerous, and intellectually debasing beliefs as 'mere possibilities' would, in my view, not only be ultimately intolerable to the devout theist, but would also be as perverse and foolish as it is sadly pathetic[238].

---

238 To me it is sad to hear adults say – as I have on too many occasions – that they don't know how they could bear to live without their faith in God; that their faith gives them the comfort, security, guidance, direction and structured discipline to live a happy, meaningful, moral (or 'good') life, or that because of their faith they are loved, watched over, provided for, and protected by a loving 'Heavenly Father,' 'saved' or rescued from 'sin' and death by a loving and forgiving 'Savior,' and accepted, watched over, and cared for by their 'brothers and sisters' in the faith. These assertions are indicative of an infantile state of mind; a state of mind which arguably circumscribes the intellect, retards our social and scientific progress as a species, and places our own well-being and survival in real jeopardy.

To such people, I want to say *please grow up*! Following Faber's specific suggestions to this end in the concluding chapter of his book (2010), what such "growing up" might entail, for those who are otherwise sufficiently honest and individuated, would be to *first* make a conscious effort to critically identify and turn away from magical thinking, practices, and behavior, including *all* forms of religious worship. In addition, growing up would require fully acknowledging our biological nature and limitations, including the fact of human fallibilism and the impossibility of certainty in knowing truth. Third, growing up requires, in Faber's words, that "we repudiate any and all indications of the omnipotence of thought in ourselves or in others," and that "[t]hose who claim to have special, superhuman powers of perception, powers that afford them knowledge of the supernatural sphere, we immediately mark as backward-looking, retrograde personalities," acknowledging "the grave narcissistic issues that reside deep within the individual who makes such extraordinary claims" (194).

Further Implications

In addition to the above summary analysis and assessment of the above so-called "spiritual re-birth" experience, I have also concluded that while this self-induced hallucinatory experience did in fact have a somewhat salutary effect in my life, such an effect was not only *not* what I thought it was, but was effectually neutralized and ultimately eclipsed over time by the regressive and self-alienating effects of both the Mormon "infantilizing process" and (as we learned in Chapter 8) its inherent, and related, "abusive dynamic." Together these two psychosocial mechanisms – which are arguably inseparable in an authoritarian patriarchal culture – can (and often do) prove to be highly toxic to psychological well-being. In relation to the Mormon faith they essentially require, again, that one must be a 'good' (obedient) and 'faithful' (loyal) 'child of god' throughout the remainder of one's life to ultimately grow up to be perfect and all- knowing and powerful like the heavenly Father and Jesus, and be "worthy" of their acceptance and approval, and ultimately united in joy with them and with one's family and loved ones for eternity. Such a requirement, of course, not only binds the believer to the faith through what amounts to as a form of psychological extortion, it also creates the earlier presented "double-bind" wherein the believer is led to believe that all the "blessings" offered and promised which form the basis of the infantilizing process are conditional. That is, if one does not receive or enjoy them in part in this life (or, as the faith's teachings would suggest, in their fullness in the next) it is due to some fault of, or deficiency in, the believer, who must then repent and work harder to be worthy. And if one alledgedly does enjoy them in part in this life, and qualifies, by inference or the believed receipt of the "more sure word of prophesy" (D&C 131:5), to receive them in full in the life to come (by conforming and remaining "true and faithful in all things" to the end of one's mortal life) he or she will have had to pay a dear price. Either way, given the likely false and clearly incoherent beliefs of the existence of the Mormon god and an afterlife, one loses.

What is such a price? Beyond paying a tithe of ten percent of gross income on all earnings throughout one's life and dedicating one's "time and talents" to a lifetime of service to build the Church (see *Appendix B*), the price one pays for the illusory infantile "blessings" one seeks can be substantial. As presented primarily in the *Introduction*, Chapter 8 and the *Personal Postscript*, such a price entails, at least from my own experience, nothing less than self-abandonment by the betrayal of one's intellectual integrity through the willful suppression of real doubt and the quiet and reasonably skeptical voice of the

---

And last, but not least, to grow up means to give up our infantile illusions of succor, joy and happiness in the bosom of a loving Parent-God and come to accept with equanimity and courage the vicissitudes and normal unhappiness of human life and the sure and unequivocal extinction of life with death. In this last regard, Faber writes, "we grow as we fully accept our mortality, as we refuse to indulge ourselves in what Ernest Becker calls in a famous phrase, 'the denial of death.'...We consider [in so doing] Christianity's denial of death (Jesus arises from the grave; salvation is available through Christ) to be a major facet of its infantilizing process and the ultimate witness to its overall failure of nerve; for in the last analysis that is what Christianity [and likewise Mormonism] boils down to as an approach to our human existence, a failure of nerve. There can be no growing up," Faber I think rightly insists, "until one honestly faces up to the ineluctable reality of his or her demise and permanent disappearance from the universe. ...Accordingly, as grown-ups, we will actively seek to explain and hopefully to diminish the denial of death whenever an opportunity to do so presents itself. And if all of this hurts, if we undergo anxiety, and sadness, and anguish, and actual psychic and physical pain as we face up to the facts, well, so be it" (195; see also Chapter 8 and the *Epilogue* of this author's present work).

intellect. It also entails, if one truly lives the religion, the abdication of one's epistemic responsibility and, more specifically in relation to mental illness, the consignment of one's life to neurotic conflictedness and one-sidedness through the eschewing and abandoning those thoughts, beliefs, needs, desires, values, and life-preferences and aspirations which conflict with, or do not conform to, the faith's conditions and requirements of 'worthiness.' Then there is the price of irrational guilt and shame likely suffered (even if without awareness or admission) by falling short of the faith's inhuman expectations (even in the watered down version of 'doing one's best with a sincere heart and real intent'), and the anguish of possibly forfeiting – through persistent, real doubt or insufficient 'valiancy' or 'righteousness' – the promised blessing of "eternal life," and the related *rescue* from relational separateness from God, family and loved ones in the next.

In my case, through the painful experience of contrition and the resulting transferential affect of forgiveness, love and acceptance which characterized the effects of my meta-conversion experience, a heightened sense of self-esteem and a greater sense of self-acceptance and compassion and sympathy for me and others ensued. Still, the Mormon framing of this purely neuropsychological experience brought with it the steep price referenced above. The price for this new, more "ideal" personality, forged – as I believed then – in "the baptism of fire," was, among other things, a conflicted and one-sided – or utterly neurotic – personality still split-off and alienated from my *natural* personality and the unintegrated "darker (human) side" of my nature. Moreover, this split was widened by the aforementioned "double-bind" at play within the faith, and as a result I became increasingly obsessive and self-absorbed in my pursuit of "greater righteousness" and consequently increasingly difficult to live with.

Looking back, my religious interpretation of this neuropsychological experience (which is also the Mormon scriptural interpretation) essentially enabled me to favorably (and necessarily) reframe certain psychological symptoms and perceived weaknesses to religious virtues and perceived strengths, obscuring them from much needed analytical view, resolution and integration. As examples, my *compulsive obsessiveness* was theologically reframed in my mind as 'faithfulness,' 'commitment' and 'dedication,' and my tendency to be *extreme* in my religious commitments was likewise positively reframed as *exact* 'obedience' and *righteous* 'zealousness.' My *regressive attachment* was also reframed as 'pure, childlike love,' 'devotion,' and a deep yearning for unity with 'God', and my deep sense of *shame* and *inferiority* was reframed as 'deep humility', 'meekness' and 'submissiveness.' Moreover, my *shame-based* neediness for recognition, acceptance and approval was reframed as 'selflessness,' while my systemic, neurotic sense of *general, existential guilt* was reframed as 'steadfastness' and a perpetual "broken heart and contrite spirit." Finally, my *grandiose* (inflated) – clearly *narcissistic* – sense of *self-importance* was reframed as being 'called', 'chosen', 'righteous', 'worthy', 'Christ-like' and having a 'special relationship with Christ' with entitlement to special privileges and 'blessings'. Such an ego-syntonic reframing of psychopathology to so-called 'spiritual' health and virtue effectually (though neither intentionally nor consciously) turned me more completely and severely against myself and those who remained agnostic, atheistic or uncommitted believers, particularly my family and those closest to me. My metaphorically "new-born" (dissociated) religious or "spiritual" self (ego) was still, in certain crucial, fundamental ways, as neurotic (one-sided and conflicted), narcissistic (grandiose and manipulative), moralistic, judgmental and compulsive and obsessive as my natural self. In some other ways, even more so.[239]

To me, the central problem in this and every case of religious conversion is, again, with the *felt* certainty of the theological *beliefs* underlying the *interpretation* of this and other affect-laden, dissociative "religious experiences," and with the false *meta-belief* that such *felt* certainty, as well as the common, regressive fantasy (and evasive fallacy) that "anything is possible," is *surely* indicative of the Truth of such beliefs and interpretation. Such a meta-belief would hold fundamentally – and, I think, falsely, incoherently and irrationally – that in this particular case and others like it, and according to Mormon theology, such regressive, infantile experiences are *somehow*, in an utterly unintelligible way, caused by a likewise unintelligible 'all-knowing', 'all-powerful' and 'all-loving and good' 'infinite', 'eternal' and 'transcendent' being ('God' or 'Christ' or the 'Holy Ghost'). And that the believed religious interpretation of such an experience, as well as its consequent or corresponding theological beliefs, are *factually* and *literally* "true" *as interpreted*.

But the theological hermeneutic of religious conversion – factually unintelligible and delusional as it is – is intended by different faiths to be as evaluative as it is explanatory and manipulative. Consequently the religious interpretation of such experiences tends, as suggested above, to shamefully and shamelessly split the personality into "worthy vs. unworthy," "righteous vs. sinful (or unrighteous)," "natural (i.e. 'carnal, sensual and devilish') vs. spiritual (i.e. 'Christ-like')" and "acceptable vs. unacceptable" polarities. It also tends to frame – through dissociation – irrational and perhaps even pathological behavior (or symptoms) and experience as being normal, rational, healthy-minded and virtuous *in the context of* a particular theology. It does so, however, to its own condemnation as both a personally damaging and potentially dangerous strategy of mind-control.

Concluding Thoughts

To be sure, there are those among devout Mormon or Christian believers who would likely take issue with my take on "the problem" of religious interpretation in general and with my psychological analysis, assessment and concerns regarding so-called conversion

---

239 It has not escaped me that many of the same reactions and attitudes which characterized my religious life pre-existed my religious conversion and have survived my deconversion. I was, as a converted Mormon, as critical and contemptuous of ignorant, complacent or uncommitted Mormons and resistant nonbelievers and disbelievers as I am now of certain Mormon (and theistic) believers. These attitudes are the same for me toward all perceived weaknesses of character, mind and will (including my own) in relation to what I consider to be matters of great value or importance. What is *not* the same for me are my naturalistic, secular, and humanistic (not "spiritual" or "eternal") values and perspectives; my criteria and methodology for evaluation (which does not involve faith or revelation); my submission to the authority of reason (not faith or God or Church leaders); and my commitment to the fact of human fallibility (not infallible certainty) in pursuit of provisional (not absolute) knowledge and truth. These changes constitute a change in direction, not attitude. The significant observation in this regard is not that my fundamental reactions and attitudes are the same, but rather that my *direction* has changed and now I can look back from the outside as a former, converted insider and make a well-informed analysis and assessment of the Mormon faith. Unlike those who were born in the faith or joined the Mormon Church but never got all the way in, or those who got in but jumped out or drifted out for different reasons, I went all the way in and came out on the other side. I think the view is different when you get to the other side. Perhaps in retrospect, the only way for some to really get all the way out (not merely inactive) is for them to get all the way in (not merely active).

experiences in particular. In doing so, there might be those who would, again, perhaps discredit the authenticity of this conversion experience, or the validity of the interpretation on the basis of ad hoc and/or question-begging assessments within the faith or the ultimate outcome. Or there might be others who additionally or instead might reject out of hand the above psychological premises and conclusions as being perhaps simplistically reductive (not all reduction is simplistic or unjustified), unwarrantedly universalizing, or disputable.

To the charge of what I term simplistic (or unjustified) reductionism – assumably in applying both Faber's work on Christianity's "infantilizing process" (2010) and my characterization of the "abusive dynamic" of the Mormon faith presented initially in Chapter 8 and applied above – I will briefly and directly reply, as Faber does, and with my own interpolations, that such a charge "will not hold up and must be dropped. There is just too much supportive material in the major presentational [and evaluative] sources of [both Christianity and Mormonism]…that we find everywhere around us, to miss the overwhelming emphasis upon infantilizing [and shaming or otherwise abusing] the worshipper" (12). Like Faber, I have sought to avoid such reductionism and have likewise been careful to test my premises and conclusions against numerous reported cases of authoritarian abuse in the Mormon and Christian faiths, including of course my own case. As I responded to the question "What if you're wrong?" in Chapter 8, the possibility is of course always present, given human fallibilism, that in some sense I don't have it quite right, or might even be wholly mistaken in places. If such is the case I truly want to know, and welcome the valid information and/or sound reasoning establishing such. Still, and again, I think there are too many well-researched and documented cases of authoritarian abuse in all theistic faiths (including Mormonism) that the assertion of an "abusive dynamic" as constructed and presented should be, on the whole, and like the assertion of an "infantilizing process," uncontroversial in the minds of all honest observers and inquirers, believers or not.

Apart from the possible concern with reductionism, there might be those who further assert that the above psychological reflections and conclusions – even if personal to me – are unwarrantedly universalized; that they do not pertain to them or commonly (if at all) to others, and are therefore disputable in that regard. The implication here perhaps is that as *truly* converted members of the Mormon Church, they have never (or rarely, if ever) questioned, doubted or wavered in their faith in God and Christ and, moreover, that they cannot personally relate to the disclosed psychological "symptoms" of mental illness presented or suggested above. Others might regard this particular conversion experience as extreme and insist that "normally" or "typically" spiritual conversion (or "rebirth") in the Mormon faith is not necessarily a single or singular event, but is usually a process which is not so dramatic or fantastic. And moreover, that (as I also, yet wrongly, believed at that time in my life) those who are again "truly" converted are *also* healed psychologically and that the natural consequences of *true* conversion are always and exclusively salutary and never pathological.

There is, as far as I know, no way to productively or effectively argue against those objections above which might be considered *red herrings* which are at least implicit *ad hominem* arguments. In the truncated, or incomplete, form hypothetically presented they would clearly be self-referential and invalid arguments and incredible – even psychologically suspicious – claims. It is difficult to imagine how fleshing them out would help much in this assessment.

Even so, it seems important to say in this regard that mental illness caused or made worse by religious belief and practice can and does manifest in children, adolescents, and adults in various, seemingly benign ways that are culturally normalized by religious conditioning and masked by various psychological defenses. Accordingly, to suffer mental illness does not necessarily mean that one is utterly dysfunctional, or that those who are mentally ill (And who among us is not so afflicted to some degree?) never have days where they *seem* to be asymptomatic or 'normal.' On the contrary, part of the *cause* of mental illness among the more moderate 'faithful' – as well as perhaps its signature manifestation among 'good,' faithful, obedient Mormons (and no doubt 'born again' Christians) – is the well-conditioned *appearance* and *sincere* attestation of 'happiness' and emotional well-being in spite of various symptoms or character disorders.[240]

Moreover, and as a relevant aside, the diagnosis of mental illness, beyond general markers or indicators, requires careful, differential diagnosis by a qualified psychiatrist or psychotherapist who has himself been well analyzed. So too does the determination of its etiology. In this regard self-analysis (if such a course is even considered), as a substitute for psychotherapy[241] with a qualified and licensed clinical psychotherapist, is

---

240 Believers are taught, of course, that personal and interpersonal difficulties are to be expected in this world of tears, toil, trials, and tribulation, and this is certainly correct as far as it goes. But they are *also* taught to believe that 'faithful' living brings health, happiness and well-being. This might at least *imply* to some, if not many, that if believers are *truly* living their faith they will not suffer from neurotic, psychotic or character disorders, or the chronic physical disorders indicative of the somatization of suppressed or repressed religious shame and guilt, and the related depression, anxiety, and compulsive self-sacrifice (or 'selflessness') caused and motivated by such religiously conditioned self-hatred. In other words, it is naturally very difficult (if not nearly impossible, short of crisis and acute dysfunctionality) for devout, functional believers (and particularly Mormon believers) to acknowledge that their metaphysically incoherent and self-hating, self-sacrificing, and abusive religious belief system has made them ill when they have essentially been conditioned to irrationally believe – *without question or doubt* – that superstitious "magical thinking," self-hate, self-sacrifice, and obedience to religious authority are necessary requirements for salvation; and that, again, the very symptoms of mental illness (or "tribulation") they suffer and endure without complaint or question are to be expected as a 'test' of their faith, as well as a proof of their faithfulness and an indicator of their righteousness. (Such an implied message is not, of course, or to my knowledge, the "official position" of the Mormon Church, and might even be officially or publicly disavowed with the formal or stated acknowledgement that (essentially) 'faithlessness' is not necessarily related to the existence of psychiatric symptoms, syndromes and disorders, or that mental illness is not necessarily caused by faithlessness or disobedience. Even so, such a disavowal does not change the at least implicit or tacit connection inherent in the very promises of the faith that faithfulness and a 'righteous' living by the rules bring peace, comfort, well-being, happiness and joy to the lives of the faithful. The mixed message is plain to suffering insiders: 'It's not your fault that you're mentally ill, but the faithful and righteous are (or should be) happy and at peace in their lives.')

---

241 Psychotherapy, as understood by this author, is, succinctly put, a *nondirective, non-moralistic relational* process that facilitates psychological healing through the *individuation* and *integration* of the personality. More specifically, it utilizes *free association, transference, dream and fantasy analysis*, and *therapeutic interaction* and *inquiry* to facilitate necessary *catharsis, insight* into symptom and character neuroses, *corrective emotional experience*, the development of *moral imagination*, and the creation of *personal meaning* related to one's personal suffering and life experience. Self-analysis and diagnosis is rarely productive, except perhaps for the more experienced and psychologically informed and oriented individuals, and only then in perhaps a very limited sense. And religious psychotherapy – or psychotherapy with a religious therapist – is, for reasons that are obvious in the context of this particular perspective, not only a contradiction in terms, but self-defeating. (For an excellent introduction into the workings of psychotherapy, see Willard Gaylin's very readable book *How Psychotherapy Really Works* (2001). Also, see Susan Vaughn's book *The Talking Cure* (1997) and, for

typically inadvisable, even for psychotherapists. This is so particularly for those who are symptomatic, are psychologically uninformed (beyond self-help, pop-psychology), and/ or have been deeply conditioned by their faith to regard psychotherapy as a course of last resort to be turned to only when 'spiritual counsel' and faithful religious practice (i.e. prayer, fasting, obedience, service, scripture study, etc.) are insufficient, and even then only when the therapist is a believer of the same faith.

All this said, and as referenced earlier, there is indeed very good reason on the basis alone of extensive clinical psychiatric case work (and plain psychological common sense) to be highly suspicious or skeptical of any or all self-referential assertions of happiness and mental health among theistic believers, or *because* of religious belief. And this is particularly so with 'faithful' Mormon believers and the Mormon religion, given its earlier assessed and asserted toxicity. From my perspective, *all* religious believers of *every* theistic faith – particularly those born and raised in an actively religious home – would do well to suspect their religion and maladaptive religious beliefs as being, at bottom, at least one very likely and significant contributor to their personal and relational frustrations, difficulties, or suffering in life, if not *the* primary or exclusive cause.

As for the question about whether or not this conversion experience is or is not "typical," I would agree that not all (or perhaps even many) members of the Mormon Church are converted in this way, while insisting that such an experience, though perhaps rare in this particular form, is in fact paradigmatic, citing again the cases of Alma the Younger and Enos in the *Book of Mormon*, to name just two.

Alternatively, regarding any and all hypothetical objections to my psychological assessment and conclusions, I think dialogue, discussion and debate could reasonably and respectfully ensue which might lead to a fruitful exchange. And regarding the claim, if it would ever be made, that the psychological effects of "true" conversion are *always* and *exclusively* salutary and *never* pathological to the believer (an extreme if not unintelligible claim to be sure), wide reflective equilibrium could only be achieved either way *if* the parties could first agree that such a claim is even justifiable. For this to be the case, the concepts embedded in the stated and believed possibility of a *literal* "spiritual conversion" to "God" and "Christ" through "faith," and by "revelation" and "confirmation" through the "Holy Spirit" would need to be intelligible, coherent and factually meaningful. Such is arguably not the case, as we have learned from our analysis in this book. Moreover, and assuming for the sake of argument, that such a claim *is* justifiable, there would also need to be agreement on the objective and universally accepted human criteria for clearly and definitively determining and differentiating "true" from "false" or *ersatz* conversion. Such agreement does not exist and is not forthcoming, even given the false or incoherent meta-belief that religious conversion is objectively real as believed. Neither, I suspect, shall it ever be.

Finally, as for the determination of whether or not the psychological effects of the so-called religious conversion experience are in fact salutary or detrimental to the "convert's" psychological well-being, I have shared my view and am certainly willing to defend it. I will leave it to the reader to explore such views for themselves and reach their

---

a more advanced introduction to the type of psychotherapy primarily advocated in this work, Rob Leiper and Michael Maltby's book *The Psychodynamic Approach to Therapeutic Change* (2004).)

own informed, analyzed and reflective conclusions.

I do think it is important to acknowledge again in closing, however, that given the fact of fallibilism, my theological interpretation and assessment of the above "conversion" experience might be false or (to be sure) incomplete. Or, as acknowledged earlier, it might not be representative of all (or even many or most) Mormon "converts." I also think it is important to acknowledge that my psychological interpretations and conclusions might arguably be too general and subjective to be of any real therapeutic value to either myself or the reader. Still, while I readily acknowledge such qualifications, I think it is nonetheless true (or so I would argue) that my theological and psychological interpretations and conclusions are indeed correct as far as they go, or at least *plausible* on the basis of scriptural exegesis, common knowledge and common sense. And I would also argue that they at least merit thoughtful and careful consideration.

Relatedly, it seems at least reasonable to conclude – following Ockham's dictum not to assume any more than what is needed to in order to explain the data – that naturalistic explanations of religious conversion experiences (and, conversely, blocked like experiences after leaving the faith) are the best, or truest, explanations. It also seems reasonable to conclude, given again the well-known and aforementioned clinical observation of renowned psychotherapist Carl Rogers that "that which is most personal is most universal," that therefore my psychological woundedness and corresponding vulnerability to Mormon dogma and hermeneutics might very likely pertain conservatively to *many* others as well, and certainly constitute neither an isolated nor even uncommon case.

In this last regard, and as emphasized in Chapter 5, if it is finally asserted *a priori* by the reader or other believers that one's own personal "testimony" or so-called spiritual "witness" of the truth of God's existence or (if one is a Christian) Christ's atonement is based on genuine spiritual experience and cannot be reduced to some neuro-psychological phenomenon, then it must be asked how specifically such an assertion of exception would (or could) be warranted or justified? More specifically, and speaking personally to the "converted" or "born again" reader, it might also be asked, and I think reasonably so, on the basis of what specific, objective, and widely accepted *non a priori* and *non question-begging* human criteria could *your* "spiritual experience" be *non-solipsistically* determined to be conclusively "genuine" as believed revelation from god, and indicative of *actual* truth on its own merits? Or in contradistinction to the experience presented above, or to those with like or identical content and described affect allegedly experienced by those of a *different* faith, or by regarded *apostates* to your faith, or by those who are either clinically psychopathological or have merely experienced an induced dissociative psychosis or a regressive, transferential hallucination in virtue of our common "basic biological situation" (Faber 2004, 2010)?

These are, to be sure, crucial questions for all who seek to *know* and not merely "believe." They are also crucial questions to those who base their so-called faith and belief in God on having experienced some kind of ecstatic, transformational and/or life-altering religious or spiritual experience, or – as in the case of Mormon believers – who have allegedly received a "personal testimony" of the existence of their God, of the atonement and saving grace of and their Lord and Savior, Jesus Christ, and of their (only true) Church by "confirmation" of such putative truth from the "Holy Ghost." These "believers," enslaved as they are – and as I was – by the real tension of their need to know and their fear of knowing, must also struggle with such questions if their faith is not a sham and their religious commitments are sincere.

Regarding, therefore, what it makes rational sense to accept as truth (or *knowledge* of truth), or to behave or say in interpreting such alleged experiences, – or in considering them as actual truth claims – has been in part the burden of this work, and of this Appendix in particular. In the end, whether or not the fundamental concepts of the Mormon faith are, as has been concluded, false and/or incoherent; and/or the beliefs of the Mormon believer are, as I have argued, irrational; and/or the Mormon faith is, as demonstrated and asserted, a toxic religion; and/or the so-called 'spiritual experiences' of Mormons with "testimonies" are, as I have maintained, factually unintelligible conceptually, and *entirely* explainable naturalistically as mere self or other-induced neuropsychological phenomena probably, if not very likely, indicative of mental illness is, of course, left for the reader to conclude on his or her own behalf. For my part, I will allow the reasoned conclusions of this work, and all other sources referenced throughout, to speak for themselves through whatever acknowledged, dismissed, or denied discomfort such conclusions might bring.

Appendix B:

TO THOSE WHO ARE INVESTIGATING "MORMONISM"*

Prefatory Note: This Internet article was written and updated by Richard Packham and is included here with his permission. I chose to include this article to present more information regarding the teachings of Mormon beliefs to investigators of the Mormon faith. Packham, like me, is an ex-Mormon. While I cannot personally attest to the complete factual accuracy of all that is claimed or presented in this article, I do think that Packham's representation of Mormon teachings and beliefs is well-documented, researched, and correct as far as it goes, although no doubt subject to evasive arguments and dismissal by apologists of the Mormon Church and its active Mormon believers. In keeping with my desire to expose what I consider to be the incoherencies and at least likely or potentially harmful and dangerous aspects of Mormon theology and culture, this article seems appropriate. (After all, echoing, in brief, questions asked in Chapters 7 and 8, why, given all that is allegedly at stake, is there so much confusion and controversy, so many contradictions, so many unanswered questions, and so much disagreement, nonbelief and disbelief about or regarding fundamental matters in a faith whose doctrines and teachings are allegedly revealed by an infallible God to his putatively "called and anointed" leaders of his only true Church?) Moreover, Packham's listed references below are extensive and offer Mormon believers, nonbelievers and investigators important counter-points to their beliefs, which are no doubt based for many, if not most, on the one-sided, official teachings of the Mormon Church. While in my view none of these references can be strictly characterized as an atheological treatment of the Mormon faith, some do raise important questions and concerns worth considering as part of a cumulative critique of Mormonism. Taken as a whole, and for those with questions and real doubts, this article and its accompanying references and resources are, I think, an important adjunct to this book and bibliography.

If you are investigating Mormonism (the "Church of Jesus Christ of Latter-day Saints" or "LDS Church"), you are probably studying it in private meetings in your home with missionaries from that church. Here are some of the key things that they are probably telling you:

- Mormonism began in 1820 when a teen-aged boy in western New York named Joseph Smith was spurred by a Christian revival where he lived to pray to God for guidance as to which church was true. In answer to his prayers he was visited by God the Father and God the Son, two separate beings, who told him to join no church because all the churches at that time were false, and that he, Joseph, would bring forth the true church. This event is called "The First Vision."

- In 1823 Joseph had another heavenly visitation, in which an angel named Moroni told him of a sacred history written by ancient Hebrews in America, engraved in an Egyptian dialect on tablets of gold and buried in a nearby hill. Joseph was told it was the history of the ancient peoples of America, and that Joseph would be the instrument for bringing this record to the knowledge of the world. Joseph obtained these gold plates from the angel in 1827, and translated them into English by the spirit of God and the use of a sacred instrument accompanying the plates called the "Urim and Thummim." The translation was published in 1830 as *The Book of Mormon*, now revered by Mormons as scripture, along with the Bible.

• *The Book of Mormon* is a religious and secular history of the inhabitants of the Western Hemisphere from about 2200 BC to about 421 AD. It tells the reader that three groups of immigrants settled the uninhabited Americas. They were led by God from their original homes in the Near East to America. The first group came from the Tower of Babel, about 2200 BC, and two other groups came from Jerusalem just before the Babylonian Captivity, about 600 BC. They had prophets of God who had been inspired with the gospel of Jesus Christ, which is thus preserved in their history, the *Book of Mormon*. Many of the descendants of these immigrants were Christians, even before Christ was born in Palestine, but many were unbelievers. Believers and unbelievers fought many wars, the last of which left only degenerate unbelievers as survivors, who are the ancestors of the American Indians. The most important event during this long history was the visit of Jesus Christ to America, after his crucifixion, when he ministered to (and converted) all the inhabitants.

• Joseph Smith was directed by revelation from God to reestablish ("restore") the true church, which he did in 1830. He was visited several times by heavenly messengers, who ordained him to the true priesthood. He continued to have revelations from God to guide the church and to give more knowledge of the Gospel. Many of these revelations are published in the *Doctrine and Covenants*, accepted by Mormons as scripture, along with the Bible and the *Book of Mormon*.

• Joseph Smith and his followers were continually persecuted for their religious beliefs, and driven from New York State to Ohio, then to Missouri, then to Illinois, where Joseph Smith was murdered in 1844 by a mob, a martyr to his beliefs. The church was then led by Brigham Young, Joseph's successor, to Utah, where the Mormons settled successfully.

• The LDS church is led today by the successors of Joseph Smith. The present president of the church is a "prophet, seer and revelator" just as Joseph Smith was, and guides the members of the church through revelations and guidance from God.

• The modern LDS church is the only true church, as restored by God through Joseph Smith. Other churches, derived from the early Christian church, are in apostasy because their leaders corrupted the scriptures, changed the ordinances of the original church, and often led corrupt lives, thus losing their authority.

• The most reliable way to determine whether the *Book of Mormon* is true, and whether the Mormon Church is "the only true church" is by sincerely asking God in prayer.

- By accepting baptism into the LDS church you take the first step necessary toward your salvation and your ultimate entrance into the Kingdom of Heaven (the "Celestial Kingdom").

WHAT THE MISSIONARIES WILL NOT TELL YOU

Until recently, the missionaries were required to present Mormonism in six "discussions", which were a series of memorized sales talks. They are now encouraged simply to "follow the spirit" in their presentations. The basic message and approach, however, is still essentially the same. A thorough, thoughtful and balanced discussion of each of the six "official" lessons as the missionaries formerly presented them to investigators is at http://www.lds4u.com, together with the techniques and strategies which the missionaries are instructed to use. (The actual texts of the discussions were also on this site at one time, but the Mormon church threatened the webmaster with a lawsuit, and he removed them; click on "next" at each window to read a summary and commentary.)

Here is a summary of important facts about the Mormon Church, its doctrine, and its history that the missionaries will probably not tell you. We are not suggesting that they are intentionally deceiving you --most of the young Mormons serving missions for the church are not well educated in the history of the church or in modern critical studies of the church. They probably do not know the all the facts themselves. They have been trained, however, to give investigators "milk before meat," that is, to postpone revealing anything at all that might make an investigator hesitant, even if it is true. But you should be aware of these facts before you commit yourself.

Each of the following facts has been substantiated by thorough historical scholarship. And this list is by no means exhaustive!   *For links to articles substantiating each of these points, see the Internet version of this article at http://packham.n4m.org/tract.htm.*

- The "First Vision" story in the form presented to you was unknown until 1838, *eighteen years* after its alleged occurrence and almost ten years after Smith had begun his missionary efforts. The oldest (but quite different) version of the vision is in Smith's own handwriting, dating from about 1832 (still at least *eleven years* afterwards), and says that only *one* personage, Jesus Christ, appeared to him. It also mentions nothing about a revival. It also contradicts the later account as to whether Smith had already decided that no church was true. Still a third version of this event is recorded as a recollection in Smith's diary, fifteen years after the alleged vision, where one unidentified "personage" appeared, then another, with a message implying that neither was the Son. They were accompanied by many "angels," which are not mentioned in the official version you have been told about. Which version is correct, if any? Why was this event, now said by the church to be so important, unknown for so long?

- Careful study of the religious history of the locale where Smith lived in 1820 casts doubt on whether there actually was such an extensive revival that year as Smith and his family later described as associated with the "First Vision." The revivals in 1817 and 1824 better fit what Smith described later.

- In 1828, eight years after he supposedly had been told by God himself to join no church, Smith applied for membership in a local Methodist church. Other members of his family had joined the Presbyterians.

- Contemporaries of Smith consistently described him as something of a confidence man, whose chief source of income was hiring out to local farmers to help them find buried treasure by the use of folk magic and "seer stones." Smith was actually tried in 1826 on a charge of money digging. It is interesting that none of his critics seemed to be aware of his claim to have been visited by God in 1820, even though in his 1838 account he claimed that he had suffered "great persecution" for telling people of his vision.

- The only persons who claimed to have actually seen the gold plates were eleven close friends of Smith (many of them related to each other). Their testimonies are printed in the front of every copy of the *Book of Mormon*. No disinterested third party was ever allowed to examine them. They were retrieved by the angel at some unrecorded point. Most of the witnesses later abandoned Smith and left his movement. Smith then called them "liars."

- Smith produced most of the "translation" not by reading the plates through the Urim and Thummim (described as a pair of sacred spectacles), but by gazing at the same "seer stone" he had used for treasure hunting. He would place the stone into his hat, and then cover his face with it. For much of the time he was dictating, the gold plates were not even present, but in a hiding place.

- The detailed history and civilization described in the *Book of Mormon* does not correspond to anything found by archaeologists anywhere in the Americas. The *Book of Mormon* describes a civilization lasting for a thousand years, covering both North and South America, which was familiar with horses, elephants, cattle, sheep, wheat, barley, steel, wheeled vehicles, shipbuilding, sails, coins, and other elements of Old World culture. But no trace of any of these supposedly very common things has ever been found in the Americas of that period. Nor does the *Book of Mormon* mention many of the features of the civilizations which really did exist at that time in the Americas. The LDS church has spent millions of dollars over many years trying to prove through archaeological research that the *Book of Mormon* is an accurate historical record, but they have failed to produce any convincing pre-Columbian archeological evidence supporting the *Book of Mormon* story. In addition, whereas the *Book of Mormon* presents the picture of a relatively homogeneous people, with a single language and communication between distant parts of the Americas, the pre-Columbian history of the Americas shows the opposite: widely disparate racial types (almost entirely east Asian - definitely not Semitic, as proven by recent DNA studies), and many unrelated native languages, none of which are even remotely related to Hebrew or Egyptian.

- The people of the *Book of Mormon* were supposedly devout Jews observing the Law of Moses, but in the *Book of Mormon* there is almost no trace of their observance of Mosaic law or even an accurate knowledge of it.

- Although Joseph Smith said that God had pronounced the completed translation of the plates as published in 1830 "correct," many changes have been made in later editions. Besides thousands of corrections of poor grammar and awkward wording in the 1830 edition, other changes have been made to reflect subsequent changes in some of the fundamental doctrine of the church. For example, an early change in wording modified the 1830 edition's acceptance of the doctrine of the Trinity, thus allowing Smith to introduce his later doctrine of multiple gods. A more recent change (1981) replaced "white" with "pure," apparently to reflect the change in the church's stance on the "curse" of the black race.

- Joseph Smith said that the *Book of Mormon* contained the "fulness of the gospel." However, its teaching on many doctrinal subjects has been ignored or contradicted by the present LDS church, and many doctrines now said by the church to be essential are not even mentioned there. Examples are the church's position on the nature of God, the Virgin Birth, the Trinity, polygamy, Hell, priesthood, secret organizations, the nature of Heaven and salvation, temples, proxy ordinances for the dead, and many other matters.

- Many of the basic historical notions found in the *Book of Mormon* had appeared in print already in 1825, just two years before Smith began producing the *Book of Mormon*, in a book called *View of the Hebrews*, by Ethan Smith (no relation) and published just a few miles from where Joseph Smith lived. A careful study of this obscure book led one LDS church official (the historian B. H. Roberts, 1857-1933) to confess that the evidence tended to show that the *Book of Mormon* was not an ancient record, but concocted by Joseph Smith himself, based on ideas he had read in the earlier book.

- Although Mormons claim that God is guiding the LDS church through its president (who has the title "prophet, seer and revelator"), the successive "prophets" have repeatedly either led the church into undertakings that were dismal failures or failed to see approaching disaster. To mention only a few: the Kirtland Bank, the United Order, the gathering of Zion to Missouri, the Zion's Camp expedition, polygamy, the Deseret Alphabet . A recent example is the successful hoax perpetrated on the church by manuscript dealer Mark Hofmann in the 1980s. He succeeded in selling the church thousands of dollars worth of manuscripts which he had forged. The church and its "prophet, seer and revelator" accepted them as genuine historical documents. The church leaders learned the truth not from God, through revelation, but from non-Mormon experts and the police, after Hofmann was arrested for two murders he committed to cover up his hoax. This scandal was reported nationwide.

- The secret temple ritual (the "endowment") was introduced by Smith in May, 1842, just two months after he had been initiated into Freemasonry. The LDS temple ritual closely resembles the Masonic ritual of that day.   Smith explained that the Masons had corrupted the ancient (God-given) ritual by changing it and removing parts of it, and that he was restoring it to its "pure" and "original" (and complete) form, as revealed to him by God. In the years since, the LDS church has made many fundamental changes in the "pure and original" ritual as "restored" by Smith, mostly by removing major parts of it.

- Many doctrines which were once taught by the LDS church, and held to be fundamental, essential and "eternal", have been abandoned. Whether we feel that the church was correct in abandoning them is not the point; rather, the point is that a church claiming to be the church of God takes one "everlasting" position at one time and the opposite position at another, all the time claiming to be proclaiming the word of God. Some examples are:

  - The Adam-God doctrine (Adam is God the Father);
  - the United Order (all property of church members is to be held in common, with title in the church);
  - Plural Marriage (polygamy; a man must have more than one wife to attain the highest degree of heaven);
  - the Curse of Cain (the black race is not entitled to hold God's priesthood because it is cursed; this doctrine was not abandoned until 1978);
  - Blood Atonement (some sins - apostasy, adultery, murder, interracial marriage - must be atoned for by the shedding of the sinner's blood, preferably by someone appointed to do so by church authorities);

All of these doctrines were proclaimed by the reigning prophet to be the Word of God, "eternal," "everlasting," to govern the church "forevermore." All have been abandoned by the present church.

- Joseph Smith's early revelations were collected and first published in 1833 in the *Book of Commandments*. God (as recorded in the *Doctrine and Covenants* Sections 1 and 67) supposedly testified by revelation that the revelations as published were true and correct. Because the *Book of Commandments* did not receive wide distribution (most copies were destroyed by angry opponents of the Mormons in Missouri, where it was published), they were republished - with additional revelations - as the *Doctrine and Covenants* in 1835 in Kirtland, Ohio. However, many of the revelations as published in Kirtland differed fundamentally from their versions as originally given. The changes generally gave more power and authority to Smith, and justified changes he was making in church organization and theology. The question naturally arises as to why revelations which God had pronounced correct needed to be revised.

- Joseph Smith claimed to have received the priesthood (the only valid priesthood recognized by God) directly from resurrected beings (angels): the Aaronic Priesthood from John the Baptist and the Mechizedek (higher) Priesthood from Peter, James and John. However, the accounts of these visitations are contradictory and questionable.

- Joseph Smith claimed to be a "translator" by the power of God. In addition to the Book of Mormon, he made several other "translations":

  - The Book of Abraham, from Egyptian papyrus scrolls which came into his possession in 1835. He stated that the scrolls were written by the biblical Abraham "by his own hand." Smith's translation is now accepted as scripture by the LDS church, as part of its Pearl of Great Price. Smith also produced an "Egyptian Grammar" based on his translation. Modern scholars of ancient Egyptian agree that the scrolls are common Egyptian funeral scrolls, entirely pagan in nature, having nothing to do with Abraham, and from a period 2000 years later than Abraham. The "Grammar" has been said by Egyptologists to prove that Smith had no notion of the Egyptian language. It is pure fantasy: he made it up.

  - The "Inspired Revision" of the King James Bible. Smith was commanded by God to retranslate the Bible because the existing translations contained errors. He completed his translation in 1833, but the church still uses the King James Version.

  - The "Kinderhook Plates," a group of six metal plates with strange engraved characters, unearthed in 1843 near Kinderhook, Illinois, and examined by Smith, who began a "translation" of them. He never completed the translation, but he identified the plates as an "ancient record," and translated enough to identify the author as a descendant of Pharaoh. Local farmers later confessed that they had manufactured, engraved and buried the plates themselves as a hoax. They had apparently copied the characters from a Chinese tea box.

- Joseph Smith claimed to be a "prophet." He frequently prophesied future events "by the power of God." Many of these prophecies are recorded in the LDS scripture *Doctrine and Covenants*. Almost none have been fulfilled, and many cannot now be fulfilled because the deeds to be done by the persons named were never done and those persons are now dead. Many prophecies included dates for their fulfillment, and those dates are now long past, the events never having occurred.

- Joseph Smith died not as a martyr, but in a gun battle in which he fired a number of shots. He was in jail at the time, under arrest for having ordered the destruction of a Nauvoo newspaper which dared to print an exposure (which was true) of his secret sexual liaisons. At that time he had announced his candidacy for the presidency of the United States, set up a secret government, and secretly had himself crowned "King of the Kingdom of God."

- Since the founding of the church down to the present day the church leaders have not hesitated to lie, to falsify documents, to rewrite or suppress history, or to do whatever is necessary to protect the image of the church. Many Mormon historians have been excommunicated from the church for publishing their findings on the truth of Mormon history.

• Trying to determine the truth by relying entirely on the feelings one gets after praying is not a reliable way to learn the truth. One can easily deceive oneself into "feeling" something that is really not true at all. The only reliable way to get to the truth is to examine verifiable facts.

• Mormonism includes many other unusual teachings which you will probably not be told about until you have been in the church for a long time. These teachings are not revealed to investigators or new converts because those people are not yet considered ready to have more than "milk" as doctrine. The Mormons also probably realize that if investigators knew of these unusual teachings they would not join the church. In addition to those mentioned elsewhere in this article, the following are noteworthy:

  ▪ God was once a man like us.
  ▪ God has a tangible body of flesh and bone.
  ▪ God lives on a planet near the star Kolob.
  ▪ God ("Heavenly Father") has at least one wife, our "Mother in Heaven," but she is so holy that we are not to discuss her nor pray to her.
  ▪ Jesus was married.
  ▪ We can become like God and rule over our own universe.
  ▪ There are many gods, ruling over their own worlds.
  ▪ Jesus and Satan ("Lucifer") are brothers, and they are our brothers - we are all spirit children of Heavenly Father
  ▪ Jesus Christ was conceived by God the Father by having sex with Mary, who was temporarily his wife.
  ▪ We should not pray to Jesus, nor try to feel a personal relationship with him.
  ▪ The "Lord" ("Jehovah") in the Old Testament is the being named Jesus in the New Testament, but different from "God the Father" ("Elohim").
  ▪ In the highest degree of the celestial kingdom [all] men will have more than one wife.
  ▪ Before coming to this earth we lived as spirits in a "pre-existence", during which we were tested; our position in this life (whether born to Mormons or savages, or in America or Africa) is our reward or punishment for our obedience in that life.
  ▪ Dark skin is a curse from God, the result of our sin, or the sin of our ancestors. If sufficiently righteous, a dark-skinned person will become light-skinned.
  ▪ The Garden of Eden was in Missouri. All humanity before the Great Flood lived in the western hemisphere. The Ark transported Noah and the other survivors to the eastern hemisphere.
  ▪ Not only will human beings be resurrected to eternal life, but also all animals - everything that has ever lived on earth - will be resurrected and dwell in heaven.
  ▪ Christ will not return to earth in any year that has seen a rainbow.
  ▪ Mormons should avoid traveling on water, since Satan rules the waters.

- The sun receives its light from the star Kolob.
- If a Gentile becomes Mormon, the Holy Ghost actually purges his Gentile blood and replaces it with Israelite blood.
- A righteous Mormon will actually see the face of God in the Mormon temple.
- You can identify a false angel by the color of his hair, or by offering to shake his hand.

YOUR LIFE AS A MORMON

If you should decide to become a member of the LDS church, you should be aware of what your life in the church will be like. Although you will find yourself warmly accepted by a lively community of healthy, active and generally supportive people, many of whom are very happy in Mormonism and could not imagine their lives without it, *there is another side*:

- You will be continually reminded that to enter the highest degree of heaven (the "Celestial Kingdom"), you will have to go through the endowment ceremony in the temple and have your marriage to your Mormon spouse "sealed." (If your spouse is not Mormon, or if you are not married, you cannot enter the highest degree of heaven.) To get permission to have these ceremonies performed in the temple, you must prove yourself to be a faithful and obedient member of the church and do everything commanded by the church authorities, from the Prophet down to the local level. You will have to undergo a personal "worthiness" interview with the local church authorities inquiring into your private life and your religious and social activities.

- You will be expected to donate at least ten percent of your income to the church as tithing. Other donations will be expected as the need arises. You will never see an accounting of how this money is spent, or how much the church receives, or anything at all about its financial condition; the church keeps its finances secret, even from its members.

- You will be expected to give up the use of alcohol, tobacco, coffee, and tea.

- You will be expected to fulfill any work assignment given to you. These assignments may be teaching, record keeping, janitorial work, cannery or farm work, helping in the Sunday nursery - any job that needs to be done. Each task you perform successfully will make you eligible for others, with more responsibility and more demands upon your time. The members who perform these jobs, even those involving sensitive pastoral counseling, receive no formal training whatsoever (there is no paid, trained clergy). You will be told that God has called you to your assignments. Many Mormons find much of their spare time taken up with church work, trying to fulfill the numerous assignments that have been given them.

- You will be expected to be unquestioningly obedient to church authorities in whatever they might tell you to do. "Follow the Brethren" is the slogan, and it means to follow without doubt or question. Discussion of whether a decree from above is correct is discouraged. You will be expected to have faith that the leaders cannot possibly lead you astray. Even if they should tell you something which contradicts what a previous prophet may have said, you will be told "A living prophet takes precedence over a dead prophet."

- You will be able to "vote" on those who have been called to positions of authority over you, but the voting will be by the show of hands in a public meeting. Only one candidate for each office will be voted on (the one "called by God"). The voting is therefore almost always unanimous in favor of the candidate.

- You will be advised not to read any material which is "not faith-promoting," that is, which may be critical or questioning of the church or its leaders, or which might place the church or its leaders in an unfavorable light.

- You will be advised not to associate with "apostates," that is, former Mormons. (You will be asked in your "worthiness" interview about this.)

- If you are unmarried, you will be encouraged to marry a good Mormon as soon as possible. When you do marry, in a wedding ceremony in the temple, your non-Mormon family members and friends will not be allowed to attend the ceremony, because only "worthy" Mormons are allowed to enter the temple.

- If you are homosexual, you will be pressured to abandon this "evil" aspect of your nature. If you do not, you will probably not be fully accepted by other church members. If you do not remain celibate, you may be excommunicated.

- If you are a male over 12 years of age and "worthy" (that is, if you are obedient, attend meetings, do not masturbate, etc.), you will be ordained to one of the levels of priesthood, and, if you continue to be faithful and obedient, you will gradually advance through the priesthood ranks. If you are female, you will receive the benefits of priesthood authority only indirectly, through your Mormon father or your Mormon husband. The role of the Mormon woman is to be a wife and mother and to obey and honor her priest husband (or father).

- If you prove yourself to be faithful, hard working and obedient, you will eventually be considered worthy to "receive your endowment" in a Mormon temple. You will not be told in advance exactly what to expect in this lengthy ceremony, except that the details of the ritual are secret (Mormons prefer to say they are just "sacred," but they treat them as though they are secret). As part of that ceremony you will be required to swear a number of oaths, the penalty for violation of which is no longer stated but until 1990 was death by various bloody methods, such as having your throat slit from ear to ear. You will be given the secret signs and passwords which are required to enter heaven. (Although most Mormons who have not received the endowment know very little about the ceremony, the entire liturgy is now available on the Internet to Mormon and non-Mormon alike.) After receiving the endowment you will be required to wear a special undergarment at all times.

- If you should ever decide that you made a mistake in joining the church and then leave it, you will probably find (judging from the experiences of others who have done so) that many of your Mormon friends will abandon and shun you. If you are unable to convince your family members to leave the church with you, you will find that the church has broken up your family and your relationship with them may never recover.

Consider very carefully before you commit yourself, and remember that any doubts you may have now will likely only increase.

Examine carefully both sides of the Mormon story. Listen to the stories of those who have been through an unhappy Mormon experience, not just those Mormons who may speak glowingly of life in the church.

The Mormon missionaries are often charming and enthusiastic. They have an attractive story to tell. At first it sounds wonderful. But remember the old saying, "If it sounds too good to be true, it probably is!" Be careful not to fall into the trap of believing something simply because you want it to be true. Mormons may tell you that those who criticize the church are lying, misquoting and distorting. If you examine the sources used by the critics, however, you will discover that most of their source material is from official or semi-official Mormon writings. You, too, should examine those sources.

Is Mormonism a "cult"? Many experts on religious cults see in Mormonism the same fundamental characteristics as cults which have entrapped the unsuspecting, even though most people think of "cults" only as small, unknown groups. Use a "cult checklist" to evaluate Mormonism, or any group, before you commit yourself. □

NOTES AND LINKS TO MORE FACTS

DISCLAIMER: Some of the links and references listed here, in addition to containing valuable material about Mormonism, also contain Christian proselytizing material. Their inclusion here is not intended as an endorsement of any religion or religious organization.

¶GENERAL REFERENCES¶

INTERNET SITES AND LISTS OF LINKS

http://www.exmormon.org/goodsite.htm Links to other sites.
http://www.mormonismi.info/jamesdavid/table.htm An alphabetical list, by topic, of Mormon-related links; many articles. Originally by James David.
http://www.lds-mormon.com Articles and links; one of the oldest and most extensive Internet sites on Mormonism.
http://www.josephlied.com Mike Norton's excellent analysis of Mormon problems.
http://utlm.org/ Many articles by Jerald and Sandra Tanner, especially from their

newsletter *The Salt Lake City Messenger*. Also several complete books are online here, including their complete book *The Changing World of Mormonism*.

http://www.2think.org/hundredsheep/mormon.shtml Text of many early Mormon publications, including the 1830 version of the *Book of Mormon* and the original *Book of Commandments*. Curt Van Den Heuvel's site.

http://www.irr.org/mit "Mormons In Transition," sponsored by the Institute for Religious Research, with many articles; Christian orientation; an on-line newsgroup, (MIT-Talk) with evangelical basis

http://www.mrm.org The "Mormon Research Ministry," an evangelical Christian group headed by Bill McKeever; many good articles on Mormonism

http://www.bcmmin.org/ The "Berean Christian Ministry," headed by John Farkas; many articles, a useful chronology of church history, and a long refutation of a Mormon scholar's attempt to discredit critics of the church.

http://www.realmormonhistory.com A collection of historical quotations from *Mormon leaders themselves* which cast doubt on Mormonism.

http://www.i4m.com/think/ "Rethinking Mormonism" - an excellent site by former Mormon "Deconstructor"

http://trialsofascension.net/mormon.html "20 Truths About Mormonism" by Jim Day, Ph. D.

http://www.TheShelf.com Convenient side-by-side listing of internet articles on both sides of controversial Mormon issues - maintained by Cora Judd

http://www.mormoninformation.com Site maintained by "Dr. Shades"

http://zarahemlacitylimits.com/ "Zarahemla City Limits" - many articles and a discussion board

http://mormoncurtain.com/ "Blogging the Exmormon World" - maintained by Michael Hoenie

http://www.zaksite.co.uk/atozelph/twosides.htm "The church is true" "The church is not true" - Chris Tolworthy's site (formerly whyprophets.com); originally a very pro-Mormon site; Tolworthy - now no longer Mormon - presents the arguments of both sides

Mormonism Disproved   Christopher Miller's website

Mormonism - Pro and Con   Online version of Ed Bliss' book (.PDF format)

http://www.helmsmansociety.com/Issues/2005/mormon052605.htm The Helmsman Society's summary of Mormonism

http://mormonthink.com/scienceweb.htm "[Mormonism's] Conflicts With Science"

WIKIPEDIA CAUTION! Be careful with articles on Mormon topics at the popular online reference site Wikipedia! Since all articles there are subject to editing by all comers, the Mormon Church regularly edits them to remove any information that criticizes the church.

For a very complete list of other websites critical of Mormonism, see Google's ranked listing HERE.

BOOKS

Listed here are only a few "must read" books. There are hundreds of others. If your local library does not own them, your librarian can obtain them for you on interlibrary loan, usually for a very small fee. Most books listed are linked to on-line reviews or order information.

No Man Knows My History: The Life of Joseph Smith by Fawn M. Brodie, 2nd ed., Knopf, New York, 1993. The most authoritative biography of Joseph Smith. Brodie is a well recognized historian.

Mormon America: The Power And the Promise. By Richard N. Ostling and Joan K. Ostling, Harper, San Francisco, 1999, ISBN 0-06-066372-3. A well-balanced and reliable overview of Mormonism's past and present.

Mormonism: Shadow or Reality by Gerald and Sandra Tanner, 5th edition, Utah Lighthouse Ministry, 1987, Salt Lake City. The Tanners have done extensive research on early Mormon history and made many rare publications available by publishing photocopies of them at a low price. This book is a good summary of the contradictions and problems of Mormonism. Available from Utah Lighthouse Ministry, where a catalog of their publications is available. Also published in a slightly smaller version as _The Changing World of Mormonism_, Moody Press, Chicago, 1981 (now online).

Inventing Mormonism: Tradition and the Historical Record by H. Michael Marquardt and Wesley P. Walters, Signature Books, Salt Lake City, 1994. A detailed examination by historians of Mormonism's origins.

Joseph Smith and the Origins of the Book of Mormon (Second edition) by David Persuitte, McFarland & Co., 2000

Farewell to Eden: Coming to Terms With Mormonism and Science by Duwayne R. Anderson, Authorhouse, 2003 - a scientist and former Mormon examines Mormonism's scientific claims

Losing a Lost Tribe: Native Americans, DNA, and the Mormon Church by Simon G. Southerton (DNA scientist, former Mormon bishop), Signature Books, 2004

An Insider's View of Mormon Origins by Grant Palmer (Mormon, retired instructor in the church's educational system); a frank disclosure of many aspects of early Mormon history.

The Pattern of the Double Bind in Mormonism by Marion Stricker; the psychological bondage of Mormonism and how to recognize and escape it.

Mormonism Pro and Con by Ed Bliss (individual chapters are online here: http://www.mormonism-proandcon.org/

For Any Latter-day Saint: One Investigator's Unanswered Questions by Sharon I. Banister, Star Bible Publications, Fort Worth, 1988. Over 600 problematical questions about Mormon history and doctrine, very clearly presented, with many photographic reproductions of the relevant Mormon books and diaries. (See my review here.) (As of May 2007 this book is out of print; click here for availability of used copies)

REFERENCES TO SPECIFIC TOPICS

THE "FIRST VISION"
http://www.irr.org/mit/fvision.html The official version, and why it is a fiction
http://www.i4m.com/think/intro/must_believe_vision.htm The church insists that belief in the validity of the "First Vision" is the basis of Mormonism
http://www.irr.org/mit/First-Vision-Accounts.html All of the early (and contradictory) accounts, from Mormon sources
http://utlm.org/topicalindexc.htm#First Vision
http://www.mrm.org/multimedia/text/first-vision.html
http://www.bcmmin.org/firstv.html and
http://www.bcmmin.org/firstv2.html
http://www.irr.org/mit/inventbk.html (a review of the book _Inventing Mormonism_)

THE 1820 REVIVAL
The question of whether there was a revival in 1820 matching Smith's story has been hotly debated by Mormon and non-Mormon scholars. See the exchange between Richard L. Bushman (Mormon) and Wesley P. Walters (non-Mormon) in _Dialogue: A Journal of Mormon Thought_, (Spring 1969) 4:1:58ff. A summary of the opposing points of view (by a Mormon scholar) is Marvin Hill, "The First Vision: A Critique and Reconciliation," _Dialogue: A Journal of Mormon Thought_, (Summer 1982) 15:31-46.

http://utlm.org/onlinebooks/mclaims1.htm
http://www.xmission.com/~research/about/index.htm (Michael Marquardt's site)
The following three links are about Marquardt's book _Inventing Mormonism_, a scholarly investigation into Mormonism's early years:
http://www.xmission.com/~research/about/contents.htm
http://www.xmission.com/~research/about/summary.htm
http://www.xmission.com/~research/about/reviews.htm

JOSEPH SMITH AND THE METHODISTS
For Smith's connection with the Methodists, see _Inventing Mormonism_, pp 54-55, citing Turner, _History of Phelp's and Gorham's Purchase_, p. 214, which relates that Smith was an informal "exhorter" at Methodist camp meetings before 1822; Pomeroy Tucker, _The Origin, Rise and Progress of Mormonism_ (NY 1867), p 18: Smith joined the "probationary class" of the Methodist church; there was no Methodist church in Palmyra until July 1821 (_Inventing Mormonism_, p 60 n 41);
http://utlm.org/topicalindexc.htm#Methodist Church

JOSEPH SMITH AND "MONEYDIGGING"
http://www.utlm.org/newsletters/no68.htm The report of Smith's 1826 arrest and court appearance for being a "glass-looker"
http://www.saintsalive.com/mormonism/necromantic.html
http://utlm.org/topicalindexc.htm#Money-Digging and Magic

BOOK OF MORMON "WITNESSES"
http://www.irr.org/mit/bomwit1.html
http://www.saintsalive.com/mormonism/testimonyof3.htm
http://www.exmormon.org/file9.htm
http://www.irr.org/mit/address1.html The book by David Whitmer, *An Address To All Believers in Christ*, testifying that God revealed to him that Joseph Smith is a fallen prophet.
(Also at http://utlm.org/onlinebooks/address1.htm
http://www.xmission.com/~research/about/docum4.htm (Martin Harris interview in Tiffany's magazine)
http://www.carm.org/lds/unveiled2.htm Affidavits of Lucy Harris and Abigail Harris about Martin Harris
http://utlm.org/onlineresources/anthon.htm (Martin Harris' visit to Professor Anthon with a copy of characters from the gold plates)
http://www.mormonthink.com/witnessesweb.htm More on the witnesses, including pro-Mormon arguments

METHOD OF TRANSLATION OF THE *BOOK OF MORMON*
http://www.irr.org/mit/address1.html (David Whitmer's *Address To All Believers in Christ*; see p. 12, 30)
http://utlm.org/topicalindexa.htm#Black hole The significance of the 116 pages of lost manuscript for testing the authenticity of the book
http://www.mormonthink.com/lost116web.htm More on the 116 lost pages
Martin Harris, *Millennial Star* 6 Feb 1882, cited in Robert N. Hullinger, *Joseph Smith's response to Skepticism*, p 9-14, Salt Lake City 1992, said that the plates were not needed, also quoted by John Clark, *Gleanings By the Way*, 1842, p 228, cited in Hullinger p 11, n 23.
http://www.mormonthink.com/transbomweb.htm More on the method of translation, with specific responses to Mormon arguments
For an official Mormon admission about Smith's use of the "seer stone" in his hat, see "Speaking Today: A Treasured Testament," by Elder Russell M. Nelson, *Ensign*, July 1993 Volume 23 Number 7 page 61

BOOK OF MORMON ARCHAEOLOGY
http://www.irr.org/mit/bomarch1.html
http://www.saintsalive.com/mormonism/bomproblems.htm
http://utlm.org/topicalindexa.htm#Archeology
http://www.bcmmin.org/bomarch.html
http://www.lds-mormon.com/bomquest.shtml

http://www.mormonthink.com/bomweb3.htm Good summary of problems, with specific responses to Mormon arguments

http://www.mindspring.com/~dwright/BOM/survey.htm "*Book of Mormon* Lands Survey" - Daniel Wright's survey of professional (non-Mormon) archaeologists and their views of Mormon claims.

http://mormonscripturestudies.com/bomor/twm/lamgen.asp Recent study by DNA expert Tom Murphy, for which he was threatened with excommunication from the Mormon church, showing that the American Indians are not Semitic

Losing a Lost Tribe by Simon Southerton, former Mormon bishop and professional DNA expert; excellent book explaining the science and how it disproves the *Book of Mormon*

"Answers to Apologetic Claims about DNA and the *Book of Mormon*" by Simon Southerton

http://www.lhvm.org/dna.htm More on DNA studies, including a video about DNA's relationship to the *Book of Mormon*'s claims

Who Are The Lamanites?, a four-part article by Kevin Mathie examining the pro and con arguments

http://www.nowscape.com/mormon/zindler1.htm "How Do You Lose a Steel Mill" by Frank R. Zindler

http://www.mormonthink.com/bomweb3.htm Summary of problems with the *Book of Mormon*, including Mormon responses

JEWISH LAW AND THE *BOOK OF MORMON*
Salt Lake City Messenger, Issue #74, February 1990, available from Utah Lighthouse Ministry
http://lds-mormon.com/feast.shtml "Feasts in the *Book of Mormon*"

BOOK OF MORMON CHANGES; OTHER CHANGES
http://www.saintsalive.com/mormonism/bomchanges.htm
http://www.bcmmin.org/bmchg.html
http://utlm.org/topicalindexa.htm#Changes Changes made in revelations after their first publication, to reflect Smith's changes in doctrine.
The original texts of the *Book of Mormon* 1830 edition and the 1833 *Book of Commandments* (predecessor to the *Doctrine and Covenants* can be found at http://www.2think.org/hundredsheep/

PRESENT MORMON DOCTRINE CONTRARY TO *BOOK OF MORMON*
http://packham.n4m.org/bomvslds.htm A concise listing, with references
http://www.mrm.org/multimedia/text/test.html
http://www.bcmmin.org/bmchg.html
http://www.mrm.org/multimedia/text/birth.html On the Virgin Birth, how Jesus was conceived.
http://www.irr.org/mit/CHANGOD.html The changing concept of God.
http://www.bcmmin.org/bcm2.html Changing doctrines of Mormonism.

THE 1825 BOOK *View of the Hebrews* by Ethan Smith
http://www.irr.org/mit/Books/View-Hebrews/viewhe1a.html (text of *View*)
http://www.2think.org/hundredsheep/voh/voh.shtml (text of *View*)
http://www.2think.org/hundredsheep/bom/written.shtml Could Joseph Smith have written the *Book of Mormon*?
http://www.lds-mormon.com/voh.shtml Parallels between *View* and the *Book of Mormon*.
http://www.irr.org/mit/bhrobert.html B. H. Roberts' conclusions.

FAILURES OF GOD-INSPIRED PROJECTS
Failure of the Kirtland Bank:
http://utlm.org/topicalindexc.htm#Kirtland Bank
Gathering of Zion:
http://packham.n4m.org/prophet.htm
Polygamy - see notes at: #POLYGAMY
Deseret Alphabet:
http://www.omniglot.com/writing/deseret.htm
http://packham.n4m.org/byoung.htm#PROPHECIES

THE HOFMANN MURDER SCANDAL
The Mormon Murders: A True Story of Greed, Forgery, Deceit, and Death by Steven Naifeh and Gregory White Smith, Weidenfeld & Nicolson, New York, 1988. The role of the Mormon church leadership in this scandal is carefully documented here.
A Gathering of Saints: A True Story of Money, Murder and Deceit by Robert Lindsey, Simon and Schuster, New York, 1988. Another book on the Hofmann scandal.
Salamander: The Story of the Mormon Forgery Murders by Linda Sillitoe and Allen Roberts, 2nd edition, Signature Books, Salt Lake City.
http://utlm.org/topicalindexb.htm#Hofmann, Mark
"Masterminds: The Anthon Forgeries" Excellent video on the Hofmann forgeries.

THE MORMON TEMPLE CEREMONY (THE "ENDOWMENT")
http://packham.n4m.org/temples.htm: "Mormon Temples and Temple Rituals" - a detailed overview of this most secret part of Mormonism.
The next five links contain the actual text of the ceremony in the various forms it has had since the early days of the church.
1931 Version: http://packham.n4m.org/endow31.htm
1984 Version: http://packham.n4m.org/endow84.htm
1990 Version: http://packham.n4m.org/endow90.htm
2005 changes: http://packham.n4m.org/endow05.htm
(See also http://i4m.com/think/temples/temple_ordinance.htm for a discussion of the significance of the 2005 changes)
http://www.lds-mormon.com/veilworker/endowment.shtml
http://utlm.org/topicalindexc.htm#Temple Ceremony
http://i4m.com/think/temples/ Several articles on temples
http://www.mrm.org/multimedia/text/garments.html A description of the sacred under-

garment which Mormons are required to wear after receiving the endowment.
http://www.nowscape.com/mormon/undrwrmo.htm More on "garments"
http://www.mrm.org/multimedia/text/temple-ceremony.html
http://www.nowscape.com/mormon/mormcr1.htm
http://www.saintsalive.com/mormonism/templechanges.htm
http://www.lds-mormon.com/veilworker/recommend.shtml The questions that are
asked in the "worthiness interview" to determine whether a member is worthy to
receive admission to the temple.

MASONIC INFLUENCE ON MORMONISM
http://www.masonicmoroni.com Paul Graham's comprehensive site, with many links
from all points of view
http://www.mormonismi.info/jamesdavid/masendow.htm
http://www.mormonismi.info/jamesdavid/masonry.htm
http://www.irr.org/mit/masonry.html
http://utlm.org/onlinebooks/changech4.htm#Joseph Smith's Magic Talisman Joseph
Smith's magical talisman
http://www.saintsalive.com/mormonism/nohelp.html
http://www.mrm.org/multimedia/text/masonic-influence.html

THE "ADAM = GOD" DOCTRINE
http://www.mrm.org/multimedia/text/theory.html
http://www.bcmmin.org/adamgod.html
http://www.bcmmin.org/evolut4.html The changes in the Mormon doctrine about God.
http://www.mrm.org/multimedia/text/adam-god.html (Text of Brigham Young's 1852
sermon)
http://packham.n4m.org/byoung.htm#ADAMGOD More statements by Brigham Young
A good discussion, with photocopy of Bruce R. McConkie's private admission that
Brigham Young did teach the doctrine, is in Tanner, *LDS Apostle Confesses Brigham
Young Taught Adam-God Doctrine*, available from Utah Lighthouse Ministry.   Similar
material is in Banister's book *For Any Latter- Day Saint*
http://www.mrm.org/multimedia/text/mcconkies-letter.html The text of McConkie's
letter admitting that Brigham Young did teach that Adam was God
See also: *Adam is God???* by Chris A. Vlachos, pamphlet available from Utah Lighthouse Ministry

POLYGAMY ("CELESTIAL MARRIAGE")
http://www.irr.org/mit/enigma.html A review of *Mormon Enigma: Emma Hale Smith*,
by Linda King Newell and Valene Tippett Avery, University of Illinois Press, 1994; a
biography of Joseph Smith's first wife, relating the development of Smith's ideas on
polygamy and her opposition to it.
In Sacred Loneliness: *The Plural Wives of Joseph Smith* by Todd Compton, Signature
Books
http://www.wivesofjosephsmith.org/home Biographies of all of Joseph Smith's wives
http://utlm.org/topicalindexb.htm#Polygamy

http://www.nowscape.com/mormon/polyg.htm

http://www.mormonismi.info/jamesdavid/denpract.htm Smith's public (and untruthful) denials of the rumors about his practice of polygamy.

http://www.mormonismi.info/jamesdavid/menwives.htm Documentation of Smith's seduction of other men's wives.

http://www.xmission.com/~country/reason/clndest2.htm An early and generally unknown revelation about polygamy

Mormon Polygamy: A History by Richard S. Van Wagoner, Signature Books, Salt Lake City. An excellent history of its theory and practice, reviewed at http://www.lds-mormon.com/polygamy.shtml.

The Works of Abraham: Mormon Polygamy Sources on Its Origin, Thought, and Practice by B. Carmon Hardy, 2007

http://www.i4m.com/think/history/joseph_smith_sex.htm "Did Joseph Smith have sex with his [polygamous] wives?"

http://www.signaturebookslibrary.org/essays/mormonpolygamy.htm Comprehensive essay on polygamy

http://www.polygamy.org Home page of *Tapestry of Polygamy*, a group of formerly polygamous women who are exposing its evils as practiced by some Mormon groups today.

http://mormonthink.com/polyweb.htm - responses to Mormon arguments and claims

http://www.i4m.com/think/polygamy/utah_census.htm "U. S. Census numbers and Mormon Polygamy"   Refutation of the claim that polygamy was practiced because of a shortage of men in early Utah

http://www.mrm.org/multimedia/video/lifting-veil-polygamy Video documentary on Mormon polygamy

THE "CURSE OF CAIN": THE CHANGING DOCTRINE ON SKIN COLOR

http://www.saintsalive.com/mormonism/africanamerican.htm

http://utlm.org/topicalindexa.htm#Blacks

http://www.exmormon.org/blacks1.htm

http://www.lds-mormon.com/racism.shtml

http://packham.n4m.org/byoung.htm#NEGRO Brigham Young's Doctrines on the Black race

http://www.mormonthink.com/blackweb.htm Summary of pro and con views

http://www.religioustolerance.org/lds_race.htm History of racism in Mormonism from the "Religious Tolerance" organization

http://jhuston.com/Documents/1978.htm   Background information on the 1978 "revelation"

THE DOCTRINE OF "BLOOD ATONEMENT" AND THE DANITES ("AVENGING ANGELS")

http://www.saintsalive.com/mormonism/bloodatonement.htm

http://utlm.org/topicalindexa.htm#Blood Atonement

http://www.exmormon.org/bloodatn.htm

http://www.exmormon.org/violence.htm

http://www.saintsalive.com/mormonism/murder.html
http://www.irr.org/mit/faulring.html
http://www.mrm.org/multimedia/text/blood-atonement.html Mormons often deny that
the doctrine was taught, but they still believe it.
"Blood Atonement" a short video on the origin and present practice

The role of violence in Mormonism is the subject of *Under the Banner of Heaven: A
Story of Violent Faith* by Jon Krakauer, Doubleday, 2003; this book was on the best-
seller lists for a number of weeks.
The authoritative work on the Mountain Meadows Massacre has been Juanita Brooks,
The Mountain Meadows Massacre, Univ. of Oklahoma Press, 1991.
Brooks is now supplemented by new evidence in Will Bagley, *The Blood of the Proph-
ets: Brigham Young and the Massacre at Mountain Meadows*, Univ. of Oklahoma
Press, 2002.
See also Sally Denton's book *American Massacre: The Tragedy at Mountain Meadows*,
Knopf 2003.
J. F. Gibbs's complete book *Mountain Meadows Massacre* is online at http://utlm.org/
onlinebooks/meadowscontents.htm
Film treatments of the Mountain Meadows Massacre:
"Burying the Past" (documentary): http://www.buryingthepast.com
"September Dawn" (fictionalized, but based on fact): http://www.septemberdawn.net

THE *BOOK OF COMMANDMENTS*
http://www.2think.org/hundredsheep/boc/boc_main.shtml The complete text of the
Book of Commandments, showing the revisions made to them in the Doctrine and
Covenants

RESTORATION OF THE PRIESTHOOD
"Priesthood Restored or Retrofit?" by Lane Thuet
THE *BOOK OF ABRAHAM*
http://www.irr.org/mit/boapage.html The complete book *By His Own Hand Upon
Papyrus* by Charles M. Larson
http://www.mrm.org/multimedia/text/abraham.html
http://www.mormonismi.info/jamesdavid/index.htm
http://utlm.org/topicalindexb.htm#Book of Abraham
http://www.xmission.com/~research/about/abraham.htm
http://www.xmission.com/~research/about/alphabet.htm The text of Smith's so-called
Egyptian Alphabet & Grammar
http://www.bookofabraham.com Comprehensive site, with message board, about the
Book of Abraham
An hour-long video about the *Book of Abraham*: "The Lost Book of Abraham" at http://
www.mrm.org/multimedia/video/lost-book-abraham

THE "INSPIRED REVISION" OF THE BIBLE
The Reorganized Church of Jesus Christ of Latter-day Saints, (RLDS, now renamed

"Community of Christ") has long used the version by Smith.
http://utlm.org/topicalindexc.htm#Inspired Revision of the Bible

THE KINDERHOOK PLATES
http://www.mormonismi.info/jamesdavid/indekind.htm
http://utlm.org/topicalindexb.htm#Kinderhook Plates
http://www.nowscape.com/mormon/kindrhk/kindrhk.htm
http://www.mormonthink.com/kinderhookweb.htm Good summary of both pro and con
views

JOSEPH SMITH'S PROPHECIES
http://packham.n4m.org/prophet.htm A listing of many of Smith's unfulfilled prophecies
http://www.saintsalive.com/mormonism/falseprophetjs.htm
http://www.mrm.org/multimedia/text/civilwar.html Joseph Smith's famous prophecy of
the Civil War
http://www.lds-mormon.com/civilwar.shtml Another article on the Civil War prophecy
http://utlm.org/onlinebooks/changech13.htm#Rocky Mountain Prophecy Joseph
Smith's prophecy about the Mormon move to the Rocky Mountains
http://www.mormonthink.com/prophetsweb.htm Lack of prophecy in the modern
church

For some of Brigham Young's failed prophecies, see:
http://packham.n4m.org/byoung.htm#PROPHECIES

JOSEPH SMITH'S DEATH
http://www.solomonspalding.com/docs/exposit1.htm The text of the *Nauvoo Expositor*,
the opposition paper which Smith destroyed, thus leading to his imprisonment and
death. It contains all the *true* accusations which Smith wanted suppressed
http://utlm.org/onlinebooks/changech17.htm#Destruction of Expositor The destruction
of the *Nauvoo Expositor*

For a detailed discussion of Smith's political ambitions, his title "king" and his secret
government, see the book by D. Michael Quinn, *The Mormon Hierarchy: [Volume 1]*
The Origins of Power, Signature Books, Salt Lake City, 1994. (Quinn was excommunicated from the Mormon church for his historical researches, but remains a believer)

MORMON FALSIFICATION OF MORMON HISTORY
http://www.xmission.com/~country/reason/mormhist.htm D. Michael Quinn's Talk "On
Being A Mormon Historian" in which he urges the church authorities to be more open
in telling the entire history of the church, without coloring it. Rather than follow his
advice, the church excommunicated him.
http://www.utlm.org/newsletters/no88.htm An evaluation of the propaganda film
Legacy, produced by the church.
http://www.bcmmin.org/persecutor.html An evaluation of the church's claim that it was

persecuted.

http://www.utlm.org/newsletters/no78.htm The uncovering of the lies told by a high-ranking Mormon official

http://www.xmission.com/~country/reason/mantle.htm A speech by Boyd K. Packer, a high-ranking church official, on how the church justifies its distortion of its history.

http://www.utlm.org/newsletters/no85.htm The recent purge of Mormon historians who told too much

http://www.exmormon.org/lying.htm A discussion of speech by Dallin Oaks, a high-ranking church official, on the need for withholding the whole truth.

http://www.exmormon.org/apology.htm

http://www.lds-mormon.com/lying.shtml

http://packham.n4m.org/gbh-god.htm The present "prophet" Gordon B. Hinckley lies about church doctrine in two interviews for the news media.

http://packham.n4m.org/lying.htm More examples of Mormon lying.

A good example of the church's distortion of history is its long cover-up of the Mountain Meadows Massacre. See Juanita Brooks, _The Mountain Meadows Massacre_, Univ. of Oklahoma Press, 1991.

PRAYING FOR TRUTH

"Testimony and Spiritual Witness" - discussion about the reliability of spiritual witness

http://packham.n4m.org/prayer.htm - prayer is not for obtaining information

http://packham.n4m.org/satan.htm - how Satan can deceive

UNUSUAL DOCTRINES
- God was once a man like us: http://packham.n4m.org/gbh-god.htm
- God has a tangible body of flesh and bone: D&C 130:22
- God lives on a planet near the star Kolob: _Book of Abraham_ 3:3-16
- God has at least one wife, our "Mother in Heaven": Joseph Fielding Smith, _Man, His Origin and Destiny_, p 348-355: "All men and women are in the similitude of the universal Father and Mother..." (More citations in _The Changing World of Mormonism_, Chapter 7)
- Jesus was married: This idea is consistent with the Mormon doctrine that marriage is required for godhood; see citations from early church leaders at _Changing World of Mormonism_, Chapter 9. The church denies that this is a doctrine of the church here.
- We can become like God and rule over our own universe. http://packham.n4m.org/gbh-god.htm
- There are many gods, ruling over their own worlds: Citations in "http://www.utlm.org/onlinebooks/changech7.htm#From%20One%20to%20Many">_The Changing World of Mormonism_, Chapter 7
- Jesus and Satan ("Lucifer") are brothers: D&C 76:25, Moses 4:1-4
- Jesus Christ was conceived by God the Father by having sex with Mary: Citations in _The Changing World of Mormonism_, Chapter 7
- We should not try to feel a personal relationship with Jesus: "Our Relationship With The Lord" by Apostle Bruce R. McConkie
- "The Lord" ("Jehovah") in the Old Testament is the same being named Jesus in the

New Testament, but not the same as "God the Father": D&C 110:2-4; Bruce R. McConkie, *Mormon Doctrine*, article "Jehovah"; 1 Nephi 19:10
-   In the the highest degree of the celestial kingdom some men will have more than one wife: D&C 132:63
-   "Pre-existence": See Joseph Fielding Smith, *Doctrines of Salvation, Vol. 1*, ch 4, esp pp 60-61
-   Dark skin is a curse from God: 1 Nephi 12:23, 2 Nephi 5:21, Alma 3:6, Jacob 3:8, 3 Nephi 2:15, Morm 5:15.
-   The Garden of Eden was in Missouri: D&C 116:1; see also D&C 107:53.
-   Animal resurrection: http://packham.n4m.org/animals.htm
-   Rainbow: http://packham.n4m.org/prophet.htm
-   Satan rules water: D&C 61
-   Sun's light is from Kolob: *Book of Abraham* Facsimile # 2, Explanation of Fig 5
-   Gentile blood is replaced: *History of the Church* 3:380, *Teachings of the Prophet Joseph Smith* p. 150
-   Seeing face of God: D&C 97:16; see also 93:1 and 88:68
-   False angel hair color: *Teachings of the Prophet Joseph Smith* p. 214; handshake: D&C 129:1-9
-   Sun receives its light from Kolob: *Book of Abraham*, Facsimile 2, Fig 5

PROHIBITION ON COFFEE, ETC. (THE "WORD OF WISDOM")
The text of the Word of Wisdom is in the *Doctrine and Covenants* Section 89
http://www.utlm.org/onlinebooks/changech18.htm Problems and inconsistencies with this revelation.
http://utlm.org/onlinebooks/mclaims8.htm#The Word of Wisdom

TITHING, CHURCH WEALTH
http://www.mrm.org/multimedia/text/tithing.html
http://www.mormonismi.info/jamesdavid/tithing.htm
On the wealth of the church, see: Anson Shupe, *Wealth and Power in American Zion*, Lewiston NY 1992, or John Heinerman and Anson Shupe, *The Mormon Corporate Empire*, Beacon, 1988.

OBEDIENCE: "FOLLOW THE BRETHREN"
http://www.xmission.com/~country/reason/cannon.htm Excerpts from *Under The Prophet In Utah* by Senator Frank J. Cannon, showing how the church leaders exert power over members.
http://www.i4m.com/think/leaders/mormon_loyalty.htm Many statements by church leaders emphasizing loyalty to the church
http://www.zionsbest.com/fourteen.html A speech by Ezra Taft Benson, a recent prophet and president, instructing members to obey the prophet without questioning and without checking his advice against scripture.
http://www.lds-mormon.com/mothink.shtml
http://www.lds-mormon.com/thinking.shtml A critical article on the church's mind control.

http://www.xmission.com/~country/reason/purge.htm The recent mass excommunications of intellectuals and historians who questioned church authority.
http://www.zionsbest.com/heresies.html Bruce R. McConkie on the heresy of evolution.

HOMOSEXUALS, MASTURBATION

http://www.affirmation.org The website of *Affirmation*, an organization for Mormons with homosexual leanings. Much information about the church's stance on sex.
http://www.affirmation.org/learning/steps_in_overcoming_masturbation.shtml A talk by Mormon apostle Mark E. Petersen, on how to prevent masturbation.
http://www.affirmation.org/learning/we_see_what_we_believe.asp A critical article by Jeffery R. Jensen, M.D., on the harm done by the church with its stance on homosexuality.
http://www.affirmation.org/learning/homosexuality_a_psychiatrists_response.asp
Another article by Dr. Jensen, criticizing the church's department of social services
http://www.zionsbest.com/only.html A speech by Boyd K. Packer on the evils of masturbation in young men, and how to prevent it.
http://www.youtube.com/watch?v=ilZt88Kt50k Video interviews with young Mormon homosexuals about their treatment
http://www.affirmation.org/learning/in_gods_name.shtml "In God's Name" by Terry Hiscox - a survey of Christian and Mormon treatment of homosexuals

POSITION OF WOMEN IN THE CHURCH

Books by two exmormon women describing their difficulties with the church's treatment of women:
Deborah Laake, *Secret Ceremonies*, Dell, 1993
Sonia Johnson, *From Housewife to Heretic*, Doubleday, 1981. Johnson was excommunicated for her activism in favor of the Equal Rights Amendment.
http://www.exmormon.org/mormwomn.htm A woman's viewpoint.
http://www.lds-mormon.com/lying.shtml How the church misrepresents its stance on the role of women.
"Mormon Women, Prozac, and Therapy" by Kent Ponder Ph.D. explores the causes for so many Mormon women being on anti-depressant medications.
http://members.shaw.ca/blair_watson/ "The Psychological Effects of Mormonism" by Blair Watson

PERSONAL STORIES BY FORMER MORMONS

http://www.exmormon.org/ has the personal stories of over six hundred people who left the church and their many different reasons for doing so.
For briefer comments from former Mormons, see http://packham.n4m.org/voices1.htm
See also these longer accounts:
Mary Ann Benson (granddaughter-in-law of Ezra Taft Benson, president of the church): http://www.exmormon.org/mormon/mormon146.htm
Steve Benson (grandson of Benson, Mary Ann's husband): http://www.lds-mormon.com/benson2.shtml and also http://www.exmormon.org/mormon/mormon418.htm

http://twincentral.com/site/pages/articles/doctrines/alt/LDS/stevebenson.htm Transcript of the Bensons' interview with two Mormon apostles
Ken Clark (former teacher in the Church Educational System): http://www.exmormon. org/whylft149.htm

For longer (booklength) accounts, see:
Suddenly Strangers: *Surrendering Gods and Heroes* by the Morin brothers.(http:// suddenlystrangers.com - click on "Excerpts")
Beyond Mormonism: *An Elder's Story* by James R. Spencer, who converted to Mormonism and left it to become a Christian minister
Martha Beck (daughter of Mormon apologist Hugh Nibley), *Leaving the Saints*, Crown, 2005, ISBN 0609609912

IS MORMONISM A CULT?
The following links are to checklists and other guidelines, to help you to evaluate whether any group (not just Mormonism) is a "cult."
http://www.csj.org/infoserv_cult101/checklis.htm
http://www.csj.org/infoserv_cult101/cult101.htm
http://www.freedomofmind.com/ The home page of Steve Hassan, an authority on cults and brainwashing.
"[Hassan's] BITE Model Applied Toward Mormonism"
http://www.caic.org.au Jan Groenveld's Cult Awareness Centre
http://www.factnet.org FACTnet, resources on psychological coercion and mind control
http://www.neopagan.net/ABCDEF.html Isaac Bonewits' cult checklist, with 18 items and worksheet.
A 12-minute video on cults in general: http://www.youtube.com/watch?v=mnNSe5XYp6E
http://members.shaw.ca/blair_watson/ "The Psychological Effects of Mormonism" by Blair Watson

*With permission from Richard Packham. Last Revision 2010

References

Adler, Jonathan E., "Faith and Fanaticism," in *Philosophers without Gods*, ed. Louise M. Antony, Oxford   Press, 2007

_____, *Belief's Own Ethics*, The MIT Press, 2006

Abanes, Richard, *One Nation under Gods*, Thunder's Mouth Press, 2003

Alston, William P., "The Perception of God," *Philosophical Topics* 16, no. 2 (Fall 1988): 23-52

_____, *Perceiving God*, Ithaca: Cornell University Press, 1991

Altemeyer, Robert, *The Authoritarian Specter*, Harvard University Press, 1996

Anderson, Duwayne R., *Farewell to Eden: Coming to Terms with Mormonism and Science*, AuthorHouse, 2003

Anderson, Lavina Fielding and Allred, Janice Merill, Case *Reports of the Mormon Alliance, Volume 1*, Mormon Alliance, 1995

_____, *Case Reports of the Mormon Alliance, Volume 2*, Mormon Alliance, 1997

Anderson, Robert, *Inside the Mind of Joseph Smith*, Signature Books, 1999

Andreadis, Athena, "Evolutionary Noise, Not Signal From Above," in Russell Blackford and Udo Schüklenk (eds.), *50 Voices of Disbelief: Why We Are Atheists*, Wiley-Blackwell, 2009, pp. 274-8

Angeles, Peter A., Ed., *Critiques of God: Making the Case against Belief in God*, Prometheus Books, 1997

Antony, Louise M., *Philosophers without Gods*, Oxford University Press, 2007

Atran, Scott, *In Gods We Trust*, Oxford University press, 1993

Bagley, Will, *Blood of the Prophets*, University of Oklahoma Press, 2004

Baker, Robert A., *Hidden Memories: Voices and Visions from Within*, Prometheus Books, 1996

Banister, Sharon I., *For Any Latter-day Saint: One Investigator's Unanswered Questions*, Star Bible Publications, 1988

Barker, Dan, *Godless*, Ulysses Press, 2008

Batson, C. Daniel and Ventis, W. Larry, *The Religious Experience*, Oxford University Press, 1982

Becker, Ernest, *The Denial of Death*, The Free Press, 1973

_____, *Escape from Evil*, Free Press, 1975

Beckwith, Francis, *The New Mormon Challenge*, Zondervan, 2002

_____, "Philosophical Problems with the Mormon Concept of God," *Christian Research Institute*, 1994

Beebe, John, *Integrity in Depth*, Fromm, 1995

Bergin, Allen E., "Values and Religious Issues in Psychotherapy and Mental Health," *American Psychologist*, April 1991, pp.394-403

_____, "Psychotherapy and Religious Values," *AMCAP Journal*, April 1980, pp. 3-11

Beversluis, John, *C.S. Lewis and the Search for Rational Theology*, Prometheus Books, 2007

Black, Max, Ed., *Philosophical Analysis*, Cornell University Press, 1950

Blackstone, William T., *The Problem of Religious Knowledge*, Prentice-Hall, 1963

Blomberg, Craig L. and Robinson, Stephen E., *How Wide the Divide: A Mormon and an Evangelical in Conversation*, InterVarsity Press, 1997

Bowlby, John, *A Secure Base: Parent-Child Attachment and Healthy Human Development*, Basic Books, 1988

Boyer, Pascal, *Religion Explained*, Basic Books, 2001

Bradlee, Ben, *Prophet of Blood: The Untold Story of Ervil Lebaron and the Lambs of God*, Putnam 1981

Bradshaw, John, *Family Secrets: What You Don't Know Can Hurt You*, Bantam, 1995

_____, *Healing the Shame that Binds You*, Health Communications, Inc., 1988

_____, *The Family: A Revolutionary Way of Self-Discovery*, HCI, 1988

Brodie, Fawn M., *No Man Knows My History*, Vintage, 1995

Brooks, Juanita, *The Mountain Meadows Massacre*, University of Oklahoma Press, 1991

Brown, Norman O., *Life against Death*, Wesleyan University Press, 1985

Browne, M. Neil and Keeley, Stuart M., *Asking the Right Questions: A Guide to Critical Thinking*, Pearson Prentice Hall, 2004

Buerger, David J., *The Mysteries of Godliness: A History of Mormon Temple Worship*, Signature Books, 2002

Burton, Robert, *On Being Certain: Believing You Are Right Even When You're Not*, St. Martins Press, 2008

Carrier, Richard, *Sense & Goodness Without God*, Authorhouse, 2005

Clarke, Isabel, Ed., *Psychosis and Spirituality*, Whurr, 2001

Clark, Thomas W., "Too Good to Be True, Too Obscure to Explain: The Cognitive Short-comings of Belief in God," in Russell Blackford and Udo Schüklenk (eds.), *50 Voices of Disbelief: Why We Are Atheists*, Wiley-Blackwell, 2009, pp. 57-64

Clifford, W. K., "The Ethics of Belief," in *Ethics of Belief and Other Essays*, Prometheus Books, 1999

Conifer, Steven J., "The Argument from Reason for the Non-existence of God," The Secular Web, 2001

Cosculluela, Victor, "Bolstering the Argument from Nonbelief," in *The Improbability of God*, Martin and Monnier Eds., Prometheus Books, 2006

Crowther, Duane S., *The Godhead*, Horizon Publishers, 2007

Damer, T. Edward, *Attacking Faulty Reasoning*, Wadsworth, 2001

Dawkins, Richard, *A Devil's Chaplain*, Mariner Books, 2004

_____, *The God Delusion*, Houghton Mifflin, 2006

_____, *The Greatest Show On Earth: The Evidence for Evolution*, Free Press, 2009

Dennett, Daniel C., *Consciousness Explained*, Little Brown, 1990

_____, *Darwin's Dangerous Idea*, Simon & Schuster, 1995

_____, *Freedom Evolves*, Viking, 2003

_____, *Breaking the Spell*, Viking, 2006

Dewey, John, *How we Think*, Dover, 1997

Doherty, Earl, *The Jesus Puzzle*, Age of Reason, 2005

Double, Richard, *The Non Reality of Free Will*, Oxford University Press, 1990

Dourley, John P., *The Illness That We Are*, Inner City Books, 1984

_____, *A Strategy For A Loss of Faith*, Inner City Books, 1992

Drange, Theodore M., *Nonbelief and Evil*, Prometheus Books, 1998

Edis, Taner, *The Ghost in the Universe*, Prometheus Books 2002

Elbert, Jerome W., *Are Souls Real?* Prometheus Books, 2000

Eller, David, *Natural Atheism*, American Atheist Press, 2004

_____, *Atheism Advanced*, American Atheist Press, 2007(a)

_____, *Introducing Anthropology of Religion: Culture to the Ultimate*, Routledge 2007(b)

Ellis, Albert, "Psychotherapy and Atheistic Values: A Response to A.E. Bergin's 'Psychotherapy and Religious Values," *Journal of Consulting and Clinical Psychology*, Vol. 48, No. 5, 635-639

Erman, Bart D., *The Orthodox Corruption of Scripture*, Oxford University Press 1985

_____, *Misquoting Jesus: The Story Behind Who Changed the Bible and Why*, HarperCollins, 2005

Everitt, Nicholas, *The Non-Existence of God*, Routledge, 2004

Faber, M.D., *Becoming God's Children: Religion's Infantilizing Process*, Praeger, 2010

_____, *The Psychological Roots of Religious Belief*, Prometheus Books, 2004

_____, *The Magic of Prayer*, Praeger, 2002

Fales, E., "Scientific Explanations of Mystical Experiences," *Rel. Studies* 32, pp. 297-313, Cambridge University Press, 1996

_____, "Do Mystics See God?" (2002), *The Secular Web*

Fine, Cordelia, *A Mind of its Own: How Your Brain Distorts and Deceives*, Norton, 2006

Fisher, Alec, *Critical Thinking, An Introduction*, Cambridge, 2001

Flanagan, Owen, *The problem of the Soul*, Basic Books, 2002

Flew, Anthony, *How to Think Straight*, Prometheus Books, 1998

Freud, Anna, *The Ego and Mechanisms of Defense*, Karnac Books, 1993

Freud, Sigmund, *The Future of an Illusion*, Norton, 1961(a)

_____, *Civilization and its Discontents*, Norton, 1961(b)

Fromm, Erich, *The Art of Loving*, Harper, 2006

Feuerbach, Ludwig, *The Essence of Christianity*, Prometheus Books, 1989

_____, *The Essence of Religion*, Prometheus Books, 2004

Fuller, Andrew R., *Psychology & Religion: Eight Points of View*, Littlefield Adams, 1994

Gale, Richard M., *On the Nature and Existence of God*, Cambridge University press, 1991
_____, "Swinburne's Argument from Religious Experience" (1994), *The Secular Web*

_____, "Why Alston's Mystical Doxastic Practice Is Subjective" (1994), *The Secular Web*

Garber, Daniel, "Religio Philosophi," in *Philosophers without Gods*, ed. Louise M. Antony, Oxford Press, 2007

Gaylin, Willard, *How Psychotherapy Really Works*, Contemporary Books, 2001

Gerson, Mary-Joan, *The Embedded Self: A Psychoanalytic Guide to Family Therapy*, The Analytic Press, Inc., 1996

Gilovich, Thomas, *How We Know What Isn't So: The Fallibility of Human Reason in Everyday Life*, Free Press, 1991

Glymour, C., "Freud's androids," in *The Cambridge Companion to Freud*, Jerome Neu, Ed., Cambridge University Press, 1991

Gold, R.D., *Bondage of the Mind: How Old Testament Fundamentalism Shackles the Mind and Enslaves the Spirit*, Aldus Books, 2008

Grossman, L., "Psychic Reality," in *International Journal of Psychoanalysis*, 77: 509-517, 1996

Guthrie, Stewart, *Faces in the Clouds*, Oxford University Press, 1993

Hagerstrom, Axel, *Philosophy and Religion*, George Allen and Unwin, 1964

Hawking, Stephen and Mlodinow, Leonard, *The Grand Design*, Bantam, 2010
Harbour, Daniel, *An Intelligent Person's Guide to Atheism*, Duckworth Publishers, 2001

Harris, Sam, *The End of Faith*, Norton, 2004

_____, *The Moral Landscape: How Science Can Determine Human Values*, Free Press, 2010

Harvey, Van A., "Religion as Creative Illusion," in *Death and Denial: Interdisciplinary Perspectives on the Legacy of Ernest Becker*, Ed. Daniel Liechty, Praeger, 2002

Hauser, Marc D., *Moral Minds*, HarperCollins, 2006

Hecht, Jennifer Michael, *Doubt, a History*, Harper, 2003

Hitchens, Christopher, *God is not Great*, Twelve, 2007

Honderich, Ted, *How free are you?* Oxford University Press, 2002

Hook, Sidney, "For an Open Minded Naturalism," *Southern Journal of Philosophy* 3, no. 1: 127-36

_____, *Religious Experience and Truth*, Sidney Hook, Ed., New York University Press, 1961

Horgan, John, "Why Freud Isn't Dead," *Scientific American* 282 (December 1996): 106-11.

Huberman, Jack, *The Quotable Atheist*, Nation Books, 2007

Hume, David, *The Natural History of Religion and Dialogues concerning Natural Religion*, edited by A. Wayne Colver and John Vladimir Price, Oxford Clarendon Press, 1976
James, William. *The Varieties of Religious Experience*, Library of America, 1987

Jaynes, Julian, *The origin of Consciousness in the Breakdown of the Bicameral Mind*, Mariner Books, 1990

Johnston, Elizabeth, *Investigating Minds*, Sarah Lawrence College, 2001

Jones, Henry E., *Religion: The Etiology of Mental Illness*, Mental Health Education, 2006

Joshi, S.T., *Atheism: A Reader*, Prometheus Books, 2000

_____, *God's Defenders*, Prometheus Books, 2003

Joyce, Richard, *The Myth of Morality*, Cambridge University Press, 2001

Kahn, Michael, *Basic Freud*, Basic Books, 2002

Kant, Immanuel, *Critique of Practical Reason*, translated and edited by Lewis White Beck, University of Chicago Press, 1949

_____, *Critique of Pure Reason*, translated by Norman K. Smith, Macmillan, 1963

Kerr, Michael E. and Bowen, Murray, *Family Evaluation*, Norton, 1988

Kirkpatrick, Lee A., *Attachment, Evolution, and the Psychology of Religion*, The Guilford Press, 2004

Kuchar, Philip, "A Rebuttal to Pardi's Criticism of ANB," *The Secular Web*, 2004
Krakauer, J., *Under the Banner of Heaven: A Story of Violent Faith*, Anchor, 2004

Krueger, Douglas E., *What Is Atheism?* Prometheus Books, 1998

Kurtz, Paul, *The Transcendental Temptation*, Prometheus Books, 1991

_____, *Science and Religion*, Prometheus Books, 2003

Lear, Jonathan, *Freud*, Routledge, 2005

Le Doux, Joseph, *Synaptic Self: How Our Brains Become Who We Are*, Viking, 2002

Leiper, Rob and Maltby, Michael, *The Psychodynamic Approach to Therapeutic Change*, Sage, 2004

Levy, Donald, *Freud Among the Philosophers*, Yale University Press, 1996

Lewis, David, "Divine Evil," in *Philosophers without Gods*, ed. Louise M. Antony, Oxford Press, 2007

Lewis, I.M., *Ecstatic Religion: A Study of Shamanism and Spirit Possession*, Routledge, 1989

Liechty, Daniel, "Freud and the Question of Pseudo Science," *Ernest Becker Foundation Newsletter*, no. 6 (1999): 7

Linden, David, *The Accidental Mind*, Harvard University Press, 2008

Loftus, John W. Ed., *The Christian Delusion,* Prometheus Books, 2010
_____, *Why I became an Atheist: A Former preacher Rejects Christianity*, Prometheus Books, 2008

_____, "Why I Am Not A Christian: A Summary of My Case Against Christianity," *The Secular Web*, 2008

Loy, David R., "The Denial of No-Self: A Buddhist Appreciation (Appropriation) of Becker," in *Death and Denial: Interdisciplinary Perspectives on the Legacy of Ernest Becker*, Ed. Daniel Liechty, Praeger, 2002

Lund, Gerald N., *Hearing the Voice of the Lord: Principles and Patterns of Personal Revelation*, Deseret Book, 2007

Mackie, J.L., *The Miracle of Atheism*, Oxford Press, 1982

_____, *Ethics, Inventing Right and Wrong*, Penguin Books, 1977

Madsen, Brigham D., *Studies of the Book of Mormon*, Signature Books, 1992

Madsen, Truman G., "The Meaning of Christ – The Truth, The Way and The Life: An Analysis of B.H. Roberts' Unpublished Manuscript," *BYU Studies*, 1975

Marquardt, H. Michael and Walters, Wesley P., *Inventing Mormonism: Tradition and the Historical Record*, Signature Books, 1994

Martin, Michael, *Atheism: A Philosophical Justification*, Temple, 1990

_____, *The Case Against Christianity*, Temple University Press, 1991

_____, "The Verificationist Challenge," in Philip L. Quinn and Charles Talaferro (eds.), *A Companion to Philosophy of Religion*, Wiley-Blackwell, 1999
_____, *Atheism, Morality, and Meaning*, Prometheus Books, 2002

_____, *The Cambridge Companion to Atheism*, Cambridge University Press, 2007

Martin, Michael and Monnier, Ricki Eds., *The Impossibility of God*, Prometheus Books, 2003

_____, *The Improbability of God*, Prometheus Books, 2006

Maslow, Abraham H., *The Farther Reaches of Human Nature*, Penguin, 1976

_____, *Toward a Psychology of Being*, Insight, 1962

Mattill, Jr., A.J., *The Seven Mighty Blows to Traditional Beliefs*, Flatwoods Free Press, 1995

Mayr, Ernst, *What Evolution Is*, Basic Books, 2001

McConkie, Bruce R., *Mormon Doctrine*, Deseret, 1979

McGraw, John J., *Brain and Belief*, Aegis 2004

McMurrin, Sterling M., *The Theological Foundations of the Mormon Religion*, University of Utah Press, 1965

McWilliams, Nancy, *Psychoanalytic Diagnosis*, The Guilford Press, 1994
Mercier, Adèle, "Religious Belief and Self-Deception," in Russell Blackford and Udo Schüklenk (eds.), *50 Voices of Disbelief: Why We Are Atheists*, Wiley-Blackwell, 2009, pp. 41-7

Metcalf, Stephen, *Hammer of the Gods: Selected Writings by Friedrich Nietzsche*, Creation Books, 1996

Milgram, Stanley, *Obedience to Authority: An Experimental View*, Harper Classic Reprint, 2009

Miller, Alice, *The Drama of the Gifted Child: The Search for the True Self*, Basic Books, 1997

_____, *For Your Own Good: Hidden Cruelty in Child-Rearing, and the Roots if Violence*, Noonday, 1990

Millet, Robert L., *Holding Fast: Dealing with Doubt in the Latter Days*, Deseret Book, 2008

Mills, David, *Atheist Universe*, David Mills 2003

Mogenson, Greg, *God is a Trauma*, Spring Publishing, 1989

Neumann, Erich, *Depth Psychology and A New Ethic*, Putnam, 1969

474 Thomas Riskas: Deconstructing Mormonism

Nielsen, Kai, "Can Faith Validate God-Talk," *Theology Today*, Vol. 20, No 2, July, 1963

_____, *Reason and Practice: A Modern Introduction to Philosophy*, Harper & Row, 1971

_____, "Eschatological Verification," Re-printed in *The Logic of God*, Edited by M. L. Diamond, Bobbs-Merrill, 1975
_____, *An Introduction to the Philosophy of Religion*, St. Martin's Press, 1982

_____, *God, Skepticism and Modernity*, University of Ottawa Press, 1989

_____, *Ethics without God*, Prometheus Books, 1990

_____, *God and the Grounding of Morality*, University of Ottawa Press, 1991

_____, *Does God Exist?* Prometheus Books, 1993

_____, *On Transforming Philosophy*, Westview, 1995

_____, *Naturalism without Foundations*, Prometheus Books, 1996

_____, *Naturalism and Religion*, Prometheus Books, 2001

_____, *Atheism and Philosophy*, Prometheus Books, 2006

_____, *Wittgensteinian Fideism?* SMC Press, 2006

_____, "On God-Talk," *Caesar, A Journal for the Critical Study of Religion and Human Values*, Vol. 2, No. 2, (Fall 2008): 32-38.

Nietzsche, Friedrich, *The Portable Nietzsche*, edited and translated by Walter Kaufmann, Viking penguin, 1982

_____, *The Antichrist*, Prometheus Books, 2000

Oaks, Dallin H., *The Lord's Way*, Shadow Mountain, 1991
Ostler, Blake T., "Review of Francis J. Beckwith and Stephen E. Parrish: The Mormon Concept of God: A Philosophical Analysis," in *FARMS*, 1996

_____, *Exploring Mormon Thought: The Attributes of God (Vol. 1)*, Gregg Kofford Books, 2001

_____, "Spiritual Experiences as the Basis for Belief and Commitment," *FAIR* website, 2007

_____, "Necessarily God Is Not Analytically Necessary: A Response to Stephen Parrish," (NGNAN) *Fair Journal* (internet source, date unknown)

Palmer, Grant H., *An Insider's View of Mormon Origins*, Signature Books, 2002

Pataki, Tamas, *Against Religion*, Melbourne: Scribe, 2007

_____, "Some Thoughts on Why I Am an Atheist," in Russell Blackford and Udo Schüklenk (eds.), *50 Voices of Disbelief: Why We Are Atheists*, Wiley-Blackwell, 2009, pp. 204-10

Paulos, John Allen, *Irreligion*, Hill and Wang, 2008

Pardi, Paul, "The Argument from Nonbelief: A Rejoinder," *The Secular Web*, 2003

Pascal, Blaise, *Pensees*, Intro. by T.S. Eliot, E.P. Dutton, 1958

Pears, D., *Motivated Irrationality*, Oxford University Press, 1984

Pereboom, Derk, *Living without Free Will*, Cambridge University Press, 2001
Persuitte, David, *Joseph Smith and the Origins of the Book of Mormon*, McFarland, 2000

Phillips, Adam, *Darwin's Worms: On Life Stories and Death Stories*, Basic Books, 2000

Pitkin, Walter B., *A Short Introduction to the History of Human Stupidity*, Simon and Schuster, 1932

Piven, J.S., *Death and Delusion: A Freudian Analysis of Mortal Terror*, IAP, 2004

_____, "Transference as Religious Solution," in *Death and Denial: Interdisciplinary Perspectives on the Legacy of Ernest Becker*, Ed. Daniel Liechty, Praeger, 2002

Plantinga, Alvin and Wolterstorff, Nicholas, eds., *Faith and Rationality*, University of Notre Dame Press, 1983

Plantinga, Alvin, "An Evolutionary Argument against Naturalism," *Logos* 12: 27-49

Pratt, Orson, *The Seer*, Eborn, 2005

Price, Robert M. and Lowder, Jeffery Jay, *The Empty Tomb*, Prometheus Books, 2005

Price, Robert M. and Sweeney, J., *The Reason Driven Life*, Prometheus Books, 2006

Proudfoot, Wayne, *Religious Experience*, University of Columbia Press, 1985

Quinn, Michael D. *The Mormon Hierarchy: Origins of Power*, Signature Books, 1994

_____, *The Mormon Hierarchy: Extensions of Power*, Signature Books, 1997

_____, *Early Mormonism and the Magic World View*, Signature Books, 1998

Ramachandran, V.S. and Blakeslee, Sandra, *Phantoms in the Brain*, William Morrow, 1998

Rank, Otto, *The Trauma of Birth*, Dover, 1993

Rawcliffe, D.H., Illusions and Delusions of the Supernatural and the Occult, Dover, 1959

Ray, Darrel W., *The God Virus: How Religion Infects Our Lives and Culture*, IPC Press, 2009

Restak, Richard, *The Infant Mind*, Doubleday, 1986

Rieff, Philip, *The Triumph of the Therapeutic*, The University of Chicago Press, 1987

_____, *Freud: The Mind of the Moralist*, University of Chicago Press, 1979

Rey, Georges, "Meta-atheism: Religious Avowal as Self-Deception," in *Philosophers without Gods*, ed. Louise M. Antony, Oxford Press, 2007

Roberts, Brigham H., *The Seventy's Course In Theology, Volume I,* S.K. Taylor, 1976
_____, *The Truth, The Way, The Life*, Signature Books, 1995

_____, *The Mormon Doctrine of Deity*, Signature Books, 2000

Robinson, Paul, *Freud and His Critics*, University of California press, 1993

Roheim, Geza, *Psychoanalysis and Anthropology*, International Universities Press, 1973

Rorty, R., "Freud and Moral Reflection," in R. Rorty, "Essays on Heidegger and Others," *Philosophical Papers*, vol. 2, Cambridge University Press, 1991

Rose, Michael R. and Phelan, John P., "Gods Inside," in Russell Blackford and Udo Schüklenk (eds.), *50 Voices of Disbelief: Why We Are Atheists*, Wiley-Blackwell, 2009, pp. 279-87

Ruchlis, Hy, *Clear Thinking*, Prometheus Books, 1990

Russell, Bertrand, *Bertrand Russell on God and Religion*, Al Seckel, Ed., Prometheus Books, 1986

Sacks, David, "In Fairness to Freud," in *The Cambridge Companion to Freud*, Jerome Neu, Ed., Cambridge University Press, 1991

Schachtel, Ernest, "On Memory and Childhood Amnesia," in *Memory Observed: Remembering in Natural Contexts*, Ulric Neisser, Ed., W.H. Freeman, 1982

Schumaker, John F., Ed., *Religion and Mental Health*," Oxford University Press, 1992

_____, *The Corruption of Reality: A Unified Theory of Religion, Hypnosis and Psychopathology*, Prometheus Books, 1995

Seymour, Michael & Fritsch, Matthias, Eds., *Reason and Emancipation: Essays on the Philosophy of Kai Nielsen*, Humanity Books, 2007

Shermer, Michael, *How We Believe: The Search for God in an Age of Science*, Freeman 2000

_____, *Why People Believe Weird Things: Pseudoscience, Superstition, and Other Confusions of Our Time*, Owl Books, 2002

_____, *The Science of Good and Evil*, Times Books, 2004

_____, "How to Think About God: Theism, Atheism, and Science," in Russell Blackford and Udo Schüklenk (eds.), *Fifty Voices of Disbelief: Why We Are Atheists*, Wiley-Blackwell, 2009, pp. 65-77

Singular, Stephen, *When Men Become Gods: Mormon Polygamist Warren Jeffs, His Cult of Fear, and the Women Who Fought Back*, St. Martins Press 2008

Slavin, Michael O. and Kriegman, Daniel, *The Adaptive Design of the Human Psyche*, Guilford Press 1992

Smith, Cameron M. and Sullivan, Charles, *The Top 10 Myths about Evolution*, Prometheus Books 2007

Smith, George H., *Atheism: The Case against God*, Prometheus Books, 1989

_____, *Why Atheism*, Prometheus Books, 2000

Smith, Joseph, Jr., *History of the Church of Jesus Christ of Latter-day Saints*," 7 Vols., Deseret Books, 1978

_____, *Lectures on Faith*, Covenant Communications, 2005

Smith, Joseph Fielding, *Doctrines of Salvation*, BookCraft, 1954

_____, *Teaching of the Prophet Joseph Smith*, Deseret Press, 1976

Solms, Mark, "Freud Returns," *Scientific American* 290 (May 2004): 82-89.

Southerton, Simon G., *Losing a Lost Tribe: Native Americans, DNA, and the Mormon Church*, Signature Books, 2004

Steele, David Ramsay, *Atheism Explained: From Folly to Philosophy*, Open Court, 2008

Stein, Murray, *Solar Conscience, Lunar Conscience*, Chiron, 1993

Stenger, Victor J., *God: The Failed Hypothesis*, Prometheus Books, 2007

_____, *The New Atheism: Taking a Stand for Science and Reason*, Prometheus Books, 2009

Stricker, M., *The Pattern of the Double Bind in Mormonism*, Universal Publishers, 2000

Stromberg, Peter G., *Language and Self-Transformation: A study of the Christian conversion experience*, Cambridge, 1993

Swartz, Harvey L., *Dialogues with Forgotten Voices: Relational Perspectives on Child Abuse Trauma and the Treatment of Severe Dissociative Disorders*, Basic Books, 2000

Swinburne, Richard, *The Existence of God*, Oxford: Clarendon Press, 1979

Talmage, James E., *Articles of Faith*, Signature Books, 2003

Taylor, Kathleen, *Brainwashing: The Science of Thought Control*, Oxford University Press, 2004

Tice, Elizabeth T., *Inside the Mormon Mind*, Pearson, 2006

Tillich, Paul, *The Courage to Be*, Yale University Press, 1980

Toscano, Paul, *The Sanctity of Dissent*, Signature Books, 1994

Trivers, R.L., *Social Evolution*, Benjamin/Cummings, 1985

Van Wagoner, Richard S., *Mormon Polygamy: A History*, Signature Books, 1992

Vaughan, Susan C., *The Talking Cure*," Owl Books, 1998

Vogel, Dan, *The Word of God*, Signature Books, 1990

_____, *Joseph Smith, The Making of a Prophet*, Signature Books, 2004

Vogel, Dan and Metcalf, Brent Lee, Eds., *American Apocrypha*, Signature Books, 2002

Wallwork, Ernest, *Psychoanalysis and Ethics*, Yale University, 1991

Wang, Xinli, "Where are Facts? - A Case for Internal Factual Realism," *Dialogos*, 82 (2003)

Ward, Ivan, Ed., *On a Darkling Plain: Journeys into the Unconscious*, Totem Books USA, 2002

Waterman, Bryan, Ed., *The Prophet Puzzle*, Signature Books, 1999

Watters, Wendell W., *Deadly Doctrine: Health, Illness, and Christian God-Talk*, Prometheus Books, 1992

Webster, Richard, *Why Freud was Wrong: Sin, Science and Psychoanalysis*, Basic Books, 1995, p. 8.

Wegner, Daniel W., *The Illusion of Conscious Will*, MIT Press, 2002

Weisberger, Andrea M., *Suffering Belief*, Peter Lang, 1999

_____, "The Argument from Evil," in *The Cambridge Companion to Atheism*, ed. Michael Martin, Cambridge University Press, 2007

Welles, James F., *Understanding Stupidity*, Mount Pleasant Press, 1995

_____, *The Story of Stupidity: A History of Western Idiocy from the Days of Greece to the Moment You Saw this Book*, Welles, 1997

Wells, G. A., *The Historical Evidence for Jesus*, Prometheus Books, 1988

Weston, Anthony, *A Rulebook for Arguments*, Hackett, 2000

White, O. Kendall, *Mormon Neo-Orthodoxy: A Crisis Theology*, Signature Books, 1987

Widtsoe, John A., *A Rational Theology," The Church of Jesus Christ of Latter-day Saints*, 1915

Wilson, Edward O., *Consilience: The Unity of Knowledge*, Vintage 1999

Wilson Jr., Emmett, "The Object in Person," *Psychoanalytic Quarterly* 71, 2002

Wolfe, David A., *Child Abuse: Implications for Child Development and Psychopathology*, Sage Publications, 1999

Worthy, Jack B., *The Mormon Cult: A Former Missionary Reveals the Secrets of Mormon Mind Control*, Sharp Press, 2008

Yalom, Irvin D., *Existential Psychotherapy*, Basic Books, 1980

_____, *When Nietzsche Wept*, Perennial Classics, 2005

_____, *Staring at the Sun: Overcoming the Terror of Death*, Jossey-Bass, 2008

The Journal of Discourses (27 Volumes)

The Standard Works (Scriptures) of the Church of Jesus Christ of Latter-day Saints (Including the *Bible*, *Book of Mormon*, *Doctrine and Covenants* (D&C), and the *Pearl of Great Price*)